217 Thursday
Leverman Hall

Personnel and Human Resource Management

Personnel and Human Resource Management

FIFTH EDITION

Randall S. Schuler
New York University

Vandra L. Huber
University of Washington

West Publishing Company
Minneapolis/St. Paul ■ New York ■ Los Angeles ■ San Francisco

Copyeditor: Cindi Gerber
Cover and Text Design: Lois Stanfield/LightSource Images
Artist: Randy Miyake/Miyake Illustration
Composition and Prepress: Parkwood Composition
Production, Printing and Binding by West Publishing Company

WEST'S COMMITMENT TO THE ENVIRONMENT

In 1906, West Publishing Company began recycling materials left over from the production of books. This began a tradition of efficient and responsible use of resources. Today, up to 95 percent of our legal books and 70 percent of our college and school texts are printed on recycled, acid-free stock. West also recycles nearly 22 million pounds of scrap paper annually—the equivalent of 181,717 trees. Since the 1960s, West has devised ways to capture and recycle waste inks, solvents, oils, and vapors created in the printing process. We also recycle plastics of all kinds, wood, glass, corrugated cardboard, and batteries, and have eliminated the use of styrofoam book packaging. We at West are proud of the longevity and the scope of our commitment to the environment.

610 Opperman Drive
P.O. Box 64526
St. Paul, MN 55164-0526

Printed in the United States of America

00 99 98 97 96 95 94 93 8 7 6 5 4 3 2 1

Library of Congress Cataloging-in-Publication Data

Schuler, Randall S.
Personnel and human resource management / Randall S. Schuler, Vandra L. Huber.—5th ed.
p. cm.
ISBN 0-314-01184-6
1. Personnel management. I. Huber, Vandra L. II. Title.
HF5549.S249 1993
658.3—dc20 92-30205

CIP

Dedication

To Susan for her immense contributions to this fifth edition in our pursuit of excellence and continuous improvement—R.S.S.

And to Michael for encouragement, Sandy and Maripi for motivation, and my parents, Fred and Twila Huber—V.L.H.

Contents

CHAPTER 6
Selection and Placement 232

CHAPTER 8
Performance Appraisal: Utilizing the Data 325

SECTION 5
Compensating/363

CHAPTER 9
Total Compensation 364

CHAPTER 14
Personnel and Human Resource Management Research 591

SECTION 7
Establishing and Maintaining Effective Work Relationships/629

CHAPTER 15
Employee Rights 630

End-of-Text Summary Cases C–1

Appendix A A–1

Name Index I–1

Subject Index I–15

Preface

Our environment is changing faster and becoming more complex, more competitive, and more global than ever. To compete in this environment—indeed, to survive in this environment—today's organizations must be more competitive, adaptive, and lean. They must think globally and they must decentralize. They must foster quality, cost reduction, and innovation. They must be willing to enter into alliances with customers, suppliers, and even competitors. To compete in this environment, the people in today's organizations must be willing and able to accomplish all of these things. For personnel and human resource managers, this translates into opportunity and excitement, because theirs is the challenge to match the ever-changing needs of organizations with quality human resources.

Managing human resources effectively requires a great deal of knowledge and expertise. Human resource managers must know what their business needs and must know the environment in which the organization is operating. They must also know about all of the personnel and human resource management activities that effective firms use in managing their human resources. Today's human resource managers must be willing and able to play more roles, must be as adaptable and flexible as the organization itself must be in order to take in stride the accelerating pace of change.

Mastering this knowledge and playing these additional roles present at once challenge and opportunity—the challenge to manage human resources better than ever, and the opportunity to significantly improve the organization's competitiveness and its bottom line. There never has been a more exciting time to get your hands around this field we call personnel and human resource management. This Fifth Edition of *Personnel and Human Resource Management* is written to help you do exactly that.

PURPOSES OF THIS BOOK

In addition to the overall goal of helping you grasp the field of personnel and human resource management, we hope this book accomplishes several specific goals, including:

- Outlining the activities of both the personnel and human resource manager and the line manager;
- Describing how world changes make effective human resource management more important than ever;

- Presenting the complexities, challenges, ethical issues, and tradeoffs involved in effectively managing human resources in today's increasingly competitive, global environment;
- Presenting issues from the perspectives of employees, employers, and society; and
- Instilling both concern and excitement for the vital field of personnel and human resource management.

THEMES

We have written this book around three central themes: (1) Applications and practical realities, (2) international comparisons, and (3) research and theory.

Practical Realities and Applications

We include many examples of companies and of personnel and human resource managers who effectively manage human resources and link them with the needs of the business. Each chapter begins with a short example of successful human resource management. More success stories are sprinkled throughout the chapters. Several in–depth features—entitled "PHRM in the News"—describe particular companies or present innovative human resource practices.

At the end of each chapter, we include two new features to help you apply your new knowledge. "Where We Are Today" offers a special summary of the knowledge of the field regarding the chapter topic. "Applied Projects" provides further opportunities for you to learn about the field.

Finally, we include short cases based on real company experiences to help you focus on specific issues. Longer cases at the end of sections and at the end of the book provide you with firsthand opportunities to deal in–depth with the broader challenges and practical realities of personnel and human resource management.

International Comparisons

As organizations become increasingly international, we must be more aware of how companies in other countries of the world manage human resources. Consequently, we include such information throughout the chapters. Comparing international management practices with domestic management practices increases our knowledge of the world and may offer alternatives for more effective personnel and human resource management in the U.S. We also include a description of human resource issues facing multinational corporations as they operate in the far-flung corners of the globe.

Research and Theory

The book extensively uses current research and theory related to the effective use and management of human resources. You will receive not only an exhaustive description of all the current human resource activities, but also an under-

ACKNOWLEDGMENTS

Providing important contributions to this Fifth Edition were Susan Jackson of New York University, Mike Burke of Tulane University, Peter Dowling of Monash University in Australia, Stuart Youngblood of Texas Christian University, Gary Florkowski of the University of Pittsburgh, and Paul Buller of Gonzaga University. The following individuals contributed useful cases: Hrach Bedrosian, Jeff Lenn, Mitchell Fields, Steve Hanks, Gaylen Chandler, Marcia Micelli, Karen Witta, Kay Stratton, Janina Latack, Kyle Steadman, Robyn Sutton, Von Madsen, and Robert McDonough.

Additional thanks should be given to the following former students at the University of Utah and University of Washington from whose class projects, cases, and research projects examples and illustrations were taken: Steve Barguss, Gregory Love, John Paul, Doyle Riley, Ann Lewis, Gaylen Chandler, and David Officer.

The following individuals also provided many good ideas and suggestions in their roles as reviewers and evaluators:

Spencer Blakeslee
Northeastern University

Jeanette A. Davey
Arizona State University

David A. Dilts
Indiana University/Purdue University–Fort Wayne

Jiing-Lib Larry Farh
Louisiana State University

Richard Grover
University of Southern Maine

Freda Z. Hartman
University of Maryland

Kenneth A. Kovach
University of Maryland

Rebecca A. Luzadis
Miami University

Joseph J. Martocchio
University of Illinois at Urbana–Champaign

Thomas H. Patten
California State Polytechnic University–Pomona

Mark A. Wesolowski
Miami University (Ohio)

Theresa Welbourne
University of Colorado

Several personnel and human resource practitioners and practicing managers also provided many good practical examples. These individuals include Calvin Reynolds, Organization Resources Counselors; Jim Walker, The Walker Group; Michael Mitchell and Jerry Goodman, Swiss Bank Corporation; Tessa Jolls, *HR Reporter;* Bill Reffett, Grand Union; Tom Kroeger, Sherwin-Williams; Jim Stahler, J.C. Penney; Chad Frost and Gary Weeda, Frost, Inc.; Steve Rutherford, Federal Express; Tom Moyers, Perdue; Stewart Cole, American Express; Dick Parker, Merck; Art Maine, Revco; Jack Berry, Coca-Cola; Denny Scott, Goldman, Sachs; Bill Maki and Horace Parker, Weyerhaeuser; John Fulkerson, Pepsi Cola International; William Hauser, Pfizer; John Lynch, North American Life Assurance; Steve Marcus, IBM; John Bradley, J. P. Morgan; Donald Brush, Barden Corporation; Sharon Ritter, American Red Cross; Robert Harris, Underwriters Laboratories; Michael Robinson, Marriott's Mark Resort; Tom Hoskison, Schnuck Markets; Greg Dawe, KSL Television; Jean Bishop, Bonneville International Broadcast Co.; and Gaylan Moffatt, Utah Transit Authority. We would also like to express special thanks to all those who granted us permission to use their materials.

The support and encouragement of Dave Rogers, chair of the Department of Management at New York University, and Dick West, Dean of the Stern School of Business at New York University, are sincerely appreciated. At New York University, Lou DeCaro provided special assistance in carefully preparing the manuscript. Also, several people at West Publishing deserve our special thanks for their help and support over many years: Richard T. Fenton, acquisitions editor; Esther W. Craig, developmental editor; M. Lynette D'Amico, production editor; and Elizabeth Grantham, promotion manager. Without their professional dedication and competence, this book would not have been possible.

Randall S. Schuler
New York City

Vandra L. Huber
Seattle

January 1993

SECTION 1

Personnel and Human Resource Management

For firms in the United States to be effective in the highly competitive environments of today and the twenty-first century, they need to devote a significant amount of time, attention, and energy to managing human resources. They also need highly effective personnel and human resource management departments. In addition, chief executive officers, managers, and nonmanagers at all levels in the organization need to be involved in managing human resources. In fact, executive officers and managers need to see themselves as actually sharing the human resource management function with the personnel and human resource managers.

At the same time, the human resource department's leader needs to be seen as one among senior management in making vital business decisions—including those involved in acquiring, deploying, and utilizing the firm's most vital resources—to best meet the needs of the business. Likewise, senior executives, managers, and nonmanagers of all levels must share with the human resource leader and staff the responsibility for developing and implementing personnel and human resource activities, programs, practices, and goals. This partnership ensures that personnel and human resource management is linked to the business and demonstrates the importance of its contribution to the organization.

Chapter 1 first describes the growing importance, excitement, challenges, and focus issues in today's personnel and human resource management. Then we set forth specific issues facing personnel and human resource departments today, including organization, staffing, budgets, careers, ethics, and professionalism. Finally, we provide a road map of where we are going in the remaining chapters of the book.

CHAPTER 1

Personnel and Human Resource Management

The fact is, the only thing that differentiates us from our competition is our people. The equipment, the building—they're all the same. It's the people who make the difference. Effective management of HR becomes an issue for everyone.

—Chuck Nielson, Vice President of HR, Texas Instruments[1]

Since 1973 this firm has added more than 90,000 employees to its payroll. It became the first service company in America to win the coveted Malcolm Baldrige National Quality Award (in 1990). Not surprisingly, since day one its basic philosophy of doing business, as stated by founder and chief executive officer Frederick W. Smith, is "People, Service and Profit." The motto of this highly successful and the nation's largest express transportation company, headquartered in Memphis, Tennessee, is "100% Customer Satisfaction."

A great deal of emphasis on people is essential to the success of the Federal Express Corporation. With a business that relies upon individuals delivering packages overnight to customers anywhere, getting 100 percent customer satisfaction comes only from managing human resources as if they really mattered. Highlighting their concern for managing human resources, Federal Express formulated a philosophy of managing people based upon these cornerstones: no layoffs, guaranteed fair treatment, survey/feedback/action, promotion-from-within, profit sharing, and an open-door policy.

Recently the company established a new pay-for-performance and pay-for-knowledge program. The program is based on interactive video training and job knowledge testing for its 35,000 customer contact employees. Basically, before couriers ever deliver a package they will have had at least three weeks of training. Because Federal Express is constantly making changes or additions to its products and services, the training curricula must constantly be updated. According to Larry McMahan, vice president of human resource development, "We can't support a customer-oriented objective without having a strong emphasis on training."

A strong emphasis, for example, means having an easily accessible 25-disk curriculum that covers topics such as customer etiquette and defensive driving available at hundreds of Federal Express locations around the country. It means having customer-contact employees take a job knowledge test every six months; the company pays each employee for four hours of study preparation time as well as for two hours of test taking. To further increase the incentive to get serious about doing well of the test, the company links its compensation plan to performance on the test. The knowledge required to do well on the tests is so job-related that performance on the tests essentially determines performance on the job. Employees who excel in applying this knowledge to job performance become eligible for additional proficiency pay.

Federal Express dedicates an enormous amount of time, money, and effort to managing its human resources because they believe it enables them to gain a competitive advantage in this highly competitive express transportation industry. They know that having the ability to satisfy customer needs enables them to succeed; and they know that managing their human resources effectively gives them this ability. Consequently, Federal Express really does manage people as if it really matters.[2]

Along with Federal Express, a growing number of outstanding companies are also managing people as if it really matters. They include Disney, Wal-Mart, L.L. Bean, Deere & Co., Levi Strauss, G.E. Medical Systems, Campbell Soup Company, U.S. West, Ben and Jerry's Homemade Inc., Texas Instruments, Household International, IBM, Apple Computer, Microsoft, Johnson and Johnson, and Merck, among many others.

Essentially they are managing people consistent with the needs of the business, yet at the same time respecting the needs of the individual and the larger society in which the company operates. They all realize that linking human resource management with the needs of the business will make their firms more competitive, profitable, able to survive and grow, and more adaptable to rapidly changing and unpredictable conditions.[3] As a consequence, they are able to offer further employment opportunities, to provide for the needs of the individual, and to contribute to the welfare of the environment.

PERSONNEL AND HUMAN RESOURCE MANAGEMENT

Of course, it is in large part the recognition of this impact from linking human resource management with the needs of the business that contributes to the increased recognition for the field of personnel and human resource management. As used here, we define **personnel and human resource management** as the use of several activities to ensure that human resources are managed effectively for the benefit of the individual, society, and the business.

Several critical themes are reflected in this definition. First, effective human resource management benefits the individual, society, and the company. Second, companies use many human resource management activities to manage their human resources. Third, the more closely and consistently human resource management is linked with the business, the more effectively human resources will be managed.

IMPORTANCE OF PERSONNEL AND HUMAN RESOURCE MANAGEMENT

Now more than ever, human resource management is recognized as being critical to the survival and success of organizations. In 1991, IBM and the internationally recognized consulting firm of Towers Perrin jointly conducted a worldwide study of nearly three thousand senior personnel and human resource management (HR) leaders and chief executive officers (CEOs). Results indicate that about seventy percent of HR managers see the human resource function as critical to the success of organizations. By the year 2000, more than ninety percent expect the HR department to be critical. While the HR respondents were perhaps a bit more positive about this trend, the CEOs were very close behind. These results are illustrated in exhibit 1.1.

While serving the very success of the business can certainly be regarded as an important goal of personnel and human resource management, it is a rather broadly conceived goal. Let us look at some more specific goals that help lead to this overall achievement of success.

GOALS OF PERSONNEL AND HUMAN RESOURCE MANAGEMENT

The three general goals or purposes traditionally associated with human resource management are attracting applicants, retaining desirable employees,

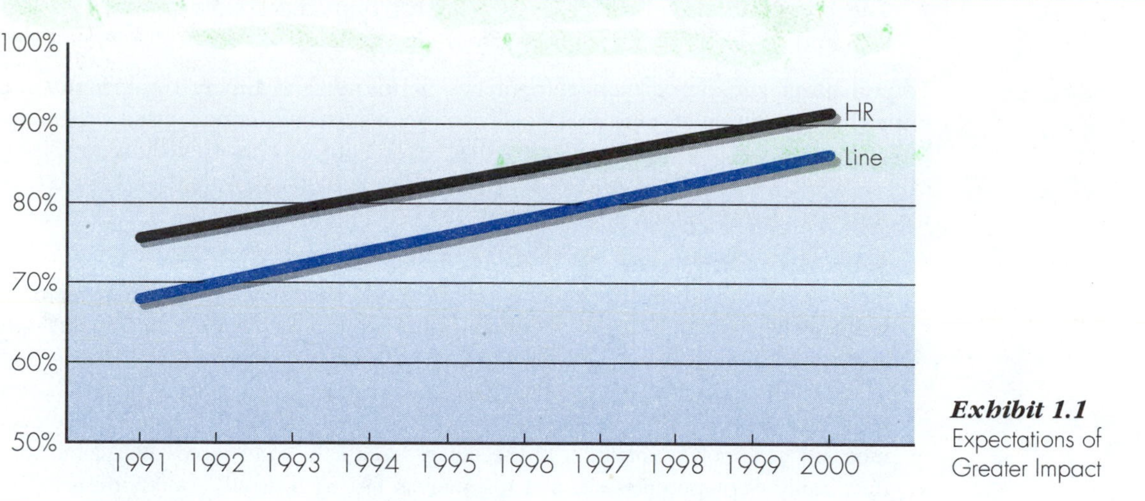

Exhibit 1.1
Expectations of Greater Impact

SOURCE: *Priorities for Competitive Advantage: A Worldwide Human Resource Study* (IBM/Towers Perrin, 1992), 27.

and motivating employees. Increasingly another goal is being added: retraining employees.

The increased attention paid to how a firm manages its human resources is attributed to the recognition that effectively managing human resources has a positive impact on the firm's overall direction and, ultimately, its bottom line. The term **bottom line** refers to the organization's survival, growth, profitability, competitiveness, and flexibility in adapting to changing conditions. Positively affecting the bottom line is a key way in which human resource departments can gain recognition and respect in organizations. In general, human resource management departments influence the bottom line through improving productivity, improving quality of work life, increasing the firm's legal compliance, gaining competitive advantage, and assuring work force flexibility—the more specific goals of managing human resources.[4]

Productivity

Without a doubt, productivity is an important goal of organizations. Human resource management can do many things to improve productivity. The most productive organizations in the U.S. know this and treat their human resource departments differently than do less productive organizations.

- They ensure that the human resource department participates in strategic decisions that affect the successful implementation of business strategies.
- They focus the current resources devoted to the human resource function on important current problems before they add new programs or seek additional resources.
- Their human resource staffs initiate programs and communicate with line managers.

- The corporate staff share responsibility for human resource policy formulation and program administration across organizational levels.[5]

Today, human resource management has a unique and timely opportunity for improving productivity, and this does not mean just increasing output. It means increasing output with higher quality than ever before. This new dual emphasis on quality and quantity is one of the many forces increasing the need for effective human resource management:

> Nobody is against quality. But to many manufacturers quality has meant something they could do to a badly designed, poorly made product to help hold it together until the buyer got it home. Some companies are now remembering that quality—in appearance, function, and durability—must be built in, not pasted on. Design and manufacturing must be united. Managers and workers at every stage of production must be motivated to contribute to the goal of quality. Above all, top management must be genuinely committed. If executives mouth the right words but signal that they really want products slapped together as fast as possible, everybody gets the message.[6]

However, although companies recognize the importance of enhanced quality and quantity, the difficulties and challenges of shifting the way people and the organization are managed are not going unnoticed.

> [S]ometimes, to their surprise, companies are also discovering that boosting quality saves money. Reducing the cost of fixing mistakes, both before and after a product is sold, can cut production costs as must as 30%. It also increases sales. The rub is that a commitment to improved quality almost always means investing more time and money now for a payoff later. Too many top executives, for a lot of reasons, have chosen not to manage for the long term. Unless it reorients its goals toward building for the future, U.S. industry has little hope of rebuilding product quality, productivity, or its competitive position in world markets.[7]

Quality of Work Life

Another important goal is responding to the needs of the employees. Many of today's employees demand a high level of involvement in their jobs. They want more control over their jobs and a chance to make a greater contribution to the organization. In response, many employers are giving their employees greater involvement and control through employee participation and communications. Communicating with employees and encouraging them to communicate their ideas are second only to increasing productivity as major roles that some chief executive officers desire to see their human resource managers play.[8]

Legal Compliance

In managing their employees, organizations must comply with many laws, executive orders, guidelines, and court decisions. Chapter 3 provides an extensive description of some of these legal requirements. A brief listing of them is also provided in Appendix A. These laws, executive orders, guidelines, and court decisions affect almost all of the activities in managing human resources. Additionally, the human resource department must be familiar with the actions of agencies such as the Occupational Safety and Health Administration, the Equal

Employment Opportunity Commission, the Office of Federal Contract Compliance Programs, the Immigration and Naturalization Services, and the various state and city equal employment commissions and human or civil rights commissions.[9] Human resource departments in U.S. multinational corporations (MNCs) must also be aware of the employment laws in other countries of the world.

If human resource departments fail to maintain awareness of current laws and regulations, both domestically and worldwide, organizations may find themselves faced with costly lawsuits and large fines. Fortunately, human resource departments can avoid these costs by constantly monitoring the legal environment for any changes, by complying with those changes, and by managing their human resources effectively.

Gaining Competitive Advantage

> Management of people is an indispensable component of sustained corporate performance and competitive advantage. Accordingly, human resource management as an area of CEO expertise rises from the third most important ranking in 1988 to the number two position in 2000.[10]

Companies can gain a competitive advantage in many ways. One way often overlooked is through their human resource management practices.

Delco-Remy uses its HR practices to produce a higher-quality product, thereby differentiating itself from its competitors. When Delco-Remy trained its employees in participative management, it succeeded in differentiating itself from all competitors in the eyes of Honda and others. Delco's Keith W. Wander describes the success of this training and the resultant competitive advantage:

> Honda of America was seeking an American battery manufacturer as a supplier to its auto plant in Marysville, Ohio. Honda wanted a plant which had a participative system of management and a reputation for producing a quality product at a competitive price. After a contact from the Delco-Remy Sales Department, two American representatives from Honda visited the Delco-Remy plant in Fitzgerald, Georgia. This visit was followed by a second one with Mr. Hoshita, President of Honda, in the group.[11]

During the second visit, members of the Operating Team (hourly employees) conducted plant tours. After the tours, Operating Team members explained to Mr. Hoshita how people were involved in the Fitzgerald business, how Fitzgerald and Honda could be mutual resources to each other because of their participative systems, and why a Delco battery was the best-built battery in the world.

Mr. Hoshita returned several months later to ask more questions of the Support Team (salaried employees) and Operating Teams. Shortly afterward, Honda of America announced Delco-Remy, Fitzgerald, as its sole supplier of batteries, based upon its culture, quality, and price, in that order of importance. To date, Honda has had zero returns of batteries and zero complaints on quality or delivery.[12]

Using human resource management to gain competitive advantage is a particularly potent weapon because it is often difficult for a competitor to respond quickly. Consequently, firms in highly competitive environments will likely seek ways to gain competitive advantage through human resources. They are likely to do it through one of four targets.

Targets. Four targets of HR practices that can be used for competitive advantage include self (the focal company), customers, distributors/servicers, and suppliers. For instance, companies such as Pepsico can train store managers (Pepsico's distributors) in merchandising techniques to help increase store sales as well as sales of Pepsico. Unifi, a textile manufacturer, helps customers with their performance appraisal systems, making their customers more competitive and, thus, better able to buy Unifi products. Mercedes has trained mechanics in service garages (their servicers) throughout the U.S. so Mercedes can offer 24-hour servicing anywhere in the United States. Nissan Motors and Honda Motors offer extensive training programs to their parts suppliers in order to enhance the quality of their products (both for them as well as the suppliers). McDonald's offers extensive training to their franchise owners (their distributors/servicers).

Work Force Flexibility

Firms in highly competitive environments must move quickly and often. This means the work force must also be able to rapidly shift and adjust to new technologies, skills, strategies, and human resource practices.

A trend in attaining work force flexibility is to train people in many skills. This keeps them ready for change and comfortable with continuous learning.[13]

Because there are so many human resource goals or purposes, you will not be surprised to know that human resource departments and their leaders and staff are expected to perform many roles.

ROLES OF THE HUMAN RESOURCE DEPARTMENT

Human resource departments in effective firms in highly competitive environments today must play many roles in the organization. The more roles they play, the more likely they will be effective in improving the organization's productivity, enhancing the quality of work life in the organization, complying with all the necessary laws and regulations related to managing human resources effectively, gaining competitive advantage, and enhancing work force flexibility.

Linking HR to the Business Role

Traditionally, many human resource departments had a relatively limited involvement in the total organization's affairs and goals. Personnel and human resource managers were often concerned only with making staffing plans, providing specific job training programs, or running annual performance appraisal programs (the results of which were sometimes put in the files, never to be used). Consequently, these HR managers were concerned only with the short-term, operational and managerial—perhaps day-to-day—human resource needs.

With the growing importance of personnel and human resource management to the success of the firm (see exhibit 1.1 again), HR managers and their departments are getting more involved in the organization. They are getting to know the needs of the business—where it's going, where it should be going—and are helping it to get there.[14] As a consequence, they and their departments are playing many more roles; linking HR to the business role is one of the newest and most important of these roles.

One consequence of playing this role is the increased involvement in the longer-term, strategic directions of the organization. With this involvement has come the linking of HR to the strategy and goals of the firm. A second consequence is the involvement of the personnel and human resource department and the use of HR activities on a long-term basis as well as the more typical medium- and short-term bases. In utilizing the activities in these three distinct time horizons, personnel and human resource departments are really operating at three organizational levels: strategic, managerial, and operational.

Operational level. At the operational (short-term) level, the human resource departments make staffing and recruitment plans, set up day-to-day monitoring systems, administer wage and salary programs, administer benefits packages, set up annual or less frequent appraisal systems, and set up day-to-day control systems. They also provide for specific job skill training, provide on-the-job training, fit individuals to specific jobs, and plan career moves.

As the personnel and human resource manager and department begin to play the role of linking HR to the business, these operational level human resource activities also get linked to the business. For example, before offering any training program, the program is first explicitly designed on the basis of specific employee skills needed by the organization for the business to succeed.

Managerial level. At the managerial (medium-term) level, personnel and human resource departments do longitudinal validation of selection criteria, develop recruitment marketing plans and establish new recruiting markets, set up five-year compensation plans for individuals, and set up cafeteria benefits packages. They also set up validated systems that relate current conditions and future potential, set up assessment centers for development, establish general management development programs, provide for organizational development, foster self-development, identify career paths, and provide career development services. All of these, of course, take some time to do; and, while these activities could be done in any human resource department, when done in those departments that are playing the role of linking HR with the business, they take on two specific characteristics. For one, they begin with an assessment of what is needed by the business. Before setting up an assessment center, the HR department identifies the types of leaders and managers needed to successfully drive the business. For another, the content of the human resource activities begins to represent the views of all employees—the managers and nonmanagers, inside and outside the personnel and human resource department.

Strategic level. At the strategic (longer-term) level, the personnel and human resource departments get involved in the broader long-term and strategic decisions (those decisions that help provide overall direction and vision) of the organization. For example, according to Kathryn Connors, vice-president of HR at Liz Claiborne,

> Human resources is part of the strategic planning process. It's part of policy development, line extension planning and the merger and acquisition processes. Little is done in the company that doesn't involve us in the planning, policy or finalization stages of any deal.[15]

This process of linking HR to the broader longer-term and strategic needs of firms is the essence of the newer HR activity called strategic human resource management.[16]

Typically, strategic business needs arise from decisions organizations make, such as what products and services to offer and on what basis to compete—quality, cost, or innovation, and/or for purposes of survival, growth, adaptability, and profitability. These decisions are typically associated with the formulation and implementation of the organization's strategy, so they are likely to reflect characteristics of the external and internal environments. The internal environment includes the nature of the business (i.e., manufacturing or service), top management's goals and values, organizational size, current and desired levels of profitability, technology, structure, and the life cycle of the business. Characteristics in the external environment that have an impact on organizational strategy and the strategic business needs include the basis upon which competitive battles are being won in the industry (e.g., cost, quality, innovation); the life cycle of the industry; social, legal, political, and cultural factors; economic conditions; scope and degree of competition; labor pool attributes; and customers.[17]

Together these aspects of the environment influence an organization's broader, longer-term, strategic needs. Thus, as personnel and human resource departments begin to play this role of linking HR to the business, they need to become knowledgeable in all these aspects of the environment; they must become strategic players. This not only helps link HR to the strategic level, but it also provides the necessary knowledge and confidence so HR can play the role in a proactive rather than reactive way. Of course, it also helps them play the enabler role much more effectively.

Enabler Role

In reality, human resource programs succeed because line managers make them succeed. The human resource department's bread-and-butter job, therefore, is to enable line managers to make things happen. Thus, in the more traditional human resource activities—such as selecting, interviewing, training, evaluating, rewarding, counseling, promoting, and firing—the human resource manager is basically providing a service to line managers. In addition, the human resource department administers direct and indirect compensation programs. It can also assist line managers by providing information about, and interpretation of, equal employment opportunity legislation and safety and health standards.

To fulfill these responsibilities, the human resource department must be accessible or it will lose touch with the line managers' needs. The human resource staff should be as close as possible to the people. A trend in this role of being accessible and of providing services and products to others (customers) is called customerization.

Customerization. Adding to the human resource department's ability to gain strategic involvement are its knowledge of the business, its creative insights into how the organization can be more effective, and its familiarity with and acceptance by top management. More and more, these qualities are being found in departments that practice customerization. **Customerization** means viewing everybody, whether internal or external to the organization, as a customer and then putting that customer first. For human resource departments, customers are typically other line and staff managers. Increasingly, customers include other organizations and even the nonmanagerial employees.

An essential underlying ingredient in this philosophy is the recognition and conceptualization of the fact that all human resource departments produce and deliver products and have customers.[18] Another essential ingredient is the realization that the products they must provide to satisfy the customer are determined with the customer. Giving the customer what is desired results in added value.

There are four major phases in the human resource customerization program: (1) gathering information, (2) developing action agendas, (3) implementing the action agendas, and (4) evaluating and revising the agendas. To do these successfully, the human resource department must learn about the business, actively seek to develop and deliver new HR products (e.g., a new performance appraisal system), and constantly seek feedback from customers. Typically, during customerization the department becomes more effective; it becomes a strategic player, it becomes more responsive, and its staff becomes more committed to the organization.[19]

Another important part of customerization is benchmarking. **Benchmarking** is a structured approach for looking outside an organization by studying other organizations and adapting the best outside practices to complement internal operations with creative, new ideas. One of the greatest values from benchmarking that firms find is learning about the practices that are used by competitors and other companies to achieve their results. As such, benchmarking provides insights into new ways of doing human resource management and challenges "business as usual" methods.

Monitoring Role

Although the human resource department may delegate much of the implementation of human resource activities to line managers, it is still responsible for seeing that activities are implemented fairly and consistently. This is especially true today because of fair employment legislation. Various state and federal regulations are making increasingly sophisticated demands on organizations. Responses to these regulations can best be made by a central group supplied with accurate information, the needed expertise, and the support of top management.

Expertise is also needed for implementing human resource activities such as distributing employee benefits. Since having human resource management experts is costly, organizations hire as few as possible and centralize them. Their expertise then filters to other areas of the organization.

In organizations with several locations and several divisions or units, tension often exists between the need to decentralize and the need for centralizing the expertise necessary to comply with complex regulations. (This is further discussed later in this chapter.) A major trend in this role of monitoring and coordinating development is the use of computer technology and human resource information systems.

Computer technology and HRIS. Managing human resources effectively requires a great deal of information. Computer technology enables organizations to combine human resource information into a single data base. This data base is often referred to as a **human resource information system (HRIS):**

> A human resource information system is logically an inventory of the positions and skills extant in a given organization. However, HRIS is more than a single aggregation mechanism for inventory control and accounting; it is the foundation for a set of man-

agement tools enabling managers to establish objectives for the use of their organization's human resources and to measure the extent to which those objectives have been achieved.[20]

There are four key advantages to utilizing computer technology in managing human resources effectively. First, the computer enables the human resource department to take a more active role in organizational planning. Forecasting techniques that are feasible would require a significant time investment without the use of computer technology. Second, the computer integrates and stores in a single data base all human resource information previously filed in separate physical locations. Thus, the human resource department can take a global view of its human resource stock and interpret it in more meaningful ways. Third, the computer speeds up the process by comparing costs and benefits of human resource activities. Fourth, HRIS and computer technology facilitate the easy storage and access of human resource records that are vital for organizations.

To comply with federal equal employment laws, organizations must follow several human resource record keeping requirements. Title VII of the 1964 Civil Rights Act says organizations must keep all employment records for at least six months. The Equal Pay Act and the Age Discrimination in Employment Act say organizations must keep records for three years. Three years, however, is not always the limit. If an employee or a government agency lodges a charge against a firm, the firm should have all of its records regarding the person making the complaint as well as records on all other employees in similar positions. The organization must also keep records on seniority, benefits, and merit and incentive plans until at least one year after the plans end.

Besides keeping records, organizations have to fill out reports. Employers of one hundred or more workers must annually file EEO-1 reports to comply with Equal Employment Opportunity laws. Multi-establishment employers need only file separate EEO-1 reports for each establishment employing fifty or more workers. Organizations with government contracts must fill out affirmative action reports that the Office of Federal Contract Compliance Programs (OFCCP) sends. Government contractors required to fill out Standardized Affirmative Action Formats (SAAFs) for the OFCCP can propose one SAAF to cover all its establishments as long as its HR activities are the same for each establishment.

Among companies using an HRIS and computer technology, relief from "telephone tag" is considered a boon; computer-assisted scheduling of meetings and even computer-based conferences are more advanced advantages. In flexible companies, managers have on-line access to systems for processing pay changes, promotions, and transfers, candidate searches, staffing requests, and other transactions that traditionally were paper driven. Some system applications provide direct computer access by employees for flexible benefit enrollments, career planning and self-assessment, job posting, and training.

In addition to internal data management, human resource professionals may benefit from having direct access to external data bases that contain information affecting their work (e.g., literature, demographic data, other company practices, legal requirements), reducing time-consuming steps.[21]

Innovator Role

Important and ever-expanding roles for the human resource department include providing up-to-date application of current techniques and developing and exploring innovative approaches to human resource problems and concerns. Benchmarking certainly helps in this innovator role.

Today, organizations are asking their human resource departments for innovative approaches and solutions on how to improve productivity and the quality of work life while complying with the law in an environment of high uncertainty, energy conservation, and intense international competition. They are also demanding approaches and solutions that can be justified in dollars and cents. To do this and to better manage the firm's human resources, HR turns to contribution assessment.

Contribution assessment. The human resource department can demonstrate its contribution to the organization in many ways. As HR departments seek to become partners with the rest of the organization in providing strategic direction, they are being proactive in providing evidence of their contributions.

While the contributions of HR departments can be assessed against many criteria or standards, the contributions can be grouped into two categories—doing the right things, and doing things right.[22]

Doing the right thing means the HR department does things which are needed by the organization to be successful. In essence, assessors ask if the department is helping the organization be more successful in areas such as competitiveness, profitability, adaptability and strategy implementation. Is it facilitating the work of line managers and the employees in their efforts to contribute to the maximum of their potential?

Doing things right means that the HR department does the right things as efficiently as possible. Of course, the organization wants to hire the best people, but they want to do it at the least cost per hire possible. The HR department wants to facilitate the work of the line managers, but they want to do it in a way that maximizes the benefit and minimizes the cost.

Within each of these two categories of criteria against which to assess departmental contribution, many more specific measures can be used. For example, within doing the right things, measures can include: knowledge of the organization's strategy; knowledge of the line managers' HR needs; development of HR plans that are consistent with the firm's strategy; and degree of involvement in the strategic planning process. Measures of efficiency, perhaps the more traditional way that HR departments have been assessed, are many. For example, just within the recruiting and selecting activity, measures include

- Number of candidates interviewed per position
- Ratio of offers accepted to offers extended
- Number of "good" hires (tenure or performance after the first year)
- Distribution of "good" hires per source
- Average tenure per hire
- Percent of hires who stay for a minimum desired period of time
- Percent of hires who are outstanding second-year performers
- Cost per hire who stays three or more years

Knowing the two major categories for assessing HR contribution is the first step. Actually doing the assessment is the second step. As implied in the list of efficiency measures for recruiting and selecting, assessment can be made by determining the cost and benefits in dollars and cents; it can also include measures of timeliness. In other words, assessment can be done using quantitative measures. While measures such as the "cost per hire who stays three or more years" might be regarded as a very specific quantitative indicator, measures such as firm productivity or profitability might be regarded as very general quantitative indicators.

Assessment can also be done using qualitative measures. For departments that want to be more customer focused, an increasingly important way to make qualitative assessments is asking the line managers for their opinions of the quality of service the HR department is delivering. Of course, line managers are just one of the HR department's constituents, so they may also ask others (e.g., the employees).

While it may be easy to categorize these measures of assessment here, in reality they are not always so clear cut. For example, the HR department may measure the satisfaction of employees (with regard to any aspect of work that is related to the HR department) with a questionnaire. In a way, this assessment gathers qualitative information in a quantitative way. You will find in the remaining chapters many examples of how HR departments assess their contributions.

Adapter Role

It is increasingly necessary that organizations adapt new technologies, structures, processes, cultures, and procedures to meet the demands of stiffer competition. Organizations look to the human resource department for the skills to facilitate organizational change and to maintain organizational flexibility and adaptability. One consequence of this adapter role is the need to be more future oriented. For example, as external environments and organizational strategies change, new skills and competencies are needed. To help ensure the right skills and competencies are available at the appropriate time, HR departments need to correctly anticipate these changes and train employees. Fostering a mind-set of continuous change and offering education programs, as is done at Motorola, help foster a flexible and adaptable work force.

A trend in this role is for the human resource department to become a role model of change and adaptability.

Flexible role model. Because human resource departments are facing the same demands as their organizations, they are streamlining and automating their operations and becoming more flexible. Not waiting for mandated cutbacks, they continuously review and evaluate expenses and implement incremental changes to become and stay lean. Flexible human resource departments aggressively seek to be perceived as "bureaucracy busters," setting an example for other staff functions and line organizations.[23]

How effective the human resource department is in playing all these roles depends upon (1) how effectively the roles for the human resource leader are played, (2) how the human resource department is organized, and (3) how well the department is staffed.

ROLES FOR THE HUMAN RESOURCE LEADER

For the human resource department to perform all these roles effectively, it needs to have a leader who is knowledgeable in the human resource activities.

Increasingly, the human resource leader must also be familiar with the needs of the business and be able to work side by side with line management as partners in topics such as mergers and acquisitions, productivity, and quality enhancement efforts. This is the essence of the Focus on Research: "New Roles and Responsibilities for Personnel and Human Resource Management." Being a member of the management team means the human resource leader assumes some new key roles. These roles and their criteria for success are illustrated in exhibit 1.2.

Exhibit 1.2
Key Roles for the HR Leader

Key Role	Some Criteria for Success (What's Expected on the Job; Measures of Success)
1. Businessperson	■ Shows concern for bottom line ■ Understands how money gets made, lost, and spent ■ Knows the market and what the business is ■ Has long-term vision of where business is headed
2. Shaper of change in accordance with business	■ Can execute change in strategy ■ Can create sense of urgency ■ Can think conceptually and articulate thoughts ■ Has sense of purpose—a steadfast focus, a definite value system
3. Consultant to organization/partner to line	■ Has ability to build commitment into action ■ Responds to organization needs ■ Recognizes importance of teamwork ■ Is capable of relationship building
4. Strategy/business planner	■ Knows plan of top executives ■ Is involved in strategy formulation of executive committee—is not an afterthought ■ Develops and sells own plans and ideas—able to get needed resources ■ Has three- to five-year focus
5. Talent manager	■ Sees the movement from an emphasis on strictly numbers or bodies needed to the type of talent and skills needed in the organization ■ Sees the emphasis on talent needed for executing future strategies as opposed to today's needs ■ Is capable of educating management ■ Knows high-potential people and anticipates their concerns—for example, who is bright but bored?
6. HR asset manager/cost controller	■ Initiates—does not wait for others to call attention to need for action ■ Can educate and sell management ■ Can creatively measure effectiveness in own areas of responsibility and other areas of organization ■ Can use automation effectively

SOURCE: Adapted from "How to Develop HR Professionals for Today's Business Environment" *HR Reporter* (August 1987), 6–7.

ORGANIZING THE HUMAN RESOURCE DEPARTMENT

In organizing the HR department, two major questions can be addressed: Where are the HR decisions made? Who is actually responsible for those HR decisions?

Centralization vs. Decentralization

Centralization means that essential decisions making and policy formulation are organized and done at one location (at headquarters). **Decentralization** means that the essential decision making and policy formulation are organized and done at several locations (in the divisions or departments of the organization).

How human resource departments are organized differs widely from one company to another, not only because of differences in type of industry, but also because of differences in the philosophy, culture, and strategic plans of the organization. For purposes of illustration, it is useful to compare the centralized human resource structure of Merck with the decentralized human resource structure of TRW. In the centralized human resource structure, large specialized corporate human resource staffs formulate and design human resource strategies and activities, which are then communicated to the small human resource staffs of operating units for implementation. High consistency and congruence with

FOCUS ON RESEARCH

New Roles and Responsibilities for Personnel and Human Resource Management

In a recent survey article of the field of human resource management, Stephen Carroll concludes that, to be effective, the human resource department must consider new roles, responsibilities, and structures.

"The new competitive pressures have forced organizations to make sure that all resources including personnel are used in such a way as to generate the maximum value to the organization in terms of contributions in return for the inducements provided." Contributing this maximum value in human resource management means new roles, responsibilities, and structures. It also means new competencies.

Organizations continue to use the traditional activities of staffing and training, and of compensation as a means of attracting and retaining employees. However, they are now emphasizing the designing and implementing of these human resource activities for the purpose of improving organizational effectiveness. Thus, the value of human resource activities is now being measured both by how well they attract and retain individuals and by how much they improve the effectiveness of the firm. For example, Carroll reports that in a firm that installed a gainsharing compensation plan, productivity increased 31 percent, variable costs were reduced by 14 percent, and absenteeism was lowered by 26 percent.

In addition to an increased concern with organizational effectiveness, Carroll reported an increased concern for linking human resource management with the needs of the business. Thus, as organizations move toward total quality management programs and the use of teams, traditional human resource activities are moving toward being concerned with team—rather than individual—work and job assignments. This concern for linking human resource management to the business is also resulting in new practices. For example, HR managers are getting involved in designing and implementing behavior-influencing systems such as compensation and performance appraisal to ensure that employees behave and perform as needed by the

Continued

corporate goals are attained. In the decentralized model, small corporate staffs manage only the human resource systems for executives and act as advisors only to operating units. Here there tends to be wider divergence in human resource practices and the flexibility for operating to address their human resource concerns as effectively as possible.[24]

Looking at the nature of the businesses of Merck and TRW, one sees how the HR structures they use are very appropriate for the types of industry. TRW, being a high-technology company with many divergent types of businesses, cannot use a consistent stable approach to HR, while Merck, with a more consistent type of product focus, is able to do so.[25]

Because of the rapidly changing and highly competitive environment, the trend seems to be toward greater decentralization and delegation of human resource responsibilities to lower human resource levels and to the operating units and managers themselves. Along with this is the trend toward less formalization of human resource policies—that is, fewer policies that are seen as bureaucratic hurdles. These conditions give the human resource department and organization the flexibility for coping with a more rapidly changing environment. The diminished bureaucratization of the HR function also can lead to a greater openness in the human resource perspectives and methods used. Of course, activities such as fair employment issues and compensation matters may have to

business. They are also getting involved with top management in strategy formulation to describe the implications of a new strategic direction on the firm's human resource capabilities.

Carroll not only finds that human resource departments are playing more roles than before, but that the HR leader is behaving more like a change agent than ever. As a result, HR leaders are making their presence felt through promoting organizational improvement programs. For example, at the Ohio-based Kiethley Instruments Company, the HR department used action research to identify needed changes in how work was performed. Working with a management team, the HR leader and the department reassigned work to teams rather than individuals and provided training so that work groups could set their own goals and solve work-related problems. The result: Productivity increased by 90 percent in four years with only a 28 percent increase in the number of employees.

Human resource management is also becoming more concerned with customers and their strategic business issues. This is changing the role and competencies of the HR leader and staff to one more businesslike than ever. Carroll found that HR professionals could make the change to this role and these competencies more easily as they interacted more with line managers and got to know their business. As they got to know the business more, they could design better HR products and be more effective in implementing them for the line managers.

Also, as HR professionals are getting closer to the customer, they are realizing that the structure of the department—or at least parts of it—may need to be decentralized, in order to best listen to and understand the needs of the customers. Of course, some types of HR activities (for example, top executive compensation) can remain more centralized. Thus, Carroll predicts that organizations of the future will have some HR activities that are centralized and some that are decentralized. At the same time, as the organizations change and restructure themselves, HR departments will have to adjust and restructure themselves, also.

The entire field of human resource management is changing in the direction of being more important and more challenging. For those in human resource management, the times were never better and are likely to get even better.

SOURCE: Based on S. J. Carroll, "New HRM Roles, Responsibilities, and Structures," in R. S. Schuler, ed. *Managing HR in the Information Age* (Washington, D. C.: SHRM/BNA Books, 1991): 204–226.

be centralized because of legal requirements and for the sake of consistency. Nevertheless, the general trend is for less formalization and less centralization. Along with this is the need for everyone to be responsible for managing human resources.

Who is Responsible for Managing Human Resources?

Everyone should be responsible for managing human resources; and, as organizations demonstrate more openness and mutuality in their human resources policies and practices, everyone is.

The HR manager and staff and line managers. Managing human resources effectively is the task of individuals who have specialized in and are primarily responsible for human resource management—HR managers and staff and line managers (those in charge of the employees who are producing the products and delivering the services of the company). These two managers are interdependent in the management of human resources. Increasingly, they will work together.

Thus, chief executive officers (CEOs), human resource managers, and all levels of senior management will be involved in managing human resources. While this is already happening in some firms, in the recent IBM/Towers Perrin worldwide HR survey, both CEOs and senior human resource managers agreed that co-involvement should be happening much more by the year 2000. Exhibit 1.3 provides more details of the type of involvement most favored. In this scenario, the HR department's leader will be counted among senior executives and will play significant roles in acquiring, deploying, and utilizing the firm's most vital resources.

Amidst other senior executives, the human resource leader will be indistinguishable from others in concern for and understanding of the needs of the business. Likewise the staff of the human resource department will appear indistinguishable from their counterparts in the firm. Sharing in the HR function, line managers, human resource staff, and nonmanagerial employees together will forge and implement human resource activities, structure, roles, policy, goals, and practices as shown in exhibit 1.3.

The employees. Employees are also taking a role in human resource management. For example, employees may be asked to appraise their own performance or that of their colleagues. It is no longer uncommon for employees to write their own job descriptions. Perhaps most significantly, employees are taking a more active role in managing their own careers, assessing their own needs and values, and designing their own jobs. Nonetheless, the human resource department must help guide this process. To these ends, the HR department must be staffed with qualified individuals.

STAFFING THE HUMAN RESOURCE DEPARTMENT

The top human resource leaders and staff members are often expected to be functional experts, capable administrators, business consultants, and problem solvers with global awareness. Management expects human resource staff "to

Percent Agreeing that Line Management Should Share Responsibility with the HR Department

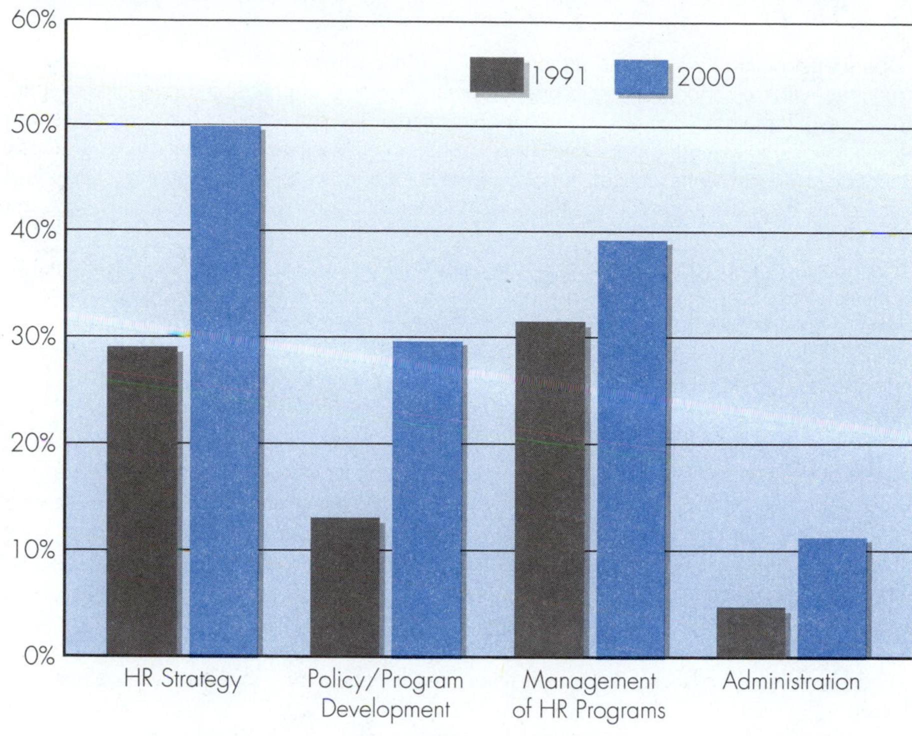

Exhibit 1.3
An Emerging Role for Line Management

SOURCE: Adapted from "Priorities for Competitive Advantages: A Worldwide Human Resource Study" (IBM/Towers Perrin, 1992), 26.

have it all." Administrative skills are also essential for efficiency. Specialized human resource expertise is also important, but particularly in combination with business knowledge and perspective. In flexible organizations, problem-solving and consulting skills are vital in guiding and supporting new management practices.

Managers would like human resource staff to work closely with them to help solve their people-related business challenges as efficiently and promptly as possible. While line managers may best understand their own people, many desire help in handling their people-related business problems. As the human resource staff becomes more capable and effective, managers find it easier to work with them as partners in dealing with these problems.

Being at the top of the organization, reporting directly to the CEO, and having business skills allow the HR leader to play a part in human resource management policy formulation and to have the power necessary to ensure fair and consistent implementation. A position profile (exhibit 1.4) illustrates the reality and the responsibilities of a senior HR leader in a large corporation today. This profile is used by a consulting firm that helps organizations find the best qualified HR person for HR jobs.

Exhibit 1.4
Senior Vice President, Human Resources

Position Profile

This position represents the personnel point of view in the strategic and operational direction of the business. The incumbent is expected to provide, with the support and concurrence of the President, a philosophy and guiding principles for managing the human resources of the company. Authority is limited to the protection of the company's interests in relation to laws and regulations pertaining to personnel. The position directly impacts all functions and areas of the company in matters of morale, management practices, employee well-being, compensation, benefits, structure, and development. The incumbent is expected to positively affect these matters through his/her personal influence and professional credibility rather than vested authority.

This position requires an incumbent with broad managerial and professional knowledge and experience. From the managerial standpoint, the Human Resources group comprises ten interrelated yet disparate functional areas: personnel relations, compensation, benefits, training, organization development, recruiting, personnel administration, field personnel services, communications and home office personnel services. The current staff consists of 75 people, including 42 professionals. The incumbent also has functional responsibility for personnel services to four distribution centers. Budget administration responsibilities approximate $29.7 million.

On the professional side, with the exception of the directors of compensation and staffing and of human resource development and the managers of benefits and of media projects, virtually all staff members have been developed inside the company. Technical and professional direction and training rest with the incumbent. The incumbent is expected to provide the company with systems, programs, and processes which effectively support business goals and organization values. The company's principal executives rely on the incumbent's personal experience, skills and resources to bring the company to current "State-of-the-Art" status.

Critical competency requirements include preventive labor relations, personnel/labor law, compensation practices, benefits practices, training and organization development practices, and employee involvement processes. The company's widespread training needs are especially important at this time. The incumbent must have highly developed consulting and communication skills.

Although the incumbent is not expected to create or invent systems and programs, he/she is expected to introduce successful practices new to and adapt them to the company's particular needs. The incumbent must be able to judge when to act and when not to act with patience and persistence. He/she must be able and willing to modify actions to gain agreement and consensus. The incumbent must be able to place the priorities of the company over those of the personnel function. At the same time, the incumbent is expected to be a strong advocate for employee interests and well-being.

Candidate Qualifications

Broad experience is required in the following areas:

- personnel/labor relations in both organized and unorganized situations, including union-free policies and practices, organizing campaigns, unfair labor practice charges, arbitrations, labor contract negotiation, and administration
- personnel policy formulation, communication and administration
- corporate culture change, including the facilitation of improved organization effectiveness
- human resource development with special emphasis on all facets of training; but also including organization planning, succession and manpower planning, performance standard/expectations, performance review, personal/management development, assessment of management potential, organization development, career pathing, and recruitment/selection process
- compensation programs, including job evaluations, wage and salary plan design and administration, short- and long-term incentive plan design and administration, bonus and gain-sharing plans
- benefit programs, including the design and administration of health care, dental, life and disability insurance, and of defined benefit/contribution plans, vacation, sick pay, holiday and other policies
- corporate communications, using print, video and other media, including booklets, newspapers and other publications, institutional and informational videos and meetings of management personnel

Continued

Exhibit 1.4 (continued)
Senior Vice President, Human Resources 

- participatory and responsive management, including use of employee and other involvement processes, project management/task force/focus group techniques, attitude surveys, and bottom-up (suggestion, coffee hours, "Express Yourself," hotline, etc.) communications
- human resource information systems, including the development and utilization of cost/time effective reports and analyses
- departmental direction, management and administration, including staff selection, training/development, and deployment; short- and long-term departmental planning, project management, program development and execution, delivery of human resource services, budget development and administration

SOURCE: Material used by the search firm, Kenny, Kindler, Hunt and Howe, New York City, from *The Changing Human Resources Function* (New York: The Conference Board, 1990), 15.

How effectively an organization's human resources are managed depends in large part upon the knowledge, skills, and abilities of the people in the human resource department, particularly the HR leader, the HR generalists, and the HR specialists (collectively referred to as HR professionals).

The HR Leader

Perhaps the most effective person who can head the human resource department is an outstanding performer in the organization (a superstar) with human resource management expertise and line management experience:

> In essence, to be a true professional in many areas of HR management, individuals virtually have to have an advanced degree in the subject and spend full time in that field. Areas like compensation have become incredibly complicated because of their close connection to strategic, legal, financial, and tax matters ... [But] with the exception of technical specialists, HR managers need to spend a significant amount of time in line-management positions. It is not enough for senior HR managers to have worked in different areas of the HR function; they must have had some line business experience so that they have a first-hand familiarity with the business operations.[26]

Even if the person is not a superstar, however, line experience gives the human resource manager an understanding of the needs of the business and the needs of the department's customers. To accomplish this, human resource professionals could rotate through various line positions over the course of a few years. Short of actually serving as a line manager, the individual could serve as a special assistant to the line manager or head up a special task force regarding a companywide project.

For decentralized organizations, the HR leader at the business unit is similar in some respects to the corporate HR leader. With smaller corporate staffs, however, the corporate person may actually manage a much smaller operation than do HR leaders in the business units. Nevertheless, the route to the corporate HR position should include rotation through the various businesses. A drawback to this method is that the same HR ideas and concepts will be carried around the organization; injecting new ideas may require the hiring of an outside person.

Whether in corporate or business units, for the human resource leader to be effective in playing the HR roles described in exhibit 1.2, the leader will need the following knowledge, skills, and abilities (competencies):[27]

- Problem-solving skills
- Business knowledge/organization sensitivity
- Knowledge of compensation techniques to reinforce business plans
- Strategic and conceptual skills
- Knowledge of succession/career-planning systems
- Established relationships and acknowledged leadership skills
- Ability to analyze data and plan from it
- Computer literacy
- Competence in HR functional areas
- Awareness of the financial impacts in the HR function as well as to the organization, particularly in areas such as pension costs, health care, and compensation

While this list of competencies is rather extensive, these will be the ones that effective HR leaders in firms in highly competitive environments will need. Some firms are now adopting procedures to identify the systematically required qualities for their HR staff.

> At Weyerhaeuser each major division, led by its human resources director, is responsible for developing a list of specific, required competencies. Of course, overlaps occur among major divisions. The HR directors help generate a slate of competencies based on their interviews with the "customers"—others in the organization—and HR professionals, and on their own requirements. The corporation is also aiming to predict future HR issues as a basis for updating human resources strategies and developing future competency requirements for HR staff.[28]

Human Resource Generalists

Line positions are also one important source for human resource generalists. A brief tour into a human resource position by a line supervisor, usually as a human resource generalist, can convey to the human resource department the knowledge, language, needs, and requirements of the line. As a result, the human resource department can more effectively fill its service role. Another source of human resource talent is current nonmanagerial employees. Like line managers, these people bring with them information about employee needs and attitudes.

Some companies have a policy of assigning line managers to work in the corporate human resource department for two or three years as a part of their career development. Indeed, in the IBM–Towers Perrin worldwide HR survey, having experience in HR is seen as critical for the careers of line managers—at least, this is what the results indicate for the year 2000. Currently the story is a bit different. In 1991, only 25 percent of the CEOs and line managers said the HR experience is critical for a line manager today. However, fully 65 percent said it would be critical in the year 2000. This latter result certainly fits the needs of CEOs in the year 2000, also. According to a major worldwide survey conducted by the Korn Ferry consulting firm and the Columbia Business School, knowledge and skill in human resource management is seen as second in importance, right behind skill and knowledge in strategy formulation. These results are shown in exhibit 1.5.

Human resource generalists should possess many of the same qualities as human resource specialists, but the level of expertise in a human resource specialty generally need not be at the same depth. After serving as a nonmanagerial human resource generalist, the next move could be to the position of manager of a human resource activity or even the manager of one of the firm's field locations. Whereas the former may result in specialization, moving to the field is likely to result in a broadening of human resource experience.

Human Resource Specialists

Human resource staff specialists should have skills related to the specialty, an awareness of the relationship of the specialty to other human resource activities, and a knowledge of the organization and where the specialized function fits. Individuals joining an organization for the first time should also have an appreciation for the political realities of organizations. Since specialists may work at almost any human resource activity, qualified applicants can come from specialized programs in law, organizational and industrial psychology, labor and industrial relations, human resource management, counseling, organizational development, and medical and health science. In addition to current specialties, human resources will need specialists in total quality management, in the new service technologies, in behavioral performance improvement systems, and in organizational change and design.

With the increase in regulatory requirements for the use of human resources and the increased expertise necessary to deal with complex human resource

Exhibit 1.5
What Traits CEOs Have—and Will Need

Percent Describing Talents Dominant Now in the CEO and Important for the CEO of 2000

Knowledge and Skills	Now	Year 2000
Strategy formulation	68%	78%
Human resource management	41%	53%
International economics and politics	10%	19%
Science and technology	11%	15%
Computer literacy	3%	7%
Marketing and sales	50%	48%
Negotiation	34%	24%
Accounting and finance	33%	24%
Handling media and public speaking	16%	13%
Production	21%	9%

SOURCE: "What Traits CEOs Have—and Will Need," *Fortune* (22 May 1989), 57.

activity, some organizations moved away from using human resource generalists and toward human resource specialists. However, with pressure to serve the customer better, some organizations are moving back to the human resource generalists. In fact, many organizations have both human resource generalists and human resource specialists. Both are valuable, and both reflect an increasing level of professionalism.

PROFESSIONALISM IN HUMAN RESOURCE MANAGEMENT

Like any profession, human resource management follows a code of professional ethics and has an accreditation institute and certification procedures. All professions share the code of ethics that human resource management follows.

1. Practitioners must regard the obligation to implement public objectives and protect the public interest as more important than blind loyalty to an employer's preferences.
2. In daily practice, professionals must thoroughly understand the problems assigned and must undertake whatever study and research are required to assure continuing competence and the best of professional attention.
3. Practitioners must maintain a high standard of personal honesty and integrity in every phase of daily practice.
4. Professionals must give thoughtful consideration to the personal interest, welfare, and dignity of all employees who are affected by their prescriptions, recommendations, and actions.
5. Professionals must make very sure that the organizations that represent them maintain a high regard and respect for the public interest and that they never overlook the importance of the personal interests and dignity of employees.[29]

Ethical HR Issues in Organizations

Increasingly, human resource professionals are becoming involved in more ethical issues. Some of the most serious issues involve differences in the way people are treated based on favoritism or relationship to top management. In a recent survey, conducted by the Society for Human Resource Management (SHRM) and the Commerce Case Clearing House (CCCH), human resource professionals identified more than forty ethical incidents, events, and situations relevant to HR activities. The ten "most serious" ethical situations reported by HR managers are shown in exhibit 1.6.

In this study, the human resource professionals agreed that workplace ethics require people to be judged solely on job performance.

> Ethics requires managers to eliminate such things as favoritism, friendship, sex bias, race bias, or age bias from promotion and pay decisions (it is, of course, also *unlawful* to take sex, race, or age into account).
>
> Is ethics a "bottom line" issue? It becomes one when we consider that by acting in an ethical manner, companies will, in fact, hire, reward and retain the best people. This will, in turn, help assure that the company has the best workforce possible to achieve its business goals.

> Certainly there are other ethical issues that do not impact the bottom line in the way favoritism *vs.* employee performance does. By adopting a definition of workplace ethics that centers on job performance, however, HR will be in a better position to persuade others in the organization that making ethical behavior a priority will produce beneficial results.[30]

Accordingly, in the following chapters we will present ethical issues relevant to human resource management in the workplace.

Professional Certification

The Society for Human Resource Management has established the Human Resource Certification Institute to certify human resource professionals.[31] The institute has the following purposes:

1. To recognize individuals who have demonstrated expertise in particular fields
2. To raise and maintain professional standards
3. To identify a body of knowledge as a guide to practitioners, consultants, educators, and researchers
4. To aid employers in identifying qualified applicants
5. To provide an overview of the field as a guide to self-development

The certification institute has two levels of accreditation: basic and senior. The basic accreditation is the Professional in Human Resources. This designation requires an examination covering the general body of knowledge and four years of professional experience. A bachelor's degree in human resource management or social sciences counts for two years of professional experience.

The senior level accreditation is the Senior Professional in Human Resources. This accreditation requires a minimum of eight years of experience, with the

Exhibit 1.6
The Ten "Most Serious" Ethical Situations Reported by HR Managers in the 1991 SHRM/CCH Survey

Situation	Percent
Hiring, training, or promotion based on favoritism (friendships or relatives)	30.7
Allowing differences in pay, discipline, promotion, etc., due to friendships with top management	30.7
Sex harassment	28.4
Sex discrimination in promotion	26.9
Using discipline for managerial and nonmanagerial personnel inconsistently	26.9
Not maintaining confidentiality	26.4
Sex discrimination in compensation	25.8
Nonperformance factors used in appraisals	23.5
Arrangements with vendors or consulting agencies leading to personal gain	23.1
Sex discrimination in recruitment or hiring	22.6

"Percent" is the percent responding with 4 or 5 on 5-point scale measuring "degree of seriousness" (5 = "very great").
SOURCE: *1991 SHRM/CCH Survey* (Chicago: Commerce Case Clearinghouse, 26 June 1991), 1.

three most recent years including policy-developing responsibility. All professionals receiving accreditation will be listed in the *Register of Accredited Personnel and Human Resource Professionals*.[32]

Budgets of Human Resource Departments

Human resource management as a field of employment is becoming very attractive. The results of a recent compensation survey indicate that salaries are generally higher for those HR individuals in larger organizations, for those with more experience, and for those with the most education.[33]

The amount of money that organizations allocate to their human resource departments continues to rise yearly. For example, the annual per-employee human resource department costs rose from $697 in 1990 to $863 in 1991. The median 1991 expenditure for the human resources function was much lower among nonbusiness organizations ($475,887) than among manufacturing companies ($563,671) and nonmanufacturing businesses ($765,842). Not surprisingly, total human resource department expenditures increase steadily with company size. Firms with fewer than 250 employees recorded a median human resource department expenditure of $194,173 in 1991, compared with $355,136 in companies with 250 to 499 employees, $532,780 among employers with 500 to 999 employees, $856,180 in organizations with 1,000 to 2,499 workers, and over $2.4 million among firms with 2,500 or more employees. However, per capita expenditures for human resource activities and staffs decline as the size of the work force increases. ($1,348 per employee for the smallest firms and $478 per employee for the largest firms).[34]

The median ratio of HR department staff to the work force is 1.1 staff member for every 100 workers. This figure is slightly higher than the median staff ratio reported in 1991 (1.0 personnel staff per 100 employees) and the same ratio of HR staff to employment recorded in 1990. The median size of the HR department is 1.7 staff per 100 workers among firms with fewer then 250 employees, and 1.2 per 100 employees among companies with 250 to 499 employees. Ratios of HR staff to total employment are substantially lower in organizations with 500 to 2,499 employees (0.8 per 100), and lowest among employers with 2,500 or more workers (0.6 per 100).[35]

Careers in Human Resource Management

Numerous career possibilities in human resources exist, although they may be somewhat altered. As described earlier, human resource specialists could remain in their fields of specialization but be selling some of their time to external organizations as consultants. Human resource generalists could remain in human resources but occasionally serve on companywide task forces for special issues such as downsizing or capital improvement projects. Human resource generalists are likely to be from three ranks: career human resource professionals with general degrees in business or psychology, former line managers who have switched over to human resources, and line managers on a required tour of duty. As human resources becomes an activity valued by line managers, required tours of duty by line managers in human resources will become more frequent. Finally, as U.S. organizations become more global, there will be increased opportunities for careers in international human resource management. A thorough description of these opportunities is provided in the PHRM in the News: "Careers in International Human Resources" feature.

FOCUS ISSUES IN PERSONNEL AND HUMAN RESOURCE MANAGEMENT

What is happening today in the field of personnel and human resource management is nothing short of revolutionary. The organizational function of human resource management is becoming more important than ever. Line managers are getting involved in human resource management, and human resource managers are becoming members of the management team. Also, because HR is seen as critical to the success of organizations, virtually everyone in the organization can make a contribution to the management of people and the success of the organization at the same time. Three focus issues accompany this excitement and challenge.

Linking with the Environment

In comparison with the past, today's and tomorrow's characterizations of human resource management reflect the more intense levels of national, regional, and global competition, projected demographic and work force figures, anticipated legal and regulatory changes, and significant technological developments. Translated through major changes in organizational strategy, structure, shape, and technology, these environmental forces require speed, quality, innovation, and globalization for firms wishing to survive the battlefield of international competition. The characterization of effective firms in highly competitive environments—the firms in which the most exciting things in human resource management are happening—reflects the corporate consensus that the requirements for successful combat will require the most effective human resource management possible. For worldwide competitiveness, organizations need world-class HR departments; thus, our second focus issue.

Becoming World Class HR

To maximize their contribution to the business, HR departments and HR professionals are striving for world-class competency. Many of the firms mentioned in this book are certainly among those firms. Basically this means that they are

- Relating HR to the needs of the business
- Being seen as a business unit within the firm (e.g., operating in the same way as other units—having customers, doing benchmarking, etc.)
- Being organized in a way that brings maximum service to the customer and maximum motivation to the HR staff
- Making the best HR products available for the customers
- Implementing HR programs that fulfill the agendas of the HR group and the customers
- Actively sharing an HR vision with the entire group

IN THE NEWS PHRM

Careers in International Human Resources

The globalization of business is occurring at a much faster pace than American economic growth. According to the U.S. Department of Commerce, the gross national product increased by 15 percent between 1985 and 1990. During that same period, U.S. exports grew by 72 percent; nearly five times as fast. Exports now constitute fifteen percent of GNP. In the late 1980's, U.S. foreign direct investment climbed by 34 percent. Even much faster at 105 percent was the growth of direct investment by foreigners in the United States. Every indication is that globalization will continue and in all probability, accelerate.

All this suggests that from a career perspective, international business is a good place to be. If corporations are to succeed in the global arena, they must manage human resources effectively. International human resource management should be one of the great growth functions of the 1990's and beyond.

How can you break into the field? What is the potential for growth? As many have already discovered, there are few recruiters at colleges and graduate schools clambering for candidates.

Entry-level positions in international human resources (IHR) are very hard to find, even with the MBA in human resources or international management. The one exception is as an expatriate compensation and benefits specialist. Expatriate compensation and benefits is currently the largest and most time-consuming IHR activity of U.S.-headquartered companies.

From a career perspective, however, there are serious limitations to entering the field through the expatriate compensation door. Most importantly, the skills developed in this area have virtually no applicability in other functions. The subject is incredibly complex, and those who master it are in high demand and under great pressure to remain within the specialty. While many in the field find expatriate compensation and benefits fascinating because of its variety and complexity, experience suggests that it is an area with limited upward mobility.

In a recent survey of 35 major U.S. multinationals, it was found that over 90 percent of senior IHR executives have had experience in other human resource functions. Nearly half have held line posi-

Continued

- Being a proactive and not reactive group
- Being involved in the key business issue discussions
- Being seen as a great place to work and an example of the desired characteristics of a great organization

Because doing all these things is not necessarily easy, many firms and their HR departments choose not to do them; some departments may say their companies are not big enough or global enough. While this may be true, their competitors couldn't care less. The way things are today, the world is the playing field for all companies. However, those firms that do strive for world-class competency usually capture the competitive advantage and the increased ability to survive and grow, to be adaptable and profitable. Those in the HR departments who are choosing to be world-class get the challenge, the excitement, and the demand of being systematic.

Being Systematic

Companies which seek to gain the maximum benefit from their personnel and human resource management activities must take a **systematic approach** to

tions and managed a business; 60 percent have had overseas assignments.

Those aspiring to upper levels of human resource management (global, international, or domestic) will have a much better chance of success if they have a degree in human resources and/or international business and enter the field through one of the domestic human resource functions, such as a human resource planning, management development, executive compensation, or industrial relations. Solid experience in two or more domestic HR areas will vastly improve the opportunities for transfer into IHR at a significant management level.

However, a major problem for those whose experience is limited to human resources is the difficulty of obtaining an overseas assignment. There are very few Americans overseas with a primary responsibility for human resource management. It is easier to gain overseas experience in other functions such as marketing, finance, and engineering. Indeed, many senior IHR executives got their overseas experience in other functions.

Is overseas experience necessary for IHR executives? Perhaps not, but it is interesting to note that the 40 percent of senior HR executives who have not worked abroad cited their lack of overseas experience as their greatest weakness.

In all probability, there will be dramatic changes in IHR management over the next decade including much more emphasis on strategic issues and support for business objectives. IHR will become a more vital management function, and greater emphasis will be placed on staffing the function with executives possessing overseas and line experience, as well as having a solid grounding in general human resources.

In the meantime, it is important to know how to pick your way through the career maze. Those who desire careers as functional specialists may find expatriate compensation and benefits fascinating and challenging. Those who aspire to higher IHR management would be well advised to acquire a solid domestic base and experience in a line function before seeking an overseas assignment. Clearly there are other options; working for a foreign multinational or consulting firm, for example. Regardless, those who will be managing IHR in the major multinationals of the future will find the challenges exciting.

Mr. Reynolds is a senior vice president of Organization Resources Counselors, Inc. (New York, NY) and directs its international personnel consulting, publications, meeting groups, and compensation services. Mr. Reynolds is on the board of the Institute for International Human Resources.

SOURCE: Calvin Reynolds, "Careers in International Human Resources," *The SHRM Student Newsletter* (January/February 1992), 1.

managing human resources. While this theme will be elaborated on throughout the remaining chapters, it is important to introduce it here. Basically, through years of intensive experience, HR professionals have realized that, to be effective, it is necessary to know what the business is, what the business needs from people, and then establish human resource management policies and practices that are consistent with the needs of the business and each other.

Human resource policy and practices that are consistent with each other and that are coordinated with each other communicate the same message to employees. A performance appraisal system that evaluates employees on the basis of the attainment of long-term goals and a compensation system that rewards employees on the basis of long-term goal attainment send the same message to the employees. On the other hand, a human resource policy that describes employees as the most valuable resource and a practice that results in constant layoffs and little training send conflicting messages to the employees.

Consistency across all human resource policies and practices results in consistency and clarity in what is expected, what is rewarded, and what is important. Consistency and clarity result in effective use of human resources and organizational effectiveness. HR departments achieve consistency and clarity when they and their leaders approach HR in a very systematic and integrated way.

PLAN OF THIS BOOK

This books intends to fulfill several specific purposes as we maintain several themes. Chapters are organized around six personnel and human resource management activities. Basically, these activities begin with the organization and its environment. To find out the types of people we want to attract, retain, motivate, and retrain, it is logical to first look at the demands and needs of the organization and environment. After this we can start planning for the organization's human resource needs. Next we will describe the jobs we have, and then we will recruit and select the people we need by matching their qualifications with the demands of the job. Once we have hired, we will be concerned with appraising employee performance, with providing feedback to improve performance, if necessary, and with providing compensation to reward their contributions and encourage even higher levels of output. To enable employees to perform, we will provide training. As technology and jobs change, we will provide retraining. As the competitive conditions in the world change, we will seek to improve the ability of the organization to compete. Throughout these activities, we will respect the rights of the employees and will provide accommodations for their safety and health. If individuals wish to belong to a union or association, we will bargain and negotiate with their representatives.

The book will follow this logical progression in personnel and human resource management as we present and describe HR activities:

- Scanning, analyzing, and planning for human resource needs
- Staffing the organization's personnel needs
- Appraising employee performance
- Compensating employee performance
- Improving employees and the work environment
- Establishing and maintaining effective work relationships

There are many terms and expressions in HR. Some get used consistently, but others take on the meaning of whomever is using them. Recognizing and appreciating the value and reality of this diversity, we constructed a short glossary of the terms used frequently in this book (exhibit 1.7).

SUMMARY

This chapter describes the six activities of human resource management, defines what is personnel and human resource management, and examines its purposes. Because of the increasing complexity of human resource management, nearly all organizations have established a human resource department. Not all of these departments, however, perform all the activities discussed in this chapter. A department's activities—and the way it performs them—depend greatly on the roles the department plays in the organization. Organizations that are most concerned with human resource management allow their departments to perform the roles to link HR to the business, provider, auditor, innovator, and adapter. When this occurs, the departments are able to link their human resource activi-

Exhibit 1.7
What is PHRM?

A Glossary of Terms Used in this Book

Recognizing some variations within and across organizations in the use and definition of words in personnel and human resource management (PHRM), this book utilizes the following definitions:

HR activities scanning, analyzing, and planning; staffing; appraising; compensating; improving; and establishing and maintaining effective work relationships

HR department/leader/staff a formal unit and individual(s) designated to be in charge of the HR function and, therefore, responsible and accountable for the organization's human resource management (HR) activities

HR function a set of activities, practices, roles, responsibilities, and structures in an organization concerned with human resource management that may be carried out by any and all employees (managers and nonmanagers)

HR issues/concerns those topics, areas, and thoughts related to human resource management

HR philosophy a general statement about the value of employees to the firm that in turn shapes the content of HR policies

HR policies general guidelines, based on the HR philosophy, that are referred to in the development of the HR practices and activities to be used by the firm

HR practices those specific actions used in attracting, motivating, retraining, and retraining employees within the general HR activities of planning, staffing, appraising, compensating, training and development, and establishing and maintaining effective work relationships

Human resources the people being attracted, motivated, retained, or retrained by an organization

Personnel and human resource management the use of several activities to ensure that human resources are managed effectively for the benefit of the individual, society, and the organization

ties to the business and demonstrate their value to their organizations by showing how their human resource activities influence productivity, quality of work life, competitive advantage, flexibility, and legal compliance—all specific goals associated with the organization's bottom-line criteria.

The remainder of this book describes each of the six broad human resource management activities, incorporating the latest issues, concerns, and illustrations. Although the following chapters treat the human resource activities separately, in reality, their effectiveness is enhanced when the activities are coordinated—and they are even more effective when coordinated with the needs of the business. When HR departments begin to coordinate their human resource activities with the business, they start to identify and select specific practices. They also begin to involve line managers and employees in the formulation and implementation of the practices.

For each of the human resource activities described above, departments can choose from many human resource practices. For example, in performance-based pay, human resource departments may choose to use a merit-pay plan or profit-sharing plan. In addition to being familiar with all the human resource practices, personnel and human resource departments need to know which ones to use depending upon the needs of the business. Thus, personnel and human resource departments need to be staffed with individuals who are aware of all the human resource activities and practices and have a knowledge and appreciation of the business. They should also be knowledgeable about the goals and roles of human resource management in organizations. When done well, personnel and human resource management can attain the specific and general human resource goals and the bottom-line indicators of company performance shown in exhibit 1.8.

We will present the first major human resource activity in section 2, "Scanning and Analyzing." First we will describe the internal and external environments in which organizations operate. Human resource management depart-

Exhibit 1.8
Objectives, Purposes, and Relationships of PHRM Activities

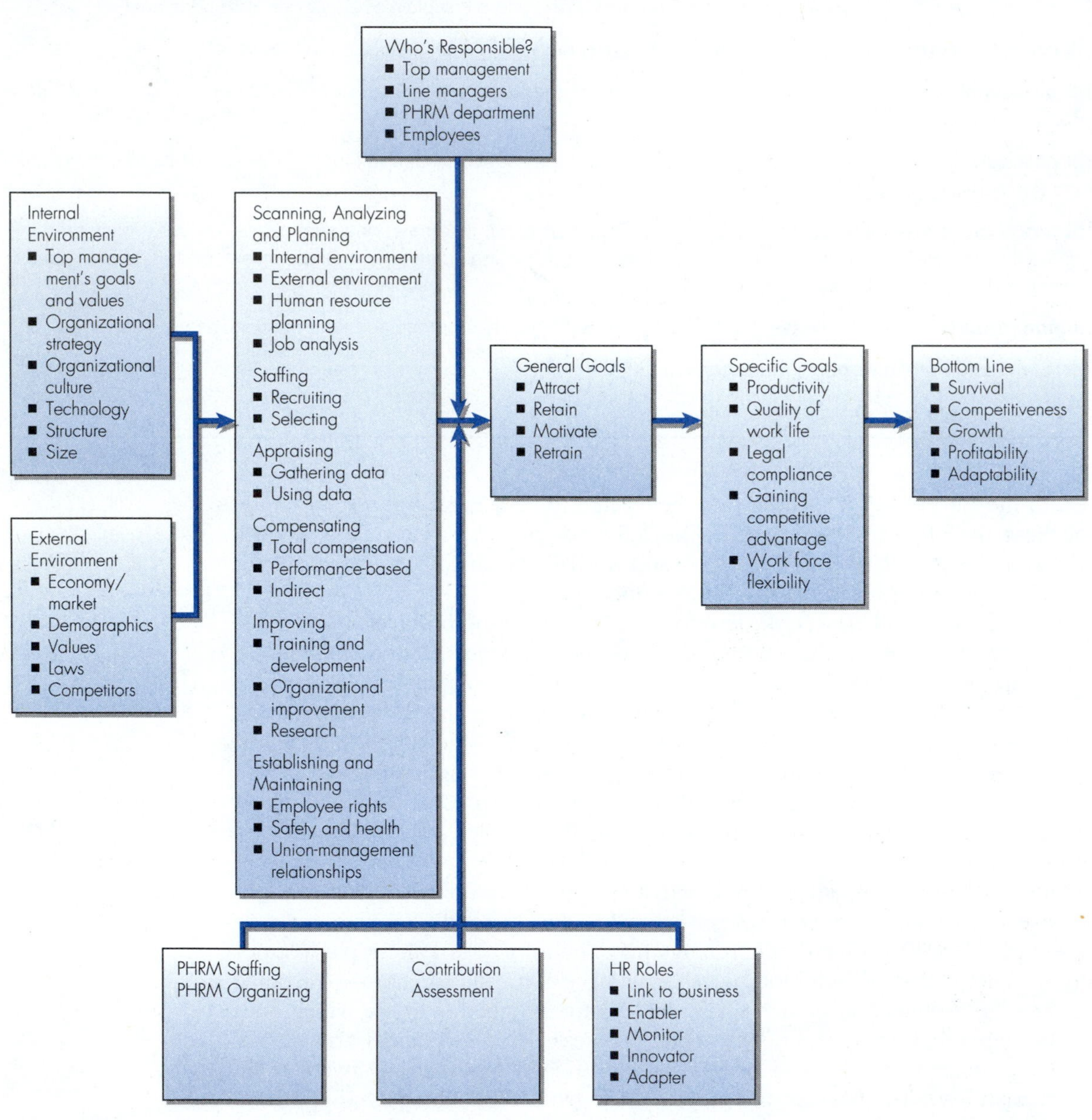

ments must constantly scan and analyze data in these environments, because using these data enables departments to more effectively carry out the other human resource activities and to more closely relate those activities to the needs of the business.

WHERE WE ARE TODAY

1. Personnel and human resource management is becoming more important as organizations seek to become more competitive, adaptable, and profitable.
2. The importance of human resource management is increasing in this era of highly competitive environments because it can increase productivity, improve the quality of work life, assist organizations in complying with legal regulations, help gain competitive advantage, and enhance worker flexibility.
3. Human resource management performs many specific activities as it basically seeks to attract, retain, motivate, and retrain employees.
4. Increasingly, human resource management seeks to perform these activities consistent with the needs of the business.
5. As human resource management gets more linked with the needs of the business, line managers as well as human resource managers are getting more involved with human resource management. Of course, this is consistent with the main job the managers have always had: getting things done through and with people. Today, however, it means more than it ever has.
6. As human resource management has become more important in organizations, it has begun to play more roles. In particular it is playing the roles of linking HR with the business, being an enabler to line managers, monitoring how others manage employees, being an innovator of human resource practices, and being an agent to help the organization and its employees adapt to changing conditions.
7. The human resource function can be organized in many ways. Basically, however, it gets down to the question, "How do we get the human resource activities as close to the action as possible?" Thus, questions of "Should we centralize or should we decentralize?" get answered by first asking "What is going on in the business?"
8. While everyone is responsible for human resource management, the human resource leader and staff (both generalists and specialists) are more effective if they play an increasing number of roles and master an increasing number of competencies. Human resource professionals are effective because of their training and experience in these roles and competencies.
9. Professionals in human resource management not only have an identifiable set of competencies and roles, they also have an identifiable professional code of ethics. These are more important than ever as firms face more ethical issues than ever.
10. Careers in personnel and human resource management are becoming more important in organizations in highly competitive environments. As such, they are becoming routes to the top executive jobs in organizations and are valued top jobs in themselves. Not surprisingly, salaries for personnel and human resource management jobs have gone up substantially over the past decade.

DISCUSSION QUESTIONS

1. What is the bottom line of an organization, and how can the personnel and human resource department have a significant impact on the organization's bottom line?
2. What evidence is there to verify the importance of managing human resources in organizations?
3. Why have the top managers of organizations attributed greater importance to human resource management?
4. What roles can the personnel and human resource department play in an organization?
5. How can personnel and human resource managers become proactive in demonstrating their effectiveness?
6. What are some concrete ways in which the human resource department can demonstrate its effectiveness to the organization?
7. What are some key issues related to the organization of an effective human resource department?
8. Why are some human resource activities centralized while others are decentralized?
9. What is the difference between human resource generalists and human resource specialists?
10. Describe the knowledge, skills, and abilities necessary for effective leadership in HR.

APPLIED PROJECTS

1. Arrange appointments and visit local companies (even the college) to interview a line manager and the human resource manager about their views of the human resource department in the organization. It is best if these interviews are done separately. The human resource manager can probably arrange the interview with a line manager for the student. Interview your working parents to solicit their opinions of human resource management and of the role it plays in the companies in which the parents work.
2. Look at the most recent issues (perhaps the last five issues) of *Fortune, Business Week, The Wall Street Journal, Personnel Journal,* and any other useful journals or papers. Present to class one story on or related to managing human resources. This project is aimed at making students aware of what the real world says about personnel (and other business topics) and of what sources students should be reading. These sources can also be useful in working on term papers, etc.

CASE STUDY

Bringing the Human Resource Department to the Business

Mike Mitchell left the Bank of Montreal to become vice president of human resources at the North American branch of the Swiss Bank Corporation (SBC) in the autumn of 1986. It was a move up for him in terms of status, responsibility, monetary compensation, and challenge. Of these, it was the challenge that was most intriguing to Mitchell. In his mid-thirties, he saw this as a perfect time to take a risk in his career. He realized that if he succeeded he would establish a prototype of "customerization" that could be marketed to other firms. In addition, success could lead to further career opportunities (and challenges). While he had a general idea of what he wanted to do and had gotten verbal support from his superiors, the senior vice president of human resources, and the president of SBC's North American branch, the details of exactly what he was going to do and how he was going to do it remained to unfold.

In 1985 the parent company of SBC (a $110-billion universal bank) headquartered in Basel, Switzerland, decided it needed a clearer statement of its intentions in order to focus its energies and resources in light of the growing international competition. Accordingly, it crafted a vision statement to the effect that the bank was going to better serve its customers with high quality products that served their needs rather than just those of the institution. While the North American operation was relatively autonomous, it was still expected to embrace this vision. The details of its implementation, however, were in local hands. For the human resources side, the hands became those of Mitchell.

While Mitchell had spent some time in human resources at the Bank of Montreal in New York, the bulk of his work experience was as an entrepreneur in Montreal, Canada. It was this experience that most influenced his thinking. Thus, when he came to the SBC, his self-image was a businessperson who happened to be working in human resources. In part because of this image, his stay at the Bank of Montreal was brief: Human resources was still a bit too conservative for his style. Too many of his ideas "just couldn't be done." In interviewing with the top managers at SBC, however, they warned him of the same general environment. Thus, he knew he would have to go slow to change nearly 1,000 employees, including his own department of ten employees, but he really didn't know what this meant. He knew, however, that he wanted to "customerize" the HR department at SBC.

Case Questions:

1. Who are Mitchell's customers? What questions will he need to ask them?
2. Detail Mitchell's game plan for success. Include items such as time frame, training needs, who will have to change, in what order will changes be made, key people (advocates) to have on his side, cost/benefit analyses, implications for line managers, and implications for his own staff and department structure.
3. What are the key factors in Mitchell's success?
4. Would you want this job? Why or why not?

NOTES

1. P. Stuart, "HR and Operations Work Together at Texas Instruments," *Personnel Journal* (April 1992): p. 64.
2. D. Filipowski, "How Federal Express Makes Your Package Its Most Important," *Personnel Journal* (Feb. 1992): 40–46; D. Filipowski, "Federal Express: A Commitment to Training has Helped Federal Express Keep Profits and Customer Satisfaction High," *Personnel Journal* (Jan. 1992): 52.
3. R. S. Schuler, ed. *Managing Human Resources in the Information Age,* Vol. 6 (Washington, D. C.: SHRM/BNA, 1991).
4. R. S. Schuler and I. C. MacMillan, "Gaining a Competitive Advantage Through Human Resource Management Practices," *Human Resource Management* (Fall 1984): 241–256.
5. R. S. Schuler and J. W. Walker, "Human Resources Strategy: Focusing on Issues and Action," *Organizational Dynamics* (Summer 1990): 5–19; C. A. Lengnick-Hall and M. L. Lengnick-Hall, *Interactive Human Resource Management and Strategic Planning* (New York: Quorum Books, 1990); R. S. Schuler, "Repositioning the Human Resource Function: Transformation or Demise?" *Academy of Management Executive,* 4 (1990): 49–60.
6. "Improve Quality," *Business Week* (8 June 1987): 158. See also O. Port, "Quality," *Business Week* (8 June 1987): 131–143; A. Bernstein, "Can America Compete?" *Business Week* (20 April 1987): 45–52. It appears that firms are competing on all fronts, i.e., quality, cost, and innovation. Increasingly, speed is becoming important as well. See M. E. Porter, *Competitive Strategy* (New York: Free Press, 1985); M. E. Porter, *Competitive Advantage* (New York: Free Press, 1985); J. Main, "The Winning Corporation," *Fortune* (26 September 1988): 50–56; B. Dumaine, "How Managers Can Succeed through Speed," *Fortune* (13 Feb. 1989): 54–59.
7. "Improve Quality," 158.
8. E. K. Burton, "Productivity: A Plan for Personnel," *Personnel Administrator* (Sept. 1981): 85–92; J. D. Hodgson, "An Impertinent Suggestion for Personnel," *Personnel Administrator* (Sept. 1981): 85–92; Y. K. Shety, "Improving Productivity: Management's Role in Declining Productivity: An Employee View," *Personnel Administrator* (Aug. 1981): 37–48; R. A. Katzell and R. A. Guzzo, "Psychological Approaches to Productivity Improvements," *American Psychologist* (April 1983): 468–472.

9. M. G. Miner, "Legal Concerns Facing Human Resource Managers: An Overview," in *Readings in Personnel and Human Resource Management,* 3d ed., ed. R. S. Schuler, S. A. Youngblood, and V. L. Huber (St. Paul: West Publishing, 1988).
10. M. G. Miner, *Reinventing the CEO* (Korn/Ferry International and Columbia University, 1989), 1.
11. Schuler and MacMillan, "Gaining Competitive Advantage Through Human Resource Management Practices."
12. Schuler and MacMillan.
13. N. Alster, "What Flexible Workers Can Do," *Fortune* (13 Feb. 1989): 62–66.
14. R. S. Schuler, "Strategic Human Resource Management: Linking the People with the Strategic Needs of the Business," *Organizational Dynamics,* Summer 1992.
15. S. Lawrence, "Voice of HR Experience," *Personnel Journal* (April 1989): 64.
16. Lawrence.
17. S. E. Jackson, R. S. Schuler, and J. C. Rivero, "Organizational Characteristics as Predictors of Personnel Practices," *Personnel Psychology,* 43 (1989) 727–86; A. K. Gupta and V. Govindarajan, "Build, Hold, Harvest: Converting Strategic Intentions into Reality," *Journal of Business Strategy* 4 (1984): 34–47; A. K. Gupta and V. Govindarajan, "Business Unit Strategy, Managerial Characteristics, and Business Unit Effectiveness as Strategy Implementation," *Academy of Management Journal* 9 (1984): 25–41; T. A. Kochan, R. B. McKersie, and P. Cappelli, "Strategic Choice and Industrial Relations Theory," *Industrial Relations* 23 (1984): 16–39; T. A. Kochan and P. Cappelli, "The Transformation of the Industrial Relations/Human Resource Function," in *Internal Labor Markets,* ed. P. Osterman (Cambridge, Mass. MIT Press, 1983), 133–62; C. A. Lengnick-Hall and M. L. Lengnick-Hall, Strategic Human Resource Management: A Review of the Literature," *Academy of Management Review* (July 1988): 454–70; A. R. McGill, "Practical Considerations: A Case Study of General Motors," in *Strategic Human Resource Management,* ed. C. J. Fombrun, N. M. Tichy, and M. A. Devanna (New York: Wiley, 1984), 149–58; R. E. Miles and C. C. Snow, "Designing Strategic Human Resource Systems," *Organizational Dynamics* (Fall 1984): 36–52; R. E. Miles and C. C. Snow, "Fit, Failure, and the Hall of Fame," *California Management Review* 26 (1984): 10–28; D. Miller, "Configurations of Strategy and Structure: Towards a Synthesis," *Strategic Management Journal* 7 (1986): 233–49; T. Peters, *Thriving on Chaos* (New York: Alfred A. Knopf, 1987); R. S. Schuler, "Personnel and Human Resource Management Choices and Organizational Strategy,"*Human Resource Planning 10:* 1 (1987): 1–18; R. S. Schuler, "Personnel and Human Resource Management Choices and Organizational Strategy," in *Readings in Personnel,* 3d ed., 1987; R. S. Schuler and S. E. Jackson, "Linking Competitive Strategies with Human Resource Management Practices," *Academy of Management Executive* 1 (1987): 207–19; R. S. Schuler and S. E. Jackson, "Organizational Strategy and Organizational Level as Determinants of Human Resource Management Practices," *Human Resource Planning* 10: 3 (1987): 125–42; J. W. Slocum, W. L. Cron, R. W. Hansen, and S. Rawlings, "Business Strategy and the Management of Plateaued Employees," *Academy of Management Journal* 28 (1985): 133–54. For more discussion of the need for the practice of HR to become more strategic and bottom-line oriented, see M. Beer, B. Spector, P. R. Lawrence, D. Q. Mills, and R. E. Walton, *Managing Human Assets* (New York: Free Press, 1984); F. K. Foulkes, *Strategic Human Resource Management* (Englewood Cliffs, N.J. Prentice-Hall, 1986); M. Magnus, "Personnel Policies in Partnership with Profit," *Personnel Journal* (Sept. 1987): 102–8; E. H. Schien, *The Art of Managing Human Resources* (New York: Oxford University Press, 1987); and D. A. Stace, "The Value-Added Organization: Trends in Human Resource Management," *Human Resource Management Australia* (Nov. 1987): 52–63.
18. "Customers for Keeps: Training Strategies," *Bulletin to Management* (31 March 1988): 8. See also R. L. Desatnik, *Managing to Keep the Customers* (San Francisco: Jossey-Bass, 1987).
19. P. Hawken, "The Employee as Customer," *Inc.* (Nov. 1987): 21–22; A. Halcrow, "Operation Phoenix: The Business of Human Resources," *Personnel Journal* (Sept. 1987): 92–109; R. S. Schuler and S. E. Jackson, "Customerizing the HR Department," *Personnel Journal* (June 1988): 36–44; R. N. Bramson, "The Secret Weapon in the War for Customers," *HR Magazine* (Jan. 1991): 65–68.
20. J. G. Milkovich, L. D. Dyer, and T. A. Mahoney, "Human Resource Planning," in *Human Resource Management in the 1980s* (Washington, D. C.: Bureau of National Affairs, 1989).
21. S. E. Ferrer and Z. B. Leibowitz, *Using Computers in Human Resources* (San Francisco: Jossey–Bass, 1991).
22. M. E. Cashman and J. C. McElroy, "Evaluating the HR Function," *HR Magazine* (Jan. 1991): 70–73; M. Mercer, *Turning Your Human Resources Department into a Profit Center* (New York: American Management Association, 1989); B. R. Ellig, "Controlling HR Costs," *Personnel* (April 1990): 20–23; W. F. Cascio, *Costing Human Resources: The Financial Impact of Behavior in Organizations,* 3d ed. (Boston: PWS-Kent, 1991); D. Ulrich, "Assessing Human Resource Effectiveness: Stakeholder, Utility and Relationship Approaches," *Human Resource Planning* 12:4 (1989): 301–16; L. Dyer, *Human Resource Management: Evolving Roles and Responsibilities* (Washington, D. C.: BNA Books, 1988), 187–227; J. Fitz-Enz, *Human Values Management: The Value-Adding Human Resource Management Strategy for the 1990s* (San Francisco: Jossey-Bass, 1990); A. S. Tsui, "A Multiple-Constituency Model of Effectiveness: An Empirical Examination at the Human Resource Subunit Level," *Administrative Science Quarterly* 35 (1990): 458–83.
23. J. Walker, "Managing Human Resources in Flat, Lean and Flexible Organizations: Trends for the 1990s," *Human Resource Planning,* 11:2 (1988): 129.
24. J. Walker, "Human Resources Roles for the '90s," *Human Resource Planning,* 12 (1989): 55.
25. S. Carroll, "HRM Roles and Structures in the Information Age," in *HRM in the Information Age,* ed. R. S. Schuler (Washington, D. C.: SHRM/BNA, 1991).
26. E. E. Lawler, III, "Human Resources Management: Meet-

ing the Challenge," *Personnel* (Jan. 1988): 25. See also R. E. Walton and P. R. Lawrence, eds., *HRM Trends & Challenges* (Boston: Harvard Business School Press, 1985); W. H. Wagel and H. Z. Levine, "HR '90: Challenges and Opportunities," *Personnel* (June 1990): 18–21.

27. E. E. Lawler, III, "Roundtable Report," *HR Reporter* (Dec. 1988): 3–6.
28. J. Walker, "What's New in HR Development?" *Personnel* (July 1990): 41; W. Galenson, *New Trends in Employment Practices: An International Survey* (Westport, Conn: Greenwood Press, 1990); Douglas W. Bray and Associates, *Working with Organizations and Their People: A Guide to Human Resource Practice* (New York: The Guilford Press, 1991).
29. S. H. Applebaum, APD, "The Personnel Professional and Organization Development: Conflict and Synthesis," *Personnel Administrator* (July 1980): 57–61; F. R. Edney, "The Greening of the Profession," *Personnel Administrator* (July 1980): 27–30, 42; F. R. Edney, "Playing on the Team," *Personnel Journal* (Aug. 1981): 598–600; L. B. Prewitt, "The Emerging Field of Human Resources Management," *Personnel Administrator* (May 1982): 81–87.
30. F. H. Applebaum, APD, *1991 SHRM/CCH Survey* (26 June 1991); M. T. Brown, *Working Ethics: Strategies for Decision Making and Organizational Responsibility* (San Francisco: Jossey-Bass, 1990); L. L. Nash, *Good Intentions Aside: A Manager's Guide to Resolving Ethical Problems* (Boston, Mass.: Harvard Business School Press, 1990); L. Tone Hosmer, *The Ethics of Management* (Homewood, Ill.: Irwin, 1991).
31. D. Yoder and H. Heneman, Jr., *PAIR Jobs, Qualifications, and Careers, ASPA Handbook of Personnel and Industrial Relations* (Washington, D. C.: The Bureau of National Affairs, 1978), 18; W. M. Hoffman, R. Frederick, and E. W. Petry, Jr., eds., *The Ethics of Organizational Transformation: Mergers, Takeovers and Corporate Restructuring* (New York: Quorum Books, 1989).
32. W. W. Turnow, "The Codifications Project and Its Importance to Professionalism," *Personnel Administrator* (June 1984): 84–100; C. Haigley, "Professionalism in Personnel," *Personnel Administrator* (June 1984): 103–106. Also contact the Institute directly by calling the Society for Human Resource Management at 1-800-331-2772.
33. *Human Resource Compensation Survey* (Dearfield, Ill.: William M. Mercer, Inc., 1990); S. Langer, "What You Earn and Why," *Personnel Journal* (Jan. 1991): 25–27.
34. Bureau of National Affairs, SHRM-BNA Survey No. 57; "Human Resource Activities, Budgets, and Staff: 1991–92," *Bulletin to Management* (25 June 1992).
35. Ibid. See also J. W. Walker, "How Large Should the HR Staff Be?" *Personnel* (Oct. 1988): 36–42.

END OF SECTION CASE STUDY

A Broader View Seizes More Opportunities

Don English, corporate vice president in charge of human resources, is now finally able to take a pause from the continuous stream of fire fighting activity he has been engaged in since he came to Bancroft ten years ago! Like many of his colleagues in other firms, Don's knowledge of human resource management came as much from doing it as anything else.

His constant fire fighting activity tended to keep him pretty narrowly focused. Because of his workload, he rarely read personnel journals or attended professional conferences. However, recently, things have been easing up. He has been able to recruit and train almost all the division managers in charge of human resources. Now they can do most of the fire fighting—at least that's what Don is planning on—and he has been doing more reading then ever before. Of course, Don has not been totally out of touch with the rest of the world or the growing importance of human resource management planning. When he started filling the slots for division personnel managers he made sure that it was a learning experience for him. Don always required job candidates to prepare a one-hour talk on the state of research and practice in different areas of personnel (e.g., selection, appraisal, compensation and training). He would even invite MBA candidates who had no course work in personnel and ask them to relate their field of interest to human resource management.

Don is planning to become the chief executive officer of Bancroft or some other firm of similar or larger size within the next five to seven years. He thinks he can achieve this if he remains in human resources and does an outstanding job. He will have to be outstanding by all standards, both internal and external to the firm. From his interviews during the past three years, Don knows that it is imperative to move human resources in a strategic direction while at the same time doing the best possible job with the "nuts and bolts" activities.

During a moment of reflection, Don begins to scratch some notes on his large white desk pad. In the middle is Bancroft. To its left are its suppliers and to its right are its customers. In his head are all the human resource practices with which he is so familiar. He has a hunch that there must be a way to use the firm's expertise in performance appraisal and training to help Bancroft be more effective. Bancroft has been learning tremendously from its five-year drive to improve quality; but, during the past year, quality gains have slowed. Bancroft must continue to improve its quality, but large internal quality gains are becoming more and more difficult as Bancroft climbs the learning curve. Don wonders: How can he help Bancroft experience the excitement of seeing large gains in quality improvement again? Don circles the list of suppliers and begins to formulate a plan that will improve his chances of becoming CEO. He now seeks your advice in exactly what to do and how to go about doing it.

Case Questions

1. Is it out of place for Don to visit Bancroft's suppliers?
2. What can Don do with his suppliers to help gain competitive advantage?
3. How can he go about doing this?
4. Is HR a very realistic path to the job of CEO?

SECTION 2

Scanning and Analyzing

Increasingly, the success in managing organizations and managing human resources depends upon knowing about and being able to anticipate what is happening in the environment of human resource management. How could you possibly plan your career without knowing the types of jobs that will be or may be available in the future or what skills and abilities they will require? To do a great job with your career planning, you would want to gather and analyze more information than just job availability. Similarly, organizations need to gather and analyze a great deal of data from the environment in order to most effectively plan how to deal with critical human resource issues in the environment.

Gathering and analyzing information from several sources is necessary for organizational survival and success. In the external environment organizations look at the events and trends in domestic and international competition, the sizes of and projections for the global and domestic population and work force, economic and organizational trends, and the legal environment. Organizations must also scan, analyze, and understand aspects of the organization itself (the internal environment) that also have a big impact on human resource management. The internal environment includes such things as the organization's strategy, culture, technology, size, and the goals and values of top management.

As we will see in the next two chapters, both environments have tremendous implications for human resource management. Fortunately, by having the information about these environments, human resource professionals can develop human resource plans to deal with them.

Planning for human resource needs involves two major activities: (1) planning and forecasting the organization's short- and long-term human resource requirements, and (2) analyzing the jobs in the organization to determine their duties and purposes and the skills, knowledge, and abilities that are needed. These two activities are essential in effectively performing many other personnel and human resource management activities. For example, they help indicate the organization's present and future needs regarding numbers and types of employees. They also help to determine how the employees will be obtained (e.g., from outside recruiting or by internal transfers and promotions) and what training needs the organization will have. These two activities can be viewed as the major factors influencing the staffing and development functions of the entire organization.

Recognizing this importance, today many of the largest corporations are relating human resource planning to corporate goals or strategies. They have come to recognize the importance of people to an organization's survival. As Walter Wriston, former Citicorp chief executive officer, commented, "I believe the only game in town is the personnel game.... My theory is if you have the right person in the right place, you don't have to do anything else. If you have the wrong person in the job, there's no management system known that can save you." In this respect, then, scanning, analyzing, and planning activities are essential if companies are to do a great job in linking human resource management with the business.

Thus, in the next three chapters of this section, we will consider the processes of scanning and analyzing by describing the external and internal environments most organizations face in their attempts to manage human resources. We will see how organizations can use this information systematically in their activities to develop human resource plans and programs to ensure that they are able to get all the people needed, at the right place and at the right time. (To complement this discussion and bring home the importance of planning to you, a career planning guide is included in chapter 4 for your immediate use.)

CHAPTER 2

Characteristics of the External and Internal Environment

Who would fight the motherhood of innovation, of empowering people to be creative? I mean, it's terrific.

—David Johnson, CEO, Campbell Soup Co.[1]

SCANNING AND ANALYZING THE ENVIRONMENT

PURPOSES AND IMPORTANCE OF SCANNING AND ANALYZING THE ENVIRONMENT

CHARACTERISTICS OF THE EXTERNAL ENVIRONMENT

Domestic and International Competition

PHRM in the News: Empowerment: Fact or Fiction?

Work Force Characteristics

Demographic Characteristics

Economic and Organizational Trends

Focus on Research: The Environment is Transforming the Human Resource Department

PHRM in the News: Flat, Lean, Flexible Organization

CHARACTERISTICS OF THE INTERNAL ENVIRONMENT

Top Management's Goals and Values

Organizational Strategy

Organizational Culture

Technology

Organizational Structure

Organizational Size

FOCUS ISSUES FOR SCANNING AND ANALYZING

Quality Enhancement

Cost Reduction

Innovation

Responsiveness to the Environment

INTERNATIONAL COMPARISONS

Worldwide Population and Educational Attainment

Mexico

Case Study: Managing Work Force Diversity: People-Related Business Issues at the Barden Corporation

For firms in the United States, small as well as large, the world market is becoming increasingly more important. Just 15 years ago exports accounted for only 15 percent of U.S. Gross Domestic Product (GDP). Today exports account for 30 percent. Some U.S. firms such as General Motors, Ford, IBM, Quaker Oats, Coca-Cola, and Dow obtain most of their earnings in the global marketplace. Of the top ten pharmaceutical companies in the world, a majority are based in America. An examination of the top 25 industrial sectors in the world reveals the U.S. has the largest firms in half of them.[2] *In the service sector alone, U.S. firms (with 150) dominate the list of the top 500 largest in the world. This is particularly important given that the worldwide service economy accounts for more than 60 percent of gross domestic product and for most of the newly created jobs in industrial economies. Clearly, then, the global environment is important to U.S. firms and is expected to become even more important in this decade.*

However, while the global marketplace is important to U.S. firms, there has been some slippage in U.S. dominance over the past decade. For example, the share of the U.S. automobile market held by the three U.S. automakers dropped from 71 percent to 62 percent. American manufacturers accounted for 94 percent of the computers sold in the U.S. in 1980 and for only 66 percent ten years later. Their share of the worldwide semiconductor market slipped from 57 percent to 36 percent during that same time. Even in the service sector, U.S. firms lead in only one category—retailing. Japan, by contrast, is tops in three: diversified services, insurance, and banking. In banking alone, Japan has a majority of the largest 50 banks in the world. When the 1980s began the two largest banks were U.S.; today only three in the top 50 are U.S., while all the top five are Japanese.

There is some evidence, however, that U.S. firms are staged for a resurgence. Firms are more productive because of the downsizing and restructuring that occurred as a result of events in the 1980s. Data on export growth indicate American firms are also making greater inroads into overseas markets. They are also establishing more productive capacity abroad and entering into more alliances than ever. For example, from a sprawling network of mostly new factories built in Mexico, the U.S. automakers are specializing in building small cars for Mexico's rapidly expanding economy.[3]

To some observers, however, much of this resurgence and revival in competitive position has been bought with borrowed funds—by selling off assets, laying off employees, and reducing wages relative to the country's major competitors. To the extent these strategies have peaked in use, the 1990s could be the decade of opportunity for firms **to continue** *to prevail in the global marketplace by more effectively managing their human resources. As Duerr has noted,*

> *... [V]irtually any type of international problem, in the final analysis, is either created by people or must be solved by people. Hence, having the right people in the right place at the right time emerges as the key to a company's international growth. If we are successful in solving that problem, I am confident we can cope with all others.*[4]

Professor Robert Reich of Harvard echoes these thoughts when he says global businesses choose to locate their factories, labs, and highest value-added work where there is a qualified supply of human resources. Increasingly, jobs go where the skills are; finished goods and even services can be produced almost anywhere and shipped to customers.[5] *Thus, at both the company level and societal level, as well as at the industrial level, the globalization of business makes the role of human resources more important than ever.*

SCANNING AND ANALYZING THE ENVIRONMENT

Almost all firms, directly and indirectly, feel the impact of the worldwide environment. This is true for large firms as well as small firms, for firms with operations around the world (what we call **multinational corporations** or **MNCs**) or with operations only in the U.S. Companies also confront issues and challenges because of the domestic environment.

Successful firms are discovering it is more important than ever to continuously be aware of the environment because it is changing so rapidly and unpredictably:

> Virtually all facets of organizational life—social, demographic, technical, legal/regulatory, and economic—are shifting at an unprecedented and accelerating rate. Anticipating and understanding these changes well enough to succeed in managing both their short-term and long-term implications is a major challenge. By meeting this challenge organizations are in a better position to avoid or minimize problems and to capitalize on opportunities.[6]

One major way organizations keep track of these changes is through environmental scanning. For us, **environmental scanning** is studying and understanding events and conditions in the environment that have an impact on how we manage human resources.

Environmental scanning has several components or steps. These steps include selecting forecasting techniques, forecasting future conditions, identifying and prioritizing major issues that affect human resource management, developing plans that anticipate those issues, and then preparing the organization for successfully dealing with them. The Honeywell Corporation in Minneapolis regularly monitors the major aspects of the external environment for their relevance to and implications for human resource management and the success of the firm. These aspects include:

- Domestic and international competition
- Work force characteristics
- Demographic characteristics
- Economic and organizational trends
- Laws, executive orders, court decisions, and government agencies

There are many other aspects of the external environment, but these have major implications for human resource management and organizational changes.

Aspects of the internal environment also have major implications for human resource management. These include the organization's strategy, structure, culture, technology and size, and top management's goals and values.

This chapter describes how these major aspects of the internal and external environments influence the effective management of human resources. Because of the significance and importance of the legal environment, the entire next chapter is devoted to that topic.

A multitude of forces and events help shape an organization's human resource management activities and practices. Consequently, these environments must be continuously scanned to effectively manage human resources.

PURPOSES AND IMPORTANCE OF SCANNING AND ANALYZING THE ENVIRONMENT

Personnel and human resource activities do not exist in a vacuum, as shown in exhibit 1.8. HR professionals can increase their effectiveness in managing human resources by scanning several aspects of the environment, not just international economic and population data. By doing this they can link the managing of human resources to the needs of the business and the demands of the external environment. While input from the scanning is useful for all HR activities, it is particularly critical for human resource planning where HR programs and initiatives take shape.

Without scanning and analyzing these environments, organizations and HR professionals are likely to be blindsided by events that will imperil their long-run success. Meaningful and timely responses to major events take time to develop and implement. Scanning and analyzing can give an organization the time it needs. Even in the short run, though, organizations must know about the environment in which they do business; for example, substantial fines and penalties are likely to be levied on firms violating one or several of the numerous employment laws.

Before continuing, please take a moment to indicate on exhibit 2.1 your evaluation of what aspects of the environment are likely to have the greatest impact on human resource management. Then describe the implications of your three highest ranked items in the year 2000+ for organizations.

CHARACTERISTICS OF THE EXTERNAL ENVIRONMENT

While many characteristics of the external environment have an impact on a firm's efforts to manage its human resources effectively, we will now consider

- Domestic and international competition
- Work force characteristics
- Demographic characteristics
- Economic and organizational trends

We will describe these characteristics and discuss their key impacts on personnel and human resource management.

Domestic and International Competition

Briefly, this synopsis shows how global is the world in which we live.

> Natural gas owned by Indonesia's oil agency, Pertamina, flows out of a well discovered by Royal Dutch Shell into a liquification plant designed by French engineers and

Exhibit 2.1
Human Resource Implications of Changes in the Environment

Many observers have predicted significant changes in the work and business environment for the twenty-first century. Some of these changes are listed below. Please choose and rank the *five* changes which you currently think have the most impact on HR management, and the *five* which you think will have the most impact in the future. For indicating your rankings, "1" indicates the highest impact, "2" indicates the next highest impact, etc.

Today	Environment	2000+
______	a. Increased national/international competition	______
______	b. Increased governmental regulation	______
______	c. Globalization of corporate business structure	______
______	d. Growth in non-traditional business structure (e.g., business alliances, joint ventures)	______
______	e. Globalization of the economy/breakdown of trade barriers	______
______	f. Increased energy costs	______
______	g. Increased reliance on automation/technology to produce goods and services	______
______	h. More sophisticated information/communication technology	______
______	i. Changing attitudes of society toward business	______
______	j. Heightened concern about pollution and natural resources	______
______	k. Heightened focus on total quality/customer satisfaction	______
______	l. Changing employee values, goals, and expectations (e.g., less loyalty to current employer)	______
______	m. Fewer entrants into the work force	______
______	n. Inadequate skills of entrants into the work force	______
______	o. Crossborder application of employee rights	______
______	p. Changing composition of the work force with respect to gender, age, and/or ethnicity	______
______	q. Greater concerns about the confidentiality of personal information	______

SOURCE: Adapted from *Priorities for Competitive Advantage: A Worldwide Human Resource Study* (IBM/Towers Perrin, 1992).

> built by a Korean construction company. The liquified gas is loaded onto U.S. flag tankers, built in U.S. yards after a Norwegian design. The ships shuttle to Japan and deliver the liquid gas to a Japanese public utility, which uses it to provide electricity that powers an electronics factory making television sets that are shipped aboard a Hong Kong–owned container ship to California for sale to American farmers in Louisiana who grow rice that is sold to Indonesia and shipped there aboard Greek bulk carriers. All of the various facilities, ships, products, and services involved in the complex series of events are financed by U.S., European, and Japanese commercial banks, working in some cases with international and local government agencies. These facilities, ships, products, and services are insured and reinsured by U.S., European, and Japanese insurance companies. Investors in these facilities, ships, products, and services are located throughout the world. This illustration is not only factual, it is typical of transactions that take place over and over again daily throughout the globe.[7]

Given this reality today for most businesses around the world, "The most important characteristic of today's business environment—and therefore the yardstick against which managerial techniques must be measured—is the new competition."[8] The new competition comes from abroad and from within the U.S. Imports of shoes, textiles, and electronics represent an ever-increasing share of the U.S. market. Fewer than ten years ago, U.S. companies dominated the office copier business in the U.S. Today their share is approximately 50 percent. All of this is occurring because of low-priced products or inventive marketing techniques, or both. In analyzing U.S. performance between 1970 and 1992, one finds that the U.S. share of markets in several other industries and the value of the dollar declined dramatically, as described in the opening paragraphs of this chapter.

Wage disparities and a fluctuating value of the dollar make it challenging for the U.S. to compete in markets requiring a great deal of labor. They also make it harder for U.S. companies to maintain employees abroad (expatriates). The successes of large U.S. multinationals such as Ford, IBM, and Dow, however, show it is possible, but that it does take a lot of hard work and a global perspective. For many firms, developing a global perspective will no longer be an option. Consequently, global organizational forms and structures will be a necessity and having the work force to staff it will be mandatory. Human resource managers can become significant players in the success of U.S. firms by aiding their organization's transition into the arena of worldwide competition. Knowledge of human resource management practices worldwide and with MNCs can help in this role.[9]

Employee performance. Increased levels of domestic and international competition are making it more difficult and yet more necessary for organizations to survive, grow, and be profitable. Human resource managers seek ways to contribute to organizational effectiveness. Improving employee performance is one way. Measuring employee performance, and seeking and ameliorating the reasons for any performance deficiencies help improve employee performance. This is the essence of gathering and using performance appraisal data, so the entire performance appraisal system takes on greater importance in organizations. This importance will continue in organizations as long as competition remains such a significant part of the external environment.

Employee empowerment. Intense levels of domestic and international competition are forcing organizations to be more productive. More effective management of human resources is seen as a way to help organizations improve their productivity. The nature of work force demographics forces many HR efforts to involve some form of employee involvement or participation. This is consistent with the preference of many individuals for a greater say in workplace decisions.

Greater involvement in workplace decisions is a growing trend. Organizations that seek to improve the quality of their products and services get their employees involved. Many **empower** employees, or give them the freedom and responsibility to make job-related decisions. They recognize employee empowerment as one way to improve quality. Many firms, such as Corning Glass and Ford, have found that improving quality is often the best way to reduce costs and improve profitability.

Is the movement toward empowerment here to stay? That is the topic of the PHRM in the News: "Empowerment: Fact or Fiction?" feature.

PHRM IN THE NEWS

Empowerment: Fact or Fiction?

As companies downsize and eliminate layers of management, more employers are setting up employee empowerment programs to help their businesses stay competitive. As with other employee involvement (EI) programs, empowerment promises improved quality, productivity, employee morale and motivation. Some employers, however, are beginning to wonder if empowerment programs really deliver what they promise.

In theory, empowered organizations give employees the skills and authority they need to make decisions that affect their jobs, decisions concerning quality and production procedures. The rationale: Employees can spot problems better than their upper-level managers. Unlike other EI techniques, such as participative management and employee suggestion systems, which concentrate on soliciting employee advice and feedback, empowerment teaches employees to initiate changes on their own.

"Empowerment means giving everyone—instead of just people with certain positions or certain job titles—the legitimate right to make judgments, form conclusions, reach decisions, and then act," noted Judith Bardwick, a management consultant and author of *Danger in the Comfort Zone* (AMACOM, 1991).

Although employee empowerment sounds more democratic than traditional autocratic management, Edward Lawler, a professor of management at the University of Southern California and an observer of EI techniques, said he sees the empowerment movement as something more than just a fight for employee independence. Lawler considers it a tool for survival in today's competitive marketplace.

"A lot of what has been argued in the past [about empowerment] came from a perspective of fairness and individual rights," Lawler said. "Today it's being argued more from the perspective of what makes an organization more effective."

But does empowerment make companies more competitive?

Officials at Ford Motor Company reportedly believe in empowerment. After watching profits and quality drop sharply in the late 1970s, management knew something had to be done. By using employee involvement and participative management programs, Ford not only listened and responded to employee problem-solving ideas, but management also encouraged employees to take the lead. As a result of these efforts, Ford experienced one of the most dramatic turnarounds of the past decade.

Some companies, however, need more convincing about empowerment's effectiveness. Many have started other EI programs with high expectations, only to watch those efforts flounder soon after they

Continued

Work Force Characteristics

Ongoing changes in the work force in the United States contribute to several human resource management concerns.

Work force educational attainment. After installing millions of dollars worth of computers in its Burlington, Vermont, factories, the IBM Corporation discovered that it had to teach high school algebra to thousands of workers before they could run the computers. David Kearns, Xerox's former chairman and CEO, has said

> … [T]he American workforce is running out of qualified people. If current demographic and economic trends continue, American business will have to hire a million new workers a year who can't read, write, or count. Teaching them how, and absorbing the lost productivity while they're learning, will cost the industry $25 billion a year for as long as it takes.[10]

start. A Carnegie-Mellon University study found that EI programs not only failed to help corporate efficiency, but may have hindered it. Large companies with EI programs in place were 46 percent less efficient than those without such programs, according to the study. Small companies were 25 percent less efficient. Therefore, companies have good reason to question what empowerment is all about.

"I think it's fair to say that there has been more talk than action [regarding empowerment]," Lawler said. "Efforts vary enormously, from some incredibly trivial things to some really significant changes. Much of what goes on, however, is in the trivial mode."

As with any new policy, however, companies cannot expect to institute a half-hearted empowerment program and hope that it will do the trick. Programs require a considerable amount of time and resources, and results will not appear overnight.

"A lot of companies haven't thought [empowerment] through enough to know that they might have to redesign not just a small part of their work space, but also their pay systems, their training systems and their overall work structures," Lawler said. "A lot of errors are being made during implementation."

In fact, many barriers to empowerment stem from top management, such as a short-term focus on profits, an entrenched style of management, a failure to position EI as a business strategy and a lack of clear objectives.

As a result, many employees doubt empowerment's effectiveness. After all, they wonder, why should an employee speak up if what he or she has to say won't make a difference or a manager resents the input? Studies have found that the lower an employee stands on the corporate ladder, the less likely it is that the employee believes in empowerment. Only 38 percent of hourly workers surveyed by the Hay Group said they felt that management encouraged their participation, and only 18 percent believed that their suggestions were put to use. On the other hand, about 60 percent of the top executives surveyed by the Wyatt Company and *Industry Week* believed that their companies' EI programs represented a fundamental shift of power and resources.

For the most part, however, businesspeople have agreed that empowerment is more than just a fad. Instead of turning their backs on unsuccessful empowerment programs, Lawler suggested that employers determine where empowerment works and where it doesn't within their company. Empowerment may not succeed in every department or in every company, but the concept has a lot of potential.

"Empowerment now is at center stage, and some practices may appear a bit faddish," Lawler said. "But I think you can see the beginning of a gradual evolution toward more democracy in the workplace."

SOURCE: K. Matthes, *HR Focus* (March 1992): 1, 6.

David Davis, chairman of Stanley Works, observes:

> … [T]he cost of incompetence in U.S. industry is higher than any of us realizes. You can't quantify it, but it shows up in missed opportunities, in bad decisions, and other ways. It's all around us.[11]

In addition to these numbers, approximately 25 percent of U.S. adults are functionally illiterate.[12] In Japan, less than 5 percent of the population is functionally illiterate.

Illiteracy is but a symptom of the larger problem afflicting the U.S. economy. The $150 billion yearly trade deficit and a foreign debt of half a trillion dollars reflect the inability of a large percentage of the American work force to compete effectively in an integrated world economy. "Much of the success of Japan stems from the fact that its blue collar workers can interpret advanced mathematics, read complex engineering blueprints, and perform sophisticated tasks on the factory floor far better than blue collar workers in the U.S.," says Merry I. White, professor of comparative sociology at Boston University and author of *The Japanese Education Challenge*.[13]

Train, train, train. As a consequence, firms

> … are energetically training and retraining their workforces. At the same time, more managers and executives are exposed to new and sometimes eccentric methods and styles of training, aimed at shaping their behavior toward more effective leadership and greater productivity. In the name of leaner, meaner, and more efficient management, corporate educators are forging ahead with no evidence beyond the promise that these emerging techniques produce long-term results.
>
> There is, however, a solid base for all the technical training and retraining that needs to be done in factories and offices. In the next five years, four out of five people in the industrial world will be doing jobs differently from the way they have been done in the last 50 years. Most people will have to learn new skills. By the year 2000, 75% of all employees will need to be retrained in new jobs or taught fresh skills for their old ones. Corporate trainers, in the interest of saving time, will explore alternative and faster methods of delivering new skills and learning, including interactive video, audiotapes, take-home videodiscs, computer-based instruction, and expert systems.[14]

Values. Stagnating productivity rates are occurring at the same time as the work ethic disappears. According to some commentators, however, the work ethic has not disappeared. People today are willing to work hard at "good" jobs, providing they have the freedom to influence the nature of their jobs and to pursue their own life-styles. People value work, but the type of work that interests them has changed. They want challenging jobs that provide them with freedom to make decisions. Increasingly, people may not seek or desire rapid promotions, especially when they involve geographic transfers, but they do seek influence and control.

A recent study compares the work values of persons more than forty years old with those less than forty years old.

- Members of the older generation, products of the World War II era, accept authority, while employees from the younger generation, who grew up during the Vietnam War, do not trust authority.
- While members of the older generation see work as a duty and a vehicle for financial support, those of the younger generation think work should be fun and a place to meet other young people.
- Employees who are over forty believe that experience is the necessary road to promotion and are willing to spend time in an "apprenticeship," with the expectation of reward for that effort. Younger employees, on the other hand, believe people should advance just as quickly as their competence permits.
- "Fairness" to the older generation means treating people with equality; for the younger generation, it means allowing people to be different.[15]

These values tend to reflect the concerns of the **baby boomers** (those born between 1946 and 1964) rather than their parents, the **traditionalists** (those born 1925–1945) who are still in the work force. The values of these parents and even some of the older baby boomers (remember, this group ranges in age from approximately 45 to 60) focus on job security, employment security, and income security. Because this older group tends to be less mobile, organizations need to be concerned with targeting training and retraining not just at the entry-level worker but at this older worker as well.[16]

As organizations begin to look at the values of their employees in the workplace, however, they realize the need to make another cut in the age categories. This is the cut of those individuals born between 1965 and 1975, the **baby busters.** According to a recent study, this group values recognition, praise, time with their managers, opportunity to learn new things, fun at work, unstructured, flexible time, and small, unexpected rewards for jobs well done. Increasingly, companies recognize that these values are different from the other groups and must be accommodated. For example, at Patagonia, the Ventura, California–based manufacturer of products for outdoor enthusiasts, a full 40 percent of 450 employees are in their twenties. Patagonia has nontraditional open offices, flexible work schedules, and flexible personal leave times for up to four months each year.

Increasingly, firms are also beginning to recognize that they need to pay more attention to the ways in which they manage employees when they have an age-heterogeneous work force. Not only do these employees have different values, they also have different perceptions of each other. Take a look at these perceptions in exhibit 2.2 and describe what you think are the implications.

A piece of the action. One value that seems to cut across employee age groups is the desire for ownership.

> The new buzzword in employee motivation is "ownership," which can mean either an equity share or just a worker's sense that [s]he counts. Says Harvard business school professor J. Richard Hackman: "If you want me to care, then I want to be treated like an owner and have some real voice in where we're going." The concept grows out of

Exhibit 2.2
How Employees Young and Old View Each Other

Traditionalists
(Born 1925–1945) See

Baby boomers as disrespectful, overly blunt, too "warm and fuzzy."
Younger workers as *very* young, impatient, unethical.

Baby Boomers
(Born 1946–1964) See

Traditionalists as caught in the by-the-book syndrome, overly cautious, conservative, inflexible.
Younger workers as selfish, manipulative, aloof.

Baby Busters
(Born 1965–1975) See

Traditionalists as old, outdated, rigid.
Baby boomers as workaholic, unrealistic, disgustingly "new age."

SOURCE: *Twentysomething: Managing & Motivating Today's New Work Force,* in C.M. Solomon, "Managing the Baby Busters," *Personnel Journal* (March 1992): 56. Used by permission.

> the "employee involvement" of the 1980s, which got off to a shaky start with quality circles that never amounted to much, then grew stronger as workers were brought into decision making.[17]

Some firms are responding.

> Ownership goes a step further by seeking to put employees in the shoes of entrepreneurs. Xerox, 3M, and Honeywell help finance startups by employees who have promising ideas in return for a minority share. Alfred West, founder and chairman of SEI Corp., a $123 million-a-year financial services company in Wayne, Pennsylvania, is planning a more radical experiment with his 1,100 workers. He intends to divide his company into entrepreneurial units, each led by a so-called champion who has been particularly effective in promoting whatever the unit does. West will give each group of employees a 20% interest in their unit. After a suitable period, he will invite an investment bank to put a price on the unit. Then West will pay members their 20%. If the unit flops, the members get nothing more than their salaries. Says West: "I'm an entrepreneur, and I want more people like that here."[18]

Along with giving employees ownership, organizations are also empowering employees. The "PHRM in the News: Empowerment: Fact or Fiction?" indicates that this is also consistent with the values of many employees, regardless of age.

Employee ownership or empowerment may appeal to many workers, but many firms may find it difficult to provide either. A common response has been to tell managers to be flexible in managing their employees. Of course, this is much harder than it sounds, so some organizations offer training to managers to help them manage work force diversity (described more later in this chapter).

Demographic Characteristics

The world. Currently there are slightly more than 5 billion people on this planet. By the year 2000 the worldwide population is projected to be around 6 billion. At current growth rates, over the next 20 years the work force in the Third World or industrializing nations alone will expand by about 700 million. Between 1990 and 2000, Asia's work force is projected to grow by 244 million, while Europe's is projected to grow by only 6 million.[19] What this means for many firms is the existence of a huge labor market worldwide. With what almost assuredly amounts to a worldwide labor surplus, a downward pressure on wages is likely to persist for some time.

United States. With a population of more than 250 million today, projections indicate that this total will slowly swell into the twenty-first century. By the year 2000, the U.S. population will reach 275 million, an increase of 15 percent over the 240 million U.S. residents in 1985. Population is expected to plateau at 330 million in 2030.[20]

This rate of gain—approximately 1 percent per year during the 1980s and .75 percent per year during the 1990s—means the U.S. population will be growing more slowly than at any time in the nation's history, with the exception of the decade of the Great Depression when the rate was also about .75 percent per year.

The slower growth of the labor force will mirror the slowing growth of the population. Between 1990 and the year 2000, the labor force will grow from 125 million to approximately 141 million.

As the total U.S. population and work force continue to grow, the projected age profile of the work force changes dramatically.

> Older people are becoming a larger segment of the population, enjoying better health and longer life, and wielding economic and political power. More than 31 million Americans—12.4% of the nation's population—are estimated to be 65 or older. By 2020, when baby boomers reach 65, old people will be 20% of the U.S. population. At that time, there will be at least 7 million Americans over age 85.[21]

These trends and other significant changes in population and work force demographics are illustrated in exhibit 2.3. The pressure for employers to deal with an anticipated huge shortage of entry-level workers has abated somewhat. In large part this is because the slowing economy has reduced the number of jobs being created and increased the number of people looking for work.

Women in the work force. During the 1990s, women are expected to continue to join the work force in substantial numbers. By the year 2000, approximately 50 percent of the work force will be women, and 61 percent of all U.S. women will be at work. Women will comprise almost three-fifths of the new entrants into the labor force between 1990 and 2000.

> For many women, especially those with more than average education and with career prospects, there is an economic and opportunity cost for bearing children that may be limiting their lifetime fertility, as well as encouraging them to postpone childbearing. Demographers now expect the average U.S. woman to bear fewer than two children, although she herself may anticipate having at least two. Many more women will be childless than had planned to be. While the consequences of these trends have yet to be fully estimated, one likely outcome is childbearing that is explicitly planned to coincide with career choices.[22]

By contrast, new entrants into the labor force will include only fifteen percent native white males in this same period of time. This figure and others illustrating the increasing heterogeneity of the U.S. labor force are shown in exhibit 2.4.

Occupational distribution. Currently, the occupational makeup of the civilian labor force reflects much higher percentages of women than men in clerical positions, and higher percentages of men than women in managerial and administrative jobs and employed as crafts workers.

At present, about twenty percent of women occupy professional and technical positions; most of those are in the nursing and teaching professions. Thus, most working females are in service, clerical (secretarial), nursing, and teaching jobs. The majority of men, on the other hand, are in semiskilled (operative), skilled (crafts workers), managerial and administrative, and professional and technical jobs.

This distribution has, in part, resulted from the notion of **job sex-typing.** That is, a job takes the image of being appropriate only for the sex that dominates the job. Consequently, once a job becomes sex-typed, it attracts only persons of that sex. Job sex-typing, combined with sex-role stereotyping, has traditionally restricted perceived job choices and preferences for both men and women. Whereas job sex-typing refers to the labeling of jobs as either "men's jobs" or "women's jobs," **sex-role stereotyping** refers to labels, characteristics,

Exhibit 2.3

How America Will Change Over the Next 30 Years

How America Will Change Over the Next 30 Years

Demographers are the first to admit the inexact nature of their science, which includes projections of U.S. population growth and changes in the country's ethnic mix. But for all the uncertainties, forecasters also warn that managers ignore such predictions at their peril. Says Margaret Regan, a partner at TPF&C, a New York City human resource firm: "The leading-edge companies take these numbers seriously, not as just crystal ball guesses. They are starting to figure out how they will get the best value out of the country's increasing diversity."

The future hasn't always turned out as some predicted. For example, the 1990 census showed that in the 1980s the black population increased less than had been forecast, reaching 30 million rather than 31 million.

Some prognostications, even though based on how the U.S. has evolved since World War II, are largely speculative, dependent as they are on unknowns like economic growth. The WEFA Group predicts unemployment will decline steadily from today's 6.6% to 4.6% by the year 2003, the lowest it has been since 1969. Other forecasts:

- The Hispanic population will be the fastest-growing segment of the labor force, making up 9.2% of the total in 2000, vs. 7.8% in 1991 (source: U.S. Department of Labor).
- The diversity of the work force will stabilize around 2020 as the birthrate among minorities plateaus (Institute for Workplace Learning).
- Immigration, estimated to reach 685,000 in 1991, will jump to 800,000 in 1993 and remain at that level well into the 21st century. In 1993 immigrants will account for 33% of the population increase (WEFA Group).

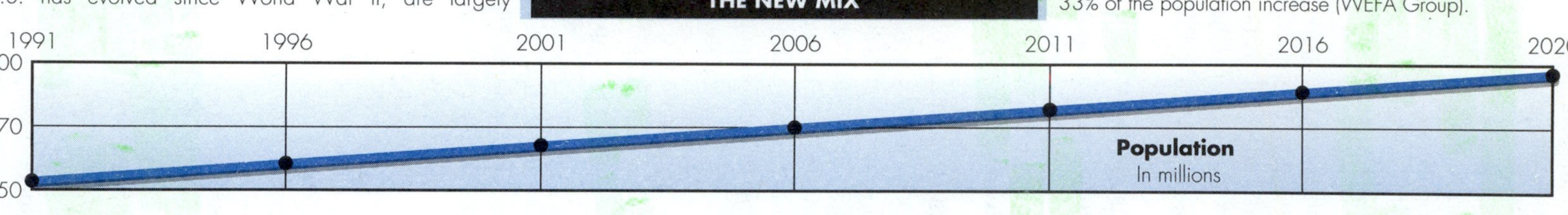

1991: 117.9 million Americans—including 54 million women—have jobs. Births reach four million, matching 1957, the peak baby-boom year. Fastest-growing city: Los Angeles, increasing by 20% from 1980 to more than nine million. Highest per capita income ($24,650): Bridgeport, Connecticut.

1996: Birthrate drops as women on average have 1.8 children, down from two in 1991. Reason: The rush to catch up and have babies is over. In the year 2000, the rate of increase in the size of the work force starts to slow to 0.9% a year from 1.4% in the 1990s.

2001: Life expectancy for men reaches 73.5, for women 80.4, compared with 72.2 and 79.2 in 1991. Medicare payments for the elderly and disabled increase 63% from 1990 to $173.9 billion in 1990 dollars.

2006 Some 15% of the Labor force is 55 or older, vs. 12% in 1991. By the year 2010, New England has the highest percentage of elderly among regions, some 14% of its total 16 million population. Of the states, Florida still has the highest proportion of oldsters, who make up nearly 20% of its 18.4 million people.

2011: Baby-boomers start to hit 65 and begin to retire in big numbers. That pushes the total of retirees from 25 million in 1991 to over 33 million, compared with 153 million working Americans. Number of women in labor force: 76.3 million, or 64% of adult female population, up from 57% in 1991.

2020: About 18% of the population is 65 or older, vs. 13% in 1991. Social Security payments reach $558.3 billion in 1991 dollars, almost double 1995's level. On average, each woman will still have 1.8 children, a constant since 1996.

SOURCE: *Fortune* (17 June 1991), 12. Used by permission.

Exhibit 2.4
New Entrants into the Labor Force

	1985 Labor Force	Net New Workers, 1985–2000
Total	**115,461,000**	**25,000,000**
Native white men	47%	15%
Native white women	36%	42%
Native nonwhite men	5%	7%
Native nonwhite women	5%	13%
Immigrant men	4%	13%
Immigrant women	3%	9%

SOURCE: *Workforce 2000* (Washington D.C.: U.S. Government Printing Office, Department of Labor, 1987).

or attributes that become attached to men and women solely because they are members of their respective sexes.

Evidence now indicates that the range of perceived job choices and preferences is expanding for both men and women. This trend has been facilitated in part by the gradual reduction of sex-role stereotyping in our society. In addition, some of the job sex-typing has been reduced through sex-neutral job titles and because of the increased number of women graduating from professional schools.

These changes, however, definitely appear to be gradual, as illustrated in exhibit 2.5. Furthermore, the real choices of women and minorities in the top levels of management still seem to be limited.

> In 1978, *Fortune* counted 10 women among the 6,400 highest paid officers and directors of major publicly-held firms. The comparable figures for 1990 were 19 of 4,012.[23]

The Work That Women Do

1890	1940	1990
1. Servant	1. Servant	1. Secretary
2. Agricultural laborer	2. Stenographer, secretary	2. Cashier
3. Dressmaker	3. Teacher	3. Bookkeeper
4. Teacher	4. Clerical worker	4. Registered nurse
5. Farmer, planter	5. Sales worker	5. Nursing aide, orderly
6. Laundress	6. Factory worker (apparel)	6. Elementary school teacher
7. Seamtress	7. Bookkeeper, accountant, cashier	7. Waitress
8. Cotton-mill operative	8. Waitress	8. Sales worker
9. Housekeeper, steward	9. Housekeeper	9. Child care worker
10. Clerk, cashier	10. Nurse	10. Cook

Exhibit 2.5
The Work That Women Do

SOURCE: *Fortune* (23 Sept. 1991), 9. Used by permission.

This is due in part to the phenomenon called the **glass ceiling**—invisible but seemingly unbreakable barriers. In today's progressive atmosphere, it may seem hard to believe glass ceilings still exist in corporate America. However, according to "Women and Minorities in Management," a recent study by researchers Mary Ann Von Glinow and Ann Morrison, women and minorities are still prevented from entering top executive ranks.

Clearly, although women have made significant inroads into management, they have fallen short of the top. Furthermore, they often do not find themselves on a path that might take them there.

Glass-ceiling programs. With the number of qualified women entering the work force growing at an astonishing rate, why is it taking so long for them to reach top positions in corporate America? According to several leading business analysts and corporate recruiters, there are many reasons for the impasse, ranging from male managers' discomfort with female executives to women's pressures of balancing work and family concerns. "Mention women in management and the instant association in the minds of most men (and women) is: Women have babies. The conclusion follows naturally that women can't be counted on to make a full-time, open-ended commitment to their careers," says Felice Schwartz, founder and president of Catalyst, a research organization that studies work-family issues.[24] Ms. Schwartz contends it costs companies more to employ women managers than men. "Given a man and a woman of equal abilities and motivation, investing in a woman is undeniably riskier."[25] The implication is that women are more likley to interrupt their careers, or forego them altogether, to pursue motherhood. In fact, one large industrial company estimates that turnover for top managerial women is approximately two and one-half times greater than for their male counterparts.[26] These perspectives can dissuade corporate decision makers from spending the time, money, and effort to groom women for top spots in their corporations and are a major factor contributing to the glass ceiling.

A second, more subtle hurdle for women to overcome is the comfort level (or lack thereof) that male managers and executives have with female executives. According to Linda Jones, president of Women in Management, a professional group of 250 female executives, "Male CEOs accept women as professionals, but they're not ready to accept them as true peers."[27] Margaret Hennig, dean of the Simmons College Graduate School of Management, believes male executives are often disturbed by the thought of a woman taking their place. "Usually, he's threatened because his identity as a male and his job are intermeshed."[28] This feeling by many advocates of women's rights is summed up in a quote by Felice Schwartz.

> ... [I]t goes against the grain of most senior executives to encourage and welcome the women, so unlike their wives, who put their career before marriage and rearing children. Talent in women is not difficult to recognize, but the very qualities that bespeak motivation—determination, drive, aggressiveness, singlemindedness—still tend to promote discomfort and uncertainty, even among male executives who have decided they should be developing female leaders.[29]

It is also conceivable that some of the barriers facing women who strive to reach positions in management have been somewhat self-imposed. For example, many women have opted for staff jobs, as opposed to line-oriented jobs—the most likely track to senior management posts. These positions were more frequently open to them than other organizational functions. In addition, women have had fewer opportunities to share information through professional networks.

Furthermore, additional factors also may have contributed to the slow growth rate of women to top positions in corporate management. Some organizations may have an influential "queen bee"—a female executive who enjoys being the only woman at the top and does her best to thwart the advancement of other women. In addition, there is a cultural belief by many Americans that the male's job is more important than his spouse's, and that it is the male's duty to be the major contributor to household income.

Two main avenues can be taken to shatter or at least raise the glass ceiling. Until recently the dominant approach has been to focus on the individual developing a "winning style" to succeed in a "man's" world. This has worked to some extent to help women advance into upper management, but it is not enough. The more long-term approach, and the one that might determine whether businesses will survive in the future, is the idea that it is management's responsibility to assure that the workplace offers no barriers to women's day-to-day activities or advancement. That way women can offer their individual talents to a company, rather than suppress them to conform to deep-rooted prejudices.

However, until management accepts women solely on their merits and value to a company, it is a practical idea for women to at least be aware of the kinds of behavior that current management prefers. "To be successful in upper management, women must constantly monitor their behavior, making sure they are neither too masculine nor too feminine."[30] Some women in upper management have achieved success by altering their behavior to what is desirable to the male management hierarchy already in place. This is helping women because male managers are becoming more comfortable with the idea of women in upper management. However, retraining women on how to "fit" into the male-dominated upper management ranks is simply not the long-term solution.

What is management's role in helping women break the glass ceiling? The overall objective is to increase an organization's effectiveness by improving management practices. "Impacting organizational norms and changing those policies and structures which inhibit utilization of females" is the goal, according to Elsie Y. Cross Associates, Inc., a consulting firm dedicated to providing companies with training to help them encourage women as well as other minorities in the workplace.[31] The "organizational norms" above refer to the idea that, in the past, many corporations sought employees who looked, acted, and dressed alike. These ideas must change not only for the employee's benefit, but to ensure that companies will be able to attract qualified employees from the ever-changing applicant pool. Training programs are of value because they provide an outside "unbiased" view of how a company can improve its practices, and the consultants can evaluate and monitor the program's progress.

Two steps are useful to educate and increase sensitivity in a corporation. First, heighten awareness of discriminatory attitudes and how this has an impact on work relationships. Second, implement strategies that will tie elimination of such barriers into incentive plans.

Several strategies can be used to increase awareness of problems concerning discriminatory attitudes and practices. Managers can be trained to work and manage in a diverse work force. For example, women are often characterized as less aggressive than their male counterparts. Managers can be sensitive to this and elicit input from all employees, not just those who speak first and loudest. Goal setting and action plans should be designed to maximize an employee's truly useful qualities. Work can be done with managers and supervisors to identify ways in which traditional performance ranking and rating systems can be improved so they are more objective and do not perpetuate disadvantage. Continuing the example above, employees can be rewarded for quality input rather than slighted for timidity or lack of confidence when presenting their ideas. Task forces made up of managers and supervisors can be formed to plan new programs and make recommendations for change based on problems discovered in the workplace. These task forces could also review and monitor such programs on a continuing basis.

Management can then be held accountable for improving utilization of females in upper management. Managers' objectives and performance appraisals should include their hiring, development, and advancement of women as well as ensuring minimum turnover of women in key positions. Compensation can be tied to achievement of these objectives. For instance, managers can be rewarded or penalized for their affirmative action plan results in hiring and/or promoting women. These plan goals can be challenging; they should represent significant utilization of women.

In addition to solving problems related to discriminatory practices, other programs can be implemented that will benefit women in indirect ways. Management can provide opportunities for women to gain experience, knowledge, and exposure as well as provide career planning. Mentorship programs can be encouraged. Some of the problems women face in climbing the ranks of management stem from the fact that, because of their growing responsibility with their company, they are forced to make trade-offs between their work and family lives. More and more companies provide initiatives such as pregnancy leave of absence and flexible hours, but fewer provide on-site child care, flexible projects, and opportunities to work at home. More comprehensive programs are necessary in order to help women balance their work and family responsibilities.[32]

Companies that have taken action to remove the glass ceiling are already seeing an impact. For example, Merck reports about 25 percent of its middle managers to be women versus approximately 10 percent in 1980,[33] and the Prudential Insurance Company has 50 percent women managers now versus 30 percent 10 years ago.[34]

While the entry of more women in the work force is creating the need for glass ceiling programs, the entry of more minorities and immigrants along with more women is creating a need for diversity management programs.

Minorities in the work force. Over the next decade, African-Americans, Hispanics, and other minorities will make up a large share of the expansion of the labor force. Nonwhites, for example, will comprise 20 percent of the net additions to the work force between 1990 and 2000, and they will be more than 15 percent of the work force by the year 2000.

Immigrants in the work force. The number of immigrants in the work force is expected to increase dramatically over the next ten years. This is the result of a significant increase in immigrant population. The Immigration Act of

1990 allocates 750,000 visas annually, up from the previous limit of 500,000. While most of these visas are granted to reunite family members, job-based immigration is 150,000, up from 54,000. The Census Bureau predicts that during the 1990s California will add almost 2 million immigrants, followed by New York, Texas, Illinois, and Florida. Once here, two-thirds or more of immigrants of work age are likely to join the labor force.

Managing diversity. The radical demographic work force transformation means business will need to develop competence in managing a very diverse workforce—African-Americans, Hispanics, Asians, males, females, young, and old.[35] "Successful organizations will react to diversity as the important business issue it is by implementing proactive, strategic human resource planning. Short-term strategies designed to circumvent the situation will keep an organization from effectively positioning itself in tomorrow's world of cultural, gender, and lifestyle diversity."[36] Top management in corporations, then, will need to emphasize to line managers two goals of "diversity competence": productivity growth and market share expansion, both domestically and internationally.

Human resource managers will typically need to focus on nine key areas in managing diversity.[37]

- **Recruitment:** A concerted effort to find quality minority hires by improved college relations programs
- **Career development:** Expose those minority employees with high potential to the same key developmental jobs that traditionally have led to senior positions for their white, male counterparts
- **Diversity training for managers:** Address stereotypes and cultural differences which interfere with the full participation of all employees in the workplace
- **Upward mobility:** Break the "glass ceiling" and increase the number of minorities in upper management through mentors and executive appointment
- **Diverse input and feedback:** Ask minority employees themselves what they need versus asking managers what they think minorities need
- **Self-help:** Encourage networking and support groups among minorities
- **Accountability:** Hold managers accountable for developing their diverse work forces
- **Systems accommodation:** Develop respect and support for cultural diversity through recognition of different cultural and religious holidays, diet restrictions, etc.
- **Outreach:** Support minority organizations and programs, thus developing a reputation as a multicultural leader

Businesses are taking the diversity issue very seriously. Digital Equipment Corporation now has a manager with the title of Manager of Valuing Differences. Honeywell, Inc., has a Director of Workforce Diversity, and Avon Products, Inc., has a Director of Multicultural Planning and Design.[38] Hewlett-Packard conducts training sessions for managers to teach them about different cultures and races and about their own gender biases and training needs,[39] and Procter & Gamble

FOCUS ON RESEARCH

The Environment is Transforming the Human Resource Department

A study entitled "A Worldwide Human Resource Study: A 21st Century Vision" was released in 1992. International Business Machines Corporation and the consulting firm of Towers Perrin surveyed almost 3,000 chief executive officers (CEOs) and human resource managers of worldwide firms in twenty countries. The firms were selected because they are effective and are in highly competitive environments. Translated into eight languages, the survey was based on the premise that characteristics of the environment have been having a major impact on the events in personnel and human resource management. A major objective of the study was to test this premise and to explore what characteristics are having the most impact today and are predicted to have the most impact in the year 2000. Of course, the researchers were also interested in knowing whether or not the characteristics with most impact would vary depending upon the country of the survey respondents.

The results of the study strongly supported the premise that the environment plays a major role in shaping personnel and human resource management around the world. While several characteristics of the environment have an impact, some are regarded as more significant than others. Which are more significant varies country by country. The results are shown in exhibit 2.6. (Compare this exhibit against

Continued

Exhibit 2.6
Geographic Differences for the Six Most Important Environmental Factors

ENVIRONMENTAL FACTORS FOR HR	RELATIVELY HIGH RATINGS IN . . .	SOMEWHAT LOWER RATINGS IN . . .
Increased National/ International Competition	Mexico, Brazil	Japan, U.S.
Focus on Quality/ Customer Satisfaction	Latin America, Australia	Japan, Korea
Changing Employee Values	Korea, Japan, Germany	Latin America, Italy
Globalization of the Economy	Latin America, Italy	Japan, U.S.
Fewer Entrants to the Work Force	Japan	Latin America, Korea, Australia
Changing Work Force Demographics	Japan, U.S.	Latin America, Korea, Australia

SOURCE: *Priorities for Competitive Advantage: A Worldwide Human Resource Study* (IBM/Towers Perrin, 1992), 13.

has implemented "valuing diversity" programs throughout the company. A mentor program designed to retain black and female managers was developed at one plant, and one-day workshops on diversity were given to all new employees.[40]

Equitable Life Assurance encourages minorities and women to form support groups that periodically meet with the CEO to discuss problems in the company pertaining to them. At Avon, several councils represent various groups, each

the evaluations you made using exhibit 2.1 at the start of this chapter.) Exhibit 2.6 shows the six environmental characteristics regarded as being most important to human resource management, overall. However, these factors were more important to some countries than others. For example, respondents in the U.S. and Japan indicated that changing work force demographics are relatively high in importance, but respondents in Korea and Australia indicated they are comparatively low in importance (but still high in the overall results).

Increased levels of national and international competition refer to more commerce and competition from firms in countries all over the world. Globalization of the economy refers to what a firm must do in order to compete on a global basis—for example, operate in all countries of the world or in just some.

Notice that results are presented with no indication of the present or the year 2000; regarding the impact of the environment, respondents said "the future is today." They said the same thing when it came to identifying the most important human resource goals. Here, worldwide, the two most important goals selected were productivity/quality/customer satisfaction and linkage of HR to the business.

In addition to indicating the most significant aspects of the environment, respondents were asked how these aspects were affecting human resource management more specifically. Basically, respondents saw the human resource department literally being transformed from a functional specialist to a business partner. The impact of this transformation on the four areas of human resource management is shown in exhibit 2.7.

Exhibit 2.7
A Model of the HR Department's Transformation

	Functional Specialist		Business Partner
Nature of HR Programs and Function	Responsive	→	Proactive
	Operational	→	Strategic
	Internal	→	Societal
Creation of HR Strategy and Policy	HR Department has Full Responsibility	→	HR Department and Line Management Share Responsibility
Organization of HR Department	Employee Advocate	→	Business Partner
	Functional Structure	→	Flexible Structure
	Reporting to Staff	→	Reporting to Line
Profile of HR Professionals	Career in HR	→	Rotation
	Specialist	→	Generalist
	Limited Financial Skills	→	Financial Expertise
	Current Focus	→	Focus on Future
	Monolingual	→	Multilingual
	National Perspective	→	Global Perspective

SOURCE: Adapted from *Priorities for Competitive Advantage: A Worldwide Human Resource Study* (IBM/Towers Perrin, 1992), 6.

having a senior manager present at meetings. These councils inform and advise top management.[41]

Thus, important work force and demographic changes are already affecting human resource management and will continue to do so throughout the 1990s. While these changes present significant challenges and opportunities, they must also be addressed in the context of several major economic and organizational trends.

Economic and Organizational Trends

National, state, and local economies can have a significant impact on managing human resources. So can the international economy, whose recent impact has increased the level of competition and has forced U.S. corporations to become more flexible, competitive, and bottom-line oriented. The impact of these economies on the HR department is described in the Focus on Research: "The Environment is Transforming the Human Resource Department." A strong economy tends to lower the unemployment rate, increase wage rates, make recruitment more necessary and more difficult, and increase the desirability of training current employees. In contrast, a weak economy tends to increase the unemployment rate, diminish demands for wage increases (and even result in wage concessions), make recruitment less necessary and easier, and reduce the need for training and developing current employees.[42] Although a weak economy may tend to diminish the importance of some human resource activities, other events in the external environment act to increase the importance of human resource management.

American executives feel a sense of vast impending change in the world and for their organizations. Many of the reasons for their feelings result from the rapidly changing demographic conditions just described and the fast-paced, highly competitive international marketplace. Executives look at these and other conditions and foresee that the 1990s will be tougher than the 1980s. They see companies being forced to develop and make decisions faster. Consequently, they are adopting more fluid structures that can be altered as conditions change. More than before, companies are living by computers, shaping strategy and structure to fit information technology. They are engaging in more mergers, joint ventures, acquisitions, downsizing, and development in order to become and stay competitive; and they are coping with a more demanding work force, increasingly characterized by its overall diversity. This, along with the increasing level of computer usage and automated facilities and techniques, is changing the nature of jobs and requiring more skilled workers at a time when functional illiteracy is on the rise.

Changing jobs and skills needed. What will the work force of 2000 be doing? The changes projected for the nation's industries will restructure U.S. occupational patterns. The jobs that will be created between now and 2000 will be substantially different from those in existence today. According to the Bureau of Labor Statistics, 23.4 to 28.6 million new wage and salary jobs will be created by 1995. Most of the job growth will be in the service-producing and not the goods-producing area. Of these, only between 1.0 and 4.6 million will be in high-technology industries. Thus, a substantial number of new jobs will be in industries other than high technology.

Exhibit 2.8 shows the occupations that will have the greatest numbers of new jobs by 2000. A number of jobs in the least-skilled job classes will disappear, while high-skilled professions will grow rapidly. Overall, the skill mix of the economy is moving rapidly upscale, with most new jobs demanding more education and higher levels of language, math, and reasoning skills (see exhibit 2.9).

Exhibit 2.8

Occupations with the Largest Job Growth, 1986–2000 (Numbers in Thousands)

Occupation	Employment 1986	Employment Projected, 2000	Change in Employment 1986–2000 Number	Change in Employment 1986–2000 Percent	Percentage of Total Job Growth 1986–2000
Salespersons, retail	3,579	4,780	1,201	33.5	5.6
Waiters and waitresses	1,702	2,454	752	44.2	3.5
Registered nurses	1,406	2,018	612	43.6	2.9
Janitors and cleaners, including maids and housekeeping cleaners	2,676	3,280	604	22.6	2.8
General managers and top executives	2,383	2,965	582	24.4	2.7
Cashiers	2,165	2,740	575	26.5	2.7
Truck drivers, light and heavy	2,211	2,736	525	23.8	2.5
General office clerks	2,361	2,824	462	19.6	2.2
Food counter, fountain, and related workers	1,500	1,949	449	29.9	2.1
Nursing aides, orderlies and attendants	1,224	1,658	433	35.4	2.0
Secretaries	3,234	3,658	424	13.1	2.0
Guards	794	1,177	383	48.3	1.8
Accountants and auditors	945	1,322	376	39.8	1.8
Computer programmers	479	813	335	69.9	1.6
Food preparation workers	949	1,273	324	34.2	1.5
Teachers, kindergarten and elementary	1,527	1,826	299	19.6	1.4
Receptionists and information clerks	682	964	282	41.4	1.3
Computer systems analysts, electronic data processing	331	582	251	75.6	1.2
Cooks, restaurant	520	759	240	46.2	1.1
Licensed practical nurses	631	869	238	37.7	1.1
Gardeners and groundskeepers, except farm	767	1,005	238	31.1	1.1
Maintenance repairers, general utility	1,039	1,270	232	22.3	1.1
Store clerks, sales floor	1,087	1,312	225	20.7	1.0
First-line supervisors and managers	956	1,161	205	21.4	1.0
Dining room and cafeteria attendants and barroom helpers	433	631	197	45.6	.9
Electrical and electronics engineers	401	592	192	47.8	.9
Lawyers	527	718	191	36.3	.9

SOURCE: *Bulletin to Management* (22 Oct. 1987), 342. Reprinted by permission from *Bulletin to Management* © 1987 by The Bureau of National Affairs, Inc., Washington, DC 20037.

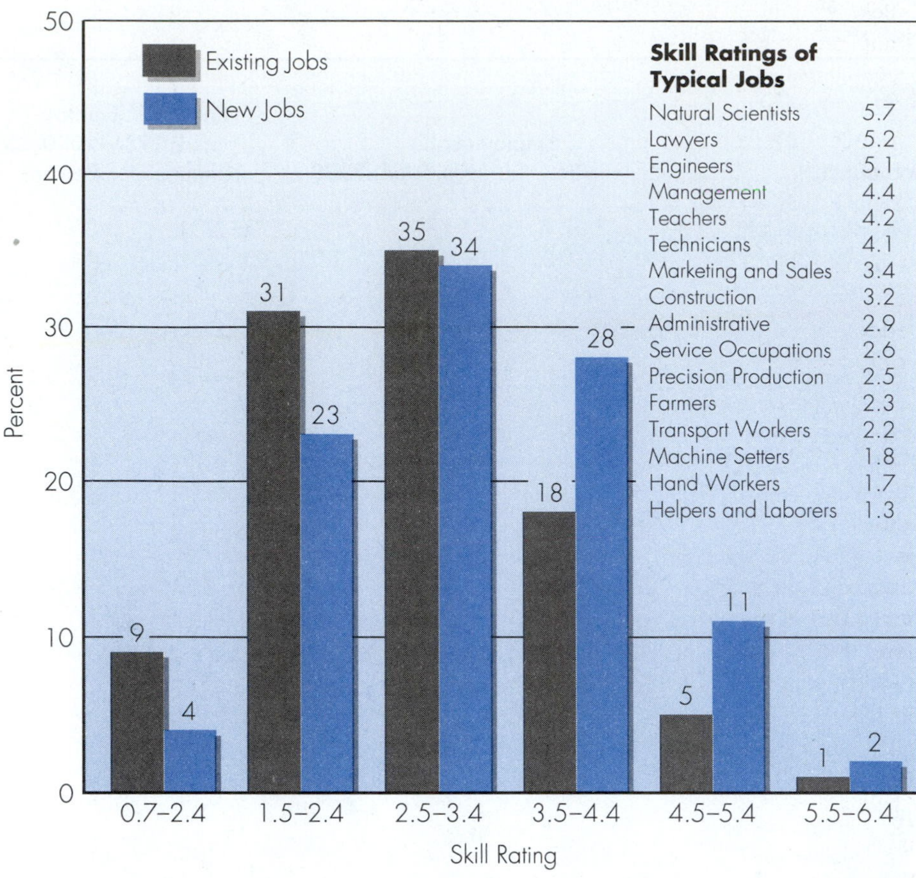

Exhibit 2.9
Low-Skilled Jobs Are Declining

SOURCE: *Workforce 2000* (Indianapolis, Ind.: Hudson Institute, 1987), 100. Used by permission from Hudson Institute, © 1987.

Skills critical to the future of the workplace are emerging, but some are or will be in short supply. Several factors are driving the shift toward new skills for work: greater use of information technologies, the move away from craft and assembly manufacture and toward computer-mediated processes, the larger amount of knowledge work in almost every occupation, new requirements for education and the ability to manage complexity, and the redesign of many jobs to include computer-based work. Frequently, several skills will be folded into one job, often with a new title and greater individual responsibility.[43]

These changes are occurring because newer jobs will require substantially more education than the current jobs. This is why the illiteracy situation is especially critical[44] and why companies

> ... are reaching into the educational system with a variety of incentives, new ideas, and cooperative agreements. In Minneapolis, for example, corporate contributions underwrote extensive participatory planning, which was used in the successful

restructure of the city's school system, particularly its inner-city high schools. In Peking, Illinois, IBM's "Writing to Read" program helped first graders, cutting the number who needed remedial teaching from 11% to 2%.[45]

The changing organization. The organization today is more global, leaner, flatter, more flexible, faster, more customer oriented, more quality focused, and more innovative as described in PHRM in the News: "Flat, Lean, Flexible Organization." Above all, today's organizations are constantly changing. Change is becoming the constant. Restructuring, retraining, and retooling are becoming the *modus operandi*. There is more employee involvement and skill utilization. At the same time, leaner and flatter organizational structures mean fewer jobs are needed. While organizations are benefiting from these trends, there is opportunity only for persons with the requisite skills, who are willing and able to retrain and retool, and for whom jobs exist.

Eliminating layers of employees continues to be an important aspect in shaping the organization. The typical target is middle management. The elimination of this group facilitates the process of decentralizing, the process so necessary to enhance the speed with which decisions can be made. Along with this trend is the use of more contingent workers. **Contingent workers** are individuals hired on a limited time basis. They are subject to dismissal on short notice and typically do not receive as many benefits as regular employees. There is also greater use of subcontracting. For example, IBM has subcontracted with Pitney Bowes to run its mailrooms, stockrooms, and reproduction operations. Companies are increasingly out-sourcing their payroll activities to payroll processing firms such as ADP. Again, these activities are being done in concert to form the new lean and trim organizations of the 1990s. For many organizations, these activities accompany programs dedicated to improving quality and facilitating innovation in an attempt to make organizations more competitive.

While it is becoming more difficult for U.S. firms to compete on the basis of cost, they can be successful by differentiating their products. Improving quality is one way of differentiating a product or service. Organizations started to focus on quality enhancement in the 1980s in response to customer preferences for quality products, largely supplied by Japan and Germany. Companies such as Xerox, L.L. Bean, and Ford became examples of what quality enhancement means and how the customer responds. Their successes serve as examples of how it can be done and of quality's importance to survival.

Companies are succeeding in their efforts to improve quality in many ways. While automation is often suggested as a way to improve quality (by getting the "unreliable" human element out of the process), examples such as the NUMMI plant in Fremont, California, and L.L. Bean demonstrate that state-of-the-art automation is not mandatory in enhancing quality. In many cases, automation is not even feasible. Alternative ways to improve quality are discussed further in chapter 13.

Perhaps the most likely way U.S. firms can compete globally is through the development of new products. Other nations can copy U.S. products and improve them, but this still takes time. The U.S. has not been a nation to copy and imitate the products of others; it has always been centered on the creative-minded individual, the entrepreneur, and the pioneer. Organizations now recognize that this focus can be used to gain a competitive advantage over others.

IN THE NEWS PHRM

Flat, Lean, Flexible Organization

Management is experiencing a radical transformation. The relative stability and predictability of business are being replaced by uncertainty, complexity, and rapid change. Intense global competition, rapidly changing technology, shifting demography, economic fluctuations, and other dynamic conditions require companies to be adaptive and swift. Companies are stripping away long-standing management policies and practices impeding flexibility and are adopting new practices to foster desired initiative, innovation, and change.

In the new environment, strategic business planning has also changed. It is becoming more tentative, short-term, and issue focused. Planning is now considered useful more as a tool for provoking thinking and discussion than as a process of determining long-term objectives and courses of action. In this context, strategies are shaped as guides to help organizations recognize and address important changes and opportunities to manage them effectively.

In the flexible organization, the planning horizon is typically no farther than three years, with concentration on the next year. For example, when Hicks Waldron became CEO at Avon, he was asked at an employee meeting what his strategic plan was. He said, "Ask me in five years. I'll tell you what it was." He has since divested Tiffany and other businesses, has acquired new beauty products companies, and has flattened, trimmed, and restructured the company. Human resource management activities have stressed keeping up with the demands of restructuring, staffing changes, and absorption of acquisitions. The experience has been similar in other companies.

Many companies address these issues through human resource planning. Human resource issues and plans are based on analysis of business unit issues, environmental trends suggesting issues of company concern, and forecasts of future staffing and development needs. Typically, human resource plans are developed as functional plans, parallel to strategic plans. In the absence of clear strategic business direction, the human resource function charts its own course, relying on the best available information. The plans provide a basis for discussion and negotiation with unit managers on priorities, activities, and allocation of time and resources. Where business strategic planning is established, human resource strategies are developed as part of this process, with human resource and management effectiveness issues addressed as any other business issues.

In the flat, lean, and flexible organization, the planning process is most valuable as an issue identification and diagnostic process and is necessary to foster management consideration of longer-range vision, strategic direction, and values. In this way, the process helps educate both staff and line on important long-range considerations affecting near-term actions. Less time and patience are given to formal aspects of planning systems and procedures, detailed data collection and analysis, forecasting, or scanning of external trends and issues. Precision and accuracy are less important than the provocation of considering issues and alternative future projections. Under conditions of rapid change, human resource strategies are long-term views intended to guide today's actions.

SOURCE: J. Walker, "Managing Human Resources in Flat, Lean and Flexible Organizations: Trends for the 1990s," *Human Resource Planning* 11:2 (1988): 125–27. Reprinted by permission of *Human Resource Planning*, © 1988.

Advanced technologies, automation, and robots. Information technology, office automation, factory automation, data communications, voice mail, and information systems are implemented together faster than ever to virtually revolutionize the ways we do work and organize. These so-called **telematics technologies** encompass

- Mainframe computers and associated information systems
- Microcomputers and word processors

- Networking technologies
- Telecommunications technologies
- Reprography and printing
- Peripherals[46]

Telematics technologies are enabling organizations to shape themselves into winners. They facilitate speed, flexibility, decentralization, and staying in close touch with the customer. For example:

> How fast is fast enough? The Limited (an upscale retail store with headquarters in Columbus, Ohio), tracks consumer preferences every day through point-of-sale computers. Orders, with facsimile illustrations, are sent by satellite to suppliers around the U.S. and in Hong Kong, South Korea, Singapore, and Sri Lanka. Within days clothing from distant points begins to collect in Hong Kong. About four times a week a chartered 747 brings it to the company's distribution center in Ohio, where goods are priced and shipped to stores within 48 hours. Says Chairman Leslie Wexner: "That's not fast enough for the Nineties."[47]

Computers can also let customers look inside an organization. The trucking firm Pacific Intermountain Express gives customers access to its computers so they can check the status of their shipments. Banks and brokerage firms are also using computers to enable customers to do their business from their homes and offices.

These technologies also enable organizations to enhance their quality by ensuring better parts and services from their supplier. Already retail chains are linked with their suppliers so that they know the timing and the nature of needed shipments. These technologies will also facilitate R&D capabilities and give managers more free time to get to know their companies better.

Automation, whether in the factory or the office, has changed and will continue to change organizational structures and culture. Because information is instantaneously available, there is little need for layers of management between the top and first-line management. Top management can bypass middle managers on their way to the first-line management, and this breaks the chain of command and can lead to ambiguity in reporting relationships.[48]

Thus, as the telematics technologies will produce better products and faster and leaner organizations, they will also undermine traditional authority structures. Blue-collar workers will become information managers by becoming computer operators at advanced plants. Traditional managers may no longer be needed.

> A few observers believe the computers in the workplace will lead to far more than better information and better products. Shoshana Zuboff, an associate professor at the Harvard Business School and author of *In the Age of the Smart Machine,* argues that computerization undermines traditional forms of authority and breaks down barriers between job categories and functions. "You have people doing work which is more abstract, more analytical," says Zuboff. "People not considered managerial in the past are managing information." Zuboff concludes that the role of the managers will have to be redefined in the Nineties. Says she: "Since managers are no longer the guardians of the knowledge base, we do not need the command-control type of executive."[49]

In summary, more telematics implementation will provide organizations with opportunities to downsize, decentralize, and make their organizations more flexible and responsible. However, organizations must also be prepared to retrain workers, out-place workers (especially managers), and redesign jobs.

CHARACTERISTICS OF THE INTERNAL ENVIRONMENT

Several aspects within organizations influence how effectively a firm manages its human resources. These aspects include top management's goals and values, organizational strategy, technology, organizational structure, organizational culture, and organizational size. Although these features are described separately here, they often influence each other. For example, top management's values help shape organizational strategy, which in turn influences several personnel and human resource management activities.

Top Management's Goals and Values

Top management determines how critical human resource management will be in organizations. If top management minimizes the importance of people to the organization's overall success, so will the line managers. In turn, those in the human resource department will perform the routine operational-level human resource activities. A likely consequence will be minimally effective human resource management in the firm.[50]

Goals and guidance. Because they are created by organizations, jobs are management's explicit statements of what they believe are the most appropriate means for accomplishing their goals. The stated goals and the subsequent standards of excellence that an organization establishes also give clear cues to employees about what is important and what behaviors are required. Thus, goals help determine the criteria against which workers and their behaviors will be evaluated. The criteria and goals, in turn, also determine the kinds of individuals who will be attracted to the organization and how they will be evaluated and promoted. Thus, organizational goals can help establish the reasons for jobs, the organization's expectations for workers, and even the legitimacy of the job demands.

Developing people. Top management's goals and values plus the support and commitment of the chief executive officer are important in the development of people.

> Grab any Wall Street analyst by the lapel and he'll tell you PepsiCo is a brilliant marketing company. Well, sure, but then ask CEO Wayne Calloway how it got that way and he'll talk not about those slick ads starring Madonna and Michael Jackson, but about what he calls the three P's, "people, people, people." Ah, touch-feely management? Anything but. Behind Calloway's alluringly alliterative slogan lies the country's most sophisticated and comprehensive system for turning bright young people into strong managers. Says he: "We take eagles and teach them to fly in formation."
>
> PepsiCo takes people development more seriously than perhaps any other American corporation. Calloway spends up to two months every year personally reviewing the performance of his top 550 managers, discussing their futures with their bosses and with the personnel department. Calloway, who says he knows most of the 550

> managers and spends anywhere from five to 30 minutes reviewing each one, states with conviction, "There's nothing I do that's more important." In all, he spends 40% of his time on people issues. He expects the people below him to do the same, so that by the end of each year every one of the company's 20,000 managers knows exactly where he or she stands.[51]

Without top management support for and commitment to developing people, the major focus of an organization is likely to be on other activities. This is particularly true when the focus is on short-term goals and immediate results. This situation allows too little time to wait for the benefits of training and development. Top management at PepsiCo began to emphasize training and development at the same time they recognized that they had to develop their people and businesses in order to be effective.

Rights and ethics. Top management shares responsibility in setting the stage for employee rights and ethical conduct because they set policy, with input from the human resource department, on the treatment of human resources and on the definition of ethical behavior. Top management's policy regarding these rights and what is ethical is important in shaping the way the organization's human resources are treated and the conduct of employees with respect to each other, customers, and to themselves.

Organizational Strategy

The essence of organizational strategy for human resource management is its creation of **strategic business needs.** These are needs that arise during the formulation and implementation of the organization's strategic intentions and directions. Once those needs are identified, **strategic human resource management** is created.

> According to Horace Parker, Director of Strategic Education at the Forest Products Company, an 18,000 person division of Weyerhaeuser in Seattle, Washington, strategic human resource management is about getting the strategy of the business implemented. For Bill Reffett, former senior vice president of personnel at the Grand Union, a 20,000 person supermarket operation on the East Coast, strategic resource management is getting everybody from the top of the organization to the bottom doing things that make the business successful.[52]

Together, these statements suggest that organizational strategy serves as a trigger for the HR activities. Specific examples of how this is done are provided in the following chapters. Thus, the impact of organizational strategy on human resource management is very significant.[53]

Organizational Culture

Organizational or corporate culture represents the organization's value system.[54] Strongly influenced by top management, corporate culture typically indicates how the organization regards its customers, suppliers, competitors, the environment, and its employees.[55] As such, corporate culture is often found in a statement of business values.

The aspect of corporate culture that refers to employees can be referred to as a company's HR philosophy. The **HR philosophy** is a statement of how the organization regards its human resources—what role human resources play in the overall success of the business and how they are to be treated and managed. This statement is typically very general, thus allowing interpretation at more specific levels of action within an organization. For example, at the Forest Products Company (FPC), part of their statement on business values describes their philosophy of what employees mean to the company and how they are to be managed:

- People are mature, responsible individuals who want to contribute.
- People hold themselves to high standards of integrity and business ethics; they are responsible stewards of the land and environment.
- Our work environment is based on mutual respect, personal satisfaction, and growth opportunities for everyone.
- People recognize that teamwork, cooperation, and a clean, safe, well-maintained workplace are essential to fulfilling our customer commitments.
- Continuing education is an ongoing commitment that involves everyone.[56]

Instead of using the term HR philosophy or HR values to describe how human resources are regarded and are to be treated and managed, some organizations just use the term **culture.** That is, "We will create a culture that recognizes how important we feel about people and how we are going to treat them." Culture often comes to be reflected in the company's HR activities. For example, companies such as Levi Strauss that have a culture of caring for and respecting the individual are likely to offer employment security and provide benefits for a variety of employee needs. In this way, many employees learn the culture of the organization through the HR activities—how it selects, what criteria it evaluates, and what it compensates most highly.

Technology

Technology generally refers to the equipment and knowledge used to produce goods and services. What we are witnessing today in organizations is a virtual discarding of yesterday's technology. For example, organizations are discarding old forms of technology such as Henry Ford's mass production. In their place are new forms, such as the "lean" production systems of Eiji Toyoda of Toyota and his production genius, Taiichi Ohno:

> Just as the mass-production principles pioneered by Henry Ford and General Motors' Alfred Sloan swept away the age of craft production after World War I, so the ideas of Toyoda and Ohno are today chipping away at the foundations of mass production. We call their system "lean" production because it uses less of everything than a comparable mass-production operation: half the human effort in the factory, half the manufacturing space, half the investment in tools, half the engineering hours to develop a new product. Lean production is built not simply on technical insight but on a precisely defined set of relationships that extends far beyond the factory floor to encompass designers, suppliers and customers.[57]

In many organizations today, employee skills are insufficient for the current jobs because of these technological changes. Consequently, organizations such as Xerox, Ford, GM, and General Electric are retraining employees. Others are providing training programs in order to have individuals who can operate the new technology.

With the pace of technology likely to accelerate, the most reasonable scenario is one of organizations continually retraining current employees and recruiting new employees with unique skills. Changing technology necessitates continual training program formulation and implementation, and employees who are willing to adapt, to be reassigned to different jobs, and to be retrained. By encouraging and supporting employees in these efforts, employers may provide employment security.[58]

centralized home office

Organizational Structure

Organizational structure describes the number of levels of employees in an organization—the number of nonmanagement and management levels, and the distribution of the decision-making process. Companies have tended to restructure themselves to be most effective in quality and cost terms. They have done this by reducing the number of levels of employees and by decentralizing the decision-making process.

decentralize

> A shrinking world has meant an expanding clock. Managers have shaped organizations that can respond quickly to developments abroad. As speed and agility become paramount virtues, we will see even more decentralization, with responsibility closer to the operating level.[59]

Controlling behavior. Technology can limit efforts to improve productivity and quality of work life by restricting job redesign programs. So can organizational structure, particularly through the design of the control structure in the organization. Because locating the person who is responsible for problems or errors is important, control structures often specify who is accountable, how things should be done, and who must give approval for doing something differently. Although this helps reduce the complexity of each job and defines the responsibility of each worker, it also sets up impersonal boundaries. The boundaries then become critical in the way people behave.

Changing control structures is just as difficult as changing technology, yet both need to be changed to facilitate job design changes. Furthermore, particular types of job designs are unlikely to be adopted if key decision makers adhere to certain philosophies. For example, if the top management or owners want to retain close control, or if they do not think employees can act responsibly, they will likely choose the scientific approach to job design rather than one of the contemporary approaches discussed in chapter 13.

Organizational Size

Organizational size is also an important factor in human resource activities. Although exceptions exist, generally the larger the organization, the more developed its internal labor market and the less its reliance on the external labor market. In contrast, the smaller the organization, the less developed its internal labor market and the greater its reliance on the external labor market.

As more reliance is placed on the internal labor market, the organization relies more on itself in deciding how much to pay people and on whether job evaluation, job classifications, and internal equity will be used. As more reliance is placed on the external labor market, the organization relies less on itself and more on what other organizations are doing when deciding issues such as pay rates and external equity.

FOCUS ISSUES FOR SCANNING AND ANALYZING

Many issues flow from our discussion of the several aspects of external and internal environments that face organizations. Four issues of considerable importance closely relate the needs of the business with human resource management.

Quality Enhancement

The need for organizations to deliver quality goods and services will continue to confront and challenge organizations. This need is being forced on organizations by domestic and international competition, of course, but also by us as consumers. We continue to demand high quality products and are willing to buy from whomever offers those products. To keep matters interesting, the ante on playing in this international arena of high quality keeps going up: What was acceptable quality yesterday is unacceptable today. Thus, organizations must continue to pursue quality enhancement with a vengeance; to successfully do so will involve human resource management.

Do you think the quality of service you get from a bank has anything to do with the treatment you get from the bank's tellers? Do you think the quality of the stereo, VCR, CD player, or car you drive has anything to do with level of motivation, dedication, training, and commitment of the individuals making these products? Of course. In both cases, quality depends on the people we are dealing with as well as on the people behind the scenes who make the products. Total quality depends upon all parts of the organization working together. Consequently, organizations are bound to give increasing attention to their human resources as they continue to seek to enhance their quality in order to survive and compete.

Cost Reduction

We all want quality; but, if there are two products with equally great quality, which will you buy? As organizations seek to enhance quality, they will also seek to reduce costs. Consequently, we are likely to see organizations continue work force reductions throughout this decade.

We are also likely to see organizations continue to shift some production outside the U.S. to take advantage of substantial wage disparities. If the worldwide population is growing dramatically and getting better educated at the same time, do you think there will also be some downward pressure on wages in the U.S. over the next several years? Workers are likely to be asked to hold down wage demands and to become more flexible in job assignments, or both, as organizations try to reduce their costs of operation. In some organizations, the cost of labor is a relatively small percentage of the total operations cost, but this tends to be less true in most of our service-oriented organizations.

Innovation

A third focus issue here is the continued need by organizations to develop new products and offer new services. This results from the same environment that necessitates quality enhancement and cost reduction. Some observers believe this is where the U.S. should concentrate its efforts to compete worldwide. If we cannot make the cheapest products or the highest quality products, at least we can develop products no one else has and get them to market faster once we have developed them. Again, though, getting innovation requires human resource management; it takes highly talented people managed very effectively to develop new products and ideas. Some U.S. firms such as Merck have shown that they can do this rather well. The challenge in the future is for more firms to do this and for those doing it to stay ahead of competitors worldwide who are trying to catch up.

Responsiveness to the Environment

Concern about quality, cost, and innovation reflects the general focus issue of being more responsive to the environment. This entire chapter, of course, is about the environment. It is filled with facts that suggest the world order is changing and will continue to change. While some trends are somewhat predictable, increasingly the changes are becoming unpredictable; and, just as they are becoming more unpredictable, they are having a greater impact on managing human resources. Speed of responsiveness will become critical. Thus, the human resource manager must continually scan and analyze the environment and respond rapidly. Results of the worldwide IBM/Towers Perrin study support this need for scanning and analyzing. Two significant conclusions of the study are that, for effective firms in highly competitive environments, the HR departments must

- be responsive to a highly competitive marketplace and global business structures, and
- be closely linked to the business.

INTERNATIONAL COMPARISONS

We selected three important sets of international comparisons for human resource management: worldwide population figures, worldwide educational attainment levels, and human resource management in Mexico.

Worldwide Population and Educational Attainment

Between now and the year 2020, the industrializing nations are expected to increase their population in an amount equal to the total population of the industrialized nations. As this happens, the average age of the population in the industrializing nations decreases, and that of the population in the industrialized nations increases. Comparing industrialized nations with those in the process of industrializing, we also see substantial differences in educational attainment levels. Data in exhibit 2.10 show the percentage of high school and college students in industrial nations has fallen and will continue to fall dramatically.[60]

Exhibit 2.10
Share of School Students by Industrialized Nations*

	Ages 15–18 (High School)	Ages 19–22 (College)
1970	44% 160 million	77% 26 million
1985	30% 280 million	51% 58 million
2000	21% 450 million	40% 115 million

*Industrialized nations include those in North America, Western Europe and the Asia-Pacific Region.

SOURCE: Compiled from W. B. Johnston, "Global Work Force 2000: The New World Labor Market," *Harvard Business Review* (Mar.–Apr. 1991), 115–29.

Together, these two sets of international comparisons suggest an increasing worldwide labor supply with a large component of highly educated individuals. From a human resource management point of view, the implications can be significant. To say the least, these trends can certainly facilitate the globalization of businesses; it may be feasible for companies to open up shop in literally any part of the world. Do **you** see any other possible implications?

Mexico

Because of the U.S.'s rapidly developing trade relationship with Mexico, it might be useful to gain more understanding of this country where, currently, more than 100,000 Mexicans work for U.S. auto companies in border plants.[61]

A significant difference exists between human resource practices in the U.S. and those practiced in Mexico. This is due to historical as well as cultural differences in the populations. Mexico's human resource practices are extremely pro-employee and heavily government regulated. The Mexican labor law is derived from the federal labor law of Mexico. Therefore, the Mexican government dictates most of what human resource professionals can do in Mexico.

Mexico is an excellent source for the study of environmental influences of human resource practices. In 1965 it established the Border Industrialization Program (BIP) in order to fight high unemployment. The maquiladoras grew from the BIP. **Maquiladoras** are "off-shore" manufacturing plants for the assembly, processing, and finishing of foreign material and components. Most of these are located along the U.S.–Mexico border, where the bulk of Mexico's economic activity takes place. The program permits duty-free import of all tools (equipment, raw materials) required for production if the final product is to be exported.

Since its inception, BIP goals have remained the same: to increase Mexico's level of industrialization; to create new jobs; to raise the domestic income level; to facilitate the transfer, absorption, and skills of technology; and to attract much-needed foreign exchange. Foreign firms' main reasons for a Mexican base are the low cost of labor, high quality, and high productivity.[62]

Social and legal structure. Mexico's social structure is similar to the family structure. One of the biggest issues in Mexico—which is also an issue in

Japan—is paternalism. In the Mexican mind, all institutions—whether government, business, or church—are like an authoritarian family structure. A plant manager, like the president of Mexico, fills an authoritarian and fatherly role, rather than a mere organizational function.

Mexican law and history reflects the Mexican view that the employer has a moral and paternal responsibility for all his employees, even when there is a union. The Mexican employee is not just working for a paycheck. Workers tend to expect to be treated as the "extended family" of the boss, thereby to receive a wider range of services and benefits than the ones provided north of the border. Examples of these benefits include food baskets and medical attention for themselves and their families (apart from social security). The medical benefits are not considered "an extra" or discretionary; in the Mexican worker's mind, they simply fulfill the employer's role and responsibilities.

Corresponding to this practice is the Mexican view that employees have a reciprocal obligation to be loyal, to work hard, and to be willing to do whatever is requested of them. American managers who accept the Mexican sense that a job is more than a paycheck and who try to fulfill their part of the "bargain" can reap the benefits of employee loyalty, including employee willingness to come to work every day and to work conscientiously.

SUMMARY

The decade of the 1990s is now and promises to be filled with rapid change, challenge, uncertainty, and intense global competition, all demanding ever higher standards of quality and rates of innovation at the same time as cost reduction. There will be a higher than ever premium on obtaining and utilizing information. This means the human resource department must scan the external environment to stay abreast of international and national economic activity, social and demographic changes, and technological trends and developments. With this information, the human resource department will create scenarios of how these external environmental forces are likely to have an impact on the organization.

For example, environmental scanning of work force demographics may indicate coming labor shortages of the domestic workers, but that any shortfalls will likely be made up by unprecedented flows of immigration. Using this and other scenarios from external environmental changes, the human resource department will need to craft organizational responses.

On the basis of what has been going on in the external environment in the past few years, HR professionals and other organizational observers see organizational success resulting from organizations that are

- Capable of rapid response
- Flexible
- Adaptable
- Focused
- Lean and cost-oriented
- Quality-oriented
- Customer-oriented
- Innovation-oriented

For these responses to be effective, they must be sufficiently anticipated, discussed, and shared with all employees, and then implemented with full support of the organization.

For the human resource department the decade of the 1990s also means scanning the internal environment to stay abreast of changes in strategies and directions of the organization, the needs and characteristics of the work force, and the needs of line managers as they seek to make their organizations more competitive, flexible, adaptable, and focused. Combining these internal, organizational characteristics with the external conditions, HR professionals suggest that successful firms in highly competitive environments are likely to have—indeed, will be required to have–employees who are

- Adaptable
- Committed
- Motivated
- Skilled/reskilled
- Highly energetic
- Good performers in diverse employee groups
- Good team players

Together, all these internal and external environmental characteristics are having a major impact. As described in the "Focus in Research" for this chapter, they are causing a virtual transformation in the operation and staffing of HR departments. This impact is reflected throughout this book; but, because the environment is ever-changing, HR professionals will forever have to keep scanning and analyzing the environments. This applies equally to the legal environment discussed in the next chapter.

WHERE WE ARE TODAY

1. For a rapidly growing number of organizations, the world is the playing field where long-term survival and success will be determined.
2. The world is changing more rapidly than ever, but the real challenge is the increasing unpredictability of those changes.
3. Rapid change and the growing unpredictability make it necessary to, if not throw out old assumptions and traditional ways of doing business, at least be willing to take a hard look at substantially modifying them.
4. We can no longer use the past in guiding us through the present and future, so it is critical to scan and analyze the environment in order to help us anticipate what might be required.
5. Increasingly, organizational success will depend upon doing a great job in human resource management. If the personnel and human resource people can get out in front of this one, they are likely to be able to make a substantial contribution to the success of their organizations.
6. Getting out in front requires scanning and analyzing environmental factors that have an impact on organizations. This helps human resource depart-

ments formulate necessary responses to the immediate environment and allows time to develop responses for big changes in the environment that require longer-term, big-impact human resource programs and initiatives.

7. The big challenges for organizations will continue to be quality enhancement, cost reduction, innovation, and rapid response (speed). These remain the key ways organizations will compete in the worldwide marketplace.
8. The worldwide demographic data indicate substantial increases in well-educated individuals. This may prove to be too tempting for organizations and, of course, represents one of the most significant HR issues for all of us.
9. In the meantime, organizations will continue to increase their involvement in secondary, elementary, and preschool education. The risk of not doing so is too great. Success, however, will depend upon the cooperation of all groups involved.
10. The worldwide economic slowdown and the pressure to reduce costs will likely force organizations to further reduce their needs for new employees. Thus, even as the number of new entrants into the labor market shrinks, many organizations are likely to enjoy a buyer's market.

DISCUSSION QUESTIONS

1. What is the impact of domestic and international competition on effectively managing human resources?
2. What work force and demographic changes are likely to have the most significant impact on human resource management? Please describe the nature of the impact.
3. How can organizations really increase decision making and power at the lower levels of the organization without upsetting the middle managers?
4. Will the trend toward employee ownership really make firms more competitive? What is the limit of this trend?
5. What will U.S. firms do to help manage the work force diversity effectively?
6. Do you expect that by the year 2000 jobs will no longer be sex-stereotyped?
7. Should U.S. employers encourage a greater influx of immigrants? What are the HR implications of this issue?
8. What impacts are economic and organizational trends having on human resource management?
9. Will employers have to do even more basic education training in order to be competitive?
10. Briefly describe how each of the aspects of the internal environment affects human resource management.

APPLIED PROJECTS

1. Pick an organization with which you are familiar. It may range anywhere from very small to very large. Then identify and describe the characteristics of its environment and their impact on its human resource management.
2. Interview four people, two from each of two different organizations. Ask them to describe their organization's culture, particularly as it relates to man-

aging people. Then compare and contrast the two people within the same organization, and then the responses from both organizations. Report for the class on the differences and your explanation for them.

3. Analyze the labor force in the local area. Report on the number employed, what type of work they have, the number unemployed, etc. Ask about the demographic characteristics of each group (e.g., their racial, sex, and age characteristics). Go to the library for this or even to a local company (or even the school, especially if it has an affirmative action program). This project should be useful for this chapter as well as chapters 5 and 6.

CASE STUDY

Managing Work Force Diversity: People-Related Business Issues at the Barden Corporation

Background

The largest segment of the business at the Barden Corporation is the Precision Bearings Division. It manufactures high-precision ball bearings in a range of sizes for machine tools, aircraft instruments and accessories, aircraft engines, computer peripherals, textile spindles, and medical and dental equipment. Currently, the division employs about 1,000 people and includes a marketing department and a small corporate staff. It was founded during World War II to manufacture the special bearings needed for the Norden bombsight. It has been non-union since that time (which gives you a hint about the culture). The following description is told by Mr. Donald Brush, Vice President and General Manager of the Precision Bearings Division.

Reporting directly to me is a small staff comprising a manufacturing manager, a quality manager, an engineering manager, a director of manufacturing planning, and a director of industrial relations. We meet together several times a week to discuss current problems, as well as short- and long-range opportunities and needs. On alternate weeks we augment this group by including the supervisory personnel who report to the senior managers listed above. I might interject here that all supervisors meet with hourly employees on either a weekly or biweekly basis to review specific departmental successes and failures, and otherwise to keep employees informed about the business and to encourage ownership of their own jobs. The managers themselves meet on call as the Employee Relations Committee to discuss and recommend approval on a wide range of issues that include the evaluation and audit of hourly and salaried positions, as well as the creation of modification of all divisional personnel policies.

A few words about our Personnel (or Industrial Relations) Department: (You will notice that the term "Human Resources" does not yet roll off our tongues easily, but we understand what it means.) There are six employees who together provide the basic services of employment, affirmative action, employee activity support, labor relations, interpretation of the plethora of federal and state laws, benefits administration, wage and salary administration, records preparation and maintenance, cafeteria supervision, and so on. There are, in addition, two people who coordinate our rather extensive training activities.

As currently organized, the Medical Department comes under the supervision of the director of industrial relations. Its authorized staff includes a medical director, the manager of employee health and safety (who is an occupational health nurse), a staff nurse, a safety specialist, and secretary/clerk.

The development and execution of plans and programs, including those of a strategic nature, almost invariably involve the active participation of Personnel. And that's how we want it to be. On the other hand, the Personnel Department doesn't run the business. By this I mean they don't hire or fire, promote or demote. The don't write job descriptions or determine salaries or wages, etc. All these things are done by the line managers with the Personnel Department providing a framework to ensure consistency and that all actions are appropriate to company goals. You might say that Personnel is our "Jiminy Cricket"—they are there for advice, consent and, importantly, as a conscience.

During the past several months we have been running into many issues that are affecting the very essence of our business: growth, profits, survival, and competitiveness. Because the issues involve our human resources, we call them people-related business issues. Would you please give us your experience, expertise and suggestions as to how we can solve them? Thanks! The following briefly describes the nature of each of the four issues.

Issue: Recruiting and Training New Hourly Employees

The need to recruit and train approximately 125 new hourly workers to respond to a surge in business in a high-cost-of-living area at a time when the unemployment rate is low is very challenging. By mid-1992 it had become evident that we had an opportunity to significantly increase our business. In order to achieve otherwise attainable goals, we have to increase our hourly work force by a net of about 125 employees (that is, in addition to normal turnover, retirements, etc.) in one year. I have asked Personnel to test the waters, recognizing the unemployment in the Danbury labor market has reached an unprecedented low of about 2.5%.

Issue: Safety and Occupational Health Issues

The need to create a heightened awareness by the work force for safety and occupational health considerations is very important. This is an evolving mission born of a dissatisfaction on our part about "safety as usual." Over the years, Barden employees have assumed that, because we are a metalworking shop, people were just going to get hurt. But we cannot afford to have people get hurt and miss work anymore. Yet, as our work force ages, the employees seem to get out of shape and become more injury and illness prone.

Issue: Spiraling Health Costs of an Aging Population

The spiraling health costs of an aging and sometimes out-of-shape work force are very costly. All employers face this. Barden's problem is a little unique in that hourly employees tend to stay with the company and retire from the company. For example, we still have several employees whose careers began with us 45 years ago shortly after the company was founded. Our average age approaches 45 for employees and their dependent spouses. Generally, our jobs do not require much physical effort, and it's easy to become out of shape and overfed. As a consequence, they get sick, use hospitals, and have accidents.

Issue: New Machines and the Development of Qualified Workers

The technological evolution of increasingly complex machinery and related manufacturing equipment, and the development of trained workers to operate and maintain these machines and equipment, are important facts of life. This process is unceasing and requires a good deal of planning for both the short and the long run. For example, what should we do in the next year or five years out in order to remain competitive in terms of cost, quality, and service? Buying and rebuilding machines is part of the story. Running them efficiently is quite another. As you know, modern equipment of this sort requires operational people who are not only knowledgeable about the turning or grinding of metals, but also conversant with computerized numerical controls. The employee who sets up and operates a $500,000 machine must be well-trained. Yet having trained people is getting more difficult.

Summary

Mr. Brush knows that these four people-related business issues all reflect the increasing diversity of the work force. Because of this, he knows these issues will be around for a long time. Therefore, he requests that you provide him with action plans that can offer long-lasting solutions (if at all possible!). He would also appreciate having any more facts related to the four issues identified.

SOURCE: This case was prepared by Randall S. Schuler who expresses his appreciation for the cooperation of Donald Brush.

Case Questions

1. How should Barden deal with its people-related business issue of recruiting and training new hourly employees?
2. What do you recommend to Barden to help address its potential health and safety issues?
3. How can Barden begin to approach its concern about rising health care costs?
4. Are qualified workers getting harder to find? What can Barden do to keep its current work force up-to-date?

NOTES

1. B. Saporito, "Campbell Soup Gets Piping Hot," *Fortune* (9 Sept. 1991): 142–48.
2. "The Fortune Global Service," *Fortune* (26 Aug. 1991): 165–88; "The Fortune Global Manufacturing" *Fortune*

(29 July 1991): 237–80.
3. "Detroit South," *Business Week* (16 March 1992): 98–103.
4. M. G. Duerr, "International Business Management: Its Four Tasks," *Conference Board Record,* 1986: 43.
5. R. B. Reich, *Tales of a New America* (New York: Vantage Books, 1987).
6. L. P. Shrenk, "Environmental Scanning," in *Human Resource Management Evolving Roles & Responsibilities,* ed. L. Dyer (Washington, D.C.: The Bureau of National Affairs, Inc., 1989): 1/88–1/123.
7. T. Peters, *Thriving on Chaos* (New York: Alfred Knopf, 1987): 123.
8. D. Q. Mills, *The New Competitors* (New York: Wiley, 1985): 19; and J. C. Grayson and C. O'Dell, *Two Minute Warning* (New York: The Free Press, 1988).
9. J. F. Coates, "An Environmental Scan: Projecting Future Human Resource Trends," *Human Resource Planning* (Dec. 1987): 219; J. Main, "The Winning Organization," *Fortune* (26 Sept. 1988): 50–56; R. S. Schuler, ed., *Managing Human Resources in the Information Age,* Vol. 6 (Washington, D.C.: SHRM/BNA, 1991).
10. W. H. Miller, "Employers Wrestle with 'Dumb' Kids," *Industry Week* (4 July 1988): 47.
11. *Training America: Learning to Work for the 21st Century* (Alexandria, Va.: American Society for Training and Development, 1989).
12. B. Nussbaum, "Needed: Human Capital," *Business Week* (19 Sept. 1988): 100; A. P. Carnevale, L. J. Gainer, and A. S. Meltzer, *Workplace Basics: The Essential Skills Employers Want* (San Francisco: Jossey-Bass, 1990); A. P. Carnevale, L. J. Gainer, and E. Schulz, *Training the Technical Work Force* (San Francisco: Jossey-Bass, 1990).
13. Nussbaum, "Needed: Human Capital," 101.
14. J. F. Coates, J. Jarratt, and J. B. Mahaffie, "Future Work," *The Futurist* (May–June 1991); J. F. Coates, J. Jarratt, and J. B. Mahaffie, *Future Work: Seven Critical Forces Reshaping Work and the Work Force in North America* (San Francisco: Jossey-Bass, 1990).
15. C. M. Solomon, "Managing the Baby Busters."
16. J. Spiers, "The Baby Boomlet is for Real," *Fortune* (10 Feb. 1992): 101–104; "Downward Mobility," *Business Week* (23 March 1992): 56–63; N. Hale, *The Older Worker* (San Francisco: Jossey-Bass, 1990).
17. N. Perry, "Saving the School: How Businesses Can Help," *Fortune* (7 Nov. 1988): 45.
18. Perry.
19. W. B. Johnston, *Workforce 2000* (Indianapolis, Ind.: Hudson Institute, 1987); G. Gallup, *Forecast 2000* (New York: Simon and Schuster, 1988); C. D. Fyock, *America's Work Force is Coming of Age* (Lexington, Mass.: D. C. Heath and Company/Lexington Books, 1990).
20. See note 19.
21. J. F. Coates, J. Jarratt, and J. B. Mahaffie, "Future Work," *The Futurist* (May–June 1991): 11.
22. Coates, Jarratt, and Mahaffie, 13.
23. *Personnel* (Dec. 1990): 17. For a discussion of these data and issues, see Johnston, *Workforce 2000;* W. H. Wagel and H. Z. Levine, "HR '90: Challenges and Opportunities," *Personnel* (June 1990): 18–19; R. R. Thomas, Jr., "From Affirmative Action to Affirming Diversity," *Harvard Business Review* (March–April 1990), 107–17; C. M. Marmer Solomon, "Careers Under Glass," *Personnel Journal* (April 1990): 96–105; J. Fierman, "Why Women Still Don't Hit the Top," *Fortune* (30 July 1990): 41–62; W. Konrad, "Welcome to the Woman-Friendly Company," *Business Week* (6 Aug. 1990): 48–52; J. Nelson Horchler, "Derailing the Mommy Track," *Industry Week* (6 Aug. 1990): 22–26; and M. J. Williams, "Women Beat the Corporate Game," *Fortune* (12 Sept. 1988): 46–52.
24. F. Schwartz, "Don't Write Women Off as Leaders," *Fortune* (8 June 1987): 185; C. Cockburn, *In the Way of Women: Men's Resistance to Sex Equality in Organizations* (Ithaca, N.Y.: ILR Press, School of Industrial and Labor Relations, Cornell University, 1991); K. A. Matthews and J. Rodin, "Women's Changing Work Roles: Impact on Health, Family, and Public Policy," *American Psychologist* (Nov. 1989): 1389–93.
25. See note 24.
26. B. Brophy, "The Truth About Women Managers," *U.S. News and World Report* (13 March 1989): 57; and F. Schwartz, "Women as a Business Imperative," *Harvard Business Review* (March–April 1992): 105–14.
27. B. Brophy and M. Linnon, "Why Women Execs Stop Before the Top," *U.S. News and World Report* (29 Dec. 1986).
28. See note 27.
29. Schwartz, 185.
30. A. Morrison, R. P. White, and E. Van Velsnor, "Executive Women: Substance Plus Style," *Psychology Today* (Aug. 1987): 18–21; 24–26.
31. E. Y. Cross Associates, "Managing Diversity," Managing Diversity Workshop Summary; S. E. Jackson and Associates, *Diversity in the Workplace: Human Resource Initiatives* (New York: The Guilford Press, 1992); J. D. Goodchilds, ed., *Psychological Perspectives on Human Diversity in America: Master Lectures* (Washington, D.C.: American Psychological Association, 1991); J. P. Fernandez, *Managing a Diverse Workforce: Regaining the Competitive Edge* (Lexington, Mass.: Lexington Books, 1991); D. Jamieson and J. O'Mara, *Managing Workforce 2000: Gaining the Diversity Advantage* (San Francisco: Jossey-Bass, 1991); L. I. Kessler, *Managing Diversity in an Equal Opportunity Workplace* (Washington, D.C.: National Foundation for the Study of Employment Policy, 1990); S. B. Thiederman, *Bridging Cultural Barriers for Corporate Success* (Lexington, Mass.: Lexington Books, 1991); R. R. Thomas, Jr., *Beyond Race and Gender: Unleashing the Power of Your Total Workforce by Managing Diversity* (New York: AMACOM, 1991).
32. K. Myers, "Cracking the Glass Ceiling,"*Information Week* (27 Aug. 1990): 38–41; G. N. Powell, "Upgrading Management Opportunities for Women,"*HR Magazine* (Nov. 1990): 67–70; D. T. Hall, "Moving Beyond the 'Mommy Track': An Organization Change Approach," *Personnel* (Dec. 1989): 23–29; E. Ehrlich, "The Mommy Track," *Business Week* (20 March 1989): 126–34; F. N. Schwartz, "Management Women and the New Facts of Life," *Harvard Business Review* (Jan.–Feb. 1989): 65–76.
33. Information provided by Jennifer Hunt, Merck & Company, as part of an MBA project, Fall 1990, New York University.

34. Information provided by Mike Penso, Prudential, Inc.
35. S. E. Jackson and Associates, *Working Through Diversity: Human Resources Initiatives* (New York: Guilford Press, 1992); S. Caudron, "U S WEST Finds Strength in Diversity," *Personnel Journal* (March 1992): 40–44.
36. B. P. Foster, "Workforce Diversity and Business," *Training and Development Journal* (April 1988): 59.
37. L. Copeland, "Valuing Diversity, Part 2: Pioneers and Champions of Change," *Personnel* (July 1988): 48; H. Jain, B. M. Pitts, and G. De Santis, eds., *Equality for All: National Conference on Racial Equality in the Workplace—Retrospect and Prospect* (Hamilton, Ont., Canada: McMaster University and IRRA, Hamilton and District Chapter, 1991); A. Dastmalchian, P. Blyton, and R. Adamson, *The Climate of Workplace Relations* (New York: Rutledge, a Division of Rutledge, Chapman and Hall, 1991).
38. See note 37.
39. J. Nelson-Horchler, "Demographics Deliver a Warning," *Industry Week* (18 April 1988): 58.
40. Copeland.
41. Copeland.
42. P. B. Doeringer and M. J. Piore, *Internal Labor Markets and Manpower Analysis* (Lexington, Mass.: D. C. Heath, 1971); P. Osterman, ed., *Internal Labor Markets* (Cambridge, Mass.: London, 1984).
43. Coates, Jarratt, and Mahaffie.
44. *Training America: Learning to Work for the 21st Century* (Alexandria, Va.: American Society for Training and Development, 1990).
45. Coates, Jarratt, and Mahaffie.
46. Coates, "An Environmental Scan..."
47. A. Kupfer, "Managing Now for the 1990's," *Fortune* (26 Sept. 1988): 44–47.
48. J. Main, "The Winning Organization," *Fortune* (26 Sept. 1988): 50–56; W. P. Powell, "Neither Market nor Hierarchy: Network Forms of Organization," *Research in Organizational Behavior,* Vol. 12 (Greenwich, Conn.: JAI Press, Inc.): 295–336.
49. Kupfer, "Managing Now for the 1990's," 47.
50. J. J. Sherwood, "Creating Work Cultures with Competitive Advantage," *Organizational Dynamics* (Winter 1988): 4–27.
51. B. Dumaine, "Those Highflying Pepsico Managers," *Fortune* (10 April 1989): 78–86.
52. R. S. Schuler, "Strategic Human Resource Management: Linking People with the Strategic Needs of the Business," *Organizational Dynamics* (Summer 1992).
53. Strategic business needs can arise even if an organization does not have a formal organizational strategy. However, these needs are more likely to be clearly focused and identified if the organization does have a strategy. For an insightful discussion of the impact of strategic intent and its implications for strategic human resource management, see: G. Hamel and C. K. Prahalad, "Strategic Intent," *Harvard Business Review* (May–June 1989): 63–76; C. K. Prahalad and G. Hamel, "The Core Competence of the Corporation," *Harvard Business Review* (May–June 1990): 79–91; J. Butler, J. Ferris, and N. Napier, *Strategy and Human Resources Management* (Cincinnati, Ohio: Southwestern, 1990); R. S. Schuler and S. E. Jackson, "Linking Competitive Strategies with Human Resource Management Practices," *Academy of Management Executives* (Aug. 1987): 207–19; J. Milliman, M. A. Von Glinow, and M. Nathan, "Organizational Life Cycles and Strategic International Human Resource Management in Multinational Companies: Implications for Congruence Theory," *Academy of Management Review* 16:2: 318–39; S. E. Jackson, R. S. Schuler, and J. C. Rivero, "Organizational Characteristics as Predictors of Personnel Practices," *Personnel Psychology* 42 (1989): 727–86; J. A. Courtright, G. T. Fairhurst, and L. E. Rogers, "Interaction Patterns in Organic and Mechanistic Systems," *Academy of Management Review* 32:4: 773–802.
54. T. E. Deal and A. A. Kennedy, *Corporate Cultures* (Reading, Mass.: Addison-Wesley, 1982); R. Pascale, "Fitting New Employees into the Company Culture," *Fortune* (28 May 1984): 28–40.
55. Deal and Kennedy.
56. Schuler, "Strategic Human Resource Management..."
57. J. P. Womack, D. T. Jones, and D. Roos, "How Lean Production Can Change the World," *The New York Times Magazine* (23 Sept. 1990): 20–24, 34, 38; A. Taylor, III, "New Lessons from Japan's Carmakers," *Fortune* (22 Oct. 1990): 165–66, 168.
58. S. Zuboff, *In the Age of the Smart Machine: The Future of Work and Power* (New York: Basic Books, 1988). Also see B. Garson, *The Electronic Sweatshop* (New York: Simon and Schuster, 1988); P. B. Doeringer, *Turbulence in the American Workplace* (New York: Oxford University Press, 1991); S. E. Forrer and Z. B. Leibowitz, *Using Computers in Human Resources* (San Francisco: Jossey-Bass, 1991); U. E. Gattiker, *Technology Management in Organizations* (Newbury Park, Calif.: Sage, 1990); A. Majchrzak, *The Human Side of Factory Automation: Managerial and Human Resource Strategies for Making Automation Succeed* (San Francisco: Jossey-Bass, 1988); P. S. Goodman, L. S. Sproull, and Associates, *Technology and Organization* (San Francisco: Jossey-Bass, 1990).
59. A. Kupfer, "Managing Now for the 1990's," *Fortune* (26, Sept. 1988): 44–47; A. Ross, "Synergistics: A Strategy for Speed in the '90's,"*Business Quarterly* (Autumn 1990): 70–74; C. A. Bartlett and S. Ghoshal, "Organizing for Worldwide Effectiveness: The Transnational Solution," *California Management Review* (Fall 1988): 54–74; M. S. Scott Morton, *The Corporation of the 1990s: Information, Technology, and Organizational Transformation* (New York: Oxford University Press, 1991).
60. W. B. Johnston, "Global Work Force 2000: The New World Labor Market," *Harvard Business Review* (March–April 1991): 115–29.
61. "Detroit South,"*Business Week* (16 March 1992): 98–103.
62. See note 61.

CHAPTER 3

Legal Environment

The Civil Rights Act, on top of the Americans with Disabilities Act (ADA), is the final kick in the pants for managers. Managers have to think differently.

—Attorney Fred Sullivan of the Springfield, Mass., firm Sullivan & Hayes.[1]

In 1979 Barbara L. Sogg, at the age of 47, had heart surgery from which she fully recovered. Unbeknownst to her at the time, her surgery was enough to cause her employer, American Airlines, to give her a "nonpromotable" status. Not until 1984 did this secret designation come into play. In March of that year, the job of general manager of American Airlines at the LaGuardia Airport in New York became open. The only one considered for the opening was Mr. Zurlo, an engineer who had been with the company for ten years less and who had far less supervisory experience than Ms. Sogg. Ms. Sogg resigned herself to being manager of flight services; but, in January of 1985, she became a bit more curious after being told her job was being eliminated because of a reorganization. Actually her job was combined with a similar job position at the JFK International Airport. That new, enlarged position was then offered to a younger woman who was the flight services manager at JFK. At this point, what would you have advised Ms. Sogg to do? What were her options?

She engaged the services of an attorney in 1985. In January, 1992, a State Supreme Court jury in New York City found that the airline had illegally discriminated against Ms. Sogg. Indeed, the airline had actually discriminated against her three times! First, it discriminated against her when it passed her over for the job of general manager at LaGuardia. Second, it discriminated against her in the 1985 reorganization as it failed to provide her and another woman, age 60, with jobs, even though they did provide jobs for the other eighteen younger workers who were displaced. Third, she was discriminated against when she was passed over for the promotion at JFK in favor of the younger woman.

The jury awarded $4.5 million in compensatory damages and found that American and its top four executives should also pay $2.5 million in punitive damages. Of the $2.5 million, Robert Crandall, CEO of the airline, was ordered to pay $125,000 and Mr. Zurlo was ordered to pay $25,000. At the trial, American said that the treatment of Ms. Sogg was not related to her age, sex or disability, but rather to her personality. Claiming that she was inflexible, insensitive, and stubborn, American said it would appeal the decision.[2]

Well, what's $7 million, you ask. Who's to say the jury was right, or that perhaps the jury was right in finding the company guilty, but the penalty was excessive? Is this just more evidence of the impact of what many call the "litigious society"? Regardless of your opinions, this is a real case, involving real money and the lives of real people. Someday you could be in this type of situation or know someone who has been or even is today. Because of the magnitude of the impact and the extensive set of laws, executive orders, court decisions, and legal agencies influencing how firms manage human resources, this entire chapter is devoted to describing the legal environment.

LEGAL ENVIRONMENT

Government's influence on human resource management in organizations is greater than ever. In some respects, the requirements of federal and state legislation have shaped the modern corporate human resource department. (Appendix A contains many laws and executive orders that impose requirements on human resource management.) Changes in aspects of the legal environment, such as new rulings by the U.S. Supreme Court, are also likely to have a significant impact on human resource management. Thus, human resource managers must continuously scan the legal environment and be familiar with these changes in order to manage their organizations' work forces more effectively. Human resource managers need to use this knowledge in developing and implementing programs in all of the human resource activities.

To convey the depth and range of impact of laws, executive orders, court decisions, and agencies—referred to as legal considerations—we will review them within the context of the human resource activities where that impact is most significant.

Job Analysis

Job analysis faces several legal constraints, largely because it serves as the basis for selection decisions, performance appraisals, compensation, and training determinations. These constraints have been articulated in the *1978 Uniform Guidelines on Employee Selection Procedures* (known by its shortened form, *Uniform Guidelines*) and several court decisions. For example, Section 14.C.2 of the *Uniform Guidelines* states that "... there shall be a job analysis which includes an analysis of the important work behaviors required for successful performance." Any job analysis should focus on work behavior(s) and the tasks associated with them.[3]

Where job analysis has not been performed, the validity of selection decisions has been successfully challenged (*Kirkland v. New York Department of Correctional Services,* 1974; *Albemarle Paper Company v. Moody,* 1975). Numerous court decisions regarding job analysis and promotion and performance appraisal also exist. For example, in *Brito v. Zia Company* (1973), the court states that the performance appraisal system of an organization is a selection procedure, and, therefore, must be validated—that is, it must be anchored in job analysis. In *Rowe v. General Motors* (1972), the court ruled that, to prevent discriminatory practices in promotion decisions, a company should have written objective standards for promotion. In *U.S. v. City of Chicago* (1978), the court stated that, in addition to having objective standards for promotion, the standards should describe the job for which the person is being considered for promotion. These objective standards can be determined through job analysis.[4]

Recruitment

Legal considerations play a critical role in the recruitment process of most companies in the U.S. Although much of the legal framework facing human resource management is directed at employment decisions concerning hiring, firing, health and safety, and compensation, legal considerations essentially begin with the organization's search for job applicants, whether inside or outside the organization. Although the fair employment laws in regard to staffing decisions (hiring, firing, demoting, transferring, and training) specifically apply only to selection, they directly affect recruitment. (Some of the laws and acts applicable to selection are discussed in the next section.) Because those laws essentially help identify who will be selected, they also identify who should be recruited. Fair employment or equal employment laws most directly relevant to recruitment are those describing affirmative action programs (AAPs).

Affirmative action programs are efforts designed to ensure proportional and fair representation of qualified employees on the basis of race, color, ethnic origin, sex, and disability.[5] As shown in exhibit 3.1, many firms have AAPs.

Affirmative action programs generally arise from three different conditions, to be described over the next several pages.

Federal contracts. If a company has a federal contract greater than $50,000 and has fifty or more employees (thereby referred to as a federal contractor), it is required to file, with the Office of Federal Contract Compliance Programs, a written plan outlining steps to be taken for correcting "underutilization"

Exhibit 3.1
Corporate Hiring Practices

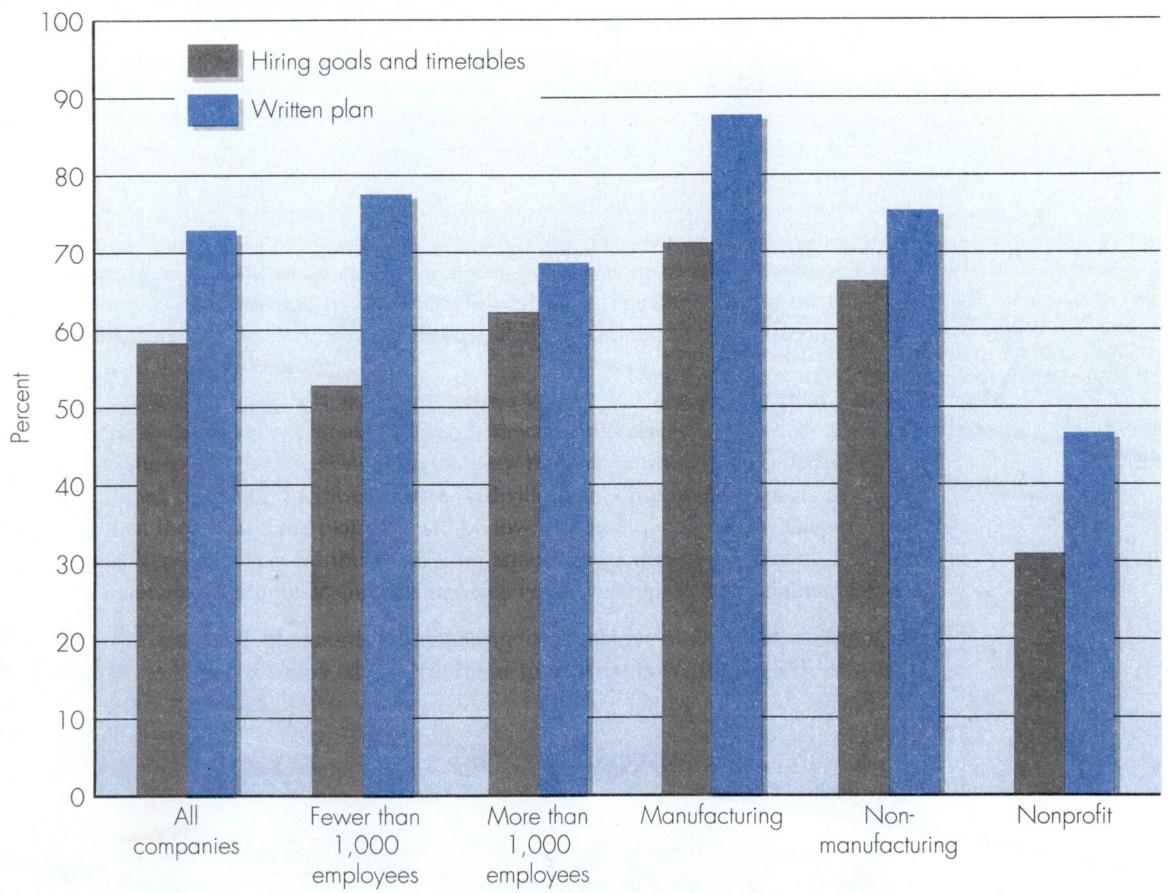

NOTE: Some written affirmative action plans are merely statements and do not include goals and timetables.
SOURCE: *Bureau of National Affairs*

in places where it has been identified. Goals and timetables are critical parts in these plans.

The specific components of affirmative action programs for federal contractors are specified by the Department of Labor in the Office of Federal Contract Compliance Programs (OFCCP). The AAPs are currently enforced by the OFCCP and the Equal Employment Opportunity Commission (EEOC) through Executive Order 11246. Affirmative action programs are designed to facilitate an organization's commitment to provide and achieve proportional representation or parity (or to correct underutilization) in its work force with the relevant labor market of protected group members. Title VII of the Civil Rights Act of 1964 includes women and Americans of African, Hispanic, Native-American, and Asian/Pacific Islands descent.

AAPs often contain several important components, including utilization and availability analyses, goals, and timetables. A **utilization analysis** determines the number of members of minorities and women employed in different jobs within an organization. An **availability analysis** measures how many members of minorities and women are available to work in the relevant labor market of an organization. If an organization is employing fewer members of minorities and women than are available, a state of underutilization exists. Males are also covered by most equal employment laws, but most examples, except of reverse discrimination, exclude them because they usually are the majority.

Relevant labor market is generally defined as the geographical area from which come a substantial majority of job applicants and employees. Published population data sources such as the Standard Metropolitan Statistical Analysis may help provide initial guidance in determining this defined area. Within a relevant labor market, availability data can be gathered from sources such as the U.S. Census, local and state Chambers of Commerce, and city and state governments. Because organizations may fill job openings for some jobs with applicants in the local area and may fill other jobs with applicants from across the nation, organizations may have several relevant labor markets. The relevant labor markets are important in both affirmative action program development and in defending cases of *prima facie* illegal discrimination. As such, they are discussed further in the next section on selection.

After the utilization and availability analyses are completed, goals and timetables are written to specify how an organization plans to correct any underutilization. Because goals and timetables become the organization's commitment to equal employment, they must be realistic and attainable. An example of a utilization plan for one job group in an organization is shown in exhibit 3.2.[6]

Federal contractors are also required to "take affirmative action to employ and advance in employment qualified handicapped individuals at all levels of employment" (Section 503 of the Rehabilitation Act of 1973). The Rehabilitation Act, as amended in 1980 and in 1990 by the Americans with Disabilities Act (ADA), names three categories of disabled persons as protected against employment discrimination:

- Any individual who has a physical or mental impairment that greatly limits one or more of life's major functions
- Any individual who has a history of such an impairment
- Any individual who is perceived as having such an impairment

Exhibit 3.2
Utilization, Goals, and Timetables

Job Group: ABC
As of: 2/14/92
Availability source: 8-factor analysis

Current Utilization

	Male	**Female**	**White**	**Black**	**Hispanic**	**Asian**	**Native American**	**Minority**	**Total**
Employees (#)	193	7	186	4	3	6	1	14	200
Employees (%)	96.5	3.5	93.0	2.0	1.5	3.0	.5	7.0	
Availability (%)	88.0	12.0	66.0	15.0	14.0	4.0	1.0	34.0	100.0
Underutilized ?	No	Yes	No	Yes	Yes	Yes	Yes	Yes	

Based on expansion of 36

Goals

	Male	Female	White	Black	Hispanic	Asian	Native American	Minority	Total
Long-range goal (%)		15.0		15.5	14.5	4.0	1.0	35.0	100.0
Long-range goal (#)		35		37	34	9	2	82	236
Annual placement (%)		22.5		21.0	19.7	7.2	1.8	49.7	

Timetables

	Male	Female	White	Black	Hispanic	Asian	Native American	Minority	Total
If 12 openings (5.1% turnover)—Employment opportunities 1st yr. = 48									
Years to goal (#)		14		15	15	1	3	15	
Hired 1st year		11		10	9	3	<1	24	
Hired 2nd year on		3		3	2		<1	6	
If 24 openings (10.2% turnover)—Employment opportunties 1st yr. = 60									
Years to goal (#)		7		11	10	1	2	9	
Hired 1st year		14		13	12	4	1	30	
Hired 2nd year on		5		5	5		<1	12	
If 47 openings (19.9% turnover)—Employment opportunities 1st yr. = 83									
Years to gaol (#)		4		5	5	1	1	4	
Hired 1st year		19		17	16	6	2	41	
Hired 2nd year on		11		10	9			23	
Projected openings 18 (7.6% turnover)—Employment opportunities 1st yr. = 54									
Years to goal (#)		10		14	14	1	2	11	
Hired 1st year		12		11	11	4	<1	27	
Hired 2nd year on		4		4	4		<1	9	

Utilization Analysis

	Male	**Female**	**White**	**Black**	**Hispanic**	**Asian**	**Native American**	**Total**
Employees (#)	193	7	186	4	3	6	1	200
Employees (%)	96.5	3.5	93.0	2.0	1.5	3.0	.5	
Availability (%)	88.0	12.0	66.0	15.0	14.0	4.0	1.0	100.0
Should have (#)	176	24	132	30	28	8	2	
Underutilized?	No	Yes	No	Yes	Yes	Yes	Yes	
Calculation type		Z		Z	Z	Z	P	
Statistical value		3.59		5.05	4.99	.54	.73	
Z or probability		0.00		0.00	0.00	.59	.36	
Significant?	No	Yes	No	Yes	Yes	No	No	
Additional needed		8		16	15			

The impairments in the first category are usually evident conditions such as amputations, Down's syndrome, paralysis, hearing or visual problems, etc. Impairments in the second category can't be readily discerned. Nevertheless, some employers shy away from applicants whose medical histories include cancer, heart disease, diabetes, and similar health problems, perhaps out of fear that a recurrence or other effects of the disease will result in increased insurance costs, a higher rate of absenteeism, and decreased efficiency. In one case, an employer refused to hire a worker who had leukemia because he was prone to infection from even minor injuries; but a Wisconsin circuit court found that the man was qualified to perform his job; therefore, the company could not refuse employment.

Notice that an employer's misconceptions can bring an individual who isn't actually disabled under the coverage of the act or a similar state law. That's what happened, for instance, when an employee was terminated because his employer thought he had epilepsy. The Washington Court of Appeals awarded the worker two years back pay and ordered him reinstated. Also included are individuals who have suffered from alcoholism and drug abuse and those suffering from acquired immune deficiency syndrome (AIDS).

Individuals who are well but test positive for the AIDS virus likely will be covered by the third category of the Rehabilitation Act. This portion of the act protects any individual who is perceived as having a disability.[7]

According to the 1990 ADA, a qualified individual with a disability is anyone who has the skill, experience, and education required for the job and can perform the "essential functions" of the job, with or without reasonable accommodation. The act permits medical exams only after the job offer has been made. The offer can be made conditional upon the results of the exam, but the employer must make reasonable accommodation. Before the job offer is made the employer can describe the essential functions to the individual, but the employer cannot inquire about any disabilities the applicant might have.

The rules further provide that employers with fifty or more employees who hold federal contracts totaling more than $50,000 must prepare written affirmative action programs for disabled workers in each of their establishments—for example, in each plant or field office. This condition must be met within 120 days after the contractor receives the federal contract. Those who hold contracts or subcontracts of less than $2,500 are not covered by this act. Those with federal contracts that range from $2,500 to $50,000 are required to include an affirmative action clause in their contracts, but they do not need a written affirmative action plan.

To aid an organization's efforts to attain its specified goals and timetables, the organization must make sure its employment policies, practices, and procedures are operating to facilitate goal attainment. This generally requires an assessment of its current policies, practices, and procedures. The assessment may reveal policies, practices, and procedures that are not operating to facilitate goal attainment if underutilization exists. If so, these policies, practices, and procedures need to be modified.

Past discrimination. This is the second way an affirmative action program may arise. A federal court may require an AAP if a discrimination suit brought against the organization through the Equal Employment Opportunity Commission has found evidence of past discrimination. An AAP under these conditions is generally part of a **consent decree,** a statement indicating the specific affirmative action steps the organization will take.

A famous affirmative action program resulting from a consent decree involved American Telephone and Telegraph (AT&T), which the EEOC found to be discriminating against women. Although AT&T did not admit nor was required to admit any act of discrimination, it entered into a consent decree after the EEOC opposed its application for a rate increase. In a more recent settlement,

> State Farm Insurance Co. agreed to set aside for women half of its new sales agent jobs in California over the next 10 years, and to pay damages and back pay to women who were refused sales jobs during a 13-year period, according to a consent decree settling a long-running sex bias case against the company.
>
> Female employees filed a class action suit in 1979, claiming that State Farm in California had discriminated against women in recruitment, hiring, job assignments, training, and termination decisions. A federal district court found the company had discriminated and was liable for damages to all women who unsuccessfully applied for or were deterred from applying for trainee agent jobs since 1974. The settlement covers 1,113 sales jobs that became vacant and were filled by men between 1974 and 1987, and is expected to result in back pay awards totaling between $100 and $300 million.
>
> The agreement provides that State Farm will use its best efforts to give women 50 percent of the trainee agent appointments each year for the next decade. The company is required to nominate one woman in each of its three California regions to serve as a recruitment administrator to train agency managers to recruit and retain qualified women. In addition, procedures are specified for the company to follow in publicizing openings for sales agent jobs.
>
> Women affected by the decree who wish to make a claim may file for damages during a four-month period beginning May 1. (*Kraszewski v. State Farm,* 1988)

By the way, in April 1992 State Farm reached a settlement with those women affected by the decree who filed for damages. The settlement was worth $157 million, the largest settlement ever brought under the Civil Rights Act of 1964.

Although goals set by consent decrees, or as part of the federal contractor's AAP, only specify percentages, in essence they are often seen as establishing quotas. That is, the goals establish that an organization must hire a certain number of women or African-Americans to correct underutilization or past discrimination in employment. Setting quotas may result in a violation of the Fourteenth Amendment, as well as against Title VII protection against all employment discrimination; for example, white males might not be hired because an organization has a quota to meet. However, the courts have generally held in favor of goals as the only way to reverse previous practices of discrimination (*Detroit Police Officers' Association v. Coleman Young,* 1979; *Charles L. Maehren v. City of Seattle,* 1979; and *City of St. Louis v. U.S.A.,* 1980).

Nevertheless, the issue of reverse discrimination is being heard. For example, the Supreme Court ruled that federal courts could not ignore a seniority-based layoff policy and modify a consent decree to prevent the layoff of black workers (*Firefighter Local Union 1784 v. Stotts,* 1984). In related cases, the Supreme Court has ruled that there are limits to the use of rigid racial and ethnic criteria to accomplish remedial objectives (*Fullilove v. Klutznick,* 1980; *Richmond v. Croson,* 1989).

Since this issue relates more directly to selection, it is addressed in more detail in the section on selection. Reverse discrimination as it relates to recruitment is discussed here as an issue in organizations establishing voluntary AAPs.

Voluntary AAPs. In addition to AAPs related to federal contracts and consent decrees, organizations may voluntarily establish goals for hiring and promoting women, members of minority groups, and handicapped individuals. The exact content of such AAPs depends on the organization and the extent to which various groups are underrepresented.

Organizations often establish their own voluntary affirmative action programs without pressure from the EEOC or OFCCP. In fact, organizations may benefit from using EEOC guidelines that support voluntary AAPs. The key considerations in an organization's establishment of a legal, voluntary AAP are that it be remedial in purpose, limited in its duration, restricted in its reverse discrimination impact—that is, it does not operate as an absolute ban on nonminorities—and flexible in implementation. When an organization's voluntary AAP has these characteristics, the risk of losing a reverse discrimination suit may be minimized. Nonetheless there is still some risk of being liable for reverse discrimination (*Martin v. Wilks,* 1989).

Selection

Legal considerations appear to be most extensive for selection. Numerous acts, executive orders, regulations, and agencies have an impact on selection practices in most organizations. They do this particularly through defining bases of illegal discrimination and serving as defenses for the same charges.

Acts. The historical development of equal employment legislation began with the **Civil Rights Act of 1866,** Section 1981, which prohibits employee discrimination based on race, color, and national origin. The **Civil Rights Act of 1871,** Section 1983, enforces the Fourteenth Amendment to the U.S. Constitution, which has been held to prohibit discrimination based on race, color, national origin, religion, sex, and age.

The **Civil Rights Act of 1964** and, in particular, **Title VII**, prohibits discrimination against individuals on the basis of sex, race, color, national origin, and religion. The **Civil Rights Act of 1991** has redefined discrimination and exposed employers to greater financial liability. Passage of this act was in part triggered by several Supreme Court decisions in the 1980s, including *Wards Cove Packing v. Atonio,* 1989. These decisions had, among other things, shifted the burden of proving discrimination to the employee. The Civil Rights Act of 1991 returned this burden to the employer.[8] Other major provisions and issues of this act are described in the PHRM in the News: "The Burden of Proof Grows Heavier" feature. Many of the terms in this feature, which outlines the basic framework for proving illegal discrimination, are discussed over the next several pages.

The **Equal Employment Opportunity Act of 1972** amended the Civil Rights Act of 1964 that had first created the Equal Employment Opportunity Commission. This 1972 amendment expanded the coverage of Title VII to include public and private employers with fifteen or more employees, labor organizations with fifteen or more members, and public and private employment agencies. Elected officials and their appointees are excluded from Title VII coverage but are still covered under the Fourteenth Amendment and the Civil Rights Acts of 1866 and 1871. The 1972 amendment also identified exceptions or exemptions to Title VII, including bona fide occupational qualifications, seniority systems, preemployment inquiries, use of job-related tests for selection, national security interests, and veterans' preference rights. Much of what is discussed under the section below on proving illegal discrimination is based upon the Civil Rights Act of 1964 and the Civil Rights Act of 1991.

The **Age Discrimination in Employment Act (ADEA) of 1967** as amended in 1978, 1986, and 1990, prohibits discrimination against employees and applicants who are more than forty years old. While age discrimination (bias) has been a significant legal issue in the U.S. for some time, it is just now becoming an issue in Europe.

> Rampant job bias against older Europeans is just starting to decline, thanks to a scarcity of young people and the spread of U.S.–style advocacy groups. Unlike America, Europe lacks tough laws broadly barring age discrimination. Employers routinely run advertisements seeking workers under 40, force staffers as young as 55 to retire, and fire people simply for being too old.[9]

As already described, the **Americans with Disabilities Act of 1990** substantially extends the coverage of the Rehabilitation Act to include the same organizations covered by the Civil Rights Act of 1991. Coverage began in 1992, with organizations making accommodations for individuals (employees and customers) with disabilities. As defined by the act, an estimated forty-five million Americans are classified as disabled. The impact of the act is regarded as the most significant since Title VII. It is likely to supersede both the **Rehabilitation Act** and the **Vietnam Era Veterans' Readjustment Act of 1974**, which protects disabled veterans and veterans of the Vietnam era.[10]

In addition to these major federal acts pertaining to equal employment opportunity, state and local governments also have their own acts that employers must follow. There are also many executive orders.

Executive orders. The equal employment opportunity acts have been supported by a number of executive orders (EOs). **EO 11246** of 1965 prohibits discrimination on the basis of race, color, religion, and national origin by federal agencies, contractors, and subcontractors. In 1966, **EO 11375** was signed to prohibit discrimination in these same organizations on the basis of sex. **EO 11478** of 1969 prescribes that employment policies of the federal government be based on merit and that the head of each agency establish and maintain a program of equal employment opportunity.

Guidelines. While acts and executive orders delineate protected classes, guidelines provide the mechanisms, such as selection tests, by which these acts and orders are implemented. The first set was issued in 1970 by the EEOC and originally intended to provide a workable set of ideal standards for employees, unions, and employment agencies. Those guidelines defined a test as being

> ... all formal, scored, qualified or standardized techniques of assessing job suitability, including ... background requirements, educational or work history requirements, interviews, biographical information blanks, interview rating scales and scored application blanks.

PHRM IN THE NEWS

The Burden of Proof Grows Heavier

The 1991 Civil Rights Act has redefined discrimination and exposed employers to greater financial liability. The law now in effect reversed several Supreme Court rulings and shifted the burden of proof for cases of intentional discrimination from the employee to the employer. In addition, workers who successfully prove they were discriminated against now can receive compensatory and punitive damages that previously were not allowed. Under the original civil rights legislation, employees could only receive reinstatement, back pay and attorneys' fees.

The total amount of compensatory and punitive damages allowed by the law is determined by the number of employees at the company and cannot exceed the following limits:

- $50,000 for companies with 15 to 100 employees;
- $100,000 for employers with 101 to 200 employees;
- $200,000 for companies with 201 to 500 employees;
- $300,000 for employers with over 501 employees.

These damages would be added on top of attorneys' fees, which can range anywhere between $40,000 and $150,000, according to professionals in the employment law field. Companies also may be responsible for paying the fees of expert witnesses called by the plaintiffs, which often range between $10,000 and $15,000.

Legal experts agree that damages will be awarded more easily now because an employee can have his or her case heard before a jury. Previously, discrimination cases were tried before judges, many of whom were considered more sympathetic to employers. Juries, on the other hand, historically have decided against businesses and awarded plaintiffs huge sums of money for damages.

"The Civil Rights Act, on top of the Americans with Disabilities Act (ADA), is the final kick in the pants for managers," said attorney Fred Sullivan of the Springfield, Mass., firm Sullivan & Hayes. "Managers have to think differently."

This new way of thinking represents a radical departure for businesses, according to Sullivan. Companies must approach their employment practices from the perspective of a jury, rather than from a managerial viewpoint. The underlying question employers need to consider regarding any potentially liable action is, "How can this be perceived differently than the way we perceive it," Sullivan added.

"The Civil Rights Act and the ADA place more limitations on recruiting as well as discharging employees," said Howard Flaxman, an attorney with the Philadelphia firm Blank, Rome, Comisky & McCauley. "The stakes are very high right now."

Continued

Following the issuance of the guidelines, the courts began using them as a sort of checklist of **minimum** standards for test validation, rather than as a flexible set of ideal standards, as intended. Concern over this trend prompted the Equal Employment Opportunity Coordinating Council to develop a set of uniform guidelines, to be used by all federal agencies, that were based on sound psychological principles and were technically feasible. As a result, the *Federal Executive Agency Guidelines* were published in 1976 followed by the *Uniform Guidelines on Employee Selection Procedure* in 1978. These Uniform Guidelines are a fourteen-thousand-word catalog of do's and don't's and questions and answers for hiring and promotion. They contain interpretation and guidance not found in earlier EEOC guidelines.

The EEOC also has published other guidelines. On November 10, 1980, the commission issued *Guidelines on Discrimination Because of Sex*. These guidelines are premised on the assumption that sexual harassment is a condition of employment if women are exposed to it more frequently than men. Six weeks

The Burden is Shifted

The stakes are higher because any employer brought before a court on a "disparate impact" discrimination case today must prove that the challenged employment practice was a result of a business necessity. In the past, companies only had to submit evidence of a business justification, and the employee was responsible for persuading the court against the employer's evidence.

The act also shifts the burden of proof to employers in dual motive cases, that is, cases in which both lawful and unlawful factors were involved. Before, a company that used an illegal factor, such as race or gender, to make an employment decision could prevail if it proved that the same decision would be made even if that factor were not considered. Now an employer must show that only lawful factors were used to make the employment decision. The employee only has to prove that his or her protected status, such as race, gender or disability, was a "motivating factor" in the decision regardless of other factors involved.

Flaxman said that such changes in the law, in addition to increased monetary awards, will provoke more litigation, particularly for marginal cases that would not have gone to court in the past. Attorneys also may be more likely to use the law as a bargaining tool to negotiate better out-of-court settlements for their clients.

An Employer's Defense

Companies now must review all of their personnel policies to protect themselves against any litigation that could result from the new law. As part of the review process, Flaxman advised employers to make sure they have established a sexual harassment policy. Businesses also need to study their disciplinary policies to ensure that every problem is dealt with through progressive and corrective actions that are thoroughly documented.

"With juries, the issue is more of fairness, not discrimination. That's the issue even though it's not supposed to be," Flaxman said. "Juries are punishing employers who appear to be almost cavalier in their attitude."

"You want to show to the jury that efforts went beyond what was normally expected," Sullivan added. "Go beyond the final warning; issue a second warning."

Hiring practices also must be reviewed to comply with the new law. Employers must make sure that the people conducting the screening process ask the proper questions and conduct the proper investigations.

Although the law encourages both parties to seek an alternative method to resolve disputes, such as arbitration, its effectiveness remains questionable. Unless the employee is legally bound by an arbitration agreement, the matter still can go to court.

Sullivan, however, said the use of a third party can be helpful in settling disputes. Many employers have resisted arbitration, believing they did not need a third party to tell them how to manage their business. "But today there is a third party—the jury."

SOURCE: B. Smith, *HR Focus*, (Feb. 1992): 1, 6.

later, the EEOC issued its *Guidelines on Discrimination Because of National Origin*. The national origin guidelines extended earlier versions of this protection by defining national origin as a **place** rather than a **country** of origin. It also revised the "speak–English–only rules." This means employers can require that English be spoken if there is a compelling business–related necessity. On September 29, 1981, the EEOC issued guidelines on age discrimination, in essence, identifying what the Age Discrimination in Employment Act meant to do and what it should mean to employers and employees.[11]

Under the *Guidelines on Discrimination Because of Religion,* an employer is obliged to accommodate the religious preferences of current and prospective employees unless the employer demonstrates undue hardship. It appears, however, that if an employer shows "reasonable attempts to accommodate," the courts may be satisfied that no religious discrimination has occurred (*State Division of Human Rights v. Rochester Housing Authority,* 1980; *Philbrook v. Ansonia Board of Education,* 1986).

Professional standards. Selection processes are also monitored by the American Psychological Association. In 1966 and again in 1974, the American Psychological Association (APA) released its *Standards for Education and Psychological Tests*. These standards were updated in 1985. In 1975 and again in 1987, the Society for Industrial-Organizational Psychology (SIOP), a division of the APA, published its *Principles for the Validation and Use of Personnel Selection Procedures.* Drawing from relevant research, these standards and principles help clarify issues regarding test fairness and discrimination.

Proving Illegal Discrimination

While the Civil Rights Act of 1991 explicitly prohibits discrimination, nowhere in the law is discrimination defined. Essentially, a jury must decide whether or not illegal discrimination has occurred. Broadly speaking, however, the act prohibits differences in the treatment of employees who belong to one of the five protected groups (based on race, color, religion, sex, and national origin). Discrimination based on age, physical and mental handicaps, or against disabled or Vietnam-era veterans is prohibited by other acts. Discrimination on all other bases or qualifications is untouched by federal law, except when discrimination on **nonprohibited** factors is disguised as legal discrimination. For example, using minimum height and weight requirements as substitute measures of physical strength may adversely affect women and certain ethnic groups (Asians, Hispanics). When this occurs, the **Civil Rights Act of 1991** is violated.[12]

***Prima facie* cases.** In a typical discrimination suit a person alleges discrimination due to unlawful employment practices. The person may first go to the Equal Employment Opportunity Commission (EEOC) office. The EEOC may seek out the facts of the case from both sides, attempting a resolution. Failing a resolution, the person may continue the case and file a suit. In the first phase of a discrimination suit, it is the obligation of the plaintiff (the person filing the suit) to establish a *prima facie* case of discrimination. A *prima facie* case of illegal discrimination is established by showing disparate impact or disparate treatment.

Disparate treatment means there is an apparent case of illegal discrimination against an **individual** while **disparate impact** is against a group. (Occasionally, the term **adverse impact** is used in making references to **effects** of disparate treatment or disparate impact.) The basic criteria for establishing a *prima facie* case of disparate impact were specified by the Supreme Court in *Griggs v. Duke Power,* and those for a disparate treatment case in *McDonnell Douglas Corp. v. Green* (1973). While a charge of disparate treatment has always required evidence of **intent to discriminate,** only more recently has the Court required the same of some disparate impact cases (*Wards Cove Packing v. Atonio,* 1989). The Civil Rights Act of 1991, however, substantially diminishes the plaintiff's burden of proof responsibility.[13]

Disparate impact. Cases of disparate impact rely on three types of statistical evidence.

One approach relies upon **comparative statistics** or comparisons of the rates or ratios of hiring, firing, promoting, transfering, and demoting for protected and nonprotected groups. The *Uniform Guidelines* suggest that disparate impact (adverse impact) has been demonstrated if the selection rate "for any racial, ethnic, or sex subgroup is less than four-fifths or 80 percent of the highest selection rate for any group." Originally, this bottom-line criterion was aimed at identifying disparate impact only for an entire set of selection procedures rather than for any single part of the procedures. This aim, however, has now been modified to apply to each part of the selection procedures as well as to the entire set (*Connecticut v. Teal,* 1982). The EEOC can examine an organization's personnel records and determine the existence of this type of illegal discrimination. The personnel records that employers are required to keep and that the EEOC can examine are called EEO-1 reports, shown in exhibit 3.3.[14]

In contrast, the argument using **demographic statistics,** a second approach, centers on a comparison of an organization's work force to the relevant labor market. This argument is rooted in the Civil Rights Act of 1964. For example, an employer's selection procedures can be shown as discriminatory (*prima facie*) if the employer's work force fails to reflect parity with the race or sex composition of the relevant labor market. Organizations may determine their relevant labor market in several ways. One is by identifying where eighty-five percent of current employees and job applicants reside. Another is to choose the labor market from which they generally select applicants. The EEOC, however, may suggest that organizations expand their labor markets; as a consequence, determining relevant labor markets is often an art rather than a science.

Once the relevant labor market has been determined, it is subject to revisions because of changing demographic characteristics of the U.S. labor force. Organizations are witnessing dramatic demographic changes based on the comparisons of the 1980 and 1990 national censuses. As a result of the demographic changes, organizations are having to redetermine their relevant labor markets to successfully defend AAPs and cases of *prima facie* claims of discrimination. *Prima facie* cases of this type are likely to be successfully defended to the extent that parity is attained (that is, the extent to which the proportions of protected group members in an organization's work force mirror the proportions in the relevant labor market).

The third basis for establishing a case of disparate impact is use of **concentration statistics.** The argument here is that a *prima facie* case of illegal discrimination exists to the extent that protected group members are located in one particular area or job category in the organization. For example, equal numbers of male and female employees may be hired into entry-level jobs in the organization, but the females may be placed predominantly in secretarial jobs. Such a situation provides a case of disparate impact.

Promotion practices can also create unbalanced demographic concentration. For example, in *Wards Cove Packing v. Atonio,* the Wards Cove Packing Company in Alaska was charged by Atonio and other minority workers (primarily Filipinos and Alaska Natives) with illegal discrimination because they were never promoted. Concentration statistics supported this claim. The Court, while not denying the accuracy of the data, stated that Atonio also had the burden of showing intentional discrimination and suggesting alternative procedures that would be equally valid but less discriminatory. This scenario, which was a significant break from past Court actions, has been essentially reversed by the Civil Rights Act of 1991 as described in the "PHRM in the News: The Burden of Proof Grows Heavier."

Disparate treatment. Illegal discrimination against an individual is referred to as disparate treatment. In contrast to the cases of disparate impact, a

Exhibit 3.3
Equal Employment Opportunity Report EEO–1

Joint Reporting Committee

- Equal Employment Opportunity Commission
- Office of Federal Contract Compliance Programs (Labor)

EQUAL EMPLOYMENT OPPORTUNITY

EMPLOYER INFORMATION REPORT EEO–1

Standard Form 100
(Rev. 5–84)
O.M.B. No. 3046–0007

100–211

Section A—TYPE OF REPORT
Refer to instructions for number and types of reports to be filed.

1. Indicate by marking in the appropriate box the type of reporting unit for which this copy of the form is submitted (MARK ONLY ONE BOX).

(1) ☐ Single-establishment Employer Report

Multi-establishment Employer:
(2) ☐ Consolidated Report (Required)
(3) ☐ Headquarters Unit Report (Required)
(4) ☐ Individual Establishment Report (submit one for each establishment with 50 or more employees)
(5) ☐ Special Report

2. Total number of reports being filed by this Company (Answer on Consolidated Report only) ______

Section B—COMPANY IDENTIFICATION *(To be answered by all employers)* — OFFICE USE ONLY

1. Parent Company
   a. Name of parent company (owns or controls establishment in item 2) omit if same as label — a.

Name of receiving office				Address (Number and street)	b.
City or town	County	State	ZIP code	b. Employer Identification No. ☐☐☐☐☐☐☐☐☐	

2. Establishment for which this report is filed. (Omit if same as label) — OFFICE USE ONLY
   a. Name of establishment — c.

Address (Number and street)	City or Town	County	State	ZIP code	d.

b. Employer Identification No. ☐☐☐☐☐☐☐☐☐ (Omit if same as label) — e.

Section C—EMPLOYERS WHO ARE REQUIRED TO FILE *(To be answered by all employers)*

☐ Yes ☐ No 1. Does the entire company have at least 100 employees in the payroll period for which you are reporting?

☐ Yes ☐ No 2. Is your company affiliated through common ownership and/or centralized management with other entities in an enterprise with a total employment of 100 or more?

☐ Yes ☐ No 3. Does the company or any of its establishments (a) have 50 or more employees AND (b) is not exempt as provided by 41 CFR 60–1.5, AND either (1) is a prime government contractor or first-tier subcontractor, and has a contract, subcontract, or purchase order amounting to $50,000 or more, or (2) serves as a depository of Government funds in any amount or is a financial institution which is an issuing and paying agent for U.S. Savings Bonds and Savings Notes?

If the response to question C–3 is yes, please enter your Dun and Bradstreet identification number (if you have one): ☐☐☐☐☐☐☐☐☐

☐ Yes ☐ No 4. Does the company receive financial assistance from the Small Business Administration (SBA)?

NOTE: If the answer is yes to questions 1, 2, or 3, complete the entire form, otherwise skip to Section G.

NSN 7540–00–180–6384

Exhibit 3.3 (continued)

SF 100 Page 2

Section D—EMPLOYMENT DATA

Employment at this establishment—Report all permanent full-time or part-time employees including apprentices and on-the-job trainees unless specifically excluded as set forth in the instructions. Enter the appropriate figures on all lines and in all columns. Blank spaces will be considered as zeros.

JOB CATEGORIES	NUMBER OF EMPLOYEES										
	OVERALL TOTALS (SUM OF COL. B THRU K)	MALE					FEMALE				
		WHITE (NOT OF HISPANIC ORIGIN)	BLACK (NOT OF HISPANIC ORIGIN)	HISPANIC	ASIAN OR PACIFIC ISLANDER	AMERICAN INDIAN OR ALASKAN NATIVE	WHITE (NOT OF HISPANIC ORIGIN)	BLACK (NOT OF HISPANIC ORIGIN)	HISPANIC	ASIAN OR PACIFIC ISLANDER	AMERICAN INDIAN OR ALASKAN NATIVE
	A	B	C	D	E	F	G	H	I	J	K
Officials and Managers 1											
Professionals 2											
Technicians 3											
Sales Workers 4											
Office and Clerical 5											
Craft Workers (Skilled) 6											
Operatives (Semi-Skilled) 7											
Laborers (Unskilled) 8											
Service Workers 9											
TOTAL 10											
Total employment reported in previous EEO–1 report 11											
(The trainees below should also be included in the figures for the appropriate occupational categories above)											
Formal On-the-job trainees — White collar 12											
Formal On-the-job trainees — Production 13											

NOTE: Omit questions 1 and 2 on the Consolidated Report.

1. Date(s) of payroll period used:
2. Does this establishment employ apprentices?
   1 ☐ Yes 2 ☐ No

Section E—ESTABLISHMENT INFORMATION *(Omit on the Consolidated Report)*

1. Is the location of the establishment the same as that reported last year?
   1 ☐ Yes 2 ☐ No 3 ☐ No report last year
2. Is the major business activity at this establishment the same as that reported last year?
   1 ☐ Yes 2 ☐ No 3 ☐ No report last year

OFFICE USE ONLY

3. What is the major activity of this establishment? (Be specific, i.e., manufacturing steel castings, retail grocer, wholesale plumbing supplies, title insurance, etc. Include the specific type of product or type of service provided, as well as the principal business or industrial activity.)

f.

Section F—REMARKS

Use this item to give any identification data appearing on last report which differs from that given above, explain major changes in composition or reporting units and other pertinent information.

Section G—CERTIFICATION *(See Instructions G)*

Check one
1 ☐ All reports are accurate and were prepared in accordance with the instructions (check on consolidated only)
2 ☐ This report is accurate and was prepared in accordance with the instructions.

Name of Certifying Official	Title	Signature	Date

Name of person to contact regarding this report (Type or print)	Address (Number and street)				
Title	City and State	ZIP code	Telephone Area Code	Number	**Extension**

All reports and information obtained from individual reports will be kept confidential as required by Section 709(e) of Title VII
WILLFULLY FALSE STATEMENTS ON THIS REPORT ARE PUNISHABLE BY LAW, U.S. CODE, TITLE 18, SECTION 1001

prima facie case of disparate treatment exists to the extent that an individual can demonstrate the following:

- The individual belongs to a minority group
- The individual applied for a job for which the employer was seeking applicants
- Despite being qualified, he or she was rejected
- After the individual's rejection, the employer kept looking for people with the applicant's qualifications

These conditions, which basically present a case of intentional discrimination, were set forth in *McDonnell Douglas Corp. v. Green* (1973). These conditions were essentially met in the case of Barbara L. Sogg in her discrimination suit against American Airlines. Her story is also an excellent follow-up to our discussion of glass-ceiling programs in chapter 2.

Once a *prima facie* case of disparate treatment discrimination has been established by any one of the four ways, the employer must be given the opportunity to defend itself.[15]

Bases for Defending Discriminatory Practices

An organization accused of illegal discrimination may be able to successfully defend its employment practices by showing one of the following:

- Job-relatedness
- Business necessity
- Bona fide occupational qualification (BFOQ)
- Bona fide seniority systems (BFSS)
- Voluntary transient affirmative action programs (AAPs)

Job relatedness. For many jobs, employee qualifications are necessary. Thus, employers are interested in measuring qualifications and establishing predictions of how employees who possess them do on the job. To demonstrate **job-relatedness,** the company must show that its selection and placement procedures (predictors, tests when used for selection decisions) are related to an employee's being successful on the job (*Watson v. Fort Worth Bank and Trust,* 1988).[16]

It's important to note, however, that any test must be related to **important components of the job** as determined through job analysis. For example, a typing test may be an appropriate selection device for a clerk-typist who spends sixty percent of his or her time on data entry. However, it may not be an appropriate selection device for a receptionist who spends less than five percent of his or her time typing.

Business necessity. Although showing the job-relatedness of a selection procedure is desirable, it may not always be possible. Some courts, recognizing this situation, have allowed companies to defend their selection procedures by showing business necessity. Whereas the job-relatedness defense often requires a demonstration of actual predictor-criterion relationships, business necessity does not. The case of *Levin v. Delta Air Lines, Inc.* (1984) was decided on the fact that pregnancy was not shown to affect the essence of the business (safe air travel), not on the fact that it failed to affect the ability of a flight attendant to provide service to the air travelers. In cases where business necessity clearly is high, demonstrating that a specific selection procedure is job-related is not necessary (see *Spurlock v. United Airlines,* 1972, and *Hodgson v. Greyhound Lines, Inc.,* 1974, in Appendix A).[17]

Bona fide occupational qualifications. Another defense against a charge of illegal discrimination is **bona fide occupational qualifications (BFOQ).** For example:

> ...[T]he EEOC sued the Massachussets State Registry of Motor Vehicles, charging that denying entry-level jobs to individuals over age 35 violated ADEA. The state argued that the 1986 ADEA amendment exempts all law enforcement officers from the scope of the Act for a seven year period, and that in any event, age is a bona fide occupational qualification for motor vehicle examiners under *Mahoney v. Trabucco,* which upheld an age-50 mandatory retirement rule for Massachusetts state troopers. EEOC countered that few motor vehicle examiners perform active law enforcement duties.
>
> Acknowledging that the issue is a close one, the court agrees with the state that motor vehicle examiners, who are authorized to carry weapons, enforce the state's motor-vehicle laws, and perform many of the same duties as state and local police officers, are properly classified as law enforcement personnel and are therefore exempt from ADEA under the 1986 amendment (*EEOC v. Commonwealth of Massachusetts,* 1987).[18]

Bona fide seniority sytems. Closely related to BFOQs are **bona fide seniority systems (BFSS).** As long as a company has established and maintained a seniority system without the intent to illegally discriminate, it is considered bona fide (*International Brotherhood of Teamsters v. United States,* 1977; *United States v. Trucking Management, Inc.,* 1981; *American Tobacco v. Patterson,* 1982). Thus, promotion and job assignment decisions can be made on the basis of seniority.[19] In a major decision the U.S. Supreme Court ruled that seniority can also be used in the determination of layoffs, even if doing so reverses effects of affirmative action hiring (*Firefighters Local Union 1784 v. Stotts,* 1984).

Voluntary affirmative action programs. As described above, organizations may establish affirmative action programs without pressure from the EEOC and OFCCP. For them to be a defense against illegal discrimination, however, the programs need to be remedial in purpose, limited in duration, restricted in impact, flexible in implementation, and minimal in harm to innocent parties. However, there is growing ambiguity as to whether or not the courts will be sympathetic to these affirmative action programs despite past decisions (*Wygant v. Jackson Board of Education,* 1986; *International Association of Firefighters Local 93 v. City of Cleveland,* 1986).

Performance Appraisal

Organizations must also pay attention to several legal considerations in the process of employee performance appraisal, as shown in exhibit 3.4.

Establishing valid performance criteria and standards. Developing performance appraisals that reflect critical performance criteria (job components

Exhibit 3.4
Prescriptions for Legally Defensible Appraisal Systems

1. Job analysis to identify important duties and tasks should precede development of a performance appraisal system.
2. The performance appraisal system should be standardized and formal.
3. Specific performance standards should be communicated to employees in advance of the appraisal period.
4. Objective and uncontaminated data should be used whenever possible.
5. Ratings on traits such as dependability, drive, or attitude should be avoided or operationalized in behavioral terms.
6. Employees should be evaluated on specific work dimensions rather than on a single global or overall measure.
7. If work behaviors rather than outcomes are to be evaluated, evaluators should have ample opportunity to observe ratee performance.
8. To increase the reliability of ratings, more than one independent evaluator should be used whenever possible.
9. Behavioral documentation should be prepared for extreme ratings.
10. Employees should be given an opportunity to review their appraisals.
11. A formal system of appeal should be available for appraisal disagreements.
12. Raters should be trained to prevent discrimination and to evaluate performance consistently.
13. Appraisals should be frequent, offered at least annually.

SOURCE: Adapted from H. J. Bernardin and W. F. Cascio, "Performance Appraisal and the Law," in *Readings in Personnel and Human Resource Management,* 3d ed., ed. R. S. Schuler, S. A. Youngblood, and V. Huber (St. Paul: West 1988), 239.

for performance appraisal) is necessary if the appraisals are to be considered valid. The U.S. Circuit Court in *Brito v. Zia Company* (1973) found that Zia Company was in violation of Title VII when a disproportionate number of employees of a protected group were laid off because of low performance scores. The critical point was that the performance scores were based on the supervisor's best judgments and opinions, not on important components of doing the job. When companies make performance-based decisions on the basis of appraisals, they are using the appraisals as employment tests; thus, the appraisals must be based upon identifiable job-related criteria (*Stringfellow v. Monsanto Corp.*, 1970; *U.S. v. City of Chicago,* 1978). The best way to determine whether the appraisal criteria are job-related is to do a job analysis (*Albemarle Paper Company v. Moody,* 1975).

Once the appropriate performance criteria are established, levels or standards marking the degree of desirability or acceptability of employee performance on each job criterion are established. To ensure that the essence of job performance is captured, several criteria may be required. In turn, a standard must be established for each criterion. Establishing criteria and standards is necessary, not just for legal considerations but also for job performance reasons. Consequently, how these criteria and standards are established is important. Accordingly, they are discussed in chapter 7.

Using valid performance appraisal forms. Once the critical job components (criteria) are established, forms that relate to those components must be used. For example, if quantity of output is a critical job criterion, appraisal forms that ask supervisors their general impressions of how personable and valuable the employees are may lead to an inappropriate appraisal; and, if used for an employment decision, such an appraisal may lead to a *prima facie* case of illegal discrimination. Appraisal forms on which the raters indicate by a check mark their evaluation of an employee on attributes such as leadership, attitude toward people, or loyalty are often referred to as **subjective forms.** In contrast, appraisals where the evaluation involves specifically defined behaviors or outcomes—such as level of output, level of specific goal attainment, or number of days absent—are often called **objective forms.**

Although the courts will allow a company to use a subjective form (*Roger v. International Paper Co.,* 1975), they generally frown upon their use (*Albemarle Paper Company v. Moody,* 1975; *Oshiver v. Court of Common Pleas,* 1979; *Baxter v. Savannah Sugar Refining Corp.,* 1974; and *Rowe v. General Motors,* 1972) because they may not produce fair or accurate evaluations. Consequently, the courts have ruled that, when disparate impact is found, all performance appraisal procedures—objective or subjective—must be shown to be job-related (*Watson v. Fort Worth Bank and Trust,* 1988).

It is also important to communicate these expectations to incumbents in advance of the evaluating period. In *Donaldson v. Pillsbury Company* (1977), a female employee who was dismissed was granted relief because she had never been shown her job description (which would have specified performance criteria).

Total Compensation

As in many activities in managing human resources, state and federal laws and court decisions have had an important effect upon total compensation.

Davis-Bacon and Walsh-Healey. The federal government has enacted several laws influencing the level of wages employers may pay, pay structures, and individual wage determinations. The first federal law to protect the amount of pay employees receive for their work was the **Davis-Bacon Act of 1931;** this act required organizations holding federal construction contracts to pay laborers and mechanics the prevailing wages of the majority of the employees in the locality where the work was performed. The **Walsh-Healey Public Contracts Act of 1936** extended the Davis-Bacon Act to include all federal contracts exceeding $10,000 and specified that pay levels conform to the industry minimum rather than the area minimum, as specified in Davis-Bacon. The Walsh-Healey Act also established overtime pay at one and one-half times the hourly rate. These wage provisions, however, did not include administrative, professional, office, custodial, or maintenance employees, or beginners, or disabled persons.

Wage deduction laws. Three federal laws influence how much employers may deduct from employee paychecks. The **Copeland Act of 1934** authorized the secretary of labor to regulate wage deductions for contractors and subcontractors doing work financed in whole or in part by a federal contract. Essentially, the Copeland Act was aimed at illegal deductions. Protection against a more severe threat from an employer with federal contracts was provided in the **Anti-Kickback Law of 1948.** The **Federal Wage Garnishment Law of 1980** also protects employees against deductions from pay for indebtedness. It provides that only twenty-five percent of one's disposable weekly earnings or thirty times the minimum wage, whichever is less, can be deducted for debt repayment.

Fair Labor Standards Act. Partially because Davis-Bacon and Walsh-Healey were limited in their coverage to employees on construction projects, the **Fair Labor Standards Act of 1938** (or the Wage and Hour Law) was enacted. This set minimum wages, maximum hours, child labor standards, and overtime pay provisions for all workers except domestic and government employees. The Supreme Court extended the coverage to include state and local government employees in 1985 (*Garcia v. San Antonio Metropolitan Transit Authority*).[20]

1. **Minimum wage.** The minimum wage began at 25¢ an hour and has reached $4.25 as of April 1, 1991. Still, subminimum wages are permitted for learners in semiskilled occupations, apprentices, handicapped persons working in sheltered workshops, and employees who receive more than $30 per month in tips (up to 40 percent of the minimum requirement may be covered by tips).

2. **Child labor.** In order to prevent abuses regarding children, the act also prohibits minors under the age of 18 from working in hazardous occupations. For nonhazardous positions, the minimum age ranges from 14 to 16, depending on the type of work to be performed and whether the employer is a child's parent.

3. **Overtime provisions.** The overtime provision of the act establishes who is to be paid overtime for work, and who is not. Most employees covered must be paid time and a half for all work exceeding 40 hours per week. These are called **nonexempt employees.** Several groups of individuals are exempt from both overtime and minimum wage provisions. The **exempt employees** include employees of firms not involved in interstate commerce, employees in seasonal industries, and outside salespeople. Three other employee groups—executives, administrators, and professionals—are also exempt from overtime pay and minimum wage laws in most organizations. Trainee managers and assistant managers, however, are excluded and should thus be paid overtime.[21]

To be exempt, professionals must spend 80 percent of their work hours in the following tasks:

- Doing work requiring knowledge acquired through specialized, prolonged training
- Exercising discretion or judgment
- Doing work that is primarily intellectual and nonroutine

The criteria for exempt status as an executive include spending at least 80 percent of work time in the following tasks:

- Undertaking management duties
- Supervising two or more employees
- Controlling or greatly influencing hiring, firing, and promotion decisions
- Exercising discretion

In both cases, a comprehensive job analysis is necessary to determine whether a job is exempt.

Equal Pay Act. While not covered in the original 1938 law, the fourth provision of the **Fair Labor Standards Act** was added as an amendment in 1963. Called the **Equal Pay Act,** this extension prohibits an employer from discriminating

> ... between employees on the basis of sex by paying wages to employees...at a rate less than the rate at which he pays wages to employees of the opposite sex...for equal work on jobs the performance of which requires equal skill, effort and responsibility, and which are performed under similar working conditions.

To establish a *prima facie* case of wage discrimination, the plaintiff needs to establish that a disparity in pay exists for males and females performing substantially equal, not necessarily identical, jobs. To determine this, the amount of skill, effort, responsibility, and working conditions required by each job must be assessed through careful job analysis. In making this judgment, job content rather than the window dressing of a job title should be examined. If jobs are found to be substantially equal, wages for the lowest paid job must be raised to match those of the higher paying position. Freezing or lowering pay of the higher paid job is unacceptable.

Four exceptions can be used to legally defend unequal pay for equal work, as specified in the Bennett amendment. They are the existence and use of (1) a seniority system, (2) a merit system, (3) a system that measures earnings or quality of production, or (4) any additional factor other than sex. To establish a *prima facie* case of discrimination, the plaintiff needs to establish that a disparity in pay exists for employees on equal jobs. If the employer can show the existence of one or more of the four exceptions, however, the differential may be found to be justified.

Title VII of the Civil Rights Act. Note that the Equal Pay Act (EPA) provides legal coverage only for equal pay for equal work. Only when men and women are performing jobs requiring equivalent skills, effort, and responsibility are they entitled to identical pay (unless there are differences in performance, seniority, or other conditions). **Title VII of the Civil Rights Act of 1964,** however, provides broader legal coverage for pay discrimination:

> Addressing the interrelationship between the Equal Pay Act and Title VII, [the] EEOC observes that while both laws prohibit sex-based wage discrimination, Title VII's prohibitions are broader. In cases where a complainant meets the jurisdictional requirements of both laws, the rules say, "any violation of the Equal Pay Act is also a violation of the Title VII." But since Title VII covers types of wage discrimination not actionable under the EPA, "an act or practice of an employer or labor organization that is not a violation of EPA may nevertheless be a violation of Title VII," according to the rules.
>
> If an employer violates both EPA and Title VII, the complainant may recover under both laws for the same period of time, as long as the individual "does not receive duplicative relief for the same wrong," according to the regulations. Relief will be computed, the rules say, "to give each individual the highest benefit which entitlement under either statute would provide (e.g., liquidated damages may be available under the EPA, but not under Title VII).[22]

Comparable worth. An important concept in compensation is comparable worth. The heart of the **comparable worth** theory is the contention that, while the "true worth" of nonidentical jobs may be similar, some jobs (often held by women) are paid a lower rate than others (often held by men). Resulting differences in pay that are disproportionate to the differences in the "true worth" of jobs amount to wage discrimination. Consequently, according to the comparable-worth advocates, legal protection should be provided to ensure pay equity.

Although several state and local governments and unions have passed comparable-worth or pay-equity legislation, comparable-worth plans have made few inroads in the private sector.[23] Internationally, comparable worth is an idea that has been around for some time.

> The International Labor Organization (ILO), the Geneva-based agency of the United Nations the U.S. joined in 1934, adopted an international convention on comparable worth almost 35 years ago. And what the ILO's experience shows is that while comparable worth may have helped reduce the gap between male and female wages in some countries that have tried it, it hasn't eliminated that gap. But neither has it led to the major economic or bureaucratic headaches that its critics prophesy.[24]

Since its adoption, more than one hundred governments—but not the U.S.—have ratified the convention. These include most of the nations of Western Europe, Canada, Australia, New Zealand, Japan, and more than seventy developing countries.[25]

Performance-Based Pay

As indicated above, Title VII applies not only to selection decisions but also to pay decisions. A supervisor may be charged with unlawful discrimination by an employee (belonging to a protected group) who feels a pay raise was denied on the basis of factors unrelated to performance. Raises not related to performance, however, can be given legally. Defensible factors influencing merit pay (when they are equally applied to all employees) include the following: position in salary range; time since last increase; size of last increase; pay relationships within the company or department; pay levels of jobs in other companies; salaries of newly hired employees; and budgetary limits. What is critical is that the same "rules of the game" must be used to give raises fairly and consistently to all employees. The same is true for incentive pay plans.

Indirect Compensation

In 1929, indirect benefits were less than 5 percent of the cost of total compensation. Today, in dramatic contrast, indirect benefits average between 35 and 40 percent. Indirect benefits grew rapidly during the Depression of the 1930s, which produced the first major legislation involving indirect benefits. **The Social Security Act,** passed in 1935, provided old age, disability, survivor's, and health benefits and established the basis for federal and state unemployment programs. **The Wagner Act,** or the **National Labor Relations Act (NLRA) of 1935,** helped ensure benefits' growth by strengthening the union movement in the U.S. Both the Social Security Act and the Wagner Act continue to play significant roles in the administration of benefits.

After World War II, the legal environment further stimulated indirect benefits. Two court cases helped to expand benefit coverage by declaring that pension and insurance provisions were bargainable issues in union and management relations. The right to bargain over pensions was established in *Inland Steel v. National Labor Relations Board,* 1948, and the right to bargain over insurance was upheld in *W.W. Cross v. National Labor Relations Board,* 1949. In the 1960s, Congress passed several acts that made this legal environment more complex.

Equal Pay Act. This act, described earlier under total compensation, mandates that employees on the same jobs be paid equally except for differences, in seniority, merit, or other conditions unrelated to sex. Direct as well as indirect compensation are included in the term paid equally. Thus, for example, women and men on the same job, other factors being equal, must receive the same level of direct and indirect compensation. Actuarial data, however, indicated that women live approximately seven years longer than men. Therefore, on the average, women will receive a greater total level of retirement benefits than men. Is this equal indirect compensation? Would it be equal if women contributed more? In *Los Angeles Department of Water v. Manhart,* 1981, the court ruled against the department's policy of having female employees contribute more to their retirement than males because women on the average live longer than men. Furthermore, when males and females make equal contributions to their pensions, their pension benefits must be equal (*Arizona Governing Committee v. Norris* 1983). Additional guarantees for equal pension-benefit treatment to surviving spouses, male and female, are contained in the **Retirement Equity Act of 1984.**

Pregnancy Discrimination Act of 1978. A trend in recent years has been to treat pregnancy as a disability, although opponents of this trend argue that pregnancy is a voluntary condition, not an involuntary sickness, and therefore should not be covered by disability benefits. The **Pregnancy Discrimination Act of 1978,** however, states that pregnancy is a disability and qualifies a person to receive the same benefits as any other disability. Applying this statute, a state appeals court in Michigan ruled that a labor contract between General Motors and United Auto Workers that provided sickness and accident benefits of up to fifty-two weeks but that limited childbearing disability to six weeks was illegal.[26]

Another issue in this area, which is not covered by the Pregnancy Discrimination Act, is whether companies must offer the same pregnancy-benefit program to wives of male employees and to husbands of female employees. The U.S. Supreme Court ruled in the *Newport News Shipbuilding and Dry Dock Co. v. EEOC,* 1983, that employers who provide health care insurance to spouses of employees that includes complete coverage for all disabilities except pregnancy are violating Title VII of the Civil Rights Act of 1964. In essence, employers must provide equal benefit coverage for all spouses.

Age Discrimination in Employment Act of 1967. Although the Social Security Act allows women to retire earlier than men (at age 62, as opposed to age 65), the U.S. Supreme Court, by refusing to hear a lower court ruling, affirmed the provisions of the **Age Discrimination in Employment Act (ADEA) of 1967** that it is illegal to require women to retire earlier than men. On the issue of mandatory retirement, now most men and women cannot be forced to retire if they are working for a private business with at least twenty persons on the payroll. One exception to this is top-level executives, who can be retired at age 70. These provisions are contained in a 1986 amendment to the act, which took effect on January 1, 1987. Employees may still choose to retire voluntarily at 65 and receive full benefits, however.

Some members of Congress seek to increase to 68 the age at which full Social Security benefits can start. Although this has not been done yet, Congress has attempted to reduce some of the burden on Social Security through a provision in the **Tax Equity and Fiscal Responsibility Act of 1982.** According to that act, employers of twenty or more workers must include those between the ages of 65 and 69 in their group health plans unless the employees specifically choose Medicare, funded by Social Security, as their primary coverage. Nonetheless, employers may still freeze pension contributions and plans for employees at age 65.

Amending ADEA is the **Older Workers Benefit Protection Act of 1990.** This prohibits discrimination in employee benefits. As a result of this act, Congress amended ADEA by defining the term "compensation, terms, conditions, or privileges of employment" to encompass all employee benefits, including benefits provided under a bona fide employee benefit plan.

ERISA and private employers' pensions. Building on the foundation of the Revenue Act of 1942, the **Employees' Retirement Income Security Act (ERISA)** was enacted to protect employees covered by private pension programs. While ERISA does not require an employer to offer a pension fund, it is designed to protect the interests of workers covered by private retirement plans. Employees are eligible for private pension fund participation after one year of service or at age 25.[27]

Because of problems over ownership of pension funds, ERISA also established provisions regarding vesting. **Vesting** refers to the time when the employer's contribution belongs to the employee. There are three basic options:

1. Full vesting after 10 years of service
2. Twenty-five percent vesting after 5 years, with 5 percent additional vesting until 10 years of service, and then 10 percent vesting for years 10–15
3. Fifty percent vesting when the employee has worked 5 years and when age and service equal 45; each additional year of service increases vesting by 10 percent

Because companies in the past have used pension funds for operating expenses, ERISA also prohibits the use of unfunded pension programs that rely on the goodwill of the employer to pay retirement benefits out of current operating funds when needed. Money paid into a pension fund must be earmarked for retirees whether paid in part by the employee as in **contributory programs** or paid solely by the employer, as in **noncontributory programs.**

In a **defined-benefit plan**, the actual benefits received upon retirement vary by age and length of service of the employee. One concern with such plans is overfunding, or having more money in the account than is needed to meet future funding requirements. Overfunding increases the likelihood of takeover bids because an acquiring company can terminate the pension program, retrieve the excess funding, and then start a new pension fund. To resolve this problem, organizations are reducing their contributions to defined budget plans or are switching to **defined-contribution plans.** In the latter approach, each employee has a separate account into which are added individual and/or organizational contributions. Growth of investments directly benefits the employee. Consequently, there is no fiscal advantage to takeover firms.[28]

Under ERISA, employers are not required to accommodate new or transfered employees who wish to deposit funds into their retirement plans. On a voluntary basis, employers can allow employees to transfer money to individual retirement accounts. When this occurs the pension funds are said to be **portable.** Increasingly, employers are making it possible for employees to transfer their retirement funds to another firm.

Because the ERISA only covered single-employer firms, the **Multi-Employer Pension Plan Amendment Act of 1980** was passed to broaden the definition of defined-benefit plans to include multi-employer plans. If any employer withdraws from multi-employer plans, they, rather than the employees, face liability for doing so and must reimburse employees for money lost.[29] Congress also has passed several tax acts that influence the administration or level of indirect compensation programs.

Economic Recovery Tax Act of 1981. A major provision of this act is that employees can make tax-deductible contributions of up to $2,000 to an employer-sponsored pension, profit-sharing, or savings account, or to an individual retirement account. The act also made it possible for employers to provide company stock to employees and pay for it with tax credits or to establish a payroll-based stock ownership plan that facilitates employee stock ownership of organizations.

Because these plans are so attractive to organizations, ten million employees have gained direct ownership of stock in their own companies as described in the opening feature on Procter & Gamble. By the year 2000, twenty-five percent or more of all U.S. workers will own part or all of their companies. Despite the potential benefits of employee stock ownership plans (ESOPs), critics contend that organizations benefit at the expense of employees.[30] In addition,

> ... Organized labor has customarily opposed the theory of employee stock ownership on the ground that the plans can make workers unnatural allies of management. But in practice, unions have embraced them because of the advantages that sale of stock to employees can give ailing enterprises, in raising capital for expansion and rewarding loyal employees—who may well be the only available buyer for a minority interest.[31]

Tax Equity and Fiscal Responsibility Act of 1982. This act sharply cut the maximum benefit and contribution limits for qualified pension plans (legally covered) and set limits for loans from such plans. The maximum individual yearly retirement benefit now stands at $94,023, and the maximum employer contribution per employee per year is $30,000. As an outgrowth of the act, some organizations have established nonqualified pension plans (not legally protected) for high-income employees. Contributions to these plans are taxable, while contributions to qualified plans are not.

Deficit Reduction Act of 1984. Along with several IRS rulings, this act makes some benefits—particularly flexible spending plans—taxable. In one form, employees are given the choice between several nontaxable benefits in return for reduced pay. In another, money is set aside initially and, if employees don't use the benefits, they receive the money. In still another, no money is set aside, but employees are reimbursed for some expenses.

Consolidated Omnibus Budget Reconciliation Act. Passed in 1985, this act assures that terminated or laid-off employees have the option to maintain their health care insurance by personally paying for the premiums. The option must also be extended to employees who lose their health benefits eligibility because their work hours have been reduced to the point where they no longer are eligible for coverage.

Tax Reform Act of 1986. Two provisions of this act affect indirect compensation. Essentially the act caps at $9,500 the amount of tax-exempt deferred contribution employees can make to a deferred pay plan. Effective January, 1989, the act also put into force provisions to reduce the disparity of benefits provided high- and low-income employees. Because of the difficulty of implementing this provision, it has been modified substantially.[32]

Training and Development

Legal considerations are relevant to several aspects of training and development. One aspect is the determination of the training and development needs of an applicant for a job. Legally an applicant cannot be eliminated from the selection pool just because he or she lacks a skill that can be learned in eight hours. Thus, it is important to determine what skills an individual needs to perform a job, what skills an applicant possesses, training programs that can remove any deficiencies, and the time necessary to complete these programs.

Another legal consideration pertains to providing training and development opportunities for current employees. Here bans on discrimination extend to on-the-job training and one-day introductions to new jobs or equipment, as well as to affirmative action and formal apprenticeship/training programs. Admission to formal training programs, however, can be limited to those under a certain age, as long as those passed over for the program are not women and minorities who have previously been denied training opportunities. Specific discriminatory training practices can often be determined by the responses to the following questions:

- Are minorities and/or women given the same training opportunities as white males? Be careful! Advertising and recruiting practices come into play here.
- Are requirements for entry into a training program (that is, tests, education, or experience) job-related, or are they arbitrary?
- Are nearly all machine functions or other specialized duties that require training performed by white or male workers?
- Does one class of trainees tend to get more challenging assignments or other special training opportunities?
- Do supervisors know what constitutes training? It could be almost any learning experience, from how to fit a drill bit to a two-week seminar on complex sales procedures.

- Who evaluates the results of instruction or training—only white males?
- Are all trainees given equal facilities for instruction? Are they segregated in any way?
- Do a disproportionate number of females and/or minorities fail to pass training courses? If so, find out if it is because they are more often unqualified or because they receive inferior instruction.

To defend against charges of discrimination, organizations can provide a reasonable defense by showing that the training programs were conceived and administered without bias. This, however, will be exceedingly difficult to demonstrate unless companies have the foresight to **document** their training practices. Thus, they should follow these guidelines:

- Register affirmative action training and apprenticeship programs with the Department of Labor. This must be done in writing. Include the goals, timetables, and criteria for selection and evaluation of trainees. Such a record will help prove job-relatedness and that there was no intent to discriminate. It can also be valuable in proving that an organization's program was not used as a pretext to discriminate.
- Keep a record of all employees who wish to enroll in your training program. Detail how each trainee was selected. Keep for at least two years or as long as training continues application forms, tests, questionnaires, records of preliminary interviews, and anything else that bears on an employee's selection or rejection.
- Document all management decisions and actions that relate to the administration of training policies.
- Monitor each trainee's progress. Provide progress evaluations, and make sure counseling is available.
- Continue to evaluate the results even after completion of training.

Keep in mind that legal considerations apply to all forms of training, including apprenticeships:

> Apprenticeship, on-the-job training, retraining, and other training programs have become increasingly important as companies grapple with new technologies in the workplace and with the uncertain economy. These programs also entail legal considerations, since they are covered by federal and state fair employment practices and separate apprenticeship statutes. Title VII of the Civil Rights Act of 1964 makes it illegal for an employer to discriminate against any individual in such manner as to deprive him or her of employment opportunities because of race, color, religion, sex, or national origin. It is a violation of Title VII to discriminate in admission to, or employment in, any apprenticeship or training program, including on-the-job training or retraining. Title I of the Americans with Disabilities Act of 1990 extended the equal employment opportunity requirements by prohibiting the denial of admission to an apprenticeship or training program on the basis of physical or mental disability.[33]

A final legal consideration of training and development is federal and state government support. This support can enable organizations to defray some training costs and receive already trained employees. It can also enable employees to obtain training and jobs. Currently, support from the federal government is funneled through block grants to states and through the Office of Federal Contract Compliance Programs under provisions in the **Job Training Partnership Act of 1982.** Under that act, grants are provided to states that in turn use the money to train economically disadvantaged youths and adults as well as workers whose jobs have been eliminated.[34]

Organizational Improvement

Certain legal considerations must be taken into account when programs to improve the organization are implemented. The National Labor Relations Act (NLRA) is particularly important for quality-of-work-life programs, especially for organizations with non-unionized workers. Section 8(a)(2) states that it is an unfair labor practice for an employer to dominate or interfere with the formation or administration of any labor organization or contribute financial or other support to it. Section 2(5) defines a "labor organization" as an "organization of any kind or any agency or employee representation committee or plan in which employees participate or which exists for the purpose, in whole or in part, of dealing with employers concerning grievances, labor disputes, wages, rates of pay, hours of employment, or conditions of work."

In cases where a union represents or could represent the employees, the employer must consider that almost all issues, including the establishment of programs to improve productivity and quality of work life, may need to be negotiated with the union. In many cases, however, employers and unions can cooperatively work together on improvement programs. When this is done, the NLRA requires employers to provide information to the union, when requested, for purposes related to the improvement program.[35]

Occupational Safety and Health

The legal considerations of occupational safety and health can be divided into four major categories: the Occupational Safety and Health Administration, worker compensation programs, the common-law doctrine of torts, and local initiatives.

Occupational Safety and Health Administration (OSHA). The federal government's primary response to the issue of safety and health in the workplace has been the **Occupational Safety and Health Act of 1970,** which calls for safety and health inspectors of organizations regardless of size, reporting by employers, and investigations of accidents and allegations of hazards. The other two organizations are the **National Institute for Occupational Safety and Health** and the **Occupational Safety and Health Review Commission (OSHRC).** The commission reviews appeals made by organizations that received citations from OSHA inspectors for alleged safety and health violations.

OSHA has the responsibility for establishing and enforcing occupational safety and health standards and for inspecting and issuing citations to organizations that violate these standards. According to *Marshall v. Barlow's, Inc.,* 1978, however, employers are not required to let OSHA inspectors enter their premises unless the inspectors have search warrants. This decision has been clarified and supported by subsequent court decisions (*Weyerhaeuser Co. v. Marshall,* 1978;

Cerro Metal Products v. Marshall, 1978; and *Marshall v. Gibson's Products, Inc.,* 1978). In *Chamber of Commerce v. OSHA,* the U.S. Court of Appeals for the District of Columbia struck down the "walkaround" pay requirement that made it mandatory for companies to pay employee wages for the time spent accompanying an OSHA inspector on the workplace.[36]

Regardless of whether organizations are inspected, they are required to keep safety and health records so OSHA can compile accurate statistics on work injuries and illnesses. These include all disabling, serious, or significant injuries and illnesses, whether or not they involve loss of time from work. Excluded are minor injuries that require only first aid treatment and do not involve medical treatment, loss of consciousness, restriction of work or motion, or transfer to another job. Falsification of records or failure to keep adequate records can result in some other substantial fines. The recordkeeping requirement was recently qualified, however.

> An employer may withhold injury and illness records from federal safety investigators if it has a legitimate need to keep the records private, and the Occupational Safety and Health Administration has failed to obtain a warrant granting it access to such documents, the Occupational Safety and Health Review Commission (OSHRC) rules. Rejecting the principle that OSHA compliance officers have unlimited rights to make warrantless examinations of an employer's records, the commission holds that the employer had a reasonable expectation of privacy in safeguarding the information in its injury records. Such documents, OSHRC points out, may contain proprietary information on operations and manufacturing processes that employers may want to keep confidential. (*Kings Island Division of Taft Broadcasting Co.,* 1987)[37]

Employers must do more than keep records. The **Access to Employee Exposure and Medical Records Regulation of 1980** requires organizations to show or give to employees, their designated representatives, and OSHA, their on-the-job medical records. This regulation also requires employers to provide access to records of measurements of employee exposure to toxic substances.[38]

The employee's right to know has been further strengthened by the **Hazard Communication Standard** that went into effect in 1986. Under this standard, employers are required to provide workers with information and training on hazardous chemicals in their work area at the time of their initial assignment and whenever a new hazard is introduced. According to OSHA, effective communication is the real key and should include information for employees on the following:

- The Standard's requirements, and operations in the workplace that use hazardous chemicals
- Proper procedures for determining the presence of chemicals and detecting hazardous releases
- Protective measures and equipment that should be used
- Location of the written hazard communication programs[39]

Workers' compensation programs. Whereas OSHA was established to provide workers protection against accidents and diseases, workers' compensation was established to provide financial aid for those unable to work because of accidents and diseases.

For years worker compensation awards were granted only to workers unable to work because of physical injury or damage (that is, due to accidents and diseases). Since 1955, however, court decisions have either caused or enticed fifteen states to allow worker compensation payment in job-related cases of anxiety, depression, and mental disorders.[40] That year, the Texas Supreme Court charted this new direction in worker compensation claims by stating that an employee who became terrified and highly anxious and unable to work because of a job-related accident had a compensable claim even though he had no physical injury (*Bailey v. American General Insurance Company,* 1955). In another court ruling (*James v. State Accident Insurance Fund,* 1980), an Oregon court ruled in favor of a worker's claim for compensation for inability to work due to job stress resulting from conflicting work assignments.[41]

Common-law doctrine of torts. Employees can obtain damage awards by suing employers; however, employees must demonstrate that the employer engaged in reckless or intentional infliction designed to degrade or humiliate. Although a few such cases have been successfully brought against employers, they appear to be the exception.[42]

Local initiatives. State, municipal, and city governments may pass their own safety and health laws and regulations that go beyond the coverage of the Occupational Safety and Health Administration. Consequently, employers need to be aware of the regulations of the local areas in which they do business. Sometimes these local initiatives offer a glimpse as to what other areas or even the federal government might do in the future. This seems to be the case with the law passed in San Francisco imposing safeguards on workers using video display terminals. The law requires the use of adjustable chairs and tables, angle-adjustable screens and keyboards, work time at tasks away from the computer, training of workers and supervisors, and the use of printer covers to reduce office noise. The local labor unions heralded the San Francisco law as a model for other cities and municipalities.

Employee Rights

Legal considerations are integral to the activity of employee rights. Because they are extensive, chapter 15 is devoted to them. Here, however, is a brief overview.

Employee rights to job security. Over the years, the major limit on employee rights to job security has been the employer's right to terminate employees for any reason. This right is known as the **termination-at-will** rule (also referred to as the **employment-at-will** rule). The termination-at-will rule was developed in the United States more than 100 years ago. One Tennessee court in 1884 explained it this way: "All may dismiss their employee(s) at will, be they many or few, for good cause, for no cause, or even for cause morally wrong without being thereby guilty of legal wrong" (*Payne v. Western & A.R.R. Co.,* 1884).

Although employees have relied on the termination-at-will rule over the years, using it today as justifiable defense is proving less legally defensible because of several recent statutes (Title VII of the Civil Rights Act of 1964, Age Discrimination in Employment Act of 1967, and Rehabilitation Act of 1973).

The National Labor Relations Act of 1935 prohibits discharge because of union-organizing activities or for the assertion of rights under a union contract, even if the employee in question had a record of poor performance (*NLRB v. Transportation Management,* 1983). When employees are represented by a union, the union contract replaces the termination-at-will doctrine and specifies the conditions under which an employee can be fired.

Court decisions such as the *Board of Regents of State Colleges v. Roth* (1972) protects workers from discharge when due process has not been given the employee. Various state acts such as Montana's Maternity Leave Act, which prohibits employers from terminating female employees because of pregnancy, also limit the employer's rights.

In summary, discharge is not a legitimate action under any circumstances for the following employee actions:

- **Whistleblowing** (e.g., opposing and publicizing policies or practices that violate antitrust laws, consumer protection laws, or environmental protection laws)
- **Complaining or testifying** about equal pay or wage/hour law violations
- **Complaining or testifying** about safety hazards and/or refusing an assignment because of the belief that the assignment is dangerous
- **Engaging in union activities,** provided the employee's behavior is nonviolent and lawful
- **Engaging in concerted activity** to protest wages, working conditions, or safety hazards

Employee rights to cooperative acceptance. Employees have brought cases of sexual harassment against employers for infliction designed to degrade or humiliate. Although a few such cases have been successfully brought against employers (*Alcorn v. Ambro Engineering,* 1970; *Contereras v. Crown Zellerbach Corporation,* 1977), they appear to be the exception. Nevertheless, with these precedents established, additional cases of sexual harassment against employers are likely. These cases and others involving employee rights are discussed in detail in chapter 15.

Unionization and Collective Bargaining

The federal government entered the labor scene in an attempt to stabilize the violent and disruptive labor situation in the 1920s and the 1930s.[43] Court actions and efforts by employers prior to this time generally suppressed the rights of workers to act collectively to protect their interests. This was consistent with classical economic theory in which the free operation of the law of supply and demand was considered essential.

> According to this theory, control of wage rates by workers artificially inflated prices, ultimately harming commerce, the community, and even workers themselves, because higher prices discouraged consumption and created unemployment. Therefore, according to many observers, the best prescription for a healthy economy was one free of either government regulation or private regulation via collective action of workers.

> Until 1935, application of these restrictive theories of law inherited from England reflected the political assumption that free competition and the sanctity of contract and property rights of individuals were fundamental values of society that must be protected.[44]

The courts protected these "fundamental values of society" by declaring that attempts by workers to band together to increase wages (that is, form a union) were conspiracies condemned by law (*Commonwealth v. Pullis, Philadelphia Cordwainers, Pennsylvania,* 1806). Later this outright condemnation was modified to include the necessity of applying a "means test" before condemning the union as an illegal conspiracy (*Commonwealth v. Hunt,* 1842). Using the means test, the courts hampered efforts at unionization.

By the 1880s, the **conspiracy doctrine** was reinforced by using civil instead of criminal law, particularly civil injunctions. The injunction maintained the status quo until the legal issues could be resolved. Injunctions are still used for this purpose. Thus, if workers attempt to join together and strike for the purpose of attaining higher wages, an injunction can be granted by the courts forcing the workers to return to work until the legality of the strike is decided. The injunction can also be granted quickly (in order to provide an equitable remedy) without the use of juries and other time-consuming legal proceedings. The impact of injunctions on unionization was particularly evident when the U.S. Supreme Court ruled that injunctions could be used to enforce **yellow-dog contracts**—that is, contracts signed by employees agreeing not to join a union (*Hitchman Coal & Coke v. Mitchell,* 1917).

Further protection for the "fundamental values of society" was provided by the **Sherman Antitrust Act,** which was passed by Congress in 1890 to limit the ability of organizations (for example, unions) to engage in acts (such as union mergers) that lessened competition. This act, as applied to unions, was upheld by the U.S. Supreme Court in *Loewe v. Lawlor* (The Danbury Hatters case), 1908. The application of the Sherman Antitrust Act to unions was reinforced by the Clayton Antitrust Act of 1914 and subsequent court decisions (*Duplex Printing Co. v. Deering,* 1921; *United Mine Workers of America v. Coronado Coal Company,* 1922).

Although this supposed protection of society was largely maintained throughout the 1920s, early legislation in the railway industry (because of the industry's impact on the public welfare) suggested it was not sacrosanct. Union activities derived support from the Arbitration Act of 1888; the Erdman Act of 1898, which outlawed yellow-dog contracts in the railway industry; and *Adair v. United States* (1921), which upheld the unconstitutionality of the yellow-dog contract. These events in the railway industry culminated in the **Railway Labor Act of 1926,** which brought about the demise of the "fundamental values of society" doctrine for all other industries. This act was passed by Congress in 1926 to prevent labor unrest in the railway industry from having serious economic consequences. It has since been expanded to include air carrier employees as well. It was the first act to protect "the fundamental right of workers to engage in labor organizing actively without fear of employer retaliation and discrimination."[45] Other objectives of the act were to avoid service interruption, to eliminate any restrictions in joining a union, and to provide for prompt settlement of disputes and grievances.

The act specified that employers and employees would maintain an agreement over pay, rules, working conditions, dispute settlement, representation, and grievance settlement. A board of mediation (later called the National Mediation Board) was created to help settle disputes by encouraging, as necessary, negotiation, then arbitration, and finally emergency intervention by the president. A second board—the National Railway Adjustment Board—was created in 1934 to deal with grievances. This board has exclusive jurisdiction over questions relating to grievances or the interpretation of agreements concerning pay, rules, or working conditions; it makes decisions and awards binding on both parties. The success of the Railway Labor Act led Congress to enact a comprehensive labor code in 1935. The purpose of the **National Labor Relations Act** was to restore the equality of bargaining power arising out of employers' general denial to labor of the right to bargain collectively with employers. Such employer refusal resulted in poor working conditions, depression of wages, and a general depression of business.

The act affirmed employees' rights to form, join, or assist labor organizations to bargain collectively, and to choose their own bargaining representative through majority rule. As stated in Section 8, the second significant portion of the act identified the following unfair labor practices on the part of the employers:

- Interference with the efforts of employees to organize
- Domination of the labor organization by the employer
- Discrimination in the hiring or tenure of employees in order to discourage union affiliation
- Discrimination for filing charges or giving testimony under the act
- Refusal to bargain collectively with a representative of the employees

Court interpretation of these unfair labor practices has made it clear that bribing, spying, blacklisting union sympathizers, moving a business to avoid union activities, and other such employer actions are illegal.

The National Labor Relations Board was established to administer this act. Its major function is to decide all unfair labor practice suits. (During the 1980s, the board's decisions did not favor the union movement.)

Employer groups criticized the National Labor Relations Act (also known as the Wagner Act) on several grounds. They argued that the act, in addition to being biased toward unions, limited the constitutional right of free speech of employers, did not consider unfair labor practices on the part of unions, and caused employers serious damage when there were jurisdictional disputes.

Congress responded to these criticisms in 1947 by enacting the **Labor-Management Relations Act,** often called the **Taft-Hartley Act.** This act revised and expanded the Wagner Act in order to establish a balance between union and management power and to protect the public interest. It introduced the following changes:

- Employees were allowed to refrain from union activity as well as to engage in it.
- The closed shop was outlawed, and employees were required to agree in writing before union dues could be deducted from their paychecks.
- Employers were ensured of their right to free speech, and they were given the right to file charges against unfair labor practices, such as coercing work-

ers to join the unions, causing employers to discriminate against those who do not join, refusing to bargain in good faith, requiring excessive or discriminatory fees, and engaging in featherbedding activities.

- Certification elections (voting for union representation) could not be held more frequently than once a year.
- Employees were given the right to initiate decertification elections.[46]

These provisions indicated the philosophy behind the act—as Senator Robert Taft put it—"simply to reduce the special privileges granted labor leaders."

From time to time amendments have been added to the Taft-Hartley Act. For example, the 1980 amendments to the act provided for an identical accommodation for employees with religious objections to union membership or support. Thus, employers and unions must respect (within reason) the religious beliefs of employees as protected by Title VII. For example, an employee may, on religious grounds, contribute to a charity in lieu of paying union dues (*Tooley v. Martin-Marietta Corp.*, 1981).

Although the Taft-Hartley Act included some regulation of internal union activities, abuse of power and the corruption of some union officials led to the passage of a "bill of rights" for union members in 1959. The **Labor-Management Reporting and Disclosure Act,** or the **Landrum-Griffin Act,** provided a detailed regulation of internal union affairs. Its provisions include the following:

- Equality of rights for union members in nominating and voting in elections
- Controls on increases in dues
- Controls on suspension and firing of union members
- Elections every three years for local offices and every five years for national or international offices
- Restriction of the use of trusteeships to take control of a member group's autonomy for political reasons
- Definition of the type of person who can hold union office
- Filing of yearly reports with the secretary of labor

The intention of this act was to protect employees from corruption or discriminatory labor unions. By providing standards for union conduct, the act eliminated much of the flagrant abuse of power and protected the democratic rights of employees to some degree. The United Mine Workers, for example, held their first election of international officers in 1969 as a result of the Landrum-Griffin Act.

Court decisions. One of the most significant court decisions of the 1980s is *First National Maintenance Corp. v. NLRB*. In this case the U.S. Supreme Court held that an employer is not obligated to bargain with the union about a decision to close a portion of its business. Consistent with this ruling, the NLRB rendered several probusiness decisions in 1984. In addition, the NLRB recently ruled that labor law is not necessarily violated when supervisors who support union activities are fired along with workers as part of an employer plan to discourage unions. In this particular case, however, the board ruled that the employer must rehire the workers fired for union activities.

The cornerstone of labor relations—the grievance-arbitration process—was established in *Textile Workers Union v. Lincoln Mills,* 1957. In that case, the U.S. Supreme Court held that the agreement to arbitrate grievances is the quid pro quo for an agreement not to strike through the years. This agreement, however, has led to the problem of unfair representation by the union of its members.[47] Over the past ten years, cases filed by employees with the NLRB against their unions for unfair representation (breach of duty) have risen to several thousand annually. Although the union's obligation of fair representation is clear, the specific duties involved have been left unclear by numerous court decisions, including *Ford Motor Co. v. Huffman* (1953) and *Hines v. Anchor Motor Freight Co.* (1976).

Finally, the U.S. Supreme Court has ruled bona fide seniority systems are protected under Section 703(h) of Title VII of the Civil Rights Act of 1964. Thus, equal employment considerations in general do not overrule seniority systems in employment decisions where a seniority system has been in existence for some time or where its intention is not discriminatory (*California Brewers Association v. Bryant,* 1980, *International Brotherhood of Teamsters v. United States,* 1977; *American Tobacco v. Patterson,* 1982).

Union-management settlements. The grievance arbitration process can have a major impact on the ways companies conduct business. In a recent settlement,

> Northern Telecom Inc. agreed to a settlement with the Communications Workers of America (CWA) to compensate workers and others who were allegedly subject to secret electronic monitoring.
>
> CWA charged that Northern Telecom used hidden bugging devices and telephone wiretaps at several locations in the company's Nashville plant between 1976 and 1989 to identify CWA supporters and thus thwart unionization drives. According to CWA, the company denied that it authorized illegal electronic surveillance but acknowledged evidence that electronic monitoring activity occurred at the plant during some periods of the alleged years.
>
> In settling the case, the company agrees to pay $50,000 to individual plaintiffs, $125,000 for attorney's fees, and $200,000 toward class claims by workers and members of the public whose conversations may have been secretly recorded over telephone lines or on the premises of the Nashville plant. The union expects that a few more than the initial three plaintiffs will be involved in the settlements. The settlement still was pending when Northern Telecom announced a new policy stating it will not conduct undisclosed monitoring of employee voice, video or data communications.[48]

Because the issue of electronic monitoring of employees is such a significant issue in the workplace today, this settlement may have far-reaching effects.

FOCUS ISSUES IN THE LEGAL ENVIRONMENT

Balance of Rights

An important issue for legal considerations in the workplace is basically, "Whose rights are more important?" The question is often one of balance; but are the rights of employees and employers equal? Can or should employees look for balance?

Take the case of employee drug testing. Employers argue they need to know; employees argue that they have a right to privacy, and, besides, it breaks the trust between worker and employer. The issue can be carried even further, to the job applicant. Do job applicants have a right to privacy? Should they have the right to refuse to be drug tested? Finally, society has an interest in this discussion, too. Does society (you and I) have a right to safety and safe products and services that a company might be providing?

This issue of balance is likely to be a factor in many issues in human resource management during the 1990s. Large organizations in particular may need to carefully assess whether the balance is right (see Focus on Research: "Can Corporate Illegalities Be Predicted?").

FOCUS ON RESEARCH

Can Corporate Illegalities be Predicted?

Ultimately, individuals behave legally, not corporations. But does this mean that the only way to understand illegal corporate behavior is by studying individual criminals? Or, can corporate crime be predicted by characteristics of the firm and the environment in which it operates? We know that some people repeatedly commit crimes, whereas other people never do. Is it also true that some firms are more likely to repeatedly break the law? One study addressed these questions by looking at corporate convictions among Fortune 500 firms during a 10-year period. Four types of convictions were studied: discrimination violations, antitrust violations, product liability violations, and a general class of "other" violations (the "other" category included a mixture of violations that were relatively uncommon). All the convictions studied were for violations of laws that were fairly clear, so in most of these cases the people involved should have known they were engaging in illegal behavior. So, for example, discrimination violations were considered in this study only if the case involved disparate treatment (intentional discrimination).

During the years studied, 88 Fortune 500 firms were convicted of 141 violations. Overall, about half of all these convictions involved illegal discrimination. Like people on the street, firms with several prior violations were more likely to be convicted than were firms with few prior violations. This suggests that the cultures of some firms—which are reinforced by selectively recruiting and promoting people with particular types of values—may encourage illegal behavior.

To address the question of whether guilty firms differ from innocent firms, the characteristics of the 88 firms with convictions for illegal behavior were compared to a randomly selected sample of 102 Fortune 500 firms that had no convictions. This comparison showed that several characteristics of firms were related to illegal behavior in general, including which industry the business was in, the degree to which resources were available, and degree of environmental turbulence. However, for discrimination in particular, the best predictor of illegalities was the size of the firm. The findings were straightforward—larger firms had more convictions. This may reflect the fact that, during the years of this study, the EEOC aggressively sought to identify and correct discriminatory practices among the nation's largest employers. Or, it may reflect the fact that there are more opportunities for discrimination to occur in large firms. In either case, the implication is that managers in larger firms need to be especially aware of the high probability of prosecution for intentional discrimination. Human resource management departments can help prevent such illegal behavior by offering training programs to inform managers about their legal responsibilities, and by insuring that the promotion and reward systems encourage fair treatment of everyone.

SOURCE: Based on M.S. Baucus and J. P. Near, "Can Illegal Corporate Behavior be Predicted? An Event History Analysis," *Academy of Management Journal* 34 (1991), 9–36.

State Employment Discrimination Coverage

A number of states are beginning to enact their own legislation covering employment discrimination. While their coverage is not contradictory to federal legislation, it can sometimes anticipate it and offer insight into what may someday be done at the federal level.

It is also important to know your own state and local legislation because it may cover companies that have too few employees to be covered by federal legislation.

State employment discrimination legislation is starting to address several issues. For example, Florida, Maine, and the District of Columbia have each adopted some type of family leave legislation, thereby allowing employees time off to care for members of the family; family leave legislation is also under consideration at the federal level at this time. As another example, the legislatures of Indiana, Louisiana, Connecticut, and Arizona have passed laws making it illegal for employers to discriminate against employees for smoking outside the workplace. Also, Illinois has amended its AIDS Confidentiality Rules to protect persons from disclosure of their AIDS test results except in certain specified instances. While this, of course, is just a sample of what is happening at the state level, it does indicate that employment discrimination coverage does exist. It also reinforces the importance of continuously scanning and analyzing the legal environment to see what legislation exists and what might exist in the near future.[49]

INTERNATIONAL ASPECTS OF THE LEGAL ENVIRONMENT

We could discuss many international aspects of legal considerations, but perhaps the two most striking and current relate to equal employment and termination. Other aspects will be covered in later chapters.

Equal Employment

As you travel the world you realize there can be substantial differences among nations. These differences often get played out at the level of employment. This is not surprising, given that

> Equal employment opportunity laws are expressions of social values with regard to employment and reflect the values of a society or country. The selection procedures of U.S. multinationals often must be defended against illegality and must take into consideration the increasingly conflicting national laws on employment. For example, mandatory retirement/hiring ages are illegal in the U.S. and some other countries but legal in still other countries. Determining which law applies where, and which has precedence, is a problem without a specific solution.[50]

It was only in 1991 that the Supreme Court decided (with *E.E.O.C. v. Arabian American Oil Co.*) that Title VII of the Civil Rights Act of 1964 has no application to U.S. employers employing U.S. citizens to work abroad. This was then essentially reversed with the passage of the Civil Rights Act of 1991.

The number of U.S. expatriates is relatively small; estimates range from 100,000 to 250,000 (of which less than five percent are female). That's one reason U.S. multinationals rely on **host country nationals (HCNs)** and **third country nationals (TCNs)** for much of their staffing needs.

Equal opportunity for female HCNs is a complex issue for MNCs. Many MNCs already experience difficulties in the recruitment and selection of HCNs, particularly in less-developed countries where relatively low educational and economic levels limit the sources of potential talent.[51] The relative status of women in some countries may further restrict employment practices, particularly equal employment objectives. In western countries, the tendency is toward opening all occupations to both sexes, mainly through the introduction of sex discrimination legislation.[52] In general, however, the less developed the country, the less equal are the sexes with regard to job opportunities and education. In fact, in many countries the customs, attitudes, or religion are hostile to the presence of women in the professions or business and in society in general, and legislation reinforces those attitudes. Several sources provide details of such legislation in several countries, including in Pakistan, Saudi Arabia, and India.[53] Even in countries where legislation states there should be equality of the sexes, the reality may not comply with the legislation. As some have stated, the cultures of countries—particularly many Asian countries—"perpetuate the scarcity of indigenous female managers."[54]

Termination

Another legal consideration of importance on the international scene regards employee termination. Many outside the U.S. think U.S. employers have it easy when it comes time to terminate employees: Seemingly, it can be done fast and without much cost. They are partially right; there are no real legal guidelines for paying people upon termination. However, in many cases (to be described in chapter 15), employers do have to give employees warning of dismissal. This contrasts sharply with the situation in Europe, where

> ... relatively high termination benefits in most European countries are set by law and include such items as termination payments and full salary for a notice period during which severed employees are usually not required to show up for work.[55]

William Mercer, a benefits consulting firm, calculates

> ... that a typical 45-year-old European middle manager, with 20 years of service and a salary of $50,000, would be entitled to termination benefits ranging from $94,000 to $130,000 in Belgium, Spain, and Italy—and from $25,000 to $38,000 in the Netherlands, Germany, and Denmark. And that doesn't include extra benefits mandated for group dismissals or embodied in union contracts.
>
> By contrast, Mercer estimates that a U.S. middle manager, earning $50,000 a year with 20 years of service, typically walks away with about 20 weeks severance pay or some $19,000. But the firm also notes that since payments are determined by individual corporate policy, such employees can be legally terminated with nothing more than a handshake.[56]

Thus, on your way to becoming more global, keep in mind the significant worldwide differences in the area of human resource management.

SUMMARY

The legal considerations described in this chapter have a major impact on managing human resources effectively—and we have only reviewed the legal considerations at the federal level! During this course you should find out what legal considerations arise from the state and city in which you live. Doing this is entirely consistent with scanning the human resource environment.

Legal considerations influence all aspects of attracting, retaining, motivating, and retraining employees in the workplace. At the same time, these considerations have a way of changing. In the example of who has the burden of proof, it took a new civil rights law to reverse a decision by the Supreme Court to restore the intention of Congress that was defined by the 1964 Civil Rights Act. Thus, it is necessary to constantly scan and analyze the legal environment.

It is also necessary to scan and analyze because a new law may be promulgated—such as the Americans with Disabilities Act of 1990—for which there may be no immediate guidelines. In the case of many laws, it may be several months before regulations are written that identify more specifically what the law means and how it is to be implemented by companies. During this interim period, companies can anticipate the provisions and be ready as soon as possible; but, again, this requires constant scanning and analyzing of the legal environment.

Now that we have provided an overview of just how extensive the legal considerations are for human resource management, it is time to move on to the next human resource activity—human resource planning. With an understanding of the external and internal environments, it is easier to proceed with human resource plans and programs to help ensure we get the right people to the right place at the right time.

WHERE WE ARE TODAY

1. Potentially providing coverage to almost 45 million Americans, the Americans with Disabilities Act is one of the most significant pieces of employment legislation on which employers will focus in this decade.
2. The Civil Rights Act of 1991 is equally significant because its coverage of equal employment extends beyond the landmark Civil Rights Act of 1964, and because it offered clarification to the Supreme Court regarding burden of proof in discrimination cases.
3. The Civil Rights Act of 1964 has had an instrumental impact on job analysis, recruitment, and selection procedures in the U.S.
4. Developing job-analysis, recruitment, and selection procedures consistent with equal employment legislation is also consistent with the needs of business, because the legislation basically directs employers to select only those individuals who are qualified to perform the job.
5. Congress passes federal employment legislation, but that legislation gets interpreted at several levels of the court system. These courts are part of the same system, but they do have judges who may interpret the legislation somewhat differently and, therefore, offer somewhat different opinions on cases. It takes some cases years to be heard before the Supreme Court in order to resolve opinions that might appear contradictory. Some cases never even get a hearing, because the Supreme Court offers to hear far less than 10 percent of the cases brought to it on appeal.
6. Federal legislation is extensive and affects virtually all personnel and human resource activities.

7. A great deal of employment legislation at the state and local levels covers employees who may not be covered by federal legislation; therefore, it is important for organizations to scan and analyze state and local legislation, too.
8. With continued pressure on organizations to reduce costs, there will be considerable attention during the 1990s on age-discrimination cases.
9. As U.S. organizations become global players, they have to scan and analyze the global legal environment. Vast differences exist in employment legislation throughout the world.
10. Employment legislation typically mirrors concerns and issues in the larger society. Because these change, it is usual to see employment legislation change. Therefore, it is important to continuously scan and analyze the legal environment.

DISCUSSION QUESTIONS

1. What legal considerations affect job analysis?
2. Based on the recent past, what changes in legal considerations do you forecast? What will be their impact on managing human resources?
3. How have the legal considerations helped the practice of personnel and human resource management?
4. Why is there such an extensive set of legal considerations?
5. Can line managers really be expected to be aware of all these legal considerations? Isn't this an important place for the HR professional?
6. What are the costs to the organization for ignoring the legal considerations?
7. Do legal considerations really force employers to hire by the quota method? Are goals really quotas?
8. Under what conditions can affirmative action programs arise?
9. What are the reasons for a *prima facie* case of illegal discrimination?
10. What are the employer's defenses against charges of illegal discrimination?

APPLIED PROJECTS

1. Select a company in your locale. Using government data that is found in the U.S. Government Depository section of many libraries, identify the relevant labor market for each of the following occupational categories: clerical, technical and professional, and managerial.
2. Report on one or two examples of sex discrimination, race discrimination, age discrimination, or discrimination against the disabled based on either your own experience or incidents reported in newspapers. In your examples, include the criteria on which employment practices and decisions should have been based in each case, as opposed to those discriminatory factors on which they were allegedly based.
3. Review cases in which employers have successfully defended against charges of alleged employment discrimination (i.e., bona fide occupational qualifications, bona fide seniority systems, business necessity, voluntary affirmative action plans, and job-relatedness). Review either the Bureau of National

Affairs' *Fair Employment Practices* cases or the Commerce Clearing House's *Employment Practices Decisions* as a source for these cases.

CASE STUDY

Equal Opportunity Selection

Karen Deft was looking forward to the monthly executive committee meeting at Commerce Bank. Commerce is a small-town bank (fifty-four employees) located in Winnsboro, South Carolina. Karen, the personnel officer of Commerce Bank, was going to make a proposal to the executive committee to change the way selection of hourly or nonexempt employees was conducted at Commerce. In the two years Karen had worked at Commerce, this would be the first major initiative she would take. Karen's strategy up to now was to lie low, learn the ropes, and not make any waves.

Karen was promoted to assistant vice-president of personnel, the first female to attain this rank during the forty-year history at Commerce. She began as a clerk in the personnel department and got her chance at an administrative position when her predecessor was promoted to vice-president in charge of trusts. Commerce was built by Melvin Hitt shortly after World War II and passed along to his two sons, Ronald and Donald, shortly before his death ten years ago. Ronald, the older brother, earned both an MBA and CPA and was groomed by the elder Hitt to assume the reins at the bank. Donald, while earning an undergraduate degree in business, had pursued no further education but was secure in his position as president of Commerce while brother Ron served as CEO.

The executive committee of the bank consisted of brothers Ron and Don and four other male vice-presidents for each of the areas of commercial/consumer loans, marketing, operations, and trusts. Karen and others at the bank frequently referred to this group as the "big six" who ultimately made policy and set the tone and direction of the bank. Karen knew that, if she was to be successful in implementing new selection procedures, she would have to sell them to the big six first.

Karen had worked hard during the past year to systematize the selection system she inherited from her predecessor. The basic problem with the old system was the failure to follow an orderly process for hiring. In addition, few if any records were kept to document the hiring process. Karen had written a policy and procedures manual that she hoped the big six would adopt.

In the policy and procedures manual, Karen spelled out a five-step process for hiring tellers. Briefly, the process called for taking an application, conducting an interview, administering a paper-and pencil test, referring the applicant to the area manager if the applicant successfully jumped all the hurdles at this step, and, finally, doing a reference check if the area manager recommended a hire decision. In practice, Karen often eliminated applicants after the interview based on poorly completed applications or admissions during the interview that the applicant had problems with the law, particularly shoplifting. Karen and her assistant, though, began to have second thoughts about the test they were administering at step three.

It seemed that many of the applicants, particularly minorities, who Karen thought would make excellent employees were eliminated at this stage. Moreover, Karen questioned whether the test was relevant to the type of work done at the bank. The 1961 copyright on the test did not bolster Karen's confidence in the test, either. Karen could sympathize with applicants who missed the cutoff for the test because of arithmetic errors committed on the math section. Karen wasn't strong in arithmetic, either, and reasoned that the widespread use of calculators reduced the criticalness of this skill.

Karen recalled from her personnel course that test manufacturers often produce evidence of test validity during the development process of the test. On a hunch, she decided to call the test company in Chicago and inquire about the existence of criterion validity for the test. The company representative informed Karen that the test had been validated and offered to send Karen a copy of the validity study done for the test. The following Monday, she received the study as promised. To her chagrin but not surprise, the study had been conducted more than twenty-five years ago and only with two Chicago banks. The bottom line for Karen was that this test would be hard to defend at

Commerce, especially given its history of eliminating a disproportionate number of minorities.

The following Monday, the executive committee met, and Karen presented her proposal for systematizing the selection process. After considerable discussion, much of it focused on the use of the test, the committee elected to table Karen's recommendation for further consideration. When Karen arrived home that evening, she was met by her husband, Jim, who warmly greeted her with, "Hi, do you want to hear about my day?" only to be abruptly cut off by Karen's reply, "No! But let me tell you about mine!" After Karen had set the scene for Jim, she got to the point of her anger and frustration. "Do you know what that jerk Donald proposed? He suggested that we administer the test only to applicants we don't know. Given that I wasn't raised in this community and a few other considerations, how am I supposed to implement such an asinine policy anyway?"

Case Questions

1. Is Commerce Bank required to validate their selection process for tellers?
2. For the selection of tellers, who makes the decision, line or staff?
3. Evaluate Donald Hitt's proposal to selectively administer the test.
4. What would you do if you were Karen?

SOURCE: Stuart A. Youngblood, Texas Christian University.

NOTES

1. B. Smith, "The Burden of Proof Grows Heavier," *HR Focus* (Feb. 1992): 1.
2. M. Zall, "What to Expect from the Civil Rights Act," *Personnel Journal* (March 1992): 46.
3. The essence of the Civil Rights Act of 1964, the Equal Opportunity in Employment Act of 1972, the Civil Rights Act of 1991, and various court decisions is that employment decisions must be made on the basis of whether the individual will be able to perform the job. To determine this, organizations should conduct job analyses to help them determine what skills, knowledge, and abilities individuals need to perform the jobs. Once this is known, selection procedures can be developed. Chapter 6 expands on the job relatedness of selection procedures. For more legal review, see D. E. Thompson and T. A. Thompson, "Court Standards for Job Analysis in Test Validation," *Personnel Psychology* 35 (1982): 865–74; B. Shaw and A. Wolfe, *The Structure of the Legal Environment: Law, Ethics, and Business,* 2d ed. (Boston: PWS-Kent, 1991); M. Moody Jennings, *Business and the Legal Environment* (Boston: PWS-Kent, 1991).
4. See, "Objective Employee Appraisals and Discrimination Cases," *Fair Employment Practices* (6 Dec. 1990): 145–46; R. J. Nobile, "The Law of Performance Appraisals," *Personnel* (Jan. 1991): 7.
5. R. D. Dickson, "The Business of Equal Opportunity," *Harvard Business Review* (Jan.-Feb. 1992): 46–53; W. Guzzardi, "A Fresh View of Affirmative Action," *Fortune* (23 Sept. 1991): 210–13; R. Turner, *The Past and Future of Affirmative Action: A Guide for Human Resource Professionals and Corporate Counsel* (Westport, Conn.: Quorum Books/Greenwood Press, 1990); S. Carter, *Reflections of an Affirmative Action Baby* (New York: Basic Books, 1991); A. J. Jones, Jr., *Affirmative Talk, Affirmative Action: A Comparative Study of the Politics of Affirmative Action* (Westport, Conn.: Praeger Publishers, 1991).
6. The steps in utilization and availability analysis are based on the eight-factor analysis (used in exhibit 2.1). For a description, see R. H. Faley and L. S. Kleiman, "Misconceptions and Realities in the Implementation of Equal Employment Opportunity," in *Readings in Personnel and Human Resource Management,* 3d ed., eds. R. S. Schuler, S. A. Youngblood, and V. L. Huber (St. Paul, Minn.: West Publishing, 1988); and Biddle and Associates, 903 Enterprise Drive, Suite 1, Sacramento, CA 95825).
7. "Hiring the Disabled: A Firm Commitment," *Fair Employment Practices* (4 Feb. 1988): 16; "Reasonable Job Accommodations for Employers and Employees," *Fair Employment Practices* (14 April 1988): 45; B. Solomon and W. H. Wagel, "Spreading the Word on New Technologies for People with Disabilities," *Personnel* (July 1988): 14–17; W. H. Wagel, "Project Ace: New Opportunities for People with Disabilities," *Personnel* (Jan. 1988): 9–15; J. M. Williams, "Technology and the Disabled," *Personnel Administrator* (July 1988): 81–83.
8. M. Zall, "What to Expect from the Civil Rights Act," *Personnel Journal* (March 1992): 46–50; B. Southard Murphy, W. E. Barlow, and D. D. Hatch, "Manager's Newsfront: Retroactivity of the Civil Rights Act of 1991 Unsettled," *Personnel Journal* (March 1992): 24; "EEOC Issues Policy on Retroactivity of Civil Rights Act of 1991," *FEP Guidelines* (March 1992): 1–2; "1991 Civil Rights Act Highlights," *FEP Guidelines* (Dec. 1991): 1–2.
9. J. S. Lublin, "Graying Europeans Battle Age Bias," *The Wall Street Journal* (14 Aug. 1990): B1; D. P. O'Meara, *Protecting the Growing Number of Older Workers: The Age Discrimination in Employment Act* (Philadelphia: The Wharton School of the University of Pennsylvania, 1989); C. S. Miller, J. A. Kaspin, and M. H. Schuster, "The Impact of Performance Appraisal Methods On Age Discrimination in Employment Act Cases," *Personnel Psychology* 43 (1990): 555–78.
10. "Americans With Disabilities Act Final Regulations," *Fair Employment Practices* (15 Aug. 1991); B. Presley Noble, "As Seen from a Wheelchair," *The New York Times* (26 Jan. 1992): F25; J. West, ed., *The Americans with Disabili-*

ties Act: From Policy to Practice (New York: Milbank Memorial Fund, 1991).

11. For more on age discrimination see A. Zakarian, "Downsizing Defense," *Personnel* (Jan. 1991): 19; P. S. Greenlaw and J. P. Kohn, "Age Discrimination in Employment Guidelines," *Personnel Journal* (March 1982): 224–28; D. H. Weiss, *Fair, Square and Legal: Safe Hiring and Firing Practices to Keep You and Your Company Out of Court* (New York: AMACOM, 1991); A. M. Ryan and M. Lasek, "Negligent Hiring and Defamation: Areas of Liability Related to Pre-Employment Inquiries," *Personnel Psychology* 44 (1991): 293–319.
12. R. D. Arvey and R. H. Faley, *Fairness in Selecting Employees* (Reading: Addison-Wesley, 1988); R. A. Baysinger, "Disparate Treatment and Disparate Impact Theories of Discrimination" in *Readings in Personnel and Human Resource Management,* 3d ed.: 162–77; P. M. Podsakoff, M. L. Williams, and W. E. Scott, Jr., "Myths of Employee Selection Systems," in *Readings in Personnel and Human Resource Management,* 3d ed.: 178–92.
13. S. Faison, Jr., "Rash of Suits Seen After Rights Act," *The New York Times* (30 Nov. 1991): 1.
14. "Go Ahead for AA Data Disclosure," *Fair Employment Practices* (29 Oct. 1987): 129. Also see R. E. Biddle, *"Ward's Cove Packing v. Atonio* Redefines EEO Analyses," *Personnel Journal* (June 1990): 56, 59–62, 64–65.
15. J. Ledvinka and V. G. Scarpello, *Federal Regulations in Personnel and Human Resource Management* (Boston, Mass.: PWS-Kent, 1990); R. A. Baysinger, "Disparate Treatment and Disparate Impact Theories of Discrimination," in *Readings in Personnel and Human Resource Management,* 3d ed., and V. L. Huber, G. B. Northcraft, and M. A. Neale, "Foibles and Fallacies in Organizational Staffing Decisions," in *Readings in Personnel and Human Resource Management,* 3d ed.
16. The phrase "being successful on the job" is used instead of the word "performance" to emphasize the notion that job-relatedness or validity refers to the relationship between the predictors and the criteria. Just as there can be several measures or indicators predicting how well an individual may do, there are several things or bases on which an individual can do well. Those bases may be performance quality, performance quantity, and absenteeism. Thus, there are three criteria, just two of which have the word "performance." So to say that job-relatedness refers to how well predictors will predict "performance" may be misleading.
17. For an excellent discussion of the impact and interpretation of the *Uniform Guidelines* and many other issues related to selection and testing, see the special issue of the *American Psychologist* (Oct. 1981).
18. "Age-35 Job Restriction Upheld," *Fair Employment Practices* (7 Jan. 1988): 2.
19. T. C. McKinney, "The Management of Seniority: The Supreme Court and the California Brewers Case," *Personnel Administration* (Feb. 1984): 8–14.
20. "Crackdown on Child Labor Violations," *FEP Guidelines* no. 299 (6 June 1990); "FLSA Amendments of 1989: Higher Federal Minimum Wage, Plus New Training Wage," *Bulletin to Management* (28 Dec. 1989): 1–3; B. Southard Murphy, W. E. Barlow, and D. D. Hatch, "A News Report for Personnel Professionals: Subminimum Training Wages Available," *Personnel Journal* (June 1990): 19.
21. G. Ameci, "Overtime Pay: Avoiding FLSA Violations," *Personnel Administrator* (Feb. 1987): 117–18; H. Stout, "Propping Up Payments at the Bottom," *The New York Times* (24 Jan. 1988): 4.
22. *FEP Guidelines* (Jan. 1985): 2. This copyrighted material is reprinted with permission of the Bureau of Business Practice, Waterford, CT 06386.
23. "Pay Equity Makes Good Business Sense," *Fair Employment Practices* (30 Aug. 1990): 103; A. Bernstein, "What's Dragging Productivity Down? Women's Low Wages," *Business Week* (27 Nov. 1989): 171; "Comparable Worth Policies that Work: The Minnesota Case," *The Urban Institute/Policy and Research Report* (Summer 1990): 10–12; G. J. Meng, "All the Parts of Comparable Worth" *Personnel Journal* (Nov. 1990): 99–104; "Market Forces: An Obstacle to Pay Equity?" *FEP Guidelines,* no. 292.
24. T. Linesenmayer, "Comparable Worth Abroad: Mixed Evidence," *The Wall Street Journal* (27 May 1986): 26.
25. See note 24.
26. "Permissible Pregnancy Practices," *Fair Employment Practices* (1 Dec. 1983): 3. The Pregnancy Disability Amendment also has other provisions; for a description of them, see S. R. Zacur and W. Greenwood, "The Pregnancy Disability Amendment: What the Law Provides, Part II," *Personnel Administrator* (March 1982): 55–58.
27. The Bureau of National Affairs, "ERISA's Effects on Pension Plan Administration," *Bulletin to Management* (9 Aug. 1984): 1–2; K. D. Gill, ed., *ERISA: The Law and the Code,* 1985 ed. (Washington, D.C.: The Bureau of National Affairs, Inc., 1985): B. J. Coleman, *Primer on Employee Retirement Income Security Act* (Washington, D.C.: The Bureau of National Affairs, Inc., 1985).
28. R. M. McCaffery, *Employee Benefit Programs: A Total Compensation Perspective* (Boston, Mass.: PWS-Kent, 1988); Bureau of National Affairs, "ERISA's Effects on Pension Plan Administration," *Bulletin to Management* (9 Aug. 1984): pp. 1–2; Coleman, *Primer on Employee;* Gill, *ERISA.*
29. J. A. LoCicero, "How to Cope with the Multi-Employer Pension Plan Amendments Act of 1980," *Personnel Administrator* (May 1981): 51–54, 68; J. A. LoCicero, "Multi-Employer Pension Plans: A Time Bomb for Employers?" *Personnel Journal* (Nov. 1980): 922–24, 932.
30. J. Case, "ESOPs: Dead or Alive?" *INC.* (June 1988): 94–100: P. Nulty, "What a Difference Owner-Bosses Make," *Fortune* (25 April 1988): 97–104.
31. Case, 95.
32. D. Schwartz, "The Last Word on Section 89," *Personnel Journal* (Jan. 1989): 48–57; R. E. Johnson and S. J. Velleman, "Section 89: Close the New Pandora's Box," *Personnel Journal* (Nov. 1988): 70–78; J. Ortman, "Section 89: Why You Should Act Now," *Personnel Journal* (Nov. 1988): 78–79.
33. *FEP Guidelines,* no. 315 (Oct. 1991): 3.
34. J. J. Laabs, "How Federally Funded Training Helps Businesses," *Personnel Journal* (March 1992): 35–37; S. B. Garland, "90 Days to Learn to Scrub? Sure, If Uncle Sam's

Paying," *Business Week* (20 Jan. 1992): 70–71; "Training for Promotions," *Federal Employment Guidelines,* no. 224 (3) (1984): 1–8; "Absenteeism and Tardiness," *Federal Employment Practices Guidelines,* no. 214(5) (1983): 1–8; S. B. Wehrenberg, "How to Decide on the Best Training Approach," *Personnel Journal* (Feb. 1983): 117–18.

35. *Chicago Raw Hide Manufacturing Co. v. NLRB,* 1955 *NLRB v. Northeastern University* 1979; *Hertzk & Knowles v. NLRB,* 1974; *NLRB v. Steamway Division of the Scott and Fetzer Co.,* 1982.

36. S. B. Garland, "This Safety Ruling Could Be Hazardous to Employers' Health," *Business Week* (20 Feb. 1989): 34; "Now OSHA Must Justify its Inspection Targets," *Business Week* (9 April 1979): 64; M. Hayes, "What Can You Do when OSHA Calls?" *Personnel Administrator* (Nov. 1982): 65–66; "Has OSHA Become Too Much of a Pussycat?" *Business Week* (11 March 1985): 82G–82J.

37. "On the Safety and Health Scene," *Bulletin to Management* (2 April 1987): 105.

38. B. Meir, "Use of Right-To-Know Rules is Increasing Public's Scrutiny of Chemical Companies," *The Wall Street Journal* (23 May 1985): 10; "OSHA's Final Labeling Standard," *Bulletin to Management* (1 Dec. 1983): 1.

39. P. A. Susser, "Update on Hazard Communication," *Personnel Administrator* (Oct. 1985): 57–61; M. G. Miner, "Legal Concerns Facing Human Resource Managers: An Overview," in *Readings in Personnel and Human Resource Management,* 3d ed., eds. R. S. Schuler, A. Youngblood, and V. Huber (St. Paul, Minn.: West Publishing Co., 1988); "Hazard Communication Training: Compliance Cues," *Bulletin to Management* (13 March 1986): 81.

40. *The Wall Street Journal,* (2 Oct. 1984): 1; Bureau of National Affairs, "State Right-To-Know Laws: Toxic Substances," *Bulletin to Management,* (22 Nov. 1984): 4–5; "Worker Right to Know," *Chemical Work* (18 April 1984): 38–44.

41. M. Novit, "Mental Distress: Possible Implications for the Future," *Personnel Administrator* (Aug. 1982): 47–54. The Civil Rights Act of 1871, Section 1983, enforces the Fourteenth Amendment providing for "equal protection of the laws" and prohibits employment discrimination on the basis of race, color, national origin, religion, sex, or age.

42. Determining responsibility is sometimes difficult because determining cause-and-effect relationships is difficult, especially when reaction such as asbestosis or hypertension take so long to develop or occur only in some people working under the same conditions as others. For a discussion, see A. D. Marcus, "Fearful of Future, Plaintiffs are Suing Firms for What Hasn't Happened Yet," *The Wall Street Journal,* (11 July 1990): B1, B8.

43. A good discussion of earlier contributions to labor law can be found in D. P. Twomey, *Labor Law and Legislation,* 6th ed. (Cincinnati, Ohio: Southwestern, 1990); R. C. Trussell, ed., *U. S. Labor and Employment Laws* (Washington, D.C.: Bureau of National Affairs, Cambridge University Press, 1987).

44. L. Balliet, *Survey of Labor Relations* (Washington, D.C.: Bureau of National Affairs, 1981): 44.

45. H. B. Frazier II, "Labor Management Relations in the Federal Government," *Labor Law Journal* (March 1979): 131.

46. See J. A. Fossum, *Labor Relations: Development, Structure, Process,* 4th ed. (Dallas, Tex.: Business Publications, 1988).

47. G. W. Bohlander, "Fair Representation: Not Just a Union Problem," *Personnel Administrator* (March 1980): 36–40, 82; J. P. Swann, Jr., "Misrepresentation in Labor Union Elections," *Personnel Journal* (Nov. 1980): 925–26.

48. *Bulletin to Management* (5 March 1992): 66.

49. *Fair Employment Practices* (16 Jan. 1992): 3.

50. P. J. Dowling and R. S. Schuler, *International Dimensions of Human Resource Management,* (Boston: PWS-Kent, 1991): 63.

51. Dowling and Schuler, 63.

52. See C. E. Landau, "Recent Legislation and Case Law in the EEC on Sex Equality in Employment," *International Labour Review* 123: 1 (1984): 53–70.

53. D. A. Ball and W. H. McCulloch, *International Business: Introduction and Essentials* (Plano, Tex.: Business Publications, 1988).

54. M. Jelinek and N. J. Adler, "Women: World-Class Managers for Global Competition," *Academy of Management Executive* 2: 1 (1988): 11–19.

55. G. Koretz, "In Europe, Cash Eases the Pain of Getting Fired," *Business Week* (16 March 1992): 26.

56. See note 55.

CHAPTER 4

Human Resource Planning and Job Analysis

All of our HR programs serve the bank's mission. If they didn't, we wouldn't have them.
—Jim Alef, Corporate Senior Vice President and Head, Human Resources, First Chicago Corporation[1]

HUMAN RESOURCE PLANNING

PURPOSES AND IMPORTANCE OF HUMAN RESOURCE PLANNING

THE HUMAN RESOURCE PLANNING PROCESS

FOUR PHASES OF HUMAN RESOURCE PLANNING

Phase 1: Gathering, Analyzing, and Forecasting Supply and Demand Data
Phase 2: Establishing Human Resource Objectives and Policies
PHRM in the News: The New Faces of Wall Street '92
Phase 3: Human Resource Programming
Phase 4: Human Resource Planning—Control and Evaluation
Roadblocks to Human Resource Planning

FOCUS ISSUES IN HUMAN RESOURCE PLANNING

Assessing Human Resource Planning
Artificial Intelligence and Planning
Ensuring Human Resources are Aligned with the Needs of the Business

SHARING THE RESPONSIBILITY: YOUR CAREER ACTIVITIES

Step 1: Conducting a Personal Appraisal
Step 2: Identifying Types of Jobs, Organizations, and Industries
Step 3: Preparing for Organizational Life
Focus on Research: If at First You Don't Succeed, Try, Try Again
Step 4: Getting Job Offers
Step 5: Choosing an Offer
Step 6: Doing Well

JOB ANALYSIS

PURPOSES AND IMPORTANCE OF JOB ANALYSIS

ASPECTS OF JOB ANALYSIS

Collecting Job Analysis Information
Job Descriptions

JOB ANALYSIS METHODS

Methods Analysis
Structured Questionnaire
Managerial Jobs
Development of Job Families
PHRM in the News: Building Competency Models

COST-BENEFIT ASSESSMENT OF JOB ANALYSIS

FOCUS ISSUES IN JOB ANALYSIS

Exemplary Job Analysis
Job Analysis and Employee Flexibility

INTERNATIONAL COMPARISONS IN HUMAN RESOURCE PLANNING AND JOB ANALYSIS

Japan
Case Study: What Human Resource Strategy Should Techtronics Pursue?
End of Section Case Study: Job Descriptions at HITEK

In 1990, Boeing Chief Executive Officer Frank Shrontz, set out to define a long-term direction and course of action for the corporation. Taken into consideration was the aerospace giant's current capabilities and capacities, the changing work force, current and future competition, forecasted economic conditions, and the Boeing heritage, as well as employee and customer needs. As a result of this process, Boeing set three fundamental goals to achieve in order for the firm to attain its mission. The goals included (1) quality, (2) profitability, and (3) growth.

A special handout was delivered to all Boeing employees and posted prominently on bulletin boards in all Boeing facilities. It explained the billion-dollar firm planned to achieve its goals through continuous improvement, a highly skilled and motivated work force, capable and focused management, technical excellence, financial strength, and a commitment to integrity.

With the overall plan in place, each of the major players in the Boeing Commercial Airplane Group (including the Fabrication Department) established its own goals and tactics to achieve those goals. The process continued on down to the work group level where goals were set for work teams and tactics outlined for achieving the goals. For example, one corporate objective is to have "a highly skilled and motivated work force." As operationalized in the Commercial Airline Division, this objective means beefing up training programs to "ensure that all employees have the knowledge, tools, and skills to implement continuous improvement." In the Fabrication Division, this objective has been brought to life with a tactical plan which includes the redesign and development of a new performance management system and the development of a joint union-management training program to increase the skills and competencies of hourly workers.[2]

This introductory feature about Boeing highlights several important aspects of human resource planning. One is that human resource planning is critical to the success of organizational strategy and planning. Second, human resource planning is tied to the nature of the organization: As the organization changes and becomes more flexible and adaptable, the human resource planning horizon becomes flexible and more adaptable. Third, line managers and human resource managers share responsibility for human resource planning. Fourth, the external environment has to be analyzed and incorporated into an organization's human resource planning.

HUMAN RESOURCE PLANNING

In general terms, **human resource planning** is the base upon which effective human resource management is constructed. Most specifically, human resource planning involves forecasting human resource needs for the organization and planning the steps necessary to meet these needs. Human resource planning consists of developing and implementing plans and programs to ensure that the right number and type of individuals are available at the right time and place to fulfill organizational needs. As such, human resource planning is directly tied to strategic business planning.[3] Because of the trend toward more strategic involvement by the human resource department (discussed in chapter 1), human resource planning is one of the fastest growing and most important areas in human resource management. It is also important because it serves so many purposes.

PURPOSES AND IMPORTANCE OF HUMAN RESOURCE PLANNING

In general, human resource planning helps ensure that organizations fulfill their business plans—plans that chart the organization's future regarding financial objectives, output goals, product mix, technologies, and resource requirements.[4] Once their business plans are determined, often with the assistance of the personnel and human resource department, "the human resource planner assists in developing workable organizational structures and in determining the numbers and types of employees that will be required to meet financial and output goals.[5] After workable structures and the requirements for needed individuals are identified, the human resource planner develops personnel and human resource programs to implement the structure and to obtain the individuals. However, line managers and supervisors are responsible for providing the necessary information for human resource planning, and for working with the human resource manager to ensure that the organization's human resources are used effectively.

More specifically, human resource planning is used to

- Reduce personnel costs by helping management anticipate shortages or surpluses of human resources and correct these imbalances before they become unmanageable and expensive
- Provide a better basis for planning employee development that makes optimum use of workers' aptitudes
- Improve the overall business planning process
- Provide equal opportunities for men and women, members of ethnic majority and minority groups, and individuals with as well as without physical disabilities in future growth plans
- Promote greater awareness of the importance of sound human resource management throughout all levels of the organization
- Provide a tool for evaluating the effect of alternative human resource actions and policies[6]

All these purposes are now more easily attained, thanks to computer technology. This technology allows vast job-related records to be maintained on each employee, in essence creating a human resource information system. These records include information on employee job preferences, work experiences, and performance evaluations. They also provide a job history of each employee in an organization and a complete set of information on the jobs and positions in the organization. In turn this information can be used for human resource planning in the interests of the individual as well as the organization.

A large number of environmental and organizational changes also make human resource planning more critical. These changes are pushing human resource management into a future-oriented, comprehensive, and integrative perspective with some fundamental attributes. This perspective

1. Considers human resource costs an investment rather than an uncontrollable expense
2. Is proactive rather than reactive or passive in its approach to developing human resource policies and resolving human resource problems
3. Is characterized by a change in role perspective from an emphasis on the completion of personnel transactions toward a future-oriented approach in which the personnel department acts as a developer of the organization's human resources
4. Recognizes that an explicit link must exist between human resource planning and other organizational functions, such as strategic planning, economic and market forecasting, and investment and facilities planning
5. Recognizes that such human resource activities as recruitment, selection, labor relations, compensation and benefits, training, organizational planning, and career management must be visualized as dynamic, interconnecting activities rather than as a series of separate and nonintegrated functions
6. Focuses on approaches that further both organizational and individual goals[7]

One organizational change that is making human resource planning more important is the growing shortage of human resources to fill certain jobs. Currently predicted are shortages in blue-collar occupations and entry-level white-collar occupations, such as tool and die makers, bricklayers, and other skilled crafts workers. In addition, shortages currently exist for shipbuilders, legal secretaries, engineers, robotics engineers, machinists, and mechanics.[8] Yet, while there are shortages of certain types of individuals, there is a growing abundance of another—those in the twenty-five-to-fifty-four-year-old age category.[9]

New retirement options available to workers are also causing a shift in concern for staffing positions, but not in the direction once expected. Workers now have options ranging from early retirement in their midfifties to retirement in their seventies. These options, coupled with the protection given to employees over the age of forty by the Age Discrimination in Employment Act, have caused organizations to devote more time to managing senior workers. As a consequence, managers are developing training programs to ensure that senior employees are kept up-to-date and provided with career counseling and preretirement planning.[10]

The increasing potential for managerial obsolescence is another critical issue. Rapid changes in knowledge are making it difficult for professionals, engineers, and managers to remain adept at their jobs. It has been speculated that entrants into the labor force in the 1990s will be retrained more than ten times during their work lives, and half of what today's managers, scientists, and professionals know will be obsolete by the year 2000.[11]

Another change is the resistance of employees to change and to relocation. The emphasis on self-evaluation, loyalty, and dedication to the organization also is growing. All these changes are making it more difficult for the organization to assume it can move its employees around anywhere and anytime it wants, thus increasing the importance and necessity of planning ahead.

All these changes also are increasing the importance of human resource management. Their implications for planning and program development are described later in the chapter.

THE HUMAN RESOURCE PLANNING PROCESS

As the introductory story about the Boeing company and the discussion in the paragraphs above illustrate, the human resource planning process takes place in a dynamic environment and in close relationship to the planning process of the business. Accordingly, the human resource planning process, in mirroring the business planning process, must consider both the longer term and the short term. In fact, firms might typically go out five years in their planning and then work back to the present. Similarly, in your own career planning you go out five, ten, even twenty years and then work back, noting what milestones must be reached along the way in order to achieve the objectives of year twenty. Of course, modifications can be made, both in your career planning and in a firm's business and human resource planning. Exhibit 4.1 shows the integration between business and human resource planning across several time horizons. At the core—and common to human resource planning regardless of the time horizon—are four phases:

1. Assess supply and demand
2. Develop objectives
3. Design and implement programs
4. Evaluate outcomes

Because of their importance, each is discussed in its application within or across any time horizon. Regardless of time horizon, the essential theme of linking back to the business remains.

FOUR PHASES OF HUMAN RESOURCE PLANNING

Determining an organization's human resource needs lies at the base of human resource planning. The two major components of this determination are identifying the human resource supply and identifying the human resource demand—the first phase in human resource planning. Although these determinations are critical, organizations have, until recently, avoided making them. Indeed, some organizations avoid or at least resist engaging in any of the four phases of human resource planning.[12] These roadblocks to human resource planning are described later in the chapter.

Human resource planning is generally accomplished in four phases, each of which is discussed below.[13]

Phase 1: Gathering, Analyzing, and Forecasting Supply and Demand Data

The first phase of human resource planning involves developing data that can be used to determine corporate objectives, policies, and plans as well as human resource objectives and policies. The data developed in Phase 1 represent information retrieved from the past, observed in the present, and forecasted for the future. Obtaining data from the past may be difficult because of inadequate or nonexistent records, and forecasting data with reliability and accuracy may be difficult because of uncertainties, especially the farther out the forecast goes.

Exhibit 4.1
Dynamic Linkages Among Components of a Fully Integrated System of Business and Human Resource Planning

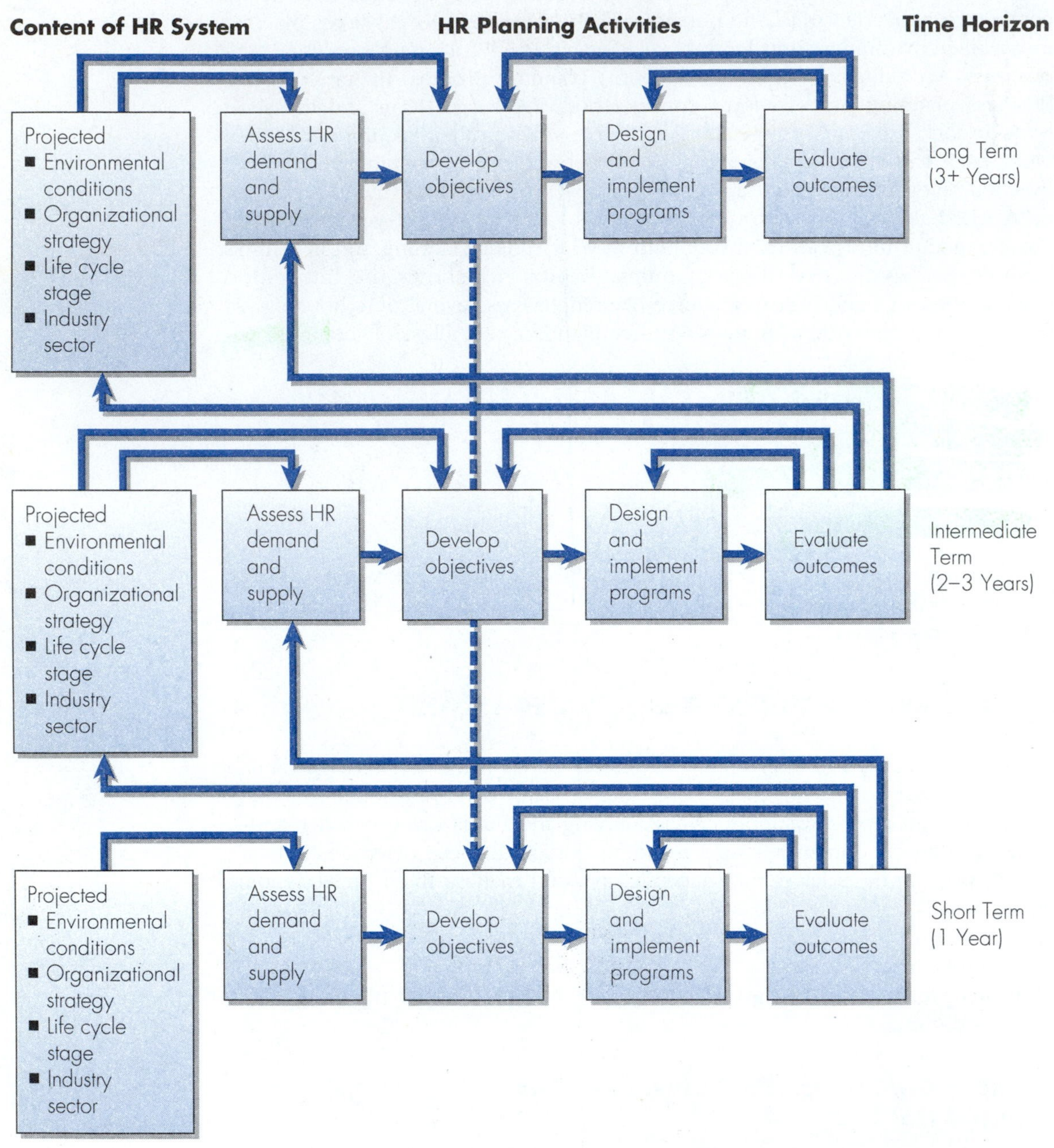

SOURCE: Adapted from S. E. Jackson and R. S. Schuler, "Human Resource Planning," *American Psychologist* (Feb. 1990), 225.

Nevertheless, this data should be provided, however tentatively. The more tentative the data, the more flexible and subject to revision they should be. Contin-

Exhibit 4.2
Procedures and Steps for Human Resource Planning and Programming

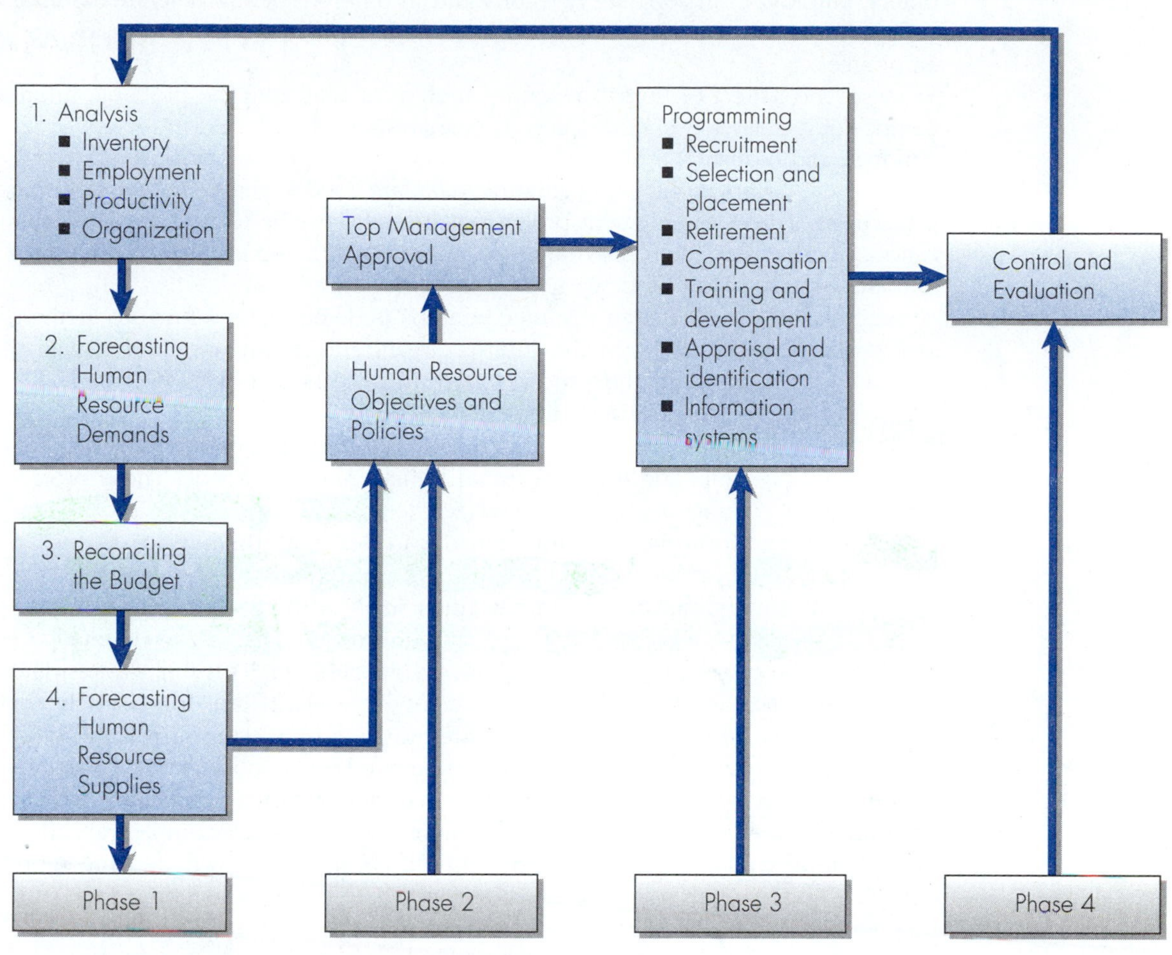

SOURCE: Adapted from E. W. Vetter, *Manpower Planning for High Talent Personnel* (Ann Arbor, Mich.: Bureau of Industrial Relations, Graduate School of Business, University of Michigan, 1967), 34.

gencies causing uncertainties in the forecasts should be incorporated, perhaps in the form of estimated ranges. Organizations in unstable, complex environments are faced with many more contingencies than are organizations in stable, simple environments.

Exhibit 4.2 shows the four steps in Phase 1. Each is important for the success of human resource planning and programming. Step 1 consists of analyzing the human resource situation in an organization; it has four aspects, all of which are applicable for the three time horizons shown in exhibit 4.1.

Analysis. One aspect of a human resource analysis is taking an inventory of the current work force and the current jobs in the organization. Both elements are needed if the organization is to determine its capability to meet current and future human resource needs.

Use of computers makes compiling inventories much more efficient and allows for a more dynamic, integrative human resource program. Through computers, employees in separate divisions and in different geographic areas find it easier to participate in the organization's network for matching jobs and employees.

A second aspect of human resource analysis is analyzing the probable future composition of society's work force. This analysis is often based on wage, occupational, and industrial groups. Historical data on work force composition, along with current demographic and economic data, are used to make human resource projections. These employment projections are not specific to any single organization, but they can often provide an organization with useful information for its human resource plans, particularly for long-term needs.

Another aspect of human resource analysis is determining labor productivity and probable productivity in the future. Organizations can use their HRISs to measure performance in the process of evaluating the productivity of specific programs, offices, or positions. Related measures are projections of employee turnover and absenteeism. These influence an organization's work force productivity at any one time and, thus, its future human resource needs. These projections might also suggest a need to analyze the reasons for turnover and absenteeism, and then form the basis for strategies to deal with them. Note, however, that at some times and for some employees, increased turnover is desirable. For example, if an organization suddenly finds itself with too many employees, increased turnover—especially among poor performers—might be welcomed.[14]

Finally, the organizational structure must be examined. This helps determine the probable size of the top, middle, and lower levels of the organization, for both managers and nonmanagers. In addition, it provides information about changes in the organization's human resource needs and about specific activities or functional areas that can be expected to experience particularly severe growth or contraction. As organizations become more technologically complex and face more complex and dynamic environments, their structures will become more complex—with more departments and a greater variety of occupations—and they will face more changes in the environment.[15]

Forecasting human resource demands. A variety of forecasting methods—some simple, some complex—can determine an organization's demand for human resources. The type of forecast used depends on the time frame and the type of organization, its size and dispersion, and the accuracy and certainty of available information. The time frame used in forecasting the organization's demand for human resources frequently parallels that used in forecasting the potential supply of human resources and the needs of the business. Comparing the demand and supply forecasts then determines the firm's short-, intermediate-, and long-term needs.

Forecasting results in approximations—not absolutes or certainties. The forecast quality depends on the accuracy of information and the predictability of events. The shorter the time horizon, the more predictable the events and the more accurate the information. For example, organizations are generally able to predict how many graduates they may need for the coming year, but they are less able to predict their needs for the next five years.

A recent study indicates that sixty percent of major firms conduct some form of human resource forecast. More than half of these firms prepare forecasts for both the short term (one year) and the long term (five years). In conducting forecasts, the emphasis is generally on predicting human resource demand rather than supply. In fact, more than half of the firms predicted *only* demand, while only one-third formally forecast supply *and* demand.[16]

Two classes of forecasting techniques are frequently used to determine the organization's projected demand for human resources. These are **judgmental forecasts** and **conventional statistical projections.**

Judgmental forecasting employs experts who assist in preparing the forecasts. The most common method of estimating human resource demand is **managerial estimates.**[17] Estimates can be made by top managers (**top-down**). Alternatively, the review process can begin at lower levels (**bottom-up**) with the results sent to higher levels for refinement. The success of these estimates depends on the quality of the information provided to the judgmental experts. Useful information can include data on current and projected productivity levels, market demand, and sales forecasts, as well as current staffing levels and mobility information.

Another way to make human resource demand judgments is called the **Delphi technique.** At a Delphi meeting, experts take turns at presenting their forecasts and assumptions to the others, who then make revisions in their own forecasts. This combination process continues until a viable composite forecast emerges. The composite may represent specific projections or a range of projections, depending on the experts' positions.

The Delphi technique has been shown to produce better one-year forecasts in comparison with linear regression analysis, but it does have some limitations. Difficulties may arise, for example, in integrating the experts' opinions. This technique, however, appears to be particularly useful in generating insights into highly unstructured or undeveloped subject areas, such as human resource planning.

A related method is the **nominal group technique.** Several people sit at a conference table and independently list their ideas on a sheet of paper.[18] The ideas presented are recorded on larger sheets of paper so everyone can see all the ideas and refer to them in later parts of the session.

The two techniques are similar in process, but the Delphi technique is more frequently used to generate predictions, and the nominal group technique is more frequently used to identify current organizational problems and solutions to those problems. Although all these judgmental forecasts are less complex and rely on less data than those based on the statistical methods discussed next, they tend to dominate in practice.[19]

The most common statistical procedures are simple linear regression and multiple linear regression analyses. In **simple linear regression analysis,** a projection of future demand is based on a past relationship between the organization's employment level and a variable related to employment, such as sales. If a relationship can be established between the level of sales and the level of employment, predictions of future sales can be used to make predictions of future employment. Although a relationship may exist between sales and employment, it is often influenced by an organizational learning phenomenon. For example, the level of sales may double, but the level of employment necessary to meet this increase may be less than double; and, if sales double again, the amount of employment necessary to meet this new doubling may be even less than that necessary to meet the first doubling of sales. An organizational learning curve can usually be determined by logarithmic calculations. Once the learning curve has been determined, more accurate projections of future employ-

Exhibit 4.3
Statistical Techniques Used to Project Staffing Demand Needs

Name	Description
Regression analysis	Past levels of various work load indicators, such as sales, production levels, and value added, are examined for statistical relationships with staffing levels. Where sufficiently strong relationships are found, a regression (or multiple regression) model is derived. Forecasted levels of the retained indicator(s) are entered into the resulting model and used to calculate the associated level of human resource requirements.
Productivity ratios	Historical data are used to examine past levels of a productivity index (P): $P = \frac{\text{Work load}}{\text{Number of people}}$ Where constant, or systematic, relationships are found, human resource requirements can be computed by dividing predicted work loads by P.
Personnel ratios	Past personnel data are examined to determine historical relationships among the employees in various jobs or job categories. Regression analysis or productivity ratios are then used to project either total or key-group human resource requirements, and personnel ratios are used to allocate total requirements to various job categories or to estimate requirements for non-key groups.
Time series analysis	Past staffing levels (instead of work load indicators) are used to project future human resource requirements. Past staffing levels are examined to isolate seasonal and cyclical variations, long-term trends, and random movement. Long-term trends are then extrapolated or projected using a moving average, exponential smoothing, or regression technique.
Stochastic analysis	The likelihood of landing a series of contracts is combined with the personnel requirements of each contract to estimate expected staffing requirements. Potential applications are mostly in government contractors and construction industries.

SOURCE: Adapted from L. Dyer, "Human Resource Planning," in *Personnel Management,* ed. K. Rowland and G. Ferris (Boston: Allyn & Bacon, 1982). Used with permission.

ment levels can be established. (See chapter 14 for a more complete description of regression analysis.)

Multiple linear regression analysis is an extension of simple linear regression analysis. Instead of relating employment to one variable, several variables are used. For example, instead of using only sales to predict employment demand, productivity data and equipment-use data may also be used. Because it incorporates several variables related to employment, multiple linear regression analysis may produce more accurate demand forecasts than does simple linear regression analysis. Apparently, however, only relatively large organizations use multiple linear regression analysis.[20]

In addition to these two regression techniques, several other statistical techniques are used to forecast staffing needs. Such techniques include productivity ratios, personnel ratios, time series analysis, and stochastic analysis. Currently, little research exists regarding the use of these techniques for human resource planning.[21] These techniques and a brief description of each are presented in exhibit 4.3. Although most of these techniques are used for forecasting the total organization's human resource demand, parts of the organization use an additional technique. The **unit demand forecasting** technique relies on labor estimates provided by the unit or functional area managers. This technique may produce forecasts of demands that, when added up for all unit managers, are discrepant with the total organization's forecasted demands. However, the technique encourages unit managers to be more aware of their employees' skills, abilities, and desires. This awareness may also produce a higher-quality forecast. Each unit may use the same statistical techniques that are used for the total organization.

Since the use of unit demand forecasting often produces discrepant forecasts, the differences must be reconciled before planning can be undertaken. The discrepancies, however, can often provide a useful basis for questioning and examining each unit's contributions as compared with its demands.

Reconciling the budget. The third aspect in the first phase of human resource planning and programming puts the whole activity into economic perspective. The human resource forecast must be expressed in dollars, and this figure must be compatible with the organization's profit objectives and budget limitations.[22] The budget reconciliation process may point up the importance of adjusting the budget to accommodate the human resource plan. This reconciliation stage also provides an opportunity to align the objectives and policies of the organization with those of the personnel and human resource department.

Forecasting human resource supplies. Although forecasted supply can be derived from both internal and external sources of information, the internal source is generally the most crucial and the most available. As with forecasting demand, two basic techniques help forecast internal labor supply: judgmental and statistical. Once made, the supply forecast can then be compared with the human resource demand forecast to help determine, among other things, action programming for identifying human resource talent and balancing supply and demand forecasts. However, most current forecasting of labor supply and demand is short-range and for the purposes of budgeting and controlling costs. Forecasts for periods of five or more years are used in planning corporate strategy, planning facilities, and identifying managerial replacements.[23]

Organizations use two judgmental techniques to make supply forecasts: replacement planning and succession planning. **Replacement planning** uses replacement charts. These charts are developed to show the names of the current occupants of positions in the organization and the names of likely replacements. Replacement charts make potential vacancies readily apparent and indicate what types of positions most urgently need to be filled. Present performance levels of current employees can be used to estimate potential vacancies. These vacancies may occur in those jobs in which the incumbents are not outstanding performers. On the replacement chart the incumbents are listed directly under the job title. Those individuals likely to fill the potential vacancies are listed directly under the incumbents. Such a listing can provide the organization with a good estimate of what jobs are likely to become vacant and indicate if anyone will be ready to fill the vacancy.

Succession planning is similar to replacement planning, except that succession planning tends to be longer term and more developmental and tends to offer greater flexibility.[24] Although succession planning is widely practiced, many employers using it tend to emphasize the characteristics of the managers and downplay the characteristics of the positions to which these managers may eventually be promoted.[25]

Statistical techniques are used less frequently than are judgmental techniques. Still, with the advent of personal computers and the need to gain a competitive edge, organizations are using more sophisticated statistical models to examine the supply of human resources. An important component of these statistical models is a **transition matrix** or **Markov matrix,** which models the flow of human resources. For example, the public accounting firm of Deloitte and Touche traditionally used a recruitment planning heuristic. However, this method did not account for attrition, expected growth of the firm, or the time needed to reach a specific job level. Now the firm uses a transition matrix similar to the one presented in exhibit 4.4. The percentages in a transition matrix indicate average rates of historical movement between job categories from one period to the next. The matrix shows, for example, that a supervisor during year T (the first year) has a 12 percent chance of being promoted to manager, a 60 percent chance of remaining a supervisor, and a 28 percent chance of exiting the firm in the following year.

These data can also be used to estimate future human resource supply and demand (see Part B of exhibit 4.4). This is done by multiplying the staffing levels at the beginning of the planning period by the probabilities of movement. In this example, the anticipated availabilities are 10, 30, 50, 85, and 130 in the five job categories. To keep staffing levels at the same level as in the initial year, the firm would need to hire 15 senior accountants and 70 accountants. Alternatively, the firm could promote 15 more accountants to senior accountant and recruit 85 accountants. This may be more cost effective. However, if new ideas are needed, the firm may wish to hire at higher levels. The transition matrix also points out rates of turnover. If the firm believes that the 30 percent turnover in partners is too high, it would need to develop strategies to correct the problem.

Markov analysis is also at the heart of **computer simulations** that examine alternative worker flows.[26] Promotion, turnover, and hiring rates can be varied

Exhibit 4.4
Transition Matrices for 1992–1996

Personnel Classification in Year T		**Personnel Classification in Year T + 1**					
A:		*P*	*M*	*S*	*Sr*	*A*	*Exit*
Partner		.70					.30
Manager		.10	.80				.10
Supervisor			.12	.60			.28
Senior				.20	.55		.25
Accountant					.15	.65	.20
B:	Beginning Staffing Levels	*P*	*M*	*S*	*Sr*	*A*	*Exit*
Partner	10	7					3
Manager	30	3	24				3
Supervisor	50		6	30			14
Senior	100			20	55		25
Accountant	200				30	130	40
		10	30	50	85	130	

and the effects on the bottom line examined. **Goal programming** is a further extension of Markov analysis.[27] The objective here is to optimize goals—in this case, a desired staffing pattern—given a set of constraints concerning such things as the upper limits on flows, the percentages of new recruits, and the total salary budget. Fortunately, software packages are available to facilitate these processes. IBM has gone so far as to develop personal-computer-based software to be used by line managers in all their facilities to simulate human resource flows for specific units or facilities.

Phase 2: Establishing Human Resource Objectives and Policies

While Markov-based analysis provides useful information, the actual strategy chosen to fill vacancies or resolve turnover problems depends on corporate goals and their linkage to human resource goals established in Phase 2 of the planning process (refer to exhibit 4.2.). The importance of an organization's objectives and policies for human resource planning seems difficult to deny; thus, it is not surprising that more and more firms are establishing human resource objectives and policies. (However, as the environment becomes more uncertain and harder to predict, these objectives and policies tend to have a shorter term outlook than previously. This also has an impact on the design of human resource management programs.)

As firms establish human resource objectives and plans, they link them closer to the needs and plans of the business. An excellent example of this and the implications this linkage can have for many aspects of human resource management are described in PHRM in the News: "The New Faces on Wall Street '92."

Phase 3: Human Resource Programming

The third phase in human resource planning—human resource programming—is an extremely important extension. After the assessment of an organization's human resource needs, action programming must be developed to serve those needs. These action programs may be designed to increase the supply of the right employees in the organization (e.g., if the forecasts in Phase 1 showed that demand exceeded supply) or to decrease the number of current employees (e.g., if the forecasts showed that supply exceeded demand). Organizations today use many alternative programs to address these purposes. These include diversity programs to make organizations more attractive to a broader array of applicants; programs to improve the socialization efforts so that good employees want to remain with the organization; and programs to downsize or "rightsize" the organization, such as early retirement incentives and generous severance packages to complement the normal attrition process. All of these programs are described in the following chapters.

Regardless which human resource program is implemented, it must be monitored and evaluated. This allows for controlling how well the program is being implemented and revising it as appropriate. Thus, control and evaluation comprise the necessary fourth phase in human resource planning.

PHRM IN THE NEWS

The New Faces of Wall Street '92

A fresh crop of recruits has arrived on Wall Street, one of the few areas in the New York region that is hiring after years of retrenchment. The new faces are older and more experienced than those hired in the past, and, if David Nelson is any example, they bring a more lucrative list of potential clients with them.

Mr. Nelson, 43 years old, was once lead guitarist for the Turtles, one of the mop-top rock groups that characterized the rebellious flavor of the late 1960's. Last year, he became a broker at Merrill Lynch & Company, and by tapping his acquaintances in the music business, he is likely to develop a fuller book of clients than most first-year brokers.

Opportunity Knocking Again

"I've already been able to make inroads with record companies that need business and financial advice," said Mr. Nelson, who talks about cash-flow, pension and insurance issues with the assurance of a knowledgeable insider. "I don't want to limit myself to the music business, but that is obviously my area of expertise."

"I wanted to make this move back in 1987," added Mr. Nelson, who worked most recently as a record producer. "But the opportunity wasn't there," he said, after the stock market crashed in October of that year.

It is now. Several brokerage firms are hiring more entry-level brokers than they did a year ago. While limited, this expansion is one of the few economic bright spots in the New York region, where 40,000 jobs are expected to evaporate in the next few years.

If a silver lining to a recession is that the quality and size of job-applicant pools swell, Wall Street firms are in the enviable position of being able to take advantage of the talent fleeing hard times in other businesses. It is not so much that the rash of new applicants are unemployed, recruiting executives say, but rather that many are finding their careers stalled in depressed areas like banking and financial consulting....

A Growing Pool

Paradoxically, Wall Street's recent success—reflected in record profits at brokerage houses and in new stock market highs—is drawing so many job seekers that despite the hiring, some firms are turning away

Continued

Phase 4: Human Resource Planning—Control and Evaluation

Control and evaluation of human resource plans and programs are essential to effectively manage human resources. Efforts in this area are clearly aimed at quantifying the value of human resources. These efforts recognize human resources as an asset to the organization. An HRIS facilitates program control and evaluation by allowing for more rapid and frequent collection of data to back up the forecast. This data collection is important not only as a means of control but also as a method for evaluating plans and programs and making adjustments.

Evaluation of human resource plans and programs is an important process not only for determining the effectiveness of human resource planning but also for demonstrating the significance of both human resource planning and the personnel and human resource department in the organization as a whole.

Possible criteria for evaluating human resource planning include the following:

- Actual staffing levels against established staffing requirements
- Productivity levels against established goals

many more applicants than they did a year ago. For Wall Street's big firms, the result is a richer choice of applicants for each available position.

"We've seen a dramatic change in the people coming in," said Robert J. Dwyer, who oversees recruitment at Dean Witter Reynolds Inc. In 1991, Mr. Dwyer said, the average broker recruited by Dean Witter was 36 years old, with six years of related experience. Only a year earlier, Dean Witter's average new broker was 26 years old, with a year of experience.

Concentrated in Retail Area

Dean Witter expects to hire 1,000 account executives this year, compared with 600 in 1991. Shearson Lehman Brothers expects to hire between 600 and 1,000 brokers, compared with 400 last year. Prudential Securities' training program has accepted more than 400 brokers this year, compared with just 97 last year.

This expansion, while limited mostly to the retail side of the business, is giving the securities industry its first boost in employment in three years....

Several brokerage firms are both expanding the training of their own retail brokers and stressing the value of building a long-term relationship with each client instead of relying on quick trading commissions.

"It's no longer 'get a hunch and sell a bunch,'" said Linda Marcelli, branch manager of Merrill Lynch's main New York office. She supervises more than 160 financial advisers, including Mr. Nelson. "It's long-term planning that we're looking for."

Prudential Securities recently hired a new executive vice president, A. Laurence Norton, to oversee recruitment, training and retention of the firm's financial advisers.

One of the advantages of the older, more seasoned crop of new brokers coming into Prudential, Mr. Norton said, is that they generally are people with some financial experience, people who have some understanding of the securities business.

"These are the kind of people who can make an impact a little quicker," Mr. Norton said. Some customers are more comfortable entrusting their investments to an older broker, he added, although more sophisticated customers tend to judge a financial consultant by rate of success and not by age.

For brokerage houses, another bonus of the higher caliber of fresh recruits is that instead of starting from scratch, new brokers often come to their jobs with a list of potential clients from their previous work.

SOURCE: S. Faison, Jr., *The New York Times* (16 March 1992): D1, D3.

- Actual personnel flow rates against desired rates
- Programs implemented against action plans
- Program results against expected outcomes (e.g., improved applicant flows, reduced quit rates, improved replacement ratios)
- Labor and program costs against budgets
- Ratios of program results (benefits) to program costs[28]

An important aspect related to evaluation, revision, and adjustment is the issue of cause and effect. The human resource management model presented in chapter 1 is based on the notion of integrated, related activities. For example, if the recruiting program is not working well, the conclusion that the program needs revision may be invalid. Perhaps the salaries offered to recruits were too low and not competitive with other organizations. Also possible is that, despite the best recruiting efforts, few acceptable applicants applied. The integrated approach makes the evaluation of any single program not only complex but also necessary on the basis of the total program.

In reality, evaluation can be so complex it tends not to get done. Indeed, many obstacles serve as roadblocks to the entire process of human resource planning.

Roadblocks to Human Resource Planning

A key roadblock to initiating human resource planning is the lack of **top management support.** Human resource managers can help remove this roadblock with data and bottom-line facts that demonstrate the effectiveness of human resource planning.

Another roadblock is the difficulty in obtaining **integration** with other personnel activities—a necessary step if human resource planning is to work. A challenge for personnel and human resource managers is to create a personnel system in which all the activities discussed in chapter 1 are integrated and coordinated in conjunction with the organization's business plan.

A third roadblock is line managers' **lack of involvement.** Failure to involve line management in the design, development, and implementation of a human resource planning system is a common oversight for first-time planners. Personnel and human resource managers are often tempted to develop or adopt highly quantitative approaches to planning, which often have little pragmatic value in solving line managers' problems. To be effective, human resource planning must be useful. An integral part of being useful is serving line managers' needs. With this important point in mind, the firm can begin developing human resource plans and programs.

FOCUS ISSUES IN HUMAN RESOURCE PLANNING

Because of their relevance for the entire area of personnel and human resource management, major issues introduced in chapter 1 are also relevant to human resource planning.

Assessing Human Resource Planning

Human resource planning can make or break an organization, especially over the long term. Without effective human resource planning, an organization may find itself with a plant or an office with no people to run it. On a broad level, then, human resource planning can be assessed on the basis of whether the organization has the people it needs—the right people at the right place, at the right time, and at the right salary.

At more specific levels, human resource planning activities can be assessed by how effectively they, along with recruitment, attract new employees, deal with job loss, and adapt to the changing characteristics of the environment. Because an important part of human resource planning is forecasting, human resource planning can be assessed by how well its forecasts (whether of specific personnel needs or of specific environmental trends) compare with reality. Several other criteria against which human resource planning can be assessed were presented earlier in the section on human resource planning control and evaluation.

Artificial Intelligence and Planning

High-level computer languages have vastly increased the ease with which complex human knowledge can be represented in computer-usable form. This is making it possible to capture and make available expert knowledge about how things work and get done through **artificial intelligence.** Artificial intelligence (AI) has gained enough momentum to be considered the second computer revolution. Advances are making possible computer programs that have reliable knowledge about important topics. The field of human resource management is no exception. Interactions with these new AI programs can closely simulate interaction with experts. This is making possible, at least in principle, the attainment of the highly desirable goal of providing "real-time" on-the-job access to people who need human resource support. From a human resource planning perspective, the advantage is that managers in the field will have optimal planning expertise available at a moment's notice.[29]

Ensuring Human Resources are Aligned with the Needs of the Business

Ensuring that business needs are met by human resources will be a significant issue through the twenty-first century. In particular, human resources must be a strategic partner to the line manager, international human resource needs must be addressed, and sufficient programs must be put in place to ensure cost efficiency management. Success in all these areas will depend upon the organization's human resource planning skills and programs.

Planning at the organizational level and individual level will continue to change into the twenty-first century. At the organizational level, there will be a greater focus on shaping and managing change. Human resource planning, as an identifier of needs and mobilizer of human resorces, will increasingly identify business needs and ways human resources can assist in meeting those needs. To deal with the rapidly changing environment, human resource planning will become more tentative and short-term focused. At the same time, long-term needs will still be important because some organizational change efforts—such as quality improvement—take time.

Human resource planning will also be done with people in mind. As labor shortages develop, there will be more concern for retaining and retraining good employees. As employee commitment and empowerment are causally linked to quality improvement, there will be an even stronger concern for retaining and retraining.

However, there will be a corresponding need to link human resource planning with business planning so that excess human resources are not created. As the external environment changes, so may the strategy and business needs of the firm. Therefore, human resource planning must cultivate work force flexibility and adaptability. To the human resource planning practice will go the responsibility for systematically orchestrating all the human resource practices to stimulate and reinforce employee flexibility and adaptability. This orchestration will become more important as the need to link human resources with the strategies of organizations grows.

Finally, businesses must ensure that the most effective human resource practices are being used. To that end, continuous and extensive environment scanning will be an important feature of successful firms in highly competitive environments in the twenty-first century.

SHARING THE RESPONSIBILITY: YOUR CAREER ACTIVITIES

We have been talking about human resource planning from the organization's perspective. Now let's talk about it from your perspective. This is not only interesting, but also very functional; increasingly, organizations want employees to share responsibility for managing their own careers.

You'll do better if you actively manage your career. "Better" can be measured by any standard you choose—job security, self-esteem, growth, comfort, success in climbing to the top of the organization, or salary level. By planning and managing, you'll increase your chances of obtaining whatever you realistically identify as most important. Exhibit 4.5 outlines a general strategy for planning and managing your career.

Personal appraisal for career self-appraisal is really the basis of career planning activities. It consists of identifying an individual's strengths and weaknesses. Itemize your own strengths and weaknesses as you do your own personal appraisal. Complete all the career planning activities shown. (If you have recently done career planning, you may wish to skim or even skip this segment and move on to "Job Analysis.")

Exhibit 4.5
Personal Career Planning Activities

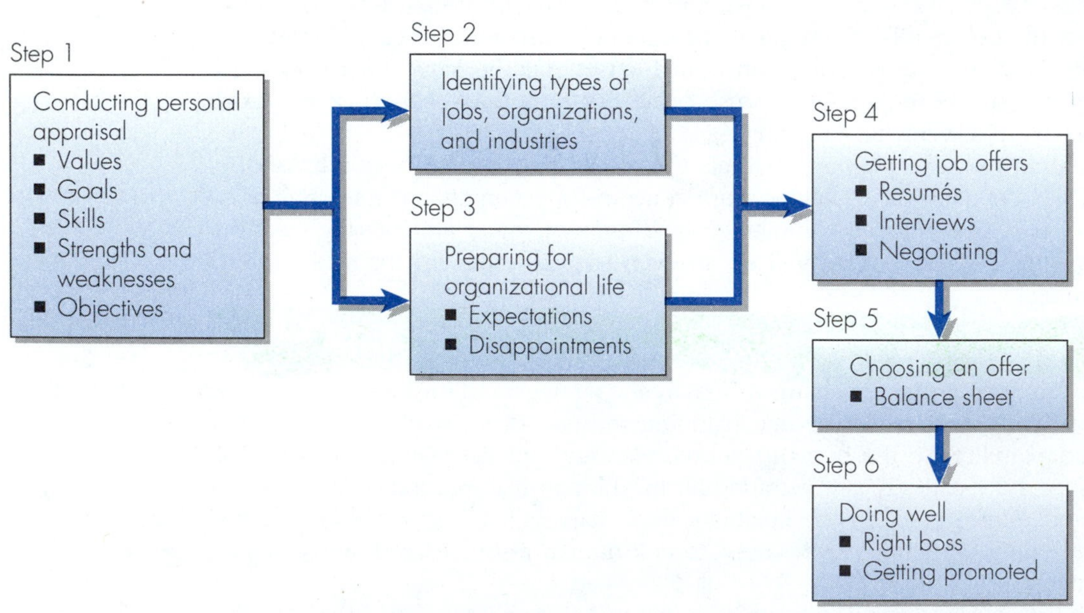

Step 1: Conducting a Personal Appraisal

This step involves taking a personal inventory of the following:

- Values
- Goals
- Skills
- Strengths and weaknesses
- Objectives

Do this step by completing the career self-appraisal exercise shown in exhibit 4.6.

Step 2: Identifying Types of Jobs, Organizations, and Industries

Because the job or jobs you choose can have such an impact on your life, it is important to analyze carefully what you want from your first job and your first company. You may want to start by first identifying industries in which you may want to work. For example, you may want to work in an industry with great potential, such as health care, computer science and/or data processing, or communications. Then gather information on a particular company within your chosen industry. Summer work experience, internships, and part-time work are valuable ways to gain exposure to new companies. Although some work experience may be boring to you, it sometimes helps if you consider them as learning experiences, as ways of getting to know yourself better. Other sources of information are newspapers and professional magazines, school placement offices, libraries, direct mail, job-search firms, friends, and family.[30]

As you think about the types of job, organizations, and industries, also weigh the relative value to you of such things as higher salary and fewer benefits versus lower salary, more benefits, and more opportunities to learn more skills.[31]

If you are skilled with your hands and you enjoy working with things, consider becoming any of the following: air-conditioning, refrigeration, and heating mechanic; appliance service person; television and radio service technician; business machine, computer, or industrial machinery service person; truck or bus mechanic; or vending machine mechanic. Research by the Department of Labor indicates that, if you do learn one of these skills, you'll have plenty of job opportunities through the 1990s. Exhibit 2.8 in chapter 2 illustrates occupations with the largest job growth potential through 2000.

Many other types of jobs can be considered. Self-employment and the more traditional entry-level jobs in larger organizations are the first step in a series through promotions to senior management positions. Within larger organizations, these traditional paths are available in many functional areas (such as personnel) and across functional areas as described in the first part of this chapter. Also, the relatively new field of internal corporate consulting offers a few job opportunities.

Management consulting has long been a springboard to lofty corporate positions for men; and, as far back as the late 1960s, a handful of women also used consulting to move up in corporations. For instance, Mary C. Falvey, 40, currently earns a salary estimated at well above $100,000 as vice-president of finance at

Exhibit 4.6
Career Self-Appraisal

Steps

1. List five goals you have for each of three categories—career, affiliations, and personal fulfillment (or create other categories).
2. Go back and *rate* them (1–little importance through 5–great importance). Which list has the most 4s and 5s?
3. Merge the three lists and *rank* all 15 goals in order of importance to you on the next sheet.
4. Select your top goal and describe it on the top of the second sheet. Then, discuss it in terms of:
   a. Personal strengths and weaknesses
   b. Obstacles to prevent achieving the goal
   c. Strategies to circumvent obstacles
   d. Are the goals realistic, attainable, and measurable?
   e. What are the rewards for achieving the goal?
   f. Do you value these rewards?

Career goals (e.g., become president by 45; become V.P. by 35, etc.): Goal Rating (1, 2, 3, 4, or 5)

1. ______________________ ________
2. ______________________ ________
3. ______________________ ________
4. ______________________ ________
5. ______________________ ________

Affiliation/Interpersonal (e.g. family, friends, clubs, group members, etc.):

1. ______________________ ________
2. ______________________ ________
3. ______________________ ________
4. ______________________ ________
5. ______________________ ________

Personal Fulfillment/Achievements (e.g., master the piano, run a marathon, get an MBA degree, etc):

1. ______________________ ________
2. ______________________ ________
3. ______________________ ________
4. ______________________ ________
5. ______________________ ________

Goal Ranking

Please list (in order of importance) the 15 goals from above.

1. ______________________
2. ______________________
3. ______________________

Continued

Exhibit 4.6
Career Self-Appraisal (Continued)

4. __________
5. __________
6. __________
7. __________
8. __________
9. __________
10. __________
11. __________
12. __________
13. __________
14. __________
15. (least important) __________

Take one important goal, restate it here, and then continue by discussing your personal strengths and weaknesses.

____

____

Personal strengths in relation to attaining the goal

1. __________
2. __________
3. __________
4. __________
5. __________

Personal weaknesses in relation to attaining the goal

1. __________
2. __________
3. __________
4. __________
5. __________

Obstacles in the way to good attainment	Strategy to overcome obstacles
1. __________	1. __________
2. __________	2. __________
3. __________	3. __________
4. __________	4. __________

Continued

Exhibit 4.6
Career Self-Appraisal (Continued)

5. ______________________ 5. ______________________

Rewards for achieving the goal (rank in terms of value)

1. ______________________
2. ______________________
3. ______________________
4. ______________________
5. ______________________

Indicators that you have achieved the goal (short and long term)

1. ______________________
2. ______________________
3. ______________________
4. ______________________
5. ______________________

Steps for achieving the goal (starting now)	Time deadline
1. ______________________	______________________
2. ______________________	______________________
3. ______________________	______________________
4. ______________________	______________________
5. ______________________	______________________

Shaklee Corp. in San Francisco. She started her career by joining the management consulting firm of McKinsey & Co. in 1967. Only in the past four or five years, however, have substantial numbers of women discovered consulting as a path to corporate achievement, a demanding but rewarding way of bypassing lower managerial jobs.[32]

At this point you may also wish to consider working for a foreign-owned firm. While there may be potential glamor in working for a British or Japanese firm and traveling abroad, there are potential drawbacks. Such drawbacks include limited promotion opportunities and the limited freedom to manage as you would like. As with any job, however, it is important to gather as much information as possible before deciding whether or not to consider a foreign-owned firm. For one thing, you may wish to consider it because there is a trend of increased foreign ownership in the U.S.[33]

Step 3: Preparing for Organizational Life

It is one thing to know the type of jobs you might want and the type of industry or organization in which you want to work, but it's an entirely different thing to

FOCUS ON RESEARCH

If at First You Don't Succeed, Try, Try Again?

When you were first learning to ride a bicycle, this may have been good advice. Does the advice still hold when you're starting off in a new career? One theory of career mobility sees winning the corporate game as more similar to winning a tennis tournament. Those who succeed go on to compete; those who do poorly in the early rounds drop out–the opportunity to "try, try again" has been lost. If careers are like tournaments, then early career experiences are critical to later achievements–you can't make up for a poor showing later in the tournament if you have already been forced out of the competition. A study conducted in a large public utility illustrates this type of career system. The job histories of all 338 managers who started their careers during a ten-year period were examined. In this company, the first hurdle proved to be the path of entry into a management job. The three paths were internal promotion from a nonmanagement job, external hire into a management job, or entry through a management training program. Career mobility was greatest for those hired as management trainees, next best was being hired from outside the company, and slowest for those promoted from within. After 18 months, 55% of trainees had moved on to other assignments, but only 38% of direct hires and 30% of internally promoted incumbents had moved to new jobs. The movement was not necessarily upward, however; in many cases, the career moves were lateral. Furthermore, those who churned through more job positions faster were rewarded within this company, perhaps because the company's strategy of acquisitions as a means of growth meant they needed to be sure they had a ready supply of managers who understood the larger system.

Another early key to success was getting placed in a high-power department for the first job assignment. Almost all job assignments (80%) after the first one were in other departments of equal power, so managers who had high-power first assignments had much better chances of later moving into other high-power departments and less chance of being placed in a low-power assignment. Job assignments in powerful departments serve the company in several ways. A department's power reflects the importance of its function in determining company effectiveness, so these assignments serve to teach the company's best talent about key success factors for the company's strategy. Also, such assignments build commitment on the part of both the new managers, who have better opportunities to develop a strong network with those already in power, and their mentors.

Companies that manage careers using a tournament model seek to use their human resources as efficiently as possible. They identify the best talent early, and then develop this (and only this) talent. This puts pressure on everyone involved: Employers must learn to correctly identify their best talent and plan to utilize it most efficiently, and employees must learn to read the early signals that tell them which career paths remain open and which are closed to those who do not succeed early.

SOURCE: Based on J. E. Sheridan, J. W. Slocum Jr., R. Buda, and R. C. Thompson, "Effects of Corporate Sponsorship and Departmental Power on Career Tournaments," *Academy of Management Journal* 33 (1990), 578–602.

know the realities of living and working in an organization. In almost any organization, you should be aware of two qualities of organizational life: organizational expectations and organizational disappointments.

Organizational expectation. Most organizations expect new employees to have certain characteristics:

- Competence to get a job done
- Ability to accept organizational realities
- High personal integrity and strength
- Capacity to grow[34]

Organizational disappointment. Although organizations have high expectations of you, they may not always live up to their end of the bargain. What they do or don't do may bring you disappointments (reality shock).[35] Here are several likely reasons:

- *Low initial job challenge.* Although some findings have indicated the usefulness of giving new recruits a challenging initial job, many organizations continue to ease the new recruit into the organization. This is consistent with the organization's perception of the new recruit as a novice.
- *Low self-actualization and need satisfaction.* The new recruit may fail to experience the autonomy and challenge necessary to grow and to develop self-esteem and competency. Some researchers have suggested that an individual may actually lose competency in the job if not given the opportunity to advance in the direction of the growth and independence characteristic of mature adults.
- *The vanishing performance appraisal, or inability to determine what are the real criteria.* New recruits come on board expecting to receive clear and unambiguous evaluations of their performance. In reality, new recruits report having little feedback on their performance, although their supervisors may claim the opposite.
- *Unrealistically high aspirations.* Most recruits have higher expectations of being able to use their skills and abilities than actually occurs. The gap between an individual's skills and the skills actually used on the job is probably increased because of the manager's belief that the new recruit is not capable of assuming responsibility.
- *Source of threat to the boss.* A new recruit's first boss plays a critical role for the recruit's future in the organization. The role tends to be negative, especially if the boss feels threatened. The threat may occur to the supervisor who is in a terminal position and can't go any further in the organization. The new recruit may be seen as a "comer" with a great deal more potential than the boss. In addition, the new recruit is probably younger and has different values and styles. As a result, the supervisor may not provide many positive experiences.
- *Amount of conflict and uncertainty in the organization.* New recruits think that rules and procedures, directions and communications will be clear, crisp, and without conflict. The reality in many situations is just the opposite.[36]

Individuals (you) can do a number of things to facilitate successful organizational entry, including the following:

- *Development of self-awareness.* This activity, known also as self-assessment, involves an inventory of values, goals, skills, strengths and weaknesses, and objectives. Individuals must develop an awareness of themselves and their preferred work environment.
- *Identification of prospective employers.* Because the job or jobs individuals choose have such an impact on their lives, they must analyze carefully what they want from their first job and their first company. Information about companies can be gathered through summer work experience, internships, and part-time work.

- *Effective job interview behavior.* "Selling" oneself to prospective employers requires a high degree of self-awareness. The interview is the individual's chance to create a favorable impression, gather additional information about the company, emphasize past accomplishments, demonstrate initiative and leadership through extracurricular activities, and practice interviewing skills (perhaps through information interviews).
- *Choice of organizations.* Although choosing the best job offer may be more art than science, individuals can construct a **career balance sheet.** Using a separate sheet of paper for each job, the positive and negative aspects of each offer can be listed. Individuals should consider how each aspect will affect them and how it will affect others, such as their spouse, friends, or family. Balance sheets help individuals make a job choice because they require individuals to organize job information in a systematic way.

Step 4: Getting Job Offers

Now that you've narrowed down (but not too much) the types of jobs, organizations, and industries you want and are prepared for organizational life, the next thing to do is get some job offers. Three aspects of getting job offers are resumé writing, interviewing, and negotiating.

Resumé writing. The standard resumé lists work experience from your current job and/or student status to those two years you spent delivering the daily paper (to show youthful vitality, industry, and responsibility for customers and money). Often it's a chronology of dates, titles, and responsibilities (whether they are previous jobs or positions held in school organizations).

Job interviewing. Step 1 has great value as preparation for job interviews. If you know yourself inside and out, you will find it easier to "sell" yourself to potential employers. Here are six suggestions for participating in job interviews.

- Sell yourself to the recruiter with the same determination you would use in selling a product or service to a customer. The interview period is brief, yet a favorable impression of your appearance, sense of purpose, and clarity of self-expression will probably weigh more heavily with the recruiter than your transcript, your resumé, or your references.
- Familiarize yourself ahead of time with the employer to be interviewed—know what the company does and what products or services it offers. Ask only pertinent questions during the interview, and suggest how your skills and abilities may benefit the organization.
- Develop your ability to communicate, but do not come on too strong or be overly confident.
- Cite academic achievements, especially if they appear to relate to the job area in which you are interested. Remember that recruiting companies often view your college work as a preparatory period. Hence, cite your academic efforts as evidence that you can attain long-range goals and objectives.
- Mention extracurricular activities that demonstrate your leadership or initiative.

- Learn the art of interviewing by accepting as many interview opportunities as you can, even with organizations you think you may not want to join. Interviews can be practiced by role playing.[37]

Negotiating. An important topic that will surely arise in your interviewing is salary. How you handle this topic could make a substantial difference in how much you get paid. Here are a few tips on how to handle this aspect in your job search:

> It's "dumb" for a job candidate to raise the question of salary early in the hiring process, says Pfizer divisional vice-president Max Hughes. And it is. Until the employer has had time to make up his or her mind to hire you, you aren't worth anything to the employer. To negotiate the highest possible salary, listen and ask questions so that you can identify the other person's needs and communicate how you can help meet them. It's best to delay the subject of salary until later in the interview. Loaded with information about your strengths, the employer should see you as a more valuable asset than when you began to talk....
>
> Inevitably, the employer who wants you on his or her team will ask, "What are your salary requirements?" Unlike some career consultants who encourage you to get the employer to name the first figure, executive recruiter Richard Irish, career consultant John Crystal, job-market analyst Richard Lathrop, and others say (and I agree) that you should name the first figure and make it high.[38]

Step 5: Choosing an Offer

Now that you have all the skills necessary to get several offers, equally necessary is the skill to choose one from among several offers. Although choosing the best offer may be more an art than a science to be taught and learned, one method that may help is the career balance sheet. On this you weigh the offers just as described above in choosing an organization.[39]

Step 6: Doing Well

Doing well involves getting what you want from the organization in which you are working. It means having things go your way. It may mean getting promoted, and it certainly means staying valuable and useful to the organization. As such, it requires that you know how to deal with your boss and how to get promoted.

The right boss. People are more likely to develop strong leadership qualities if they work for a boss who has something to teach, who is on the move, and who is capable of taking others along. The preference for being on a winning team is a survival mechanism. People are less dependent and uncertain if they're allied with bosses who are strong leaders. Consequently, it pays to try to be in a position to select your boss. This is especially true for your first boss. You can enhance your chances of working for the boss of your choice by being an outstanding performer and by becoming a critical subordinate for your boss, but one who doesn't threaten the boss.[40]

Getting promoted. Getting promoted is much easier when you

- Have credibility with senior managers. Managers with credibility can take greater risks and make more mistakes because they have the known ability to produce results. It's necessary to have credibility with superiors before developing it with subordinates. For example, a manager was brought in from the outside to run a division that designs aerospace equipment. He could barely get information he needed from headquarters—he had few connections and no clout. And his subordinates had a better idea of what was going on. Without the support of top management, his subordinates thought little of him.[41]
- Have a reputation as being an expert. When a manager has the reputation of being an expert, others tend to defer to that manager on issues involving his or her expertise. This is important in large organizations where many people have only secondhand knowledge about one's professional competence.[42]
- Be the first in the position. A manager who is the first in a new position, takes risks, and succeeds is more likely to be rewarded than a manager who does something second. While excellent performance on routine tasks is usually valued, being innovative is a big plus.[43]
- Know and use networks. Knowing about and using networks can be critical to your job success. Essentially a **network** is a collection of friends and acquaintances, both inside and outside one's workplace, that can be counted on for some kind of help. Networks can provide many kinds of help including information, services, support, and access.

While getting promoted is certainly still possible, it is becoming more difficult to do it rapidly. The days of the "fast track" appear to be all but over for most employees.[44] Thus, you need to prepare yourself for getting as much out of each job as possible.

JOB ANALYSIS

Job analysis is the process of describing and recording the purpose of a job, its major duties and activities, the conditions under which it is performed, and the necessary skills, knowledge, and abilities (SKAs).[45] As shown in exhibit 4.7, job analysis collects information that forms the essentials of job descriptions that, in turn, tell workers what is expected. Of course, job analysis has several purposes in organizations.

PURPOSES AND IMPORTANCE OF JOB ANALYSIS

Job analysis is necessary for legally validating the methods used in making employment decisions, such as selection, promotion, and performance appraisal. Job analysis is also important because it

- Aids the supervisor and the employee in defining each employee's duties and related tasks
- Serves as a reference guide to move employees in the correct work-related direction

Exhibit 4.7
Relationships and Aspects of Job Analysis

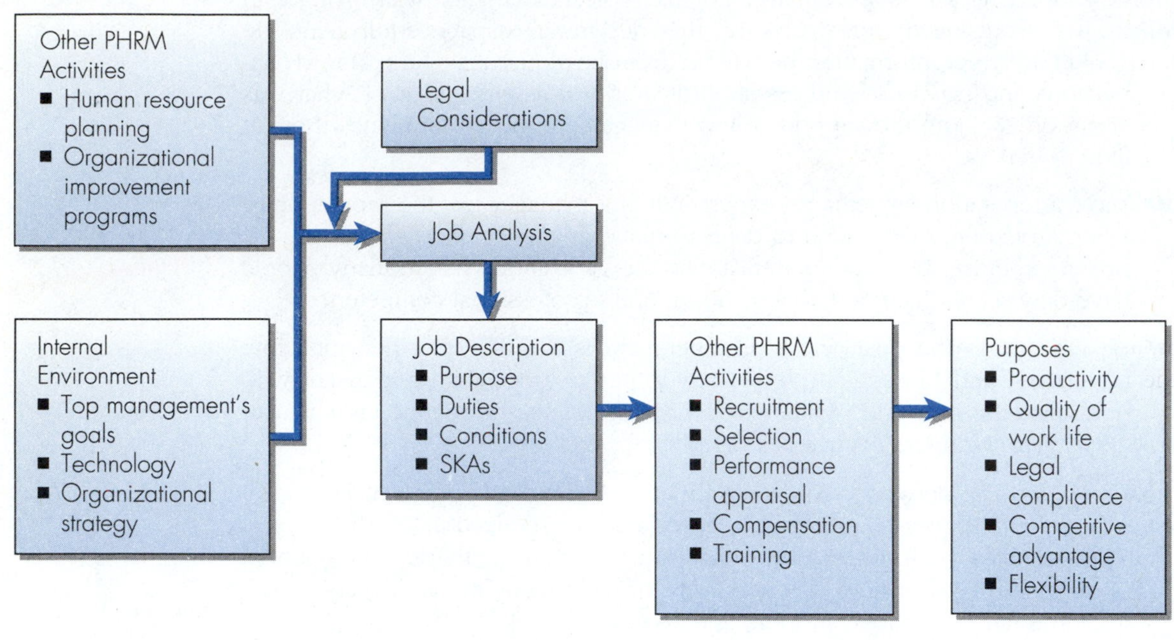

- Prescribes the importance of and time requirements for a worker's effort
- Provides job applicants with realistic job information regarding duties, working conditions, and job requirements
- Provides a justification for the existence of the job and where it fits into the organizational structure
- Identifies reporting relationships for supervisors and subordinates
- Guides change in work design and task management
- Determines the relative worth of jobs to maintain external and internal pay equity
- Ensures that companies do not violate the Equal Pay Act of 1963
- Provides selection information necessary to make employment decisions[46]
- Serves as a basis for establishing career development programs and paths for employees
- Identifies worker redundancies during mergers, acquisitions, and downsizing
- Guides supervisors and incumbents in writing references and preparing resumés, respectively, for employees leaving and seeking new employment[47]

ASPECTS OF JOB ANALYSIS

Renewed interest in job analysis has been spurred in part by organizational efforts to become more competitive and profitable and in part by the need to comply with the *Uniform Guidelines*.[48] Interest has also grown because job analysis serves many purposes and has an extensive set of system relationships in organizations. As a consequence, organizations want to know about all aspects of job analysis, starting with collecting job analysis information.

Collecting Job Analysis Information

As defined earlier, job analysis is the process of describing and recording many aspects of jobs. These aspects vary greatly, often depending on the purposes to be served. Because gathering information on these aspects is necessary to comply with the *Uniform Guidelines,* one must know who collects the information and how it is collected.

Choice of analyst. Job analysis can be conducted by those in the PHRM department, outside consultants, supervisors, or incumbents, or by means of instrumentation—or by combinations of these. Because each person sees the job from a different perspective, job analysis outcomes may differ, depending on the information source. For example, supervisors and incumbents rate the worth of incumbent jobs more positively than do outside job analysts; and, while supervisors and incumbents usually agree about whether an incumbent performs specific tasks and duties, incumbents tend to see their jobs as requiring greater skill and knowledge than do supervisors or outside job analysts.

One reason for these differences is that job-specific information is more salient to incumbents who perform the work than to outsiders who observe or interview incumbents. Differences may also be due to a **self-enhancement bias.** Because job analysis is related to many important human resource outcomes (e.g., performance appraisal, compensation), incumbents, and to a lesser extent, their supervisors, may exaggerate job duties in order to maximize organizational rewards and self-esteem.[49]

While incumbent ratings may be slightly enhanced, there are still good reasons to include them in the job analysis process. First, they are the source of the most current and accurate information about the job. Second, by including incumbents in the analysis process, supervisors and incumbents gain a shared perspective of job expectations.

In choosing a job analyst, attention should be paid to the analyst's education and training, degree of job familiarity, and cost of involvement. If incumbents do not have the reading and writing skills necessary to complete task inventories or write job descriptions, it is essential that outside experts intervene. For example, the Position Analysis Questionnaire (PAQ) requires postcollege-level reading comprehension and extensive training. To train all employees in PAQ procedures would be inordinately costly.

Communication about job analysis. The launching of a job analysis program is often unpopular. It is not only time consuming but also potentially threatening to incumbents who perceive that it may lead to changes in job responsibilities, compensation, and training. To defuse resentment and misunderstanding, management should convey to employees the purpose of the job analysis program, who will be involved, and exactly what will happen as a result of the program.[50] Employee involvement also increases perceptions of procedural fairness and reduces resistance to change.

Methods of gathering information. Information is gathered by a number of methods, including (1) interviews with job incumbents, (2) conferences with job analysts/experts, (3) observations by job analysts, (4) diaries kept by job incumbents, (5) structured and unstructured questionnaires filled out by incumbents or by observers, such as supervisors or job analysts, (6) critical incidents written by incumbents or others who know the jobs, and (7) mechanical devices, such as stopwatches, counters, and films. Here again, multiple methods can provide more information that can be used for a variety of purposes. However, the cost is usually high in terms of employees' time spent recording, coordinating, and storing all the information.

Job Descriptions

Job descriptions are generated from the data gathered through job analyses. On the basis of job descriptions, performance appraisal forms can be developed, and job classification systems can be established for job evaluation and compensation purposes. Because job descriptions identify the education and training needed to perform a job, it is also possible to design appropriate recruitment, selection, and training and development programs. Typically, a single document describes job duties and underlying tasks. The final job analysis documents should probably include the following:

- **Job title** refers to a group of positions that are identical with regard to their significant duties. In contrast, a **position description** refers to a collection of duties performed by a single person. A company with fifty accounting assistants has fifty accounting positions but probably fewer than five discernible jobs. Job titles can be deceptive; jobs in different departments or in different organizations may erroneously carry the same title but different duties. Thus, in determining whether jobs are similar for purposes of pay or selection procedures, an analyst should focus on the degree of overlap in job duties rather than on the similarity in job titles.[51]
- **Department** or division in which the job is located should be listed.
- **Date** the job was analyzed will cue job analysts as to when the description was and should be updated.
- **DOT code** is a standard job code published in the *Dictionary of Occupational Titles* by the Department of Labor. It provides some desirable but not essential information for validation reports pertaining to the job.
- **EEO-1/AAP categories** are the reporting categories in which the job calls for annual Equal Employment Opportunity (EEO) reporting and Affirmative Action Plans (AAPs).
- **Name of incumbent and name of job analyst** are useful for record-keeping purposes. However, for job evaluation purposes, incumbent names should not be included because they may inappropriately bias evaluators.

- **Job summary** is an abstract of the job; it can be used for job posting, recruitment advertisements, and salary surveys.

- **Supervision received and given** identifies reporting relationships. If supervision is given, the duties associated with that supervision should be detailed under **work performed.**

- **Work performed** identifies the duties and underlying tasks that make up a job. A task is something that workers perform or an action they take to produce a product or service. Duties are a collection of tasks that recur and are not trivial. For maximum informational use, duties should be prioritized in terms of the time spent as well as the importance; a duty may take little time to complete but be critical to job success. Weighted duty statements prioritize work for incumbents, are useful in establishing performance standards, and may be important for determining whether job accommodations for individuals protected under the Americans with Disabilities Act are reasonable. A concise weighted listing of job duties is also important to determine whether jobs are exempt from overtime provisions of the Fair Labor Standards Act and whether two jobs with different job titles are similar in skill, effort, responsibility, and working conditions, as provided by the Equal Pay Act.[52]

- **Job requirements** delineate the experience, education, training, licensure, and specific knowledge, skills, and abilities needed to perform a job. **Knowledge** relates to a body of information in a particular subject area that, if applied, makes adequate performance of the job possible (e.g., knowledge of Pascal; knowledge of OSHA regulations). The terms **skill** and **ability** are often used interchangeably and relate to observable capabilities to perform a learned behavior (e.g., operating a drill press).

  Job requirements should be limited to the **minimum qualifications** a new employee can be expected to bring to the job. Minimum qualifications are likely to be prime focal points for EEO investigations because abuses are common and the potential for adverse impact is great. For example, requiring a high school diploma is unnecessary for the position of janitor. A janitor may, however, need basic reading skills to identify cleaning agents. Thus, an appropriate requirement would be the ability to read labels and instructions, not a high school diploma. Similarly, requiring an M.S. degree in social work may be an inappropriate qualification for the position of child welfare worker if individuals without the degree have been shown to perform the job as well as those with the degree. An M.S. degree *may* be necessary if required by state law. Job requirements are also controversial when employers impose artificially high minimums to reduce the number of applicants to be processed, to justify high salaries, or to enhance the prestige of the job or organization. Acceptable minimum qualifications should also not be incumbent-specific. If an incumbent has a college degree, yet the job requires only a high school diploma, only the high school diploma should be listed as required.

- **Job context** deals with the environment that surrounds the job. For example, work may be conducted outdoors (construction worker), in close quarters (film editor), in remote areas (forest ranger), in high temperatures (chef), or in low temperatures (meat cutter). It may involve extensive standing (sales clerk), sitting (data entry clerk), or exposure to fumes (fiberglass fabricator), noise (drill press operator), electrical shocks (electrician), diseases (laboratory technician), or stress (pension fund manager). Information on these job components provides an understanding of the setting in which work is conducted.[53]

Job descriptions should employ a terse, direct writing style, using present tense and active verbs. Each sentence should reflect an objective, either specifically stated or strongly implied.

Omit any words that impart unnecessary information. Use words that have only one connotation and that specifically describe how the work is accomplished. Task descriptions should reflect the assigned work performed and worker traits ratings.[54] Begin each task statement with an action verb (e.g., controls, sets up).

Keep in mind that the job should be described in enough detail that the reader can understand (1) what is to be done (the domains, behaviors, results, and duties), (2) what products are to be generated (the job's purposes), (3) what work standards are applied (e.g., quality and quantity), (4) under what conditions the job is performed, and (5) the job's design characteristics. Design characteristics are included so individuals might select and be placed in jobs that match or suit their personalities, interests, and preferences; nevertheless, organizations generally do not include job design characteristics in their job descriptions. Exhibit 4.8 is an example of a job analysis document.[55]

JOB ANALYSIS METHODS

This section summarizes the most common methods of job analysis. Methods analysis focuses on job efficiency. Task listings and inventories [e.g., the Position Analysis Questionnaire (PAQ) and the Job Element Inventory (JEI)] are structured questionnaires that can be analyzed by computer. Three other methods designed to meet specific human resource information needs are also described. Finally, we examine three methods that focus specifically on managerial work.

Methods Analysis

Methods analysis focuses on analyzing **job elements,** the smallest identifiable components of a job. The need for methods analysis often results from (1) changes in tools and equipment, (2) changes in product design, (3) changes in materials, (4) modifications of equipment and procedures to accommodate physically disabled workers, and (5) health and safety concerns.

While human resource managers have downplayed the importance of methods analysis in recent years, it is still widely used in manufacturing settings. In fact, the increased use of new technologies, collectively referred to as **programmable automation,** has increased the need for methods analysis. These new processes include **computer-aided design (CAD), computer-aided manufacturing (CAM), computer-aided engineering (CAE), flexible manufacturing systems (FMS),** group technology, robotics, and **computer-integrated manufacturing (CIM).** Unfortunately, manufacturers have acquired new equipment much in the way a family buys a new car. Drive out the old, drive in the new, enjoy the faster, smoother, more economical ride—and go on with life as before. With the new technology, however, "as before" can mean disaster. Executives are discovering that acquiring an FMS or any of the other advanced manufactur-

Exhibit 4.8
Position Description (Exempt)

Functional Title: Corporate Loan Assistant
Function Code:
Incumbent:

Department: Corporate Banking
Division:
Location: Head Office
Date: June 1991

Note: Statements included in this description are intended to reflect in general the duties and responsibilities of this classification and are not to be interpreted as being all inclusive.

Relationships

Reports to: Corporate Account Office A or AA; or Sr. Corporate Account Officer B or BB

Subordinate staff: None

Other internal contacts: Various levels of management within the Corporate Banking Department

External contacts: Major bank customers

Summary Statement

Assist in the administration of commercial accounts, to ensure maintenance of profitable Bank relationships.

Domains

A. Credit Analysis (Weekly)
Under the direction of a supervising loan officer: Analyze a customer company's history, industry position, present condition, accounting procedures, and debt requirements. Review credit reports, summarizing analysis and recommending course of action for potential borrowers; review and summarize performance of existing borrowers. Prepare and follow-up on credit communications and reports and Loan Agreement Compliance sheets.

B. Operations (Weekly)
Help customers with banking problems and needs. Give out customer credit information to valid inquirers. Analyze account profitability and compliance with balance arrangements; distribute to customer. Direct Corporate Loan Note Department in receiving and disbursing funds and in booking loans. Correct internal errors.

C. Loan Documentation (Weekly)
Develop required loan documentation. Help customer complete loan documents. Review loan documents immediately after a loan closing for completeness and accuracy.

D. Report/Information System (Weekly)
Prepare credit reports, describing and analyzing customer relationship and loan commitments; prepare for input into Information System. Monitor credit reports for accuracy.

E. Customer/Internal Relations (Weekly)
Build rapport with customers by becoming familiar with their products, facilities, and industry. Communicate with customers and other banks to obtain loan-related information and answer questions. Prepare reports on customer and prospect contacts and follow-up. Write memos on significant events affecting customers and prospects.

F. Assistance to Officers (Monthly)
Assist assigned officers by preparing credit support information, summarizing customer relationship, and accompanying on calls or making independent calls. Monitor accounts and review and maintain credit files. Coordinate paper flow to banks participating in loans. Respond to customer questions or requests in absence of assigned officer.

G. Assistance to Division (Monthly)
Represent bank at industry activities. Follow industry/area developments. Help Division Manager plan division approach and prospect for new business. Interview loan assistant applicants. Provide divisional back-up in absence of assigned officer.

Continued

Exhibit 4.8
Position Description (Exempt) (Continued)

H. Knowledges and Skills (Any item with an asterisk will be taught on the job)
Oral communications skills, including listening and questioning. Intermediate accounting skills. Writing skills. Researching/reading skills to understand legal financial documents. Organizational/analytical skills. Social skills to represent the Bank and strengthen its image. Sales skills. Knowledge of Bank credit policy and services.* Skill to use Bank computer terminal.* Knowledge of bank-related legal terminology. Independent work skills. Work efficiently under pressure. Courtesy and tactfulness. Interfacing skills. Knowledge of basic business (corporate) finance. Skill to interpret economic/political issues.

I. Physical Characteristics
See to read fine print and numbers. Hear speaker twenty feet away. Speak to address a group of five. Mobility to tour customer facilities (may include climbing stairs). Use of hands and fingers to write, operate a calculator.

J. Other Characteristics
Driver's license. Willing to: work overtime and weekends occasionally; travel out of state every three months/locally weekly; attend activities after work hours; wear clean, neat businesslike attire.

SOURCE: Used by permission of Biddle and Associates.

ing systems is more like replacing that old car with a helicopter. If you fail to understand and prepare for the revolutionary capabilities of these systems, they will become as much an inconvenience as a benefit—and a lot more expensive.

The new manufacturing technologies can shock a business organization because they require a quantum jump in a manufacturing organization's precision and integration. Automated machine tools can produce parts to more exacting specifications than can the most skilled human machinist, but to do so they need explicit, unambiguous instructions in the form of computer programs.

The new hardware provides added freedom, but it also makes possible more ways to succeed or fail. It therefore requires new skills on the part of managers—an integrative imagination, a passion for detail. To prevent process contamination, for example, it is no longer possible to rely on people who have a "feel" for their machines, or just to note on a blueprint that operators should "remove iron filings from the part." When using the new automated machine tools, everything must be stated with mathematical precision: Where is the blower that removes the filings, and what's the orientation of the part during operation of the blower?[56]

Thus, it is increasingly important to study and document work processes. A variety of techniques are available for conducting methods analysis.

Flow process charts. These charts are used to examine the overall sequence of an operation by focusing on either the movement of an operator or the flow of materials. For example, flow process charts have been used in hospitals to track patient movements, in grocery stores to analyze the checkout process, in small-batch manufacturing facilities to track material flows from machine to machine, in banks to examine the sequence associated with document processing, and in general to track supervisor-incumbent interactions during a performance appraisal interview.

Worker-machine charts. These are useful for envisioning the segments of a work cycle in which the equipment and the operator are busy or idle. The analyst can easily see when the operator and the machine are working jointly or independently. One use of this type of chart is to determine how many machines or how much equipment an operator can manage. A gang process chart is an extension of worker-machine charts. Rather than focusing on the operations of a single operator and a machine, this chart simultaneously plots the man-machine interfaces for a team of workers. Such charts are particularly useful for identifying individuals' utilizations of equipment and for pinpointing bottlenecks in interdependent tasks.

Methods analysis. Also called **motion study,** this technique has its origins in industrial engineering and the work of Frederick Winslow Taylor and Frank Gailbreth. In essence, work measurement determines standard times for all units of work activity in a given task or job. Combining these times gives a standard time for the entire job. Exhibit 4.9 summarizes the formulas associated with methods analysis. **Observed time** is simply the average of observed times. **Normal time** is the observed time adjusted for worker performance; this is accomplished by determining a **performance rating** (PR) for observed performance. The PR is an estimation of the difference between the normal rate at which a worker could be expected to perform and the observed rate. The adjustment is necessary because workers may deliberately slow down or speed up the processes when observed. For instance, a PR of 1.20 indicates that an observed pace is much faster than normal. By comparison, a PR of .80 indicates that observed performance is slower than normal (a likely occurrence if the job is being studied to set rates of pay).

Standard time is the normal time adjusted for normal work interruptions. These delays may include personal delays (getting a drink of water, going to the washroom) and variable allowances specific to the job (mental or physical effort, lighting, atmospheric conditions, monotony, and detail). Industrial engineers have developed tables listing the allowances for different work delays.

To demonstrate the calculations associated with time study, an example follows:

Observations:

1. 4.50	PR	=	1.10 (Observed performance is faster than normal)					
2. 4.32	Allowance	=	15%					
3. 4.15	OT	=	T/n	=	21.18/5	=	4.23
4. 4.12	NT	=	OT × PR	=	4.23(1.10)	=	4.65
5. 4.09	ST	=	NT(1 + A)	=	4.65(1.15)	=	5.35
21.18							

In explaining these equations, it should be emphasized that there are several different formulas for determining standard time (see exhibit 4.9). For example, if the allowance is expressed as a percentage of the normal time, then ST = NT(1 + A). Alternatively, if the allowance is expressed as a percentage of total time, then ST = NT/(1 − A). In both cases, the performance rating and allowance factors are judgment calls made by such experts as trained, licensed industrial engineers or psychologists.

Exhibit 4.9
Summary of Time Computations

Variable	Formula	Note
Observed Time	$OT = t_i/n$	
Normal Time	$NT = OT*PR$	
Standard Time	$ST = NT(1 + A)$	Allowance as a % of NT
	or	
	$ST = NT/(1 - A)$	Allowance as a % total time

Where

A = Allowance percentage
n = Number of observations
NT = Normal time
OT = Observed or average time
PR = Performance rating
ST = Standard time
t_i = Time observed for the ith observation

Standard times can be used as a basis for wage incentive plans (incentives are generally given for work performance that takes less than the standard time), cost determination, cost estimates for new products, and balancing production lines and work crews.[57] Establishing standard times is a challenge of some consequence because the time it takes to do a job can be influenced as much by the individual doing the job as by the nature of the job itself. Consequently, determining standard times often requires measurement of the "actual effort" the individual is exerting and the "real effort" required. This process often involves trying to outguess someone else.

Work sampling is not only a technique for determining standard times but also another form of methods analysis. Work sampling is the process of taking instantaneous samples of the work activities of individuals or groups of individuals.[58] The activities observed are timed and then classified into predetermined categories. The result is a description of the activities by classification of a job and the percentage of time for each activity.

Work sampling can be done in several ways. The job analyst can observe the incumbent at predetermined times; a camera can be set to take photographs at predetermined times; or, at a given signal, all incumbents can record their activity at that moment.

Work sampling was utilized in a recent study that examined the differences between successful managers and effective managers. **Successful managers** are those who move up formal hierarchies quickly, while **effective managers** are those who have achieved high levels of quality and quantity of work performance and satisfaction. Managers in general were found to spend their time in the following activities: traditional management (32 percent), routine communication (29 percent), human resource management (20 percent), and networking (19 percent). Successful managers spent more time on networking activities and less on human resource management activities than did effective managers. The latter spent additional time on routine communication and human resource management.[59]

Structured Questionnaire

Task inventories. In contrast to the multiple methods that are used in work sampling to gather job data, the task inventories method of job analysis is based solely on a structured questionnaire. As such, task inventories are a listing of tasks for the occupations (jobs) being analyzed, with a provision for some type of response scale for each task listed. Using such a questionnaire, the job incumbent, supervisor, or job analyst performs the job analysis by checking the appropriate scale responses for each task listed. Suppose a specific secretarial job were to be analyzed using a task inventory with only three tasks. A part of the questionnaire might look like that shown in exhibit 4.10. Because the task inventory method is based on a structured questionnaire, it is easy and quick to score and analyze. The results can be readily processed by computer and used for recruitment, selection, and compensation.

Because the development of task inventories requires large samples of employees and complex statistical analysis, their use is usually limited to organizations that employ many people in the same occupation (police, firefighters, data entry clerks). As a consequence, the use of task inventories is fairly widespread in city and state governments and the military, which typically have many incumbents performing the same job.[60]

Position Analysis Questionnaire (PAQ). The PAQ is a structured questionnaire containing 187 job elements and 7 additional items relating to amount of pay that are for research purposes only. The PAQ is organized into six divisions, each of which contains some of the 187 job elements. The divisions and a sample of elements include the following:

Exhibit 4.10
Sample of a Task Inventory Questionnaire

	Is Task Done?	**Importance**	**Time Spent**
	1. Yes 2. No	1. Extremely unimportant 2. Very unimportant 3. Unimportant 4. About medium importance 5. Important 6. Very important 7. Extremely important	1. Very much below average 2. Below average 3. Slightly below average 4. About average 5. Slightly above average 6. Above average 7. Very much above average
Prioritize typing requirements	① ②	① ② ③ ④ ⑤ ⑥ ⑦	① ② ③ ④ ⑤ ⑥ ⑦
Type address labels	① ②	① ② ③ ④ ⑤ ⑥ ⑦	① ② ③ ④ ⑤ ⑥ ⑦
Type business correspondence	① ②	① ② ③ ④ ⑤ ⑥ ⑦	① ② ③ ④ ⑤ ⑥ ⑦

- **Information input:** Where and how does the worker get the information used in performing the job? Examples are the use of written materials and near-visual differentiation.
- **Mental processes:** What reasoning, decision-making, planning, and information-processing activities are involved in performing the job? Examples are the level of reasoning in problem solving and coding/decoding.
- **Work output:** What physical activities does the worker perform, and what tools or devices are used? Examples are the use of keyboard devices and assembling/disassembling.
- **Relationships with other people:** What relationships with other people are required in performing the job? Examples are instructing and contacts with the public or customers.
- **Job context:** In what physical or social contexts is the work performed? Examples are high temperature and interpersonal conflict situations.
- **Other job characteristics:** What other activities, conditions, or characteristics are relevant to the job?[61]

Each element is also rated on one of six rating scales: (1) extent of use, (2) importance to the job, (3) amount of time, (4) possibility of occurrence, (5) applicability, and (6) other.

Using these six divisions and six rating scales, the nature of jobs is essentially determined in terms of communication, decision making, and social responsibilities; performance of skilled activities; physical activity and related environmental conditions; operation of vehicles and equipment; and processing of information. Using these five dimensions, jobs can be compared and clustered. The job clusters can then be used for staffing decisions and developing job descriptions and specifications.

While task inventories limit comparisons of jobs within occupations, the PAQ is more general and can be applied to a variety of jobs and organizations without modification. Responses to the items are analyzed by computer to produce a job profile that indicates how a particular job compares with other jobs with regard to the six elements detailed above. The PAQ data base also contains information about the relationships among PAQ responses, job aptitudes, and labor market pay rates. These scores can then be used to set qualification or compensation levels for jobs. Thus, the PAQ is a potential selection and job evaluation tool, as well as a job analysis tool.

Using the PAQ to set qualification cutoff levels is less subjective than using a supervisor's opinion. However, there is no direct evidence that obtaining a given test score makes an applicant more likely to perform well. Care is also needed in using the PAQ to set compensation rates because the worth of jobs is not determined independently of the labor market. Thus, jobs highly valued by an organization but less valued in a labor market would be paid the lower market rate. Another concern with the PAQ is that it must be bought from a consulting firm; consequently, direct costs appear high. Finally, a postcollege reading comprehension level is required to respond to the items. Thus, the PAQ is not well suited to job analysis situations in which job incumbents or supervisors serve as raters.[62]

Job Element Inventory (JEI). Closely modeled after the PAQ, the 153-item Job Element Inventory has a readability index estimated to be at the tenth-grade level and is explicitly designed for completion by incumbents. For example, the PAQ item "Dirty Environment (situations in which workers and/or their clothing easily becomes dirty, greasy—environments often associated with garages, foundries, coal mines, highway construction, furnace cleaning)" is "Work where you easily become dirty" on the JEI. The dimensional structure of the JEI is similar to that of the PAQ. The advantage of this instrument lies in the cost savings associated with having incumbents rather than trained analysts complete the instrument.[63]

Functional Job Analysis (FJA). The U.S. Training and Employment Service (USTES) developed functional job analysis to describe concerns (people, data, and things) and to develop job summaries, job descriptions, and employee specifications.[64] FJA was designed to improve job placement and counseling for workers registering at local state employment offices. Today, a number of private and public organizations use many aspects of FJA.[65]

FJA is both a conceptual system for defining the worker activity dimensions and method of measuring worker activity levels. Its basic premises are as follows:

- A fundamental distinction must be made between what gets done and what workers do to get things done. Bus drivers do not carry passengers; they drive vehicles and collect fares.
- Jobs are concerned with data, people, and things.
- In relation to things, workers draw on physical resources; in relation to data, on mental resources; and in relation to people, on interpersonal resources.
- All jobs require workers to relate to data, people, and things to some degree.
- Although workers' behavior or the tasks they perform can apparently be described in an infinite number of ways, only a few definitive functions are involved. Thus, in interacting with machines, workers feed, tend, operate, and set up; in the case of vehicles or related machines, they drive or control them. Although these functions vary in difficulty and content, each draws on a relatively narrow and specific range of worker characteristics and qualifications for effective performance.
- The functions appropriate to dealing with data, people, or things are hierarchical and ordinal, proceeding from the complex to the simple. Thus, to indicate that a particular function—say, compiling data—reflects the job requirements is to say that it also includes lower-function requirements, such as comparing, and excludes higher-function requirements, such as analyzing.[66]

Exhibit 4.11 lists the worker functions associated with data, people, and things. The USTES has used these worker functions as a basis for describing more than thirty thousand job titles in the *Dictionary of Occupational Titles* and for creating job families (groupings of jobs) based on similar data, people, and things. The USTES even provides a simple job description for most job titles.

A human resource manager who has to prepare job descriptions and specifications might start with the *Dictionary of Occupational Titles* to determine gener-

Exhibit 4.11
Functions Associated with Data, People, and Things

Data	People	Things
0 synthesizing	0 mentoring	0 setting up
1 coordinating	1 negotiating	1 precision working
2 analyzing	2 instructing	2 operating-controlling
3 compiling	3 supervising	3 driving-operating
4 computing	4 diverting	4 manipulating
5 copying	5 persuading	5 tending
6 comparing	6 speaking-signaling	6 feeding-offbearing
	7 serving	7 handling
	8 taking instructions-helping	

SOURCE: Adapted from U.S. Department of Labor, Employment Service, Training and Development Administration, *Handbook for Analyzing Jobs* (Washington, D.C.: Government Printing Office, 1972), 73.

al job analysis information. The *Handbook for Analyzing Jobs* is used for more specific resource planning, recruitment, selection, placement, performance evaluation, training, and job design.

Critical Incidents Technique (CIT). A job analysis technique frequently used for developing behavioral criteria is the critical incidents technique (CIT). The CIT requires those knowledgeable about a job to describe to a job analyst the critical job incidents (i.e., those incidents observed over the past six to twelve months that represent effective or ineffective performance). Sometimes the job analyst needs to prompt those describing the incidents by asking them to write down five key things an incumbent must be good at in the job to be analyzed or to identify the most effective job incumbent and describe that person's behavior.[67]

Those describing the incidents are also asked to describe what led up to the incidents, what were the consequences of the behavior, and whether the behavior was under the incumbent's control. After the critical incidents (often several dozen for each job) have been gathered, task statements are written by the job analyst. Incumbents then rate tasks on frequency of occurrence, importance, and the extent of ability required to perform them. These ratings can then be used to identify key job dimensions.

Job dimensions, which may reflect only a subset of all the critical incidents obtained, can then be used to describe the job. They can also be used to develop performance appraisal forms, particularly behavioral anchored ratings scales and behavioral observation scales (described in chapter 7). Additionally, critical incidents can be used to develop job-specific situational questions for selection purposes (described in chapter 6).

With this job analysis method, as with others, the major disadvantages are the time required to gather the incidents and the difficulty of identifying average performance, because these methods often solicit performance extremes (e.g., ineffective or effective, or very bad or very good) and omit examples of average performance. This disadvantage, however, can be overcome by obtaining examples of multiple levels of performance.

Guidelines-Oriented Job Analysis (GOJA). GOJA was developed in response to the *Uniform Guidelines*—hence its name.[68] The several steps in GOJA each involve the job incumbents. Before any of these steps begin, the incumbents indicate their names, their length of time on the job, their experience, and the location of the current job.

In the first step, incumbents list their job domains. Related duties in a job often fall into broad categories. A category with related duties is called a **domain.** For example, a secretary may type letters, contracts, and memos. Since these duties are related, they are put into the same domain—call it typing. Jobs typically have several domains.

After the domains are identified, the incumbents list the critical duties typically performed for successful job performance in each domain. **Duties** are observable work behaviors that incumbents are expected to perform. Often each domain contains several duties.

Once the critical duties are identified, the incumbents indicate how frequently the duties are performed. Then each duty's degree of importance is determined.

The fourth step is the incumbents' determination of the skills and knowledge required to perform each duty. Only those skills and knowledge that cannot be learned or acquired in eight hours or less are included. This is consistent with the *Uniform Guidelines.* Not selecting an applicant who could have learned the necessary skills in less than eight hours is not a defensible (job-related) practice. This is discussed further in chapter 6.

The fifth step is determining the physical characteristics incumbents need to perform their job duties. Here the incumbents respond to five open-ended statements, each related to a physical characteristic.

The sixth and final step is a description of other characteristics necessary to perform the job, such as a listing of any legally required licenses or degrees. It may also inquire about the necessity to work overtime and travel and, if so, when, where, and how frequently.

The result of the six GOJA steps are a job description; a set of individual skills, knowledge, and abilities needed to perform the job; and a basis for developing job-related selection procedures and performance appraisal forms. As with the CIT, GOJA, because it focuses on behaviors, is useful for developing performance appraisal forms and spotting training needs.[69] In addition, because skills (physical and mental) and knowledge are identified, selection procedures can also be developed as described in chapter 6. As with the CIT, GOJA enhances employee understanding and validity of the job analysis because job incumbents are involved in the process. This involvement, however, takes time.

Managerial Jobs

A number of special concerns arise in analyzing managerial jobs. One is that managers adjust job duties to fit their styles rather than adjust their styles to fit the job. Also, it is difficult to identify what a manager does over time because activities vary from hour to hour and day to day. As immediate situations or exceptions arise, the content of a manager's job changes. Despite these complications, several methods have been developed to analyze managerial jobs.

Management Position Description Questionnaire (MPDQ). Although the Functional Job Analysis approach is complete, using it well requires considerable training, and its nature is quite narrative. The narrative portions tend to be less reliable than more quantitative techniques, such as the Management Position Description Questionnaire.[70] The MPDQ relies on the checklist method to analyze jobs. It contains 197 items related to managers' concerns, responsibilities, demands, restrictions, and miscellaneous characteristics. These 197 items have been condensed into the following 13 job factors:

- Product, market, and financial planning
- Coordination of other organizational units and personnel
- Internal business control
- Products and services responsibility
- Public and customer relations
- Advanced consulting
- Autonomy of action
- Approval of financial commitments
- Staff service
- Supervision
- Complexity and stress
- Advanced financial responsibility
- Broad personnel responsibility

The MPDQ is designed for managerial positions, but responses to the items vary by managerial level in any organization and also in different organizations. The MPDQ is appropriate for determining the training needs of employees moving into managerial jobs, evaluating managerial jobs, creating job families and placing new managerial jobs into the right job family, compensating managerial jobs, and developing selection procedures and performance appraisal forms.

Supervisor Task Description Questionnaire (STDQ). While MPDQ can be used to describe, compare, classify, and evaluate management jobs at all levels, the STDQ is limited to the work of first-line supervisors. The questionnaire describes 100 work activities of first-line supervisors in areas such as

- Working with subordinates
- Planning subordinates' work
- Work planning and scheduling
- Maintaining efficient production and quality
- Maintaining safe and clean work areas
- Maintaining equipment and machinery
- Compiling records and reports

A study of more than 250 first-line supervisors in 40 plants showed that these job responsibilities were universal, regardless of technology or product type.[71]

The Hay Plan. A large number of organizations use another method of analyzing managerial jobs—the Hay Plan. Although less structured than the MPDQ and STDQ, it is systematically tied into a job evaluation and compensation system. Thus, use of the Hay Plan allows an organization to maintain consistency not only in how it describes managerial jobs but also in how it rewards them. The Hay Plan's purposes are management development, placement, and recruitment; job evaluation; measurement of the execution of a job against specific standards of accountability; and organization analysis.

The information gathered relates to four aspects of the incumbent's job: objectives, dimensions, nature and scope of the position, and accountability objectives.

Because the Hay Plan is based on information gathered in an interview (as opposed to the checklist method used by the MPDQ), the plan's success depends on the interviewer's skills. Interviewers can be trained, however, enabling the information to be used for job descriptions, job evaluation, and compensation. The Hay Plan results in one organization can be compared with those in other organizations to ensure external pay comparability. This plan is discussed further in chapter 9.

Development of Job Families

The initial results of job analyses are typically many separate and unique job descriptions and employee specifications—as many as there are unique jobs. Often, however, these unique jobs are not greatly different from each other. That is, employees who perform one job can most likely easily perform several others. Those jobs are also likely to be of similar value to the organization. This is why organizations group jobs into families or classes. Jobs are placed in the same family to the extent that they require similar job specifications or have similar tasks and are of similar value to the organization (as determined by a job evaluation study as described in chapter 9).[72]

There is no one best way to construct job families.[73] One newer way to do so, however, is through the job competency framework. This is based on identifying the **competencies** (knowledge, skills, abilities, attitudes, and personality) that individuals need to perform jobs.[74] Aerojet General Corporation uses competency models for key jobs in the organization, as described in the PHRM in the News: "Building Competency Models." Jobs requiring similar competencies for excellent performance can be grouped into the same job family.

Other ways to construct families can include all the methods of job analysis described earlier in this chapter.

COST-BENEFIT ASSESSMENT OF JOB ANALYSIS

A variety of standards have been proposed for analyzing the usefulness of job analysis methods. These include (1) versatility for analyzing a variety of jobs, (2) standardization in procedures for data collection and analysis, (3) user acceptability and involvement, (4) training required by those involved in using the method, (5) ease of immediate application, (6) time required for completing the method and obtaining results, (7) reliability and validity, and (8) utility or overall benefit of using the method in relation to other methods and the costs incurred in their use.[75]

Unfortunately, even leading organizations do not employ elaborate and formalized evaluation processes. The majority of them, however, do rely on a job

PHRM IN THE NEWS

Building Competency Models

"Our objective in HR is to be able to have more employees who are capable of delivering superior performance on the job," Donatelli (an Aerojet General Corp. official) said. "We have made quite an investment in taking steps to identifying competency models for key jobs in our organization to help us:

- make better candidate selections, based on facts about what characteristics are necessary to be successful in a particular job;
- know whether we have the needed skills inside the organization—or whether we need to recruit outside;
- know our training needs;
- have realistic expectations for performance evaluations;
- make realistic assessments for promotional possibilities; and
- affect our compensation policies and performance incentives.

"Because the research for building a competency model for a specific job takes about six months, we have been careful to target our efforts to focus on key jobs where we can see meaningful results for our investment—what we call 'jugular jobs.' The more important the job, the more important and sophisticated competencies are to effective business performance. To date, we have identified three jobs which we have built competency models for—models that are all specific to Aerojet.

"In competencies we look at include knowledge, skills, self-concept, character traits and motivation. We take the following steps to define a competency application:

1. We nominate individuals to serve on an expert panel—those who know and can evaluate performance of a job.
2. We interview the expert panel to gain nominations and to use a data-based interview with nominated job incumbents. It takes about two hours for each interview.
3. We get transcripts of interviews, and analyze them thematically and for content. The content is analyzed by expert coders.
4. A committee of three expert coders cross-validates patterns, practices and characteristics identified in the transcripts. They must reach consensus on their conclusions.
5. The expert coders then provide a definition of competency indicators.
6. The competency indicators are put into conceptual clusters. For example, our management competency model has four clusters:

- Commitment to Work Achievement
- Diagnostic and Problem-Solving Skills
- Interpersonal Management
- Leadership and Management

"Each cluster has defined practices associated with it, plus examples of the application of these practices on the job. Practices are behaviors associated with successful—or unsuccessful—execution of the job. For example, we identified a total of 26 practices associated with management at Aerojet.

"By the time we have built a competency model, we know what is required for success in a job—through facts, experience of successful incumbents, and examples of behaviors on the job."

SOURCE: *HR Reporter* (August 1987): 5. Reprinted by permission from *HR Reporter*, © 1987.

analysis manual and analyst training to standardize procedures. Regardless of outcome standards, statistical analyses are sometimes conducted to assess the reliability of results and user acceptance is assessed through surveys. Thus, leading organizations still fall short of theoretical recommendations for analyzing job analysis procedures.[76]

FOCUS ISSUES IN JOB ANALYSIS

Exemplary Job Analysis

Organizations that do job analysis well share several characteristics.

First, their job analysis process is formal and highly centralized in a specific human resource unit—usually compensation. The system is formalized to the extent that a structured effort is made to conduct job analysis and update job descriptions for specific purposes. Too strong a linkage between job analysis and a particular application limits the broad use of job analysis information to create an integrated system of human resource management practices. However, locating job analysis functions with the application it must serve ensures that information will be maximally used and that the program will not be eliminated during a period of financial retrenchment.

Second, flagship job analysis programs rely on highly detailed structured questionnaires—including task inventories, the PAQ, semistructured position description questionnaires for job evaluation, or some combination of these—to collect job information. Semistructured interviews are relied on to construct questionnaires and fill in information gaps. The programs also rely on elaborate software to analyze the data collected by the inventories. These human resource information systems can create and access large data banks. They can also generate a variety of products, such as job descriptions and job analysis summary sheets.

Third, organizations use consultants at some point in the development of the job analysis program. This is important because the development of an organization-specific, structured questionnaire is extremely time consuming and complicated. Off-the-shelf job evaluation procedures, such as the PAQ or the MPDQ, require extensive training and consequently involve outside experts.[77]

Fourth, these organizations attempt to make only general estimates of costs and benefits of job analysis. Precise quantification of benefits is often not even attempted. Estimates of costs may be made, but only in rudimentary ways. For example, custom-designed qualitative job analysis plans entail direct costs of between $250,000 and $500,000 for development expertise, at least one human resource professional's time for one year, and about twenty-four months to complete, from design through installation. The installation of a computerized job analysis system for one county government required a full-time project director, three to seven job analysts, and a systems analyst.[78] Compared with these costs, the PAQ and the MPDQ are relatively inexpensive; computer processing costs between five dollars and twenty-five dollars per position. Costs associated with the JEI are even less because incumbents complete the instrument with little or no training.

Assessment of the job analysis methods used by these organizations suggests that, overall, no method is clearly superior to others. Thus, the challenge is finding the best or most appropriate way to analyze jobs. Because jobs can be analyzed in so many ways, first identifying what purposes are to be served becomes important. This knowledge is useful because the different ways to analyze jobs serve different purposes, such as helping to develop tests for selection, identifying criteria for performance appraisal, and assessing training needs. Once the purposes are decided, the possible ways can be narrowed down. A final selection can then be made with the consideration of several practical concerns.

Job Analysis and Employee Flexibility

Today's environment requires organizations that are adaptable and individuals who are flexible. At the same time, organizations also need highly repetitive and reliable behavior in order to produce and deliver high quality goods and services, and individuals typically need to know what's expected and need some degree of certainty and predictability in their life.

Job analysis methods were developed in a time when everything was a bit more stable and predictable. People could be hired to do a particular job. This arrangement was convenient for management and workers, except when management wanted the workers to change or do something "not in their job descriptions."

The focus issue today is on how organizations can get the flexibility without worker resistance, yet at the same time satisfy workers' need to know. Organizations such as Nissan Motor Manufacturing and Honda are hiring applicants to work for the company rather than hiring them to do a specific job. Of course, the organization has specific jobs. Consequently, the job rather than the individual gets a job description. As the worker moves from job to job, the description stays with the job. In this way, the worker knows what is expected, and management gets flexibility to move workers around as needed and gets high-quality performance from individuals doing the job.

INTERNATIONAL COMPARISONS IN HUMAN RESOURCE PLANNING AND JOB ANALYSIS

Not all countries practice job analysis and human resource planning in precisely the way this chapter has described. In more than forty countries, including Korea, Japan, Germany, England, Australia, and the former Soviet Union, a type of time-and-motion study called MODAPTS is utilized to assess the elements that make up manufacturing, government, banking, and dental jobs. Little known in the U.S., MODAPTS is fundamentally simple. It is based on the assumption that the time taken for any body movement can be expressed in terms of a multiple of the time taken for a simple finger move. The time for a finger move is called a MOD (set at 129 milliseconds). The code of a MODAPTS move consists of a mnemonic character (G = Grasp) and a number, which is the MOD value of that movement. Thus, a hand move becomes M2 (.129 second × 2).

The MODAPTS system answers four questions:

- What is a reasonable time for a "normal" (nondisabled for the task) person to carry out a defined task?
- What is a reasonable output for a "normal" person in a given time period?
- What are the relative efficiencies of two or more ways of performing the task?
- When a particular person takes longer than "normal" to perform a specific task, what is the degree of deficiency?

An advantage of MODAPTS is that a series of twenty-one "workability" tests have been developed to assess the functional capabilities of workers against the performance standard of a "nondisabled" individual. The results of the test can be used to place people on tasks that maximize their strengths, to train workers in areas of identified deficiencies, to redesign jobs to minimize worker deficiencies, and to determine if a performance loss is due to injury or handicap. Testing materials cost less than fifty dollars, and even individuals suffering from cerebral palsy can be tested.[79]

Japan

Japanese organizations select individuals on the basis of their fit with the company rather than on the basis of how they can do a particular job. In essence, individuals are organizational applicants rather than job applicants, as in the U.S. Consequently, job analysis takes on much less significance. If an individual is unable to perform a job, training is provided.

The Japanese system of lifetime employment also contrasts sharply with human resource management practices in the U.S. Described as *shushin koyo,* or lifetime employment, the practice comes close to a guarantee that, once an employee joins a company, he will stay with it until retirement age. The employee will not decide halfway through his career to move to another company, nor will the employer decide to dismiss him before retirement, except under extreme circumstances. (In Japan, lifetime employment has not generally applied to women workers who, for the most part, have left their jobs once they were married or pregnant.)

With lifetime employment, human resource planning takes on more importance, especially in a dynamic global environment in which products and competitors are constantly changing. Training and development programs must be accurately planned so employees will be prepared for new tasks and new environments. Thus, human resource plans must be more closely linked to the plans of the business.

Though neither required by law nor formalized by a written contract, lifetime employment is encouraged by and endorsed by the Ministry of Labor and Nikkeiren (the Japan Federation of Employers' Associations) and is practiced by major employers. Lifetime employment does not appear to be practiced within smaller companies, such as vendors and small parts suppliers, although it is not uncommon for a major corporation to provide extra benefits to valued employees within vendor companies as a means of encouraging lasting relationships with important suppliers. Although lifetime employment has been a cornerstone in Japanese employment practices, increasing levels of international competition, shrinking profit margins, and slowing economic growth are making the practice less feasible than before.[80]

SUMMARY

Human resource planning is needed because of societal changes: (1) changes in population and labor force characteristics, such as age, sex, and race composition, job preferences, and job openings; (2) changes in general economic conditions and the increased use of automation and robots; (3) changes in social values, especially those regarding work, mobility, and retirement; and (4) changes in legislation and the level of government activity. (You may wish to review these changes in chapters 2 and 3 before going on to chapter 5.)

These changes mean that personnel and human resource departments must develop strategic and operational plans for all phases associated with using human resources. By moving it into a more vital position in total organization management, human resource management can begin to play the several roles described in chapter 1, one of which is linking HR to the business role, to ensure that the organization's human resources are used as effectively as possible. A major roadblock to human resource planning is lack of top-management support. Support, however, can be gained by showing top management the potential gains of planning.

The department must pay careful attention to accomplishing each of the four phases of human resource planning. The first phase determines present and future resources in order to develop a forecast of human resource needs. The second phase ensures that human resource objectives and policies are compatible with the organization's overall objectives. Action programs must be developed and implemented in the third phase. The fourth phase controls and evaluates each program in order to help ensure its effectiveness. Based on the results of the evaluation, the program can then be modified as necessary.

The creation and maintenance of organizations today requires that the worker-job interface be understood and managed. The belief that the way jobs are organized and perceived by job incumbents affects job attitudes and behaviors is a compelling reason for understanding job analysis.

Job analysis provides information about what jobs are about and what individuals need in order to perform them. Information can be collected by several individuals using several methods; together, they provide the information for job descriptions and job specifications. These go a long way toward linking the individual to the organization and the job analysis activity to all other human resource activities.

The choice of a job analysis method should be a product of purpose, as defined by the type of human resource issue to be served, and practical concerns. Regardless of the approach, bear in mind that job analysis serves as the backbone of nearly all the human resource activities described in the succeeding chapters. The value of job analysis will become even more apparent in the following two chapters on staffing.

WHERE WE ARE TODAY

1. It is impossible to have the right people at the right place at the right time without engaging in great human resource planning.
2. Increasingly, human resource planning objectives must be closely linked with the needs of the business.
3. The human resource needs of organizations are becoming more difficult to fill. Organizations can no longer assume that the person they need will walk through the door just when that person is needed.
4. Just as human resource planning is becoming a necessity for organizations, career planning is becoming a necessity for individuals.
5. Career planning is an important process and should be regarded as something to do more than once. Conservative estimates are that most people will work for more than five different organizations in their lifetimes.
6. As organizations start to identify who they need to hire, they always go back to the job description and job specifications. This is where it all begins, when we get right down to it.
7. A challenge in organizations today is to utilize job descriptions that tell people what is expected without making the employees inflexible to change.

8. Organizations can gain employee flexibility by hiring individuals to work for the company rather than hiring them to do particular jobs. The workers still know what is expected because, as they move from job to job, the job itself retains its description. Thus, in these organizations the term job description really means what it says.
9. The development of job families and the use of competencies also facilitates an organization's need to have more worker flexibility. The development of job families can also facilitate the development of complementary performance appraisal forms and compensation plans.
10. As the benefits of worker participation in many human resource activities are recognized, and as technologies and work methods continuously change, workers will get more involved in revising their job descriptions.

DISCUSSION QUESTIONS

1. If human resource planning is so difficult, why do companies still engage in it?
2. What are the major changes in the demographic, occupational, industrial, and geographic mix of the U.S. labor force? What impact could these changes have on human resource planning and job analysis? (Refer again to chapter 2.)
3. What is the difference between judgmental and statistical forecasting? Give examples of how both techniques could be used to forecast human resource demand and supply for an organization.
4. Human resource planning can identify future organizational personnel and human resource needs and establish programs for eliminating discrepancies, at the same time balancing individual and organizational interests. What other specific purposes does human resource planning have?
5. Discuss the roadblocks to human resource planning and how each might be removed.
6. Provide a step-by-step overview of the four phases of human resource planning.
7. Discuss and review the important considerations in selecting job analysis methods.
8. Are jobs static? That is, will a job change over time? If so, what might cause the job to change? What implications does this have for job analysis?
9. Do you think the existence of job analysis might make a PHRM function (such as recruitment, performance appraisal, or compensation) less legally vulnerable? Explain.
10. Despite the de-emphasis on scientific management in organizations, why is it important that today's organizations have a firm understanding of the elemental motions that comprise many jobs?
11. Why have special job analysis procedures been developed for managerial jobs?
12. Can the reliability of job analysis information be compromised by the individual who provides it? If so, in what way? What can be done to minimize any biasing effects caused by job analysis sources?
13. Why aren't organizations conducting cost-benefit analyses of job analysis when methods exist to evaluate such programs?

APPLIED PROJECTS

1. Contact a personnel and human resource manager in a local company and interview the manager regarding the nature of the company's human resource planning effort. Find out what type of human resource planning is done (short-, mid-, or long-range) and how often it is done. Are forecasts subjective estimates, or are quantitative models used? What kind of personnel information system does the company have (if any), and how is it used in making forecasts? Ask who in the company is involved in the human resource planning efforts (e.g., the line managers) and how planning efforts affect other human resource activities in the company. Describe the nature of the company's planning effort in a written report. Report to the class.
2. Obtain one or more job descriptions from local companies (e.g., businesses, hospitals, or service organizations) and analyze them in terms of completeness as described in chapter 4. To what extent do they provide information regarding performance standards, worker activities, equipment used, job context, job characteristics and job specifications, or personal requirements? Find out what job analysis methods were used by the company to collect the information in the descriptions, who provided the information, and how long ago the information was collected. Suggest specific improvements.
3. This exercise will give you experience in conducting a job analysis as well as in writing a job description.

   To complete this project:
   a. Select a job that you are interested in knowing more about or might like to perform during some stage of your career. You should not pick semi-skilled or skilled jobs but professional jobs (e.g., manager, financial analysis, chemical engineer, museum curator, dietician).
   b. Select a method to conduct your job analysis.
   c. Select a person or persons to interview, observe, etc. Identify and give the telephone number of the individual(s) you interview.
   d. Conduct your job analysis.
   e. Type up a complete job description for the position. Rank the job duties in order of their importance. Indicate the amount of time spent on each task. Also, indicate the criticality of error if this task is performed incorrectly.
   f. On a separate typed sheet, explain the method of job analysis you used, why you chose it, and what are its strengths and weaknesses.
   g. Respond to this question: From the perspective of (1) an employee and (2) a manager, why is it important to have an accurate, up-to-date, job description for the position being analyzed?

CASE STUDY

What Human Resource Strategy Should Techtronics Pursue?

You are the CEO of Techtronics, a ten-year-old mature firm which manufactures computer chips. Because of foreign competition and cheap labor overseas, the business is very competitive. Approximately

75 percent of your firm's costs are salary related. In order to gain a competitive edge, it is critical that you manage your human resources carefully.

To assist you in analyzing your human resource flow, the director of administrative services, Christine Stephens, has prepared a matrix of Techtronics' employee flows for the past year. Listed on the left are the five levels in the organization and the number of employees at each level at the beginning of 1992. The remainder of the table lists employee flows across the different levels for the year. At the administration level, 150 administrators worked for the company at the beginning of 1992. At the end of the year, 120 of the original 150 remained. Thirty employees quit. Ten employees were promoted from midlevel management positions and one from engineering. Consequently, at the end of 1992, there were 131 persons at the administrative level. Your task is to analyze the remaining flows and develop a strategy to meet Techtronics' staffing needs for 1993.

Case Questions

1. How many employees are needed at each level to maintain current staffing levels?
2. What strategies can you pursue at Techtronics to fill all the available positions?
3. Which is preferred? Why?
4. Is turnover a problem at Techtronics? Why or why not?
5. Assume that Techtronics is forced to cut back its work force by 15 percent at all levels except management. At the management level, a 10 percent cutback is anticipated. In light of this, are there surpluses or shortages at other levels? What strategies are available to Techtronics to deal with this impending crisis?

	Number at Start of 1992	Movement of Employees Through the Year					
		Adm.	*Mid.*	*Eng.*	*Tech.*	*Prod.*	*Exit*
Administration	150	120	0	0	0	0	30
Midlevel Managers	300	10	225	5	0	0	60
Engineers	500	1	34	350	5	0	110
Technicians	700	0	20	10	500	100	70
Production Workers	1200	0	0	20	30	800	350

NOTES

1. S. Candon, "Strategic HR at First Chicago," *Personnel Journal* (Nov. 1991): 56.
2. Based on personal conversations between V. Huber and employees at Boeing, and on newspaper accounts. For example, see R. W. Stevenson, "Will Aerospace be the Next Casualty?" *The New York Times* (15 March 1992): 1 & 6.
3. N. L. Bloom, "HRM's Planning Pays Off: Down-to-Earth Strategies for Your System's Success," *Personnel Journal* (April 1988): 66–70; E. H. Burack, "A Strategic Planning and Operational Agenda for Human Resources," *Human Resource Planning* 11, no. 2 (1988): 63–69; L. Dyer, "Strategic Human Resources Management and Planning," in *Research in Personnel and Human Resources Management* 3 (Greenwich, Conn.: JAI Press, 1985): 1–30; G. L. Manis and M. S. Leibman, "Integrating Human Resource and Business Planning," *Personnel Administrator* (March 1988): 32–38; G. Milkovich, L. Dyer, and T. Mahoney, "The State of Practice and Research in Human Resource Planning," in *Human Resource Management in the 1980s,* ed. S. J. Carroll and R. S. Schuler (Washington, D. C.: Bureau of National Affairs, 1983).
4. S. E. Jackson and R. S. Schuler, "Human Resource Planning: Challenges for Industrial/Organizational Psychologists," *American Psychologist* (Feb. 1990): 223–39; M. London, E. S. Bassman, and J. P. Fernandez, eds., *Human Resource Forecasting and Strategy Development* (Westport, Conn.: Quorum Books, 1990); E. H. Burack, "Linking Corporate Business and Human Resource Planning: Strategic Issues and Concerns," *Human Resource Planning* 8 (1985): 133–46; D. Ulrich, "Strategic Human Resource Planning," in *Readings in Personnel and Human Resource Management,* 3d ed., R. S. Schuler, S. A. Youngblood, and V. Huber (St. Paul, Minn.: West, 1988): 57–71.
5. L. Dyer, "Strategic Human Resources Management and Planning," 57–58.
6. D. B. Gehrman, "Objective-Based Human Resource Planning, "*Personnel Administrator* (Dec. 1982): 71–75; J. W. Walker, "Managing Human Resources in Flat, Lean and Flexible Organizations: Trends for the 1990s," *Human Resource Planning* 11, no. 2 (1988): 125–32.
7. J. Laurie, "Gaining Acceptance for Your HRD Plan," *Personnel* (Dec. 1982): 896–7; J. P. Muczyk, "Comprehensive Manpower Planning," *Managerial Planning* (Nov./Dec. 1981): 36–41; C. F. Fuss, Jr., "Manpower Planning Systems: Part I," *Personnel Journal* (Jan. 1982): 40–45; C. F. Ross, "Manpower Planning Systems, Part II," *Personnel Journal* (Feb. 1982): 119–23.

8. A. Etzioni and P. Jargonwsky, "High Tech, Basic Industry, and the Future of the American Economy," *Human Resource Management* (Fall 1984): 229–40; L. Greenhalgh, R. B. McKersie, and R. W. Gilkey, "Rebalancing the Workforce at IBM: A Case Study of Redeployment and Revitalization," *Organizational Dynamics* (Spring 1986): 30–47; P. H. Mirvis, "Formulating and Implementing Human Resource Strategy: A Model of How to Do It, Two Examples of How It's Done," *Human Resource Management* (Winter 1985): 385–412.
9. J. F. Coates, "An Environmental Scan: Projecting Future Human Resource Trends," *Human Resource Planning* 10, no. 4 (1987): 209–19; G. F. Gallup, *Forecast 2000: George Gallup, Jr. Predicts the Future of America* (New York William Morrow, 1984).
10. R. W. Goddard, "How to Harness America's Gray Power," *Personnel Journal* (May 1987): 33–40; J. A. Kingson, "Golden Years Spent under Golden Arches," *The New York Times* (6 March 1988): 26; "Older Minorities in Work and Retirement," *Working Age* (May/June 1988): 1. For information on senior workers, write to the American Association of Retired Persons, 1909 K Street, N.W., Washington, DC, 20049.
11. D. W. Allen, "We Don't Know What 50% of the Jobs Will Be in the Year 2000," in *The Changing Composition of the Workforce: Implications for Future Research and Its Applications,* ed. A. S. Glickman (New York: Plenum Press, 1982); S. B. Wehrenberg, "Training Megatrends," *Personnel Journal* 62, no. 4 (1981): 279–80.
12. C. Mackey, "Human Resource Planning: A Four-Phased Approach," *Management Review* (May 1981): 17–22.
13. For an extensive description of each of these phases, see E. H. Burack, "A Strategic Planning Operational Agenda for Human Resources," *Human Resource Planning* 11, no. 2 (1988): 63–68; L. Dyer, "Studying Human Resource Strategy: An Approach and An Agenda," *Industrial and Labor Relations Review* 23 (1984): 156–69; L. Dyer and N. D. Heyer, "Human Resource Planning at IBM," *Human Resource Planning* 7, no. 3 (1984): 111–26; "Manpower Planning and Corporate Objectives: Two Points of View," *Management Review* (Aug. 1981): 55–61; A. O. Manzini, "Integrating Human Resource Planning and Development: The Unification of Strategic, Operational and Human Resource Planning Systems," *Human Resource Planning* 11, no. 2 (1988): 79–94; G. S. Odiorne, "Developing a Human Resource Strategy," *Personnel Journal* (July 1981): 534–36; J. A. Sheridan, "The Relatedness of Change: A Comprehensive Approach to Human Resource Planning for the Eighties," *Human Resource Planning* (1979): 123–33; N. M. Tichy and C. K. Barnett, "Profiles in Change: Revitalizing the Automotive Industry," *Human Resource Management* (Winter 1985): 467–502.
14. For a discussion, see D. R. Dalton, "Absenteeism and Turnover in Organizations," in *Applied Readings in Personnel and Human Resource Management,* ed. R. S. Schuler, J. M. McFillen, and D. R. Dalton (St. Paul, Minn.: West, 1980).
15. M. D. Hawkins, "Micros and Mainframes: Emerging Systems to Support HRP's Newer Roles," *Human Resource Planning* 11, no. 2 (1988): 125–32.
16. M. J. Feuer, R. J. Niehaus, and J. A. Sheridan, "Human Resource Forecasting: A Survey of Practice and Potential," *Human Resource Planning* 7, no. 2 (1988): 85–97.
17. For a description of managerial estimates, see J. W. Walker, *Human Resource Planning* (New York: McGraw-Hill, 1980).
18. For a more extensive discussion of group techniques, including the nominal group technique, see A. C. Delbecq, A. H. Van deVen, and D. H. Gustafson, *Group Technique for Program Planning* (Glenview, Ill.: Scott, Foresman, 1977); D. H. Gustafson, R. K. Shukla, A. Delbecq, and G. W. Walster, "A Comparative Study of Differences in Subjective Likelihood Estimates Made by Individuals, Interacting Groups, Delphi Groups and Nominal Groups," *Organizational Behavior and Human Performance* 9 (1973): 280–91; J. K. Murnigham, "Group Decision Making: What Strategy Should You Use?" *Management Review* (Feb. 1981): 56–60.
19. H. Kahalas, H. L. Pazer, J. S. Hoagland, and A. Leavitt, "Human Resource Planning Activities in U.S. Firms," *Human Resource Planning* 3 (1980): 53–66.
20. D. M. Atwater, E. S. Bress, R. J. Neihaus, and J. A. Sheridan, "An Application of Integrated Human Resource Planning Supply-Demand Model," *Human Resource Planning* 5 (1982): 1–15; E. P. Bloom, "Creating an Employee Information System," *Personnel Administrator* (Nov. 1982): 67–75; Milkovich, Dyer, and Mahoney, "The State of Practice…" G. Milkovich and T. Mahoney, "Human Resources Planning and PAIR Policy," in *PAIR Handbook,* vol. 4, ed. D. Yoder and H. Heneman (Berea, Ohio: American Society of Personnel Administration, 1976).
21. J. R. Hinrichs and R. F. Morrison, "Human Resource Planning in Support of Research and Development," *Human Resource Planning* 3 (1980): 201–10; Milkovich, Dyer, and Mahoney, "The State of Practice…."
22. P. S. Bender, W. D. Northup, and J. F. Shapiro, "Practical Modeling for Resource Management," *Harvard Business Review* (March/April 1981): 163–75.
23. M. London, E. S. Bassman, and J. P. Fernandez, eds., *Human Resource Forecasting and Strategy Development: Guidelines for Analyzing and Fulfilling Organizational Needs* (Westport, Conn.: Quorum Books, 1990); S. E. Forrer and Z. B. Leibowitz, *Using Computers in Human Resources: How to Select and Make the Best Use of Automated HR Systems* (San Francisco: Jossey-Bass, 1991); "Resource Planning: Forecasting Manpower Needs," *Personnel Journal* (Nov. 1981): 850–57; N. Scarborough and T. W. Zimmerer, "Human Resources Forecasting: Why and Where to Begin," *Personnel Administrator* (May 1982): 55–61.
24. J. Fraze, "Succession Planning Should be a Priority for HR Professionals," *American Society for Personnel Administration/Resource* (June 1988): 4; G. L. McManis and M. S. Leibman, "Succession Planners," *Personnel Administrator* (Aug. 1988): 24–30.
25. T. P. Bechet and W. R. Maki, "Modeling and Forecasting: Focusing on People as a Strategic Resource," *Human Resource Planning* 10, no. 4 (1987): 209–19; J. Carnazza, *Succession Replacement Planning: Programs and Practices* (New York: Center for Research in Career Develop-

ment, Columbia Business School, 1982); Dyer, "Strategic Human Resources"; S. H. Zanski and M. W. Maret, "A Markov Application to Manpower Supply Planning," *Journal of the Operational Research Society* 31 (1980): 1095–102.

26. G. T. Milkovich and F. Krzystofiak, "Simulation and Affirmative Action Planning," *Human Resource Planning* (1979): 71–80.
27. E. S. Bress, D. Burns, A. Chernes, and W. W. Cooper, "A Goal Programming Model for Planning Officer Accessions," *Management Science* (1980): 773–82.
28. H. L. Dahl and K. S. Morgan, "Return on Investment in Human Resources," unpublished manuscript, Upjohn Company, 1982.
29. A. O. Putnam, C. R. Bell, and J. B. Van Zwieten, "Artificial Intelligence and HRD: A Paradigm Shift," *Training and Development Journal* (Aug. 1987): 28–31.
30. S. Sloan Faber, *Family Weekly* (18 Jan. 1981): 11.
31. See note 30.
32. "The Consulting Springboard," *Business Week* (17 Aug. 1981): 101–104.
33. J. J. Fucini and S. Fucini, *Working for the Japanese* (New York: The Free Press, 1990); S. Moffat, "Should You Work for the Japanese?" *Fortune* (3 Dec. 1990): 107–108, 112, 116, 120; W. Zellner, "Help Wanted, Room To Advance—Out the Door," *Business Week* (30 Oct. 1989): 42.
34. E. H. Schein, "How to Break in the College Graduate," *Harvard Business Review* (March/April 1964): 70; D. T. Hall and Associates, *Career Development in Organizations* (San Francisco: Jossey-Bass, 1986).
35. G. F. Dreher and R. D. Bretz, Jr., "Cognitive Ability and Career Attainment: Moderating Effects of Early Career Success," *Journal of Applied Psychology* (1991): 392–97; G. F. Dreher and R. A. Ash, "A Comparative Study of Mentoring Among Men and Women in Managerial, Professional, and Technical Positions," *Journal of Applied Psychology* (1990): 539–46; A. Howard and D. W. Bray, *Managerial Lives In Transition: Advancing Age and Changing Times* (New York: The Guilford Press, 1988); K. G. Smith, E. A. Locke, and D. Barry, "Goal Setting, Planning, and Organizational Performance: An Experimental Simulation," *Organizational Behavior and Human Decision Processes* (1990): 118–34; D. E. Berlew and D. T. Hall, "Some Determinants of Early Managerial Success," Working paper 81–64 (Cambridge, Mass.: Sloan School of Management, MIT, 1964); R. A. Webber, "Career Problems of Young Managers," *California Management Review* (1976): 19–33.
36. D. T. Hall, "Careers and Socialization," *Journal of Management* (1987): 301–21; J. L. Pierce and R. B. Dunham, "Organizational Commitment: Pre-Employment Propensity and Initial Work Experiences," *Journal of Management* (1987): 163–74.
37. J. H. Conley, J. M. Hueghi, and R. L. Minter, *Perspectives on Administrative Communication* (Dubuque, Iowa: Kendall/Hunt, 1976): 172; W. J. Morin, "The Four Interviewer Breeds: How to Tame Them," *The New York Times Recruitment Survey* (11 Oct. 1981): 59, 62; J. T. Yenckel, "Careers: Facing the Interview," *The Washington Post* (20 Oct. 1981): D5.
38. S. Chastain, "On the Job: The Winning Interview," in *Winning the Salary Game: Salary Negotiations for Women,* eds. D. Littman and C. Stegel (New York: Wiley, 1980).
39. I. Janis and D. Wheeler, "Thinking Clearly about Career Choices," *Psychology Today* (May 1978): 67–76, 121–22.
40. B. Rose Ragins and J. L. Cotton, "Easier Said than Done: Gender Differences in Perceived Barriers to Gaining a Mentor," *Academy of Management Journal* 34, no. 4 (1991): 939–51; W. Whitely, T. W. Dougherty, and G. F. Dreher, "Relationship of Career Mentoring and Socioeconomic Origin to Managers' and Professionals' Early Career Progress," *Academy of Management Journal* 34, no. 2 (1991): 331–51; B. Rose Ragins and E. Sundstrum, "Gender and Power in Organizations: A Longitudinal Perspective," *Psychological Bulletin* 1 (1991): 51–88; A. L. Ball, "Mentors & Proteges: Portraits of Success," *Working Woman* (Oct. 1989): 134–42; D. Jacoby, "Rewards Make the Mentor," *Personnel* (Dec. 1989): 10–14.
41. "Living with the New Guidelines on Sexual Harassment," *People and Business* (July 1981): 3
42. See note 41.
43 See note 41.
44. "Farewell, Fast Track," *Business Week* (10 Dec. 1990): 192–200.
45. F. J. Landy and J. Vasey, "Job Analysis: The Composition of SME Samples," *Personnel Psychology* 44 (1991): 27–50; A. M. Hyland and P. M. Munchinsky, "Assessment of the Structural Validity of Holland's Model With Job Analysis (PAQ) Information," *Journal of Applied Psychology* (1991): 75–80; P. D. Geyer, J. Hice, J. Hawk, R. Boese, and Y. Brannon, "Reliabilities of Ratings Available From the *Dictionary of Occupational Titles," Personnel Psychology* 42 (1989): 547–81; B. Schneider and A. M. Konz, "Strategic Job Analysis," unpublished manuscript, University of Maryland, College Park, 1988. More traditional definitions of job analyses are found in S. E. Bemis, A. H. Belenky, and D. A. Sodner, *Job Analysis* (Washington, D.C.: BNA Books, 1983); E. J. McCormick, "Job and Task Analysis," in *Handbook of Industrial and Organizational Psychology,* ed. M. D. Dunnette (Chicago: Rand McNally, 1976): 651–96; E. J. McCormick, *Job Analysis: Methods and Applications* (New York: AMACOM, 1979); C. P. Sparks, "Job Analysis," in *Personnel Management,* ed. K. M. Rowland and G. R. Ferris (Boston: Allyn & Bacon, 1982): 78–100; and C. P. Sparks, "Job Analysis," in *Readings in Personnel and Human Resource Management,* ed. R. S. Schuler, S. A. Youngblood, and V. Huber, 3d ed. (St. Paul, Minn.: West, 1988). In these sources, job analysis is the process of determining, by either structured or unstructured methods, the characteristics of work, often according to a set of prescribed dimensions, for the purpose of producing job descriptions and job specifications. See J. V. Chorpade, *Job Analysis: A Handbook for the Human Resource Director* (Englewood Cliffs, N.J.: Prentice-Hall, 1988).
46. The essence of the Civil Rights Act of 1991 and various court decisions is that employment decisions must be made on the basis of whether the individual will be able to perform the job. To determine this, organizations should conduct job analyses to help them determine the

skills, knowledge, and abilities needed to perform the jobs. Once this is known, selection procedures can be developed. Chapter 3 expands on the job relatedness of selection procedures.

47. For more discussion of the purposes of job analysis, see R. A. Ash and E. L. Levine, "A Framework for Evaluating Job Analysis Methods," *Personnel* (Nov./Dec. 1980): 39–53; S. Gael, *Job Analysis: A Guide to Assessing Work Activities* (San Francisco: Jossey-Bass, 1983); P. C. Grant, "What Use is a Job Description?" *Personnel Journal* (Feb. 1988): 45–53; E. L. Levine, *Everything You Always Wanted to Know about Job Analysis* (Tampa, Fla.: Mariner Publishing, 1983); E. Prien, "Multi-Domain Job Analysis," paper presented at the National I-O and OB Graduate Student Convention, April 23–25, 1982, University of Maryland; Sparks, "Job Analysis," in *Personnel Management* , 81–88; and Sparks, "Job Analysis," in *Readings in Personnel and Human Resource Management,* 3d ed.
48. See Bemis, Belenky, and Soder, *Job Analysis;* Gael, *Job Analysis;* Sparks, "Job Analysis."
49. R. D. Arvey, "Sex Bias in Job Evaluation Procedures," *Personnel Psychology* 39 (1986): 315–35; A. P. O'Reilly, "Skill Requirements: Supervisor-Subordinate Conflict," *Personnel Psychology* 26 (Spring 1973): 75–80.
50. R. L. Brady, L. N. Persson, and S. E. Thompson, *Comparable Worth Compliance Handbook: A Wage and Salary Handbook* (Stanford, Conn.: Bureau of Law and Business, 1982); V. Huber, "Comparison of Supervisor-Incumbent Job Evaluation Ratings," working paper, University of Washington, 1989.
51. R. D. Arvey, "Sex Bias in Job Evaluation Procedures," 315–35; D. Doverspike, B. Racicot, and C. Albertson, *The Role of Information Processing Variables in the Decision Making Process in Job Evaluation: Results of Empirical Studies on Sex Prototypes, Person Prototypes and the Effects of Training,* First Annual Conference on HRM Decision Making, October 1986, Buffalo, N.Y.; M. K. Mount and R. A. Ellis, "Investigation of Bias in Job Evaluation Rating of Comparable Worth Study Participants," *Personnel Psychology* (1987): 85–96; D. P. Schwab and R. Grams, "Sex-Related Errors in Job Evaluation: A 'Real World' Test," *Journal of Applied Psychology* (1986): 533–39.
52. Equal Employment Opportunity Commission, "Uniform Guidelines on Employee Selection Procedures," *Federal Register* 43 (1978): 38, 290–315; J. Ledvinka and V. G. Scarpello, *Federal Regulation of Personnel and Human Resource Management,* 2nd ed. (Boston: Kent Publishing, 1991).
53. P. C. Grant, "What Use is a Job Description?" 45–53; *How to Analyze Jobs* (Stanford, Conn.: Bureau of Law & Business, 1982); V. L. Huber, "Job Descriptions," in *Cases in Personnel/Human Resources Management,* ed. E. Stevens (Plano, Tex.: BPI, 1986): 278–86; M. A. Jones, "Job Descriptions Made Easy," *Personnel Journal* (May 1982): 31–34; L. Levine, *Everything You Always Wanted to Know About Job Analysis;* R. J. Plachy, "Writing Job Descriptions That Get Results," *Personnel* (Oct. 1987): 56–63.
54. See note 53.
55. "Job Analysis," *Employee Relations Law Journal* (1981): 586–87.
56. R. H. Hayes and R. Jaikumar, "Manufacturing's Crisis: New Technologies, Obsolete Organizations," *Harvard Business Review* (Sept./Oct. 1988): 77–85.
57. E. E. Adam, Jr., and R. J. Ebert, *Production and Operations Management* (Englewood Cliffs, N.J.: Prentice-Hall, 1986); V. L. Huber and N. L. Hyer, "The Human Factor in Cellular Manufacturing," *Journal of Operations Management* 5 (1985): 213–28; V. L. Huber and T. S. Lee, "Job Design: The Airplane Assembly Exercise," *Organizational Behavior Teaching Journal* 7 (1987–1988): 80–91; B. W. Nieble, *Motion and Time Study* (Homewood, Ill.: Richard D. Irwin, 1976); W. J. Stevenson, *Production/Operations Management* (Homewood, Ill.: Richard D. Irwin, 1986).
58. McCormick, *Job Analysis.*
59. F. Luthans, R. M. Hodgetts, and S. A. Rosenkrantz, *Real Managers* (Cambridge, Mass.: Ballinger Publishing, 1988).
60. McCormick, *Job Analysis,* 117–35.
61. E. J. McCormick and J. Tiffin, *Industrial Psychology,* 6th ed. (Englewood Cliffs, N.J.: Prentice-Hall, 1974): 53. Reprinted by permission of Prentice-Hall, Inc. The Position Analysis Questionnaire (PAQ) is copyrighted by the Purdue Research Foundation. The PAQ and related materials are available through the University Book Store, 360 West State Street, West Lafayette, IN 47906. Further information regarding the PAQ is available through PAQ Services, Inc., P.O Box 3337, Logan, UT 84321. Computer processing of PAQ data is available through the PAQ Data Processing Division at that address.
62. For discussion of the PAQ, see E. T. Cornelius III, A. S. DeNisi, and A. G. Blencoe, "Expert and Naive Raters Using the PAQ: Does It Matter?" *Personnel Psychology* (Autumn 1984): 453–64; and J. B. Shaw and J. H. Riskind, "Predicting Job Stress Using Data from the Position Analysis Questionnaire," *Journal of Applied Psychology* (May 1983): 253–61.
63. R. J. Harvey, F. Friedman, M. D. Hakel, and E. T. Cornelius, "Dimensionality of the Job Element Inventory, A Simplified Worker-Oriented Job Analysis Questionnaire," *Journal of Applied Psychology* 73 (1988): 639–46.
64. McCornick, *Job Analysis.*
65. McCormick, "Job and Task Analysis," in *Handbook of Industrial and Organizational Psychology,* 111.
66. S. A. Fine, "Functional Job Analysis: An Approach to a Technology for Manpower Planning," *Personnel Journal* (Nov. 1974): 813–18. See also Department of Labor, *Dictionary of Occupational Titles,* vol. 2, 3d ed. (Washington, D.C.: U.S. Government Printing Office, 1965); Department of Labor, *Dictionary of Occupational Titles,* vol. 2, 3d ed. (Washington, D.C.: U.S. Government Printing Office, 1965); Department of Labor, Manpower Administration, *Handbook for Analyzing Jobs* (Washington, D.C.: U.S. Government Printing Office, 1972); Department of Labor, *Task Analysis Inventories: A Method of Collecting Job Information* (Washington, D.C.: U.S. Government Printing Office, 1973); and J. Markowitz, "Four Methods of Job Analysis," *Training and Development Journal* (Sept. 1981): 112–21.
67. J. C. Flanagan, "The Critical Incident Technique," *Psychology Bulletin* 51 (1954): 327–58; G. P. Latham and K. N. Wexley, *Increasing Productivity through Performance Appraisal* (Reading, Mass.: Addison-Wesley, 1981).

68. GOJA is a specific technique developed by a consulting firm, as is the Hay Plan. GOJA is from Biddle and Associates and is described here with their permission. Although GOJA was developed in response to the *Uniform Guidelines,* this does not mean that it is the only technique that complies with the guidelines. According to the guidelines (Section 14A), "Any method of job analysis may be used if it provides the information required for the specific validation strategy used" (i.e., content, construct, or empirical). See also G. A. Kesselman and F. E. Lopez, "The Impact of Job Analysis on Employment Test Validity for Minority and Non Minority Accounting Personnel," *Personnel Psychology* (Spring 1979): 91–108; and L. S. Kleiman and R. H. Faley, "Assessing Content Validity: Standards Set by the Court," *Personnel Psychology* (Fall 1978): 701–13.
69. When job analysis techniques are used for more than just descriptions and employee specifications, they are often referred to as *integrated techniques.* The Guidelines-Oriented Job Analysis is an example.
70. W. W. Tornow and P. R. Pinto, "The Development of a Managerial Job Taxonomy: A System for Describing, Classifying, and Evaluating Executive Positions," *Journal of Applied Psychology* 61 (1976): 410–18. See also W. F. Cascio, *Applied Psychology in Personnel Management,* 2d ed. (Reston, Va.: Reston, 1982): 61.
71. B. E. Dowell and K. N. Wexley, "Development of a Work Behavior Taxonomy for First Line Supervisors," *Journal of Applied Psychology* 63 (1978): 563–72.
72. For an excellent description of issues related to job family or classes, see M. K. Garwood, L. E. Anderson, and B. J. Greengart, "Determining Job Groups: Application of Hierarchical Agglomerative Cluster Analysis in Different Job Analysis Situations," *Personnel Psychology* (1991): 743–62; J. Hogan, "Structure of Physical Performance in Occupational Tasks," *Journal of Applied Psychology* (1991): 495–507.
73. E. L. Levine, F. Sistrunk, K. J. McNutt, and S. Gael, "Exemplary Job Analysis Systems in Selected Organizations: A Description of Process and Outcomes," *Journal of Business and Psychology* (1988): 3–21.
74. *HR Reporter* (Aug. 1987): 3.
75. R. A. Ash and E. L. Levine, *Personnel* (Nov./Dec. 1980): 53–59; E. L. Levine, R. A. Ash, and N. Bennett, "Exploratory Comparative Study of Four Job Analysis Methods," *Journal of Applied Psychology* (1980): 524–35; E. L. Levine, R. A. Ash, and F. Sistrunk, "Evaluation of Job Analysis Methods by Experienced Job Analysts," *Academy of Management Journal* (1983): 339–48.
76. F. Krystofiak, J. M. Newman, and G. Anderson, "A Quantified Approach to Measurement of Job Content: Procedures and Payoffs," *Personnel Psychology* (Summer 1979): 341–57.
77. See note 73.
78. N. Gambordella and W. G. Alvord, *Ti-CODAP: A Computerized Method of Job Analysis for Personnel Management,* (Prince Georges County, Md.: April 1980); G. Milkovich and J. M. Newman, *Compensation* (Plano, Tex.: BPI, 1987).
79. J. Shervington, "Return of the Handicapped to Employment," *Australian Occupational Therapy Journal* 30 (1983): 20; M. D. Shinnick and D. L. Gerber, "A Common Language for Analyzing Work," *Journal of Systems Management* (April 1985): 8–13; Y. Yokomizo, *Research Reports* (Waseda, Japan: Waseda University Press, 1982).
80. This section on Japan is adapted in a large part from M. S. O'Conner, "Report on Japanese Employee Relations Practices and Their Relation to Worker Productivity," prepared for the study mission to Japan, 8–23 November 1983. M. S. O'Conner's permission to reproduce this material is appreciated. K. J. Duff, "Japanese and American Labor Law: Structural Similarities and Substantive Differences," *Employee Relations Law Journal* (Spring 1984): 629–41; R. Marsland and M. Beer, "The Evolution of Japanese Management: Lessons for U.S. Managers," *Organizational Dynamics* (Winter 1983): 49–67; and E. Zussman, "Learning from the Japanese: Management in a Resource-Scarce World," *Organizational Dynamics* (Winter 1983): 68–76.

END OF SECTION CASE STUDY

Job Descriptions at HITEK

Jennifer Hill was excited about joining HITEK Information Services after receiving her MBA. Her job involved examining compensation practice, and her first assignment was to review HITEK's job descriptions. She was to document her work and make recommended changes, which would include reducing more than six hundred job descriptions to a manageable number.

Background

To its stockholders and the rest of the outside world, HITEK is a highly profitable, highly aggressive company in the computer business. In addition to its numerous government contracts, it provides software and hardware to business and individuals. From its inception in the late 1970s, it has maintained its position on the leading edge by remaining flexible and adaptable to the turbulent environment in which it operates. It is a people-intensive organization that relies enormously on its human resources; therefore, it is in HITEK's best interests to establish policies and procedures that nurture productivity and enhance the satisfaction of its employees.

Because the computer industry is growing at an incredible pace, opportunities for placement are abundant, and the competition for high-quality human resources is tremendous. HITEK has grown about 30 percent in the last three years, and its management knows that, as easily as it attracts new employees, it can lose them. However, its turnover rate (14 percent) is about average for its industry.

HITEK remains relatively small at one thousand employees, and it prides itself on its "small team company culture." This culture is maintained partly by the use of a computer mail system that can put any employee in touch with anyone at HITEK and by the utilization of open office spaces. The relatively flat lean

Exhibit 1
HITEK's Organizational Chart

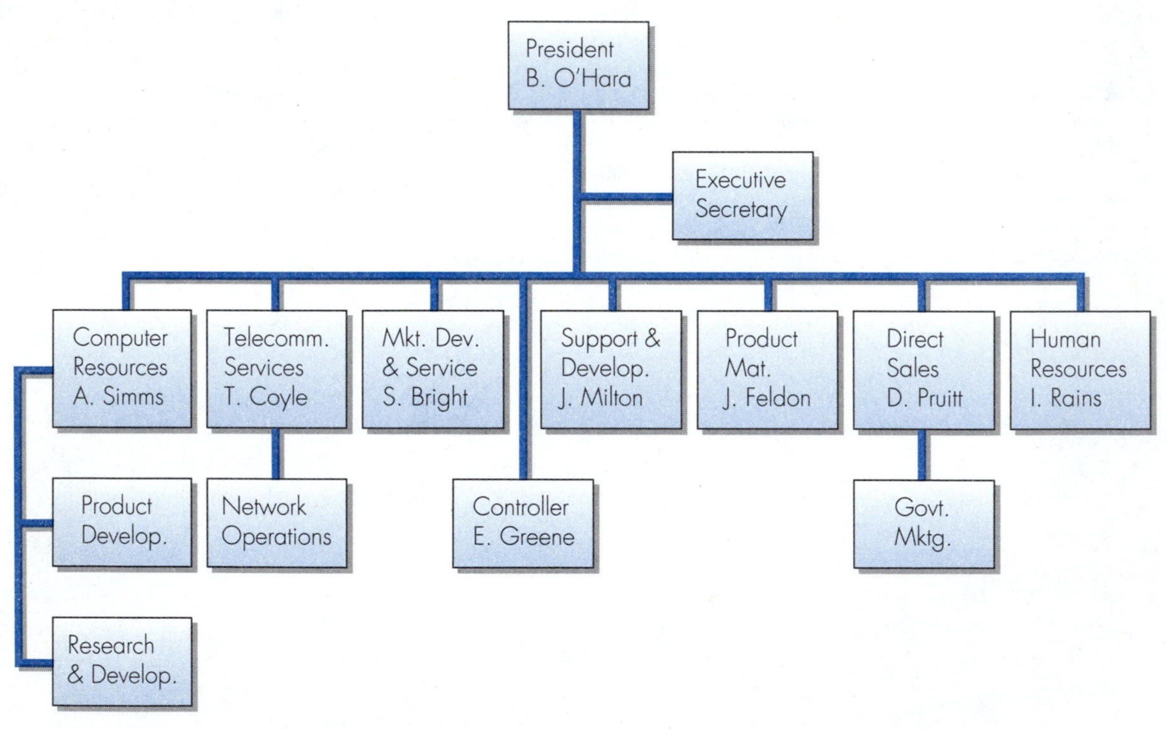

organizational structure (see exhibit 1) and the easy accessibility of all corporate levels also promotes an open-door policy. All in all, employees enjoy working for HITEK, and management is in touch with the organization's "pulse."

With the notable exception of the human resource department, there are few rules at HITEK. Work in a department is often shared by all levels of employees, and positions are redefined to match the specific skills, abilities, and interests of the incumbent. "Overqualified" and "overachieving" individuals are often hired but are then promoted rapidly. Nothing is written down; and if newcomers want to know why something is done a certain way, they must ask the person(s) who created the procedure. There is extensive horizontal linkage between departments, perpetuating the blurring of distinctions between departments.

The Human Resource Department

The human resource department stands in stark contrast to the rest of HITEK. About thirty people are employed in the department, including the support staff members, or about one human resource employee per thirty-three HITEK employees. The vice president for human resources, Isabel Rains, rules the department with an "iron fist." Employees are careful to mold their ideas to match Rains perspective. When newcomers suggest changes, they are told that "this is the way things have always been done" because "it's our culture." Most of the human resource functions are bound by written rules and standard operating procedures; and, because department employees know their job descriptions well, there is little overlap in duties.

With the exception of one recruiter, all twelve of the incumbents whose positions are represented in exhibit 2 are women. Only half of them have degrees in industrial relations or PHRM, and only one-fourth have related experience with another company. Most of them have been promoted from clerical positions. In fact, some employees view the vice-presidency as a "gift" given to Isabel, a former executive secretary, the day after she received her bachelor's degree at a local college. In other departments, it is widely believed that professional degrees and related experience lead to expertise.

One incident that conveyed the department's image to Jennifer Hill occurred during her second week on the job. While preparing a job description with Dave Pruitt, Jennifer explained that she would submit the job description to Janet Voris for final approval. Dave became confused and asked, "But Janet is only a clerical person; why would she be involved?"

Exhibit 2
The Structure of the Human Resource Department at HITEK

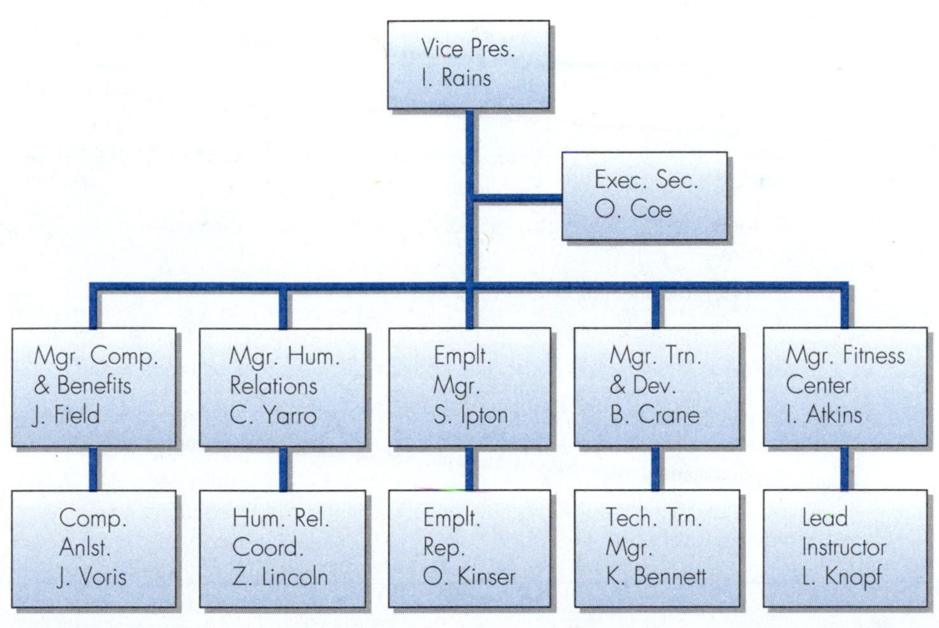

Jennifer Hill's Duties

At HITEK, the pool of job descriptions had grown almost daily as newcomers were hired, but many of the old job descriptions were not discarded, even when obsolete. Other job descriptions needed updating. Jennifer spent some time thinking about how to proceed. She considered the uses of the job descriptions and what steps she would need to take to accomplish all that was expected of her. Support from within the department was scarce because other employees were busy gathering materials for the annual review of HITEK's hiring, promotion, and development practices conducted by the Equal Employment Opportunity Commission.

After six harried months on the job and much frustration, Jennifer had revised all the descriptions that were still needed (examples of "old" and "new" job descriptions appear in exhibits 3 and 4). She was also beginning to develop some strong opinions about how the human resource department functioned at HITEK and what needed to be done to improve its effectiveness and its image. She decided to arrange a confidential lunch with Billy O'Hara.

SOURCE: Written by M. P. Miceli, Ohio State University, and Karen Wijta, Macy's.

Case Questions

1. What are the goals of HITEK? Of the human resource department? Why does the conflict create problems for HITEK?
2. Organization members can draw from several kinds of power, such as referent power and reward power. Is the human resource department powerful? Why is is important for HITEK to maintain a professional, competent human resource function?
3. Jobs change frequently at HITEK. Shouldn't the human resource department simply discontinue the practice of job analysis and stop writing job descriptions?
4. What steps should Jennifer Hill take in performing the tasks assigned to her? How do your answers to the earlier questions affect your answer?
5. Is the "new" job description (exhibit 4) better than the "old" one (exhibit 3)? Why or why not?
6. What should Jennifer suggest to the president concerning the image and operation of the human resource department?

Exhibit 3
An "Old" Job Description

Associate Programmer

Basic Objective	Perform coding, testing, and documentation of programs, under the supervision of a project leader.
Specific Tasks	Perform coding, debugging, and testing of a program when given general program specifications. Develop documentation of the program. Assist in the implementation and training of the users in the usage of the system. Report to the manager, management information services as requested.
Job Qualifications	Minimum: (a) BA/BS degree in relevant field or equivalent experience/knowledge; (b) programming knowledge in FORTRAN; (c) good working knowledge of business and financial applications. Desirable: (a) computer programming experience in a time-sharing environment; (b) some training or education in COBOL, PL1, or assembler languages.

Exhibit 4
A "New" Job Description

Associate Programmer

General Statement of Duties	Performs coding, debugging, testing, and documentation of software under the supervision of a technical superior. Involves some use of independent judgment.
Supervision Received	Works under close supervision of a technical superior or manager.
Supervision Exercised	No supervisory duties required.
Examples of Duties	(Any one position may not include all the duties listed, nor do listed examples include all duties that may be found in positions of this class.) Confers with analysts, supervisors, and/or representatives of the departments to clarify software intent and programming requirements. Performs coding, debugging, and testing of software when given program specifications for a particular task or problem. Writes documentation for the program. Seeks advice and assistance from supervisor when problems outside of realm of understanding arise. Communicates any program specification deficiencies back to supervisor. Reports ideas concerning design and development back to supervisor. Assists in the implementation of the system and training of end users. Provides some support and assistance to users. Develops product knowledge and personal expertise and proficiency in system usage. Assumes progressively complex and independent duties as experience permits. Performs all duties in accordance with corporate and departmental standards.
Minimum Qualifications	Education: BA/BS degree in relevant field or equivalent experience/knowledge in computer science, math, or other closely related field. Experience: No prior computer programming work experience necessary. Knowledge, Skills, and Abilities: Ability to exercise initiative and sound judgment. Knowledge of a structured language. Working knowledge in operating systems. Ability to maintain open working relationship with supervisor. Logic and problem-solving skills. System flowchart development skills.
Desirable Qualifications	Exposure to BASIC, FORTRAN, or PASCAL; some training in general accounting practices and controls; effective written and oral communication skills.

SECTION 3

Staffing

Once the environment has been scanned and analyzed, plans and programs are established to deal with the key issues in human resource management. Of course, one of the key issues is getting the people we need in order to run the company as effectively as possible. So many companies need people that each company finds it must do a great job marketing itself as a topnotch career opportunity. The more people who know about it, the more might apply for work at the company; and the more who apply, the more likely the selected applicant will perform well once hired.

Getting individuals interested in applying for a job at a company is the essence of recruitment. Doing recruitment effectively results from knowing how the individual views recruitment as well has how the organization views recruitment. Thus, it is important for human resource management to know the needs of the applicants and the needs of the business. Whether the needs of the applicant or the business get priority sometimes depends upon the situation. When there are more applicants than jobs, there is a buyer's market, and the needs of the business might win out. When there are more jobs than applicants, there is a seller's market, and the needs of applicants might win out.

Because conditions vary, effective firms find that it pays to be consistent—to develop a great set of recruitment procedures and use them consistently. While this may result in being more accommodating to individuals than some firms might wish, it might also mean being attractive to more candidates regardless of employment and economic conditions.

Once all these decisions have been made, the appropriate recruiting procedures can be put in place. All of these issues and ideas associated with recruitment are described in the first of the two chapters in this section on staffing.

After job applicants have been recruited, the organization and the applicants must decide whether to offer the job and whether to accept the offer, respectively. The organization must develop and utilize procedures for selecting the individuals who are most likely to perform well once hired. The hiring decision is very important, and, organizations find that it pays to develop selection procedures that are as job-related as possible. From our discussion in chapter 3, you also know that many legal considerations apply in the process of selecting from among job applicants. However, in the selection process, the individual also must do some selecting. "Is this the right organization? Will I be happy with the job and the opportunities to work here? Will my career be advanced if I accept the job offer?" Because the individual—you—is the only one who can answer these questions, it helps to have as many aids as possible as you make your selection. That is why we included a career management exercise for your use in chapter 4. The organization's concerns with selection and placement are found in chapter 6.

Recruitment

Ask Bill Gates what the most important thing he did last year was and he answers: "I hired a lot of smart people."

—William H. Gates, III Chairman, Microsoft[1]

Microsoft is one of the biggest success stories in America today. In the past seventeen years Bill Gates, founder and chairman, has virtually grown the company from infancy to 10,000 employees. According to Jeff Raikes, an eleven-year veteran and the vice-president, Microsoft is "high horse-power, high energy." Just two years ago the company had only 5,000 employees. Today, with revenues approaching $3 billion, Microsoft is hiring almost one hundred people per week. Acknowledging that [Gates] is the biggest single influence on the corporate culture, the question that might come to mind to an outside observer is, "Where does he get the time to get involved in hiring?" Working sixteen hours a day does give him some time to get involved, but still he could easily spend his time on many other things. The answer, of course, is that he believes in this stuff. He believes that people make the difference. Consequently, finding and hiring the best people is the number one priority of Microsoft. They recruit at 137 campuses four times per year, review 120,000 resumés per year, interview 7,400 [recruits] and eventually hire 2,000 of them. And they succeed while having a reputation for paying below-market wages![2]

Perhaps what this feature about Bill Gates and Microsoft illustrates most clearly is the importance a great company places on getting the right people into the organization. It is so important that the chairman gets personally involved in the firm's recruiting and selection. Of course, this also means that other top managers do the same. Together, the top managers devote so much time and attention to recruiting and selection because they believe it is vital to the long-run survival and success of the business. If recruiting and selection are important enough to involve Bill Gates, then they might be important enough for us also to consider. There's a lot to consider. That's why this chapter is devoted entirely to recruitment, and chapter 6 is devoted entirely to selection.

RECRUITMENT

Recruitment involves searching for and obtaining qualified job candidates in such numbers that the organization can select the most appropriate person to fill its job needs. In addition to filling job needs, the recruitment activity should be concerned with satisfying the needs of the job candidates.[3] Consequently, recruitment not only attracts individuals to the organization but also increases the chance of retaining the individuals once they are hired. Of course, the recruitment activity must be done in compliance with legal regulations. Thus **recruitment** is the set of activities used to obtain a pool of qualified job applicants. In other words, recruitment gets the organization its human resources, now recognized as critical to survival and competitiveness. Consequently, we discuss many aspects of recruiting after first more specifically identifying its purposes and importance.

PURPOSES AND IMPORTANCE OF RECRUITMENT

The general purpose of recruitment is to provide an organization with a pool of potentially qualified job candidates. The specific purposes of recruitment are as follows:

- To determine the organization's present and future recruitment needs in conjunction with human resource planning and job analysis
- To increase the pool of qualified job applicants at minimum cost to the organization
- To help increase the success rate of the selection process by reducing the number of obviously underqualified or overqualified job applicants
- To help reduce the probability that job applicants, once recruited and selected, will leave the organization after only a short period of time
- To meet the organization's responsibility for affirmative action programs and other legal and social obligations regarding work force composition
- To increase organizational and individual effectiveness in the short and long term
- To evaluate the effectiveness of various techniques and locations of recruiting for all types of job applicants.[4]

Important activities that are part of recruitment include:

1. Determining the organization's long- and short-range needs by job title and level in the organization
2. Staying informed of job market conditions
3. Developing effective recruiting materials
4. Developing a systematic and integrated program of recruitment in conjunction with other human resource activities and with the cooperation of the line managers
5. Obtaining a pool of qualified job applicants
6. Recording the number and quality of job applicants produced by the various sources and methods of recruiting
7. Following up on applicants—those hired and not hired—in order to evaluate the effectiveness of the recruiting effort
8. Accomplishing all of these activities within a legal context as described in chapter 3

The result of all this is the identification of a pool of potentially qualified applicants from which to select and place job applicants. These relationships are shown in exhibit 5.1.

SOURCES AND METHODS FOR OBTAINING JOB APPLICANTS

We now examine the internal and external sources where potentially qualified job applicants can be found and the internal and external methods used to recruit them. First, we will examine internal sources and methods of search. Then we will examine external sources and methods and conclude with an assessment of multiple methods.[5]

Exhibit 5.1
Relationships and Aspects of Recruitment

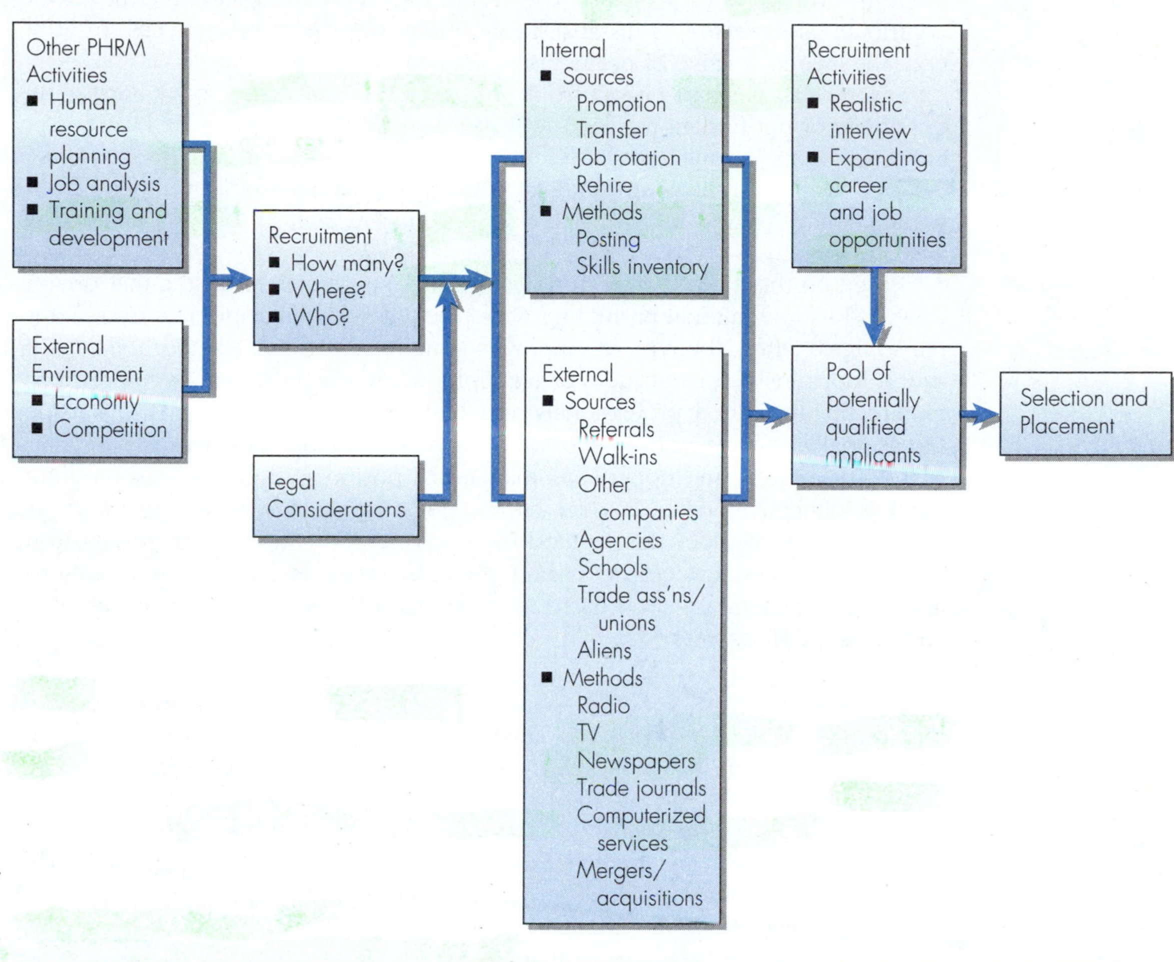

Internal Sources

Internal sources include present employees who become candidates for promotions, transfers, job rotation, as well as ex-employees, who are available for rehires and recalls.

Promotions. The case for **promotion from within** rests on sound arguments. Internal employees can be better qualified. Even jobs that do not seem unique require familiarity with the people, procedures, policies, and special characteristics of the organization in which they are performed. Employees are likely to feel more secure and to identify their long-term interests with an organization that provides them the first choice of job opportunities. Availability of promotions within an organization can also motivate employees to perform.

Internal promotion can also be much less expensive to the organization in terms of time and money. By comparison, the outside recruit is often brought in at a higher salary than that earned by people already in similar positions, and the costs to the company of relocating the new recruit and his or her family may range from $50,000 to $500,000. The result, especially if the new recruit fails to contribute as expected, is dissatisfaction among the current employees. In addition, the incentive value of promotions diminishes.

Several disadvantages result from a promotion-from-within policy. First is the possibility of not finding the best-qualified person. Then, even if the best person is found, he or she may not take the promotion for personal reasons, such as a desire to stay in familiar surroundings. Other disadvantages of a promotion-from-within policy include infighting and inbreeding—a lack of varied perspectives and interests.

Based on these advantages and disadvantages, it is not surprising that organizations do some internal promoting while they also obtain applicants from external sources. Often, the type of employee sought determines whether the organization looks inside or outside. For example, many organizations are more likely to hire highly trained professionals and high-level managers from the outside. Occasionally, the criterion for promotion is personal judgment. This is particularly true for middle- and upper-level managerial positions. Because personal judgment is difficult to defend under current legal guidelines, many organizations have had to reconsider this method of promotion. The use of test results from managerial assessment centers is one alternative to personal impressions. Since assessment centers are used more as a selection than a recruiting device, they are discussed in chapter 6.

Transfers. Another way to recruit internally is by transfering current employees without promotion. Transfers are often important in providing employees with the broad-based view of the organization necessary for future promotions.

Once affirmative action and equal employment requirements are met, the basis used to select the internal candidates for transfer must be decided. The choice is often seniority versus merit. Unions seem to prefer seniority, while some organizations prefer transfer based on ability. Where seniority systems exist, decisions can be made on that basis even if the results appear contrary to affirmative action and equal employment guidelines (*California Brewers Association v. Bryant,* 1980; *International Brotherhood of Teamsters v. U.S.,* 1977).

Job rotation. Whereas a transfer is likely to be permanent, job rotations are usually temporary in nature. Job rotation has been used effectively to expose management trainees to various aspects of organizational life. Job rotation has also been used to relieve job burnout for employees in high-stress occupations. For example, the Utah Department of Social Services has a job rotation program in which human service workers swap jobs with workers in other divisions or with employees in federal agencies for periods of up to one year. At the end of the contracted year of service, employees have the opportunity to return to their original positions or remain in the new position. Such programs give employees different perspectives (e.g., federal government) as well as give them the opportunity to try out new positions without fear of failure. Management, on the other hand, gets a chance to preview the employee prior to making a long-term commitment.

A relatively new disadvantage for both job rotation and transfers is the cost of relocation. For the first time at the Mitre Corporation, a Bedford, Massachusetts, systems engineering firm with 6,000 employees, real estate has become a consideration in selecting a candidate to fill a job.[6] This has been largely due to the housing slump in the U.S. With housing actually worth less than before, companies must pay employees for the housing loss they experience when they sell their homes in order to relocate.

Rehires and recalls. Each week thousands of employees are temporarily laid off from work and more are recalled to former jobs. The rehire of former employees or employees temporarily laid off is a relatively inexpensive and effective method of internal recruiting. Unlike new job candidates, the organization already has information about the performance, attendance, and safety records of these employees. Because they are already familiar with job responsibilities, rehires may be better performers than recruits from other sources. Additionally, they tend to stay on the job longer and have better attendance records.

In considering rehiring as a recruitment strategy, organizations need to weigh the costs against the benefits. Rehiring and recalls are particularly beneficial to organizations that have seasonal fluctuations in the demand for workers (e.g., department stores, canneries, construction jobs, ski resorts). For example, canneries in eastern Washington state recall large numbers of employees—some who have been employed for more than 20 years—each summer and fall during the apple harvest. This helps reduce employment costs. The down side of this recruitment approach is that employee commitment may be low. By the time of the recall, a qualified recruit also may have found alternative employment—possibly with a major competitor. Finally, because of turnover, an organization's contribution to unemployment compensation programs is likely to increase.

Internal Methods

Internal applicants for job vacancies can be located by posting a notice on the bulletin board, word of mouth, company personnel records, promotion lists based on performance, potential ratings obtained from assessment activities, seniority lists, and lists generated by the skills inventory in an organization's HRIS. Frequently used methods include job posting and skills inventories.

Job posting. This method of prominently displaying current job openings extends an open invitation to all employees in an organization. It serves the following purposes:

- Provides opportunity for employee growth and development
- Provides equal opportunity for advancement to all employees
- Creates a greater openness in the organization by making opportunities known to all employees
- Increases staff awareness of salary grades, job descriptions, general promotion and transfer procedures, and what comprises effective job performance
- Communicates organization goals and objectives and allows each individual the opportunity to help find a personal fit in the organization job structure[7]

Although job postings are usually found on bulletin boards, they also appear in company newsletters and are announced at staff meetings. Sometimes specific salary information is included, but job grade and pay range are more typical. Job posting is also beneficial for organizations because it improves morale, provides employees opportunity for job variety, facilitates a better matching of employee skills and needs, and fills positions at a low cost.[8]

These benefits, of course, are not always realized. Job-posting problems include the following:

- Conflicts are sometimes created if an "heir apparent" in the department is passed over in favor of an outside candidate.
- Conversely, the system may lose credibility if it appears that the successful candidate within the department has been identified in advance and the managers are merely going through the motions in considering outsiders.
- The morale of the unsuccessful candidates may suffer if feedback is not carefully handled.
- Choices can be more difficult for the selecting manager if two or three equally qualified internal candidates are encountered.

Skills inventories. Aiding internal job posting and employee recalls are skills inventories. Most organizations have skill-related information buried in personnel files. When needed, much time and effort may be required to get at it. A formal skills inventory aggregates this information through the use of a human resource information system. Any data that can be quantified can be coded and included in a skills inventory.

Common information includes name, employee number, job classification, prior jobs, prior experience, and salary levels. The results of formal assessments, such as those attained in assessment centers, during work sample tests, and with job interest inventories, are usually included. Skills inventories also should include information regarding the employee's job interests, geographical preferences, and career goals. This information is often overlooked, yet it can ensure that potential job assignments meet individual as well as organizational goals.

Skills inventories are only as good as the data they contain. They also are time consuming and somewhat costly to maintain. Still, skills inventories help ensure that *any* individual who has the necessary qualifications for a position is considered.[9]

External Sources

Recruiting internally does not always produce enough qualified applicants. This is especially true for rapidly growing organizations or those with a large demand for high-talent professional, skilled, and managerial employees. Therefore, organizations need external sources.

Recruiting from the outside has a number of advantages, including bringing in people with new ideas. It is often cheaper and easier to hire an already trained professional or skilled employee, particularly when the organization has no immediate demand for scarce labor skills and talents. External sources can also supply temporary employees who provide the organization with more flexibility to expand or contract the work force than would permanent employees.

In general, organizations need to use both internal and external sources of recruitment. A summary of the advantages and disadvantages of each source appears in exhibit 5.2.

Employee referral program. **Employee referral programs** are word-of-mouth advertisements in which current employees refer applicants from outside the organization. Because of the involvement of current employees, this recruiting method blends internal with external recruitment and is a low cost-per-hire means of recruiting.[10] Informal referrals consist of informing current employees about job openings and encouraging them to have qualified "friends and associates" apply for positions. Formal referral programs, on the other hand, reward employees for referring skilled applicants to organizations. The financial incentive may be as little as $15 or as much as $2,000 for referring someone with a critical skill such as robotics engineering or specialized nursing care. Financial incentives can be linked to the completion of an application, acceptance of employment, or the completion of work for a specified period of time on the part of the recruit.

Compared with other external recruiting methods, employee referrals generally result in the highest one-year survival rates for most occupations. One explanation for the success of employee referral programs is that employees provide a balanced view of organizational life. Another explanation is that employees tend to recruit applicants who are similar to them in skills, interests, and abilities. Since the employee is already integrated in the organization culture, this matching process increases the likelihood that applicants also will fit into the environment. On first blush, referring individuals who are similar in type (age, sex, race, and religion) is beneficial. However, such referrals—particularly if they are required for employment—may be detrimental with regard to equal employment opportunity obligations.[11]

Exhibit 5.2
Sources of Job Applicants

Internal

Advantages	Disadvantages
Morale of promotee	Inbreeding
Better assessment of abilities	Possible morale problems of those not promoted
Lower cost for some jobs	"Political" infighting for promotions
Motivator for good performance	Need strong management development program
Have to hire only at entry level	

External

Advantages	Disadvantages
"New blood," new perspectives	May not select someone who will "fit"
Cheaper than training a professional	May cause morale problems for those internal candidates
No group of political supporters in organization already	Longer "adjustment" or orientation time
May bring competitors' secrets, new insights	May bring in an attitude of "This is the way we used to do it at XYZ Company"
Helps meet equal employment needs	

SOURCE: R. L. Mathis and J. H Jackson, *Personnel: Contemporary Perspectives and Applications*, 5th ed. (St. Paul, Minn.: West Publishing Co., © 1992). Reproduced by permission. All rights reserved.

Walk-ins. As illustrated in exhibit 5.3, the use of walk-ins in recruiting is especially prevalent for clerical and service job applicants. Managerial, professional, and sale applicants, however, are seldom walk-ins.

In the walk-in method, individuals become applicants by walking into an organization's employment office. This method, like employee referrals, is relatively informal and inexpensive and is almost as effective as employee referrals in retaining applicants once hired.[12] Unlike referrals, nonreferred applicants may know less about the specific jobs available and may come without the implicit recommendation of a current employee. This may be a disadvantage in comparison with referrals, since current employees may be reluctant to refer or recommend unsatisfactory applicants.

Because this method tends to be a passive source of applicants, it may not provide sufficient numbers to fulfill affirmative action and equal employment requirements. These problems can be reduced by using open house events to attract all types of walk-ins from the nearby community. Open house events, however, may not be appropriate for every organization and, even if useful, other sources will probably be necessary as well.

Employment agencies. Public and private employment agencies are a good source of temporary employees—and an excellent source for permanent ones. American public employment agencies are under the umbrella of the U.S. Training and Employment Service. The Service sets national policies and oversees the operations of state employment services, which have branch offices in many cities. The Social Security Act provides that, in general, any worker who has been laid off from a job must register with the state employment agency in order to be eligible for unemployment benefits. The agencies then have a roster of potential applicants to assist organizations looking for job candidates.

State employment agencies provide a wide range of services, most of which are supported by employer contributions to state unemployment funds. The agencies offer counseling, testing, and placement services to everyone. They provide special services to individuals, military veterans, minority groups, and college, technical, and professional people. The state agencies also make up a nationwide network of job and applicant information in the form of job banks. These job banks have one drawback, however; the Service and its state agencies do not actually recruit people but only passively assist those who come to them. In addition, those who do come in are often untrained or only marginally qualified for most jobs.

Private employment agencies (sometimes called head-hunting or search firms) tend to serve two groups of job applicants—professional and managerial, and unskilled. The agencies dealing with unskilled applicants often provide job candidates that employers would have a difficult time finding otherwise. Many of the employers looking for unskilled workers do not have the resources to do their own recruiting or have only temporary or seasonal demands for them.

Private agencies play a major role in recruiting professional and managerial candidates.[13] These agencies supply services for applicants of all ages; however, most applicants have had some work experience beyond college. During the past ten years, the executive recruiting industry has grown phenomenally. Some estimates suggest that the search firm industry now generates more than $200 million in billings. The fees charged by these agencies range up to one-third of the first year's total salary and bonus package for the jobs to be filled.

Exhibit 5.3
Organizational Recruiting Sources and Methods by Occupation

	Percent of Companies					
	Any Job Category*	**Office/ Clerical**	**Production/ Service**	**Professional/ Technical**	**Commissioned Sales**	**Managers/ Supervisors**
(Number of companies)	(245)	(245)	(221)	(237)	(96)	(243)
Internal Sources						
Promotion from within	99%	94%	86%	89%	75%	95%
Advertising						
Newspapers	97	84	77	94	84	85
Journals/magazines	64	6	7	54	33	50
Direct mail	17	4	3	16	6	8
Radio/television	9	3	6	3	3	2
Outside Referral Sources						
Colleges/universities	86	24	15	81	38	45
Technical/vocational institutes	78	48	51	47	5	8
High schools/trade schools	68	60	54	16	5	2
Professional societies	55	4	1	51	19	37
Community agencies	39	33	32	20	16	9
Unions	10	1	11	1	—	1
Employee referrals	91	87	83	78	76	64
Walk-in applicants	91	86	87	64	52	46
Employment Services						
State employment services	73	66	68	38	30	23
Private employment agencies	72	28	11	58	44	60
Search firms	67	1	**	36	26	63
U.S. Employment Service	22	19	20	11	7	7
Employee leasing firms	20	16	10	6	2	**
Computerized resume service	4	**	—	4	—	2
Video interviewing service	2	**	**	1	—	1
Special Events						
Career conferences/ job fairs	53	20	17	44	19	19
Open house	22	10	8	17	8	7
Other	9	5	5	7	6	7

*Percentages for each job category are based on the number of organizations that provided data for that category, as shown by the number in parentheses.

SOURCE: Reprinted by permission from *Personnel Policies Forum,* Survey No. 146, Recruiting and Selection Procedures, 4–5 (The Bureau of National Affairs, Inc., Washington, D.C., 1988).

Even if the search is successful, the cost may be much greater than the fees charged. In the prescreening process, for example, the search firm may have erred in rejecting a candidate who would do well. These errors pose additional costs to the organization.[14] The organization, however, can help minimize these costs by closely monitoring the search firm's activities. Note also that these agencies may prescreen applicants who are already working with other organizations. Consequently, in addition to the expense, this method of dealing with a potential candidate is apt to be secretive and counter to the openness that is desirable in an organization's employment process. Whatever the method, it is nevertheless still subject to equal employment guidelines.

Other companies. Companies such as General Electric and Procter & Gamble are noted for their management development programs and their systematic way of developing people through job assignments. While this practice results in great managers, it also serves as a fertile source of job applicants for others.

> So many companies have been rejuvenated by the arrival of a new chief executive drawn from the management of the General Electric Company that many investors feel as if they have hit a jackpot when their companies announce such recruiting coups.
>
> Companies that hire G.E. executives usually get managers who have experience running businesses that would be among the nation's largest companies if they were independent. Most have also been through G.E.'s widely admired management training courses and have absorbed G.E.'s global perspective.[15]

While employees in these outstanding companies may be contacted by private employment agencies, increasingly they are as likely to be contacted directly by the company that wants them.

Management development programs are expensive, and some firms do not have them because they think it is foolish to basically train managers for others. This view may be shortsighted for two reasons. First, the developing firm still gets its "pick of the litter," and second, having a good reputation for development serves as a powerful recruiting tool for younger job applicants.

Temporary help agencies. At the same time that private recruiting agencies provide applicants for full-time positions, temporary help agencies bring in more than $3 billion in business. More than three thousand temporary help offices annually employ more than 2.5 million people.[16] Their use is growing as skilled and semiskilled individuals find it preferable to work less than a forty-hour week or on a schedule of their own choosing. Temporary employees (or temps) also have the chance to work in a variety of organizations; consequently, they can satisfy preferences for schedule flexibility and workplace variety. Furthermore, temps may receive higher pay than the organization's permanent staff, although they also generally forego receiving any benefits.

Organizations are using temporary help agencies more than ever because some hard-to-get skills are available nowhere else. (This is especially true for small companies that are not highly visible or cannot spend time recruiting.) In addition, many organizations need people for only a short time. Getting them without an extensive search—while retaining the flexibility to reduce their work force without costly layoffs and potential unemployment compensation payments—is an obvious advantage.[17]

Trade associations and unions. Unions for the building trades and maritime workers assume responsibility for supplying employers with skilled labor. This practice takes many labor decisions, such as job assignment, out of company hands. The Taft-Hartley Act, however, restricts these "hiring hall" practices to a limited number of industries.

Trade and professional associations are also important sources for recruiting. Their newsletters and annual conferences often provide notice-of-employment opportunities. Annual conferences can also give employers and potential job applicants an opportunity to meet. Communities and schools have adopted this idea and now bring together large numbers of employers and job seekers at **job fairs.** Of course, with only a limited time for interviews, such fairs serve only as an initial step in the recruitment process. Nevertheless, they provide an effective means for both employers and individuals.

Schools. Schools can be categorized into three types: high schools, vocational and technical schools, and colleges and universities. All are important sources of recruits for most organizations, although their importance varies depending on the type of applicant sought. For example, if an organization is recruiting for managerial, technical, or professional applicants, then colleges and universities are the most important source. These institutions become less important when an organization is seeking plant/service and clerical employees (see exhibit 5.3).

Recruiting at colleges and universities is often an expensive process, even if the recruiting visit eventually produces job offers and acceptances. Approximately thirty percent of the applicants hired from college leave the organization within the first five years of their employment. This rate of turnover is even higher for graduate management students. Some people attribute this high rate of turnover to the lack of job challenge provided by organizations. Organizations claim, however, that people just out of college have unrealistic expectations. Partly because of the expense, organizations are now questioning the necessity of hiring college graduates for some of their jobs. Another reason for this reevaluation is the potential legal burden that an organization must assume if adverse impact results. In this event, the organization may have to show that a college degree is related to performance of the job.

Nevertheless, college placement services are helpful to an organization recruiting in particular fields—such as engineering and microelectronics—and those seeking highly talented and qualified minorities and women. In addition, organizations are making campus visits to recruit college alumni, not just those about to graduate. Outreach programs by colleges and universities that provide placement services for their alumni enhance the attractiveness of the campus to employers, who benefit by having a broader and more experienced pool of applicants from which to recruit.

Aliens. As indicated in chapter 2, real shortages of some job applicants exist, including professionals such as chemical engineers, nurses, and geologists. As a result, employers seek to recruit aliens—often overseas or in college placement offices.[18] Organizations use aliens for operations in the U.S. and abroad.

PHRM IN THE NEWS

Genius for Hire: The Soviet's Best, At Bargain Rates

The millions of scientists and engineers of the former Soviet Union, once feared and respected throughout the world for their big rockets and thermonuclear bombs, for their mathematical rigor and breakthroughs in fields like nonlinear optics, are now desperate amid a crumbling economy. Many have been thrown out of work. The lucky ones who still do science often help support themselves and their families by moonlighting. Inevitably, a growing number who can afford to do so are leaving to work in the West. And those left behind can often be hired for a song.

That point was driven home last week as a top team of more than 100 fusion scientists at the Kurchatov Institute of Atomic Energy in Moscow signed a contract to go to work for Uncle Sam. The cost to American taxpayers for one year's effort was an amazingly low $90,000. So eager was the team to work for the United States that it fired up its world-class apparatus for exploring the feasibility of nuclear fusion even before the contract was signed.

"There are some areas of science where the old Soviet Union was a world leader," he said. "There were centers of excellence. If those dry up and disappear, it's a loss not just for Russia and former Soviet republics but for world civilization."

It was the Russian chemist Dmitri Mendeleev who came up with the periodic table of the elements in the 19th century. In the early 20th century, Ivan Pavlov probed the riddle of behavior. Soviet scientists put the first satellite and man into space. Pytor Kapitsa, Nikolai Basov and Lev Landau won Nobel prizes for physics.

Dr. Mohamed S. El-Genk, a nuclear engineer at the University of New Mexico, recently brought experts from the Kurchatov Institute in Moscow for a semester in Albuquerque, even though he says it is better to fund them at home in Russia. "If you bring them over here, there's a chance they won't want to go back," he said. "You'll be draining the country of its talent."

Scientists left behind are signing Western contracts as fast as they can to supplement dwindling incomes. A Russian computer scientist, Boris A. Babayan, is setting up a laboratory in Moscow for Sun Microsystems Inc., based in Mountain View, Calif., that will employ his team of about 50 software and hardware designers. Mr. Babayan created the supercomputers used by the Soviets to design nuclear arms. Sun Microsystems will pay each of his team's members a few hundred dollars a year—ample pay by Moscow standards.[19]

SOURCE: *The New York Times* (15 March 1992): E3.

When they work abroad, aliens serve as **host-country nationals** (persons working in their own country, which is not the country of the parent company) or **third-country nationals** (persons working in a country that is neither their own country nor the country of the parent company). In either capacity, alien employees are critical for any company operating internationally. Perhaps a novel way to use aliens as host-country nationals is the practice of U.S. firms contracting out work to Russian scientists. This practice not only represents a global solution to a domestic skill shortage, but also an economical way to get highly skilled workers. This practice is described in the PHRM in the News: "Genius for Hire..." feature.

Aliens are so critical that U.S. companies have made increased efforts to ensure that their alien employees either are or become legal. Under the 1986 Immigration Reform and Control Act and the Immigration Act of 1990, it is unlawful for employers to hire aliens who are not authorized to work in the U.S.

External Methods

Many organizations looking for applicants of all types engage in extensive advertising on radio and television, in the local paper, and in national newspapers such as *The Wall Street Journal.*

Radio and television. Of the approximately $2 billion spent annually on recruitment advertising, only a tiny percentage is spent on radio and television. Companies are reluctant to use these media because they fear media advertising will be too expensive or that it will make the company look desperate and damage the firms's conservative image.

Yet, organizations are desperate to reach certain types of job applicants such as skilled workers. In reality, of course, there is nothing inherently desperate about using radio and television. Rather, the implied level of desperation depends on what is said and how it is delivered. Recognizing this, organizations are increasing their recruitment expenditures for radio and television advertisements, with favorable results.[19]

Newspapers and trade journals. Newspapers have traditionally been the most common method of external recruiting. They reach a large number of potential applicants at a relatively low cost per hire. Newspaper ads are used to recruit for all types of positions, from unskilled to top managerial. The ads range from matter-of-fact to creative.

Trade journals enable organizations to aim at a much more specific group of potential applicants than do newspapers. Ads in trade journals are often more creative and of a higher quality. Unfortunately, long lead times are required, so the ads can become dated.

Whatever the medium, preparing ads requires considerable skill. Many organizations hire advertising firms to do this rather than attempt to do it themselves. Selecting an advertising agency must be done with the same care used to select a private recruiting agency.[20]

Computerized services. A newer and much less common external method is the computerized recruiting service. This service works both as a place to list job openings and a place to locate job applicants.

> Personnel officers using a Job/Net terminal "can find people in fifteen minutes that it would take eight hours to find going through paper resumes," says Janice Kempf, a vice-president and cofounder. M/A Com, a microwave and telecommunications company in Burlington, Massachusetts, recently hired a $30,000 quality-control engineer through Job/Net. "If we paid an agency fee, it would have been $6,500 to $7,000," says Richard L. Bove, the staffing and development manager. He adds that the service lets him see more resumes of qualified people and lets him choose people who don't require expensive relocation.[21]

Acquisitions and mergers. Another method of staffing organizations is mergers and acquisitions. In contrast to the other external methods, this one can facilitate the immediate implementation of an organization's strategic plan by acquiring a company with skilled employees. This ready pool may enable an organization to pursue a business plan—such as entering a new product line—that would otherwise be unfeasible using standard recruiting methods. The need to displace employees and to integrate a large number of them rather quickly into a new organization, however, means that the human resource planning and selection process becomes more critical than ever.[22]

Multiple Sources and Methods

Growing labor and skill shortages described in chapter 2 and in the opening feature mean organizations need to use new solutions for their recruiting needs in addition to using multiple external and internal sources and methods. They are using sources and methods not used before, including advertising in movie theaters, using handicapped agencies, and trying to entice retired senior citizens back to work. For its restaurant staff positions, McDonald's has used a variety of recruiting approaches depending on the type of employee. First, rather than rely on its traditional labor pool, McDonald's has looked to new groups to hire, such as retirees and mothers with young children. To attract these groups, the firm offers flexible working hours. With young people, particularly from inner city locations, the firm was able to recruit and hire but was unable to retain those employees. The company found that inner city teenagers often would work for a few months and then quit; the teenagers worked long enough to earn money to buy specific items, such as new clothes. To retain such employees, McDonald's sought ways to make the jobs more fun. In some parts of the country, for example, the young people were allowed to choose the music played in the restaurant or to wear favorite clothes on particular days, rather than the standard McDonald's uniforms. Such flexibility in company practices has made it a more attractive employer for different groups in the work force. Finally, to attract employees who could become future managers, McDonald's sponsors summer internships and management training programs for minority students.

Its recruitment of franchise operators, particularly those for overseas restaurants, has been easier because of the opportunities the company offers to those managers. For overseas franchisees, in particular, the company offers an opportunity to be an entrepreneur, uncommon in many countries outside the U.S. Thus, "recruitment" varies greatly depending on the area and type of employee the firm needs.[23]

As companies face increased skill shortages, they are becoming more skillful at recruiting. To do this, they look at the recruiting process from the applicant's perspective so they can better design new recruiting programs as suggested in the Focus on Research feature.

JOB SEARCH FROM THE APPLICANT'S PERSPECTIVE

For organizations to attract more potentially qualified candidates, they need to know *what* attracts and *how* candidates are attracted. In essence, knowing how candidates are attracted means understanding where they get their information regarding job availability.

Sources Used

As discussed in the previous section, different types of candidates learn about jobs through different sources. Still, informal methods—referrals from friends and relatives, direct applications—top the list of sources used by recruits across all jobs. Additionally, these sources result in the highest one-year job survival rates. However, individuals who get help from friends and relatives in obtaining jobs tend to accept lower wages. It would appear that recruits give in to friends and relatives who apply pressure to accept job offers.

More formal sources, such as classified advertisements and private employment agencies, have lower survival rates but are used more often by managerial and clerical employees. Because the recruiter's fee is contingent on the salary

FOCUS ON RESEARCH

Do Recruiters and Recruiting Practices Really Make a Difference?

Imagine that you own a toy company. With the baby boomlet in full swing, orders are growing at a fast pace. To keep up, you need to expand your manufacturing facility and hire a couple good managers. When you offer the best applicants a job, what will determine whether they say "yes"? Does it make a difference whom you choose to do the job of recruiting, or can you just give this task to whomever is most easily spared? Does the recruitment process itself really make much difference?

To develop a better understanding of how job applicants view recruiting practices, one team of researchers decided to conduct intensive, open-ended interviews with a few job hunters. The researchers asked placement directors from four colleges of a large university to identify job seekers who were as different from each other as possible in terms of sex, race, grade point average, and so on. Forty-one job seekers were identified and then interviewed early in the campus recruiting season and again near the end, 8 to 10 weeks later. These interviews were recorded, transcribed and then content-analyzed.

The results showed that job seekers' early perceptions of how well they fit a job were affected most by job and company characteristics, then by contacts with recruiters, and then by contacts with other people in the company besides recruiters. Important job and company characteristics included status of the functional area the job was in, company reputation and management ethics as presented in the media, attitudes toward the product, and personnel practices—such as whether they were hiring new managers and at the same time laying some people off. By the end of the recruiting season, most people reported that the recruiters made a big difference in how they felt about a job. By this time, the average job seeker in the study had completed 18 interviews, made more than 6 site visits, and received 3 offers.

In many instances, recruiters made jobs that initially appeared unattractive seem attractive. Positive impressions were created by the status of recruiters and whether recruiters made applications feel "specially" treated. On the other hand, almost all job seekers reported that some recruiters and/or recruiting practices created poor impressions and made some jobs seem less attractive. Timing was especially important here, with slow or late decisions being a major reason for negative impressions. Recruiters were viewed as more important by job seekers who had more job offers to choose from. Also, women (compared to men) viewed recruiters as more important. Many women (50%) reported some "offensive" interactions with recruiters, including remarks made about their personal appearance, negative comments about "minority" groups other than women (e.g., older workers), and receiving mail addressed to "Mr." even after the initial interview. Another interesting finding was that the best applicants were more likely than weaker applicants to interpret recruiting practices as indications of what the employing *organization* was like rather than assuming the practices were just a poor reflection on the particular recruiter involved.

Clearly, this study suggests that every employer should select recruiters carefully and put their best foot forward when they begin their hiring process.

SOURCE: Based on S. L. Rynes, R. D. Bretz, Jr., and B. Gerhart, "The Importance of Recruitment in Job Choice: A Different Way of Looking," *Personnel Psychology* 44 (1991): 487–523.

level accepted, it can be speculated that salaries secured through private employment agencies may be higher than those obtained through other methods. This occurs because the recruiter as well as the applicant will be pushing for a higher salary.[24]

Intensity

Individuals also differ in the intensity with which they search for employment opportunities. Several factors are related to job-search intensity.

Financial need. Intensity is inversely related to financial security. Employed job seekers spend fewer hours on job searches than do unemployed workers. There is also a negative relationship between the weekly hours spent on a job search and the level of unemployment compensation received. Also, the duration of unemployment compensation benefits is positively related to the duration of employment. One explanation for these results is that, as financial stress decreases, job seekers are able to hold out longer for better employment or higher wages. If employed, their job search may even be passive, with no search unless they are contacted by a search firm.[25]

Self-esteem. Job applicants who have a high need for achievement tend to launch more intensive job searches than do applicants who have less drive. Additionally, high-self-esteem job seekers apply for more jobs than they intended to (prior to the search) and more than low-self-esteem individuals apply or intend to apply for. One reason for this is that job applicants with high self-esteem may have greater feelings of self-efficacy (beliefs about their competency) in terms of job search activities and job competence.[26]

Training. For individuals low in self-esteem or lacking job search skills, training has been found effective. Interventions that encourage job seekers to locate as many alternatives as possible and that provide them with skill building (e.g., grooming tips, resumé preparation, letter writing) lead to more job opportunities and, more important, job placements. In one study, the placement rate following two months of search was 90 percent for trained job seekers, compared with 55 percent for untrained job seekers. Thus, for displaced workers, an important organizational strategy will be to provide job search training coupled with skill building. This will increase the likelihood that the displaced workers' job searches will be successful.[27]

Evaluating Job Offers

Just as organizations have ideal requirements for job applicants, recruits have preferences for jobs. Several factors, including occupational choice and organizational choice, influence applicants' evaluations of job options.

Occupational choice. Choosing an occupation involves a narrowing process which begins in childhood and continues through adulthood. While almost any occupation to which a child is exposed may be a potential choice, people have narrowed their job choices to one or two by young adulthood. These choices are influenced by economic factors, including the realities of the labor market; psychological factors, such as individual needs, interests, and abilities; and sociological factors, including exposure to the occupation. The process draws to a close when an organization offers a position that most clearly meets these needs.[28]

Organizational choice. Most individuals make an occupational choice and then choose an organization within that occupation. As noted in chapter 3, the number of functionally illiterate individuals is substantial. For these individuals, organizational choice may dictate occupational choice. Still, several factors affect organizational choice.

While it has often been assumed that job seekers generate as many options as possible and simultaneously evaluate them, job search activities are usually not this intense. In fact, job seekers typically have only a hazy notion of their options.[29] Thus, the objective of most job seekers is to find a minimally acceptable, rather than optimal job. As a result, job opportunities are usually evaluated **sequentially.** If a job meets minimum qualifications, it is accepted; if it does not, the sequential search process continues.

The exception is job search activities after college. In high-demand fields (e.g., nursing and engineering), new graduates often have more than one offer to consider **simultaneously.** Traditionally, organizations provide these individuals with job information and give them time to consider various job options. Increasingly, however, organizations are adopting strategies that bring high-potential students to the company's attention earlier in the process to ensure acceptance of its job offers.[30]

Organizational choices are also affected by job attributes. An important job attribute is an individual's **noncompensatory reservation wage** (the minimum pay necessary to make a job offer acceptable). Prior compensation levels, the length of unemployment, and the availability of accurate salary information all affect an individual's reservation wage. There is also evidence that males have higher reservation wages than females. One reason is that females have been found to undervalue their work abilities. Reservation wages of males also may be higher because they are exposed to more job opportunities.[31]

Once a reservation wage is met, job seekers adopt a **compensatory approach** in which trade-offs are made between different job attributes, including higher levels of compensation. In the largest study ever undertaken, more than 50,000 male and female applicants to the Minnesota Gas Company were asked to rank the importance of ten job attributes. For both sexes there was a tendency for individuals to rank the importance of company and co-workers higher for themselves than for others, while benefits, hours, and pay were ranked lower. Job applicants agreed that pay was important to others but were less willing to admit that it was important to them. For females, the type of work was ranked as most important, while job security was ranked higher by males.[32]

INCREASING THE POOL OF POTENTIALLY QUALIFIED APPLICANTS

As the previous sections indicate, recruitment goes beyond choosing between internal and external sources. To gain a competitive edge, organizations must also understand and meet the needs of job seekers. To increase the likelihood that high-potential employees will be successfully recruited, hired, and retained, organizations can adopt a variety of strategies.

Conveying Job and Organizational Information

The traditional approach to recruitment involves matching the job applicant's skills, knowledge, and abilities with the demands of the job. The more recent approach to recruitment is also concerned with matching the job applicant's personality, interests, and preferences with the job and with organizational characteristics. For effective human resource management, getting the job applicants to stay is as important as recruiting job applicants who can do the job. Both objectives are facilitated by (1) devoting attention to the job interview, (2) having a job-matching program, (3) carefully timing recruitment procedures, and (4) developing appropriate policies regarding job offer acceptances.

Job interview. The interview is a vital aspect of the recruitment process. A good interview provides the applicant with a realistic preview of what the job will be like. It can definitely be an enticement for an applicant to join an organization, just as a bad interview can turn away many applicants.

The quality of the interview is just one aspect of the recruitment process. Other things being equal, the chances of a person's accepting a job offer increases when interviewers show interest and concern for the applicant. In addition, college students feel most positive toward the recruitment interview when they can take at least half of the interview time to ask the interviewer questions and when the interviewer does not embarrass them or put them on the spot.

The content of the recruitment interview is also important. Organizations often assume that it is in their best interests to tell a job applicant only about the positive aspects of the organization. However, studies by the life insurance industry have reported that providing realistic (positive and negative) information actually increases the number of eventual recruits. In addition, those who receive realistic job information may be less likely to quit once they accept the job. The type of interview that conveys positive and negative information is referred to as a **realistic job interview.**

> A realistic preview can be given as part of the recruitment process before an individual has accepted a job, or as part of the orientation or socialization process that takes place after job acceptance. Such previews can take many forms, including written descriptions of the job, film or video tape presentations, and samples of the actual work. Although they may differ in form or mode of presentation, all realistic job previews are alike in presenting all relevant aspects of a job as accurately as possible. Since new or potential employees usually have inflated ideas or expectations about what a job involves, a realistic preview usually *reduces* these overly optimistic expectations. In effect, even though it presents a complete and accurate picture, a realistic preview primarily serves to acquaint new or prospective employees with the previously unknown *negative* aspects of a particular job.[33]

Assuming that job applicants pass on initial screening, they should be given the opportunity to interview with a potential supervisor and even with co-workers. The interview with the potential supervisor is crucial, because this is the person who often makes the final decision.

Job matching. Job matching is a systematic effort to identify people's knowledge, skills, and abilities, and their personalities, interests, and preferences, and then match them to the job openings. Increasing pressure on organizations to effectively recruit, select, and place new and current employees may make an automated job matching system worthwhile. For example, Citibank's job matching system for nonprofessional employees evolved from an automated system designed to monitor requisition and internal placement processes. The system is used to identify suitable positions for staff members who wish to transfer or who are seeking another job because of technological displacement or reorganization. The system also ensures that suitable internal candidates won't be overlooked before recruiting begins outside the organization. Thus, the system appears to not only help recruit people and ensure that they stay, but also to provide a firm basis for job-related recruitment and selection procedures. (Job relatedness is an important part of legal compliance, as discussed in chapter 3.)

Timing of recruitment procedures. In markets where recruiting occurs in well-defined cycles (as in college recruiting), organizations can enhance their chances of obtaining high-potential candidates through early entry into the recruitment process. For example, high-technology companies begin the recruitment process by involving high-potential juniors in summer internships or cooperative education programs. Progressive organizations are also bypassing traditional second-semester campus interviews and inviting high-potential candidates directly to corporate headquarters early in the senior year. Most major accounting firms have job offers out and accepted by year-end. Such strategies are designed to induce commitment from top graduates before exposure to competing firms. Organizations that rely on traditional second-semester interviews and long selection processes may find themselves in a less competitive position than that of their more aggressive recruiting rivals.[34]

Policies regarding job offer acceptance. Employers can also influence job applicants' selection decisions through the amount of time they allow individuals to ponder their offers. Given unlimited time to ponder a job offer, most job seekers will delay decision making until they have heard from all the organizations in the job search net. While potentially advantageous to the job seeker, the lack of a deadline places the organization at a distinct disadvantage. Unless job openings are unlimited, the organization cannot extend an offer to a second-choice candidate until a decision is made by the preferred candidate. Conversely, job applicants may want to delay making a commitment until they have completed all interviews. Thus, most organizations have recall policies, and job seekers find themselves in the dilemma of having to accept or reject a minimally acceptable alternative before receiving an offer from a preferred alternative. The short- and long-term effects of time deadlines need further investigation before definitive conclusions can be drawn about their effectiveness.

Expanding Career Options and Opportunities

By providing career opportunities, career management programs, and work-family interface programs, organizations can enhance their attractiveness. This results in increased numbers of job applicants and a greater ability to retain key employees.

Career opportunities. The decision to provide career opportunities involves several choices for the organization. First, should the organization have an active policy of promotion from within? Second, should the organization be committed to a training and development program to provide sufficient candidates for internal promotion? If the answers to these questions are "yes," then the organization must identify career ladders consistent with organizational and job requirements and employees' skills and preferences.

An organization may identify several career paths for different groups or types of employees. This concept is based on the premise that an organization cannot afford to recruit applicants for jobs at the lower rungs of the ladder when they already possess those skills necessary for jobs at the higher rungs. This actually occurs, however, with many people recruited from college. Although they are essentially overqualified for their first jobs, the organization hires them for more difficult "future" jobs. This approach is partially to blame for the higher turnover rate of new college graduates and is also a cause for concern regarding legal compliance. Employers may claim that a college degree is necessary for an entry-level managerial job when they may actually consider the degree necessary for the second or third job. Such a policy can lead to discriminatory barriers for recruitment and promotion.

One way to reduce the possibility of discriminatory barriers is for an organization to establish career ladders and paths. When organizations have career ladders and paths with clearly specified requirements anchored in sound job analyses, they can present better legal defenses for their recruitment policies. In essence, organizations establish a case of long-term job relatedness. Organizations with clearly defined career ladders may also have an easier time attracting and recruiting qualified job applicants and a better chance of keeping employees.

Providing clearly defined global career paths and career ladders may also help firms remain competitive. Remaining competitive for many U.S. firms now means being globally competitive. This may mean developing more expatriates to help run the businesses overseas. While offering clear career paths for expatriates would seem to be necessary to encourage individuals to become expatriates, it appears that few U.S. firms have done this as yet. In a survey of human resource managers at 56 multinational companies based in the U.S.,

- 56 percent say a foreign assignment is either detrimental to or immaterial in one's career;
- 47 percent say their returning expatriates aren't guaranteed jobs with the company upon completion of their foreign assignments;
- 65 percent say their expatriates' foreign assignments are not integrated into the company's overall career planning;
- 45 percent view returning expatriates as a problem because they are so hard to fit back into the company; and
- 20 percent consider their company's repatriation policies adequate to meet the needs of their returning expatriates.[35]

Perhaps the development of career paths for expatriates will become a trend in the 1990s.

Career management programs. Providing career management programs is helpful for all employees, and can be particularly helpful for those who are not members of the majority group in an organization. For example, many companies realize that, in order to help women and people of color advance, they must develop programs to break the "glass ceiling." This nonphysical barrier has blocked career advancement for these individuals. Some companies, however, are working hard to change this situation, including through mentoring programs. For example, according to Gordon Smyth, senior vice president of employee relations at Du Pont,

> Mentoring is informal. We urge people who are good at it to do it. We have tried to encourage other people to get good at it. One of the best things you can do is know your people; they'll tell you whether they are getting any help.
>
> One of the most helpful things that we are working on lately in addressing the glass ceiling problem is to define it as a corporate and not a departmental or divisional problem. Most units say they have a management position candidate, but chances are the candidate is a white male. We come in now and say that there may be other candidates somewhere else that are minorities or female. It is in the corporate interest to place those people in that position. It has to be done carefully. You have to have a good person who can do the job.[36]

In the fast-paced world of product brand management, Quaker Oats is experimenting with the idea of a "part-time brand manager." Rather than lose a valuable brand manager after the birth of her son, the company agreed to let the manager work three days per week, an unprecedented move in such a line position. The company is evaluating the pilot program on a quarterly basis, using the objectives that the manager negotiated with senior managers. After two years, the program has been quite successful.

As the full force of the baby boomers works its way into the working world, Quaker Oats and its employees have also come to view careers in new ways. The company's "pyramid" has flattened to the point where one manager, after six promotions in nine years, has remained in the same job for three years. While his initial reaction at staying in one place was frustration that he was not viewed as successful, the advantages of staying in one job are becoming more evident. A manager can see the results (both good and bad) of earlier decisions, rather than moving on before learning of their implications. In addition, a manager can take the time to create a team and more thoroughly develop subordinates. Finally, Quaker Oats is using more lateral moves as a way to broaden manager experience, allowing people to become knowledgeable about many aspects of the company, which can have benefits when and if those managers do move into senior management positions.[37]

Organizations can also improve their ability to retain and utilize the career contributions of their more senior employees. Individuals in later career stages must continue to be productive and eventually prepare for retirement. Retirement is a major career transition for many employees because it represents the culmination of forty or more years of work involvement. However, older individuals may be viewed as less productive, less versatile, unopen to new ideas, and less adaptable.[38] Such stereotypes may make continued effective performance even more difficult.

Organizations can help employees in later career stages in a number of ways including:

- Carefully examining human resource policies and procedures affecting older workers

- Surveying the needs of older workers
- Providing realistic retirement previews
- Developing retirement programs
- Implementing flexible work patterns and options[39]

Organizations must also consider the legal issues that affect the treatment of older workers. The Age Discrimination in Employment Act forbids discrimination in hiring, placement, compensation, promotion, and termination for individuals aged 40 and over. Treating these workers fairly makes good business sense and also helps to avoid costly litigation.

Work-family interface programs. Balancing work and family demands has become an increasingly important organizational issue. The "traditional" family—with a husband who is the breadwinner, a wife who is a full-time homemaker, and two children—is coming to reflect a minority of U.S. households. With the dramatic influx of women into the workforce and the growing number of dual-career and two-earner couples, individuals are finding it difficult to avoid conflict between work and family areas. Since work and family have been treated as separate worlds in the past, many people feel that conflict is not supposed to happen, that they are the only people experiencing such problems, and that the organization will not be impressed if family problems are causing poor job performance. Perhaps the most significant aspect of work-family programs is the recognition that work and family life are interdependent and that family issues can affect work performance and career development.

In fact, career development can now be viewed as a family affair. Organizations can provide a setting for employees to discuss work-family issues and to identify coping strategies that can reduce the conflict.[40] In a more direct way, organizations can provide child care assistance, flexible work schedules, and career and life planning activities. They can also provide assistance by securing new jobs for working spouses of employees they are relocating or transfering. According to the Conference Board,

> More than one-half of American corporations currently offer some sort of re-employment assistance to spouses of transferred employees. Nearly 500,000 employees are transferred annually, with an average cost per transfer of $41,000. Aid to spouses adds $500 to $2,000 to that figure. Much of this largesse is impelled by changes in the U.S. family and emerging trends in the workforce, the report says, pointing out that "about 70 percent of all American couples represented in the workforce are dual earners."[41]

Typically, companies providing spouse job information materials use that material in addition to other approaches. For example,

- U.S. West gives working partners a choice of either a self-guided workbook with audio tapes or up to $2,500 to apply to job search costs, such as employment agency fees, interview trips, and job counseling. While the printed information is aimed at satisfying the needs of most spouses, the reimbursement option can be used by those facing more difficult job transitions.
- Compaq Computer Corp. supplements its information package with a "Career Corner" at the company's relocation resource center. The company also par-

ticipates in a consortium of Houston employees who cooperate in circulating spouse resumés. Compaq provides the materials to all its married transferees, even if not requested.

- Johnson & Johnson offers personal counseling to supplement its package of in-depth information on job search techniques to relocating families.[42]

Finally, as companies recognize the work-family connection, more than ever they will provide some kind of child care service for their employees. (Because child-care service is such a critical employee benefit, it is discussed in detail in chapter 11.)

Offering Alternative Work Arrangements

This may be the decade in which Americans free themselves from the tyranny of the time clock. Already, more than ten million workers have taken advantage of several types of alternative work arrangements. The growing number of single-parent families, the high costs of commuting, the desire for larger blocks of personal time, and the desire of older workers to reduce their hours all suggest that alternative work arrangements can reduce the stresses caused by the conflict between job demands, family needs, leisure values, and educational needs. Thus, organizations can expect to reduce absenteeism and turnover by offering alternatives to their standard work arrangements.[43]

Standard work schedules. In the 1860s the average work week was 72 hours—twelve hours a day, six days a week. It was 58 in 1900, and is approximately 40 hours a week today. Standard work schedules for the typical week include day, evening, and night sessions as well as overtime, part-time, and shift work longer than a 40-hour week. Someone who does shift work might report from 7:00 AM to 4:00 PM one week, and from 4:00 PM to midnight the next. Since the end of World War I, shift-work systems have become more prevalent in industrialized countries. Currently, about twenty percent of all industrial workers in Europe and the U.S. are on shift-work schedules. The percentage of employees on part-time schedules has also increased steadily, from approximately fifteen percent in 1954 to more than twenty-five percent today.

All of these standard work schedules have advantages and disadvantages. Initially, employees may select a given schedule, but after that the days of the week (five) and the hours of the day (eight) are generally fixed. Because employee preferences and interests change over time, what had once been an appropriate work schedule may no longer be so. If alternative arrangements are not provided, the employee may leave the organization. Furthermore, the organization may have a difficult time attracting similar types of employees. As a result, it pays to give employees a choice between a nonstandard and standard schedule, as well as a choice of hours, days, and total number of hours to work per week.

Flextime schedules. Flextime, a nonstandard work schedule, is popular with organizations because it decreases absenteeism, increases employee morale, induces better labor-management relations, and encourages a high level of employee participation in decision making, control over the job, and discretion. Simply stated, **flextime** is a schedule that gives employees daily choice in the timing of work and nonwork activities. Consideration is given to **band width** or maximum length of the workday. This band (often ranging between ten and sixteen hours) is divided into core time and flexible time. **Core time** is when the employee has to work; flexible time allows the employee the freedom to choose the remaining work time.

Among the advantages of flextime is its ability to increase overall employee productivity. It also allows organizations to accommodate employee preferences, some of which may be legally protected, such as reasonable religious obligations. On the other hand, flextime forces the supervisor to do more planning, sometimes makes communications difficult between employees (especially with different schedules), and complicates keeping records of employees' hours. Furthermore, most flextime schedules still require employees to work five days a week.

Compressed work weeks. An option for employees who want to work fewer than five days is **compressed work weeks.** By extending the workday beyond the standard eight hours, employees generally need to work only three to four days to equal a standard forty-hour week. At two General Tire and Rubber plants, some employees work only two twelve-hour shifts each weekend and yet are considered full-time employees.

Compressed work weeks are becoming especially popular for certain occupations, such as nursing, because they fit employees' needs. At the same time, compressed work weeks permit an organization to make better use of its equipment and decrease turnover and absenteeism. Scheduling and legal problems may accompany such arrangements, but legal exceptions can be made, and scheduling can become a joint negotiation process between supervisors and employees.

Permanent part-time and job sharing. Traditionally, part-time work has meant filling positions that lasted only for a short time, such as those in retail stores during holiday periods. Now some organizations have designated permanent part-time positions. A **permanent part-time** work schedule may be a shortened day schedule (for example, from 1:00 to 5:00 PM) or an odd-hour shift (for example, from 5:00 to 9:00 PM). Organizations can also use part-time schedules to fill in the remainder of a day composed of two ten-hour shifts (representing a compressed work week).[44]

Job sharing is a particular type of part-time work. In **job sharing,** two people divide the responsibility for a regular full-time job. Both may work half the job, or one could work more hours than the other. Traditional part-time workers generally receive little or no indirect compensation, but workers on permanent part-time and job-sharing schedules often do. The benefits of these workers are not equal to those of full-time workers but are prorated according to the amount of time they work.

Both permanent part-time and job sharing provide the organization and individual with opportunities that might not otherwise be available. They offer staffing flexibility that can expand or contract to meet actual demands, using employees who are at least as productive, if not more so, than regular full-time employees. Individuals benefit from being able to enjoy permanent work with less than a full-time commitment to the company.

Industrial and electronic cottages. To provide individuals with even more choices in how to arrange their work and work schedules, companies are allowing employees to work at home. Work-at-home arrangements can be made for those with a full-time commitment to the company and for those wanting only part-time employment. Increasingly, individuals are working at home by means of computer terminals linked to the mainframes at their regular office or plant. In essence the employee's home then becomes an **electronic cottage.**

Of course, some employees even work on the road: in their cars using the car phone (perhaps the epitome of "tele-communicating"), and in hotel rooms and airplanes, using lap-top computers.

Individuals can also take home work that involves assembly, such as small toys. After a batch is done, the worker takes it to the regular plant and turns it in for more parts. In this example, the home becomes an **industrial cottage.**[45]

The use of industrial and electronic cottages is increasing. These arrangements offer workers another choice as well as more freedom. One drawback is the difficulty of protecting the health and safety of the employee at home. Another is ensuring that workers are still paid a fair wage for their work. State and federal laws can also restrict home work. For example, a federal law prohibits commercial knitting at home. The restrictions must be dealt with carefully if expanding cottages are to remain viable options.

Providing Employment Security

> Sony Corporation has had a plant in San Diego for many years. Several years ago the company encountered a sudden decline in sales. Soon the San Diego plant was piling up inventory and then had to begin reducing production. Where were costs to be cut?
>
> The American managers of the plant requested permission from headquarters in Japan to begin work force reductions. They received a refusal. They renewed the request, pointing out that sales were way down and that significant losses would soon appear on the bottom line. To this, Akio Morita, the founder of Sony, replied, "Think of the opportunity."
>
> "What opportunity?" the American managers persisted. "We are going to be drowning in red ink."
>
> "Think of the opportunity," Morita repeated. Then he explained. "If we keep the American work force with us through these difficult times, then they will understand that we are really committed to them. And they will be committed to us."[46]

There was no layoff. The company absorbed the losses for a while until business recovered. Since then the San Diego plant has performed very well, in some instances outperforming Sony's plants in Japan—the first foreign facility of Sony to do so.

Other organizations, small as well as large, have also thought of the opportunity arising from offering employment security. It can mean avoiding: low employee involvement and loyalty; severance pay; higher unemployment compensation taxes; continuation of health and other benefits for a period after the layoff; legal and administrative expenses; and the expense of rehiring and training workers when recalled. Add to these the potential costs of lower productivity and the lack of ability to compete in world markets.

Offering employment security is probably unwise if an organization is already overstaffed or pursuing a strategy of liquidation or disinvestment. As several major computer firms found out in the 1980s, full-employment or job-security provisions are easy to maintain during periods of growth but difficult to endure during economic downturns.

A solution is to have a core of full-time employees with job guarantees. This core work force can be augmented by contingent or buffer employees. According to Audrey Freedman, an economist with the Conference Board, one out of every four workers today actually is a contingent worker. They include freelancers and contract workers, temporary office and accounting personnel, and part-timers. Because the size of the work force can be quickly reduced or increased to match business needs, the deployment of buffer employees increases staffing flexibility. Since contingent workers receive no pensions, vacations, or holiday pay, and since there is no obligation to train them, they also cost less. This situation is applauded by business strategists concerned with costs because it enormously reduces labor costs per unit of output, yet it can also be successful in maintaining and enhancing the level of commitment of the core work force.

REDUCING THE NEED FOR APPLICANTS: SOCIALIZATION

The problem of increased labor shortages can be partly solved by effectively managing the socialization process. **Socialization** is the process a company uses to expose new employees to the company's culture and ways of doing things. When done successfully, it results in intensely loyal employees. Companies that have perfected the socialization process include IBM, Procter & Gamble, and Morgan Guaranty Trust.

Often the socialization process begins before the employee is hired. At Procter & Gamble (P&G), for example, an elite cadre of line managers trained in interviewing skills probes applicants for entry-level positions in brand management for qualities such as the "ability to turn out high volumes of excellent work." Only after successfully completing at least two interviews and a test of general knowledge is the applicant flown to P&G headquarters in Cincinnati, where the applicant confronts a day-long series of interviews. If the applicant passes this extensive screening process, he or she is confronted with a series of rigorous job experiences calculated to induce humility and openness to new ways of doing things. Typically, this phase of socialization involves long hours of work at a pressure-cooker pace. Throughout this phase and others of the socialization process, the new employee is constantly made aware of transcendent company values and organizational folklore, including the emphasis on product quality and the dedication and commitment of employees long since retired. This intense socialization results in increased commitment to the success of the company, willingness to work long hours, and decreased absenteeism and turnover.[47]

The intensity of the socialization often depends on employees' backgrounds. Organizations usually recruit from familiar sources that have supplied good applicants in the past. They may also recruit individuals who are already socialized but by other organizations. However, recruitment and selection processes are not likely to produce new employees who know the values, norms, and behavior patterns of the organization. When this is the case, more extensive socialization efforts must be conducted. Of the several possible formalized methods of socialization, two deserve particular attention: orientation programs and job assignments.

Orientation Programs

Orientation programs are frequently used to brief new employees on benefits programs and options, to advise them of rules and regulations, and to provide them with a folder or handbook of the policies and practices of the organization:

> A first-rate orientation system for new-hires can reduce turnover rates, decrease employee learning time, and improve quality and productivity throughout the organization, according to Edmund McGarrell, Jr., supervisor of special projects at Corning Glass Works. Addressing the American Management Association's 56th Annual Human Resource Conference, which was held in New Orleans, McGarrell stresses that the company's orientation process is designed to provide new-hires with "red carpet treatment" that will turn them into highly skilled, involved, and committed employees.[48]

Of course, orientations can be used for an even more encompassing purpose: to make someone feel he or she is a member of a big, happy family. This is the case at the Walt Disney Company. Every newly hired "cast member" participates in an orientation and training program at "Disney University." Cast members first receive an overview of Walt Disney Company and learn about its traditions, history, achievements, and philosophy. In addition, cast members learn about the key Disney "product"—happiness—and their roles in helping to provide it. Next, each cast member learns about the benefits (health, social, recreational) of being part of the Disney "family," gains more direct information about his or her role in the production, and has a tour of the complex. Tailored to reflect the needs of each type of cast member and group, the initial orientation and subsequent training has a theme of bringing cast members into the family and developing a team sense, as well as a focus on courtesy to guests, on safety, and on putting on a good "show" (entertainment).[49]

More typically, orientation programs usually contain information about equal employment opportunity practices, safety regulations, work times, coffee breaks, the structure and history of the organization, and perhaps the products or services of the organization. Usually, however, the orientation program does not tell employees about the politics of the organization—for example, that the organization may soon be going out of business, that it may be merging with another company, or even that an extensive layoff may soon occur.[50]

The orientation program conveys some information about the norms, values, attitudes, and behaviors appropriate for new employees, but much of the socialization is left to informal day-to-day interactions among employees. Nevertheless, orientation programs are useful for factual information, and a handbook can be used to tell employees where to get additional information after orientation is over.

Orientation programs are almost always coordinated by the human resource director of the organization. The program is often run by a staff member of the human resource department, with some participation by line managers or representatives from other departments or divisions in the organization.

When organizations are large, orientation programs often are conducted every week. Some organizations even have two orientation sessions one week apart. Typically, these programs are run for groups of new employees. Although this is an efficient method, it tends to negate each employee's sense of identity and importance. Therefore, each employee is often assigned to a trainer or buddy (sometimes the immediate supervisor) who can answer further questions and introduce the new employee to other employees in the work unit or department.

Orientation programs may last longer than one or two days. The orientation program at Corning Glass Works, for example, lasts fifteen months. Exhibit 5.4 shows the critical components of the program at Corning. However, most orientation programs last only a few hours, and are done within the first week or two of employment. Occasionally, an orientation follow-up takes place a year or so later. Most employees take longer than just one or two weeks to acquire all the information contained in the orientation program. Because orientation programs do only part of the job of socialization, other methods are also used.

Job Assignments

The important socializing aspects of **job assignments** are the characteristics of the initial job, the nature of early experiences on the job, and the first supervisor. The initial job often determines the new employee's future success. The more challenge and responsibility the job offers, the more likely an employee will be successful with the organization.[51] A challenging (but not overwhelming) job assignment implies that the organization believes the employee can do well and that the organization values him or her. Many times, organizations give new employees simple jobs or rotate them through departments to get a feel for different jobs; but employees may interpret these practices to mean the organization does not yet trust their abilities or loyalties.

Closely related to the first job are employees' initial experiences, which are often provided by supervisors. These types of experiences help prepare new employees for the acquisition of the appropriate values, norms, attitudes, and behaviors. Supervisors of new employees can serve as role models and set expectations. The positive influence that the supervisor's expectations can have on the new employee is referred to as the **Pygmalion effect.** A supervisor who believes the new employee will do well will convey this belief to the employee, who will be apt to live up to those expectations.[52]

Another way to improve the effectiveness of the socialization process and the chances of getting employees to stay is by developing skills in managing work force diversity. Because this can also increase an organization's applicant pool, skill in managing work force diversity is an important trend affecting recruitment and involving many other human resource activities. Recall the new recruitment measures used by McDonald's, described earlier in the chapter.

FOCUS ISSUES IN RECRUITMENT

Key focus issues in recruitment include managing work force diversity, assessment of recruiting, contract recruiting, and applicant rejection management.

Managing Work Force Diversity

The radical demographic work force transformation, described in chapter 2, means that business must develop knowledge and understanding in managing a very diverse work force.

Exhibit 5.4
Critical Components of the Orientation Program at Corning Glass Works

- Pre-arrival period—The supervisor gets the office ready and, based on discussions with the new-hire, creates a preliminary management-by-objectives [MBO] list.
- First day—Following breakfast with the supervisor, the new-hire goes through personnel processing, attends a half-day "Corning and You" seminar, tours the facility, and meets co-workers.
- First week—This time is set aside for getting settled in the department or office and for one-on-one discussions with the supervisor and co-workers. Performance expectations and other general job-related matters are discussed, and details of the MBO plan are formalized.
- Second through fourth weeks—Regular assignments begin. The new-hire also attends a special employee benefits seminar.
- Second through fifth months—Assignments increase and progress is reviewed biweekly with the supervisor. The employee also attends six two-and-one-half-hour seminars on such topics as quality and productivity and reviews these with the supervisor.
- Sixth month—The new employee reviews the MBO list with the supervisor and receives a performance review.
- Seventh through 15th months—MBO and performance and salary reviews are conducted.

McGarrell says that since initiating the system in 1982, Corning has reduced its turnover rate by 69 percent, shortened employee learning time by one month, and saved more than $500,000 in recruiting and training costs.

SOURCE: *Bulletin to Management* (9 May 1985), 1,2. Reprinted by permission from *Bulletin to Management* (Washington, D.C.: The Bureau of National Affairs, Inc., 1985).

> Successful organizations will react to diversity as the important business issue it is by implementing proactive, strategic human resource planning. Short-term strategies designed to circumvent the situation will keep an organization from effectively positioning itself in tomorrow's world of cultural, gender, and lifestyle diversity.[53]

Increasingly, organizations are casting the topic of work force diversity in terms that define it as an important business issue.

> Bill Fuller, human resources director at the Bank of Boston Corporation, describes companies that value diversity as winners and points out that the costs of programs that support diversity do not compromise a company's ability to maximize profits. On the contrary, companies that value diversity are also financially successful; indeed, some of the companies that lead in valuing differences rank among the United States' most profitable. Fuller says, "In the valuing diversity company, you see employees who are less risk averse, who play to win rather than not to lose, and as a result you see more creativity, more leadership, more innovation.
>
> Kevin Sullivan of Apple makes an observation that may capture the attention of white male managers who resist diversification efforts. Before joining Apple in 1987, Sullivan worked at Digital Equipment Corporation—where he noted that over 40% of the salespeople were women and minorities. "When white male managers understand that 40% of their sales force is responsible for about a billion and a half dollars in orders," he observes, "it becomes an obvious bottom-line management goal to keep them happy, motivated, and productive!"
>
> More managers are realizing that valuing diversity is a business and economic issue, not just one of morality. As Effenus Henderson, director of international human

> resources at Weyerhaeuser Company points out, "Competing requires full utilization of all our resources. If we develop only white males, we're not really developing our resources, and that is a complete waste. Human resources will provide critical leverage in a more competitive business environment—if we can't effectively recruit, train, and motivate we will lose out. We won't be able to compete in the marketplace."[54]

As a consequence, human resource managers are focusing on several key areas in managing diversity.

- *Recruitment:* Exerting a concerted effort to find quality minority hires by improved college relations programs
- *Career development:* Exposing those minority employees with high potential to the same key developmental jobs that have led traditionally to senior positions for their white, male counterparts
- *Diversity training for managers:* Addressing stereotypes and cultural differences that interfere with the full participation of all employees in the workplace
- *Diversity training for employees:* Helping employees understand the corporate culture requirements for success in the firm, and career choices open to them
- *Upward mobility:* Breaking the "invisible (or) glass ceiling" and increasing the number of minorities in upper management through mentors and executive appointment
- *Diverse input and feedback:* Asking minority employees themselves what they need versus asking managers what they think minorities need
- *Self-help:* Encouraging networking and support groups among minorities
- *Accountability:* Holding managers accountable for developing their diverse work forces
- *Systems accommodation:* Developing respect and support for cultural diversity through recognition of different cultural and religious holidays, diet restrictions, etc.
- *Outreach:* Supporting minority organizations and programs, thus developing a reputation as a multicultural leader[55]

Businesses are taking the diversity issue very seriously. Digital Equipment Corporation has a manager with the title of Manager of Valuing Differences. Honeywell Inc. has a director of work force diversity, and Avon Products, Inc., has a director of multicultural planning and design.[56] According to Stona Fitch, vice-president of manufacturing for Procter & Gamble,

> The first companies that achieve a true multicultural environment will have a competitive edge. Diversity provides a much richer environment, a variety of viewpoints, greater productivity. And not unimportantly, it makes work much more fun and interesting.[57]

Assessing Recruitment

The recruitment activity is supposed to attract the right people at the right time within legal limits, so that people and organizations can select each other in their best short- and long-run interests. This is how recruitment should be assessed. More specific criteria for assessing recruitment are shown in exhibit 5.5, grouped by the stage of the recruitment process to which they are most applicable.

Recruitment is not concerned just with attracting people; it is concerned also with attracting those whose personalities, interests, and preferences will most likely be matched by the organization and who have the skills, knowledge, and abilities to perform adequately. Another criterion by which to assess recruiting is legal compliance. Job applicants must be recruited fairly and without discrimination.

In order to assess the utility of recruitment practices, each method of recruitment can be valued, or "costed out," in terms of its short- and long-term benefits and costs. For example, for each occupational group, the proportion of potentially qualified applicants hired by each method could be used to determine the **selection ratios** of alternative methods. The method resulting in the largest number of qualified applicants at the lowest per-hire cost may be deemed the most effective in the short run. The important costs to compare are those associated with hires versus those associated with nonhires. As noted earlier, if an organization is spending more than two-thirds of its recruiting budget on individuals who never join the company, the recruiting program needs serious revamping. The items reviewed should include the salaries of recruiters and line managers involved in interviewing and selection; all expenses for mailing, telephone, and recruiting materials; administrative support costs; and all recruiting advertising charges, including receptions, videos, and programs.[58]

Exhibit 5.5
Some Criteria for Assessing Recruitment

Stage of Entry	Type of Criteria
Pre-entry	Total number of applicants Number of minority and female applicants Cost per applicant Time to locate job applicants Time to process job applicants
Offers and hires	Offers extended by source Total number of qualified applicants Number of qualified female, minority, and handicapped applicants Costs of acceptance versus rejection of applicants
Entry	Initial expectations of newcomers Choice of the organization by qualified applicants Cost and time of training of new employees Salary levels
Post-entry	Attitudes toward job, pay, benefits, supervision, co-workers Organizational commitment Job performance Tenure of hires Absenteeism Referrals

Contract Recruiting

In response to employment cycles and the need for cost containment, a trend toward contract recruiting has developed. A contract recruiter is a consultant who accepts temporary assignments with companies (typically three to six months), becomes an integral part of the staff, and addresses problems relating to recruitment.

Although employment activity accounts for a majority of their assignments, contract recruiters are increasingly involved in a variety of human resource issues, ranging from compensation and benefits to employee relations and to equal access and equal opportunity programs.

Contractors are available immediately, without the need to hire a full-time employee or the expense of employee benefits. Unlike regular employees, a contractor is easily replaced without the trauma of an employee termination. For example, GTE, in Needham, Massachusetts, won a major contract, assuring the government that 1,200 professionals would be on board within sixteen months. At the peak of recruiting, twelve recruiting contractors worked full-time as an instant employment staff, establishing a recruiting and selection system. The number diminished to two at the end of the sixteen months. Before leaving, the consultants recruited, hired, and trained their own replacements.

With the switch to a service economy, financial service, insurance, and health care organizations are also expected to use contract recruiting. Recently, Fidelity Investments opened up a new consumer division in Salt Lake City. Rather than rely on a corporate staff to recruit applicants, the firm trained human resource graduate students in Fidelity's selection procedures. En masse, these contract recruiters were able to select sufficient job candidates that Fidelity's new office could be operational within two months. Similarly, companies such as Kendall have used contract recruiters to reduce the cost per hire. During downsizing, Kendall has used contractors for outplacement counseling rather than recruiting.[59]

Rejection with Tact

When a new Toyota plant opened in Georgetown, Kentucky, the applicant pool reached 40,000 for 2,700 assembly-line openings. Thousands more applied for the 300 office jobs.[60] For "high-demand" organizations, there's a new challenge to recruiting—rejection with tact.

Consider a hundred applicants who apply for one position with a bank. Only one applicant out of one hundred will be accepted, leaving ninety-nine potential employees and/or customers. If these rejected candidates feel angry at the rejecting organization, they may never again purchase goods or services from the organization. If procedures are viewed as unfair, too lengthy, or too impersonal, rejected candidates may also share their dissatisfaction with friends and associates.

While research on the rejection process is in its infancy, several characteristics of rejection letters make a difference. Statements that (1) are friendly (e.g., thank you for applying, good luck in the future), (2) include a personalized address and correct salutation (Ms., Mrs., and Miss—versus Mr. to all), and (3) summarize the applicant's job qualifications leave positive impressions. Including statements about the size and excellence of the application pool and the person who was offered the job (e.g., the person had ten years experience and was certified in arbitrage) reduce disappointment and increase perceptions of fairness.

Including a statement that the applicant's resumé will be kept on file increases the likelihood that the applicant will continue to use the organization's services or buy its products. While no court challenges have been launched, promises made in rejection letters (e.g., to keep the resumé on file) can serve as binding contractual obligations. Thus, a promise to keep an application on file should be made only if the organization intends to do just that. The timeliness with which rejection letters are mailed also seems important. Not only should a recruitment and selection timetable be specified to applicants, but also the organization should meet its self-imposed deadlines.[61]

INTERNATIONAL COMPARISONS

Japan

The recruitment of graduates takes place once a year only although this is changing somewhat. In a company's direct recruitment, college professors play dominant roles. Company Y may ask Professor X to recommend so many students with special qualifications in certain fields. The selection process depends on the students' future occupational class. Students who major in the social sciences, law, or the humanities will enter administrative *(jimukei)* jobs, such as planning, human resources, sales, or purchasing. Students majoring in technical disciplines will enter technical jobs *(gijitsukei)*. The selection procedures differ for each of the two occupational classes.

Aspiring administrators are asked to apply directly to employers for jobs. Following the formal application, the candidate is asked to appear for a set of interviews with company employees, managers, and executives. The basic criteria for hiring—besides an employee's potential or ability—are "balanced" personality and moderate views. The evaluation of job candidates is often supplemented by background checks assigned to private investigators who interview the candidate's neighbors and acquaintances, check local police records, and examine the family history. Those who pass the last round of interviews are invited to sit for the company entrance examination. Officially this exam should determine who is best qualified for the job, but in many corporations over 90 percent of candidates are preselected on the basis of earlier interviews. The exam usually asks essay questions on such topics as family background, career/life objectives, or the applicant's strengths and weaknesses. A number of firms are actually using the exam as an assessment tool to determine the career interests of new employees.[62]

The reliance on intermediaries (i.e., college professors) for selection decisions, especially when evaluating technical candidates, serves a number of purposes. First, it is difficult to evaluate a student's technical potential on the basis of a short interview only, when the majority of interviewers have little up-to-date technical background. If a company waited for a written examination, it would not preselect and would risk losing the best candidates to the competition. Second, because of the competition for graduates, recruiters cultivate good relations with college professors, who then recommend individual firms to the students. In this way, the firms expect to get their "fair share" of talent and simultaneously prevent a self-defeating bidding war that would not only raise the starting salaries for selected jobs, but more critically would disrupt the carefully balanced compensation structures of internal labor markets. Moreover, specific seminars (courses taken with a professor's permission) are seen as more selective than others and, thus, develop an "elite" reputation. And last, college grades are not an important selection tool. What matters are the educational credentials of the school from which the student is graduating. Given the intense and rigorous competition to enter first-tier schools, the companies rely on the university entrance examination as an indicator of the employee's "latest ability."

During the 1970s, many factors in Japanese management practice demanded modification. Economic growth rates were declining and automation was broadly implemented. At this point, Japanese companies began hiring significantly fewer workers in entry-level positions. This resulted in the average age of employees increasing as they moved up the seniority ladder. In turn, pressure was added on average wage costs. The most powerful and negative effect of this era was the low morale caused by few opportunities for real advancement.

The Japanese responded to these problems quickly instead of ignoring them. They increased their flexibility in employment. This was accomplished with temporary transfers of surplus employees to other companies that are part of the "extended organization." This form of organization, called *Keiretsu,* is a vertical linkage of companies that are mutual suppliers and customers.[63]

Mexico

Mexican employers in the Maquiladora region recruit, hire, and fire personnel as the need arises. There is always an abundance of applicants, which allows for screening for those who are most apt for what is mostly assembly-work jobs. Mexican workers accept this screening because of the relatively good wages and benefits they can get at maquiladoras compared with other manufacturing-based employment opportunities. The work week in this industry is normally 48 hours. Overtime at one and a half times the hourly rate is paid for time in excess of 48 hours.

Since the cost of newspapers makes help wanted advertisements useless, recruitment is done primarily by approaching people and asking them to apply. Therefore, it is common to find many family members working at the same maquiladora.

Another significant aspect of employee retention and recruitment involves the need for workers to feel they are part of the operation. The plant will be populated by people oriented to traditional Mexican values and social structure. In order to achieve this, employers make certain to celebrate numerous holidays, and it is common for companies to throw parties for a variety of events.[64]

SUMMARY

Recruitment is a major activity in an organization's program to manage its human resources. After human resource needs have been established and job requirements have been identified through job analysis, a recruiting program can be established to produce a pool of job applicants. These applicants can be obtained from internal or external sources.

For recruitment to be effective, it must address not only the needs of the organization but also those of society and the individual. Society's needs are most explicitly defined by various federal and state regulations in the name of equal employment opportunity. Individuals' needs figure prominently in two aspects of recruiting: attracting candidates and retaining desirable employees.

Keeping legal considerations firmly in mind, the organization must recruit sufficient numbers of potentially qualified applicants so that the individuals selected are adequately matched to jobs. This matching will help ensure that the individuals will perform effectively and not leave the organization. An organization can attract and retain these job applicants by numerous methods and through various sources. Although some methods and sources are more effective than others, the ones chosen are often necessarily determined by the type of applicant sought.

As with other human resource activities, recruitment assessment is essential. Recruitment can be assessed by evaluating the associated benefit and cost criteria. For example, the benefits of reduced turnover or enhanced performance can be assessed and compared with the costs of the program to recruit job applicants. Costs of sources and methods can also be assessed and weighed against the benefits, such as the ease of recruiting or the number of qualified applicants obtained. After these assessments are made, recruiting methods and sources can be revised as appropriate. As with the recruitment assessment, however, the revision should be made with consideration for selection, the other half of the staffing function. This is necessary because the two activities are interdependent, as is made more apparent in the next chapter.

WHERE WE ARE TODAY

1. Recruiting is increasingly seen as an essential activity in a company's ability to successfully compete.
2. The downsizing efforts of firms across the country are creating a large pool of potentially very qualified and experienced individuals.
3. During the 1990s, however, firms are still expected to experience a shortfall in qualified entry-level job applicants.
4. Because of the growing diversity of job applicants and the work force, we will see more firms introduce major diversity management programs.
5. Organizations that are successful in getting good employees devote considerable time and attention to their recruiting efforts.
6. By the end of this decade, 25 percent of the work force is expected to be spending a substantial portion of their working time away from the official location of the company, i.e., in their homes, cars, hotels, airports, and airplanes.
7. Managing workers who are not in close physical proximity to either the organization or their bosses may become a focus issue in this decade.
8. Taking an active role in the management of your own career activities is becoming a necessity for your career survival and success.

9. As organizations seek to improve levels of quality and customer service, they realize it is important to effectively socialize and orient employees to the vision and goals of the organization.
10. To help the organization make the right investments in recruiting, human resource managers are demonstrating the tremendous contribution effective recruiting makes to the firm.

DISCUSSION QUESTIONS

1. What are the purposes of recruitment? How do these purposes affect other organizational activities?
2. Just-in-time inventory is a concept that enables manufacturers to assemble products from parts that are delivered as needed rather than kept in inventory, which is costly. Could this concept be applied to the recruitment function and the management of human resources? Explain.
3. How does human resource planning contribute to effective recruitment? What are the roles of the line manager and human resource manager in each of these activities?
4. Why do some organizations use mostly external searches, whereas others use mostly internal searches?
5. The search for job applicants involves finding not only the right number but also the right kind of applicants. Are some recruitment sources "richer" than others—that is, do they yield more information about the kind of applicant needed? Can you give examples?
6. What impact has the legal environment had on organizational recruitment? Has this impact been positive or negative for organizations? Explain (Refer back to chapter 3.)
7. Assessment of recruitment activities requires an estimate of costs as well as benefits. Choose an organization with which you are familiar, and describe how you would measure and compare the costs and benefits of the recruitment methods used in that organization.
8. How can organizations increase their attractiveness to potential job applicants?
9. How can organizations increase the chances that applicants will stay once hired?
10. Why is it so important to reject with tact?

APPLIED PROJECTS

1. Outline information that would be contained in a realistic job preview for prospective college students. This information would be communicated to prospective students in their admission interviews. Prepare such a preview for undergraduate and graduate students.
2. Given that work organizations will be competing for a diverse pool of labor in the near future, it will be critical for organizations to manage diversity effectively. Assume you are a human resource professional in charge of recruiting clerical employees from a labor pool consisting of a large percent-

age of single parents. What programs might the organization develop and implement to attract qualified single parents to work for this organization? Outline the content of these programs and the rationale for them. Keep in mind the relevant legal constraints that influence managing human resources.

CASE STUDY

The New Recruit

Stan Fryer, project leader at General Instruments (GI), knew today would be one of those proverbial Mondays that managers so often fear. Stan's boss and group manager at GI, Harry Hoskinsson, had left town on business the previous Friday and would not return until the following week. General Instruments, a defense contractor, employs nearly one thousand engineers and designs and manufactures a number of electronic systems for nuclear submarines. Recruiting qualified engineers has been difficult for GI because of the competitive market in Palo Alto and the fairly substantial cost-of-living increase for anyone relocating to the area.

Stan's immediate problem this morning concerned a new engineer recruit, June Harrison, a single, 23-year-old systems engineer who was hired three weeks ago upon graduation from San Diego State. Much to Stan's surprise, June had submitted a letter of resignation, stating personal reasons as the cause of her departure. In addition to the letter of resignation, Stan also had a memo from June's supervisor, Lou Snider, describing the events leading up to June's resignation.

As Stan reconstructed these events, it seemed that June was expecting overtime payment in this week's paycheck because of the extra hours she had put in over the previous three weeks. Lou Snider, however, had neglected to file the proper payroll paperwork so that June could receive her overtime in the current pay period. This did not surprise Stan, given Lou's prior history of not getting the job done in other supervisory positions at GI. Apparently, Harry Hoskinsson had spoken to Lou about filing so much overtime for his section, so Lou decided to spread out some of the overtime charges over several pay periods.

What Lou hadn't realized was that June had finally secured an apartment in Palo Alto (she had been renting a room in a nearby hotel) and had committed herself to make a three-month payment and deposit with her paycheck and the additional overtime payment she was expecting. When June realized what was going to happen, she called Harry Hoskinsson to set up a meeting to discuss how she could cover her housing expense. June remembered that, when she was being recruited, Harry had emphatically told her to contact him if she ever needed anything or had any problems settling into her new job at GI. Harry was in a bit of a rush to make a staff meeting, so he agreed to see June early the following day. When June reported to Harry's office the next morning, she was understandably upset when Harry's secretary told her that Harry had left town on a business trip. With that, she returned to her office and drafted her resignation letter.

As Stan contemplated how to resolve his "Monday morning" problem, he recalled the speech Harry had given him two years ago when he joined GI. Harry had made clear his distaste for young engineers who tended to live beyond their means and to count on bonuses and overtime as if they were regular and assured components of their paycheck. Nonetheless, Stan decided, despite Harry's speech, that GI must try to arrange for a loan covering June's housing expenses and, more important, to persuade her to reconsider her hasty decision.

No sooner had Stan decided on a course of action when June appeared in his doorway. She had done some thinking over the weekend after talking with another GI project engineer, a "temporary" employee hired only for the duration of his project. It seemed that "temporary" employees earned about twenty percent more than comparable permanent employees at GI, although they received considerably fewer benefits (such as retirement and health insurance). June made a proposal to Stan: She would retract her resignation letter if GI would permit her, in effect, to quit and be rehired as a temporary project engineer. Otherwise she planned to leave GI and accept a standing offer she had received from an engineering firm in her home city of San Diego. As Stan listened, he wondered how Harry would handle this situation. To Stan, June's proposal sounded like blackmail.

Case Questions

1. Should June have resigned over the overtime issue?
2. Should GI accept June's proposal of hiring her as a temporary employee?
3. How could the recruiting process for June have been done better?
4. Was the socialization process for June lacking something? What?

NOTES

1. "Microsoft: Bill Gates's Baby is on Top of the World. Can It Stay There?" *Business Week* (24 Feb. 1992): 60–65.
2. See note 1.
3. "Employer Recruitment Practices," *Personnel* (May 1988): 63–65; B. Schneider and N. Schmitt, *Staffing Organizations,* 2d ed. (Glenview, Ill.: Foresman, 1986), J. A. Breaugh, *Recruitment: Science and Practice,* (Boston: PWS-Kent, 1992).
4. S. L. Rynes, "Recruitment, Job Choice, and Post-Hire Consequences: A Call for New Research Directions," *Handbook of Industrial and Organizational Psychology,* eds. M. D. Dunnette and L. M. Hough (Palo Alto, Calif.: Consulting Psychologists Press, Inc., 1991): 399–444; D. Arthur, *Recruiting, Interviewing, Selecting and Orienting New Employees,* 2d ed. (New York: AMACOM, 1991); S. E. Jackson, J. F. Brett, V. I. Sessa, D. M. Cooper, J. A. Julin, and K. Peyronnin, "Some Differences Make a Difference: Individual Dissimilarity and Group Heterogeneity as Correlates of Recruitment, Promotions, and Turnover," *Journal of Applied Psychology* (1991): 675–89; "Employer Recruitment Practices;" and Schneider and Schmitt.
5. Only promotions and transfers are considered as internal sources for recruitment. Recruiting by demotions is done infrequently. For an informative discussion, see A. Patton, "When Executives Bail Out to Move Up," *Business Week* (13 Sept. 1982): 13, 15, 17, 19.
6. A. Swasy, "Housing Slump Boosts Relocation Costs," *The Wall Street Journal* (21 Aug. 1990): B1.
7. T. Rendero, "Consensus," *Personnel* (Sept.-Oct. 1980): 5.
8. J. R. Garcia, "Job Posting for Professional Staff," *Personnel Journal* (March 1981): 189–92; G. A. Wallrop, "Job Posting for Nonexempt Employees: A Sample Program," *Personnel Journal* (Oct. 1981): 796–98; L. S. Kleiman and K. J. Clark, "An Effective Job Posting System," *Personnel Journal* (Feb. 1984): 20–25.
9. W. Glueck, *Personnel: A Diagnostic Approach* (Plano, Tex.: Business Publications, Inc., 1982).
10. B. Stoops, "Employee Referral Programs: Part I," *Personnel Journal* (Feb. 1981): 98; Stoops, "Part II," *Personnel Journal* (March 1981): 172–73.
11. See note 10.
12. P. J. Decker and E. T. Cornelius, "A Note on Recruiting Sources and Job Survival Rates," *Journal of Applied Psychology* 64 (1974): 463–64; D. P. Schwab, "Recruiting and Organizational Participation," in *Personnel Management,* eds. K. M. Rowland and G. R. Ferris (Boston: Allyn and Bacon, 1982), 103–28.
13. S. L. Rynes and A. E. Barber, "Applicant Attraction Strategies: An Organizational Perspective," *Academy of Management Review* (1990): 286–310; R. E. Herman, *Keeping Good People: Strategies for Solving the Dilemma of the Decade* (New York: McGraw-Hill, 1991); K. Groll Connolly and P. M. Connolly, *Competing for Employees: Proven Marketing Strategies for Hiring and Keeping Exceptional People* (Lexington, Mass.: Lexington Books, 1991); C. L. Cooper and I. T. Robertson, eds., *International Review of Industrial and Organizational Psychology* 1991, vol. 6 (New York: John Wiley & Sons, 1991); S. L. Rynes, R. D. Bretz, Jr., and B. Gerhart, "The Importance of Recruitment in Job Choice: A Different Way of Looking," *Personnel Psychology* 44 (1991): 487–522; J. M. Grant and T. S. Bateman, "An Experimental Test of the Impact of Drug-Testing Programs on Potential Job Applicants' Attitudes and Intentions," *Journal of Applied Psychology* (1990): 127–31; K. R. Murphy, G. C. Thornton III, and D. H. Reynolds, "College Students' Attitudes Toward Employee Drug Testing Programs," *Personnel Psychology* 43 (1990): 615–31; T. J. Hutton, "Increasing the Odds for Successful Searches," *Personnel Journal* (Sept. 1987): 140–52; M. S. Taylor and T. J. Bergmann, "Organizational Recruitment Activities and Applicants' Reactions at Different Stages of the Recruitment Process," *Personnel Psychology* (Summer 1987): 265–85.
14. For a detailed discussion of these errors in recruiting decisions, see S. Rubenfeld and M. Crino, "Are Employment Agencies Jeopardizing Your Selection Process?" *Personnel* (Sept.-Oct. 1981): 70–78.
15. B. J. Feder, "Companies Find Rewards in Hiring G. E. Executives," *The New York Times* (9 March 1992): D1, D4.
16. "The Disposable Employee is Becoming a Fact of Corporate Life," *Business Week* (15 Dec. 1986): 52–54.
17. This form of recruiting is not without problems; see N. Jones-Parker and R. H. Perry, eds., *The Executive Search Collaboration: A Guide for Human Resource Professionals and Their Search Firms* (Westport, Conn.: Quorum Books, 1990); B. Lozano, *The Invisible Work Force: Transforming American Business with Outside and Home-based Workers* (New York: The Free Press, 1989); B. Meier, "Some 'Worker Leasing' Programs Defraud Insurers and Employers," *The New York Times* (20 March 1992); 1; D. C. Feldman, "Reconceptualizing the Nature and Consequences of Part-Time Work," *Academy of Management Review* (1990): 103–12; D. R. Dalton and D. J. Mesch, "The Impact of Flexible Scheduling on Employee Attendance and Turnover," *Administrative Science Quarterly* 35 (1990): 370–87.
18. M. A. Camuso, "The Employment Recruiting Trip—6 Stages to Success," *Personnel Journal* (Nov. 1984).

19. J. Bredwell, "The Use of Broadcast Advertising for Recruitment," *Personnel Administrator* (Feb. 1981): 45–49; R. Stoops, "Radio Recruitment Advertising, Part II," *Personnel Journal* (July 1981): 532; "Affirmative Action in the 1980's: What Can We Expect?" *Management Review* (May 1981): 4–5; R. Stoops, "Television Advertising," *Personnel Journal* (Nov. 1981): 838; R. Stoops, "Reader Survey Supports Market Approach to Recruitment," *Personnel Journal* (March 1984): 22–24.
20. R. Stoops, "Recruitment Ads that Get Results," *Personnel Journal* (April 1984): 24–26; R. Siedlecki, "Creating a Direct Mail Recruitment Program," *Personnel Journal* (April 1983): 304–307; B. S. Hodes, "Planning for Recruitment Advertising: Part I," *Personnel Journal* (May 1983): 380–84; and J. P. Bucalo, "Good Advertising Can Be More Effective than Other Tools," *Personnel Administrator* (Nov. 1983): 73–78.
21. *The Wall Street Journal* (8 Feb. 1983): 35. Reprinted by permission of *The Wall Street Journal*. Copyright Dow Jones & Company, Inc., 1983. All rights reserved.
22. D. M. Schweiger, J. M. Ivancevich, and F. R. Power, "Executive Actions for Managing Human Resources Before and After Acquisitions," *Academy of Management Executive* (May 1987): 127–38.
23. Information for the story about McDonald's came from Joel Dreyfuss, "Get Ready for the New Work Force," *Fortune* (22 April 1990): 165–81; Resener, Debes, Lloyd, and R. Turner, "From Singapore to Sao Paulo, A Network of True Believers," *Business Week* (13 Oct. 1986): 80–81; R. J. Vandenberg and V. Scarpello, "The Matching Model: An Examination of the Processes Underlying Realistic Job Previews," *Journal of Applied Psychology* 75, no. 1: 60–67; S. Rynes and B. Gerhart, "Interviewer Assessments of Applicant 'Fit': An Exploratory Investigation," *Personnel Psychology* 43 (1990): 13–35; J. P. Wanous, "Installing A Realistic Job Preview: Ten Tough Choices," *Personnel Psychology* 42 (1989): 117–34; J. Powell Kirnan, J. A. Farley, and K. F. Geisinger, "The Relationship Between Recruiting Source, Applicant Quality, and Hire Performance: An Analysis by Sex, Ethnicity, and Age," *Personnel Psychology* 42 (1989): 293–308; R. A. Dean and J. P. Wanous, "Effects of Realistic Job Previews on Hiring Bank Tellers," *Journal of Applied Psychology* (Feb. 1984): 61–68; B. M. Meglino and A. S. DeNisi, "Realistic Job Previews: Some Thoughts on Their More Effective Use in Managing the Flow of Human Resources," *Human Resource Planning* 10, no. 3 (1987): 157–67; and B. M. Meglino, A. S. DeNisi, S. A. Youngblood, and K. J. Williams, "Effects of Realistic Job Previews: A Comparison Using an Enhancement and Reduction Preview," *Journal of Applied Psychology* (May 1988): 259–66.
24. C. Rosenfield, "Job Seeking Methods Used by American Workers," *Monthly Labor Review* (Aug. 1975): 39–42; D. P. Schwab, "Organizational Recruiting and the Decision to Participate," in *Personnel Management,* eds. K. M. Rowland and G. R. Ferris (Boston: Allyn & Bacon, 1982): D. Schwab, S. L. Rynes, and R. J. Aldag, "Theories and Research in Job Search and Choice," in *Research in Personnel and Human Resource Management* (Greenwich, Conn.: JAI Press, 1987), 136–37; M. S. Taylor and D. W. Schmidt, "A Process-Oriented Investigation of Recruitment Source Effectiveness," *Personnel Psychology* 36 (1983): 343–54.
25. P. Burgess and J. Kingston, "UI Benefit Effect on Compensated Unemployment," *Industrial and Labor Relations Review* 20 (1981): 258–70; H. J. Holzer, "Job Search by Employed and Unemployed Youth," *Industrial and Labor Relations Review* 40 (1987): 600–601.
26. R. Kanfer and C. L. Hulin, "Individual Differences in Successful Job Search Following Lay-Off," *Personnel Psychology* 63 (1985): 835–47.
27. N. H. Nazrin, T. Flores, and S. J. Kaplan, "Job-Finding Club: A Group-Assisted Program for Obtaining Employment," *Behavior Research Therapy* 13 (1975): 17–27; J. J. Zandy and L. F. James, "A Review of Research on Job Placement," *Rehabilitation Counseling Bulletin* 30 (1977): 451–61.
28. J. O. Crites, *Vocational Psychology* (New York: McGraw-Hill, 1969); J. P. Wanous, *Organizational Entry: Recruitment, Selection, and Socialization of Newcomers* (Reading, Mass.: Addison-Wesley, 1980); K. G. Wheeler and T. M. Mahoney, "The Expectancy Model in the Analysis of Occupational Preference and Occupational Choice," *Journal of Vocational Behavior* 19 (1981): 113–22.
29. Schwab, Rynes, and Aldag, 129–66.
30. G. T. Milkovich and J. Newman, *Compensation* (Plano, Tex.: BPI, 1984); Schwab, Rynes and Aldag, 129–66.
31. C. E. Jergenson, "Job Preference: What Makes a Job Good or Bad?" *Journal of Applied Psychology* 63 (1978): 267–76; B. Major and E. Konar, "An Investigation of Sex Differences in Pay in Higher Education and Their Possible Cause," *Academy of Management Journal* 4 (1986): 777–92; Schwab, Rynes and Aldag, 129–66.
32. Jergenson; Schwab, Rynes, and Aldag; and S. L. Rynes, H. Heneman III, and D. P. Schwab, "Individual Reactions to Organizational Recruiting: A Review," *Personnel Psychology* 33 (1980): 529–42.
33. R. D. Arvey and J. G. Campion, "The Employment Interview: A Summary and Review of the Recent Literature," *Personnel Psychology* 35 (1982): 281–322; J. A. Breaugh, "Realistic Job Previews: A Critical Appraisal and Future Research Directions," *Academy of Management Review* (Oct. 1983): 612–23; Dean and Wanous; M. D. Hakel, "Employment Interviewing," in *Personnel Management,* eds. K. M. Rowland and G. R. Ferris (Boston: Allyn & Bacon, 1982), 153–54; Meglino and DeNisi; B. M. Meglino, A. S. DeNisi, S. A. Youngblood, and K. J. Williams; G. N. Powell, "Effects of Job Attributes and Recruiting Practices on Applicant Decision: A Comparison," *Personnel Psychology* (Winter 1984): 721–32; S. L. Rynes and H. E. Miller, "Recruiter and Job Influences on Candidates for Employment," *Journal of Applied Psychology* (Feb. 1983): 147–56.
34. Meglino and DeNisi. See also S. M. Colarelli, "Methods of Communications and Mediating Processes in Realistic Job Previews," *Journal of Applied Psychology* (1984): 633–42.
35. *The Wall Street Journal* (11 Dec. 1989): B1. See also J. J. Laabs, "The Global Talent Search," *Personnel Journal* (Aug. 1991): 38–44.
36. A. Halcrow, "Voice of HR Experience," *Personnel Journal* (May 1989): 38.

37. From D. Kirkpatrick, "Is Your Career on Track?" *Fortune* (2 Jul. 1990): 38–48; E. Ehrlich, "The Mommy Track," *Business Week* (20 March 1990): 126–34.
38. W. A. Campione, "The Married Woman's Retirement Decision: A Methodological Comparison," *Journal of Gerontology* (1987): 381–86; B. Rosen and T. H. Jerdee, *Older Workers: New Roles for Valued Resources* (Homewood, Ill.: Dow Jones-Irwin, 1985).
39. N. J. Beutell, "Managing the Older Worker," *Personnel Administrator* (Aug. 1983): 31–40; N. J. Beutell and O. C. Brenner, "Employee Retirement Decisions," *Personnel Review* (1987): 31–33; M. Cahill and P. R. Salomone, "Career Counseling and Worklife Extension: Integrating the Older Worker into the Labor Force," *The Career Development Quarterly* (1987): 188–96.
40. N. J. Beutell and J. H. Greenhaus, "Balancing Acts: Work-Family Conflict and the Dual Career Couple," in L. Moore, *Not as Far as You Think: The Realitites of Working Women* (Lexington, Mass.: Lexington Books, 1986); M. R. Frone and R. W. Rice, "Work-Family Conflict: The Effect of Job and Family Involvement," *Journal of Occupational Behavior* (1987): 45–53.
41. "Relocating Dual Career Couples," *Bulletin to Management* (4 Oct. 1990): 320. Also see "Relocating Two-Earner Couples," The Press Conference Board, 845 Third Avenue, New York, NY 10022; M. Moravec and B. McKee, "Designing Dual-Career Paths and Compensation," *Personnel* (Aug. 1990): 4–9; C. Trost, "How One Bank is Handling a 'Two Track' Career Plan," *The Wall Street Journal* (13 March 1989): B1, B8; Z. B. Leibowitz, B. H. Feldman, and S. H. Mosley, "Career Development Works Overtime at Corning, Inc.," *Personnel* (April 1990): 38–46; O. C. Brenner, "Career Repotters: To Know Them Could be to Keep Them," *Personnel* (Nov. 1988): 55–59; J. R. Bratkovich, B. Steele, and T. Rollins, "Develop New Career Management Strategies," *Personnel Journal* (Sept. 1990): 98–107.
42. "Relocating Dual Career Couples," 320.
43. M. Goss, "The Thirty-Hour Work Week," *Management Review* (July 1985): 40–42; S. Zedeck, S. E. Jackson, and E. Summers, "Shiftwork Schedules and Their Relationship to Health, Adaptation, Satisfaction, and Turnover Intention," *Academy of Management Journal* (June 1983): 297–310; S. E. Jackson, S. Zedeck, and E. Summers, "Family Life Disruptions: Impact of Job-Induced Functional and Emotional Interference," *Academy of Management Journal* (Sept. 1985): 574–86.
44. S. J. Mahlin, "Peak-Time Pay for Part-Time Work," *Personnel Journal* (Nov. 1984): 60–65; S. R. Sacco, "Are In-House Temporaries Really an Option?" *Personnel Administrator* (May 1985): 20–24.
45. D. Kroll, "Telecommunicating: A Revealing Peek Inside Some of the Industry's First Electronic Cottages," *Management Review* (Nov. 1984): 18–23.
46. D. Q. Mills, *The New Competitors* (New York: The Free Press, 1985, 69–70).
47. J. Van Ahn, "The Voice of Experience," *Personnel* (Jan. 1991): 17; J. P. Meyer, S. V. Paunonen, I. R. Gellatly, R. D. Goffin, and D. N. Jackson, "Organizational Commitment and Job Performance: It's the Nature of the Commitment that Counts," *Journal of Applied Psychology* (1989): 152–56; G. H. Ironson, P. C. Smith, M. T. Brannick, W. M. Gibson, and K. B. Paul, "Construction of a Job in General Scale: A Comparison of Global, Composite, and Specific Measures," *Journal of Applied Psychology* (1989): 193–200; J. E. Mathieu, "A Cross-Level Nonrecursive Model of the Antecedents of Organizational Commitment and Satisfaction," *Journal of Applied Psychology* (1991): 607–18; M. Tait, M. Youtz Padgett, and T. T. Baldwin, "Job and Life Satisfaction: A Reevaluation of the Strength of the Relationship and Gender Effects as a Function of the Date of the Study," *Journal of Applied Psychology* (1989): 502–507; R. Pascale, "Fitting New Employees into the Company Culture," *Fortune* (28 May 1984): 28–40.
48. Bureau of National Affairs, "Orientation Goals: Better Learning, Reduced Turnover," *Bulletin to Management* (9 May 1985): 1–2.
49. See note 24.
50. P. Popovich and J. Wanous, "The Realistic Job Preview as a Persuasive Communication," *Academy of Management Review* 7 (1982): 570–78; M. R. Louis, "Managing Career Transitions: A Missing Link in Career Development," *Organizational Dynamics* (Spring 1982): 68–78.
51. D. Berlew and D. T. Hall, "The Socialization of Managers: Effects of Expectations on Performance," *Administrative Science Quarterly* (Sept. 1966): 297–323.
52. J. S. Livingston, "Pygmalion in Management," *Harvard Business Review* (July-Aug. 1969): 81–89.
53. L. Copeland, "Valuing Diversity, Part 2: Pioneers and Champions of Change," *Personnel* (July 1988): 48–49.
54. See note 53.
55. See note 53.
56. See note 53.
57. See note 53.
58. J. W. Boudreau, "Utility Analysis for Decisions in Human Resource Management," *Handbook of Industrial and Organizational Psychology,* 2d ed., eds. M. D. Dunnettee and L. M. Hough (Palo Alto, Calif.: Consulting Psychologists Press, Inc., 1991): 621–746; J. W. Boudreau and S. L. Rynes, "Role of Recruitment in Staffing Utility Analysis," *Journal of Applied Psychology* (May 1985): 354–66; D. F. Caldwell and W. A. Spivey, "The Relationship Between Recruiting Source and Employee Success: An Analysis by Race," *Personnel Psychology* (Spring 1983): 67–72; D. Dennis, "Are Recruitment Efforts Designed to Fail?" *Personnel Journal* (Sept. 1984): 60–67; P. Farish, "Cost Per Hire," *Personnel Administrator* (Jan. 1985): 16; D. A. Levinson, "Needed: Revamped Recruiting Services," *Personnel* (July 1988): 50–52; M. London and S. A. Stumpf, "Effects of Candidate Characteristics on Management Promotion Decisions: An Experimental Study," *Personnel Psychology* (Summer 1983): 241–60; and Taylor and Schmidt.
59. J. S. Lord, "Contract Recruiting: Coming of Age," *Personnel Administrator* (Nov. 1987): 49–53.
60. R. Koenig, "Toyota Takes Pains and Time Filling Jobs at Its Kentucky Plant," *The Wall Street Journal* (1 Dec. 1987): 1.
61. M. J. Aamodt and D. L. Peggans, "Rejecting Applicants with Tact," *Personnel Administrator* (April 1988): 58–60; B. Adair and D. Pollen, "No! No! A Thousand Times No!" *The Washington Post* (25 Sept. 1985): 5.

62. V. Puick, "White Collar Human Resource Management in Large Japanese Manufacturing Firms," *Human Resource Management* 20, no. 2; 264; "Learning from Japan," *Business Week* (27 Jan. 1992): 52–60.

63. Puick.

64. I. Peritz, "Montreal Firm Found Cheap Labor, Lax Rules in Mexico," *The Gazette* (16 March 1992): A1, A7.

CHAPTER 6

Selection and Placement

I am the ultimate believer in people first, strategies second. To me, strategy starts with the person you hire.

—Jack Welch, CEO General Electric[1]

General Electric Company's dramatic changes during the 1980s and early 1990s reflect a company adjusting to an increasingly competitive environment in innovative and successful ways. The firm's management of human resources during the period offers an example of how a firm can successfully mesh its human resource policies with the needs and strategy of the business.

During the 1970s, GE's highly regarded "financial wizard," Chief Executive Officer Reginald H. Jones, built the firm into one of the strongest financial performers in the U.S. He also led a diversification effort that put the company into the products of about one hundred different businesses, ranging from appliances and light bulbs to coal mines, TV sets, and computer chips. Company earnings per share rose an average of 4.9 percent yearly. In the process of building a profitable and diverse conglomerate, however, Jones also built a massive organization that became mired in bureaucracy. Reporting requirements, for example, were legendary. One manager finally had to stop computers from generating seven daily reports on sales of hundreds of thousands of products; the paper from just one of the reports stood twelve feet high!

In 1981, at age 45, Jack Welch assumed the post of GE's chief executive officer. In picking Welch as his successor, Jones supported Welch's objectives of making the $27-billion GE a "world class competitor," able to thrive in an increasingly global marketplace. In taking the helm of a strong yet somewhat complacent firm, one of Welch's key challenges was to "instill in ... managers a sense of urgency when there is no emergency."[2] Welch's first goal was to prepare the company to meet the challenges of the 1980s and 1990s. Welch saw the world marketplace as a tough and increasingly competitive playing field that would eventually be dominated by a few large firms. To compete in such a world, Welch believed GE had to identify and operate only in markets in which it could be the first or second player worldwide. Such a move led to major restructuring: GE exited all but about fourteen businesses, reducing its labor force by 25 percent; during the 1980s, about 100,000 employees left GE through layoff, attrition, or divestiture of businesses.

In addition to the external competitive forces driving change, GE's increasingly diverse work force also poses a challenge. Like other American firms, GE faces a situation in which employees with "different career objectives, different family aspirations, [and] different financial goals" operate in one firm. Welch wants them to "share directly in [GE's] vision, the information, the decision-making process, and the rewards."[3] In practical terms, this means Welch and his 200 highest ranking managers must build a commitment to the changes resulting from restructuring among the other 99 percent of the company's 300,000 employees.

Welch has viewed effective human resource management as part of the solution to make GE well-positioned for the next century. He argues that the company needs new ways of doing business, and that includes human resource management. In planning and staffing business units for the future, for example, Welch says the company must seek managers who are "business leaders," able to "create a vision, articulate the vision, passionately own the vision, and ... relentlessly drive it to completion."[4] He also considers it extremely important for business leaders to be open and willing to change. Welch considers the process of identifying and preparing future leaders to be so important that he regularly *reviews files of selected employees—from the time they join the firm—to get a sense of their potential for future positions.*

This story about General Electric highlights many aspects of selection that will be discussed in this chapter, including (1) how to collect information on job applicants, (2) how to make selection and placement decisions, (3) how to use selection to improve the profitability of the company, and (4) how to tie selection into the basic philosophy of a company. Other aspects of selection and placement (to be described in chapter 14) include how to validate tests used in making selection decisions and how to make the entire set of selection and placement procedures more useful. These concerns, along with the extensive legal environment of selection decisions, are the essence of selection and placement.

SELECTION AND PLACEMENT

Selection is the process of gathering legally defensible information about job applicants in order to determine who should be hired for long- or short-term positions. **Placement** is concerned with matching individual skills, knowledge, abilities, preferences, interests, and personality to the job. Effective selection and placement involve finding the match between organizational needs for qualified individuals and individual needs for jobs in which they are interested.[5]

Line managers play an important role in the selection and placement activity. They help identify the need for staffing through the organization's human resource planning activity, assist with job analysis, and evaluate employee performance.

The personnel and human resource department, however, should be responsible for gathering information and should arrange interviews between job applicants and managers for several reasons:

- Applicants have to go to only one place to apply for a job and have a better chance of being considered for a greater variety of jobs.
- Outside sources of applicants can clear employment issues through one central location.
- Operating managers can concentrate on their operating responsibilities—especially helpful during peak hiring periods.
- Hiring is done by specialists trained in staffing techniques so selection is often better.
- Costs may be cut because duplication of effort is avoided.
- With increased government regulation of selection, it is important that people who know about these rules handle a major part of the hiring process.

PURPOSES AND IMPORTANCE OF SELECTION AND PLACEMENT

Selection and placement procedures provide the essence of an organization—its human resources. Selecting employees who are likely to perform well may result in substantial productivity improvements and cost savings.

Selection and placement are critical to any organization. Serving the organization's needs and providing effective selection and placement mean attaining several purposes, including

- To contribute to the organization's bottom line through efficient and effective production.
- To ensure that an organization's financial investment in employees pays off. For example, hiring an employee with a starting salary of $25,000, annual cost of living adjustments (COLAs) of only 1.5 percent, and no benefits results in an investment of $128,000 in that employee in five years and $578,092 in twenty years.
- To evaluate, hire, and place job applicants in the best interests of both the organization and the individual.
- To minimize multi-million dollar verdicts and settlements in litigation brought by victims of criminal, violent, or negligent acts perpetrated by employees who should not have been hired or kept in their jobs.[d]
- To enable organizations to fulfill their strategies, as suggested by the Jack Welch opening quotation.
- To help fulfill hiring goals and timetables specified in affirmative action programs.

To serve these purposes effectively, selection and placement must be congruent with the internal environment and integrated with other personnel and human resource activities (see exhibit 6.1).

CONSIDERATIONS IN CHOOSING SELECTION TECHNIQUES

In choosing the right selection devices to use, several technical factors need to be considered, including the choice of predictors and criterion scores and the relative usefulness of different devices.

Predictors

Selection decisions in organizations are generally made on the basis of job applicant's predictor scores. These scores predict how well applicants, if hired, will perform. Uses and combinations of these scores are discussed later in this chapter.

Selection decisions are often made in steps. Exhibit 6.2 shows a typical example of the steps and the predictors used in the selection process. While a wealth of selection techniques (background information, paper-and-pencil tests, work simulations, physical tests, interviews) can be used to predict job performance, the usefulness of these depends on their reliability and validity.

Reliability. The reliability of a measurement device is the degree to which it produces dependable or consistent results. Unreliable measurements produce one set of results at one time and a different set of results at another. When a selection device yields equivalent results time after time, it is considered reliable.

Exhibit 6.1
Relationships and Aspects of Selection and Placement

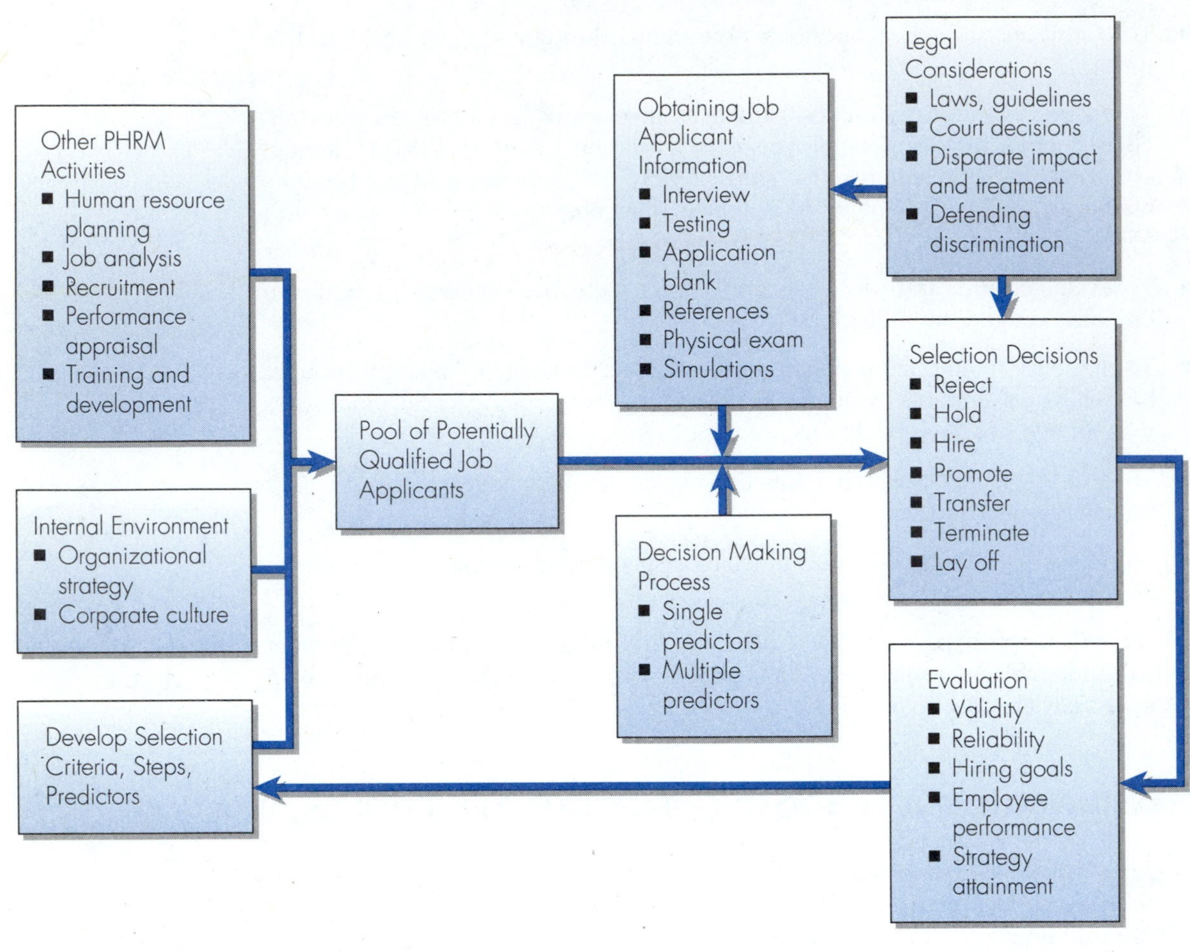

For example, tests of physical attributions (height, weight, hearing) tend to be more reliable than tests of personality characteristics (neuroticism, flexible thinking, emotional stability).

Two types of reliability are relevant to selection. Consider a cognitive ability test administered to a hundred job applicants. It would be reliable if you retested these job applicants and received similar results the second time. This form of reliability is called **test-retest reliability. Interrater reliability** focuses on the consistency of ratings by different individuals. For example, unstructured interviews tend to be unreliable, with multiple interviewers perceiving the same applicant dissimilarly.[7]

Validity. The term validity refers to how well a measure actually assesses an attribute. The validity of a measure is not absolute; rather, it is relative to the situation in which the selection device is being used. For example, a test of

Exhibit 6.2
Possible Steps in the Selection Process

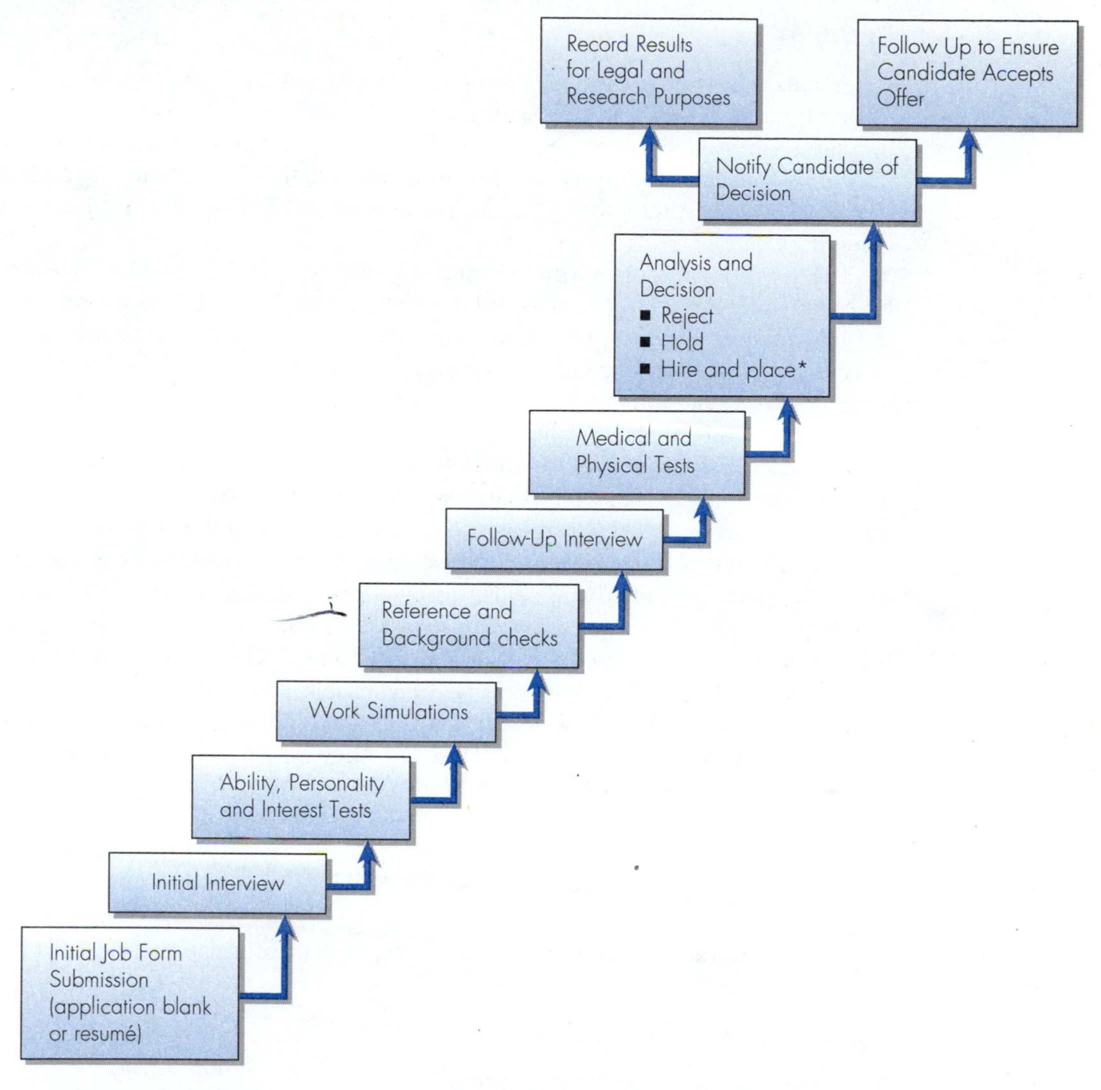

*Note that these decisions could be made in previous steps in the selection process; however, they would be based on less information.

aggression may be a valid predictor of police performance, but it may be useless in predicting job success for machinists. Chapter 14 discusses in more depth the different approaches to validating selection devices.

Mathematically, validity refers to the correlation between the predictor score (selection device) and a criterion (job performance, job rating, number of absences, tardiness, or worker compensation claims). Recall from basic statistics that a correlation coefficient can range from -1.00 to 1.00. The closer the correlation coefficient is to the absolute value of 1.00, the more valid the selection device. For example, work simulation tests have been shown to have average validity coefficients up to .47. This is substantially higher than the average validity coefficients of .14 for interview.[8]

Criteria

Criteria describe the critical elements of job performance. For example, in the corporate loan assistant's job, having a good record of accurately documenting decisions is probably more critical than keeping the office desks clean and organized. Establishing the exact criteria and their relative importance is critical to developing valid predictors and having a valid performance appraisal system (see chapter 7).

The performance criteria help determine the type of information that should be obtained from job applicants and, to some extent, the method used to gather the information. For example, if absenteeism is an appropriate criterion, a check of references on employment history may be used. If quantity of performance is identified as a criterion, a written test measuring an applicant's skills, knowledge, and abilities may be used.[9]

As described in chapter 4, the job analysis is at the base of determining appropriate, relevant, and important criteria. Compare the relationship between the job dimensions of the corporate loan assistant in exhibit 4.8 and the skills, knowledge, and abilities necessary to perform the job duties in exhibit 6.3. The job incumbents identified the skills, knowledge, and abilities needed to do the job and the job dimensions as discussed in chapter 4. The dimensions were identified as the essence of the job—the job criteria. The method by which the skills, knowledge, and abilities are to be measured is indicated in exhibit 6.3. Note that several methods are used for some knowledge and skills (for example, bank services). When the methods are used, they become the predictors of how well the applicant will preform the job criteria.

TYPES OF JOB APPLICANT INFORMATION

Organizations can gather selection and placement information from job applicants related to the following categories:

- Skills, knowledge, and abilities
- Personality, interests, and preferences
- Other characteristics

Skills, Knowledge, and Abilities

Gathering and using information on the individual are generally used to match an individual's skills, knowledge, and abilities with the job demands. This match is subject to legal constraints and traditionally has been of major interest to organizations because it is aimed at predicting how well the individual is likely to perform on the job.

Information related to skills, knowledge, and abilities can be used to demonstrate job-relatedness. However, any skills, knowledge, and abilities that can be learned in fewer than eight hours or taught on the job should not be measured

Exhibit 6.3
Selection Plan Matrix

For: Corporate Loan Assistant Date: ____________

Practices, Procedures, and Tests Used in Selection

1 2 3 4 5 6 7 8 9 10 11 12 13

Coding A	**B**	**Short Title**	**R = Rank**		**SAF**					**DAI**	**BI/ REF**		**PAF**
		Knowledge/Skills											
MQ		1. Communication	R		X					X	X		X
MQ		2. Math			X					X	X		X
MQ		3. Writing			X					X	X		X
MQ		4. Reading			X					X	X		X
MQ		5. Researching			X					X	X		X
MQ		6. Organizing	R		X					X	X		X
MQ		7. Listening	R		X					X	X		X
MQ		8. Social skills			X					X	X		X
MT		9. Sales	R		X					X	X		X
MQ		10. Interpret	R		X					X	X		X
WT		11. Bank policy											X
MT		12. Bank services	R		X					X	X		X
WT		13. Computer											X
WT		14. Credit report											X

MQ = Minimum Qualification. *MT* = May be Trained or acquired on the job (desirable). Preference may be given to those who possess this knowledge/skill. When used on a physical characteristic, MT means a reasonable accommodation can be made. WT = Will be Trained or acquired on the job. Not evaluated in the selection process. *WT* = Will be Trained or acquired on the job because it can be learned in a brief orientation, i.e., 8 hours or less. Not evaluated in the selection process. *MQ/MT* = Lower level is Minimum Qualification; higher level May be Trained or acquired on the job (desirable). *MQ/WT* = Lower level is minimum Qualification; higher level Will be Trained or acquired on the job. WT part is not measured in the selection process. *MT/WT* = Lower level May be Trained or acquired on the job; higher level Will be Trained or acquired on the job. WT part is not measured in the selection process. *R* = Rank. Applicants may be ranked by how much they possess. This is differentiating among those who possess more and who will probably perform the duties better. Not all the differentiating knowledge, skills, physical characteristics, and "other characteristics" are ranked. *SAF* = Supplemental Application Form. *WKT* = Written Knowledge Test. *ST* = Skills Test. *PCD* = Physical Capability Demonstration. *SOI* = Structured Oral Interview. *DAI* = Departmental Appointment Interview. *BI/REF* = Background Investigation/Reference Check. *ME* = Medical Examination. *PAF* = Performance Appraisal Form.

SOURCE: Biddle & Associates, Inc. Used with permission.

or used in making selection decisions. Furthermore, if job applicants need only a specified minimum level of a skill, knowledge, or ability, then the only information that should be obtained is whether or not the applicants meet the minimum levels. If having a higher level of skill, knowledge, or ability is likely to result in better performance, then information about a person's level above minimum should be obtained so that applicants can be ranked.

When making decisions in the area of firing, demotion, layoff (where a bona fide seniority system does not exist), or discipline, measuring the employees' task or job performance rather than their skills, knowledge, and abilities is appropriate. If physical abilities are being measured, consideration must be made for job accommodation. If reasonable accommodation cannot be made for a disability that interferes with performing the essential duties of the job, the applicant can be rejected.

Personality, Interests, and Preferences

Information about an individual's personality, interests, and preferences should also be gathered. If used appropriately in combination with information about job rewards and characteristics of the firm—such as culture and strategy—this information can increase employee satisfaction and reduce absenteeism and voluntary turnover. It may also improve the quality of employee performance by increasing job involvement and motivation.[10]

A firm may rely on the levels of an applicant's skills, knowledge, and abilities in making the selection decision: however, information about an applicant's personality, interests, and preferences can be useful in placing the individual in a particular part or section of the organization as suggested in the Focus on Research feature. Later, as an individual climbs the corporate ladder, personality, interests, and preferences can be used for placement as well as selection.

Other Characteristics

Employers can also gather information about other characteristics, such as terms and conditions of employment. These include licenses required by law; willingness to travel or work split shifts, weekends, or under adverse conditions such as confined facilities and high noise levels; uniform requirements; business-related grooming codes; tools required on the job and not provided by the employer; required training to be taken on the job; and driver's licenses. These characteristics may be required as minimum qualifications for a job. Very rarely are they used to rank applicants. Applicants either possess them or they do not. Although these characteristics offer no indication as to how candidates will do on the job, applicants who are unwilling to comply with them can be disqualified from consideration.

TECHNIQUES FOR OBTAINING JOB APPLICANT INFORMATION

A variety of selection techniques are available for obtaining applicant information. As exhibit 6.4 shows, each selection technique varies in terms of costs, the number of firms using them, and their usefulness as predictors.[11]

Application Blanks and Background Information

Application blank. Premised on the assumption that past behavior is a good predictor of future performance, the application blank is a form seeking information about the applicant's background and present status. Usually this information is used as an initial or preemployment screen to decide if the candidate meets the minimum job requirements. While not prohibited per se, many

FOCUS ON RESEARCH

Born Happy or Good Human Resource Management?

Good employers invest time and energy trying to select employees who fit the culture of their organization, and they try to place employees in jobs that match their skills and interests. They invest in training supervisors how to motivate their subordinates and how to socialize new workers to the values of the company. The assumption is that good management helps create a happy and productive workforce. Yet, studies that have followed employees over long periods of time suggest that job satisfaction is pretty stable—when employees change jobs and even when they change occupations, they report similar levels of satisfaction. Could it be that genetic factors account for this stability? A study of 34 pairs of identical twins who had been separated within a year after birth and then raised apart suggests the answer may be yes.

To investigate how much influence genetics have on the attitudes, personalities, and behaviors of people, psychologists often study identical (monozygotic) twins, who have the same genetic structure. By studying identical twins raised apart, researchers can estimate the relative influence of genetics versus the environment. The twins in this study, who had eventually been reunited as adults, completed questionnaires that assessed their job histories and job satisfaction. Using a complex statistical analysis, the researchers were able to estimate the magnitude of genetic influences on job experiences.

The results revealed that about 30% of the variation in people's job satisfaction scores was due to genetic effects. Consistent with what the researchers expected to find, genetics influenced job satisfaction with intrinsic aspects of the work (such as challenge), but genetics did not impact job satisfaction with extrinsic aspects of work (such as pay). One explanation for the effects of genetics on job satisfaction is that twins, who could be expected to have similar physical and mental abilities, would be likely to work in similar types of jobs. This possibility was supported by the results, which showed that genetics influenced the complexity, motor skills, and physical demands of the jobs people were employed in. However, the similarity of the jobs held by twins was not the sole reason for twins reporting similar levels of job satisfaction. Some influence of genetics was found for job satisfaction even after the similarity of the twins' jobs had been taken into account. Furthermore, a subsequent study (by Keller and associates) found that genetics may also partly determine people's work values, including how much they value achievement, autonomy and safety.

What are the implications of this research? One implication is that there may be limits on the ability of companies to enhance intrinsic job satisfaction. Another implication is that a person's current satisfaction and work values help predict their future satisfaction and work values. If this is the case, then employers might ensure they have a satisfied workforce by selecting applicants who express satisfaction with their previous employer. How do *you* think these results should be used by employers?

SOURCE: Based on R. D. Arvey, T. J. Bouchard, Jr., N. L. Segal, and L. M. Abraham, "Job Satisfaction: Environmental and Genetic Components," *Journal of Applied Psychology* 74 (1989), 187–92. See also: L. M. Keller, R. D. Arvey, T. J. Bouchard, Jr., N. L. Segal, and R. V. Dawes, "Work Values: Genetic and Environmental Influences," *Journal of Applied Psychology* 77 (1992), 79–88.

traditional questions are now considered "red flags" of discrimination and should be avoided because of their *potential* for producing adverse impacts.[12]

- *Demographic information.* Questions related to race should be strictly avoided. Because characteristics related to age, sex, religion, and national origin are difficult to prove as BFOQs, questions regarding them should also be avoided. Proof of age and citizenship can be required after hiring.
- *Commitments.* Questions about marital status, dependents, spouse's job, and child-care arrangements need to be asked of *both* men and women and given

Exhibit 6.4
Comparison of Costs and Benefits of Various Common Selection Devices

Type of Test	Cost/Applicant	% of Firms Using Device	Validity
Cognitive ability test	$5.00–$100.00	42	.53
Situational interview	25.00–50.00	5–20	.54
Work sample test	50.00–500.00	75	.44
Assessment center	50.00–2000.00	6	.44
Biodata	5.00–25.00	11	.37
Background check	100.00–500.00	8–15	.26
Experience rating	5.00–50.00	(no data)	.18
Standard interview	25.00–50.00	70	.07
Interest inventory	25.00–50.00	5	.10
Education rating	5.00–50.00	(no data)	.10
Personality test	1.00–100.00	5	.10–.25
Handwriting analysis	50.00–250.00	5	.00
Polygraph test	25.00–50.00	6	.00
Drug screening	35.00–90.00	25	(varied estimates)
Alcohol screening	10.00–35.00	13	(varied estimates)
Genetic screening	35.00–450.00	1	(varied estimates)

SOURCE: Bureau of National Affairs, "Employee Selection Procedures," ASPA–BNA Survey No. 45 (5 May 1983); J. E. Hunter and R. F. Hunter, "Validity and Utility of Alternative Predictors of Job Performance," *Psychological Bulletin* 96, no. 1 (1984): 93; T. Jantz, "Initial Comparisons of Patterned Behavior Description Interviews Versus Unstructured Interviews, *Journal of Applied Psychology* 67 (1982): 577–80; J. D. Olian, "New Approaches to Employment Screening: Body Over Mind," in *Readings in Personnel and Human Resource Management,* 3d ed., ed. R. S. Schuler, S. A. Youngblood, and V. L. Huber (St. Paul, Minn.: West, 1988), 206–16.

equivalent weight if they are asked at all. It is acceptable to ask if applicants have any social, family, or economic responsibilities that would prevent them from performing job duties.

- *Arrests and convictions.* Inquiries about arrest records are not permissible under *any* conditions because minorities are often arrested (not necessarily convicted) more frequently than whites. An employer may ask about convictions.
- *Disabilities.* Disabilities may be considered after the job offer is made. Follow closely the guidelines contained in the Americans with Disabilities Act.
- *Physical requirements.* Height and weight measurements are acceptable for a *few* jobs. Care should be taken to ensure that physical requirements (such as height and weight) are valid because they tend to discriminate against Hispanics, Asians, and women.
- *Affiliations.* Avoid catchall questions about organization affiliations (e.g., country clubs, fraternal orders, lodges). However, it is acceptable to ask about *professional* memberships that relate to specific jobs.

The accuracy of applicant-generated information is also a concern. Verified Credentials, Inc., reports that almost thirty percent of the resumés it checks contain false information. Distortions vary from a wrong starting date for a prior job to inflated college grades to actual lies involving degrees, types of jobs, and former employers. The most common distortions relate to length of employment and previous salary.[13]

Biographical information blank. In addition to the application blank, or even as a substitute for it, employers may administer a biographical information blank (BIB). A BIB generally requests *more* information from the applicant than does an application blank. For example, in addition to requesting information about name, present address, references, skills, and type of education, the BIB may request the applicant to indicate a degree of preference for such things as working split shifts, being transfered, working on weekends, or working alone. Exactly which items are asked should be based on the nature of the job. If the job does require split-shift work, a BIB item that indicates any preference for split shifts may be a good predictor of turnover.[14]

Biodata tests appear to be good predictors of job success (see exhibit 6.5) and generally have less adverse impact on minorities than do many standard tests. Consider the settlement reached in a discrimination suit against the Suffolk County (N.Y.) police department, one of the nation's largest police forces. The police department's unvalidated qualifying examination had an adverse impact on African-Americans, Hispanics, and females. Under the consent decree that settled the suit, the county agreed to offer the chance to take a biodata test to women and minorities who had taken the earlier test.

This new biodata test calls for applicants to answer autobiographical questions on such subjects as academic achievement, work attitudes, physical orientation, and self-perception. According to Frank Erwin, president of Richardson, Bellows, Henry & Co., which developed the selection device, biodata tests reduce by more than half the scoring differences that routinely result between whites and minorities on traditional general aptitude or intelligence tests (*United States v. Suffolk County, 1986*).

Education and experience evaluations. As part of the initial application process, applicants often complete a form that details their educational achievements and work experience. Validity evidence indicates that education requirements are predictive of job tenure (the average correlation of performance is .10). Like education, experience requirements may be useful in selecting individuals for high-level, complex jobs but not for jobs that require short learning periods (the average correlation is .18)

What is questionable is the *extent* of education and experience required for a specific job. In order to narrow down the application pool, some organizations impose inordinately high experience requirements (e.g., five years or more). Similarly, higher levels of education than needed are required for many jobs. These requirements serve as artificial barriers to minority applicants, who generally have less opportunity to acquire education and experience than do whites.[15]

Handwriting analysis. In addition to the completed application blank, an employer may request a special handwriting sample. Handwriting analysis, or graphology, is used by eighty-five percent of all European companies and is catching on in the U.S. An estimated 2,000 to 2,500 U.S. employers use graphology as a selection device.[16]

Despite the testimonials, there is no scientific evidence that graphology can predict job performance. In one controlled study of sales success, applicants provided handwriting samples, and graphologists predicted job success. While there was limited evidence of interrater agreement on observed character traits, there was no relationship between the assessments and three measures of job performances (sales productivity and self- and supervisory performance ratings). Graphology also is costly ($50–$250), considering its poor predictive ability. Therefore, it is not recommended as a selection device.

Reference verification. Because some job applicants falsify their past and current qualifications, employers are stepping up efforts to check references thoroughly. Instead of relying on unstructured reference letters, which are always positive, some organizations are using outside investigators to verify credentials, others are personally contacting prior employers to get reference information firsthand, and still others have structured the reference process to acquire only job-specific information (goals, accomplishments, degree of supervision).

One reason for the increased rigor in reference checking is that reference checks, if done correctly, are quite predictive of performance. Another reason revolves around the recent spate of negligent hiring lawsuits. Consider the following typical case:

> A woman raped by a cable television installer...sued the installer's employers—a cable television franchise and its independent contractor. She claimed that they gave the installer a master key to her apartment, which he used to enter her dwelling on the night of the attack. Because his employers gave him a master key to the apartments, the woman argued that they owed their customers a special duty to ensure that he was not a violent criminal. But they had failed to check his criminal record. The employers settled out of court for $250,000.[17]

Unfortunately, it is getting more difficult to get information because of the potential for defamation of character suits (discussed in chapter 15). Previous employers are becoming "street-smart" and consequently are limiting the type of information they give out about former employees. However, reference checks of an applicant's prior employment record are not an infringement on privacy if the information provided relates specifically to work behavior and to the reasons for leaving a previous job.

Written Tests

Written testing is another important procedure for gathering, transmitting, and assembling information about applicants. The most common types of written tests measure ability (cognitive, mechanical, and psychomotor); personality, interests and preferences; and achievement.

Cognitive ability tests. Ability tests measure the potential of an individual to perform, given the opportunity. Used in the U.S. and Europe since the turn of the century, these devices are useful and valid (see exhibit 6.4). Recent studies further suggest that they are equally valid for African-American and white applicants and that their use can be generalized to different jobs in different situations. Exhibit 6.5 shows sample items for measuring seven types of cognitive abilities.

Exhibit 6.5
Samples of Cognitive Ability and Psychomotor Tests

Verbal Comprehension involves understanding the meaning of words and their relationship to one another. It is measured by such test items as

Which one of the following words means most nearly the same as *dilapidated:*
(1) new (2) injured (3) unresponsive (4) run-down (5) lethargic

Word Fluency involves the ability to name or make words, such as making smaller words from the letters in a large one or playing anagrams. For example,

Using the letters in the word "measurement," write as many three-letter words as you can in the next two minutes.

________ ________ ________
________ ________ ________

Number Aptitude involves speed and accuracy in making simple arithmetic calculations. It is measured by such test items as

Carry out the following calculations:

$$\begin{array}{r} 429 \\ +762 \\ \hline \end{array} \qquad \begin{array}{r} 7983 \\ -6479 \\ \hline \end{array} \qquad 721 \; 3 \; 52 = \_\_\_\_ \qquad 4920 \div 6 = \_\_\_\_$$

Inductive Reasoning focuses on the ability to discover a rule or principle and apply it to the solution of a problem. The following is an example:

What number should come next in the sequence of five numbers?
1 3 6 10 15
(1) 22 (2) 21 (3) 25 (4) 18

Memory relates to having the ability to recall pairs of words or lists of numbers. It is measured by such test items as

You have 30 seconds to memorize the following pairs. When the examiner says stop, turn the page and write the appropriate symbols after each of the letters appearing there.
A @ C # E Δ G ?
B > D * F + H $

Perceptual Speed is concerned with the ability to perceive visual details quickly and accurately. Usually these tests are timed and include such items as

Make a check mark in front of each pair below in which the numbers are identical. Work as fast as you can.
1. 755321 753321
2. 966441 966641
3. 334579................334579

Motor Skill—Aiming involves the ability to respond accurately and rapidly to stimuli. For example,

Place three dots in as many circles as you can in 30 seconds.
O O O O O OO O O

SOURCE: Modified from M. Dunnette, *Personnel Selection and Placement* (Monterey, Calif.: Brooks/Cole Publishing, 1966), 47–49.

Tests have also been developed to measure special abilities. For example sensory tests measure the acuity of a person's senses, such as vision and hearing. These tests may be appropriate for such jobs as wine taster, coffee bean selector, quality control inspector, and piano tuner. Clerical tests focus primarily on perceptual speed. However, specific tests such as the Minnesota Clerical Tests measure these skills in a job-relevant context. Standard Oil has developed a cognitive ability test of management reasoning and judgment, while other firms have developed programmer aptitude tests.[18]

Psychomotor tests. Many jobs involve not only a wide range of cognitive abilities but also psychomotor skills. For example, a bank teller needs the motor skills necessary to operate a computer or a ten-key calculator and the finger dexterity to manipulate currency.

There are a variety of psychomotor abilities, each of which is highly specific and shows little relationship to other psychomotor abilities *or* to cognitive abilities. For example, control precision involves finely controlled muscular adjustments (e.g., moving a lever to a precise setting), whereas finger dexterity entails skillful manipulation of small objects (e.g., assembling nuts and bolts).

Ability tests, then, are useful for selecting applicants in many occupations. However, only some categories of ability tests may be predictive of job performance in a specific position.

Personality tests. Personality refers to the unique blend of characteristics that define an individual and determine his or her pattern of interactions with the environment. While most people believe personality plays an important role in job success or failure, personality tests generally have not been found viable for employee selection. One reason is that personality variables have not been consistently defined. What we have, then, is a diverse group of testing devices, each of which was designed to accomplish a different goal, but all of which are called personality inventories. The various tests are *not* equivalent, however, in their construction, their measurement goals, or their underlying theoretical bases.[19] Consequently, inventories often yield different, incompatible, or even conflicting results.

Another problem is that the wrong types of personality measurements have generally been used for human resource selection. The widely used Minnesota Multiphasic Personality Inventory (MMPI) is designed to identify areas of maladjustment. While an appropriate selection device for high-stress jobs (e.g., police, nuclear power plant employees, air traffic controllers), it is not an appropriate selection device for most jobs because the absence of psychopathology does not guarantee the presence of competence. Consequently, an employee can be well adjusted but hopelessly mediocre in performance.

Finally, in highly structured situations controlled by regulations, rules, and guidelines, an individual's personality is unlikely to have an effect. However, in less structured organizations in which individuality and creativity are encouraged, personality attributes are likely to make the difference between job success and job failure.[20]

While less predictive of job success than cognitive ability tests, carefully developed personality assessments can be inexpensive additions to the selection process for a few jobs. One common multidimensional test of personality that appears useful is the **Ghiselli Self-Description Inventory.** It includes sixty-four pairs of trait adjectives (equal in social desirability to prevent faking).[21] For each pair, a person is asked to choose the most or least descriptive adjective. Responses are then scored across thirteen personality dimensions (e.g., supervisory ability, decisiveness, achievement motivation) that relate to managerial competence. Ghiselli was able to show that successful managers perceive themselves quite differently than do unsuccessful managers on these dimensions. Sample items from the Ghiselli Personality Inventory are as follows:

In each of the pairs of words listed below, check the one you think MOST describes you.

1 _____ capable	2 _____ persevering	3 _____ unaffected
_____ discreet	_____ independent	_____ alert

Interest and preference inventories. While applicants may have the ability to perform in jobs that interest them, interest inventories assess applicants' preferences for different types of work and work situations.[22] Such inventories are useful in matching people to jobs they will enjoy.

Representative items from an interest inventory include the following:

For each set, write an "M" next to the activity you most like and an "L" next to the item you least prefer.

1 _____ go to a concert	2 _____ work in the garden
_____ play tennis	_____ go hiking
_____ read a book	_____ paint a picture

Test batteries. It is often beneficial to administer a battery of tests to applicants. The most widely used is the General Aptitude Test Battery (GATB), which measures cognitive abilities—verbal, numerical, spatial, intelligence, form perceptions, clerical perceptions, motor coordination, finger and manual dexterity—and has been found to be useful in matching individuals to a wide array of jobs. As a result of its widespread use, the GATB attracted attention because of the practice of race-norming.

Because African-Americans tend to score 16% to 20% lower than the average of GATB test takers, and Hispanics score 8% to 10% lower, many state employment agencies have engaged in "race-norming," a practice by which African-Americans' and Hispanics' GATB scores were compared only to others in their ethnic groups. Congress outlawed race-norming as part of the Civil Rights Act of 1991, recently signed into law.[23]

Alternatively, an organization can construct its own test battery. For example, Sears has used tests of ability (American Council on Education Psychological Test), values (Allport-Vernon Study of Values), and interest (Kuder Preference Record) since the 1940s to select managers. Similarly, Standard Oil of New Jersey relies on cognitive ability (Miller Analogies, Nonverbal Reasoning, Management Judgment), personality (MMPI), and an individual background survey. Because batteries are difficult to develop, they are usually designed for organizations under the guidance of industrial psychologists.[24]

Achievement tests. Achievement tests predict an individual's performance on the basis of what he or she knows. Validation is required of any test used by any organization; even so, validated achievement tests may exclude applicants who have not had equal access to the opportunities to acquire the skills. Also, not all achievement tests are actual work samples of the job; some are less job-related than others.

Paper-and-pencil achievement tests tend to be less job-related because they measure facts and principles, not the practical use of them. For example, you could take a paper-and-pencil test measuring your knowledge of tennis and pass with flying colors and yet play very poorly. Such achievement tests continue to be used in many areas because of their widespread applicability. For example, admission to the legal profession is through the bar exam and admission to the medical profession is through medical boards. Paper-and-pencil tests are used in these cases because they are—or are assumed to be—related to performance in the actual job. Job-relatedness is, of course, a necessary legal defense for the use of paper-and-pencil tests (as well as all other tests).

Recognition tests, which are examples of past performance, are often used in advertising and modeling to select applicants. The applicants bring to the job interview portfolios or samples of the work they have done. However, portfolios contain no clues as to the conditions or circumstances under which they were done. Some organizations may also insist on seeing written samples from school work for jobs where written expression may be important.

Work Simulations

Work simulations, often referred to as work sample tests, require applicants to complete verbal or physical activities under structured "testing" conditions. Rather than measure what an individual knows, they assess the individual's ability to do. Still, work sample tests are somewhat artificial because the selection process itself tends to promote anxiety and tension.[25] Exhibit 6.6 shows three sets of work simulation tests.

Because they replicate the actual work, work sample tests are not easy to fake. As a result, they tend to be more valid than almost all other types of selection devices. Additionally, they do not have an adverse impact on minority applicants. Unfortunately, because simulation tests are job specific, they are usually expensive to develop unless large numbers of applicants are to be examined. However, by placing work sample tests at the end of a selection process, the number of applicants tested is smaller and the price lower.

Assessment centers. This selection device evaluates applicants or current employees with regard to how well they might perform in a managerial or higher level position. More than twenty thousand companies now utilize this method and its use grows each year because of its validity in predicting whether job applicants will be successful or unsuccessful.[26]

An assessment center usually involves six to twelve people who have been chosen or have chosen to attend it. It is most often conducted off the premises by the organization for one to three days. The performance of the attendees is usually rated by managers in the organization who are trained assessors. Typically, the purpose of an assessment center program is to help determine potential promotability of applicants to a first-line supervisor's job.

At a typical assessment center, candidates undergo evaluation using a wide range of techniques. One important activity is the in-basket exercise, which creates a realistic situation designed to elicit typical on-the-job behaviors. Situations and problems encountered on the job are written on individual sheets of paper and set in the in-basket. The applicant is then asked to arrange the papers by priority. Occasionally the applicant may need to write an action response on the piece of paper. The problems or situations described to the applicant involve different groups of people—peers, subordinates, and those outside the organiza-

Exhibit 6.6
Examples of Physical, Verbal, and Mental Work Sample Tests

Physical	
Dental students	Carving dexterity
Machine operators	Lathe; drill press; and tool dexterity
Meat scalers	Meat weighing
Mechanics	Belt and pulley installation; gear box repair; motor installation and alignment; sprocket reaming
Miners	Two-hand coordination
Pilots	Rudder control; direction control; complex coordination
Administrative assistants	Word processing on specific equipment; dictation; filing
Mental	
Magazine editors	Writing skills; page layout; headline writing
Administrators	Judgment and decision making
Engineers	Processing mathematical data
Administrative assistants	Letter composition; proofreading
Verbal	
Telephone operators	Role play of telephone contacts
Communication specialists	Oral fact-finding
Construction supervisors	Construction error recognition
Administrative assistants	Telephone screening

SOURCE: Adapted from J. J. Asher and J. A. Sciarrino, "Realistic Work Sample Tests: A Review," *Personnel Psychology* 27 (1974), 519–33.

tion. The applicant is usually given a set time limit to take the test and is often interrupted by phone calls meant to create more tension and pressure.

Other tests used in managerial selection are the leaderless group discussion (LGD) and business games. In the LGD, a group of individuals is asked to discuss a topic for a given period of time. At IBM's assessment center, participants must make a five-minute oral presentation about the qualifications of a candidate for promotion. During the subsequent group discussion, they must defend their nomination of the candidate with five or more other participants. Participants are rated on their selling ability, oral communication skill, self-confidence, energy level, interpersonal competency, aggressiveness, and tolerance for stress. LGD ratings have been shown to be useful predictors of managerial performance in a wide array of business areas. Additionally, prior experience in LGD does not affect current LGD performance. Business games are living cases. That is, individuals must make decisions and live with them, much as they do in the in-basket exercise.

Because in-baskets, LGDs, and business games tend to be useful in managerial selection, they are often used together in an assessment center.[27] As candidates go through these exercises, their performance is observed by a specifically trained team of observers or assessors drawn from the local management group. After the candidates have finished the program, these assessors meet to discuss the candidates and prepare performance evaluations based on their combined judgments of the candidates in such areas as organizing and planning, analyzing, making decisions, controlling oral communications, conducting interpersonal relations, influencing, and exhibiting flexibility. The composite performance on the exercises and tests is often used to determine an assessment center attendee's future promotability. It may also be used to develop the organization's human resource planning and training needs, as well as to make current selection and placement decisions. This rating is generally given to the attendee, who in turn can use it for his or her own personal career planning purposes.

Assessment centers have been used effectively in manufacturing companies, government, military services, utility companies, oil companies, the foreign services, and educational institutions. Assessment centers appear to work because they reflect the actual work environment and measure performance on multiple job dimensions. Additionally, more than one *trained* rater with a common frame of reference evaluates each participant's behavior. In terms of cost effectiveness, assessment centers are often criticized as costing too much ($50 to over $2,000 per applicant). However, annual productivity gains realized by selecting managers via assessment centers average well above administrative costs.[28]

Selection and Placement Interview

Job offers go to applicants who *appear* most qualified because it is often impossible to determine from available data who really is most qualified. Though appearances can be deceiving, the job interview and the perceptions gained from it still comprise the tool most heavily used to determine who gets the job offer.[29] As shown in exhibit 6.2, the interview is important at both the beginning and the end of the selection procedure.

The reliability and usefulness of the interview really depend on several factors.

Degree of structure. The unstructured interview involves little preparation. The interviewer merely prepares a list of possible topics to cover and, depending on how the conversation proceeds, asks or does not ask them. While this provides for flexibility, the digressions, discontinuity, and lack of focus may be frustrating to the interviewer and interviewee. More important, unstructured interviews result in inconsistencies in the information collected about the candidates.

Alternatively, in a structured interview all the applicants are asked the same questions in the same order. While structuring the interview restricts the topics that can be covered, it ensures that the same information is collected on all candidates. As a result, managers are less likely to make snap and possibly erroneous judgments.

A compromise that still minimizes snap judgments is the semistructured interview. Questions are prepared in advance, and the same questions are asked of all candidates; responses are recorded. However, follow-up questions are allowed to probe specific areas in depth. This approach provides enough flexibility to develop insights, along with the structure needed to acquire comparative information.

Job relevance. At one extreme, interviewers focus on generalities about qualifications. Such questions help interviewers form an overall impression of the candidate's competence but are not predictive of success in a specific job. A better approach is to use job analysis to generate questions about specific job skills and duties. For example, the critical incident method of job analysis (see chapter 4) can be used to develop **situational questions.** (Exhibit 6.7 illustrates how critical incidents are then transformed into job-specific situational interview questions.)

Systematic scoring. Job interviews also vary in the degree to which results are scored. At one extreme, an interviewer merely listens to responses, forms an impression, and makes an accept, reject, or hold decision. Alternatively, raters are given specific criteria and a scoring key to evaluate responses to each question (see exhibit 6.7). This latter approach is more rational because it helps ensure that applicants are evaluated against the same criteria. Systematic scoring

Exhibit 6.7
Steps in Developing Job-Related Situational Interview Questions

1. Generate the critical incident of good or poor behavior.

"This employee always calls in sick at the last minute for personal reasons."

2. Rewrite the incident as a situational interview question.

"Your husband and children are all sick with the 24 hour flu. Your husband urges you to stay home and take care of them. It's two hours before your shift starts. What do you do?"

3. Develop a weighted scoring key.

Managers and incumbents brainstorm possible answers to the question and then rank them in terms of their appropriateness. Assuming a weight of 5 percent for the situational question above, responses could be scored as follows:

5 "I would call the doctor and see if there is any medication I could get for them before going to work. If it's the flu, there really isn't much I can do by staying home, so I'd go to work as usual. I might call them on break to check on how they are doing."
4 "I'd call the substitution board and see if someone could fill in for me. If not, I'd go to work."
3 "I'd call my supervisor immediately, explain the situation, and stay home and take care of my family. My family comes first."
2 "I'd see if my family got any better in the next two hours. If not, I'd call my supervisor and let him know I won't be coming in due to family sickness."
1 "Because we're allowed so many sick days a year, I'd call my supervisor at the start of my shift and say I was sick."
0 "I'd stay home and take care of my family."

4. Develop similar questions and scoring keys for all important job duties.

One of the only three female employees in your group says she is being sexually harassed by some of the male workers. She says the continuous stream of lewd jokes, sexist comments, and pats on the behind are very upsetting. The other two women have not complained. How would you respond?

5. Total the scores for all questions to arrive at an overall suitability score.

SOURCE: Adapted from: G. P. Latham, L. M. Saari, E. D. Pursell, and M. A. Campion, "The Situational Interview," *Journal of Applied Psychology* 65 (1980), 422–27.

also tends to minimize halo bias, in which an interviewer judges an applicant's entire potential on the basis of a single characteristic, such as how well the applicant dresses or talks.

Number of interviewers. Typically, applicants are interviewed by one person at a time. Unfortunately, managers sometimes overlap in their coverage of some job-related questions and miss others entirely. An applicant may have not four interviews, but one interview four times. This is a time-consuming process in which the interviewer's *and* applicant's impressions may vary, depending on what was discussed in one-on-one interviews. This problem can be overcome by using a **panel interview** in which several individuals simultaneously interview one applicant. Because all decision makers hear the same responses, panel interviews produce more consistent results. On the other hand, panel interviews are expensive because many people are involved. However, if applicants are to be interviewed by more than one manager and nonmanager anyway, panel interviewing may be more efficient and reliable and as cost effective as individual interviews.

Training. Left on their own, interviewers tend to form their own impressions based on whatever criteria are most important or salient to them. For example, an applicant might be rejected by one interviewer for being "too aggressive" but accepted by another for being "assertive." Consequently, it is important to train interviewers so they interpret information consistently.

Frame of reference training, which is also used to reduce inconsistencies in performance ratings, involves teaching interviewers (raters) a common nomenclature for defining the importance of each component of behavior that is to be observed in the interview.[30] This can be accomplished by having potential interviewers develop items and scoring approaches such as those in exhibit 6.7. Alternatively, an interviewer's ratings for "practice" interview questions can be compared to normative ratings given by other interviewers. Such training brings perceptions into closer congruence with those of the rest of the organization.

Medical, Physical, and Polygraph Tests

Although not all organizations require medical exams or physical tests, such tests are being given in increasing numbers. One consequence is a concern about genetic screening as a part of the physical examination process.

Physical examination. Because of its high cost, the physical examination is often one of the final steps in the selection process. Many employers give common physical exams to all job applicants, whereas special exams are given to only a subset of all applicants.[31] For example, production job applicants may receive back X-rays, while office job applicants may not. According to the *Uniform Guidelines,* physical examinations should be used to screen out applicants when the results indicate that job performance would be adversely affected.

Guidelines for assessing physical abilities have been developed that detail the sensory, perceptual, cognitive, psychomotor, and physical requirements of most jobs (e.g., police, firefighters, electrical power plant workers, telephone line workers, steel mill laborers, paramedics, maintenance workers, and workers in numerous mechanical jobs). When applied carefully, then, these physical requirements (not physical examinations per se) are extremely useful in predicting job performance, worker's compensation claims, and absenteeism. However, arbitrary physical requirements can be a curse, screening out women and minorities who could do a job if given the opportunity. To accommodate workers with disabilities, organizations should also explore whether equipment can be "reasonably" adapted to facilitate these workers. Guidelines on inexpensive adaptations for most types of machinery are available from the federal government.[32] This concern is particularly relevant for employees now since the passage of the Americans with Disabilities Act of 1990. In fact, the Act is giving employers an opportunity to review their entire set of policies regarding job applicants and employees with disabilities.

Genetic screening. In 1985, there were 390,000 reported cases of job-related illness and 100,000 job-related deaths. Many of these illnesses and deaths were attributable to chemical hazards. Genetic screening identifies individuals who are hypersensitive to harmful pollutants in the workplace. Once identified, these individuals can be screened out of chemically dangerous jobs and placed in positions in which environmental toxins do not present specific hazards.[33]

While cost-effective genetic tests have not yet been developed, one percent of major firms already use genetic screening, and fifteen percent are considering genetic tests in the future. As scientific research on genetic screening continues, the debate over the ethics of basing employment decisions on immutable traits is likely to grow. It also seems probable that pressure will be exerted on organizations to develop engineering controls that minimize or eliminate workplace pollutants. These controls would be the preferred alternative to genetic screening, a selection criterion over which an individual has no control.[34]

Drug and alcohol testing. Alcohol and drug abuse are said to cost U.S. industry more than $100 billion annually. However, there is some evidence that alcohol and drug abuse may be plateauing. In a recent study conducted by the Smith Kline Beecham Clinical Laboratories,

> [all] regions of the country showed declines in drug use for 1991. The most dramatic was in the West where 7.3 percent of employees and applicants tested positive in 1991, down from 12 percent in 1990.
>
> Marijuana and cocaine continue to be the most commonly detected drugs. Of all workers and applicants screened, 56,000 (2.6 percent) tested positive for cocaine and 61,000 (3.1 percent) tested positive for marijuana. Among the individuals testing positive for drugs, 29 percent were positive for cocaine (up 4.7 percent from 1990) and 34.6 percent were positive for marijuana (up 0.8 percent from 1990).[35]

Nevertheless, alcohol and drug abuse persist, and its impact on individuals and society can be significant.[36] Consequently, firms are likely to continue drug testing. Federal contractors have no choice. According to the Drug Free Workplace Act of 1988, firms that do business with the federal government must have written drug use policies. Regardless of what methods are used for drug testing, a key issue in adopting a drug policy is establishing a disciplinary procedure.

> If a drug policy does not state specifically that disciplinary actions will be taken when an employee tests positive for drug use, there's no reason to test. Drug testing doesn't make sense if you're not willing to take disciplinary action based on a confirmed pos-

itive test result. A policy calling for discipline in such a circumstance doesn't have to require termination. Rehabilitation can be required as an alternative.[37]

AIDS testing. AIDS victims are protected by the Rehabilitation Act of 1973 (*Chalk v. U.S. District Court for Central District of California,* 1987). Because AIDS is such a major challenge in today's workplace, organizations are establishing guidelines concerning it. Companies such as IBM, AT&T, and Johnson & Johnson have endorsed these guidelines:

- People with AIDs or who are infected with HIV, the AIDS-causing virus, are entitled to the same rights and opportunities as people with other serious illnesses.
- Employment policies should be based on the scientific evidence that people with AIDS or HIV infection do not pose a risk of transmitting the virus through ordinary workplace contact.
- Employers should provide workers with sensitive and up-to-date education about AIDS and risk reduction in their personal lives.
- Employers have the duty to protect the confidentiality of employees' medical information.
- Employers should not require HIV screening as part of general preemployment or workplace physical examinations.[38]

Lie detector tests. With the passage of the Employee Polygraph Protection Act of 1988, employers are restricting their use of polygraph or lie detector tests. In passing the law, supporters of polygraph restriction claim the tests are accurate only two-thirds of the time and are far more likely to be inaccurate for honest employees. The new law restricts preemployment screening and random use of the device. Other provisions of the law are as follows:

- Permits private security firms and drug companies to continue to administer polygraph tests to job applicants and employees
- Exempts federal, state, and local government employers from the ban on polygraph testing
- Prohibits employers from disciplining, discharging, discriminating against, or denying employment or promotions to prospective or current workers solely on the basis of polygraph test results
- Provides that employers that violate any provision of the law may be assessed a civil penalty of up to $10,000[39]

Honesty tests. Partly as a response to regulatory prohibitions on employers' use of polygraphs, the use of paper-and-pencil honesty tests has increased.

> A record 2.3 million employment applicants were given "honesty" tests last year, up from one million in 1981, estimates James Walls, a marketing vice president at Stanton Corp., a psychological testing concern.
>
> Stanton's own evaluations underscore why employers are using the tests more frequently. Thirty-two percent of the employment applicants the company screened last year admitted on signed statements that they had stolen from a previous employer, up

from 12 percent two decades ago. Similarly, a recent survey of 9,000 employees by the Justice Department found that one-third admitted stealing from their current or previous employers.

"More and more employees today have a negative attitude toward their employers," says E. John Keller, a security consultant at Arthur Andersen & Co., the accounting firm. "There's a direct correlation between low morale and high theft."...

Sometimes simply giving a test can help solve a company's problems. A convenience food-store chain recently gave an honesty test to a few hundred employees, who were given instructions on how to correct the test themselves. Their exposure to the test and the process of self-correction, according to Mr. Keller, prompted an immediate two-thirds reduction in inventory theft.[40]

Despite endorsements from industry, many honesty tests have not yet been subject to careful validation and, therefore, are not recommended as a selection device. Depending on the cutoff score an organization chooses to use, anywhere from 25 to 75 percent of job applicants will fail an honesty test. Thus, many people will suffer negative employment repercussions as a result of these tests.[41]

METHODS OF USING INFORMATION FOR SELECTION AND PLACEMENT DECISIONS

As shown above, a variety of devices are available to make selection decisions. The choice of devices depends on job relatedness, related costs, and time constraints. If more than one predictor is used, a decision must be made regarding the order in which selection devices will be administered and how information from the various sources should be combined. Additional considerations center on controlling bias associated with making selection decisions.

Remember, organizations want to make decisions that are correct. In other words, they want to maximize the number of true decisions and minimize the number of false decisions. True decisions include rejecting a candidate who would have been a bad performer or hiring a candidate who turns out good. False decisions include rejecting a good candidate or hiring a bad candidate.

The Single Predictor Approach

When only one piece of information is used to make selection decisions, personnel and human resource managers are using the single predictor approach. Single predictors are useful for unskilled, simple, or repetitive jobs in which one duty is most important or time consuming. It makes obvious good sense, for example, to require a candidate for a secretarial job to simply pass a typing test, and generally, the equal-opportunity establishment accepts such tests.

The Multiple Predictor Approach

When there is more than one selection device, information can be combined in three ways.

Multiple hurdles. In a multiple hurdles approach an applicant must exceed fixed levels of proficiency on all the predictors in order to be accepted. A score lower than the cutoff score on one predictor (test) cannot be compensated for by a higher-than-necessary score on another predictor. Underlying this approach is the assumption that a specific skill or competency is so critical that inadequacy guarantees the person will be unsuccessful on the job. This assumption legitimately applies for some physical ability requirements (visual acuity for pilots) and for state mandated licensing requirements (state licensure for nurses).

Previously, organizations believed they could construct multiple hurdles systems and escape liability by applying what is called the **bottom-line rule.** The rule premises that an adverse impact found in one component of a selection process (written examination) can be neutralized by favorable treatment overall. The Supreme Court, however, ruled that the bottom-line rule is no defense when adverse impact is shown for *any* component in a selection process (*Connecticut v. Teal,* 1982). For example, unless a written examination that has adverse impact can be shown to be job-related, its use is in violation of Title VII.

Compensatory approach. Since most jobs do not have truly absolute requirements, a compensatory approach is commonly used. This approach assumes that good performance on one predictor *can* compensate for poor performance on another (e.g., a low score for a written examination can be compensated for by a high score on an interview). With a compensatory approach, no selection decisions are made until the completion of the entire process. Then, a composite index that considers performance on all predictors is developed.

Combined approach. Many organizations also use a combined approach in which one or more specific requirements (e.g., pass the state bar or the CPA examination) must be met. Once these hurdles are jumped, then performance on the remaining predictors are combined into an overall measure of job suitability. Consider college recruiting. Many organizations only interview college students with GPAs that exceed a specific level (first hurdle). To be offered a plant visit, the candidate must first pass a campus interview (second hurdle). At corporate headquarters, the applicant may take aptitude tests, participate in an assessment center, and be interviewed. A composite index that takes into consideration performance in all three areas is used to make the final selection (compensatory).

SELECTION AND PLACEMENT DECISIONS

Selection and placement decisions seek to put the right person in the right job.[42] The right person may be found outside or inside the organization. Whether a person is "right" depends on the match between the person's skills, knowledge, and abilities and the job skill demands and on the match between the person's personality, interests, and preferences and the job and organizational characteristics. An organization may want job applicants to fill newly created jobs or jobs that have become vacant as a result of retirement, transfer, or voluntary termination (turnover). Vacancies may also be created by demotions and discharges. Because demotions and discharges are an important part of managing human resources, they are discussed in chapters 8 and 15. Remember, however, that as far as equal employment laws are concerned, all decisions about initial hiring, transfer, promotion, demotion, layoff, termination, and admittance to training programs are regarded as selection decisions.

The final selection and placement decision may be to hire a new job applicant or hire (transfer) one from within the organization. The decision may also be not to hire a particular applicant or set of applicants, but rather to go out and do more recruiting. The decision could also be to "put on hold" for some applicants who are qualified but for whom no jobs are currently open. Although generally not thought of as such, the final selection and placement decision could be to demote or terminate an employee. These decisions should be viewed as part of selection and placement because they are subject to the same legal considerations as hiring, transfer, and promotion decisions.

Selection decisions can also be made to bring in candidates from outside to fill higher level jobs in the organization. Although this may not raise a legal concern, it may lower employee morale if internal candidates feel passed over. Thus, organizations may prefer to promote from within. Also, as the 35-to-54 age group increases in the 1990s, transfers may become the alternative to promotions, at least in providing challenge and variety to valued employees.

Promotion and Transfer Decisions

"Going outside is the exception rather than the rule, and promotion from within is a standard practice in most organizations."[43] However, some job vacancies, particularly for highly skilled jobs, are filled by outside sources. This may also occur when the organization has been caught by surprise and has no internal individual ready to take the job, or when the focus of the organization changes. To help reduce surprises, organizations have managerial succession programs. In these programs, current managers identify employees who may one day be able to take over their jobs. Of course, this only identifies current employees, some of whom may not have the necessary style to fit an organization's structure. The result may be the need to search outside to find an individual who really fits the organization:

> This practice of careful selection to ensure better fit between company and employee is also a critical personnel practice at Goldman Sachs. There every partner interviews every MBA job applicant to ensure that new employees "fit" the company.[44]

Types of promotion and transfer. Promotions can occur within a department, a division, or an entire organization. They also can occur between two nonmanagerial positions (for example, from Typist I to Typist II), between managerial positions, and between a nonmanagerial and a managerial (or supervisory) position.

Although promotions generally refer to vertical moves in the organization, promotions may occur when an employee moves to another job at the same level but with more pay or status. However, this type of promotion may violate federal wage guidelines and equal pay regulations, and should be made advisedly. Although such a move could be regarded as a transfer, a transfer generally refers to a move at the same level and at the same pay.

Making promotion and transfer decisions. On the one hand, immediate supervisors may have limited control in deciding who to promote or transfer. Nevertheless they must search for qualified candidates and make a choice when a vacancy arises. This process is probably carried out in close consultation with one or more higher level supervisors who ultimately have to approve the choice.

On the other hand, immediate supervisors may have almost total control over promotion and transfer decisions. When a new job is being created, they may be able to determine exactly who will be promoted by writing the job description to fit only one person. This is not necessarily a fair practice, but it is common. Remember, however, that promotion decisions are just another selection decision and, as such, must be made without illegal discrimination.

Identifying candidates for promotion and transfer. Candidates may be identified by word of mouth, inspection of the organization's personnel records, promotion lists based on performance or managerial ratings, and formal programs for identifying potential candidates for promotion, such as assessment centers. The human resource information system is valuable here because it can store a vast amount of information on employees and help speed the process of identifying potential candidates. It can also ensure fairness in the process by giving everyone a chance regardless of where they are currently working or for whom they are working.

Comparing candidates. Different methods for identifying candidates can also be used to evaluate and compare candidates. Although many companies administer a battery of tests to assess mental ability, personality, and interests, one study concluded that tests are ignored more often than not as decision-making aids for internal promotions. Instead, job experience, performance history, and assessment center results are often used to evaluate internal candidates. Interviews are used as well, although they are used more widely for candidates from external sources. A powerful sponsor (often a manager at a higher level in the organization who "adopts" and looks out for an employee at a lower level) can help ensure that an individual's strengths are noted by others. A final basis for comparing candidates is seniority.

Making the final choice. Making a decision is difficult if different types of information are available for competing job applicants. Even if this is the case, however, all of the candidates can be screened quickly, and only those with obvious potential retained as candidates. Those who survive can then be evaluated. Although this may not result in selection of the best candidate, the one who is chosen should at least perform adequately.

Managers who favor a particular inside candidate may use the **confirmation approach.** To make the selection process appear legitimate, a manager may select several candidates, in addition to the favorite, for others to evaluate. The catch is that the other candidates are far less qualified than the favorite. The whole selection process becomes superficial, allowing only one "real" choice.

Why not the best? All too often, the best people are not the ones who are promoted or transfered.[45] First, staff people are often not considered for line jobs. Many organizations promote only line managers to upper management. Exceptions to this tradition are occurring, however; IBM has a company policy of promoting managers in and out of line and staff jobs.

Second, decentralized departments and divisions operate like independent organizations. When vacancies occur, a department or division tends to select only from its own employees and not from the total organization. Decentralization can also result in a separate performance appraisal system for each division;

even if divisions did obtain candidates from other divisions, they could be hard to evaluate.

A third reason the most qualified person may be overlooked is discrimination. Ignoring women and minorities means selecting managers, sometimes illegally, from a small percentage of the employees. Ignoring older employees also results in reducing the pool from which employees are selected for promotion. Because these older employees may be members of the age-protected group (over forty years of age), excluding them from promotions or job transfers may also be illegal.

In addition, the best persons may not be promoted because subjective, personal criteria are used in selection rather than objective criteria. Subjective criteria include how well they are liked by the manager, how they dress, and how popular they are. Finally, many competent managers are refusing promotion if it means moving to another location. Increasingly, members of dual-career families refuse promotions involving a geographical change because it may require a career sacrifice on the part of the other person. In addition, some managers refuse promotions because they are more interested in pursuing leisure than work.

Biases in Human Resource Decision Making

In addition to deciding on the order in which selection devices will be administered, managers should make a conscious effort to minimize biases associated with selection. Because of information processing limitations, managers tend to overutilize inferential strategies. As a result, their selection decisions may be biased in a number of different ways. Exhibit 6.8 lists some of the biases that affect selection decisions.

Training. Despite the susceptibility of human resource decision makers to these biases, distortions can be minimized in several ways. First, selection biases can be prevented or reduced by direct frontal assault—training decision makers to be aware of and to compensate for their susceptibility to judgmental influences. At a minimum, such training programs need to alert decision makers to the possibility of bias, offer alternative approaches, and give feedback regarding the frequency of bias in their judgments. Unfortunately, because of the range of decision biases, such training may be lengthy and costly.

Decision aids. Alternatively, selection biases can be reduced with decision aids. Decision aids may be as simple as a scoring key for interview questions or as complex as mathematically derived regression equations that indicate how the results from multiple selection devices should optimally be combined. Decision aids provide an "organizational memory." Because the procedures insulate the decision from the biases of the decision makers, decision aids reduce inappropriate cognitive influences for *any* decision maker who uses them.

Unfortunately, few organizations rely exclusively on decision aids: Managers do not easily accept the fact that mathematical models provide better predictions than do humans. They contend that the fine nuances of good decision making simply cannot be captured adequately by decision models. This argument is personified in discussions about the viability of the interview as a selection device. Even though the interview is less reliable and less valid than are cognitive ability tests, managers persist in using the interview as a primary selection device.

Exhibit 6.8
Description of Cognitive Biases Affecting Selection Decisions

Bias	Definition
1. Illusion of completeness	Decision makers perceive an information set as complete, even in the absence of important information or considerations. Consequently, decisions will be made with incomplete information. For example, a secretary will be selected on the basis of a typing test, even though typing accounts for only 15 percent of work duties.
2. Overconfidence	Decision makers tend to be overconfident in their fallible judgments when answering moderately to extremely hard questions. Personnel and human resource managers have greater confidence in their selection decisions than objectively they should. Recall that if selection devices (e.g., cognitive ability tests) have a validity coefficient of only .5 they account for only 25 percent of the reason someone performs well or poorly on a job.
3. Confirmatory bias	Information that confirms one's hypothesis is taken at face value, while potentially uncomfirmatory evidence is subjected to highly critical and skeptical scrutiny. For example, during the initial phase of an interview, a manager makes a judgment about the suitability of an applicant. Information that confirms this judgment is retained, while unconfirming information is more likely to be ignored.
4. Base rate fallacy	Decision makers tend to ignore prior probabilities (base rates) when any—even worthless—situational information is available. For example, in determining whether to use a specific test, managers may fail to consider how many applicants could perform adequately if no test were used. As a result, they may view a test as more useful than it actually is.
5. Law of small numbers	In estimating probabilities, people tend to ignore the importance of sample size and attribute greater stability to results attained from small samples than is warranted. For example, personnel and human resource managers have inappropriately believed that small samples were sufficient to validate a test. Similarly, they have assumed that a 30-minute interview is a representative sample of an applicant's overall job behavior.
6. Framing	Decision makers are likely to treat risks concerning perceived gains differently from risks associated with perceived losses. In the face of losses, they are risk seeking; in the face of gains, risk averse. For example, managers may not narrow down applicant pools sufficiently if they adopt a reject versus an accept selection strategy.
7. Illusion of validity	A good fit between the predicted outcome and input information produces unwarranted confidence. Information that appears consistent (redundant) is weighted more heavily than it should be. For example, managers may erroneously believe that two tests that are highly correlated (e.g., perceptual speed and error detection) predict better than a single predictor or uncorrelated predictors.
8. Anchoring and adjustment	The number of openings to be filled may inappropriately anchor selection decisions. That is, when there is more than one opening to be filled, marginal candidates may be viewed as qualified; if there is only one opening, managers adjust their evaluations upward so that fewer candidates are considered qualified. Consequently, evaluations of candidates are based on the number of openings rather than on the qualifications of the candidates.
9. Career fixation	Following an initial judgment about an applicant's qualifications, an employee is later perceived as incapable of possessing or developing expertise in other areas. As a result, the employee may be pigeon-holed in a particular career track, even when qualified for other positions.

SOURCE: Adapted from V. L. Huber, G. B. Northcraft, and M. Neale, "Foibles and Fallacies in Organizational Staffing Decisions," in *Readings in Personnel and Human Resource Management,* 3d ed., ed. R. S. Schuler, S. A. Youngblood, and V. L. Huber (St. Paul, Minn.: West, 1988), 193–205.

The argument usually forwarded is that tests really can't assess interpersonal skills (e.g., communication, likeability). Nor can they assess whether the applicant will fit within the organization's culture.

Thus, it appears that removing the possibility of human bias by removing humans from the process may be too large a step at this time.[46]

In sum, when developing a selection process, several questions need to be answered.

- Which predictors are most valid?
- Are predictors correlated with one another? (If so, only one should be used.)
- In what order will predictors be administered?
- How will predictors be scored (multiple hurdles, compensatory, or combined)?
- What strategies will be used to minimize bias in selection decisions?
- Were the desired results attained?

FOCUS ISSUES IN SELECTION AND PLACEMENT

Assessing Selection and Placement Decisions

The quality and effectiveness of selection and placement decisions depend on whether the organization hires applicants who turn out to be good performers. If the organization can select and place applicants who turn out to perform well, organizational productivity will benefit. In addition, if the organization does not select and place applicants who would have performed poorly, organizational productivity will also benefit. The critical point is that, when an organization makes selection and placement decisions based on activities that benefit organizational productivity, it makes those decisions using predictors that are valid and serve its legal considerations. Using predictors that do not result in selection and placement decisions that benefit productivity is counterproductive and generally is not consistent with legal considerations. Consequently, organizations must use valid predictors. They must also be concerned with the overall costs of the selection devices and weigh these against the benefits.

Because developing valid predictors is a critical activity in personnel research, strategies to validate single and multiple predictors are described in chapter 14. However, obtaining and using valid predictors comprise only part of making effective selection and placement decisions. The other parts include the base rate, the selection rate, the selection ratio, and the overall dollar costs and benefits of the decisions. These are also described in chapter 14.

Computer Technology

On any given day, a personnel and human resource department will probably evaluate a number of candidates for a variety of positions. Deciding which predictors are relevant (valid) for a particular case and administering a multitude of predictors (tests) make personnel's work challenging. Effective management of predictors is critical in the face of extensive laws and regulations. Doing all of these tasks effectively requires a great deal of information. Computer technology can enhance personnel's ability to coordinate the scheduling, administration, and evaluation of predictors by processing this information in a variety of ways.

For example, personnel could quickly do a validation study by correlating the current job performance data with any of several predictors, if these data were stored in a human resource information system and analyzed by computer. With an HRIS and computers, the utilization rates for affirmative action programs, as discussed in chapter 3 can also be determined quickly and easily. Results of tests to measure job applicants' skills, knowledge, and abilities, as well as personality, interests, and preferences, can be stored in an HRIS and used together with job analysis data (also in the HRIS) to make better selection and placement decisions. This same information can then be used to help plot career paths for employees when they are hired.

Computers are also being used to reduce first impression biases inherent in the interview. Computer-aided interviewing uses a computer to present a structured interview directly to an applicant, without an interviewer present. Although it does not replace the face-to-face interview, it complements it by providing a base of information about each applicant before the interviewer meets the applicant. This provides a first impression based on information that is job relevant rather than anecdotal.

Computer interviewing is also faster. An applicant can complete a one-hundred question computer-aided interview in about twenty minutes. The same information would require a face-to-face interview of more than two hours. In addition to time savings, computer-aided interviewing provides an automatic record of answers so that they can be compared across applicants. More important, computer-aided interviews have been validated in a number of settings, including manufacturing and service industries.[47]

Linking Selection and Placement with the Business

Top management. Organizations are increasingly realizing that people make a difference and that different types of people are required to run different types of organizations. Reginald H. Jones, former chairman and CEO of the General Electric Company, has noted that "businesses with different missions require quite different people running them."[48] As a result, particular characteristics, skills, abilities, values, and perspectives of executives need to match particular types of business strategy.[49] For example, a recently released study by the Hay Group reports that, when a business is pursuing a growth strategy, it needs top managers who are likely to abandon the status quo and adapt their strategies and goals to the marketplace. Because insiders are slow to recognize the onset of decline and tend to persevere in strategies that are no longer effective, top managers need to be recruited from the outside. Outsiders, of course, are not always helpful. When a business is pursuing a mature strategy, what is needed is a stable group of insiders who know the intricacies of the business.

Getting the right workers. The qualities and characteristics of the top executives matter; so do those of all the other employees. Companies that are trying to enhance their competitiveness by improving quality seem to agree that the employees at the front line—for example, the production workers on the line—are key to the success of improving and delivering quality. Furthermore, these same companies seem to agree that it takes a different type of employee to really perform well in this situation. Thus, those companies are willing to devote considerable time and effort in selecting those individuals who are most likely to fill the bill of a production worker in a high-quality manufacturing environment that is organized around work teams. To that end, some organizations have developed and use a rather extensive set of selection methods to hire a production worker, including those listed in exhibit 6.9.

As firms come to believe that particular human resource practices are necessary for their success, they tend to believe that widespread application is possible, even necessary. We will see this in our discussion of Disney in the next segment on international aspects.

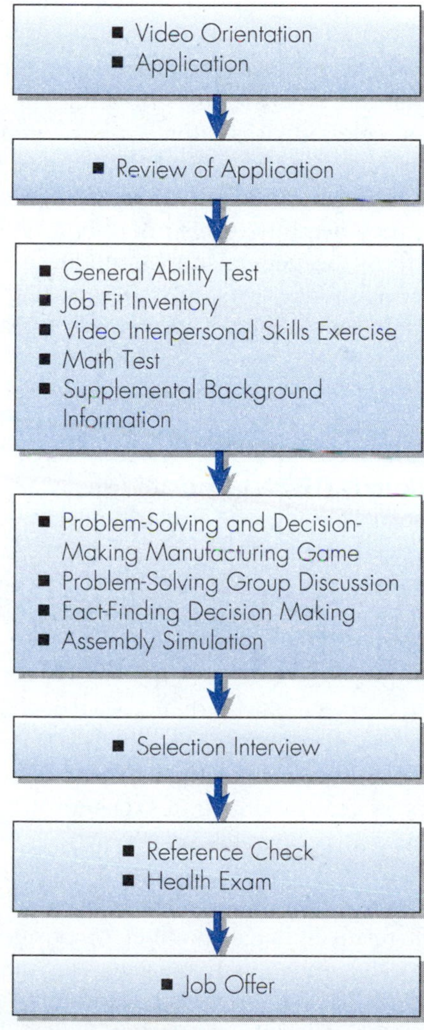

Exhibit 6.9
Selection Methods for Hiring Production Workers

INTERNATIONAL ASPECTS OF EMPLOYEE SELECTION

Selecting Expatriate Employees

The number of American expatriate employees is relatively small, but their importance to companies operating in the international markets is relatively large. Without effective expatriate employees—managers and nonmanagers—U.S. companies are essentially unable to operate successfully abroad. Nevertheless, the ineffectiveness of expatriate employees is alarmingly commonplace. Consequently, American-based multinational companies not only need to obtain candidates for expatriate positions but also must ensure those employees are effective on the job.

A key in selecting any employee is knowing what the job entails. In general, expatriate managers are involved in six major categories of relations: (1) internal relations with their co-workers, (2) relations with their families, (3) relations with the host government, (4) relations with their home government, (5) external relations with the local culture, and (6) relations with the company's headquarters.

Expatriate managers perform their daily activities in the context of the parent company's headquarters, the host country's government, the parent company's government, and a local culture that is often quite different from their home culture. In addition, expatriate managers typically operate in a culture with a different language—a major obstacle for many of them.[50] Thus, for expatriate managers to be successful, they need the skills not only to perform the specific type of job but also to perform the general duties required by these six categories. Using these criteria for selection, as well as for structuring a related management development program, can go a long way toward increasing the likelihood of expatriate managerial success.[51]

Related to the selection of expatriate employees—also called **parent country nationals (PCNs)**—is the more general issue of staffing operations abroad. Typically, expatriate employees fill only a few positions. Most of the employees are **host country nationals (HCNs)** who are usually selected using host country practices. The practice of using one's own human resource practices abroad is referred to as **ethnocentrism**. Allowing operations in different countries to develop and use their own human resource practices is called **polycentrism.** Developing practices that can be applied in all countries, with modest adjustments to local conditions, is called **geocentrism**.

As firms go global they may go through a period of trial and error, seeing what works and what doesn't. Firms that have been successful because of their human resource practices may be inclined to insist those practices be used elsewhere and may adapt only after getting feedback from the locals. The PHRM in the News feature illustrates Disney's experience in Europe. Remember that Disney-Tokyo operates with practices very similar to those in the United States. Will Disney need to adapt more French practices for Euro Disneyland to be successful?[52]

A growing but still relatively small number of positions are filled by **third country nationals (TCNs),** individuals from neither the host country nor the country of the parent firm. They are often selected by the parent firm using practices similar to those used in selecting expatriates.[54]

International Comparisons

Staffing activities in Japan and Germany present alternatives that could be used in the U.S.; Canada provides useful comparisons in regard to equal employment and human rights legislation.

Japan. The emphasis on seniority or years of service as a determinant of job promotion has led many observers of the Japanese economy to conclude that it (seniority) promotes a slow progression of employees through the ranks. However, several Japanese specialists have argued that the impact of seniority on promotion has been exaggerated. With promotion being awarded on the basis of merit evaluation, seniority is necessary but not a sufficient condition of success. Most companies, such as ELCO and STEELCO (2 major steel-producing industries), set up minimum tenure requirements for a position or minimum tenure in a grade before the next promotion or both. As a result, career progression lines are rigid and chances to recover after a slippage in ratings and a missed promotion are limited. In this sense, the Japanese promotion system is more of a "tournament" among different players than one based exclusively on seniority.

Promotion is gradual when one compares this system to ours. In fact, in one company it takes sixteen years to be promoted from the lowest management position of Supervisor to that of General Manager. Moreover, if a Supervisor is passed over in two successive years for promotion, his/her chance to reach the level of Senior Manager is altogether eliminated. Promotions are most likely to occur in situations where the organization is expanding rapidly.[55]

The degree of competitiveness that is viewed in this tournament atmosphere of job promotion can be said to undermine the fundamentality of the cooperative effort. However, the appraisal system of the Japanese serves as a check on these possible outcomes; what is rewarded most are "credibility" and "ability to get things done in cooperation with others." The competition with colleagues can be acute, but its focal point is cooperation—building cooperative networks with the same people who are rivals for future promotion.

Canada. In Canada, most companies use techniques of recruiting and selection similar to those in the U.S. At the same time, they face significantly different equal employment legislation or, more broadly, human rights legislation. Relatively comprehensive human rights legislation now exists at the federal level and in each of Canada's ten provinces. This legislation follows a common pattern but has specific deviations in each jurisdiction.

The typical Canadian human rights statute prohibits discrimination based on race, color, religion, ancestry, place of origin, material status, sex, age, or physical handicap, when such discrimination involves employment or trade union membership, services or accommodations that are available to the public, residential or commercial rentals, or public notices.[56] The statute is enforced by a human rights commission whose staff investigates and conciliates complaints of statute violations. If the commission staff is unable to conciliate a complaint successfully, an ad hoc tribunal or board of inquiry of one or more members may be appointed to hold a public hearing. The commission normally takes the lead in supporting the complaint at this hearing. If the tribunal finds that discrimina-

IN THE NEWS PHRM

A Disney Dress Code Chafes In the Land of Haute Couture

NOISY-LE-GRAND, France—Should the French have to shave their beards or scrap their lacy tights for a Mickey Mouse job?

The Walt Disney Company, which is in the midst of hiring some 12,000 people to maintain and populate its Euro Disneyland theme park near Paris, thinks so. But in making detailed rules on acceptable clothing, hair styles and jewelry, among other things, part of its terms of employment, the company finds itself caught in a legal and cultural dispute.

A Court is Investigating

The controversy has risen above the usual labor squabble as critics in the press, at universities and elsewhere have joined in asking how brash Americans could be so insensitive to French culture, individualism and privacy. Most of the critics, and many people on the street, seem amazed, if not amused, that Disney found it necessary to put such a subjective and personal hygiene code in writing, and to make its violation a firing offense for everyone from the actors portraying Mickey and Minnie who greet visitors to the chambermaids cleaning hotel rooms.

Disney executives say the planned April 12 opening of the $4.2 billion complex in Marne-la-Vallée, 20 miles east of Paris, is unlikely to be delayed by the conflict, which is being investigated by a district court. But they insist that any ruling that bars them from imposing squeaky-clean employment standards could threaten the image and long-term success of the park.

"For us, the appearance code has a great effect from a product-identification standpoint," said Thor Degelmann, vice president for human resources for Euro Disneyland, which has its headquarters in Noisy-le-Grand. Mr. Degelmann, an American from Los Angeles, is in charge of hiring for the theme park.

"Without it, we wouldn't be presenting the Disney product that people would be expecting," he added. "It would be like going to see a production of 'Hamlet' in which everyone looked different than you expected. Would you ever go again?"

The rules, spelled out in a video presentation for job applicants and detailed in a guidebook, "Le Euro Disneyland Look," go way beyond height and weight standards. They require men's hair to be cut above the collar and ears, with no beards or mustaches. Any tattoos must be covered.

Women must keep their hair in one "natural color" with no frosting or streaking, and they may make only "limited use" of makeup like mascara. False eyelashes, eyeliner and eyebrow pencil are completely off limits. Fingernails can't pass the ends of the fingers.

As for jewelry, women can wear only one earring in each ear, with the earring's diameter no more

Continued

tion has occurred, it can formulate a remedial order. The legislation varies as to whether the tribunal issues the order or recommends the order to either the human rights commission or a designated cabinet minister, who in turn has the authority to issue it. Normally, the order can be enforced by court proceedings and is appealable to a court. Violations of the statutes are also subject to the ordinary penal process, although consent of either the human rights commission or a designated cabinet minister is usually necessary to begin prosecution.

Some uncertainty exists as to what operations are subject to the federal statute and what operations are subject to the appropriate provincial statute. Federally regulated industries such as banks and interprovincial transportation and communications, are clearly subject to the federal statute. Unlike most comparable federal legislation, however, nothing in the federal statute expressly limits it to such industries, although tribunals under the statute have held that it is implicitly so limited. All other operations are clearly subject to the provincial statutes. The federally regulated industries have sometimes assumed that they are not subject to

than 2 centimeters (about three-quarters of an inch). Neither men nor women can wear more than one ring on each hand.

Further, women are required to wear "appropriate undergarments" and only transparent pantyhose, not black or anything with fancy designs. Similar rules are in force at Disney's three other amusement parks in the United States and Japan.

Though a daily bath is not specifically mentioned in the rules, the applicants' video depicts a shower scene and informs applicants that they are expected to show up for work "fresh and clean each day."

Assault on Europe Is Seen

But beyond whatever legal proscriptions arise, it is clear that many French people feel stung by the whole episode. Roger Blanpain, a professor of labor law and president of the International Industrial Relations Association, based in Geneva, said Disney's code represented a frontal assault on French and European social standards.

"A certain kind of underwear?" he asked. "There's a limit, and that's going too far."

He insisted that Euro Disneyland management "should have been aware of the environment it was operating in and shown more sensitivity."

Mr. Degelmann, however, said the company was "well aware of the cultural differences" between the United States and France, and as a result had "toned down" the wording in the restrictions from the original American version.

He said the conflict resulted from a "lack of understanding" about the nature of a Disney park, and said that many other companies, particularly airlines, maintained appearance codes just as strict. "We happened to put ours in writing," he added.

5 Percent Drop Out

A generalized code, he said, was required because employees in "backstage" positions might be asked any given day to assume a job that would involve contact with the public, and therefore all workers needed to maintain an appearance appropriate for that possibility.

In any case, he said he knew of no one who had refused to take a job because of the rules, and he said that no more than 5 percent of the people showing up at the walk-in casting center for interviews, nearly 400 a day, had decided not to proceed after viewing the 15-minute video, which details transportation and salary as well as the appearance code. But Stephane Baudet, a 28-year-old trumpet player from Paris, said in an interview that he refused to audition for a job in a Disney brass band when he learned he would have to cut his ponytail, which flaps a few inches over his collar. He said he was also dissuaded by the long hours and low pay—6,000 francs ($1,150) a month, or about 20 percent more than the French minimum wage.

"Some people will turn themselves into a pumpkin to work at Euro Disneyland," he said. "But not me."[53]

SOURCE: *The New York Times* (25 Dec. 1991): 1, 48.

the provincial statutes, but some case law indicates that the provincial statutes also apply to federally regulated industries.

In addition to protecting basic human rights, the federal statute prohibits discrimination on the basis of criminal conviction where the person has been pardoned.[57] In the case of the physically handicapped, employment discrimination is prohibited, but not other forms of discrimination, and employers are not compelled to renovate their premises to accommodate the handicapped. A unique feature of the federal statute in the area of sex discrimination is that employers are required to provide equal pay for work of equal value. This contrasts with the provincial legislation, which does not affect pay differentials between different jobs as long as there is no ongoing practice of denying access to these jobs because of sex. Penal proceedings for discrimination under the federal statute are possible only where a person violates the terms of an agreed settlement of a complaint. Otherwise, enforcement must proceed through the hearing procedure and, if necessary, court enforcement of the resulting decision.

SUMMARY

This chapter examines what are selection and placement procedures and how they relate to other personnel activities. Organizations want to ensure that they hire job applicants with the abilities to meet job demands. Increasingly, they also want to ensure that job applicants will not only perform well but also will stay with the organization. Thus, organizations may want to attain a match between the job applicant's needs and the rewards offered by the job qualities and organizational context.

To match individual knowledge, skills, and abilities to job demands and to match individual personalities, interests, and preferences to job and organizational characteristics, organizations need to gather information about job applicants. The three most common methods—interviewing, testing, and application blanks—must operate within legal regulations. These legal regulations are not intended to discourage the use of these methods but rather to ensure that information is collected, retained, and used in recognition of an individual's rights to privacy and an organization's right to select individuals on the basis of legal considerations. Consequently, the types of information and the methods used to obtain information for selection vary according to the type of job for which the applicants are being selected. For example, assessment centers are apt to be used for managerial jobs, and physical ability tests are apt to be used for manufacturing and public health and safety jobs. Exactly how many predictors are used may depend in part on the type of job, but this is also likely to depend on the selection ratio, the costs associated with the selection tests in comparison with their benefits, and the degree of validity and reliability of the predictors being used. Because these are important concerns in personnel research, they are described in more detail in chapter 14.

Increasingly, U.S. organizations are operating in other countries. For example, over forty percent of the five hundred restaurants that McDonald's opens each year are overseas. Because the globalization of many U.S. companies is just beginning, gaining information about managing expatriates and learning how other countries manage their employees are likely to be of interest for some time.

WHERE WE ARE TODAY

1. Increasingly, the staffing activity is being seen as critical for organizational success and survival. Therefore, greater active involvement of top management in staffing is likely to occur.
2. It is in the interest of firms to attract as many potentially qualified applicants as possible so as to increase their chances of finding the best people for the jobs available.
3. To enhance the firm's ability to take advantage of a large applicant pool, it is important for the firm to engage in very systematic and job-related selection practices. While this takes time, the company will benefit tremendously.
4. Recent federal legislation related to civil rights and disabilities will have a significant impact on the staffing practices of organizations. The HR department needs to be out in front on this.

5. Getting line managers and nonmanagers involved in staffing decisions can increase the feeling of ownership in the final hiring decisions. As organizations begin to utilize teams more, they will likely give more involvement in staffing decisions to the line managers and nonmanagers in the teams.
6. An evolving role for the HR manager in tomorrow's organizations will be one of helping line managers and nonmanagers in their staffing decisions.
7. People need to be trained in selection biases in order to make them aware of the biases and develop strategies to reduce those biases in their hiring practices.
8. Because people still prefer to use the interview as a way to gather data and make staffing decisions, HR professionals should spend time working with managers and nonmanagers in interview techniques to help increase their reliability and validity.
9. As organizations see the value and need for getting the right people into their organizations, they will spend more time with their staffing practices and are likely to spend more time testing job applicants. The cost of making false decisions is typically too great for organizations to be willing to incur.
10. Organizations going global need to staff their international operations with expatriates and with third-country and local-country nationals. Determining the balance among these three, and then deciding how to select and socialize them, will become more critical as firms see they have to operate truly globally to survive and succeed.

DISCUSSION QUESTIONS

1. A frequent diagnosis of an observed performance problem in an organization is "Joe was a selection mistake." What are the short- and long-term consequences of these so-called "selection mistakes"? Can you relate this question to your own experiences with organizations?
2. Successful selection and placement decisions are dependent on other human resource activities. Identify these activities, and explain their relationships to selection and placement.
3. Given all of the weaknesses identified with the interview, why is it a popular selection device? How could you improve the interview to overcome some of these weaknesses?
4. What is genetic screening? Is this a means to assess an applicant's skills, knowledge, and abilities or personality, interests, and preferences? How might the rights of the employer conflict with the rights of the individual when genetic screening is used for selection and placement decisions? How would you resolve this conflict?
5. What factors should companies consider when selecting expatriate managers?
6. Explain the difference between single and multiple predictor approaches to making selection decisions. What approach does your instructor use in evaluating performance in your human resource management course? Is it compensatory or noncompensatory? Multiple hurdle or multiple cutoff?
7. How do organizations typically make selection, promotion, and transfer decisions?
8. Why are the best people often not the ones hired for the job?

9. Discuss the actual costs of hiring applicants as well as the potential costs that might be incurred if an incorrect selection decision is made.
10. How do the selection and recruitment strategies used in Japan and Canada differ from those used in the U.S.?

APPLIED PROJECTS

1. Use the format presented in chapter 4 for writing a job description to prepare a job description for a job you are interested in performing. Detail a selection process for the position. Your report should describe the following:
   a) Selection procedures to be used. If you will use a cognitive ability test identify which one. If you will use a situational interview, describe the questions that will be asked. If you will use a personality test, identify the specific test.
   b) Provide a rationale for the choice of each selection device.
   c) Provide the order in which the selection devices will be administered and the rationale for the ordering.
   d) Specify how information will be combined (compensatory, multiple hurdles, or a combination). Detail how the selection devices will be scored.
   e) Indicate expected selection ratios for each stage in the process in which candidates would be screened out.
   f) Finally, specify the costs associated with your selection process.
2. One source of illegal discrimination and waste of human resources comes from job specifications (minimum ability, experience, and/or education standards) which are higher than necessary for adequate job performance. Thus, it is necessary that specifications be as accurate as possible and that applicants be evaluated on how well they meet these specifications. Talk with a personnel and human resource manager of a company and ask how he or she arrives at the job specifications for various jobs. Report to the class about what you learn. You may wish to invite the person to class and have him or her describe to the class the job specification and job description procedures used by the company.

CASE STUDY

Aztec: Staffing with the Right People

John Blair, the human resource manager at Aztec Industries, a medium sized electronics company, was just told by company president Martha Klein that Aztec had just received a very large contract from Sony Corporation of America. Both know that success in filling this order is likely to mean a great deal of business in the future. While this is certainly an opportunity, Blair's concern is with finding and hiring two hundred new qualified employees needed to work on the Sony contract, one that needs to be filled within twenty-four months.

In the past, Aztec's growth rate required adding only twenty-five new employees per year. With Dallas nearby, Blair never found it difficult to find enough people to fill the job openings. Nonetheless, some of the new employees quit or failed to perform adequately. Blair knew, however, that things were different now. Never had the company needed to hire so many people so quickly, and never had the company been concerned about meeting the high standards of a major customer. In addition, a majority of the new jobs had to be filled with semi-skilled and skilled employees. Previously, the majority of new hires filled unskilled jobs, jobs that simply involved a six-step process in assembly. Consequently, when he needed job applicants before he just advertised in the *Dallas Tribune* and filled most of the openings on a "first-come, first-served" basis.

Blair realizes that he must abandon his previous selection policy of hiring the first person who walks through the door. He knows it will be necessary to find out the skills of the job applicants and place them into the jobs they are qualified to perform; but performing the job is not Blair's only concern. He realizes that other behaviors such as absenteeism, cooperation, loyalty, concern for quality, flexibility, and willingness to retrain are important in the successful fulfillment of the Sony contract. He sees this as possibly the time to systematically develop an entire set of human resource practices and get line managers more involved in the process. First things first, however; he needs to hire two hundred new qualified applicants.

Case Question

1. What are all the activities Blair must do in order to be successful here?

NOTES

1. J. Welch, quoted in J. W. Peters, "Strategic Staffing: A Key Link in Business and Human Resource Planning," *Human Resource Planning* 11, no. 2 (1988): 155.
2. L. Landro, "GE's Wizards Turning from the Bottom Line to Share of the Market," *The Wall Street Journal* (12 July 1982): 1.
3. N. Tichy and R. Charan, "Speed, Simplicity, and Self-Confidence: An Interview with Jack Welch," *Harvard Business Review* (Sept.-Oct. 1989): 116.
4. Tichy and Charan, 113.
5. F. L. Schmidt, D. S. Ones, and J. E. Hunter, "Personnel Selection," *Annual Review of Psychology* 43 (1992): 627–70; A. Tziner, *Organization Staffing and Work Adjustments* (Westport, Conn.: Praeger, 1990); N. Schmitt and I. Robertson, "Personnel Selection," *Annual Review of Psychology* 41 (1990): 289–319; R. D. Gatewood and H. S. Feild, *Human Resource Selection,* 2d ed. (Hinsdale, Ill.: Dryden Press, 1990); J. P. Campbell, "An Overview of the Army Selection and Classification Project (Project A)," *Personnel Psychology* 43 (1990): 231–39; D. E. Bowen, G. E. Ledford, Jr., and B. R. Nathan, "Hiring for the Organization, Not the Job," *Academy of Management Executive* 5, no. 4 (1991): 35-51; D. F. Caldwell and C. A. O'Reilly III, "Measuring Person-Job Fit with a Profile-Comparison Process," *Journal of Applied Psychology* 75, no. 6 (1990): 648–57; C. A. O'Reilly III, J. Chatman, and D. F. Caldwell, "People and Organizational Culture: A Profile Comparison Approach to Assessing Person-Organization Fit," *Academy of Management Journal* 34, no. 3 (1991): 487–516; M. A. M. Fricko and T. A. Beehr, "A Longitudinal Investigation of Interest Congruence and Gender Concentration as Predictors of Job Satisfaction," *Personnel Psychology* 45 (1992): 99–117; L. E. Albright, "Staffing Issues," in *Human Resource Management in the 1980s,* ed. S. J. Carroll and R. S. Schuler (Washington, D.C.: Bureau of National Affairs, 1983); R. D. Arvey and R. H. Faley, *Fairness in Selecting Employees* (Reading, Mass.: Addison-Wesley, 1988); H. S. Feild and R. D. Gatewood, "Matching Talent with the Task," in *Human Resource Management: Perspectives and Issues,* ed. G. O. Ferris and K. M. Rowland (Boston: Allyn & Bacon, 1988); M. D. Hakel, "Personnel Selection and Placement," *Annual Review of Psychology* 37 (1986): 351–80; N. Schmitt and B. Schneider, "Current Issues in Personnel Selection," in *Research in Personnel and Human Resource Management,* ed. K. M. Rowland and G. D. Ferris (Greenwich, Conn.: JAI Press, 1983); B. Schneider, "The People Make the Place," *Personnel Psychology* (Autumn 1987): 437–54.
6. M. Miner, "Legal Concerns Facing Human Resource Managers: An Overview," in *Readings in Personnel and Human Resource Management,* 3d ed., ed. R. S. Schuler, S. A. Youngblood, and V. L. Huber (St. Paul, Minn.: West, 1988): 40–56.
7. F. N. Kerlinger, *Foundations of Behavioral Research* (New York: Holt, Rinehart and Winston, 1986).
8. R. D. Arvey and R. H. Faley, *Fairness in Selecting Employees,* 2nd ed. (Reading, MA: Addison-Wesley, 1988).
9. For an excellent discussion about criteria for selection and placement decisions, see Schmidt, Ones, and Hunter, "Personnel Selection."
10. The basis for the statements and suggestions here include "Educational Requirements," *Fair Employment Practices Guidelines* 186, no.1 (1980); "Experience Required" *Fair Employment Practices Guidelines* 190, no. 5 (1981); "The Importance of Record Keeping," *Fair Employment Practices Guidelines* 185, no. 12 (1980); "Personnel Guidelines for Managers and Supervisors," Biddle & Associates, 1982.
11. R. D. Arvey and R. H. Faley, *Fairness in Selecting Employees* ...
12. R. S. Lowell and J. A. DeLoach, "Equal Employment Opportunity: Are You Overlooking the Application Form?" *Personnel* 59 (1982): 49–55; E. C. Miller, "An EEO Examination of Employment Applications," *Personnel Administrator* 25 (1980): 63–69.

13. D. G. Lawrence, B. L. Salsburg, J. G. Dawson, and Z. D. Fasmen, "Design and Use of Weighted Application Blanks," *Personnel Administrator* (March 1982): 53–57, 101.
14. C. J. Russell, J. Mattson, S. E. Devlin, and D. Atwater, "Predictive Validity of Biodata Items Generated from Retrospective Life Experience Essays," *Journal of Applied Psychology* 75, no. 5 (1990): 569–80; H. R. Rothstein, F. L. Schmidt, F. W. Erwin, W. A. Owens, and C. P. Sparks, "Biographical Data in Employment Selection: Can Validities be made Generalizable?" *Journal of Applied Psychology* 75, no. 2 (1990): 175–84; M. A. McDaniel, "Biographical Constructs for Predicting Employee Suitability," *Journal of Applied Psychology* 74, no. 6 (1989): 964–70; A. Childs and R. J. Klimoski, "Successfully Predicting Career Success: An Application of the Biographical Inventory," *Journal of Applied Psychology* (Feb. 1988): 3–8.
15. See note 11.
16. K. K. Sackheim, *Handwriting Analysis and the Employee Selection Process* (Westport, Conn.: Quorum Books, 1990); "Handwriting Analysis," *Bulletin to Management* (8 May 1986): 152. Reprinted by permission from *Bulletin to Management*, copyright 1986 by the Bureau of National Affairs, Inc., Washington, D.C. 20037; G. Ben-Shakar, et al., "Can Graphology Predict Occupational Success? Two Empirical Studies and Some Methodological Ruminations," *Journal of Applied Psychology* (Nov. 1986): 645–853.
17. "Background Checks," *FEP Guidelines,* no. 266 (1987): 1; "Paper and Pencil Measures of Potential," in *Perspectives of Employee Staffing and Selection,* eds. G. Dreher and P. Sackett (Homewood, Ill.: Richard D. Irwin, 1983): 349–67.
18. C. Sparks, "Paper and Pencil Measures of Potential" in *Perspectives of Employee Staffing and Selection,* eds. Dreher and Sackett, 349–67.
19. R. Hogan, B. N. Carpenter, S. R. Briggs, and R. O. Hansen, "Personality Assessment and Personnel Selection," in *Perspectives of Employee Staffing and Selection,* 21–51; "The Future of Personality Tests in Employment Settings," *Psychological Science Agenda* (Jan./Feb. 1992): 2–3.
20. M. R. Barrick and M. K. Mount, "The Big Five Personality Dimensions and Job Performance: A Meta-Analysis," *Personnel Psychology* 44 (1991): 1–26; D. V. Day and S. B. Silverman, "Personality and Job Performance: Evidence of Incremental Validity," *Personnel Psychology* 42 (1989): 25–36; T. Newton and T. Keenan, "Further Analyses of the Dispositional Argument in Organizational Behavior," *Journal of Applied Psychology* 76, no. 6 (1991): 781–87; J. A. Chatman, "Matching People and Organizations: Selection and Socialization in Public Accounting Firms," *Administrative Science Quarterly* 36 (1991): 459–84; P. Warr and M. Conner, "Job Competence and Cognition," *Research in Organizational Behavior* vol. 14 (1992): 91–127; R. P. Tett, D. N. Jackson, and M. Rothstein, "Personality Measures as Predictors of Job Performance: A Meta-Analytic Review," *Personnel Psychology* 44 (1991): 703–42; H. M. Weiss and S. Adler, "Personality and Organizational Behavior," *Research in Organizational Behavior,* eds. B. Straw and L. L. Cummings (Greenwich, Conn.: JAI Press, 1984): 1–50.
21. E. E. Ghiselli, *Explorations in Managerial Talent* (Pacific Palisades, Calif.: Goodyear Publishing, 1971); G. S. Taylor and T. W. Zimmer, "Viewpoint: Personality Tests for Potential Employees: More Harm than Good," *Personnel Journal* (Jan. 1988): 60.
22. J. Hogan, "Interests and Competencies: A Strategy for Personnel Selection," in *Readings in Personnel and Human Resource Management,* 3d ed., eds. R. S. Schuler, S. A. Youngblood, and V. L. Huber (St. Paul, Minn.: West, 1988): 484–95.
23. J. J. Laabs, "Legalities," *Personnel Journal* (Feb. 1992): 109; J. A. Hartigan and A. K. Wigdor, eds., *Fairness in Employment Testing: Validity Generalization, Minority Issues, and the General Aptitude Test Battery* (Washington, D.C.: National Academy Press, 1989).
24. R. T. von Mayrhauser, "The Mental Testing Community and Validity: A Prehistory," *American Psychologist* (Feb. 1992): 244–53; J. P. Guilford and W. S. Zimmerman, *Guilford Zimmerman Temperament Survey* (Orange, Calif.: Sheridan Psychological Services, 1976); F. L. Schmidt, J. E. Hunt, R. McKenzie, and T. Muldrow, "The Impact of Valid Selection Procedures on Workforce Productivity," *Journal of Applied Psychology* 64 (1979): 609–26; Sparks, "Paper and Pencil Measures," in *Perspectives on Employee Staffing and Selection,* 349–67; A. K. Wigdor and W. R. Garner, eds., *Ability Testing: Uses, Consequences, and Controversies, Parts I and II* (Washington, D.C.: National Academy Press, 1982).
25. For an extensive review of and guide to these tests, see L. P. Plumke, "A Short Guide to the Development of Work Sample and Performance Tests," 2d ed. (Washington, D.C.: U. S. Office of Personnel Management, Feb. 1980). Note the interchangeability of the terms *work sample* and *performance tests.*
26. S. J. Motowidlo, M. D. Dunnette, and G. W. Carter, "An Alternative Selection Procedure: The Low-Fidelity Simulation," *Journal of Applied Psychology* 75, no. 6 (1990): 640–47; W. Arthur, Jr., G. V. Barrett, and D. Doverspike, "Validation of an Information-Processing-Based Test Battery for the Prediction of Handling Accidents Among Petroleum-Product Transport Drivers," *Journal of Applied Psychology* 75, no. 6 (1990): 621–28; J. S. Schippmann, E. P. Prien, and J. A. Katz, "Reliability and Validity of In-Basket Performance Measures," *Personnel Psychology* 43 (1990): 837–59; S. L. Cohen, "Pre-Packaged vs. Tailor-Made: The Assessment Center Debate," *Personnel Journal* (Dec. 1980): 989–95; L. C. Nichols and J. Hudson, "Dual-Role Assessment Center: Selection and Development," *Personnel Journal* (May 1981): 350–86; J. C. Quick, W. A. Fisher, L. L. Schkade, and G. W. Ayers, "Developing Administrative Personnel Through the Assessment Center Technique," *Personnel Administrator* (Feb. 1980): 44–46, 62; J. S. Shippman, G. L. Hughes, and E. P. Prien, "Raise Assessment Center Standards," *Personnel Journal* (July 1988): 69–79.
27. For the LGD, see M. M. Petty, "A Multivariate Analysis of the Effects of Experience and Training upon Performance in a Leaderless Group Discussion," *Personnel Psychology* 27 (1974): 271–82. For business games, see B. M. Bass and G. V. Barnett, *People, Work, and Organizations,* 2d ed. (Boston: Allyn & Bacon, 1981).

28. B. B. Gaugler, D. B. Rosenthal, G. C. Thornton, and C. Bentson, "Metanalysis of Assessment Center Validity," *Journal of Applied Psychology* 72 (1987): 493–511; R. Klimoski and M. Brickner, "Why Do Assessment Centers Work? The Puzzle of Assessment Center Validity," *Personnel Psychology* 40 (1987): 243–60; A. Tziner and S. Dolan, "Validity of an Assessment Center for Identifying Female Officers in the Military," *Journal of Applied Psychology* 67 (1982): 728–36.

29. C. L. Martin and D. H. Nagao, "Some Effects of Computerized Interviewing on Job Applicant Responses," *Journal of Applied Psychology* 74, no. 1 (1989): 72–80; W. L. Tullar, "Relational Control in the Employment Interview," *Journal of Applied Psychology* 74, no. 6 (1989): 971–77; A. Peek Phillips and R. L. Dipboye, "Correlational Tests of Predictions from a Process Model of the Interview," *Journal of Applied Psychology* 74, no. 1 (1989): 41–52; T. Hoff Macan and R. L. Dipboye, "The Relationship of Interviewers' Preinterview Impressions to Selection and Recruitment Outcomes," *Personnel Psychology* 43 (1990): 745–68; M. M. Harris, "Reconsidering the Employment Interview: A Review of Recent Literature and Suggestions for Future Research," *Personnel Psychology* 42 (1989): 691–726; R. A. Fear and R. J. Chiron, *The Evaluation Interview,* 4th ed. (New York: McGraw-Hill Publishing Co., 1990); A. H. Eagly, R. D. Ashmore, M. G. Makhijani, and L. C. Longo, "What is Beautiful is Good, But...: A Meta-Analytic Review of Research on the Physical Attractiveness Stereotype," *Psychological Bulletin* 110, no. 1 (1991): 109–28; M. E. Heilman, C. J. Block, R. F. Martell, and M. C. Simon, "Has Anything Changed? Current Characterizations of Men, Women and Managers," *Journal of Applied Psychology* 74, no. 6 (1989): 935– 42; M. S. Singer and C. Sewell, "Applicant Age and Selection Interview Decisions: Effect of Information Exposure on Age Discrimination in Personnel Selection," *Personnel Psychology* 42 (1989): 135–54; M. A. Hitt and S. H. Barr, "Managerial Selection Decision Models: Examination of Configural Cue Processing," *Journal of Applied Psychology* 74, no. 1 (1989): 53–61; B. R. Nathan and N. Tippins, "The Consequences of Halo 'Error' in Performance Ratings: A Field Study of the Moderating Effect of Halo on Test Validation Results," *Journal of Applied Psychology* 75, no. 3 (1990): 290–96; M. E. Heilman, J. C. Rivero, and J. F. Brett, "Skirting the Competence Issue: Effects of Sex-Based Preferential Selection on Task Choices of Women and Men," *Journal of Applied Psychology* 76, no. 1 (1991): 99–105; D. Arthur, *Recruiting, Interviewing, Selecting and Orienting New Employees,* 2d ed. (New York: AMACOM, 1991); A. Feingold, "Good-Looking People are Not What We Think," *Psychological Bulletin* 111, no. 2 (1992): 304–41; R. D. Arvey, H. E. Miller, R. Gould, and P. Burch, "Interview Validity for Selecting Sales Clerks," *Personnel Psychology* (Spring 1987): 1–12; M. A. Campion, E. D. Pursell, and B. K. Brown, "Structured Interviewing: Raising the Psychometric Properties of the Employment Interview," *Personnel Psychology* (Spring 1988): 25–42; T. W. Dougherty, R. J. Ebert, and J. C. Callendar, "Policy Capturing in the Employment Interview," *Journal of Applied Psychology* (Feb. 1986): 9–15; R. A. Fear, *The Evaluation Interview,* 3d ed. (New York: McGraw-Hill, 1984); M. D. Hakel, "Employment Interviewing," in *Personnel Management,* ed. K. M. Rowland and G. Ferris (Boston: Allyn & Bacon, 1982): 129–55; S. P. James, I. M. Campbell, and S. A. Lovegrove, "Personality Differentiation in a Police-Selection Interview," *Journal of Applied Psychology* (Feb. 1984): 129–34; G. P. Latham and L. M. Saari, "Do People Do What They Say? Further Studies on the Situational Interview," *Journal of Applied Psychology* (Nov. 1984): 569–73; S. D. Maurer and C. Fay, "Effect of Situational Interviews and Training on Interview Rating Agreement: An Experimental Analysis," *Personnel Psychology* (Summer 1988): 329–44; S. M. Raza and B. N. Carpenter, "A Model of Hiring Decisions in Real Employment Interviews," *Journal of Applied Psychology* (Nov. 1987): 596–603; D. D. Rodgers, "Personnel Computing: Computer-Aided Interviewing Overcomes First Impressions," *Personnel Journal* (April 1987): 148–52; J. A. Weekley and J. A. Gier, "Reliability and Validity of the Situational Interview for a Sales Position," *Journal of Applied Psychology* (Aug. 1987): 484–87. H. J. Bernardin and R. W. Beatty, *Performance Appraisal: Assessing Human Behavior at Work* (Boston: Kent, 1984): 258–60; W. C. Borman, "Format and Training Effects on Rating Accuracy Using Behavior Scales," *Journal of Applied Psychology* 3 (1979): 103–15.

30. H. J. Bernardin and R. W. *Beatty, Performance Appraisal: Assessing Human Behavior at Work* (Boston: Kent, 1984), 258–60; W. C. Borman, "Format and Training Effects on Rating Accuracy Using Behavior Scales," *Journal of Applied Psychology* 3 (1979): 103–15.

31. The role of the medical doctor in providing the physical exam is an important one. With it, however, is attached responsibility to the employer rather than the employee. See M. S. Novit, "Physical Examinations and Company Liability: A Legal Update," *Personnel Journal* (Jan. 1981): 47–52.

32. E. A. Fleishman, "Some New Frontiers in Personnel Selection Research," *Personnel Psychology* 41, no. 4 (1988): 679–702; E. A. Fleishman, *The Structure and Management of Physical Abilities* (Englewood Cliffs, N.J.: Prentice-Hall, 1964); D. L. Gebhardt and C. E. Crump, *Joint Mobility Evaluation Manual for Entry Level Natural Gas Industrial Jobs* (Bethesda, Md.: Advanced Research Resources Organization, 1983); D. L. Gebhardt, D. C. Meyers, and E. A. Fleishman, "Development of a Job-Related Medical Evaluation System," *San Bernardino County Medical Standard News* 1 (1984): 1–2; D. C. Meyers, M. C. Jennings, and E. A. Fleishman, *Development of Job-Related Medical Standards and Physical Tests for Court Security Officers,* ARRO Final Report #3062/r81–3 (Bethesda, Md.: Advanced Research Resources Organization, 1981).

33. Olian, "New Approaches to Employment Screening," in *Readings in Personnel and Human Resource Management,* 3d ed., 206–16.

34. R. Cropanzano and K. James, "Some Methodological Considerations for the Behavioral Genetic Analysis of Work Attitudes," *Journal of Applied Psychology* 75, no. 4 (1990): 433–39; Office of Technology and Assessment, *The Role of Genetic Testing in the Prevention of Occupational Disease* (Washington, D.C.: U.S. Government Printing Office,

1983); Z. Haranyi and R. Hutton, *Genetic Prophecy: Beyond the Double Helix* (New York: Bantam Books, 1981).

35. "Employee Drug Abuse," *Bulletin to Management* (15 March 1992): 71; J. Normand, S. D. Salyards, and J. J. Mahoney, "An Evaluation of Preemployment Drug Testing," *Journal of Applied Psychology* 75, no. 6 (1990): 629–39.
36. M. A. Konovsky and R. Cropanzano, "Perceived Fairness of Employee Drug Testing as a Predictor of Employee Attitudes and Job Performance," *Journal of Applied Psychology* 76, no. 5 (1991): 698–707; Drug Testing: Conference Policy Pointers," *Bulletin to Management* (7 Aug. 1986); 261–62. For more information see B. Heshizer and J. P. Muczyk, "Drug Testing at the Workplace: Balancing Individual, Organizational and Societal Rights," *Labor Law Journal* (June 1988): 342–57; P. L. Hunsaker and C. M. Pavett, "Drug Abuse in the Brokerage Industry," *Personnel* (July 1988): 54–58; M. F. Masters, G. Ferris, and S. L. Ratcliff, "Practices and Attitudes of Substance Abuse Testing," *Personnel Administrator* (July 1988): 72–78; J. P. Muczyk and B. P. Heshizer, "Mandatory Drug Testing: Managing the Latest Pandora's Box," *Business Horizons* (March/April 1988): 14; M. Rothman, "Random Drug Testing in the Workplace: Implications for Human Resource Management," *Business Horizons* (March/April 1988): 23; W. H. Wagel, "A Drug-Screening Policy That Safeguards Employees' Rights," *Personnel* (Feb. 1988): 10–11.
37. "Drug Policy Pointers," *Bulletin to Management* (7 Jan. 1988): 8. Used by permission of *Bulletin to Management*, copyright 1988.
38. "The AIDS Epidemic and Business," *Business Week* (23 March 1987): 122; "AIDS Focus: Employee Rights and On-Site Education," *Bulletin to Management* 10 (March 1988): 74.
39. B. Kleinmutz, "Lie Detectors Fail the Truth Test," *Harvard Business Review* 63 (1985): 36–42; S. Labato, "Business and the Law: New Rules Limit Lie Detectors' Use," *The New York Times* (28 Nov. 1988): 22; "Preemployment Polygraph Testing Restricted," *Bulletin to Managment* (30 June 1988): 201; L. Saxe, D. Dougherty, and T. Cross, "The Validity of Polygraph Testing," *American Psychologist* 40 (1985): 355–56.
40. T. F. O'Boyle, "More Honesty Tests Used to Gauge Workers' Morale," *The Wall Street Journal* (11 July 1985): 27.
41. L. R. Burris, "Integrity Testing for Personnel Selection: An Update," *Personnel Psychology* 42 (1989): 491–529; J. W. Jones, ed., *Preemployment Honesty Testing: Current Research and Future Directions* (Westport, Conn.: Quorum Books, 1991); P. R. Sackett and M. M. Harris, "Honesty Testing for Personnel Selection: A Review and Critique," *Personnel Psychology* 37 (1984): 221–46.
42. M. Bazerman, *Judgement in Management Decision Making* (New York: Wiley, 1985) M. Bazerman, "Norms of Distributive Justice in Interest Arbitration," *Industrial Relations Review* 38 (1985): 558–70; Huber, Northcraft, and Neale, "Foibles and Fallacies in Organizational Staffing Decisions," in *Reading in Personnel and Human Resource Managment,* 3d ed., 193–205; P. Slovic, "Toward Understanding and Improving Decisions," in *Human Performance and Productivity,* ed. W. C. Howell and E. A. Fleishman (Hillsdale, N.J.: Erlbaum, 1982).
43. M. London, "What Every Personnel Director Should Know about Management Promotion Decisions," *Personnel Journal* (Oct. 1978): 551.
44. R. S. Schuler and I. C. MacMillan, "Gaining a Competitive Advantage through Human Resource Management Practices," *Human Resource Management* (Fall 1984): 248.
45. D. D. McConkey, "Why the Best Managers Don't Get Promoted," *The Business Quarterly* (Summer 1979): 39–43. *The Business Quarterly* is published by the School of Business, the University of Western Ontario, Canada.
46. Bazerman, *Judgement in Management Decision Making...*
47. Rodgers, "Personnel Computing..."
48. C. Fombrun, "An Interview with Reginald Jones," *Organizational Dynamics* (Winter 1982): 46.
49. A. K. Gupta, "Contingency Linkages Between Strategy and General Manager Characteristics: A Conceptual Examination," *Academy of Management Review* 9 (1984): 339–412; A. K. Gupta and V. Govindarajan, "Build, Hold, Harvest: Converting Strategic Intentions into Reality," *Journal of Business Strategy* 4 (1984): 34–37; D. C. Hambrick and P. A. Mason, "Upper Echelons: The Organization as a Reflection of Its Top Management," *Academy of Management Review* 9 (1984): 193–206; J. D. Olian and S. L. Rynes, "Organizational Staffing: Integrating Practice with Strategy," *Industrial Relations* 23 (1984): 170–83; A. D. Szilagyi and D. M. Schweiger, "Matching Managers to Strategies: A Review and Suggested Framework," *Academy of Management Review* 9 (1984): 626–37.
50. P. J. Dowling and R. S. Schuler, *International Dimensions of Human Resource Management* (Boston: PWS-Kent, 1990).
51. M. A. Conway, "Reducing Expatriate Failure Rates," *Personnel Administrator* (July 1984): 31–38; J. S. Lublin, "More Spouses Receive Help in Job Searches when Executives Take Positions Overseas," *The Wall Street Journal* (26 Jan. 1984); J. D. Heller, "Criteria for Selecting an International Manager," *Personnel* (May-June 1980): 47–55; R. L. Tung, *The New Expatriates* (Cambridge, Mass.: Ballinger, 1988); K. D. Stuart, "Teens Play a Role in Moves Overseas," *Personnel Journal* (March 1992): 72–77; A. K. Gupta and V. Govindarajan, "Knowledge Flows and the Structure of Control within Multinational Corporations," *Academy of Management Review* 16, no. 4 (1991): 768–92.
52. On April 12, 1992, Disney opened its doors to what it expects to be an 11-million-visitors-per-year business. Believing that its current practices are important to its success, Disney did not adapt its HR practices very much; S. Toy, "Mouse Fever is About to Strike Europe," *Business Week* (30 March 1992): 32.
53. Information for the case was taken from P. L. Blocklyn, "Making Magic: The Disney Approach to People Management," *Personnel* (Dec. 1988): 28–35; L. Gubernick, "The Mouse that Soared," *Business Week* (8 Jan. 1990): 160; C. Knowlton, "How Disney Keeps the Magic Going," *Fortune* (4 Dec. 1989): 111–32; C. M. Solomon, "How Does Disney Do It?" *Personnel Journal* (Dec. 1989): 50–57; S. Toy and C. Green, "Roy Disney's Adventures in Tomor-

rowland," *Business Week* (5 Aug. 1985): 66–67; G. E. Willigan, "The Value-Adding CFO: An Interview with Disney's Gary Wilson," *Harvard Business Review* (Jan.-Feb. 1990): 85–93; and S. Greenhouse, "Playing Disney in the Parisian Fields," *The New York Times* (17 Feb. 1991): 1, 6.

54. M. E. Mendenhall, E. Dunbar, and G. R. Oddou, "Expatriate Selection, Training and Career-Pathing: A Review and Critique," *Human Resource Management* (Fall 1987): 331; M. Jelinek and N. J. Adler, "Women: World-Class Managers for Global Competition," *Executive* (Feb. 1988): 11–20; P. Dowling and R. S. Schuler, *International Human Resource Management* (Boston: PWS-Kent, 1990); J. S. Black, M. Mendenhall, and G. Oddou, "Toward a Comprehensive Model of International Adjustment: An Integration of Multiple Theoretical Perspectives," *Academy of Management Review* 16, no. 2 (1991): 291–317; H. B. Gregersen and J. S. Black, "Antecedents to Commitment to a Parent Company and a Foreign Operation," *Academy of Management Journal* 35, no. 1 (1992): 65–90.

55. *Developing Effective Global Managers for the 1990s* (New York: Business International Corporation, 1991).

56. Some, but not all, of the statutes define "age" so as to limit the effect of this particular ground of discrimination. Such definitions normally have an upper limit at age sixty-five, but the lower limit varies from nineteen to forty-five. This section on human rights in Canada was prepared by Robert J. Kerr, Professor of Law, University of Windsor, for use in this book.

57. Canadian Human Rights Act, *Statutes of Canada* (1976–1977), chapter 33.

END OF SECTION CASE STUDY

The Tall Pines Hotel and Conference Center*

Gordon McGregor sorted through his morning mail to find the report from Natalie Sharp about the open house sponsored by the hotel for job applicants. With the sounds of hammering and the smell of fresh paint all around, he was eager to get a picture of his new staff as he neared the opening of the hotel in about two months. He pushed aside samples of carpeting left by a subcontractor this morning to read the five-page report from Natalie.

As hotel manager, Gordon was faced with the last of the major hurdles in getting Tall Pines open—the filling of about 315 positions ranging from bellhops and butchers to clerks and chambermaids. The grand opening scheduled for May first made it imperative to bring his full staff on board and get them trained and operational quickly. He had brought in most of his managerial and supervisory staff over the past six months. Many had come from other hotels in the nationwide chain. Some he had worked with in other parts of the chain in his fifteen years in the system, so there was a sense of excitement about being together as a team to create something brand new. Today marked the beginning of the final phase of his plan to manage his own hotel successfully.

The Tall Pines Hotel

Gordon had been involved in the planning of the hotel for about two years. Corporate management had selected the site four years ago on the basis of a careful study by its market research staff of the southeastern part of the United States. They were interested in launching a new concept in hotels and had chosen the city of Riverton (pop. 95,000), located in the suburbs of Roosevelt City, a major city in the Southeast. The entire metropolitan area had grown dramatically since the early 1960s to a total population of about 1.9 million, with further growth forecast for the next fifteen years before a leveling off would occur.

Riverton comprised about half the area and two-thirds the population of one of the counties that surrounded Roosevelt City. Growth in population, wealth, and industry had been concentrated in the suburban counties, although there was new interest in the revitalization of the old downtown area. Riverton had been especially aggressive in its plan to attract new industry with the creation of an economic development committee, which had been successful in enticing a number of high-technology firms to open offices or build small facilities within the city limits. Many offices had moved from Roosevelt into the suburbs to take advantage of lower taxes, new buildings, and a pool of skilled workers. Shopping centers, restaurants, and housing developments mushroomed to meet the demands of the population shift.

Corporate management saw the opportunity to fill a niche in the suburbs because of lack of hotel and conference space. They purchased an eighteen-acre tract on a major highway that entered Roosevelt City from the south on the west side of Riverton. It was to be developed as a campuslike setting with the preservation of two major pine groves and the expansion of a natural lake. The hotel had been constructed in line with these plans to include 350 rooms, two swimming pools, three restaurants, small shops, and a small exercise and weight room. An outdoor jogging trail was being completed as well. The conference center was built to cater to corporate meetings with secretarial services, teleconferencing facilities, and even access to personal computers. The entire facility was oriented toward comfortable stays of extended periods as well as overnight lodging.

An architect of national reputation had designed the building to become a focal point for the surrounding area. Twin towers jutted through the pines to provide the foundation for a five-story atrium. The glass enclosure provided light and freshness to the restaurants and public space below. The building was striking as viewed from the interstate in both directions, standing boldly against the horizon and rising from the pine groves. Tall Pines was a particularly appropriate name for the entire center, which could act as a comfortable retreat from both city activity and corporate life.

The building had also been controversial. The Riverton Board of Architectural Review was besieged by complaints about the design. But support from the city council and the mayor dissolved the opposition quickly. Projections of a $3.8 million payroll and annual tax bills of $350,000 for the city and $420,000 for the state made the entire project highly appealing. The board voted unanimously to accept the architectural plans.

Natalie Sharp, Director of Personnel

Last November, Gordon had hired Natalie Sharp to become his director of personnel. She had worked for two other hotel chains after college and then been hired three years ago to help with the opening of a new one-hundred-room hotel in the Southwest. She had done an outstanding job of staffing this hotel set in the center of the older city undergoing major renovation. Corporate management was enthusiastic about her potential and had urged Gordon to consider her for the job. Two days of interviews at Tall Pines confirmed this potential as well as the experience he needed in opening a new hotel.

Natalie was given the responsibility for the entire staffing process, although Gordon had made it clear that his department managers had the final authority for those working in their departments. Supervisory personnel were hired with Natalie confirming managerial decisions and working out job descriptions, salaries, and other specifics for each position.

Her major task was the recruitment and hiring program for the bulk of the staff to ready the hotel for opening on May first. She and Gordon had met in the middle of January to review her plan. She had worked closely with the state Department of Employment Services as well as Riverton's Employment Options Office to arrange for a Job Fair on February fifteenth. Held at a local school on a Saturday, the fair was designed to attract candidates and provide a screening session and even some first-round interviews. Tall Pines would provide a good package of benefits on top of a competitive wage:

- Blue Cross/Blue Shield
- Paid vacation (after one year)
- Pension plan (vested after seven years)
- On-site job training
- Educational benefits

Natalie had convinced Gordon that although minimum wage would be the controlling factor for many entry-level positions, the promise of raises in six months was needed as an inducement for retention of good employees.

Natalie believed that the primary pool of candidates would be found in Roosevelt City and Riverton. The figures provided by a local governmental agency supported her belief that a number of people would apply for the various positions to be filled.

Local Unemployment Rates*

Metropolitan area	**3.7%**
Roosevelt City	**8.1**
Riverton	**5.0**
All suburbs	**3.7**

*December figures.

An advertising campaign directed toward the larger metropolitan area, coupled with state and city support, should yield at least double the number of candidates needed for each position. Natalie had shown Gordon a series of articles in the *Metro Star*, the major daily, about a large hotel opening last year in the center of Roosevelt City. Over 11,000 applications were made for 350 positions; the articles included pictures of long lines of people trying to get through the door for interviews. Tall Pines would find an eager group ready to work at its hotel.

The Disappointing Report

The note of optimism of last month was missing from the short report on yesterday's Job Fair. Just over 200 people had applied for the 315 positions. Of these, only 75 had been screened and interviewed. Most had little experience in the hotel business but seemed capable of on-the-job training. The applicants were mostly from the surrounding towns in the county and Riverton, with a few from Roosevelt City.

Natalie had done an informal survey of her small cadre of interviewers late in the afternoon. Applicants had concerns about wage scales and transportation. Unskilled workers with some experience found it difficult to believe that they would start at minimum wage, saying that they could get more at many fast-food chains. Three employees from Big Tex, a regional hamburger chain, had come to the fair together and reported that the chain had just upped starting salaries for counter help to seventy-five cents above minimum wage. Natalie's follow-up call to Big Tex, as well as her conversation with a representative of the county chamber of commerce, had confirmed that many employers were offering hourly wages in excess of minimum wage simply to fill empty positions.

The concerns about transportation were more difficult to bring into focus. Natalie pieced together a picture of Tall Pines being out of the way for most people using public transportation. A few asked about whether the hotel planned to provide bus transportation into Roosevelt City. It had taken them nearly an hour from home with a transfer from a subway stop onto a bus, which dropped them off about three blocks away. Riverton residents indicated that it took thirty minutes to get over from the east side of the city, which meant crossing the interstate because the bus route ended there. Location clearly was a factor in keeping applicants away.

The Stream of Telephone Calls

Gordon's optimism about his gala opening was suddenly deflated by this report. Natalie's conclusion was concisely stated in one sentence:

I have arranged another Job Fair in ten days with the hope that our results will be better this time.

He wondered whether there would be enough candidates for the remaining positions and whether there would be enough time to train them after all of the necessary personnel paperwork had been completed.

His thoughts were interrupted by a call from his secretary indicating that a reporter was on the line from the *Riverton Telegram,* asking questions about the Job Fair. He directed the call to Natalie's office. A call from the *Metro Star* was also redirected. But he did take a call from the Riverton mayor's office to assure them that the hotel had the hiring situation under control with the opening still set for May first. Later in the afternoon, the director of one of the associations scheduled to hold a conference at the hotel during the first week called to ask about the opening. Bad news travels fast! thought Gordon as he hung up with another set of assurances to the anxious director.

Natalie sailed into the office to report on the two phone calls from the press. Both had received information about the disappointing turnout at the Job Fair and were interested in both the reasons and the impact on the opening. She thought that it would be difficult to assess the impact of the publicity until the morning editions were out. Gordon suggested a breakfast meeting with the hotel's top staff to discuss the problem and work toward a solution.

The Breakfast Staff Meeting

Both papers covered the story with short articles hidden away in the second sections. The *Telegram* headline read:

NEW HOTEL NEEDS 240 WORKERS

It briefly described the low turnout at the Job Fair with a listing of the positions still available. A quote from Natalie indicated that another fair would be held in the near future. The story was done in a generally favorable light with emphasis on new business within Riverton, which the hotel should attract.

The *Star* headline was more critical:

NEW SUBURBAN HOTEL SURPRISED TO
FIND FEW APPLY FOR 315 JOBS

The new twin towers were pictured along with a sheet from the fair that listed the jobs available at the hotel. Natalie was quoted about the continuing search to be carried out as well as the types of benefits offered by Tall Pines. A representative of the Roosevelt City Office of Job Services was quoted: "It's not so much that people here won't look in the suburbs; it's that once you cross over that city line, there is a mental barrier about being away from home. Employers have to offer good jobs, good transportation, and a lot of encouragement to get people to apply." A union office spokesman wondered whether people were discouraged because Tall Pines is a nonunion hotel. A man who had been offered a second interview at the fair indicated that he would rather work close to his home in Roosevelt City, but had been out of work for four months and needed the job.

Gordon and Natalie agreed that neither article gave a negative perspective on hotel management, but questions could be raised about postponement of the opening. Clearly, it was important to follow up with the Riverton mayor's office as well as meeting planners who had scheduled the hotel opening for May and June to assure them that the situation would be under control. Contact with the Roosevelt City office of Job Services was mandatory now.

At the meeting, Gordon asked Natalie to review her report as well as the press clippings for the assembled department heads. They both answered a number of questions about the Job Fair and the type of applicants at the fair. Gordon suggested that they delay the discussion about the future until later in the meeting so that all of the facts surrounding the problem could be sorted through carefully. It became clear that many departments could operate for the first two weeks in May on a reduced staffing pattern using supervisory personnel to fill in. But a full staff was essential to accommodate the anticipated increase in business.

The meeting then turned to a brainstorming session to help Natalie develop a strategy for attracting people who would be good candidates to fill the remaining positions. The group agreed that four areas merited further consideration:

- *Advertising campaign*
  Directed particularly toward Roosevelt City and Riverton with focus on benefits of working at Tall Pines.
- *Upgrade of wage scale*
  Additions to minimum wage for entry-level jobs in order to be competitive. Necessity for incentive pay to retain good employees.
- *Transportation system*
  Necessity for assistance to workers coming from both Riverton and Roosevelt City in particular because of their reliance on public transportation.
- *Cooperation with public agencies*
  Cultivation of relationships with a number of agencies to identify other applicant pools.

Gordon asked Natalie to make use of these ideas in the development of a plan to fill the 240 remaining positions. He assured the managers that he would call them the next day with a finalized plan to meet the objective of full staffing by May first. In the meantime, he would handle the public relations aspect of the issue through his office. The meeting adjourned with an agreement that any hotel was only as good as its personnel.

Reflections Over Lunch

As manager of Tall Pines, Gordon enjoyed a number of perquisites unavailable in other jobs. Today, he was delighted to initiate one of those—access to the best meals from the hotel kitchens. Jack Sanders, the sales and convention manager, wheeled in a cart of delectable dishes prepared by one of the French chefs interviewing for the position as head chef. Expecting to join Gordon for lunch, he set a small table for two and uncorked a bottle of wine. As he settled into one of the chairs and pulled out his napkin, Gordon interrupted: "Sorry, Jack. This is a working lunch for me with all of this hiring mess on my mind. You're welcome to take a plate back to your office, but I need to be alone to get a handle on this situation." Jack excused himself, a full plate and wineglass in hand, while Gordon settled into his chair.

The meal was excellent, with the wine chosen for its appropriate balance with the food. Gordon thought about his fortunate managerial situation—no fast-food lunches, no traveling throughout the week, and no narrow job responsibilities. All of these were left behind for any hotel manager. There was a sense of excitement about what lay in store for him both here at Tall Pines and within the larger national organization as it expanded.

But the past day had drowned out much of that excitement. What seemed so close to completion was now filled with a number of questions. Could Tall Pines attract a good staff? Could they be trained and on the job by May first? How costly was it going to be to pay a competitive wage? Could he instill within the staff a sense of pride about Tall Pines? Could the hotel open on May first?

The smell of paint, the carpet samples, and even the faint sound of hammers now came into fuller focus as he asked the last question. Where had he gone wrong in the development of his plan to open the hotel? Why didn't he foresee a potential problem about staffing earlier? Getting the right people seemed like the easiest of his plans to implement. Now it looked like an impossible task. With a cup of coffee in hand, he moved back to his desk to begin the process of solving the problem he faced.

*By D. Jeffrey Lenn, School of Government and Business Administration, George Washington University. This case is based on an actual situation, but the names, location, and other significant data have been altered to provide anonymity. Its purpose is not to focus on effective or ineffective management but to provide a basis for teaching and discussion.

SECTION 4

Appraising

Employees want to know what they are supposed to do, what's expected of them, what are the standards of performance, how they're doing—and they want advice for doing even better the next time around. This is where appraising in personnel and human resource management enters.

During the recruiting and the selection activities, individuals get information on what job they are supposed to do. They may even begin to get information on what's expected of them and what are the standards of performance. This is increasingly the case in companies that do a great job in their staffing activities. However, even in these companies, the newly recruited and selected applicants—and, in some cases, even the current employees—may not know exactly what's expected of them or the standards of performance. In contrast with the staffing activities wherein the human resource manager and the line manager may work closely together, line managers may be on their own when appraising their employees. Of course, the human resource managers may contribute to the design of performance appraisal forms, and they may try to ensure that the supervisors turn their forms in on time. For the most part, though, the line manager is conveying to the employees what's expected, telling them what are the standards of performance and what they can do to improve their performance.

Appraising employee performance is discussed here in two chapters. Chapter 7 covers the issues involved in gathering information used for appraising the performance of employees. First we'll discuss all the purposes of performance appraisal and describe the major forms companies use to appraise employee work. Chapter 8 addresses the issues associated with using that information to help employees improve their performance. We will describe the basic conflicts in doing performance appraisal and giving feedback, and conclude by offering strategies managers and their organizations can use for improving employee performance.

CHAPTER 7

Performance Appraisal: Gathering the Data

At the heart of PepsiCo's Darwinian system are two distinctly different types of management evaluations. One is designed to weed out the weak and the other to nurture the strong.

—Michael Jordan, CEO of Frito-Lay[1]

The term mystery shopper may conjure up images of a detective meticulously examining a firm's products for taste clues or pulling out a magnifying glass to look for the secret ingredient; but Au Bon Pain Co.'s mystery shoppers are nothing like this caricature. Instead, the mystery shoppers who are paid $10 a visit are part of the Boston-based restaurant chain's team-based performance appraisal program. According to Ron Shaich, Au Bon Pain's co-chief executive, the program is designed to ensure that the company meets its corporate mandate of attaining excellence in product, environment, and service. "If you've got customers, you ought to be looking at what you do through a customer's eyes," he contends.

With 1,600 people on its payroll and another 400 employed by franchises, evaluating performance was not an easy task for the restaurant chain—that is, until the $70-million-plus firm implemented its mystery shopper program. Now, an anonymous noncompany-affiliated customer buys a meal and fills out a behavior-based appraisal on a specific restaurant, its food, and its service. Prior to actually evaluating performance, all shoppers (they're recruited by newspaper advertising) receive a three-hour training session on the company's customer service philosophy and are given samples of the food as it should be prepared so they can effectively evaluate how it was prepared.

Armed with a 60-question evaluation form, mystery shoppers visit each store three times over four weeks, during breakfast, lunch, and dinner. Shoppers spend at least 20 minutes (30 is average) during their visits. There are more visits if a district manager is concerned about the service or cleanliness of a particular unit. While other hospitality firms shop more or less frequently than does Au Bon Pain's, the important thing, Shaich contends "is that the appraisal be systematic and statistically significant."

Figuring out what to target in the area of food, environment, and service wasn't simple. The number of questions on the evaluation form has been whittled down from a high of 200 to the current 60. Some questions—such as, "Does the rail in front of the counter have smudge marks on it?"—were pulled in favor of those more critical to measuring quality and service, such as "Note a small piece of trash (straw, napkins, etc.) or an area of crumbs or other minor spills on the floor. Check Yes if cleaned within 10 minutes." There are also areas that the mystery customers cannot evaluate. District managers check up on such things as whether the chicken is being kept at 140 degrees, and in-house managers monitor the performance of bakers, prep people, and clean-up crews. The mystery shopper doesn't observe the former and doesn't interact with the latter.

PEGS Formula

The current system is entitled PEGS—Product, Environment, and Great Service—and focuses on the 12 specific criteria Au Bon Pain feels are most important to attaining its corporate mission. Questions assess everything from food availability to length of waiting time to restating the order when it's handed to the customer. PEGS scores are tallied (10 of 12 criteria met) and transformed into a percentile ranking (83.3 percent).

According to Joy Pomeroy, the company's first store manager and current head of Retail Quality Control, the program has significantly improved customer service because employees now know what is expected of them and receive feedback on how well they met expectations. Overall site performance scores have risen from an average of 72 percent to 82 percent. Approximately 20 people from *stores receive rave reviews each week. That's about what it was when the program was launched.*[2]

Au Bon Pain's mystery shopper program shows how the performance appraisal process can help an organization implement its business objectives. Additionally, it typifies the way strategic plans can be linked to performance planning for individual employees as well as for business units. Au Bon Pain's performance appraisal process is strategic since it helps the company meet its customer service and food quality objectives. As designed, Au Bon Pain's appraisal process incorporates many of the components of an effective performance management system—that is, one that is capable of eliciting peak performance among employees at all levels. Performance expectations are communicated to employees in advance. The goals are difficult but attainable. Individual and strategic business unit goals are intertwined. Raters are trained and have an opportunity to observe performance. Feedback is immediate, precise, and behaviorally based. Additionally, valued rewards are linked to performance outcomes.

PERFORMANCE APPRAISAL

Although employees may learn about how well they are performing through informal means, such as favorable comments from co-workers or superiors, **performance appraisal** is defined here as a formal, structured system of measuring, evaluating, and influencing an employee's job-related attributes, behaviors, and outcomes, as well as level of absenteeism, to discover how productive the employee is and whether he or she can perform as or more effectively in the future, so that the employee, the organization, and society all benefit.[3]

In this chapter, we will define performance appraisal more completely, delineate system objectives, and review components of an effective appraisal system. We will also examine the determinants of performance appraisal strategy. The chapter concludes with proposals on how to gain a competitive edge through performance management. Because performance appraisal is so important in linking with the business, chapter 8 focuses on using appraisal information, especially the appraisal interview, to implement strategy and gain a competitive edge.[4]

PURPOSES AND IMPORTANCE OF PERFORMANCE APPRAISAL

Historically, information from performance appraisals has been used as a basis for administrative decisions. However, a recent study identified twenty different uses for performance information which can be grouped into four categories: (1) between person, (2) within-person development, (3) for systems maintenance, and (4) to document human resource decisions.[5]

As shown in exhibit 7.1, salary administration and development feedback rank as the top uses; criteria for validation studies, determining organizational training needs, and reinforcing the authority structure are less frequent uses.

How well the performance appraisal system achieves these objectives depends on how successful the organization is in integrating performance plan-

Exhibit 7.1
Top Twenty Uses of Performance Appraisal Information

Use	Rating	Rank
Between-Person Evaluation		
Salary administration	5.6	2
Recognition of individual performance	5.0	5
Identification of poor performance	5.0	5
Promotion decisions	4.8	8
Retention/termination decisions	4.8	8
Layoffs	3.5	13
Within-Person Development		
Performance feedback	5.7	1
Identification of individual strengths/weaknesses	5.4	3
Determination of transfers and assignments	3.7	12
Identification of individual training needs	3.4	14
Systems Maintenance		
Development of individual corporate goals	4.9	7
Evaluation of goal attainment by individuals, teams, and strategic business units	4.7	10
Human resource planning	2.7	15
Determination of organizational training needs	2.7	15
Reinforcement of authority structure	2.6	17
Identification of organizational development needs	2.6	17
Human resource system auditing	2.0	20
Documentation		
Documentation of HRM decisions	5.2	4
Meet HRM legal requirements	4.6	11
Criteria for validation research	2.3	19

Ratings were based on a 7-point scale measuring the impact of appraisal on different organizational decisions and action, where 1 = no impact, 4 = moderate impact, and 7 = primary determinant.
SOURCE: Based on J.N. Cleveland, K.R. Murphy, and R.E. Williams, "Multiple Uses of Performance Appraisal: Prevalence and Correlates," *Journal of Applied Psychology* (Feb. 1989) 130–35.

ning with the organization's strategy—that is, in linking performance appraisal with the needs of the business. One reason organizations are not always as successful as they would like to be at integrating performance planning with organizational planning is that managers are seldom proficient in the basics of performance planning. Most managers spend far more time acquiring technical competencies (i.e., accounting, marketing, operations management) for entry into an organization than they do learning to manage. An effective performance management system aids the manager in achieving his or her corporate mandate of getting things done through other people.

Another reason organizations feel their performance management systems are not working effectively is that managers rarely see any payoff for conducting performance evaluations. A recent study showed that, in most organizations, it simply does not matter whether a manager does a good or a poor job of appraising employee performance. In fact, there is usually so much paperwork and are so many unpleasant confrontations with employees that managers tend to avoid the process entirely. Another often cited reason performance appraisals fall short of achieving strategic objectives is that organizations do not specify who is responsible for managing human resources. At the heart of the debate is whether performance management falls in the domain of human resource departments or line departments.[6]

There are, however, a variety of reasons for integrating performance appraisal with the strategy formulation and organizational planning processes. First, strategic performance appraisal aligns the goals of the individual with those of the organization; that is, it embodies the description of actions and results employees must exhibit to make a strategy come alive.[7]

Second, such a process provides a means of planning and measuring the contribution of each work unit and each employee; and third, performance evaluation contributes to the administrative actions and decisions that enhance and facilitate strategy, such as assessing current skill levels of employees. This type of information is useful during strategic transformation, which requires new or different skill mixes. For example, when Kodak made a strategic shift, it recognized Kodak would need engineers familiar with photoprocessing and electronics who could carry out new corporate objectives and move Kodak into new markets. Kodak's strategic alternatives ranged from developing skills in existing employees to acquiring engineers from the outside. On first blush, hiring engineers from the outside was appealing; yet, a more careful analysis showed it would be more cost effective to train existing employees—namely, the chemists who would be surplused with the implementation of the new strategy—to handle engineering responsibilities. In making this decision, Kodak recognized that its chemists already had a strong scientific background. More important, the chemists had a detailed knowledge of the photoprocessing industry and a well-grounded commitment to Kodak. A human resource cost-benefit analysis clinched the decision. Kodak set up corporate-sponsored technical training. An arrangement was made with a nearby university for the chemists to earn their engineering degrees. For Kodak, this strategic decision was easier to make because information was available via their appraisal process regarding the competencies of current employees.

Finally, a performance appraisal system aligned with the needs of the business is important for its potential to identify the need for new strategies and programs. At Pepsi-Cola International, the overall business goal is to accelerate corporate growth ahead of global market growth. To achieve this objective, regular climate surveys or upward evaluations are conducted. Performance information recently pointed to a deficiency in corporate training. To address this deficiency, the multinational firm established an umbrella organization to deliver training programs around the world. Performance data also were the catalyst for the development of Pepsi-Cola International's "Designate Program." This program brings non–U.S. citizens to the U.S. for a minimum of eighteen months of training in the domestic U.S. Pepsi system. The program was developed to provide in-depth experiential training that would build a skill base among employees working in overseas markets. Having a knowledgeable, trained work force was viewed a necessary first step in attaining Pepsi-Cola International's overall growth objective and its underlying business goal of developing talented people to drive the growth in Pepsi brands.[8]

COMPONENTS OF A PERFORMANCE MANAGEMENT SYSTEM

The preceding sections emphasize the importance of evaluating subordinate, work team, and business unit performance in relationship to the goals of the organization and to the legal requirements.[9] This section discusses components of a **performance management system.** In essence, a performance management or appraisal system involves

- Determining the needs of the business, particularly its strategic objectives
- Linking performance appraisal planning with organizational planning
- Conducting a job analysis to identify job duties and responsibilities for which criteria need to be developed
- Choosing an appropriate and valid performance appraisal method to assess job behaviors or outcomes
- Developing a process for conveying job expectations to incumbents prior to the appraisal period
- Establishing a feedback system relating to job performance
- Evaluating how well the performance appraisal system is doing in relation to its stated objectives

How well the system works depends on the organization's culture, its strategic objectives, and the characteristics of the rater and the incumbent.

To develop a performance management system, decide (1) what to evaluate, (2) when to conduct appraisals, and (3) who should evaluate performance. These decisions are discussed below. Rating formats will be reviewed in a subsequent section.

What to Evaluate

A valid performance appraisal system grows out of a comprehensive job analysis that identifies important job duties and tasks. Once these are delineated, performance criteria can be developed. **Criteria** are evaluative dimensions against which an incumbent's, a team's, or a work unit's behavior or performance are measured. They are the performance expectations one strives for in order to achieve the corporate mission.

Types of performance criteria. One of the most important decisions relating to performance appraisal centers on the type of performance criteria. There are three basic categories of performance criteria.

Trait-based criteria focus on the personal characteristics of an employee. Such factors as loyalty, dependability, communication ability, and leadership skill exemplify traits that are often assessed during the appraisal process. This type of performance criteria asks a lot about what a person is, but fails to focus on what a person accomplishes or does not accomplish on the job. While trait-based appraisal instruments can be constructed easily, they are not generally valid. As indicated in the appraisal and law sections, what is assessed in a performance appraisal system must be related directly to the job. Unfortunately, the link between traits and performance is often weak. This is due to the influence of situational factors. Traits also are difficult to accurately define. To one person dependability may mean showing up to work on time every day; to another person it may mean staying late when the boss requests it; to a third person, it may mean not using sick days even when you are really sick. Because of these concerns, trait-based criteria are not generally defendable in the courts.

Behavior-based criteria focus on how work is performed. Such criteria are particularly important for jobs which involve interpersonal contact. For example, how a counselor opens a discussion with a marital couple experiencing interpersonal trauma is critical to the success of the counseling session. A salesperson needs to use enough verbal persuasion to close an important sale, but not so much that the customer panics and flees.

Behavioral criteria are particularly useful for employee development. With behaviors clearly identified, an employee is more likely to exhibit those acts that lead to peak performance. Behavioral criteria are less appropriate for jobs in which effective performance can be achieved using many different behaviors. Still, the identification of the most appropriate behaviors will serve as a guideline for most employees' actions. Since they relate specifically to what the employee does on the job, behavioral criteria tend to be legally defendable.

With the increased emphasis on productivity and international competitiveness, **outcome-based criteria** have risen in popularity. This type of criteria focuses on what was accomplished or produced rather than on how it was produced. Outcome criteria are appropriate when it is not important how results are achieved, but they are not appropriate for every job. For example, the number of cases handled annually by a lawyer can easily be counted. However, such a performance indicator would not indicate the quality of legal counsel given or the resolution of the cases. Second, it may be impossible to indicate in advance how many cases can be handled or how much time a given case may take.

Another concern is that the easy-to-measure aspects of a job are often assessed rather than the more important but more evasive aspects of the job. It is far easier to assess the number of word processing errors made than it is to assess the administrative assistant's skill in screening office calls and visitors.

A results-at-all-cost mentality may also plague outcome-based appraisals. For example, a collection agency used outcome criteria (money collected) as its sole measure of performance. While large sums of money were collected, the agency ended up being sued because collection agencies used threats and punitive measures to amass collections.

Closeness to organizational goals. Depending on the organization's strategy and its ability to measure performance, criteria can be developed that relate either to individual or group job behavior or outcomes or to overall organizational effectiveness. Consider an assistant vice-president job in a bank. Behavioral criteria for this job may include "Phones arbitrageurs/traders within ten minutes of order receipt." By comparison, outcome criteria refer to the product or output produced—for example, "Generates $5 million in sales each month." Organizational effectiveness involves an inferential leap; it entails aggregating individual and group outcomes in order to determine how well the organization is functioning. For example, an organizational effectiveness criterion for the bank at which the assistant vice-president works might relate to total profitability of the bank for a specific quarter.

Single or multiple criteria. If coordinating market activities is the only job duty, then only criteria that relate to this single duty are needed. More often, however, jobs are multidimensional, composed of many different duties and related tasks. For the assistant vice-president job, the primary duty of "Coordinating market activities" is accompanied by other duties, such as "Stays abreast of current events" and "Closes out daily market activities." If job analysis identifies all these duties as important, all should be measured by the performance appraisal instrument.

If the form used to appraise employee performance lacks the job behaviors and results important and relevant to the job, the form is said to be **deficient.** If the form appraises anything either unimportant or irrelevant to the job, it is **contaminated.** Many performance appraisal forms actually used in organizations measure some employee attributes and behaviors that are unrelated to the employee's job. These forms are contaminated and are in many cases also deficient.

Weighting of criteria. For jobs involving more than one duty, there is another decision to be made. How should these separate aspects of performance be combined into a composite score that will facilitate comparisons of incumbents? One way is to weight each criterion equally. The simplest, but most accurate approach is to use weights generated through job analysis. Individual weights can also be determined for each criterion, relative to its ability to predict overall performance. Multiple regression also can be utilized to determine appropriate weights for each job dimension.

When to Conduct Appraisals

In addition to identifying appropriate criteria, we must identify the time period for which performance is to be assessed and the timing of appraisal.

Cycle length. On average, most organizations require formal performance review sessions at six-month to one-year intervals. This makes some sense since it fits with the natural rhythm of the organization. However, there are reasons to believe that performance of some jobs should be evaluated more or less frequently. Some writers contend that the evaluation period should correspond to the time span of the job, the length of time it takes to recognize the performance level of someone who is doing a job. In the case of some simple, lower level jobs, the time span may be as short as a few minutes; in the case of a senior level management job, the appropriate time period may be as long as several years. In an advertising agency, account executives receive evaluation feedback after each presentation. In a research firm searching for a genetic marker, the time period would be much longer.[10]

Assessing performance on a cycle that roughly approximates the characteristics of the job can be advantageous. If performance is assessed before it can be reasonably measured, misassessment is likely. If the time period is too long, motivation and performance may suffer significantly. This is particularly detrimental in the case of a poor performer. If the time period is too long, the employee will not know what needs to be done to improve performance until it is too late.

The evaluation period may also depend on the purpose of the appraisal. To meet communication and evaluation purposes, the focus should be on **current** employee performance during a **single** performance period. For promotion and training decisions, an examination of performance across multiple appraisal periods may be of use. If performance is steadily increasing or is consistently high, a promotion may be justified. If performance remains consistently low, training may be necessary.

Timing of appraisal. In many organizations performance appraisals are conducted according to when the individual joined the organization. This approach is referred to as **the anniversary model**. This approach spreads the workload throughout the year, so the appraisal task is not overwhelming. However, it typically does not tie individual or team performance to the overall performance of the organization. Consequently, the strategic benefits of the appraisal process are compromised. Research also suggests that ratings given to employees early in the year are higher or more lenient than ratings given later. This is particularly so when raters/appraisers are allocated a specific number of high and a specific number of low ratings. A third drawback is that the organization does not know how the supervisor is appraising performance and subsequently can't determine how well the total organization is performing until the year is over and all evaluations have been completed.

The other approach is called a **focal-point system** in which every employee is appraised at approximately the same time in the year (usually the end of the fiscal or calendar year). The major advantage of the focal point system is that comparisons between employees can be made. Supervisors can look at all individuals, report to them, and get a sense of how their performance compares during the same time period. Similarly, top management can compare the performance of different strategic business units to assess how well corporate objectives are being met. Such comparative information is particularly important if performance information is to be used in evaluation decisions. The major disadvantage of focal-point reviews is that they produce a tremendous workload at one time. This burden can, however, be reduced in two ways: first, by having clear criteria against which to evaluate performance, and second, by ensuring that subordinates share the responsibility with their supervisor for defining performance criteria and documenting accomplishments relative to performance standards.

Who Should Conduct Appraisals

Sources of performance data include supervisors, peers or team members, subordinates, self-appraisal, customers, and computer monitoring. While many of these can be used to gather data, the relevance of each source needs to be considered before choosing the rating method.

Critical in determining who should conduct an appraisal is the amount and type of work contact the evaluator has with the person being evaluated. The quantity and quality of **task acquaintance** may vary with organizational level as well as with proximity of the worker and the rater.[11] As a result, team members, customers, and subordinates see different facets of an individual's task behavior than are seen by supervisors. For example, a customer is more likely to observe the behavior (e.g., greeting the customer, closing the sale) of a sale's representative than a first-level supervisor. On the other hand, a supervisor will have access to more information about results and comparative sales performance than will customers. The important point is that no one—not even the employee—has complete information. A worker may know what he or she has done but not be aware of the results of those behaviors. Thus, we often need to involve multiple raters in the evaluation process.

Appraisal by superiors. The superior is the immediate boss of the subordinate being evaluated. The assumption is that the superior knows the subordinate's job and performance better than anyone else. However, appraisal by the superior has drawbacks. First, because the superior may have reward and punishment power, the subordinate may feel threatened. Second, evaluation is often a one-way process that makes the subordinate feel defensive. Thus, little coaching takes place; justification of actions prevails. Third, the superior may not have the necessary interpersonal skills to give good feedback. Fourth, the superior, by giving punishments, may alienate the subordinate.

Because of the potential liabilities, organizations often invite other people to share in the appraisal process. Allowing other people who have knowledge of job performance to gather performance data increases the reliability and perceived fairness of the appraisal process. Additionally, it creates a greater openness in the performance appraisal system, thus helping to enhance the quality of the superior-subordinate relationship. The increase in information is not without cost. Evaluations obtained from other sources bypass natural lines of authority (organizational hierarchy) or reverse the usual authority structure (subordinate evaluations) and may be prohibited by contractual agreements (union-management contracts).[12]

Self-appraisal. The use of self-appraisal, particularly through subordinate participation in setting goals, was made popular as an important component of MBO, or management by objectives. Subordinates who participate in the evaluation process may become more involved and committed to the goals. Subordinate participation may also help clarify employees' roles and reduce role conflict.[13]

At this time, self-appraisals are effective tools for programs focusing on self-development, personal growth, and goal commitment. However, self-appraisals are subject to systematic biases and distortions when used for evaluations. There is evidence that self-ratings are more lenient or higher than those obtained from supervisors. Self-ratings will correspond more closely to supervisory ratings when extensive performance feedback is given and when incumbents know that their performance ratings will be checked against objective criteria.[14]

According to Roger Flax, president of Motivational Systems, a New Jersey management and sales training company, self-appraisals are particularly useful in small companies (but not necessarily in all cultures, as described in the Focus on Research: "How Do We Rate Performance?").

> There's a lot of assuming that in small companies employees are motivated so there's not a lot of formal appraisal. One answer may be the employee initiated appraisal in which employees are told they can ask for a review from their manager. The on-demand appraisal doesn't replace a conventional semi-annual review, but it promotes an attitude of self-management among workers and often makes critiques more honest.[15]

Flax suggests employees ask for as many reviews as they feel they need. Listed below are seven questions he believes employees should ask themselves and their managers in their self-initiated appraisals.

- On a scale of one to ten, how does my performance rate?
- What are the strongest elements of my work?
- What are the weakest elements?
- Why didn't I get a ten (highest rating)?
- Where can I go in my job or career in the next eighteen months to four years?
- What skills, training, or education do I need to get to that point?
- What specifically can we agree on that I can do, beginning tomorrow?

Team-member appraisal. A recent survey of 3,052 U.S. organizations revealed that only five percent include team-member appraisal in their programs. Still, the use of team-member appraisals is likely to increase in light of corporate America's focus on employee participation and empowerment. One reason is that appraisals by one's peers have been shown to be useful predictors of performance. This is particularly true in the area of interpersonal relations. An individual may be on his or her best behavior when interacting with the boss or customers but is more likely to behave naturally in his or her work group. Second, peer appraisals are useful when teamwork and participation are needed. Standard performance appraisals conducted on an individual basis do not contribute to the teambuilding efforts that are an important element in today's participative management style.

Team-member involvement in the appraisal process can take many different forms. Jamestown Advanced Products Inc., a small metal fabrication firm, recently had to deal with the issue of employee tardiness. According to team members, assessment of the problem, one person's late arrival disrupted everyone else's schedule, reduced team performance, and consequently lowered financial bonuses. Traditionally, a tardy employee lost some wages but could still receive a quarterly performance bonus. Team members thought this wasn't fair. The work team was encouraged to set performance standards for themselves and to identify consequences for low performance. After the team batted around the issue of how much lateness or absenteeism employees could tolerate and how punitive they should be, the team reached agreement. Employees could be tardy—defined as one minute late—or absent without notice no more than five times a quarter. Beyond that, they would lose their entire bonus.

In addition to defining performance expectations, Jamestown team members commonly serve as evaluators; the co-worker who is at an individual's side all day has an excellent opportunity to observe that individual's behavior. Common performance dimensions on which team members have evaluation expertise include

1. Attendance and timeliness (attends scheduled group meetings)
2. Interpersonal skills (willing to give and take on issues; not unreasonably stubborn)

FOCUS ON RESEARCH

How Do We Rate Performance? Let Me Count the Ways

Are self-evaluations of performance always lenient? Do workers in collective cultures, which discourage boasting about individual accomplishments, evaluate performance the same way as American workers do? Or, is the leniency bias merely a product of Western culture's emphasis on individuality? As the world economy becomes globalized and more multinational firms find themselves operating in many different countries, these questions become more important. Also, a growing portion of the U.S. labor force includes people with non-Western cultural backgrounds. How will this diversity impact the performance evaluations used by companies to make important decisions?

In Western cultures, subordinates tend to evaluate themselves more favorably than do their supervisors. This effect occurs across different types of employees (clerical, managerial, blue collar), for different types of rating scales, and for appraisal done for different purposes. Leniency in self-ratings is consistent with the notion that people view themselves in a positive light. The tendency to have a positive self-image and to project a positive self-image to others is common in Western culture, which stresses individual achievement, self-sufficiency and self-respect. In contrast, collectivistic cultures encourage interpersonal harmony, interdependence, solidarity and group cohesiveness. They deemphasize individual achievement in the interest of interpersonal harmony.

Are workers in collectivistic cultures more modest than their American counterparts when it comes to rating their own job performance? To find out, an international team of researchers examined the performance ratings of over 900 pairs of supervisors and their subordinates. The ratings of people working in the Republic of China (Taiwan) were compared to those of American supervisors. In conducting this cross-cultural research, English language versions of the rating scales were translated into Chinese and then back-translated into English to be sure that a good translation had been achieved.

When Chinese workers evaluated their own job performance and their own desire to work, they gave themselves lower ratings than did their supervisors. Their ratings were also lower than the ones American workers gave to themselves. Consistent with the belief of collectivistic cultures that wisdom comes with age, younger workers rated themselves lower than did their supervisors, and the self-ratings of younger workers were lower than those of older workers.

The researchers concluded that the use of self-ratings by multinational firms may create bias against Chinese employees and against other employees from collectivistic cultures. Such employees may rate themselves lower than equally performing Anglo-Americans. Also, Chinese employees may be reluctant to engage in impression management behaviors and self-promotion (for example, making sure their supervisor knows about their accomplishments). As a result, their supervisors may give them lower ratings than they deserve. If the ratings are used for evaluation purposes, the result may be unintended discrimination and unfair treatment, as well as lower morale and ineffective use of the best talent.

SOURCE: Based on J. Farh, G. H. Dobbins, and B. S. Cheng, "Cultural Relativity in Action: A Comparison of Self-Ratings Made by Chinese and U.S. Workers," *Personnel Psychology* 44 (1991), 129–47.

3. Group supportiveness (offers ideas/suggestions for the group to use on the project, supports group decisions)
4. Planning and coordination (contributes input to assist other team members in performing their assignments)[16]

Firms such as Jamestown have learned that team members may also provide useful information for evaluating how well the team *as a whole* is functioning. Exhibit 7.2 contains questions that may be used by firms to assess overall team productivity, cohesiveness, and motivation (drive). Using this instrument, comparisons between groups can be made to determine the relative degree of productivity, cohesiveness, and drive. Within groups, comparisons can also be made by examining group ratings at specific intervals, to determine which perform effectively and which ones are dysfunctional.

Upward or reverse appraisals. While some organizations such as Johnson & Johnson and Sears have been surveying employees for their opinions of management for years, upward appraisals are still catching on. Major firms including Amoco, Cigna, and Du Pont use subordinates' ratings of how their bosses manage to help improve operations, to make their organizations less hierarchical, and to develop managers into better managers.[17] While subordinates often do not have access to information about all dimensions of supervisory performance, they do have frequent access to information about supervisor-subordinate interactions. When asked, subordinates usually complain that they do not get enough feedback. They want a pat on the back for doing well and honest criticism—even when it "hurts"—when they haven't performed well. Employees also complain that their supervisors pay only lip service to their input that suggestions are not taken seriously and are seldom acted upon. Subordinates also want their supervisor to go to bat for them more—singing their praises to others in the company—particularly when it comes to salary, promotion, or assignments. A fourth common complaint is that their supervisors don't delegate and give them enough responsibility.

One drawback is that subordinates may not always evaluate performance objectively or honestly. This is particularly likely if subordinates feel threatened (e.g. "If I give my boss a low rating, she will reciprocate and give me a low rating, too"). To protect anonymity, evaluations need to be made by at least three or four subordinates and turned in to someone other than the supervisor being evaluated.

Computer monitoring. A more recent trend in performance appraisal is the gathering of performance data by computers.

> Advances in computer technology make it possible for employers to continuously collect and analyze information about work performance and equipment use. More and more managers are using this type of data to help plan workloads, reduce costs, and find new ways to organize work.[18]
>
> Computer-generated statistics form the basis for the work evaluations of up to six million office workers, mostly in clerical occupations or jobs whose duties are largely repetitive. Similarly, some employers are using "service observations"—the practice of listening in on telephone conversations between employees and customers—to ensure that customers receive correct and courteous service.[19]

Although this method may be fast and seemingly objective, it has raised a number of critical issues in the management and use of human resources. One of the most critical is the employee's right to privacy, and the ethical issues surrounding that right. These are discussed more extensively in chapter 15 on employee rights.

Appraisal by customers. Another source of appraisal information comes from customers or clients of job incumbents. As the chapter introduction illus-

Exhibit 7.2

Representative Appraisal Questions to Measure Team or Work Group Cohesiveness, Drive, and Perceived Productivity

Cohesiveness

1. People in this work group pitch in to help one another.
2. People in the work group don't get along with one another. (R)
3. People in this work group take an interest in one another.
4. There is a lot of team spirit among members of my work group.
5. The members of my work group regard each other as friends.
6. The members of my group are very cooperative with one another.
7. My group's members know that they can depend on each other.
8. Group members stand up for one another.
9. Members of my group work together as a team.

Drive

10. My group tackles a job with enthusiasm.
11. The group I work with has quit trying. (R)
12. The group is full of vim and vigor.
13. The work of my group seems to drag. (R)
14. My group works hard on any job it undertakes.
15. The group shows a lot of pep and enthusiasm.

Productivity

16. My group turns out more work than most groups in the company.
17. My group turns out as much work as our supervisor expects.
18. My group has an excellent production record.
19. My group gets a job done on time.
20. This work group has an excellent production record.

Items are scored on a 1–7 scale with "1" being strongly disagree and "7" being strongly agree. Items marked with an (R) should be reverse scored.

SOURCE: Based on R.M. Stogdill, *Group Productivity, Drive and Cohesiveness.* (Columbus, Ohio: Bureau of Business Research, 1965).

trated, appraisals by customers are appropriate in a variety of contexts. For example, a medical clinic in Billings, Montana, routinely has patients rate desk attendants and nursing personnel on such features as courtesy, promptness, and quality of care. Domino's Pizza hires mystery customers who order pizzas and then evaluate the performance of the telephone operator and delivery person. Doyle Ripley, owner of a carpeting firm in Utah, uses a customer checklist to monitor the on-site performance of carpet installers (see exhibit 7.3). According to Doyle Ripley,

> When you've got installers out on jobs everywhere, it's impossible to check their work. The advantage of our appraisal instrument is that it educates customers regarding what to look for in a quality installation job. Simultaneously, it provides us with inexpensive performance feedback. From the installer's perspective, the system works well because any problems can be resolved immediately without being recalled back to the job.

To encourage customers to return the surveys, Ripley holds a monthly drawing for free carpet shampooing. Installers with the highest ratings are recognized monetarily and praised verbally.

PERFORMANCE APPRAISAL FORMATS

Rating forms should not be equated with rating systems. The development of a raing form comes only after systematic job analysis, the identification of criteria and appropriate raters, and decisions about the timing of appraisals. While direct output measures of performance are available for some jobs, by far the most widely used performance measurement systems are judgmental. The simplest classifications are the norm-referenced, absolute standards, and output formats, each of which is supplemented by essays.[20]

Norm-Referenced Appraisals

For many types of human resource decisions, the fundamental questions often are "Who is the best performer in the group?" or "Who should be retained, given that we have to cut our work force?" or "Who should be assigned a specific task?" For these types of decisions, norm-referenced performance formats are appropriate.

Straight ranking. In straight ranking, the superior lists the incumbents in order, from best to worst, usually on the basis of overall performance. Incumbents can also be ranked with regard to their performance of specific duties. Rankings such as these are appropriate only in small organizations. As the number of incumbents increases, it becomes difficult to discern differences in the performance of incumbents—particularly average incumbents. Alternative ranking can help.

Alternative ranking. The first step in alternative ranking is to put the best subordinate at the head of the list and the worst subordinate at the bottom. The superior then selects the best and worst from the remaining subordinates; the best is placed second on the list, the worst next to last. The superior continues to choose the best and worst until all subordinates are ranked. The middle position on the list is the last to be filled by this method.

Paired comparisons. The paired comparison approach involves comparing each incumbent to every other incumbent, two at a time, on a single standard to determine who is "better." A rank order of the individuals can be obtained by counting the number of times each individual is selected as the better of a pair. An advantage of this approach over traditional ratings is that it overcomes the problem of an "evaluation set." That is, it forces the rater to compare the performance of each incumbent to all other incumbents, one by one.

Several potential problems exist with paired comparisons. If the number of incumbents is large, the number of comparisons may be unmanageable. [There are $N[(N-1)/2]$ total comparisons, where N is the number of individuals. Thus, for 25 incumbents, there are 300 comparisons if only overall performance is evaluat-

Exhibit 7.3
Customer Evaluation Form

Name ________________________________ **Date** ______________

Address ____

Your business and satisfaction are important to us. To help ensure quality installation and service, we would appreciate your help in completing this postage paid evaluation form and returning it to our store. Each statement is intended to describe and point out things to look for in a quality installation. This completed evaluation form will qualify you for our monthly drawing, good for two free rooms of carpet cleaning, which can be used within one year from the date of this drawing.

Please circle Y if the installer met the statement or N if the installer did not meet the statement.

1. Y N The installer consulted with the customer on the location of all seams and placed them in the most desired areas.
2. Y N All seams were located in closets or low traffic areas other than doorways.
3. Y N Seams are not visible.
4. Y N The seams feel secure.
5. Y N The installer installed carpet avoiding property damage (i.e., scratches or mars on baseboards, walls, or doors).
6. Y N The installer stretched the carpet tight enough to avoid all wrinkles, waves, and bubbles.
7. Y N The installer trimmed and tucked all carpet edges flush with walls and/or metal stripping.
8. Y N The installer cleaned up the entire area leaving no scraps.
9. Y N The installer went over the job with the customer and ensured satisfaction.

Additional Comments: (Use the back of this form if necessary) ______________________

____

____

____

For office use only

SCORE ______

(Y = 3, N = 0)

SOURCE: Modified from a project report submitted by Doyle Riley, Steve Barfuss, Gregory Love, and John Paul. University of Utah, 1987.

ed.] Intransitivity in judgment is another problem. It occurs if incumbent A is rated better than B, and B is rated better than C, but C is rated better than A.

A problem with all three methods discussed so far is that each person is assigned a unique rank. This suggests that no two subordinates perform exactly alike. Although this may be true, many supervisors believe that some incumbents perform so similarly that individual differences cannot be discerned.

Forced distribution method. The fourth method, forced distribution, was designed to overcome this complaint. The term forced distribution is used because the superior must assign only a certain proportion of subordinates to each of several categories on each factor. A common forced distribution scale may be divided into five categories, with a fixed percentage of all subordinates in the group falling within each of these categories. Typically, the distribution follows a normal distribution; for example,

	Lowest 10%	Next 20%	Middle 40%	Next 20%	Highest 10%
Number of Employees	5	10	20	10	5

A problem with this method is that a group of subordinates may not conform to the fixed percentages.

Comments on norm-referenced methods. Regardless of the approach, all norm-referenced methods are based on the assumption that performance is best captured or measured by one criterion—overall performance. Because this single criterion is a global measure and is not anchored in any objective index, such as units sold, the results can be influenced by ratee subjectivity. As a consequence, the rankings lack behavioral specificity and may be subject to legal challenge.[21] Peer comparisons were used in the *Watkins v. Scott Paper Co.* (1976), *Albemarle Paper Co. v. Moody* (1975), and *Brito v. Zia Co.* (1973) cases. The courts ruled against the companies in all three decisions, saying the comparisons were not based on objective performance criteria (or that the companies failed to establish that they were).

Another critical problem facing the rater is that no information regarding the absolute level of performance is available. Because these methods yield ordinal rather than interval data, managers do not know whether the best performer in a group is actually outstanding, average, or poor, or whether two individuals with adjacent ranks are quite similar or quite different.

Absolute Standards Formats

With norm-referenced methods of evaluation, the rater is forced to evaluate the ratee, team, or strategic unit in relation to similar others. In contrast, absolute standards formats allow the evaluator to assess performance in relation to trait or behavioral criteria. Consequently, it is possible for ratees to receive identical ratings.

Graphic rating scales. The graphic rating scale is the most widely used form of performance evaluation. Introduced in the 1920s, graphic rating scales were touted as useful because direct output measures were not needed and the rater was free to make as fine a discrimination as desired. The scales as originally developed and as used today consist of trait labels and unbroken lines with various numbers positioned along the line and sometimes with descriptive adjectives below.

As shown in exhibit 7.4, graphic rating scales vary considerably in terms of the clarity with which the trait of performance dimension is delineated, the number of rating categories, and the specificity of the anchors associated with rating categories. Scales A through C require the rater to define the dimension. This obviously leads to different interpretations by different raters. While scales D and E do a better job of defining work quality, they still provide latitude for disagreement. Scale F is problematic in a different way; although it provides the most extensive definition of work quality, raters must consider more than one aspect of performance quality. Additionally, this scale provides no anchors for the scale values.

The primary advantage of graphic rating formats is simplicity. The major disadvantage is the lack of clarity and definition. This makes their legal defensibility questionable. Even when raters are trained, they still might not define a specific trait similarly.[22]

Dissatisfaction with graphic rating scales has led to the development of other absolute standards formats which utilize behavioral, rather than trait, criteria. The most systematic of these approaches relies on critical incidents to replace ambiguous graphic scale anchors. The critical-incident method of job analysis was discussed in-depth in chapter 4. These formats are discussed next.

Exhibit 7.4
Samples of Graphic Rating Scale Formats

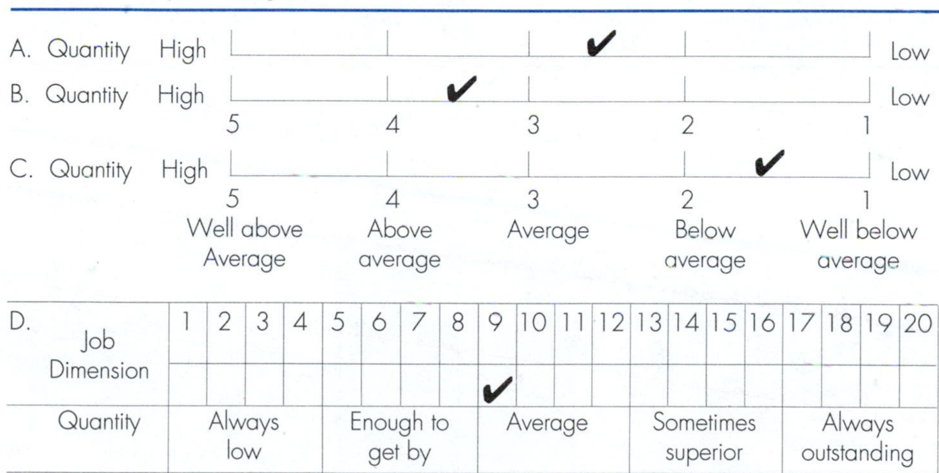

A. Quantity High ✔ Low

B. Quantity High ✔ Low
5 4 3 2 1

C. Quantity High ✔ Low
5 Well above Average | 4 Above average | 3 Average | 2 Below average | 1 Well below average

D. Job Dimension	1	2	3	4	5	6	7	8	9	10	11	12	13	14	15	16	17	18	19	20
									✔											
Quantity	Always low				Enough to get by				Average				Sometimes superior				Always outstanding			

E. Quantity of Work is the amount of work an individual does in a workday.

		X		
Does not meet minimum requirements	Does just enough to get by	Volume of work is satisfactory	Industrious; does more than is required	Superior work production record

F. Quantity In rating work quantity, give careful consideration to such items as amount of work produced in terms of the specific job, employee's application to the job, effect of employee on the general flow of work, and skill in handling special assignments. For *supervisors*, work quantity also includes skill in getting work out. Poor, 1–6; Average, 7–18; Good, 19–25

Score **18**

Behaviorally anchored rating scales. A major breakthrough in utilizing critical incidents to evaluate incumbent performance was the development of behaviorally anchored rating scales (BARS). These scales were developed to provide results that subordinates could use to improve performance. They were also designed to allow superiors to be more comfortable in giving feedback. The development of a BARS generally corresponds to the first steps in the critical-incidents method of job analysis (i.e., collecting incidents describing competent, average, and incompetent behavior for each job category). These incidents are then grouped into broad overall categories or dimensions of performance (e.g., administrative ability, interpersonal skill). Each dimension serves as one criterion in evaluating subordinates. Using these categories, another group of individuals lists the critical incidents pertinent to each category. Exhibit 7.5 shows an example of one such criterion or category—transacting loans—and the critical incidents listed as pertinent to it. This exhibit also shows the next step: the assignment of a numerical value (weight) to each incident in relation to its contribution to the criterion.

Armed with a set of criteria with behaviorally anchored and weighted choices, superiors rate their subordinates with a form that is relatively unambiguous in meaning, understandable, justifiable, and relatively easy to use. Yet the form has its limitations. Because most BARS forms use a limited number of performance criteria (e.g., seven), many of the critical incidents generated in the job analysis stage may not be used. Thus, the raters may not find appropriate categories to

Exhibit 7.5
Sample Behaviorally Anchored Rating Scale for One Dimension of the Work Performance of Corporate Loan Assistant

Transacting Loans

Scale	Behavioral anchor
10	Credit reports are always completed without error.
9	Prepares follow-up documentation in a timely manner.
8	Provides services desired but not asked for by customers.
7	Customers praise the help of the assistant.
6	Assists customers with loan applications.
5	Develops loan documentation accurately.
4	Prepares credit reports without having to be told.
3	Provides information to customers, even if not asked.
2	Fails to help other banks participating in loans.
1	Loan applicants complain about the loan interview.

describe the behaviors—the critical incidents—of their subordinates.[24] Similarly, even if the relevant incidents are observed, they may not be worded in exactly the same way on the dimension; the rater may thus be unable to match the observed behaviors with the dimension and anchors.

Another concern with BARS is that it is possible for an incumbent simultaneously to display behavior associated with high and low performance. For example, the corporate loan assistant could prepare follow-up documentation in a timely manner and also receive complaints from loan applicants about rudeness and inappropriate questioning. In a situation such as this, it is difficult for the rater to determine whether the rating should be high or low.

Mixed standard scales. Mixed standard rating scales were developed to eliminate some of the problems associated with BARS. Like BARS, critical incidents underscore the development of these scales. The format consists of sets of three statements that describe high, medium, and low levels of performance for a specific performance dimension. These items have been scaled using a process similar to that employed in the development of the BARS scales. The behavioral examples for each dimension are arranged randomly on the rating sheet. Unlike BARS, in which scale values are known, no values are attached to the behavioral incidents. Instead, the rater makes one of three responses to each example.

A score on each performance dimension is calculated on the basis of the pattern of results. Exhibit 7.6 shows an example of a mixed standard scale (MSS) developed to evaluate the performance of grocery store checkers.

Once gathered, these ratings are then transcribed by the human resource department (usually via computer) into numerical ratings, with more points given for "+" than for "0" or "-" respectively. For example, a checker who receives "+" ratings for all three store maintenance items might receive a rating of 9 (3 points for each "+") on that dimension; a checker who receives two "0"s and a "+" might receive a rating of 7 (2 points for each "0" and 3 points for the one "+" on the same dimension).

The advantage of the MSS format is that the rater is not dealing with numbers. Consequently, some of the most common errors associated with rating are overcome. Additionally, analysis of rater response patterns can identify raters whose use of the scales is haphazard. A drawback of mixed standard scales is that scale values are not known. Consequently, developmental information is lost. Still, once developed, MSSs are relatively easy to use.[25]

Behavioral observation scales. A more recent development in behavioral scales is called the behavioral observation scale (BOS). Like the behavioral methods already discussed, these scales are derived from critical incidents of job behavior. BOS scales differ, however, in that job experts are *not* asked what level of performance they illustrate. Instead, job experts are asked to indicate the *frequency* with which job incumbents engage in the behaviors. Scores are obtained for each behavior by assigning a numerical value to the frequency judgment. For example, a score of 2 may be assigned if it is almost always observed. These scores can be summed to get an overall rating. Exhibit 7.7 includes examples of BOS scales. Note that the examples of ineffective performance are reverse-scored.

Exhibit 7.6
Representative Mixed Standard Scale Items for Grocery Store Checkers

Name ______________________ **Rater** ______________________

Store ______________________ **Date** ______________________

Mark each of the following statements in one of three ways:
"+" Indicates the checker performs better than this statement
"0" Indicates the checker performs exactly like this statement
"–" Indicates the checker performs worse than this statement

______ 1. Arrives late to work for one shift per week (T)
______ 2. Averages 23 items per minute when checking (C)
______ 3. When business is slow, hangs around the check stand talking to other checkers (M)
______
______ 4. Arrives late to work once a month (T)
______ 5. When business is slow, cleans the check stand, helps with light stocking, or performs other tasks (M)
______ 6. Averages 18 items per minute when checking (C)
______ 7. Arrives late for work two shifts per week (T)
______ 8. Averages 36 items per minute when checking (C)
______ 9. When business is slow, cleans check stand (M)

"T" = Tardiness; "C" = Checking; "M" = Maintenance

The advantages of BOS include the following. (1) It is based on a systematic job analysis. (2) Its items and behavioral anchors are clearly stated. (3) In contrast with some other methods, it allows participation of employees in the development of the dimensions (through the identification of critical incidents in the job analysis), which facilitates understanding and acceptance. (4) It is useful for performance feedback and improvement because specific goals can be tied to numerical scores (ratings) on the relevant behavioral anchor (critical incident) for the relevant performance criterion or dimension. (5) BOS appears to satisfy the *Uniform Guidelines* in terms of validity (relevance) and reliability.

The limitations of BOS are connected with some of its advantages, especially the time and cost for its development as compared with graphic rating formats. While the behavioral orientation of these scales appears, on the surface, to be an advantage, there is evidence that raters do not respond to these scales in terms of behaviors. Rather they use their overall, subjective evaluations to guide their behavior ratings. There is also evidence that most raters do not have sufficient time or ability to accurately assess the frequency with which behaviors are observed. The accuracy demanded for accurate BOS ratings may best be achieved through computer monitoring.[26]

Comments on absolute standard formats. The utilization of these formats is expected to increase for two reasons. First, the service sector of the economy is growing rapidly. For service jobs, how the work is performed is critical to job success and is often viewed as the way to gain a competitive edge. Second, employee development is increasing in importance. Behavioral formats, unlike graphic or norm-referenced formats, provide useful information for modifying the behavior of employees. On the other hand, absolute standards formats are difficult and time-consuming to develop. The exception is graphic rating formats which are simple to develop but not generally legally defendable. From a cost-

Exhibit 7.7

Sample Behavioral Observation Scale Items for a Maintenance Mechanic

In completing this form, circle
0–if you have no knowledge of the employee's behavior
1–if the employee has engaged in the behavior 0–64% of the time
2–if the employee has engaged in the behavior 65–74% of the time
3–if the employee has engaged in the behavior 75–84% of the time
4–if the employee has engaged in the behavior 85–94% of the time
5–if the employee has engaged in the behavior 95–100% of the time

Customer Relations

Item						
1. Swears in front of customers (e.g. operators, vendors) (R)	0	1	2	3	4	5
2. Blames customer for malfunction (R)	0	1	2	3	4	5
3. Refers to customer by name or asks for his/her name when first introduced	0	1	2	3	4	5
4. Asks operator to demonstrate what s/he was doing at the time of the malfunction	0	1	2	3	4	5

Team Work

Item						
1. Co-workers complain about the rudeness of this worker (R)	0	1	2	3	4	5
2. Verbally shares technical knowledge with other technicians	0	1	2	3	4	5
3. As needed, consults fellow workers for their ideas on ways to solve specific problems	0	1	2	3	4	5
4. Given an incomplete assignment, leaves a clear, written tie-in for the next shift to use	0	1	2	3	4	5
5. Works his/her share of overtime	0	1	2	3	4	5

Planning

Item						
1. Estimates repair time accurately	0	1	2	3	4	5
2. Completes assigned jobs on time	0	1	2	3	4	5
3. Is able to set job priorities on a daily or weekly basis	0	1	2	3	4	5
4. Even when the job is not yet complete, cleans up area at the end of the shift	0	1	2	3	4	5
5. Identifies problems or potential problems that may affect repair success or completion time	0	1	2	3	4	5

Planned Maintenance Repairs (PMR)

Item						
1. Executes planned maintenance repair requiring no follow-up	0	1	2	3	4	5
2. Adjusts equipment according to predetermined tolerance levels; no errors	0	1	2	3	4	5
3. Replaces components when necessary rather than when convenient or easy	0	1	2	3	4	5
4. Takes more time than allotted to complete a PMR (R)	0	1	2	3	4	5

SOURCE: Adapted from V.L. Huber, *Validation Study for Electronics Maintenance Technician Positions* (Washington, D.C.: Human Resource Development Institute, AFL-CIO, 1991). Prepared under Grant No. 99-9-0264-98-090-02 from the Employment and Training Administration, U.S. Department of Labor.
(R) denotes item is reverse scored.

benefit perspective, the development of behavioral formats should be restricted to jobs which have a large number of incumbents or for which the job processes are critical to job success. Even then, relying exclusively on behavioral formats may mean that the real essence of many jobs, especially managerial and highly routine jobs, is not captured. For these types of jobs actual outputs produced, regardless of the behaviors used to obtain them, may be more important. When these conditions exist, output-based formats may be better.

Output-Based Formats

Output-based formats focus on job products as the primary criteria. These approaches to performance evaluation rely upon job analysis to identify critical job duties and tasks. Once duties are identified, the level of proficiency that an employee must attain is determined. There are four variants of output-based appraisal formats: (1) management by objectives, (2) performance standards, (3) the direct index measure, and (4) accomplishment records. Regardless of the format, effective output criteria should include the seven characteristics listed in exhibit 7.8.

Management by objectives. Management by objectives (MBO) is a widely used management system in both private and public sector settings.[27] MBO is a method of appraisal that begins with the establishment of goals or objectives. After appropriate goals have been established for the upcoming performance period, the superior and subordinate need to delineate an appropriate strategy for goal attainment. Experienced and high-performing managers can develop their strategies on their own; the freedom to perform the job in the way they think best is reinforcing in and of itself. However, for less experienced or low-performing incumbents, the supervisor may need to intervene. Clearly delineating how the goal is to be attained reduces ambiguity and makes goal attainment more likely. Strategy development includes outlining the steps necessary to attain

Exhibit 7.8
Components of Effective Output-Based Performance Criteria

- *Specificity.* Identify how well the behavior must be performed or how high the output must be to be considered acceptable. Specificity reduces variability in performance and in ratings.
- *Timeliness.* Identify the deadline for completion of the task or the attainment of the output level.
- *Conditions.* Any qualifications associated with attaining the standard (e.g., whether the production schedule is adhered to) need to be pointed out because many factors beyond the control of the incumbent may hamper goal attainment.
- *Prioritization.* Incumbents need to understand which standards are most important. Supervisors and incumbents can weight them, or weights can be derived from the job description.
- *Consequences.* Specify the consequences of attaining or not attaining the specified level of performance.
- *Goal congruence.* For managers performing similar jobs, it is important to assign comparable goals.

the objective. Additionally, it is important to identify any constraints that may block the attainment of the objective. Finally, it is important to specify the responsibilities of the incumbent and those of the supervisor.

At the conclusion of the performance period, actual performance is evaluated relative to the agreed-on objectives. Here, it is important to develop an appropriate scoring algorithm. Because people do not synthesize multidimensional data well, *each* objective should be scored *separately*. Scoring algorithms can be either simple (indicating whether the objective was or was not met) or complex (signaling how far above or below the objective actual performance was). After evaluation, the superior and subordinate jointly explore the reasons goals were not attained or were exceeded. This step helps determine training needs and development potential.

The final step is to decide on new goals and possible new strategies for goals not previously attained. At this point, subordinate and superior involvement in goal setting may change. Subordinates who successfully reach the established goals may be allowed to participate more in the goal-setting process the next time.[28]

Management must clearly be committed to the process if the MBO system is to be effective. When management is committed and there is a cascade of goals from the top down, productivity gains average 56 percent. Additionally, there is a substantial reduction (more than 20 percent) in supervisory complaints and an increase in employee satisfaction. However, without management commitment and a shared vision, productivity gains average a meager 6 percent. Management must recognize, though, that MBO systems do not lead to immediate increases in productivity. On average, it takes about two years after implementation for MBO systems to work effectively.[29]

Finally, it is important to remember that the **objectives** are only guidelines that facilitate two-way communication. They can and should be changed if the job changes or the situation changes. In some organizations, superiors and subordinates work together to establish goals; in others, superiors establish goals for work groups or individuals; in still others, the goals are derived from time and motion studies (Recall this job analysis technique was discussed in Chapter 4). **Goals** can refer to desired outcomes to be achieved, means for achieving the outcomes, or both. Goals may be related to routine activities that comprise day-to-day duties or to the identification and solution of problems that hamper individual and organizational effectiveness; they may also be innovative or have special purposes.[30]

Performance standards approach. While similar to MBO, the performance standards approach uses more direct measures of performance and is usually applied to nonmanagerial employees. Standards, like objectives, need to be specific, time bound, conditional, prioritized, and congruent with organizational objectives. Compared with objectives, there are generally more standards, and each is more detailed. Exhibit 7.9 includes some performance standards for a plumber. This particular format specifies the average expected behavior as well as the level of performance that would be considered exceptional. Notice that each standard is rated separately and multiplied by an importance weight.[31]

Direct index approach. The direct index approach differs from the other approaches primarily in how performance is measured. This approach measures

Exhibit 7.9
Representative Performance Standards for a Plumber

Duty	Meets Standard When (Score as 1)	Exceeds Standard When (Score as 2)	Performance Attained	Pts. × Weight	Total
1. Completes job assignments	Averages five routine drain-cleaning jobs per day	Averages seven or more drain-cleaning jobs per day	Performed an average of six routine jobs per day	1 × 30%	30
2. Operates equipment in a safe manner	Wears required safety equipment (boots, gloves, safety belts)	Always wears required safety equipment (boots, gloves, safety belts) to prevent job injury from cleaning agents	Wore safety equipment on all jobs that were spot-checked	2 × 10%	20
3. Diagnoses the problem at the job site	Recall reports indicate at least an 80% accuracy rate in diagnosing problems on first visit	Recall reports indicate a 90% accuracy rate in diagnosing problems on the first visit	Only 42 recalls out of 720 jobs	2 × 30%	60
4. Completes paperwork in a timely manner	Job reports are turned in the day of the job 80% of the time	Job reports are turned in the day of the job 90% of the time	30% of reports filed the next day or later	0 × 10%	00
5. Maintains good customer relations	80% of customers rated plumber as "good" in customer relations-survey	80% of customers rated the plumber as "very good" or "excellent" in customer relations; no dissatisfied customers	90% of customers rated the plumber as "good," 10% were dissatisfied	1 × 20%	20

Unacceptable: 80% or below the standards
Satisfactory: 81% to 120% of standards
Outstanding: 121% or more of standards

Total 130 points
Overall Performance is Highly Satisfactory

SOURCE: Modified from a project report submitted by Linda Smith, Deridra Lacy, Lori Rosendahl, and Abutalib Kaba, University of Utah.

performance by objective, impersonal criteria, such as productivity, absenteeism, and turnover. For example, a manager's performance may be evaluated by the number of the manager's employees who quit or by the employees' absenteeism rate. For nonmanagers, measures of productivity may be more appropriate. These measures of productivity can be broken into measures of quality and measures of quantity. Quality measures include scrap rates, customer complaints, and number of defective units or parts produced. Quantity measures include units of output per hour, new customer orders, and sales volume. Exhibit 7.10 provides some examples of direct indexes for several jobs.

Accomplishment records. A relatively new type of output-based appraisal is called an accomplishment record. It is suitable for professionals who claim "my record speaks for itself" or who claim they can't write standards for their job because every day is different. With this approach, professionals describe their achievements relative to appropriate job dimensions on an accomplishment record form. The professional's supervisor verifies the accuracy of the accomplishments. Then a team of outside experts evaluates the accomplishments to determine their overall value. While time-consuming and potentially costly because outside evaluators are used, this approach has been shown to be predictive of job success for lawyers. It also has face validity because professionals believe it is appropriate and valid. Exhibit 7.11 shows an example of an accomplishment rating for using knowledge. (This accomplishment was rated as 4.5 on a 6.0 scale.)[32]

Exhibit 7.10
Examples of Direct Indexes of Performance

Salesperson	Dollar volume of sales over a fixed period Number of new customers Delinquent accounts collected Net sales/month in territory Penetration of the market
Manager	Number of employee grievances Cost reductions Unit turnover Absenteeism Unit safety record Timeliness in completing appraisals Employee satisfaction with supervisor Division productivity Diversity of new hires
Police officer	Number of arrests for felony offenses Number of shots fired in the line of duty Number of complaints Clearance rates Average response time
Scientist	Number of patents Number of grants Number of technical articles Number of solo-authored manuscripts
Computer scientist	Number of coding signoffs Response time for requests Number of lines of code written Bytes of compiled code
Administrative assistant	Number of letters prepared Word processing speed Number of errors in filing Number of jobs returned for reprocessing Number of calls screened

Exhibit 7.11
Accomplishment Record for Using Knowledge

Using Knowledge

Interpreting and synthesizing information to form legal strategies, approaches, lines of argument; developing new configurations of knowledge, innovative approaches, solutions, strategies; selecting the proper legal theory; using appropriate lines of argument, weighing alternatives, and drawing sound conclusions.

Time period: 1992
General statement of what you accomplished:
I developed three new legal theories which could be used to justify jurisdiction in areas previously thought to be foreclosed as a result of a Supreme Court decision on equal employment.

Description of exactly what you did:
I located and analyzed every judicial opinion discussing the "fair employment" jurisdiction, and demonstrated that sound legal arguments could be developed to support firm's action.

Awards or formal recognition:
The CEO sent me a note thanking me for my efforts.

The information was verified by: Ima Worker, Director,
Rating 4.5

SOURCE: Adapted from L. Hugh, "Development of the Accomplishment Record Method of Selecting and Promoting Professionals," *Journal of Applied Psychology* 69 (1984), 135–46.

Comments on output-based formats. With the increased emphasis on performance enhancement, the use of output-based appraisal continues to increase. The major advantage of these formats—when done correctly—is that they provide clear, unambiguous direction to employees regarding desired job outcomes. When exceptional performance also is specified (See exhibit 7.11), these scales can motivate the average as well as exceptional employee. Recent research indicates that, when the criteria used in output-based rating formats is specific, extraneous factors such as the ratee's prior evaluation, the order of evaluation, salary, and even personal characteristics such as gender are less likely to bias judgments. When standards were vague—failing to specify an exact level of performance or a time time period—these factors biased performance ratings.

The disadvantages of these formats are that they require time, money, and cooperation to develop. Second, the essence of job performance may not be captured completely by output-based criteria. Consequently, important job behaviors may be ignored in the evaluation process. The production of desired products or output may also induce unintended competition among employees. The latter problem can be overcome if the output-based appraisal system is carefully designed, building on job analysis and utilizing training for raters. Under these conditions, output-based formats are highly useful decision tools. Results can be used to make between-employee comparisons and to develop employees, as well as to document organizational actions.

RATING JUDGMENTS, BIASES, AND REMEDIES

Despite the prevalence of performance appraisal systems, many people are dissatisfied with them. This disillusionment centers on the vulnerability of these measures to intentional as well as unforeseen bias. According to current thought, the quality of performance judgments is dependent upon the information processing capabilities or strategies of the decision maker.[33] As shown in exhibit 7.12, the decision maker must first attend to and recognize relevant information. This information must then be aggregated and stored in the rater's short-term memory. Because of long appraisal periods, information must be condensed further and stored in long-term memory. When a judgment needs to be made, information relevant to the category to be rated must be retrieved from memory and a comparison made between observed behaviors and the rater's standards. Finally, a rating must be made based on aggregated data retrieved from memory and any additional information the rater intentionally or unintentionally chooses to include. Ratings at this point may be revised depending on the reaction of the incumbent or higher level managers. Unfortunately, raters' memories are quite fallible. Consequently, they fall prey to a variety of reading errors, including deviations between the "true" rating an employee deserves and the actual rating assigned.[34]

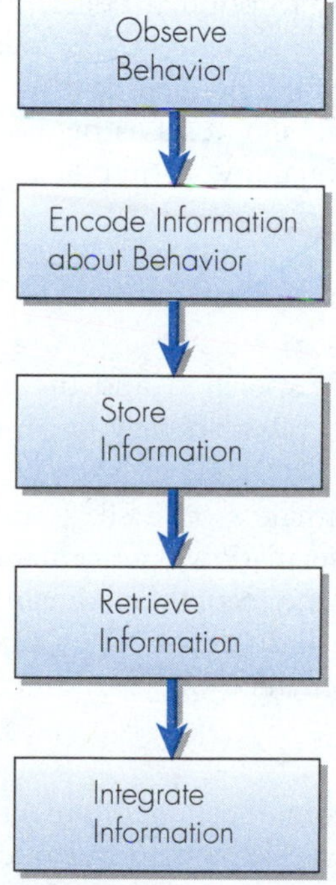

Exhibit 7.12
Basic Cognitive Model of the Performance Appraisal Rating Process

Ratee and Rater Characteristics

The characteristics of ratee and rater can inappropriately affect judgments at various stages of the evaluation process.

Ratee characteristics. As one might expect, the actual level of performance attained by a ratee has the most influence on performance ratings. However, other ratee characteristics also directly affect performance ratings, particularly when performance criteria are not precise. The gender of the ratee and the "gender" of the job interact, so that males receive higher ratings than females in male-dominated jobs but equivalent evaluations in traditionally female jobs. Due to **perceptual congruence,** ratees tend to receive higher ratings from same-race raters. Also, managers often associate job tenure with job competency. As a result, they tend to give higher ratings to senior employees. The exception is in government merit systems, where less senior employees receive higher ratings to advance them up the merit pay system. Age and education level tend not to affect ratings.

Rater characteristics. Characteristics of the rater exert a more subtle and indirect influence on performance judgments. Limited data suggest that female raters are more lenient than male raters. When performance standards are used, female raters also tend to give more extreme ratings to high and low performers than do male raters. For the average performer, gender of the rater doesn't make a difference.

Younger and less experienced raters and raters who have received low evaluations themselves rate more strictly than older, more experienced, and/or high-performing raters do. Contrary to popular belief, supervisors who have previously held the job in question rate accurately. The personality of the rater may also affect judgment accuracy. Self-confidence, low anxiety, intelligence, social skills and insight, and emotional stability tend to be associated with better judgments. Finally, the quality, not the quantity, of interaction between a rater and a ratee affects ratings positively.[35]

Rating Errors

When criteria are not clearly specified and there are no incentives associated with rating accuracy, a variety of errors may occur during the rating process.

Halo and horn. Performance on a single dimension may be so outstanding or so important that it overshadows performance of other tasks. Consequently, a rater will often evaluate the incumbent similarly on all dimensions of performance. This effect is called a **halo error.** The opposite of a halo error is a **horn error,** when negative performance on one dimension supersedes any positive performance.[36]

Leniency. A second common and often intentional rating error is called leniency. In order to avoid conflict, a manager rates all employees in a particular work group higher than they should be rated objectively. This is particularly likely when there are no organizational sanctions against high ratings, when rewards are not part of a fixed and limited pot, and when dimensional ratings are not required. Some strategies to eliminate this bias in particular are discussed in a later section.

Strictness. At an opposite extreme is the error of strictness in which ratees are given unfavorable ratings, regardless of performance level. Inexperienced raters who are unfamiliar with environmental constraints on performance, raters with low self-esteem, and raters who have received a low rating are most likely to rate strictly. Rater training that includes reversal of supervisor-incumbent roles and confidence building will reduce this error.

Central tendency. Rather than use extremes in ratings, some raters tend to evaluate all ratees as average, even when performance actually varies. This bias is referred to as the error of central tendency. Raters with large spans of control and little opportunity to observe behavior are likely to rate the majority of incumbents in the middle of the scale rather than too high or too low. This is a "play it safe" strategy. Central tendency may also be the byproduct of the rating method. The forced distribution format *requires* that most employees be rated average.

Primacy and recency effects. As noted earlier, the typical appraisal period (six months to a year) is far too long for any rater to adequately retain in memory all performance-relevant information. As a cognitive shortcut, raters may fall prey to primacy and recency effects. As explained in chapter 5, raters may use initial information to categorize a ratee as either a good or a bad performer. Subsequently, information that supports the initial judgment is amassed, and unconfirming information is ignored. Because special attention is paid to information initially collected, this bias is referred to as the **primacy bias.**

Conversely, a rater may not pay attention to employee performance throughout the appraisal period. As the appraisal interview draws near, the rater searches for information cues about the value of performance. Unfortunately, only recent behaviors or outputs are salient. As a result, recent events are weighted more heavily than they should be. Called the **recency of events error,** this bias can have serious consequences for a ratee who performs well for six months or a year but then makes a serious or costly error in the last week or two before he or she is evaluated.

Contrast effects. If criteria are not clear or if ranking systems are used, contrast effects will occur. When compared to weak employees, an average employee will appear outstanding; when evaluated against outstanding employees, an average employee will be perceived as a low performer. Again, the solution is to have specific performance criteria established prior to the evaluation period; then any employee with adequate performance receives an acceptable rating.

Escalation of commitment. This costly error results when managers are unable to cut their losses. Consider a situation in which you personally hired a new middle-level manager. Although you expected excellent performance, early reports suggest that she is not performing as expected. Should you fire her? After all, you can't afford to "carry" a low performer. On the other hand, you have invested in her training, and she may just be learning the ropes. Research indicates that if you made the initial hiring decision, you are likely to escalate your commitment and invest in her a bit longer. You may even go so far as to provide her with additional training so that she can succeed. On the other hand, if you did not make the initial decision, your investment is lower and you are more likely to recommend immediate termination. According to decision experts, when faced with negative feedback about a prior decision, the decision maker feels the need to reaffirm the wisdom of having invested time and money. Further commitment of resources somehow justifies the initial decision.[37] This bias, which may have some beneficial consequences, can be managed by setting limits in advance on involvement and commitment.

Anchoring and adjustment bias. Past decisions affect current performance ratings in yet another way. Recall that when ratings are used for performance or pay decisions, they should be based on current performance. Unfortunately, prior performance information often anchors judgments about current performance, and adjustments away from that value will be insufficient. The tendency to use prior information inappropriately to make current judgments is referred to as the anchoring and adjustment bias. This bias can be controlled by limiting access to prior rating information and by having clear, concise performance standards and performance output data available to judge current performance.

Self-fulfilling prophecy. The anchoring and adjustment bias may also partially account for the phenomenon of self-fulfilling prophecies: candidates evaluated positively tend to perform better in the future than do those initially evaluated low. Such judgments have been shown to affect supervisor-incumbent interactions. High performers receive more and more positive feedback and believe in their ability more than do low performers. Consequently, they perform better and/or receive higher evaluations.[38]

Strategies for Increasing Rater Accuracy

Even the most valid and reliable appraisal forms may not be effective when so many extraneous factors impinge on the process. However, several strategies can be utilized to minimize appraisal inaccuracies.

Carefully design the appraisal system. As an initial step, the appraisal process should include the following steps:

- Each performance dimension addresses a single job activity, rather than a group of activities.
- Overall ratings are not used. Instead, ratings are made on a dimension-by-dimension basis and summed to determine the overall rating.
- The rater can observe the behavior of the ratee on a regular basis while the job is being accomplished.
- Terms like *average* are not used on a rating scale because different raters have various reactions to such terms.
- The rater does not have to evaluate large groups of employees.

- Raters are trained to avoid such errors as leniency, strictness, halo, central tendency, and recency of events.
- Raters are trained to share a common frame of reference.[39]

In sum, performance ratings tend to be more accurate when the rating criteria, the record of performance accomplishments, and the rating scales are precise. Recent research also suggests that, when all three factors are in place, raters are not only more accurate in their ratings but also more confident with their ratings.[40]

Provide memory aid. The use of behavior diaries or critical-incident files has been shown to be a useful memory aid. The emphasis here is on recording behaviors or outcomes (good or bad) that relate to an employee's or work group's performance. The rationale in doing so is that it is often difficult for raters to remember all of the relevant behaviors they observe or outcomes that occur, particularly when the assessment period is six months to a year in length. By consulting a behavioral diary or a critical-incident file before rating, evaluations are expected to be more accurate; recency and primacy errors are likely to be reduced.

Train raters. In addition to the above suggestions, rating accuracy can be improved through careful training that focuses on improving the observation skills of raters and providing feedback and coaching. **Frame-of-reference training** is also useful. A comprehensive frame-of-reference training program might include the following steps.

1. Raters are given a job description and instructed to identify appropriate criteria for evaluating the job.
2. When agreement is reached, raters view a tape of an employee performing a job.
3. Independently, they evaluate the videotaped employee's performance, using the organization's appraisal system.
4. The ratings are compared to each other and to those of job experts.
5. With a trainer as a facilitator, the raters present the rationales for their ratings and challenge the rationales of other raters.
6. The trainer then helps raters to reach consensus regarding the value of specific job behaviors and overall performance.
7. A new videotape is shown, followed by independent ratings.
8. The process continues until consensus is achieved.[41]

Organizations that cannot afford to develop videotapes or that use MBO performance standards can accomplish similar results using written performance profiles instead of videotapes of behavior.

Increase self-efficacy. Raters also should be trained to be critical. This is best accomplished by increasing the rater's self-efficacy, or beliefs that he or she can rate accurately and can handle the consequences associated with giving negative feedback. Self-efficacy can be increased through observing someone else's success in handling the appraisal process, practice in performing the behaviors, and coaching and feedback on how to do it better.

Reward accurate and timely appraisals. Another potential cause of rating inaccuracy—particularly leniency—is rater motivation. Without rewards, raters may find it easier to give high ratings than accurate ratings.[42] If this is the case, a straightforward strategy for increasing rater motivation is to base supervisory evaluations partly on the ability to evaluate employees accurately. That is, salary increases, promotions, and assignments to key positions should depend partly on the manager's performance as a rater. Ratings done in a timely manner as well as a fair manner (measured by employee attitude surveys) should be rewarded. Human resource audits can be performed in which a random sample of supervisory ratings are examined for thoroughness, completeness, and timeliness.

Diffusion of responsibility. Often, the ratee believes that the rater is solely responsible for a poor evaluation and any subsequent loss of rewards; the rater may also believe this. Research suggests that this source of negative effect can be minimized through the diffusion of responsibility. Rather than rely on the judgment of one rater, use multiple raters. While an incumbent may be able to shrug off negative information from one rater, this is less likely when multiple raters are involved.[43] From the rater's perspective, the diffusion of responsibility frees one to rate more accurately than if one is solely responsible.

ASSESSING APPRAISAL SYSTEM EFFECTIVENESS

Although the appraisal form or method is just one component of a performance appraisal system, the performance appraisal system often centers on that form. Attention is therefore often focused on assessing the available appraisal forms in order to to choose the best one.[44]

Which Form is Best?

Determining the best appraisal form prompts the question: What criteria should we use to *decide* what is "best?"

Research on the question of which form is best, reinforces the necessity of first identifying the purposes the organization wants and needs to serve with performance appraisal. Each form can then be assessed in relation to the following criteria:

- *Supports the business:* Is developed on the basis of the strategy and plans of the organization
- *Developmental usefulness:* Motivates subordinates to do well, provides feedback, and aids in human resource planning and career development
- *Evaluational usefulness:* Used in promotion, discharge, layoff, pay, and transfer decisions and, therefore, must provide the ability to make comparisons across subordinates and departments

- *Economic:* Can be assessed in terms of cost for development, implementation, and use
- *Freedom from error:* Is free from errors due to biases such as halo, leniency, and central tendency, and is reliable and valid
- *Interpersonal:* Allows superiors to gather useful and valid appraisal data that facilitate the appraisal interview
- *Practicality:* Can be developed or implemented with ease
- *User acceptance:* Accepted by users as being reliable, valid, and useful
- *Procedural and distributive fairness:* Appraisal procedures as well as outcomes are perceived as fair by incumbents and supervisors.

Utility of the Appraisal Process

Finally, the best appraisal system is one that supports the formulation and implementation of an organization's strategy in a cost-effective manner. No rational manager is interested in rating accuracy or performance feedback for altruistic purposes along. Performance appraisal is an important but costly human resource activity that affects a wide range of organizational and individual decisions. The same techniques used to assess the value of employment testing (see chapter 14) can be applied to assess the potential benefits of accurate ratings, as well as timely and structured feedback, and procedurally fair appraisal processes.

The utility of human resource activities can often be expressed in dollar terms. In recent years, several studies have been undertaken to determine the utility of replacing a poorly designed performance appraisal system with one that provides valid feedback to workers.[45]

The following example illustrates how utility analysis can be used.

A city government had been using trait-based performance appraisals. In place of this system, the city was considering an output-based MBO system. While the MBO process was intuitively appealing, managers were concerned about costs. The MBO system demanded thorough job analysis and regular updating of job descriptions, participative goal setting, and extensive documentation. These costs were estimated at $1,000 per person. By comparison, the trait-based appraisal process was relatively simple and took little time to complete for a per-person cost of only $100. Thus, the MBO system was ten times as costly as the trait system. Five hundred managerial, technical, and professional employees were to be evaluated with the new MBO system. These employees earned an average salary of $45,000 and stayed in their jobs an average of 8.6 years.

The research reviewed earlier on the effectiveness of MBO systems showed that the average validity for the MBO system was .63 since the city manager and counsel members were all highly committed to the new appraisal process. The validity of trait-based criteria are much lower, estimated to be as low as –.15 and only as high as .15. Recall that trait evaluations can be subjective and unreliable. Given these values, a utility analysis indicated that the current appraisal system may cost the city as much as $4.1 million in lost productivity (probably due to grievances, absenteeism, lower motivation); at best, the trait system might yield gains in productivity valued at $4 million. By comparison, the MBO system that includes goal setting, participation, and feedback could be expected to yield productivity gains valued at $12 million. Put another way, the MBO system could be viewed as being three or more times as effective as the trait system in bolstering productivity. While utility analysis such as this can be quite convincing (one of the authors actually used it to convince city fathers to adopt the new system), it is erroneous to conclude that the MBO system will actually produce an extra $8 to $16 million to spend. Since model parameters were estimated, the actual gain in productivity may be more or less than predicted. What is important, however, is that the new system could be expected to have higher utility and should yield substantial gains in productivity over the old system.

FOCUS ISSUES IN PERFORMANCE APPRAISAL DATA GATHERING

As mentioned earlier in this chapter, when subordinates are empowered and responsible for their own behavior, the management of performance becomes easier. An extension of this philosophy is self-management, which requires employees to manage their own behavior. Another significant trend includes the debate over the fundamental reasons for doing performance appraisal.

Self-Management

Self-management is a relatively new approach to resolving performance discrepancies. It teaches people to exercise control over their own behavior. Self-management begins by having people assess their own problems and set specific (but individual) hard goals in relation to those problems. Once goals are set, the employees discuss ways in which the environment facilitates or hinders goal attainment. The challenge here is to develop strategies that eliminate blocks to performance success. Put another way, self-management teaches people to observe their own behavior, compare their outputs to their goals, and administer their own reinforcement to sustain goal commitment and performance.[46]

The power of self-management in organizations is only beginning to be recognized. In a recent study, twenty unionized government employees with habitual attendance problems identified and learned to overcome personal obstacles to job attendance. During eight thirty-minute, one-on-one sessions they identified the reasons for using sick leave (legitimate illness, medical appointment, job stress, job boredom, difficulties with co-workers, alcohol and drug issues, family problems, transportation difficulties, and employee rights). After identifying problem behaviors, the employees identified the conditions that elicited and maintained the problem behavior and, more important, identified specific coping strategies. This completed the self-assessment phase of the program.

Next, distinct goals to increase attendance by a specified amount over a specified period of time were set. These were coupled with the development of individual day-by-day strategies to attain the long-term goal. The employees were then taught to record their own attendance, the reason for missing work, and the steps that were to be followed to get to work. Finally, they identified powerful rewards (e.g., self-praise, purchase of a gift) and punishers (clean the oven, do the laundry) that could be self-administered. The employees practicing self-management attended work thirteen percent more (fifty-five hours in twelve weeks) than did other employees with similar past attendance problems. A follow-up study showed that the improvement in attendance persisted for over a year.[47]

The concept of self-management is also important in programs of empowerment. In order for employees to work effectively in a firm that delegates power and responsibility, they need to have the basic skills of self-management. Also, as organizations move from individual-based systems to group- or team-based systems of human resource management, the concept of self-management extends to self-managed work groups. These are discussed in chapter 13 under "Organizational Improvements." Self-management also applies to the question: "Why do performance appraisal at all?"

Disappearance of Performance Appraisal?

If companies want employees to work together in teams in their pursuit of a total quality management strategy, they must adjust several human resource activities. One of the important ones is the performance appraisal system. Typically, the basis for appraisal begins to reflect team-oriented criteria rather than solely individual-oriented criteria. Longer-term criteria become included with more traditional, shorter-term criteria. Peer review becomes included along with traditional supervisory review.

As is usually the case, these changes do not take place with one big bang; they take place gradually. People need to get familiar with the new ways. Just as important, organizations need to experiment with what they are doing. New ways of doing things generally have to be adapted to specific conditions facing a given company. In the instance of performance appraisal, companies may continue to make the types of changes described in the above paragraph. Then they may go on to ask, "Do we even need performance appraisal?"

Firms have used performance appraisal systems for a long time now. It is unlikely that they will abandon them wholesale, but some are at least starting to ask, "Why do we do appraisals?" As firms address these questions, they may see that they do it more to *control* than to develop or improve employee performance—and they do it because they assume they need to. If employee goals are different from organizational goals, then—the assumption goes—firms have to monitor and control what employees do. In some cases, firms are finding that the assumption is wrong: Employees can have goals that coincide with the organization's. W. Edwards Deming, a father in the field of quality management and statistical process control, acts on the assumption that employees will do their best when management treats them accordingly. In fact, he argues that, in terms of performance problems, *management*—not the employees—is largely responsible for the problems. This questioning could eventually result in the disappearance of performance appraisal as most organizations use it today. PHRM in the News: "Take This Job and Love It" offers an excellent description of these possibilities.

SUMMARY

Human variability is a fact of life, especially of organizational life. From a personnel and human resource management point of view, organizations attempt to

PHRM IN THE NEWS

Take This Job and Love It

With profits declining and competition on the rise, the International Business Machines Corporation wants to make sure all of its employees are pulling their weight. So the computer giant is making it easier for its people to get fired. Under one of the most intricately structured appraisal systems in the nation, 10 percent of Big Blue's vaunted work force will get flunking grades in their annual reviews this year, marking for many the first step toward dismissal. Another 10 percent, deemed by their bosses to be superstars, could earn bonuses of $50,000 or more.

By contrast, Eastman Kodak's Eastman Chemical Company has stopped grading employees. To eliminate a tier of managers and push responsibility down the line, Eastman recently did away with the top jobs in marketing, production and product development. Now, decisions in manufacturing, for instance, and solutions to, say, waste treatment problems, are hammered out in monthly meetings by the heads of the company's three major plants. Because the new team structure makes it difficult to evaluate individual performance, Eastman Chemical is likely to adopt a system of peer review.

Pressured by the recession to thin their ranks while improving products and services to remain competitive, companies across the country are grappling anew with how to get the most from their troops. And a growing minority are scrapping the all-American merit system—championed by companies like I.B.M.—in favor of a more egalitarian approach based on teamwork, where peer pressure rather than the carrot-and-stick approach, drives motivation.

Companies as diverse as the General Motors Corporation and Eastman Kodak are experimenting with a pass/fail approach to performance evaluation as a way to replace the traditional star system. They are gradually being won over to the notion that rewarding a handful of "winners" and holding them up as the keys to corporate innovation and success brands the majority of employees as losers, hurting morale and cooperation.

The Trouble With Rating

"The merit rating nourishes short-term performance, annihilates long-term planning, builds fear, demolishes teamwork, and nourishes rivalry and politics," said W. Edwards Deming, a management expert whose principles for attaining higher quality are inspiring performance appraisal reforms.

Some experts, in fact, believe the merit system, and the way it measures and rewards individual initiative, is in fundamental conflict with the search for quality and solutions to competitive problems.

In his upcoming book "The Economics of Trust," John O. Whitney, a former chief operating officer of Pathmark supermarkets and now a management professor at Columbia University, writes: "If we continue with our traditional measurements and rewards, our relative productivity will continue its decline, our quality will suffer, and our ability to compete will wither away."

Traditionalists, for whom the star system is as logical as Darwin's theory of natural selection, argue that abandoning it would breed complacency rather than discovery. "You start with your culture, where your history and practices have positioned you," said Walton E. Burdick, senior vice president of personnel at I.B.M., who contends that performance appraisal systems must reflect the ingrained culture of individualism long fostered by American companies.

Moreover, he said, in defense of I.B.M.'s recent actions, "The destiny of this corporation is dependent on the quality of the employees. We're still a compassionate caring company, but in a global competitive environment, making the bottom 10 percent uncomfortable is good business."

But proponents of no-fault performance appraisals counter that the country has outgrown the corporate

Continued

select and *control* individual variability. Chapter 6 addressed how selection and placement decisions enable organizations to staff positions for effective performance. This chapter and the next discuss how organizations control performance variability through the performance appraisal system.

star system. It used to be easy to give merit raises to most employees, but as competitive pressures have tightened salary budgets, companies have been forced to make hair-splitting distinctions between individual performances.

Earl Conway, director of corporate quality at Procter & Gamble, said that as companies "get better and better at selecting and training individuals, it's going to get harder and harder to make distinctions between the overall quality of individual performance." That's especially true as they encourage employees from different departments and with widely varying expertise to work in teams.

In response, a cluster of companies are overhauling the way they manage, evaluate and compensate workers to foster cooperation. Rather than passing judgment on individual performance, some companies are trying a pass/fail approach on the premise that individuals can be only as effective as the systems within which they work. In this setting, the boss is a trouble-shooter who helps employees improve the system and create an environment conducive to change.

They hope that the teamwork that results will have as big an impact on overall corporate productivity as it did on manufacturing in the 80's, when it helped improve such things as car assembly at the Ford Motor Company. And in their view, it is a better way to capitalize on the strengths of a uniquely diverse work force. Although diversity may be difficult to manage, it is a resource that can give United States companies an edge over most foreign competitors because it provides the same creative potential that has made cross-functional problem-solving among the most important innovations of the decade, Mr. Conway said.

The Zytec Way

Indeed, as companies turn to teamwork to foster innovation and speed decision-making, they are driven to reassess the way they supervise and reward performance. Take the Zytec Corporation, a maker of customized power supplies in Eden Prairie, Minn. After being spun off in 1984 by the Control Data Corporation and without a single outside customer to its name, Zytec overhauled its performance appraisal and compensation system with an eye toward building the sort of collaborative environment it deemed was needed to quickly churn out products for customers.

For the last few years, the vast majority of Zytec employees have earned the same percentage pay increases. The company has eliminated bonuses and executive perquisites, and it maintains a narrow 14-fold differential between the salary of the chief executive and the lowest paid manufacturing worker.

Like Powertrain, Zytec, in its only concession to the old star system, agreed to let managers petition for extra money for a few exceptional employees. "The system isn't perfect," said Ronald D. Schmidt, chief executive, referring to the difficulty of keeping the exceptional category below 5 percent of the work force. "But it certainly hasn't hurt us any."

Last year, the privately held company won the Malcolm Baldrige Award for Quality and made nearly $2 million on more than $74 million in sales. Since 1988, it has slashed the time it takes to develop a new product by 50 percent, cut product development cost by nearly as much, and increased sales per employee to $100,000, 20 percent above the industry average.

The recession and the need to pare personnel, however, confronts these pioneers with new challenges. G.M., for instance, looking to eliminate more than 20,000 jobs, has given the Powertrain division six months to cut 800 jobs. The division is canvassing employees for ideas and is considering everything from leaves-of-absence to job-sharing to transferring work once done by outside contractors to in-house personnel—but not trying to identify poor performers.

Says Mary Jenkins, director of human resource planning at Powertrain: "When we're done, we don't want people wondering how a colleague lost their job. If it isn't done carefully, people who remain could be very negatively affected."[48]

SOURCE: A. Gabor, The New York Times (26 Jan. 1992): 1,6.

Performance appraisal is not a single act or a particular form used to evaluate job behavior. Rather, it is a system or a set of processes and procedures that evolve over time. A performance appraisal system is premised on the beliefs that individuals will vary in performance over time and that individuals can exert some influence over their performance. Thus, an effective performance appraisal system must generally serve two purposes: (1) an evaluative role to let people know where they stand and (2) a developmental role to provide specific information and direction so individuals can change (improve) their performance. Performance appraisal is, therefore, linked to other important human resource activities such as compensation, promotion decisions, human resource planning, development and training, and validation of selection systems for legal compliance. Increasingly, it is also being linked to the strategy and plans of the business.

Because performance appraisal is linked to so many other human resource activities, it is important to understand why performance appraisal data are gathered, as well as how this information is used. Legal considerations have also heightened the need for organizations to review this process. Special emphasis is placed on the need for job analysis as a means of developing job-related performance criteria. In general, the more subjective the performance appraisal approach, the more vulnerable the performance appraisal system to legal challenge. Although various approaches to performance appraisal exist, they can be classified into three broad categories: norm-referenced, absolute standards, and output-based. The choice of the best approach is really a function of several criteria: the purpose of the performance appraisal system (evaluation and/or development), the costs of developing and implementing of the system, the degree to which rater errors are minimized, and user acceptance of the system.

Despite the most well-laid plans for a performance appraisal system, human resource professionals are often frustrated by the failure of line managers to apply and use the performance appraisal system consistently. A number of obstacles can contribute to rater resistance to a performance appraisal system: raters may not have the opportunity to observe subordinates' performance; raters may not have performance standards; raters as human judges are prone to errors; and raters may view performance appraisal as a conflict-producing activity and therefore avoid it. For these reasons and others, it is important to examine not only why and how performance appraisal data are gathered but also, as the next chapter explores, how they are used.

WHERE WE ARE TODAY

1. Performance appraisal information has multiple uses including employee evaluation, employee development, systems maintenance, documentation, and the fulfillment of the firm's strategic objectives.
2. Performance appraisals often don't work because managers are not proficient at conducting appraisals and because they rarely see any payoffs for accurate appraisals.
3. A strategically aligned performance management system aligns the goals of the individual and work team with those of the organization. It facilitates the measurement of individual, team, or unit contributions and serves as a source of input for administrative actions, and it can help identify the need for new strategies or programs.
4. Ensuring that rating errors are minimized and employees are evaluated on work behavior or outputs rather than traits is critical for a legally-defendable appraisal system.

5. In setting up an appraisal system, managers need to make decisions about what to evaluate, when to conduct appraisals, who will do the evaluation, and what rating format to use.
6. Rating methods can be categorized as norm-referenced, absolute standards, or output-based; the latter two are more legally defendable than the former.
7. Graphic rating scales are simple and easy to use but do not provide useful developmental information. They also are legally questionable if used to make important evaluation decisions.
8. Output-based criteria should be specific, time-bound, and weighted, and should specify the conditions and consequences of performance.
9. Cognitively, the rating process is complex. It involves the observation of behavior or outcomes, and then encoding, storing, retrieving, and integrating the information.
10. The careful design of the appraisal system, the availability of memory aids, rater training, self-efficacy, rewards for accurate and timely appraisal, and the diffusion of rating responsibility are all strategies to improve the accuracy of performance evaluation.

DISCUSSION QUESTIONS

1. How can performance appraisal forms be developed so supervisory errors in performance appraisal can be minimized?
2. Why does employee performance vary even after employees have successfully passed rigorous organizational selection and placement procedures? How can a performance appraisal system address this performance variability?
3. Assume the identity of each of the following persons: a subordinate, a superior, a personnel professional. Then answer this question: What purpose can a performance appraisal system serve for you? Are the purposes served by the performance appraisal system for each of these three people congruent or conflicting? Explain.
4. Why is job analysis essential for the development of a performance appraisal system?
5. Managers often complain that a performance appraisal system puts them in a bind. On the one hand, they are supposed to give feedback to help improve future performance; on the other hand, they are supposed to allocate rewards (pay raises or promotions). How would you respond to this complaint?
6. What are the three major approaches to performance appraisal? Can you give an example of each approach?
7. What is BARS? BOS? Mixed standard? What advantages are offered by each of these performance appraisal approaches? What disadvantages?
8. Performance appraisal approaches often differ based on whether behavior or the results of behavior are evaluated. Can you cite examples from organizations with which you are familiar in which one approach might be preferred over the other? Explain why.
9. Teachers often complain that students should not be used to evaluate teacher performance. Argue the position that students should be used. What potential rater errors are students likely to commit? How can these be mini-

mized? Are the rater errors that students might commit similar to the type of rater errors that teachers might commit when evaluating student performance?

10. For legal considerations, a well-developed performance appraisal system can provide measurable criteria of job success, which can then be used as a test to validate selection procedures. Under what circumstances could the criterion—in this instance, the performance appraisal—be an actual test, or a predictor of future job success?

APPLIED PROJECTS

1. Assume you want to convince top management that your firm's performance appraisal processes should be strategically linked to the overall business plan. What arguments would you use to convince top management to use performance information strategically? What arguments would you use to build a case against strategic linkages?
2. You are the Vice President of Operations for a 1,000-person, computer hardware firm that makes and markets specialized computer circuit boards. You have been asked to develop an appropriate performance appraisal system for the firm's 500-plus software and hardware engineering professionals. What type(s) of appraisal system(s) would you recommend and why? What arguments could you make to convince the CEO and the board of directors to adopt your new appraisal system?
3. Assume your company, an international consulting firm, puts you in charge of developing an output-based appraisal system. Develop a flow chart (timelines included) detailing the steps that will be taken and the decisions that will be needed to develop the new appraisal system.

CASE STUDY

Performance Appraisal at Essex

Percy Sharp sat at his desk, looking over the performance appraisal form he had just completed on Bob Maxwell, one of his insurance underwriters. Bob was on his way to Percy's office for their annual review session. Percy dreaded these appraisal meetings, even when he did not have to confront employees with negative feedback.

A couple of years before, Essex Insurance Ltd., which had experienced very rapid growth, decided to implement a formal appraisal system. All supervisors had been presented with the new appraisal form, which included five different subcategories in addition to an overall rating. Supervisors were asked to rate employees on each dimension using a scale from 1 (unacceptable) to 5 (exceptional). They were also advised to maintain a file on each employee into which they could drop notes on specific incidents of good or poor performance during the year to use as "documentation" when completing the appraisal form. They were told they could only give an overall rating of "1" or "5" if they had "substantial" documentation to back it up. Percy had never given one of these ratings because he wasn't diligent about recording specific incidents in employee files; he believed it was just too time-consuming to write up all of the documentation necessary to justify such a rating. There were a couple

2# no get feed back

of employees in his department who deserved a "5" rating, in Percy's opinion, but so far no one had complained about the appraisals they received from Percy.

Bob was one of Percy's "exceptional" workers. Percy had three or four specific examples of exceptional performance in Bob's file but, looking over the form, he could not clearly identify the category in which they belonged. "Oh well," Percy said to himself, "I'll just give him 3s and 4s. I don't have to justify those, and Bob has never complained before." One of the categories was "Analyzing Work Materials." Percy had never understood what that meant or whether it was relevant for the job of insurance underwriter. He had checked "3" (satisfactory) for Bob, as he did on all the evaluations he did. He understood the meaning of the other categories—Quality of Work, Quantity of Work, Improving Work Methods and Relationships with Co-workers—although he was confused as to what a "3" or a "4" indicated about each category.

Bob knocked on Percy's door and came in. Percy looked up and smiled. "Hi, Bob. Sit down. Let's get through this thing so we can get back to work, OK?

Case Questions

1. Does Percy feel very comfortable giving Bob his performance appraisal?
2. What problems do you see with the appraisal system Percy is using?
3. What are Bob's likely reactions to being told by Percy that he scored 3s and 4s even though he is one of Percy's exceptional workers?
4. What suggestions do you have for improving the performance appraisal system at Essex?

NOTES

1. B. Dumaine, "Those Highflying Pepsico Managers," *Fortune* (10 April 1989): 78–86.
2. L. Brokaw, "The Mystery-Shopper Questionnaire," *Inc.* (June 1991): 94–97.
3. H. S. Feild and W. H Holley, "The Relationship of Performance Appraisal System Characteristics to Verdicts in Selected Employment Discrimination Cases," *Academy of Management Journal* 25 (1982): 392–406; D. L. DeVries, A. M. Morrison, S. L. Shullman, and M. L. Gerlach, *Performance Appraisal on the Line* (Greensboro, N.C.: Center for Creative Leadership, 1986).
4. J. N. Cleveland, K. R. Murphy, and R. E. Williams, "Multiple Uses of Performance Appraisal: Prevalence and Correlates," *Journal of Applied Psychology* 74 (1989); K. R. Murphy and J. N. Cleveland, *Performance Appraisal: An Organizational Perspective* (Boston, Mass.: Allyn & Bacon, 1991).
5. N. Napier and G. Latham, "Outcome Expectancies of People Who Conduct Performance Appraisal," *Personnel Psychology* 1986: 827–37; C. E. Schneier, "Implementing Performance Management and Recognition and Rewards (PMRR) Systems at the Strategic Level: A Line Management Driven Effort," *Human Resource Planning* (1989): 205–20.
6. J. E. Butler, G. R. Ferris, and N. K. Napier, *Strategy and Human Resource Management* (Cincinnati, Ohio: South Western Publishing, 1991); R. D. Pritchard, *Measuring and Improving Organizational Productivity: A Practical Guide* (New York: Praeger, 1990); R. D. Pritchard, S. D. Jones, P. L. Roth, K. K. Stuebing, and S. E. Ekeberg, "The Evaluation of an Integrated Approach to Measuring Organizational Productivity," *Personnel Psychology* 42, (1989): 69–115; S. B. MacKenzie, P. M. Podsakoff, and R. Fetter, "Organizational Citizenship Behavior and Objective Productivity as Determinants of Managerial Evaluations of Salesperson's Performance," *Organizational Behavior and Human Decision Processes* 50 (1991): 123–50; J. Hogan and R. Hogan, "How to Measure Employee Reliability," *Journal of Applied Psychology* 47, no. 2 (1989): 273–79; T. McDonald, "The Effect of Dimension Content on Observation and Ratings of Job Performance," *Organizational Behavior and Human Decision Processes* 48 (1991): 252–71; B. M. Staw and R. D. Boettger, "Task Revision: A Neglected Form of Work Performance," *Academy of Management Journal* 33, no. 3 (1990): 534–59; J. A. Weekley and J. A. Gier, "Ceilings in the Reliability and Validity of Performance Ratings: The Case of Expert Raters," *Academy of Management Journal* 32, no. 1 (1989): 213–22.
7. M. Rozek, "Can You Spot a Peak Performer?" *Personnel Journal* (June 1991): 77–78.
8. J. Fulkerson and R. S. Schuler, "Managing Worldwide Diversity at Pepsi-Cola International," in *Diversity in the Workplace: Human Resources Initiatives,* ed. S. E. Jackson (New York: Guilford Publications, 1992).
9. Bernardin and Cascio, "Performance Appraisal and the Law," in *Readings in Personnel and Human Resource Management,* 3d ed.; R. Giles and C. Landauer, "Setting Specific Standards for Appraising Creative Staffs," *Personnel Administrator* (March 1984): 35–47; C. J. Hobson and F. W. Gibson, "Policy Capturing as an Approach to Understanding and Improving Performance Appraisal: A Review of the Literature," *Academy of Management Review* (Oct. 1983): 640–49; C. J. Hobson and F. W. Gibson, "Capturing Supervisor Rating Policies: A Way to Improve Performance Appraisal Effectiveness," *Personnel Administrator* (March 1984): 59–68; J. S. Kane, "Measure for Measure in Performance Appraisal," *Computers in Personnel* (Fall 1987): 31–39.
10. A. M. Mohrman, S. M. Resnick-West, and E. E. Lawler, III. *Designing Performance Appraisal Systems* (San Francisco: Jossey-Bass, 1989): 119–20; R. Johnson and R. D. Bretz,

Jr., *Research and Applications of the Processes of Performance Appraisal: An Annotated Bibliography of Recent Literature, 1981–1989* (Monticello, Ill.: Vance Bibliographies, 1991).

11. P. O. Kingstrom and L. E. Mainstone, "An Investigation of Rater Ratee Acquaintance and Rater Bias," *Academy of Management Journal* 28 (1985): 641–53; K. R. Murphy, "Dimensions of Job Performance," in *Testing: Theoretical and Applied Perspectives,* ed. R. Dillion (New York: Praeger, 1992).
12. Murphy and Cleveland, *Performance Appraisal: An Organizational Perspective.*
13. H. J. Bernardin and J. Abbot, "Predicting (and Preventing) Differences Between Self and Supervisory Appraisals," *Personnel Administrator* (June 1985): 151–57; A.S. Tsui and C. A. O'Reilly III, "Beyond Simple Demographic Effects: The Importance of Relational Demography in Superior-Subordinate Dyads," *Academy of Management Journal* 32, no. 2 (1989): 402–23; B. B. Gaugler and A. S. Rudolph, "The Influence of Assessee Performance Variation on Assessor's Judgments," *Personnel Psychology* 45 (1992): 77–98; W. C. Borman, L. A. White, E. D. Pulakos, and S. H. Oppler, "Models of Supervisory Job Performance Ratings," *Journal of Applied Psychology* 76, no. 6 (1991): 863–72; R. A. Jako and K. R. Murphy, "Distributional Ratings, Judgment Decomposition, and Their Impact on Interrater Agreement and Rating Accuracy," *Journal of Applied Psychology* 75, no. 5 (1990): 500–505; S. J. Ashford, "Self-Assessments in Organizations: A Literature Review and Integrative Model," *Research in Organizational Behavior,* vol. 11 (1989): 133–74; T. H. Shore, L. McFarlane Shore, and G. C. Thornton III, "Construct Validity of Self- and Peer-Evaluations of Performance Dimensions in an Assessment Center," *Journal of Applied Psychology* 77, no. 1 (1992): 42–54; S. Fox, Z. Ben-Nahum, and Y. Yinon, "Perceived Similarity and Accuracy of Peer Ratings," *Journal of Applied Psychology* 74, no. 5 (1989): 781–86; L. Klebe Trevino and B. Victor, "Peer Reporting of Unethical Behavior: A Social Context Perspective," *Academy of Management Journal* 35, no. 1 (1992): 38–64; J. L. Farh, G. H. Dobbins, and B. S. Cheng, "Cultural Relativity in Action: A Comparison of Self-Ratings Made by Chinese and U.S. Workers," *Personnel Psychology* 44 (1991): 129–47.
14. J. L. Farh and J. Werbel, "Effects of Purpose of the Appraisal and Expectation of Validation on Self Appraisal Leniency," *Journal of Applied Psychology* 71 (1986): 527–29; R. P. Steel and N. K. Ovalle, "Self Appraisal Based on Supervisory Feedback," *Personnel Psychology* 37 (1984): 667–85; P. R. Sackett, C. L. Z. DuBois, and A. Wiggins Noe, "Tokenism in Performance Evaluation: The Effects of Work Group Representation on Male-Female and White-Black Differences in Performance Ratings," *Journal of Applied Psychology* 76, no. 2 (1991): 263–67; D. A. Waldman and B. J. Avolio, "Race Effects in Performance Evaluations: Controlling for Ability, Education and Experience," *Journal of Applied Psychology* 76, no. 6 (1991): 897–901; P. R. Sackett and C. L. Z. DuBois, "Rater-Ratee Race Effects on Performance Evaluation: Challenging Meta-Analytic Conclusions," *Journal of Applied Psychology* 76, no. 6 (1991): 873–77; E. D. Pulakos, L. A. White, S. H. Oppler, and W. C. Borman, "Examination of Race and Sex Effects on Performance Ratings," *Journal of Applied Psychology* 74, no. 5 (1989): 770–80; B. S. Klaas and A. S. DeNisi, "Managerial Reactions to Employee Dissent: The Impact of Grievance Activity on Performance Ratings," *Academy of Management Journal* 32, no. 4 (1989): 705–17; J. W. Smither, H. Collins, and R. Buda, "When Ratee Satisfaction Influences Performance Evaluations: A Case of Illusory Correlation," *Journal of Applied Psychology* 74, no. 4 (1989): 599–605.
15. "Measuring Performance: Employee Initiated Reviews," *Inc.* (July 1991): 80. Also see P. Lanza, "Team Appraisals," *Personnel Journal* (March 1985): 50; J. D. Coombe, "Peer Review: The Emerging Successful Application," *Employee Relations Law Journal* (Spring 1984): 659–71; J. S. Kane and E. E. Lawler III, "Methods of Peer Assessment," *Psychological Bulletin* 3 (1978): 555–86; G. M. McEvoy, P. F. Buller, and S. R. Roghaar, "A Jury of One's Peers," *Personnel Administrator* (May 1988): 94–98; and L. Reibstein, "More Firms Use Peer Review Panel to Resolve Employees' Grievances," *The Wall Street Journal* (3 Dec. 1986): 25.
16. Discussions between company officials and the second author. Also see C. A. Norman and R. A. Zawacki, "Team Appraisals—Team Approach," *Personnel Journal* (Sept. 1991): 101–104; J. Fitz-Enz and J. Rodgers, "Get Quality Performance from Professional Staff," *Personnel Journal* (May 1991): 22–24; L. Thornburg, "Performance Measures that Work," *HR Magazine* (May 1991): 35–38; T. Slater, "Get it Right the First Time," *Personnel Journal* (Sept. 1991): 35–40.
17. Bernardin and Abbott, "Predicting Differences..."
18. "Electronic Monitoring: Employee Rights Invaded?" *Bulletin to Management* (8 Oct. 1987): 322–27; J. Chalykoff and T. A. Kochan, "Computer-Aided Monitoring: Its Influence on Employee Job Satisfaction and Turnover," *Personnel Psychology* 42 (1989): 807–34; G. Bylinksy, "How Companies Spy on Employees," *Fortune* (4 Nov. 1991): 131–32, 136, 140; J. R. Larson, Jr., and C. Callahan, "Performance Monitoring: How it Affects Work Productivity," *Journal of Applied Psychology* 75, no. 5 (1990): 530–38.
19. "Electronic Monitoring..."
20. R. J. Greene, "A '90s Model for Performance Management," *HR Magazine* (April 1991): 62–65.
21. W. F. Cascio and H. J. Bernardin, "Implications of Performance Appraisal Litigation for Personnel Decisions," *Personnel Psychology* 34 (1981): 211–26
22. R. Jacobs and S. W. J. Kozlowski, "A Closer Look at Halo Error in Performance Ratings," *Academy of Management Journal* (March 1985): 201–212; L. M. King, J. E. Hunter, and F. L. Schmidt, "Halo in a Multi-Dimensional Forced Choice Performance Evaluation Scale," *Journal of Applied Psychology* 65 (1980): 507–516.
23. G. Latham and K. Wexley, *Improving Productivity Through Performance Appraisal* (Reading, Mass.: Addison-Wesley, 1981).
24. In some forms of BARS, the anchors are stated as expected behaviors (e.g., the person could be expected to develop loan documentation accurately). When expected behaviors are included, the BARS form is more appropri-

ately labeled BES—a Behavioral Expectation Scale. For further discussion, see F. J. Landy and J. L. Farr, "Performance Rating," *Psychological Bulletin* (Jan. 1980): 72–107; K. R. Murphy and J. I. Constans, "Behavioral Anchors as a Source of Bias in Rating," *Journal of Applied Psychology* (Nov. 1987): 573; and S. Zedeck, "Behavioral Based Performance Appraisals," *Aging and Work* 4 (1981): 89–100.

25. H. J. Berardin and R. W. Beatty, *Performance Appraisal: Assessing Human Behavior at Work* (Boston: Kent, 1984); F. J. Landy and J. L. Farr, *The Measurement of Work Performance: Methods, Theory and Applications* (New York: Academic Press, 1983).
26. G. Latham and K. Wexley, "Behavioral Observation Scales for Performance Appraisal Purposes," *Personnel Psychology* 30 (1977): 255–68.
27. T. H. Poister and G. Streib, "Management Tools in Government: Trends Over the Past Decade," *Public Administration Review* 44 (1984): 215–23; S. R. Ruth and W. W. Brooks, "Who's Using MBO in Management?" *Journal of Systems Management* (1982): 1–17.
28. E. A. Locke and G. P. Latham, *A Theory of Goal Setting & Task Performance* (Englewood Cliffs, N.J.: Prentice-Hall, 1990); J. R. Hollenbeck, C. R. Williams, and H. J. Klein, "An Emperical Examination of the Antecedents of Commitment to Difficult Goals," *Journal of Applied Psychology* 74, no. 1 (1989): 18–23; P. C. Earley, T. Connolly, and G. Ekegren, "Goals, Strategy Development and Task Performance: Some Limits on the Efficacy of Goal Setting," *Journal of Applied Psychology* 74, no. 1 (1989): 24–33; R. E. Wood and E. A. Locke, "Goal Setting and Strategy Effects on Complex Tasks," *Research in Organizational Behavior* vol. 12 (1990): 73–109; C. E. Shalley, "Effects of Productivity Goals, Creativity Goals, and Personal Discretion on Individual Creativity," *Journal of Applied Psychology* 76, no. 2 (1991): 179–85; S. Siero, M. Boon, G. Kok, and F. Siero, "Modification of Driving Behavior in a Large Transport Organization: A Field Experiment," *Journal of Applied Psychology* 74, no. 3 (1989): 417–23; T. R. Mitchell and W.S. Silver, "Individual and Group Goals When Workers are Interdependent: Effects on Task Strategies and Performance," *Journal of Applied Psychology* 75, no. 2 (1990): 185–93; R. Rodgers and J. E. Hunter, "Impact of Management by Objectives on Organizational Productivity," *Journal of Applied Psychology* 76, no. 2 (1991): 322–36; P. C. Earley, G. B. Northcraft, C. Lee, and T. R. Lituchy, "Impact of Process and Outcome Feedback on the Relation of Goal Setting to Task Performance," *Academy of Management Journal* 33, no. 1 (1990): 87–105; D. C. Anderson, C. R. Crowell, M. Doman, and G. S. Howard, "Performance Posting, Goal Setting and Activity-Contingent Praise as Applied to a University Hockey Team," *Journal of Applied Psychology* (Feb. 1988): 87; M. Erez and R. Arad, "Participative Goal-Setting: Social, Motivational, and Cognitive Factors," *Journal of Applied Psychology* (Nov. 1986): 591; J. R. Hollenbeck and H. J. Klein, "Goal Commitment and the Goal-Setting Process: Problems, Prospects, and Proposals for Future Research," *Journal of Applied Psychology* (May 1987): 212; J. R. Hollenbeck and C. R. Williams, "Goal Importance, Self-Focus, and the Goal-Setting Process," *Journal of Applied Psychology* (May 1987): 204; J. S. Kane and K. A. Freeman, "MBO and Performance Appraisal: A Mixture That's Not a Solution, Part 1," *Personnel* (Dec. 1986): 26–36; J. S. Kane and K. A. Freeman, "MBO and Performance Appraisal: A Mixture That's Not a Solution, Part 2," *Personnel* (Feb. 1987): 26 –32; T. Matsui, T. Kakuyama, and M. L. U. Onglatco, "Effects of Goals and Feedback on Performance in Groups," *Journal of Applied Psychology* (Aug. 1987): 407; C. E. Shalley, G. R. Oldham, and J. F. Porac, "Effects of Goal Difficulty, Goal-Setting Method, and Expected External Evaluation on Intrinsic Motivation," *Academy of Management Journal* (Sept. 1987): 553; R. E. Wood, A. J. Mento, and E. A. Locke, "Task Complexity as a Moderator of Goal Effects: A Meta-Analysis," *Journal of Applied Psychology* (Aug. 1987): 416; P. F. Drucker, "What Results Should You Expect? A Users Guide to MBO," *Public Administration* 23 (1976): 23–26; G. S. Odiorne, *MBO II: A System of Managerial Leadership for the 80s* (Belmont, Calif.: Pitman Publishers, 1986).
29. For a comprehensive review see R. Rodgers and J. E. Hunter, "Impact of Management by Objectives on Organizational Productivity," *Journal of Applied Psychology* 76, no. 2 (1991): 316–22.
30. See note 29.
31. L. Baird, *Managing Performance* (New York: Wiley, 1986); J. J. Carlyle and T. F. Ellison, "Developing Performance Standards," *Performance Appraisal: Assessing Human Behavior at Work,* ed. H. J. Bernardin and R. W. Beatty (Boston: Kent, 1984); 343–47; E. A. Locke, "Toward a Theory of Task Motivation and Incentives," *Organizational Behavior and Human Performance* 3 (1968): 157–89.
32. L. Hugh, "Development of the Accomplishment Record Method of Selecting and Promoting Professionals," *Journal of Applied Psychology* 69 (1984): 135–46.
33. J. W. Fredrickson, "The Comprehensiveness of Strategic Processes: Extension, Observations and Future Directions," *Academy of Management Journal,* (1984), 445–66.
34. DeNisi and Williams, *"Cognitive Approaches to Performance Appraisal,"* in *Readings in Personnel and Human Resource Management,* 109–56. D. R. Ilgen and J. M. Feldman, "Performance Appraisal: A Process Focus," in *Research in Organizational Behavior,* ed. B. Staw and L. Cummings (Greenwich, Conn.: JAI Press, 1983), 141–97.
35. Bernardin and Beatty, *Performance Appraisal;* Landy and Farr, *The Measurement of Work Performance;* G. B. Northcraft, V. L. Huber, and M. A. Neale, "Sex Effects in Performance-Related Judgments," *Human Performance* (1988): 1–14; V. L. Huber, M. A. Neale, and G. B. Northcraft, "Judgment by Heuristics: Effects of Ratee and Rater Characteristics and Performance Standards on Performance-Related Judgments," *Organizational Behavior and Human Decision Processes* (Oct. 1987): 149–69.
36. M. H. Bazerman, R. I. Beekun, and F. D. Schoorman, "Performance Evaluation in a Dynamic Context: A Laboratory Study of the Impact of a Prior Commitment to the Ratee," *Journal of Applied Psychology* (Dec. 1982): 873–76; B. E. Becker and R. L. Cardy, "Influence of Halo Error on Appraisal Effectiveness: A Conceptual and

Empirical Reconsideration," *Journal of Applied Psychology* (Nov. 1986): 662; R. L. Cardy and G. H. Dobbins, "Affect and Appraisal Accuracy: Liking as an Integral Dimension in Evaluating Performance," *Journal of Applied Psychology* (Nov. 1986): 672; W. H. Cooper, "Internal Homogeneity, Descriptiveness, and Halo: Resurrecting Some Answers and Questions about the Structure of Job Performance Rating Categories," *Personnel Psychology* (Autumn 1983): 489–502; M. E. Heilman and M. H. Stopeck, "Being Attractive, Advantage or Disadvantage: Performance-Based Evaluations and Recommended Personnel Actions as a Function of Appearance, Sex, and Job Type." *Organizational Behavior and Human Decision Processes* 35 (1985): 202–15; R. L. Heneman and K. N. Wexley, "The Effects of Time Delay in Rating and Amount of Information Observed on Performance Rating Accuracy," *Academy of Management Journal* (Dec. 1983): 677–86; K. Kraiger and J. K. Ford, "A Meta-Analysis of Ratee Race Effects in Performance Ratings," *Journal of Applied Psychology* (Feb. 1985): 56–65; C. E. Lance and D. J. Woehr, "Statistical Control of Halo: Clarification from Two Cognitive Models of the Performance Appraisal Process," *Journal of Applied Psychology* (Nov. 1986): 679; K. N. Wexley and E. D. Pulakos, "The Effects of Perceptual Congruence and Sex on Subordinates: Performance Appraisals of Their Managers," *Academy of Management Journal* (Dec. 1983): 666–76.

37. G. Northcraft and G. Wolf, "Dollars, Sense and Sunk Costs: A Life Cycle Model of Resource Allocation," *Academy of Management Review* 9 (1984): 225–34.
38. M. Bazerman, *Judgment in Managerial Decision Making* (New York: Wiley, 1986); Bazerman, Beekun, and Schoorman, "Performance Evaluation in a Dynamic Context," 873–76; Huber, "Comparison of the Effects of Specific and General Performance Standards"; G. B. Northcraft, M. A. Neale, and V. L Huber, "The Effects of Cognitive Bias and Social Influence on Human Resources Management Decisions," in *Research in Personnel and Human Resource Management,* ed. G. Ferris and K. M. Rowland (Greenwich, Conn.: JAI Press, 1988), 157–89; Northcraft and Wolf, "Dollars, Sense, and Sunk Costs," 225–34.
39. R. L. Dipboye, "Some Neglected Variables in Research on Discrimination in Appraisals," *Academy of Management Review* (Jan. 1985): 118–25; M. R. Edwards and J. R. Sproull, "Rating the Raters Improves Performance Appraisals," *Personnel Administrator* (Aug. 1983): 77–82; J. L. Gibson, J. J. Ivancevich, and J. H. Donnelly, *Organizations: Behavior, Structure, Processes,* 3d ed. (Dallas: Business Publications, 1979): 361; B. R. Nathan and R. A. Alexander, "The Role of Inferential Accuracy in Performance Rating," *Academy of Management Review* (Jan. 1985): 109–17; R. M. McIntyre, D. E. Smith, and C. E. Hassett, "Accuracy of Performance Ratings as Affected by Rater Training and Perceived Purpose of Rating," *Journal of Applied Psychology* (Feb. 1984): 147–56.
40. V. L. Huber and T. Deharpport, "Rating Inputs and Scales: Effects of Cued Judgments on Performance Appraisal and Raise Decisions," (Working Paper: University of Washington, 1989); V. L. Huber, "Comparison of Specific and General Performance Standards on Performance Appraisal Decision," *Decision Sciences* 20 (1989): 545–57
41. Henderson, *Performance Appraisal.*
42. Murphy and Cleveland, *Performance Appraisal: An Organizational Perspective,* 190–210; C. G. Banks and K. R. Murphy, "Toward Narrowing the Research-Practice Gap in Performance Appraisal," *Personnel Psychology* 38 (1985): 335–45; Northcraft, Neale and Huber, "The Effects of Cognitive Bias and Social Influence."
43. K. R. Murphy, "Difficulties in the Statistical Control of Halo," *Journal of Applied Psychology* 67 (1982): 161–64; L. Hirshhord, Meaning in the New Team Environment (Reading, Mass.: Addison-Wesley, 1991); Murphy and Cleveland, *Performance Appraisal: An Organizational Perspective.*
44. H. J. Bernardin and R. W. Beatty, *Performance Appraisal: Assessing Human Behavior at Work* (Boston: Kent, 1984); W. F. Cascio, *Applied Psychology in Personnel Management,* 3d ed. (Reston, Va.: Reston, 1988); F. J. Landy and D. A. Trumbo, *Psychology of Work Behavior,* rev. ed. (Homewood, Ill.: Dorsey, 1980).
45. F. J. Landy and J. L. Farr, *The Measurement of Work Performance: Methods, Theory and Applications* (San Diego, Calif.: Academic Press, 1983); Murphy and Cleveland, *Performance Appraisal: An Organizational Perspective.*
46. For an excellent discussion of the application of discipline in organizations, see R. D. Arvey and J. M. Ivancevich, "Punishment in Organizations: A Review, Propositions, and Research Suggestions," *Academy of Management Review* 5 (1980): 123–32.
47. C. Frayne and G. Latham, "Application of Social Learning Theory to Employee Self-Management of Attendance," *Journal of Applied Psychology* 72 (1987): 387–92; F. Kanfer, "Self Management Methods," in *Helping People Change: A Textbook of Methods,* eds. P. Karoly and A. Goldstein (New York: Pergamon Press, 1980): 334–89; P. Karoly and F. Kanfer, *Self Management and Behavior Change: From Theory to Practice* (New York: Pergamon Press, 1986).
48. A. Gabor, *The New York Times* (26 Jan. 1992): 1, 6; R. D. Gatewood and A. B. Carroll, "Assessment of Ethical Performance of Organization Members: A Conceptual Framework," *Academy of Management Review* 16, no. 4 (1991): 667–90; R. G. Eccles, "The Performance Measurement Manifesto," *Harvard Business Review* (Jan.-Feb. 1991): 131–37.

CHAPTER 8

Performance Appraisal: Utilizing the Data

The quality of work from motivated people is light-years ahead of what you get from people not well motivated.

—Frank Popoff, President[1]

It's 8 a.m. in the morning in Park City, Utah, a ski resort community thirty miles southwest of Salt Lake City. Debbi Fields, founder and CEO of Mrs. Fields' Cookies, has just arrived at her office. Sipping herbal tea and nibbling on a Mrs. Fields' muffin, she turns on her desktop computer, presses a few keys and calls up the cookie emporium's Retail Operations Intelligence (ROI) system. The state-of-the-art computer software system networks all retail outlets to the company's headquarters and allows corporate officials to communicate with all store managers and vice versa. Simply stated, the system allows store managers, district managers, and regional directors across the country to have daily contact via computer with Debbi and the rest of the company's top administrative staff.

Clicking through a couple of menus, Debbi finds what she's looking for—yesterday's sales figures for all 650 cookie emporium outlets, including those in Hong Kong, Tokyo, Singapore, and Sydney. Since the ROI system tracks sales continuously through cash registers, a summary report of the preceding day's performance test results appears on the screen within seconds. By pressing a few more keys on the computer, Debbi can tell which stores did the best, which did the worst, or which stores met their sales projections and which stores didn't. Armed with this information, Debbi begins her favorite task of the morning—calling store managers to congratulate them on their performance. According to Paul Quinn, vice president of management information systems, "People can't believe that she knows so quickly how they did the day before. It makes them feel as if she's watching and that she cares."

In addition to sales reporting and analysis, the twenty modules or applications of the ROI system allow Debbi's management philosophy and skills to filter throughout the company to help sell cookies. When the company was started in Palo Alto, Debbi set hourly sales quotas for herself and baked up the day's inventory based on daily experience. It was also her policy (and still is) not to sell a product that's more than two hours old, Quinn pointed out. Through the ROI's production planning module, store managers know how many units of a particular cookie they can expect to sell to meet projections from hour to hour, how much dough must be prepared, and when to bake to maximize sales and minimize loss. To further assist managers in meeting their sales goals, the system charts hourly progress versus projections and makes suggestions on how to keep selling cookies.

Information obtained via the ROI system also can be used to motivate managers and staff. For example, Janet Oskinski, manager of a Mrs. Fields' store in Costa Mesa, California, provides her employees with individualized, daily bonus reports to let them know how close they are to reaching their goals. The computer even flashes reinforcing messages such as "Congratulations, you're doing great" as employees reach performance milestones.

The system also is a decision aide and can help diagnose performance ailments and develop high-potential employees. This is done by strategically integrating all human resource functions via the ROI. For example, after a store manager conducts an initial screening interview, a half-hour computer interview is administered to each applicant and then computer-analyzed. By automating and standardizing the selection process via computer, the company can select the employees who are most likely to be successful.

Once hired, employees participate in the ROI skill assessment. This module tests employees to make sure they're qualified to do their jobs. Immediate grading with online tutorials for questions incorrectly answered are provided. If any performance deficiencies are found, additional computer-aided training is provided. The computer also provides refresher courses for existing employees. For example, when an employee wasn't performing as effectively on the job as he could be, store manager Janet Oskinski directed him to work on the computer located in the back of the store for a few hours. "When he returned, his performance improved," Oskinski explained, adding that you can tell employees that they need to sell more, but if they don't know how to do it they won't perform as expected. "Computer training assures that trainees know the ingredients of a successful sale as well as other aspects of the cookie business."

According to Randy Fields, president of Mrs. Fields' parent company (Debbi's husband too!), the ROI system was designed to keep the corporation administratively lean and flat. Nanette Mathieu, director of operations, was promoted from a store manager to her current position in just four years. Much of the knowledge she now possesses was acquired via the ROI system. The ROI system also freed her to do what she does best—manage people. "If you're supposed to be the expert and the manager who's going to build sales, the last thing you should be doing is sitting at your desk working numbers. You should be developing your team."

Since implementing the new system in 1985, sales at Mrs. Fields' have continued to increase. Employee turnover is also substantially lower than for other companies in the fast-food industry at all levels.[2]

As the Mrs. Fields' example shows, companies are finding out that their best chance for attaining individual, team, and organizational peak performance lies with the establishment of a strategically aligned performance management system. While performance management systems are as individual as the goals and objectives of organizations, successful systems incorporate several key components which minimize conflicts and maximize performance potential. At Mrs. Fields', employees are selected who have a high likelihood of success. High-potential employees are then trained to handle job responsibilities. Goals are set and coupled with feedback via the computer or management (e.g., personal calls from Mrs. Fields). Individualized training is available to correct performance deficiencies, and employees are empowered to increase their own skills by completing ROI training modules on their own. Finally, employees at all levels are rewarded for meeting performance targets.

Building on this model, this chapter discusses the inherent conflicts in the strategic management of performance as well as strategies to resolve those conflicts. Next, we will discuss the components of appraisal processes that evoke peak performance, paying special attention to the appraisal interview and the appraisal context. Then we will discuss how to diagnose performance problems and how to improve performance, and we will conclude by discussing performance appraisal in other countries.

SOURCES OF CONFLICT IN PERFORMANCE APPRAISAL

Performance appraisal touches on one of the most emotionally charged activities in business life—the assessment of a person's contribution to an organization.

The signals a person receives about this assessment have a strong impact on self-esteem and on subsequent performance. Unfortunately, performance appraisal draws poor reviews from employees, employers, and experts. Appraisal processes are problematic for several reasons.

Lack of Strategic Integration

Performance appraisal processes often lead to conflict because the goals of the appraisal process often are not aligned with an organization's overall objectives. One reason is that human resources traditionally have not been given the same priority as other resources with respect to strategic planning. As a consequence, the performance management system usually evolves separately in response to strategic initiatives rather than in anticipation of them. A second reason is that building such linkages takes time and resources that organizations may be unwilling to commit unless there is an immediate payoff.[3]

When the performance management system *is* strategically integrated, it is more likely that an organization will move from where it is to the desired future. For example, Metropolitan Property and Casualty Insurance Company of Warwick, Rhode Island, decided to evaluate its performance appraisal system as part of a realignment in strategic mission. To begin the process the company established employee focus groups to review and evaluate the existing system.

Although concerns about the appraisal process had led to the decision to review the system, the focus groups found that the extent of dissatisfaction was far greater than expected. Rather than supporting the strategies of the organization, stakeholders viewed the appraisal process as demotivating. Employees particularly abhorred the fact that the appraisal was something done *to* them by the manager rather than with them. Additionally, they felt the perspective of appraisals was backward, focusing on the past rather than providing direction for the future. Timing was also an issue, and the assessment of performance every six to twelve months was viewed as nonsensical and inaccurate. With this information in mind, Metropolitan Property and Casualty conducted an environmental scan to find out what exemplary firms were doing.

Armed with both types of information, an employee-management team created a new performance management system. Called "Focus on Achievement," the new program was built upon the organization's vision: "We will provide an environment in which individuals effectively utilize their skills and creativity and receive recognition for their contributions." Exhibit 8.1 summarizes the differences between Metropolitan's old system and its new strategically aligned system. At the heart of the system is a shift in emphasis from evaluation to development.

Viewing performance management as an ongoing process, Metropolitan launched its "Focus on Achievement" program by reviewing its organizational goals and strategies with all employees at the beginning of the year and at the beginning of each year thereafter. Then each employee develops a personalized achievement plan which includes a statement of individual vision—what he or she values in the company, and what he or she wants to become and achieve on the job during the next year. Job responsibilities are reviewed to identify possible "throwaways," or activities that can be eliminated in order to enhance effectiveness. The employees develop personal action plans in which they specify primary customers, assign stretch goals, and identify effectiveness indicators. Then the employee reviews the proposed plan with the supervisor. During the

Exhibit 8.1
Components of a Strategically Aligned Appraisal System

Old vs. New Methods

	Performance Appraisal	**Focus on Achievement**
Goal	Evaluation	Achievement
Manager	Controls program	Partnership
Employee	Passive	Initiator
View	Rearview mirror	Prospective
Outcome	Performance rating	Improved performance
Timing	Once a year	Ongoing
Links	None	Corporate goals
Rewards	Based on rating	Based on contribution
Theme	Control	Sharing
Criteria	Determined by manager	Suggested by and mutually determined with employee
Customer	No input	Provides input
Development plan	Sometimes included	Essential element
Individual vision	Not discussed	Basis for the plan
Atmosphere	Often confrontational	Supportive

SOURCE: Adapted from "A New Focus on Achievement," *Personnel Journal* (Feb. 1991), 73–75.

year checkpoint meetings may be called by the employee or manager. At year end, employees are recognized for their achievements. However, an employee who established an ambitious plan but didn't fully achieve it may receive greater recognition than someone who exceeded a simpler plan.[4]

Power and Politics

By definition, a performance appraisal system has legitimate power to influence job incumbents. That is, higher ranking employees typically evaluate employees in lower and less powerful positions. Additionally, formal organizational consequences such as monetary rewards, promotion. and dismissal, as well as informal consequences such as public criticism, and special privileges, are linked to appraisals. If this power is used inappropriately, conflicts arise between superiors and subordinates.

Because appraisals are conducted within a political system,[5] the process can influence the behavior of evaluators. Exhibit 8.2 provides examples of politically motivated rating practices that can occur. These behaviors are categorized in terms of whether they are defensive or assertive and whether they are tactical or strategic. Tactical behaviors are enacted to secure some short-term political goal and are episodic with a clear beginning and end. In comparison, strategic behaviors involve a longer time frame and are used to develop characteristics that will yield long-term results.[6]

	Tactical	Strategic
Defensive	*Deflated Ratings* ■ Attribute poor unit performance to individual subordinate problems (e.g., committee work) ■ Self-handicapping for anticipated poor unit performance ■ To keep valuable employees who would otherwise be promoted or transferred ■ To control greater proportions of discretionary funds by restricting merit awards *Inflated Ratings* ■ To avoid complaints about poor supervision/performance appraisal process ■ To avoid personal confrontations with subordinates over lower than expected ratings.	*Deflated Ratings* ■ Attribute poor unit performance over several periods to subordinate's lack of ability ■ Attribute poor unit performance to subordinate's lack of ability in order to increase future unit evaluations and to claim greater personal responsibility for future effectiveness *Inflated Ratings* ■ To attend to other supervisory responsibilities by avoiding potential subordinate PA rating grievances.
Assertive	*Deflated Ratings* ■ To comply with superior demands for high work standards ■ To comply with informal demands of superiors for a normal distribution of ratings ■ To increase the perceived coercive power of the supervisor, i.e., "slacking off" results in punishment or fewer rewards *Inflated Ratings* ■ To enhance image of work unit effectiveness as a form of self-enhancement ■ To motivate employees to reciprocate with higher performance ■ To promote troublesome individuals out of the work unit ■ To inflate subordinate ratings of leadership or supervisory competence	*Deflated Ratings* ■ To increase perceptions of esteem/competence by superiors by maintaining high standards *Inflated Ratings* ■ To increase or maintain subordinate liking ■ To claim credit for aggregated unit excellence under conditions of ambiguous criteria ■ To increase the perceived reward power of the supervisor, i.e., hard work is financially rewarded ■ To increase prestige with rates by making them eligible for more merit increases

Exhibit 8.2
Examples of Rater Rating Practices to Minimize Conflict in Appraisals

SOURCE: P. Villanova and H.J. Bernardin "Impression Management in the Context of Performance Appraisal," in *Impression Management in the Organization*, eds. R.A. Giacalone and P. Rosenfeld (Hillsdale, N.J.: Lawrence Erlbaum, 1989), 299–314. Reprinted by permission.

According to a recent study, the main reason managers distort ratings is to avoid conflict with subordinates. They may also believe high ratings will be reciprocated during upward appraisals. Politically astute managers may rate their subordinates higher than deserved in order to appear successful themselves, to enlist subordinate cooperation for future work, to enhance their popularity, or to compare favorably with other supervisors. Conversely, managers may be motivated to give out strict ratings in order to create an image as a task master, to signal a change in leadership, or to motivate employees to work even harder.[7]

A low rating also may have negative consequence (firing, demotion) for the employee, a consequence for which the manager may not want to be personally responsible. As a career military officer put it, "The political environment in the Armed Forces has been such that an officer MUST have ALL superior ratings or he or she won't move up. ANY glitch in your ratings and you're out or plateaued. Therefore, we all play the game: My commanding officer gives me high ratings and I do the same for my men and women. While the military is trying to change all this, it's going to take a cultural revolution before any significant progress will be made."

Conflict in Stakeholder Goals

Goal conflict between the various constituents who have stakes in the appraisal process may also be a problem. From organizational and individual goals come three sets of conflicts. One is between the organization's evaluative and developmental goals. When pursuing the evaluative goal, superiors have to make judgments affecting their subordinates' careers and immediate rewards. Communicating these judgments can lead to the creation of an adversarial, low-trust relationship between superior and subordinate. This, in turn, precludes the superior from performing a problem-solving, helper role that is essential if the organization wants to serve the developmental goal.

A second set of conflicts arises from the various goals of the individuals who are being evaluated. On the one hand, these individuals want valid feedback that gives them information about how to improve and where they stand in the organization. On the other hand, they want to verify their self-image and obtain valued rewards. In essence, the goals of individuals imply a necessity to be open (to give valid feedback for improvement) yet to be protective (to maintain a positive self-image and obtain rewards).

The third set of conflicts arises between the individual's goals and those of the organization. One conflict is between the organization's evaluation goal and the individual's goal of obtaining rewards. Another conflict is between the organization's developmental goal and the individual's goal of maintaining self-image.[8]

Perceptual Focus

Another reason performance appraisals are problematic is that supervisors and subordinates view the process from different perspectives. For the subordinate, the perceptual focus is outward, keying on the environmental factors (the supervisor, lack of supplies, co-workers) that impinge on his or her performance. The perceptual focus of the supervisor is on the subordinate and his or her motivation and ability. These differences in perceptual focus are called **actor and observer differences** and can lead to conflict when it comes to identifying the causes of poor or good performance. This perceptual problem is accentuated by the tendency to account for performance in a self-serving manner. In order to protect one's ego, an employee is likely to attribute the causes of his or her own poor performance to external factors (difficult task, unclear instructions, lack of necessary equipment) and attribute successful performance to one's motivation and ability.

The ramifications of actor-observer differences in appraisal were uncovered in a recent study. Subordinates and their supervisors universally agreed on the general causes of job success and failure. However, when it came to the subordinate's job, there was absolutely *no* agreement on the causes of good *or* poor performance.[9]

High Performers All

One key reason performance appraisal is viewed negatively centers on the self-evaluation of employees. The overwhelming majority of employees believe they perform better than seventy-five percent of their peers. Thus, when confronted with information suggesting they performed adequately, but not outstandingly, employees don't perceive the evaluation as fair or the rewards as equivalent to their contributions. As a result, organizational commitment and job satisfaction drop and remain low for as long as a year after evaluation.

While one would expect positive feedback to increase job satisfaction, this doesn't occur either. Because employees believe their performance is high, the receipt of positive feedback merely maintains their current level of satisfaction and commitment. Thus, no matter what a supervisor does, the best he or she can accomplish is to maintain the status quo.[10]

Consequences of Inherent Conflicts

Among the several consequences of the inherent conflicts just described are ambivalence, avoidance, defensiveness, and resistance. Some of these consequences and the inherent conflicts are implicit in the discussion of the contextual impact on performance appraisal data gathering, particularly that of the superior-subordinate relationship discussed in chapter 7.

Ambivalence is a consequence for both superiors and subordinates. Superiors are ambivalent because they must act as judge and jury in telling subordinates where they stand, both because the organization demands it and because the subordinates want it; yet they are uncertain about their judgments and how the subordinates will react to negative feedback. This feeling is intensified when superiors are not trained in giving feedback. Subordinates are equally ambivalent because they want honest feedback, yet they also want to receive rewards and maintain their self-image (That is, they really want only positive feedback). Additionally, if they are open with their superiors in identifying undeveloped potential, they risk the chance that the superiors may use this to evaluate them unfavorably.

DESIGNING APPRAISAL PROCESSES TO ATTAIN PEAK PERFORMANCE

As this chapter's Focus on Research feature points out, the appraisal system as well as the appraisal interview must be designed to minimize appraisal conflicts,

yes/No

attain perceptual congruence, and maximize peak performance among individual workers and work teams.[11] This section will present strategies that have proven useful for maximizing the effectiveness of the appraisal process.

Use Appropriate Performance Data

The first step in reducing conflict and perceptual difference is to utilize performance data that focus on specific behaviors or goals. As noted previously, performance expectations need to be communicated at the beginning of the appraisal period.

Performance data that focus on personal attributes or characteristics are likely to prompt more defensiveness because they are more difficult for the superior to justify and because more of the subordinate's self-image is at stake. As Marilyn Moats Kennedy, managing partner of Career Strategies, a management consulting company in Wilmette, Ill., says,

> It's important to critique the behavior of an employee, not the employee himself.
>
> If you bark, "You have a bad attitude," to your receptionist, for example, you'll likely find yourself facing a very defensive employee. You'll probably get better results if you say, "When someone steps up to your desk: I'd like them to get the distinct impression that you're delighted to see them"[12]

The delivery of performance information also should be **well-timed.** In general, immediate feedback is most useful. Delays may be necessary if the recipient is not yet ready to receive the performance information. Feedback also should involve the **amount of information the receiver can use** rather than what the evaluator would like to give. Overloading a person with information reduces the possibility that he or she will use it effectively. An evaluator who gives more data than can be used is most likely satisfying a personal need (e.g., don't hold anything back) rather than helping the other person.[13]

Ensure Fairness

To minimize the emotionally charged atmosphere that surrounds the performance appraisal process, managers also need to take steps to ensure that the process is perceived as fair and equitable. Appraisal programs are viewed as fair to the extent that there is

- *Consistency.* Performance standards are applied consistently to all incumbents. Allowances are not made frequently for workers with special problems, nor are high performers expected to carry more than their own weight.
- *Familiarity.* The use of diaries to record worker outputs, frequent observation of performance, and management by "wandering around" increase a supervisor's job knowledge and consequently create the impression that the supervisor and the appraisal are fair.
- *Solicitation of input.* Information regarding performance standards as well as strategies to attain them, needs to be solicited *prior* to evaluation. More important, this information should be used constructively.
- *Opportunity to challenge or rebut the evaluation.* Consistent with the problem-solving interview (to be discussed in the next section), employees need to be able to challenge or rebut evaluations.

FOCUS ON RESEARCH

System or Supervisor: What Causes the Conflict in Appraisals?

Research on performance appraisal processes has focused on a number of areas, including the appraisal instrument, rater training, cognitive processes, and bias in judgments. However, the context in which performance appraisal is conducted has received comparatively limited study. Contextual factors are not explicitly related to the nature of the rater, ratee, or rating instrument but are part of the context in which the rating occurs. This research void is problematic because the environment has an important influence on behavior in general and on performance judgments specifically. Depending on the rating context, raters may be strict or lenient, and may complete appraisals in a timely manner or may not do them at all. Also the system may be perceived as fair or unfair. Therefore, the context in which appraisals are conducted may be related to performance appraisal process satisfaction.

To understand the relative importance of the rating context, a field study was conducted by two human resource researchers from Auburn University. The first part of the study was designed to identify the contextual factors most important to the appraisal process. More than five hundred employees of a textile firm (ninety-five % male) responded to a two-part questionnaire. The first part of the survey contained items relating to the performance appraisal system; the second part of the survey related to the appraisal interview. Using a statistical process called factor analysis, the researchers identified three important components of an appraisal system or context. Complexity referred to how well employees understood how the appraisal process worked. The second factor focused on implementation of the appraisal process and included such things as the training provided and how the system was introduced. The third critical factor was follow-up and monitoring to ensure that supervisors discussed appraisal results with their subordinates.

Regarding the appraisal interview, four factors were found to be particularly important. They included (1) participation of the incumbent in the appraisal discussion; (2) goal setting clarity and specificity for subsequent performance; (3) amount of criticism about performance; and (4) salary linkage, defined as explaining the relationship between performance and salary. Since all of these factors are under the control of the supervisor, the researchers named this second set of variable supervisory session variables.

Next, the researchers set out to determine if the set of system contextual variables were more predictive of appraisal system satisfaction than were the supervisory session variables and, conversely, whether the supervisory session variables were more predictive of session satisfaction than the former. Mul-

Continued

It is also important to ensure that outcomes based on of the appraisal process are distributed fairly. For example, in a merit-based system ratings need to be based on the levels of performance attained, and recommendations for salary increases and promotions need to be based on these ratings.[14]

Empower Employees

Part of the difficulty in managing the appraisal process is collecting and maintaining information on all employees. As the span of control increases in size, this task grows to unmanageable levels. One way to resolve this problem, while simultaneously increasing perceptions of fairness, is to shift the responsibility for performance record keeping to the job incumbent. To carry out this process, incumbents first need training in writing performance standards and in collecting and documenting performance information. In addition, the two-way communication process discussed above needs to operate effectively, so that incumbents

tiple regression was used to test specific hypotheses. As hypothesized, the set of supervisory session variables (as compared with the set of system contextual variables) was more highly correlated with the satisfaction of employees with the appraisal interview. Conversely, the set of system contextual variables was more strongly related to employees' appraisal system satisfaction than were the supervisory session variables.

The researchers also demonstrated that the linkage between pay and performance should be explicit and should be discussed in the appraisal interview. This finding is inconsistent with early research on the appraisal interview. Based on a series of studies at General Electric in the 1960s, practitioners have generally assumed that the development and evaluation objectives of performance appraisal are at cross purposes. Thus, practitioners have traditionally separated salary discussions from nonevaluative appraisal feedback because of presumed negative repercussions of mixing the two. Contrary to the older study, employees in this study were *more* satisfied with the performance appraisal system when it was clear to them how pay was linked to performance. In fact, system credibility (process satisfaction) eroded if subordinates perceived that organizational reinforcements (e.g., raises, promotions, recognition) were not related to the appraisal they received.

The findings also indicated clearly that organizations should train managers to rate accurately and also should train them to set specific, difficult, but attainable performance goals, to give specific feedback, and to establish clear linkages between pay and performance. Managers must be appraised of the crucial role performance appraisal serves in meeting organizational goals. Results also indicated that organizations need to monitor their appraisal systems to ensure that employees have review sessions with their managers at specific times. Third, it is not enough to simply have an employee sign off on an appraisal form to indicate that an appraisal interview has occurred, because employees might feel pressured to sign off.

Together, these results indicate that managers and subordinates should be queried routinely (e.g. with an attitude survey) about their appraisal session experiences.

Regarding satisfaction with the appraisal process, the research showed that organizations need to remove excessive complexity from appraisal systems, properly introduce the system into organizations, ensure that supervisors conduct appraisal sessions, and link salary adjustments directly with appraisal results. If such actions are neglected, the effectiveness of the appraisal system will likely be substantially undermined, the researchers concluded.

SOURCE: Based on W.F. Giles and K.W. Mossholder, "Employee Reactions to Contextual and Session Components of Performance Appraisal", *Journal of Applied Psychology* 75 (1990), 371–77.

feel free to renegotiate performance standards that have become obsolete or unattainable due to constraints.

Delegating responsibility offers several advantages in terms of performance planning, goal setting, and record keeping. First, subordinates are no longer passive participants, reacting to supervisor directives. Second, because it is now their responsibility to identify performance hurdles and bring them to the attention of their manager, defensiveness is reduced. Third, the supervisor is free to manage and coach rather than police. Finally, the subordinate feels ownership of the process.

At Southwest Texas Methodist Hospital, employees are empowered to call a "powwow" any time there is a problem to be resolved. Powwows are brief, impromptu problem-solving meetings designed to improve patient care, increase productivity, and involve employees in the decision process. As operationalized, a powwow must focus only on patient care or job-related issues and can be called by simply announcing it. The employees who are involved complete all work that cannot wait and join the powwow. The person calling the powwow acts as the leader and is responsible for stating the problem, leading the discussion, and assuring that the powwow is brief (less that five minutes). The leader also must inform a supervisor about the problem and the solution. Powwows also can be a policy-making forum and may result in changes in written policies and procedures.[15]

Provide an Appropriate Degree of Participation

Recently, many companies have viewed worker participation as *the* performance elixir. It was felt, and still is by some managers, that allowing workers the opportunity to set or participate in the development of their own goals will result in higher commitment and consequently better performance. Research however, has shown that participation in and of itself does not lead to higher levels of performance. Participation in the appraisal process is useful if it helps employees identify an appropriate strategy to attain peak performance. Participation may also help employees understand how their jobs contribute to organizational success. According to Henry Givray, vice president of Smith Buckline and Associates in Chicago,

> As we move forward into a period of growth we need to get more people participating in the company's direction who are more capable of solving problems. You achieve that result by having management share information with more people in the organization while staying focused on a clear, compelling vision of what you want the organization to be.[16]

Establish Interlocking Goals

To resolve the problem of goal conflict among stakeholders, new goals can be established that integrate the needs of all parties' concerns. For example, retailers have historically had different performance management systems for buyers and sellers. Buyers usually are evaluated on gross margins, managers on sales and management (people usage, service, etc.)

At Neiman-Marcus, the two systems are merged to give the buyer and the department manager a stake in both ends of retailing. According to Craig Innes, senior vice president of human resources, Neiman-Marcus,

> Buyers and managers receive a monthly Base Profit Contribution Report. The buyer's report lists all the gross margin components, including handling and merchandise preparation. The buyer can use this information to negotiate with the manager. The manager's report lists all the expenses involved in selling such as draw versus commission pay. This information allows the manager to determine that sales productivity is covering the cost of selling. Our profit contribution reporting system works because it merges the goals of buyers and sellers and forces them to look at the business more holistically.[17]

Conduct Problem-Solving Interviews

While performance management is an ongoing process, the appraisal interview serves a unique role and can have a major impact on minimizing conflict.

Advance preparation. To signal employees that performance matters, the interview needs to be scheduled in advance. In setting up the interview, agreement should be reached regarding the purpose and content of the interview. For example, will the subordinate have an opportunity to evaluate the performance of the supervisor, or will the evaluation be one-way? Will the interview be restricted to evaluating past performance, to mapping out a strategy for future performance, or both? By discussing these issues before the actual interview, both participants have time to prepare. If subordinates are empowered, advance notice will give them sufficient time to update their performance records and do a self-review.

Interview content. Initiating and carrying out an effective interview session requires both **coaching** and **counseling** skills. Additionally, a supervisor needs to be able to listen and reflect back what his or her subordinates are saying with regard to performance, its causes, and its outcomes. Too often, however, the interview process breaks down and the supervisor ends up **telling** employees how well or poorly they are doing and **selling** them on the merits of setting specific goals for improvement. This may be efficient, but subordinates may become frustrated in trying to convince their superiors to listen to justifications for their performance levels. As a result, they may discount feedback and become entrenched in past behavior.

A more effective approach is to view the appraisal interview as a **problem-solving strategy**. Here, an active and open dialogue is established between superior and subordinate. This approach to performance management centers on sharing perceptions and identifying solutions to problems. Goals for improvement are established mutually by superior and subordinate. Because this type of interview is generally more difficult for most superiors to do, prior training in problem solving is usually necessary and beneficial. Training in giving and receiving feedback is also useful.

Appropriate follow-up. Even with appropriate planning and careful structuring, **follow-up** is essential to ensure that the behavioral contract negotiated during the interview is fulfilled. Because changing behavior is hard work, there is a tendency for supervisors, as well as subordinates, to put the agreement on the back burner. Consequently, a supervisor may wish to verify that the subordinate **knows what is expected,** has a **strategy** to perform as desired, and **realizes the consequences** of good or bad behavior.

Additionally, it is important to immediately **reinforce** any new behavior on the job that matches desired objectives. If there is a delay in reinforcement, it is less likely that new behavior will become a habit. Reinforcement can be as simple as a pat on the back or a compliment (That was nice work, George) or as tangible as a note placed in the employee's file indicating performance improvement.[18]

DIAGNOSING PERFORMANCE

The interview provides a mechanism by which performance information can be exchanged, but it is only one component of an effective behavioral change process. That is, for performance appraisal processes to work well, the information on which the interview is based must be accurate. This means performance gaps need to be identified as soon as possible and the cause of the deficiency accurately pinpointed.

Identifying Performance Gaps

As discussed in chapter 7, employee job performance is appraised in terms of behaviors and outcomes. These also help identify performance gaps. To identify performance gaps, however, they are used somewhat differently. For example, goals can be used to identify performance deficiencies by determining how well an employee does in relation to the goals set. If an employee had a performance goal of reducing the scrap rate by ten percent but reduced it by only five percent, a performance gap exists. The discrepancy between actual and set goals can thus be used to spot performance gaps. This method is valid if the goals are not contradictory and can be quantified in measurable terms, and if the subordinate's performance can be measured in the terms in which the goals are set.[19]

In addition to comparing performance to appropriate goals, the performance levels of individuals, units, or departments can be compared with one another. For example, organizations with several divisions often measure the overall performance of each division by comparing it with that of all other divisions. The divisions ranked at the bottom then are identified as problem areas because they have performance gaps. Whether ranking individuals or units, identifying performance gaps by means of comparisons prevents an effective diagnosis of performance gaps.

Gaps can also be identified by comparisons over time. For example, a manager who sold one thousand record albums last month but only eight hundred this month appears to have a performance gap. Although performance has declined, does this gap represent a deficiency that should be or can be corrected? The month in which one thousand albums were sold may have occurred during the peak buying season. During the month in which only eight hundred albums were sold, the employee may have had to attend an important conference vital to longer-run record sales.

Finally, gaps can be spotted by symptoms. Exhibit 8.3 includes a checklist of symptoms associated with performance problems. While the checklist does not identify the causes of the performance discrepancies, more than one "yes" indicates a need to probe deeper. Regardless of the method used to discover if a performance deficiency exists, once detected, managers want to remove it. If they hope to improve their employee's performance, however, they must begin by examining the causes underlying any actual gaps.

Identifying Causes of Performance Deficiencies

To uncover the reasons for performance deficiencies, a number of questions can be asked, based on a model of the determinants of employee behavior in organizations.[20] This model enables the personnel manager to diagnose performance deficiencies and correct them in a systematic way. In general, the model says that employees perform well if the following determinants are present:

- Ability
- Interest in doing the job

Exhibit 8.3
Checklist for Identifying Performance Problems

Read each question. If you are thinking "yes" in response to a question, place a check mark next to that item. If not, leave it blank.

Do Peers Complain That

_______ 1. She is not treating them fairly?
_______ 2. He is not carrying his own weight?
_______ 3. She is rude?
_______ 4. He is argumentative and confrontational?
_______ 5. She is all talk and no action?

Do Customers

_______ 1. Always ask for someone else to help them?
_______ 2. Complain about her attitude?
_______ 3. Complain that he has made promises to them that he's never fulfilled?
_______ 4. Say she is bad-mouthing you, the organization, or its products?
_______ 5. Complain that he is too pushy?

Do You

_______ 1. Find it difficult to get your own work done because you spend so much time with him on his problems and mistakes?
_______ 2. Worry about what she will say to customers and clients?
_______ 3. Check his work often because you are afraid of mistakes?
_______ 4. Do work yourself that you should have delegated to her?
_______ 5. Assign work to others because they can do it faster or better than he can?
_______ 6. Hear about her mistakes from your boss or others?
_______ 7. Sometimes find out that he has lied to you or stretched the truth?
_______ 8. Seldom think of her when you're deciding who should get an important assignment?

Does He/She

_______ 1. Infrequently complete assignments on time?
_______ 2. Often show up to work late or not at all?
_______ 3. Always have an excuse for poor performance?
_______ 4. Wait to be assigned additional work rather than asking for more work when an assignment is completed?
_______ 5. Rarely complete assignments in the way you want?
_______ 6. Ignore suggestions for improvement?

- Opportunity to grow and advance
- Clearly defined goals
- Certainty about what is expected
- Feedback on how well they are doing
- Rewards for performing well
- Punishments for performing poorly
- Power to get resources to do the job[21]

Exhibit 8.4 shows these determinants and the specific questions to ask in pinpointing the causes of performance deficiencies. Negative responses indicate that the item is probably a cause. Based on a series of such responses, the likely causes of a performance deficiency can be established.

STRATEGIES FOR IMPROVING PERFORMANCE

When performance deficiencies are found and the causes of the deficiency identified, companies can do many things to improve.

Positive Reinforcement Systems

A positive reinforcement system lets employees know how well they are meeting specific goals and rewards improvements with such things as pay, time off, praise, or recognition. This approach to improvement encourages desirable job behaviors by establishing appropriate performance goals and setting up rewards contingent on achieving them. A basic premise of positive reinforcement is that behavior can be understood and modified by its consequences. That is, performance is elicited because of the consequence of getting rewards. Positive reinforcement systems can be designed in many different ways and have been shown to be effective across a wide variety of situations and problems. For example, cash rewards, paid leave for perfect attendance, bonuses for unused sick leave, lotteries, and profit sharing have all been utilized successfully to control absenteeism.[22]

While the "carrots" associated with traditional positive reinforcement programs work well, there may be a hitch. Dave Wiegand, president of Advance Network Design, Inc., a California telecommunications company, used to get employees to do what he wanted by using traditional weekly, monthly, and quarterly bonuses. "We'd start a program to motivate a certain behavior and see results. But when we stopped a program, we'd lose the behavior," Wiegand recalls.

To rectify this problem, Wiegand started a new awards system: No regular bonuses. Instead employees are rewarded on an intermittent basis. Now his employees don't know who will get bonuses. During 1990, 15 awards totaling more than $9,000 were distributed at two meetings. One executive received a five-day family vacation to Disney World because his department's sales exceeded expectations by 70 percent. An unusually dependable receptionist was awarded a $75 clock radio. For increasing his department's revenues by 40 percent in two months, a manager earned a $375 suit and pearl jewelry for his wife. Citing company statistics to back up his claims, Wiegand says,

> Intermittent reinforcement is far more cost effective than defined bonus plans. Since 1988, our sales force has shrunk from 12 to 4 people while productivity has increased. Previously, top sales people generated $110,000 in annual new revenue. In 1990 the top sales personnel *each* averaged more than $500,000 in new revenue.[23]

Employee Assistance Programs

As the PHRM in the News feature "Today's EAPs..." indicates, **employee assistance programs (EAPs)** are specifically designed to assist employees with chronic personal problems that hinder their job performance and attendance.

Exhibit 8.4
Diagnosing the Causes of Performance Deficiencies

Check those factors affecting an individual's performance or behavior that apply to the situation you are analyzing.

	Yes	No
I. *Knowledge, Skills, and Abilities*		
A. Does the incumbent have the skill to perform as expected?	_______	_______
B. Has the incumbent performed as expected before?	_______	_______
C. Does the incumbent believe he or she has the ability to perform as desired?	_______	_______
D. Does the incumbent have the interest to perform as desired?	_______	_______
II. *Goals for the Incumbent*		
A. Were the goals communicated to the incumbent prior to the performance period?	_______	_______
B. Are the goals specific?	_______	_______
C. Are the goals difficult but attainable?	_______	_______
III. *Uncertainty for the Incumbent*		
A. Has desired performance been clearly specified?	_______	_______
B. Have rewards or consequences for good or bad performance been specified?	_______	_______
C. Is the inbumbent clear about his or her level of authority?	_______	_______
IV. *Feedback to the Incumbent*		
A. Does the incumbent know when he or she has performed correctly or incorrectly?	_______	_______
B. Is the feedback diagnostic so the incumbent can perform better in the future?	_______	_______
C. Is there a delay between performance and the receipt of the feedback?	_______	_______
D. Can performance feedback be easily interpreted?	_______	_______
V. *Consequences to the Incumbent*		
A. Is performing as expected punishing?	_______	_______
B. Is nonperformance more rewarding?	_______	_______
C. Does performing as desired matter?	_______	_______
D. Are there positive consequences for performing as desired?	_______	_______
VI. *Power for the Incumbent*		
A. Can the incumbent mobilize the resources to get the job done?	_______	_______
B. Does the incumbent have the tools and equipment to perform as desired?	_______	_______

SOURCE: This format is based on R.F. Mager and P. Pipe, *Analyzing Performance Problems, or "You Really Oughta Wanna"* (Belmont, Calif.: Fearon Pitman, 1970).

While EAPs that provide assistance with alcohol and drug abuse are most common, organizations have also established EAPs to help employees cope with marital/family problems, mental disorders, financial problems, stress, eating dis-

PHRM IN THE NEWS

Today's EAPs Make the Grade

No matter how you try to measure them, EAPs are making the grade in the 1990s: Not only do more companies have successful programs, but those programs are addressing more types of problems and saving companies more money than ever.

Overall, American organizations invest as much as $798 million annually in EAPs. But for every dollar employers invest, recovery of loss is estimated at $5. That's $3.9 billion recovered from loss annually, according to statistics compiled by the Employee Assistance Professionals Association (EAPA), based in Arlington, Va. Recovery from loss is money that otherwise would have been spent on absenteeism, sick benefits and work-related accidents.

In fact, a survey of 50 companies published in *American Management Magazine* showed that EAPs were responsible for substantial cost reductions, including declines of 33 percent in the use of sickness benefits, 65 percent in work-related accidents, 30 percent in worker's compensation claims and 74 percent in time spent on supervisor reprimands. Individual worker absenteeism traceable to alcohol abuse dropped 66 percent.

Tailored Solutions

EAPs were originally created to battle alcoholism, but have since expanded to address family, financial and legal problems.

Thus, demographics—and geography—play a large role in determining the type of EAP a company adopts. No two are the same. Carpenter Technology in Reading, Pa., for example, happens to be located about 100 miles from Atlantic City, N.J. "Our proximity allows for a whole lot of gambling in the casinos. And Eastern Pennsylvania's got a wealth of horse tracks where a lot of our employees spend a lot of money and time," said Gregory DeLapp, EAP administrator for the company's 3,600 employees. On the financial end, you've got everything from problems related to plastic financing to the other extreme, which is owing money to all the wrong people, for gambling debts." The company's EAP helps employees stop seeking short-term solutions such as cash advances or loans and achieve a long-term solution through counseling or referral.

#1 Problem: Marital

Marital and family relationship problems tend to be the most common problems employees bring to their EAPs, even though substance abuse continues to have more of an effect on job performance and costs more to treat. In fact, marital and family problems account for 40 to 50 percent of the referrals that EAPs receive, said Keith McClellan, president of the Employee Assistance Society of North America (EASNA), based in Oak Park, Ill.

But even though EAPs have evolved over the years, they haven't strayed too far from their roots. "We had a good salesman recently who was referred by his boss because he went to a company function that served alcohol, and he began to drink too much," recalled Susan Swan-Granger, executive director of Employee Assistance of Central Virginia. "He also began to talk too much, and he put his foot in his mouth a couple of times to his boss and to his vice president. And the next day, he didn't even remember it. They could have terminated him for insubordination, but they didn't. Instead they insisted that he refer himself to the EAP."

And that, perhaps, best demonstrates the continuing ideals of EAPs; they rehabilitate rather than punish—for that, they earn an A.[24]

SOURCE: S. Feldman, "Today's EAPs Make the Grade," *Bulletin to Management* (Feb. 1991), 3. Used by permission of the Bureau of National Affairs.

orders, weight control, and smoking cessation and to provide dependent care programs, bereavement counseling, and AIDS support group meetings.

To be successful, an employee assistance program should possess the following attributes:

- Top management backing
- Union or employee support

- Confidentiality
- Easy access
- Trained supervisors
- Trained union steward, if in a union setting
- Insurance
- Availability of numerous services for assistance and referral
- Skilled professional leadership
- Systems for monitoring, assessing, and revising

Even though EAPs are designed to provide valuable assistance to employees, many employees in need fail to use the programs unless faced with the alternative of being fired. When so confronted, however, the success rate of those attending EAPs is high. As discussed in the article, the results can mean substantial gains in employee job performance and reductions in absenteeism that far outweigh the costs of an EAP.[25]

Self-Managed Work Teams

Self-management is a relatively new approach to resolving performance discrepancies. It teaches people to exercise control over their own behavior. Self-management begins by having people assess their own problems and set specific (but individual) hard goals in relation to those problems. Once goals are set, the employees discuss ways in which the environment facilitates or hinders goal attainment. The challenge here is to develop strategies that eliminate blocks to performance success. Put another way, self-management teaches people to observe their own behavior, compare their outputs to their goals, and administer their own reinforcement to sustain goal commitment and performance.[26]

At Johnsonville Foods, a Wisconsin sausagemaker, self-management is part of the company's overall philosophy. According to Ralph Stayer, CEO,

> We believe that the management of performance problems is the concern of people who have to work with other individuals, peers. We think any work area should set up its own standards and rules and enforce them.[27]

Self-management is effective here for at least two reasons. When employees have greater control over what they do, they typically invest more of themselves in it. Additionally, hierarchical control is replaced with social or group control over behavior.[28] Think about it. You're part of a five-member work group whose pay is determined by your collective efforts. You come in two hours late one day. Which would you prefer, the boss chastising you or all of your peers shaking their heads and mumbling about how you let them down?

While self-management has proven effective in the management of a variety of performance problems, its implementation can be tricky—particularly for the manager. Managers often perceive a threat of loss of power and ultimately importance as they realize that their subordinates are to become to a large extent their own managers. Second, managers soon recognize that their repertoire of skills is at least in part obsolete. According to Jim Kouzes, president of Tom

Peters Group, self-management entails coaching on the part of the manager. "If you want people to do what's right, teach them what's right and then show them by your own behavior."[29]

Negative Behavioral Strategies

While most employees want to conduct themselves in a manner that is acceptable to the organization and their fellow employees, problems of absenteeism, poor work performance, and rule violation do arise. When informal discussions or coaching fails to neutralize these dysfunctional behaviors, formal disciplinary action is needed. The objective of punishment is to decrease the frequency of an undesirable behavior. Punishments can include material consequences, such as a cut in pay, a disciplinary layoff without pay, a demotion, or, ultimately, termination. More common punishments are interpersonal and include oral reprimands and nonverbal cues, such as frowns, grunts, and aggressive body language.[30]

Punishment is commonly used by many organizations because it can achieve relatively immediate results. Additionally, punishment is reinforcing to supervisors in that they feel they have taken action. Discipline (i.e. punishment) is an effective management tool for the following reasons:

- Discipline alerts the marginal employee that his or her low performance is unacceptable and that a change in behavior is warranted.
- Discipline has vicarious reinforcing power. When one person is punished, it signals other employees regarding expected performance and behavioral conduct.
- If the discipline is viewed as appropriate by other employees, it may increase their motivation, morale, and performance.

Punishment can also have undesirable side effects. For example, an employee reprimanded for low performance may become defensive and angry toward the supervisor and the organization. As recent news reports attest, this anger may result in sabotage (destroying equipment, passing trade secrets) or retaliation (shooting the supervisor). Second, punishment frequently leads to only the short-term suppression of the undesirable behavior, rather than its elimination. Another concern is that control of the undesirable behavior becomes contingent on the presence of the punishing agent. When the manager is not present, the behavior is likely to be displayed. Finally, the employee may not perceive the punishment as unpleasant. For example, an organization with a progressive disciplinary procedure may send an employee home without pay for being late one too many times. If this occurs at the beginning of the fishing season, the employee may relish the excuse not to go to work.

The negative effects of punishment can be reduced by incorporating several principles, including the following:

- Provide ample and clear warning. Many organizations have clearly defined disciplinary steps. For example, the first offense might elicit an oral warning; the second offense, a written warning; the third offense, a disciplinary layoff; the fourth offense, discharge.

- Administer the discipline as quickly as possible. If a long time elapses between the ineffective behavior and the discipline, the employee may not know what the discipline is for.
- Administer the same discipline for the same behavior for everyone every time. Discipline has to be administered fairly and consistently.
- Administer the discipline impersonally. Discipline should be based on a specific behavior not a specific person.

Because the immediate supervisor or manager plays the integral role in administering discipline, the personnel and human resource department and the organization should do the following to increase the discipline's effectiveness:

- Allow managers and supervisors to help select their own employees.
- Educate managers and supervisors about the organization's disciplinary policies, and train them to administer the policies.

When Nothing Else Works

Helping employees—especially the problem ones—to improve their work performance is a tough job. It is easy to get frustrated and to wonder if you are just spinning your wheels. Even when we want our efforts to work, they sometimes don't. Still, when you conclude that "nothing works," you are really saying that it is no longer worth your time and energy to help the employee improve. This conclusion should not be made in haste because the organization has already invested a great deal of time and money in the selection and training of its employees. However, some situations may require more drastic steps, including when

- Performance actually gets worse
- There is a little change in the problem behavior—but not enough
- There is no change in the problem behavior
- Drastic changes in behavior occur immediately, but improvements don't last

If, after repeated warnings and counseling, performance does not improve, then four last recourses are available.

Transferring. Sometimes there is just not a good match between an employee and a job. If, however, the employee has useful skills and abilities, it may be beneficial to transfer him or her. Transferring is appropriate if the employee's skill deficiency would have little or no impact on the new position. The concern with transfers is that there must be a job available for which the problem employee is qualified.

Restructuring. Some jobs are particularly unpleasant or onerous. For these positions, the solution may be redesigning the job, rather than replacing the employee. It may also make sense to redesign a position to take advantage of an employee's special strengths. If an employee has extraordinary technical expertise, it may be advantageous to utilize this expertise, rather than having the employee perform routine maintenance tasks.

Firing. While human resource policies vary across organizations and industries, firing is generally warranted for dishonesty, habitual absenteeism, substance abuse, and insubordination, including flat refusals to do certain things requested and consistently low productivity that cannot be corrected through training. Unfortunately, firing, even for legitimate reasons, is unpleasant. In addition to the administrative hassles, documentation, and paperwork involved, supervisors often feel guilty about being the "bad guy," and the thought of sitting down with an employee and delivering the bad news makes most supervisors anxious. As a result, they continue to put off the firing and justify it by saying that they won't be able to find a "better" replacement. Still, when one considers the consequences of errors, drunkenness, or "being high" on the job, firing may be cost effective. Employee rights regarding firing will be discussed in chapter 15.

Neutralizing. Neutralizing a problem employee involves restructuring that employee's job in such a way that his or her areas of needed improvement have as little impact as possible. Because group morale may suffer when an ineffective employee is given special treatment, *neutralizing should be avoided* whenever possible. However, it is a fact of organizational life that neutralizing may be practical when the firing process is time-consuming and cumbersome or when an employee is close to retiring. In neutralizing the employee, a manager shouldn't harass the employee, hoping that he or she will quit or transfer, but instead should assign the employee noncritical tasks in which he or she can be productive.[31]

Arbitration. While arbitration has long been used in unionized environments, its popularity is spreading. The National Conference of Commissioners on Uniform State Laws has suggested a new employment statute that would let most fired employees take their case to a neutral arbitrator. Arbitration here is viewed as an effective alternative to costly legal suits that often evolve following the last step in the disciplinary process—termination. Any legal action will likely occur at the state level.

FOCUS ISSUES IN GATHERING AND UTILIZING PERFORMANCE APPRAISAL INFORMATION

Linking Appraisal to the Business

A major theme in our discussion of all the personnel and human resource activities is linking with the business. As with many things in life, it's easier said than done. For performance appraisal this is particularly true, because it can mean starting over:

> What gets measured gets attention, particularly when rewards are tied to the measures. Grafting new measures onto an old performance system or making slight adjustments in existing plans accomplishes little. Enhanced competitiveness depends on starting from scratch and asking: "Given our strategy, what are the most important measures of performance?"[32]

In going back to square one, many decisions need to be made. Decisions must be made regarding how tight and complete the linkage will be. For example, will appraisal practices be standardized across organizational units, or will each unit be free to develop its own appraisal system? Standardization allows comparisons across units but may not provide the flexibility needed in large, diverse organizations. Another decision concerns the security of the information. Questions need to be answered regarding who will have access to performance-related information and how that information will be stored (in a centralized system or in individual files). As organizations decentralize, they realize it is necessary to pass control of the firm's human resources from corporate headquarters to the units in which most employees work. Centralized personnel files become less useful and less justifiable; but with unit control over files, the individual risks getting holed away in one unit, never able to take advantage of career opportunities in other units. In addressing these decisions and others in performance appraisal, we may benefit from looking at what's happening in other countries.

INTERNATIONAL COMPARISONS IN PERFORMANCE APPRAISAL

To understand what is distinctive about the U.S. culture, forty international managers (all non-U.S. nationals who were familiar with the U.S. business culture) were interviewed and asked to identify cultural aspects that underlie the U.S. system of management. Thirty-six of the forty international managers felt that a strong commitment to the philosophy of meritocracy is a distinctively American societal value. **Meritocracy** emphasizes fairness, evaluating people on their work-related contributions. The managers also noted the short-term orientation in America as emphasized by annual appraisals based solely on current performance.

In other cultures, meritocracy is not so firmly established as a guiding principle. In its place is more concern for status, family ties, and loyalty to one's supervisor or organization rather than for the adequacy of current job performance. In other cultures, recent performance is not always the most important criteria. Behavior over time, loyalty and the potential for the future are emphasized much more.[33]

There is also evidence that U.S. managers believe in a "Master of Destiny" viewpoint where, if a person works hard and has the ability and motivation to perform, he or she will be able to advance in a company. A more fatalistic view predominates in many other countries. That is, persons are born into a certain class and they are not able, no matter what they do, to improve their standing. In such a culture, there may be no need for a performance management system.[34]

Americans also have very specific ideas about performance appraisal criteria. For example, Peter Drucker writes that "An employer has no business with a man's personality. Employment is a specific contract calling for specific performance and for nothing else."[35] As will be discussed in the following sections, other societies base performance judgments much more on the "whole man or woman" than on actual job performance.

Pacific Rim Countries

While actual practices vary by country, most Pacific Rim countries utilize informal and formal appraisal processes to develop and reward employee performance. However, there appears to be less reliance on sophisticated formalistic systems than in U.S. companies. That is, most dialogue on performance occurs informally on either a one-on-one or group basis, rather than in a formal review session.

Korea. In Korea, performance appraisal systems are in place in almost all large and most small companies. Since promotions are based primarily on seniority, performance appraisal is conducted primarily for purposes of counseling and development. The scope of performance appraisal does vary across enterprises with some enterprises approaching the process formally, almost ritualistically, and other enterprises approaching it very informally.

One reason appraisal practices vary in scope is that many Koreans believe the cooperative nature of work makes it impossible to differentiate performance levels among employees with any degree of accuracy. As a result, factors such as seniority, loyalty, proper attitude, and initiative are at least as important as actual job performance.

Practices at a company called Sunkyong are representative of the more formalized approach to appraisal in Korea. The appraisal process begins with an extensive self-assessment inventory that is completed by the employee. Results are discussed with the employee's immediate supervisor and later with the supervisor's supervisor. Extensive peer assessments are also used. In other companies, however, the appraisal review consists of nothing more than informal individual counseling sessions.[36]

People's Republic of China (PRC). Since the 1978 cultural revolution, management practices in China have undergone significant changes. Most notable is a shift from a Stalinist system of industrial management (centralization, detailed plans, standard operating procedures) to a new motivational system that emphasizes responsibility and performance. Since 1984, the imperative has been to calculate profit prior to action rather than action before calculation.

At the enterprise level, these changes were accompanied by a move from participatory management in the Yan'an tradition (pluralistic decision making and tight control) to a new structure of collective leadership. According to a PRC Decision Document of 1984, "Modern enterprises must have a minute division of labor, a high degree of continuity in production, strict technological requirements and a high degree of cooperation." This document also prescribes that enterprises must specify in explicit terms the requirements for each work post and the duties of each worker and staff.

As a result of these reforms, there is an increasing emphasis on performance in Chinese enterprises. In the past, profits reverted directly to the state. Since the cultural revolution, a portion of profits can be held out and distributed to employees. Even by western standards, performance bonuses—even for low-level workers—are high, averaging as much as one-third of one's annual salary. Still, the allocation of these rewards is based upon organizational rather than individual performance.

Regarding a shift in values, a recent study found that objective performance was the most important determinant of performance ratings of both U.S. and

Chinese decision makers. However, unlike Americans, Chinese were significantly influenced by employee loyalty/dependability when making performance judgments. Apparently, traditional Chinese cultural values of defining performance in broad terms still linger.[37]

Performance evaluation in China also includes one unique facet: self-criticism. The format of these meetings, called "Hsiao-tsu" sessions, are advocated by the central committee of the national government. The official objective is to create more cohesive groups through identifying insensitive and other dysfunctional behaviors. As operationalized, they appear to serve as upward appraisal sessions in which lower ranking employees can make perceived or real mistreatments known to management.[38]

Japan. On first blush, performance appraisal would seem to be an unnecessary control mechanism for the Japanese enterprise which emphasizes job rotation, slow promotion, and group, rather than individual, loyalty. As William Ouchi, a cross-cultural management expert notes, Japanese employees are controlled in a subtle, indirect manner which contrasts greatly with the explicit formal control system used in the U.S.[39]

Still, an increasing number of Japanese firms are using formal appraisals to evaluate the contribution of employees and to develop them into better employees. However, the concept of performance has a different meaning in Japan than in Western countries. For example, merit ratings are based on educational attainment and job ability factors such as communication skills, cooperativeness, and sense of responsibility, rather than on work results. The Japanese concept of performance includes not only the achievement of results but the expenditure of a good-faith effort.[40]

SUMMARY

Ineffective employee performance, whether anyone wants to admit it or not, plagues all organizations at least some of the time. For a performance appraisal system to be effective, it must not only permit the gathering of performance appraisal data; it must also enable the manager to *use* this information. Organizations that have developed an effective performance appraisal system, therefore, directly influence productivity, quality of work life, and legal compliance through the gathering and use of performance appraisal data.

Because of the dual appraisal purposes of evaluation and development, conflicts are inevitable. These conflicts, if unaddressed, will cripple the effectiveness of any performance appraisal system. Recognition of their sources, however, suggests how performance feedback can be given to reduce them. From a design perspective, an effective performance appraisal system can avoid inherent conflicts by (1) separating evaluation from development, (2) focusing on behavior rather than on subjective traits, (3) distinguishing evaluation of current performance from future performance, and (4) using multiple appraisals to improve reliability and validity.

Although many motivation theories exist to explain human performance in organizations, a single diagnostic framework has been provided to help you, the appraiser, get at the "root cause" of the performance problem. Using this framework to understand performance gaps forms a basis for choosing different strategies to improve performance. From a developmental perspective, strategies that involve participation and job clarification encourage self-directed improvement. Ultimately, problem employees may require outside assistance through counseling or EAPs. Control of behavior can also be achieved by linking rewards to behavior or using group or organizational norms (as suggested by the discussion of socialization in chapter 5). In some cases it may be necessary to neutralize the negative behavior or in extreme cases to fire the employee, but these strategies should be used only when all else fails. Because all organizations experience performance problems, it is crucial that the performance appraisal system—the process of gathering and feeding back appraisal data—function to improve individual performance. Performance assessment also plays a vital role in other key personnel and human resource activities, particularly compensation and training, topics explored in the chapters ahead.

WHERE WE ARE TODAY

1. The best chance for attaining individual, team and organizational peak performance lies with the establishment of a strategically aligned performance management system.
2. Organizational politics, conflicts in stakeholder goals, and differences in the assessment of performance are potential sources of conflict.
3. To minimize conflicts, the supervisor should actively involve the incumbent in the appraisal interview, set specific goals, keep criticism to a minimum, and establish a clear link between performance and pay.
4. Appraisal systems are fair to the extent that there exists: consistency in the application of evaluation criteria, familiarity with performance, solicitation of input from participants, and opportunity to challenge or rebut the evaluation.
5. Empowering incumbents can ease administrative burdens, reduce defensiveness, and free the supervisor to manage and coach.
6. Effective appraisal interviews are preplanned, focus on problem solving, and are followed up with action.
7. A positive reinforcement system lets employees know how well they are meeting specific goals and rewards improvements with such things as pay, time off, praise, or recognition.
8. EAPs were originally created to battle alcoholism but have expanded to address family, financial, and legal problems that impinge on work performance.
9. Self-management teaches people to observe their own behavior, compare their outputs to their goals, and administer their own reinforcement to attain peak performance.
10. Before implementing an "American-style" appraisal process overseas, undertake a comprehensive analysis of its chance of success and the consequences in that culture.

DISCUSSION QUESTIONS

1. Suppose you have decided that an employee is not working out and must be fired. What performance appraisal approach would you want to use to support this decision? Why?
2. An observer of the performance appraisal process once commented that, when it comes to appraisal, all organizations experience a "shortage of bastards." What do you suppose this comment means? Does this comment relate to the inherent conflicts associated with appraisals? Explain.
3. What considerations are there in designing an effective performance appraisal system?
4. With what causes are performance deficiencies associated, and what are the respective strategies used to correct those performance deficiencies?
5. What are the critical issues in determining the utility of a specific performance appraisal system?
6. Assume you are supervising employees who fall into one of three categories: (1) effective performers with lots of potential for advancement, (2) effective performers who lack motivation or ability (or both) for potential advancement, and (3) currently ineffective performers. It is performance appraisal time, and you must plan interviews with subordinates from each of these three categories. How will your interviews differ? How will they be similar?
7. Assume you are a professor counseling a student with a grade complaint. Describe how you would conduct this session using the problem-solving approach. Why?
8. If subjective, trait-oriented approaches are legally vulnerable, why do you suppose organizations persist in using them?
9. What are the advantages of self-management for the organization? For the individual?
10. Discuss the ramifications of neutralizing employees' performance.

APPLIED PROJECTS

1. Mary James was seen smoking a cigarette in her car about forty minutes before her scheduled time to leave; a male co-worker was seen at the same time sitting in his car. "It isn't fair to fire me when a male co-worker received a day's suspension for the same offense," shrieked Mary James, trying to explain why she was in her car at the time. But she was never heard.

   "Your co-worker has a much better work record than you," retorted the supervisor. "He's never had an attendance problem. You were suspended for another attendance infraction two months earlier and knew that the next incident would result in discharge. Therefore, you're fired."

   Based on your knowledge of appraisal procedures, was the discharge fair, or should Mary James be reinstated?
2. Steve Young is a 40-year-old vice-president of marketing for a large corporation. He recently promoted a promising young regional sales manager, Linda Thomas, to assistant vice-president of sales for the western states. While Linda is viewed as a "real comer" in the organization, Young feels she is

focusing too much on meeting monthly quotas when she should be focusing on the big picture. He wants to get her on the right wavelength but isn't sure what he should do. Based on your knowledge of appraisal processes, outline a specific plan of action.

3. Your company has decided to go international and plans to open offices in several foreign countries. You plan to employ host country nationals for all but the top few positions. Before implementing a performance appraisal system, what questions would you want to ask?

CASE STUDY

Evaluating the Performance of Nurses Aides at Sunshine Manor

Sunshine Manor is a privately owned long-term health care facility whose primary objective is to create an atmosphere for its residents that adds life to their years, not just years to their lives. The staff of Sunshine Manor consists of fifty employees in addition to the administrator and general manager. Sunshine Manor also contracts with a local physician, physical therapist, and nurse consultant for special services. Sunshine Manor has adequate facilities for fifty residents and provides around-the-clock care.

The staff works three eight-hour shifts and some four-hour shifts depending on the mix of nurses aides and LPNs. One LPN is scheduled during each shift, with six nurses aides during the daytime and three during the evening shifts. Nursing staff and nurses aides rotate regularly so aides do not report directly to any one nurse. Director of Nursing Marilyn Gest makes all job assignments and is responsible for selecting, training, and appraising all nurses and nurses aides. Currently, there are ten nurses and twenty-five nurses aides.

Employees are evaluated at the end of their first six months and once a year thereafter. Performance appraisal is done for feedback and employee development purposes only. However, low ratings occasionally have been used to justify terminating an employee. Pay raises are indirectly linked to appraisal results. Input from performance appraisal is one of the factors used by the owner of the nursing home, Fred Sweet, to determine raises. It isn't, however, the only factor. Fred has been known to give a pretty girl a little extra in her paycheck to keep her happy. Need also seems to be a factor. The more in need employees are, the more likely they are to get a pay raise. These practices have undermined the effectiveness of Sunshine Manor's performance appraisal system. As it is, performance appraisal generally is viewed as a big joke by all employees at Sunshine Manor.

As shown in exhibit 1, employees are rated on ten dimensions (responsibility, independence, punctuality, self-starting ability, teamwork, enthusiasm, absenteeism, organization, judgment, and personal appearance). Traditionally, Marilyn has had each employee rate his or her own performance *prior* to the annual review. She does the same thing independently. Then they get together and discuss the results. Generally, employees are quite honest about their own abilities. In fact, they usually rate themselves lower than Marilyn does. This has always made her job easy. That is until today.

Today she is meeting with Theresa Sawyer, a new employee, to go over her six-month evaluation. As usual, she had Theresa complete the appraisal independently. The results were surprising. Whereas, Marilyn felt Theresa was performing satisfactorily in most areas, she definitely felt Theresa needed to work on punctuality. On three occasions in the last two weeks, Marilyn had had to find Theresa and tell her to get back to her work station after her lunch or rest break. She would usually find Theresa talking to Charlie Hill, a jolly 85-year-old in Ward D. Theresa and Charlie seemed to have formed a special attachment to one another. While Charlie was a sweet guy, he was one of twenty patients assigned to Theresa, and Theresa was spending far too much time with him and neglecting other patients. Marilyn also felt that Theresa's dress was unprofessional. There were always buttons missing from her uniform.

Marilyn wasn't sure she knew how to address these issues in the appraisal interview. As a result of all this, Marilyn gave Theresa an overall rating of 2 (see exhibit 2), leaving plenty of room for her to develop her skills

Exhibit 1
Sunshine Manor Nursing Home Performance Appraisal Form

Name ______________________________ **Date** ______________

Score each factor using the following key:
1–poor, 2–below average, 3–average, 4–above average, 5–excellent

_______ 1. *Responsibility.* Identifies and takes appropriate nursing measures to meet the physical and emotional needs of the patient.

_______ 2. *Independence.* Works independently, but will request assistance if needed.

_______ 3. *Punctuality.* Is punctual and reports to work on time. Returns from lunch and breaks within allotted time.

_______ 4. *Self-starter.* Completes assignments. Is a self-starter.

_______ 5. *Teamwork.* Assists others when asked and offers independently to help. Is liked by peers.

_______ 6. *Enthusiasm.* Shows interest in the patients and the job. Never bad-mouths the company in front of patients or their families.

_______ 7. *Absenteeism.* Has no more than three call-ins during a six-month period. Calls in at least two hours before the shift starts.

_______ 8. *Organization.* Organizes work responsibilities carefully. Sets priorities. Does what is told when told once.

_______ 9. *Judgment.* Has good judgment.

_______ 10. *Personal appearance.* Always dresses in proper uniform. Uniform and hair are neat. Shoes are polished.

Overall Evaluation ______________

Employee Comments:

Employee Strengths:

Employee Weaknesses:

Supervisory Comments:

______________________ ______________________ __________
Employee's Signature Supervisor's Signature Date

in the future. While her appraisal ratings were low, Marilyn didn't want to fire Theresa. The nursing home was short of nurses aides, and this one at least showed up to work each day. Still, she wasn't sure what to do next.

Case Questions

1. What type of appraisal instrument is currently being used by Sunshine Manor? Is it a good appraisal device to meet the organization's objectives? Why or why not?
2. What types of rating errors are Theresa and Marilyn committing? What could be done to reduce these errors?
3. Why do you think the ratings by Theresa and Marilyn differ so drastically?
4. How would you approach the appraisal interview if you were Marilyn?
5. How would you go about improving Theresa's performance in the critical areas?
6. What would you recommend to improve the appraisal system at Sunshine Manor?

Exhibit 2
Comparison of Theresa's and Marilyn's Ratings

Dimension	Theresa's Ratings	Marilyn's Ratings
1. Responsibility	5	3
2. Independence	4	2
3. Punctuality	5	1
4. Self-starter	5	2
5. Teamwork	4	1
6. Enthusiasm	4	2
7. Absenteeism	4	3
8. Organization	4	3
9. Judgment	5	3
10. Personal appearance	5	0

NOTES

1. E. Faltermayer, "Is this Layoff Necessary?" *Fortune* (1 June 1992): 86.
2. J. September, "Mrs. Fields' Secret Weapon," *Personnel Journal* (Sept. 1991): 56–58.
3. R. W. Beatty and C. E. Schneier, "Strategic Performance Appraisal Issues," in *Readings in Personnel and Human Resource Management,* eds. R. Schuler, S. Youngblood, and V. Huber (St. Paul, Minn. West Publishing, 1988): 256–66; J. N. Cleveland, K. R. Murphy, and R. E. Williams, "Multiple Uses of Performance Appraisal: Prevalence and Correlates," *Journal of Applied Psychology* 74, no. 1 (1989): 130–35; R. D. Prichard, *Measuring and Improving Organizational Productivity: A Practical Guide* (New York: Praeger Publishers, 1990).
4. "A New Focus on Achievement," *Personnel Journal* (Feb. 1991): 73–75.
5. E. Lawler, "Control Systems in Organizations," in I. M. Dunnette, ed., *Handbook of Industrial/Organizational Psychology* (Chicago: Rand McNally, 1986).
6. P. Villanova and H. J. Bernardin, "Impression Management in the Context of Performance Appraisal, " in R. A. Giacalone and P. Rosenfeld, eds., *Impression Management in the Organization* (Hillsdale, N. J.: Lawrence Erlbaum, 1989): 299–314.
7. C. O Longnecker, H. Sims, and D. Gioa, "Behind the Mask: The Politics of Employee Appraisal," *Academy of Management Executive 1* (1987): 183–93; J. Greenberg, "Inflated Performance Evaluation as a Self-Serving Bias," working paper, Ohio State University, 1984; H. J. Bernardin and P. Villanova, "Performance Appraisal," in E. Locke, ed., *Generalizing from Laboratory to Field Settings* (Lexington, Mass.: Heath/Lexington, 1986): 43–67.
8. M. Beer, "Performance Appraisal: Dilemmas and Possibilities," *Organizational Dynamics* (Winter 1981): 26; A. Zander, "Research on Self-Esteem, Feedback and Threats to Self-Esteem," in *Performance Appraisals: Effects on Employees and Their Performance,* ed., A. Zander (New York: Foundation for Research in Human Behavior, 1963).
9. V. Huber, P. Podsakoff, and W. Todor, "An Investigation of Biasing Facts in the Attributions of Subordinates and Their Supervisors," *Journal of Business Research* 14 (1986): 83–97.
10. D. T. Hall, *Careers in Organizations* (Glenview, Ill.: Scott, Foresman, 1976).
11. R. F. Catalenello and J. A. Hooper, "Managerial Appraisal," *Personnel Administrator* (Sept. 1981: 75–81; T. Rendero, "Consensus," *Personnel* (Nov./Dec. 1980): 4–12; R. S. Schuler, "Taking the Pain Out of the Performance Appraisal Interview," *Supervisory Management* (Aug. 1981): 8–13; K. S. Teel, "Performance Appraisals: Current Trends, Persistent Progress," *Personnel Journal* (April 1980): 296–301; "Training Managers to Rate Their Employees," *Business Week* (17 March 1980): 178–79; K. N. Wexley, "Performance Appraisal and Feedback, " in *Organizational Behavior,* ed. S. Kerr (Columbus, Ohio: Grid, 1979): 241–62.
12. C. Hymowitz, "Bosses: Don't be Nasty (and Other Tips for Reviewing Worker Performance), *The Wall Street Journal* (17 Jan. 1985): 35.
13. D. R. Ilgen, C. D. Fisher, and M. S. Taylor, "Consequences of Individual Feedback on Behavior in Organizations," *Journal of Applied Psychology* 64 (1979): 349–71; D. R. Ilgen and C. F. Moore, "Types and Choices of Performance Feedback," *Journal of Applied Psychology* (Aug. 1987): 401; B. L. Davis and M. K. Mount, "Design and Use of Performance Appraisal Feedback System," *Personnel Administrator* (March 1984): 91–107; B. C. Florin-Thuma and J. W. Boudreau, "Performance Feedback Utility in Managerial Decision Processes," *Personnel Journal* (Winter 1987): 693; T. R. Mitchell, M. Rothman, and R. C. Liden, "Effects of Normative Information on Task Performance," *Journal of Applied Psychology* (Feb. 1985): 66–71;

J. L. Pearce and L. W. Porter, "Employee Responses to Formal Performance Appraisal Feedback," *Journal of Applied Psychology* (May 1986): 211.

14. J. Greenberg, "The Distributive Justice of Organizational Performance Evaluation," in *Research in Negotiations in Organizations,* eds. M. Bazerman, R. Lewicki, and B. Sheppard (Greenwich, Conn.: JAI Press, 1986): 25–41; J. Greenberg, "Using Diaries to Promote Procedural Justice in Performance Appraisal," *Social Justice Review* (1987): 20–37.
15. D. Jamieson and J. O'Mara, *Managing Workforce 2000* (San Francisco: Jossey-Bass, 1991): 125–26.
16. M. Rozek, "Teach Your Employees to be Peak Performers," *Personnel Journal* (June 1991): 78.
17. "Starting Fresh at Neiman-Marcus," *HR Reporter* (April 1988): 1–2.
18. For a discussion of these characteristics for an effective appraisal interview, see Beer, "Performance Appraisal," 34–35; *Bulletin to Management* (18 Oct. 1984): 2, 7; and P. Wylie and M. Grothe, *Problem Employees: How to Improve Their Performance* (Belmont, Calif.: Pitman Learning, 1981).
19. E. W. Morrison and R. J. Bies, "Impression Management in the Feedback-Seeking Process: A Literature Review and Research Agenda," *Academy of Management Review* 16, no. 3 (1991): 522–41; J. R. Larson, Jr., "The Dynamic Interplay between Employees' Feedback-Seeking Strategies and Supervisors' Delivery of Performance Feedback," *Academy of Management Review* 14, no. 3 (1989): 408–22; T. E. Becker and R. J. Klimoski, "A Field Study of the Relationship between the Organizational Feedback Environment and Performance," *Personnel Psychology* 42 (1989): 343–78; W. F. Giles and K. W. Mossholder, "Employee Reactions to Contextual and Session Components of Performance Appraisal," *Journal of Applied Psychology* 75, no. 4 (1990): 371–77; R. A. Baron, "Countering the Effects of Destructive Criticism: The Relative Efficacy of Four Interventions," *Journal of Applied Psychology* 75, no. 3 (1990): 235–45; B. R. Nathan, A. M. Mohrman, Jr., and J. Milliman, "Interpersonal Relations as a Context for the Effects of Appraisal Interviews on Performance and Satisfaction: A Longitudinal Study," *Academy of Management Journal* 34, no. 2 (1991): 352–69.
20. This section is adapted in part from R. F. Mager and P. Pipe, *Analyzing Performance Problems or "You Really Oughta Wanna"* (Belmont, Calif.: Fearon Pittman, 1970).
21. R. D. Arvey, G. A. Davis, and S. M. Nelson, "Use of Discipline in an Organization; A Field Study," *Journal of Applied Psychology* (Aug. 1984): 448–60; J. Brockner and J. Guare, "Improving the Performance of Low Self-Esteem Individuals: An Attributional Approach," *Academy of Management Journal* (Dec. 1983): 642–56; D. N. Campbell, R. L. Fleming, and R. C. Grote, "Discipline Without Punishment at Last," *Harvard Business Review* (July/Aug. 1985): 162–78; D. Cameron,"The When, Why and How of Discipline," *Personnel Journal* (July 1984): 37–39; D. R. Ilgen and J. M. Feldman, "Performance Appraisal: A Process Focus," in *Research in Organizational Behavior* vol. 5, eds. B. M. Staw and L. L. Cummings (Greenwich, Conn.: JAI Press, 1983); R. C. Liden and T. R. Mitchell, "Reactions to Feedback: The Role of Attributions," *Academy of Management Journal* (June 1985): 291-304; T. R. Mitchell, S. G. Green, and R. E. Wood, "An Attributional Model of Leadership and the Poor Performing Subordinate: Development and Validation," in *Research in Organizational Behavior* vol. 3, eds. L. L. Cummings and B. M. Staw (Greenwich, Conn.: JAI Press, 1981); D. Tjosvold, "The Effects of Attribution and Social Context on Superiors' Influence and Interaction with Low Performing Subordinates," *Personnel Psychology* (Summer 1985): 361-76.
22. "Strategies for Improving Job Attendance," *Bulletin to Management* (10 March 1988): 80. Also see D. R. Dalton and D. J. Mesch, "On the Extent and Reduction of Avoidable Absenteeism: An Assessment of Absence Policy Provisions," *Journal of Applied Psychology* 76, no. 6 (1991): 810–17; D. A. Harrison and C. L. Hulin, "Investigations of Absenteeism: Using Event History Models to Study the Absence-Taking Process," *Journal of Applied Psychology* 74, no. 2 (1989): 300–316; D. W. Organ, "The Motivational Basis of Organizational Citizenship Behavior," *Research in Organizational Behavior* vol. 12 (1990): 43–72.
23. "Incentives: The Element of Surprise," *Inc.* (July 1991): 79.
24. See W. F. Scanlon, *Alcoholism and Drug Abuse in the Workplace* (Westport, Conn.: Praeger Publishers, 1991); D. Klinger with N. O'Neill, *Workplace Drug Abuse and AIDS: A Guide to Human Resource Management Policy and Practice* (Westport, Conn.: Quorum Books, 1991); A. J. Gelenberg and S. C. Schoonover, *The Practitioner's Guide to Psychoactive Drugs* (New York: Plenum Medical Books, 1991); W. F. Banta and F. Tennant, Jr., *Complete Handbook for Combating Substance Abuse in the Workplace* (Lexington, Mass.: Lexington Books, 1989); R. Thompson, Jr., *Substance Abuse and Employee Rehabilitation* (Washington, D.C.: BNA Books, 1990); K. B. O'Hara and T. E. Backer, *Organizational Change and Drug-Free Workplaces: Templates for Success* (Westport, Conn.: Quorum Books, 1991).
25. "Productivity and Performance EAP-Improved," *Bulletin to Management* (23 July 1987): 1; R. W. Hollman, "Beyond Contemporary Employee Assistance Programs," *Personnel Administrator* (Sept. 1981): 37–41; D. Masi and S. J. Freidland, "EAP Actions and Options," *Personnel Journal* (June 1988): 61–67.
26. C. Frayne and G. Latham, "Application of Social Learning Theory to Employee Self-Management of Attendance," *Journal of Applied Psychology* 72 (1987): 387–92; F. Kanfer, "Self-Management Methods," in *Helping People Change: A Textbook of Methods,* eds. P. Karoly and A. Goldstein (New York: Pergamon Press, 1980): 334–89; P. Karoly and F. Kanfer, *Self-Management and Behavior Change: From Theory to Practice* (New York: Pergamon Press, 1986).
27. R. Stayer, "How I Learned to Let My Workers Lead," *Harvard Business Review* (Nov.-Dec. 1990): 66–83.
28. C. Manz, D. E. Keating, and A. Donnellon, "Preparing for an Organizational Change to Employee Self-Management: The Managerial Transition," *Organizational Dynamics* (Feb. 1990): 15–27.
29. Manz, Keating, and Donnellon, "Preparing an Organizational Change..." For a good discussion of positive strate-

gies see A. W. Bryant, *Personnel Psychology* 43 (1990): 117–34.

30. B. S. Klass and H. N. Wheeler, "Managerial Decision Making about Employee Discipline: A Policy-Capturing Approach," *Personnel Psychology* 43 (1990): 117-34; R. Folger, M. A. Konovsky, and R. Cropanzano, "A Due Process Metaphor for Performance Appraisal," *Research in Organizational Behavior* vol. 14 (1992): 129–77. Also see note 21.
31. P. Wylie and M. Grothe, *Problem Employees: How to Improve Their Performance* (Belmont, Calif.: Pittman Learning, 1981).
32. R. G. Eccles, "The Performance Measurement Manifesto, " *Harvard Business Review* (Jan.-Feb. 1991): 131-32.
33. J. Sargent, "Performance Appraisal 'American Style': Where it Came From and Its Possibilities Overseas," working paper, University of Washington, Sept. 1991; A. Nimgade, "American Management as Viewed by International Professionals," *Business Horizons* (Nov.-Dec. 1989): 98–105.
34. N. Adler, *International Dimensions of Organizational Behavior* 2d ed. (Boston, Mass.: PWS-Kent, 1991); W. H. Newman, "Cultural Assumptions Underlying U.S. Management Concepts," in *Management in an International Context* (New York: Harper & Row, 1972).
35. P. Drucker, *Management: Tasks, Responsibilities and Practices* (New York: Harper & Row, 1973): 424–25.
36. R. Steers, Y. K. Shin, and G. Ungson, *The Chaebol: Korea's New Industrial Might* (Reading, Pa.: Harper & Row, 1990): 121–22.
37. V. Huber, G. Northcraft, M. Neale, and X. Zhao, "Cognitive Similarity and Cultural Dissimilarity: Effects on Performance Appraisal and Compensation Decisions of Chinese and Americans," working paper, University of Washington, 1991.
38. S. Carroll, "Asian HRM Philosophies and Systems: Can They Meet Our Changing HRM Needs," in R. Schuler, S. Youngblood, and V. Huber, eds., *Readings in Personnel and Human Resource Management* (St. Paul, Minn.: West Publishing, 1988): 442–55.
39. W. Ouchi, *The M-Form Society* (Reading, Mass.: Addison-Wesley, 1984).
40. T. Mroczkowski and M. Hanaoka, "Continuity and Change in Japanese Management," *California Management Review* (Winter 1989): 39–52.

END OF SECTION CASE STUDY

Assessing Performance of Couriers at PAP

The Pacific Association of Pathologists, Inc. (PAP), is a regional medical laboratory founded in 1987 as a for-profit pathology laboratory. Since its inception, PAP has secured contracts with five of six hospitals in the Seattle area and has expanded its scope to the western United States. By centralizing laboratory operations, using the latest in computerized assessment, and achieving quick turnaround, PAP has gained economies of scale. As a result, PAP has grown to four times its original size and now has 321 employees.

One of PAP's major problems when moving from traditional hospital environments to a regional service was the need to transport specimens from draw sites to the central operation. To meet this need, PAP employs couriers who are responsible for picking up and transporting specimens and other items between PAP and its clients. The courier position is an entry-level position requiring little education or training. The position does require the ability to meet rigid deadlines and a safe driving record.

Since incorporation, the demand for couriers has increased six times: couriers now number thirty, compared to the original five hired in 1987. Unfortunately, turnover has been equally high. It is not uncommon for a courier not to show up for a shift. PAP has also fired ten couriers for poor performance in the past three years. Because pickups have to occur on schedule, PAP has had to rely on overtime, with some couriers working more than sixty hours a week. The inconsistency in service has resulted in PAP losing one of its hospital contracts. Additional complaints about slow service, rudeness, and lack of knowledge on the part of couriers have filtered in from private physicians and veterinarians served by PAP.

Because PAP's competitive advantage lies in its ability to provide quick, efficient, off-site laboratory services, Kyra Burns, personnel and human resource manager, has targeted courier services as one of her first priorities. Since being hired two months ago, she has rewritten and standardized the courier's job descriptions (see exhibit 1). Next she plans to tackle PAP's performance appraisal system (see exhibit 2). However, corporate officers are resisting her plans. The following comment is typical of management's view: "It's a low-skill 'dime-a-dozen' position. All the couriers do is drive, and if they don't work out, the company can simply replace them."

Kyra had found out that courier overtime has cost PAP $100,000 this past year, or about 25 percent of total payroll for couriers. The selection of new couriers has taken more than 250 hours of time and has cost more than $50,000. The problem of improving courier performance is exasperating because 70 percent of the couriers' time is spent driving to and from PAP—out of the supervisor's sight. Therefore, it is difficult to get a clear picture of what is actually going on at client sites. Another potential problem is that the couriers report to more than one supervisor. Besides the immediate courier supervisor, couriers also report to the administrative technologist over the Courier Department and to a medical doctor who coordinates medical services.

At the heart of the performance problem is PAP's current performance appraisal system. As exhibit 2 shows, the instrument includes ratings in six categories (quality, quantity, timeliness, attendance, responsibility, and cooperation). Some of the complaints from supervisors are that feedback is not specific to the employee's job and that many of the levels on the behavioral checklist are not mutually exclusive. Thus, supervisors are forced to check two of the behavioral scores within one area. For example, when evaluating responsibility, raters sometimes are forced to check two areas: (1) reluctant at times to accept delegated responsibility and (2) self-starter who seeks out more effective ways to achieve results or seeks additional responsibilities.

There are also problems with rater bias. For the twenty out of thirty couriers who were rated during the last performance appraisal period, the average score was 3.8, which is significantly above the expected average level of 3.0. No couriers received a score lower than 2.0. While high scores may have been justified in some cases, high scores were given even to employees whom the managers wanted to fire. This made it difficult to justify firing individuals for performance deficiencies. However, when compared with the average score for all employees at PAP, couriers received *lower* individual scores than did all other employees (average of 4.1) Couriers who receive a high rating on one dimension tend to receive high ratings on all others. To make matters worse, the human resource budget is limited, with little money available for revising the performance appraisal system or for training raters.

Armed with this gloomy report, Kyra sat at her desk, pondering where she should go from here.

Case Questions

1. What rating biases are associated with the current appraisal format?

Exhibit 1
Position Description

Title: Courier

Position Summary

Under the direction of lead courier/dispatcher, administrative technologist, and medical supervisor, provides timely and efficient transport of specimens, slides, mail supplies, and company personnel to and from PAP and its affiliated clients. Acts as a liaison in a public relations capacity by providing clients with needed information and handling customer complaints.

Supervision Received

Lead courier dispatcher. When asked, takes direction from medical supervisor and administrative technologist.

Supervision Given

None

Duties

1. Drives to and from PAP and its clients.
2. Locates the appropriate pick-up and/or receiving areas.
3. Picks up, sorts, and properly packages items for transport.
4. Delivers items to the appropriate receiving area.
5. Adjusts time schedule and driving routes to accommodate state pick-ups.
6. Creates a favorable public relations environment.
7. Properly handles and delivers interdepartmental mail.
8. Maintains equipment such as coolers, radios, and automobiles in working condition. Reports problems within one hour.
9. Keeps an accurate daily log of activities such as dispatch time, arrival time, breaks, and lunch.
10. Handles cash for COD pick-ups and makes change for petty cash.

Skills and Abilities

Ability to: (1) closely follow a prescribed time schedule; (2) drive safely and effectively in heavy traffic and in poor road conditions; (3) determine and follow the quickest route between designated contact points; (4) make independent decisions about scheduling; (5) handle client relations when presented with conflicting client demands; (6) read, write, and speak English; and (7) lift and carry packages and boxes weighing up to 50 pounds.

Requirements

21 years of age or older

Good driving record as shown by a current motor vehicle record

Class C driver's license

Good visual acuity

Willing to handle or be exposed to blood, urine, feces, tissue, and other samples from humans and animals

Willing to work overtime as required.

---

2. Will changing the appraisal format alleviate the problems with courier performance? Why or why not?
3. Assuming the current appraisal system needs to be changed, what type of rating format would you recommend using to assess the performance of couriers?
4. Who should evaluate the performance of couriers?
5. What can be done to increase the commitment of PAP managers to performance appraisal?
6. Discuss the relationships among selection, appraisal, and training and their implications for improving the performance of couriers.

SOURCE: Modified from a project report by Kyle Steadman, Robyn Sutton, and Von Madsen, University of Utah, 1986.

Exhibit 2
Employee Performance Appraisal Form

Employee Name ______________________ **Date** ______________________
Department Couriers **Position** Lead Courier

Ratings Factors **List Comments, Strengths, Areas For Improvement**

Quality of Work refers to accuracy and margin of error:

_______ 1. Makes errors frequently and repeatedly.
_______ 2. Often makes errors.
_______ 3. Accurate; makes occasional errors.
_______ 4. Accurate; rarely makes errors.
_______ 5. Is exacting and precise.

Quantity of Work refers to amount of production or results:

_______ 1. Usually does not complete workload as assigned.
_______ 2. Often accomplishes part of a task; others must help.
_______ 3. Handles workload as assigned.
_______ 4. Turns out more work than requested.
_______ 5. Handles unusually large volume of work.

Timeliness refers to completion of task, within time allowed:

_______ 1. Duties not completed on time.
_______ 2. Often late in completing tasks.
_______ 3. Tasks completed on time.
_______ 4. Tasks usually completed in advance of deadlines.
_______ 5. Completes all tasks always in advance of time frames.

Attendance and Punctuality refers to adhering to work schedule as assigned:

_______ 1. Takes longer or more frequent breaks than most; usually tardy or absent.
_______ 2. Takes longer or more frequent breaks than most; often tardy or absent (comment).
_______ 3. Usually assures that breaks do not cause inconvenience; normally not tardy or absent.
_______ 4. Makes a point of being on the job and on time.
_______ 5. Extremely conscientious about attendance and punctuality.

Responsibility refers to completing assignments and projects:

_______ 1. Usually does not assume responsibility for completing assignments.
_______ 2. Reluctant at times to accept delegated responsibility.
_______ 3. Accepts and discharges delegated duties willingly.
_______ 4. Accepts additional responsibility.
_______ 5. "Self-starter" who seeks out more effective ways to achieve results or seeks additional responsibilities.

Cooperation with others refers to working and communicating with supervisors and co-workers:

_______ 1. Has difficulty working with others; is usually unwilling to perform assignments, and rarely assists others.

_______ 2. Sometimes has difficulty working with others and often complains when given assignments.
_______ 3. Usually is agreeable and obliging; generally helps out when requested.
_______ 4. Works well with others; welcomes assignments, and is quick to offer assistance.
_______ 5. An outstanding teamworker; always assists others and continually encourages cooperation by setting an excellent example.

Performance Summary (include strong areas and areas for future emphasis in improving performance or developing additional job skills):

Employee Comments/Concerns:

Signatures:

Reviewed by Human Resource Director _______________ **Date:** _______________
Employee _______________ **Date:** _______________
Supervisor _______________ **Date:** _______________

SECTION 5

Compensating

For most people work is a central activity in their lives. It can provide structure, meaning, and purpose. However central or important work is for them, most are still unlikely to work if the company doesn't pay them, and they are more likely to work for one company than another if one pays more than the other, all other things being equal. In some circumstances, of course, individuals may work for less than they could get with another company or in another occupation. For the most part, though, individuals work for a particular company because of the compensation they expect to receive for their contributions.

Once on the job, employees generally want to work hard and do a good job. They also want fair pay and feedback from the boss. Consequently, companies and their human resource managers usually try to ensure that their employees are paid fairly, both in terms of what others in the company are being paid and what others with similar jobs in other organizations are being paid. The first chapter of this three-chapter section on compensating employees will discuss issues associated with establishing equitable pay plans to attract, retain, and motivate individuals.

Employees will also work more if they are paid more for their additional work; thus, organizations are increasingly establishing compensation plans that tie additional compensation to additional work. Even here, employees are concerned with fairness and equity, so companies must design performance-based pay plans around performance appraisal systems that are valid and accepted by the employees. These plans can be designed for individuals, groups, or even organizational performance achievements. Because of the growing use of these plans, they are discussed extensively in the second of the three chapters of this section.

While employees are concerned about getting paid regularly, they are also concerned about the "not so little things." These can include medical benefits (one of the biggest concerns of all Americans), insurance benefits, and perks such as larger offices and named parking spaces. Because these aspects of total compensation are very important to individuals and very costly to organizations, we discuss them in our third and final chapter on compensating employees.

CHAPTER 9

Total Compensation

There are two things people want more than sex and money ... recognition and praise.

—Mary Kay Ash, Chairman Emeritus, Mary Kay Cosmetics[1]

When a telecommunications system malfunctions, the pressure to restore service is intense. Every second without a dial tone can cost the customer lost sales and adverse customer relations. If for example a catalog sales company such as Eddie Bauer loses its telephone system, the business is unable to receive telephone orders, verify delivery addresses, check on incoming orders, contact suppliers, etc. Under such conditions, the next best thing to a telephone system that is never interrupted is one that is quickly restored.

Recognizing the competitive advantage to be gained from fast, reliable service, Northern Telecom set increased customer service as its number one objective. To determine the best way to launch this strategic initiative, Telecom examined its customer service ratings in thirteen key areas. Overall, customer service rated a respectable 72 on a scale of 0 to 100; but two customer service factors—installation and technical support—were identified as opportunity areas. Customer ratings on these two dimensions averaged 70, only slightly below average; however, both management and employees knew that customer service could be improved to enhance Telecom's reputation as a high-quality supplier.

Telecom zeroed in on two things: 1) shortening the time required to install new equipment, and 2) diagnosing troubleshooting, and repairing service outages on the initial call. Success in both areas was seen as a function of having a versatile, flexible, and knowledgeable cable field service work force. Since increased spending on skills training is only wise if employees stay with the company and apply their knowledge, Telecom established a second objective of building a highly skilled and committed work force. Telecom also needed to resolve a concern with pay inequity. Traditionally, company divisions used different salary structures, pay grades, and career ladders. Because technicians and engineers from different divisions often found themselves on the same job, pay equity was continually being questioned.

After researching different approaches to attain these objectives, Telecom's planning team settled upon skill-based pay to drive its strategic initiative. While skill-based pay (SBP) was not the only possible solution, a shift to a totally different approach to pay allowed Telecom to meet their last objective—pay fairness—while avoiding the difficult task of adjusting one division's pay to agree with another's; previous attempts to combine pay plans had failed in the company. The resulting program was named "Fast Forward." Fast refers to Telecom's focus on time-based solutions, and "Forward" describes the direction to be advanced by the company and employees when skills are developed. The theme of reciprocity—the company will do well if employees do well and vice versa—was used to better link business objectives to employee rewards.

Here's how the program was designed. A development team identified skill requirements for the three major job families to be included in the plan. The skill sets for technicians, for example, were built from existing equipment–installation procedure manuals. By comparison, the skill hierarchy for the technical support engineering job family had to be developed from scratch. Seven key dimensions of work were identified: hardware, software, customer database, documentation, network interface, written communication, and interpersonal interaction. For each dimension, managers ranked-ordered skills from most to least difficult. Then they bundled skills into four separate blocks, one for each level/title in the technical support engineer job family. Because Telecom's jobs are dynamic, job bundles are routinely reviewed to keep the inventory current.

The fundamental difference between Telecom's "Fast Forward" pay plan and its predecessor is that employees now progress through a job ladder at their own pace, based on their ability to learn new skills. Under the old job-based system, an employee could not advance unless there was an opening at the higher level and the employee had sufficient seniority. Under Fast Forward, technicians gradually progress from level to level, on average every six months. Career ladders can be branched by moving from associate status to technical support status.

The second development step involved determining rates of pay for Fast Forward skill bundles. This is no easy task, since pay data to fit a whole job family rather than individual jobs must be extracted from traditional pay surveys. Determining the minimum rate of pay for a job bundle was relatively easy since the salary range could be matched to the labor market entry-hire rate. After considering various alternatives, the maximum was established on the basis of the average rate of pay for tasks at the senior job level. Applying these guidelines to the technical family produced a salary range with a 270 percent spread. (Job-based pay ranges typically are 30 percent to 60 percent). Fast Forward's broad pay range was broken into segments called "target pay zones" that corresponded to the skill blocks (e.g., associate, field technician, field test technician).

With SBP, salary increases typically are given only for skill accomplishment. Because quality of service was important, the Fast Forward program was modified to include merit pay. Employees are reviewed annually on their individual anniversary dates for increases based on performance rather than on skill flexibility. Merit increases advance salary up to an employee's skill-target high, but not beyond.

The final component of Telecom's SBP plan is a skill assessment/certification program, the process for evaluating employee skill levels to determine skill grade advancement. The assessment process developed for technicians was relatively straight-forward compared with the one developed for technical support engineering. The former involved a simple hierarchy of skills; the latter included abstract problem-solving and interpersonal abilities.

When an employee believes he or she has mastered a specific skill level, a preassessment discussion with the supervisor is held. Next, skill accomplishments are documented for review by the assessment committee. A "qualified" rating is given to an employee who can perform a skill unaided; a "perform" rating is assigned to those who need some direction; and a "trained" designation is used to note that the employee has received instruction. To earn a certificate, participants must not only learn but must demonstrate their proficiencies on the job. Obviously, an extensive training system supports Telecom's SBP program.

What's been the outcome of Fast Forward? Since it was implemented two years ago, Telecom's overall customer satisfaction rating has increased to 75, with high gains in installation ratings (from 70 to 74). Turnover among the highly mobile technician work force has been reduced from 16 percent to 7 percent. Complaints about salary differences have all but disappeared now that all employees are paid on the same system.[2]

Northern Telecom's Fast Forward pay system represents three recent and very important issues in compensation management. Faced with major challenges to their survival, more companies than ever view compensation as a strategy to drive their business. That is, organizations have recognized that compensation not only can attract, motivate, and retain employees, but also can enhance organizational competitiveness, survival, and profitability. The second issue is that an increasing number of firms are replacing traditional job-based pay (JBP) systems in which employees are paid for the particular jobs they are performing with skill-based pay (SBP) systems in which employees are paid for the range, depth, and types of skills they demonstrate. Third, the use of SBP traditionally has been restricted to high-involvement, continuous-process manufacturing plants. As the Northern Telecom case illustrates, SBP plans and other new pay plans are flexible enough that they can be used in a wide variety of industries, including service firms that employ white-collar professionals.

Other issues in total compensation are important also: How are wages really determined? How do we know when people are paid fairly? How do we decide the wage rate for a given individual? Chapters 9–11 address these and many other issues in compensating employees.

TOTAL COMPENSATION

Total compensation involves the assessment of employee contributions in order to distribute fairly and equitably direct and indirect organizational rewards in exchange for those contributions. As exhibit 9.1 shows, extrinsic rewards can be categorized as direct or indirect compensation. **Direct compensation** includes an employee's **base salary** (which may be determined using SBP or JBP methods) and **performance-based pay. Indirect compensation** consists of federal- and state-mandated protection programs, private protection programs, health care benefits, paid leave, and life cycle benefits.

The next three chapters discuss the process of compensation and how it can be linked with the organization's strategy. This chapter begins with a discussion of compensation's purposes and importance, and then describes its overall role in developing and linking human resource management to the organization's strategy. Next we present various ways to attain internal and external pay equity. Then we examine issues associated with compensation administration (e.g., resolving equity imbalances, participation, pay secrecy, and pay satisfaction). Chapter 10 continues the discussion of total compensation but focuses on individual equity, including the mix of various elements of total compensation. Compensation for specific groups (sales people and executives) also will be delineated. In conclusion, chapter 11 focuses on employee benefits and the role they play in fulfilling organizational objectives. Some compensation issues in other countries also will be reviewed.

PURPOSES AND IMPORTANCE OF TOTAL COMPENSATION

Total compensation is important because it can serve several major purposes.

- *Attract potential job applicants.* In conjunction with the organization's recruitment and selection efforts, the total compensation program can help assure that pay is sufficient to attract the right people at the right time for the right jobs.

Exhibit 9.1
Components of Total Compensation

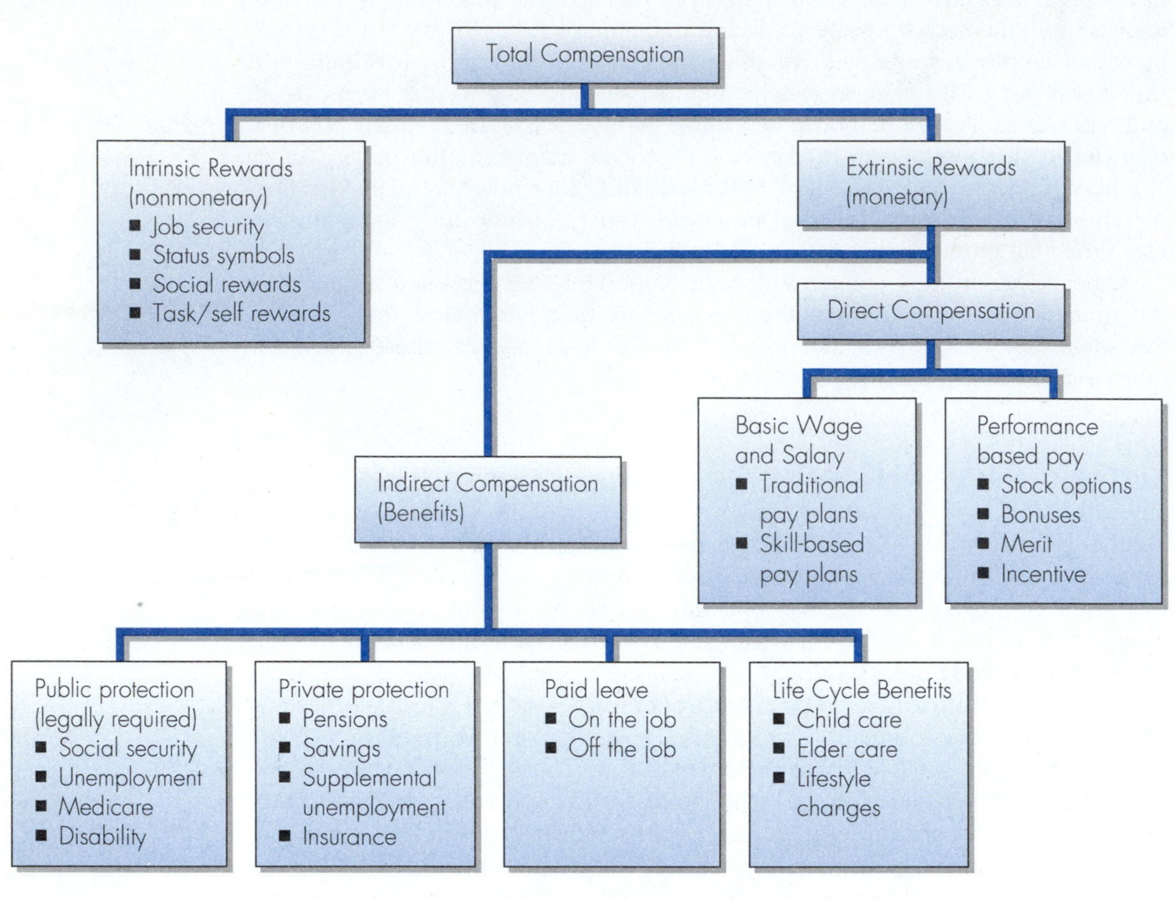

- *Retain good employees.* Unless the total compensation program is perceived as internally equitable and externally competitive, good employees (those the organization wants to retain) are likely to leave.
- *Gain a competitive edge.* Total compensation can be a significant cost of doing business. Depending on the industry, labor costs range from ten to eighty percent of total costs. To gain a competitive advantage, an organization may choose to automate or to relocate to areas where labor is cheaper.
- *Motivate employees.* While nonmonetary awards may influence an employee's motivation, performance-based pay has been shown to be the *most* effective motivator. Still, because of individual differences and preferences, organizations must determine the correct blend of monetary and nonmonetary rewards.[3]
- *Administer pay within legal regulations.* Because several legal regulations are relevant to total compensation, organizations must be aware of them and avoid violating them in their pay programs.

- *Facilitate organizational strategic objectives.* The organization may want to create a rewarding and competitive climate, or it may want to be an attractive place to work so that it can attract the best applicants. Total compensation can attain these objectives and can also further other organizational objectives, such as rapid growth, survival, and innovation, as implied in the opening feature of Northern Telecom.
- *Reinforce and define structure.* The compensation system of an organization can help define the organization's structure, status hierarchy, and degree to which people in technical positions can influence those in line positions.

Obviously, these objectives are interrelated. When employees are motivated, the organization is more likely to achieve its strategic objectives. When pay is based on the value of the job, the organization is more likely to attract, motivate, and retain its employees. Nonmonetary rewards become more important in attaining the above objectives as monetary rewards decrease.

No other human resource activity has more relationships with other human resource activities and with the internal and external environments than does total compensation. Exhibit 9.2 illustrates these relationships, along with the administrative issues and processes in total compensation.

LINKING TOTAL COMPENSATION TO THE NEEDS OF THE BUSINESS

Being strategic about compensation implies developing programs that support the needs of the business and are sensitive to anticipated environmental pressures. To do this, businesses must make a series of critical decisions regarding the distribution of total compensation among its basic elements—base pay, incentives, and benefits.

Linking with the Business Strategy

The first decision relates to the linkage between compensation and business strategy. As the opening case study of Northern Telecom showed, the implementation of a compensation system can signal a shift in business strategy or can play a less prominent role during organization changes. In some cases, compensation programming is fully integrated with the business planning process. In other cases, the system is designed to merely accommodate or complement the strategy. High-risk–high-return incentive plans at financial investment firms represent the former. The adoption of a new pay system in *support* of a strategic initiative represents the latter; here, the pay plan is an afterthought, designed to complement rather than drive the business strategy.[4]

Internal Pay Structure

The second decision relates to establishing an internal pay structure that is perceived as fair and equitable. **Internal equity** requires employers to set wage rates for jobs within their companies that correspond to the relative internal value of each job. At Northern Telecom, pay differences were based on the skill level of employees. This is a relatively new approach to attaining internal pay equity. More traditionally, employees are paid for the particular jobs they per-

Exhibit 9.2
Relationships, Administrative Issues, and Processes of Total Compensation

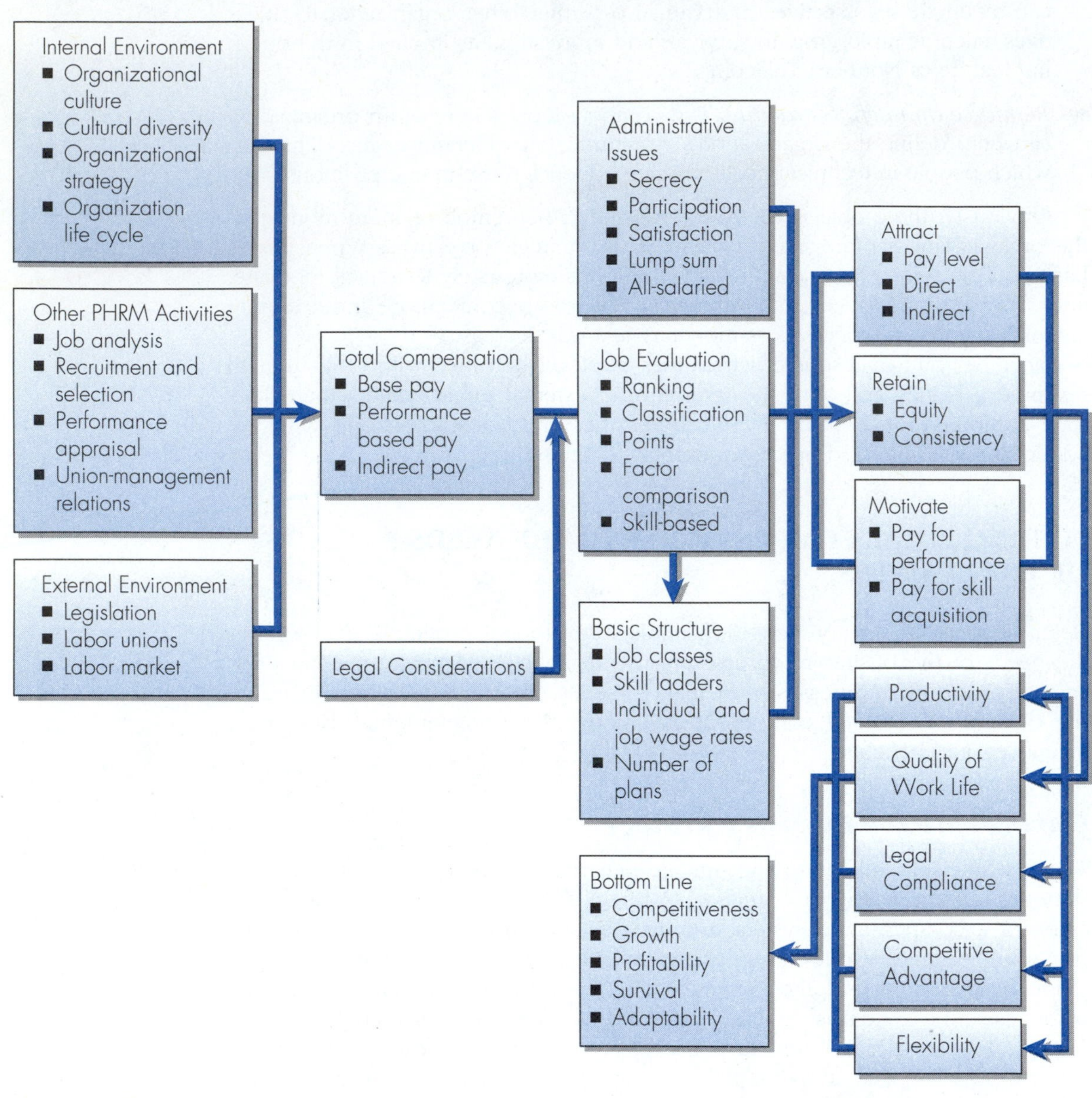

form. This is accomplished by developing a job hierarchy wherein jobs of greater value receive greater rewards. The premise underlying a strategic perspective is that considerable discretion exists to design different pay hierarchies even in organizations with similar technologies. For example, Bonneville International, a Utah broadcast group, has a single pay structure for all nonexempt employees; the system applies to all divisions. One of Bonneville's competitors, however, takes a decentralized approach to pay, and each division has its own pay structure and rates.[5]

External Equity Considerations

From a strategic perspective, external equity refers to positioning a firm's compensation relative to its competitors. At the most basic level, the options are to lead, lag, or match the pay rates of labor market competitors. In the competitive 1990s, external equity has become more complex, with firms considering the mix of pay forms as well as the risk-return tradeoff. To support a high-volume strategy, sales representatives at one company may receive low base salaries ($20,000) with a $40,000 bonus potential. Conversely, high base salary ($50,000) coupled with merit pay is more likely to support a customer service objective. In addition to the mix of pay, these two competitive positions differ in risk-return tradeoff. The former pay plan shifts most of the risk to the employee, while the latter leaves a greater portion of risk with the company. How effective either strategy is in attaining corporate objectives is unknown until the policies are implemented.[6]

Compensation Administration Policies

Fourth, the process used to administer compensation is also linked to business strategy. Business-related choices here include the amount of information to be disclosed to employees, the involvement of employees in the development of the plan, and the nature of a dispute-resolution process. For example, should the business provide broad policies or specific details about how the pay structure was developed? A high-involvement firm may involve employees directly in the development of the pay plan, including the evaluation of their jobs; other firms may have outside consultants evaluate jobs or may even evaluate jobs via the computer using an automated expert system.

Performance Focus

The policies for granting pay increases based on performance have business implications. General Dynamics' top twenty-five executives receive a large bonus each time its stock price rises ten dollars a share and stays there for ten days. While executives have to wait a while for the money, this plan has drawn widespread criticism among union leaders and Wall Street analysts because it seems to encourage management to focus on short-term gains at the expense of long-term profitability. The proportion of pay that is placed at risk, the degree of pay differentiation among peak and competent employees, the relative emphasis on individual versus team versus corporate performance all have strategic implications.[7]

In sum, a strategic perspective on compensation is based on the belief that fitting compensation systems to organizational conditions and objectives makes a difference. If matched appropriately, compensation policies and practices can have desired effects on employee behavior and on the overall performance of the organization. The effectiveness of linking compensation with the business is, however, moderated by the external and internal environments.

IMPACT OF EXTERNAL ENVIRONMENT

Several factors in the external environment directly affect the critical decisions in linking compensation with the needs of the business: legislation, unions, and the labor market.

Legislation

Compensation systems, like other human resource activities, need to be responsive to state and federal laws and court decisions. A legislative change such as an increase in the minimum wage affects lower paid employees, while the 1986 Tax Reform Act is said to have a significant effect on executive and middle-management compensation.

Pay policies still navigate many unchartered waters. Exhibit 9.3 summarizes pay system guidelines that have emerged in relation to the enforcement of the Fair Labor Standards Act and its 1963 Equal Pay Act Amendment.

As discussed in chapter 3, the Equal Pay Act provides legal coverage to males and females performing substantially equal work. Only when men and women perform jobs requiring equivalent skills, effort, responsibility, and working conditions are they entitled to identical pay (unless there are differences in performance, seniority, or other conditions). Title VII of the Civil Rights Act of 1964, however, provides broader legal coverage for pay discrimination.

> Addressing the interrelationship between the Equal Pay Act and Title VII, [the] EEOC observes that while both laws prohibit sex-based wage discrimination, Title VII's prohibitions are broader. In cases where a complainant meets the jurisdictional requirements of both laws, the rules say, "any violation of the Equal Pay Act is also a violation of Title VII." But since Title VII covers types of wage discrimination not actionable under the EPA, "an act or practice of an employer or labor organization that is not a violation of EPA may nevertheless be a violation of Title VII," according to the rules.
>
> If an employer violates both EPA and Title VII, the complainant may recover under both laws for the same period of time, as long as the individual "does not receive duplicative relief for the same wrong," according to the regulations. Relief will be computed, the rules say, "to give each individual the highest benefit which entitlement under either statute would provide (e.g., liquidated damages may be available under the EPA, but not under Title VII)."[8]

Labor Unions

The presence of a union in a private-sector firm is estimated to increase wages by 10 to 15 percent. Union presence also adds about 20 to 30 percent to the cost of employee benefits. There also is evidence that the wage differential between unionized and nonunionized firms is greatest during recessionary periods and smallest during inflationary periods. Whether the increased wage costs in unionized firms translate into higher output is widely debated. Some researchers contend that, by improving employee satisfaction, lowering turnover, and decreasing absenteeism, the net productivity impact of unions is positive. Others, however, contend the gains in productivity are not equivalent to the increased compensation costs.[9]

Unions also have pushed for wage escalation clauses. Wage escalation clauses are designed to increase wages automatically during the life of a contract. One way unions have accomplished this is to tie wage increases to changes in the consumer price index. While **cost of living adjustments (COLAs)** were popular in the 1960s and 1970s, the number of workers covered by COLAs declined during the 1980s and early 1990s—primarily because the consumer price index has decelerated in recent years.

Exhibit 9.3
Enforcement of Fair Labor Standards Act and Equal Pay Act Provisions

1. Conduct a *systematic job analysis* to identify skill, effort, responsibility, and working conditions of jobs.
2. Use an *established job evaluation system* to determine whether jobs are similar. Remember, they need to be substantially equal and not identical or comparable.
3. *Examine job content, not job titles.* Titles may be biased (e.g., beautician or barber, orderly or nurse's aide).
4. *Examine total compensation* including indirect benefits *and* direct pay.
5. *Exempt employees are not exempt from equal pay stature.* Those performing substantially equal work need to be paid the same rates of pay.
6. Pay trainees different rates of pay only if the *training program is bona fide.*
7. If a violation is found, *raise the pay of the lower-paid job.* Do not lower the pay of the higher-paid job.
8. *Keep records* including job descriptions, job evaluations, minimum wage information, overtime, and hours of employment.
9. *Don't hide behind a union contract.* If a violation is found, the employer, not the union, foots the bill because the employer pays the wages.
10. Remember, *males and females can sue* under the Equal Pay Act.

Another way unions have affected compensation practices is through the establishment of two-tiered wage systems that vary the rates of pay with hiring date. As operationalized, a contract is negotiated which specifies that employees hired after a specific date will receive lower wages than their higher-seniority peers working on the same or similar jobs. Two-tiered pay systems increased in use during the 1980s because unions viewed them as less painful than wage freezes and salary cuts for existing employees.[10] However, remember that all employees hired after the contract is ratified receive wages which are as much as 50 to 80 percent lower than peers in the higher tier. American Airlines, Greyhound, McDonnell Douglas, and Ingersol Rand are representative of firms that have had two-tiered wage systems to help reduce total fixed costs.[11]

Form of pay deals basically with the question of how the economic package is to be allocated between wages and benefits. Unions have also played a role here. For example, the International Association of Machinists opted to set aside ten cents an hour for skill retraining rather than take a five-cent-an-hour increase in direct pay. According to Seattle Local President Tom Baker, union members were more concerned with long-term job security than short-term gains in salary. With the establishment of the $12 million annually funded Career Mobility program, union members are being retrained for higher level jobs, which also happen to pay better.

A different, but equally useful, strategy was employed at Crown Zellerbach Corporation. To reduce fixed labor costs without reducing total wages of unionized workers, the International Woodworkers of America and management opted for an incentive pay plan. Under this system, workers earn about three dollars more an hour than before on straight wages. Because the incentive plan shifted greater risk to the workers, the company also gave the union a greater say in work-related decisions. Thus, workers gain in involvement and salary, and the company gains in fixed-cost salary reductions.[12]

Probably the strongest traditional as well as emerging influence of unions on wage structures relates to the quality of the union-management relationship. Some unions may want to take an active part in job evaluation to ensure that their interest in a rational wage structure is preserved. Others seek to preserve customary relationships and job security and resist changes in job content and concomitant wage rates. "Scanlon plans," which will be discussed in the next chapter, were developed by a union leader but only work when there is a high degree of trust between the union and management. Skill-based pay programs such as the one described in the opening company profile are more likely to work if the union is willing to trade job and financial security for the work assignment flexibility that skill-based pay demands.

Labor Market

The labor market influences the wage and salary structure basically through the supply of labor. Shortages in the labor market (internal or external) provide those who are qualified to fill the jobs an opportunity to negotiate better terms of employment. A part of this negotiation is for a relative increase in pay that is higher than the increase for other groups. The juggling act between labor supply and demand has ramifications for internal as well as external pay equity. Externally, the firm must pay a higher rate of pay for workers who are in short supply than for workers for which there are no shortages. This creates problems—particularly if the two jobs are of equivalent internal value to the organization.

Although many organizations use wage survey results to help set pay levels for jobs, they should be aware that paying what the market will bear—e.g., paying women and minorities less because they are willing to accept less—is no excuse for wage discrimination (*Marshall v. Georgia Southwestern College,* 1981). Nonetheless, paying one employee more than another for the same job is not necessarily illegal if market conditions differ for the two employees. Organizations also need to be concerned over the issue of price fixing. If organizations exchange market data on their own and set pay rates based on this information, the organizations may be charged with price fixing and collusion.

Market data can be used directly or indirectly to set rates of pay. Indirectly, rates of pay for benchmark jobs are used to establish pay rates for all other jobs. Alternatively, a job evaluation study of existing jobs can be conducted first; then internal rates of pay are compared to existing rates of pay.

IMPACT OF INTERNAL ENVIRONMENT

Organizational Culture

Organizations differ in the values, norms, and expectations that make up their culture. An organization's compensation system is an important signal of what is valued by an organization. For example, in a hierarchy-based reward system, qualitative criteria, which are subjectively weighted and evaluated by a supervisor, are used to allocate rewards. As a result, a **clan-type culture** emerges in which loyalty is exchanged for the organization's long-term commitment to the individual. In this culture, members share a sense of pride in the "fraternal network."

By comparison, when rewards are objectively and explicitly linked to performance, a **market culture** evolves. In this culture, the relationship between the individual and the organization is contractual with obligations specified in advance. The market culture is not designed to generate loyalty, cooperation, or a sense of belonging. Members do not feel constrained by norms, values, or allegiance to accepted ways of doing things. The market culture does, however generate personal initiative, a strong sense of ownership, and responsibility.[13]

Cultural Diversity

Even though an organization has a predominant reward culture (e.g., market culture), the diversity of today's work force demands a more flexible approach to compensation. David Jamieson, president of the Jamieson Consulting Group, and Julie O'Mara, President of O'Mara and Associates, summarize the problems associated with compensation in the 1990s.

> The value of money, response to public recognition, the desire for professional and peer respect, and the need for challenging assignments all vary according to lifestyle and culture. The importance of these rewards to individuals affects their motivation, productivity and satisfaction. A greater variety of rewards is clearly called for in an era of cultural diversity.[14]

Attention to cultural diversity in rewards also has increased as more and more organizations become transnational and emphasize global over national perspectives. Such firms face the difficult task of administering rewards in multiple cultures, each of which emphasizes different values and reward priorities.

Consider compensation practices in the People's Republic of China. Here, a person of good character is expected to be less occupied with the self than with the group and to be more concerned with citizenship behaviors (altruism, attendance, and conscientiousness) that benefit group more than individual outcomes. All workers, to reinforce this culture, regardless of rank or occupation, receive an identical basic wage (e.g., forty yuan a month). Workers also get subsidies for rent, transportation, food, sanitation, retirement, education, and general welfare. Only minimal differentials are given for differences in job responsibility and seniority. Performance-based pay, which accounts for as much as one-third of total pay, is based on the performance of the organization, not of the individual worker. This compensation mix contrasts sharply with pay practices in less collective or less clan-based Western countries.[15]

Organizational Strategy

A recent study by the American Compensation Association indicates that two-thirds of all firms implementing changes in their pay system do so because of fundamental changes in the way they view and define their markets. That is, the selection of the right compensation mix is highly dependent on what a company needs from its employees to match its strategy initiative, (be that strategy for entrepreneurial development, for dynamic growth, to extract profit, for liquidation/divestiture or for turnaround).[16]

General Dynamics is pursuing a **turnaround strategy.** Faced with a shrinking market, the company eliminated more than 10,000 jobs through layoffs and attrition, drastically cut spending on plants and equipment, and sold several non-military subsidiaries. To support this strategy, top executives were offered short- as well as long-term incentives linked to stock prices. Employee involvement at the top was high. However, at lower levels, General Dynamics employed a **liquidation/divestiture strategy.** Here, wages were frozen and jobs eliminated. Participation in compensation activities was held to a minimum, perks were limited and a standard, fixed severance package with no incentives was offered.

Tandem Computers, Inc., in comparison, has pursued an **entrepreneurial strategy.** To encourage employees to be innovative, to take more risks, and to be willing to assume responsibility, compensation practices are flexible, contain many perks and long-term incentives (incentive stock options or stock appreciation rights), and encourage high employee participation. Tandem's compensation philosophy is to reward people fairly but not necessarily equally. While stock options are awarded equally to every employee, cash bonuses are awarded only to top performers. A "night on the town" is given to people who make a special contribution. To further recognize employee contributions, peak performers (selected by their supervisor and peers) annually attend a special retreat at a resort. The retreat creates a place for top performers to relax, network, become acquainted, and brainstorm on key issues facing the business.[17]

Organization Life Cycle

The choice of a specific compensation mix also is constrained by an organization's life cycle. The concept of organization life cycle is adapted from the concept of product life cycle developed in marketing and relates growth in sales revenues to the age of the organization. Organizations (like products) go through different stages of development: start-up, growth, maturity, and decline.

As suggested in exhibit 9.4, growth is rapid during some stages and slow during other stages of the life cycle. During the **start-up phase** the emphasis is on product and market development. The HR focus is on attracting key contributors and facilitating innovation. Still, risk is high, sales growth is slow, and earnings are low. As a result, base salary and benefits are usually below the market. However, broad-based short- and long-term incentives are offered to stimulate employees to innovate. Sales growth is rapid, with moderate increases in earnings during the **growth stage.** To keep up, the organization must grow rapidly to satisfy increased demand for products and/or services. The human resource focus is on rapid recruitment and training to develop the human capital. Bonuses offered for innovation and sales growth and stock options offered to encourage employees to think about the long-term growth of the company.

Because the market is saturated with the product, growth is slower and more orderly during the **mature stage.** High entry costs and exit barriers keep the number of competitors low, so organizations can focus on profitability. During this stage, the HR emphasis is on consistency and the retention of peak performers. Profit sharing, cash bonuses, and stock awards tied to short- or long-term growth may be utilized to retain key contributors. Base pay and benefits usually are competitive.

During the **decline stage,** the human resource focus shifts to cutback management as market share declines. Incentives of any kind are unlikely to be awarded. Base salary and benefits are, at best, competitive and may drop below market levels as management attempts to cut back expenditures.[18]

Exhibit 9.4
Potential Pay Mixes for Different Stages of Organizational Life

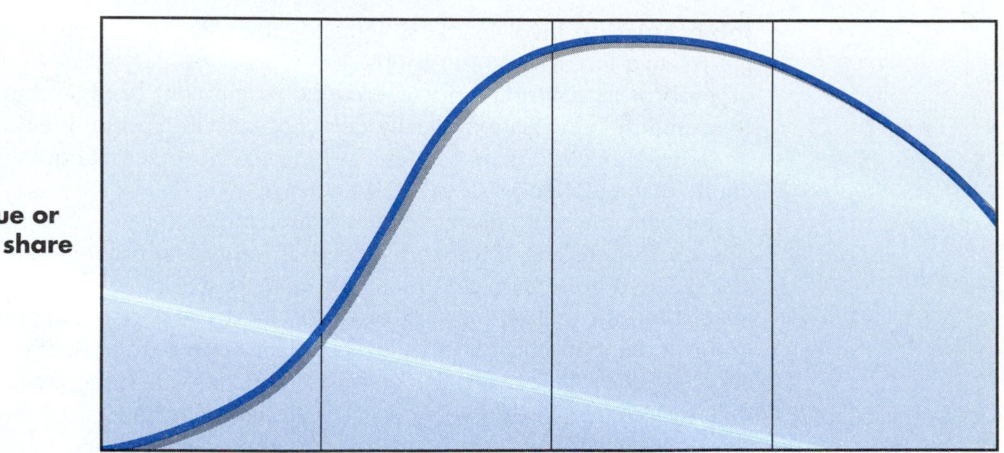

ORGANIZATION CHARACTERISTICS	Life-Cycle Stage			
	Start-Up	**Growth**	**Mature**	**Decline**
HRM Focus	Innovation, Attract Key Contributors	Recruiting, Training	Retention, Consistency	Cutback Management
Risk Profile	High	Moderate	Low	Moderate to High
COMPENSATION STRATEGY				
Short-Term Incentives	Stock Bonus	Cash Bonus	Profit Sharing, Cash Bonus	Unlikely
Long-Term Incentives	Stock Options (broad participation)	Stock Options (limited participation)	Stock Purchase	Unlikely
Base Salary	Below Market Level	At Market Level	At or Above Market Level	At or Below Market Level
Benefits	Below Market Level	Below Market Level	At or Above Market Level	At or Below Market Level

SOURCE: D.B. Balkin and L.R. Gomez-Mejia, "Compensation Systems in High Technology Companies," *New Perspectives on Compensation* (Englewood Cliffs, N.J.: Prentice-Hall, 1987), 269–77.

Organization life cycles have received wide attention as a heuristic device, but the concept has critics. More than one set of compensation policies may be appropriate for any given cycle. Additionally, organizations often have more than one product, each at a different stage of development. Due to this complexity, it may be impossible to cleanly classify a firm and its compensation mix according to its stage of development.[19]

INTERNAL EQUITY: DETERMINING THE RELATIVE WORTH OF JOBS

Job evaluation involves the systematic, rational assessment of jobs to determine the relative internal worth of jobs. Job worth normally relates to the importance of a job or its contribution to the overall attainment of organizational objectives. By design, job evaluation usually does not take into account either market forces or individual performance; these belong to the external-equity and employee-equity management processes respectively.

As with any administrative procedure, job evaluation invites give and take. Consensus building is often required among stakeholders (incumbents, managers, HR representatives, union officials) to work out conflicts that inevitably arise about the "relative" worth of jobs to an organization. Still, the application of group judgments through the job evaluation process normally produces a pay structure that is more congruent with organizational values regarding job worth than a structure based solely on external market valuations of worth.[20] Choosing among job evaluation processes depends on several factors.

- *Legal and social background.* The choice of job evaluation methods may be limited by collective bargaining arrangements or by what is legally acceptable.
- *Organizational structure.* In small firms, simple systems such as ranking may be appropriate. However, in a multiplant enterprise, plans may be more complex.
- *Management style.* Management style can vary from autocratic to democratic. This style will primarily affect the scope of worker participation in the design and application of a job evaluation scheme.
- *Labor-management relations.* No job evaluation scheme can succeed unless the workers accept it. Indeed, the results of many job evaluation programs have been totally rejected because of union opposition. To prevent this, organizations may choose a plan that provides for participation.
- *Cost in time and money.* Job evaluation, like other HR activities, costs time and money. There is up-front cost in developing a tailor-made plan. Canned programs may also be costly in terms of dollar cost and user acceptance. Usually job evaluation takes between six and twelve months for firms employing more than 500 employees.[21]

Establishing a job evaluation system involves several major decisions. They include deciding whether to use a single plan or multiple plans, choosing an appropriate job evaluation approach, and setting up a process to drive the plan.

Single Plan Versus Multiple Plans

One of the first decisions is whether to use one or multiple job evaluation plans to evaluate jobs in an organization. Traditionally, job evaluation plans have varied depending on the job family (e.g., clerical, skilled craft, professional). This approach is premised on the assumption that the work content of various job families is too diverse to be captured by one plan. For example, manufacturing jobs may vary in terms of working conditions and physical effort, while professional jobs may not differ in terms of these compensable factors. Proponents of multiple plans contend that these are necessary to capture the unique job characteristics of job families.

Proponents of pay equity advocate a single pay plan. Their argument is premised on the assumption that universal compensable factors relate to *all* jobs. Only when jobs are evaluated using the same criteria can the relative value of *all* jobs be determined. When separate plans are used, it is much easier to discriminate against specific classes of jobs (e.g., clerical versus skilled). To prevent this, universal factors need to be utilized.

It is also possible, but difficult, to develop firm-specific job evaluation systems with universal factors. Some companies, such as Control Data and Hewlett-Packard, use a set of core factors and another set of factors unique to particular occupational groups.

Traditional Job Evaluation Methods

Job evaluation methods differ in several respects. Some methods evaluate the whole job, while others evaluate jobs using compensable factors. Job evaluation approaches also vary with regard to the type of output produced. For example, the factor comparison method evaluates jobs directly in dollar worth, while the point evaluation system requires conversion of points to dollars. Five of the most frequently utilized job evaluation systems will be discussed. We will also discuss skill-based pay, introduced in the opening company profile of Northern Telecom.

Ranking method. The least specific job evaluation method is **ranking.** One approach to ranking relies on the market value of each job. Alternatively, jobs can be ranked on the basis of such factors as difficulty, criticality to organizational success, and skill required.

This method is convenient when there are only a few jobs to evaluate and when one person is familiar with them all. As the number of jobs increases and the likelihood of one individual knowing all jobs declines, detailed job analysis information becomes more important, and ranking is often done by committee. Especially when a large number of jobs are to be ranked, key or benchmark jobs are used for comparison.

One difficulty in the ranking method is that all jobs must be different from each other. Making fine distinctions between similar jobs is often difficult, so disagreements often arise.

Job classification method. The job classification method is similar to the ranking method, except that classes or grades are established and the job descriptions are then slotted into classes that cover the range of jobs. Pay grade classification standards specify in general terms the kinds and levels of responsibilities assigned to jobs in each grade, the difficulty of the work performed, and the qualifications required of incumbents. According to compensation experts George Milkovich and Jerry Newman;

> Classes can be conceived as a series of carefully labeled shelves on a bookshelf. The labels are the class descriptions which serve as the standard against which the job descriptions are compared. Each class is described in such a way that it captures sufficient work detail and yet is general enough to cause little difficulty in slotting jobs.[22]

No matter how lengthy and comprehensive the pay grade narratives, the placement of a specific position into a pay grade is often difficult. Two steps can be taken to make this process easier. First, it is essential that job descriptions be accurate and complete. Second, the slotting of jobs can be simplified by including benchmark jobs that fall into each class. **Benchmark jobs** are common across a number of different employers. Because the job content is relatively stable, external wage rates for these jobs are used for setting internal pay. Benchmark jobs can serve as reference points or judgment anchors against which the content of nonslotted jobs can be compared.

A particular advantage of the job classification method is that it can be applied to a large number and a wide variety of jobs. As the number and variety of jobs in an organization increase, however, the classification of jobs tends to become more subjective. This is particularly true when an organization has a large number of plant or office locations and, thus, jobs with the same title may differ in content. Because evaluating each job separately is difficult in such cases, the job title becomes a more important guide to job classification than job content.[23]

Factor comparison. Approximately ten percent of employers evaluate jobs using the factor comparison approach. This approach to job evaluation represents a significant change from ranking and classification because compensable factors are utilized to determine job worth. **Compensable factors** are job attributes that provide the basis for evaluating the relative worth of jobs inside the organization. While organizations differ in their choices, compensable factors should be work related and acceptable to all stakeholders in the compensation process. Factor comparison differs from other job evaluation processes because it systematically links external market rates of pay with internal, work-related compensable factors.

To begin the process, define the compensable factors. Then, choose benchmark jobs, as discussed above. Use a compensation committee to allocate wage rates for each benchmark job to each compensable factor. As shown in exhibit 9.5 the $12 salary for drill press operator equals $3 for skill, $3 for effort, $4 for responsibility, and $2 for working conditions. After all benchmark jobs are slotted across compensable factors, determine the rate of pay for nonbenchmark jobs. To do this, compare jobs against each benchmark job to determine whether they are of greater or lesser value. Total wage for the nonbenchmark jobs is the sum of slotted wages across all compensable factors.

Although the factor comparison method is a quick way to set wage rates, it has the potential to perpetuate traditional pay differentials between jobs because the wage rates for other jobs are determined against externally anchored pay rates. Another concern is that the relationship among jobs may change as external rates of pay shift for benchmark jobs. In spite of these limitations, the factor comparison method of job evaluation is a definite improvement over ranking and classification.

Point rating method. The most widely used method of job evaluation is point rating or the point factor method. This consists of assigning point values for previously determined compensable factors and then adding them to arrive at the overall worth of the job. Compensable factors may be adapted from existing point evaluation plans or may be custom designed to reflect the unique values of an organization. Regardless how they originate, factors should be **weighted** relative to their importance. For example, a research and development firm may assign more points to education and experience factors than a

Exhibit 9.5

Factor Comparison Ratings for Benchmark Positions in a Small-Batch Manufacturing Facility

Pay/Hour	Skill	Effort	Responsibility	Working Conditions
$5.25	Parts Insp.			
5.00				
4.75				
4.50	Crane Opr.			Com. Labor
4.25		Com. Labor	Crane Opr.	
4.00			Drill/Press	
3.75		Crane Opr.		
3.50		Parts Insp.	Parts Insp.	
3.25		Riveter		
3.00	Drill/Press	Drill/Press		Watchman
2.75		Watchman		Crane Opr.
2.50				
2.25	Riveter			Riveter
2.00				Drill/Press
1.75			Watchman	
1.50				Parts Insp.
1.25	Watchman		Riveter	
1.00	Com. Labor		Com. Labor	
.75				
.50				
.25				

manufacturing facility would assign. Conversely, the manufacturing facility may assign more points to a working conditions factor than would an accounting firm. The point evaluation system presented in exhibit 9.6 has six compensable factors. The total number of points in this system is 1000 (sum of highest degree points), which represents the maximum points that can be allocated to any job being evaluated. The minimum number of points is 225 (sum of lowest degree points). This system places a premium on problem solving—260 points maximum—followed by impact (profits generated or lost) at an assigned 240 points maximum. By comparison, the working conditions factor was weighted at only 50 points.

Once factors are chosen and weighted, the next step is to construct scales reflecting the different degrees within each factor. Exhibit 9.7 shows descriptions for five degrees of the problem-solving factor mentioned above. Notice that each degree is anchored by a description of the typical tasks and behaviors associated with that degree. Once factors and underlying degrees are delineated, a job's worth can be assessed. Typically, a compensation committee is chosen to assess job worth. The committee includes a cross section of stakeholders (e.g., management, union, hourly workers, various job families) who are trained in the use of the job evaluation process. They independently evaluate each job and then come together to discuss their evaluations. Debate continues until consensus is reached on the value of each job.

As with other job evaluation plans, the point factor method incorporates the potential subjectivity of the job analyst. As such, it has the potential for wage dis-

Exhibit 9.6
Sample Point Evaluation System

Compensable Factor	First Degree	Second Degree	Third Degree	Fourth Degree	Fifth Degree
1. Job Knowledge	50	100	150	200	
2. Problem Solving	50	100	150	205	260
3. Impact	60	120	180	240	
4. Working conditions	10	30	50		
5. Supervision needed	25	50	75	100	
6. Supervision given	30	60	90	120	150

crimination. Bias or subjectivity can enter (1) in the selection of the compensable factors, (2) in the assignment of relative weights (degrees) to factors, and (3) in the assignment of degrees to the jobs being evaluated. At stake here are equal pay and job comparability. To make sure its point factor evaluation system is free from potential bias and is implemented as objectively as possible, an organization may solicit the input of the job incumbent, the supervisor, and job evaluation experts, as well as the staff of its personnel department.[24]

Hay Guide Chart-Profile Method. One of the most widely used job evaluation systems in the world combines the best characteristics of the point evaluation and factor comparison methods of job evaluation. Used by more than 5,000 employers worldwide (130 of the 500 largest U.S. corporations), the Hay Guide Chart-Profile is particularly popular for evaluating executive, managerial, and professional positions, but is also widely used for many others including technical, clerical, and manufacturing positions.

Operationally, the Hay system relies on three primary compensable factors—problem solving, know-how, and accountability (see exhibit 9.8 for definitions). Point values are determined for each job, using the three factors and their subfactors. Additionally, jobs are compared to one another on the basis of each factor. The former approach parallels traditional point evaluation processes, and the latter parallels factor comparison methods.

According to Hay Associates, a major advantage of its system centers on its wide acceptance. Because organizations worldwide use the system, Hay can provide clients with comparative pay data by industry or locale. Another advantage of the system is that it has been legally challenged and found acceptable by the courts.

Still, the Hay Guide Chart-Profile Method, like any "canned" or standardized system, may not reflect an organization's true values. Thus, an organization needs to consider whether the Hay system's problem-solving, know-how, and accountability factors are truly congruent with the firm's values. For example, when the Hay system is used to evaluate the job of an airline pilot, the pilot's job usually receives between 289 and 333 points (the point range typically associated with a first-line supervisor). The problem is that pilots with major airlines often make six-figure salaries, but no first-line supervisors make comparable salaries. A better way to evaluate airline jobs is to specifically design a job evaluation for such jobs. This can be done by selecting compensable factors that are appropriate for an airline and weighting the factors in a way that is appropriate to the specific application.[25]

Skill-Based Job Evaluation

A growing number of organizations, academics, and consultants assert that the conventional job evaluation processes delineated above are easily abused and ill-suited to the needs of today's organizations. Critics contend that conventional job-based evaluation approaches

- Support rigid hierarchical organizations that suppress employee motivation and creativity
- Assume that people are commodities who can be made to "fit" defined roles
- Are inappropriate in today's flatter organizations where small, flexible teams of multiskilled people make better economic sense than a larger number of single-skilled individuals
- Are inappropriate in the service sector, where future success lies in the knowledge workers possess rather than in the jobs they are assigned.[26]

Because of these concerns, companies such as Northern Telecom (described earlier), General Foods, General Motors, Honeywell, Mead Paper, Procter and Gamble, and Anheuser-Busch are implementing **skill-based pay** (alternatively called **pay-for-knowledge** or **multiskilled pay**) to gain a competitive advantage.

Skill-based pay (SBP) rewards employees for the range, depth, and types of skills they are capable of using. This is a very different philosophy from the conventional job-based approaches described above. It moves the compensation of workers toward the approaches used to evaluate many types of professionals. For example, research and development firms have used maturity curves since

Exhibit 9.7
Example of a Compensable Factor and Related Degree Statements

Problem solving:
This factor examines the types of problems dealt with in your job. Indicate the one level that is most representative of the majority of your job responsibilities.

Degree 1: Actions are performed in a set order per written or verbal instruction. Problems are referred to supervisor.

Degree 2: Solves routine problems and makes various choices regarding the order in which the work is performed within standard practices. May obtain information from varied sources.

Degree 3: Solves varied problems that require general knowledge of company policies and procedures applicable within area of responsibility. Decisions made based on a choice from established alternatives. Expected to act within standards and established procedures.

Degree 4: Requires analytical judgment, initiative, or innovation in dealing with complex problems or situations. Evaluation not easy because there is little precedent or information may be incomplete.

Degree 5: Plans, delegates, coordinates, and/or implements complex tasks involving new or constantly changing problems or situations. Involves the organization of new technologies or policies for programs or projects. Actions limited only by company policies and budgets.

Exhibit 9.8
Hay Compensable Factors

Mental Activity (Problem Solving)	Know-How	Accountability
The amount of original, self-starting thought required by the job for analysis, evaluation, creation, reasoning, and arriving at conclusions Mental Activity has two dimensions: ■ The degree of freedom with which the thinking process is used to achieve job objectives without the guidance of standards, precedents, or direction from others ■ The type of mental activity involved; the complexity, abstractness, or originality of thought required Mental Activity is expressed as a percentage of Know-How for the obvious reason that people think with what they know. The percentage judged to be correct for a job is applied to the Know-How point value; the result is the point value given to Mental Activity.	The sum total of all knowledge and skills, however acquired, needed for satisfactory job performance (evaluates the job, not the person) Know-How has three dimensions: ■ The amount of practical, specialized, or technical knowledge required ■ Breadth of management, or the ability to make many activities and functions work well together; the job of company president, for example, has greater breadth than that of a department supervisor ■ Requirement for skill in motivating people Using a chart, a number can be assigned to the level of Know-How needed in a job. This number—or point value—indicates the relative importance of Know-How in the job being evaluated.	The measured effect of the job on company goals Accountability has three dimensions: ■ Freedom to act, or relative presence of personal or procedural control and guidance; determined by answering the question, How much freedom has the job holder to act independently?—for example, a plant manager has more freedom than a supervisor under his or her control ■ Dollar magnitude, a measure of the sales, budget, dollar value of purchases, value added, or any other significant annual dollar figure related to the job ■ Impact of the job on dollar magnitude, a determination of whether the job has a primary effect on end results or has instead a sharing, contributory, or remote effect Accountability is given a point value independent of the other two factors.

NOTE: The total evaluation of any job is arrived at by adding the points (not shown here) for Mental Activity, Know-How, and Accountability.

the 1950s to evaluate the contribution of engineers and scientists. With the maturity curve method, a series of curves is developed to provide differing levels of worth for individuals with the same years of experience. The distribution of rates of pay within any one interval indicates the level of performance. The underlying principle for this approach to pay is that professionals with more experience and knowledge are more valuable to the organization. Similar approaches are used to pay elementary and secondary school teachers and apprentices in skilled crafts, who receive pay increments based on educational levels and seniority.

SBP is premised on the same assumption that a person who can do more things or knows more is of greater value and should be paid according to skill criteria, not according to job assignment. The important distinction between SBP and the maturity curve approach is that, with maturity curves, pay increases are usually given at particular time intervals. With SBP, they are given only after the worker has actively demonstrated the ability to perform specific competencies.

SBP systems also differ in a variety of ways from conventional job-based pay (JBP) evaluations. These differences are summarized in exhibit 9.9. Under JBP, an employee receives the pay that is attached to his or her job regardless of whether the employee ever develops the competencies to perform the job effectively. In SBP, base pay is not attached to the job per se. Employees must be certified as competent in the skills required for the job in order to receive a pay

Exhibit 9.9

Comparison of Skill-Based Pay Components with Conventional Job Evaluation

Component	Skill-Based Evaluation	Job-Based Evaluation
1. Determination of Job Worth	Tied to evaluation of skill blocks	Tied to evaluation of total job
2. Pricing	Difficult because the overall pay system is tied to the market	Easier because wages are tied to benchmark jobs in the labor market
3. Pay Ranges	Extremely broad; one pay range for entire cluster of skills	Variable depending on type of job and pay-grade width
4. Evaluation of Performance	Competency tests	Performance appraisal ratings
5. Salary Increases	Tied to skill acquisition as measured by competency testing	Tied to seniority, performance appraisal ratings, or actual output
6. Role of Training	Essential to attain job flexibility and pay increases for all employees	Necessitated by need rather than desire
7. Advancement Opportunities	Greater opportunities; anyone who passes competency test advances	Fewer opportunities; no advancement unless there is a job opening
8. Effect of Job Change	Pay remains constant unless skill proficiency increases	Pay changed immediately to level associated with new job
9. Pay Administration	Difficult because many aspects of pay plan (training, certification) demand attention	Contingent upon the complexity of job evaluation and pay allocation plan

SOURCE: Adapted from G. E. Ledford, "Three Case Studies on Skill-Based Pay: An Overview," *Compensation and Benefits Review* (Apr. 1990): 11–23; H. Tosi and L. Tosi "What Managers Need to Know about Knowledge-Based Pay," *Organizational Dynamics* (Winter, 1986).

increase. When an employee changes jobs under JBP, the employee's pay usually changes automatically and immediately to the level assigned to the job (to be discussed further in chapter 10). Pay changes are not automatic with SBP. The employee must demonstrate proficiency before receiving an increase. Traditionally, seniority or time in grade often plays a large role in JBP systems; more time in the job is assumed to correspond to greater value. With SBP, value is more closely aligned with skill than seniority. Skill-based pay also facilitates more rapid advancement than job-based pay. All employees, rather than just a few, are encouraged to attain the top rate in a SBP system.

Implementing a SBP program is also different from implementing conventional job evaluation systems. As described in the Northern Telecom example, the design of the SBP plan must develop a set of skill blocks, define progression paths through the skill blocks, and formulate maximum and minimum times that employees may remain in any particular skill block. Issues such as training and certification are more complex and much more important in SBP than in JBP. Finally, internal equity—the fairness of pay levels within the organization—is more important in SBP than it is in JBP. This is because pay for each step in the progression is set in relation to the pay of all other steps, not in relation to the external market rate for each pay grade.

While SBP is relatively new, preliminary research has identified a number of consequences of skill-based pay. First, SBP creates an environment that facilitates worker rotation. This may serve to reduce absenteeism and may ease job assignment pressures for management. Because workers are motivated to learn higher-level skill jobs, employees will likely be paid more than the job evaluation rate of a specific job to which he or she is assigned. However, overall compensation costs may be lower because of work force flexibility and higher productivity.[27]

Overall Assessment

The strengths and weaknesses of job evaluation to attain internal pay equity were recently summarized by Helen Murlis and David Fitt, directors of Hay Management Consultants. They contend that "job evaluation is not a wholly scientific process since it relies on evaluators making judgments about jobs based on facts presented to them. Once this reality is accepted, the true value of formal job evaluation can be seen for what it is: a means of improving objectivity and attaining perceptions of internal equity."[28]

The acid test of any scheme's validity is whether it produces results that are acceptable both to job holders and managers, and are perceived as fair and reasonable. Formal job evaluation schemes can contribute to this aim by providing a vehicle for genuine participation by managers, employees, or union representatives in the process and enabling the results to be communicated and justified to employees more rationally than can pay and job relationships determined solely by subjective management opinion.

EXTERNAL EQUITY: BUILDING A COMPETITIVE WAGE STRUCTURE

Whatever method is used to determine internal equity, the next step is to develop a wage structure or an order of pay rates for jobs or skill clusters in the organization. For the pay structure to be equitable, rates of pay must be internally consistent and comparable with those in the external market. Achieving both objectives involves several steps, including (1) conducting an external market wage survey, (2) setting the wage policy, and (3) developing a wage structure including ranges, flat rates, or incentives.

Conducting a Wage Survey

Whereas job evaluation helps ensure internal equity, wage surveys provide information to help ensure external equity. Both types of equity are important if an organization is to be successful in attracting, retaining, and motivating employees.[29]

In conducting a wage survey, an organization first needs to select appropriate benchmark jobs. Benchmark jobs should have relatively stable job content. They should also represent the entire job structure under study and, if at all possible, all functions. The point in using benchmark jobs is to anchor the comparisons in the external market with descriptions of similar work in the organization.

Next, the organization must define the relevant labor market for each benchmark job. Three factors are commonly used to determine the relevant market: the occupation or skill required, the geographic location (willingness to relocate or commute), and the other employers competing for labor. The relevant geographic labor market for a vice president of sales for Microsoft Corporation may be the entire U.S. By comparison, the relevant labor market for an accounts receivable clerk is the Greater Seattle area, because competent workers can be found in that limited geographic area. Once the labor market is defined for each benchmark job, survey data must be collected. In some cases, the company may conduct its own wage and salary survey; however, it is much less costly to purchase a survey from a consulting firm or to use public domain labor market data distributed by the U.S. Department of Labor.

After collecting appropriate wage and salary information, the external market pay policy line is determined by calculating the relationship between job points and market pay for the benchmark jobs. The equation below represents the external-pay-policy-line equation generated through linear regression:

External pay = $630 + $2 (points)

Using this equation, a receptionist job valued at 331 points would be worth $1,292.00 a month [$630 + $2 (331)]; a senior engineer position valued at 1,066 points would be worth $2,762.00 on the external market.

Deciding on a Pay Policy

Once an external pay policy line has been calculated, an organization has data sufficient to set its *own* pay policy line. Some of the factors that influence the choice of a pay policy include the pay rates paid by major competitors, the firm's profits or losses, surpluses or shortages of qualified workers, stage of firm development, strength of union demands, and organizational culture.[30]

Regardless of the potency of these factors, there are three prevalent pay-level policies. The rationale behind a **lead policy** is to maximize the ability to attract and retain quality employees and to minimize employee dissatisfaction with pay. A lead policy signals employees that they are valued by the firm. However, a concern is whether the additional pay actually attracts and retains the *best* or merely the *most* applicants. It is also uncertain how much a firm needs to lead others to gain a distinct competitive advantage. Finally, there is a tendency for pay rates of other firms to escalate and eventually match the leader's rate of pay.

By far the most common approach is to **match the competition.** While this approach does not give an employer a competitive advantage, it does ensure that the firm is not at a disadvantage. One way to maximize a match policy is to implement annual pay adjustments prior to major recruiting periods. By doing so, the organization essentially leads the market for the first half of the year and lags the market during the last half of the year.

The final approach is a **lag policy.** This approach may hinder a firm's ability to attract potential employees unless other factors (job security, benefits, locale, job content) compensate for the low pay.[31]

Regarding the effectiveness of these strategies for attracting applicants, there is little evidence to recommend one policy over another. The most important consideration is whether the pay policy is congruent with your HR strategy. For example, KSL Television in Salt Lake City, Utah, has a corporate objective of being a broadcast leader in the Intermountain West. In support of this objective, executives of the television station set their pay policy line at 1.05 percent of the market. According to Jean Bishop, vice-president of human resources,

> ...The cost of replacing and training a highly skilled engineer, a technical operator, or producer is substantial. We wanted to be proactive in our efforts to attract and retain these people. On the other hand, we didn't want to position our pay line higher than anticipated productivity increases would support. Therefore, leading the market by 5 percent was considered appropriate. It is high enough to signal our employees and competitors that we are a leader but not so high that our revenues can't support it.

By comparison, Luther Child Center, a not-for-profit agency in Everett, Washington, has set a goal of matching its competitors in pay and in benefits. "We were losing some of our best therapists to our competitors. When we conducted a market survey, we found that our compensation package was not competitive. While we'd like to be a pay leader, our funds are restricted, so we've settled on matching rates of pay," HR Director Janet Allen explained.

Developing a Pay Grade Structure

Once the firm's pay policy line has been set, a pay grade structure can be developed.

Job-based pay grade structure. Exhibit 9.10 shows a pay grade structure for a conventional job-based pay system. The boxes shown are associated with a spread of job evaluation points (the job class) and a range of pay (the pay grade).[32] In essence, several different jobs may be within one box, but they are similar in terms of job evaluation points, if not in content. The boxes may be the same size or vary in height but generally ascend from left to right. This reflects increased job worth and the association of higher pay levels (shown on the vertical axis) with more valued jobs. The pay levels are established using market information to help ensure external equity.

Exhibit 9.10
Graph for a Job-Based Wage Structure

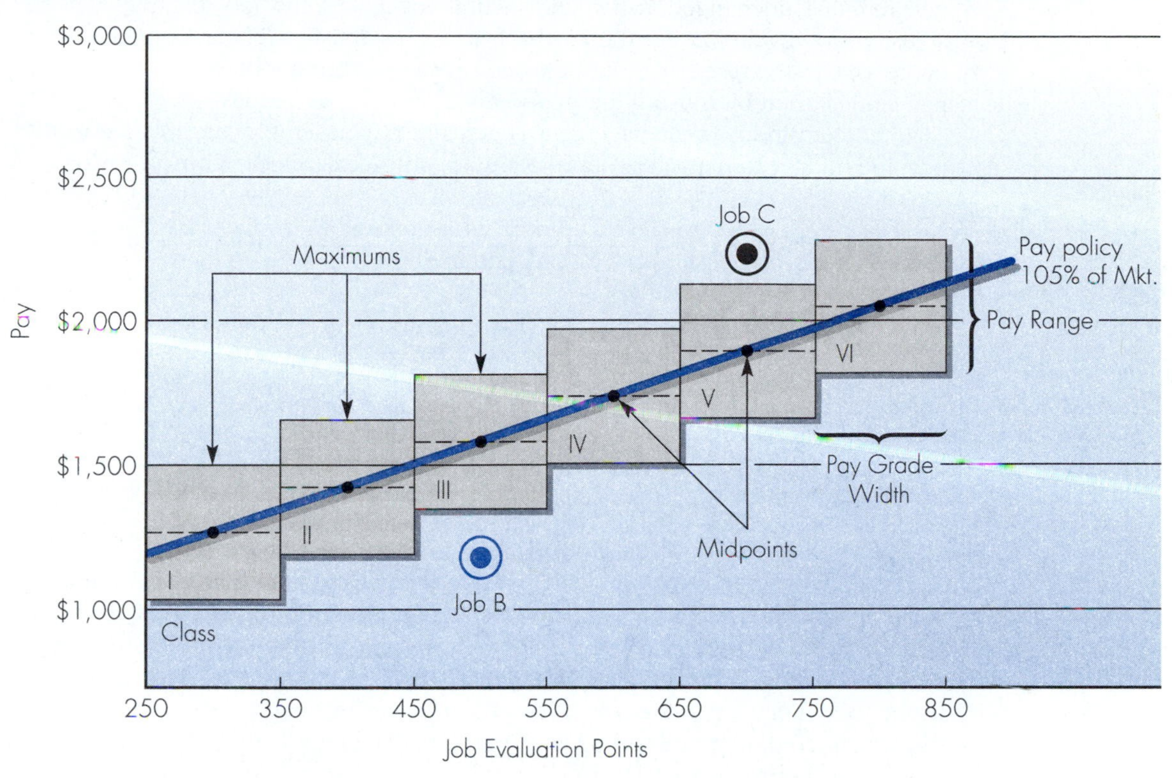

In establishing pay ranges, the corporate pay line generally serves as the pay grade midpoint. Pay grade maximums and minimums are generally set at a percentage above and below that amount. The difference between the two is the pay range. Some common ranges above and below pay grade midpoint include

- Nonexempt: Laborers and trades Up to 25%
- Nonexempt: Clerical, technical, paraprofessional 15–50%
- Exempt: First-level management; professionals 30–50%
- Exempt: Middle and senior management 40–100%

For the firm depicted in exhibit 9.10, six equal-interval pay grades were established; each has a **width** of 100 points. Each grade has a **pay range** of $500. For pay grade II, the range goes from $1,125 (minimum) to $1,625 (maximum) a month; the midpoint is $1,375 a month. For pay grade VI (750 to 850 points), the minimum pay is $1,750 a month and the maximum is $2,225, with a midpoint of $2,000 a month.

Occasionally, jobs fall outside the established pay grades (Jobs B and C in exhibit 9.10). When a job falls *below* the established pay grade (Job B in pay grade III), it is *blue circled*, and usually a wage adjustment (sweetener) is made to bring the job within the established pay grade. Sometimes, though, a job will be overpaid (Job C in pay grade V). One means of dealing with this is to *red circle* the job. That is as long as the current incumbent remains in the job, the pay rate remains unchanged; when the incumbent leaves the job, the rate will be adjusted downward to put the job back in the established grade. Sometimes the entire salary structure has to be adjusted upward to bring jobs within established pay grades, thereby moving the midpoints up for all pay grades.

To determine how management is actually paying employees relative to the pay line midpoint, managers often rely upon an index called a **compa-ratio:**

$$\text{Compa-ratio} = \frac{\text{Average rate of pay for employees in pay class}}{\text{Range midpoint}}$$

A compa-ratio of less than 1.00 means that, on average, employees in the pay grade are being paid below the midpoint. Translated, this means that managers are paying below the intended policy. One valid reason may be that employees are newly hired or poor performers. Alternatively, employees could be promoted so rapidly that they don't reach the upper half of the pay range. A compa-ratio greater than 1.00 means the organization is paying more than the stated policy on average.

Pay grades for skill-based pay. The establishment of external equity is more complex with skill-based pay systems than with job-based pay systems. As experienced at Northern Telecom, it simply was not possible to compare directly any particular pay levels in the firm's SBP plan with pay levels of other firms using JBP. While organizations using SBP rely on the market to set pay levels, the data is used to set minimum, maximum, and average pay levels for the *entire job family*, not to peg each particular skill step in the pay system to jobs found in the outside markets. Exhibit 9.11 depicts the salary guidelines for Northern Telecom's field technician job family. Notice there are five competency levels with an overall pay range of 270 percent. Target high rates are suggested maximum rates of pay for employees at a specific competency level.

As with JBP, organizations employing SBP differ in their pay policies relative to the external market. According to Peter LeBlanc, director of compensation, Northern Telecom matched the market by setting the minimum of the salary range at the labor market entry rate. The maximum was established on the basis of the average rate of pay for the senior job in the firm's traditional benchmark ladder.

HR officials at a Honeywell, Inc., ammunitions plant in Joliet, Illinois, adopted a different policy. Traditionally, the ammunition industry has been a low-wage industry. However, average wages in the local area of the Honeywell plant were relatively high, due partly to the number of unionized, industrial plants in the region. According to HR manager William Tyler, "This meant that paying wages that were competitive in the local labor market risked making the organization uncompetitive in its business market." SBP was viewed as a way out of this pricing nightmare. Entry wages were pegged at a rate that was low for the area but competitive within the industry. Pay rates rose sharply as employees reached higher skill levels. That is, each new skill was worth an additional 90¢ an hour. With a total of five levels, this produced a pay range of $4.50. According to Tyler, Level 3 was pegged at slightly above the area average, and Level 4

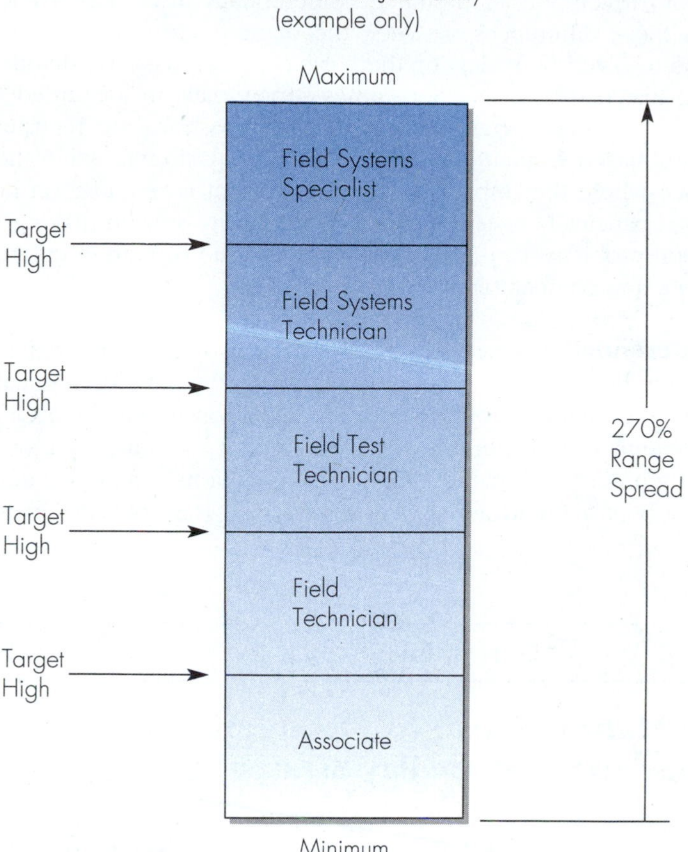

Exhibit 9.11
Salary Administration Guidelines for a Sample Skill-Based Pay Job Family

was priced at well above the area average. Company officials believed that, by the time employees reached Level 4, employees would be so productive that the facility could afford to pay them at a high rate.[33]

ADMINISTRATIVE CONTROL: BALANCING INTERNAL AND EXTERNAL EQUITY

Among the several contemporary issues in wage and salary administration, four are of particular importance. (1) How can differences in the order in which jobs are ranked on internal (job evaluation) and external (wage surveys) factors be reconciled if they do not agree? (2) To what extent should employees be able to participate in determining job value? (3) What are the advantages and disadvantages of pay secrecy? (4) What is needed for employees to be satisfied with their pay?

Reconciling Internal and External Equity Imbalances

As discussed in this chapter's Focus on Research, external and internal data as well as a firm's compensation strategy differentially affect job worth decisions. Sometimes these differences between the market rate and the job evaluation rank can be resolved by reviewing the basic decisions associated with evaluating and pricing that particular job. Sometimes survey data are discarded; sometimes benchmark job matches are changed. Other times, jobs are reevaluated using point or skill-based evaluations. Often, this reanalysis will solve the problem; but, in cases where the disparity persists, judgment is required on how best to resolve discrepancies between market and internal worth. In making these decisions, several problems can arise including the issue of market differentials, pay compression, and comparable worth.

Pay differentials. One way the discrepancy between internal and external pay equity can be resolved is to establish temporary market differentials.

Consider the dilemma confronting KSL Television in Salt Lake City, Utah. To resolve problems of pay inequity, the broadcast firm conducted a job evaluation study and then collected market data for key positions. The job evaluation positioned the job of a broadcast engineer technician (624 of 1,200 points) in pay

FOCUS ON RESEARCH

What Matters Most: Job Evaluation, Wage Surveys, or Pay Strategy?

Researchers have long recognized the existence of large differentials in pay for the same job, even in a single local labor market. While the magnitude of interfirm differentials for the same job title—as much as 300 percent—make it unlikely that the difference in pay is due to job content alone, the causes of these differentials have not been well understood. This is a serious omission in our knowledge of compensation, because job pay decisions are critical strategic concerns affecting whether firms will lead, lag, or match the market, whether pay structures will be steep or flat, whether particular jobs will receive unique compensation treatment and whether internal or external considerations will drive job rates.

To better understand the sources of pay differentials, researchers Carolyn Weber and Sara Rynes examined how compensation managers from a wide variety of industries determine pay rates for jobs. A policy capturing approach was utilized in which 411 trained compensation analysts were provided simulated information about current job pay, market survey rates and job evaluation results. The analysts were instructed to assign new pay rates in dollars per month to nine jobs on the basis of the following pieces of information: job title and description, current pay rate, median market survey rate and job valuation points. The primary objective of the study was to determine how compensation managers make job pay decisions when alternative sources of information about job worth suggest different outcomes. To make the simulation realistic, conflicting information was built into the simulation via the market survey and job evaluation data. Both stimuli were varied in terms of whether the data indicated the job to be priced was over or under valued. The compensation experts were told to evaluate the nine jobs "according to the same priorities that would be used in their own organization." Information was also collected on whether the firms which employed the compensation analysts tried to meet, lead or follow the market and whether they were unionized.

Consistent with expectation, both job evaluation (internal equity) and market survey information (exter-

Continued

grade VI. The pay range for this grade was set at $20,000 to $26,000, well below the average rate of pay of $28,900 in the external market. This discrepancy persisted even following a check of the job evaluation and wage survey data. Because engineers with broadcast experience are difficult to find, KSL executives considered reassigning the job to a higher pay grade. (They'd done this in the past.) While this would provide a "quick fix," the long-term consequences—particularly if other employees found out about the reclassification—could be disastrous, threatening the validity of the entire pay compensation system. To preserve the integrity of the system while meeting market demands, KSL left engineering jobs in appropriate grades but paid a market differential. As long as the external market rate of pay was higher than the station's policy line, engineers would receive a $2,900 market differential; when the labor market imbalance corrected itself, the differential would be eliminated.

Pay compression. Pay compression is a second potential consequence of internal and external imbalances. Compression results when wages for those jobs filled from outside the organization are increasing faster than the wages for jobs filled from within the organization. As a result, pay differentials among jobs become very small, and the traditional pay structure becomes compressed. Consider the dilemma faced by fast food restaurants who traditionally pay wages at

nal equity) figured prominently in compensation managers' job pay decisions. However, compensation managers relied *more* on market information than the job evaluation information. According to the researchers, most employers do not openly communicate the details of their job evaluation ratings, thus employees are more likely to know about market rates than job evaluation rates. Hence, they are more sensitive to deviations from market practices than job evaluation results. Still, the preeminence of market rates in setting job pay is problematic for those who advocate the use of job evaluation to attain pay equity.

An organization's pay strategy also played a prominent role in the setting of wages in two ways. Managers from market leading firms and internally oriented firms assigned significantly *higher* pay levels to jobs than those from market meeting and externally oriented firms. Put another way, internally oriented respondents were distinguished more by their reluctance to act on market data than by any tendency to place greater emphasis on job evaluation.

There was also evidence that pay policies vary by industry. Public utilities and services were less likely to report external orientations than were diversified and multiple classification organizations. The researchers also found that unionized organizations were more likely to be pay leaders and expanding organizations were more likely to be laggers or meeters than market leaders. Public sector compensation managers were more likely to be market followers. Unionization also affected pay policies. That is, unionization was associated with market leadership pay strategies. Still, these organizational variables affected assigned pay levels *less* than pay strategies themselves.

Weber and Rynes concluded that most compensation is administered in such a way that decisions about job pay (internal and external equity) precede and hence severely constrain decisions about individual pay (employee equity). While some experts have suggested that the whole notion of paying for jobs is fast becoming obsolete, the persistence of basic job pay-setting techniques in the face of vast changes in labor and product market conditions suggests that job pay decisions are likely to remain important determinants of individual earnings for some time to come.

SOURCE: Based on C. Weber and S.L. Rynes, "Effects of Compensation Strategy on Job Pay Decisions," *Academy of Management Journal* 34 (1991), 86–109.

or near the minimum wage. When Congress increased the minimum wage to $4.25 in 1991, these firms had to decide whether to shift the entire wage structure upward in order to maintain differentials or to allow pay differences to narrow. Compression is also an issue in professional work (engineers, lawyers, professors) where new graduates command salaries equal to or above those of professionals with more experience.

Comparable worth. The continuing debate over comparable worth also is related to internal-external equity differences. A general definition of comparable worth is that jobs should be paid commensurate with their "value." While this definition seems innocuous, debate over the issue has raged in the U.S. since World War II and reached a head in the 1980s as attempts were made to change provisions of the Equal Pay Act. Pivotal to the debate are two questions:

1. Who determines the worth of jobs (e.g. government, labor market, management, courts)?
2. What criterion of value (job evaluation or labor market) should be used to determine the worth of jobs?

Comparable worth theory contends that, while the true worth of jobs may be similar, some jobs (often held by women) are paid at a lower rate than others (often held by men). Since the resulting differences in pay are disproportionate to the differences in the true worth of jobs, this practice amounts to wage discrimination. Consequently, legal protection under the Equal Pay Act (discussed in-depth in chapter 3 and earlier in this chapter) can be demonstrated. This interpretation of pay equity goes beyond the intent of the Equal Pay Act. In the final argument prior to passage, the legislature actually substituted "equal" pay for "comparable" because the former would invite too broad an interpretation of the act.[34]

The key to attaining comparable worth is to use a single job evaluation plan to evaluate the worth of all jobs within a unit. Jobs may differ in their rankings for specific compensable factors. However, if total points are equal, wage rates must also be equal. Also, the wage-to-job evaluation point ratio should be based on wages paid to male-dominated jobs rather than to female-dominated jobs; typically, male-dominated job wages are higher.

While comparable worth is not the rule of the land in the U.S., the concept has been around for some time internationally.[35]

> With all the sound and fury about comparable worth—the idea that men and women should get paid the same for work of equal value even if their jobs are different—it's easy to get the impression that the idea is both recent and uniquely American. But the truth is, it's neither.
>
> The International Labor Organization, the Geneva-based U.N. specialized agency the U.S. joined in 1934, adopted an international convention on comparable worth almost 35 years ago. And what the ILO's experience shows is that while comparable worth may have helped reduce the gap between male and female wages in some countries that have tried it, it hasn't eliminated that gap. But neither has it led to the major economic or bureaucratic headaches that its critics prophesy.
>
> In 1951 the ILO adopted Convention No. 100 requiring "equal remuneration for men and women workers for work of equal value." Governments that ratify the convention must promote "objective appraisal of jobs" whenever that would help assure equal pay for different jobs having equal value.

> Since its adoption, more than 100 governments—but not ... the U.S.—have ratified the convention. These include most of the nations of Western Europe, Canada, Australia, New Zealand, Japan, virtually all of the [former] Soviet bloc, and more than 70 developing countries.[36]

In the province of Ontario, Canada, the Pay Equity Act of 1987 is currently being phased into practice (1990–1994). What distinguishes this law from earlier laws is its proactive imposition of comparable worth wage scales on the private sector. Less obvious, but of equal importance, is its focus on jobs as opposed to individual employees. The valuations and comparison called for by the statute pertain to job classes, not workers themselves. Therefore, the workers who stand to benefit are those employed in female-dominated job classes which are underpaid in comparison with comparable male-dominated job classes.

In terms of implementation, T. Eaton Company has 15,000 employees in 580 jobs and has traditionally used three different job evaluation systems. To comply with the new legislation, the firm switched to a single computer-scored job evaluation process. According to William F. Robinson, compensation manager, the result will cost the company quite a few million dollars annually in equity adjustments, but the switch has increased internal communication and identified compensation inequities that had gone undetected in the past.[37] This chapter's PHRM in the News: "Achieving Pay Equity" details the issues associated with attaining pay equity.

Participation Policies

Job evaluation judgments, like other human resource decisions, can be made by a variety of raters including compensation professionals, managers, and job incumbents. An important decision is who should be involved in the development of a job evaluation system and in the determination of job worth.

Traditionally, compensation professionals and managers had the most involvement in the design of compensation systems. Recently, however, there has been an emphasis on employee involvement in job evaluation. For example, sixty-four percent of all labor agreements require incumbent involvement. Employee participation in job evaluation also is a key feature of what is called "new pay." New pay gives employees ownership over their work outcomes. For example, the Polaroid Corporation, having established its policy of openness, involves employees in making salary decisions. Employees are also involved in the job evaluation process to get a broad understanding of the process by which job value is established.

One of the most common ways to increase involvement is to establish a job evaluation committee composed of management, nonmanagement, and union representatives. Individuals on such a committee should be knowledgeable about a wide range of jobs. It may also be useful to co-op antagonists. Involving representatives from all areas improves communication, and increases the likelihood that the organization's values are reflected in the job evaluation system. The involvement of multiple parties does, however, increase the potential for conflict. For example, managers may try to distort job evaluation ratings of a favorite or superstar employee so that pay can exceed the maximum permitted for a job of that value. Conversely, compensation professionals will want to preserve pay equity at all costs. However, managers and employees are less likely to accept the results of a job evaluation study when they were not consulted.

PHRM IN THE NEWS

Achieving Pay Equity: Not Simple, but Not so Costly

Pay equity is a policy that provides businesses the competitive edge to meet the challenges of the next century, declares the National Committee on Pay Equity. A consistent, fair pay policy whereby all workers are paid equally for work of equal value produces a more productive and better-motivated workforce, which, in turn, promotes recruitment and retention of good workers....

"Smart employers recognize that future profits depend on current investment in their most vital resource: their people," ... says the coalition of labor, women's, and civil rights groups in its report, "Pay Equity Makes Good Business Sense."

Women and men of color are concentrated in lower-paying jobs. Additionally, when women and men of color occupy traditionally white-male-dominated positions—even after accounting for legitimate reasons for pay differences such as differing skills, work experience and seniority—women and men of color are still paid less, contends the pay equity committee's publication.

On the basis of every dollar paid to white men in 1988, white women were paid 65 cents, black women were paid 61 cents, and Hispanic women were paid 55 cents, the report notes. Black men were paid 75 cents and Hispanic men were paid 65 cents for every dollar paid to white men.

Discriminatory wage practices account for between one quarter and one half of this disparity in wages, says the report.

What Is Pay Equity?

Pay equity, also known in the U.S., Canada, and Europe as equal pay for work of equal value, is broader than "equal pay for equal work." Pay equity is a means of eliminating race, ethnicity, and gender as wage determinants within job categories and between job categories, the report says.

Many businesses pay women and men of color less than white males. This result is often unintentional and due in part because personnel systems and wage structures retain historical biases and inconsistencies that are, in fact, discriminatory, explains the report.

A pay equity policy examines existing pay policies that underpay women and men of color and activates steps to correct the discrimination.

How to Achieve Pay Equity

A comprehensive audit is the first step in implementing a pay equity policy, explains the committee's report. The audit should examine the following areas for inequities and needed changes:

- Job evaluation;
- Market pricing;
- Pay administration; and
- Recruitment.

In the area of pay administration, the audit should scrutinize each individual component of a business's system including: salary range design, salary grades, pay differentials, and the determination of hiring rates. Additional items to be examined for inequities include promotion rates, merit increases, incentive programs, and performance and seniority factors in the pay system.

Pay Equity Is Not Costly

Following the lead of public employers, many private sector businesses are already incorporating pay equity analyses in their annual budget proposals. "The cost of pay equity adjustments," reports the committee, usually has been "between 2 and 5 percent of payroll."

In no cases have the wages of any workers been lowered in order to achieve pay equity, reports the committee, because the objective of pay equity is to remedy wage inequities for underpaid workers, not to penalize another group of employees.

SOURCE: "Pay Equity Makes Good Business Sense," National Committee on Pay Equity, 1201 Sixteenth Street N.W., Suite 420, Washington DC 20036. Reprinted by permission.

In addition to involving employees in the development of a job evaluation system and the determination of job worth, a newer method of employee participation allows employees to set their own wage rates. One way of doing this is to let employees vote on who should get a raise. At Romac, a pipe-fitting plant, employees request their pay raises by completing a form that includes information about their current pay level, previous raise, raise requested, and reasons they think a raise is deserved. The employee then "goes on board." His or her name, hourly wage, and photograph are posted for six consecutive working days. The employees then vote, and the majority rules. Although top-level managers can't vote, they can veto a raise. This, however, hasn't happened yet because management has learned that employees can responsibly set their own wages if they trust management and have a sufficient understanding of the "cost of doing business."[38]

Pay Secrecy

According to organizational etiquette, asking others their salaries is generally considered gauche. In a study of E.I. du Pont de Nemours, all employees were asked if the company should disclose more payroll information so everyone would know everyone else's pay. Only 18 percent voted for an open pay system. Managers also favor pay secrecy because it makes their lives easier. Without knowledge of pay differentials, employees are less likely to confront their supervisor about inequitable pay. Consequently, managers do not have to defend or justify their actions.[39]

Despite these common perceptions, there are several reasons *for* open communication about pay practices. First, some research indicates that employees misperceive the pay levels of other employees. They tend to overestimate the pay of those with lower-level jobs and to underestimate the pay of those with higher-level jobs. Because pay differentials are designed to motivate employees to seek promotion, this misperception may be detrimental to employee motivation. After all, why should an employee in training gain experience and accept greater responsibility for meager increases?

A second, more practical reason for an open pay policy is that considerable resources have been devoted to developing a fair and equitable system. For managers and employees to gain an accurate view of the system, they must be informed.

Finally, and potentially most important, pay is a powerful motivator only when its linkage to performance is explicitly stated and known to employees. For an employee to perform well, he or she must know what performance is desired, what will be the reward for performing well, and what is the consequence for performing poorly.

Regarding what should be communicated, many employers specify the range for an incumbent's job and other jobs in a typical career path. In addition to ranges, some organizations detail the typical increases associated with low, average, and top performance. A concern in communicating the latter is that the organization may not be able to maintain the same pay schedule in the future. If increases are lower in subsequent years, some employees may be dissatisfied. Still, if it is made clear that the size of the bonus pool is contingent on the profitability of the organization, this problem can be avoided.

Satisfaction with Pay

If organizations want to minimize absenteeism and turnover through compensation, they must make sure employees are satisfied with their pay. Because satisfaction with pay and motivation to perform are not necessarily highly related, organizations must know the determinants of pay satisfaction. With this knowledge, organizations can develop pay practices more likely to result in satisfaction with pay. Three major determinants of satisfaction with pay are pay fairness, pay level, and pay administration practices.[40]

Pay fairness. Pay fairness refers to what people believe they deserve to be paid in relation to what others deserve to be paid. The tendency is for people to determine what they and others deserve to be paid by comparing what they give to the organization with what they get out of the organization. In comparing themselves with others, people may decide whether they are being paid fairly. If they regard this comparison as fair or equitable, they are more likely to be satisfied. If they see this comparison as unfair, they are likely to be dissatisfied.

Fairness can also be increased by providing "voice" and due process to employees. Thus it is important for organizations to establish **formal appeals procedures.** These appeals procedures vary in the degree of formality and in how independent the process is from traditional lines of authority. Union contracts often prescribe a formal system in which complaints are first filed with the immediate supervisor. If a satisfactory resolution is not attained, the appeal moves forward to a higher level of management. IBM has an open-door policy in which employees are free to write to *any* manager, including the CEO. Each letter is answered personally.

Pay level. Pay level is an important determinant of pay satisfaction. People compare their pay level with what they believe they should receive. The result of the comparison is satisfaction with pay if the "should" level of pay equals the actual level of pay. Pay dissatisfaction results if the actual level is less than the "should" level.

Increasingly, pay-level satisfaction is being related to differences in pay levels for employees at different levels in the organization. A study of 216 firms by consultants Sibson and Co. showed that total compensation for top executives increased 9.5 percent in 1989 while pay gains for workers lagged behind inflation.[41] This disparity in wages is summarized in exhibit 9.12. Observes David Sirota, chairman of the corporate polling firm Sirota and Alper,

> CEOs say "We're a team. We're all in this together, rah, rah, rah." But employees look at the differences between their pay and the CEO's. They see top management's perks—oak dining rooms and heated garages, vs. cafeterias for the hourly guys and parking spaces half a mile from the plant. And they wonder: "Is this togetherness?"[42]

As the disparity in pay levels widens between top management and everyone else, the wonder grows.

Pay administration practices. What does the preceding discussion suggest for pay administration practices? First, if the employer is to attract new employees and keep them satisfied with their pay, the wages and salaries offered should approximate the wages and salaries paid to other employees in comparable organizations (i.e., external equity must exist).

Second, the pricing of jobs can enhance pay satisfaction when it is perceived as embodying a philosophy of equal work or equal pay for jobs of comparable worth. The determination of equal pay for equally valued work can be aided by sound job evaluations.

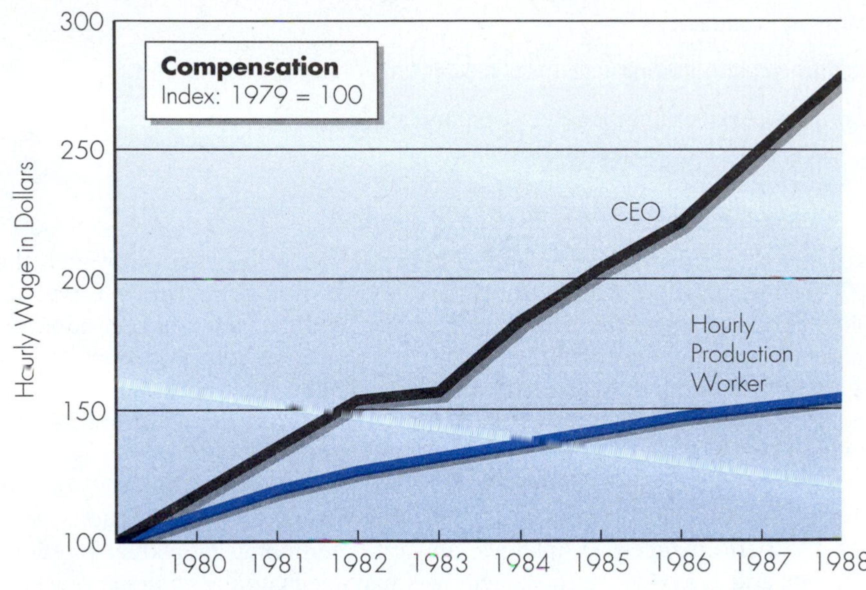

Exhibit 9.12
Comparison of Increases in CEO Pay to Pay of Hourly Workers

SOURCE: A. Farnham, "The Trust Gap," *Fortune* (4 Dec. 1989), 56.

Third, pay-for-performance systems must be accompanied by a method for accurately measuring the performance of employees and must be open enough so employees can clearly see the performance-pay relationship. This is discussed further in chapter 10.

Fourth, compensation rates and pay structures should be continually reviewed and updated if necessary. Over time, the content of a job may increase or decrease, thus distorting the relationship between its true worth and its job-evaluated worth.

A final pay administration practice involves maintaining trust and consistency. Employees must perceive that the organization is looking out for their interests as well as its own. Without trust and consistency, pay satisfaction is low, and pay becomes a target for complaints regardless of the real issues.

FOCUS ISSUES IN TOTAL COMPENSATION

Compensation is a dynamic, challenging, and exciting personnel and human resource activity. It is also a valuable activity for positively influencing the bottom line of organizations, as illustrated by the following description of two trends in compensation. Chapters 10 and 11 provide further descriptions of compensation trends.

Assessment

The effectiveness of total compensation should be assessed against a program's objectives.

- Attract potentially qualified employees
- Motivate employees
- Retain qualified employees
- Administer pay within legal constraints
- Facilitate organizational strategic objectives
- Reinforce and define structure

To achieve these purposes, employees generally need to be satisfied with their pay. This means the organization's pay levels should be competitive, that employees should perceive internal pay equity, and that the compensation program should be properly administered.[43] It also means compensation practices must adhere to the various state and federal wage and hour laws. It suggests that the notion of comparable worth should be considered in pay administration practices. Consequently, an organization's total compensation can be assessed by comparing its pay levels with those of other organizations, by analyzing the validity of its job evaluation method, by measuring employee perceptions of pay equity and performance-pay linkages, and by determining individual pay levels within jobs and across jobs. These activities may facilitate the strategic objectives of an organization.

Attracting, motivating, and retaining employees are worthy purposes of total compensation and can facilitate organizational objectives. Attaining them at a lower rather than higher cost of total compensation also can facilitate an organization's strategic objectives. This can be done by replacing nondeductible pay expenditures (e.g., expensive perquisites such as cars and club memberships) with deductible pay expenditures, such as contributions to employee stock ownership plans. This replacement must be done with consideration for the differential impact of alternative pay expenditures on attracting, motivating, and retaining employees. These differentials being relatively minimal, replacing nondeductible forms of compensation with deductible forms can increase the effectiveness of the total compensation dollar.

Total compensation is composed of base pay, performance-based pay, and indirect pay, so the discussion here represents only the first part of the total assessment. Chapters 10 and 11 cover the other two parts necessary for total assessment.

Computer Technology and HRIS

Computer technology combined with compensation data in an HRIS can be instrumental in managing total compensation and ensuring equity. The four components of total compensation are direct monetary, indirect monetary, direct nonmonetary, and indirect nonmonetary rewards (see exhibit 9.1). In ledger format, human resource specialists can maintain the value (cost) of total compensation in several configurations. For example, total compensation can be computed for each employee and the average for each position, or department. In addition, specific components of total compensation can be calculated and used for projecting and establishing salary and benefits budgets for appropriate organizational units. In conjunction with job evaluation, the human resource department can determine whether compensable factors are being assigned monetary values systematically or randomly. This may serve as an initial step in minimizing inequitable compensation.

Performance appraisal information is closely related to the compensation activity. Based on a particular performance rating, an individual receives a salary increase. Computer technology can link the HR department with other departments to facilitate projecting departmental salary budgets. By having each department manager submit projected performance ratings for each employee, the human resource department can use the computer to project anticipated salary increases associated with performance (assuming salary increases are a function of performance ratings). The HR department can also estimate salary increases that can be paid upon various proposed salary budget increases.

INTERNATIONAL ASPECTS OF TOTAL COMPENSATION

As the environment for many business firms in the U.S. becomes more global, international compensation becomes a more significant factor in total compensation.[44]

Objectives of International Compensation

When developing international compensation policies, a multinational corporation (MNC) seeks to satisfy several objectives. First, the policy should be consistent and fair in its treatment of all categories of international employees. The interests of the MNC are best served if all international employees are relatively satisfied with their compensation package and perceive that they are treated equitably. Second, the policy must work to attract and retain personnel in the areas where the MNC has the greatest needs and opportunities. Third, the policy should facilitate the transfer of international employees in the most cost-effective manner for the MNC. Fourth, the policy should be consistent with the overall strategy and structure of the MNC. Finally, compensation should serve to motivate employees. Some professional international HR managers would say that motivation is the major objective of their compensation programs.[45]

Compensation in Multinational Corporations (MNCs)

In general, the first issue facing MNCs when designing international compensation policies is whether to establish an overall policy for all employees or to distinguish between PCNs (parent country nationals) and TCNs (third country nationals). This differentiation may diminish in the future, but it is currently very common for MNCs to distinguish between these two distinct groups.

There is even a tendency for MNCs to differentiate among types of PCNs. Separate types of policies may be established based on the length of assignment (temporary transfer, permanent transfer, or continual relocation) or on the type of employee. Cash remuneration, special allowances, benefits, and pensions are determined in part by such classification. Short-term PCNs, for example, whose two- or three-year tours of duty abroad are interspersed with long periods at home, may be treated differently from career PCNs who spend most of their time working in various locations abroad. Both of these groups are different from TCNs, who often move from country to country in the employ of one MNC (or several) headquartered in a country other than their own (for example, a Swiss banker may be in charge of a German branch of a British bank). In effect, these are the real global employees, the ones who can weave together the far-flung parts of a MNC. As the global MNC increases in importance, it is likely that the TCNs will become more valuable and thus be able to command levels of compensation equivalent to PCNs.

For PCNs, the most widely used policy emphasizes "keeping the expatriate whole"—that is, maintaining salary level relative to the PCN's colleagues plus compensating for the costs of international service.[46] The basis of this policy implies that foreign assignees should not suffer a material loss due to their transfer. This can be accomplished through the utilization of what is known as the balance-sheet approach. The balance-sheet approach to international compensation is a system designed to equalize the purchasing power of employees at comparable position levels living overseas and in the home country, and to provide incentives to offset qualitative differences between assignment locations.[47]

Five major categories of outlays cover all of the types of expenses incurred by PCNs and their families.

1. *Goods and services:* Home-country outlays for items such as food, personal care, clothing, household furnishings, recreation, transportation, and medical care
2. *Housing:* The major costs associated with the employees' principal residence
3. *Income taxes:* Payments to federal and local governments for personal income taxes
4. *Reserve:* Contributions to savings, payments for benefits, pension contributions, investments, education expenses, social security taxes, etc.
5. *Shipment and storage:* The major costs associated with shipping and storing personal and household effects

Thus, MNCs seek to develop international packages that are competitive in all of the following aspects of compensation:

Base Salary

- Home rate/home currency
- Local rate/local currency
- Salary adjustments or promotions—home or local standard
- Bonus—home or local currency, home or local standard
- Stock options
- Inducement payment/hardship premium—percent of salary or lump-sum payment, home or local currency
- Currency protection—discretion or split basis
- Global salary and performance structure

Taxation

- Tax protection

- Tax equalization
- Other services

Benefits

- Home-country program
- Local program
- Social security program
- Car

Allowances

- Cost-of-living allowances
- Housing standard
- Education
- Relocation
- Perquisites
- Home leave
- Shipping and storage

While all these aspects of international compensation are unlikely to come into play for every expatriate, expatriates are still rather expensive. Exhibit 9.13 shows a breakdown of just how expensive they can be. Thus, firms want to be global but face rather high compensation bills if they need to staff with expatriates. Some of these aspects of international compensation may not apply to TCNs or HCNs (host country nationals), but all do apply to PCNs.

To illustrate some of the issues MNCs face, consider the base salary decision. The term base salary acquires a somewhat different meaning when employees go abroad. At home, base salary denotes the amount of cash compensation that serves as a benchmark for other compensation elements (for example, bonuses and benefits). For PCNs, base salary is the primary component of a package of allowances, many of which are directly related to base salary (foreign service premium, cost-of-living allowances, housing allowances, and tax protection, for example) as well as the basis for in-service benefits and pension contributions.

When applied to TCNs, base salary may mean the prevailing rate paid for a specific skill in the employee's home country. Typically, companies use local compensation levels as guidelines when developing HCN compensation policies. Conditions that force compensation policies to differ from those in the U.S. include inflation and cost of living, housing, security, school costs, and taxation. For example, it is far less costly to recruit a construction engineer from Spain or Taiwan to work in the Middle East than from the United Kingdom or the U.S.

> More than half of American companies now tie base salaries to the home countries of the third-country national they employ, rather than to U.S. or host-country salary structures, according to a survey of 117 international companies by Organization Resources Counselors Inc. The number of companies doing this has risen from 38% to more than 52% in just two years, and the trend includes those with small as well as

Exhibit 9.13
The Price of an Expatriate

An employer's typical first-year expenses of sending a U.S. executive to Britain, assuming a $100,000 salary and a family of four.

Direct Compensation Costs	
Base Salary	$100,000
Foreign-service premium	15,000
Goods and services differential	21,000
Housing costs in London	39,000*
Transfer Costs	
Relocation allowance	5,000
Airfare to London	2,000
Moving household goods	25,000
Other Costs	
Company car	15,000
Schooling (two children)	20,000
Annual home leave (tour)	4,000
UK personal income tax	56,000
Total	$302,000

NOTE: Additional costs often incurred aren't listed above, including language and cross-cultural training for employee and family and costs of selling home and cars in the U.S. before moving.

*Figures take into account payments by employee to company based on hypothetical U.S. income tax and housing costs.

SOURCE: *The Wall Street Journal* (11 Dec. 1989), 4. Reprinted by permission.

> large PCN populations. The primary objective is cost saving, since base pay levels of most other countries are currently below those of the U.S.[48]

The base salary of a PCN is usually paid either in the home currency at the home rate or in the local currency at a rate equivalent to the rate paid locally for the same job. Similarly, salary adjustments and promotional practices may be fashioned according to either home-country or local standards. In some select cases, global salary and performance structures have been implemented.

Strategic Imperatives

To succeed in an ever-changing international environment, MNCs must look beyond next year's goals and develop clear but flexible long-term compensation strategies.

> An effective managerial reward system should be linked to long-term corporate strategy and should anticipate changes in employees' valence for different organizational rewards. On the one hand, multi-national settings make the complex task of developing such a system even more difficult; on the other hand, the fact that the corporation operates in many different environments permits the establishment of unique reward programs, unavailable in more conventional environments.[49]

In addition, MNCs need to match their compensation policies with their staffing policies and general human resource management philosophies. If, for example, a MNC has an ethnocentric staffing policy (that is, staffing with an expert chosen by headquarters), its compensation policy should be one of keeping the PCN whole. If, however, the staffing policy follows a geocentric approach (that is, staffing a position with the "best person," regardless of nationality) there may be no clear "home" for the TCN, and the MNC will need to consider establishing a system of international base pay for key managers paid in a major reserve currency such as the U.S. dollar or the Deutschmark. This system allows MNCs to deal with considerable variations in base salaries for managers, such as that noted in the following recent report:

> In Switzerland, a department head working for a medium-sized company earns $60,000. The same executive in Germany earns only $49,000. But in the U.S., the equivalent job pays only $45,000, according to a survey by Business International Corporation. However, the gap increases as U.S. executives climb the corporate ladder. At the highest levels, CEOs in the U.S. average $727,000 while those in Switzerland average only $214,000 and in Germany only $171,000.[50]

In addition to pay practices that vary from country to country, MNCs must deal with salary management systems that differ radically from west to east. European and North American MNCs usually base compensation on the type of work individual employees or classes of employees perform and the skill required for each defined job position. In Hong Kong and Singapore, individual performance and skill can dramatically affect compensation. Japanese companies tend to pay employees according to their age and seniority as well as group or company performance, offering little or no pay differentials for individual performance or exceptional skills. Latin American firms often continue to pay aging, nonproductive workers as much as they do young, vigorous ones because they cannot force them to retire without making additional payments on top of termination indemnities. Clearly, a company cannot ignore the compensation practices of the countries in which it operates. Ignorance of local custom invites disaster; knowledge of the laws, practices, and employer obligations in each country should form the basis for all international compensation.

Compensation Practices in Other Countries

Cash is, of course, the basis of compensation everywhere, but "pay" often includes additional noncash elements. In France, for example, subsidized transportation services and company restaurant lunches or luncheon vouchers are common. Workers in the Philippines receive a measure of rice, with better-quality rice provided to skilled and professional workers. In many countries, flour, grain, or potatoes are provided as pay supplements. Consumer product companies may offer their employees a choice of cash or the cash equivalent of their pay in company products at a discounted price. Employees are free to resell these products at a profit, thereby increasing their actual earnings. Voluntary noncash or "in kind" payments are made because they are tax effective. In some countries they may come to be regarded as acquired rights—payments to which employees are legally entitled.

The Netherlands. Job evaluation has been used in the Netherlands since the 1950s when the government introduced a national job evaluation plan as part of its postwar reconstruction of the economy. The original plan set the weights of compensable factors equal in all industries. If jobs were found to be of similar point value, they received identical wages, regardless of their contribution to the national economy.

Currently more than 80 percent of manual jobs and more than 40 percent of nonmanual jobs are evaluated using point ratings. However, more than 40 different point evaluation systems are in use that differ in factors, weights, and degrees.

Great Britain. Job evaluation has been widely used in Great Britain for many years. In fact, some novel approaches to job evaluation—time span of discretion and decision banding—were invented there. The Equal Pay Act of 1970, which put the burden on companies to prove that wage differentials were *not* due to gender, stimulated the growth of job evaluation. By 1980, more than 80 percent of British firms were using job evaluation to obtain a fair pay structure, establish a job hierarchy, and meet the obligations of their Equal Pay Act.

European Economic Community. With the advent of the European Economic Community in 1992 came the movement toward a common currency called the ECU (European Currency Unit). This currency (with a value of approximately $1.40) is already being used by some European firms. This will facilitate the mobility of workers across nations. Having a similar impact is the movement toward Europay. **Europay** is a practice of developing a common policy and common set of pay practices regardless of national origin and extent of location throughout Europe. This practice, primarily targeted for top management, recognizes the need to treat European operations as truly one market and their employees as truly European.

Australia. In Australia, compensation occurs in the context of both a powerful labor union movement that covers almost half of the work force and a long-established, centralized conciliation and arbitration system that plays a central role in national wage determination. These two factors together make appraisal and compensation practices in Australia very different from those in the U.S.

The key institution in the Australian industrial relations system is the Australian Conciliation and Arbitration Commission (ACAC), which has its statutory basis in the Conciliation and Arbitration Act of 1904. In addition to settling industrial disputes, the ACAC has over time become the mechanism by which national wage policy is implemented.[51] ACAC and its permanent staff are legally independent of the government of the day but clearly must seriously consider the government's views. In April, 1983, the Labor federal government signed an accord with the labor unions whereby the government supported the unions' request to the ACAC for quarterly national wage increases to match changes in the consumer price index in return for broad compliance with the government's macroeconomic strategy to reduce inflation and unemployment.[52]

In early 1987 the indexed wages system was replaced by a more flexible two-tiered system of wage determination. The first tier of the new system provides for a maximum level of wage increases for all employees over a period, consistent with economic and social factors. The second tier of the system allows for enterprise-level bargaining between unions and employers through which wage increases can be negotiated in exchange for increased efficiency arrangements (e.g., agreements to introduce new technology, more flexible work practices, a reduction of demarcation disputes between unions, and changes in training/skill formation systems). These second-tier agreements must be ratified by the ACAC. For many companies and unions, this has been their first experience with enterprise-level bargaining without the facilitation of the ACAC.

Even with the introduction of a more flexible wage determination system, labor unions in Australia have tended to oppose individual performance appraisal.[53] The reality for most employers is that they must pay all workers performing a similar job the award rate determined by the ACAC, plus any over-award benefits that may have been negotiated between the employer and the unions. A traditional U.S.–style, individually oriented appraisal and compensation system only appears with managerial-level employees who are not covered by an industry award.

Japan. The Japanese are fond of saying there are three sacred treasures of the Imperial House. The first of these is lifetime employment. The second, which stems from lifetime employment, is the traditional seniority system, which determines not only wages but also the timing of promotions. Under this system, an employee rarely works under someone with less seniority in service length, assuming both have similar educational backgrounds. This system has its roots in the traditional *Oyabun-Kobun,* or parent-child relationship, which attaches great respect to the older or senior member of the family (company). The third treasure of the Imperial House is the enterprise (or company) union.

During the past several years much consideration has been given to the argument that, if wages are paid on the basis of seniority only, then those who have more ability may not always work hard. Accordingly, the predominant method for determining wage increases is now one that incorporates both seniority and merit. The annual incremental rate for wage increases, which differs by enterprise, is generally about two to four percent. The amount of the increment is determined by a merit rating, seniority, job responsibility, and work requirements.

Initially, individual companies pay almost the same starting salary for new employees hired on graduation from either high school or college. After that, an employee's annual earnings increase according to the merit rating system. In addition, earnings will increase annually—even if an employee's job responsibilities remain unchanged—until the age of mandatory retirement, now commonly sixty years of age.

Japanese basic hourly wages are among the highest in the world. Starting in about 1955, Japanese trade unions initiated a concerted, industrywide campaign known as the "spring offensive," during which many of the trade unions took simultaneous, instead of independent, actions in demanding wage hikes. Today, approximately eighty percent of the organized workers negotiate wage hikes in the spring. As a result, wage decisions in the major industries, such as steel, influence the outcomes of other industries. This has resulted in relatively standardized wage increase rates throughout Japanese industry.

A distinguishing feature of the Japanese wage system is the provision for a semiannual bonus or wage allowance that is separate from the annual incremental rate. Usually paid without exception, even in times of recession, the bonus amount is closely related to both the general economy and the profitability of the company. Generally, the equivalent of five to six months' salary is paid in bonuses at midsummer and at the end of the year.

In addition to basic salary, Japanese workers customarily receive compensation in the form of housing or a housing allowance, daily living support (including transportation, meals, and workers' uniforms), cultural and recreational benefits, and medical and health care.[54]

SUMMARY

Organizations are being forced to develop strategic compensation practices in light of a cost-conscious, competitive business environment that demands high quality and a continuous flow of new products. Compensation programs must be consistent with the organization's culture and strategic objectives. In addition, compensation practices must adhere to the Fair Labor Standards Act and Equal Pay Act. Concern over comparable worth is also causing organizations to consider the manner in which rates of pay are determined for male- and female-dominated positions.

Job evaluation is a systematic, rational assessment of the value of jobs that is designed to establish internal equity in jobs. Ranking and job classification methods focus on evaluating the whole job. These methods are premised on intuitive judgments about job worth. Preferable methods include point evaluation and factor comparison systems, both of which evaluate jobs using compensable factors.

In conducting a job evaluation study, a decision needs to be made regarding whether to custom-design or buy a system. While it may be more expedient to buy a standardized system, such a system may not reflect organizational needs and values. To ensure systemwide equity, a single job evaluation plan is usually preferred over multiple plans. Another important decision is who should evaluate the worth of jobs. The greater the involvement of incumbents, the more likely they are to accept the results of the job evaluation study. Alternatively, an organization can choose a pay-for-knowledge or skill-based pay system in which pay increases with job skill or flexibility.

Once the worth is determined, jobs must still be priced. Although job evaluation procedures are important in establishing worth, they are more relevant to establishing relative job value than actual wage rates. To help establish actual wage rates, organizations often use market survey data, especially for those jobs that have identical or nearly identical counterparts in the marketplace. Doing market surveys for pricing jobs that are not found in other organizations should be done with caution. It involves subjectivity and, therefore, is open to potential wage discrimination charges. Organizations should be careful in using market rates that perpetuate wage differentials that are obviously discriminatory. Fair evaluations should be conducted to help reduce that likelihood.

In establishing wages, organizations can rely upon job evaluations and market surveys and can use inputs from the employees themselves. Employees can responsibly set their own wages. In the few companies that have tried it, employees have set their own wages without management altering the procedures or changing decisions. The method is most successful in organizations where employees and management have mutual trust and where employees are provided with information to help them understand the financial status of the company.

Establishing wages and determining which job evaluation method to use, though important, are only two components of compensation. Other components include selecting the best performance-based pay plan and obtaining benefit from indirect compensation. Chapters 10 and 11 discuss these important components of compensation.

WHERE WE ARE TODAY

1. The issues involved in linking total compensation to the needs of the business are some of the most complex and extensive in the entire field of personnel and human resource management.
2. As a consequence, individuals often specialize in compensation and stay in that specialization for their entire career.
3. This also helps explain why there are so many consulting firms that specialize in compensation (or, more generally, "comp and benefits").
4. Because so many aspects of the environment have an impact on total compensation, it pays to become familiar with them to help predict what different firms might be able to pay you.
5. Internal equity is a very important issue in total compensation. It pays for you to know the methods used by organizations and the one used by your firm.
6. As firms allow their employees more participation in HR activities, you may find yourself one day evaluating a colleague on how well he or she has learned the skills required in order to receive additional compensation.
7. It's wise to become familiar with your firm's pay-grade structure, including how it was established and the rationale for the various job classifications or families.
8. Eliminating pay inequity is at the heart of comparable worth, but particularly across different jobs of equivalent value or worth to the organization. Here's where the type of job evaluation system often comes under close scrutiny.
9. International compensation is generally the first human resource activity in which firms operating globally get involved.
10. If you elect to become an expatriate, you will be amazed at the complexity of the choices and the calculations required in order to at least "make you whole."

DISCUSSION QUESTIONS

1. What purposes can total compensation serve? Can the purposes vary across different organizations? Explain.
2. What forms of pay and rewards make up total compensation?
3. What are four basic wage issues that any job evaluation system must address?
4. Describe the basic mechanics of the common job evaluation methods.
5. How do firms establish the actual pay levels for each job?

6. Are the CEOs of U.S. firms overpaid relative to firms in other countries? How can you defend this?
7. What are the components of the typical expatriate's compensation package?
8. How do the base salaries of expatriates differ from the base salaries of employees in the United States?
9. What are the advantages of skill-based evaluation over traditional evaluation methods?
10. How can an organization's total compensation package be assessed?

APPLIED PROJECTS

1. The head of engineering comes to you, the compensation analyst, and demands that you allow him to pay a "hot-shot" more than the current pay range allows. The manager contends that we'll loose this particular person, if we don't pay her what she's worth. You know that individuals are difficult to find, however, your company has a firm policy about pay ranges.
2. You are head of administrative services for Kitsap County, Washington. Your county has just completed a pay audit. Much to your surprise, the county's pay audit study reveals that the rates of pay currently being paid four jobs (ferry operator, accounting clerk, accountants and dog catchers) exceeds significantly the rate of pay dictated by the external market. One strategy is to freeze the wages of employees in these jobs. However, County Commissioners are afraid of the voters' reaction if they find out that public sector employees are being paid above average wages. What do you do about this dilemma and why?
3. You are a member of the management team for a major accounting firm (200 accountants). Traditionally, accountants in the firm have been salaried but have been awarded overtime or time off for excess work during tax season. You've heard about skill-based pay and are thinking that it may be appropriate for your firm. Discuss the pros and cons of implementing skill-based pay in an accounting firm. Bottom line, would you make the switch or not?

CASE STUDY

Planned Parenthood at Midwest City

Mary Johnson, executive director of Planned Parenthood of Midwest City (PPMC), sat at her desk sifting through miscellaneous compensation and budget documents. A major agenda item at the next PPMC board meeting was salary recommendations for the coming year. "This just isn't going to do the job," she thought as she looked at the old salary scale. "It really needs to be revised."

The present salary scale had been adopted by the board four years previously. While designed to last a number of years, inflationary pressures had rendered it useless. Cost-of-living adjustments had moved some employees right off the scale, and the gap between lower- and higher-paid employees appeared to be widening. "In spite of our efforts to keep pace with inflation, Ann, Ellen, and Kathryn still feel underpaid," she thought. "I think it's time to revamp the whole system."

PPMC is a private, nonprofit organization which provides educational, counseling, and clinical services to the community. Located in a small university town, PPMC employs nine full- and part-time employees. Numerous volunteers also provide services without pay to the agency. Funding for PPMC comes from multiple sources: the federal government (48 percent), local sources and patient fees (45 percent), and other sources (7 percent). Last year's annual budget was $213,755. A slight increase (5 to 7 percent) in funding is projected for the coming year, assuming federal funding is authorized by Congress. Mary Johnson has been with PPMC for ten years and has served as the executive director the past nine years.

Mary began organizing the relevant documents she had gathered. Taking a file folder from her drawer, she organized the documents as follows: First was a list of present employees, their position, years of service, present pay level, and hours of work (see exhibit 1). Next she added a copy of the organization chart (see exhibit 2) and summarized job descriptions in the file. "I want the pay system to be perceived as equitable by employees," she thought. "Pay levels should reflect varying levels of job responsibilities and skills, as well as reporting relationships."

Exhibit 1
PPMC Employee Summary (Fiscal Year 1989)

Name[1]	Position	Years PPMC	Years Position	FTE*	Salary
Mary Johnson	Executive Director	10	9	.8	$18,843
Peter Martin	Administrative Director	10	9	.6	9,427
Ann Mitchell	Clinic Manager	14	3	1.0	12,570
Sarah Watson	Education Director	4	3	1.0	13,750
Janet Smith	Nurse Practitioner	1	1	1.0	21,969
Rick Winters	County Coordinator	8	2	.5	5,864
Ellen Peters	Clinical Asst. II	3	3	1.04	11,345
Kathryn Woo	Clinical Asst. I	10	5	1.0	10,837

* 1 FTE = 35 hours/week
[1] Note medical director is excluded from the plan.

The next item she placed in the folder was a salary survey reflecting pay ranges of other planned parenthood clinics in the region (see exhibit 3). While the job titles in the survey didn't match those used at PPMC in all cases, Mary felt if was useful to compare pay levels at PPMC with other clinics whenever possible.

"One thing I don't have in my life," Mary mused, "is comparative wage information from other organizations in Midwest City that employ personnel in positions similar to ours. Perhaps the state employment service has that information. I'll have to get it from somewhere. I want our salaries to be sufficient and fair. Yet, as a nonprofit organization, I don't feel we should pay the highest wages in the community."

Other desired outcomes began to flow into Mary's mind: "I want the system to be objective and systematic. I want it to be flexible and adjustable from year to year." Mary liked the idea of pay ranges, allowing her flexibility in accounting for experience and years of service when determining specific pay levels. Ranges played a vital role in her ability to project salary costs one or two years into the future. "If possible, I'd also like to be able to reward team productivity. We've had some success with productivity bonuses in the past."

"In developing a pay plan," reasoned Mary, "I want to make sure it fits with our other personnel policies." All employees at PPMC are paid on a salaried basis and work 35 hours a week. PPMC has a fairly liberal fringe-benefits package and has received awards for its innovative personnel policies.

"Another criteria," thought Mary, "is that the pay system must meet federal and state wage and salary guidelines. Finally," she thought, "I don't want anyone to receive a pay cut as a result of changing the system, yet the cost of the system should not exceed budget projections."

Case Questions

1. What should be the objectives of Planned Parenthood's compensation program?

Exhibit 2
PPMC Organization Chart

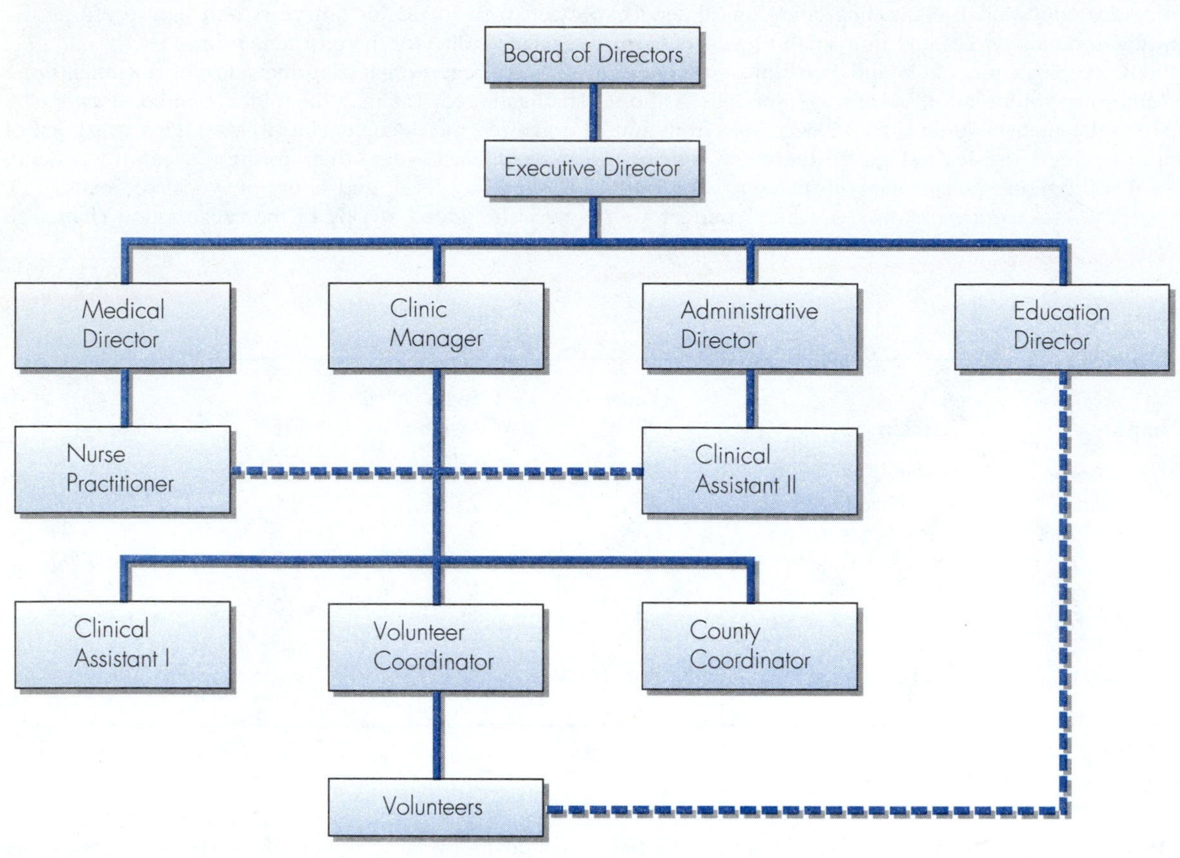

2. What are the advantages and disadvantages of using market rates to set the pay for all PPMC employees?
3. Discuss the merits of using a job classification versus a point system to determine the worth of the PPMC's jobs.
4. Are there legitimate reasons for the three employees to be dissatisfied? Why or why not?
5. What strategies are available to Mary to alleviate the pay dissatisfaction of PPMC's three employees?
6. How should Mary go about developing a fair and equitable compensation system for Planned Parenthood?
7. What salary adjustments, if any, do you recommend if PPMC is to be competitive with other agencies? Justify your answers.

SOURCE: Steve Hanks, Utah State Univ. and Gaylen Chandler, Univ. of Utah

Exhibit 3
Planned Parenthood Regional Salary Survey[1]

Position	Average Low Salary[2] (Range)[4]	Average Current Salary[3] (Range)	Average High Salary[2] (Range)	Average Years in Position (Range)
Executive Director	$18,240 ($17,600–$19,800)	$21,673 ($17,722–$24,750)	$25,961 ($19,800–$30,800)	3.04 years (.58–9 years)

Continued

Exhibit 3 (Continued)
Planned Parenthood Regional Salary Survey[1]

Position	Average Low Salary[2] (Range)[4]	Average Current Salary[3] (Range)	Average High Salary[2] (Range)	Average Years in Position (Range)
Director of Administration/Fiscal	$13,868 ($13,750–$13,985)	$16,693 ($15,711–$17,674)	$19,575 ($18,150–$21,000)	7.50 years (5–9 years)
Clinic Director	$13,875 ($11,000–$18,150)	$18,250 ($12,570–$25,967)	$19,640 ($15,400–$26,530)	3.38 years (2–6 years)
Educator	$11,825 ($11,000–$13,300)	$14,453 ($12,584–$16,170)	$17,372 ($16,245–$19,925)	3 years (1–6 years)
Nurse Practitioner	$18,168 ($16,020–$20,020)	$20,979 ($18,280–$23,140)	$24,060 ($22,000–$25,740)	3.5 years (1–10 years)
All-Purpose Person[5]	$9,090 ($8,000–$10,810)	$10,831 ($8,500–$12,575)	$13,059 ($10,000–$16,240)	4.44 years (.33–10 years)
Records Clerk[6]	$9,075 ($8,800–$9,350)	$11,297 ($11,100–$11,350)	$13,200 ($12,700–$13,400)	2.13 years (1.25–3 years)
Secretary[6]	$8,980 ($8,580–$9,350)	$11,125 ($9,650–$12,600)	$12,526 ($10,725–$13,650)	.61 years (.08–1.25 years)

[1] Salary survey data taken from eight planned parenthood clinics in the Midwest region, having total annual budgets under $275,000. Survey data is based on a thirty-five-hour work week. The County Coordinator position was not included in the regional salary survey, so no regional data are available.

[2] Average Low and Average High Salaries summarize the low and high points on the pay scale for each position.

[3] Average Current Salary is the average reported salary for current job incumbents.

[4] Range is the statistical range of responses in each category.

[5] Job descriptions of PPMC's Clinical Assistant I and the All-Purpose Person position surveyed above are similar.

[6] PPMC's Clinical Assistant II position involves 50 percent records clerk duties and 50 percent secretarial duties.

NOTES

1. D. L. Costley and R. Todd, *Human Relations in Organizations,* 4th ed. (St. Paul, Minn.: West Publishing Company, 1991): 187.
2. P. V. LeBlanch, "Skill-Based Pay Case Number 2: Northern Telecom," *Compensation and Benefits Review* (March-April 1991): 39–56. Also see G. E. Ledford, Jr., "Three Case Studies on Skill-Based Pay: An Overview," *Compensation and Benefits Review* (March-April 1991): 11–23; G. E. Ledford, W. R. Tyler, and W. B. Dixey, "Skill-Based Pay Case Number 3: Honeywell Ammunition Assembly Plant," *Compensation and Benefits Review* (March-April 1991): 57–77.
3. C. Alderfer, *Existence, Relatedness, and Growth* (New York: Free Press, 1972); J. Campbell and R. Pritchard, "Motivation Theory in Industrial and Organizational Psychology," in *Handbook of Industrial and Organizational Psychology,* ed. M. Dunnette (Chicago: Rand McNally, 1976); W. H. Griggs and S. Manning, "Money Isn't the Best Tool for Motivating Technical Professionals," *Personnel Administrator* (June 1985): 63–78; V. Vroom, *Work and Motivation* (New York: Wiley, 1964).
4. For an excellent review of strategic compensation, see E. E. Lawler III, *Strategic Pay: Aligning Organizational Strategies and Pay Systems* (San Francisco: Jossey-Bass, 1990); F. K. Foulkes, *Executive Compensation: A Strategic Guide for the 1990s* (Boston: Harvard Business School Press, 1991); C. L. Weber and S. L. Rynes, "Effects of Compensation Strategy on Job Pay Decisions," *Academy of Management Journal* 34, no. 1 (1991): 86–109; M. L. Rock and L. A. Berger, *The Compensation Handbook: A State-of-the-Art Guide to Compensation Strategy and Design* (New York: McGraw-Hill, 1991); L. R. Gomez-Mejia and D. B. Balkin, *Compensation, Organizational Strategy, and Firm Performance* (Cincinnati, Ohio: South-Western Publishing, 1992); R. G. Ehrenberg, ed., *Do Compensation Policies Matter?* (Ithaca, N.Y.: ILR Press, 1990). For a dis-

cussion of approaches to HR strategy see, J. E. Butler, G. R. Ferris, and D. Smith Cook, "Exploring some Critical Dimensions of Strategic Human Resource Management," in R. Schuler, S. Youngblood, and V. Huber, eds., *Readings in Personnel and Human Resource Management* (St. Paul, Minn.: West 1988): 3–13; E. Lawler, *Pay and Organizational Development* (Reading, Mass.: Addison-Wesley, 1981); L. Dyer, "Strategic Human Resource Management and Planning," in K. Rowland and G. Ferris, eds., *Research in Personnel and Human Resource Management* (Greenwich, Conn.: JAI Press, 1985): 1–30.

5. G. Milkovich, "A Strategic Perspective on Compensation Management," in *Research in Personnel and Human Resources Management;* M. J. Wallace, Jr., and C. H. Fay, *Compensation Theory and Practice* (Boston, Mass.: PWS-Kent, 1988); S. Carroll, "Business Strategies and Compensation Systems," in D. B. Balkin and L. R. Gomez-Mejia, eds., *New Perspectives in Compensation* (Englewood Cliffs, N.J.: Prentice-Hall, 1987); B. Gerhart and G. T. Milkovich, "Organizational Differences in Managerial Compensation and Financial Performance," *Academy of Management Journal* 33, no. 4 (1990): 663–91.
6. G. Milkovich and J. Newman, *Compensation* (Plano, Tex.: Business Publications, Inc., 1990); S. Rynes and G. T. Milkovich, "Wage Surveys: Dispelling some Myths about the 'Market Wage,'" *Personnel Psychology* (Spring 1986): 71–89.
7. R. L. Heneman, "Merit Pay Research," in Rowland and Ferris, eds., *Research in Personnel and Human Resources Management:* 203–65; J. Newman, "Selecting Incentive Plans to Complement Organizational Strategy," in Balkin and Gomez-Mejia, eds., *New Perspectives on Compensation:* 214–25; R. M. Steers and G. R. Ungson, "Strategic Issues in Executive Compensation Decisions," in *New Perspectives on Compensation:* 294–309; G. Milkovich, "A Strategic Perspective on Compensation Management," in *Research in Personnel and Human Resources Management:* 263–88; M. J. Wallace, Jr., and C. H. Fay, *Compensation Theory and Practice* (Boston, Mass.: PWS–Kent, 1988).
8. "Final Equal Pay Interpretations Issued by EEOC," *Fair Employment Practices* (4 Sept. 1986): 108.
9. H. C. Bentiam, "Union–Non-Union Wage Differential Revisited," *Journal of Labor Research* 8 (1987): 381; D. Lewin, "Public Sector Labor Relations: A Review Essay," in D. Lewin, P. Feuill, and T. Kochan, eds., *Public Sector Labor Relations: An Analysis and Readings* (Glen Ridge, N.J.: Thomas Horton and Daughters, 1977): 166–84; R. Flanagan, R. Smith, and R. Ehrenberg, *Labor Economics and Labor Relations* (Glenview, Ill.: Scott Foresman, 1984).
10. M. Bowers and R. Roderick, "Two-Tiered Pay Systems: The Good, the Bad and the Debatable," *Personnel Administrator* 32 (1987): 101–12; Towers, Perrin, Forster and Crosby, "Survey of Company Experiences with Two-Tier Wage Systems" (Washington, D.C.: Towers, Perrin, Forster and Crosby, 1986).
11. R. Freeman and J. Medoff, *What Do Unions Do?* (New York: Basic Books, 1984); T. A. Kochan, H. C. Katz, and R. B. McKersie, *The Transformation of American Industrial Relations* (New York: Basic Books, 1986).
12. R. S. Schuler and I. C. MacMillan, "Gaining Competitive Advantage through Human Resource Management Practices," in *Readings in Personnel and Human Resource Management:* 14–23.
13. J. Kerr and J. W. Slocum, Jr., "Managing Corporate Culture through Reward Systems," *Executive* (May 1987): 99–108; J. Kerr and J. W. Slocum, Jr., "Linking Reward Systems and Organizational Cultures," in *Readings in Personnel and Human Resource Management:* 297–311.
14. D. Jamieson and J. O'Mara, *Managing Workforce 2000: Gaining the Diversity Advantage* (San Francisco, Calif.: Jossey-Bass, 1991): 108.
15. V. L. Huber, G. B. Northcraft, M. A. Neale, and X. Zhao, "Cognitive Similarity and Cultural Dissimilarity: Effects on Performance Appraisal and Compensation Decisions of Chinese Americans," working paper, University of Washington, 1990.
16. R. Schuler, "Managing Resource Management Choices and Organizational Strategy," in *Readings in Personnel and Human Resource Management:* 24–39; E. Lawler and J. A. Drexler, "The Corporate Entrepreneur," working paper, Center for Effective Organizations, University of Southern California, 1984; E. Lawler, "The Strategic Design of Reward Systems," in *Readings in Personnel and Human Resource Management:* 253–69.
17. D. Jamieson and J. O'Mara, *Managing Workforce 2000 ...*
18. D. B. Balkin and L. R. Gomez-Mejia, "Entrepreneurial Compensation," in *Readings in Personnel and Human Resource Management*: 14–23; D. B. Balkin and L. R. Gomez-Mejia, "The Strategic Use of Short-Term and Long-Term Pay Incentives in the High Technology Industry," in Balkin and Gomez-Mejia, eds., *New Perspectives on Compensation:* 237–49.
19. G. Milkovich, "A Strategic Perspective on Compensation Management," in *Research in Personnel and Human Resources Management:* 263–88.
20. E. R. Livernash, "Internal Wage Structure," in G. W. Taylor and F. C. Pierson, eds., *New Concepts in Wage Determination* (New York: McGraw-Hill, 1957): 143-72; P. Cappelli and W. F. Cascio, "Why Some Jobs Command Wage Premiums: A Test of Career Tournament and Internal Labor Market Hypotheses," *Academy of Management Journal* 34, no. 4 (1991): 848–68; S. R. Rynes, C. L. Weber, and G. T. Milkovich, "Effects of Market Survey Rates, Job Evaluation, and Job Gender on Job Pay," *Journal of Applied Psychology* 74, no. 1 (1989): 114–23; D. Gleicher and L. Stevans, *A Classical Approach to Occupational Wage Rates* (Westport, Conn.: Praeger Publishers, 1991).
21. G. Milkovich and J. Newman, "Job Evaluation: Perspectives and Design," *Compensation* (Homewood, Ill.: BPI-Irwin, 1990).
22. G. Milkovich and J. Newman, "Job Evaluation...": 109.
23. R. Sneigar, "The Comparability of Job Evaluation Methods in Supplying Approximately Similar Classifications in Rating One Job Series," *Personnel Psychology* (Summer 1983): 371–80.
24. D. Doverspike, "An Internal Bias Analysis of a Job Evaluation Instrument," *Journal of Applied Psychology* (Nov. 1984): 648–50; S. L. Fraser, S. F. Cronshaw, and R. A.

Alexander, "Generalizability Analysis of a Point Method Job Evaluation Instrument: A Field Study," *Journal of Applied Psychology* (Nov. 1984): 643–47.

25. A. J. Candrilli and R. D. Armagast, "The Case for Effective Point Factor Job Evaluation, Viewpoint 2," *Compensation and Benefits Review* (1990): 49–54.
26. H. Murlis and D. Fitt, "Job Evaluation in a Changing World," *Personnel Management* (May 1991): 39–43.
27. G. E. Ledford, "Three Case Studies on Skill Based Pay: An Overview," *Compensation and Benefits Review* (April 1990): 11–23; H. Tosi and L. Tosi, "What Managers Need to Know About Knowledge-Based Pay," *Organizational Dynamics* (Winter 1986): 52–64.
28. *Bulletin to Management* (14 Jan. 1988): 10.
29. Milkovich and Newman, *Compensation*.
30. G. E. Ledford, Jr., W. R. Tyler, and W. B. Dixey, "Skill-Based Pay Case Number 3: Honeywell Ammunition Assembly Plan," *Compensation and Benefits Review* (April 1990): 57–77.
31. D. W. Belcher and T. J. Atchison, *Compensation Administration*, 2d ed. (Englewood Cliffs, N.J.: Prentice-Hall, 1987); J. Franklin, "For Technical Professionals: Pay for Skills and Pay for Performance," *Personnel* (May 1988): 20–28; J. C. Kail, "Compensating Scientists and Engineers," in *New Perspectives on Compensation:* 278–81; G. T. Milkovich, "Compensation Systems in High-Technology Companies," in *New Perspectives on Compensation:* 269–77; Milkovich and Newman, *Compensation;* C. F. Schultz, "Compensating the Sales Professional," in *New Perspectives on Compensation:* 250–57.
32. R. Henderson, *Compensation Management* (Reston, Va.: Reston Publishing, 1985).
33. W. R. Tyler, W. B. Dixey, "Skill-Based Pay Case Number 3: Honeywell Ammunition Assembly Plant," *Compensation and Benefits Review* (March-April 1991): 57–77.
34. K. K. Romanoff, K. Boehm, and E. Benson, "Pay Equity: Internal and External Considerations," *Compensation and Benefits Review* vol. 18 (1986): 17–25; T. J. Bergmann and F. S. Hills, "A Review of the Causes of Solutions to Pay Compression," in *New Perspectives on Compensation:* 112-23.
35. Hearings on H.R. 8898, 10266, Part I, 87th Congress, 2d Session (1962); M. Gold, *A Dialogue on Comparable Worth* (Ithaca, N.Y.: ILR Press, 1983).
36. J. R. Bellace, "A Foreign Perspective," *Comparable Worth: Issues and Alternatives* (Washington, D.C.: Equal Employment Advisory Council, 1980): 123–45.
37. K. A. Kovach and P. E. Millspaugh, "Comparable Worth: Canada Legislates Pay Equity," *Academy of Management Executive* 4, no. 2 (1990): 92–101; M. R. Killingsworth, *The Economics of Comparable Worth* (Kalamazoo, Mich.: W. E. Upjohn Institute for Employment Research, 1990); M. A. Hill and M. R. Killingsworth, eds., *Comparable Worth: Analyses and Evidence* (Ithaca, N.Y.: ILR Press, 1989); Y. Haberfeld, "Employment Discrimination: An Organizational Model," *Academy of Management Journal* 35, no. 1 (1992): 161–80; V. L. Huber, "Comparison of Supervisor-Incumbent and Female-Male Multidimensional Job Evaluation Ratings," *Journal of Applied Psychology* 76, no. 1 (1991): 115–21; J. L. Barnes-Farrell, T. J. L'Heureux-Barrett and J. M. Conway, "Impact of Gender-Related Job Features on the Accurate Evaluation of Performance Information," *Organizational Behavior and Human Decision Processes* 48 (1991): 23–35; E. Frankel Paul, *Equity and Gender: The Comparable Worth Debate* (New Brunswick, N.J.: Transaction Books, 1989).
38. M. Zippo, "Roundup," *Personnel* (Sept.-Oct. 1980): 43–45.
39. E. E. Lawler, III, *Pay and Organizational Development* (Reading, Mass.: Addison-Wesley, 1981).
40. V. Scarpello, V. Huber, and R. J. Vanderberg, "Compensation Satisfaction: Its Measurement and Dimensionality," *Journal of Applied Psychology* (May 1988): 163–71; R. W. Rice, S. M. Phillips, and D. B. McFarlin, "Multiple Discrepancies and Pay Satisfaction," *Journal of Applied Psychology* 75, no. 4 (1990): 386–93.
41. "Labor Letter," *The Wall Street Journal* (17 July 1990): 1.
42. "Executive Pay: Compensation at the Top is Out of Control—Here's How to Reform It," *Business Week* (30 March 1992): 52–57; G. S. Crystal, *In Search of Excess: The Overcompensation of American Executives* (New York: Norton, 1992); G. Colvin, "How to Pay the CEO Right," *Fortune* (6 April 1992): 61–69; A. Franham, "The Trust Gap," *Fortune* (4 Dec. 1990): 56–58.
43. A "properly administered" compensation program implies several qualities of total compensation, including that the job evaluation process is valid, pay structures are fairly and objectively derived, pay is administered in a nondiscriminatory way, compensation policies are communicated so as to be understood, administrative costs are contained, it has sufficient motivational value, and it is supported by top management. For a discussion of these, see R. E. Azevedo and J. M. Beaton, "Costing the Pay Package: A Realistic Approach," in *New Perspectives on Compensation:* 143–50; S. B. Henrici, "A Tool for Salary Administrators: Standard Salary Accounting," *Personnel* (Sept.-Oct. 1980): 14–23; and J. C. Horn, "Bigger Pay for Better Work," *Psychology Today* (July 1987): 54–57.
44. The following materials are adapted from P. Dowling and R. S. Schuler, *International Dimensions of Human Resource Management* (Boston: PWS-Kent, 1990): 117–35. Also see three excellent articles entitled, "Compensating Your Overseas Executives, Part 1 *Compensation Review* (May-June 1990), Part 2 (July-Aug. 1990), and Part 3 (Jan.-Feb. 1991); K. I. Kim, H. J. Park, and N. Suzuki, "Reward Allocations in the United States, Japan, and Korea: A Comparison of Individualistic and Collectivistic Cultures," *Academy of Management Journal* 33, no. 1 (1990): 188–98; A. R. Thomann, "Flex-base Addresses Pay Problems," *Personnel Journal* (Feb. 1992): 51–52, 55.
45. C. Reynolds, "High Motivation and Low Cost through Innovative International Compensation," *Proceedings of ASPA's 40th National Conference* (Boston, Mass., 1989).
46. See B. W. Teague, *Compensating Key Personnel Overseas* (New York: The Conference Board, 1972), for a discussion of the concept of keeping the expatriate "whole."
47. This discussion of the "balance sheet" approach is based on C. Reynolds, "Compensation of Overseas Personnel," in J. J. Famularo, ed., *Handbook of Human Resources Administration,* 2d ed. (New York: McGraw-Hill, 1986).
48. *HR Reporter Update* (Feb. 1987): 2.

49. V. Pucik, "Strategic HRM in Multinational Corporations," in H. V. Wortzel and L. H. Wortzel, eds., *Strategic Management of Multinational Corporations* (New York: John Wiley, 1985): 430.
50. *HR Reporter Update* (Jan. 1987): 5.
51. For a detailed discussion of wage determination in Australia, see S. Deery and D. Plowman, *Australian Industrial Relations,* 2d ed. (Sydney: McGraw-Hill, 1985): Chapter 11.
52. F. Bairstow, "The Trend toward Centralized Bargaining—A Patchwork Quilt of International Diversity," *Columbia Journal of World Business* 20, no. 1 (1985): 75–83.
53. M. Derber, "Reflections on Aspects of the Australian and American Systems of Industrial Relations," in W. A. Howard, ed., *Perspectives on Australian Relations* (Melbourne: Longman Cheshire, 1984).
54. M. S. O'Connor, *Report on Japanese Employee Relations Practices and Their Relationship to Worker Productivity,* a report prepared for the study mission to Japan, November 8–23, 1980. Her permission to reproduce this material is appreciated. Also see, *Employment and Employment Policy* (Tokyo: Japan Institute of Labor, 1988).

CHAPTER

Performance-Based Pay

Companies were laying off workers, asking workers for sacrifices, while at the same time their CEOs were significantly increasing their own salaries. When there is no relationship between pay and profitability of the company, you are in an anticompetitive position.

—U.S. Senator Carl Levin[1]

Landscape maintenance is a dirty-hands, low-margin industry with no barriers to entry or lack of competition, according to Dennis Dautel and Rex Gore, owners of Clean Cut Inc., a $1.8-million landscape maintenance business in Austin, Texas. In this competitive environment, customer service and repeat business are critical components of organizational survival. The problem, however, is to motivate employees to view these issues as important as management does.

Clean Cut team leaders are not MBAs but lunch-bucket guys with a talent for supervising people. They're more interested in an incentive compensation plan that is simple and gives more short-term rewards than in one that makes long-term promises. However, a straight profit-sharing plan can encourage supervisors to shortchange customers; profits go up, but the company's reputation and long-term prospects for repeat business suffer. On the other hand, long-term incentive plans—such as employee stock ownership plans or stock option plans—don't offer any immediate rewards for good work; they sound complicated, too. Such plans also may be viewed by owners as "giving away the company store."

Faced with the problem of motivating their managers to pay closer attention to the short-term profitability of the jobs they were overseeing and to customer service for long-term growth, Dautel and Gore devised a "phantom equity" incentive plan. Clean Cut team leaders use a portion of the profits their crews generate to buy a "take" in their own team's growth. Here's how the plan works.

> *Let's say that George, a team leader, decides to buy into the phantom-equity plan. For the past six months his team has generated, on average, $24,000 a month in revenues. Dautel and Gore propose to value any team's business at twice its monthly revenues. So George's team's business is worth $48,000. Plus, it's only fair, Dautel says, to add to the price the depreciated cost of the capital equipment assigned to the team. George's team currently uses, say, $12,000 worth of trucks, trailers, mowers, and so on. In total, George will be buying into a business currently valued at $60,000. George decides to "buy" a 25% share, worth $15,000.*
>
> *In a paper transaction, Clean Cut lends George the $15,000 to be paid back over five years. Neglecting any interest (to keep the example's calculations simple), George owes the company $250 a month for five years. The money will come out of his 25% share of the team's profits.*
>
> *Now, let's say it's 10 years later. George is ready to retire and wants to cash out by selling his "equity"—his share of the team's business. By keeping his customers happy and adding on new accounts, he's built his monthly revenues up to $40,000. Assuming that the capital-equipment numbers haven't changed (again, to keep the example simple), the business George's team does is worth $92,000 (two times $40,000, plus $12,000). When George retires, the company buys back his 25% share for $23,000 ($92,000 times 0.25). George never used a dime from his own pocket to buy his share of the business, yet he was able to enjoy extra income out of profits while he was working, and he was able to retire with a nice nest egg.*[2]

This chapter's opening company profile illustrates several important aspects of performance-based pay. First, regardless of their size, organizations see performance-based pay as necessary for company survival in a highly competitive business. Second, performance-based pay plans must be straightforward and understandable. Third, incentive compensation must be customized to fit the organization's culture and to meet important goals. The phantom stock plan described above may be appropriate for team leaders of Clean Cut. However, different types of individual team, or organizational incentive systems may better help other firms meet their objectives.

Building on the foundation of chapter 9, this chapter focuses on performance-based pay—specifically, on the purposes and importance of performance-based pay to attaining organizational objectives. We will review theoretical considerations in linking pay to performance. Then we'll discuss the mix of various elements of total compensation (base pay, incentive or merit pay, cost-of-living adjustments, and stock options, to name some) used to attain organizational objectives. Finally, we'll examine compensation for special groups, including executives and sales personnel.

PERFORMANCE-BASED PAY

External and internal equity, as discussed in the previous chapter, focus on the value of jobs in the labor market and to the organization, respectively. Together, they establish the base pay for specific jobs in an organization. In contrast, performance-based pay centers on valuing the performance contribution of an individual, a team, or an organization unit. The emphasis here is on the value of the performance contribution rather than the value of the job.

PURPOSES AND IMPORTANCE OF PERFORMANCE-BASED PAY

Performance-based pay serves a multitude of important purposes in today's firms.

Attain Strategic Goals

An organization could pay all individuals in a job or pay grade a single rate of pay (e.g., midpoints described in chapter 9). For several reasons, this usually is not done. As compensation experts Marc Wallace and Charles Fay note, organizations that wish to pay strategically need pay differentials available within an individual job to reinforce strategic initiatives.[3] For example,

> In early 1989, the Fibers Department of E.I. DuPont de Nemours and Co. initiated a major shift from straight hourly or salary-based pay to one in which employees' compensation rests on their unit's overall performance. As an effort to view employees as "stakeholders" of the firm's future and to build a sense of teamwork, the compensation plan bases pay on the department's profits and losses. One employee described it as a shift from being paid for "coming to work" to being paid for how well a business unit succeeds.
>
> The plan pays employees based on how well their department meets its performance goals. Thus, employees in the fibers department could receive one to twelve percent above their base pay, depending upon the department's performance; this also means fibers department employees could receive up to 6 percent more in pay than their counterparts in other departments.[4]

Reinforce Organizational Norms

Differentials also provide a firm with an important tool for reinforcing organizational norms. That is, those who comply with organizational requirements are rewarded; those who do not are not rewarded. For example, Airborne Express of Seattle, Washington, revised their incentive packages to directly link pay to the corporate goals of growth, profitability, service, cost control, and productivity. According to Dick Goodwin, vice president of human resources for the overnight delivery and international freight-forwarding company, "We tend to attract young, aggressive managers at Airborne and we encourage internal competition to the point of publicly ranking peers on sales volume and revenue performance. Our incentive system supports these norms."[5]

Motivate Performance

Money is one of the most powerful motivators available to a manager because it is valued directly as a reward and because it facilitates the purchase of items that are valued. Its potential to motivate is unquestionable.

Consider the effect of a 25¢ reward at Creole Foods of Opelousas, Louisiana. When Alex Chachere took over as president, he found a lethargic work force content to ship fewer than 3,500 cases per month, far below the company's potential; so he devised a bonus plan. Every month that shipments topped 7,000 cases, workers would divide up an additional 25¢ per case. If the cost of sales stayed under 50 percent, they would get another 10¢. Chachere expected them to reach these targets in a year or so. The first month they shipped about 8,000 cases. Last year, the company's 28 employees averaged 30,000 cases per month, and Chachere paid $77,000 in bonuses. "That's a lot of money," he admits, "but the day we discontinue the bonuses is the day I quit."[6]

Similarly, American Greeting Corp. says that even its cost-of-living increases are now tied to merit, and bonuses are based on each unit's results. About 2,500 executives at Aetna Life & Casualty Co. vie for bonuses under a new "Superior Pay for Superior Performance" program. Bank of America increased by 29 percent the number of managers whose salary depends in part on performance. Hewlett-Packard Co. and Bechtel Group Inc. base all salary increases on merit.[7]

Recognize Differential Contributions

As noted in chapter 6 on selection, the difference in performance between a peak- and low-performing employee *averages* 3 to 1 and can be as much as 20 to 1.[8] Thus, a fourth objective of performance-based pay is to recognize and reinforce the differential contribution of high versus low performance. Good pay and larger increases help retain employees, and good performers are the ones managers most want to keep. Additionally, it has been shown that an employee who is rewarded for good performance will be more likely to continue performing well than one who is not appropriately rewarded.[9]

Still, few employees—particularly middle managers—ever see performance pay. While nine out of ten managers believe the best way to allocate scarce payroll dollars is to provide significant rewards to their top performers, only one-third of employees believe their pay is related to their performance.[10] The problem is that many plans are ill-conceived. Bonuses are not large enough nor sufficiently linked to performance to be motivational. Now, we'll examine the obstacles to the effective administration of performance-based rewards as well as other initial administrative issues associated with employee equity.

PERFORMANCE-BASED PAY OBSTACLES

Although performance-based pay systems can substantially improve productivity, many obstacles in their design and implementation may suppress their potential effectiveness. However, organizations can identify these obstacles and remove them. The following discussion of the obstacles pertains equally to both merit pay and incentive pay.

The many obstacles in the design and implementation of performance-based pay systems can be grouped into three general categories: (1) difficulties in specifying and measuring job performance, (2) problems in identifying valued rewards (pay being one of many rewards), and (3) difficulties in linking rewards to job performance.[11]

Before job performance can be rewarded firms must specify what job performance is, determine the relationships between levels of job performance and rewards, and accurately measure job performance. These activities are often difficult because of the changing nature of work, its multidimensional nature, technological developments, lack of supervisory training, and the manager's value system.

A second set of obstacles applies to monetary and nonmonetary rewards. These obstacles highlight the importance and value of using rewards other than pay to reward desired behaviors. Rewards other than pay may have more motivational value, especially for employees whose pay increments may be largely consumed by increased taxes. Managers must learn which rewards are most valued by employees and contingently administer on a timely basis those that are most reinforcing. This process is filled with potential problems.

The third set of obstacles involves the difficulties in linking rewards to job performance. The causes of these difficulties include the creation of inappropriate contingencies, the use of an inaccurate performance appraisal measure, and existing employee opposition. Employee opposition is often a major obstacle to successful implementation of performance-based pay, especially incentive plans; yet perceptions that employees may have about incentives plans are usually inaccurate (e.g., incentive plans can result in work speedups or can work you out of a job). Incentive plans appear to work best and overcome these obstacles when

- The plan is clearly communicated
- The plan is understood, and bonuses are easy to calculate
- The employees have a hand in establishing and administering the plan
- The employees believe they are being treated fairly
- The employees have an avenue of appeal if they believe they are being treated unfairly
- The employees believe they can trust the company; therefore, they believe they have job security
- The bonuses are awarded as soon as possible after the desired performance

Au Bon Pain, the restaurant chain discussed in chapter 7, provides an example of how a firm can overcome performance obstacles and link pay directly to performance. Recall that Au Bon Pain uses mystery customers to evaluate the performance of its restaurants and their employees. To establish a direct relationship between performance and rewards, managers whose employees score 100 percent in all 12 categories that are evaluated receive an on-the-spot bonus of 20 "Club Excellence Dollars"—dubbed CDs. These dollars can be traded like green stamps for items in a company catalog. Most items are in the $10 to $70 range and include such things as Au Bon Pain sunglasses and portable cassette players. Performance scores also help determine shift and district managers' eligibility for monthly cash profit-sharing bonuses.

Employees receive 10 CD points if they score 100 percent in six areas of customer interaction: overall willingness to serve, customer greeting within three seconds, pleasant parting, etc. Additionally, winners' names are posted on the store's bulletin board next to a list of the criteria, and all winners receive personal letters of congratulations from company officials. Customer service reminders are also included periodically with paychecks to reinforce high performance. On the downside, a score of less than 78 percent (individual or store) cancels out any bonus for the month.

LEGAL CONSIDERATIONS

Assuming the obstacles detailed above are overcome, a viable performance-based pay system can be developed. By definition, pay discrimination based on performance (not job status) is an inevitable and appropriate outcome of a properly administered performance-based pay system. Performance-based compensation is intended to create behaviors that lead to the accomplishment of organizational goals. Rewards that are administered contingently (that is, according to performance) cause increases in subsequent employee performance and expressions of satisfaction among high performers.[12] They encourage low performers to perform at a higher rate or to exit the organization. The legal issue, then, is not whether to discriminate in pay but how to administer performance-based pay so it does not unfairly discriminate against protected-group members.

As indicated in chapter 3, Title VII of the Civil Rights Act of 1964 applies not only to selection decisions but also to pay decisions. The Equal Pay Act of 1963 (an amendment to the broader Fair Labor Standards Act) specifically prohibits discrimination on the basis of gender for jobs that are substantially equal in skill, effort, responsibility, and working conditions.

Under both laws a supervisor may be charged with unlawful discrimination by an employee (in a protected group) who believes that a pay *raise was denied* on the basis of factors unrelated to performance. Raises not related to performance, however, can be *given* legally. Defensible factors (when they are equally applied to all employees) include the following:

- Performance
- Position in salary range
- Time since last increase
- Size of last increase

- Pay relationships within the company or department
- Pay levels of jobs in other companies
- Salaries of newly hired employees
- Budgetary limits

What is critical for both merit and incentive pay is that the same rules are used to give raises fairly and consistently among all employees.

ADMINISTRATIVE CONCERNS WITH PERFORMANCE-BASED PAY

There are several concerns associated with attaining employee equity through performance-based pay. Firms must decide the basis upon which adjustments to pay will be made, what portion of total pay will be based on performance, and at what level of aggregation rewards will be distributed.

Basis for Pay Adjustments

A primary concern is determining the basis on which employees in the same job will receive different salaries and salary increases. For example, should pay be advanced based on organizational tenure, performance, or a combination of both? Adjustments based on time send a message that, if employees play by the rules and avoid risks and obvious violations, the system will take care of them.

One of the simplest approaches to salary increases is the general increase. Typically found in unionized firms, a contract is negotiated which specifies an across-the-board adjustment for each year of the contract. There is no direct relationship with performance.

Job seniority. General increases may also be granted on the basis of job or organizational seniority. For example, a pay grade might be divided into eight equal steps, and employees move up a step for each year of job seniority. Alternatively, a stretch-out policy may be employed where low-seniority employees receive increases more frequently (every eight months if seniority is less than two years) than high-seniority employees (every eighteen months if seniority is greater then six years). Underlying this approach is the assumption that new workers are brought in at a pay rate below the fully competent level.

In some cases, seniority pay may reinforce corporate strategy. For example, Orrefors, a Swedish manufacturing firm has positioned itself in the marketplace as a high-end producer or unique handmade glass products. To attract and retain the highly talented crafts people its needs, Orrefors implemented a pay system that links salary increases with tenure and, presumably, skill level. The company argues that glassmaking demands a long apprenticeship period—often a decade of learning. Young people frequently are unwilling to remain in a job so long without a financial incentive. Thus, those willing to learn the craft of glassmaking and who remain with the company for that period will receive increasingly higher wages.[13]

Maturity curves. An alternative approach, the maturity curve, is popular in high technology and in research and development firms. The maturity curve approach uses years of applicable experience since receiving the B.S. degree as the x-axis and the rate of pay (dollars) as the y-axis. The theory behind factoring in the number of years since degree is that professional employees normally must have certain qualifications before they are hired and a certain amount of experience to be fully competent. With a maturity curve approach, a series of curves can be developed to provide differing levels of worth (performance ratings) for individuals with the same years of experience.[14] This helps reduce the perception that employees are almost entitled to increases.

On the other hand, performance-based pay (depending on the amount) sends a message that there are no entitlements; the strong will prosper, and the weak will not. Organizational cultures that promote risk taking—rather than stability and growth through tried and true methods—encourage the use of performance-based pay systems. Exhibit 10.1 details some questions to ask when considering whether to implement a performance-based pay system.[15]

Methods for Linking Pay to Performance

A second concern is how pay will be linked to performance. As shown in exhibit 10.2, three options are available. These techniques differ in regard to (1) the level of guaranteed base pay, (2) the relationship of base pay to the market, (3) the amount of performance pay, (4) the method used to allocate performance pay, (5) the permanency of performance-based pay, and (6) the portion of total pay that is at risk.

Traditional pay plans. With traditional pay plans, base pay (entitlement to be received regardless of performance) is set at the market rate. A small pool of money is set aside to reward performance. Under such plans, performance usually is not directly assessed. Instead, firms use indicators of performance (standards, behavioral descriptors) as measured through the performance appraisal processes discussed in chapters 7 and 8. Because performance measurement is

Exhibit 10.1
Ten Questions to Answer before Implementing a Performance-Based Pay System

1. Is pay valued by employees?
2. What is the objective(s) of the performance-based pay system?
3. Are the values of the organization conducive to a performance-based pay system?
4. What steps will be taken to ensure that employees and management are committed to the system?
5. Can performance be accurately measured? If not, what type of appraisal system will be used?
6. How frequently will performance be measured or evaluated?
7. What level of aggregation (individual, group, organization) will be used to distribute rewards?
8. How will pay be tied to performance (e.g. merit increase, bonus, commission, incentive)?
9. Does the organization have sufficient financial resources to make performance-based pay meaningful?
10. What steps will be taken to control and monitor the system?

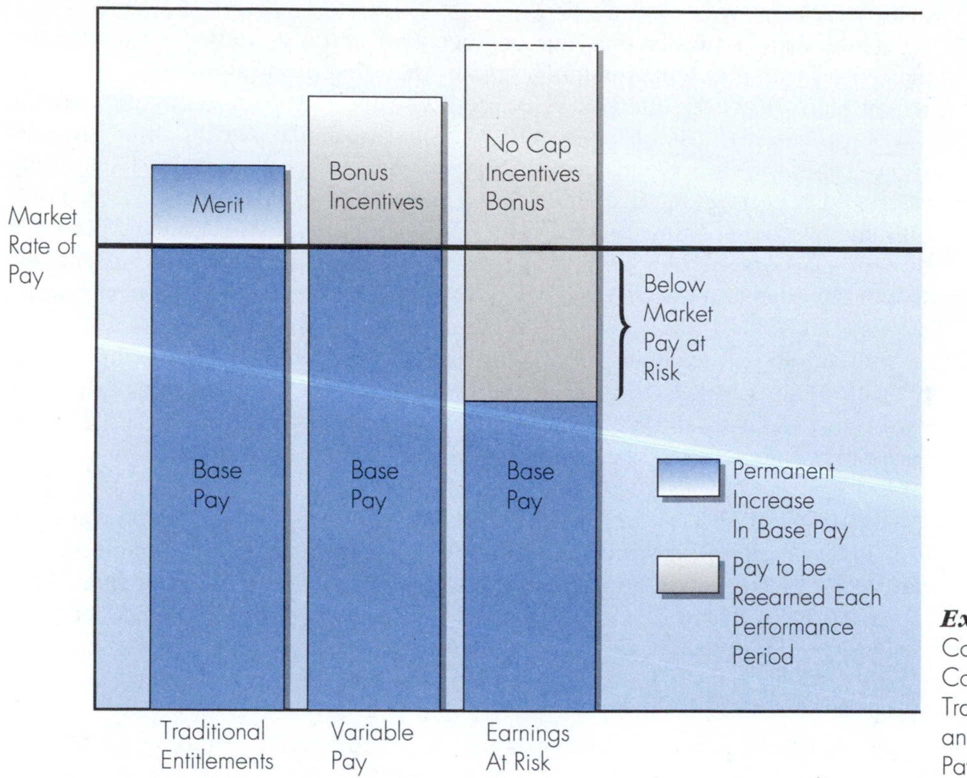

Exhibit 10.2
Comparison of Total Compensation under Traditional, Variable, and Earnings-at-Risk Pay Plans

less accurate, the size of a merit-pay adjustment typically is smaller than that awarded under the variable and earnings-at-risk plans to be discussed next.

A recent survey indicated that 72 percent of blue-collar workers and 56 percent of white-collar workers prefer straight wages over *any* type of incentive pay plan.[16] Even if subsequent performance remains the same or declines, merit increases awarded in a preceding year are permanent and cannot be revoked. Therefore, traditional pay entails little risk for the employee. From the organization's perspective, traditional pay plans are costly and risky. They permanently increase wage costs without guaranteeing permanent increases in performance.

Variable pay plans. Like traditional pay systems, variable pay plans peg base pay at the market rate. Additional compensation is available through incentives or bonuses, for peak performance. **Incentive** pay is compensation that is tied to specific goals established and communicated to participants before the start of the performance period. The emphasis is on specific actions performed in pursuit of the goals. By contrast, a **bonus** is payment based on an after-the-fact assessment of events when no specific actions were called for. The company assesses its performance and allocates a portion of profits to employees in the form of a bonus. While a bonus may increase loyalty and performance, the relationship is less direct and, consequently, less strong than with incentive pay.

That is, employees do not know in advance what performance and what level of that performance will be rewarded.

While there typically is a cap on incentive earnings under a variable pay plan, the earning potential is much greater than that associated with a traditional pay plan. However, the risk associated with the pay plan is that the variable pay supplement must be re-earned *each* performance period. For example, since 1983, Boeing Company employees have received bonuses totaling approximately 31 percent of their gross pay instead of wage increases. For a full-time worker making $12 an hour, these bonuses totaled about $7,740. If the annual bonuses had been wage increases instead, the *additional* income would have been about $25,940 more than the total received in base salary and bonuses.[17]

Still, traditional variable-pay systems provide an "upside earnings opportunity" with minimal risk to the employee. In the worst-case scenario, the employee earns what the market pays for the job. However, there is always the potential to earn more if goals are exceeded.[18]

Earnings at risk. Traditional and variable-pay systems provide rewards for individual or group performance as a *supplement* to historically guaranteed base pay amounts that equal the market rate. By comparison, **earnings at risk (EAR)** plans involve reductions in base pay to below-market levels. In essence, employees must earn their way back to the level that would have been guaranteed under a traditional, or variable pay plan, but have the potential for unlimited earnings.

According to Cathe Johnson, manager of compensation planning for Motorola's semiconductor business sector, "When base pay for the job lags the market, there is no longer a safety net. Additional earnings are possible if goals are exceeded, but income will be lost if goals are not met. The worst case scenario is that if the employee does not reach his or her performance goals, the standard of living will be lowered."[19]

As explained in this chapter's Focus on Research feature, such plans may not be acceptable to employees who are used to more traditional reward structures that assure earnings stability. Thus, organizations must weigh the goal of attaining strategic initiatives through performance-based pay against the costs of implementing such systems in a nonsupportive culture.

Level of Aggregation

A third administrative issue concerns the level of aggregation at which performance will be measured (individual, work team, department, plant, strategic business unit, organization) and at which performance pay will be administered. One factor influencing the aggregation level is the ease with which performance can be objectively measured. If individual performance can only be evaluated by subjective supervisory ratings, then it may be appropriate to move to a higher level of aggregation (e.g., team or strategic business unit). Moving to a higher level tends to yield more objective measures of performance (e.g., labor costs, profits, cost savings). The trade-off, however, is that the tie to individual performance is less direct.

Technical constraints may dictate the appropriate level of aggregation. Individual incentives are less appropriate when work flows are interdependent (as in small-batch manufacturing or the development of an advertising campaign) or when the work flows are machine-paced (as on an assembly line). Systems in which work outputs are conditional on the receipt of information or materials from someone else also are good candidates for team- or organizational-level plans.[20]

A third factor affecting the choice of aggregation level relates to the type of behavior an organization needs to attain its strategic initiatives. As discussed previously, Airborne Express wants its sales force to be entrepreneurs. Therefore it utilizes individual incentive plans that are associated with greater competition, increased performance pressure, and greater risk taking.[21] Team incentive plans, on the other hand, reinforce behaviors that promote collective rather than individual success. In addition, they offer the benefits of group reinforcement to ensure that all team members help to attain objectivess. While the perceived connection between pay and performance is weaker, this may be offset by an increase in cooperation. Team and organizational incentive plans also are less costly and less difficult to administer than individual pay systems.

Timing of Performance-Based Pay

Generally speaking, the more quickly rewards follow desirable behavior, the more potent the rewards are in evoking subsequent desirable behavior. Delayed rewards may (1) decrease desired behavior (because the employee doesn't see an immediate consequence), (2) increase dissatisfaction and frustration among high performers, and (3) increase undesired behavior that occurs during the interval between performance and the receipt of the reward.

As noted in the section on obstacles, the administration of performance-based pay frequently is delayed from several weeks to a year. As a result, employees end up receiving pay at a time far removed from the accomplishment that earned the rewards.

Several practical reasons could cause the delay. Task cycles may not be conveniently equal to calendar cycles, or performance information may not be readily available. Also, the delay may be part of a cost-containment strategy; the longer the company delays paying the incentive, the longer it can use the money for its own purposes.

One way to minimize the problems associated with delayed rewards entails developing performance contracts. Upon completion of agreed-upon work at an agreed-upon date, the performance pay is distributed. If the time frame is too short to be managed, then feedback or supervisory recognition can be provided intermittently until the formal reward can be delivered.[22]

However, it can be advantageous to delay the distribution of performance pay. For example, the Utah firm, Exhibit Systems, builds one-of-a-kind industrial displays. Traditionally, the company paid its sales people at the time a contract was signed. The immediacy of the reward, however, created problems. According to Dennis Peterson, a partner in the firm, "Once the sales person received his commission, he moved on to the next sale. We received complaints from our designers that the sales reps were not cooperating. Production workers also complained that the reps were slow in providing specifications for displays." The company also was running a large number of accounts receivables.

To alleviate these problems, the commission plan was redesigned. Sales representatives now receive one-half of their commission when the industrial dis-

FOCUS ON RESEARCH

Lowering Floors and Raising Ceilings: Effects of an Earnings-at-Risk Plan on Pay Satisfaction

Traditional variable pay systems (such as incentives, bonus, or gain sharing) provide rewards for individual or group performance as a supplement to historically guaranteed base pay amounts. Because base pay is pegged to the market, traditional variable pay systems provide an "upside earnings opportunity" with minimal risk to the employee. At the worst, the employee would earn what the market pays for the job but nothing above that amount. Earnings at risk plans involve *reductions* in base pay and employees are placed in the position of earning their way back to the level that would have been guaranteed under a traditional pay system. Regardless of the employee's performance level, the amount of pay an employee can be *certain* of earning will be lower than it was before the implementation of an earnings-at-risk (EAR) system.

EARs have gained popularity in many industries including retail banking because of their potential to reduce fixed costs and ensure long term employment stability. As operationalized in banks, EARs cut base pay levels to below market levels and reward employees for selling bank products (e.g., new accounts, loan packages and even insurance) rather than merely servicing customer accounts. While these systems result in a wider range of possibilities for total take-home pay (no upper limit on earnings), they do add elements of risk and uncertainty which may be foreign to a retail banking culture. In contrast to real estate sales, and garment manufacturing, the conservative retail banking industry has traditionally placed a relatively high value on commitment and longevity rather than productivity. Thus, the implementation of an EAR plan may meet with employee resistance and dissatisfaction.

Because little research has been devoted to examining the effects of EAR pay programs, Seattle-based researchers Karen Brown and Vandra Huber examined pay satisfaction before and after the introduction of an EAR plan in a retail bank. The two researchers wanted to understand whether an EAR system differentially would affect pay process as well as pay outcome satisfaction. Additionally, they wanted to determine the antecedents to pay satisfaction before and after implementing an EAR system.

The research was conducted in a large publicly held bank in a western region of the U.S. where the economy is very stable. The bank was in extremely good financial health at the time of the study and was not associated with the savings and loan industry which had experienced downturns. All branch employees were surveyed at two points in time, just prior to the implementation of a reduced base EAR pay plan and six months after the plan had gone into effect and just before the beginning of a new fiscal year.

Surveys were mailed to bank employees along with a letter from bank officials encouraging employees to complete the survey. A total of 101 employees responded to both surveys. At the time that the first survey was distributed, a traditional "upside earnings" variable pay plan was in place. Employees received a base salary set at the market rate. In addition they were eligible for quarterly bonuses based on branch performance determined by the net present value of each bank product. Six months after the EAR pay system was implemented a second survey was distributed. Six months was chosen because it provided enough time for employees to sufficiently

Continued

play has been built and the customer has signed off on it. The remainder of the commission is paid when the account is paid in full. Now, Peterson notes, sales people work closely with designers and construction teams to ensure the product is built to customer specifications. Additionally, the plan encourages sales personnel to play an active role in collecting accounts receivable.

In sum, many design issues need to be considered to attain employee equity and corporate objectives. The next two sections will review in greater detail the

experience the pay system but not so much time that turnover, known to be high in retail banking, would result in a substantial degradation of the employee population base.

A statistical process called multivariate analysis of variance was used to examine the changes in pay process and pay outcome satisfaction before (time 1) and after the implementation of the EAR system (time 2). This analysis showed that implementing an EAR pay plan had a significant effect on both aspects of pay satisfaction. Employees were moderately satisfied with pay outcomes (how much they earned) before the EAR system was implemented (average = 4.43) but were significantly less satisfied once it was in place (average = 3.05). The change in pay administration procedures also led to a significant decline in pay process satisfaction (Time 1 average = 3.77; Time 2 average = 2.88). Under the old system employees were significantly more satisfied with their pay outcomes than with the pay process. Under the new system, employees were equally dissatisfied with pay outcomes and pay process. Apparently the new incentive system was viewed so negatively that it washed out differences in process and outcome ratings found under the old system.

To determine if the changes in pay satisfaction would occur even when total pay did not decrease, a second set of analyses were conducted. Here, only respondents for whom pay had either stayed the same or increased were included. Again, both pay process satisfaction and pay outcome satisfaction declined. Apparently, changing a pay system even when one benefits from the change leads to dissatisfaction. Because satisfaction decreased for wage gainers as well as for wage losers, the opportunity for receiving higher pay appears to have been overshadowed by the reduction in the steady portion of their pay checks upon which they had come to rely.

The study found that process and outcome satisfaction were tied to an individual's reward for effort beliefs. When employees perceive that they are not getting sufficient rewards for their job efforts, dissatisfaction with the way pay was administered as well as the level of pay received increased. A second important variable is pay system understanding. An employee's understanding of how pay is tied to performance is more important than the actual mechanics of the plan. Under the old system, understanding was related to both pay process and outcome satisfaction. When the new system was implemented, understanding affected satisfaction with the pay process. The researchers concluded that if the EAR system had been explained better or differently, pay satisfaction may not have declined to the extent that it did.

Tenure was also found to be a significant predictor variable. Employees with greater tenure were more dissatisfied with the new pay system than employees with less tenure. The authors noted that as the workforce continues to age, it may be more and more difficult for service organizations to convince their employees that riskier pay plans are in everyone's best interests. In sum, the implementation of an EAR system must be handled with great care and strong consideration must be given to its fit with the organization and its employees.

Based on the high dissatisfaction associated with the EAR pay system, the bank returned to the variable pay system that had been in place at the time of the first survey. Base pay was raised to match the market and variable pay was administered in the form of bonuses.

SOURCE: Based on K.A. Brown and V.L. Huber. "Lowering Floors and Raising Ceilings: A Longitudinal Assessment of the Effects of an Earnings-At-Risk Plan on Pay Satisfaction," *Personnel Psychology* (June 1992): 297–312.

formulas for allocating pay. The last section of the chapter focuses on the issues surrounding compensation for special groups.

TRADITIONAL PERFORMANCE-BASED PAY

Traditional performance-based pay has been the cornerstone of public and private compensation systems for many years. It is best exemplified by merit pay plans.

Merit Pay Plans

While general increases are on the decline, more than eighty percent of all organizations still use some form of merit pay.[23] Merit pay plans differ along several dimensions. First, some plans include other factors (cost of living, job or organizational seniority, comparability in the pay grade) than just performance in the pay adjustment formula. Second, plans differ in the way the merit increase is calculated. Some plans award an absolute amount; other plans award a percentage of base salary; still others rely on merit grids (to be discussed separately). Third, merit increases may be distributed more often than once a year or delayed in times of budget crisis.[24]

While the concept of merit pay has been implemented in a variety of ways, all merit pay plans share two characteristics. First, some portion of employees' pay is based on their rated performance in a previous time period. Second, the merit increase awarded in one evaluation period carries over into the base salary for future evaluation periods.

Performance assessment. Fundamental to an effective merit pay system is a credible and comprehensive performance appraisal system. Without a reliable assessment of performance, it is impossible to relate pay to performance in a way that is motivating. As discussed in chapters 7 and 8, performance appraisal processes are often subjective. The criteria may be contaminated or deficient. Supervisors all too frequently evaluate incumbents according to preconceived biases. Regardless of the appraisal form (e.g., behavior, output, trait), rating errors such as leniency and halo are rampant. In fact, one study found that over a two-year period, the average rating given by managers using a five-point rating scale increased significantly from 3.36 to 3.60 on a five-point scale.[25]

As noted in chapter 8, supervisors and employees seldom agree on evaluation results. When pay hinges on evaluation results, confrontation and mistrust often escalate.[26] A related concern is that appraisals in general—and merit pay systems specifically—emphasize individual rather than group goals. This may promote an "every-man-for-himself" attitude that does little to boost productivity—particularly in the team-oriented 1990s.

Size of merit increase. Under merit pay plans, pay raises are recommended by the department head for the employee being supervised. This is usually carried out within the constraints of a merit pool budget. In 1982, the median increase granted to merit recipients was 8.8 percent. The difference between the median raise and high raise was 5.5 percent; the difference between the median and low raise was 3.9 percent. In recent years, merit budgets have declined steadily and for the past four years have averaged 5 percent. Since the total of all increases cannot exceed the budget percentage for the department, the decline in merit pay pools is problematic. As Charles Peck, a compensation expert with the Conference Board noted,

> Merit increases tend to be expensive and, contrary to their intent, not strongly related to performance. Usually everybody gets something. This so dilutes the salary increase budget that the top performer's increase is not large enough to be significant (especially after it is prorated over the number of pay periods in the year and subjected to withholding). On the other hand, the poor performer is getting more than he or she

should have, which is nothing. If the concept of pay for performance is rigorously applied, there must be zero pay for zero performance.[27]

In illustration, the typical merit pay difference between satisfactory and excellent performance at the $40,000 level averages $17 per week after taxes.[28] The result of all this is that the employees who are most dissatisfied are the ones the company least wants dissatisfied—the top performers.

Merit increase guidelines. Three types of merit increase guidelines are commonly used to tie pay to performance. The simplest and easiest to understand specifies pay increase percentages for different levels of performance.

Performance Rating	(1) Unacceptable	(2) Below Average	(3) Competent	(4) Above Average	(5) Superior
Merit Increase	0%	2%	4%	6%	8%

To give supervisors some latitude, increase ranges may be included for each performance category (e.g., 0–1% for unacceptable performance; 2–3% for below average, and so on). Another option is to vary the timing of increases (e.g., every eight months for high performers and as long as every fifteen months for low performers).

A more complex system involves the development of a merit pay grid. As shown in exhibit 10.3, this approach considers the individual's position in the salary range as well as performance. Holding performance rating constant, an employee whose current base pay is low (first quartile of pay range) would receive a larger percentage increase in pay than an employee whose current base salary is higher (fourth quartile). Although the percentage of merit increase is greater in the lower quartiles, the absolute size of the merit increase is often larger in the higher quartiles, provided the merit budget is large enough and the grid is designed correctly.

Still, because employees confuse market adjustments and performance pay, they may not perceive the merit pay grid approach as fair. That is, equally performing employees do not get equal percentage increases in pay. While employee education may help to minimize this problem, a more practical approach is to

Exhibit 10.3
Sample Merit Pay Grid

	Current Position in the Salary Range			
Performance Rating	**First Quartile**	**Second Quartile**	**Third Quartile**	**Fourth Quartile**
1. Unacceptable	0%	0%	0%	0%
2. Below Average	2%	0%	0%	0%
3. Competent	8%	6%	4%	2%
4. Above Average	10%	8%	6%	4%
5. Superior	12%	10%	8%	6%

decouple performance and market pay adjustments and award each type of increase separately.

Overall Assessment

According to Edward E. Lawler, one of the nation's experts on reward system design, merit increases do not work well because they are plugged into antiquated pay systems. In the early 1900s, many jobs were in manufacturing and agriculture and involved the production of relatively simple, high-volume products. This is not the case today. "If we've learned anything in 40 years of researching reward systems, it's that merit pay is a terrible way to increase productivity—particularly for the service, information-processing, and high technology-based industries of the 1990s."[29] Still, most U.S. workers are paid under merit systems and like them.

VARIABLE-PAY PLANS

Top executives have long received bonuses and incentives based on company financial results. Now variable and earnings-at-risk pay plans are being used more frequently to reward rank and file employees, too. Sibson and Company found that 53 percent of compensation plans included variable pay in 1990, up from 46 percent in 1989. Another report showed that more variable-pay plans have been adopted in the past five years than in all of the past two decades.[30]

There are several reasons for the stepped-up interest in variable pay. First, production improvements are necessary if the U.S. intends to retain a leadership role in an increasingly global market. America's shift to a service economy also promotes interest in variable pay. In service companies, compensation can account for up to 80 percent of a firm's operating budget; consequently, variable pay is spreading into banks (such as the one studied by Brown and Huber in the "Focus on Research..."), hospitals, and other labor-intensive service providers.

A third reason for increased interest is the discrepancy between the level of top executive compensation and the levels paid other workers. Company-wide incentive plans allow *all* workers a direct share in company prosperity. Finally, there is a growing awareness that traditional pay plans do a terrible job of linking pay to performance. If organizations are to achieve their strategic initiatives, then pay needs to be linked to performance in such a way that it aligns the goals of the employee and organization.

While endless variations on the theme exist, seven new performance-based pay approaches predominate and will be reviewed in this section. Exhibit 10.4 summarizes the characteristics as well as the advantages and disadvantages of each. These plans can be implemented as variable-pay or earnings-at-risk plans. Recall that earnings-at-risk pay plans differ from variable-pay plans in two respects—the level of guaranteed base pay and the presence or absence of a cap on variable earnings.

Performance Bonuses

With increased emphasis on cost-effective human resource practices, firms are questioning the traditional practice of granting annual salary or merit increases.

Exhibit 10.4
Definition and Characteristics of Variable Pay Programs

Plan Type	How It Works	Advantages	Disadvantages
Lump-Sum Bonus **5% of Total Pay**	Payment in lieu of merit increase; not added to base salary	Company can control fixed wage costs and benefits; more visible reward than merit increase	May be based on subjective appraisal; may be resented by employees because not everyone gets something
Instant Incentive **3% of Total Pay**	Special payment to an individual for a noteworthy achievement (e.g., devising a cost-saving plan)	Allows employee to benefit from cost savings ideas; easy to administer	Emphasize quantity not quality; individual rewards may be too small to encourage employee participation
Individual Incentive **10–20% of Total Pay**	Payment based on measured individual performance, such as a piece-work system	Produces high rate of productivity; links labor costs to performance; easy to explain and administer	Promotes competition, standards difficult to calculate; inappropriate for interdependent tasks
Restricted Stock/Stock Options **15% of Total Pay**	Grants of stock subject to restrictions or stock option grants to employees ordinarily not eligible for such awards	Increases loyalty; provides retirement income; enables employee to share in firm's success	May focus on short-term earnings, not long-term profitability; difficult to explain; lose motivation power in economic downturns
Small-Group Incentives **10% of Total Pay**	Uniform award to all members of a group based on achievement of predetermined goals	Ups productivity; also promotes teamwork, utilizes reinforcing power of co-workers, and creates goal interdependence	Promotes competition between groups; workers may resent low performers
Profitsharing **6% of Total Pay**	Uniform payment to all employees based on corporate profits; payments can be made in cash or deferred into a retirement fund	Plan guaranteed to be affordable; unites company and employees' financial interests; provides retirement income in some cases; raises productivity.	Annual payment may lead workers to ignore long-term performance; forces company to open their books; employees may see payments as gifts
Gainsharing **3% of Total Pay**	Plans to measure productivity of a unit or organization and to share the value of productivity gains	Employees learn more about business; links labor costs to firm performance; improves performance	Requires measurable standards; difficult to administer; not workable if trust is low; may pay bonuses even when unprofitable

Consider an employee who performs outstandingly one year and is given a 15 percent merit pay increase. The next year, for whatever reason, the employee may not perform as well, or even adequately. While subsequent performance may decrease, the original salary increase is a permanent cost for the organization. Merit increases administered in this way may also demotivate other employees because the employee who had performed well previously may have a higher base pay rate than the employee who is currently performing well. As a result, the low performer may receive a larger increase than the better-performing employee whose base pay is lower.

To rectify this situation, firms such as B.F. Goodrich, Timex, and Westinghouse are replacing merit increases with one-time semiannual, or quarterly performance bonuses. These bonuses may be distributed in one lump sum or in the traditional way (divided up into parts for each check). Performance bonuses are most popular for executives. Recent surveys indicate that approximately 90 percent of executives receive bonuses that account for about 50 percent of their total pay.

Bonuses also have replaced merit increases in 32 percent of all firms using variable pay for rank and file employees.[31] For example,

> ... [F]actory workers at Nucor's five steel mills earn meager base wages ($5.80 to $9.02) per hour, less than half the typical union. Yet bonuses based on the number of tons of acceptable quality steel produced, bump total pay to more than $32,000, about $2,000 more than unionized counterparts. Workers who are late lose their bonus for the day; workers who are more than 30 minutes late lose their bonus for the week.
>
> Department managers at Nucor earn yearly bonuses based on return on plant assets and plant managers receive bonuses based on return on equity. At year end the company distributes 10 percent of pretax earnings to employees.. As a result of this, Nucor turned out more than twice as much steel per employee than larger steel companies.[32]

Bonuses hold several advantages over salary increases. First the bonuses increase the meaning of pay. The lump-sum payment of $5,000 is more striking than a before-tax increase of $100 a week. A wise employee can leverage the value of the bonus further by investing it carefully. This may not be possible when increases are spread throughout the year. Second, bonuses maximize the relationship between pay and performance. Unlike permanent salary increases, an employee must perform above average year in and year out to continue receiving bonuses. A major constraint with this, as well as any performance-based pay system, is measurement. If subjective appraisal criteria are used, the fairness of the system will be undermined, and the motivational potential of the bonus will be lost.

Occasionally, traditional merit pay and bonus plans are combined. For example, reasoning that excellence is the standard, not the exception, a broadcast firm set its pay policy line at 105 percent of the external market. Pay grade minimums were also established so entry-level trainees with no experience could be paid less. Merit increases were awarded until the employee's base salary reached the pay grade midpoint. Then annual salary increases were replaced with an annual performance bonus for all excellent or above-average employees. Depending on the employee's base salary, these bonuses ranged from $1,000 to $5,000.

Instant Bonuses

Unlike other performance-based pay systems described in this section, instant bonuses are not based on formulas, special performance criteria, or goals. Sometimes called "lightning strikes" or "recognition" bonuses, these performance awards are designed to recognize the exceptional contribution of employees. Utilized by 95 percent of all firms, instant bonuses recognize length of service (88 percent), special achievement (64 percent), and innovative ideas (42 percent). Often certificates, plaques, cash, savings bonds, or flower arrangements are used. To recognize **longevity,** most companies give pins or other jewelry (e.g., $30 pin for five years and $300 watch for twenty years). Longevity awards are also being used in the health services as a strategy to retain professionals in critical demand areas. A hospital may offer a cash bonus ($1,000) to any nurse who joins its staff and works for a full year. Typically, the cash award is cheaper than the recruitment, selection, and training costs associated with a new hire.

Achievement bonuses emphasize overall performance or performance on a particular project in the areas of safety, customer service, productivity, quality, or attendance. Recipients typically are nominated by peers or supervisors to receive awards including gifts, savings bonds, dinner certificates, and cash incentives ranging from $150 to more than $1,000 (43 percent). Data IO, an electronics manufacturing company in Redmond, Washington, makes extensive use of bonuses. For example, all members of a computer-aided electronics software development team (e.g., engineers, technical writers, shipping group, quality assurance) garnered $60 dinner certificates when the product was released. Two high achievers in the groups also earned weekend trips for two to San Francisco (airline and motel valued at $1,500). On other occasions, recognition plaques, mugs, T-shirts, and pen sets have been distributed. Monthly, an employee is recognized for his or her contribution to Data IO. Recognition brings with it a parking place by the front door, an engraved plaque, and verbal recognition in a company meeting.

According to the National Association of Suggestion Systems, its 900 members received nearly one million **suggestions** from their employees, resulting in savings over $2 billion in 1990. Crowley Maritime Corporation's "Ship Us an Idea" is typical of most suggestion plans. The shipping company receives an average of 20 suggestions a month from its 1,000 employees. Employees earn between $50 to $150 for most ideas and may earn up to 10 percent of the cost savings for significant ideas. A presidential award of $1,000 is given annually for the best idea. According to Moon Hui Kim, program developer, the benefits far outweigh the $6,000–$10,000 annual program administration costs.[33]

Individual Incentives

Individual incentives are among the oldest and most popular form of incentive plan. In this type of plan, individual standards of performance are established and communicated in advance; rewards are based on individual output. Individual incentives are used by a significant minority (35 percent) of all companies in all industry groups except utilities. Utility firms have been slower to implement such plans due to their history of regulation that limits work force autonomy.

While a variety of individual incentive plans exist, they differ in terms of the method of rate determination. When the work cycle is short, units of production generally serve as the method of rate determination. For longer-cycle jobs, the standard is typically based on the time required to complete a unit. Individual incentive systems also vary with regard to the constancy with which pay is a function of production level. One option is to pay a consistent amount at *all* production levels (e.g., twenty-five cents per carton). Alternatively, pay may vary as a function of production level. For example, employees may be paid twenty-five cents a carton up to 1,000 units a day. When this threshold is passed, the incentive rises to twenty-seven cents a carton.

Individual incentive plans also share a common job analysis foundation. As discussed in chapter 3, time-and-motion studies are often employed to determine how wages are tied to output. The challenge is to identify a "normal" rate of production.[34]

Piecework plan. Piecework is the most common type of individual incentive pay plan. In this plan, employees are guaranteed a standard pay rate for each unit of output. Under the **straight piecework plan,** employees are guaranteed a standard pay rate for each unit of production. For example, if the base pay of a job is $40 per day and the employee can produce at a normal rate twenty units a day, the piece rate may be established at $2 per unit. The incentive pay rate is based on the standard output and the base wage rate. The "normal" rate is more than what the time and motion studies indicate but is supposed to represent 100 percent efficiency. The final rate also reflects the bargaining power of the employees, economic conditions of the organization and industry, and what the competition is paying.

In a **differential piece rate plan,** there is more than one rate of pay for the same job. This plan can be operationalized in different ways. The Taylor Differential Plan consists of a higher rate of pay for work completed in a set time period. For production per unit that takes longer than the established time to complete the job, the rate of pay is lower. Merrill Lynch, one of the largest stock brokerage firms in the country, instituted a commission plan similar to Taylor's plan. Sales personnel having higher sales volume receive higher rates of commission than do sales personnel with lower volume.

The success of any piece rate system depends on more than just paying individuals for more work. Its success is dependent on how employees are treated and the level of employment security provided. These ideas are illustrated at Lincoln Electric.

> Lincoln Electric, in Cleveland, is a 93-year-old manufacturer of welding machines and motors—a company that might seem to be an unlikely candidate for survival, let alone success. Its biggest customers have been in such cyclical markets as oil, steel, and construction, and during the downturns, Lincoln, like other machinery-makers, has taken some licks. But, its managers argue, it has remained solvent—and keeps bouncing back—because of its approach to managing and rewarding people.
>
> For more than 50 years, the combination of pay by output, bonus, and job security has worked like a charm. Lincoln's employees produce an average of two to three times what their counterparts produce at competitive plants, including those in Japan. Hard workers who don't mind overtime have been known in a good year to gross more than $80,000, with bonus.[35]

Standard hour plan. The standard hour plan is the second most common type of incentive plan. This approach is based on setting a standard time per unit of production. Tasks are broken down by the amount of time it takes to complete them. This can be determined by historical records, time-and-motion studies, or a combination of both. The time to perform each task then becomes a "standard."

Consider a standard time of 2 hours and a rate of pay of $12 an hour. In this system, a worker receives $24 for each unit of work completed (regardless of the actual time needed to complete the unit). If a worker completes six units in an eight-hour day; the worker would receive 6 X $24 or $144. This is substantially more than $96, the standard rate of pay for eight hours (based on 4 units).

Rewarding indirect labor. While individual piece-rate systems work well for direct-labor personnel, it is more difficult to reward personnel who support and make possible the productivity improvements of the direct laborer. The problem is that these workers often assist a number of direct laborers. They may sort, feed, and prepare raw materials or remove and inspect finished materials. One approach is to provide the same percentage of increase above normal as is earned by the *average* direct laborer.

Top executive plans. Individual incentives are also commonly used to award top-level managers. Utilizing a formula in which the attainment of corporate or unit goals are weighted, these plans relate incentives to the attainment of corporate or strategic business unit (SBU) goals. In addition to cash, incentive pay includes such things as restricted stock grants (free shares given to the CEO for staying with the company), performance shares or performance units (free shares or cash for achieving multiyear goals), and stock-option grants.

Debate over the effectiveness of executive incentives has raged for many years. For one thing, executive pay seems excessive relative to the pay of rank and file employees and of CEOs in other countries. In 1992 there was a ratio of 40 to 1 in the U.S. between the pay of CEOs and rank and file employees, compared with 17 to 1 in Germany and only 10 to 1 in Japan. Among the top 200 U.S. firms, CEO pay (base and incentives) averaged $1.3 million in 1990, an increase of 5.4 percent over the preceding year. At the extreme, Steven J. Ross, co-CEO of Time Warner, Inc., earned a base salary of $3.3 million. Incentive pay awarded through a stock-option grant boosted his overall pay to $39 million for 1990. By comparison, David D. Glass, CEO of Wal-Mart, the nation's hottest retailer, got a comparatively miniscule option grant ($250,000) besides his cash pay of $630,000.[36]

According to compensation experts Michael Jensen and Kevin J. Murphy, "the relentless focus on how much CEOs are paid diverts public attention away from the real problem—how CEOs are paid." After studying the pay of CEOs in 1,400 companies over an eight-year period, the researchers contend that the "incentive" compensation of top executives is virtually independent of corporate performance and is no more variable than that of hourly workers.

To rectify the problem, the researchers recommend greater performance variability in executive pay, restructuring incentive pay so that salaries, bonuses, and stock options provide big rewards for superior performance and big penalties for poor performance. This can be accomplished by ensuring that CEOs own substantial amounts of company stock and face the real prospect of being fired as a result of poor performance. Unfortunately, current incentive pay for CEOs too often is treated like an entitlement program rather than as a way to motivate outstanding performance.[37]

Team-Based Incentives

Team incentives fall somewhere between individual-incentive and whole-organizational plans such as gainsharing and profitsharing (to be discussed next). The goals are tailored specifically to what the work team needs to accomplish. Strategically, they link the goals of individuals to those of the work group (typically ten people or fewer) to achieve financial goals. According to Judy Huret, a principal with Towers Perrin in San Francisco, team incentives improve employees' "line of sight" regarding what they need to do as a group to enhance profits. For example,

> An insurance company was encountering friction between two different departments—data processing and claims. The claims people said the data processing staff never met its deadlines. The data processing people said the claims people kept changing their minds and made unreasonable demands. When the company instituted a team incentive plan, senior management facilitated a discussion between the two departments and informed them that their incentive award would be linked to how well they worked together to meet customer needs.
>
> The claims group then clearly outlined the specifications and timetable necessary to meet customer service needs and discussed them with data processing. Data processing developed a detailed project plan and shared it with claims. Now that both groups understand the ultimate objective, they can work together to achieve a common goal. The amount of their incentive award will depend on how quickly and how well the team goal is met.[38]

Given that the prerequisites listed in exhibit 10.5 are met, team-based incentives offer four major advantages compared with individual incentive systems. First, the mere presence of group members who have some control over rewards evokes more vigorous and persistent behavior than when individuals work alone. Second, the likelihood that conflicting contingencies (peer pressure) will evoke counterproductive control over behavior is reduced. Third, the strength of

Exhibit 10.5
Prerequisites for the Effective Administration of Group Incentives

1. Everyone who's on the team, including indirect laborers and support staff members, is eligible.
2. Team performance is measurable.
3. Performance standards are communicated to team members in advance of the performance period.
4. The incentive system is easy to understand.
5. Team members receive regular feedback on their progress towards performance targets. "War rooms," including graphs, charts, and statistical analyses, provide on-going useful feedback.
6. Team members must believe they can affect performance outcomes.
7. Organizational culture must be congruent with team problem solving and participation.

the rewards is increased since they are now paired with group-administered rewards (praise, camaraderie). Research also suggests that the performance of a group is higher than that attained by individual group members (although not as high as the best person in the group). Finally, the performance of another group member (usually the high performer) can serve as a model, encouraging other team members to imitate successful behavior.[39]

While team-based incentives are promising, administrative responsibilities are as great as those associated with individual incentive plans. Job analysis is still necessary to identify how to structure the teams and to ensure workloads are equivalent between teams. There may also be unintended side effects, including competition between groups, that may or may not compliment goal attainment. A second concern is social loafing, where group performance declines because team members (consciously or subconsciously) lower their inputs, believing that others in the group will pick up the slack. Social loafing is particularly likely to occur if group cooperation is overly emphasized.[40]

Profit Sharing

Introduced first in the Gallatin glasswork factory in New Geneva, Pennsylvania, in 1794, profit-sharing plans are now on the increase. The Bureau of Labor Statistics found that 19 percent of all full-time employees participated in profit-sharing plans in 1990, up from 16 percent in 1989. As defined by the Council of profit Sharing, these plans include any program under which an employer pays or makes available to regular employees special current or deferred sums based on the profits of business in addition to their regular pay.[41] The median payment under a profit-sharing plan is 6 percent, which is slightly higher than the typicaly merit increase of 5 percent.

According to a Conference Board study, profit-sharing plans are designed to enable employees to share in the organization's success and to promote teamwork. Most plans emphasize "motivating employees to improve profits." Since goals are not set in advance of the performance period, gainsharing plans fall into the broad category of bonus disbursements. That is, employees are rewarded only after a company has been successful. As noted earlier, the motivational potential of bonus plans is more questionable than incentive plans because employees are unlikely to know the relationship between their performance and the profitability of the firm.[42]

Particularly prevalent in financial services and manufacturing firms, profit-sharing plans typically involve placing a portion of an organization's profits into a pool for distribution to eligible employees. The portion of profits to be shared is either fixed by the terms of the plan or is determined annually by the board of directors. In some cases stated profit objectives must be attained before profit sharing kicks in. In other cases, a differential formula is used (similar to differential piece-rate plans discussed earlier). For example, 5 percent of the first $10 million goes into the fund and 7 percent of profits over $15 million. Another example would be to tie gains to the operating income of the firm (e.g., it must increase 3 percent above the prior year before funding will begin).

Profit-sharing plans fall into three categories. **Current distribution plans** provide for between 14 and 33 percent of corporate profits to be distributed quarterly or annually to employees. While this approach can be relatively complex,[43] **"first dollar" profit-sharing plans** are much simpler. In these plans a fixed percentage of pre- or post-tax annual profits goes into a pool for distribution to eligible employees.

The most prevalent type of plan—**deferred profit-sharing plans**—increased from 100,000 in 1969 to more than 450,000 in 1989. With these plans, profits are invested on behalf of employees. The employee is free to draw out the money upon retirement. In the interim, loans for emergencies can be made from contributions. About 20 percent of firms with profit-sharing plans have **combined plans.** Here a portion of profits is distributed immediately to employees; the remaining amount is set aside in a designated account.

One-fifth of profit-sharing plans *require* participants to make contributions (2 to 10 percent of their salaries). Other plans allow, but do not require, employees to contribute up to 8 percent of their salaries. In all deferred plans, contributions are invested on behalf of the employee. Participants can choose between company stock, guaranteed investment contracts, fixed-interest securities, and diversified investments.

While base salaries are often lower with profit-sharing plans, total compensation tends to be equal to or better than that received in non-profit-sharing firms. In nonmanufacturing profit-sharing firms, employees actually earn 60 cents an hour more than other workers. A portion of the employee's total pay is at risk; however, it is not much more than would be at risk in a merit pay system.

In addition to the risk factor, a second concern is that, unlike pension plans, deferred plans (specifically) are not closely regulated. As a result, the possibility that the deferred compensation funds will be inappropriately invested or used for other purposes is potentially higher than for traditional pension funds. To dispel employee fears around this issue, sponsoring companies have begun to add provisions (e.g., insurance) to their plans that reduce risk to their workers.

From the employer's perspective, profit-sharing plans help contain wage costs. A recent study by Rutgers University's Institute of Management and Labor Relations reported that profit-sharing firms were typically more productive than non-profit-sharing firms. Since profit sharing is based on company performance, when business declines, the company is not obligated to make any payouts.[44] For example, Ford Motor Company employed profit sharing as a means of regaining profitability.

> When negotiations on a new collective bargaining agreement took place, the automakers asked the union for wage concessions. In exchange for such concessions, the automakers offered profit sharing to their employees. As the auto industry recouped in the mid 1980s, the benefits from those agreements began to pay off. Not only did auto workers regain lost wages from previous concessions but they also received large profit sharing allocations from auto makers.[45]

As corporate profits declined in the 1990s, employee profits—like corporate profits—declined proportionately.

Gainsharing Plans

Gainsharing plans are premised on the assumption that it is possible to reduce costs by eliminating wasted materials and labor, developing new or better products or services, or working smarter. Typically, all employees in a work unit or firm are involved in a gainsharing plan.[46]

The median gainsharing payout is 3 percent, substantially less than the average 5 percent merit increase. Still, gainsharing plans represent one of the fast-growing types of performance pay, with 13 percent of all firms currently using them and another 14 percent of firms anticipating the use of them in the next few years.[47] Three generations of gain-sharing plans are reviewed here.

First generation plans. Two types of plans—Scanlon and Rucker—were developed in the Depression Era of the 1930s. Both plans focus on cost savings relative to historical standards. The Scanlon and Rucker plans are built around the following four principles:

- A management philosophy emphasizing employee participation
- A formula to share the benefits of productivity-generated saving between employees and the employer
- Employee committees to evaluate ideas
- A formal system for gathering and implementing employee suggestions on ways to increase productivity or reduce costs[48]

Even though Scanlon and Rucker plans share a common philosophy, these plans differ in one important aspect: Scanlon plans focus only on labor cost savings. For example, assume the historical cost of labor is $1 million for a year. If actual labor costs are less than anticipated costs (e.g., $800,000), a portion of the money saved ($50,000) is placed in a set-aside fund in case labor costs soar in subsequent quarters. The remaining savings are split between the company and the employees ($150,000).[49] In contrast, a Rucker plan ties incentives to a wide variety of savings. A ratio is calculated that expresses the value of production required for each dollar of total wages.

Both plans are appropriate in small, mature firms employing fewer than 500 employees. Since standards are based on past performance, simple and accurate measures of performance are needed. Because of the heavy involvement of all employees, the culture must be open, trusting, and participative.[50]

Second generation plans. Beginning in the 1960s, a second generation of gainsharing plans began to emerge. These plans differ from first generation plans in several respects. First, they focus on labor *hours* saved, rather than labor costs saved. Detailed time-and-motion studies are conducted to develop engineered standards of physical production. Because of the depth of analysis required, employees typically are not involved in the development of the plan. This may reduce perceptions of fairness.

Unlike in first generation plans, nonproduction workers are included in the measurement of the organization's productivity and in the distribution of variable pay, realized from cost savings. **Improshare,** developed by industrial engineer, Mitchell Fein, is typical of second generation plans. It has been adopted in a wide array of firms including service-sector firms such as hospitals and financial institutions.

Third generation plans. According to Marc Wallace, who studied new pay practices in 46 firms, a third generation of gainsharing plans is emerging that "is so different from first and second generation models that the term gainsharing may no longer be appropriate." Third generation plans encompass a much broader range of organization goals. They have definite terms which support the current business plan. As the business plan changes over time, so does the incentive plan. Also, the plan includes all employees, making no distinctions between direct and indirect labor.[51] For example, the manager of a gold mine

> ... believed that costs could be reduced in three areas: the mining of the ore; the milling, or processing, of the ore; and administration. If costs were reduced for a sustained period, profits would increase. He also knew he could not simply tell the mine staff to save money without involving them in the process. Because he thought they probably had some good ideas on how to reduce costs, he wanted to reward them for putting these ideas to work.
>
> Working with his human resource manager, the mine manager developed an incentive plan with five components.
>
> | Component | Weight | How Measured |
> |---|---|---|
> | 1. Overall mine results | 20% | Judgment of the manager |
> | 2. Mining cost | 30 | Cost per ton |
> | 3. Milling cost | 25 | Cost per ton |
> | 4. Administrative cost | 15 | Cost per ounce |
> | 5. Individual performance | 10 | Judgment of the supervisor |
> | | 100% | |
>
> Every mine employee was measured on the same basis for the first four components. The manager and supervisors met with all the employees to brainstorm how they could work together to achieve the cost-reduction goals. After considerable brainstorming, the employees had a clear sense of which ideas were worth pursuing and which ones would yield only marginal improvement. They then set to work, as a team, on those actions with the biggest potential payoff. The fifth component, individual performance, allowed the participant's supervisor to provide an additional reward for special individual achievement.[52]

Characteristics of Successful Variable Pay Plans

Wallace's research also identified several common characteristics of successful variable pay plans. First, they are based on a clear vision of the organization's strategy and culture. That is, they tie rewards (individual, team, or organizational) to business priorities. They provide sufficient time for implementation—one to two years—and they keep score, indicating expected results through clearly measurable goals and evaluating accomplishments against those goals. Finally, the plans are continually audited and controlled to ensure that they stay on course. "A one or two degree correction one month out is much easier to accomplish than a 40 degree correction 12 months out," Wallace noted.

Successful plans provide a wide margin for employees to exercise discretion and add value to the firm. This was accomplished by having fewer management levels and fewer job titles; but broader, simpler definitions of employee work responsibilities were the rule, rather than the exception. Programs were flexible, focusing more on the needs of the business rather than adherence to a performance formula. Finally, successful plans provide a sunset so rewards aren't viewed as entitlements, and employees celebrated when they were successful.

Exhibit 10.6 lists questions to evaluate the effectiveness of variable pay plans. In terms of costs, a firm should expect to spend more than $40,000 on a task force to complete the initial study, including the development of communication materials, and administrative and implementation costs. Gainsharing plans also involve significant additional cost to administer the data base and generate the reports upon which payouts depend. According to Wallace, firms typically underestimate the time and money it takes to develop stable, accurate standards for tracking performance and calculating awards.[53]

Stock Options

While more than sixty percent of all firms with revenue greater than $100 million offer stock options to top-tier managers, a growing number of firms are now offering stock in various forms to lower-tier employees. A 1990 Conference Board Study found that one-third of all firms now utilize restricted stock and stock options as a component in their variable-pay plans.

Stock-option plans. With stock-option plans, stockholders vote to create a pool of shares—usually about five percent of the total number outstanding—out of newly issued shares. Over a period of years, employees are given the right to buy stock in the future at today's price. Most options last ten years with executives typically allowed to exercise half their options after two years and the entire grant after three.

In theory, options are supposed to motivate an employee to make a company's stock more valuable. The backbone of executive compensation programs,

Exhibit 10.6
How to Tell a Live Plan from a Dead One

Does the plan capture attention? Are employees talking more about their work and the incentive program? Are they celebrating early successes under the plan?

Do employees understand the plan? Could you walk up to a participant, ask how the plan works, and get a technically correct answer? Do employees know what they need to accomplish in order to earn payments?

Does the plan communicate about the business? Has the plan contributed to knowledge about the business? Do employees have a better understanding of how their individual and collective efforts impact the bottom line?

Does the plan pay out when it should? Are payouts occurring for actual results against goals and being withheld when they are not met? Or is the plan becoming another entitlement by paying out under all circumstances?

Is the business unit performing better? Can we point to the operation of the reward plan and conclude that we are actually performing better as a result? Are profits up? Have we gained market share?

SOURCE: M. J. Wallace, *Rewards and Renewal: America's Search for Competitive Advantage Through Alternative Pay Strategies* (Scottsdale, Ariz.: American Compensation Association, 1990), 15.

the awarding of stock options is premised on the assumption that the plans encourage executives to "think like owners." After all, they profit only if the stock price goes up. However, critics of stock options contend that companies without options plans do as well as companies with them. According to management consultant James H. Carbone, "Options don't really make managers walk in the owner's moccasins. Only after executives exercise options do they truly become owners. Until then, they have no capital at risk. If the stock sags, they can expect a new grant the next year at a lower price."[54]

Even with the above criticisms, stock options flourish—particularly in high-growth companies. The primary reason is that stock options are the only major form of compensation that never show up as a cost on a company's profit and loss statement. Under generally accepted accounting principles, granting options is never recorded as a cost to the company. Instead the money paid for option shares and the tax break the company may get (based on the spread between the strike price and the exercise price) show up only on the balance sheet. As a result, employees can earn millions from options at no apparent cost to the company. Consider Disney's Michael Eisner. From 1985 through 1990 he received options on 4,040,000 shares. By 1990, he exercised 683,000 shares for a profit of $32,588,275.

Several other advantages make stock options particularly well-suited to high-growth companies. Stock options avoid both earnings charges and the need for immediate cash outlays. When the options are exercised, the company doesn't have to lay out any money but does receive back the value of the initial stock purchase price. This money can then be used to meet business objectives. Third, the company receives a tax deduction for the amount of income realized by the executive—producing additional cash through tax savings. In comparison, companies that give cash incentives must charge against earnings for financial reporting purposes.[55]

Restricted stock grants. An alternative approach entails the award of stock at no or very low cost. In most cases, employees are required to work a set period of time—usually three to five years—before they are vested in the plan.

Restricted stock is a potent program for attracting and retaining executives. Microsoft Corporation uses stock grants to attract and retain peak performers. The software leader's policy of "getting it right" demands that the firm have top-notch, creative programmers. Finding and retaining such talent is difficult given the tight national market and Microsoft's stringent hiring requirements. Once the firm finds its programmers, it relies on incentive pay to motivate and retain them. Rather than get high salaries (Gates' base salary is only $190,000 yearly) or perks (no company cars), Microsoft evaluates programmers yearly and places them on one of six levels. As a programmer reaches the top two levels—the equivalent of becoming a partner in a law firm—there is a big celebration and the employee receives significant stock awards. Does the program pay off? Employees think so—particularly the more than a dozen who are now millionaires. A stock grant in 1985 of $1,000 was valued at $30,000 in 1992.[56]

Phantom stocks. As described in this chapter's opening profile, a third option involves the awarding of phantom stocks. Here participants receive a cash payment equal to the full value of stock in the future, not just the appreciation.

An advantage of phantom stocks is that private companies such as Clean Cut can establish these programs even though the company is not publicly traded.

Phantom stocks are also useful to retain key performers in a merger. Consider the dilemma faced by Fine Organics Corporation, an $8.2-million chemical manufacturer in Lodi, New Jersey. The company was buying two small companies and wanted to retain key personnel in the acquired company without diluting the ownership control by broadening the base of regular shareholders. Company officials considered setting up a second tier of stock options without voting rights but, because Fine Organics had been incorporated as an "S" corporation, Internal Revenue Service regulations prohibited the introduction of a second-tier plan. According to CEO William Reidy,

> We were trolling about for some kind of compromise solution and heard about phantom stock. The basic scheme was simple. Instead of real stock, we'd give peak performers a document that, at the time it was issued, had a value of zero. As the book value of combined equity, namely Fine Organics and the acquired company, increases, the amount of the increased value is added to the original zero value. At an agreed-upon point, the employee can cash in the phantom stock for the gain in value.[57]

In implementing these plans, it is important to keep the financial terms simple. If publicly traded, the value can be tied to the book value of stock. If not, it can be based on the board of directors assessed value. In selling the plan to employees, Reidy advises presenting the plan as a win-win benefit. One benefit, for example, is that there is no tax bill associated with the receipt of phantom shares. Phantom stock, unlike regular stock grants, are considered a form of deferred compensation by the IRS.[58]

FOCUS ISSUES IN PERFORMANCE-BASED PAY

We discussed focus issues in assessment and computer technology in chapter 9 but they are also useful to discuss here. We will also discuss CEO pay a bit more.

Assessing Performance-Based Pay Systems

Regardless of organizational conditions and considerations, performance-based pay systems can be assessed on the basis of three criteria: (1) the relationship between performance and pay—that is, the time between performance and the administration of the pay (the actual time and the time as perceived by employees),[59] (2) how well the plan minimizes the perceived negative consequences of good performance, and (3) whether the plan contributes to the perception that rewards other than pay (such as cooperation and recognition) also stem from good performance.[60] The more the plan minimizes the perceived negative consequences, and the more it contributes to the perception that other good rewards are also tied to performance, the more motivating it is likely to be.

Exhibit 10.7 uses three objective measures to determine the level of job performance to be rewarded: sales or units made (productivity), cost effectiveness or savings below budget, and traditional supervisor ratings. As discussed in chapter 7, more objective measures tend to clarify what is rewarded and what is not. This may produce more keen competition with other workers, result in

Exhibit 10.7
Effectiveness of Performance-Based Pay Systems

	Type of Plan	Performance Measure	Tie Pay to Performance	Minimize Negative Side Effects	Tie Other Rewards to Performance
Merit	Individual	Productivity	+2	0	0
		Cost effectiveness	+1	0	0
		Superior's rating	+1	0	+1
	Department	Productivity	+1	0	+1
		Cost effectiveness	+1	0	+1
		Superior's rating	+1	0	+1
	Organization-wide	Productivity	+1	0	+1
		Cost effectiveness	+1	0	+1
		Profit	0	0	+1
Incentive	Individual	Productivity	+3	-2	0
		Cost effectiveness	+2	-1	0
		Superior's rating	+2	-1	+1
	Department	Productivity	+2	0	+1
		Cost effectiveness	+2	0	+1
		Superior's rating	+2	0	+1
	Organization-wide	Productivity	+2	0	+1
		Cost effectiveness	+2	0	+1
		Profit	+1	0	+1

SOURCE: E.E. Lawler III, *Pay and Organizational Effectiveness* (New York: McGraw-Hill, 1971), 165. Reprinted with permission.

more social ostracism, and lead workers to perceive that good job performance may reduce the work available to them.[61]

The overall evaluation of plans suggests that, when compared with individual-level incentive plans, department and organization-wide incentive plans are not as effective in relating individual performance to pay, but they do result in fewer negative side effects (the exception is with intergroup competition) and in additional benefits besides pay, such as esteem, respect, and social acceptance from other employees.

Computer Technology

Much of the time spent in compensation planning is lost to pencil pushing and number crunching, not planning. Computer technology can accommodate performance-based pay planning and administration in the following ways. First, administration may be conducted by establishing a merit pay plan grid on a computer system. The computer can be programmed to post the appropriate percentage increases. Second, budget planning is facilitated simply by manipulating the percentage values on the grid, automatically changing each individual's pay. As in total compensation, performance-based planning may be considered by department, by position, or in other meaningful ways. In addition, these values may be equally useful to top management. Because time is a cost to the organization, the ability to analyze this information with a minimal time investment represents a substantial cost efficiency.[62]

Computer technology facilitates the management and manipulation of data that can be used to formulate projections concerning salary structure proposals, compa-ratios, compensation cost/amount of revenue generated ratios, total cost of selected configurations of benefits packages, and the cost of compensation in the future under different rates of inflation. These calculations may be made on an individual employee, group, or overall organizational basis. Selected information may be further extracted to make summary reports and projections for areas other than the personnel department, such as a budget sheet for the comptroller.

Computer technology can also be applied to compensation planning by analyzing the various monetary components that make up compensation. These include, for example, base salary, performance-based salary, seniority bonus, performance bonus, profit sharing, and cost of benefits.

CEOs: Performance-Based Pay?

Over the past several years this question has been asked by many people, many times. More recently it has been asked by people such as Senator Carl Levin and the writers and staff of national business magazines such as *Fortune* and *Business Week*.[63] The implicit answer is often "No." The *real* issue is what to do about it. For some people this focal issue raises an ethical question: "Should CEOs get paid a hundred times more than the workers who are actually making and selling the goods and services of the company?" For others it is a business issue: "Is the firm really getting the most bang from its buck when it gives its CEOs extremely high compensation packages?" We raise these questions here because you might want to discuss CEO pay with others. The issue is emotional and one which will probably exist for some time, with or without government intervention. From the perspective of the CEO who receives a large compensation package, carefully read the PHRM in the News: "Coke's Chairman Defends $86 Million Pay and Bonuses." Of course, this entire situation is unlikely to occur in a country such as the People's Republic of China.

INTERNATIONAL COMPARISONS IN PERFORMANCE-BASED PAY

People's Republic of China

During Mao's tenure, the evaluation of individual performance and the use of performance-based pay systems were denounced as capitalistic and incompatible with communist ideology. Instead, job security was absolute, and compensation administration was egalitarian. To be eligible for a wage increase, a worker's political standing, attitude toward labor, experience, and achievements had to be appraised democratically by colleagues. Under strict guidelines, raises were allocated in such a manner as to be equivalent. By the time of the economic reforms in the 1980s, the lowest-paid workers earned approximately 35 yuan a month, and the highest-paid official, including the premier, earned only 450 yuan, a differential of only 12 times, which is far less than the differential in the U.S.[64]

PHRM IN THE NEWS

Coke's Chairman Defends $86 Million Pay and Bonus

Atlanta, April 15—The chairman of the Coca-Cola Company, whose 1991 pay and stock bonus was estimated to be worth more than $86 million, today delivered his first public defense of his compensation by noting that the company's stock price had increased fourteenfold over the last 10 years.

He also noted that under Coke's rules, the stock bonus, valued at $83 million, could have been doubled.

In a long address at Coca-Cola's annual shareholders meeting, Roberto C. Goizueta, the company's chairman and chief executive, rattled off a glittering array of statistics that showed the nation's No. 1 soft-drink maker outpacing most measures of corporate investment performance.

$50 Billion in Wealth

"Our stock outperformed the other 29 stocks in the Dow Jones industrial average in the past decade," he said. "The end result has been the creation of $50 billion of additional wealth for the share owners of our company in the same time period."

And to cap off the highlights, Mr. Goizueta (pronounced Got-SWET-ta) used the occasion to announce that Coca-Cola's first-quarter profits climbed 19.4 percent, to $383.1 million, or 58 cents a share, from $320.9 million, or 48 cents a share, a year earlier. Revenues rose 11.7 percent, to $2.77 billion from $2.48 billion.

But in the ballroom of the Georgia World Congress Center here, filled with nearly 4,000 Coke shareholders, Mr. Goizueta was preaching to the converted. Shareholders interrupted his remarks with applause four times and when it came time for questions from the floor, not one shareholder offered a critical opinion of his pay or his stewardship of the company. In fact, two shareholders publicly praised him.

The strong first-quarter performance prompted some analysts to increase their earnings estimates for the company. Emanuel Goldman, an influential beverage industry analyst at Paine Webber Inc., raised his 1992 earnings estimate for Coca-Cola by 3 cents a share, to $2.89 and increased the 1993 estimate by 5 cents a share, to $3.45. Last year, Coke earned $1.62 billion, or $2.43 a share.

Mr. Goizueta's compensation included $3.14 million in salary and bonuses and a restricted stock grant of one million shares of Coca-Cola stock. The

Continued

With the economic revolution, it was decided that an enterprise's performance should be directly linked to the amount of profits generated. This was particularly true in the free economic zones where capitalistic principles were encouraged. The mandated philosophy became "from each according to his ability, to each according to his work" and "more pay for more work, less pay for less work."

There is limited evidence that the Chinese have made this philosophical shift. In one recent study, the Chinese relied primarily on supervisory assessments or performance to allocate pay raises. Peer evaluations as well as individual needs were also still considered when granting raises. In another study, performance was the most important determinant of performance appraisal ratings and pay decisions. Another recent study indicates employee performance is the most important determinant of performance ratings and pay raises among the Chinese *and* Americans. Consistent with new Chinese management, lower performance results in lower performance ratings *and* lower pay. However, remnants of the past Chinese regime and its values still persist. Chinese decision makers still consider dependability, loyalty to the enterprise, and job experience as important and tend to reward employees who display these behaviors. The bottom line in set-company's stock closed today at $83.375 a share, up $1.375, on the New York Stock Exchange, so the stock grant is valued at $83.375 million.

Compensation Defended

In an interview before today's meeting, Herbert A. Allen, a Coke director who is chairman of the board's compensation committee, defended Mr. Goizueta's compensation. "Allowing for the size of the company, their performance is probably the best in America and the best in the world," Mr. Allen said of Coca-Cola's executives. "The compensation package is therefore going to be competitive with the best."

Mr. Goizueta noted that the company's 1989 restricted stock award plan "authorizes awarding a maximum of 10 million shares of our common stock, but not more than 20 percent of this total to a single individual."

"In other words," he said, "the plan specifically authorizes awarding up to two million shares to one person."

He also noted that the stock plan was approved by shareholders three years ago by a 93 percent majority of the shares voted at the annual meeting.

Overseas Sales Rise

In reporting its earnings today, Coca-Cola said unit case sales in Latin America increased 7 percent during the quarter, including a 57 percent gain in Argentina. It also said case sales increased 12 percent in Japan.

But Mr. Goizueta emphasized that the company was looking for even stronger growth in Eastern Europe and the former Soviet Union, and in India, a market that Coca-Cola is planning to re-enter after a 15-year absence.

"For the first time since we left India in 1977, our product will soon be available to the 860 million inhabitants of the world's second-most-populous country," Mr. Goizueta said.

He said the company sold 100 million cases of soft drinks in the eastern part of Germany in 1991 and expected to sell 120 million cases there in 1992.

Mr. Goldman, the analyst, said he had raised his Coca-Cola earnings estimates because of strong earnings gains in Latin America and Japan from price increases.

"About 21 percent of Coke's world-wide earnings come from Japan alone," Mr. Goldman said. "Coke can continue to look for very strong earnings from Japan."

SOURCE: Jerry Schwartz, "Coke's Chairman Defends $86 Million Pay and Bonus," *The New York Times* (16 April 1992), D1, D11. Used by permission.

ting up ventures in the People's Republic of China is to modify U.S. pay-for-performance systems, so that a portion of pay is based on loyalty and job seniority.[65]

SUMMARY

Performance-based pay systems continue to attract the attention of many personnel and human resource managers, and line managers continue to ask whether pay can be used as a motivator with their employees. The success of many incentive plans indicates that pay can motivate job performance, although many problems can arise because of the myriad issues associated with the implementation of performance-based pay systems.

Despite the potential motivational value of performance-based pay systems, most organizations continue to choose essentially nonperformance-based plans. Some organizations believe that performance-based pay systems are not possible because of the lack of appropriate conditions or because of the cost. However, if organizations can measure performance, and if everyone thinks the system is fair and tied to the objectives of the organization, paying for performance should increase profitability.

Which performance-based pay plan to use must be determined by several factors, such as the level at which job performance can accurately be measured (individual, department, or organization), the extent of cooperation needed between departments, and the level of trust between management and nonmanagement. However, there may be limits on a specific organization's decision to use performance-based pay, which may include management's desire to have performance-based pay, management's commitment to take the time to design and implement one or several systems, the extent to which employees influence the output, the extent to which a good performance appraisal system exists, the existence of a union, and the degree of trust in the organization. Whether the organization is public or private influences the decision, too. Generally, only private organizations utilize incentive systems. Both types, however, can and do use merit pay systems. A final major consideration is the extent to which employees will understand and accept the plan.

To this point we have been discussing compensation from the viewpoint of what goes into your pocket. There is, however, a substantial component of total compensation which may miss your pocket altogether. However, if an organization didn't offer it, you probably wouldn't work for it. Indirect compensation is the subject of the next chapter.

WHERE WE ARE TODAY

1. Employee equity centers upon valuing the performance contribution of an individual, a team, or an organizational unit, rather than the value of the job.
2. Performance-based differentials are useful to attain strategic goals, reinforce organizational norms, motivate performance, and recognize differential contributions.
3. Performance pay works best when the plan is clearly communicated and understandable, when employees are involved in developing and administering the plan and have an appeals process, and when employees receive awards as soon as possible after desired performance occurs.
4. Under the Equal Pay Act, pay differentials based on performance, seniority, merit systems, and position in salary range are allowable when applied equally to all employees.
5. With traditional pay plans, base pay is set at the market rate and a small pool of money is set aside to reward performance. As such, traditional pay plans tend to reinforce equality and longevity.
6. Although merit pay plans are widely used, the link between performance and pay is weaker with merit than with incentive or bonus pay plans.
7. The shift to a service economy, cost accountability, and a focus on linking employee with firm profitability are all responsible for stepped-up interest in variable-pay plans.
8. Choosing between incentives and bonuses hinges on whether performance goals can be identified in advance of the performance period. Since base pay is set below the market rate, earnings-at-risk pay plans entail greater pay risk for employees but control the fixed-wage costs for the employer.
9. Choosing between individual, team, and organizational incentives depends on the level at which performance can be accurately measured and on whether teamwork and cooperation are needed.

10. Are CEOs paid too much? Should their pay be linked only to performance on the upside but not the downside? These questions elicit strong opinions. Where do you stand on these issues?

DISCUSSION QUESTIONS

1. What conditions are necessary for effective performance-based pay systems (i.e., systems that enhance the organization's strategic goals)?
2. What obstacles are there in specifying and measuring job performance?
3. How can an organization determine whether merit pay is administered accurately across all employees or across all its units and divisions?
4. Describe a performance-based pay system that you have directly experienced. Did the system work? If not, why not?
5. Under what conditions would you expect a performance-based pay system to have the greatest likelihood of success?
6. Debate the following assertion. If selection and placement decisions are done effectively, individual performance should not vary by a great deal; therefore, a performance-based pay system is not needed.
7. What are the challenges in setting up an international compensation program?
8. What is your overall assessment of variable pay?
9. Assume you are the manager of a small job shop that employs machinists in drilling, punch press, and grinding positions. Bottlenecks have been a concern in production. Design a compensation program to address this problem.
10. How can performance-based pay plans be assessed?

APPLIED PROJECTS

1. Interview two or three employees (of one of the companies in the area) to learn whether they are paid on the basis of their performance and, if so, on what basis do they get paid. If they are not so paid, find out if the employees would like to be paid for performance and, if so, under what type—merit or incentive-based plans. Identify the type of person who prefers performance-based pay and the type who does not.
2. Do a library project to learn about the types and numbers of companies offering performance-based pay. An excellent start for this project is an AMA survey report entitled, "Paying for Performance and Position" by James W. Steele. You can get this report from the library or by writing: AMACOM, 135 West 50th Street, New York, NY 10020.

CASE STUDY

Productivity, Compensation, and Layoffs at St. Luke's Hospital

St. Luke's Hospital, located in a large southern city, is a 295-bed community hospital offering a full line of health care services. These services range from maternity to hospice care and vary in complexity from simple surgery to advanced cardiac care. The hospital is supported by an associated system of health care centers. These centers include physician-staffed clinics, emergency rooms, an industrial accident clinic, and two urgent care clinics. They are designed to act as entry points to the health care system for those individuals who do not have a regular physician or access to regular health care.

While St. Luke's is part of a nation-wide corporation of health care facilities, corporate control is minimal. Individual hospitals have a high degree of autonomy. The CEOs of the individual hospitals are all members of the Catholic religious order. As a result, St. Luke's traditionally has been run with close attention by the sister in charge. While innovative in the use of new technology, a conservative approach to employee relations has prevailed at St. Luke's. Attempts to unionize nursing personnel have been blocked, but there have been a number of close calls, with the last vote barely losing despite the hospital's competitive base pay structure.

The main competitors to St. Luke's include the flagship hospital of the Southwest Health Care Association, Providence Hospital, and the University Medical Center. Both are located a short distance from St. Luke's. Due to deregulation, a variety of special care facilities for ambulatory, adult and juvenile mental health, and alcoholism problems have sprung up in the community over the last four years. These have divided the market further.

This increase in competition has occurred at the same time as changes in the way providers are being paid have occurred. Third-party payers, both public and private, have realized that the least cost-efficient method of health care is an extended hospital stay. Consequently, the length of stay for a patient has dropped from a national average of approximately 6 days to 4.5 days.

At St. Luke's, the *number* of patients admitted to the hospital has remained at former levels. However, the average length of stay has decreased from 5.7 days to 4.0 days in two years. Because the majority of services are provided during the first two days of a patient's stay, the cost of the patient's stay has not declined at the same rate as the revenue from that stay has. As a result, a series of low-profile layoffs in selected revenue areas, such as radiology and physical therapy, occurred in 1989. In general, these were accomplished through retirements and layoffs of temporary and part-time personnel.

Because the downturn now appears permanent, St. Luke's administration believes its financial reversal will be permanent. It estimates it will have to trim its annual budget by ten percent or increase revenues by the same amount. Because of the negative consequences of the prior layoffs, the board of directors wants to avoid another round of layoffs if at all possible.

As one nurse summed up the current situation, "You can't get blood out of a turnip. We can't provide quality care and be expected to handle bigger and bigger patient loads. They're asking us to do a lot more with a lot less and they aren't even compensating us for the extra work we now do. They never consult us or involve us. They just act. And we're tired of not being involved in decisions that affect us. Nobody knows how or why the prior cuts were made. They were made and now we're expected to live with them. We just can't go on this way and still be expected to deliver quality care."

To deal with the current situation, Tom Lee, director of administrative services, was considering some form of new pay to motivate staff and simultaneously solve his budget concerns. For example, he'd recently read about a bank that implemented an earnings-at-risk pay plan in which base salaries were reduced significantly to cut fixed costs and employees were given the opportunity to earn large incentives for exceeding performance goals. While the plan sounded interesting, he wondered just what type of goals could be set in hospitals and whether employees would buy into reductions in their pay without reductions in work load. After all, nothing like this had ever been tried in a hospital.

Another option he'd heard about was Improshare. Here, performance measurement formulas are developed for all work groups. While several hospitals had purportedly tried such plans, he'd heard that implementation was expensive and cumbersome. Because Improshare relied on time-and-motion type studies to set performance standards, the plans also were not flexible to dynamic jobs such as those at St. Luke's.

A third option was a Scanlon plan in which employees would share in labor cost savings. These plans were usually implemented in unionized environments, and St. Luke's wished to avoid unionization at *all* costs. For this plan to be successful, there also needed to be a high level of employee-management trust and participation. Lee wasn't sure that the culture at St. Luke's was right for such a plan—particularly with the low morale caused by the earlier layoffs. Still, Beth Israel Hospital in Boston, Massachusetts, has had a Scanlon plan in place since the late 1980s.

Given the current financial crisis, Lee knew he had to do something and do it soon. The question was what. At a minimum, he knew he had to involve employees in the development of the plan. The pay plan had to be capable of attracting, motivating, and retaining employees. It also had to be fiscally sound if it was to meet the board of directors' demand for cost containment. Third, it had to be easy to understand

and communicate to employees. Staff members ranged from highly educated medical personnel (nurses, pharmacists, laboratory technicians) to low-skilled workers (e.g., laundry, dietary, and nurses aides).

If he decided to use a performance pay plan he also needed to determine who should be involved and at what level performance should be assessed. Physicians, for example, were not paid by the hospital, they were merely affiliated with it; yet they were critical to the success of St. Luke's. Department attempts at labor or cost containment could be measured but were often dependent on other units. For example, X-ray may exceed its budget if physicians order too many X-rays or overload the department in work on specific days.

SOURCE: Robert McDonough, Fidelity Investment.

Case Questions

1. Describe the culture at St. Luke's Hospital.
2. Summarize the major problems at St. Luke's Hospital.
3. Is performance-based pay a viable option? Why or why not?
4. How should Lee go about determining which, if any type of variable pay would be appropriate for St. Luke's?
5. Evaluate the three options—earnings-at-risk, Improshare, and the Scanlon plan—in light of what you know about St. Luke's.
6. Design a performance-based pay plan (it may or may not be one of those considered by Lee), and delineate a schedule of implementation for the hospital.

NOTES

1. J. Byrne, "Executive Pay," *Business Week* (30 March 1992): 56.
2. M. J. Wallace and C. H. Fay, *Compensation Theory and Practice* (Boston, Mass.: PWS-Kent, 1988).
3. See note 2.
4. J. E. Santora, "Dupont Builds Stakeholders," *Personnel Journal* (Dec. 1989): 72–75; R. P. McNutt, "Achievement Pays Off at Dupont," *Personnel* (June 1990): 5–10.
5. "Clarified Carrots," *HR Reporter* (May 1987). Personal correspondence with Dick Goodwin.
6. "Compensation: Growth Bonuses," *Inc.* (Feb. 1988): 100.
7. G. Milkovich and J. Newman, *Compensation* (Plano, Tex.: BPI, 1987); D. Q. Mills, *The New Competitors* (New York: Wiley, 1985).
8. N. H. Mackworth, "High Incentives Versus Hot and Humid Atmospheres in a Physical Effort Task," *British Journal of Psychology* (1947): 90–102; P. M. Podsakoff, M. L. Williams, and W. E. Scott, Jr., "Myths of Employee Selection Systems," in R. Schuler, S. Youngblood, and V. Huber, eds., *Readings in Personnel and Human Resource Management* (St. Paul, Minn.: West Publishing, 1988): 178–92.
9. L. C. Cumming, "Linking Pay to Performance," *Personnel Administrator* (May 1988): 47–52; T. Rollins, "Pay for Performance: Is it Worth the Trouble?" *Personnel Administrator* (May 1988): 42–46.
10. D. Filipowski, "Perspectives: Is Pay Linked to Performance?" *Personnel Journal* (May 1991): 39.
11. P. M. Podsakoff, C. N. Greene, and J. M. McFillen, "Obstacles to the Effective Use of Reward Systems," in *Readings in Personnel and Human Resource Management:* 275–90; T. R. Hinkin, P. M. Podsakoff, and C. A. Schriesheim, "The Mediation of Performance-Contingent Compensation by Supervisors in Work Organizations: A Reinforcement Perspective," in D. Balkin and L. Gomez-Mejia, eds., *New Perspectives on Compensation* (Englewood Cliffs, N.J.: Prentice-Hall, 1987): 196–210; R. K. Miller, "Discrimination is a Virtue," *Newsweek* (21 July 1980): 15.
12. See also K. E. Foster, "Does Executive Pay Make Sense?" *Business Horizons* (Sept./Oct. 1981): 47–58; "Pay at the Top Mirrors Inflation," *Business Week* (11 May 1981): 58–59; "Surge in Executive Job Contracts," *Dunn's Business Month* (Oct. 1981): 86–88; D. B. Thompson, "Are CEOs Worth What They're Paid," *Industry Week* (4 May 1981): 65–74.
13. C. Babski, "Turning Glass into Art—and Profits, Too," *The New York Times* (5 June 1988): F4.
14. R. Henderson, *Compensation Management: Rewarding Performance* (Englewood Cliffs, N.J.: Prentice-Hall, 1989): 298; J. C. Kail, "Compensating Scientists and Engineers," in *Current Trends in Compensation Research and Practice:* 278–81.
15. "Compensation," in *Readings in Personnel and Human Resource Management:* 291–97; J. Kerr and J. W. Slocum, Jr., "Linking Reward Systems and Organizational Culture," in *Readings in Personnel and Human Resource Management:* 297–308.
16. "Change Pay Practices: New Developments in Employee Compensation," Bureau of National Affairs (Washington, D.C.: 1988).
17. Association of Machinists and Aerospace Workers.
18. M. J. Wallace, *Rewards and Renewal: America's Search for Competitive Advantage through Alternative Pay Strategies* (Scottsdale, Ariz.: American Compensation Association, 1990); M. J. Wallace Jr., *Compensation Theory and Practice*.
19. Wallace, *Rewards and Renewal: America's Search for Competitive Advantage...*
20. J. Newman, "Selecting Incentive Plans to Complement Organizational Strategy," in D. Balkin and L. Gomez-Mejia, eds., *Current Trends in Compensation Research and Practice* (Englewood Cliffs, N.J.: Prentice-Hall, 1987): 14–24.

21. J. Kerr, "Diversification Strategies and Managerial Rewards: An Empirical Study," *Academy of Management Journal* 28 (1985): 155–79; G. Milkovich and J. Newman, *Compensation* (Homewood, Ill.: BPI-Irwin, 1990); E. E. Lawler III, *Pay and Organizational Development* (Reading, Mass.: Addison-Wesley, 1981).
22. T. R. Hinking, P. M. Podsakoff, and C. A. Schriesheim, "The Mediation of Performance Contingent Compensation by Supervisors in Work Organizations: A Reinforcement Perspective," in *Current Trends in Compensation Research and Practice:* 196–210; G. Milkovich and J. Newman, *Compensation:* 337.
23. C. Peck, *Pay and Performance: The Interaction of Compensation and Performance Appraisal* (New York: The Conference Board, 1984); C. Peck, *Variable Pay: New Performance Rewards* (New York: The Conference Board, 1990).
24. R. Heneman, "Merit Pay Research," in Rowland and Ferris, eds., *Research in Personnel and Human Resource Management* vol. 8 (1990): 204–263; R. Heneman, *Pay for Performance: Exploring the Merit System* (New York: Pergamon Press, 1984).
25. D. Filipowski, "Perspectives: Is Pay Linked to Performance?" *Personnel Journal* (May 1991): 39.
26. L. Gomez-Mejia and D. Balkin, "Merit Pay Perspectives," in *Current Trends in Compensation Research and Practice:* 159–61; H. A. Levine, "Performance Appraisals at Work," *Personnel* 62 (1986): 63–71.
27. C. Peck, *Variable Pay: New Performance Rewards:* 4.
28. Filipowski, "Perspectives: Is Pay Linked to Performance?"
29. R. Henderson, *Compensation Management: Rewarding Performance:* 298.
30. Press release, Sibson & Company, Princeton, N.J. (5 Sept. 1989): C.
31. G. S. Crystal, "How Much CEOs Really Make," *Fortune* (17 June 1991): 72–80; M. C. Jensen and K. J. Murphy, "CEO Incentives–It's Not How Much You Pay, but How," *Harvard Business Review* (May-June 1990): 138–49; H., Fox and C. Peck, *Top Executive Compensation,* Report 875 (New York: The Conference Board, 1986); C. Peck, *Variable Pay: New Performance Rewards:* 6.
32. "Incentive Compensation," *Fortune* (19 Dec. 1988): 50–58.
33. J. Birnbaum, "Recognition Programs are Widespread," *HR News* (Nov. 1991): 2.
34. D. W. Belcher and T. J. Atchison, *Compensation Administration* 2d ed. (Englewood Cliffs, N.J.: Prentice-Hall, 1977); Henderson, *Compensation Management;* Milkovich and Newman, *Compensation.*
35. A. W. Bergerson, "Employee Suggestion Plan Still Going Strong at Kodak," *Supervisory Management* (May 1977): 32–33; V. G. Reuter, "A New Look at Suggestion Systems," *Journal of Systems Management* (Jan. 1976): 6–15; M. A. Tather, "Turning Ideas into Gold," *Management Review* (March 1975): 4–10.
36. G. S. Crystal, "How Much CEOs Really Make," *Fortune* (17 June 1991): 72–80.
37. M. Jensen and K. J. Murphy, "CEO Incentives—It's Not How Much You Pay but How."
38. J. Huret, "Paying for Team Results," *HR Magazine* (May 1991): 39–43.
39. G. P. Latham and V. L. Huber, "Schedules of Reinforcement: Lessons from the Past, Issues for the Future," *Journal of Organizational Behavior Management* (in press).
40. R. T. Hamblin, C. Hathaway, and J. Wodarski, "Group Contingencies, Peer Tutoring and Accelerating Academic Achievement," in E. A. Ramp and B. L. Hopkins, eds., *A New Direction for Education: Behavior Analysis* (Lawrence, Kans.: University of Kansas Press, 1971); L. A. Hayes, "The Use of Group Contingencies for Behavioral Control: A Review," *Psychological Bulletin* 83 (1976): 628–48.
41. Henderson, *Compensation Management.*
42. Profit Sharing Plans and Provisions," *Bulletin to Management Datagraph* (Washington, D.C.: Bureau of National Affairs (20 June 1991); "Employee Benefits Report," *Profit Sharing* (Washington, D.C.: U.S. Chamber of Commerce, Feb. 1990): 6–7; B. Graham-Moore and T. L. Ross, *Gainsharing: Plans for Improving Performance* (Washington, D.C.: BNA Books, 1990); M. Poole and G. Jenkins, *The Impact of Economic Democracy: Profit-Sharing and Employee-Sharing Schemes* (New York: Routledge, 1991); J. L. Pierce, S. A. Rubenfeld, and S. Morgan, "Employee Ownership: A Conceptual Model of Process and Effects," *Academy of Management Review* 16, no. 1 (1991): 121–44; M. J. Roomkin, *Profit Sharing and Gain Sharing* (Metuchen, N.J.: IMLR Press, 1990).
43. C. Peck, *Variable Pay: New Performance Rewards.*
44. "Profit Sharing Productivity," *Profit Sharing* (Nov. 1988): 13.
45. M. Sorge, "Ford Touts Profit Sharing to UAW," *Automative News* (6 Aug. 1984): 6.
46. R. Henderson, *Compensation.*
47. C. Peck, *Variable Pay: New Performance Rewards:* 6.
48. B. E. Moore and T. L. Ross, *The Scanlon Way to Improved Productivity: A Practical Guide* (New York: Wiley, 1978); R. J. Schulhof, "Five Years with a Scanlon Plan," *Personnel Administrator* (June 1979): 55–63; L. S. Tyler and B. Fisher, "The Scanlon Concept: A Philosophy as Much as a System," *Personnel Administrator* (July 1983): 33–37.
49. *Changing Pay Practice: A BNA Special Report* (Washington, D.C.: 1988): 68.
50. B. Graham-Moore and T. Ross, *Productivity Gainsharing* (Englewood Cliffs, N.J.: Prentice-Hall, 1983); R. J. Bullock and E. E. Lawler, "Gainsharing: A Few Questions and Fewer Answers," *Human Resource Management* 23 (1984): 23–40.
51. M. J. Wallace, *Rewards and Renewal...:* 41.
52. H. Huret, "Paying for Team Results": 41.
53. M. J. Wallace, *Rewards and Renewal...:* 14–16.
54. T. A. Steward, "The Trouble with Stock Options," *Fortune* (1 Jan. 1990): 93–95.
55. J. D. McMillan and C. Young, "Sweetening the Compensation Package," *HR Magazine* (Oct. 1990): 36–39.
56. "Microsoft: Bill Gates's Baby is on Top of the World. Can It Stay There?" *Business Week* (24 Feb. 1992): 60–65.
57. "Incentives: The ABCs of Phantom Stock," *Inc.* (May 1991): 100–102.
58. J. McMillen, K. Allen, and R. Salwen, "Private Companies Offer Long-Term Incentives," *HR Magazine* (June 1991): 63–66.

59. L. Abramson, "Boost to the Bottom Line," *Personnel Administrator* (July 1988): 36–39; A. D. Anderson, "In the Office: See How They Run," *New York Times* (3 Jan. 1988): 13; G. Kramon, "The 'Wellness' Discount Plans," *New York Times* (22 Sept. 1987): D2; R. P. Sloan and J. C. Gruman, "Does Wellness in the Workplace Work?" *Personnel Administrator* (July 1988): 42–48.

60. E. E. Lawler III, *Pay and Organizational Development* (Reading, Mass.: Addison-Wesley, 1981); N. B. Winstanley, "Are Merit Increases Really Effective?" *Personnel Administrator* (April 1982): 37–41.

61. M. P. Miceli, I. Jung, J. P. Near, and D. B. Greenberger, "Predictors and Outcomes of Reactions to Pay-for-Performance Plans," *Journal of Applied Psychology* 76, no. 4 (1991): 508–21; J. W. Harder, "Equity Theory Versus Expectancy Theory: The Case of Major League Baseball Free Agents," *Journal of Applied Psychology* 76, no. 3 (1991): 458–64; S. R. Collings, "Incentive Programs: Pros and Cons," *Personnel Journal* (July 1981): 571–75; R. B. Goettinger, "Compensation and Benefits," *Personnel Journal* (Nov. 1981): 840–42. For a case study illustration of merit pay assessment issues, see S. C. Freedman, "Performance-Based Pay: A Convenience Store Case Study," *Personnel Journal* (July 1985): 30–34; and J. R. Terborg and G. R. Ungson, "Group Administered Bonus Pay and Retail Store Performance: A Two-Year Study of Management Compensation," *Journal of Retailing* (Spring 1985): 63–77.

62. W. H. Wagel, "A Software Link between Performance Appraisals and Merit Increases," *Personnel* (March 1988): 10–14.

63. "Executive Pay: Compensation at the Top is Out of Control—Here's How to Reform It," *Business Week* (30 March 1992): 52–58; G. Colvin, "How to Pay the CEO Right," *Fortune* (6 April 1992): 60–69.

64. R. L. Tung, "Patterns of Motivation in Chinese Industrial Enterprises," *Academy of Management Review* 6 (1981): 481–89; M. Warner, "Managing Human Resources in China: An Empirical Study," *Organizational Studies* 7 (1983): 353–66.

65. V. L. Huber, G. Northcraft, M. Neale, and X. Zao, "Comparison of Appraisal and Pay Decisions of Chinese and Americans: A Management Revolution in the Making?", paper presented at the Eastern Academy of Management's International Conference, Hong Kong, June 1989; G. Northcraft, M. A. Neale, and V. L. Huber, "Behind the Great Wall: A Comparison of Pay Allocation Values of Americans and Chinese," paper presented at the 1987 National Meeting of the Academy of Management, New Orleans, La.

CHAPTER 11

Indirect Compensation: Benefits and Services

Business is spending $800 billion on health care, and we're not getting our money's worth.

—Dr. Mary Jane England, President
Washington Business Group on Health[1]

The bad news comes in a telephone call to Daniel P. Heslin, the employee-benefits director of the Rockwell International Corporation. Doctors attending to an employee report that she has leukemia. They want to do a bone marrow transplant. The cost: more than $100,000. Will Rockwell pay?

Experts at various medical centers tell Rockwell it is customary not to perform such a transplant on people older than forty because the chances for success are slim. The patient is fifty, and she is very weak. Rockwell's insurance administrator, the Metropolitan Life Insurance Company, recommends denying payment; but the final decision belongs to Rockwell. Like a growing number of large firms, Rockwell is self-insured. The insurance company administers the plan. But Rockwell must decide how to distribute its health care investment.

Like his counterparts at companies across the country, Heslin has become accustomed to such tough issues. In an attempt to aggressively control skyrocketing medical costs (rising about twenty percent per year), the role of the American benefits manager has become one of a pin-striped referee in a game where the field keeps expanding and the calls get tougher.

"As a society, we want the best and it's hard to say no—particularly to someone who is dying," Heslin said. Indeed, in the case of the worker with leukemia, Metropolitan eventually withdrew its opposition and Rockwell agreed to pay for the treatment. The rationale was that the company would refuse payment only if the procedures were clearly excluded by the plan or were clearly not medically necessary. The bone-marrow transplant was performed. The patient died six weeks later.

Heslin's job is a daunting one in several other ways. Each of Rockwell's businesses has its own benefits arrangement, and there are a lot of businesses, with about 350,000 employees, retirees, and dependents in almost every state and twenty foreign countries. The vastness of the program is complicated by the fact that Rockwell is trying to slow the growth of medical costs. By 1990, Rockwell was spending about half a billion dollars a year on health benefits. That's a substantial amount of money, yet Rockwell's health care costs are lower than those of most companies. That is, Rockwell's health care costs rose approximately 13.5 percent in 1990; the national average was a 20-percent increase over the previous year.

To contain costs, Rockwell's strategy is to pay medical expenses related to injuries or illness and exclude those deemed nonessential, cosmetic, experimental, or covered under the less-comprehensive provisions of Rockwell's vision or dental plans. Rockwell pays for heart, pancreas, and bone marrow transplants and for expensive tests like magnetic resonance imaging and CAT scans. However, it won't pay for other things such as in-vitro fertilization, sex change operations, some treatments for temporamandibular joint syndrome (a jaw disorder), and it has eliminated payment for radial keratomy, an operation on the cornea to correct nearsightedness.

Rockwell's strategy makes sense in theory, but it does pose some ethical dilemmas. For example, the employee of impeccable health habits who is having trouble conceiving a child must pay her own way for some fertility treatments, while the employee whose illness is related to potentially modifiable habits like smoking, heavy drinking, or bad diet still has expenses covered by the company.

The final decision on what Rockwell will cover rests with Robert H. Murphy, senior vice president for organization and human resources—the boss of Heslin's boss—who reports to Rockwell's chairman. Like many executives in charge of benefits, Heslin and his colleagues do not have medical backgrounds. They rely on the insurance company, the company medical department, and consultants for expertise. Heslin received his B.S. in business administration and worked in human resources at three different companies before joining Rockwell seventeen years ago as a regional benefits manager.

Heslin also is in charge of life insurance, vacation and leave time, plus pensions and saving plans. "But these days, easily 55 percent of my time goes to health care," he said, "up from about 20 to 25 percent six years ago." Much of the additional time is devoted to developing strategies to control medical costs. For example, outside consultants review each mental health and substance-abuse case to determine how long a hospital stay is warranted. "The idea is to prevent [the need for] the miraculous cure that always comes after 28 days, just as the hospital insurance runs out," Heslin said. "We are not looking to roll back the benefits but to channel them into more effective care."

The importance of aggressively handling long-term catastrophic cases is driven home by a study conducted by a Dallas consulting firm that helps Rockwell analyze its costs. It found that five percent of employees accounted for half the health care dollars spent. Excluding the catastrophic cases, health care costs would have risen only 11 percent.

Rockwell also is trying to save money by being more flexible. Consider the potentially high cost of a head-injury case that causes paralysis. Rather than paying for long-term hospitalization, Rockwell will pay to buy wheelchair ramps and a specially equipped van so an employee can live at home. A second strategy employed by Rockwell to handle soaring costs involves larger employee contributions to health care. Rockwell employees now contribute about $500 annually for their health coverage. Employees also must cover a $250 deductible and bear 30 percent of the cost up to $2,500. (Deductibles in most firms are $100 with cost sharing set at 10–20 percent.) Such out-of-pocket costs are hard to accept for employees who still think a faceless insurance company—and not Rockwell itself—is paying the bill. To correct this misperception, Rockwell has launched a major communications campaign designed to teach workers that the insurance company is merely the claims administrator; the company pays the bills.[2]

As the Rockwell profile indicates, employers and employees are vitally concerned with indirect compensation. Aside from its high value, it is a form of compensation on which employees generally do not have to pay income taxes. However, as the cost of indirect benefits grows in proportion to the total pay cost, organizations are becoming more concerned about the number and type of benefits they provide, the management of benefits, and cost containment. As a result, benefits management has moved off the back burner and into the fireline of strategic management.

This chapter will discuss indirect compensation—or, as they are also called, employee benefits and services—and the role indirect compensation plays in fulfilling organizational objectives. First, we'll outline the objectives and organizational and environmental influences affecting the strategic management of benefits. Next, we'll review public and private protection programs, such as workers' compensation and health care, respectively. We'll also examine life cycle benefits including such things as child and elder care, and financial planning. Due to the increased aging of the work force, a separate section covers pensions and retirement-related benefits. The chapter concludes with a discussion of administration issues, including cost-benefit analyses and some international comparisons.

INDIRECT COMPENSATION: BENEFITS AND SERVICES

Benefits and services that organizations provide include:

- Public protection programs
- Private protection programs
- Health care benefits
- Paid leave
- Life-cycle benefits

Several of these categories are mandated by federal and state governments and must therefore be administered within the boundaries of laws and regulations. Many others are provided voluntarily by organizations and vary with the organization.

While the specific elements of plans vary, employee benefits and services are generally defined as in-kind payments employees receive for their membership and/or participation in the organization. **Employee benefits and services** provide protection against health and accident-related problems and insure income at the end of one's work cycle. Legally required payments include Social Security, unemployment compensation, and workers' compensation; private protection programs include health care, life insurance, and disability insurance. Retirement income is provided via pensions and savings plans. Benefits programs also include pay for time not at work (e.g., vacations, holidays, sick leave and absence pay, breaks, and wash-up and clean-up time). A growing category of benefits relates to changing lifestyles. These benefits enable the employee to enjoy a better lifestyle or to meet social or personal obligations while minimizing employment-related costs. Discounts, education assistance, and child and elder care fall into this category.

PURPOSES AND IMPORTANCE OF INDIRECT COMPENSATION

Benefits and services have been provided by firms in order to attract and retain valued employees. Until recently, employers provided them relatively generously; the tide has shifted for several reasons. First, benefits and services are a major, increasingly costly part of total compensation. In 1929, total wages were estimated at $50.4 billion and total benefits payments were $1.5 million (5 percent of total pay). By 1990, benefits had risen to be more than 38.4 percent of wages and salaries, or roughly $6 per payroll hour or $12,402 per year per employee. While these numbers are large and represent substantial dollars for employers, there are major differences across industries. These differences, along with the various types of benefits and services provided, are illustrated in exhibit 11.1.

Exhibit 11.1

Employee Benefits as a Percentage of Payroll by Type of Benefit and Industrial Sector

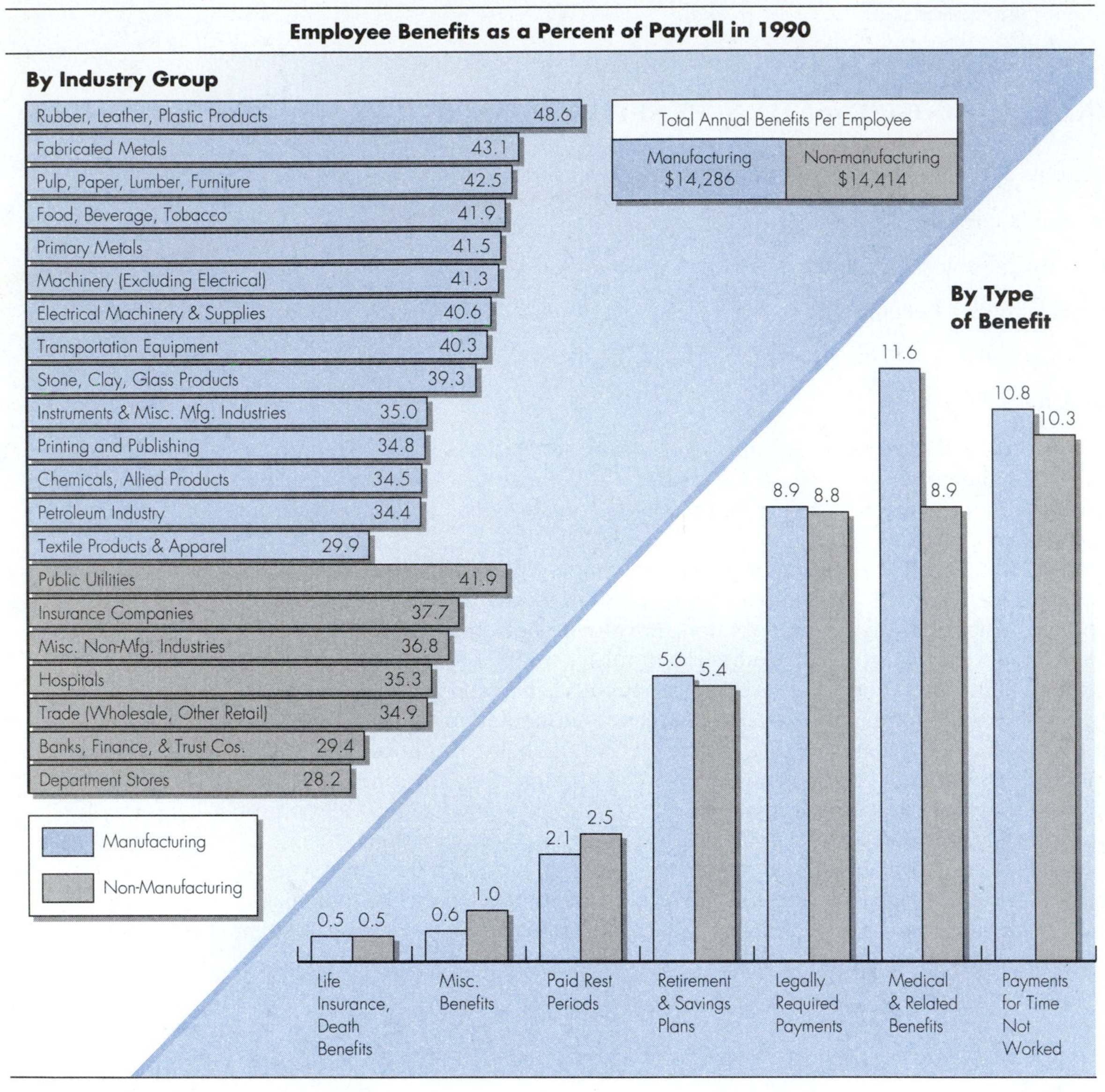

SOURCE: U.S. Chamber of Commerce *Bulletin to Management Datagraph* (16 Jan. 1992), 13.

Regardless of the type of worker or sector of the economy, the cost of benefits to organizations is enormous. While wages and salaries have increased 40-fold over the past 50 years, benefits increased even more—500 times.[3] Unfortunately, a majority of workers fail to recognize the magnitude of these costs and are dissatisfied with what they receive. A 1991 Employee Benefits Service found that employees believe the cost of their benefits equaled only 17 percent of their total salary, and more than 5 percent believed their benefits cost their company nothing. Another study found that satisfaction with basic benefits—medical, dental, life insurance, disability, and pension and savings plans—dropped 44 percentage points in the past decade, from an 86 percent favorable response in 1982 to 41.5 percent in 1990.[4]

External Influences

The skyrocketing growth in the type and cost of employee benefits can be traced to several environmental trends.

- *Wage controls.* The imposition of wage controls during World War II and the Korean Conflict forced organizations to offer more and greater benefits in place of wage increases to attract new employees.
- *Expansion of Social Security.* In 1935, the Social Security Act covered 60 percent of all workers. Subsequently the scope of benefits and the percentage of eligible workers has increased substantially. Now 95 percent of all workers are covered and receive disability and health benefits in addition to retirement pay.
- *Union bargaining.* From 1935 into the 1970s, unions were able to gain steady increases in wages and benefits for their members. As currently conceptualized, practically all benefits are mandatory bargaining items which require an employer to bargain in good faith on union proposals to add benefits.
- *Federal tax policies.* Income tax legislation has had and continues to have a critical influence on the design of benefits packages. As noted in chapter 10, employers are interested in benefits expenses that include pretax business costs; employees want to receive benefits without the burden of increased taxation.
- *Social legislation.* A variety of laws including the Age Discrimination in Employment Act, the Health Maintenance Organization Act of 1973, and the Employee Retirement Income Security Act have been passed that significantly affect the administration of benefits.
- *Inflation.* Employee benefits managers, more so than compensation managers, must anticipate the effects of inflation on medical service, education, and pension benefits. For example, double-digit inflation in the 1980s eroded the purchasing power of retirees and resulted in adjustment in the level of benefits.
- *Competition.* Most companies label their benefit packages as "competitive." Due to increased competition, many companies are going beyond mere statements and developing innovative packages of benefits to attract and retain employees. Wellness programs, health screenings, and employee assistance programs are examples of new benefits options. Flexible benefit plans or cash options instead of benefits are responses to external competitive pressures.

Internal Influences

The scope of employee benefits has also been affected by organizations and their stakeholders. Initiatives such as major medical insurance, long-term disability plans, and child and elder care allowances reflect a general concern for employee needs. All were implemented by organizations in response to employee needs. Provisions such as education assistance benefits, employee assistance programs, and wellness programs have been inspired by employer objectives to improve productivity and worker skills. More recently, benefits such as subsidies for buying American-made cars and matching funds for charitable giving have been prompted by private businesses' concern to "buy American" or to be "socially responsible."

Employee demand for benefits is evident in a recent poll conducted by the Employee Benefits Research Institute (EBRI) and the Gallup Organization. Four out of five Americans (84 percent) consider employee benefits such as pensions, health and life insurance, vacations, and sick leave "very important" or "important" in deciding whether to accept or reject a job. While only 15 percent had ever changed or quit a job based on benefits provided, if given a choice between two identical jobs—only one of which offered benefits—respondents said they would require a medium amount of $10,000 to accept the job without benefits.[5]

Employee wants. Traditionally, employers have adopted a "father knows best" attitude toward benefits; the company assumed it knew what was the most appropriate coverage for its employees. In the 1990s this attitude is being replaced with one of high employee involvement and choice, as described in the PHRM in the News: "A Farewell to Paternalism." Employee attitude surveys administered by the company or by unions contain questions regarding employee benefits preferences. Choice accounts that provide various benefits options and allow employees, rather than the company, to allocate benefits dollars are increasingly popular.

Human resource philosophy. An organization's fundamental beliefs about its employees and the employer-employee relationship set the stage for benefits management. The benefits manager must understand the underlying basis of the philosophy and the extent to which management supports human resources generally and benefits specifically. For example, some firms adopt an egalitarian approach to benefits and services by insisting that the same set of benefits be provided to all employees. Other firms adopt a more competitive approach, varying benefits with organizational level. For example, some firms still have executive lunches and executive parking areas. Many of the U.S. automakers give larger purchase entitlements with rank (e.g., a Ford Escort for lower level managers, a Thunderbird for top executives; two weeks severance pay for lower-level workers, substantial gold parachutes for top officials). Again, these choices cue employees as to the organization's culture and values.

Business objectives. As described in chapter 4, comprehensive planning typically involves assessing external threats and internal factors, setting and prioritizing goals, establishing timetables, and integrating benefits planning with human resource planning specifically and with the organizational planning process generally. In a study of nonunion firms, Fred K. Foulkes identified benefits as one of the key policy areas that reflect top management's belief in individual worth and equity and as a key area to achieve organizational objectives.[6] Exhibit 11.2 provides some examples of business objectives and possible responses from the benefits area.

IN THE NEWS

A Farewell to Paternalism

Recruiters and outplacement consultants say they have seen unmistakable signs of a pickup in the job market over the past two months. But many people returning to the work force—or simply changing jobs—will find a dramatic change because of the restructuring and recession companies have been through in the last few years: Most of the old paternalism is gone.

Because the uncertainties of employment—and the prospects of a long and lean retirement—are more apparent now, employers have new reasons for wanting employees to take responsibility for their own welfare. A study of 14 corporations released last September by the Conference Board, a New York–based business research group, found that companies "expect employees to share more responsibility for their careers and future financial security."

It is easy to be cynical about companies dumping more responsibilities on their employees. And employees are resisting the change, according to Helen Dennis, co-author of the Conference Board study. But in the long run, it's better for everyone if employees are firmly in charge of their own needs in three areas: career planning, financial planning and retirement planning.

"It's good for the employer, but it's absolutely critical for the employee," said Ms. Dennis, a gerontologist who teaches at the University of Southern California in Los Angeles. Ms. Dennis, who has worked with more than a thousand corporate executives to help them prepare for retirement, says that those in paternalistic companies often don't make a good transition to retired life.

In fact, employees in paternalistic companies generally do less to take care of themselves because they believe the company will pick up the slack. "In paternalistic companies, financial awareness and savings levels are very low," said Roger C. Hindman, a partner in the tax technology group at Price Waterhouse in Chicago.

Many companies are developing tools to help employees make the transition to a higher level of self-reliance. The tools include training programs, software packages to help plan for retirement and financial planning services. For example, the Shell Oil Company in Houston hired Mr. Hindman to give employees retirement planning seminars. "Most people who come to work for a big corporation like Shell say: 'I don't have to worry, everything will be there when I need it,'" said Guy Mason, Shell's pensioner relations manager. "That's not always true and it will not be true in the future."

Whether a company is offering assistance or not, employees need to get involved in their own futures, the experts say.

Many companies are beginning to be much more straightforward with employees about what they will provide in benefits, too, rather than shrinking from talking about reductions. "In the decade of the '90s there will be a lot more realism in employee benefits programs," Mr. Hindman said.

For example, Mr. Hindman uses a software program to help employees of his clients project what they will need for retirement and what they might have available. "Companies like Goodyear that have been paternalistic in the past tell us that they want to educate their employees because they're not going to be enriching their programs in the future," Mr. Hindman said.

One of the things Mr. Hindman points out to employees is that most pension benefits from private companies are not indexed for inflation. Today, when people spend 25 or 30 years in retirement, that has a tremendous impact on their income level and they must plan for it.

SOURCE: Mary Rowland, "A Farewell to Paternalism," *The New York Times* (8 Mar. 1992): F16.

PUBLIC PROTECTION PROGRAMS

Protection programs are designed to assist the employee and his or her family if and when the employee's income (direct compensation) is terminated and to alleviate the burden of health care expenses. Protection programs required by

Exhibit 11.2
Business Objectives and Potential Benefits Responses

Business Objective	Benefits Response
1. By year end, unify company acquired from merger from independent subsidiary to integrated division status	Perform analysis of immediate versus gradual transfer of subsidiary employees into corporate benefits plan. Make recommendations by end of first quarter.
2. To develop a working environment that is founded on integrity, open communication, and individual growth	Develop an employee career counseling system which provides employees with an opportunity to assess skills and develop competencies. Have it operational by July 1. Establish a tuition-reimbursement program by fall.
3. To establish the division as a recognized leader in support of its community	Establish a corporate-giving matching fund by 1993.
4. Complete downsizing of milling unit by end of third quarter	Develop various termination subsidies such as severance pay, outplacement assistance, and early retirement benefits by end of first quarter.
5. To cut accident rates 10 percent by year end	Establish an employee assistance program by year end. Set up free literacy training program to ensure that all employees can read job safety signs.

federal and state government are referred to as public programs, and those voluntarily offered by organizations are called private programs.

Social Security System

Public protection programs are the outgrowth of the Social Security Act of 1935. The act initially set up systems for retirement benefits, disability, and unemployment insurance. Health insurance, particularly Medicare, was added in 1966 to provide hospital insurance to almost everyone age 65 and older.

Funding of the Social Security System is provided by equal contributions from the employer and employee under terms of the Federal Insurance Contribution Act (FICA). Initially, employee and employer paid 1 percent of the employee's income up to $3,000. Currently, they pay tax on the first $53,400 of the employee's income at the rate of 6.2 percent (for retirement and disability) and on the first $125,000 at the rate of 1.45 percent (for hospital insurance via Medicare).

The average Social Security benefit for a single person is about $6,500; for a married couple it is about $12,000 per year, with adjustments routinely made for increases in the consumer price index. The maximum benefits from Social Security are now around $900 a month for a person who retired in 1988. Retired people age 65 to 69 can also earn about $9,000 annually without sacrificing benefits; beneficiaries under age 65 can earn about $6,500.[7]

Unemployment Compensation Benefits

To control costs, the Social Security Act dictates that unemployment compensation programs be jointly administered through the federal and state governments. Because income levels vary from state to state, unemployment compensation also varies by state. With the exception of Alabama, Alaska, and New Jersey, only employers contribute to the unemployment fund. All profit-making organizations pay a tax on the first $7,000 to $10,000 of wages paid to each employee. The contribution rate for employers, however, varies according to the number of unemployed people drawing from the fund. Consequently, during periods of high unemployment, employers make larger contributions than they do during periods of stable employment.

To be eligible for benefits an employee must

- Have worked a specified number of weeks (set by the state)
- Be able and available to work
- Be actively looking for work
- Not be unemployed due to a labor dispute (except in Rhode Island and New York)
- Not have been terminated for gross misconduct
- Not have terminated voluntarily

The length of time an employee may receive benefits is a function of how long the employee had worked prior to termination, but the standard maximum is 26 weeks. Extended benefits of up to 13 weeks are provided during periods of high unemployment or when jobs are lost due to foreign competition. The level of benefits ranges from 50 to 70 percent of base salary up to a maximum weekly amount that varies by state (around $225). With the passage of the Tax Reform Act of 1986, unemployment compensation became *fully taxable,* making actual benefit levels much lower.[8]

Medicare

When Medicare became operational in 1966, benefits managers felt this program would be a cure-all, satisfying the health care needs of older Americans. Managers anticipated significant cost savings by coordinating private medical programs with Medicare. Unfortunately, this has not proved to be true. In the era of early retirements to reduce staffing levels, organizations have discovered that the assurance of continuing health coverage is a critical factor in an individual's decision to elect retirement. Because 80 percent of retirements occur before the age of 65 (the age for Medicare eligibility), there is a gap in health care coverage that must be subsumed by organizations. Medicare has progressively shifted cost responsibility to subscribers and, as a result, retirees over age 65 are demanding supplemental health benefits from their former employers.

Because employers' liabilities for post-retirement health benefits are estimated in the *trillions* of dollars and are expected to increase, the Financial Accounting Standards Board (FASB) has specified that these liabilities be included in corporate financial statements. A partial consequence is that organizations have begun avoiding promises of specific levels of benefits for future retirees.

Disability and Workers' Compensation

Of the more than 6.4 million job-related injuries reported annually in the private sector, about half are serious enough for the injured worker to lose work time, experience restricted work activity, or both. Additionally, 332,000 new occupational illness cases were reported in 1990, up from 284,000 in 1989. Almost 60 percent of these illnesses were associated with repetitive motions such as vibration, repeated pressure, and carpal tunnel syndrome, and a majority require medical care and result in lost work time.[9]

When such injuries or illnesses occur as a result of on-the-job concerns, workers may be eligible for workers' compensation benefits. Administered at the state level and fully financed by employers, workers' compensation benefits are provided for temporary and permanent disability, disfigurement, medical expenses, and medical rehabilitation. Survival benefits are provided following fatal injuries.

While specific terms and conditions vary by state, workers' compensation benefits are provided regardless of fault in an accident. Awards can consist of lump-sum monetary benefits (e.g., $10,000 for the loss of an eye), the payment of medical benefits, or long-term payments tied to the worker's income level. Currently, most states award employees who are unable to work at least two-thirds of their gross salary before they were injured. Employee contributions to the state-managed programs are contingent on their accident rates. The average premium an employer paid for an employee was more than $500 in 1991. This represents a five-fold increase in 20 years.

There are several reasons for the increase in premiums. Even though the economy has been moving from manufacturing to service, the number of claims has doubled in the past decade. In 1990 the average number of lost work days was 78 days per incident. Some of the increase is due to real and debilitating diseases that science recently has linked to the work place (e.g., carpal tunnel syndrome, asbestosis). Increases are also due to worker compensation fraud; a recent study estimates that 20 percent of all workers' compensation claims are fraudulent.[10] To deal with phony claims, state-owned or state-managed worker compensation insurers are utilizing a variety of strategies ranging from case monitoring, videotaping, and media blitzes to prosecution.

Proactive workers' compensation administrators also are applying a variety of health care cost-containment strategies to workers' compensation, such as

- Developing networks of preferred provider organizations
- Specifying fees for treating workers' compensation claimants
- Limiting payments to medically necessary or reasonable procedures
- Requiring pre-certification of hospital admissions
- Establishing concurrent review of inpatient hospital stays
- Routinely auditing hospital and health care bills[11]

Employers also are jumping on the cost-containment bandwagon. For example, Sprague Electric Co. in Concord, New Hampshire, assembles a team consisting of the worker's supervisor, a rehabilitation counselor, and the firm's personnel and human resource manager. Using videotaped demonstrations of the employee's job and physician input, the team identifies components of the jobs the worker can still perform, as well as appropriate accommodations that need to be made.[12]

Burns of Boston, a Rhode Island-based photo frame and album manufacturer, has adopted a comprehensive approach. In 1989, when an employee was injured it took an average of nine months to close the case. According to Michael Fitzgerald, former human resource director, "Active injury management didn't exist, nor did an effective support program for returning injured workers to work. More important, injured employees many times didn't receive a comprehensive first-day injury evaluation."[13] To make the necessary changes, the company hired a workers' compensation consulting firm and formed a management design team. The result was a five-step process to bring about organization awareness of the problems and associated costs of workers' compensation and how the problems could be solved. Between 1989 and 1990, the average number of lost-time work days used by employees fell from 681 to 45, a 93 percent decrease.

The results of the study identified several areas of concern. Because Burns lacked an early-return-to-work program, it took much longer for workers' compensation cases to be resolved. In addition, injured employees returned to work much later than the medical severity of their injury would warrant. Consequently, Burns' frequency (number of injuries per 100 employees) and severity (number of lost work days per 100 employees) were 166 percent and 249 percent above the national average. The implementation of an active, modified-duty, return-to-work program recouped $378,480 in lost-time dollars in one year.

The company also established a cross-functional management team to oversee the management of worker health and safety. Tangible goals were set in all areas of workers' compensation management. Safety inspections and training were stepped up in support of these strategic objectives. The safety committee became an active enforcer of safety rules and was empowered to recommend changes to procedures that would increase safety. Other tactics included the establishment of a safety incentive program; safety results by department were posted and updated daily, and prizes were awarded when safety milestones were surpassed.

Burns also committed to get the injured employee a same-day medical evaluation. The worker's supervisor was required to accompany the individual to the treating physician on the first visit. Transportation was available for follow-up treatments. "Although it was a cost to the company, providing transportation removed any barrier between the injured employee and the medical community. Having same-day access to medical providers assured prompt evaluations by qualified medical personnel and return to work," Fitzgerald explained. To assertively manage workers' compensation costs, he recommends four things:

1. Actively manage your workers' compensation insurance carrier by using all of the services it can provide.
2. Aggressively review cases each quarter until you're satisfied that open cases are being resolved and closed appropriately.

3. Request that your carrier's loss control representative visit your office or plant location to evaluate your safety awareness program.

4. Ensure that a company representative attends every workers' compensation hearing. Your presence gives incredible weight to any claims challenge and shows the hearing officer the company's concern for speedy case resolution.[14]

PRIVATE PROTECTION PROGRAMS

Private protection programs are offered by organizations but are not required by law. They include retirement income plans, capital accumulation plans, savings and thrift plans, and supplemental unemployment benefits and guaranteed pay. Some firms also are offering work options for retirees including temporary full-time and permanent part-time employment.

The various retirement income plans can be classified in terms of whether they will be qualified or nonqualifited. A **qualified plan** means that the pension plan covers a broad, nondiscriminatory class of employees, meets Internal Revenue Code requirements, and consequently receives favorable tax treatment. For example the employer's contributions to the plan are tax deductible for the current year and employees pay no taxes until retirement. **Nonqualified plans** do not adhere to the strict tax regulations and cover only select groups of employees. As described in chapter 10, they are often utilized to provide supplemental retirement benefits for key executives.[15]

Pension Plans

The largest category of private protection plans are pensions. Four out of five employees in medium and large firms are covered by some type of private pension or capital accumulation plan and rely on these plans to provide future security. A less known fact is that the 20 largest pension funds (13 of them fund public employees) hold one-tenth of the equity capital of America's publicly owned companies. All told, institutional investors—primarily pension funds—control close to 40 percent of the common stock of the country's largest businesses. Pension funds also hold 40 percent or more of the medium-term and long-term debt of the country's bigger companies. Thus, employees via their pension funds have become America's largest retirement bankers, lenders as well as business owners.[16]

Defined benefit plans. With a defined benefit pension plan, the actual benefits received on retirement vary by age and length of service of the employee. For example, an employee may receive $50 a month for each year of company service. As delineated in exhibit 11.3, defined plans are preferred by paternalistic employers and unions because they produce predictable, secure, and continuing income. Another advantage of defined benefit plans is that they are carefully regulated by Employees' Retirement Income Security Act. In addition to the reporting, disclosure, fiduciary standards, plan participation rules, and vesting standards, defined benefit plans must adhere to specific funding level requirements and be insured against plan termination due to economic hardship, misfunding, or corporate buyouts.

Exhibit 11.3
Comparison of Defined Benefit and Defined Contribution Pension Funds

Aspect	Defined Benefit	Defined Contribution
1. Definition	Benefits vary by age and length of service according to a formula. Set amount received.	Each employee has an account to which personal, corporate or both contributions are made.
2. Source of Funding	Majority funded entirely by company contributions. Some public-sector funds require employee participation.	Employer and employee both contribute to the plan. Formulas are 50–50 or higher employer to employee contribution.
3. Prevalence	20 percent of new plans. Majority of existing plans.	80 percent of new plans. Minority of existing plans.
4. Supporting Culture	Paternalistic, mature, union.	Competitive, participative, start-up.
5. ERISA Control	Must meet ERISA funding requirements. Must have termination insurance. Excise tax on asset reversions.	No set funding requirement. No plan termination insurance.
6. Advantages to Employee	Guaranteed level of retirement income.	No set retirement income. Based on profitability of investments.
7. Disadvantages to Employee	Pension may not be enough to maintain standard of living.	Contributions restricted, early withdrawals penalized, loans limited. Must contribute funds to activate.
8. Advantages to Employer	Contributions are tax deductible. Rewards long-term employee.	Less costly. Less risky.
9. Disadvantages to Employer	Difficult to determine how to credit employees before fund was started. May be underfunded.	Contributions increase as employees' income goes up.

SOURCE: Adapted from R.M. McCaffery, *Employee Benefit Programs: A Total Compensation Perspective* (Boston, Mass.: PWS-Kent, 1992).

The Pension Benefit Guaranty Corporation (PBGC) administers the required insurance program and guarantees the payment of basic retirement benefits to participants if a plan is terminated. The PBGC also can terminate pension funds that are seriously underfunded. In July, 1991, they moved to do exactly that with Pan Am's pension fund. The airline had missed three required funding contributions over the past year. According to James Lockhart, executive director for PBGC, "We had to act immediately to keep the pension insurance safety net strong for workers and retirees and stem the rising costs for companies with well-funded pension plans."

When a plan is terminated, employees who had participated in the plan are guaranteed to receive what they had contributed. In the case of Pan Am, this covers 34,000 participants, including 11,000 retirees enrolled in Pan Am's Cooperative Retirement Income Plan and 750 participants in the Defined Benefit Plan for Flight Engineers. According to Lockhart, PBGC will lose more than $600 million due to the mismanagement of this plan alone. Losses like this explain why PBGC's long-term deficit now tops more than $2 billion and why retirement programs are feared to be the next "savings and loan crisis" of the 1990s.[17]

Defined contribution plans. Eighty percent of new plans are defined contribution plans. With this type of plan, each employee has a separate account to which employee and employer contributions are added. Typically, the employee must activate the plan by agreeing to contribute a set amount of money; the employer then matches the percentage contribution to a specific level. Defined contribution plans are more prevalent in competitive, participative organizations.

The two most common types of defined contribution plans are money purchase and tax-deferred profit-sharing plans. With **money purchase plans,** the employer makes fixed, regular contributions for participants, usually a percentage of total pay, to a fund. Employees may also make voluntary contributions. The maximum amount is equal to 25 percent of earned income, up to a maximum of $30,000 for all defined contribution plans. Monies are held in trust funds, and the employee is given several investment options that differ in terms of the degree of risk and growth potential. At retirement, accumulated funds are used to provide annuities. In some cases, lump-sum distributions may be made.

One of the largest money purchase plans is the Teachers Insurance and Annuity Association–College Retirement Equity Fund (TIAA-CREF). More than 1.4 million faculty and administrative staff members from nearly 4,500 organizations participate in this program. Enrollees can choose to allocate contributions across four distinct CREF investment accounts (stock, money market, bond market, or a social choice). An allocation to TIAA is a premium for a contractually guaranteed amount of future life time annuity income.

Tax-deferred profit-sharing plans were discussed in chapter 10 and provide for employee participation in profit sharing using a predetermined formula. Monies contributed to these plans are set aside until retirement when the employees can cash in their profits. From the employer's perspective, tax-deferred profit-sharing plans are useful because they may deduct up to 15 percent of participants' compensation (up to an income level of $200,000) for profit-sharing contributions. Additionally, they pass on the investment risk to the employee.[18]

Supplemental Plans

In addition to Social Security and standard pension plans, large firms often offer a supplemental defined contribution plan or savings plan. Currently, 30 percent of all employees participate in supplemental plans. Such plans serve as the third leg of the retirement income stool; they also provide additional retirement income or serve as a source for accumulating funds to meet short-term needs and goals, according to benefits expert Robert M. McCaffery. These plans take one of two forms: savings plans that work as defined contribution plans, and deferred employee stock-ownership plans as discussed in chapter 10.

As provided under Section 401(a) of the Internal Revenue Code, a key feature of a savings plan is that the employee must elect to participate in the program by setting aside a small percentage of pay. Other features of the plan include loan provisions and limited in-service withdrawal for hardship or for employment termination. Participants can elect to receive their entire contribution in a lump sum upon retirement or termination.

Individual Retirement Accounts

Under current law, an employee who is not an active participant in an employer-sponsored pension plan during any part of a year may contribute up to $2,000 unconditionally to an Individual Retirement Account (IRA), with an additional $250 allowed for a spousal account. The latter provision applies only if a joint tax return is filed. Employees who are involved in employer-sponsored pension plans also may participate, providing their income does not surpass limits set by the IRS.

Guaranteed Pay Plans

A relatively new type of income guarantee involves providing guaranteed pay to nonexempt employees who are laid off. Such plans protect employee income during periods of involuntary unemployment. In automotive, steel, and related industries, the protection project is in the form of supplemental unemployment benefits plans. Such plans provide income safety nets by providing corporate-financed unemployment benefits—up to 85 percent of regular take-home pay for up to three years.

For example, the 1990 contract between General Motors and the United Auto Workers guarantees laid off workers in 1991 unemployment pay of $457 a week. A decade ago, benefits would have been restricted to one year or until the supplemental funds ran out. Currently more than 100,000 Big Three autoworkers are covered under these plans. Unions negotiated for this form of job security in exchange for the work assignment flexibility management wanted. As the layoffs in 1992 have shown, these benefits were quite valuable to automotive workers.

According to Harley Shaiken, a professor of labor studies at the University of California at San Diego, "This new type of benefit is unprecedented in union history. What they won is very important and it does provide some very real protection." On the downside, economists contend that blue-collar workers get more protection than the companies can prudently afford. In the fourth quarter of 1990, General Motors lost about $1.4 billion, the largest quarterly net operating loss ever sustained by a car company. One big reason is that labor, for the first time, is a fixed cost. In essence the auto companies are committed to paying hourly workers for extended periods even if they don't work.

Autoworkers, on the other hand, say they feel sorry GM is losing so much money; but they feel workers shouldn't bear all the pain of recessions, especially now that GM and other automakers are preaching teamwork and asking employees to help raise quality and cut costs. As one worker put it, "GM is asking us to give more effort and this contract pays [for] that contribution. If GM says the workers are the most important thing, then they should treat us like that."

Paid idleness affects workers in different ways. "Let them tell me I could retire with full benefits and I'd be gone," says Richard Pearson, chief steward at UAW Local 7, which represents workers in a closed Chrysler plant. "Anytime you get something for nothing, it's good." Jimmy Bishop, a laid-off Chrysler worker, has used his spare time to go back to school. The 53-year-old has learned to drive an 18-wheel truck, retiled the basement, replaced the windows, and reroofed the garage. "But when you're used to doing something every day, and then all of a sudden it's stopped, it's almost like being in prison." One Chrysler union local cites 51 deaths since the plant closed eight months previous, a toll that officials of the plant's employee assistance program attribute in part to the stress of being out of work.[19]

HEALTH CARE BENEFITS

Coverage for medical expenses including hospital charges, physician charges, and other medical services is the core of a group health plan and will be discussed first. Organizations also may provide wellness programs, employee assistance programs, and short- and long-term disability insurance. Because the cost is far below what employees would pay on their own, health benefits—particularly medical insurance—represent an important, although costly, benefit. Unfortunately, most employees underestimate the cost of health benefits to the organization and view coverage as an entitlement rather than a costly benefit. In a recent study more than 80 percent of all workers said their employers are obligated to provide health care for them, but almost half of all employees did not know what their health insurance cost their employer.

In reality, health care costs more than $500 billion or 12 percent of the nation's gross national product (GNP). Employer-funded health care costs, like workers' compensation, double every five years. In 1990 health insurance cost employers an average of $149 per employee per month.[20] To fund rising health care costs, businesses are passing the cost on to consumers. For example, Detroit automakers estimate that $500–$700 is added to the retail price of each automobile to pay for employee health care costs.[21] Exhibit 11.4 delineates what five different companies had to sell to cover the cost of a simple appendectomy. According to Walter Williams, CEO of Bethelem Steel, attempts to stem the tide of rising health care costs have amounted to little more than "band-aids."

Medical Care Approaches

Employers can finance and provide medical expense benefits to employees and their dependents in four different ways. The most widely used source for financing group medical benefits involves insurance companies. However, a variety of other approaches are gaining in popularity as business attempts to thwart rising costs.

Insurance companies. Insurance carriers offer a broad range of health care services from which employers can select coverage. Premiums are set and are adjusted depending on usage rates and increases in health care costs. The insurance company administers the plan, handling all the paperwork, approvals, and problems. Proponents of this approach argue that insurers protect the plan

Exhibit 11.4
What Companies Must Sell to Pay for an Appendectomy

Company	Product
1. Dayton Hudson	39,000 Ninja Turtle action figures
2. Atlantic Richfield	192,000 gallons of gas
3. Southern California Edison	1 year's electricity for 330 households
4. Anheuser-Busch	11,627 6-packs of 12-ounce Bud
5. Goodyear Tire & Rubber	461 radial tires for passenger cars

SOURCE: "CEOs Seek Help on Health Costs," *Fortune* (3 June 1991), 12.

sponsor against wide fluctuations in claims experience and costs and offer opportunities for participation in larger risk pools. Insurance companies also have administrative expertise related to certification reviews, claim audits, coordination of benefits, and other cost-containment services.

On the downside, the insurance company, not the employer, makes decisions regarding covered benefits. Such decisions may go against the corporation's ethics and sense of social responsibility. Recall that the Rockwell Company was advised against covering the bone-marrow transplant by the insurance company that administers its health care plan. Because the firm was self-insured it could ignore the advice and do what it felt was ethical. Companies who subscribe to a specific insurance plan do not have this luxury. The insurance company would make all the tough calls. However, the tendency would be towards conservatism to contain their costs (not the employer's costs).

Provider organizations. Blue Cross/Blue Shield associations are nonprofit organizations that operate within defined geographic areas. While Blue Cross plans cover hospital expenses, Blue Shield plans provide benefits for charges by physicians and other medical providers. Typically, these associations negotiate arrangements with their member hospitals and physicians to reimburse the hospital or physician at a discounted rate when a subscriber incurs a charge. As originally established, the rate represents full payment for the service and there is no additional charge. However, recently skyrocketing costs in health care have resulted in deductibles ($50 to $250 per year per person) and cost sharing (10 to 20 percent) on the part of employees.

Health maintenance organizations. A survey of almost 2,000 firms found that 63 percent of all organizations now offer health care through health maintenance organizations (HMOs). Health care costs with HMOs have risen only 15.7 percent a year compared to increases above 20 percent for traditional health care plans. About one-third of all eligible employees participate in HMO plans. By 1990, 36 million employees participated in HMOs.[22]

The growth in HMOs was stimulated by the passage of the **Health Maintenance Organization (HMO) Act of 1973.** This act requires that companies with at least 25 employees living in an HMO service area must offer membership in that organization to employees as an alternative to regular group health coverage, provided the HMO meets federal qualification requirements. HMO amendments of 1988 relaxed many of the federal rules governing HMOs and specifically repealed the dual-choice alternative, effective in October, 1995. This shift in legislative direction is designed to make the HMO field more competitive and, as a result, employers more receptive to using HMOs.

One of the most effective HMOs is the Group Health Cooperative in Seattle, Washington, which had more than 470,000 members (one of every eight residents in the Puget Sound area) in 1991. This HMO reported a surplus of $19 million in 1990 and has been widely cited for providing high-quality and cost-effective care for its members. Still, Group Health has its problems. Unions have consistently targeted the HMO for actions and have routinely struck over wages and benefits that they believe should be increased, given the large surplus of funds.[23]

Preferred provider networks. Preferred Provider Organizations (PPOs) are a relatively new option in health care delivery. Introduced in the 1980s, these plans covered 55 to 60 million participants in 1990. With these programs, employers contract directly—or indirectly through an insurance company—with a provider organization to secure agreements from health care providers (physicians, dentists, laboratories, hospitals) to deliver services to group health plan participants on a discounted basis. Because these plans are relatively unregulated with respect to rate setting and requirements, employers have a great deal of flexibility in structuring an arrangement.

Unlike HMOs, employees are not required to use PPO providers exclusively. However, there are usually incentives (lower deductibles or cost sharing) when a PPO is utilized. For example, the employer may cover all health care costs provided by a PPO but only 80 percent of the cost of care provided by physicians outside of the PPO network. A concern with PPOs in the 1990s is the potential for antitrust legislation since these plans involve agreeing on standard charges for health care services.[24]

Self-funded plans. A growing number of companies are opting for self-funded plans as a way to control medical plan costs and gain relief from state insurance regulations. By eliminating or reducing insurance protection, the employer saves on carrier retention charges (the amount of money not utilized to pay claims). This includes such things as state premium taxes, administrative costs, risk and contingency expenses, and reserve requirements. Typically, the employer creates a voluntary employee beneficiary association and establishes a tax-exempt trust. The trust's investment income is tax exempt as long as it is used to provide benefits to employees and their dependents.

Cost-containment strategies. To further control costs, firms are also employing a variety of cost-containment strategies. While no strategy can hold the line on soaring medical costs, these strategies represent employers' best efforts to date to control costs. Some of the more common strategies include

- *Hospital utilization programs* that review the necessity and appropriateness of hospitalization prior to admission and/or during a stay.
- *Coordination of benefits* with other providers to prevent duplicate payment for the same health care service.
- *Data analysis* to determine the most viable cost management approach. Simulations and experience-based utilization assumptions are utilized to develop models.

- *Managed care.* Many employers now are active participants in case management. Interventions include requirements for second opinions and peer reviews.
- *Cost sharing with employees.* By raising deductibles and contribution levels, employers hold the line on overall expenses.

A new variation on cost sharing involves premium rebates to employees who stay healthy. For example, Baker-Hughes, a Texas drilling and tool company that employs close to 40,000 people, rewards employees who are nonsmokers by reducing their annual insurance contribution by $120. The company estimates that the plan has saved $2 million a year in health-related costs.

Other examples include Southern California Edison in Rosemead, California, which gives $10 for employees and $10 for spouses off the monthly contribution to its health plan if they agree to be tested for smoking, weight, cholesterol, blood pressure and blood sugar—and to participate in a helpful program if they fall short.

At Blue Cross and Blue Shield, the discounts for nonsmokers are offered not only for people buying health insurance individually but, in Wisconsin and Idaho, to small employee groups in which the percentage of smokers is below a certain point.

But sometimes employers can go too far. The Circle K Corporation's decision, later dropped, to deny coverage to employees with problems related to alcohol, drugs, and AIDS was widely criticized.

Indeed, while he advocates programs that include financial incentives, the director of the United States Office of Disease Prevention, Dr. J. Michael McGinnis, said he was concerned about the potential for discrimination. In the worst case, companies may be in violation of the Americans with Disabilities Act if individuals with specific disabilities are treated differently than other employees without the disability. There are also ethical dilemmas. While employees may consider it fair to give premium rebates for healthy lifestyles, most would not tolerate raises in premiums for genetically linked conditions. According to Michael Carter, senior vice president of Hay/Huggins, a consulting firm specializing in health care cost containment, "Companies shouldn't include anything in their plan which isn't under the employee's control."[25]

Wellness Programs

Frustrated with efforts to manage health care costs for employees who already are sick, a growing number of employers are taking proactive steps to prevent health care problems. Moving beyond employee exercise classes and stress management classes, a handful of firms are implementing well designed wellness programs, which are producing significant savings on the bottomline.

For example, the Adolph Coors Company based in Golden, Colorado, has spent the past 10 years fine-tuning its wellness program. For every dollar spent on wellness, Coors sees a return of $6.15 including $1.9 million annually in decreased medical costs, reduced sick leave, and increased productivity. According to William Coors, chairman and CEO, the secret to Coors's success is really no secret. "Wellness is an integral part of the corporate culture."

Coors's commitment to wellness includes a health-risk assessment, nutritional counseling, stress management, and programs for smoking cessation, weight loss, and orthopedic rehabilitation. "When employees hear health warnings and statistics on the television, the warnings are always about someone else. When they read a personalized assessment that indicates a genuine risk of heart attack based on heredity, cholesterol, and high blood pressure, the warnings take on new significance," says D. W. Edmonton, Ph.D., director of the University of Michigan Fitness Research Center.

Overweight Coors employees learn about the long-term risks associated with obesity through a health-hazard survey. They're educated about the effect of excess weight on the cardiovascular, endocrine, and musculoskeletal systems. Then an individual plan is developed. The individualized program may include individual counseling, group classes, and medical programs such as Optifast. The company even gives employees a financial incentive if they participate in the program and achieve and maintain their weight loss goal during a twelve-month period. To further encourage involvement, classes are held on-site.

According to Max Morton, manager of Coors Wellness Services, a successful wellness program must contain several key elements including support and direction from the CEO which manifests itself in company values statements. For example, Coors's value statement reads, "We encourage wellness in body, mind and spirit for all employees." In addition, the program needs to be accessible to all employees and their families. By making wellness a family affair, Coors creates the support necessary at home to maintain healthy lifestyles. When designing the program, employee input is necessary to determine components as well as to plan program logistics. Morton also recommends in-house and external evaluations to ensure that programs are meeting their objectives. Finally, ongoing internal communication keeps employees aware of the company's unwavering commitment to wellness.[26]

Efforts by other companies include a variety of wellness programs. For example, Bell of Pennsylvania and Diamond State Telephone have provided mammography tests for their female employees and spouses of male employees—more than 3,700 employees in two states. The company maintains a mobile unit that travels to worksites in Pennsylvania and Delaware. In 1990, more than 25 New England companies joined together to provide regular mammography screenings for their female employees using a mobile van coordinated by the Yale University Comprehensive Cancer Center. Participating firms included the Hartford Insurance Companies, Aetna Life and Casualty, General Electric, and GTE. Since 1968, Campbell Soup Company has offered blood pressure screening for its employees at 25 plants through the country. Company doctors provide follow-up and prescribe medication for hypertension as needed.

Employee Assistance Programs

Whereas wellness programs attempt to prevent health care problems, employee assistance programs **(EAPs)** are specifically designed to assist employees with chronic personal problems that hinder their job performance and attendance. EAPs are often used with employees who are alcoholics, have drug dependencies, or who have severe domestic problems that interfere with competency on the job. EAPs also provide assistance to help employees cope with mental disorders, financial problems, stress, eating disorders, smoking cessation, and to provide dependent care programs, bereavement counseling, and AIDS support group meetings. Because the job may be partly responsible for these problems, some employers are taking the lead in establishing EAPs to help affected workers.[27]

Even though EAPs are designed to provide valuable assistance to employees, many employees in need fail to use the programs unless faced with the alternative of being fired. When so confronted, however, the success rate of those attending EAPs is high. The results can mean substantial gains in employee job performance and reductions in absenteeism. For example,

> Employees experienced an increase in work productivity and a decrease in lost work time, health insurance claims, and accidents after participating in the employee assistance plan at Detroit Edison Co...
>
> For the 67 employees receiving EAP treatment, the total number of lost work days dropped 29 percent, from 476 days before treatment to 341 days following treatment, the study reports. The study also finds that after EAP participation:
>
> - Combined lost work time was reduced by 18 percent—from 117 instances to 97 instances.
> - The cost of health insurance claims declined 26 percent—from a total $36,472 to $27, 122.
> - Work suspensions dropped from five to three; written warnings decreased from eight to seven; and the number of job-related accidents went from seven to three.[28]

Thus EAPs serve as an important form of indirect compensation that benefits the individual and the firm.

PAID LEAVE

Paid leave is not as complex to administer as benefits from protection programs, but it is the more costly, accounting for more than 10 percent of the total payroll. If absenteeism policies are not designed correctly, costs may escalate even further. The two major categories are time not worked *off* the job (holidays, vacations, sick days) and time not worked *on* the job (rest periods, wash-up times, lunches).

Off the Job

The most common paid off the job components are vacations, sick leave, holidays, and personal days. The challenge in administering these benefits is to contain the costs of these programs while seeking better ways to package them.

Vacations. Vacations are granted because employees need time to recuperate away from the physical and mental demands of work. It is also believed that vacation time is an appropriate reward for service and commitment to the organization. Recently, a small number of firms have granted sabbaticals to employees (similar to those in academia) which after a stated period of service can be used for self-improvement, community work, or teaching. Tandem Computers, which has been granting six-week sabbaticals plus normal vacation time at full pay, claims that in the short term such programs have a negative impact on productivity, but in the long term they enhance productivity.

Length of vacations tends to vary by industry, locale, company size, and profession. Some firms believe that longer vacations for more senior employees help to counterbalance salary compression problems. However, there are no hardcore data to suggest that employees view this as a fair exchange.

In setting up vacation programs, several issues need to be addressed. (1) Will vacation pay be based on scheduled hours or on hours actually worked? (2) Under what circumstances can an employee be paid in lieu of a vacation? (3) Can vacations be deferred, or will they be lost if not taken? (4) What pay rate applies if an employee works during a vacation? The trend is toward vacation banking, with employees able to roll over a specified period of unused vacation days into a savings investment plan.[29]

Holidays. Employees in the U.S. average about ten paid holidays a year. However, the actual days vary by industry and locale. For example, in some southern states Jefferson Davis's and Robert E. Lee's birthdays are observed, in Utah there is Mormon Pioneer Day, and in Alaska there is Steward's Day.

Trends in union contract negotiations are to include floater holidays that meet employee preferences, as well as personal holidays in recognition of the employee's birthday. Conversely, other organizations are cutting back on the number of paid holidays because they are an investment with marginal return. Companies are also moving toward established holiday pay policies such as "In order to be eligible for holiday pay, an employee must perform work on the day before and the day after the holiday." Obviously these policies are intended to deter absenteeism.

Paid absences. On any given day, one million American workers who are otherwise employed will *not* attend work; they will be absent. In the U.S. the absenteeism rate ranges from 2 to 3 percent of total payroll. However, some organizations report absenteeism in excess of 20 percent. An estimated 400 million person days are lost each year as a result of employee absenteeism. This is almost 10 times the number of person days lost to strikes over a ten-year period.[30]

In comparison with other countries, the U.S. is midrange. Japan and Switzerland have lower absenteeism rates; Italy, France, and Sweden report substantially higher rates. The problem in Italy became so severe at one point that police began arresting some of the habitual absentees, charging them with fraud.[31]

What makes absenteeism so problematic is the cost of employee replacement. It has been estimated that for every 1 percent change in the national absence rates, the gross national product goes down by $20 billion. Absenteeism at General Motors has been estimated to cost $1 billion annually.[32]

While there are many reasons employees do not attend work (health, family problems, transportation difficulties), there is evidence that absences are proportional to the number of paid days off offered by an organization. That is, as the number of paid days off increases, the number of days of actual absence increases proportionally. As pay rates rise, absenteeism also increases, with employees potentially "buying" time off. Consequently, because of lax policies, many organizations unwittingly not only tolerate or accept absenteeism but actually reward it. Their policies make it easier to be absent than to come to work.[33]

Negative strategies to control absenteeism include disciplinary procedures against employees who are absent weekly, once every two weeks, without a physician's excuse, before or after a holiday, after payday, without calling in, or for personal business. Absences for these reasons are subject to employee discipline ranging from oral warnings for first offenses to discharge. Unfortunately, these policies appear to be generally ineffective in controlling absenteeism among habitual offenders.

Programs that reward attendance—cash prizes, bonuses, conversion of a proportion of unused absence days to vacation days—appear more promising. To prevent unscheduled absenteeism, organizations have also moved to personal days. The logic here is that employees must notify officials in advance that they will be absent. As discussed earlier, self-management programs for habitual offenders also offer some hope for controlling excessive absenteeism.

On the Job

Pay for time not worked on the job includes rest periods, the lunch period, wash-up time, and clothes-change and get-ready times. Together these are the fifth most expensive indirect compensation benefit.

Another benefit that is growing in popularity is paid time for physical fitness. This is clearly pay for time not worked, but organizations often offer it because of its on-the-job benefit—healthy workers.

LIFE CYCLE BENEFITS

In response to a growing number of single parents, two-earner families, employees with aging parents in need of care, and nontraditional families, employers are expanding their benefits packages to address new priorities. As shown in exhibit 11.5, only a handful of firms currently offer these benefits. However, employers realize that a failure to address these needs in the near future will restrict their ability to compete. Three categories of life cycle–related benefits—child care, eldercare, changing lifestyle—will be discussed in greater detail below.

Child Care Services

Recognizing that child care is a shared responsibility, more and more employers are providing child care assistance to their employees. In fact, a survey of more than 10,000 firms employing 10 or more workers showed that 63 percent of all employers offer some benefits, schedule help, or services relating to child care. As this chapter's Focus on Research feature explains, employee preferences for various child care options vary. Thus, in order to be competitive, firms minimally need to survey their employees to find out their preferences and may need to offer a variety of options to meet their needs.

Dependent care reimbursement accounts. Dependent care reimbursement accounts have become the most prevalent type of child care benefit in the 1990s. These accounts allow employees to pay for qualified expenses with pretax dollars subject to a use-it-or-lose-it rule. While they benefit employees greatly, they entail minimal administrative costs for the sponsoring organization. The maximum amount an employee can channel into one of these accounts is $5,000 a year. For an employee to participate in a reimbursement account, the child must be under the age of thirteen. Additionally, the expense must be necessary to permit an employee to work, both husband and wife to work, or a spouse to attend school full-time.

For the employee, these accounts offer potential tax advantages. Consider a single parent with a four-year-old daughter. He anticipates child care expenses

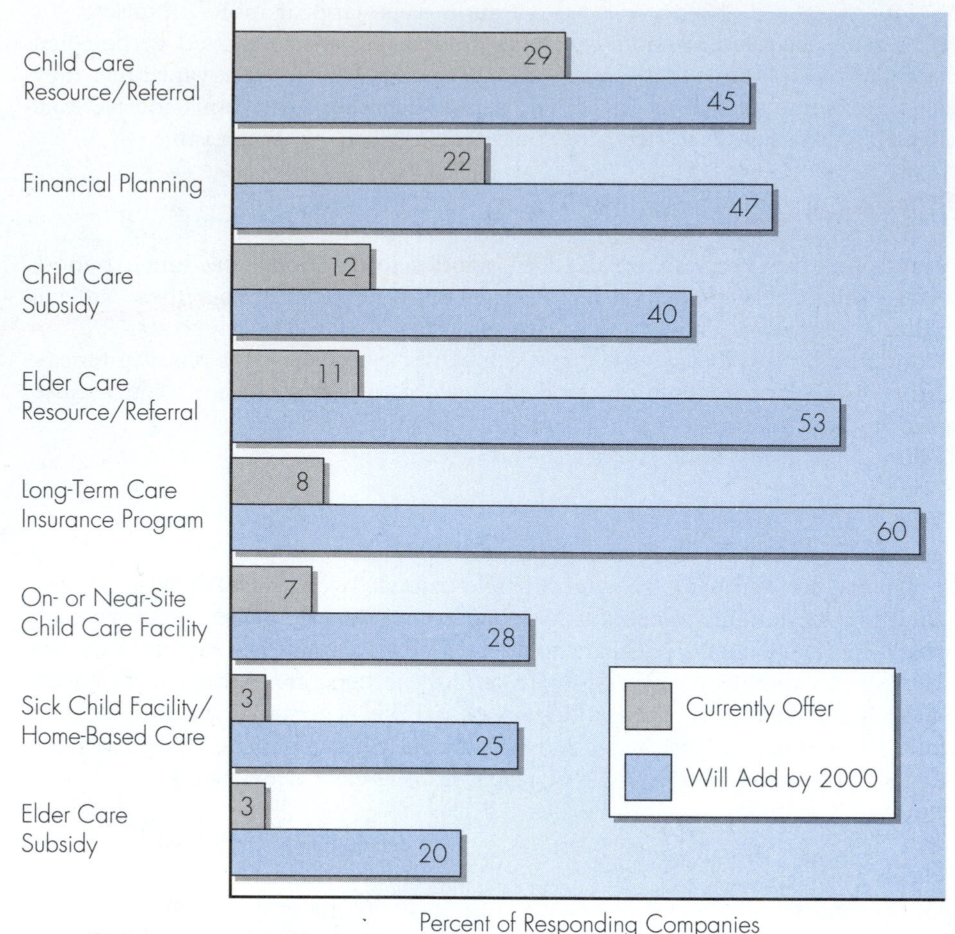

Exhibit 11.5
Prevalence of Selected "Life Cycle" Benefits for 1990 and by Year 2,000

SOURCE: International Foundation of Employee Benefit Plans

of $5,000 in the next year. His projected salary for the next year is $35,000. Listed below is the employee's disposable income without and with an employee financed dependent care reimbursement account.

	Without Account	With Account
Gross Salary	$35,000	$35,000
Pre-elected payroll deduction	0	- 5,000
	35,000	30,000
Estimated taxes (federal income tax and Social Security)	- 3,115	- 2,670
Net salary	31,885	27,330
Payment from account		+ 5,000
Available income	31,885	32,330
Payment to child care center	- 5,000	- 5,000
Disposable income	$26,885	$27,330

As shown, the employee has $445 *more* in disposable income using a dependent care reimbursement account.[34]

Resource and referral programs. Twenty-nine percent of firms offer child care information and referral assistance. These company-sponsored programs counsel employees about day care options and refer them to prescreened local providers. Prescreening helps to ensure the centers in the network meet minimum care standards and are financially responsible.

The program offered by the Eastman Kodak Company is typical. The leading manufacturer of photographic products, chemicals, and health care products contracted with Work/Family Directions, Inc., a national organization that specialized in child care resources and issues to maintain its Child Care Resource and Referral Program. To provide Kodak employees with detailed information and referrals, Work/Family Directors established contracts with community-based child care agencies through the country. Because not all areas have sufficient child care services, Kodak also has provided start-up costs to develop child care programs in areas of short supply. During the program's first eighteen months, Kodak's funding resulted in the addition of 650 family day care homes in communities where Kodak employees live.

Other firms also are providing referral services. AT&T has set up a $5 million Family Care Development Fund to sponsor family care projects. IBM, which develops, manufactures, and distributes computers and office equipment, offers referral services in 250 communities. In the first three years of operation, the IBM program had 14,000 families using the care network. Seventy percent of the children enrolled in IBM's programs are under three years of age.

Steelcase employs a child care administrator whose staff evaluates day care centers and family care homes. An employee survey of users indicates that more than 90 percent of the employees who use the Steelcase program feel more relaxed and productive at work.[35]

At the 3M Company in St. Paul, Minnesota, Working Parent Resource Fairs are held biannually to give employees the chance to peruse a range of parent or child related services. "In the spring parents look for what to do with kids during the summer," Suzanne T. Osten, child care administrator noted. "We hold the fair early to give them time to plan ahead." Typically more than 600 employees attend the four-hour fair (cost is only $2,000) which features exhibitors from 67 organizations. Exhibits range from church social services, Parents Without Partners, the Minnesota Council for the Gifted and Talented, Minnesota Safe Kids Project, and Science Museum of Minnesota. Employers are given time off from work to attend the fair and shop for services.[36]

On-site care facilities. By 1989 there were more than 1,100 employer-sponsored on-site or near-site care centers in operation. In San Francisco, office and hotel complexes with more than 50,000 square feet must either provide an on-site facility or pay into a city child care fund. Although the operation of such centers can be costly, a growing number of employers now accept the burden of operating and funding such centers as a social and business necessity.

Consider the comments of Dick Parker, director of administrative services for Merck & Co., at groundbreaking ceremonies for its $8 million child care center:

> You don't provide child care just because you want to be a good guy. You do it for business reasons. Merck decided to build the center for three reasons: retention,

FOCUS ON RESEARCH

Child Care Assistance: Diversity, Preferences, and Outcomes

Historically companies have viewed child care as a "women's issue" and not as a mainstream human resource issue. However, a growing number of firms have come to realize that work/family conflicts can directly affect employee attitudes and performance. To address this concern, U.S. firms (12%) are providing child care assistance ranging from referral programs to employer-sponsored child care centers to dependent care reimbursement accounts. Unfortunately, little research has been focused on child care needs of specific employee groups. For example, little is known about the types of employees who will most likely utilize the services and whether child care assistance actually affects attitudes and behaviors. Second, it is not well understood whether employees have diverse needs or unilateral needs.

To understand the complexity of the child care problem and the diversity of child care assistance needs, Ellen Kossek, a Michigan State University researcher, assessed the dependent care needs of 200 employees with dependent children under the age of 12. All respondents were employed at a public utility. In addition to surveying employees about their current child care arrangements, attitudes, and demographic backgrounds, they were asked to rank nine child assistance options. The options included: job sharing or part-time work; information referral assistance; family day care networks which consist of licensed day care homes organized by the employer; sick care; on-site or near-site centers; voucher system which provides financial assistance in purchasing care of choice; flexible spending accounts; parental level; and education seminars. While most of these programs currently are offered by less than 1 percent of all employers, the number of firms opting for some form of child care assistance beyond referral systems is expected to swell to 40 percent by the year 2000. Thus, it is important to understand the problem domain.

The results of the survey revealed several interesting findings that can be used by managers attempting to address work-related concerns associated

Continued

recruitment, and productivity. Child care will become more and more of a recruitment issue in the future. If employees are worried about their child care services that will affect their productivity and retention.[37]

Linda Fitzpatrick, director of human resources for Gentech, a pharmaceutical company in the San Francisco area, makes a similar point noting that, "Providing a near site center makes good business sense. Not only is the center a great recruiting tool but we've found that employees come back to work sooner after maternity leave because they know that their child is receiving quality, nearby care." Gentech's center is open from 6:45 AM to 7:00 PM and accepts children from six weeks to six years of age. The building is maintained by Gentech but the program is operated by an independent child care group. Employees pay between $390 and $490 per month (depending on age). The company offers a 50 percent scholarship to employees who earn less than $25,000.

Campbell Soup Company's child care center is located across the street from its corporate headquarters and cares for 110 children. Contending that on-site care cuts absenteeism, reduces distractions for employees, and helps with hiring, the company picks up 40 percent of the weekly expense for each child. The Hacienda Child Development Center in Pleasanton, California, serves multiple employers (e.g., Hewlett-Packard, Computerland, Prudential Insurance Company). Operating costs are funded from parent fees and business fees. Employees working in the Hacienda Business Park receive a discount on monthly rates.

with child care problems. As might be expected, employees who were having problems with child care arrangements held significantly less favorable attitudes towards balancing family and work responsibilities.

Despite the advances made towards equality in the work force, problems with child care arrangements had a bigger impact on female than male employees. Women considered quitting their jobs more often because of child care, felt it was not easy to combine work and family responsibilities and believed that child illnesses created more problems at work than [did] male employees. In terms of child care preferences, gender explained only one option—job sharing and part-time work.

While diversity was found in child care preferences, the most preferred benefits were sick care and on- or near-site care. Single parents had a significantly greater preference for sick care compared to other employee groups. Referral and information and a voucher system for assistance with care costs were also preferred. Employees with infants expressed a higher preference for employer support of a family day care network of licensed provider homes than employees with older children.

The researchers concluded that employers would be well advised to conduct a needs assessment prior to adopting any specific child care program. Unfortunately, many companies have jumped on the "child care corporate bandwagon" without delineation of how such programs fit with their human resource strategy or work force profile. Assuming there are scarce organizational resources available to attack the child care problem, adding programs based on current labor market data will better ensure that the policies added will be needed and used. The study also suggested that employers might strongly consider offering part-time work, job sharing, parental leave and, where feasible, work at home arrangements, which may enable employees to use familial care to a greater extent.

SOURCE: Based on E. E. Kossek, "Diversity in Child Care Assistance Needs: Employee Problems, Preferences, and Work-Related Outcomes," *Personnel Psychology* 43 (1990): 769–91.

Family leave. Although a family leave policy has yet to become federal law, an increasing number of companies are offering paid and unpaid family leave. A recent survey conducted by *Working Mother* magazine notes that cutting-edge firms protect a woman's job for at least six weeks after childbirth, and more than two-thirds of the companies with leave policies guarantee a woman's job for at least twelve weeks.

US Sprint offers a Family Care Leave of Absence to support family adjustments and prevent high-performing employees from leaving the company. Leaves may be as short as a few weeks to several years. In determining the need for long leaves, US Sprint considers the employee's situation and contribution to the company. Recently, Paul Covington, manager of the program, granted a year's leave of absence to an employee who had given birth to her third child and wanted to extend her disability leave to be home with her children. Covington justified the leave on the basis of her high performance and company dedication. "Her peers adamantly supported the leave and shared my belief that we should do whatever we could to keep her. So we gave her the time off." Covington has monthly meetings with the employee by telephone and she comes in once each quarter. "We don't want her to feel alienated from the company during her leave."

IBM offers up to three years of personal leave including six to eight weeks paid leave for recovery from childbirth. New mothers or fathers—natural and adoptive—may be granted up to three years of unpaid leave with the option of working part-time during the period. Throughout the leave, employees continue to receive full benefits. A percentage of adoption expenses is also reimbursed.[38]

While federal family care legislation is not yet a reality, some state and local governments—for example, Dade County, Florida—have already moved ahead.[39] With these initiatives and examples from several European nations, family care legislation at the federal level could be seen within the next few years.

Elder Care

Twenty-eight percent of employees over the age of 30 currently spend an average of 10 hours a week giving care to an older relative. For a significant faction, this commitment equals a second job. Some 12 percent of workers who care for aging parents are forced to quit their jobs to do so. With the continued graying of the U.S. population, more and more employers are considering ways to assist workers who are caring for elderly relatives. Assistance ranges from information and referral programs to specialized care insurance.

Information and referral programs. In 1990, only 11 percent of employers offered elder care information and referral programs to link up employees with community resources that already exist; by the year 2000, the number could exceed 50 percent. Like the dependent care programs discussed previously, company-operated elder care referral programs are designed to assist the care giver in identifying appropriate community resources.

The program offered by First Interstate Bank of California is representative of today's referral programs. Two years ago, an employee survey revealed that about 8 percent of bank employees provide care for one or more elderly or disabled relatives, and 25 percent said they expected to do so by 1993. Further, 30 percent of supervisors said their subordinates' caring for elderly family members had a negative impact on operations due to increased anxiety and health problems, requests for time off, and leaves of absence.

To address this concern, the company investigated setting up its own elder care program. According to Julia Gettinger, manager of work and family programs at the bank, "If a company the size of ours were to do an independent elder care resource and referral program, it could cost up to $100,000 a year. The bank's commitment was substantial, but it wasn't $100,000." To address the need for elder care assistance *and* stay within the budget, First Interstate entered into a public-private partnership with the County Division on Aging. The agency is a member of a nationwide elder care resource and referral system. Linked into the system, First Interstate employees call a toll-free number and talk to a counselor about what resources they need and in what city they're needed. The counselor calls back with a list of potential resources including at-home care for the elderly, day care centers, and support groups for the care giver.[40]

Elder care centers. Recognizing that elder care is not always available, a small but growing number of firms are offering on-site or corporate-financed elder care centers. The Stride Rite Corporation, a leading marketer of high-quality footwear for children and adults, is a leader in this venture. Stride Rite has had an on-site child care center since 1971. In 1990 the firm opened the Stride Rite Intergenerational Day Care Center which houses 55 children between the ages of 15 months and 6 years and 24 elders who are over the age of 60. Group activities include reading and writing stories, cooking and eating, card games, and field trips, and routinely bring elders and children together. Employees pay a percentage of their annual household income through payroll deduction.[41]

Long-term care insurance. One of the newest and fastest growing options is long-term care (LTC) insurance. While only 8 percent of firms currently offer this benefit, nearly 70 percent of companies are expected to offer this elder care option by the year 2000. This type of insurance covers medical, social, custodial, and personal services for people who suffer from chronic physical or mental illnesses or disabling injury or disease over an extended period of time. Typically, coverage is offered to employees on an employee-pay-all basis. Premium rates are age-based and in some plans there is a maximum age (typically 79) for participation. Benefit maximums are related to care site (nursing home versus day care center) and include lifetime limits.[42]

Changing Lifestyles

With demographic and value shifts, there is now a wider array of lifestyle choices. As a consequence, a rising percentage of workers—unmarried couples, divorced people, single parents—do not fit into conventional benefits packages. Recognizing that people are assets to the organization and that the world of work can never be fully separated from the rest of one's life, cutting-edge companies are redesigning their benefits packages to address the needs of all employees.

Adoption benefits. In 1989 the Communications Workers of America (CWA) negotiated a benefit plan with AT&T that provides a $2,000 allowance per adoption. That agreement is expected to serve as a model for other unions to follow as part of their bargaining strategy for the 1990s. An adoption benefit plan is a company-sponsored program that financially assists or reimburses employees for the costs associated with the adoption of a child. The most frequently covered benefits include adoption agency fees, attorney fees, and court costs. Some plans also include paid or unpaid leave, and a handful cover pregnancy care expenses for the birth mother.

IBM has had an adoption assistance program since 1972. According to Harold P. Kneed, Jr., director of employee benefits, the plan filled a perceived need. "IBM was already assisting in the medical expenses associated with child birth, yet provided no assistance to those families where the family was enlarged through adoption. The adoption program provides a degree of equity."[43]

Benefits for spousal equivalents. Some companies must now grapple with the demands of same-sex partners for "spousal" benefits. At AT&T, a lesbian is suing for pension benefits she says are owed upon the death of her partner, a former AT&T manager. The company contends that benefits are only available to widows and widowers. A Boston-based flight attendant has filed a union grievance, demanding free travel perks for his partner. The company says only legally married spouses are eligible. At the University of South Maine, an arbitrator dismissed a nursing school professor's claim for health insurance for her partner. The university refused coverage, despite policy provisions that forbid discrimination based on sexual orientation.

The picture is somewhat different at the Lotus Development Corporation. After a two-year debate, the Cambridge, Massachusetts, software company modified its insurance and benefits policy to offer the partners of homosexual employees the same benefits accorded heterosexual spouses. According to Russell J. Campanello, vice president for human resources, "This is fair and equal." Lotus's decision did not come easily. In 1989, three workers began petitioning Lotus for spousal benefits. Even after Lotus agreed, it took the company and the three employees two years to develop a workable policy. The insurance carrier that pays Lotus's claims above $140,000 was reluctant to take on more homosexual enrollees, largely because of potential AIDS-related bills. After researching the actual costs carefully, Lotus convinced the carrier that the cost was not a seven-digit dollar issue but about the same as treating a coronary patient, Campanello said.

Premiums for the 12 "spousal equivalents" currently enrolled in the program cost Lotus about $30,000, none of which is tax deductible because the IRS doesn't recognize unmarried partners. Participating employees pay about $1,350 in taxes a year on the premium's benefits. To be eligible, a couple must live together and share financial obligations. If they break up, the employee must wait one year before registering a new partner. In addition to health care, the plan includes life insurance, relocation expenses, bereavement leave, and a death benefit. Unlike Ben and Jerry's Homemade Inc. and *The Village Voice,* Lotus does not offer the same same benefits to unmarried partners of heterosexual employees because these couples have the option of marriage while homosexuals do not.[44]

Educational expense allowances. Faced with skill obsolescence, downsizing, and retraining demands, 69 percent of all medium and large firms provided some form of educational expense assistance in 1989. Most plans cover registration fees, and some assist with graduation fees, laboratory expenses, entrance examinations, professional certification, and activity fees. Typically, these programs require a relationship between the course and some phase of company operations. For example, National Healthcorp, which is headquartered in Murfreesboro, Tennessee, offers tuition assistance to any aide who wishes to become a nurse. The company will pay for up to two years of school in exchange for the aide's promise to stay on staff that long after graduation.

Educational assistance also has become a negotiated benefit for unions. During collective bargaining negotiations in 1982, the Ford Motor Company and the United Automobile Workers agreed that jointly developed and provided training and retraining programs should be made available to UAW-represented workers. Funded with five cents for every hour worked by every hourly worker, the program provides a variety of benefits. These include a tuition assistance program that provides workers with up to $2,000 per year; a skills enhancement program that focuses on basic education and English as a second language; preretirement counseling; a life/education planning program that provides career counseling to eligible employees; and the college and university options program that facilitates college entry and success.[45]

Relocation and housing assistance. As housing costs continue to soar, more employers are considering housing assistance as an employee benefit. Seventy-five percent of surveyed New Jersey employers with 500 or more employees attributed hiring and retention problems to the high cost of housing;

71 percent of surveyed California manufacturers said high housing costs were limiting their business expansion abilities.

Relocation assistance traditionally has consisted of financial help for travel expenses and the cost of moving possessions. If needed, the company might also pay for storage of furniture for a limited time as well as temporary housing. However, a growing number of firms are also offering a greater variety of allowances and services for transferred employees and high-demand new hires. These benefits include cost allowances for selling a house, search expenses for finding a new residence, assistance in finding employment for a spouse, and temporary living expenses.

Colgate-Palmolive, for example, helps its workers buy homes by paying points and origination fees on mortgages of up to $191,250 and a portion of these costs on more expensive homes. According to Daniel Bagely, a 32-year-old toxicologist, the Colgate program saved him about $2,000 up front. He also figures he'll save at least $5,000 in interest payments over the 15-year-period of his mortgage because the mortgage lender gives Colgate employees favorable rates. To date 380 employees have utilized the Colgate-Palmolive program detailed above.

An interesting approach is being tried in Santa Barbara, California. Concerned about attracting and retaining key personnel in this expensive real estate area, a consortium of 15 firms in the area struck a bargain with a local lender. In exchange for the low-interest loans, the employers agree to certain corporate banking arrangements with the lender. First Federal Savings and Loan in Raleigh, North Carolina, has developed a forgivable down payment loan program for its employees. With this arrangement, an employer advances an employee a portion of the money needed for a down payment, and the loan is forgiven when the employee completes some predetermined length of service.

Recent federal initiatives are helping to pave the way for housing assistance. The Federal National Mortgage Association or Fannie Mae plans to invest $1 billion in employer-sponsored housing programs. The mortgage guarantee agency has developed several programs to aid lower-paid employees in buying homes. In one plan, the employer loans the employees the difference between what they have and what they need in the way of down-payment money to qualify for a loan. Fannie Mae then guarantees the mortgage as a way of encouraging banks to lend the balance to the borrower. Housing assistance is also becoming a negotiated benefit. In June, 1991, the AFL-CIO and the Federal Home Loan Mortgage Corporation reached agreement on a plan to make home buying easier for low- and moderate-income families.[46]

ADMINISTRATIVE ISSUES

Although organizations tend to view indirect compensation as a reward, recipients do not always see it that way. This causes organizations to become concerned with their package of indirect compensation benefits and how they are administered.

Determining the Benefits Package

The benefits package should be selected on the basis of what's good for the employee as well as for the employer. Knowing employee preferences can often help determine what benefits should be offered. For example, employees in one company indicated a strong preference for dental insurance over life insurance, even though dental insurance was only one-fourth the cost to the company. As workers get older, the desire for higher pension benefits steadily increases. This is also the case for employees with rising incomes. Employees with children prefer greater hospitalization benefits than do those without.[47]

Providing Benefit Flexibility

When employees can design their own benefits packages, both they and the company benefit. At least that's the experience at companies such as Ex-Cello, TRW, the Educational Testing Service (ETS), and Morgan Stanley.[48] At ETS, the company provides a core package of benefits to all employees, covering basic needs such as personal medical care, dental care, disability, vacation, and retirement. In addition, each individual can choose, cafeteria-style, from optional benefits or can increase those in the core package. Employees are allowed to change their packages once a year. At Morgan Stanley, about two-thirds of its eligible employees elected their own benefit package over the standard no-choice plan. The options themselves were developed by the employees, working in small discussion groups. That providing benefit flexibility is so effective is not surprising. What is surprising is that so few organizations provide such flexibility.

A recent benefits survey showed that workers want to choose how to pay for their benefits and would modify their benefits if given the opportunity. Among the most preferred benefits are preventive medical care, wellness programs, vision care, and deferred compensation plans. One-third of all employees would prefer expanded medical and dental benefits over other types of benefits.[49]

Communicating the Benefits Package

Considering that most benefits program objectives are not currently attained, assessment of communication effectiveness would probably produce unfavorable results. This may be partly due to the communication techniques used. Almost all organizations use impersonal, passive booklets and brochures to convey benefits information; only a few use more personal, active media, such as slide presentations and regular employee meetings. An especially good technique is one that communicates the total compensation components every day. This can be done through giving employees calendars. Each month of the calendar shows a company employee receiving a compensation benefit. For example, one month may feature a photo of an employee building a new home made possible through the company's incentive program and savings plan. Another month may feature the usefulness of the company's medical plan.

Through communicating the benefits package and providing employees with benefit flexibility, the positive image of indirect compensation can be increased. Hewitt Associates found that 72 percent of employees who understand their compensation program perceived it as fair, while only 36 percent of employees who did not understand the system said it was fair. Information about how to file claims and where to get services tend to bring more employees into the positive camp.[50]

Assessing Benefit Costs

Several purposes of indirect compensation were listed at the beginning of this chapter. The impact of the indirect benefits in fulfilling these purposes is half of the equation for measuring the effectiveness of the benefits package. The other half involves determining the costs. Determining the effectiveness of the indirect benefit program also involves a comparison of the costs and effects.[51]

An organization can determine the dollar value of the costs of indirect compensation in the following ways:

- Total costs of benefits annually for all employees
- Cost per employee per year divided by the number of hours worked
- Percentage of payroll divided by annual payroll
- Cost per employee per hour divided by employee hours worked

These costs can then be compared with the effects, such as reduced turnover, less absenteeism, or an enhanced company image among employees. The dollar value of these in turn can be determined, enabling the organization to compare its dollar costs of benefits directly against its dollar savings of benefits.

After the company determines these cost/effect (or cost/benefit) ratios, it can further assess the available alternatives.[52] By way of example, let's look at the hypothetical example of how a 5,000-employee company faced the business problem of constantly rising medical coverage costs. This self-insured firm realized that no relief would be in sight if its medical insurance practices continued.

If the company paid the average amount per employee for health care costs, then it spent about $1,800 annually for each of its 5,000 employees, meaning that the cost of the business problem was $9,000,000. The solution could be a cost-containment program similar to the one implemented by Chrysler. That program enabled Chrysler to reduce its annual health care costs by $300 per employee. The company would spend around $730,000 as the cost of the solution. While that may seem like a hefty figure, it could be quite worth it. If this company realizes an annual $300 per employee cost reduction, an approximately 17 percent decrease, then its improvement benefit would amount to $1,500,000. This figure is how much less the company would spend under the new cost-containment program.

Comparing the improvement for the company with the cost of the solution generates a 2.1:1 cost/benefit ratio. This certainly would be a fine use of company funds to reduce costs.[53]

FOCUS ISSUES IN INDIRECT COMPENSATION

Major issues in indirect compensation focus on reducing indirect compensation costs. Using computer technology to aid the assessment process can enable organizations to contain, if not reduce, these indirect compensation costs. If they can't be reduced, at least the costs can be linked with the needs of the business.

Computer Technology and HRIS

Computer technology can be applied to indirect compensation planning to analyze its various components. These include such items as health and medical benefits, vacation time, sick time, pensions, and profit sharing. The key here is planning. Given budgeted values for salary and bonuses, projections of spending and allocation can be determined with regard to budget restrictions. In addition, including information about actual benefits usage may reveal that a significant amount of money is being spent on a benefit that is not widely used. Thus, companies can maximize the value of limited funds by offering employees only the most relevant benefits.

With an HRIS and computer technology, an organization can more easily implement and administer a flexible or cafeteria-style benefit package. The computer can quickly cost out different benefit combinations that employees may select. As a consequence, equity can be more easily attained across employees. The costs of indirect compensation can be more strictly controlled and even reduced with compensation information in an HRIS.[55]

Linking with the Needs of the Business

A trend in indirect compensation is to use it to gain competitive advantage for the organization. This ranges from using pension funds to fend off corporate takeovers to taking steps to engage in strategic planning for compensation.[56]

Organizations can take several steps in strategic compensation planning. First, employers should conduct an external survey to determine if their compensation programs are at a level that will attract and retain talented labor. Exit interviews with employees who have resigned are beneficial to determine if compensation or benefits affected their decisions to leave. It is important also to understand the financial advantages of different methods of financing benefits. Examining these issues will help an organization use its benefits packages strategically.

INTERNATIONAL COMPARISONS IN INDIRECT COMPENSATION

Canada

In Canada, the sharpest contrasts with the U.S. concerning compensation are found in indirect compensation, particularly pensions; yet even these differences appear relatively minimal. For example, Canada has the Canada Pension Plan (CPP) and the Quebec Pension Plan in the province of Quebec, both of which are similar to the U.S. Social Security system. CPP is a mandatory plan for all employees except federal workers. Like the Social Security system, CPP pays retirement benefits, disability pensions, benefits for children of disabled contributors, orphans' benefits, and pension benefits to survivors' spouses. Canada also has private pension plans, although fewer than 40 percent of all employees are covered by these plans. The administration of these plans is governed by the Pension Benefits Act, which is less extensive in its regulation of private pension plans than is the U.S. Employees' Retirement Income Security Act.

Family Leave Legislation

Perhaps one of the most widely followed debates in the U.S. concerns legislation on family leave. As mentioned earlier, some states have passed such legislation while, at the federal level, debate continues over numerous provisions for such legislation. However, passage of some type of bill could take place at any time. When and if it does, you may want to compare it with what other countries are doing today. Exhibit 11.6 provides this information.

SUMMARY

Unlike in the past, the growth in indirect compensation has been double that of direct compensation. This doubling has occurred despite the lack of evidence that indirect compensation helps to attain the purposes of total compensation. Money, job challenge, and opportunities for advancement appear to serve the purposes of compensation as much as, if not more than, pension benefits, disability provisions, and services, especially for employees aspiring to managerial careers.

This is not to say, however, that employees do not desire indirect benefits. Organizations are offering them at such a rapid rate in part because employees desire them. Unfortunately, the specific indirect benefits offered by an organization are not always valued by all employees, and all employees may not even know what benefits are offered. As a result, some organizations now solicit employee opinions about their preferences for compensation programs. Organizations are also becoming more concerned with the communication of their benefits programs. Current evidence suggests that employees' lack of awareness of the contents and value of their benefit programs may partially explain why the programs are not perceived more favorably.

These benefits do not come without costs. To ensure that an organization is getting the most from its indirect compensation, thorough assessments must be made of what the organization is doing, what other organizations are doing, and what employees prefer to see the organization doing. To improve the motiva-

FAMILY LEAVE POLICIES AROUND THE WORLD

As debate over federal family leave legislation continues in the United States, other industrialized nations have established policies.

Country	Duration of leave (weeks)	Number of paid weeks and percent of normal pay (paid by government and/or employer)
Canada	17–41	15 weeks/60%
France	18	16 Weeks/90%
Germany	14–26	14–19 Weeks/100%
Japan	12	12 Weeks/60%
Sweden	12–52	38 Weeks/90%

Source: Women at Work, International Labour Office, Geneva, Global Survey.

Exhibit 11.6
Family Leave Policies Around the World

tional value of indirect compensation, organizations should try to provide what employees want. As with direct compensation, employees apparently will continue to want more benefits like the ones they now have, as well as some they presently do not have. For example, employees want greater private retirement benefits, more health and insurance coverage, and more time off. Demands for dental coverage, eye care, and legal services will probably increase. Greater educational and career development opportunities are also likely to be demanded by employees.

As more U.S. firms move into international markets, the need to understand international compensation and appraisal trends increases in importance. While practices in countries such as Britain and Canada are quite similar to those in the U.S., the same cannot be said for Pacific Rim countries and the East European controlled-economy countries. The former rely on seniority more than does the U.S., and many of the latter still have wage rates set by the government.

WHERE WE ARE TODAY

1. Because of the growing costs of benefits and services, employers are trying to manage them more effectively than ever.
2. The result of this may be more effective administration of benefits and services, more burden sharing (co-payments), and more benefits and service reduction or even elimination.
3. To compete and get the best people, though, firms still have to provide the benefits people want and need.
4. Certainly, an important part of your job selection process may be to consider what benefits and services firms provide and how likely they are to continue offering them.
5. To improve the effectiveness of the benefits and services offered, employers are giving employees greater choice and responsibility. Thus, you will need to become very aware of this entire area of benefits and services—what you need and what they cost.
6. As firms begin to have more diverse work forces, they will begin to offer more choice in order to attract the people they need.
7. As benefits and service diversity increases, firms will face the need to ensure that all employee groups get equivalent choices, both in terms of number and value.
8. The government may get more involved in benefits and services with the provision of family leave legislation. While this will tend to level the playing field, it will also remove a competitive advantage from the firms that now offer family leave benefits.
9. Health care cost containment will continue to be a major issue for firms and the society. As this rolls out, more firms may encourage their employees to pursue certain lifestyles. This may create some tension and disagreement within firms and provoke debate at the national level.
10. As with the other human resource activities, you can benefit from knowing what other countries are doing for their workers.

DISCUSSION QUESTIONS

1. How are unemployment benefits derived, and what is the status of unemployment compensation?
2. In what sense is indirect compensation "indirect"?
3. Describe the various components of indirect compensation.
4. Distinguish between public and private protection programs, and give examples of each.
5. How have legislation and the changing nature of the work force created the tremendous Social Security benefit burden that most employers and workers confront when they witness the size of the FICA deduction from their paycheck?
6. How would you rationalize the costs to an organization of providing a physical fitness facility and program for their work force? How would you assess and compare benefits and costs?
7. For each of the various forms of indirect compensation, describe what incentives employers and the employees have for minimizing the cost of the benefit.
8. In theory, flexible benefits sound great. In practice, this may not be so. Describe the problems that could be encountered in administering a flexible benefits program.
9. What are the components of an effective benefits communication program?
10. What factors should be considered in establishing a compensation program in a foreign country?

APPLIED PROJECTS

1. Interview a personnel/human resource manager in a local company and ask about their benefits program: how has it changed in the past several years, what methods are used to communicate the program to employees, how they measure the effectiveness of the benefits, how do they know what the employees want, and what are the future of benefits in the company?
2. Go to local companies or the university to learn about their pension plans. Discuss with the benefits manager the 1) characteristics of the plan; 2) the benefits it provides, to whom, when, and how; 3) the level of vesting; 4) whether it is contributory or noncontributory; 5) how its benefits are communicated; and 6) how ERISA has affected their plan.

CASE STUDY

You're Darned If You Do and Darned If You Don't

Sally Yuen, director of PHRM for Dough Pineapple's Maui cannery, returned to her office deep in thought. She'd just spent the last hour and a half in a lengthy and somewhat heated discussion with cannery manager Danny Sackos regarding the latest turnover crisis among cannery employees. Shrugging her shoulders, Sally wondered if Sackos was right. Maybe the current turnover problem was her fault—well, the fault of her department, that is. According to Sackos, if she'd done a better job in selecting employees in the first place, Dough Pineapple (DP) would not be in the current mess. "You hired quitters," he argued, pointing to the high turnover among temporary *and* permanent full-time employees. But then Sally wondered if it really was her fault.

DP maintained a regular work force of 200 employees. Depending on the harvest, as many as 150 temporary employees were also employed. Temporary workers were paid higher base salaries than regular employees ($6.25 an hour). However, they were not eligible for any benefits, including vacation leave, day care, and sick leave. If they were sick, they had to take time off without pay. They also could not participate in DP's highly successful profit-sharing program and matching pension fund.

Full-time, regular cannery workers were paid $5.00 an hour ($10,400 annually). While DP's hourly rate was below the industry average of $6.00 an hour ($12,480 annually), employees more than recouped this amount in performance bonuses. To date, they were the only cannery on the islands to have a state-of-the-art incentive pay program. In fact, they were the only cannery that shared organizational profits with employees at all.

Last year, employees received approximately $2,000 each. This amount was lower than usual due to a hurricane that destroyed almost all of one harvest. Since the program was implemented in 1986, bonuses had averaged $8,000 per employee. And this year they were expected to be back on target. Sally anticipated handing out bonuses in the range of $10,000 each. Employees had the option of taking the money in one lump sum, in quarterly installments, or in even distributions throughout the next year. According to company policy, employee bonuses would be announced at the semiannual employee's meeting, which was to be held in six weeks.

Sally also was proud of DP's benefits. Employee benefits as a percentage of payroll averaged 30 percent in the industry. DP's percentage was 45 percent. All full-time employees with one year's seniority (tenured) were eligible to participate in DP's extensive benefit program, which included such innovations as an on-site day care center (Sally's brain child, which took her two years to get approved) and an employee assistance program, including free legal assistance. The company also matched dollar for dollar employee contributions to a retirement fund and offered two college scholarships annually to employees' children. Sally was particularly proud of DP's fitness center which could be used by any "tenured" employees and their families. Swimming lessons were provided free of charge to family members.

Vacation days also were above the industry average. Employees with one to two years of seniority earned one-half day of paid vacation per month, three-fourths day per month with three to five years seniority, and one day per month with more than five years of service. Personal days accrued at the same rate for tenured employees. To prevent abuse, employees calling in absent before or after a holiday or after a payday are charged with an absence of 1.5 days. Employees with less than one year's service and temporary employees are not reimbursed for absences. The failure of any employee to call in to report an absence at least four hours before his or her shift starts is grounds for disciplinary procedures.

By having a core of permanent, tenured employees, DP is assured of having enough employees to meet average production demands. By paying temporary employees base salaries slightly above the labor market average, DP has traditionally had its pick of new employees. The system was cost effective because the salaries of temporary employees were only 18 percent over the base pay for cannery employees and well under the estimated hourly rate (with benefits) for permanent tenured employees (estimated at $7.98 an hour).

With all this going for DP, Sally wondered where things had gone wrong. Maybe Sackos was right, and she just hadn't picked the right kind of employees. Shaking her head in bewilderment, she had her assistant Mark George interview some employees to see what was going on. Additionally, he prepared a report on causes of turnover at DP (see exhibit 1).

According to Mark, the following comments are representative of the feelings of full-time permanent employees:

- "Sure, it's a great place to work, but I'm tired of those young kids walking in off the street and making more than I do."
- "I know, I know, we're eligible to get bonuses, but they just can't make up for a weekly salary—at least not when you have three kids to support."
- "I worry that things are going to be the same as last year. I hung in there and look what I got, a lousy $2,500. The bottom line is that I still made less than temporary employees and those at the other canneries. I don't like it one bit."

The following comments are typical of the views of permanent untenured workers (2 years seniority):

- "I got really steamed last month when they docked my pay for being sick. I mean, I was really sick. I hadn't gone out with the girls or anything. I was down flat in bed with the flu. Why should I work hard here if I can't even get a lousy day off when I'm sick?"
- "I've worked here seven months already, and I'm pulling my own weight around here. Know what

Exhibit 1
Turnover among Employees

Reason	Higher Pay	Better Benefits	Supervision	Moving	Better Job	Job Security	Fired
Group							
Permanent							
<1 year	40	22	1	2	3	1	2
1–2 years	10	0	3	3	2	4	1
>2 years	1	0	5	4	4	2	0
Temporary							
<6 months	10	45	4	3	10	17	3
6–12 months	12	23	1	0	2	32	2
>1 year	5	15	2	3	15	19	0

NOTE: An employee could list more than one reason for quitting.

I mean? Well, it doesn't seem right that I should be paid less than those part-timers."

Among temporary workers, the view was,

- "Yeah, we make a good rate of pay but that's not everything. My wife had to have a C-section last month. Without insurance, it cost me a bundle."
- "I work just as hard as everyone else, so why shouldn't I have the same benefits? I'm getting up there in years. It'd be nice to have a little bit set aside."

In reading these comments, it seemed to Sally that she couldn't win for losing. Maybe the most current employee attitude survey would be of help. At least it was worth a try (see exhibit 2). All she knew was that if they didn't come up with a strategy soon, DP would not meet its canning quotas, and the employee bonuses would be lost forever.

Case Questions

1. Do you agree with Sackos that selection procedures are flawed, causing the high turnover? Why or why not?
2. What does the employee attitude survey tell you that is helpful in understanding the turnover problem at DP?
3. What should Sally's bottom-line response be to resolve the current crisis?

Exhibit 2
Results of the Employee Attitude Survey

	Permanent			
	<1 year	**1–2 years**	**>2 years**	**Temporary**
Satisfaction with:				
1. Pay level	2.1	2.3	2.4	3.4
2. Pay system	1.5	2.4	3.2	3.3
3. Benefits	1.0	3.2	4.1	1.1
4. Supervision	3.4	4.1	3.7	3.3
5. Job	2.4	2.7	3.1	2.3
6. Co-workers	3.3	4.0	4.7	2.3
7. Work environment	3.4	4.1	3.6	2.7

NOTE: 1 - very dissatisfied, 5 = very satisfied.

NOTES

1. K. DeWitt, "The Corporate Role in Prenatal and Maternal Health Care," *The New York Times* (1 May 1992): D6.
2. G. Kramon, "Rockwell's Point Man in the Health Care Campaign," *The New York Times* (7 April 1991): 5.
3. "Americans on Benefits: Keep Them Coming," *HR Reporter* (Feb. 1991): 4–5.
4. "Effective Employee Benefits," *Inc.* (May 1991): 19; "Dissatisfaction on the Increase," *HR Focus* (Dec. 1991): 13.
5. "Americans on Benefits: Keep Them Coming": 4–5; R. M. McCaffery, *Employee Benefits Programs: A Total Compensation Perspective* (Boston, Mass.: PWS-Kent, 1988): 14–30.
6. F. Foulkes, *Personnel Policies in Large Nonunion Companies* (Englewood Cliffs, N.J.: Prentice-Hall, 1980): 209–29.
7. "Changes in the Social Security Law," *Bulletin to Management Datagraph,* 14 Jan. 1988, p. 12; B. Keller, "Another Stab at Pension Reform," *New York Times,* 15 July 1984, p–1. R. C. Murphy and R. E. Wallace, "New Directions for the Social Security System," *Personnel Journal* (Feb. 1983): 138–41.
8. *Bulletin to Management Datagraph* (Washington, D.C.: Bureau of Labor Statistics, 19 Dec. 1991): 396–98; B. DeClark, "Cutting Unemployment Insurance Costs," *Personnel Journal* (Nov. 1983): 868–72; McCaffery, *Employee Benefits Programs;* B. S. Murphy, W. E. Barlow, and D. D. Hatch, "Unemployment Compensation and Religious Beliefs," *Personnel Journal* (June 1987): 36–43; L. Uchitelle, "Jobless Insurance System Aids Reduced Number of Workers," *The New York Times* (26 July 1988): 1.
9. "Workers' Compensation: Total Disability Benefits," *Bulletin to Management Datagraph* (19 May 1988): 156–57.
10. P. Kerr, "Fraud Pushes Worker's Comp. Near Crisis," *Seattle Times* (29 Dec. 1991): A4.
11. *Managing Workers' Compensation Costs* (William M. Mercer Company, 1991); A. Tramposh, *Avoiding the Cracks: A Guide to the Workers' Compensation System* (New York: Praeger Publishers, 1991).
12. "Injured Workers: Cost-Cutting Rehabilitation Option," *Bulletin to Management* (15 Oct. 1987): 330, 335.
13. M. W. Fitzgerald, "How to Take on Workers' Compensation and Win," *Personnel Journal* (July 1991): 31–33.
14. See note 12.
15. McCaffery, *Employment Benefits Programs...:* 130–31.
16. P. F. Drucker, "Reckoning with the Pension Fund Revolution," *Harvard Business Review* (March-April 1991): 106–14.
17. B. Leonard, "Agency Protects Pan Am Pension Benefits," *HR News* (Sept. 1991): A1, 10.
18. "Pension Issues: A 50 Year History and Outlook," Newsletter 33, no. 3, Martin E. Segal Company, February 1990; T. F. Duzak, "Defined Benefit and Defined Contribution Plans: A Labor Perspective," in *Economic Survival in Retirement* (New York: Salisbury Publishing, 1990): 69; U. S. Department of Labor, Bureau of Labor Statistics, *Employee Benefits in Medium and Large Firms, 1989* (Washington, D.C.: U.S. Government Printing Office, June 1990).
19. G. A. Patterson, "Hourly Auto Workers Now on Layoff Have a Sturdy Safety Net," *The Wall Street Journal* (29 Jan. 1991): A1, A2.
20. "Perspectives: Health Care Costs," *Personnel Journal* (July 1990): 12.
21. "CEOs Seek Help on Health Costs," *Fortune* (3 June 1991): 12.
22. M. Freudenheim, "Health on a Budget," *The New York Times* (2 Sept. 1991): 1.
23. E. Eckholm, "Rescuing Health Care," *The New York Times* (2 May 1991): B12; P. Moore, *Evaluating Health Maintenance Organizations: A Guide for Employee Benefits Managers* (Westport, Conn.: Quorom Books, 1991).
24. McCaffery, *Employee Benefits...:* 130–31.
25. "An Incentive a Day Can Keep Doctor Bills at Bay," *Business Week* (29 April 1991): 22.
26. S. Caudron, "The Wellness Pay Off," *Personnel Journal* (July 1990): 55–60; "How Healthy are Corporate Fitness Programs?" *The Physician and Sports Medicine* (March 1989). Also contact Wellness Councils of America (WELCOA), 1823 Harney St., Ste. 201, Omaha, NE 68102, (402) 444-1711.
27. C. M. Steele and R. A. Josephs, "Alcohol Myopia: Its Prized and Dangerous Effects," *American Psychologist* (Aug. 1990): 921–33; P. M. Roman, ed., *Alcohol Problem Intervention in the Workplace: Employee Assistance Programs and Strategic Alternatives* (Westport, Conn.: Quorum Books, 1990); W. J. Sonnenstuhl and H. M. Trice, *Strategies for Employee Assistance Programs: The Crucial Balance* (Ithaca, N.Y.: ILR Press, 1990); G. M. Farkas, "The Impact of Federal Rehabilitation Laws on the Expanding Role of Employee Assistance Programs in Business and Industry," *American Psychologist* (Dec. 1989): 1482–90; "Debunking Myths About Self-Quitting: Evidence From 10 Prospective Studies of Persons Who Attempt to Quit Smoking by Themselves," *American Psychologist* (Nov. 1989): 1355–65; E. J. Busch, Jr., "Developing an Employee Assistance Program," *Personnel Journal* (Sept. 1981): 708–711; M. Douglass and D. Douglass, "Time Theft," *Personnel Administrator* (Sep. 1981): 13; H. J. Featherston and R. J. Bednarek, "A Positive Demonstration of Concern for Employees," *Personnel Administrator* (Sept. 1981): 43–47; R. C. Ford and F. S. McLaughlin, "Employee Assistance Programs: A Descriptive Survey of ASPA Members," *Personnel Administrator* (Sept. 1981): 29–35; R. T. Hellan and W. J. Campbell, "Contracting for AEP Services," *Personnel Administrator* (Sept. 1981): 49–51; R. W. Hollman, "Beyond Contemporary Employee Assistance Programs," *Personnel Administrator* (Sept. 1981): 37–41; D. Masi and S. J. Freidland, "EAP Actions and Options," *Personnel Journal* (June 1988): 61–67.
28. L. Abramson, "Boost to the Bottom Line," *Personnel Administrator* (July 1988): 36–39; A. D. Anderson, "In the Office: See How They Run," *The New York Times* (3 Jan. 1988): 13; G. Kramon, "The 'Wellness' Discount Plans," *The New York Times* (22 Sept. 1987): D2; R. P. Sloan and

J. C. Gruman, "Does Wellness in the Workplace Work?" *Personnel Administrator* (July 1988): 42–48.

29. McCaffery, *Employee Benefits Programs...*
30. G. Latham and N. Napier, "Practical Ways to Increase Employee Attendance," in P. Goodman and R. Atkins, eds. *Absenteeism: New Approaches to Understanding, Measuring and Managing Employee Absence* (San Francisco: Jossey-Bass, 1984); R. Steers and S. Rhodes, "Major Influences on Employee Attendance: A Process Model," *Journal of Applied Psychology* 63 (1978): 391-407.
31. D. Scott and S. Markham, "Absenteeism Control Methods: A Survey of Practices and Results," *Personnel Administrator* 27 (1982): 73–86.
32. C. R. Deitsch and D. A. Dilts, "Getting Absent Employees Back on the Job: The Case of General Motors," *Business Horizons* (Fall 1981): 52–58.
33. J. Chadwick-Jones, N. Nicholson, and C. Brown, *Social Psychology of Absenteeism* (New York: Praeger, 1982).
34. McCaffery, *Employee Benefits Programs...*: 172–73; M. B. Scott, "How Companies Help with Family Care," *Employee Benefit Plan Review* (May 1990): 12.
35. D. Jamieson and J. O'Mara, *Managing Workforce 2000...*: 148–49; "International Foundation of Employee Benefits Plans," *Nontraditional Benefits for the Work Force of 2000: A Special Report* (Brookfield, Wis.: IFEBP, 1990).
36. S. Overman, "3M Arranges Summer Child Care," *HR Magazine* (March 1991): 46–47.
37. C. M. Loder, "Merck and Co. Breaks New Ground for Employee Child Care Centers," *The Star Ledger* (May 1990): 12; "Companies Cited for Supporting Working Mothers," *HR Focus* (Dec. 1991): 13; S. J. Goff, M. K. Mount, and R. L. Jamison, "Employer Supported Child Care, Work/Family Conflict, and Absenteeism: A Field Study," *Personnel Psychology* 43 (1990): 793–809; S. Zedeck and K. L. Mosier, "Work in the Family and Employing Organization," *American Psychologist* (Feb. 1990): 240–51; S. Scarr, D. Phillips, and K. McCartney, "Working Mothers and Their Families," *American Psychologist* (Nov. 1989): 1402–09; E. Ernst Kossek, "Diversity in Child Care Assistance Needs: Employee Problems, Preferences, and Work-Related Outcomes," *Personnel Psychology* 43 (1990): 769–91; E. Ernst Kossek, *Childcare and Challenges for Employers* (Horsham, LRP Publications, 1991); S. L. Grover, "Predicting the Perceived Fairness of Parental Leave Policies," *Journal of Applied Psychology* 76, no. 2 (1991): 247–55.
38. Jamieson and O'Mara, *Managing Workforce 2000...*: 148–49; International Foundation of Employee Benefits Plans, *Nontraditional Benefits for the Work Force of 2000....*
39. B. P. Noble, *The New York Times* (22 March 1992): F25.
40. E. Smith, "First Interstate Finds an Eldercare Solution," *HR Magazine* (July 1991): 152; A. E. Scharlach, B. F. Lowe, and E. L. Schneider, *Elder Care and the Work Force* (Lexington, Mass.: Lexington Books, 1991); L. Crawford, *Dependent Care and the Employee Benefits Package* (Westport, Conn.: Quorum Books, 1990).
41. Jamieson and O'Mara *Managing Workforce 2000...*: 150.
42. International Foundation of Employee Benefits Plans, *Nontraditional Benefits for the Work Force of 2000: A Special Research Report.*
43. D. Weeks, *Rethinking Employee Benefits Assumptions* (New York: The Conference Board, 1978): 88; McCaffery, *Employee Benefits Programs: A Total Compensation Perspective:* 176–77.
44. "Lotus Opens a Door for Gay Partners," *Business Week* (4 Nov. 1991): 80–81.
45. "National Healthcorp," *Fortune* (29 July 1991): 110; L. A. Ferman, M. Hoyman, J. Cutcher-Gershenfeld, and E. Savoie, *Joint Training Programs: A Union-Management Approach to Preparing Workers for the Future* (Ithaca, N.Y.: ILR Press, 1991).
46. J. Reese, "Mortgage Help as a Job Benefit," *Fortune* (3 June 1991): 13; "Housing Aid—Benefit of the 90s?" *Bulletin to Management* (5 Sept. 1991): 280; *Employer-Assisted Housing Programs* (Lincolnshire, Ill.: Hewitt Associates, 1991).
47. K. P. Shapiro and J. A. Sherman, "Employee Attitudes Benefit Plan Designs," *Personnel Journal* (July 1987): 49–53; A. Barber, R. B. Dunham, and R. A. Formisano, "The Impact of Flexible Benefits on Employee Satisfaction: A Field Study," *Personnel Psychology* 45 (1992): 55–75; C. A. Baker, "Flex Your Benefits," *Personnel Journal* (May 1988): 54–60; J. E. Burkholder, "Cafeteria-Style Benefits: No Free Lunch," *Personnel* (Nov. 1987): 13–16; "Flexible Benefit Plans Finding Acceptance," *Bulletin to Management* (28 April 1988): 136; "Flexible Comp Programs: Health Care Cost-Cutting Tool," *Bulletin to Management* (12 March 1987): 82; "Personnel Shop Talk," *Bulletin to Management* (14 Jan. 1988): 10.
48. K. P. Shapiro and J. A. Sherman, "Employee Attitudes Benefit Plan Designs," *Personnel Journal* (July 1987): 49–53.
49. "Employees Would Change Benefits If Possible," *Bulletin to Management* (15 Aug. 1985): 1–2. Reprinted by permission from *Bulletin to Management,* copyright 1985, by The Bureau of National Affairs, Inc., Washington, D. C.
50. "Cost, Communication, and Compliance Concerns," *Bulletin to Management* (21 March 1985): 7; "Pay Off," *The Wall Street Journal* (8 July 1982): 1; R. Foltz, "Communiqué," *Personnel Administrator* (May 1981): 8; R. M. McCaffery, "Employee Benefits: Beyond the Fringe?" *Personnel Administrator* (May 1981): 26–30; T. F. Casey, "One-to-One Communication of Employee Benefits," *Personnel Journal* (Aug. 1982): 572–74; "Employee Benefits: Attitudes and Reactions," *Bulletin to Management* (11 April 1985): 1.
51. "Employees Would Change Benefits If Possible," *Bulletin to Management* (15 Aug. 1985): 1–2. Reprinted by permission from *Bulletin to Management,* copyright 1985, by The Bureau of National Affairs, Inc., Washington, D.C.
52. R. B. Dunham and R. A. Formisano, "Designing and Evaluating Employee Benefit System," *Personnel Administrator* (April 1982): 29–36.
53. M. Mercer, *Turning Your HR Department into a Profit Center* (New York: AMACOM, 1989): 91.

54. P. Farish, "Interactive Pension Data," *Personnel Administrator* (July 1985): 10–12; E. M. Fowler, "Employees, Benefits and Computers," *The New York Times* (16 Feb. 1988): 3; R. D. Huff, "The Impact of Cafeteria Benefits on the Human Resource Information System," *Personnel Journal* (April 1983): 282–83; "IRS Benefit Regulations Call for Strict Record-Keeping," *Resource* (Feb. 1985): 1, 9; J. L. Krakauer, "Slash Health Care Costs with Claims Automation," *Personnel Journal* (April 1985): 88–91; H. D. Spring, "Medical Benefit Plan Costs," *Personnel Administrator* (Dec. 1984): 64–72.

55. L. Asinof, "Excess Pension Assets Lure Corporate Raiders," *The Wall Street Journal* (11 Sept. 1985): 6; "Business Reduces Pension Funding to Cut Costs, Fend Off Takeovers," *The Wall Street Journal* (11 Oct. 1984): 35; P. F. Drucker, "Taming the Corporate Takeover," *The Wall Street Journal* (30 Oct. 1984): 30; R. J. Greene and R. G. Roberts, "Strategic Integration of Compensation and Benefits," *Personnel Administrator* (May 1983): 79–82; "Total Compensation Strategies," *Bulletin to Management* (4 Oct. 1984): 8.

END OF SECTION CASE STUDY

What She Had In Mind

Ending months of speculation, Bev's employer, National Drug, has just announced a merger with one of the country's leading food and drug chains. That evening, all local personnel from National were scheduled for their first meeting with the regional manager of the acquiring firm. The purpose of the meeting was to introduce the "new and improved" benefits package to be applied to employees of both firms within a month.

"Great, it arrived on time," said Bev, referring to a letter she just received from Steelko Manufacturing, Inc. The letter included the benefits brochure of the company where she interviewed for a pharmacist position a week earlier. It was a slow evening at National Drug, and Bev had filled all the day's prescriptions, so she sat down to read Steelko's brochure. It was a pleasant coincidence that the brochure arrived the same day of the meeting, allowing for a fresh comparison.

Beverly Cox

Bev was twenty-two when she graduated from the University of Illinois School of Pharmacy. She passed the license exam the same year and joined Medicare Drug in a small town near her farming parents. In a year, she received an offer from another pharmacy but Medicare countered it and promoted her to head of their branch office in Peoria, Illinois. In 1984, an independent pharmacist in Peoria convinced Bev to leave Medicare. Soon after she joined his pharmacy, Medicare went out of business. In July of 1985, Bev applied for a position at National Drug and was hired for the job at their firm in Bloomington, Illinois. Two years later, she was promoted to head National's other pharmacy in Bloomington.

A year later, Bev got to know Jerome Cox, a frequent prescription customer, and in another year they married. Jerry is a mechanical engineer who lived through several unlucky experiences. He is a veteran of two wars, Korea and Vietnam; currently he suffers frequent and increasing back pain from an earlier helicopter crash. From his first marriage, Jerry has a seventeen-year-old son, Bob, who lives with him and Bev. During the last four years, Jerry has been laid off twice and is currently out of a job due to economic conditions. Because Jerry's unemployment compensation will be running out soon, Bev decides to fill in for two part-time jobs during her days off. One of these jobs is forty miles north. The family has been discussing the possibility of spinal surgery for Jerry but the cost is formidable given their current economic condition.

Bob is a junior in high school and wants to go to an engineering school when he graduates in a year and a half. Although the family prefers not to leave Bloomington before Bob's graduation, Bev decides to assess each situation separately.

Steelko's Package

Steelko's plant, where Bev interviewed, is located in a university town similar to Bloomington. However, the university is more nationally recognized for its engineering reputation. Jerry is quite familiar with the city and the university because it is his alma mater.

Steelko itself is a heavy manufacturing company with an international reputation in earth-moving equipment and tractor business. Recently, Steelko's local administration decided to have their own in-plant pharmacy so employees and workers could buy their medicine at cheaper rates.

During Bev's interview with Steelko, they told her that their personnel conducted a market analysis for the pharmacist position and the salary they offer for the position will be competitive. When she told them that she now makes $16.65 per hour, they observed that although it is higher than average market they will meet it. What they stressed the most was their benefit package that was recently beefed up by headquarters. They promised to send a copy as soon as it arrived from print.

It was an impressive detailed brochure. Without noticing, Bev thumbed through the booklet to see whether it contained something for dependents. She then read it more carefully from the beginning.

Health Care Coverage

This coverage will help you pay most of the medical, hospital, surgical, and physicians' charges you and your dependents incur during the year. Each benefit year, you pay the first $200 of covered medical expenses per covered person as a deductible. After that, this coverage pays 80 percent of your covered medical expenses for the remainder of the benefit year for that person. You pay the remaining 20 percent of these covered medical expenses, called your "copayment." Your Medical Expense Coverage has a special feature called an excess expense limitation. This feature limits the amount you pay during a benefit year for covered medical expenses. *It does not limit expens-*

es for mental and nervous conditions. If you or your covered dependents do not have coverage under any other group plans, the most you will need to pay is $700 during a benefit year for you and your covered dependents. Once you have paid $700, this coverage pays all remaining covered medical expenses for the benefit year up to the annual and lifetime maximums. The annual maximum is $500,000 per person. Each person is covered for up to $1,000,000 during their lifetime.

Dental Expense Coverage

Maximum Benefit:

For orthodontic treatment ... $650.

For other covered dental expenses ... $1,000 per calendar year (orthodontic treatment will not be charged against this maximum).

Vision Expense Coverage

Vision examination ... once every 24 months.

Lens or lenses for eyeglasses and frames for eyeglasses ... once every 24 months.

Reasonable and customary charges up to maximum benefits.

Organ Transplant Coverage

Benefits for donation and receipt of an organ.

Medicare Part B Premium Reimbursement

You are reimbursed for your Medicare Part B premium.

Employee Benefits Security Fund

Your account in this Fund offers money to help pay your share of health care expenses. You have an account if you had hospital expense or Comprehensive Medical Expense Coverage for at least one full calendar month in the prior benefit year. If you have comprehensive Medical Expense Coverage on the first day of the benefit year, your Fund account will be credited with $700 *provided you were both at work at least one day in each calendar month and covered for Health Care Coverage* the full prior benefit year. If you had Health Care Coverage for the full prior benefit year but were not at work at least one day each month, a lower amount will be credited to your Fund account. All of the money credited to your Fund account in any benefit year is available to help pay for qualified medical expenses incurred by you or one of your covered dependents during that benefit year. You will receive any remaining balance in your Fund account as taxable compensation.

Disability Benefits in General

You will be paid Short Term Disability benefits during your total disability for up to twenty-six weeks. Based on your continuous service at the start of your disability absence, the Full Benefit (100 percent of your base weekly salary) will be paid for two to twenty-six weeks. The Partial Benefit (60 percent of your base weekly salary) will be paid for those weeks the Full Benefit is not paid. Extended Term Disability benefits are equal to 60 percent of your base weekly salary. These benefits begin after Short Term Disability benefits end. Payments can continue for a maximum of seventy-eight weeks during your total disability. To be eligible, you must have two or more years of continuous service. Long Term disability benefits range from 50 percent to 60 percent of your base monthly salary, depending on your years of continuous service. To be eligible, you must have three or more years of continuous service.

Retirement

Your Retirement Plan pension will be based on your years of pension service and on your average earnings during your final years of pension service.

Besides paying a pension benefit to you, the Plan may provide a lifetime monthly pension to your spouse following your death, whether you die before or after retirement.

In addition, the Plan may pay benefits to you even if you leave before you are eligible for retirement. For example, if you leave after completing at least ten years of pension service, you have a right to a pension benefit, which can begin as early as age fifty-five.

Steelko pays the entire cost of all the benefits provided under the Rules. You are not required to make any contributions.

Savings Plan

The Savings Plan gives you a convenient and systematic way to save and invest for your future. Like other personal savings and investment accounts, a separate account is set up in the Steelko Savings Plan in your name. Money you save each month is credited to this account.

But there are some big differences from other types of savings open to you. In your Steelko Plan:

Steelko matches some of your savings with a contribution that is invested solely in Steelko common stock.

You direct the way your savings are invested.

You can transfer money from one type of investment to another ... "manage" your account to reach your individual goals.

You pay no taxes on Company contributions or on any earnings your account enjoys until you withdraw them.

The full value of your Plan account will be paid to you when you retire. If you have been saving steadily, the value of your account can substantially boost your retirement income. If you leave Steelko *before* you retire, you'll receive the value of your *own savings*—meaning you'll get back what you've saved plus (or minus) any earnings (or losses) on it. You will also get the value of Company contributions that have been in the Plan for three or more full calendar years.

If you die *before* you retire or leave, the full value of your account will be paid to your beneficiary. If you die *after* retirement but before you have received the full value of your account, the beneficiary you've chosen will receive the remaining balance.

Our Savings Plan is primarily designed to help you save for your *long-range* goals; it's an ideal source of retirement income in addition to our Retirement Plan and Social Security. However, you can make withdrawals of your savings while you're still employed by the Company. *All things considered, Steelko's Savings Plan offers you an extraordinary opportunity to expand your savings.*

Stock Ownership

The Steelko Ownership Plan is actually an arrangement between you and an investment firm. The Company's role is to make the regular payroll deductions that Plan participants have authorized. The Company turns these payroll deductions over to the investment firm, which uses them to buy Steelko's common stock. You can ask your investment firm to hold the shares purchased for you in an account set up in your name, or in your and your spouse's name. At your request, you can have a certificate for the shares in your Plan account delivered to you at any time.

You have control over the distribution of stock held in your Stock Ownership Plan account. You can sell your shares or have the certificates transferred to you whenever you want. If you have a joint account, you and your spouse share control of the stock.

Company-Paid Life Insurance

Your insurance goes into effect on the first day you are actively at work with the Company.

You have Life Insurance equal to $30,000 or one times your annual compensation, whichever is more.

If you die or suffer loss of limbs or eyesight as a result of an accidental injury, you or your beneficiary can receive benefits up to two times your annual compensation. The amount of benefit will depend on your loss.

Travel Accident Policy

This policy pays benefits if your accidental death occurs while you are on a business trip.

Your insurance is $100,000 or $2^1/_2$ times your annual compensation, if that is more, up to a maximum of $1,500,000.

This insurance also provides these benefits: one-half the death benefit for the loss of one hand, foot, or eye and the same amount as the death benefit for the loss of any two of them, if they result from an accident that occurs while you are on a business trip.

Optional Insurance

This Plan allows you to purchase additional Life Insurance. You pay for this additional insurance at group rates.

The amount of your Contributory Life Insurance can be one, two, three, or four times your annual compensation.

Dependent Life Insurance

Steelko also offers a Dependent Life Insurance Plan. You pay for the insurance you elect at group rates that vary according to your age.

You can cover your spouse and each dependent child by electing one of these options:

Option 1
- Spouse..$10,000
- Each Dependent Child.................$ 2,000

Option 2
- Spouse..$20,000
- Each Dependent Child.................$ 4,000

Your Vacation Benefits in General

Each year you earn from one to four weeks of regular vacation ... paid time off ... according to the length of time you've been with Steelko. After you've been with Steelko for one year, you also earn from 1.4 weeks to 3 weeks of additional vacation benefits ... generally taken in cash ... also according to your service.

In addition, Steelko observes nine regularly scheduled holidays plus one locally selected holiday for ten paid holidays each year.

Steelko pays the full cost of your regular paid vacation, additional vacation benefits, and holidays.

Holiday Schedule

Steelko recognizes ten paid holidays each year:

New Year's Day
President's Day
Good Friday
Memorial Day
Independence Day
Labor Day
Thanksgiving Day
The day after Thanksgiving
The day before Christmas
Christmas Day

OR

Instead of one of the above holidays, a locally selected holiday.

Ordinarily, your office or plant will be closed on these holidays. If a holiday falls during a week when you are on vacation, you are allowed an added day of vacation. Each year you will be told in advance when the holidays will be.

Bev finished reading Steelko's brochure, attended to some customers, and it was time for the meeting with the regional manager of the acquiring firm. The meeting was at a hotel nearby, and on the way she was deep in thought. If Steelko's salary is competitive, the comparison between the two positions may boil down to comparing their benefit packages. However, National applied a store incentive system that was unmatched by Steelko. At National, every store is given a quota that is based on its performance in recent years. If the store exceeds the quota, the pharmacists may claim extra pay up to $3000 a year. Last year Bev made half that amount.

The meeting started with the regional manager assuring pharmacists that the store incentive system would remain intact. Then he went on to explain the new package. He said, "The package provides employees and their dependents with substantial protection and encourages them to become careful health consumers." The last part of the sentence was apparently included by design. The benefit brochure that he handed out started with a letter from the Executive Vice-President of the firm. In the letter, the VP stated: "Changes have been made in the design of many of our company medical plans to encourage containment of controllable costs and to move toward reasonable uniform treatment of eligible employees throughout our family of companies." Bev noticed that the language of the brochure was more informal than they were used to in National's correspondence. She also noticed that a section on "Health Care Tips" was included.

Benefit Package of the Acquiring Firm

Note: The benefits described in this package are highlighted only. The actual plan documents will govern should there be any questions concerning your benefits.

Health Plan

Our Health Plan pays up to $1,000,000 in lifetime benefits to you, your spouse, and each covered dependent child (up to age twenty-six).

Once your covered medical expenses for one year exceed the annual deductible of $150 per person (or $450 per family), the Plan pays 80 percent of expenses for most covered medical and hospital services, including charges for:

Physician's service
Hospital room and board at semi-private room rate
Hospital services and supplies
In-hospital doctor's visits
Surgery
Maternity
Emergency care.

You will receive a booklet that describes these and other covered services in detail.

Special incentives To promote the cost-conscious use of health care services, the Plan offers financial incentives to stay out of the hospital unless medically necessary. The Plan pays 100 percent of covered expenses for these outpatient services, with no deductible required:

Outpatient surgery, including surgeon's fees
Diagnostic testing, including pre-admission tests
Birthing rooms and licensed birthing centers
Home health care.

The claims administrator may also review hospital procedures and treatment prior to your admission to determine appropriateness of care (Pre-admission Review).

Your maximum costs The Plan limits the amount of money you have to pay "out-of-pocket" each year on covered charges. If you have paid $1,000 (for individual coverage) or $2,000 (for family coverage) plus the applicable deductible, the Plan pays 100 percent of remaining eligible expenses for that year.

Coordination of health care benefits You or a dependent may also be entitled to health benefits from another source that pays part or all of the cost of certain medical expenses. If this is the case, benefits under this Plan may be limited when you receive benefits from other sources.

When there is a claim for an employee, our Plan will pay benefits first. If you have family coverage, when a qualified member of your family has a claim that is covered by another group plan, the other plan may have the primary payment responsibility. We want to make sure that even if they are not primary, your family members still get a total benefit equal to the full benefits covered by the Plan. For this reason, we will pay the difference between the primary Plan's benefits and this Plan's reasonable and customary benefits. In no case will the combined payment be greater than what our Plan would have paid if it had had primary payment responsibility.

To illustrate, let's assume you have already met your family deductible when your spouse incurs further covered expenses totaling $800.

Total Eligible Expense	$800
Allowable from our Benefit Amount	$640

Minus Payment from Spouse's Plan	$580
Equals Payment from our Health Plan	$ 60

Converting your coverage If you leave the Company, you may convert your coverage to an individual policy if you apply within thirty days. Because you can do so without providing evidence of good health, this may be an important benefit. Also, preexisting conditions would be covered in the conversion policy. Be sure to request a conversion application form when you terminate.

Health care These benefits are part of the Health Plan and provide you and your eligible family members with important protection. The benefits described here are covered after you satisfy the deductible.

Well physical examination The Plan pays 80 percent of covered charges toward the cost of a well physical examination, up to a maximum of $100 per exam.

The frequency of routine well physical examinations is limited to:

Once every five years under age forty
Once every two years age forty and over

This benefit is available to employees and all covered dependents who are at least five years old.

Psychiatric treatment In-hospital: You are covered at 80 percent for up to a maximum of forty-five days each year, or a lifetime maximum of ninety days.

Outpatient: The Plan pays 80 percent for the first ten visits in a calendar year. The maximum payment for each visit is $70. After ten visits, the Plan pays 50 percent for the rest of the year. The maximum outpatient benefit for a calendar year is $1,500 per person with a lifetime maximum benefit of $7,500.

Substance abuse (drug/alcohol) Although treatment can be as an inpatient, outpatient, or a combination of both, only one course of treatment per individual's lifetime is allowed. The maximum total lifetime benefit is $11,000.

Inpatient: If you are confined in an approved treatment facility for alcohol or drug abuse, the Plan pays 80 percent for a maximum of one confinement. The maximum lifetime benefit is $8,000 per individual.

Outpatient: After the deductible, the Plan pays 80 percent towards charges for an approved substance abuse program. The maximum lifetime benefit is $3,000.

Vision care The Plan pays 80 percent of covered charges. The maximum benefit per calendar year is $100 per person; you are limited to:

One exam per calendar year
One pair of lenses and/or frames in a two-calendar-year period unless you have a significant prescription change.

Prescription Drugs No deductible required. The Plan provides benefits on an 80 percent copayment basis for the cost of all eligible drugs prescribed by a physician or dentist that are dispensed from a licensed pharmacy. Your cost for each eligible prescription filled is 20 percent of the retail charge. The Plan pays the balance of the retail charge.

If you buy your prescription drug at one of our stores, after showing appropriate identification, you pay only your 20 percent share. However, if your prescription is filled elsewhere, you must pay the full amount and then submit a claim form for reimbursement.

Enrollment To cover you and your family members for Health Care, return the enrollment card in the back of this folder to your manager or supervisor.

Dental Benefits

Your Health Plan includes separate Dental Benefits that provide some protection against the high cost of dental care. Your benefits emphasize preventive care—and are designed to encourage you to stop problems before they occur.

Deductibles Before the Dental benefits payments begin to pay for expenses you or your covered family members incur, you must pay an annual deductible of $25 for regular exams and cleanings, and $50 for other services. This $50 deductible is reduced by a deductible already paid during the year for exams and cleaning. However, if the combined deductibles of covered family members reach $100 during the calendar year, no further deductibles will be required on any members for the rest of that year.

Coverage for routine and preventive care After the $25 annual deductible has been satisfied, the Plan pays 80 percent of the expenses for routine and preventive care, including routine cleaning and maintenance and usual repairs.

Coverage for other services For other dental expenses (except orthodontia), you must first pay the $50 deductible each year for each person covered. The Plan will then pay 50 percent of the expenses for unusual procedures that are generally elective or nonrecurring (such as inlays, crowns, and fixed bridgework).

Maximum benefit The Dental Plan provides a $1,500 maximum benefit plan each year for each person covered by the Plan. The Plan also includes a lifetime dental maximum of $7,500 for each person.

Coverage for orthodontia The Plan provides for orthodontia with no deductibles. The Plan pays 50 percent of covered orthodontia charges.

The maximum lifetime payment for orthodontia charges is $1,750 per person.

Health care tips "An apple a day keeps the doctor away."

If controlling health care costs were as simple as eating apples, the public would not be spending over $400 billion a year on medical and dental expenses. Nor would the cost of health care have *doubled* every five years.

The spiraling costs of health care have become a national concern. No longer can we expect others to shoulder the entire burden of health care costs for us. We now realize the burden of skyrocketing health care costs must be shared, and we are learning that, as individuals, we can help lessen the burden of excessive medical costs. In the following paragraphs we'll explore ways we can cut expenses—from becoming educated health care consumers to staying healthy.

Alternate treatment facilities Although hospitals can save lives by providing important acute medical care, in less critical situations the need for hospitalization must be considered carefully. Evidence suggests that for many conditions, other treatment facilities covered by your Plan may provide more effective care. For example:

Skilled Nursing Facilities offer twenty-four-hour nursing care for the patient recovering from a serious illness or injury.

Home Health Care Services can provide quality medical treatment in a more convenient and economical setting.

Hospice Programs may be a more appropriate place for the supportive care of terminally ill patients. Qualified facilities can give the same quality care as hospital inpatient, while protecting your health. Hospice programs provide a coordinated program of inpatient, outpatient, and home care.

Birthing Centers offer quality natal care as an alternative to hospitals.

Outpatient Facilities, including surgicenters and doctor's centers, can give the same quality care as hospital inpatient, while reducing the cost of protecting your health.

Auditing your hospital bills A surprisingly effective way to help control costs is simply to check (audit) your hospital bill. Studies show that it's not unusual for duplicate charges or charges for services and supplies never received to show up on a hospital bill. As the patient, only you will know if services were not performed. Hospitals are usually receptive to reviewing bills as it is good public relations and it helps in maintaining accurate records.

To make your audit easier, record the services you receive each day while you're in the hospital. When you're discharged, ask for an itemized bill. Compare your list and the bill. Then ask your hospital's patient account representative about any charges you don't understand.

Health habits You can do more for your health than your doctor can. By defining and applying solid, workable health goals, you can make permanent changes in your life. Lifestyle changes in the areas of exercise, smoking, stress, and eating and drinking habits are long-term commitments that will allow you to live longer, feel better, and have more energy to share with family and friends. As an added benefit, practicing good health habits is the best way to control medical costs.

Smart consumer behavior We should be cost-conscious about the health care services we use. Of course you will not want to take shortcuts where your health is concerned, but here are some suggestions that may help you receive better care while avoiding unnecessary expenses:

1. When your doctor recommends non-emergency surgery—before you agree to it—get a second opinion on the need for surgery.
2. Insist on a full, understandable explanation of your medical condition and the proposed treatment plan.
3. Use outpatient services whenever you can. Some hospitals have special ambulatory surgical centers for minor walk-in surgery. These can save you the trouble and expenses of overnight hospitalization. Use free standing surgicenters to handle minor surgeries, tests, or other procedures on an outpatient basis.
4. Avoid being admitted to the hospital on Friday or Saturday if your condition is not likely to be dealt with until Monday and if there is no medical reason for you to be hospitalized over the weekend.
5. Many hospitals run a battery of tests simply as a precaution. Some of them may not be necessary. Verify their necessity with your doctor. Also, you may be able to have preadmission tests done on an outpatient basis.
6. Ask for generic drugs. They can often be substituted for brand-name drugs, sometimes at less than half the cost.
7. Review all bills closely. You are not required to pay for any services you did not receive. Check

to make sure all charges are accurate. If you have a question about a charge, ask for verification.

8. Shop around. Do not be afraid to discuss fees in advance.
9. Practice preventive medicine. Have regular checkups.

Life Insurance

Life insurance is a key part of your coverage with us. The financial security it provides for your family's future is important. Our Plan also provides your dependents with life insurance coverage.

What it's worth Effective January 1, 1992, the benefit amount for our Life Insurance Plan is equal to three times your base yearly salary rounded up to the next full thousand dollars. This benefit is paid for in full by the Company.

For example, if your salary is $25,700, three times this amount is $77,100; rounded up to the nearest thousand your benefit is $78,000.

If you receive a raise, your new benefit amount goes into effect on the date your raise is effective. If for some reason your pay is reduced, your benefit amount will not be reduced as long as you are still a salaried employee.

If your life insurance amount provided by the Company exceeds $50,000, a charge from the IRS imputed income tables will be added to your W-2.

Dependent coverage Your dependents are covered under the Plan for the following amounts:

$2,000 for your spouse
$1,000 for each eligible dependent child.

Coverage at age 65 Once you reach the age of 65 (while actively working), your life insurance coverage is reduced by 35 percent. Coverage for your dependents remains unchanged.

Converting your coverage If you retire or leave the company, you can convert to an individual policy by applying within thirty-one days. Because you can do so without providing evidence of good health, this may be an important benefit. Be sure to request a conversion application form when you terminate.

Enrollment Be sure to complete the enrollment card in the back of this folder to designate your beneficiary and enroll your dependents.

Your designated beneficiary will receive your life insurance benefit in the event of your death. As your circumstances change, you may wish to update your beneficiary designation.

Completed cards should be returned to your manager or supervisor.

Accidental Death, Dismemberment, and Total Disability Insurance

Accidental Death, Dismemberment, and Total Disability Insurance effective January 1, 1992, is a special kind of benefit that covers you for certain major injuries or death caused by an accident. When you elect this coverage, you can also receive coverage for your dependents.

The Plan covers you for accidents that happen on and off the job, twenty-four hours a day, anywhere in the world—regardless of your health history.

What it's worth You can purchase coverage for yourself in $10,000 amounts from $10,000 to $250,000. This is called your Principal Sum.

When you purchase this coverage, you may also elect family coverage. Your family member's Principal Sum is as follows:

Spouse—40 percent of your Principal Sum
Each eligible child—10 percent of your Principal Sum
Spouse with no children—50 percent of your Principal Sum
Eligible children (when there is no spouse)—15 percent of your Principal Sum.

If you or a covered family member becomes totally and permanently disabled due to an accident, the Principal Sum for that person will be paid.

Also, partial or full benefits may be payable if you or a covered family member should become dismembered as a result of an accident. The amount of this benefit will depend upon the extent of the injury.

Enrollment When enrolling for this coverage, you need to make the following decisions:

Do you need single or family coverage?
What amount of coverage will be required?
Whom will you select as your beneficiary?

You must complete and return the enrollment card in the back of this folder to receive this benefit. Completed cards should be returned to your manager or supervisor.

Employee Stock Ownership Plan

All eligible participants will receive shares of our Company Common Stock through this program. This Plan has been designed to enable you to share in the growth and prosperity of the Company and to provide you with an opportunity to accumulate capital for the future.

Eligibility You will be eligible to participate in this Plan after completing one year of service (a twelve-month period in which you complete at least 1,000 hours). If you do not complete 1,000 hours during the first twelve months of employment, we will review your hours each calendar year to determine whether you have completed 1,000 hours. When you meet your eligibility requirements, complete 1,000 hours, and are employed as of December 31, you will receive your full share for that year.

Benefits Each year the Company will make contributions to the Plan. The maximum total company contribution allowed by law is one-half of one percent (0.5%) of the *total* compensation paid to all qualified members. This total contribution will be evenly shared with all qualified members. This means that each of you will receive the same benefit from this Plan, regardless of your actual compensation.

The full value of your account will be paid to you in a lump sum of cash or shares as requested when you retire or if you leave the Company before retirement. You are automatically vested in your account. Your account will primarily be in the Company stock; however, there may also be accumulated dividends and cash waiting to be invested in stock.

If you should die while actively employed, your beneficiary would receive the total value of your account. If you should become permanently and totally disabled, you will receive a lump sum payout of your entire account.

Voting rights Participants with allocations will be entitled to direct the manner in which their company stock is voted.

Enrollment You are automatically enrolled. To designate your beneficiary, you must complete the enrollment card in the back of this folder. Completed cards should be returned to your manager or supervisor.

Monthly Investment Plan

The Company provides each of you with an opportunity to purchase our Company Common Stock through payroll deductions. The purchase of Company stock will be made through an investment firm.

Common Stock will be purchased at market prices. The Company will pay brokerage charges to purchase stock and reinvest dividends from shares in your account. Charges made by the investment firm for the sale of Company Stock or any purchases not made through payroll deductions will not be paid by the Company.

Eligibility When you reach the age of majority (usually eighteen) in your state of residence, you may participate in this Plan.

Benefits You may purchase Company Common Stock with a minimum payroll deduction of $1 each week or $4 each month. Your payroll deductions will then be delivered to Merrill Lynch to purchase Company stock at current market rates. Remember, the Company will be paying the brokerage fees for the purchase of your stock. There is no limit to the amount of stock you can purchase through deductions.

Long-Term Disability Plan

As a salaried employee of our Company, you can elect coverage under the Long-Term Disability Plan. The LTD Plan is designed to provide you with a continuing income when a disabling illness or injury prevents you from working. If you do not elect this coverage, you will automatically receive the Short-Term Disability Plan described below.

Plan coverage For the first six months of disability, the Company pays you your full salary (less any amounts due you from other sources). After you have been disabled for six months, the Plan provides you with an income equal to 60 percent of your base monthly salary up to a maximum benefit of $5,000 per month. This benefit payment continues for the period of your disability to age sixty-five. If you become disabled after age sixty-two, benefits continue for the number of months specified by the Plan's schedule.

What is "total disability"? The meaning of total disability changes with the length of time that you're disabled.

For the first twenty-four months, total disability means you're unable to do your regular job. After you've been receiving the usual benefit for twenty-four months, total disability means you can't do any job that you'd normally be suited for by your training and experience.

You cannot receive disability benefits if you're doing any kind of work for pay, unless the work is part of a special rehabilitation program.

Payments from this Plan after the first six months are tax free because you pay the entire premium for your coverage.

Coordination with other benefits Your disability may entitle you to benefits from sources other than the LTD Plan, such as Workers' Compensation or Social Security. These other benefits are considered when determining your LTD benefit. The Plan provides that you will receive a 60 percent disability (up to $5,000) when combining benefits from all sources.

Special note: The insurance company requires that you apply for Social Security and appeal any first denial. If you do not follow this procedure, the benefit to which you might be entitled will automatically be subtracted from the Plan's benefit, even if you are not actually receiving Social Security payments.

Your Social Security benefit offset amount is frozen at the level you're eligible for when you're disabled. Any later increases in Social Security benefits except for changes in the number of your dependents will increase the total disability benefit paid to you.

If the total sum of all these other benefits, taken together, is less than your 60 percent guaranteed benefit, then your LTD Plan makes up the difference. And if you have no sources other than LTD, your disability plan provides you with the entire 60 percent guaranteed monthly benefit.

Short-Term Disability Plan

Our Short-Term Disability Coverage provides you with a continuing income during short periods when you cannot work. This benefit is only for eligible persons who have not elected the Long-Term Disability Plan.

Plan coverage You begin to receive a short-term disability benefit after your regular pay ceases. Your regular pay will continue in full for the week in which you are disabled plus the next full week.

The Plan pays 60 percent of your regular weekly pay up to a maximum of $277 per week. You can receive short-term disability benefits for up to fifty-two weeks. However, you must first submit medical certification of your disability in order to receive benefits. Then you will need to submit continuing verification of your disability.

Benefits from other sources Any disability benefits you receive from Social Security or state disability programs are subtracted from your short-term disability payment.

Any disability that is the result of an injury or illness sustained on the job is not covered under this Plan since these causes of disability are covered by Workers' Compensation.

If you are disabled for more than the fifty-two weeks allowed under this plan, Social Security will continue to pay you a benefit depending on the laws in effect at that time. If you become disabled, check with your local Social Security office to determine whether or not you're eligible for benefits.

When you apply for disability benefits, you will be referred to the proper state agency for necessary vocational rehabilitation service. If you refuse this training without good cause, you will forfeit your disability benefits.

The meeting was longer than Bev expected and she had to call home twice. Driving home, the comparison of the two packages occupied her mind almost totally. She didn't notice she was still thinking about the benefit packages until her husband's sleepy voice came from under the covers as she went to sleep: "Is that you dear?" She answered with the first smile of the day, "Were you expecting someone else?"

SOURCE: A. Magid M. Mazen, Professor, Department of Management, Suffolk University. Printed by permission.

SECTION 6

Improving

Even with the best staffing procedures, the most useful forms of performance appraisal and performance feedback, and the best methods of compensation, employees still may not perform at their highest levels. Employees may be deficient in one or more skills and abilities really needed to do the job. This may result because the employee has changed jobs, because the jobs have changed through new technologies, or simply because the deficiency wasn't picked up by the staffing procedures. Nevertheless, these skill and ability deficiencies need to be removed. While some deficiencies may be corrected in a rather short period of time, others may take longer. Consequently, we typically find companies offering a variety of training programs (short-term) as well as a variety of development programs (longer-term). We will discuss both in the first of three chapters on improving.

Many companies today recognize that simply offering a variety of training and development programs may not be enough. That is, companies realize they must improve employees *and* organizational effectiveness. To this end, companies are using a variety of organizational improvement programs. These range from surveying the employees to know what is going on to restructuring the entire company. Within this broad range are programs to redesign jobs to make them more exciting, challenging, and effective. Also within this range are programs to improve teamwork skills. Because so many of the programs companies are now using for organizational improvement have significant implications for human resource management, those programs are the subject of the second of our three chapters in this section.

Human resource management can also improve organizations in other ways. One way is to constantly gather data from employees and customers on how they perceive things are going. Organizational surveys can be used to monitor how things are going, to point the direction for specific improvement, and to communicate with employees. More traditional forms of personnel research can also be used. For a long time organizations have relied on personnel research to improve employee and organizational effectiveness by improving employee selection techniques and procedures. This ranges from test validation studies for employees at all levels to the development of assessment centers to identify future managerial candidates. Consequently, the last of our three chapters on improving will discuss the activities in personnel research.

Training and Development

What sets us apart is that we train people to be merchants. We let them see all the numbers so they know exactly how they're doing within the store and within the company; they know their cost, their markup, their overhead, and their profit. It's a big responsibility and a big opportunity.

—Sam Walton, past chairman, Wal-Mart[1]

The changing face of competition, both domestic and global, was staring directly into the window of the headquarters of the Forest Products Company (FPC) of the Weyerhaeuser Corporation in Seattle. It was a face that reflected the trend away from the large-firm, commodity lumber business and toward the small mills that tailor-made products to meet customer demands. Interestingly, these small mills owed their existence, in large part, to the sale of machinery by the larger firms when they were faced with the depressed housing market in the early 1980s. As a consequence of being able to buy this machinery at depressed prices, these small, nonunion, owner-operated, entrepreneurial, customer-oriented mills were able to not only be the most market-oriented but also the lowest cost operations.

Charley Bingham, the CEO of the FPC, decided that going out of business was not an alternative; but something needed to be done, preferably sooner than later. Together, the top dozen managers decided that a massive reorganization was called for, accompanied by a radical change in strategy. According to Bingham, the change in strategy went something like this: "Approximately 80 percent of our sales dollars in 1982 represented products sold as commodities. By 1995 we resolved that we must reverse the proportions."[2]

The massive reorganization mirrored the dramatic decentralization at headquarters. The three operating units, of which FPC was one, were given free reign on how to do their business. Given this scenario, Bingham and his top team decided to create an organization capable of acting and responding just like their competitors. Thus, they created two hundred profit centers, and each center was largely responsible for its own bottom line.

This restructuring soon proved to be only a step in the right direction. The ability of the organization to implement its new strategy was being undermined by pervasive poor morale. In addition, many middle managers—those needed to actually carry out the change—were pessimistic about the possibility of sustained future success. Silently, they even questioned their own ability to operate the profit centers.

Together with Horace Parker, director of strategic education at FPC, the rest of the top team came to realize they needed a total transformation of the organization. In particular they realized that all the managers would need a new knowledge base, skill levels, style of leadership, and team orientation. In other words, the success of the change would depend in large part upon the success of the training and development practices to change the skills, knowledge, and styles of FPC's managers.[3]

Training and retraining are critical to organizations because they provide the skills needed both now and in the future. Together, training and retraining ensure the skills and employee commitment needed for high-quality goods and services and, thus, competitiveness and survival. Because training and development are both important and costly, companies want each to be as effective as possible. The program launched by the Forest Products Company is an example of what companies are doing to train their employees. The success of programs such as FPC's will help determine how competitive U.S. businesses will be in the 1990s and beyond. Of course, there are many other reasons for training and development.

This chapter examines the purposes and importance of training and development programs—from basic literacy to computer-integrated manufacturing, from job enrichment to total quality management and global thinking. It discusses the types of needs analysis that must be conducted to determine who should receive training, what skills are necessary, and at what level they should be taught. Implementing a successful training and development program involves creating appropriate conditions for training to occur and selecting the type of program that matches needed skills and skill levels. These are described, along with techniques by which to assess training programs. International issues and comparisons in training and development conclude the chapter.

TRAINING AND DEVELOPMENT

Employee training and development is any attempt to improve current or future employee performance by increasing an employee's ability to perform.[4] The need for training and development may arise for many reasons. Job applicants with insufficient skills may be hired; technological changes may be introduced resulting in new job skills; organizations may redesign jobs and thus require employees to learn more skills; employees may be transferred or promoted to jobs requiring new skills and knowledge; or the company may decide to develop a new product requiring technologies not before used by the employees. In some of these cases, the need for training and development can be immediate; in others the need can be anticipated and planned.

PURPOSES AND IMPORTANCE OF TRAINING AND DEVELOPMENT

A major purpose of training and development is to remove performance deficiencies, whether current or anticipated, that cause employees to perform at less than the desired level. Training and development thereby enables employees to be much more productive. Training for performance improvement is particularly important to organizations with stagnant or declining rates of productivity. It is also important to organizations that are rapidly incorporating new technologies and consequently increasing the likelihood of employee obsolescence. Furthermore, as in the example of the Forest Products Company, training and development are vital if organizations are to be able to adapt and be competitive.

Training and development can also increase the level of commitment of employees to the organization and increase their perceptions that the organization is a good place to work. Increased commitment can result in less turnover and absenteeism, thus increasing an organization's productivity.[5] Increasingly recognized is that training and development can benefit society by enabling individuals to be productive and contributing members of organizations.

However, while training and development are important, managers may view them as too costly and the payoffs too distant. Thus, the support and commitment of leaders such as Sam Walton and of Wayne Calloway of PepsiCo are often critical for the success of an organization's training and development efforts.[6]

Without top management support and commitment to training, the major focus of an organization is likely to be on activities other than training. This is particularly true when the focus is on short-term goals and immediate results; this situation allows too little time to wait for the benefits of training and development. Top management at PepsiCo began to emphasize training and development at the same time they recognized that they had to develop their people and businesses in order to be effective.

This is happening at many companies across America today, and, as they discover, training and development are relatively complex and challenging activities. This is due in part to the multitude of relationships training and development have with other human resource activities, as shown in exhibit 12.1.

DETERMINING TRAINING AND DEVELOPMENT NEEDS

Training can be conducted for a variety of reasons. In some organizations, attendance at an executive training program is a reward for past performance. In

Exhibit 12.1
Training and Development Processes, Procedures, and Relationships

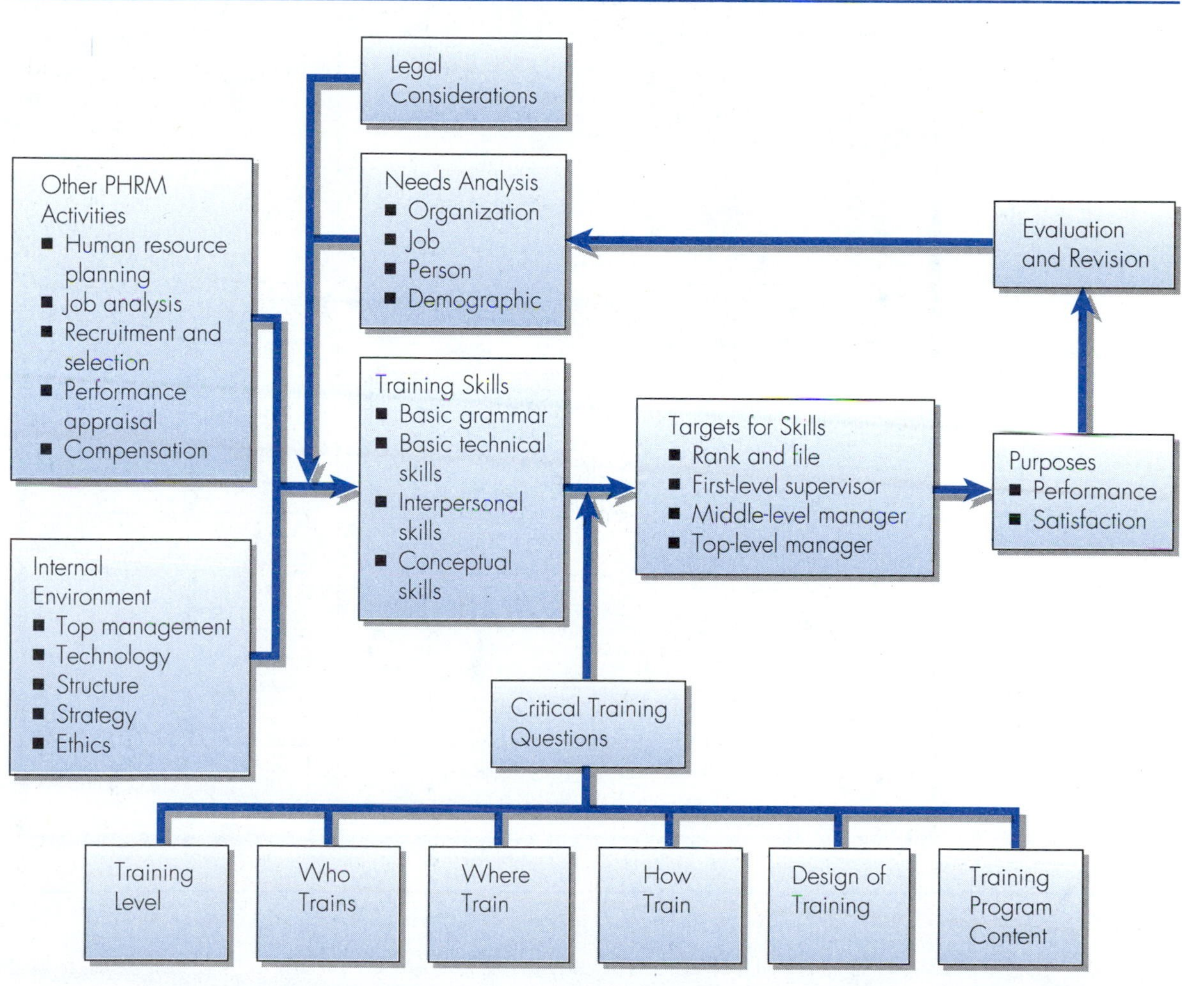

other organizations, participation in a training program is an organizational ritual that signals to the employee who is promoted and the members of his or her former work group that a switch in stature has occurred (a rank-and-file employee is now a manager). However, most often training is conducted to rectify skill deficiencies and provide employees with job-specific skills.[7]

A first step in establishing a viable training program is needs assessment, which determines the training and development needs of the organization. While less than one-third of all U.S. companies currently conduct formal needs assessment, its importance cannot be emphasized enough.[8] Without determining the need for training, there is no guarantee that the right training will be provided for the right trainees. This process is detailed in exhibit 12.2

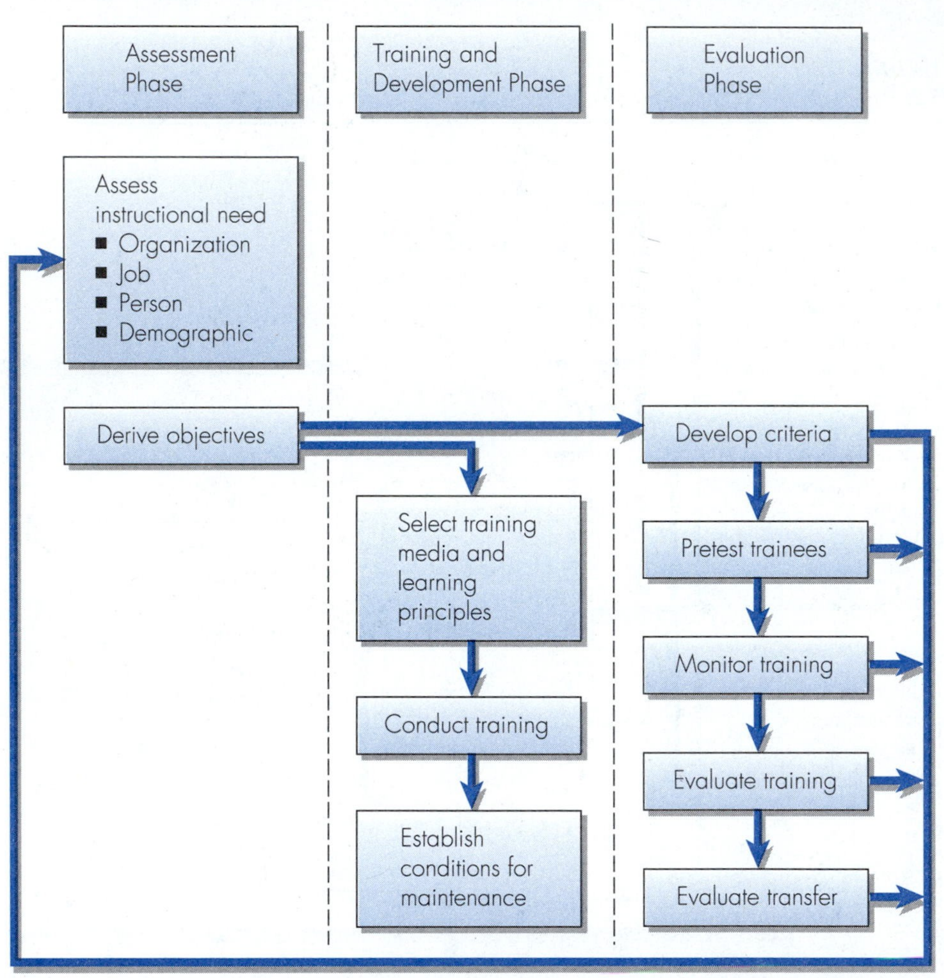

Exhibit 12.2
Model for an Instructional System

SOURCE: Adapted from I. Goldstein, *Training: Program Development and Evaluation,* 8. Copyright © 1974 Wadsworth, Inc. Reprinted by permission of the publisher, Brooks/Cole Publishing Company, Monterey, Calif.
Note: Many other models for instructional systems are used in the military, in business, and in education. Some of the components of this model were suggested by these other systems.

Organizational Needs Analysis

Conducting an organizational needs analysis is the first step in effective needs assessment. It begins with an examination of the short- and long-term objectives of the organization and the trends that are likely to affect these objectives. According to one expert, attaining organizational objectives should be the ultimate concern of any training and development effort. Organizational needs analysis also can include a human resource analysis, analyses of efficiency indices, and an assessment of the organizational climate.[9]

This analysis should translate the organization's objectives into an accurate estimate of the demand for human resources. Efficiency indices, including cost of labor, quantity of output, quality of output, waste, and equipment use and repairs, can provide useful information. The organization can determine standards for these indices and then analyze them to evaluate the general effectiveness of training programs and to locate training and development needs in departments.

Job Needs Analysis

The content of present or anticipated jobs should be examined through job needs analysis. For existing jobs, information on the tasks to be performed in each job (information contained in job descriptions), the skills necessary to perform those tasks (from job qualifications), and the minimum acceptable standards (gleaned from performance appraisal) are gathered. This information can then be used to ensure that training programs are job-specific and useful. For anticipated jobs, expert information and predictions can be made relevant to the content and complexity of future jobs (or existing jobs as they evolve). For example, it is predicted that the

> … next generation of manufacturing managers will need to know computer-aided design and computer-aided manufacturing (CAD/CAM), computer-integrated manufacturing (CIM), group technologies, flexible manufacturing, "just-in-time" inventory control, manufacturing resource planning (MRP), robotics, and a whole litany of other techniques and technologies in manufacturing.
>
> They're going to have to understand systems thinking, as more and more of the major corporations move toward the globalization of their manufacturing to achieve the competitive advantages of economies of scale, vertical integration, and offshore production.
>
> They'll have to develop different perspectives on managing a work force as the concepts of lifestyle employment, worker participation, and job enrichment extend further and further through the American enterprise system.
>
> Perhaps most importantly, they are going to have to have a well-developed understanding of corporate strategies, not only to find those organizations and subunits of organizations in which they will be most comfortable and successful, but also to be able to take an important role in determining and directing those strategies. The demands on manufacturing managers—on their skills, abilities, and training—are going up, but so too are their status and importance in manufacturing-based industries.[10]

Armed with these predictions, training and development specialists can begin to design training programs for manufacturing managers of the future.

Person Needs Analysis

After information about the necessary skills and their importance and the minimal acceptable standards of proficiency has been collected, the analysis shifts to the person. A person needs analysis can be accomplished in two different ways. Employee performance discrepancies may be identified either by comparing actual performance with the minimum acceptable standards of performance or by comparing an evaluation of employee proficiency on each required skill dimension with the proficiency level required for each skill. The first method is based on the actual, current job performance of an employee; therefore, it can be used to determine training needs for the current job. The second method, on the other hand, can be used to identify development needs for future jobs.[11]

In examining various methodologies for determining employee training needs, a continuing problem concerns the ambiguity of the word "need." Need can be an expression of preference or demand and not an observable discrepancy produced by a lack of skill. At this level, several different approaches can be used to identify the training needs of individuals.

Output measures. Performance data (e.g., productivity, accidents, customer complaints), as well as performance appraisal ratings, can provide evidence of performance deficiencies. Person needs analysis can also consist of work sampling and job knowledge tests that measure performance capability and knowledge.[12]

Self-assessed training needs. The self-assessment of training needs is growing in popularity. A recent study of training practices in major U.S. firms showed that between fifty and eighty percent of all corporations allow managers to nominate themselves to attend short-term or company-sponsored training or education programs. Self-assessment can be as informal as posting a list of company-sponsored courses and asking who wants to attend or as formal as conducting surveys regarding training needs.[13] Exhibit 12.3 shows sample questions from a managerial self-assessment survey.

Self-assessment is premised on the assumption that employees, more than anyone else, are aware of their skill weaknesses and performance deficiencies. Therefore, they are in the best position to identify their own training needs. One drawback of self-assessment is that individuals who are fearful of revealing any weaknesses may not know or be willing to report accurately their training needs. Consequently, these individuals may not receive the education necessary to remain current in their fields. On the other hand, managers forced to attend programs that they believe they do not need or that do not meet their personal training needs are likely to become dissatisfied with training and lack the motivation to learn and transfer skills.

Attitude surveys. Attitude surveys completed by a supervisor's subordinates and/or by customers also can provide information on training needs. For example, when one supervisor receives low scores regarding his or her fairness in treatment as compared with other supervisors in the organization, this may indicate that the supervisor needs training in that area.[14] Not only does this format provide information to management about service, but also results can be used to pinpoint employee deficiencies.

Exhibit 12.3
Sample Questions from a Self-Administered Training Needs Survey

Please indicate in the blanks the extent to which you have a training need in each specific area. Use the scale below.

To what extent do you need training in the following areas?

To no extent 1	2	3	4	To a very large extent 5

Basic Management Skills (organizing, planning, delegating, problem solving)

_______ 1. Setting goals and objectives
_______ 2. Developing realistic time schedules to meet work requirements
_______ 3. Identifying and weighing alternative solutions
_______ 4. Organizing work activities

Interpersonal Skills

_______ 1. Resolving interpersonal conflicts
_______ 2. Creating a development plan for employees
_______ 3. Identifying and understanding individual employee needs
_______ 4. Conducting performance appraisal reviews
_______ 5. Conducting a discipline interview

Administrative Skills

_______ 1. Maintaining equipment, tools, and safety controls
_______ 2. Understanding local agreements and shop rules
_______ 3. Preparing work flowcharts
_______ 4. Developing department budgets

Quality Control

_______ 1. Analyzing and interpreting statistical data
_______ 2. Constructing and analyzing charts, tables, and graphs
_______ 3. Using statistical software on the computer

SOURCE: Modified from J. K. Ford and R. A. Noe, "Self Assessed Training Needs: The Effects of Attitude toward Training, Managerial Level and Function," *Personnel Psychology* 40 (1987), 40–53.

Surveys can also be completed by employees and their bosses. For managers, such surveys can be used to identify which skills are important for managerial effectiveness. Differences in opinions can serve as a basis of discussion about what is really necessary for managerial success in today's environment. Based on the results of a recent survey, differences in opinions may not be totally surprising. This survey is described in the PHRM in the News: "Managers Fall Short of Their Supervisors' Expectations." Generally, the results of attitude surveys contribute important input into training program design.

Competency-based assessment. A type of needs assessment growing in popularity is competency-based assessment. This approach involves five major steps:

Step 1: *Develop Broad Competency Categories.* The initial step is to develop a set of broad competency areas, i.e., to determine the critical skills that employees at a given level or job classification in the organization need to be most effective.

PHRM IN THE NEWS

Managers Fall Short of Their Supervisors' Expectations

Managers and their bosses agree on the qualities that a successful manager must have, but managers generally don't live up to those expectations, according to a nationwide survey of 600 managers by Personnel Decisions Inc. (PDI), a Minneapolis-based firm of organizational psychologists. The study also discovered that both managers and their bosses are slow to recognize some of the new demands placed on managers by the evolving business environment.

Participating managers and their supervisors were asked to list what they thought were the most critical management skills. Managers then were rated by their supervisors and peers on how well they exhibit those skills. The study also included self-assessments by each manager to produce the ratings.

The most important skill, according to an overwhelming majority of managers and their supervisors, was the ability to *act with integrity*. Other key skills were ranked in the following order: *using sound judgment, providing direction, motivating others, managing execution, demonstrating adaptability, fostering teamwork, driving for results, thinking strategically* and *focusing on customer needs*. The study noted that managers and their supervisors ranked these attributes very similarly; however, the managers' performance in all these categories did not measure up to the importance both they and their bosses placed on each characteristic.

"In general, managers have not yet caught up with the changing demands in the business world," said Susan H. Gebelein, PDI vice president. "These changes require managers to exhibit participative—rather than autocratic—leadership, to build trust and influence others without direct challenge, and to champion change. For many, these skills are new, so they are just learning them."

Although some "new" skills have gained importance, other more traditional skills remain crucial to management, such as *using sound judgment, managing execution*, and *driving for results*. Other skills rated as less important, however, actually are critical factors for success in the changing global business environment, Gebelein noted. In fact, the skill that received the lowest rating was *recognizing global*

Continued

Step 2: *Develop Specific Competencies*. Once broad categories are selected, the next step is to further define each and develop a list of more specific competencies.

Step 3: *Develop a Resource Guide and a Competency Rating Form*. The third step involves the development of resource guides or competency manuals that will aid employers and employees in developing skills.

Step 4: *Prepare a Developmental Plan for Each Employee*. Once each employee has been evaluated, the next step would be for the boss to work with each of his/her subordinates to develop a specific improvement plan.

Step 5: *Evaluate Employee Progress and Develop a New Plan*. Periodic assessment of an employee's progress skill development is essential.[15]

Demographic Needs Analysis

In addition to organizational, job, and person analyses, organizations also should conduct demographic studies to determine the training needs of specific populations of workers.[16] For example, Frito Lay conducted a special assessment to determine the training needs of women and minorities in its sales force. According to Dave Knibbe, Frito Lay management development director, the needs assessment was critical to see if there were ways in which the organization could facilitate more rapid career advancement for these employees.

implications. Also, despite the continued support and emphasis by management experts, two other skills found their way into the bottom five: *promoting corporate citizenship* and *using financial data*.

SOURCE: *HR Focus* (March 1992), 22.

Importance of Management Skills

Management Skill	**Self-rated Importance**	**Supervisor-rated Importance**
Act with integrity	44.0	44.0
Use of sound judgment	38.5	39.5
Provide direction	38.5	37.5
Motivating others	38.0	37.5
Demonstrating adaptability	38.0	39.0
Fostering teamwork	37.0	36.5
Drive for results	36.5	35.5
Think strategically	33.0	32.0
Focus on customers	32.5	32.0
Use technical/functional expertise	32.5	34.0
Prepare written communications	32.0	30.5
Use financial/qualitative data	30.0	31.5
Promote corporate citizenship	26.0	25.0
Recognize global implications	22.5	22.0

Lowest Importance = 10 **Highest Importance = 50**

SOURCE: *Personnel Decisions Inc.*

Research indicates that different groups have different training needs. For example, first-line supervisors need more technical training (record keeping, written communications), while mid-level managers rate PHRM courses as most important for meeting their needs, and upper-level managers rate conceptual courses (goal setting, planning skills) as critical to their development.[17] In a study of male and female managers, male managers were found to need training in listening, verbal skills, nonverbal communication, empathy, and sensitivity; women managers, on the other hand, needed training in assertiveness, confidence building, public speaking, and dealing with male peers and subordinates.[18]

SETTING UP TRAINING AND DEVELOPMENT PROGRAMS

Successful implementation of training and development programs depends on selecting the right programs for the right people under the right conditions.

Who Participates in Training?

Once a training need has been established, a decision must be made regarding *who* will be trained. This is because, for most programs, only one target audience is in attendance, and the training program is designed to address only one topic.[19]

Also important here is the decision as to *how many* employees are to be trained simultaneously. If only one or two employees are to be trained, then on-the-job approaches such as coaching are generally cost effective. If large numbers of individuals need to be trained in a short period of time, then programmed instruction may be the most viable option.

Who Conducts the Training?

Training and development programs may be taught by one of several people, including

- The supervisor
- A co-worker, such as a lead worker or a buddy
- An internal or external subject area expert
- The employee

Which of these people is selected to teach often depends on where the program is held and which skill(s) is being taught. For example, basic job skills are usually taught by the immediate job supervisor or a co-worker, whereas a basic organizational orientation is usually handled by a member of the PHRM staff. Interpersonal skills and conceptual, integrative skills for management are usually taught by university professors or consultants. However, technical skills may be taught by either internal or external subject matter experts.

A concern with using immediate supervisors or co-workers as trainers is that, while they may perform adequately, they may not be able to instruct anyone in proper work procedures. It is also possible that they will teach workers their own shortcuts rather than correct procedures. On the other hand, immediate supervisors or co-workers may be more knowledgeable than anyone else about work procedures. If co-workers or managers are to be used as trainers, they should receive training in how to train and be given sufficient time on the job to work with trainees.[20]

Subject area experts may have specific knowledge but may not be familiar with procedures in a specific organizational culture. As a result, they may be respected for their expertise but mistrusted because they are not members of the work group. Still, if no one in the immediate work environment possesses the knowledge needed, or if large numbers of individuals need to be trained, the only option may be to hire experts.

Self-paced instruction is also an option. Learning at one's own pace is both an advantage and a disadvantage of self-paced instruction. Trainees benefit because they learn at a speed that maximizes retention. However, if there are no incentives for the trainee to complete the instruction in a specified period of time, training may be placed on a back burner.

What Types of Skills are to be Acquired?

In addition to using appropriate training techniques, the training program must have content congruent with the types of skills being taught. In general, skills fall into three broad areas; as discussed below.

Basic skills. As noted in chapter 2, organizations are increasingly concerned about illiteracy. Consequently, it is estimated that training programs designed to correct basic skill deficiencies in grammar, mathematics, safety, reading, listening, and writing will increase in the 1990s. For example:

> Ask most business executives how they would like to improve their reading on the job, and they will probably answer, "I would like to read faster. I can't keep up with all the reading material that comes across my desk." Employers..., such as Scott Paper Company, Providence National Bank, Western Electric Company, and Getty Oil, have appreciated this need and have implemented [reading] programs for their employees.[21]

Training that expands or maintains the technical expertise of employees is a subset of basic job skills training. Due to rapid changes in technology and the implementation of automated office, industrial, and managerial systems, technological updating and skill building have become a major thrust in training to keep technical skills current.[22]

Interpersonal skills. Skills in communications, human relationships, performance appraisal, leadership, and negotiations are increasingly in demand. In fact, this type of training tops the list of training needs for first- and middle-level managers. The development of interpersonal skills is also important for those employees who interface with the public (e.g., receptionist, sales associates).[23]

Conceptual integrative skills. Strategic and operational planning, organization design, and policy skills are needed by organizational planners as well as by top management. Adapting to complex and changing environments is often a part of top- and middle-management responsibilities, and conceptual training helps such employees to make new associations. It is at the heart of today's emphasis on creativity and entrepreneurship.

Where is the Training Conducted, and How?

Decisions also need to be made regarding where the training will take place. This decision may be constrained by the type of learning that is to occur (basic, interpersonal, or conceptual), as well as by cost and time considerations. Exhibit 12.4 summarizes the various approaches to training according to the locale of the training.

On-the-job. A frequently used approach is to train workers on the job. On-the-job training (OJT) occurs when an employee is taught a new job under the direct supervision of an experienced worker or trainer. The trainee is expected to learn the job by observing the experienced employee and by working with the actual materials, personnel, and/or machinery that comprise the job. The experienced employee/trainer is expected to provide a favorable role model and to take time from regular job responsibilities to provide job-related instruction and guidance.

One advantage of OJT is that transfer of training is high. That is, because trainees learn job skills in the environment in which they will actually work, they will be more apt to apply these skills on the job. Assuming the trainer works in the same area, the trainee receives immediate feedback about performance. However, such on-site training is appropriate only when a small number of individuals need to be trained and when the consequence of error is low. The quali-

Exhibit 12.4
A Summary of the Advantages and Disadvantages of On-the-Job, On-Site, and Off-the-Job Training Programs

On-the-Job	**Advantages**	**Disadvantages**
Job instruction training	Facilitates transfer of learning No need for separate facilities	Interferes with performance Damages equipment
Apprenticeship	No interference with real job performance Provides extensive training	Takes a long time Expensive May not be related to job
Internships or assistantships	Facilitates transfer of learning Gives exposure to real job	Not really a full job Learning is vicarious
Job rotation	Exposure to many jobs Real learning	No sense of full responsibility Too short a stay in a job
Supervisory assistance	Informal Integrated into job Inexpensive	Effectiveness rests with supervisor Not all supervisors may do it
On-Site But Not On-the-Job		
Programmed instruction	Provides for individualized learning and feedback Faster learning	Time-consuming to develop Cost effective only for large groups
Videotapes	Conveys consistent information to employees in diverse locations More portable than film	Costly to develop Don't provide for individual feedback
Videodisks	Stores more information than tapes Allows for fast forward Portable	Extremely costly to develop Courseware is limited
Interactive	Training draws on more senses Self-paced learning and feedback	Costly to develop and implement Requires diverse staff to develop
Telecommunications training	Provides for latest insights and knowledge Speeds up communications Standardized	Costly and difficult to set up Not feasible for small firms
Off-the-Job		
Formal courses	Inexpensive for many No interference with job	Require verbal skills Inhibit transfer of learning
Simulation	Helps transfer Creates lifelike situations	Can't always duplicate real situations exactly
Role playing	Good for interpersonal skills Gives insights into others	Can't create real situations exactly; still playing
Sensitivity training	Good for self-awareness Gives insights into others	May not transfer to job May not relate to job

ty of the training also hinges on the skill of the manager or lead employee conducting the training.[24]

The disadvantages of on-the-job training can be minimized by making the training program as systematic and complete as possible. **Job instruction training (JIT)** represents such a systematic technique. JIT was developed to provide a guide for giving on-the-job skill training to white- and blue-collar employees as well as technicians.[25] Because JIT is a technique rather than a program, it can be adapted to training efforts for all employees in off-the-job as well as on-the-job programs.

JIT consists of four steps: (1) careful selection and preparation of the trainer and the trainee for the learning experience to follow; (2) a full explanation and demonstration by the trainer of the job to be done by the trainee; (3) a trial on-the-job performance by the trainee; and (4) a thorough feedback session between the trainer and the trainee to discuss the trainee's performance and the job requirements.[26]

Another method for minimizing the disadvantages of on-the-job training is combining it with off-the-job training. Apprenticeship training, internships, and assistantships are based on this combination. **Apprenticeship training** is mandatory for admission to many of the skilled trades, such as plumbing, electronics, and carpentry. These programs are formally defined by the U.S. Department of Labor's Bureau of Apprenticeship and Training and involve a written agreement "providing for not less than 4,000 hours of reasonably continuous employment ... and supplemented by a recommended minimum of 144 hours per year of related classroom instruction." The Equal Employment Opportunity Commission does not prevent the nation's 48,000 skilled trade (apprentice) training programs from excluding anyone age forty to seventy because apprenticeship programs are part of the educational system aimed at youth.[27] To be most effective, the on- and off-the-job components of the apprenticeship program must be well-integrated and appropriately planned and must recognize individual differences.

Somewhat less formalized and extensive than apprenticeship training are the internship and assistantship programs. **Internships** are often part of an agreement between schools and colleges and local organizations. As with apprenticeship training, individuals in these programs earn while they learn, but at a rate that is less than that paid to full-time employees or master crafts workers. The internships, however, function as a source not only of training but also of realistic exposure to job and organizational conditions. **Assistantships** involve full-time employment and expose an individual to a wide range of jobs. However, because the individual only assists other workers, the learning experience is often vicarious. This disadvantage is eliminated by programs of job or position rotation and multiple management.[28]

Job rotation programs are used to train and expose employees to a variety of jobs and decision-making situations. Although job rotation provides employee exposure, the extent of training and long-run benefits it provides may be overstated. This is because the employees are not in a single job for a long enough period to learn very much and are not motivated to work hard because they know that they will move on in the near future. As a personal career planning strategy, you may want to avoid job rotation and opt instead for job assignments that are more fixed but that provide a greater challenge.

The final and most informal program of training and development is **supervisory assistance or mentoring.**[29] This method of training is a regular part of the supervisor's job. It includes day-to-day coaching, counseling, and monitoring of workers on how to do the job and how to get along in the organization. The effectiveness of coaching, counseling, and monitoring as a technique for training and development depends in part on whether the supervisor creates feelings of mutual confidence, provides opportunities for growth to employees, and effectively delegates tasks. Mentoring programs, in which an established employee guides the development of a less-experienced worker or "protege" can increase employees' skills, achievement, and understanding of the organization.

> At NCR Corp., proteges are usually chosen from among high-potential employees in middle or entry-level management, says James E. McElwain, vice president for personnel resources. Each executive is encouraged to select two people to mentor, and must decide how to develop the relationships, McElwain notes. Executives counsel their proteges on how to advance and network in the company, and sometimes offer personal advice, he says.[30]

On-site but not on-the-job. Another option is to conduct the training at the work site but not on the job. On-site training is appropriate for required after-hours training programs and for training programs in which contact needs to be maintained with work units but OJT would be too distracting or harmful. On-site training is also appropriate for voluntary after-hours training programs and for programs that update employees' skills while allowing them to attend to their regular duties.

For example, when a major Northeast grocery store chain switched to computerized scanners, it faced the problem of training thousands of checkers spread out across three states. The cost of training them off site was prohibitive. Yet management also was fearful about training employees on the job, lest their ineptness in learning to use the scanners would offend customers. To solve the problem, the grocery chain developed a mobile training van that included a vestibule model of the latest scanning equipment. Checkers were trained on site but off the job in the mobile unit. Once the basic skill of scanning was mastered, employees returned to the store, and the trainer remained on site as a resource person. According to one store manager, the program was effective because employees could be trained rapidly and efficiently. Yet, because the training was not conducted on the job, no customers were lost due to checker errors or slowness.

New technologies have rapidly increased the options available to organizations that want to provide on-site training. **Programmed instruction** (PI) is one of the oldest on-site training methods. Here, the instructional material is broken down into frames. Each frame represents a small component of the entire subject to be learned, and each frame must be learned successfully before going on to the next one.

An advantage of PI is that large numbers of employees can be trained simultaneously, with the learner free to explore the material at his or her own pace. Additionally, PI includes immediate and individualized feedback. The downside is that programming computers for PI is involved and time consuming. While the development of several authoring systems in the 1980s eased the burden of developing PI modules, instruction still must be carefully planned. It is estimated that one hour of programmed instruction requires fifty hours of development work. Consequently, this approach is effective only if "canned" programs (e.g., word and data-base tutorials) are used or if large numbers of employees are to be trained so that development costs for an original program can be justified.

Videotaped presentations can be used on site or off site and have generally replaced films as the visual medium of choice for organizational training. At its most basic level, video training includes taped instruction that can be stopped and stated at any point. Because videotapes are less expensive than traditional training films, their use has increased rapidly in recent years. In fact, it is estimated that organizations will spend $7 billion on video-based education in 1990.

An advantage of videotape is that instruction can be standardized. For example, Pizza Hut faced the burden of training 10,000 employees in various locales on such matters as competing with Domino's Pizza in the home delivery market, new products (e.g., pan pizza), safe driving, and customer service. Professionally prepared video presentations were mailed out to its individual locations, and the training was then provided on site to each shift of workers. Cost savings over traditional off-site or on-site training were substantial.

Organizations with large budgets for training are replacing videotapes with **videodisks.** A videodisk relies on a laser beam instead of a needle to pick up images and project them on a television screen. While more expensive to produce than simple videotape programs, videodisks provide higher-quality images, quicker starts and stops, and greater durability than do tapes. Because disks are much smaller than tapes, they are also easier to transport and utilize. The newness of videodisk technology and the lack of standardized courseware make these systems cost ineffective for small companies. Still corporations such as NCR and Kodak are relying on videodisks for training in business, computer logic, mechanics, and new technology. For example, Kodak uses videodisks to keep its scientists and engineers updated on technological advances.[31]

Interactive video training (IVT) combines the best features of PI with the best attributes of videotape and/or videodisk instruction. Interactive video programs present a short video and narrative presentation (via tape or disk) and then require the trainee to respond to it. Usually, the video program is attached to a personal computer, and the learner responds to video cues by using the keyboard or by touching the screen. This sequence—packaged program, learner response, and more programmed instruction—provides for individualized learning.

Interactive video has been used by a variety of organizations. Kodak developed an IVT system to train office personnel in the use of a new word processing system. The Kodak system relied on two computer screens. On one screen a model demonstrated how to use the software package (via videodisk); written instructions, as well as the trainee's word processing output, were displayed on the adjacent screen. Support staff could complete their training on site. If portions were forgotten, that segment could be repeated merely by walking over to the on-site training center and calling up the module of concern.

Interactive video training has been used to train 400,000 General Motors workers in occupational health and safety procedures, and it has been used to train Dow Chemical employees in how to deal with petrochemical hazards. Electrical workers have learned how to solve complex wiring problems by tracing patterns on touch-sensitive screens. The U.S. Army has found interactive video training (IVT) so effective that it installed 48,000 IVT units at army bases and had developed more than 5,000 hours of course work by 1989.[32]

One of the more elaborate IVT programs was developed by the American Heart Association to teach cardiopulmonary resuscitation (CPR). The IVT program includes a demonstration via a computer of correctly performed CPR. After observing the model and receiving verbal and written instructions, the trainee is asked to perform the same manipulations on a "computerized" dummy. Computer sensors inside the dummy record the location, intensity, and frequency of pressure applied. Consequently, rapid and accurate computer-generated feedback can be provided. In particular, the computer is programmed to provide instructions on how to perform better (e.g., apply more pressure to the left, lighter strokes, more rapid strokes). While development costs were high, CPR training time is cut in half by use of the IVT program.[33]

On the downside, development and equipment costs associated with IVT are high. Hardware alone can cost between $6,000 and $12,000 and master videodisk costs between $2,000 and $5,000. For sophisticated programs, more than 500 hours can be spent on developing one hour of interactive video training, with costs running as high as $150,000. A sizable and diverse staff is also needed to make IVT work. Instruction designers, script writers, programmers, video producers, and subject experts are all needed. Still, IVT offers fast, effective training and, as its popularity increases, IVT's development and hardware costs should drop, making IVT more affordable to small organizations.

Another innovation for on-site training involves **telecommunications training** using video satellite networks. In 1987, the Public Broadcasting System (PBS) entered the field of satellite training with the establishment of the National Narrowcast System (NNS). Produced in cooperation with the American Society for Training and Development (ASTD), the network offers more than five hours of daily programming via microwave to subscribing businesses, public agencies, and colleges and universities. Contractors are free to tape programs for six months to one year, and the system has nine training tracks targeted for specific groups (e.g., sales, supervision, computer literacy, effective communications).

The major advantage of telecommunications training is its potential for speeding up communications within large corporations. A cost study conducted by Kodak estimates that a new product training program beamed via satellite to three cities costs $20,000. However, Kodak also estimates that it would cost five to six times that amount to send engineers and managers on the road to do the same training. More important, six weeks of training time was saved, which is invaluable in a competitive industry.[34]

Off-the-job. When the consequence of error is high, it is usually more appropriate to conduct training off the job. For example, most airline passengers would readily agree that it is preferable to train pilots in flight simulators rather than have them apprentice in the cockpit of a plane. Similarly, it is usually useful to have a bus driver practice on an obstacle course before taking to the roads with a load of school children.

Off-the-job training is also appropriate when complex skills need to be mastered or when there is need to focus on specific interpersonal skills that might not be apparent in the normal work environment. For example, it is difficult to build a cohesive work team when members of management are constantly interrupted by telephone calls and subordinate inquiries. Team building is more likely to occur during a management retreat when there is time to focus on establishing relationships.

However, the costs of off-the-job training are high. There also is concern over transfer of knowledge to the work place. As research has shown, the more dissimilar the training environment is from the actual work environment, the more likely it is that trainees will *not* be able to apply knowledge learned to their jobs. For example, the transfer-of-knowledge problem is minimal for vestibule training, in which trainees work in an environment that is comparable to the actual work environment. However, it may be difficult to apply teamwork skills learned during a wilderness survival program or on a float trip down the Colorado River to a job because the training environment is dissimilar to the actual work environment.

The **formal course method** of training and development can be accomplished either by oneself—using programmed instruction, computer-assisted instruction, reading, and correspondence courses—or by others, as in formal classroom courses and lectures. Although many training programs use the lecture method because it efficiently and simultaneously conveys large amounts of information to large groups of people, it does have several drawbacks.

- It perpetuates the authority structure of traditional organizations and hinders performance because the learning process is not self-controlled.
- Except in the area of cognitive knowledge and conceptual principles, there is probably limited transfer of the actual skills and abilities required to do the job.
- The high verbal and symbolic requirements of the lecture method may be threatening to people with low verbal or symbolic aptitude.
- The lecture method does not permit individualized training based on individual differences in ability, interests, and personality.

Because of these drawbacks, the lecture method is often complemented by other training methods.

Simulation, a training and development technique that presents participants with situations that are similar to actual job conditions, is used for both managers and nonmanagers.[35] A common technique for nonmanagers is the **vestibule method,** which simulates the environment of the individual's actual job. Because the environment is not real, it is generally less hectic and more safe than the actual environment; as a consequence, the potential exists for adjustment difficulties in going from the simulated training environment to the actual environment. However, the arguments for using the simulated environment are compelling: It reduces the possibility of customer dissatisfaction that can result from on-the-job training; it can reduce the frustration of the trainee; and it may save the organization a great deal of money because fewer training accidents occur. Even though these arguments may seem compelling, not all organizations, even in the same industry, see the situation the same way. Some banks, for example, train their tellers on the job, whereas others train them in a simulated bank environment.

An increasingly popular simulation technique for managers is the **assessment center method.** This is discussed in chapter 6 as a device for selecting managers. Assessment centers are also especially useful for identifying potential training needs. Whether used for training or selection, they appear to be a valid way to make employment decisions.[36] In fact, certain aspects of the assessment center, such as the management games and in-basket exercises, are excellent for training and need not be confined to these programs.

Regardless of where they are used, **management or business games** almost always entail various degrees of competition between teams or trainees. In contrast, the **in-basket exercise** is more solitary. The trainee sits at a desk and works through a pile of papers found in the in-basket of a typical manager, prioritizing, recommending solutions to problems, and taking any necessary action in response to the contents.[37]

Although the in-basket exercise tends to be an enjoyable and challenging exercise, the extent to which it improves a manager's ability depends in part on what takes place after the exercise. The analysis of what happened and what should have happened in both the business games and the in-basket exercise, when done by upper-level managers in the organization, should help trainees learn how to perform like managers. The opportunity for improvement may be drastically reduced if the trainees are left to decide what to transfer from the game or exercise to the job.

Whereas the simulation exercises may be useful for developing conceptual and problem-solving skills, two types of **human relations** or process-oriented training are used by organizations. **Role-playing** and **sensitivity training** develop managers' interpersonal insights—awareness of self and of others—for changing attitudes and for practices in human relations skills, such as leadership or the interview.

Role-playing generally focuses on emotional (that is, human relations) issues rather than on factual ones. The essence of role-playing is to create a realistic situation, as in the case discussion method, and then have the trainees assume the parts of specific personalities in the situation. The usefulness of role-playing depends heavily on the extent to which the trainees get into the parts they are playing. If you have done any role-playing, you know how difficult this can be and how much easier it is to do what amounts to simply reading the part. However, when the trainee does get into the role, the result is a greater sensitivity to the feelings and insights that are presented by the role.

Another method of training and development is **sensitivity training.** Individuals in an unstructured group exchange thoughts and feelings on the "here and now" rather than the "there and then." Although the experience of being in a sensitivity group often gives individuals insight into how and why they and others feel and act the way they do, critics claim that these results may not be beneficial because they are not directly transferable to the job.[38]

Other methods organizations use to increase employees' feelings about the here and now and their own self-esteem include programs that involve physical feats of strength, endurance, and cooperation. These can be done on wilderness trips to the woods or mountains or even the water.

> Everyone goes overboard during strategic planning meetings of the Meridian Group. But that doesn't bother Harvey Kinzelberg, 43, chairman of the $250-million-a-year Illinois computer-leasing firm, the nation's third largest. On the contrary, he requires it. Twice a year Kinzelberg charters a boat in the Caribbean, puts his top executives aboard, and leads them in a five-day brainstorming session cum scuba-diving expedition ... As often as three times a day, the company's managers pause from strategizing, strap on air tanks and face masks, and go for a plunge in the briny.
>
> Kinzelberg claims the downward bound excursions focus his executives' attention on business by eliminating the ... distractions of the office. More important, he says, they foster team spirit ... "In the potentially life-threatening environment underwater," he explains, "you realize that you depend on everyone else in the company not just for your livelihood in business but for your life as well."

> Excursions in the deep also provide the benefits of a different perspective, says Kinzelberg ... After spearing and killing a large barracuda, as he did on a recent dive, Kinzelberg finds that the sharks he faces in business seem like small fries.[39]

MAXIMIZING TRAINEE LEARNING

Even when the training technique is appropriate, learning may not take place if the training is not structured appropriately. Exhibit 12.5 details learning factors that affect the success of training. As shown, prior to training, the environment must be made ready for learning to occur. During training, steps need to be taken to increase self-efficacy and retention of knowledge. After training, the work environment must be monitored to ensure that what was learned is retained.

Setting the Stage for Learning

Prior to launching a training program, a trainer or manager needs to consider how information will be presented. Additionally, he or she must consider the beliefs of trainees regarding task-specific competencies.

Clarity of instructions. Research has demonstrated that learning will not occur unless task instructions are clear and precise. As noted when discussing performance standards (chapters 7 and 8), an employee must know what is expected in order to perform as desired. Giving clear instructions includes establishing appropriate behavioral expectations. As with performance standards (see chapter 7), statements of training expectations should be specific, and conditions

Exhibit 12.5

Learning Principles to Increase the Effectiveness of Training

Setting the Stage for Learning

1. Provide clear task instructions.
2. Model appropriate behavior.

Increasing Learning during Training

1. Provide for active participation.
2. Increase self-efficacy.
3. Match training techniques to trainees' self-efficacy.
4. Provide opportunities for enactive mastery.
5. Ensure specific, timely, diagnostic, and practical feedback.
6. Provide opportunities for trainees to practice new behaviors.

Maintaining Performance after Training

1. Develop learning points to assist in knowledge retention.
2. Set specific goals.
3. Identify appropriate reinforcers.
4. Train significant others in how to reinforce behavior.
5. Teach trainees self-management skills.

under which performance is or is not expected (e.g., given receipt of information) should be identified, along with the behavior to be demonstrated.

To set the stage for desired performance, it is also useful to specify up front what the reward will be for performing as desired. A trainee is more likely to be motivated if he or she knows that successful performance can lead to positive reinforcement (promotion, pay raise, recognition) or can block the administration of negative reinforcement (e.g., supervisory criticism, firing).[40]

Use of behavioral models. Even when instructions are clear, desired behavior still may not occur if the trainee does not know how to perform as desired. This problem can be overcome through behavioral modeling. **Behavioral modeling** is a visual demonstration of desired behavior. The model can be a supervisor, co-worker, or subject area expert, and the demonstration can be live or videotaped. The important thing is to show employees what needs to be done *prior* to their performance.[41]

Care is needed in choosing an appropriate behavioral model. If the model makes the task look too simple, trainees may lose confidence or quit the first time they encounter a difficulty. Thus, models should show not only how to achieve desired outcomes but also how to overcome performance obstacles.

Factors Increasing Learning during Training

While employees should be responsible for their own learning, organizations can do much to facilitate this.

Active participation. Individuals perform better if they are actively involved in the learning process. Participation may be direct (hands on) or indirect (role-plays and simulations). The important point is to hook the trainee on learning. Through active participation, trainees stay more alert and are more likely to be confident.

Self-efficacy. Even with modeling, learning may not occur if people judge themselves low in self-efficacy. Self-efficacy is defined as a trainee's beliefs about a task-specific ability. If individuals dwell on their personal deficiencies relative to the task, potential difficulties may seem more formidable than they really are. On the other hand, people who have a strong sense of self-efficacy are more likely to be motivated to overcome obstacles.

The choice of an appropriate training method is critical to self-efficacy. In a recent study, a group of trainees was taught how to use computer spreadsheets. People low in self-efficacy performed better when one-on-one tutorials were conducted; individuals with high self-efficacy (they believed they could easily learn how to use spreadsheets) performed better when appropriate behavior was merely modeled. Consequently, before choosing training techniques, the level of self-efficacy for each trainee should be determined.[42]

Enactive mastery. Self-efficacy increases when experiences fail to validate fears and when skills acquired allow for mastery of once-threatening situations. This process is called enactive mastery. To facilitate task mastery, trainers should arrange the subject matter so that trainees experience success. While this may be easy when tasks are simple, it can be quite difficult when tasks are complex.

Solutions include segmenting the task, shaping behavior, and/or setting proximal goals. Task segmentation involves breaking a complex task into smaller or simpler components. For some jobs (e.g., laboratory technician), the components (e.g., drawing blood, culturing a specimen, running a blood chemistry machine) can be taught individually and in any order. In others, segments must be taught sequentially because Task B builds upon Task A and Task C builds upon Task B (e.g., using mathematics, driving a car, conducting an effective interview.)[43]

Shaping includes rewarding closer and closer approximations to desired behavior. For example, in teaching managers how to conduct a selection interview, trainees can be reinforced for making eye contact and for developing situational questions.

The setting of proximal or intermediary goals also increases mastery perceptions. Consider a software developer with an overall objective of developing a new word processing package. Proximal goals might include meeting a project specifications deadline, developing algorithms for fonts by a set deadline, developing an algorithm for formatting paragraphs, and so on. These proximal goals all lead to the attainment of the distal or overall objective.[44]

Plenty of feedback. In order for individuals to master new concepts and acquire new skills, they must receive accurate diagnostic feedback about their performance. When feedback is not received or is inaccurate, the wrong behaviors may be practiced. While feedback can be provided by a supervisor, coworkers, customers, computers, or the individual performing the task, it must be specific, timely, behaviorally and not personally based, and practical. If a performance discrepancy exists, the feedback should also be diagnostic and include instructions or modeling of how to perform better.[45]

Practice, practice, practice. While an individual may be able to perform as desired one time, the goal of training is to ensure that desired behavior occurs consistently. This is most likely to occur when trainees are able to practice and internalize standards of performance. Practicing the wrong behaviors is detrimental. Therefore, practice must follow specific feedback.

It should be stressed that, for some jobs, tasks must be overlearned. **Overlearning** includes the internalization of responses so that the trainee doesn't have to consciously think about behavior before responding. For example, if a plane is losing altitude rapidly, a pilot must know immediately how to respond. There isn't time to think about what should be done. The emergency routine must be second nature and internalized.

Maintaining Performance after Training

Once training has occurred, the environment needs to be monitored to ensure that new behaviors will continue. Several steps can be taken to ensure this.

Development of learning points. First, new skills and information are more likely to be retained when learning points are developed. Learning points summarize key behaviors—particularly those that are not obvious—and serve as cognitive cues back on the job. While learning points can be written by trainers, trainee-generated learning points—even if they are of lower quality—enhance recall and lead to better skill acquisition and retention.[46]

Reinforcement. Learning new behaviors is difficult and threatening. To ensure that trainees continue to demonstrate the skill they have learned, behavior must be reinforced. Reinforcement can be positive (praise, financial rewards) or negative (if you perform as desired, I will quit screaming at you), but it must be performance contingent.[47]

Train significant others. To ensure that reinforcers are appropriately administered, trainers must also train significant others to look for and reinforce desired changes. If a person labeled a troubled employee continues to be viewed as a problem employee, there is no incentive for the person to display new behavior. If, however, a supervisor or co-worker responds positively to the change in behavior, the frequency with which the new behavior will be displayed is likely to increase.

Set specific goals. It is also useful to set specific goals for subsequent performance. These goals should be challenging but not so difficult as to be perceived as impossible. Without goals, people have little basis for judging how they are doing.[48]

Self-reinforcement. Because it is not always possible for significant others to reinforce an individual worker, a long-term objective should be to teach employees how to set their own goals and administer their own reinforcement. When people create self-incentives for their efforts, they are capable of making self-satisfaction contingent on their own performance. Obviously, the challenge here is to ensure that personal goals are congruent with organizational goals. As noted in previous chapters, this leads to self-management.[49]

Follow-up. A final principle to remember is follow-up. Once a participant leaves the training program, the personnel and human resource manager should provide a means of follow-up to help ensure that the participant will do what was taught. All too often, participants who want to change their current behavior get back to work and slip into the old patterns. This in turn results in a significant loss of effectiveness of the training program. One approach to help prevent this from happening is the **contract plan.** Its simplicity is a key factor in its success. Each participant writes an informal agreement near the end of a training program, stating which aspects of the program he or she believes will have the most beneficial effect back on the job and then agreeing to apply those aspects. Each participant is also asked to choose another participant from the program to whom a copy of the contract is given and who agrees to check up on the participant's progress every few weeks.

Although incorporating these principles of learning is desirable, many training and development programs do not have them or are designed without considering individual differences, motivation, learning curves and plateaus, and without reinforcement, feedback, and goal setting. Nevertheless, application of these principles of learning can increase the chances of successfully implementing a training and development program. Successful implementation also depends on selecting where the program is conducted.

ASSESSING TRAINING AND DEVELOPMENT PROGRAMS

The assessment of training and development programs is a necessary and useful activity, as illustrated in the Focus on Research: "Goals for Learning: Help or Hinderance?" Without an evaluation of results, it is impossible to tell if a training and development program met its objectives.

Assessment Criteria

Many ways of evaluating training and development programs have been proposed. Among the many options are changes in productivity, attitude survey results (covering, for example, satisfaction with supervisor, job satisfaction, stress, role conflict, and knowledge of work procedures), cost savings, benefit gains, and attitudes toward training.[50]

While different evaluation methods have been proposed through the years, most training experts agree that evaluation should include at least four components:

1. *Reaction to Training*. Did the trainees like the program? Was the instruction clear and helpful? Do they believe that they learned the material?
2. *Learning*. Did they acquire the knowledge and skills that were taught? Can they talk about things they couldn't talk about before? Can they demonstrate appropriate behaviors in training (role-play)?
3. *Behavior or Performance Change*. Can trainees now do things they couldn't do before (e.g., negotiate, conduct an appraisal interview)? Can they demonstrate new behaviors on the job? Is performance on the job better?
4. *Produce Results*. Were there tangible results in terms of productivity, cost savings, response time, quality, or quantity of job performance? Did the training program have utility?

The choice of criteria hinges on the level at which the training evaluation is to be conducted. For example, a short attitude survey could be used to assess the response of trainees to the course. However, such a survey would not provide information regarding learning, behavior, and results. In fact, when learning has been stressful or difficult, the trainees' reaction may even be negative.

If the objective is to assess what was learned, then paper-and-pencil tests can be used to determine knowledge acquisition. Additionally, it is possible to analyze the content of responses to such training exercises as in-basket tests, role-plays, or case analyses. While this may indicate that learning has occurred, it will not reveal whether learning has been transferred to the job.

To assess whether behavior or performance has changed, output measures, performance evaluation reports, and employee attitude surveys provide better information. For example, if employees report more positive attitudes toward supervisory communications *after* they complete an interpersonal skills program, it may be deduced (assuming other hypotheses can be ruled out) that the training resulted in behavioral change. Finally, bottom-line results might be assessed by examining work-group or unit output measures or by conducting a utility analysis, which will be discussed in depth in chapter 14.

FOCUS ON RESEARCH

Goals for Learning: Help or Hindrance?

With rapid changes in technologies and the gap between the skills needed by employers and those available in the workforce growing wider, organizations will be spending more resources than ever before on training. To maximize their ability to compete, employers will be looking for the best training methods available. What are the ideal training conditions for teaching adults new skills? Do individual differences in basic abilities levels influence the learning process? Specific and difficult goals are known to encourage good performance on tasks that people are familiar with, and they are used frequently as part of management-by-objectives. Can goals be used effectively to speed the learning process as well?

These questions were addressed in experiments involving 1,010 U.S. Air Force trainees. The task for these trainees was to learn Air Traffic Control. Using a simulator, they practiced landing DC10s, prop planes, 747s and 727s. To do the task well, trainees had to learn to manage four runways, 12 different hold patterns, and a queue stack of planes requesting permission to land. As they were learning, wind speeds, wind directions, and ground conditions (e.g., icy, wet, dry) changed randomly. Performance scores reflected how many planes landed safely, how many rule violations occurred, and how many planes ran out of fuel and crashed.

To study how goals influenced learning, goals were set at different stages of their learning. In the first experiment, trainees with no goals were compared to those given a specific and difficult goal very early in their training, when they were simply trying to understand the task and the rules. The early goals had no positive effect on performance, and there was some indication that they interfered with learning. In the second experiment, goals were set later in the learning sequence, after trainees understood the task but while they were still honing their skills. These later goals proved to be effective: Trainees with difficult goals landed more planes safely. These results suggested that goals influence learning of complex tasks differently depending on when they are set. If they are set too early, they can interfere with performance because they detract attention from the task at hand. Instead of focusing on the task, people spend too much time monitoring their behavior. For complex tasks, it appears to be better to set performance goals later in the learning process, after trainees have mastered some of the basic skills but while they are practicing to achieve higher levels of performance. At this stage, additional performance improvement depends mostly on skills practice rather than on cognitive activity. This means that the monitoring behaviors that people engage in when they are trying to achieve a difficult goal do not interfere with performance at this stage of learning. Finally, a third study found that the beneficial effects of goals were greater for low-ability trainees than for high-ability trainees. This suggests that to deliver effective training programs, trainers need to take into account the basic abilities of trainees and the trainees' learning stage, especially if they set goals for trainees. If trainers ignore these factors, they may inadvertently create conditions that actually interfere with the learning process.

SOURCE: Based on R. Kanfer and P. L. Ackerman, "Motivation and Cognitive Abilities: An Integrative/Aptitude-Treatment Interaction Approach to Skill Acquisition," *Journal of Applied Psychology* 74 (1989), 657–90.

Evaluation Designs

In addition to determining the appropriate criteria to evaluate the program, the personnel and human resource manager must select an evaluation design. Evaluation designs are important because they help the personnel manager determine if improvements have been made and if the training program caused the improvements. In addition to aiding in the evaluation of training programs, evaluation designs can (1) aid in evaluating any personnel and human resource program to improve productivity and the quality of work life and (2) aid in evaluating the effectiveness of any personnel and human resource activity. Combining the data collection tools (i.e., organizational surveys) discussed in chapter 14 with knowledge of evaluation designs is essential for human resource departments to demonstrate their effectiveness—and that of specific programs and activities—to the rest of the organization. Because the combination of data collection and evaluation design is vital for the human resource department, evaluation design is discussed in more detail here. Review the assessment sections of all the other chapters to see how these evaluation designs might be used with data collection techniques to help measure personnel and human resource effectiveness.

The three major classes of evaluation designs are pre-experimental, quasi-experimental, and experimental.[51] Although each can be used to evaluate the effectiveness of a human resource program, it is preferable to use the **experimental design,** which is the most rigorous. Evaluation using the experimental design allows the training manager to be more confident that

- A change has taken place—for example, that employee productivity has increased;
- The change is caused be the program or human resource activity; and
- A similar change could be expected if the program were done again with other employees.

Because of many organizational constraints, however, the training manager is generally not able to use the experimental design and must settle for a moderately rigorous **quasi-experimental design.** Even when quasi-experimental designs are feasible, most evaluations that are done rely on the **pre-experimental design.** This design is used often because it is easier and quicker. Unfortunately, this design is a poor one for most purposes. Exhibit 12.6 illustrates all three designs. This exhibit is also used to convey how programs can be evaluated using these designs and what is required. In exhibit 12.6, X indicates that the program was administered. T_1 indicates that a measure is taken of the variable against which the program is to be evaluated (e.g., productivity or the level of accidents). T_2 indicates that a second measure is taken on the same variable after training has occurred. Then the results of T_1 and T_2 are compared. Note that the two designs in the experimental class are different from those in the other two classes because all the individuals used in the evaluation are randomly assigned. Thus, if there are differences between T_1 and T_2, the training manager can be more confident that the changes were due to the program (X) and that the results can be repeated in future programs.

As indicated, although using the experimental design is desirable, many organizations find it difficult to randomly assign employees to training programs. Organizations generally want all employees in a section trained, not just a few who are randomly selected. Consequently, the pre-experimental design is more typical of the type of evaluations that organizations use.

FOCUS ISSUES IN TRAINING AND DEVELOPMENT

As with other human resource activities, two important focus issues are evident in training and development. One is the trend to establish company schools to provide specific education to employees. The other relates to the strategic importance of training and development.

Exhibit 12.6
The Three Major Classes of Evaluation Designs Used to Help Determine Program Effectiveness

Pre-experimental	Quasi-experimental	Experimental
1. One-shot case study design X T_2	1. Time-series design $T_1T_2T_3$ X $T_4T_5T_6$	1. Pretest/post-test control group design T_1 X T_2 T_1 T_2
2. One-group pretest/post-test design T_1 X T_2	2. Nonequivalent control groups T_1 X T_2 T_1 T_2	2. Solomon four-group design T_1 X T_2 T_1 T_2 X T_2 T_2

SOURCE: Based on I. Goldstein, *Training: Program Development and Evaluation*, 2d ed. (Monterey, Calif.: Brooks/Cole Publishing Company, 1986), 157–67.

Company Schools and Executive Development

Company schools focus on the education of employees and sometimes customers. McDonald's Hamburger University, which was begun in 1961, is among the oldest corporate universities. Started in a basement, the center now trains more than 2,500 students annually in the fine details of restaurant and franchise operations. General Electric, which has been an advocate of training and development for years, has an up-to-date facility in Croton-on-Hudson, New York, that it uses for divisional and group training. Corporate schools have also been developed by such diverse firms as AT&T, Ford Motor Company, United Airlines, Chase Manhattan, Kodak, and Digital Equipment.

Motorola dedicated its $10-million Galvin Center for Continuing Education in 1986. The facility contains 88,000 square feet of classrooms, individual instruction centers, an auditorium, lounges, dining facilities, and a fitness center. Affiliated with the National Technological Union, a consortium that teaches by satellite, Motorola offers courses leading to three master's degrees.

More recently, Motorola opened Motorola University, where it spends $24 million a year to teach Total Quality Management (TQM) to its own employees. They also teach TQM to faculty from business and engineering schools.[52]

Like a growing number of corporations, Motorola is committed to company-based education. In fact, recent research suggests that sixty-five percent of all major firms offer some form of executive education. In 1985, eighteen corporate colleges offered degrees, and hundreds of other corporations had course offerings leading to degrees.

Many firms are now affiliated with the National Technological Institute of Fort Collins, Colorado, which provides training for engineers via satellite transmission. Professionals from leading universities, such as Georgia Tech, Boston University, and MIT, teach classes at twenty-four cooperating colleges of engineering. The companies involved provide courses both live and on tape to suit the convenience of the students. Students interact with instructors via teleconferencing and electronic mail.

Returning to the opening story on the Weyerhaeuser Corporation, we have another example of company schools. Within FPC, chief executive Charles Bingham, and his executive team, along with the director of strategic education, Horace Parker, decided that a major strategic repositioning was going to be made using executive development.

> To meet this need, the executive team took a risk. They decided to revitalize a complex organization. In 1986, the FPC Executive Team launched the Leadership Institute.
>
> How the organization was sold on the worth of an executive development program is an important lesson. The trump card used in closing the deal was to involve the executives at various levels of the organization in the planning stages. During those stages, they came to see, as did the executive team, that an intensive development program such as the Leadership Institute was not an expensive frill but a prerequisite for survival. The Leadership Institute, top management was convinced, would be a powerful catalyst that could accelerate the normal process of change—of everything from a corporate culture to how a salesperson deals with customers.[53]

Working with others in human resource management and the top management team, FPC instituted a leadership institute where managers could come to discuss the new strategy and its implications for them. In addition, the institute offers training to managers to help them acquire needed skills, knowledge, and leadership styles. Thus far, this major change at FPC appears to be on track to meet its goal for 1995. Success clearly has been due in large measure to the quality of the human resource management activities and to the skilled leadership of those at the company.

In summing up the future in corporate education, some business educators speculate that advanced and specialized training will be a way of life for the careerist of the future. While some company schools will concentrate on the operational mechanics of the business they operate, others will provide more general management education, even global education. Almost without exception the charges for training will be paid for by the home organization of the trainees, making corporate education a business within a business.[54]

Linking with the Needs of Customers

Organizations can use their training and development activities to link with the needs of customers. For example,

> ... designing, manufacturing and operating increasingly complex high-technology systems demands advanced knowledge and hands-on expertise. That's why Siemens—one of the world's leading manufacturers of high-technology equipment—conducts a variety of training programs for many of its 27,000 employees, as well as for its customers, all across America.
>
> Siemens USA courses are designed to meet the special needs of customers and their markets. For example, on-the-job training for customers ensures that all the capabilities of the company's technologically advanced systems are fully utilized, and all their benefits are fully realized. Similarly, the special classes for Siemens engineering, manufacturing, service and administrative personnel are designed to sharpen skills, enhance professional knowledge, and improve service expertise and effectiveness.
>
> Constant, specialized training is one of the ways Siemens is fulfilling their commitment to keep customers and employees ahead of the competition in a fiercely changing, tough and complex high-technology marketplace.[55]

IN THE NEWS PHRM

Making Dreams Come True

Walt Disney said that it takes people to make a dream come true—dreamers as well as doers—and he founded Disney University (Anaheim, CA) as a place for developing Disney people. When Disneyland was launched in 1955, its creator wanted customers to feel like invited guests. Disney believed in training staff people to have good guest relations practices—and Disney pioneered a highly successful concept.

Today, guest relations programs in service companies are common—and Disney is working to build on its experience to maintain its service edge. Disney University continues to play a key role in this process, with its focus on "cast members," Disney's term for employees who are expected to play their part, and play it well.

"Disney University serves multiple functions," Bill Ross, manager, Disney University, said. "HR planning and development, cast communications (internal publications, formal communication programs), cast activities (social, recreational, and interpersonal communication programs), and audio visual programs are all handled out of the University.

"Each Disneyland unit has a dotted line relationship to Disney U, so that we can provide centralized hr services, yet have a strong link to individual entities. At Disneyland, we have about 6,000 employees.

International Focus

"Putting together our PHRM planning group is one of our newest hr efforts. Within the last two years, we've computerized information on our salaried employee population so that we can submit the criteria for a particular position, and generate the names of candidates through the computer. This system has also allowed us to pinpoint some of our development needs.

"We've found this capability particularly helpful since we've launched Tokyo Disneyland and our Euro-Disney project.

"We relocated about 200 executives to Japan—some for short stays, some for long. Given the expanded scope of our operations, we need to know all we can about the talent we have to draw on.

"We've been focusing on our need to become more internationalized. We are undertaking extensive training of Japanese managers, and our managers in the U.S., so that we can better understand cultural issues. We know that we can cross cultural lines—but we want to understand the issues to enhance our chances for success. We have established an International Fellowship with that goal in mind.

"We've also worked on providing a support system for those who return to the U.S. after a tour abroad. We recognize them for their efforts, we lis-

Continued

Similarly, in the low-margin, highly competitive world of department-store sales,

> Seattle-based Nordstrom has turned exacting standards of customer service into a billion-dollar annual business. The rapidly expanding chain, which has 46 stores in California, Washington, Oregon, Alaska, Montana and Utah, has drilled its staff incessantly with the venerable dogma that the customer is always right. Result: the chain's sales, 73% derived from women's retailing, passed the $1 billion mark for the first time in 1985 and reached an estimated $1.6 billion for 1986. Sales per square foot of space, a basic retail performance yardstick, is about double the average for the industry.
>
> A major ingredient in Nordstrom's success is the quality of the salesclerks. They are paid about 20% better than those of competitors, and they are well trained and encouraged to do almost anything within reason to satisfy customers. In Seattle, a store salesclerk personally ironed a customer's newly bought shirt so that it would look fresher for an upcoming meeting. Thomas Skidmore, vice president of a Los

ten to their descriptions of their experiences, and we review what took place here while they were gone. After all, they are not returning to the same organization that they left—things change. And the manager who has served abroad has changed, too.

"We make every effort to reinforce the whole fabric of the organization. For example, when Epcot Center was launched in 1982, the dedication ceremonies were telecast here in Anaheim—and shared with all sites.

Guest Courtesy—Inside Disney

"We believe that, for our cast members to treat our guests in a friendly and helpful way, they themselves must be treated that way. We look at guest courtesy as something that must extend to those within the organization, too.

"When cast members join Disneyland, they are treated as VIP's—they are personally greeted, and everyone is on a first-name basis. We reinforce good guest relations through our orientation process, training, performance appraisal system, and we circulate guest compliments and complaints. Our biggest challenge is to stay in touch with the changing values of both our guests and our cast members.

"We look at how our guests define service—both first-time visitors and repeat visitors. We look at the environment itself, since elements such as temperature have a definite effect on people's perceptions of their experience. We encourage those behind the scenes to be conscious of courtesy, too—for example, we have a campaign called "Put a Smile in your Voice" that emphasizes telephone courtesy. And for our Christmas party, cast members and their families come to the park—and management mans the park for that day. Cast members experience the park as a guest—and management experiences the cast members' jobs. There is a management program that focuses on guest courtesy, as well.

"We have a two-person team whose sole job is to evaluate the level of courtesy that exists in the organization. We poll guests daily, and circulate results.

"We show examples of good and bad guest relations in our training program, based on the information we gather. We teach cast members to understand outcomes—their goal is to focus on what they want the guests to experience. There are many ways to get to that goal—but the end result is what counts.

"Our training teaches them to enhance skills to initiate a relationship, to take the first step in approaching guests who might look puzzled or in need of help. In the service business, we are fortunate to get a second chance when something goes wrong: a guest may have an unfortunate experience in the ticketline, but a helpful interchange in a restaurant that helps compensate. We want to avoid the first mistake—but make sure we take advantage of all opportunities for a second chance."

SOURCE: "Making Dreams Come True," *HR Reporter* (Jan. 1987), 2–3. Used with permission from *HR Reporter*.

> Angeles—area real estate brokerage, tells of bringing back a squeaky pair of year-old shoes to a local Nordstrom outlet, hoping merely for repairs. Instead, he got a new pair of shoes free.[56]

While this description of the salesclerks might imply an endorsement by everyone concerned of Nordstrom's ability to manage its human resources, some, including union representatives, have suggested that Nordstrom's methods are not without fault.

Training in Business Ethics

In a recent survey of more than 1,000 members of the American Management Association,

> Seventy-three percent of managers surveyed said they probably would resign if their boss insisted that they carry out some action they strongly believed was unethical.

> This percentage is a decrease from the almost 80 percent of managers who responded the same way in 1981.
>
> Most of the recent participants agreed that corporate codes of ethics and ethics workshops were helpful to understand issues and help guide them through their daily decision making. However, more than three-quarters of these managers noted that their companies did not offer such workshops. Almost half said that their firms did not have a written code of ethics.[57]

As more companies recognize the need for promoting moral excellence, however, they have started providing training in ethical behavior. For example, Chemical Bank has included ethics discussions in its training programs. According to Karen Alphin, employee communications director, Chemical Bank's "Decision-Making and Corporate Values" program addresses issues that are of interest not just to bankers but also to ethical individuals. Convinced of the need for "a conversation about ethics," Polaroid Corporation set up a major internal conference that brought philosophers, ethicists, and business professors to the company for lectures and discussions of ethical concepts.[58]

As the need for ethical behavior increases, more organizations may reconsider their training programs and offer courses in ethics. When this happens, the first program participants are likely to be the managers and supervisors:

> As in the earlier study, today's managers reported that the actions of their supervisors were the most important factors that influenced ethical and unethical behavior. "Managers set the ethical tone for our organization" was an almost unanimous refrain. About one-third of surveyed managers agreed that their bosses engaged in unethical behaviors and noted that their bosses were less concerned about ethics than they were.[59]

In addition to more training programs in ethics, we are also apt to see more programs for globalizing.

INTERNATIONAL ASPECTS OF TRAINING AND DEVELOPMENT

Managing for Globalization

> A few things seem certain, and one is that "globalization" will continue to be an inescapable buzzword. Businesses will operate in an ever more interconnected world. With continuing advances in computers and communications, world financial markets will meld. Manufacturing prowess will appear almost suddenly in new Taiwans and South Koreas.
>
> A shrinking world will mean an expanding clock. Managers will have to shape organizations that can respond quickly to developments abroad. As speed and agility become paramount virtues, we will see even more decentralization, with responsibility closer to the operating level.[60]

Organizations are having to develop a world or global structure and perspective. Human resource policies need to mirror the necessary organizational characteristics. According to E. Jeffrey Stoll, director of Merck's corporate personnel relations,

> Because 50% of our business is from overseas, we must be globally competitive in terms of human resources, internationally and domestically. If not, then we won't be where we want to be five years from now.[61]

Expatriate, third-country, and host-country human resource policies must be articulated to create a worldwide work force. The expatriate assignment increasingly needs to be made an attractive one for the best employees to pursue. Assignments anywhere have to be seen as vital components of the whole. According to Jerry Junkins, the CEO of Texas Instruments, overseas managers must look beyond their own fiefdoms to consider the capabilities and needs of the company as a whole. Junkins now has all the members of the company's worldwide management group working together. TI's worldwide strategy meetings

> ... ensure that the company knows enough about its customers' needs to invest in the manufacturing technologies that will satisfy the greatest numbers of buyers, no matter where they come from. The strategy seems to be working: After steep losses in 1985, TI has posted seven consecutive quarters of profit. In the troubled semiconductor business, that counts as a win.[62]

Expatriate training. The training and development of expatriates (U.S. citizens working abroad for a U.S. company) presents special problems. Management development of expatriates should take up where selection leaves off. Although only a few companies provide expatriate training, it is critical. The basic aspects of expatriate development include the following:

- Development of expatriates before, during, and after foreign assignments
- Orientation and training of expatriate families before, during, and after foreign assignments
- Development of the headquarters staff responsible for the planning, organization, and control of overseas operations[63]

This range of training is aimed at bringing about attitudinal and behavioral changes in the expatriates, their families, and the staff (here and abroad) responsible for the multinational operations.

One form of training that is regarded as useful for expatriate preparation is cross-cultural training.

> Cross-cultural training is perhaps the main growth area in the training field, and more and more companies include it as a part of predeparture programs. The primary beneficiaries of this new emphasis on cross-cultural training are departing executives themselves. But companies stress that spouses and children may benefit as much or even more than executives from this type of instruction, since it is they who are "out" in the local community daily and need to be sensitive to and knowledgeable about the culture. In contrast, most of an executive's time is spent in the somewhat insulated office environment. Therefore, more and more companies have begun offering the training to families as well as executives.[64]

Although important, the number of expatriates in any one firm is limited. Thus, many firms offering cross-cultural training use outside vendors.

> Cross-cultural programs usually take the form of a three-to-five-day immersion course in the assigned country's values, customs and traditions. Although a few companies ... teach these courses themselves, more often than not (and especially in the US) firms use outside consultants for such instruction. Most consultants have a basic training module for each country, which they tailor to a client company's particular requirements. [The consulting firm of] Moran, Stahl & Boyer, ... for example, begins

with a basic program, which becomes more specific depending on client needs. Its three-day predeparture program covers everyday life in the country in question, area studies, doing business in the country, the role of women in the foreign culture, as well as culture shock and the stress executives and their families are likely to experience. Sessions make use of nationals of the country and are designed to prepare executives and their families for situations they will actually encounter.[65]

By having such an extensive management development effort for expatriates, multinational companies can help increase the effectiveness of their expatriate managers. Such a program can also increase the likelihood of getting more domestic managers to apply for expatriate positions. To really make expatriate positions attractive, however, multinational companies must also offer commensurate salaries.[66] This in turn makes is expensive for these companies to have expatriate managers. For example, it would currently cost a company almost $200,000 a year to maintain an expatriate manager in Japan, whereas such a middle-level manager would earn about $60,000 at home. In addition to providing an attractive salary to expatriate managers, multinational companies also need to provide an attractive package of indirect compensation, including such things as 401(k) plans.[67]

Although the selection and development of expatriate managers is a large and expensive undertaking, doing both well can help multinational companies operate and compete more effectively abroad; and, as the economies of nations become more interconnected, it becomes increasingly necessary for companies, especially those in the United States, to operate as multinational firms. Hence, the importance of expatriate development will continue to grow, for international as well as for domestic reasons.

International Comparisons

Training in Japan. Given the "policy" of lifetime employment in Japan, training is a vital aspect of Japanese corporate strategy. Recall that employees are promoted within the company; consequently, their jobs change, as do the products and the technology associated with production; so education is necessary. This thought is expressed at Hitachi in the following phrase: "The essence of enterprise is people." "Matushita produces capable people before it produces products," is another phrase that reflects the emphasis on training.[68]

Trainees can be categorized under three headings: (1) newly hired employees, (2) general employees, and (3) managers. One of the reasons Japanese companies prefer to hire only new school graduates is that a virgin work force can be readily assimilated into each company's unique environment as a community. This assimilation process begins with a lecture by the owner of the corporation wherein the owner attempts to instill in the new recruits the corporate philosophy and objectives. Almost always the message is evident: "We are in this together." The phrase comes from the Japanese phrase *ichiren takusho,* and it has taken on the meaning that, for better or worse, people must work together and share the same fate.

On-the-job training is intensive, taking the forms of apprenticeship and lectures. The length of training varies from company to company, but the norm is from three to eight months. In Matushita, the orientation and training of new employees from universities take place in the head office, and the schedule is as follows:

- Lectures in the head office (3 weeks)
- Training in retail stores (3 months)
- Training in production (1 month)
- Lectures on cost accounting (1 month)
- Lectures on marketing (2 months)[69]

Trainees are encouraged to voice their opinions. Mistakes are viewed as part of the learning process; avoiding recurrence is what matters. In on-the-job training, teaching is done by example, and initiative is encouraged; often the new employee is given full responsibility for a small project.

One of the best uses of on-the-job training is demonstrated by Fujitsu, the computer manufacturer. It recruits engineers from top universities and immediately places them in the design division to design large mainframe computers. After two or three years in the design division, these young engineers are transfered to the manufacturing division to produce the computers they themselves designed. Then, after three or more years in manufacturing, these engineers are sent out as systems engineers or engaged in technical sales to operate, service, and sell the computers they designed and manufactured.[70]

The advantage of this training is quite obvious. These engineers are involved with the product from beginning to end. They are best equipped to manufacture, sell, and service the product because, quite simply, they know the computer inside and out; and the feedback they get from customers in the form of complaints helps them to design better machines.

Job rotation (in-company) is yet another method Japanese companies use for training and development of people. Unlike the typical short-term programs for job rotation common in the U.S., in Japan job rotation is a process that continues until retirement, and promotes flexibility in the work force. It also helps develop the middle or upper managers into "generalists" with broader perspectives on the experience of the company's business and with wider human contacts and friendships that are vital for generating consensus. For example, Toyota's policy is to rotate employees once every three years; Canon has an implicit policy of choosing the head of a section from among those members of staff that have served in at least three different departments.

The merits of this type of employee developmental strategy include:

1. It enables the firm to reassign production and office workers more freely.
2. Japanese employees (because of their job security) are more receptive to organizational changes and the introduction of new technology or machinery.
3. Wider experience within the firm tends to nurture the goals of the total firm, rather than those of specific subunits.
4. It can produce high-quality managers. The job rotation system allows an employee to build wider interpersonal relationships that may result in freer information exchange.[71]

Furthermore, it should be pointed out that a socialization and re-socialization process occurs at each point of entry for the employee whether he/she be a new employee or transferring from another department. This socialization process is usually supplemented by off-the-job training in the form of technical training and language classes. Managers are trained mainly by this method, and the primary purpose of this instruction is to improve one's skills in negotiation, leadership, human relations, and conceptual skills. These classes are sponsored both by the divisions and by the head offices.[72]

Training in Germany. Germany is one of the world's largest exporting nations. Its economy is based upon providing high-priced, high-quality goods. German executives say a key factor in their industrial success is a sophisticated work force. "You need highly qualified people when you produce high-quality goods," says Hans-Peter Kassai, chief economist with Daimler-Benz.[73]

A relatively unique feature of training and development for employees in Germany is an extensive and successful apprenticeship system. The three-and-a-half-year apprenticeship program gives employees wide expertise on many machines. The program costs about $15,000 per apprentice and, each year, German companies spend about $20 billion on their programs. Apprenticeship training for almost a half million German students begins at age fifteen when compulsory schooling ends. At that point, youths select one of several programs. By comparison, in the U.S. many machine operators receive just a week or two of training.[74]

Even though the programs are costly, German firms believe apprenticeship pays off because workers end up being more loyal. Once apprentices become permanent employees, they often stay for years, giving stability and maturity to the work force.

SUMMARY

Rapidly changing technology, illiteracy, and foreign competition are putting pressure on organizations to train effectively. This requires careful attention to the three phases of training and development: assessment, program development and implementation, and evaluation. The four types of needs analysis (organizational, job, person, and demographic) discussed in this chapter are designed to systematically diagnose the short- and long-term human resource needs of an organization. When there is a difference between actual performance and desired performance, there is a training need.

Following effective needs analysis, a training program must be designed and implemented. In setting up a training program, there are legal considerations issues to consider as described in chapter 3. Decisions on who will be trained, who will train, and where the training will occur must be made before an appropriate training method can be selected. Cost considerations, coupled with the types of skills to be acquired (basic, interpersonal, or conceptual) and the location of the training (on-the-job, on-site, or off-the-job), have important effects on selection of an appropriate training method.

Regardless of the method chosen, the content of the training should be designed to maximize learning. Factors to consider include clear instructions, proper role models, active participation, feedback, and practice. These should be viewed in relationship to the trainees' self-efficacy or competency beliefs. It is also important to examine the work environment to ensure that new behaviors will be reinforced rather than punished.

The last major phase of training and development is the evaluation phase. Not only should the reaction to training be assessed, but also the degree of learning, the change in job behavior, and organizational outcomes should be examined against program objectives. Research design principles should guide the evaluation process.

Regarding the future of training and development, new technology in training is making it possible to train more individuals faster and more effectively. To provide specialized training needed in today's technologically oriented environment, companies are establishing their own corporate schools. Topics of growing importance include linking training to the needs of the business, ethics, globalization, and cross-cultural understanding.

Now that organizations recognize the need for more than just individual training and development, they are designing and implementing programs for total organizational improvement, the topic of the next chapter.

WHERE WE ARE TODAY

1. Increasingly, organizations such as Wal-Mart see training and development as a key to gaining and sustaining a competitive advantage—that is, surpassing and staying ahead of their competitors.
2. As firms seek to shake off their more traditional models of management and styles of leadership, they realize it takes a major commitment from top management for management training programs to succeed.
3. For two reasons, organizations are taking a larger role in the educational system of America and in the training and retraining of their employees. First, the educational system is failing to prepare a sufficiently qualified work force for most firms' needs. Second, firms keep changing and adapting new technologies and strategies that require different skills and abilities.
4. Because events and conditions are changing so rapidly, it is imperative for companies to anticipate their job and skill needs and then immediately begin to design the necessary training and development programs.
5. As organizations seek to utilize more team-based approaches to management, they will offer more training programs to develop individuals' group interaction skills.
6. Similarly, as firms realize the necessity for adopting total quality management programs, they will offer more training programs in statistical process control, group decision making, problem solving skills, and problem identification and diagnosis.
7. Training and development is a major business in the U.S. Many consulting firms can provide training and development to organizations. Companies, however, need to be sure they are paying for what they really need.
8. As with other human resource activities, a systematic approach to designing, implementing, and evaluating training and development programs helps increase the chances of success.
9. Ethics in business is becoming a more widely discussed issue in our society. As this continues, we are likely to see more firms roll out training programs in ethics.
10. As the globalization trend continues, firms will pay more attention to the training and development needs of their third-country and host-country nationals as well as their expatriates.

DISCUSSION QUESTIONS

1. Describe and explain the three major phases of any training and development program.
2. How do companies decide whether to invest in training? What factors would influence a company not to invest in training?
3. Reflect for a moment on your own work experience. What benefits did your former (or present) employer receive by training you? Why didn't your employer just hire someone who could perform the job without training?
4. What legal considerations influence training and development decisions? How can training and development programs avoid potential legal problems? (Review chapter 3 for a legal refresher.)
5. What relationships do training and development have with other activities of human resource management?
6. What design principles can enhance the learning that takes place in training and development programs?
7. As a first-line supervisor, what indicators would you need in order to decide whether a low-performing subordinate was a selection mistake or merely in need of training? Can you illustrate this dilemma with an example from your own organizational experience?
8. Discuss the strategic role of training and development activities.
9. You have been asked to train employees to use personal computers. What factors would you consider in designing the program?
10. Why do organizations often overlook or lack proper evaluation of employee training and development programs?

APPLIED PROJECTS

1. Describe a job experience in which you had to improve or master a certain skill or behavior. Describe: (a) the learning process or training situation through which mastery was or was not gained; (b) whether and how the process was facilitated by the learning principles presented in this chapter; and (c) which, if any, of the learning principles was more or less important during the learning experience.
2. Evaluation of a college or university course represents an important aspect of training. Develop a set of questions to facilitate evaluation of this course.

CASE STUDY

Walton Memorial Hospital: Starting Up the Training Activity

Dennis Springer sat at his desk looking at the notes he'd scrawled on a yellow legal pad. Today was his first day on the job. He marveled at his emotions: they seemed to vacillate between total exhilaration and stark terror. He could hardly believe he'd finally landed a job for which he'd earned a degree, yet he wondered if he could accomplish what Walton management wanted him to do. As a matter of fact, he wasn't totally sure management knew what it wanted.

Dennis was the new training manager at Walton Memorial Hospital, a primary care hospital with 257 patient beds. Affiliated with the hospital were an onsite outpatient clinic and four small clinics located in outlying rural communities. The hospital and clinics combined to employ a work force of approximately 1,100 employees.

Dennis began his training at Oregon State University, where he completed a teaching degree. He then went to the University of Utah, where he studied human resource management, completing a master's degree. During his last year at the university, Dennis picked up an internship working part time for Linda McAlisster, training manager with the university's Personnel Office.

While Dennis had never really thought about a career in training, he found it fit well with his teaching background, and Linda was a wonderful mentor, involving him in all aspects of the training process. It is often difficult for new graduates to break into the training field. However, because of his hands-on experience at the university, Dennis had been successful in landing the position at Walton Memorial.

Medical inservice training for nursing personnel had been conducted at Walton Memorial for a number of years. However, management and general employee training represented new endeavors. "I'm really excited about starting up my own program," thought Dennis. "It's nice not to be locked into someone else's system."

Dennis's most pressing challenge at present was determining where to begin. "I've learned that effective training must have a purpose and should focus on real training needs," he thought. "What should my major objectives be? What are the most pressing needs?" On the legal pad in front of him, he began to write down some of the things he'd learned about Walton Memorial during the selection process that resulted in his hiring.

Walton Memorial Hospital had a long and rich history, spanning over one hundred years. Its founder, Dr. Benjamin Walton, was a country doctor, known for his kindness and his "unusual gift" for healing. In the post–Civil War years, students came from as far away as Europe to study with Dr. Walton.

Management's decision to hire a training manager was triggered by events of the previous year. The health care industry was rapidly changing. Declining levels of Medicare reimbursement combined with rising health care costs to bring Walton Memorial its first financial crisis since the Great Depression. Just two weeks before Christmas, 135 employees had been laid off. Walton Memorial had always been a source of stable employment in the community, and many of those laid off felt betrayed by Walton management. Employee morale seemed to be at an all-time low.

Another factor impacting on Walton Memorial's financial condition was the erosion of its patient base by a small, private, doctor-owned hospital which was offering competitive services. This smaller hospital was viewed by many in the community as more personal and caring than Walton Memorial.

Shortly after the layoff, representatives of the Service Employees International Union began a campaign to organize a union at Memorial. In hearings before the National Labor Relations Board regarding which employees were eligible to join the union, it became apparent that many of Walton Memorial's first-line supervisors didn't perceive themselves as a part of the management team. The hospital's labor counsel advised management that, if they wished to retain a nonunion work force, they should begin immediately to upgrade the skills of their first- and second-level supervisors. Effective managers at these levels can do much to quell union organizing efforts.

As to which problems demanded immediate attention, there were significant differences of opinion. The director of human resources felt poor employee morale was due to poor interpersonal skills on the part of management. Further, she was concerned that employees weren't being as helpful or as friendly to patients as they should be. The hospital administrator echoed these concerns. The lab director felt that the greatest problem was a lack of motivation on the part of hospital employees. Ms. DePuell, the director of nursing, had recently attended a seminar on the Managerial Grid and the Johari Window and wanted these topics taught to her people. The chief of staff, a physician, wanted training for those who transported patients between the nursing floors and outpatient areas of the hospital. "They're always getting lost," he complained. Finally, the director of hospital security had expressed concern that employees and supervisors were unfamiliar with fire and disaster procedures.

Dennis began to wonder if he would be able to meet this diverse set of expectations. Further, he wasn't sure that all these problems were really training problems and, if they were, which should be addressed first. "Well, I've got to start somewhere," thought Dennis. "The Executive Committee is expecting my training recommendations in four weeks!"

Case Questions

1. How should Dennis determine training needs for the hospital?
2. Is training the solution for morale problems? Why or why not?

3. What are the advantages and disadvantages with "canned" training programs such as the managerial grid and the Johari Window?

SOURCE: Steven H. Hanks, Utah State University.

NOTES

1. J. Huey, "America's Most Successful Merchant," *Fortune* (23 Sept. 1991): 54; W. Zellner, "O.K., So He's Not Sam Walton," *Business Week* (16 March 1992): 56–58; B. Saporito, "Is Wal-Mart Unstoppable?" *Fortune* (6 May 1992): 50–62; J. Huey, "Wal-Mart: Will it Take over the World?" *Fortune* (30 Jan. 1989): 52–64. (Sam Walton died April 5, 1992, at the age of 74.)
2. J. Bolt, *Executive Development* (Boston: Ballinger, 1989).
3. J. Bolt, *Executive Development*. Also see R. S. Schuler, "Strategic Human Resource Management: Linking the People with the Strategic Needs of the Business," *Organizational Dynamics* (Summer 1992): 18–32.
4. J. W. Pfeiffer, ed., *The 1991 Annual: Developing Human Resources* (San Diego: University Associates, 1991); L. A. Ferman, M. Hoyman, J. Cutcher-Gershenfeld, and E. J. Savoie, eds., *New Developments in Worker Training: A Legacy for the 1990s* (Madison, Wis.: Industrial Relations Research Association, 1990); R. R. Sims, *An Experimental Learning Approach to Employee Training Systems* (Westport, Conn.: Quorum Books, 1990); M. Silberman, *Active Training* (Lexington, Mass.: Lexington Books, 1990); J. E. Morrison, ed., *Training for Performance* (New York: John Wiley & Sons, 1991); M. London, *Managing the Training Enterprise: High-Quality, Cost-Effective Employee Training in Organizations* (San Francisco: Jossey-Bass, 1989); A. P. Carnevale, L. J. Gainer, and J. Villet, *Training America: The Organization and Strategic Role of Training* (San Francisco: Jossey-Bass, 1990); L. Nadler and Z. Nadler, eds., *The Handbook of Human Resource Development* (New York: John Wiley & Sons, 1990); M. Silver, *Competent to Manage: Approaches to Management Training and Development* (New York: Routledge, 1991); I. L. Goldstein and P. Gilliam, "Training System Issues in the Year 2000," *American Psychologist* (Feb. 1990); 134–43; S. I. Tannenbaum and G. Yukl, "Training and Development in Work Organizations," *Annual Review of Psychology* 43 (1992): 399–441; W. R. Scott and J. W. Meyer, "The Rise of Training Programs in Firms and Agencies: An Institutional Perspective," *Research in Organizational Behavior,* Vol. 13 (1991): 297–326; R. E. Snow and J. Swanson, "Instructional Psychology: Aptitude, Adaptation, and Assessment," *Annual Review of Psychology* 43 (1992): 583–626; I. L. Goldstein, "Training in Work Organizations," *Annual Review of Psychology* 31 (1980): 229–72; G. P. Latham, "Human Resource Training and Development," *Annual Review of Psychology* 39 (1988).
5. R. E. Ganger, "HRIS Logos on to Strategic Training," *Personnel Journal* (Aug. 1991): 50–54; B. J. Martin, P. J. Harrison, and E. Ingram, "Strategies for Training New Managers," *Personnel Journal* (Nov. 1991): 114–17; T. R. Horton, "Training: A Key to Productivity Growth," *Management Review* (Sept. 1983): 2–3.
6. B. Dumaine, "Those Highflying PepsiCo Managers," *Fortune* (10 April 1989): 78–79.
7. W. Finn, "No Train, No Gain," *Personnel Journal* (Sept. 1991): 95, 98; T. J. Von der Embse, "Choosing a Management Development Program: A Decision Model," *Personnel Journal* (Oct. 1973): 908; W. McGehee and P. W. Thayer, *Training in Business and Industry* (New York: Wiley, 1961); M. L. Moore and P. Dutton, "Training Needs Analysis."
8. L. Saari, T. Johnson, S. McLaughlin, and D. Zimmerle, "A Survey of Management Training and Education Practices in U.S. Companies," *Personnel Psychology* 41 (1988): 731–45.
9. W. F. Joyce and J. W. Slocum, "Climates in Organizations," in S. Kerr, ed., *Organizational Behavior* (San Francisco: Grid, 1979); W. F. Joyce and J. Slocum, "Climate Discrepancy: Refining the Concepts of Psychological and Organizational Climates," *Human Relations* 35 (1982): 951–72; B. Schneider, "Organizational Climates: An Essay," *Personnel Psychology* 28 (1975): 447–79; B. Schneider, "Organizational Climates: Individual Preferences and Organizational Realities Revisited," *Journal of Applied Psychology* 60 (1975): 459–65; B. Schneider and A. E. Reichers, "On the Etiology of Climates," *Personnel Psychology* 36 (1983): 19–40.
10. J. Lynch and D. Orne, "The Next Elite: Manufacturing Supermanagers," *Management Review* (April 1985): 49.
11. J. W. Walker, "Training and Development," in R. Schuler and S. Carroll, eds., *Human Resource Management in the 1980s* (Washington, D.C.: Bureau of National Affairs, 1983); I. I. Goldstein, *Training: Program Development and Evaluation* (Monterey, Calif.: Brooks/Cole, 1986); Wexley and Latham, *Developing and Training*.
12. L. A. Berger, "A DEW Line for Training and Development: The Needs Analysis Survey," *Personnel Administrator* (Nov. 1976): 51–55.
13. R. B. McAfee and P. J. Champagne, "Employee Development: Discovering Who Needs What," *Personnel Administrator* (Feb. 1988): 92–93.
14. Latham, "Human Resource Training and Development."
15. E. L. Bernick, R. Kindley, and K. Petit, "The Structure of Training Courses and the Effects of Hierarchy," *Public Personnel Journal* 13 (1984): 109–119.
16. C. Berryman-Fink, "Male and Female Managers' View of the Communication Skills and Training Needs of Women in Management," *Public Personnel Management* 14

(1985): 307–314; Latham, "Human Resource Training and Development;" F. D. Tucker, "A Study of Training Needs of Older Workers: Implications for Human Resources Development Planning," *Public Personnel Management* 14 (1985): 85–95.

17. M. E. Gist, A. G. Bavetta, and C. K. Stevens, "Transfer Training Method: Its Influence on Skill Generalization, Skill Repetition, and Performance Level," *Personnel Psychology* 43 (1990): 501–523; N. Schmitt, J. R. Schneider, and S. A. Cohen, "Factors Affecting Validity of a Regionally Administered Assessment Center," *Personnel Psychology* 43 (1990): 1–12; M. J. Kruger, and G. D. May, "Two Techniques to Ensure that Training Programs Remain Effective," *Personnel Journal* (Oct. 1985): 70–75; E. E. Lawler III, "Education Management Style and Organizational Effectiveness," *Personnel Psychology* (Spring 1985): 1–17; M. London and S. Stumpf, "Individual and Organizational Career Development in Changing Times," in D. T. Hahl, ed., *Career Development in Organizations* (San Francisco: Jossey-Bass, 1986).
18. J. Main, "The Executive Yearn to Learn," *Fortune* (3 May 1982): 234–48; M. M. Starcevich and J. A. Sykes, "Internal Advanced Management Programs for Executive Development," *Personnel Administrator* (June 1982): 27–28.
19. T. Hornberger and R. Trueblood, "Misused and Underrated: Reading and Listening Skills," *Personnel Journal* (Oct. 1980): 809–812. Reprinted with the permission of *Personnel Journal*, Costa Mesa, Calif.: All rights reserved.
20. M. E. Gist, C. Schwoerer, and B. Rosen, "Effects of Alternative Training Methods on Self-Efficacy and Performance in Computer Software Training," *Journal of Applied Psychology* 74, no. 6 (1989): 884–91; "AMA Designs Training Program for Use on Personal Computers," *AMA Forum* (Dec. 1983): 29–30; W. C. Heck, "Computer-Based Training—The Choice is Yours," *Personnel Administrator* (Feb. 1985): 39–46; V. L. Huber and G. Gray, "Channeling New Technology to Improve Training," *Personnel Administrator* (Feb. 1985): 49–57; G. Kearsley, *Computer-Based Training: A Guide to Selection and Implementation* (Reading, Mass.: Addison-Wesley, 1983); S. Schwade, "Is it Time to Consider Computer Based Training?" *Personnel Administrator* (Feb. 1985): 25–35.
21. C. H. Deutsch, "Vocational Schools in a Comeback," *The New York Times* (21 July 1991): F21; "Training Bosses," *Time* (7 June 1982): 61.
22. K. H. Cowdery, "Training Inner-City Youth to Work," *Personnel Journal* (Oct. 1991): 45–48; C. Marmer Solomon, "New Partners in Business," *Personnel Journal* (April 1991): 57–67.
23. Goldstein, *Training: Program Development and Evaluation.*
24. B. M. Bass and J. A. Vaughan, *Training in Industry: The Management of Learning* (Belmont, Calif.: Wadsworth, 1966): 88.
25. L. A. Ferman, M. Hoyman, J. Cutcher-Gershenfeld, and E. J. Enfeld, *Worker Training: A Legacy for the 1990s* (Madison, Wis.: Industrial Relations Research Association, 1990); A. P. Carnevale, L. J. Gainer, and A. S. Meltzer, *Workplace Basics Training Manual* (San Francisco: Jossey-Bass, 1990); T. T. Baldwin, R. J. Magjuka, and B. T. Loher, "The Perils of Participation: Effects of Choice of Training on Trainee Motivation and Learning," *Personnel Psychology* 44 (1991): 51–65; A. P. Carnevale, L. J. Gainer, and E. Schulz, *Training the Technical Work Force* (San Francisco: Jossey-Bass, 1990); Goldstein, *Training: Program Development...*
26. "Planning the Training Program," *Personnel Management,* BNA Policy and Practice Series, no. 41 (Washington, D.C.: Bureau of National Affairs, 1975): 205; see also Bass and Vaughan, *Training in Industry:* 89–90; and J. M. Geddes, "Germany Profits by Apprentice System," *The Wall Street Journal* (15 Sept. 1981): 33.
27. S. Overman, "Apprenticeships Smooth School to Work Transitions," *HR Magazine* (Dec. 1990): 40–43; K. Matthes, "Apprenticeships Can Support the 'Forgotten Youth,'" *HR Focus* (Dec. 1991): 19; Bass and Vaughan, *Training in Industry;* Goldstein, *Training: Program Development...;* D. T. Hall, *Careers in Organizations* (Santa Monica, Calif.: Goodyear 1976); J. R. Hinrichs, "Personnel Training," in M. D. Dunnette, ed., *Handbook of Industrial and Organizational Psychology* (Chicago: Rand McNally, 1976): 854.
28. M. W. McCall, Jr., M. M. Lombardo, and A. M. Morrison, *The Lessons of Experience: How Successful Executives Develop on the Job* (Lexington, Mass.: Lexington Books, 1989); T. Delone, "What Do Middle Managers Really Want from First-Line Supervisors?" *Supervisory Management* (Sept. 1977): 8–12; W. E. Sasser, Jr., and F. S. Leonard, "Let First Level Supervisors Do Their Job," *Harvard Business Review* (March-April 1980): 113–21; L. R. Sheeran and D. Fenn, "The Mentor System," *Inc.* (June 1987): 138–42; The Woodlands Group, "Management Development Roles: Coach, Sponsor, and Mentor," *Personnel Journal* (Nov. 1980): 918–21.
29. R. F. Morrison and J. Adams, eds., *Contemporary Career Development Issues* (Hillsdale, N.J.: Lawrence Erlbaum Associates, 1991); A. Saltzman, *Down-Shifting: Reinventing Success—on a Slower Track* (New York: Harper Collins, 1991); S. L. Willis and S. S. Dubin, eds., *Maintaining Professional Competence: Approaches to Career Enhancement, Vitality and Success Throughout a Work Life* (San Francisco: Jossey-Bass, 1990); J. A. Schneer and F. Reitman, "Effects of Employment Gaps on the Careers of M.B.A.'s: More Damaging for Men than for Women?" *Academy of Management Journal* 33, no. 2 (1990): 391–406; J. H. Greenhaus, S. Parasuraman, and W. M. Wormley, "Effects of Race on Organizational Experiences, Job Performance Evaluations and Career Outcomes," *Academy of Management Journal* 33, no. 1 (1990): 64–86; N. Nicholson and M. West, *Managerial Job Change: Men and Women in Transition* (Cambridge, England: University of Cambridge Press, 1988); S. J. M. Freeman, *Managing Lives: Corporate Women and Social Change* (Amherst, Mass.: The University of Massachusetts Press, 1990).
30. S. Bartlett, "Our Intrepid Reporter Wheels and Deals Currencies," *Business Week* (1 Feb. 1988): 70–71; N. Madlin, "Computer-Based Training Comes of Age," *Personnel* (Nov. 1987): 64–65.
31. Huber and Gray, "Channeling New Technology"; G. S. Odiorne and G. A. Rummler, *Training and Development: A Guide for Professionals* (Chicago: Commerce Clearing

House, 1988); D. Torrence, "How Video Can Help," *Training and Development Journal* (Dec. 1985): 122–30; M. Piedmont, "Put Computer Software Training $$$ To Better Use," *HR Focus* (Nov. 1991): 13.
32. Odiorne and Rummler, *Training and Development*.
33. Huber and Gray, "Channeling New Technology."
34. Odiorne and Rummler, *Training and Development*.
35. G. C. Thornton III and J. N. Cleveland, "Developing Managerial Talent through Simulation," *American Psychologist* (Feb. 1990): 190–99; G. Waddell, "Simulations: Balancing the Pros and Cons," *Training and Development Journal* (Jan. 1982): 75–80.
36. For an excellent discussion of assessment centers, see Thornton, G. C., III, *Assessment Centers* (Reading, Mass.: Addison-Wesley, 1992); V. R. Boehm, "Assessment Centers and Management Development," in K. M. Rowland and G. Ferris, eds., *Personnel Management* (Boston: Allyn & Bacon, 1982): 327–62; R. B. Finkle, "Managerial Assessment Centers," in M. D. Dunnette, ed., *Handbook of Industrial and Organizational Psychology* (Chicago: Rand McNally, 1976): 861–88; I. T. Robertson and S. Downs, "Work-Sample Tests of Trainability: A Meta-Analysis," *Journal of Applied Psychology* 74, no. 3 (1989): 402–410; V. J. Marsick and K. Watkins, *Informal and Incidental Learning in the Workplace* (New York: Routledge, 1991).
37. S. Carey, "These Days More Managers Play Games, Some Made in Japan, as a Part of Training," *Wall Street Journal* (7 Oct. 1982): 35.
38. J. P. Campbell, M. D. Dunnette, E. E. Lawler III, and K. E. Weick, Jr., *Managerial Behavior, Performance, and Effectiveness* (New York: McGraw-Hill, 1970); B. Mezoff, "Human Relations Training: The Tailored Approach," *Personnel* (March/April 1981): 21–27.
39. "Downward Bound," *Fortune* (15 Aug. 1988): 83.
40. V. L. Huber, "A Comparison of Goal Setting and Pay as Learning Incentives," *Psychological Reports* 56, (1985): 223–35; V. L. Huber, "Interplay between Goal Setting and Promises of Pay-for-Performance on Individual and Group Performance: An Operant Interpretation," *Journal of Organizational Behavior Management* 7, no. 3/4 (1986): 45–64.
41. Latham, "Human Resource Training and Development;" C. A. Frayne, *Reducing Employee Absenteeism through Self-Management Training: A Research-Based Analysis and Guide* (Westport, Conn.: Quorum Books, 1991); A. Bandura, "Self Efficacy Mechanisms in Human Agency," *American Psychologist* 37 (1982): 122–47; A. Bandura, *Social Foundations of Thought and Action* (Englewood Cliffs, N.J.: Prentice-Hall, 1986); M. Gist, "Self Efficacy: Implications for Organizational Behavior and Human Resource Management," *Academy of Management Review* 12 (1987): 472–85; M. Gist, C. Schwoerer, and B. Rosen, "Modeling versus Nonmodeling: The Impact of Self Efficacy and Performance in Computer Training for Managers," *Personnel Psychology* (1989); Latham, "Human Resource Training and Development."
42. S. J. Ashford and A. S. Tsui, "Self-Regulation for Managerial Effectiveness: The Role of Active Feedback Seeking," *Academy of Management Journal* 34, no. 2 (1991): 251–80; S. I. Tannenbaum, J. E. Mathieu, E. Salas, and J. A. Cannon-Bowers, "Meeting Trainees' Expectations: The Influence of Training Fulfillment on the Development of Commitment, Self-Efficacy and Motivation," *Journal of Applied Psychology* 76, no. 6 (1991): 759–69; M. E. Gist, "The Influence of Training Method on Self-Efficacy and Idea Generation among Managers," *Personnel Psychology* 42 (1989): 787–805; Bandura, "Self Efficacy Mechanisms"; Bandura, *Social Foundations of Thought and Action*.
43. Huber, "Interplay between Goal Setting and Promises of Pay-for-Performance."
44. V. L. Huber, G. P. Latham, and E. A. Locke, "The Management of Impressions through Goal Setting," in *Impression Management in the Organization,* ed. R. A. Giacalone and P. Rosenfield (Hillsdale, N.J.: Erlhaun, 1989) D. R. Ilgen, C. D. Fisher, and M. S. Taylor, "Consequences of Individual Feedback on Behavior in Organizations," *Journal of Applied Psychology* 64 (1979): 349–71; E. A. Locke, "Effects of Knowledge of Results, Feedback in Relation to Standards, and Goals on Reaction-Time Performance," *American Journal of Psychology* 81 (1968): 566–75.
45. P. Hogan, M. Hakel, and P. Decker, "Effects of Trainee-Generated vs. Trainer-Provided Rule Codes on Generalization in Behavioral Modeling Training," *Journal of Applied Psychology* 71 (1986): 469–73.
46. W. Honig, *Operant Behavior* (New York: Appleton-Century-Crofts, 1966); Huber, "Interplay between Goal Setting and Promises of Pay-for Performance;" J. S. Russel, K. Wexley, and J. Hunter, "Questioning the Effectiveness of Behavior Modeling Training in an Industrial Setting," *Personnel Psychology* 34 (1984): 465–82.
47. "A Comparison of Goal Setting and Pay"; V. L. Huber, E. Locke, and G. Latham, *Goal Setting: A Motivational Technique that Works* (Englewood Cliffs, N.J.: Prentice-Hall, 1984).
48. C. Frayne and G. Latham, "The Application of Social Learning Theory to Employee Self-Management of Attendance," *Journal of Applied Psychology* 72 (1987): 387–92; Latham, "Human Resource Training and Development."
49. J. Fierman, "Shaking the Blue-Collar Blues," *Fortune* (22 April 1991): 209–210, 214, 216, 218; S. R. Siegel, "Improving the Effectiveness of Management Development Programs," *Personnel Journal* (Oct. 1981): 770–73.
50. For extensive description of training and development assessment, see M. J. Burke and R. R. Day, "A Cumulative Study of the Effectiveness of Managerial Training," *Journal of Applied Psychology* (1986): 232–45; "Cost-Effective Training Techniques," *Bulletin to Management* (21 Aug. 1986): 284; H. E. Fisher and R. Weinberg, "Make Training Accountable: Assess Its Impact," *Personnel Journal* (Jan. 1988): 73–75; J. Fitzenz, "Proving the Value of Training," *Personnel* (March 1988): 17–23; J. K. Ford and S. P. Wroten, "Introducing New Methods for Conducting Training Evaluation and for Linking Training Evaluation to Program Redesign," *Personnel Psychology* (Winter 1984): 651–66; V. S. Kaman and J. D. Mohr, "Training Needs Assessment in the Eighties: Five Guideposts," *Personnel Administrator* (Oct. 1984): 47–53; D. L. Kirkpatrick, "Four Steps to Measuring Training Effectiveness," *Personnel Administrator* (Nov. 1983): 19–25; D. F. Russ-Eft and J. H.

CHAPTER 13

Organizational Improvement

Getting all the people involved in making a change is absolutely necessary for the change to be successful.

—Bill Reffett, Senior Vice-President, Human Resources, Grand Union[1]

Zenger, "Common Mistakes in Evaluating Training Effectiveness," *Personnel Administrator* (April 1985): 57–62; H. W. Smith and C. E. George, "Evaluating Internal Advanced Management Programs," *Personnel Administrator* (Aug. 1984): 118–31; and W. G. Thomas, "Training and Development Do Make Better Managers!" *Personnel* (Jan. 1988): 52–53.

51. F. O. Hoffman, "A Responsive Training Department Cuts Costs," *Personnel Journal* (Feb. 1984): 48–53; D. L. Kirkpatrick, "Four Steps to Measuring Training Effectiveness"; H. W. Smith and C. E. George, "Evaluating Internal Advanced Management Programs"; S. B. Wehrenberg, "Evaluation of Training: Part I," *Personnel Journal* (Aug. 1983): 608–10; S. B. Wehrenberg, "Evaluation of Training: Part II," *Personnel Journal* (Sept. 1983): 698–702.
52. "B-School Faculty Quality Training," *Fortune* (13 Jan. 1992): 14. Also see W. Wiggenhorn, "Motorola U: When Training Becomes an Education," *Harvard Business Review* (July-Aug. 1990): 71–83.
53. J. Bolt, *Executive Development* (New York: Harper & Row, 1989); A. A. Vicere and K. R. Graham, "Crafting Competitiveness: Toward a New Paradigm for Executive Development,"*Human Resource Planning* 13, no. 4 (1990): 281–296; J. K. Berry, "Linking Management Development to Business Strategies," *Training and Development Journal* (Aug. 1990): 20–22.
54. Odiorne and Rummler, *Training and Development.*
55. Used by permission of Siemens, Siemens, USA, New Brunswick, New Jersey.
56. "Pul-eeze! Will Somebody Help Me?" *Time* (Feb. 1987): 49.
57. B. Z. Posner and W. H. Schmidt, "Values of American Managers: Then and Now," *HR Focus* (March 1992): 13.
58. "Ethics Exams: Focus for Too Few?" *Bulletin to Management* (19 Feb. 1987): 64; R. W. Goodard, "Are You an Ethical Manager?" *Personnel Journal* (March 1988): 38–47; "Policy Guide," *Bulletin to Management* (18 Dec. 1986): 420; "Values and Ethics," *HR Reporter* (March 1987): 3.
59. Posner and Schmidt, "Values of American Managers: Then and Now."
60. J. W. Walker, "Managing Human Resources in Flat, Lean and Flexible Organizations: Trends for the 1990s," *Human Resource Planning* 11, no. 2 (1988): 124–132.
61. K. Labich, "The Innovators," *Fortune* (6 June 1988): 50–64.
62. See note 61.
63. A. Rahim, "A Model for Developing Key Expatraite Executives," *Personnel Journal* (April 1983): 315.
64. *Developing Effective Global Managers for the 1990s* (New York: Business International, 1991): 38.
65. See note 64.
66. C. G. Howard, "How Best to Integrate Expatriate Managers in the Domestic Organization," *Personnel Administrator* (July 1982): 27–33; A. Kupfer, "How to be a Global Manager," *Fortune* (14 March 1988): 52–58; M. E. Mendenhall, E. Dunbar, and G. R. Oddou, "Expatriate Selection, Training and Career-Pathing: A Review and Critique," *Human Resource Management* 26, no. 3 (Fall 1987): 331–45; F. Rice, "Should You Work for a Foreigner?" *Fortune* (1 Aug. 1988): 123–34; N. Shahzad, "The American Expatriate Manager," *Personnel Administrator* (July 1984): 23–28.
67. J. C. Roberts, "Section 401(k) and the Expatriate Employee," *Personnel Administrator* (July 1984): 18–21. For related issues, see R. L. Tung, *The New Expatriates* (Boston: Ballinger, 1988).
68. T. Kono, *Strategy and Structure of Japanese Enterprises* (New York: M. E. Sharpe, Inc., 1984): 318.
69. T. Kono, *Strategy and Structure...*: 320.
70. P. J. Dowling and R. S. Schuler, *International Dimensions of Human Resource Management* (Boston, Mass.: PWS-Kent, 1990). Also see J. S. Black and M. Mendenhall, "Cross-Cultural Training Effectiveness: A Review and a Theoretical Framework for Future Research," *Academy of Management Review* 15, no. 1 (1990): 113–136.
71. S. Sethi, *The False Promise of the Japanese Miracle: Illusions and Realities of the Japanese Management System* (Pitman Publishing Co., 1984).
72. This presentation from S. Dolan and R. Schuler, *Canadian Human Resource Management,* 2d ed. (Toronto, Canada: Nelson Publishers, 1993).
73. *Bulletin to Management* (14 July 1988): 3.
74. S. Greenhouse, "An Unstoppable Export Machine," *The New York Times* (6 Oct. 1988): D7.

While the margins on fresh pastries are more than double those on packaged donuts and cakes, the pastry business is, well, just that—another business. It's another business from the business of running a grocery store—at least, if "grocery store" is defined as the traditional low-margin, high-volume, limited-selection, space-driven, discount-driven, 40,000-square-foot grocery store. However, if it is defined as a high-margin, high-volume, expanded-selection, customer-driven, service-oriented, 40,000-square-foot grocer store, can we then sell fresh pastries?

"Of course," said the top team at the Grand Union, a New Jersey–based retail grocery operation with stores up and down the East Coast, but primarily in its home state. Five years ago the top team decided that competing with the new 100,000-square-foot stores was not a viable merchandising strategy; their competitors' volume and the size of their parking lots were so much greater. Competing with them would not be possible because it would mean moving from all Grand Union's current, space-bound locations and uprooting relationships with all its current customers, suppliers, and communities. Obviously, even the world's greatest pâtisserie *wouldn't be able to do enough volume to justify 40,000 square feet.*

The top team got back to the basic questions: What business are we in? Who are our competitors? Given that we aren't moving the stores, what do our customers want?

Once they answered the above questions, the company's top team members decided to embrace the newer definition of grocery store: a customer-driven, service-oriented store with an expanded selection of items. From an individual store perspective this would mean the elimination of many of the current items to make room for more brand items and higher margin items. The latter meant having a deli section (with the smells of barbecued chicken), an expanded fresh fruit section (more tropical fruits), a variety of small, ethnic food booths (for eating in or taking home), and, yes, a pastry shop.

All this sounded great to Bill Reffett, senior vice-president of human resources for Grand Union's 20,000 employees. Asked by the others on the top team if he could "deliver the people on this one," he answered, "No problem." Bill knew the success of the store's new quality strategy depended upon changing employee behaviors. He also knew that changing behaviors meant changing the store's human resource practices.[2]

This case on Grand Union illustrates many important points. One is that firms are seeking to improve themselves through quality improvements. This is happening in both service-oriented and manufacturing-oriented firms. Federal Express became the first service-oriented firm to win the race to quality improvement. This was in 1990 when Cadillac and IBM, both manufacturing-oriented firms, also won. In organizational improvement efforts to increase quality, employee behaviors typically need to change. For those new behaviors to last, many human resource priorities need to be changed as well. Consequently, the importance of managing human resources grows and will continue to grow in the 1990s. Thus, the more you know about programs for organizational improvement, the more effective your career will be. This chapter is intended to provide you with this knowledge. We return to the Grand Union case later in this chapter.

ORGANIZATIONAL IMPROVEMENT

As firms strive to be more competitive worldwide, they seek all ways possible to improve themselves. Increasingly they look to their personnel and human resource department for answers to questions such as these. How can we get our people more motivated to improve their productivity? Can we improve our quality without changing the current work force? What do our employees now think about our mission and values? Do they see themselves as part of one organization?

These questions help define what is meant by **organizational improvement.** Basically it comprises any organizational attempt to enhance the ability of the firm to attain its bottom-line objectives of competitiveness, profitability, adaptability, survival, and growth that, for its success, depends upon the more effective utilization of the firm's human resources.

The attempt to improve the Grand Union represents a typical example of what many firms are doing today to improve their bottom-line objectives. The need to do this is highlighted in the discussion of the purposes and importance of organizational improvement.

PURPOSES AND IMPORTANCE OF ORGANIZATIONAL IMPROVEMENT

Domestically and internationally, competition is growing more intense each year. The need has never been greater for organizations to continually improve. Many organizations in the 1990s will have little choice: They will either continually improve or go out of business (or they may get bought up by another business or may be forced to merge in order to survive). With this situation comes the increased recognition by line managers and human resource managers that success in improving organizations depends upon the HR department doing things it may not have done before. As HR departments seek to implement their own programs for organizational improvements, they set examples of organizational change for other departments and, thus, the entire organization.

Organizational improvement programs that the HR department can implement range from linking human resource practices with the needs of the business to conducting organizational surveys. Programs that link human resource practices to the business can be particularly effective if they help (1) improve the quality of the organization's products or services, (2) increase its ability to be innovative, and/or (3) reduce its costs. Especially with regard to linking HR with strategy, we use the expression "human resource practices." These represent specific ways of practicing each HR activity. Within each HR activity there are many HR practices, some of which are more effective for one strategy than others. It generally depends upon what role behaviors are needed from the employees to implement the strategy of the business. Selecting the right practices can increase the chances of successfully implementing a firm's strategy. Other organizational improvement programs include job redesign, teamwork, and empowerment; automation and advanced technologies; and organizational surveys.

The results of these improvement programs can directly benefit the organization, the employees, and the customers. Reaching general and specific goals of human resource management enhances the likelihood of improving the organization's bottom line. That is, as improvement programs are implemented, they serve to improve the firm's ability to attract, retain, motivate, and retrain the best individuals. As this occurs, improvements occur in productivity, quality of work life, legal compliance, competitive advantage, and work force flexibility. As a further consequence, the firm increases its competitiveness, profitability, and adaptability, making it more likely to survive and grow. These components are illustrated in exhibit 13.1.

ORGANIZATIONAL IMPROVEMENT PROGRAMS

While there are many programs to improve organizations, the ones we describe here have a significant impact on human resource management. Alternatively, their success often depends in large part on how effectively human resources are managed. All programs also provide a significant role for the human resource manager. In fact, it is through success in developing and implementing

Exhibit 13.1

Components and Programs of Organizational Improvements

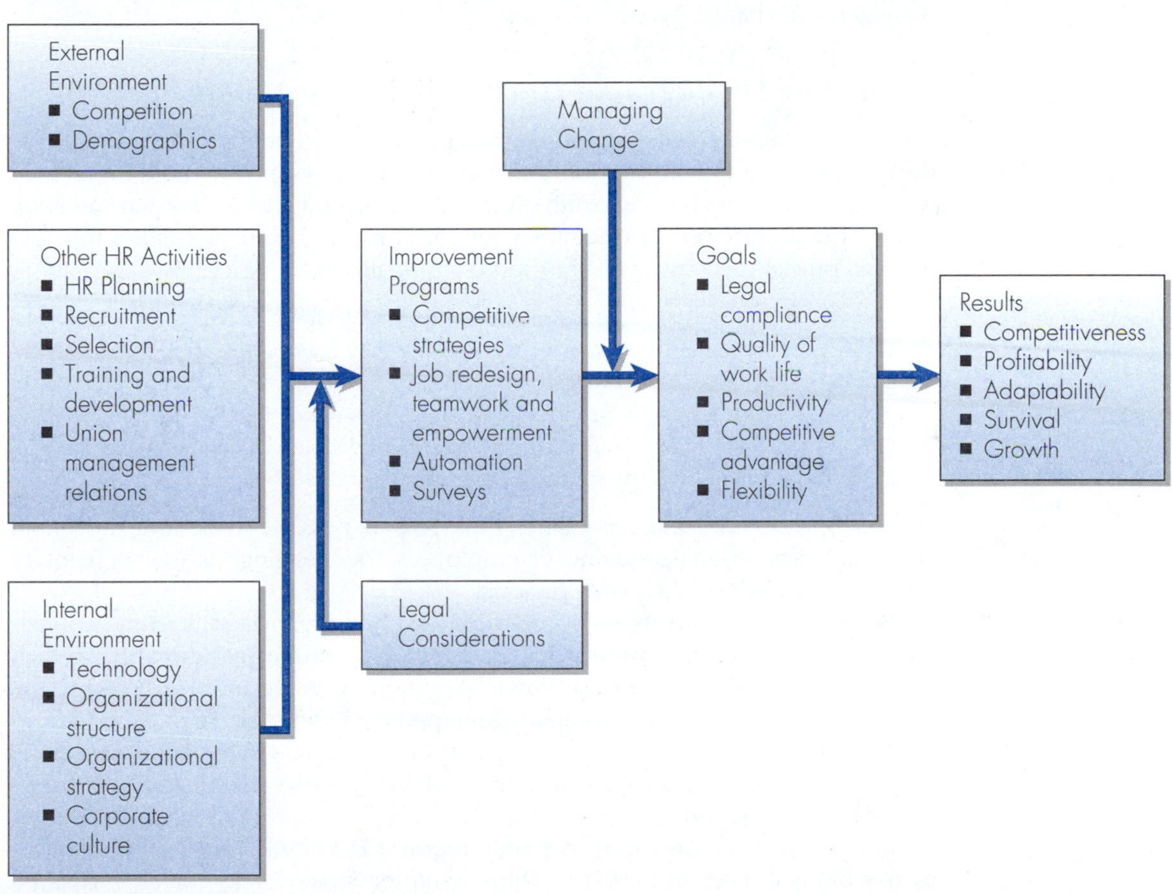

organizational improvement programs that HR managers further demonstrate their importance to the organization. Their success in implementing organizational improvement programs often depends upon doing a great job with several of the human resource activities, all at the same time and in a very systematic and coordinated way.

This will be particularly apparent in the first set of organizational improvement programs to be described. These are strategies for enhanced competitiveness. As the economy changes, and as the nature and level of competition change, jobs and organizations also change. The changes described in chapters 1, 2, and 3 are likely to continue to spread to more and more firms in the U.S. during the 1990s. For human resource managers, this decade offers tremendous opportunities. They can help organizations be successful in pursuing competitive strategies to be more innovative, improve quality, or reduce costs[3]—the three strategies for enhanced competitiveness.

While many programs to create a highly competitive organization have significant implications for human resource management, and vice versa, it is perhaps in the efforts to enhance innovation and quality and to reduce costs where the implications are most extensive and significant to the business.[4] Other programs for organizational improvement to be described are more focused than those strategies for enhancing competitiveness. They include job redesign and teamwork, automation and technological developments, organizational surveys, and managing the change process.

Innovation Strategy and Human Resource Management

Because the imperative in an **innovation strategy** is to be the most unique producer, conditions for innovation and entrepreneurial behavior must be created for organizations to be competitive through new product and service development. These conditions can be rather varied. They can be created either formally through official corporate policy or more informally:

> Innovation [and new venture development] may originate as a deliberate and official decision of the highest levels of management or they may be the more-or-less "spontaneous" creation of mid-level people who take the initiative to solve a problem in new ways or to develop a proposal for change. Of course, highly successful companies allow both, and even official top management decisions to undertake a development effort benefit from the spontaneous creativity of those below.[5]

For example, to encourage as many employees as possible to be innovative, 3M developed an informal doctrine of employees "bootlegging" fifteen percent of their time to work on their own projects.

Because these innovations occur within existing organizations, some companies call them **intrapreneurship** (in contrast to **entrepreneurship,** which refers to the creation of start-up firms).[6] According to a report by Ameritech, the midwest regional telephone company, intrapreneurs add more than $2 million to Ohio Bell's net income. Employees submit their ideas to reduce expenses, bring in new revenues, or develop new lines of business to the Ohio subsidiary's "Enter-Prize" program.

In a recent Dow Chemical corporate report, CEO Frank Popoff said management's job is to liberate people to think intrapreneurially. This can be facilitated by creating a climate in which people can be "change-oriented," with decision making at the lowest level.[7]

Creating a change-oriented climate and an organization where innovation becomes the norm can be done by crafting together a set of human resource practices that stimulate and reinforce intrapreneurial behavior. For example, Frost, a small Grand Rapids, Michigan, manufacturer of overhead conveyer trolleys used in the automobile industry, combines automation and human resource practices to implement an innovation strategy. Employee identification with the firm was increased by giving each employee ten shares of closely held corporate stock and calling them "shareholder-employees." Shared ownership was further increased through employee stock purchases deposited to a 401(k) savings plan. By making their future depend on firm profitability, Frost provides employees a long-term perspective—a perspective necessary for innovation.

Frost's compensation package was also restructured to strike a balance between employee concern for results—i.e., productivity—and the process by which goods get manufactured. The company instituted a quarterly bonus that is based on companywide productivity and established a "celebration fund" that managers can tap at their discretion to reward significant employee performance achievements. While most rewards are as simple as a lunch with owner Chad Frost, or, at most, a weekend for an employee and spouse at the local Marriott Hotel, one employee was granted his unusual request for a belly dancer performance at the office!

Frost encourages cooperative behavior—also necessary for innovation—in a number of ways. Most of the offices have no doors. Chad Frost's "office," for example, is simply a large open area at the end of a hallway, which allows employees easy access. Major executive perks, including reserved parking spaces, have been eliminated. Frost encourages employees to broaden their skills by paying for extensive training programs, both at the company and at local colleges; but Frost goes even further, identifying the development of additional skills as advancement in its own right. This is partly out of necessity, since Frost has compressed the company's eleven previous levels of hierarchy into just four in order to speed decision making.[8]

By changing the human resource practices, Frost treats employees in a way that gets them to perform in ways necessary to foster creativity and innovation. Employees have more skills, they can focus on the longer term, they cooperate with each other, and information flows easily to where it is needed because status differences are minimal. In addition, their financial future is tied to the success of Frost, so they want Frost to win so they can win. Everyone helps each other because they want to and because cooperative behavior is rewarded. However, this type of organizational climate only comes when many of the human resource practices are changed in a manner that gets employees to behave in ways necessary for the innovation strategy to be successfully implemented.

Quality-Improvement Strategy and Human Resource Management

To improve quality, organizations must approach the situation in the same way as they do to improve innovation: They need to be systematic in changing their human resource practices. The practices selected are different because the behaviors needed from the employees to improve quality are somewhat different from those needed to improve innovation.

In a **quality-improvement strategy,** the objective is to improve quality. Xerox, Baldrige award winner for quality, defines **quality** as "being right the first time, every time."

The implications of quality improvement for managing people are significant. The "total quality approach" at Corning is about people, according to James Houghton, the chief executive officer. At Corning, good ideas for product improvement often come from employees. In order to carry through on their ideas, Corning workers form short-lived "corrective action teams" to solve specific problems:

> Employees [also] give their supervisors written "method improvement requests," which differ from ideas tossed into the traditional suggestion box in that they get a prompt formal review so the employees aren't left wondering about their fate. In the company's Erwin Ceramics plant, a maintenance employee suggested substituting one flexible tin mold for an array of fixed molds that shape the wet ceramic product baked into catalytic converters for auto exhausts.[9]

At Corning, then, quality improvement involves getting employees committed to quality and continual improvement. While policy statements emphasizing the "total quality approach" are valuable, they are also followed up with specific human resource practices. At Corning and elsewhere, feedback systems are in place; teamwork is permitted and facilitated; decision making, autonomy, and responsibility are a part of everyone's job description; and job classifications are flexible.

The Ford Motor Company, which has become a leader in quality-improvement programs, follows the principles of W. Edwards Deming, one of the fathers of quality and the person for whom the Deming Award for Quality in Japan is named. The fourteen points listed below guide Ford's programs.

- Create consistency and continuity of purpose.
- Refuse to allow commonly accepted levels of delay for mistakes, defective material, defective workmanship.
- Eliminate the need for and dependence upon mass inspection.
- Reduce the number of suppliers. Buy on statistical evidence, not price.
- Search continually for problems in the system and seek ways to improve it.
- Institute modern methods of training, using statistics.
- Focus supervision on helping people to do a better job. Provide the tools and techniques for people to have pride of workmanship.
- Eliminate fear. Encourage two-way communication.
- Break down barriers between departments. Encourage problem solving through teamwork.
- Eliminate the use of numerical goals, slogans, and posters for the work force.
- Use statistical methods for continuing improvement of quality and productivity, and eliminate all standards prescribing numerical quotas.

- Remove barriers to pride of workmanship.
- Institute a vigorous program of education and training to keep people abreast of new developments in methods, materials, and technologies.
- Clearly define management's permanent commitment to quality and productivity.[10]

Thus, pursuing quality improvement requires dedication, commitment, and employee involvement.

Of course, there is no one best way or one best set of human resource practices to use in pursuing total quality. For most organizations, the human resource management component is only one of several that a company must manage effectively in improving quality. This is made clearer when you look at the criteria used to evaluate companies competing for the Baldrige award—companies such as Federal Express, Xerox, the Cadillac division of General Motors, and IBM. Exhibit 13.2 shows the seven components used in scoring the 1991 Baldrige Award contestants. While the fourth component is the only one directly showing human resource activities, the customer satisfaction component is directly associated with human resource utilization.[11] This was certainly the case at Grand Union. Let's return now to see how Bill Reffett improved the quality of service through human resource practices.

Grand Union strategy. Under the guidance of the senior vice-president of human resources, Bill Reffett, Grand Union developed a human resource philosophy that said the employee was a valuable, long-term source of competitive advantage and that all efforts would be made to provide exciting jobs and promotion opportunities (promotion-from-within) and continual retraining as needed. The firm described this philosophy as developmental. It was clearly recognized at this point that the role behaviors needed from all employees would change in order to match the needs of the new business.

While the physical size of the stores remained the same, employees were added because of the new sections and the need for additional staff. The new business meant it was important to keep employees longer so that they could get to know the customer and the store.[12] Consistent with the new business, the traditional command and control relationship across all levels was modified to accommodate a more self-directed, self-managed approach. Similarly, individual orientation was modified to be more team oriented to better serve the customer. The developmental HR philosophy was carried through to this level because this was the glue that kept all the employees together.

Key issues were addressed by formalizing all the activities that were occurring to support the new business. Success depended on managing the business systematically, including human resources. While there was formality in the establishment of new HR practices, there was allowance for adapting to local conditions. Regardless of location, however, decision making authority was pushed down in the organization. Store managers and their staff could make more decisions in the interests of the customer and the needs of the business.

Needed role behaviors. Grand Union directed major effort toward identifying the needed role behaviors of supervisors and the remaining staff in the stores. The HR process required the intense involvement of the employees, with

Scoring the 1991 Baldrige Award

1.0 Leadership (100 points)
- 1.1 Senior Executive Leadership (40)
- 1.2 Quality Values (15)
- 1.3 Management for Quality (25)
- 1.4 Public Responsibility (20)

2.0 Information and Analysis (70 points)
- 2.1 Scope and Management of Quality Data and Information (20)
- 2.2 Competitive Comparisons and Benchmarks (30)
- 2.3 Analysis of Quality Data and Information (20)

3.0 Strategic Quality Planning (60 points)
- 3.1 Strategic Quality Planning Process (35)
- 3.2 Quality Goals and Plans (25)

4.0 Human Resource Utilization (150 points)
- 4.1 Human Resource Management (20)
- 4.2 Employee Involvement (40)
- 4.3 Quality Education and Training (40)
- 4.4 Employee Recognition and Performance Measurement (25)
- 4.5 Employee Well-Being and Morale (25)

5.0 Quality Assurance of Products and Services (140 points)
- 5.1 Design and Introduction of Quality Products and Services (35)
- 5.2 Process Quality Control (20)
- 5.3 Continuous Improvement of Processes (20)
- 5.4 Quality Assessment (15)
- 5.5 Documentation (10)
- 5.6 Business Process and Support Service Quality (20)
- 5.7 Supplier Quality (20)

6.0 Quality Results (180 points)
- 6.1 Producer and Service Quality Results (90)
- 6.2 Business Process, Operational, and Support Service Quality Results (50)
- 6.3 Supplier Quality Results (40)

7.0 Customer Satisfaction (300 points)
- 7.1 Determining Customer Requirements and Expectations (30)
- 7.2 Customer Relationship Management (50)
- 7.3 Customer Service Standards (20)
- 7.4 Commitment to Customers (15)
- 7.5 Complaint Resolution for Quality Improvement (25)
- 7.6 Determining Customer Satisfaction (20)
- 7.7 Customer Satisfaction Results (70)
- 7.8 Customer Satisfaction Comparison (70)

1,000 Total Points

Exhibit 13.2
Scoring the 1991 Baldrige Award

SOURCE: National Institute of Standards and Technology

guidance provided by the senior vice-president of human resources. Together, they identified needed supervisory (department and store managers) and staff role behaviors based on what they saw as characterizing a customer-driven service grocery store. Then they compared these to the status quo.

Supervisory roles. Supervisory role behaviors were identified and redistributed. What occurred here was very important. The firm recognized the distinction between supervisors as an employee job category, and supervisory responsibilities associated with the supervisory role. Recognizing this distinction made it easier to decide how to redistribute the supervisory roles and responsibilities to enhance the level of customer service. Exhibit 13.3 illustrates those items identified as being supervisory responsibilities that could be and were redistributed.

Staff roles. The nonsupervisory employees also addressed the question, "What does this new business orientation mean for us at the store?" Because the focus was on the customer, they first asked, "How do we currently interact with the customers?" This resulted in a before-and-after analysis of relationships with customers. The "before" analysis resulted in the following list:

- We do not know customer desires
- We make limited use of customers
- We are space-driven, not customer-driven
- We have traditional departments, low margins, high quit rates
- We feel no ownership of service
- We lack management skills

In contrast, the employees felt that the change would require:

- Having focus groups with customers
- Being customer-driven
- Including service as part of the product
- Adding high-margin departments
- Having stores coordinate efforts, exchange best practices
- Expanding management skills

Exhibit 13.3
Supervisory Responsibilities that can be Distributed

Absence control	Personnel recordkeeping
Performance appraisal	Quality circle leadership
Staff deployment	Work planning/allocation
Discipline	Quality control
Shift rotation planning	Recruitment
Employee welfare	Team briefing
Grievance handling	Team building
Health and safety	Communicating
Induction training	

SOURCE: Adapted from R. Schuler, "Strategic Human Resource Management: Linking the People with the Strategic Needs of the Business," *Organizational Dynamics* (AMACOM: New York, Summer 1992), 26.

In addition, these employees asked, "From the broader, store viewpoint, what characteristics reflect a solutions-oriented, customer-driven, service operation?" This question resulted in the list of characteristics for the store shown in exhibit 13.4.

Based on these characteristics, they analyzed the needed role behaviors vis-à-vis the customer and concluded that substantial changes were in order. The before-and-after role behaviors for the major job categories in a store are listed in exhibit 13.5.

New human resource practices. In the final stage, the employees identified HR practices that had to be formulated to match the business, based on the role behaviors needed from the employees, especially those in direct contact with customers. The analysis and formulation resulted in several HR practices that represented significant change. Those practices most affected and how they changed are illustrated in exhibit 13.6. While these changes in HR practices were in part driven by what the employees thought was necessary for the business, it was in large part driven by what they thought would enable them to perform as needed by the customer.

In summary. This Grand Union case highlights the several strategic human resource management activities that were affected by the strategic business needs resulting from a change in organizational strategy. It also suggests the apparent necessity for making changes in these HR activities in a rather consistent manner.

The Grand Union case also highlights the involvement of all employees in the HR process of identifying needed role behaviors and the HR practices they think are likely to encourage them to perform these roles. The line employees, more than the human resource manager, may be better able to identify the HR practices needed because they are closer to the action and know what is needed to successfully implement a strategy, and they know how they will respond to alternative HR practices.

Of course, pursuing a strategy of quality improvement requires more than just a set of human resource practices; but these practices are essential in getting

Exhibit 13.4

Organizational Characteristics of a Customer-Driven Service Organization

- Just-in-time inventory
- Just-in-time working commitment
- Team-oriented
- Multi-skilled—Technical, process, interpersonal
- Flexibility
- Trust, harmonious employee relations
- Communications
- Egalitarianism
- Distributed leadership
- Responsibility for customers
- Standard operating procedures
- Continuous improvement
- No-fault policies
- Job grade reduction
- Rewards for small improvements/suggestions
- Supplier and customer involvement
- Site visits, comparisons, benchmarks
- Customer knowledge

SOURCE: Adapted from R. Schuler, "Strategic Human Resource Management: Linking the People with the Strategic Needs of the Business," *Organizational Dynamics* (AMACOM: New York, Summer 1992), 28.

Exhibit 13.5
Customer-Driven Employee at Grand Union

Behaviors Before the Change	Behaviors After the Change
Bag Packers	
Ignore customers Lack of packing standards	Greet customers Respond to customers Ask for customers' preferences
Cashiers	
Ignore customers Lack of eye contact	Greet customers Respond to customers Assist customers Speak clearly Call customers by name
Shelf Stockers	
Ignore customers Don't know store products/location	Respond to customers Help customers with correct information Knowledgeable about product location
Department Workers	
Ignore customers Limited knowledge	Respond to customers Know products Know store
Department Managers	
Ignore customers Ignore workers	Respond to customers Reward employees for responding to customers
Store Managers	
Ignore customers Stay in booth	Respond to customers Reward employees for service Appraise employees on customer service

SOURCE: Adapted from R. Schuler. "Strategic Human Resource Management: Linking the People with the Strategic Needs of the Business," *Organizational Dynamics* (New York: AMACOM, Summer 1992), 29.

the employee behaviors of consistency, accuracy, reliability, and concern for quality so necessary for quality improvement. Changes in the design of the organization—particularly the reduction of layers of management, or decentralization—helps to get and maintain these behaviors. By decentralizing, organizations move decision making farther down the organization. This enhances employee involvement in the company and improves productivity.

While improving quality improves an organization's ability to be competitive, the organization still may take other measures to survive and be competitive. On the other hand, it may just pursue other measures to be competitive rather than improve innovation or quality. In particular, it may pursue a cost-reduction strategy.

Exhibit 13.6
Human Resource Management Practices Affected by Change

Human Resource Planning

Longer term focus
Tie to the needs of the business

Staffing

More socialization
More opportunities

Performance Appraisal

Customer service measures used
Feedback provided

Compensation

Relates to performance appraisal
Awards and celebration

Training and Development

More skill training
Customer service training

SOURCE: Adapted from R. Schuler, "Strategic Human Resource Management: Linking the People with the Strategic Needs of the Business," *Organizational Dynamics* (New York: AMACOM, Summer 1992), 30.

Cost-Reduction Strategy and Human Resource Management

A **cost-reduction strategy** aims to reduce costs. This can be done by **downsizing** or eliminating employees.[13] This, of course, has already happened at some companies, even the rather large and global ones such as IBM, General Electric, Ford, GM, and Dow, and it appears likely to continue throughout the 1990s, in European nations as well as in the U.S.

Along with downsizing, firms are **subcontracting** or **outsourcing**—finding other firms to do some of the work they used to do. For example, IBM uses Pitney Bowes to run its mail rooms, stockrooms, and reproduction operations. Companies are increasingly outsourcing their payroll activities to firms such as ADP. Kodak sold its mainframes to IBM and then hired IBM to do its data processing for the next ten years.[14]

Firms are also using **contingent workers**—individuals who are employed during good economic times and released during downturns. During these economics cycles, the employees who stay are called **core employees.** By having a pool of contingent workers, firms can adjust their payroll costs quickly and still retain the loyalty of the core employees.

In summary, the human resource implications of the three competitive strategies of innovation, quality improvement, and cost reduction will become even more important in the 1990s. Particularly critical in these programs is the design of the employees' jobs. For example, in quality-improvement programs, jobs often become more complex, precisely defined, and team oriented. To facilitate innovation, jobs may be more complex, but less precisely defined. In cost-reduction programs, jobs become more narrowly defined or scientifically designed. Actually, the choice of job designs is rather extensive, and programs of redesign may be done apart from broader companywide programs to pursue an innovation, quality-improvement, or cost-reduction strategy.

With this in mind, let us examine some of the major choices in job design. Because our purpose is for organizational improvement, we discuss them as choices in job *re*design; and, because teamwork and empowerment are becoming such important components of job redesign programs, they are described along with job redesign.

Job Redesign, Teamwork, and Empowerment

Jobs can be designed in many different ways, four of which are discussed here. Other methods of designing jobs are essentially combinations of these four major approaches.

Scientific approach. Under the scientific approach, job analysts (typically, industrial engineers) take special pains to design jobs so that the tasks performed by employees do not exceed their abilities. The jobs designed by scientific management often result in the work being partitioned into small, simple segments. These tasks lend themselves well to time-and-motion studies and to incentive pay systems, each aimed at obtaining high productivity. The scientific approach to job design still is an important part of many present organizational structures described in chapter 2.[15]

Through meticulous human engineering and close scrutiny of its 152,000 employees, United Parcel Service (UPS) has grown highly profitable, despite stiff competition from Federal Express and others. According to Larry P. Breakiron, the company's senior vice-president of engineering, "Our ability to manage labor and hold it accountable is the key to our success."[16] In other words, in the business where "a package is a package," UPS succeeds as a result of its work standard/simplification method. This method has been the key to gains in efficiency and productivity increases since the privately held company was founded in 1907. As early as the 1920s UPS engineers cut away the sides of UPS trucks to show how the drivers performed. The engineers then made changes in techniques to enhance worker efficiency.

Time-and-motion studies also enable the company to closely monitor the performance of workers. At UPS, more than 1,000 industrial engineers use time study to set standards for a variety of closely supervised tasks. In return, the UPS drivers, all of whom are Teamsters, earn wages of approximately $15 per hour—a dollar or so more than the drivers at other companies. Because of the company's success, it can also offer job security to those employees who perform at acceptable levels.

Individual contemporary approach. Concerned over the human costs associated with the scientific approach, organizations began searching for alternative job design approaches. Following the era of time-and-motion, Hackman and Oldham developed their job characteristics model. As shown in exhibit 13.7, five positive personal and work outcomes—high motivation, high-quality work performance, increased satisfaction, low absenteeism, and low turnover—result

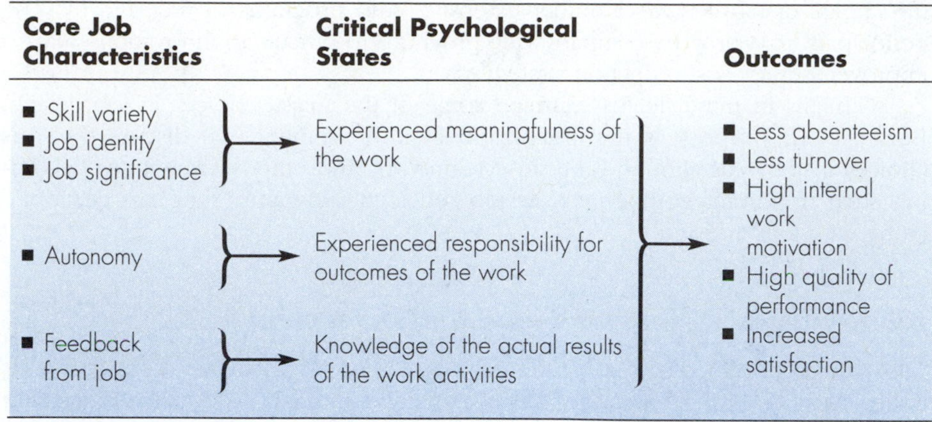

Exhibit 13.7
The Impact of the Core Job Characteristics on Employee Psychological States

SOURCE: Adapted from J. R. Hackman and G. R. Oldham, *Work Redesign* (Reading, Mass.: 1980), 77. Reprinted with permission.

when an employee works in an environment in which work is meaningful, there is knowledge of results, and there is responsibility for work outcomes.

According to researchers, these three critical psychological states evolve from five core job dimensions: (1) skill variety (the degree to which tasks are performed that require different abilities and skills); (2) job identity (the degree to which a whole and identifiable piece of work with a visible outcome is produced); (3) job significance (the degree to which the job has substantial importance); (4) autonomy (the degree of freedom and discretion allowed in work scheduling and procedures); and (5) feedback (the amount of direct and clear information about performance effectiveness). When people value feelings of accomplishment and growth, enriching jobs can lead to positive outcomes.[17]

Several different strategies can be used to stimulate core job characteristics. For example, **job rotation** doesn't change the nature of a specific job, but it does increase the number of duties an employee performs over time. This increases task variety and also may boost job identity and scope of purpose because the employee is performing several jobs.

Job enrichment is the opposite of the scientific approach that seeks to reduce the number of duties; it involves combining subparts of a job. The resulting job is enlarged and often involves more skill variety. Task identity can also be improved when the employee completes a whole and identifiable piece of work.

Horizontal loading involves adding more duties with the same types of task characteristics; **vertical loading** means creating a job with duties that have many different characteristics. The former approach may increase skill variety, but it's also likely to foster resentment because the employee is expected to do more of the same. Vertical loading is more promising because it closes the gaps between planning, doing, and controlling the work. As a result, it affects job autonomy, skill variety, and possibly feedback.

Client relationships can be established by placing quality control closer to the worker and providing summaries of performance to workers. When this occurs, task significance, skill variety, and feedback are increased. For example, Exhibit Systems of Salt Lake City designs industrial displays for trade shows. Its manufacturing team goes to trade shows and sets up displays; thus, any problems are directed to the workers—not to an intermediary or the account manager.

Finally, organizations can open communication channels by placing quality closer to the worker and by providing summaries to workers. Emery Air Freight improved performance substantially by having employees mark a checklist each time they used appropriate containers.

Team contemporary approach. Whereas the individual contemporary and scientific approaches design jobs for individuals, the team-contemporary approach designs jobs for teams of individuals. The final designs generally show a concern for the social needs of individuals as well as the constraints of the technology. Here, teams of workers often rotate jobs and may follow the product they are working on to the last step in the process. If the product is large—for example, an automobile—teams may be designed around sections of the final car. Each group then completes only a section and passes its subproduct to the next team. In the team-contemporary design, each worker learns to handle several duties, many requiring different skills. Thus, they can satisfy preferences for achievement and task accomplishment and some preferences for social interaction.

Some recent manufacturing innovations draw from this approach for their success. For example, **cellular manufacturing** rearranges the traditional job shop layout by clustering different machines together and gives work teams a "whole" piece of work to complete. **Zero inventory systems** are premised on the assumption that, rather than allow inventory to build up in queues, production should stop until the bottleneck or work problem is solved. Workers pitch in to solve the problem, rather than waiting for solutions.

As organizations gain experience with teams, they tend to give them more freedom and discretion. This can result in **self-managed teams** of the kind described in the "PHRM in the News: An Approach with Staying Power." Basically, here the *teams* become empowered. Thus, you can observe self-management and empowerment at both the individual and team levels. While the team-based approach has much going for it, there may be times when it is not as feasible as the individual-based approach.[18] There are also times when other human resource practices can be used along with teams as described in the "Focus on Research."

Ergonomics approach. Ergonomics is concerned with trying to design and shape jobs to fit the physical abilities and characteristics of individuals so they can perform the jobs. The ergonomic approach is being used to redesign jobs to accommodate women as well as disabled individuals. Often this serves equal employment opportunity and affirmative action objectives. This approach is even helping to serve as an alternative to retirement. Studies have shown that, when jobs are designed along ergonomic principles, worker productivity is greater.

In a recent study done by the National Institute for Occupational Safety and Health (NIOSH), two groups of employees working under an incentive pay system were compared. The group working on jobs designed according to ergonomic principles was twenty-five percent more productive than the group

IN THE NEWS

PHRM

An Approach With Staying Power: Self-managed teams helped an A.T.&T. plant survive

MICHAEL GREENSTEIN has a passion for charts–or "metrics," as he calls them—that goes well beyond most people's. The lanky Mr. Greenstein, engineering and quality manager at the A.T.&T. submarine systems plant in Clark, N.J., curled himself into a comma to trace the upward trend of a chart fastened near the floor. "Just look at the metrics," he said, as he applauded the employees who have driven up the yields on housing seals for the underwater fiber-optic cable repeater made at the 318-employee plant.

As far as Mr. Greenstein is concerned, the banks and banks of metrics lining the walls at Clark like spidery, high-tech graffiti make the case for the sort of team approach the plant adopted two years ago. An assessment of the metrics reveals, Mr. Greenstein says, that the Clark plant, which A.T.&T. had planned to close, has reduced the cost of its only product by more than 30 percent.

That type of result has given the team approach a reputation for legs not enjoyed by more evanescent management philosophies. "Its growth has been explosive," said John Simmons, president of Participation Associates in Chicago. "No one has a good fix on the numbers," he acknowledged, but "In the last year or two alone, thousands of companies have started team programs."

The team, in one form or another, has endured since workers, in a radical break with the assembly-line tradition, began mimicking Japanese quality circles in the late 1970's. Mr. Greenstein's metrics indicate how far the notion of worker participation and team integration has evolved.

The Clark plant looks more like an orderly suburban community college than a manufacturing plant and Mr. Greenstein's universe is well-traversed by a paper trail of memos and meeting notes. He thinks perhaps the plant, in a part of New Jersey cluttered with now-shuttered industrial plants, survived in part because its parent in New York wasn't paying much attention. An early-retirement program announced in

Continued

working on the jobs designed without these principles. Along with several unions, NIOSH is also actively involved in redesigning jobs using ergonomic principles to help reduce the incidence and severity of **carpal tunnel syndrome,** a condition characterized by numbness, tingling, soreness, and weakness in the hands and wrists. It is caused or aggravated by jobs requiring repetitive hand motions, such as those used by meat cutters. Companies such as Armco, Inc., and Hanes Corporation[19] are using ergonomic principles to successfully redesign jobs to eliminate these motions.

Which design to use. Exhibit 13.8 shows some of the advantages and disadvantages to consider in selecting a job design. The decision of which job design to implement is a complex one and includes the following steps:

1. Recognize a need for a change and gather prechange data for evaluation.
2. Determine that job redesign is the appropriate change.
3. Diagnose the organization, work flow, group processes, and individual needs.
4. Determine how, when, and where to change jobs.
5. Provide for training and support if necessary.

1989 left the plant with virtually new management, which knew its survival was in question.

"The new managers allowed us to make a radical change rather than incremental ones," Mr. Greenstein said. He arrived at Clark in 1990 as a novice team-builder and soon became its principal missionary. He visited several plants where the team approach was in place before developing his own model. "I stole ideas from everywhere I went," he said.

At the program's core is a contract between top management and the self-managed teams at Clark that details the team's responsibilities and obligations. The 14 teams are cross-functional and vertically integrated—management jargon for people with different job categories and at different levels of the work hierarchy.

A team of 10 or 12 might include, for example, engineers, designers, a production supervisor and lab technicians who actually put the pieces together. To a certain degree, this violates the natural order of the universe. "It is not natural for engineers to work in teams," said Frank Petrock, an expert in organizational change who runs the General Systems Consulting Group in Ann Arbor, Mich., who held workshops at Clark in "jump-starting" the team approach.

It is also often difficult for workers typically regarded as low on a company's food chain—technicians, for example—to speak out. "It's getting better," said Edward Headington, one of the team leaders. "We see more and more of the shop people voicing their opinions. Actually, I think they were voicing them before they were heard."

A big complaint is about meetings, the occupational hazard of the white-collar workplace. Self-management requires "open communication" (code for "more meetings"). But the teams have been able to use the minutes of meetings, which are read by supportive management on up the line at Clark and beyond, to orchestrate their way around resistance to team goals.

The approach seems to have support at the shop level. "I knew this is what we had to do," said Herman T. Piraneo, a material management analyst who has been with A.T.&T. for 43 years. "Now, when you resolve a problem, you feel great." There is at least one empirical indication that the team experiment is working: the plant that once was scheduled to close this summer has several years of orders on file.

SOURCE: B.P. Noble, "An Approach with Staying Power," *The New York Times* (8 Mar. 1992), F23.

6. Make the job changes.
7. Evaluate the change by comparing postchange data with prechange data.[20]

Following these steps may not always result in a successful redesign, but it will increase the chances for success. It will also give you information on what *not* to do the next time so that future redesign programs are even more likely to succeed. Next time, however, you may wish to make an organizational improvement by automation and technological change.

Automation and Technological Developments

Information technology, office automation, factory automation, data communications, and voice communication are becoming implemented together faster than ever. Sometimes referred to as **telematics technology,** they are revolutionizing the ways we do work and organize.[21] Singly or together, these technologies are facilitating the following capabilities within organizations:

- Networking across organizational units and countries
- Control over time and space
- Higher productivity and amplification of human cognitive functions

FOCUS ON RESEARCH

Getting Everyone Involved: Principles for Effective Organizations

According to Ed Lawler, Director of the Center for Organizational Effectiveness at the University of Southern California, "the enormous changes in corporate structure and needs over the past decade have necesitated a refocusing of management approaches," Lawler's research over the past decade has focused on exactly what it means for organizations to adapt new management approaches. Recently he summarized and updated this research, and while his research has been mainly focused on modern manufacturing plants, he concludes now that the following principles of management apply in any product or service organization wanting to be highly effective. He generally defines effectiveness in terms of high quality, customer-driven organizations that survive and flourish by staying ahead of competitors with new and better products and services.

Based upon the extensive research that he and his colleagues have done over the years, Lawler suggests that there are several aspects of management that effective organizations share today. One of the first is an organization design that makes extensive use of self-managing teams and a relatively limited number of hierarchical levels of management. These two features facilitate individuals working in teams that are responsible for and serving an identifiable customer or producing a whole product. In turn, this enables individuals to feel that they have control over a real business. Thus, in effective organizations, individuals really feel a sense of ownership in what they are doing and a sense of responsibility and accountability for how effective their organizations are. Organizations are even designed to enable teams to have contact with suppliers. For example, the Digital Equipment plant at Enfield, Connecticut allows teams to deal directly with suppliers and deal directly with customers for the electronic boards that the teams make.

Continued

- New extensions of human action
- New levels of efficiency and productivity or energy and materials conservation
- New power to centralize and decentralize
- Blurring of organizational distinctions
- Promotion of monitoring, evaluation, and simulation
- Erosion of hierarchical relationships
- Shifting power
- Shifting authority
- Integration
- New mischief or vulnerabilities
- Promote autonomy or dependency[22]

Not too far down the road the computer will emerge as a full-fledged management aid, helping to coordinate the daily tasks of administration. The programs to do that, developed after years of studying human behavior are called **groupware.** Action Technologies of Emeryville, California, markets a program named the Coordinator, based on the principle that all managerial interaction can be sorted into "offers," "counteroffers," "commitments," and "requests." The Coordinator keeps track of such

Today's effective organizations do not restrict the use of teams to the production floor only, but extend the team concept to all areas of the organization. This broader use of self-managed teams further flattens the organization by reducing the number of supervisors and managers throughout the operation.

The use of teams is extended in the effective organization so that cross-functional teams work together. This cross-function integration might combine manufacturing, product engineering and product design functions. This might not only produce a better product but also a better understanding by all employees of the needs of the business. This understanding is enhanced with information technology that allows workers in the manufacturing area to have direct access to marketing and sales and even answer questions from customers as they produce the products and services.

In today's effective organizations, reward systems compensate individuals for being in teams, for gaining more skill-based competencies, for learning and continuous improvement, and for business and organizational performance. Of course, the teams themselves have a significant input in compensation decisions, such as deciding when employees have attained mastery of needed skill-based competencies. Some of these important competencies are related to the use of information and data technology. The effective organization today is networked with computers and relies extensively upon videos for learning and television screens to link employees in various parts of the firm.

Along with all the above aspects of the effective organizations are: (a) the use of total quality management tools and principles, such as problem solving approaches and continuous commitment to process and product improvement; (b) continuous and widely available training for all employees on topics ranging from technical job details to business strategy; and (c) commitment from individuals to organization involvement, continuous learning and constant improvement.

SOURCE: Based on E. Lawler, "The New Plant Approach: A Second Generation Approach," *Organizational Dynamics* (American Management Association: New York, Summer 1991), 5–14.

transactions, minds deadlines, sends reminders, arranges meetings, and sorts electronic mail. It also lets users organize themselves easily into ad hoc work groups. Coordination Technology, a young company in Trumbull, Connecticut, that will launch its own groupware next year, uses it to manage the temporary groups that form to deal with specific assignments and then dissolve.[23]

The impact of the telematics technology revolution is also being seen in manufacturing advances.[24] The revolution within industrial manufacturing includes the emerging technologies of

- Robotics
- Computer-aided design, computer-aided manufacturing, and computer-aided engineering
- Lasers and optics
- Biotechnologies
- Polymers and alloys
- Advanced ceramics
- Computer-integrated manufacturing[25]

Robots are accompanying the increase of factory automation. Annual sales of robots are expected to be twenty thousand units by the end of the century, com-

Exhibit 13.8
A Summary of Some Advantages and Disadvantages of the Four Job Design Approaches

Approach	Advantages	Disadvantages
Scientific	Ensures predictability Provides clarity Fits abilities of many people Can be efficient and productive	May be boring May result in absenteeism, sabotage, and turnover
Individual Contemporary	Satisfies needs for responsibility, growth, and knowledge of results Provides growth opportunity Reduces boredom Increases quality and morale Lowers turnover	Some people prefer routine predictability May need to pay more, since more skills are needed Hard to enrich some jobs Not everyone wants to rotate
Team Contemporary	Provides social interaction Provides variety Facilitates social support Reduces absenteeism problem	People may not want interaction Requires training in interpersonal skills Group may be no better than weakest member
Ergonomics	Accommodates jobs to people Breaks down physical barriers Makes more jobs accessible to more people	May be costly to redesign some jobs Structural characteristics of the organization may make job change impossible

pared with the current rate of five thousand units. Estimates are that, by 1995, robots will displace about five percent of the work force. Although most employees are expected to remain with their current employers, substantial retraining will be required. The costs of this training will be offset by lower labor costs, enhanced product quality, fewer defects, and a better flow of materials.

Eventually, almost eighty percent of the white-collar jobs in the U.S. will be at least partially automated, including those of managers, professionals, and clerical staff. In fact, the biggest gains in office productivity are predicted to come from automating the jobs of professionals and managers and making vastly greater use of technology to manage people.[26]

Automation, whether in the factory or the office, has had and will continue to have the impact of changing organizational structures. Because information is instantaneously available, there is little need for layers of management between the top and first-line management. Automation also causes a significant change in organizational culture. It permits top management to bypass middle managers on their way to the first-line management. This breaks the chain of command and can lead to ambiguity in reporting relationships. This is nicely illustrated by this story of how Mrs. Fields Inc.'s chairman, Randy Fields, uses technology to manage people.

> Fields sees the computer as the most powerful tool around for managing people. For keeping the corporate staff lean. For organizing ideas. For enabling employees to communicate directly with the CEO in her Park City, Utah, headquarters. For automating most routine paperwork and decision making. Since technology is capable of doing so much, says Randy, CEOs should "understand it just like they understand operations."

Wise use of technology, he says, is one of the reasons for Mrs. Fields' growth into an international retailer with sales last year of $180 million....[27]

Available technologies have an impact on other significant relationships and events within the traditional organizational structure, too.

> Let us assume that a division director puts out some foolish memorandum on Thursday afternoon. What did you do in the old days? You sat around and you groused, and wondered when he was going to retire. Nothing happens. But, when you have got electronic mail, tomorrow morning 17 denunciations may be in his electronic mailbox. And if the fool was stupid enough to put a code on his mailbox to shield himself from his underlings, that young person just hired from the University of Illinois would crack that code for breakfast. There no longer is a mechanism for shielding the superior from the wrath of his underlings.
>
> And this is a crisis for middle and upper management. After all, how do you get to be upper management? You get to be upper management by being macho man in the workplace, who can make tough decisions under limited information and terrible time pressures, etc. What does the technology tell us? Technology says macho man is obsolete. If you need more information, sit at your desk and punch the keys. You want to try out some alternatives, sit at your desk and punch the keys. Many reasons why a senior manager is in his senior management position are eroded, assaulted, or demolished by this new technology. The emerging manager of the future will be less of a decision maker and more a moderator of a collegial process in which he will announce to those participating, "Well folks, after these past two weeks, it looks like we agree that..."
>
> Other things will happen. Suppose your headquarters is in Chicago and the expert who has the information that you, the VIP, want, is in San Francisco. You are not going to go down, down, down the chain of command, across the country, and up, up, up the chain of command. Electronically you will go right out to the expert, and get what you want. Being 100% American, the last thing you will say as you sign off, is "Charlie, if anything develops, let me know." You have just wiped out the chain of command. Unless Charlie is a timid fool, if anything develops, he will go directly back to the V.P. Technology is now shifting the priorities in the corporation from where you stand in the hierarchy to what you know.[28]

Some observers suggest that telematics will also be used to redesign jobs à la Frederick Taylor in the name of scientific management.[29] In *The Electronic Sweatshop,* Barbara Garson expressed concern that the computer's ability to monitor behavior will lead to oppressive control of employees. She suggested that some fast-food restaurants are using their computer systems to create jobs that virtually remove the need for employees to think and, therefore, to grow on the job. In essence, she sees telematics as leading to the de-skilling of jobs. While some may say this is necessary because of the nature of the work force, others say that it only perpetuates the de-skilling of the U.S. work force and, thus, the eventual decline of U.S. industry.[30]

Although the challenges for human resource managers from the telematics revolution are significant, other characteristics of this revolution must be considered. For instance, work can now go directly to the worker. The need for more daycare services can be addressed in part by allowing workers to do their work at home, linking up as needed to the company's computers. While this has implications for supervision and training, it also has legal and ethical implications. The human resource manager needs to monitor the legal events regarding the utilization of homework activities and the limits of liability for worker safety and health. The ability to have individuals work at home also facilitates the use of subcontractors and contingent employees because work can be more easily bundled and let out to individuals. This can lead to lower labor costs since individuals could bid for jobs as contingent employees with essentially no benefits packages.

Thus, the possibilities are enormous for organizational improvements for survival and competitiveness through automation and advanced technology, but the same possibilities involve tremendous human resource implications. This suggests that any such program be considered and/or implemented carefully and systematically. Consideration may start with something as basic as an organizational survey.

Communicating with Employees: Organizational Surveys

Improving communications with employees facilitates the transmission of employee ideas into product improvements and organizational changes. At the same time, it enhances employee job involvement, participation, and sense of being in control. In addition, training programs can be established to improve supervisory communications, and the human resource department can conduct organizational surveys.

What do we measure? In each of the applications of human resource data discussed in the previous chapters, the data gathered have been either measures of job performance itself or predictors of job performance, such as tests and background characteristics; but the human resource manager often needs other types of data. For example, in order to develop ways to improve employee performance, the human resource manager needs to measure how the employees perceive their environment, including the consequences of job performance, quality of feedback, and aspects of goal setting. It is equally necessary to gather data on employees' perceptions of quality of work life and employee stress. This is not to say that the objective qualities of the job are not important. However, with both objective and perceptual data, the human resource manager can begin to make other changes for organizational improvement.

It is also important to know how employees react to the environment and job qualities. Many of these reactions, which include physical measures such as blood pressure and heart rate, are symptoms of employee stress. Because one human resource management criterion is employee health, systematically gathering this type of information may become more common in the 1990s.

In general, then, organizational surveys can measure the following:

- *Employee perceptions:* role awareness, role conflict, qualities of the job, and interpersonal qualities, such as those of the supervisor and group members
- *Employee reactions:* feelings (such as satisfaction) and physiological responses, such as heart rate and blood pressure
- *Behaviors:* employee performance, absenteeism, and turnover

Conducting an organizational survey. Important steps for the human resource manager—or an outside consultant—to consider when conducting an organizational survey include careful planning, actual data collection, and ensuring employee participation.[31] These become necessary after top management has given its support for the survey.

As the first step, the human resource manager must consider the following:

- Specific employee perceptions and responses that should be measured
- Methods that will be used to collect the data, including observations, traditional questionnaires, interviews, personnel records or electronically
- Reliability and validity of the measures to be used
- People from whom the data will be collected—all employees, managerial employees only, a sample of employees, or only certain departments within the organization
- Timing of the survey and the way to make the survey part of a longer-term effort
- Types of analyses that will be made with the data
- Specific purposes of the data—for example, to determine the reasons for the organization's turnover problem

This last consideration is important because, by identifying the problem, the human resource manager can determine which models or theories will be relevant to the survey. Knowing which to use tells the human resource manager what data are needed and what statistical techniques will be necessary to analyze the data.

The next step is the actual collection of data. Three things are important here. Decide who will administer the questionnaire—the line manager, someone from the human resource department, or someone from outside the organization. Decide where, when, and in what size groups the data will be collected. Both these considerations are influenced by the method used to gather the data. For example, if a questionnaire is used, larger groups are more feasible than if interviews are conducted. Finally, take steps to ensure employee participation in the survey. This can be done by gathering the data during company time and by providing feedback—for instance, by promising employees that the results of the survey will be made known to them.

The actual feedback process is the third step in the survey. As part of this process, the data are analyzed according to the purposes and problems for which they were collected. The results of the analysis can then be presented by the human resource department to the line managers, who in turn discuss them with their employees. The feedback sessions can be used to develop solutions to any problems that are identified and to evaluate the effectiveness of programs that may already have been implemented on the basis of an earlier survey.

The extent to which employees actually participate in the development of solutions during the feedback process depends on the philosophy of top management. Organizations willing to survey their employees are also usually willing to invite employee participation in deciding how to make things better. This willingness allows organizational surveys to be used most effectively.

Because of the value of knowing what employees think, more and more firms are surveying their employees. Chief executive officers (CEOs), in particular, see surveys as a valuable way of communicating with employees.[32] This is illustrated in "PHRM in the News: CEOs Think That Morale is Dandy."

While giving a survey could be regarded as an organizational improvement in itself, it is more likely to be regarded as a fundamental part of doing an organizational improvement program. It is fundamental in that it gets employee participation, a critical aspect in managing the process of organizational improvement and change. Clearly, a significant trend in organizational improvement programs is to see a great deal more attention paid to the process of managing change.

Managing the Change Process

Programs for improving quality, stimulating innovation, or redesigning jobs represent important changes for most organizations. Consequently, it is important that they be managed effectively.

> Managing change is "one of the cutting-edge areas" for HR managers today, says Linda Ackerman, president of Linda S. Ackerman Inc. in Oakland, Calif. Most employees are traumatized by complex change, she observed, noting that managers have a responsibility to guide the changes process and minimize its effects on employees.[33]

The change process, regardless of whether it is human resource quality improvement or installing automation, appears to benefit from employee communication and participation, modification of the corporate culture, and support from top management. The more extensive the change, the more people and more parts of the organization significantly changing, the more likely it is for human resource practices to change at all levels of the organization and the more likely it is that the change will occur over time in stages.

Increasingly, efforts for improving organizations combine several of the programs described above. For example, Burroughs Wellcome used an organizational survey to identify improvement needs and define what human resource practices had to be changed to improve white-collar productivity.[34]

Executive Education. Human resource practices are being modified based on changes in the strategy of the organization, and the changes themselves are being orchestrated more frequently by human resources. Organizations such as Xerox, Weyerhaeuser, Northern Telecom, and General Foods implement programs of strategic change through management and executive education programs. Here the top management teams come together and identify what needs to be done to be more competitive. The need for executive education, which is becoming increasingly common in U.S. businesses today, was recognized at the Forest Products Company (FPC) of the Weyerhaeuser Company described in chapter 12. Recall that FPC and its parent, Weyerhaeuser, had to act fast to survive. Action was not only fast, it had a major impact on how the entire company was structured. As a result, FPC established an extensive executive development program and its own leadership institute.

While not all organizations are establishing leadership institutes as a part of their organizational change programs, many are using executive development as a vehicle by which to coordinate and implement the change. This is likely to continue as a major way to manage the change process in the 1990s.

PHRM IN THE NEWS

CEOs Think That Morale is Dandy

To make use of a phrase that has been growing rapidly in popularity these past few weeks: When it comes to the managerial morale crisis, CEOs just don't seem to get it. That's the clear implication of *Fortune's* poll of 212 chief executives of America's largest companies, conducted by the opinion research firm Clark Martire & Bartolomeo. Fully 91% of the top brass believe that morale in their companies is just fine. And 59% think that satisfaction among middle managers is either "excellent" or "very good," with only one CEO in ten conceding that morale at that level is fair or poor. While many middle managers and the people who conduct surveys of their attitudes say that their enthusiasm for work has declined in the past three to five years, 58% of chief executives think morale has gotten *better* over that period of time. About one-quarter of the CEOs in the survey said morale has stayed the same, and just 16% have noticed a decline.

All this despite the fact that most chief executives report they are making a herculean effort to stay in touch and to keep people in the picture and on board. They are communicating with employees in regular meetings, conducting employee surveys, and churning out newsletters and informational videos. "We've tried to build an organization that's congruent with the highest side of human nature," says William J. O'Brien, 59, CEO of Hanover Insurance Co. in Worcester, Massachusetts. "The fundamental movement in business in the next 25 years will be in the dispersing of power, to give meaning and fulfillment to employees in a way that avoids chaos and disorder."

W. Thomas Stephens, 49, chairman of Manville Corp., with its history of asbestos problems, likens a session with employees to an "old-time revival meeting. We had a psychiatrist in to do a study for us, and we learned that, in times of stress, communication has to increase exponentially or you won't survive."

Richard F. Teerlink, 55, CEO of Harley-Davidson, explains, "It's a matter of top management getting out and talking with people, not at people ... We're making progress, but we still have a long way to go." Says Alan G. Hassenfeld, 43, CEO of toymaker Hasbro in Pawtucket, Rhode Island: "We have a program called 'Write to the top' in which everyone is encouraged to write to me about anything that's on their minds, and it's read only by me. We are meeting more often with senior management in small group settings, and they in turn are doing the same with middle management."

Nearly 60% of the chief executives say they conduct employee surveys regularly, and most of those bosses claim they augment the surveys with frequent personal contact. But some concede that restructuring still takes a toll on employee attitudes. "We've worked hard at bottom-up, two-way communication," says Richard A. Clarke, 61, chairman of Pacific Gas & Electric in San Francisco. While removing layers of management has been good for that, it hasn't helped middle-management morale. So in addition to employee surveys and a twice-a-year video presentation to all 80 PG&E locations, Clarke holds monthly brown-bag lunches where managers can ask questions or air gripes. The lunches "develop a good dialogue," Clarke says.

With all those chief executives out there communicating like crazy and believing that their efforts are giving morale a shot in the arm, why are middle managers and professionals still feeling unappreciated and cut off? Could it be that when the boss asks for an employee's opinion on the really tough issues, the employee is less than candid? Some who have pondered the question think so. Manhattan consultant Dee Soder recalls hearing a conversation between two middle managers about an anonymous employee survey they were being asked to fill out. Said one to the other: "Oh, come on, you're not going to write down what you *really* think, are you?" That, says Soder, is a common attitude, and one that defeats the purpose of doing surveys at all.

Consultant and author Robert Kriegel agrees. "Most middle managers really do not want to rock the boat," he says. "They tell their bosses what they think their bosses want to hear, and then go home and seethe privately." Kriegel says this is a shame, since in his view many top executives really do want to know what their subordinates are thinking. The *Fortune* poll of chief executives strongly suggests that he is right. Could it be that those middle managers who don't speak up have no one to blame but themselves?

SOURCE: T. Welsh, "CEOs Think That Morale Is Dandy," *Fortune* (18 Nov. 1991), 83–84.

ROLE OF THE HUMAN RESOURCE DEPARTMENT

The role of the HR department in improving quality can be considerable, as illustrated in the Grand Union example. In general, it can

- Assist in the formulation of the firm's strategic direction and needs
- Identify the human resource philosophies or culture consistent with the business needs
- Develop and implement human resource policies and activities consistent with the human resource culture
- Ensure that the human resource process is consistent with the other human resource activities

If, as in the case of the Grand Union, organizational change creates new strategic needs, the human resource department can play a critical role in the change process by establishing a human resource initiative, i.e., a specific program that is responsible for formulating and implementing the major strategic change. The initiative can involve

- Establishing a senior human resource council and executive operating committee
- Naming a major initiative that rallies all employees to the change
- Developing a leadership program that ensures that the change clearly includes the top management (this is often called a senior management development program)

In the development of the senior management program (and other programs that facilitate the change throughout the organization), a director of executive development or strategic education, such as Horace Parker of FPC, often takes the lead. This individual knows the top team perhaps better than any other human resource person. This being the case, this person can then orchestrate the entire change process—and thus the entire strategic human resource management function.[35]

Within the human resource department there can be further division of roles and responsibilities. This often involves clarifying the relationship between the corporate human resource department and the business unit or division human resource departments. Taking a very proactive stance, the corporate human resource department can:

- Assist senior managers in formulating change
- Become a model of change
- Develop and guide divisional human resources
- Change organizational structure
- Serve as a clearinghouse
- Serve as trainer for other human resource staff
- Do benchmark analysis

- Develop HRIS capability
- Audit competencies

The activities of the divisional human resource departments then reflect the activities that are established by the corporate human resource department. However, where the corporate human resource department abdicates responsibility to the divisions, or where the divisions just seize the initiative, the divisions can essentially perform the roles just ascribed to the corporate human resource department. The examples of Grand Union and FPC offer examples of both of these situations. They show that, while there is variation in the sharing of the roles between the corporate human resource department and the divisional human resource departments, there should be little variation in *whether* these roles are performed. Indeed, in the extreme case, many of these roles could be performed by the line managers with or without the assistance of others. Similarly, there should be little variation in deciding *whether* to demonstrate the value of an organizational improvement program.

FOCUS ISSUES IN ORGANIZATIONAL IMPROVEMENT

*Demonstrating Contribution**[36]

A major business problem confronted a $10-million printing company. Specifically, for a number of years the company enjoyed a profitable market niche doing a particular type of specialty printing. The other printing companies caught onto this great moneymaking specialty and began encroaching on the company's market. Within five years, the company's profit margins had shrunk tremendously.

Because of these factors, the company confronted the need to increase profits in an increasingly competitive market niche. Equipment was not the problem since the company's production lines used the latest models of efficient, high-speed printing and binding equipment. Office and administrative work was computerized. Work force quality also was not the problem. Indeed, most employees were highly experienced in their jobs and had worked for the company for more than ten years. Furthermore, the way to increased profits was not in improving workers' motivation, since the work force exhibited good morale and an admirable work ethic. In fact, the employees never felt a need for a union, although most competing firms in their region were unionized.

Since the company's goal was to improve profits, there was no actual cost of the problem, as shown in exhibit 13.9. The firm's president and its human resources director discussed the business problem and possible human resources oriented solutions. They decided to try a one-day team-building session as the solution to the problem, because the two of them wondered whether the department heads could collaborate better or differently in order to improve company profits.

The team-building session was conducted by a management psychologist with expertise in team-building. The day-long session was held in a meeting room at a local hotel. Participants included the company president and all ten department heads.

*The following section "Demonstrating Contribution," is reprinted by permission of the publisher, from TURNING YOUR HUMAN RESOURCE DEPARTMENT INTO A PROFIT CENTER, pp. 173–177,

Exhibit 13.9
Model for Using Team-building to Improve Profits

Business Problem

A printing company wants to produce more profits in its increasingly competitive market.

Cost of the Problem

No specific cost, since the company's goal is to improve profitability and not to overcome a specific problem in the usual sense.

Solution to Business Problem

1-day team-building session

Participants included the company president and all 10 department heads. An outside team-building expert conducted the session.

Cost of Solution

$4,650
Costs included:

A. Participants' daily salary and benefits
= Number of participants × Average daily salaries and benefits
= 11 participants × $300/day
= $3,300

B. Consultant's fee = $1,000

C. Hotel, meals and refreshments = $350

Cost of solution
= $3,300 + $1,000 + $350
= $4,650

$ Improvement Benefit

$520,000/year in increased sales or $130,000/year in increased profits

Improvement in sales
= Amount of increased sales per week × Number of weeks per year
= $10,000/week × 52 weeks/year
= $520,000/year in increased sales

Improvement in profits
= Amount of improvement in sales per year × Percentage of sales that is profit
= $520,000/year × 25% = $520,000/year × .25
= $130,000/year in increased profits

Cost-Benefit Ratio

112:1 for increased sales
$520,000: $4,650 for increased sales
or
28:1 for increased profits
$130,000: $4,650 for increased profits

SOURCE: M. Mercer, *Turning Your Human Resources Department into a Profit Center* (New York: AMACOM, 1989) 174–75.

The president kicked off the session by saying that its purpose was for the assembled company managers to figure out how to work better together in such a way that the company could measurably better its profit picture. After this introduction, the consultant led the group through three main steps:

1. Identifying the group's four primary problems that, if surmounted, would help the group perform better
2. Letting each participant give feedback and suggestions to all other participants on their positive points and their interpersonal areas needing improvement
3. Planning how to overcome each of the top four group problems the team identified in the beginning of the session

The cost of the solution was $4,650 for the one-day team-building session. This cost included the salaries and benefits of the company president and the ten department heads, the management psychologist's fee, plus the cost of the meeting facilities, meals, and refreshments.

A fascinating—and ultimately quite profitable—phenomenon occurred during the second step of the session. It surfaced that the sales director and the production director typically did not communicate very well. The sales director thought the production director was annoyingly detail-oriented and took too long to get needed answers. The production director felt the sales director was too pushy and loud. Because of these interpersonal problems, the two of them conversed as little as possible at the company.

While discussing this interaction difficulty and its effect on their work, the sales director suddenly gasped, "Oh, my goodness! I had no idea that the equipment could print materials two inches longer and bind printing three inches wider than we normally do now. We've been turning down at least $10,000 a week in orders for exactly that kind of extra-long and extra-wide printing!"

The company could take in orders for at least $520,000 per year if it just produced this very long and wide printing. That was the improvement benefit in terms of sales. Since so few other printing companies printed such specifications, the profit margin on that sort of printing was twenty-five percent or more. The over half-million dollars in increased sales translated into at least $130,000 per year in added profits for the company.

Indeed, the first action this group decided to take after the team-building session was to begin accepting orders immediately for the extra-long and extra-wide printing. An interesting sidelight to this situation is that this same eleven-person group met each and every Friday morning for a weekly management meeting. During all of these meetings, this problem had never come up. Without the team-building session, it may never have been acknowledged, and the firm never would have been able to take profitable action in overcoming this readily solvable business problem.

In terms of the cost-benefit ratio, this team-building session turned out to be a huge success. The $4,650 investment made to conduct the session produced $520,000 annually in new sales plus $130,000 in new profits. These financial improvements could be repeated year after year. The $4,650 investment could pay for itself 112:1 for increased sales or 28:1 for increased profits during just the first year after the team-building session. Given that these improvements would be repeated for a number of years, the cost-benefit ratio over a longer period of time would be even more extraordinary.

Quality Saves Money

Quality, quantity, and price have improved in unison for most successful global competitors. One may claim that Japanese automobiles have increased dramatically in price over the past few years, but economic analysis reveals the majority of price increases for U.S. buyers can be attributed to restricted supply induced by trade restrictions. In fact, prices might have dropped had the U.S. not imposed quotas and tariffs as it did during the 1980s. In contrast to the traditional view, the world-class companies of all nations find that improved quality results in lower costs and improved productivity. David T. Kearns, former CEO of Xerox, describes their early discoveries as Xerox began to systematically focus on quality:

> Pretty early in the process we realized the cost of nonconformance [to quality specification in manufacturing] was costing us 20% of revenues. The opportunity was enormous.[37]

Motorola's Chief Executive George M. Fisher says, "Americans used to fall into the trap that high quality costs more. But high quality and low cost go hand in hand."[38] At Motorola, quality improvement yielded 25 to 30 percent reductions in costs.

Notable leaders in the worldwide quality improvement process echo similar estimates. Joseph M. Juran estimates that about a third of the U.S. economy is expended on rework due to low quality. W. Edwards Deming suggests the cost of poor quality is in the area of 30 percent of current production. Some obvious costs come in the form of rework, detection (inspection and monitoring), scrap, warranty, and repairs. However, manufacturing may not be the largest source of quality problems. Richard Beutow, Quality Director at Motorola, guesses that 90 percent of the errors made by Motorola employees have nothing to do with manufacturing; they have to do with filling out forms correctly, acting quickly, and providing service.[39] Even within manufacturing, the costs of quality do not arise from production. Juran and other experts estimate that no more than 20 percent of defects can be traced to production; the other 80 percent come from design or purchasing policies that value low prices over higher quality.

Increasingly, product and service liability—direct and in the form of insurance costs—consume a huge portion of organizations' budgets. In businesses ranging from maternity medical services and alpine skiing to private aircraft and waste hauling, liability costs can account for over half of the consumer's price. Nevertheless, Deming contends that, for most companies, these direct costs account for a small share of the real costs to individual companies; their biggest costs come from customer dissatisfaction and defection to competitors. This leads to a lost customer base and a lost future for many companies. Those costs are uncountable but critical.

Quality improvement can reduce costs in another way, too. Because quality improvement typically involves greater employee commitment and utilization, fewer employees are needed to produce the same level of output. For example, L. L. Bean's sales have increased tenfold; the number of employees has risen only fivefold. Thanks to a quality-improvement program and a cooperative work force, Toyota is producing 3.5 million vehicles a year with 25,000 production workers—the same number of workers it took to produce 1 million vehicles in 1966. Not only are Toyota workers more productive, but rejects for poor quality are fewer. This further reduces the labor needed for and reduces costs as well.

Without much doubt, the march to quality will continue. Not only do customers want quality, but competitors are willing to offer it; and, far from adding to total costs, total quality management (TQM) can actually reduce costs.[40]

INTERNATIONAL COMPARISONS

Germany

In Germany, workers perform in "work islands" where they can avoid boredom by rotating jobs, socializing, and working in cycles of up to twenty minutes rather than a few seconds. In assembling electronics products, automobiles, and appliances, the Germans appear to be well ahead of other countries in modifying or reducing the conventional assembly line and its simple, repetitive jobs. This enlightened position in alternative job design utilization is a product of the work humanization movement in Germany, initially funded by the German government in 1974 and maintained by the cooperative relationship between labor and management. Many companies also furnish their own funds for work design innovation projects.

Although each company's project may result in different types of job design, common emphasis is placed on enlarging assembly jobs by adding more complex tasks. One goal is to ensure the job cycle is more than one and one-half minutes, the point below which employees have been found to become dissatisfied with the job. As a consequence of the experiments in various companies, three major ways are being used to modify the traditional assembly line and its jobs. In **group assembly,** workers rotate jobs as they follow the product from the first to the last step in the assembly process. This is the notion of the "work island," where workers have the opportunity to socialize and are tied together by a group incentive pay plan. With **individual work stations,** work is done by the individual in a cycle time of ten to fifteen minutes. During this time, the worker assembles a major subcomponent of the total product (for example, an electric motor for a washing machine). Finally, **assembly lines** are being modified to make work easier and lighter. Where the assembly line cannot be easily replaced, as in automotive assembly, the line has been altered so that the worker stands on platforms moving at the same speed as the car.[41]

Sweden

The Volvo quality-of-work-life projects have been implemented in several plants in Sweden, but the most famous is at Volvo's assembly plant in the city of Kalmar. This plant, in operation since 1972, uses work teams instead of the traditional assembly line and allows employees to design and organize their own work. The plant was built in response to employees' job hopping, absenteeism, apathetic attitudes, antagonism, and an extremely low level of unemployment in Sweden.

Volvo's quality-of-work-life project made substantial improvements by changing the technology for assembling cars. Although changing the technology of an organization is not easy or inexpensive, Volvo proved that it can be done successfully. In fact, changing the technology may be the only way to satisfy the needs and values of employees. As P. G. Gyllenhammar of Volvo reported in the *Harvard Business Review:*

> When we started thinking about reorganizing the way we worked, the first bottleneck seemed to be production and technology. We couldn't really reorganize the work to suit the people unless we also changed the technology that chained people to the assembly line.[42]

Now car assembly is done in work groups of about twenty people. The change in technology has been accompanied by a new climate of cooperation, partnership, and participation, and by an improved physical working environment.

Employee participation through councils and committees resulted in increased employee involvement and further improvements in the work itself. This participation is implemented in accordance with a 1977 Swedish law calling for full consultation with employees and full participation by their representatives in decision making from board level to the shop floor.

A quality-of-work-life project has also been instituted at Volvo's major plant in Torslanda. Here, participation and autonomous groups are the two dominant techniques.

A technique used in both plants at the discretion of the workers is job rotation at Torslanda. This is done within the relatively autonomous work groups. Today approximately seventy percent of the assembly workers engage in job rotation. Again, P. G. Gyllenhammar of Volvo observes: "There will always be a few people, however, especially older ones, who don't want to change (jobs) at all." This recognition and acceptance of employee differences is an important factor in the long-run success of quality-of-work-life projects in general.[43]

SUMMARY

One of the key words for the 1990s is competitiveness. To survive and be profitable, organizations will need to continually be competitive. To be competitive, organizations will need to continually improve. Domestic and international competition is so intense that anything less than a full commitment to continual improvement—what the Japanese call *kaizen*—will signal economic decline. Even organizations that may not face international competition still face an increasingly competitive domestic economy.

More than ever, competitiveness depends on an organization's success in managing its human resources effectively. In some cases this means linking its human resource practices to the competitive strategy of the business. In other cases it may mean redesigning jobs and creating effective teamwork structures. In any case, it means that the HR manager must know what the business is about. He or she must take an active role in knowing what are the products and strategies of the business and what technologies are available to redesign jobs, if necessary.

By taking an active role in managing organizational improvements, the HR manager gains more credibility as a businessperson. This, in turn, enables the HR manager to become a player on the management team. The entire HR department can thus be seen as more valuable to the entire organization. As this occurs, programs for organizational improvement become more acceptable to line managers, thus making successful implementation more likely. The result of all this is organizations that are more competitive, employees who are more involved in their work, and customers who are more satisfied with the products and services of the organizations.

In addition to using the programs for organizational improvement identified in this chapter, firms can also improve by changing specific human resource practices such as the tests used in employee selection and placement. Usually this kind of work is done by human resource specialists working in personnel research. Thus, we investigate this activity in the next chapter entitled Personnel Research.

WHERE WE ARE TODAY

1. Human resource management plays an important part in the successful implementation of competitive strategies, such as those to improve quality, reduce costs, or facilitate innovation.
2. Human resource management facilitates the implementation of competitive strategies by describing what employees need to do and then rewarding them for doing it. This is more complex than it sounds, because it takes a great deal of analysis to decide what employees really need to do to help implement the strategy and then to decide which human resource practices signal and reward those role behaviors needed from the employees.
3. Increasingly, organizations are redesigning jobs to give employees more decision-making authority and responsibility as well as the chance to develop and utilize more skills and abilities. These responsibilities and opportunities are certainly critical in programs to empower employees, individually and in teams.
4. Firms anticipate that empowered employees will be more motivated to make decisions and work effectively. They also anticipate that employees will make better decisions than their managers might make, conceding that "No one knows the job better than the people doing it."
5. Especially for quality-improvement programs, organizations are encouraging their employees to work in teams; and, just as they are empowering individuals, they are empowering teams. As a result we hear about self-managing teams, empowering teams, and self-directed teams. You likely will be working in a team in your organization—if not now, in the near future.
6. Top management can stay in touch with the thoughts, attitudes, and feelings of their employees by surveying them on a regular basis. Of course, this entails a responsibility to respond to the employees. Failure to give feedback to them about what top management thinks is likely to reduce the effectiveness and participation rate of employees in future surveys.
7. An increasingly important role for human resource managers is managing the process of change. This role is important to organizations because the need to constantly change and adapt is greater than ever.
8. A major way human resource managers are facilitating the change process is through the use of executive and management development programs. These programs give managers a chance to discuss what the organization needs and how they will go about achieving those needs.
9. Gone are the days of certainty and predictability. Life in organizations today is one of constant flux. If technology is not changing, the competition or something else is changing. The best way to deal with this environment is to assume that change is the constant, and to remain flexible and adaptable.

10. Human resource management can make significant and measurable contributions to organizations. This is true for organizational improvement programs and for all other programs in human resource management.

DISCUSSION QUESTIONS

1. What is the importance of organizational improvement programs?
2. What are the essential human resource aspects of the three competitive strategies?
3. What are the human resource implications for firms pursuing a high-quality strategy?
4. How do job enrichment programs differ from job rotation programs?
5. What important factors influence the choice of job redesign approaches?
6. Automation of office systems since the advent of microcomputers has resulted in some companies permitting employees (for example, computer programmers) to work at home. What are some of the advantages and disadvantages of this arrangement? How would you overcome the disadvantages?
7. How can automation and advanced technology really improve the competitiveness of organizations?
8. Why is it so important to pay attention to the process of managing change?
9. What are the strengths and limitations of organizational surveys?
10. What are the human resource implications if firms want to remain competitive in the 1990s?

APPLIED PROJECTS

1. A fast-food chain has invited you in to make suggestions to improve its quality of customer service. Top management believes improving service will mean that prices and margins can be increased. While they understand that such things as the type of food and the physical appearance of the restaurants may need to change to improve the quality of service, they want you to tell them about the human resource implications. What are your suggestions, and what are the HR implications?
2. Productivity is a key concern to organizations. Go to companies and find out what they are doing to improve (if they are) productivity. Describe the role of personnel and human resource management in the companies' efforts to improve productivity, and describe what specific things personnel and human resource management has done to improve productivity. Visit as many different types of companies as possible so that efforts to improve productivity in different work environments can be shared in class.

CASE STUDY

How May We Serve You?

Jean Marie Stora has been with IFM for ten years. During his time with the firm he has seen sales go from $25 billion to $54 billion, all through internal growth except for two acquisitions that together added about $10 billion in sales. Because he has been director of marketing in the French country operation for the past three years, he takes some pride in thinking that his market instincts have served him and IFM well. It was well known that, when he took over the French marketing operation of this large, multinational consumer products and food conglomerate headquartered in Zurich, the French market was the most challenging because of competitors like BSN. His desire for challenge and his desire to see IFM overtake its competitors in Europe made the marketing job in France that much more appealing. In three years Stora turned the French market around and increased IFM's presence in four major product groups by more than anyone thought possible. As a consequence of his success, he was ready to take on another challenge. His desire coincided with the unexpected resignation of the vice-president in charge of personnel for all European operations.

The European operations of IFM represent more than seventy-five percent of worldwide sales. Unfortunately, its percentage of the total profits is less than fifty percent. Thus, while he was doing well in France in terms of *both* sales and profits, IFM in Europe was only gaining in terms of sales. His evaluation of the situation and what was happening in Europe convinced him that the personnel job would be not only the most challenging job he could take, but also the most important to the firm. His ten years of marketing experience in the U.S. with a major consumer products company combined with his ten years with IFM persuaded him that, unless the firm focused even more on quality service, it would not increase profits.

Stora knows that quality service means higher margins. He also knows that moving all their products and services upscale has great implications for personnel management. Only one person, however, sees the situation the same way. The other person, Pablo Gomez, is the director of personnel in the firm's Spanish operation. Personnel had always played a very minor role in the operations of the firm. Neither headquarters nor country managers thought personnel could do much for them—it never had done much more than administer the payroll and car schemes.

Still, Stora is determined to apply his marketing savvy to the personnel area. Thinking that personnel could market its products and services just like the firm did, he reasons that all he has to do is to ask the customers what they want and then provide them with products and services they really value. This is what he wants to see happen in his own operation and in the country operations. He is getting into his new job, but now he's not sure exactly where to start or what to do.

SOURCE: © Randall S. Schuler, New York University.

Case Questions

1. In his new position, who are Stora's customers? How can Stora better serve their needs?
2. Are the members of corporate personnel capable now of better serving their customers?
3. What are the implications for the country personnel directors of the change to a more customer-oriented personnel department? How can Stora get the country personnel directors to change?
4. Will the firm have to change its HR practices? Describe how.

NOTES

1. This material from the Grand Union is based on interviews with Bill Reffett, senior vice-president of human resources, during March 1989. The material here only refers to human resource management related changes that were made. Changes, of course, were also made in purchasing, merchandising, and operations. Reffett is now with Korn Ferry International.
2. See note 1.
3. R. S. Schuler and S. E. Jackson, "Linking Competitive Strategies and Human Resource Management Practices," *Academy of Management Executive* (Aug. 1987): 207–219.
4. J. Main, "The Winning Organization," *Fortune* (26 Sept. 1988): 50–56. Also see B. Schneider, *Organizational Climate and Culture* (San Francisco: Jossey-Bass, 1990); D. R. Denison, *Corporate Culture and Organizational Effectiveness* (New York: John Wiley & Son, 1990); J. R. Lincoln and A. L. Kalleberg, *Culture, Control and Commitment: A Study of Work Organization and Work Attitudes in the United States and Japan* (New York: Cambridge University Press, 1990); E. H. Schein, "Organizational Culture," *American Psychologist* (Feb. 1990): 109–119; G. E. Neuman, J. E. Edwards, and N. S. Raju, "Organizational Development Interventions: A Meta-Analysis of Their Effects on Satisfaction and Other Attitudes," *Personnel Psychology* 42 (1989): 461–89; M. K. Moch and J. M. Bartunek, *Creating Alternative Realities at Work: The Quality of Work Life Experiment at FoodCom* (New York: Harper & Row, 1990); B. M. Meglino, E. C. Ravlin, and C. L. Adkins, "A Work Values Approach to Corporate Culture: A Field Test of the Value Congruence Process and Its Relationship to Individual Outcomes," *Journal of Applied Psychology* 74, no. 3 (1989): 424–32; S.

Thiederman, *Bridging Cultural Barriers for Corporate Success* (Lexington, Mass.: Lexington Books, 1991), R. M. Kanter, B. A. Stein, and T. Jick, *The Challenge of Organizational Change* (The Free Press, 1992).

5. R. M. Kanter, "Supporting Innovation and Venture Development in Established Companies," *Journal of Business Venturing* (Winter 1985): 47–60.
6. H. DePree, *Business as Unusual* (Zeeland, Mich.: Herman Miller, 1986); K. Labich, "The Innovators," *Fortune* (6 June 1988): 50–64.
7. E. M. Fowler, "Productive Ideas from Employees," *The New York Times* (28 Aug. 1987): 21.
8. S. P. Galante, "Frost Inc. Technological Renewal and Human Resource Management: A Case Study," *Human Resource Planning,* 10, no. 1: 57–67.
9. Main, "The Winning Organization": 51.
10. W. E. Deming, *Quality, Productivity and Competitive Position* (Cambridge, Mass.: MIT Center for Advanced Engineering Study, 1982); W. E. Deming, *Out of Crisis* (Cambridge: MIT Press, 1986): 23–24. Also see R. S. Schuler and D. Harris, *Managing Quality* (Reading, Mass.: Addison-Wesley, 1992); C. B. Adair-Heeley, *The Human Side of Just-In-Time: How to Make the Techniques Really Work* (New York: AMACOM, 1991); K. A. Brown and T. R. Mitchell, "A Comparison of Just-In-Time and Batch Manufacturing: The Role of Performance Obstacles," *Academy of Management Journal* 34, no. 4 (1991): 906–917; W. A. Band, *Creating Value for Customers: Designing and Implementing a Total Corporate Strategy* (New York: Wiley, 1991); M. Beer, R. A. Eisenstat, and B. Spector, *The Critical Path to Corporate Renewal* (Boston: Harvard Business School Press, 1990); T. R. Horton and P. C. Reid, *Beyond the Trust Gap: Forging a New Partnership Between Managers and Their Employers* (Homewood, Ill.: Irwin, 1990); G. K. Suri, A. Singh, and S. Akhtar, eds., *Quality of Worklife and Productivity* (New Dehli, India: National Productivity Council, 1991); G. Merli, *Total Manufacturing Management: Production Organization for the 1990s* (Cambridge, Mass.: Productivity Press, 1990); T. H. Berry, *Managing the Total Quality Transformation* (New York: McGraw-Hill, 1991); M. Walton, *Deming Management at Work* (New York: Putnam, 1990), J. M. Juran, *Juran On Quality by Design* (The Free Press, 1992).
11. D. A. Garvin, "How the Baldrige Award Really Works," *Harvard Business Review* (Nov.-Dec. 1991): 80–95.
12. For more detail on using human resource management in service organizations see V. Johnston and H. Moore, "Pride Drives Wal-Mart to Service Excellence," *HR Magazine* (Oct. 1991): 79–80, 82; J. E. Santora, "Pacific Bell Primes the Quality Pump," *Personnel Journal* (Oct. 1991): 63–66; D. E. Bowen, R. B. Chase, and T. G. Cummings & Associates, *Service Management Effectiveness* (San Francisco: Jossey-Bass, 1990); S. W. Brown, E. Gummesson, B. Edvardsson, and B. Gustavsson, *Service Quality* (Lexington, Mass.: Lexington Books, 1991); R. B. Chase and E. B. Bowen, "Service Quality and the Service Delivery System: a Diagnostic Framework," in S. W. Brown, E. Gummesson, B. Edvardsson and B. Gustavvson, eds., *Service Quality:* 157–78; K. D. Denton, "The Service Imperative," *Personnel Journal* (March 1990): 66–74; F. Luthans and T. R. V. Davis, "Applying Behavioral Management Techniques in Service Organizations," in D. E. Bowen, et al., *Service Management Effectiveness* (San Francisco: Jossey-Bass): 126–51; Japan Human Relations Association, ed., *The Service Industry Idea Book: Employee Involvement in Retail and Office Improvement* (Cambridge, Mass.: Productivity Press, 1990).
13. A. B. Fisher, "Morale Crisis," *Fortune* (18 Nov. 1991): 70–72, 76, 80; R. L. Bunning, "The Dynamics of Downsizing," *Personnel Journal* (Sept. 1990): 69–74; C. Hymowitz, "When Firms Cut Out Middle Managers, Those at Top and Bottom Often Suffer," *The Wall Street Journal* (5 April 1990): B1; L. D. Foxman and W. L. Polsky, "Make the New Company Work After Downsizing," *Personnel Journal* (Nov. 1988); E. R. Greenburg, "Downsizing and Worker Assistance: Latest AMA Survey Results," *Personnel* (Nov. 1988): 49–53; W. H. Wagel, "New Beginnings for Displaced Workers: Outplacement at G.E.," *Personnel* (Dec. 1988): 12–17; W. W. Tornow, "Contract Redesign," *Personnel Administrator* (Oct. 1988): 97–101.
14. D. Kirkpatrick, "Why Not Farm Out Your Computing?" *Fortune* (23 Sept. 1991): 103–104, 109, 112.
15. D. R. Ilgen and J. R. Hollenbeck, "The Structure of Work: Job Design and Roles," in M. D. Dunnette and L. M. Hough, eds., *Handbook of Industrial and Organizational Psychology,* vol. 2 (Palo Alto, Calif.: Consulting Psychologists Press, Inc.): 165–208; W. C. Howell, "Human Factors in the Workplace," in Dunnette and Hough, eds., *Handbook of Industrial and Organizational Psychology:* 209–270; R. Ford, *Motivation through Work Itself* (New York: American Management Association, 1969); Garson, *The Electronic Sweatshop* (New York: Simon and Schuster, 1988).
16. "United Parcel Service Gets Deliveries Done by Driving Its Workers," *The Wall Street Journal* (22 April 1986): 1, 23. Also see J. Huey, "The Best Cities in America," *Fortune* (4 Nov. 1991): 52–63.
17. M. A. Campion and C. L. McClelland, "Interdisciplinary Examination of the Costs and Benefits of Enlarged Jobs: A Job Design Quasi-Experiment," *Journal of Applied Psychology* 76, no. 2 (1991): 186–98; Y. Fried, "Meta-Analytic Comparison of the Job Diagnostic Survey and Job Characteristics Inventory as Correlates of Work Satisfaction and Performance," *Journal of Applied Psychology* 76, no. 5 (1991): 690–97; C. S. Wong and M. A. Campion, "Development and Test of a Task Level Model of Motivational Job Design," *Journal of Applied Psychology* 76, no. 6 (1991): 825–37; R. W. Griffin, "Effects of Work Redesign On Employee Perceptions, Attitudes, and Behaviors: A Long-Term Investigation," *Academy of Management Journal* 34, no. 2 (1991): 425–535; G. R. Oldham, C. T. Kulik, and L. S. Stepina, "Physical Environments and Employee Reactions: Effects of Stimulus-Screening Skills and Job Complexity," *Academy of Management Journal* 34, no. 4 (1991): 929–38; M. A. Campion and C. J. Berger, "Conceptual Integration and Empirical Test of Job Design and Compensation Relationships," *Personnel Psychology* 43 (1990): 525–53; T. D. Taber and E. Taylor, "A Review and Evaluation of the Psychometric Properties of the Job Diagnostic Survey," *Personnel Psychology* 43 (1990): 467–500;

L. Yorks and D. A. Whitsett, *Scenarios of Change: Advocacy and the Diffusion of Job Redesign in Organizations* (Westport, Conn.: Praeger Publishers, 1989); K. W. Thomas and B. A. Velthouse, "Cognitive Elements of Empowerment: An 'Interpretive' Model of Intrinsic Task Motivation," *Academy of Management Review* 15, no. 4 (1990): 666–81; M. A. Campion, "Ability Requirement Implications of Job Design: An Interdisciplinary Perspective," *Personnel Psychology* 42 (1989): 1–24; M. A. Campion and P. W. Thayer, "Development and Field Evaluation of an Interdisciplinary Measure of Job Design," *Journal of Applied Psychology* (Feb. 1985): 29–43; Y. Fried and G. Ferris, "The Dimensionality of Job Characteristics: Some Neglected Issues," *Journal of Applied Psychology* 71, no. 3 (Aug. 1986): 419–26; J. R. Hackman, G. R. Oldham, R. Janson, and K. Purdy, "A New Strategy for Job Enrichment," *California Management Review* (Summer 1975): 57–71; J. R. Hackman, J. L. Pearce, and J. C. Wolfe, "Effects of Changes in Job Characteristics on Work Attitudes and Behaviors: A Naturally Occurring Quasi-Experiment," *Organizational Behavior and Human Performance* 21 (1978): 289–304; J. Thomas and R. Griffin, "The Social Information Processing Model for Task Design: A Review of the Literature," *Academy of Management Review* (Oct. 1983): 672–82.

18. J. Hoerr, "The Payoff from Teamwork," *Business Week* (10 July 1989): 56-62; G. W. Bohlander and A. J. Kinicki, "Where Personnel and Productivity Meet," *Personnel Administrator* (Sept. 1988): 122–30; J. Holusha, "Beating Japan at its Own Game," *The New York Times* (16 July 1989): 3:1; "Can You Compete?" *Business Week* (17 Dec. 1990): 60–132; J. Hoerr, "Is Teamwork a Management Plot? Mostly Not," *Business Week* (20 Feb. 1989): 70; E. E. Lawler III and S. A. Mohrman, "With HR Help, All Managers Can Practice High-Involvement Management," *Personnel* (April 1989): 26–31; M. Bassin, "Teamwork at General Foods: New and Improved," *Personnel Journal* (May 1988): 62–70; B. Dumaine, "Who Needs a Boss?" *Fortune* (7 May 1990): 52–60; A. S. Blinder, "Want to Boost Productivity? Try Giving Workers a Say," *Business Week* (17 April 1989): 10; "Manufacturers Urged to Increase Worker Responsibility," *Bulletin to Management* (13 Sept. 1990): 1; A. Taylor III, "Back to the Future at Saturn," *Fortune* (1 Aug. 1988): 63–64, 68, 72; "A Quality Overview," *HR Reporter* (Nov. 1990): 1, 7; S. Worchel, W. Wood, and J. A. Simpson, eds., *Group Process and Productivity* (London: Sage Publications, 1992); R. S. Wellins, W. C. Byham, and J. M. Wilson, *Empowered Teams: Creating Self-Directed Work Groups that Improve Quality, Productivity and Participation* (San Francisco: Jossey-Bass, 1991); W. Watson, L. K. Michaelson, and W. Sharp, "Member Competence, Group Interaction, and Group Decision Making: A Longitudinal Study," *Journal of Applied Psychology* 76, no. 6 (1991): 803–809; P. S. Goodman and D. P. Leyden, "Familiarity and Group Productivity," *Journal of Applied Psychology* 76, no. 4 (1991): 578–86; R. E. Cole, *Strategies for Learning: Small Group Activities in American, Japanese and Swedish Industry* (Berkeley: University of California Press, 1989); J. J. Fucini and S. Fucini, *Working for the Japanese: Inside Mazda's American Auto Plant* (New York: The Free Press, 1990); J. E. Mathieu and S. S. Kohler, "A Cross-Level Examination of Group Absence Influences on Individual Absence," *Journal of Applied Psychology* 75, no. 2 (1990): 217–20; D. Gladstein Ancona, "Outward Bound: Strategies for Team Survival in an Organization," *Academy of Management Journal* 23, no. 2 (1990): 334–65; C. J. G. Gerswick, "Marking Time: Predictable Transitions in Task Groups," *Academy of Management Journal* 32, no. 2 (1989): 274–309; J. L. Cordery. W. S. Mueller, and L. M. Smith, "Attitudinal and Behavioral Effects of Autonomous Group Working: A Longitudinal Field Study," *Academy of Management Journal* 34, no. 2 (1991): 464–76; J. L. Komaki, M. L. Desselles, and E. D. Bowman, "Definitely Not a Breeze: Extending an Operant Model of Effective Supervision to Teams," *Journal of Applied Psychology* 74, no. 3 (1989): 522–29; E. L. Deci, J. P. Connell, and R. M. Ryan, "Self-Determination in a Work Organization," *Journal of Applied Psychology* 74, no. 4 (1989): 580–90; Y. Yasuda, *40 Years, 20 Million Ideas: The Toyota Suggestion System* (Cambridge, Mass.: Productivity Press, 1990); R. J. Magjuka and T. T. Baldwin, "Team-Based Employee Involvement Programs: Effects of Design and Administration," *Personnel Psychology* 44 (1991): 793–812; D. M. Schweiger, W. R. Sandberg, and P. L. Rechner, "Experiential Effects of Dialectical Inquiry, Devil's Advocacy, and Consensus Approaches to Strategic Decision Making," *Academy of Management Journal* 32, no. 4 (1989): 745–72.

19. "Ergonomics Training Eases Man-Machine Interface," *Management Review* (Oct. 1984): 55.

20. S. L. Perlman, "Employees Redesign Their Jobs," *Personnel Journal* (Nov. 1990): 37–39; A. Aldag and A. P. Brief, *Task Design and Employee Motivation* (Glenview, Ill.: Scott, Foresman, 1979); Griffin, *Task Design;* R. E. Kopelman, "Job Redesign and Productivity: A Review of the Evidence," *National Productivity Review* (Summer 1985): 237–55; B. Schneider, A. Reichers, and T. M. Mitchell, "A Note on Some Relationships Between the Aptitude Requirements and Reward Attributes of Tasks," *Academy of Management Journal* 25 (1982): 567–74.

21. J. F. Coates, "An Environmental Scan: Projecting Future Human Resource Trends," *Human Resource Planning* (Dec. 1987): 219–29.

22. See note 21.

23. J. Dreyfuss, "Catching the Computer Wave," *Fortune* (26 Sept. 1988): 78–82.

24. Main, "The Winning Corporation."

25. Coates, "An Environmental Scan."

26. D. L. Tarbania, "Automation in the Office: Users Expand Its Role at All Levels," *AMA Forum* (Nov. 1984): 29–30.

27. S. D. Solomon, "Use Technology to Manage People," *INC.* (May 1990): 124. Also see T. D. Wall, J. M. Corbett, R. Martin, C. W. Clegg, and P. R. Jackson, "Advanced Manufacturing Technology, Work Design, and Performance: A change Study," *Journal of Applied Psychology* 75, no. 6 (1990): 691–97; J. W. Dean, Jr., and S. A. Snell, "Integrated Manufacturing and Job Design: Moderating Effects of Organizational Inertia," *Academy of Management Journal* 34, no. 4 (1991): 776–804.

28. Coates, "An Environmental Scan."
29. Main, "The Winning Organization."
30. B. Garson, *The Electronic Sweatshop*. Also see S. Zuboff, *In the Age of the Smart Machine: The Future of Work and Power* (New York: Basic Books, 1988).
31. R. B. Dunham and F. J. Smith, *Organization Surveys* (Glenview, Ill.: Scott, Foresman, 1979): 91–97. Also see W. H. Read, "Gathering Opinion On-Line," *HR Magazine* (Jan. 1991): 51–53.
32. Dunham and Smith, *Organization Surveys:* 13.
33. *Bulletin to Management* (14 July 1988): 3.
34. J. Nadel, D. Naasz, and T. Scullen, "HR Conference Report," *Bulletin to Management* (1 Nov. 1990): 3–4.
35. J. F. Bolt, *Executive Development* (New York: Harper & Row, 1989): 140.
36. This example from M. W. Mercer, *Turning Your Human Resources Department into a Profit Center* (New York: AMACOM, 1989): 173–77. Used by permission. Also see R. D. Pritchard, *Measuring and Improving Organizational Productivity: A Practical Guide* (New York: Praeger Publishers, 1990).
37. "Quality at Xerox," *The New York Times* (9 Nov. 1989): D1.
38. J. Therrien, *Fortune.*
39. *Fortune* (24 Oct. 1990): 168.
40. Schuler and Harris, *Managing Quality ...*
41. This is based on the description by J. M. Geddes, "Germany Profits by Apprentice System" *The Wall Street Journal* (15 Sept. 1981): 22.
42. P. G. Gyllenhammar, "How Volvo Adapts Work to People," *Harvard Business Review* (July/Aug. 1977): 106.
43. See note 42.

CHAPTER 14

Personnel and Human Resource Management Research

You can't give 'em what they want without asking.

—Wayne Wilson, Corporate Vice President, Human Resources, Blue Cross, Western Pennsylvania[1]

Today sixty-five percent of CEOs in large, successful firms in highly competitive environments agree that the personnel and human resource department is critical to success of the business. These same CEOs see this increasing to eighty-five percent in the year 2000.

Results from another study predict that knowledge of human resource management will be the second most valuable knowledge after strategic management for CEOs in the year 2000. Thus, spending some time in a job in the human resource department is becoming critical for individuals who want to become CEOs.

When Wayne Nelson, corporate vice-president of human resources for Blue Cross of Pennsylvania, asked his line managers how they liked the training programs being offered by the HR department, the managers asked "What training programs?"

When Bill Reffett at the Grand Union grocery store operation asked the customers what they wanted, they said: "Better selection, more helpful clerks and a place where the people are friendly and the store looks pleasant."[2]

Of course, the point in all this is that, without personnel and human resource management research, we wouldn't know these things. With knowledge from research, firms such as Blue Cross of Pennsylvania go back to the drawing board and ask how they can better serve their customers, the line managers. The result can be a much better delivery of human resource products and services. In turn, this can result in a much more successful organization, especially since most CEOs think the quality of the firm's human resource management really does influence the success of the organization. Knowing that customers want better service enables human resource leaders such as Bill Reffett to make major organizational changes by modifying and aligning human resource practices with the needs of the customers and, thus, the business.

In essence, personnel and human resource management research provides the knowledge to apply to the practical situation and the knowledge to further improve the existing human resource activities discussed throughout this book.

PERSONNEL AND HUMAN RESOURCE MANAGEMENT RESEARCH

Personnel and human resource management research is the process of gathering data, interpreting its meaning, applying it to further research or application, and then evaluating practices and programs in order to make necessary revisions. Because it has application to all the activities described in the previous chapters, personnel and human resource management research is conducted using a variety of methods and procedures. This chapter reviews those methods and procedures, discusses areas in which researchers are currently addressing unresolved questions, and describes recent research findings.

This chapter extends our discussion of organizational surveys in chapter 13. There we discussed surveys as a means of communicating with employees; those surveys were classified as a means of organizational improvement. Surveys such as Wayne Nelson's at Blue Cross of Western Pennsylvania can also be used for research purposes, with the intention of improving organizational conditions. In fact, personnel and human resource management research generally is a systematic effort to improve conditions in organizations. Research can range from doing test-validation studies to help an organization do a better job of selecting applicants to gathering survey data from customers and employees in order to deliver better quality goods and services. Being systematic, it is typically based on the empirical research process.

THE EMPIRICAL RESEARCH PROCESS

Individuals and organizations possess numerous beliefs about why people perform as they do. The question in such cases is, "Which beliefs are true?" One way to test our beliefs is to conduct research. Understanding the research process helps individuals solve human resource problems in organizations; understand and apply the research results of others; assess the accuracy of claims made by others concerning the benefits of new procedures, programs, equipment, and so on; and evaluate the soundness of the theory relating to the performance of individuals in organizations.[3]

Exhibit 14.1 shows the five basic steps needed to conduct sound empirical research. Initially, the researcher will need to identify or be alerted to a problem and formulate a question or set of questions that will address the problem. At approximately the same time, the researcher will translate the research question into a testable **hypothesis**—a tentative statement about the relationship between two or more variables. Typically in personnel research, one variable is referred to as the **independent** or **predictor variable.** Examples of predictor variables are scores on selection tests or judgments of interviewers. The predictor

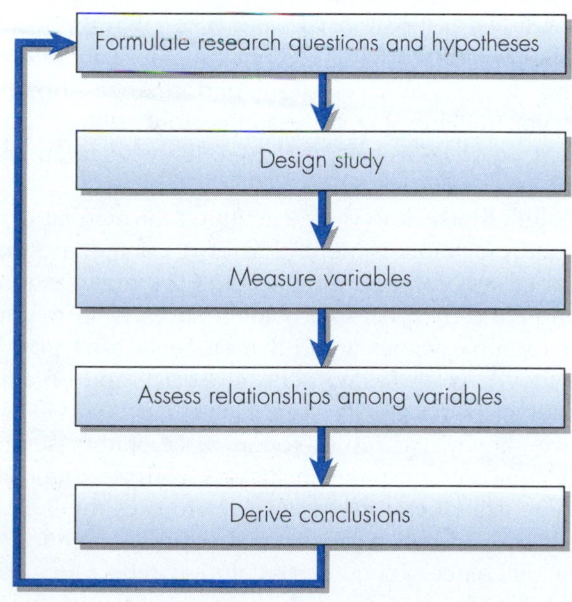

Exhibit 14.1
The Empirical Research Process

variable is often hypothesized to have some effect on or relationship with a **dependent variable** or **criterion.** The criterion is frequently a measure of job performance, such as an accident rate, reject rate, supervisory performance rating, training score, or absenteeism or turnover rate.

The second major step—the design of the research study—focuses on the development of a strategy to examine the validity or truth of the hypothesis. Next, the researcher implements the study and obtains scores (numerical values) on the variables being examined. These scores are then collected and statistically analyzed to determine the observed relationship between or among the variables. Finally, conclusions are drawn as to whether or not the hypothesized relationships were supported, as well as to the implications of the results. The conclusions derived from the study often provide useful information for formulating new research questions.

Human resource problems can be examined in a variety of ways. Some research is theoretical, designed to determine appropriate ways to measure constructs and variables important to understanding human resource activities in organizations. To acquire basic knowledge about personnel activities, research can be conducted in the laboratory. A field experiment is conducted in an organization but, as with laboratory research, one or more independent variables are manipulated to determine the effect on a dependent variable. Researchers also conduct field studies that do not involve the manipulation of variables, but rather the systematic examination of relationships between different variables (e.g. satisfaction and performance, commitment and absenteeism).

Laboratory Research

In a laboratory study, the environment is carefully controlled to ensure that extraneous factors do not influence the results. Laboratory research also allows the researcher to control the assignment of subjects to experimental conditions. In this way, such factors as age, gender, job experience, and prior performance can be carefully controlled. Laboratory research also gives the researcher control over all variables that influence the dependent variable. Laboratory research has provided basic knowledge about selection, performance appraisal processes, compensation decision making, human resource forecasting, and negotiations. Recently, it has been used extensively to acquire knowledge about how personnel decisions are made.

Despite the wealth of basic knowledge acquired through laboratory research, many researchers and practitioners are critical of it, contending that it simplifies complex issues and fails to consider the effects of the organizational context on behavior. Others are concerned because student subjects are often used instead of employees. For example, critics argue that students can't possibly think like managers; nor do they have the same political, social, and organizational pressures on them as managers do.

Proponents have shown that results found in laboratory settings are somewhat stronger, but point to the same conclusions as those found in applied settings. They also argue that laboratory research overcomes the limitation of study-specificity. That is, because each organizational setting is unique, it is difficult to determine whether differences found across studies reflect "real differences" or artifacts of the situation. By controlling the environment (via the laboratory), a body of knowledge can be built up that isn't muddled by contextual variables.[4]

Regarding student subjects, their usefulness depends on the type of decision being made. That is, they make decisions like any other naive decision maker. However, their use may not be appropriate if the objective of the study is to identify the simplifying rules used by experienced managers to make decisions. Still, researchers have shown that experts, like amateurs, fall prey to some common decision biases.[5]

Realistic materials. To overcome these concerns, laboratory researchers have done three things. First, many laboratory studies are carefully designed to mimic organizational events and contingencies. Consequently, experimental materials are carefully designed to parallel those used in actual settings (organizations).

Consider a recent laboratory study that examined the effects of decision context and anchoring bias (discussed in chapter 6) on selection decisions. Student subjects evaluated the resumés and letters of applicants submitted in response to an advertisement by an actual computer company. Some subjects were told there were three openings for computer technicians; others were told there was only one opening. Some of the subjects were told they could compare one candidate to another (simultaneous evaluation); others were told to evaluate one candidate after another (sequential evaluation).

The number of openings was found to affect judgments about job suitability when the decision maker compared one candidate with another but not when candidates were evaluated sequentially. Additionally, the study showed that if rapid decisions are needed, then evaluating candidates sequentially (one at a time) rather than simultaneously is more expeditious. The downside of sequential evaluations was that the first candidates to be evaluated were evaluated more leniently than they objectively should have been. The study provided a number of insights about hiring goals that would not have been acquired if the study had been conducted in an actual organization where information is less controlled.[6]

Managers as decision makers. Another strategy is to use organizational decision makers, rather than students, as subjects. For example, a recent study examined the effects of rater and ratee characteristics on performance appraisal, pay, training, and promotion decisions. While prior research had examined the effects of single variables (tenure, gender, pay grade), studies had neglected examining the constellation of variables that affect these judgments. The subjects were 229 administrative, professional, and technical managers who worked for a northeastern city government. The study was conducted as part of a training session on performance appraisal. To add realism, the organization's actual performance manual and its rating and pay system, as well as performance information gleaned from personnel files, were used as experimental materials. Performance profiles were constructed that varied in terms of four ratee characteristics (performance level, current pay, job tenure, and prior rating). Each manager evaluated five performance records selected from a pool of 480 profiles. In addition, information about the raters (sex, age, tenure, prior performance rating, and experience) was obtained.

The study showed that characteristics of the ratee directly affect evaluations, while characteristics of the subjects (raters) indirectly affect judgments. For example, ratees who received higher evaluations in the past got better evaluations in the present, regardless of the actual level of their performance. Female raters, more experienced raters, and raters who themselves had received higher ratings in the past all recommended larger pay increases for good performance than their colleagues did.[7]

Policy capturing. Finally, personnel and human resource researchers have begun using policy capturing, a method that requires subjects to make holistic evaluations of multi-attribute alternatives. This type of research is considered a major step forward because it parallels closely the complexity of HR decision making in actual organizations. Policy capturing studies have examined job choices of applicants, performance appraisal judgments, and compensation decisions. In a study of managerial salary-raise decision making, it was found that five factors (performance level, performance consistency, tenure, current salary, and external job offers) affected raise decisions but that decision makers placed different degrees of importance on these factors.[8]

Field Experiments

A field experiment is conducted in an organization, rather than a laboratory. As in laboratory studies, the researcher manipulates one or more independent variables and tries to maintain as much control as possible over the situation. While much more difficult to set up than laboratory studies, field experiments can utilize actual events in the organization as their foundation. Field experiments are particularly useful for understanding the effects of a specific organizational event on behavior. They can include such things as the introduction of new technology, a switch in management, or the implementation of a new performance-appraisal or pay system. As mentioned in chapter 12, field experiments are also helpful in assessing the usefulness of training programs.

For example, the safety project in two food processing plants described in chapter 16 is a field experiment in which one group received training on safety behaviors and another group did not. The study then compared the incidents of safe behavior in the two environments. Another field experiment examined the influence of training method and trainee age on the acquisition of computer software skills. For the latter study, an announcement offering the training was placed in a newsletter. Without the subjects' knowledge, two different types of training (tutorial and modeling) were conducted. Subjects were divided into age groups (younger and older), and their computer skill mastery was assessed. Older trainees exhibited lower performance than younger trainees did in both training environments. The study provided a number of insights regarding strategies managers can use to help older workers overcome technological obsolescence.[9]

Another interesting field experiment involved unionized workers employed by a state government that had problems with work attendance. Twenty workers were taught principles of self-management. Compared with twenty untrained workers with similar attendance problems, the employees given training in self-regulation were better able to manage personal and social obstacles to job attendance; the training raised their self-efficacy beliefs that they could control their behavior. The advantage of studies such as this one over laboratory research is that effects were found in the organization where a multitude of outside factors could impinge on or reduce the effectiveness of training. That training led to better attendance despite the environmental conditions is noteworthy.[10]

Correlational Field Studies

While the two strategies discussed above (laboratory and field experiments) are useful in determining the effects of specific variables on others or the consequences of organizational interventions, they may not lend themselves well to studying the broad research questions that frequently confront the researcher. Consequently, researchers conduct correlational field studies, which do not involve the manipulation of variables. This type of study does, however, allow the researcher to systematically measure numerous variables and examine the relationships between these variables. In most cases, correlational field studies gather data through questionnaires or interviews. An important consideration of the researcher using the field study is to intrude as little as possible on the organization, department, or individuals being studied. Organizational surveys and test-validation studies (to be discussed later) are examples of two types of field studies.

Correlational field studies have been used to examine a variety of issues. For example, researchers Thomas Lee and Richard Mowday were interested in identifying the factors that affect an employee's decision to voluntarily leave an organization. Relying on a theoretical model (see exhibit 14.2), they generated hypotheses about the relationship between the variables. For example, one hypothesis predicted that there would be a relationship between a person's efforts to change a situation and job satisfaction, commitment, and involvement. Another hypothesis predicted that a person's intentions to leave would be related to job satisfaction, commitment, involvement, and the importance of nonwork influences, attitudes, and turnover intentions.

A questionnaire containing items measuring constructs in the model was mailed to a random sample of the fourteen thousand employees who worked at a major financial institution in the western United States. There were questions about how well their expectations about work were met, the importance of job information, organizational characteristics (e.g. job content, co-workers), organizational experiences, job satisfaction, and the influence of nonwork factors on their job values. They also were asked about intentions to leave, job search activities, and perceptions of job opportunities. Job performance was measured by a single supervisory rating of overall job performance taken from company records.

The researchers collected the surveys and waited nine months. At this time the company generated a list of persons who had left and their reasons for leaving. Of the 445 employees who had completed the original questionnaire, eight percent had quit. Using mathematical procedures to be described in the next section, they examined the relationships between the variables and tested the hypotheses. Results indicated that met expectations, job values, job attitudes, intention to leave the organization, and actual leaving were related. More important, the study found general support for the interrelationships proposed in the model. The study also showed that an employee's intention to stay or leave was the best predictor of actual turnover. For the manager concerned about employee turnover, the study clearly indicates that it is important to meet employee expectations and to ensure that employees are satisfied and that their commitment is high.[11]

Another study grew out of concern about the rapid growth in benefit costs and the low return on this investment. A team of three researchers first conduct-

Exhibit 14.2
The Steers and Mowday Model

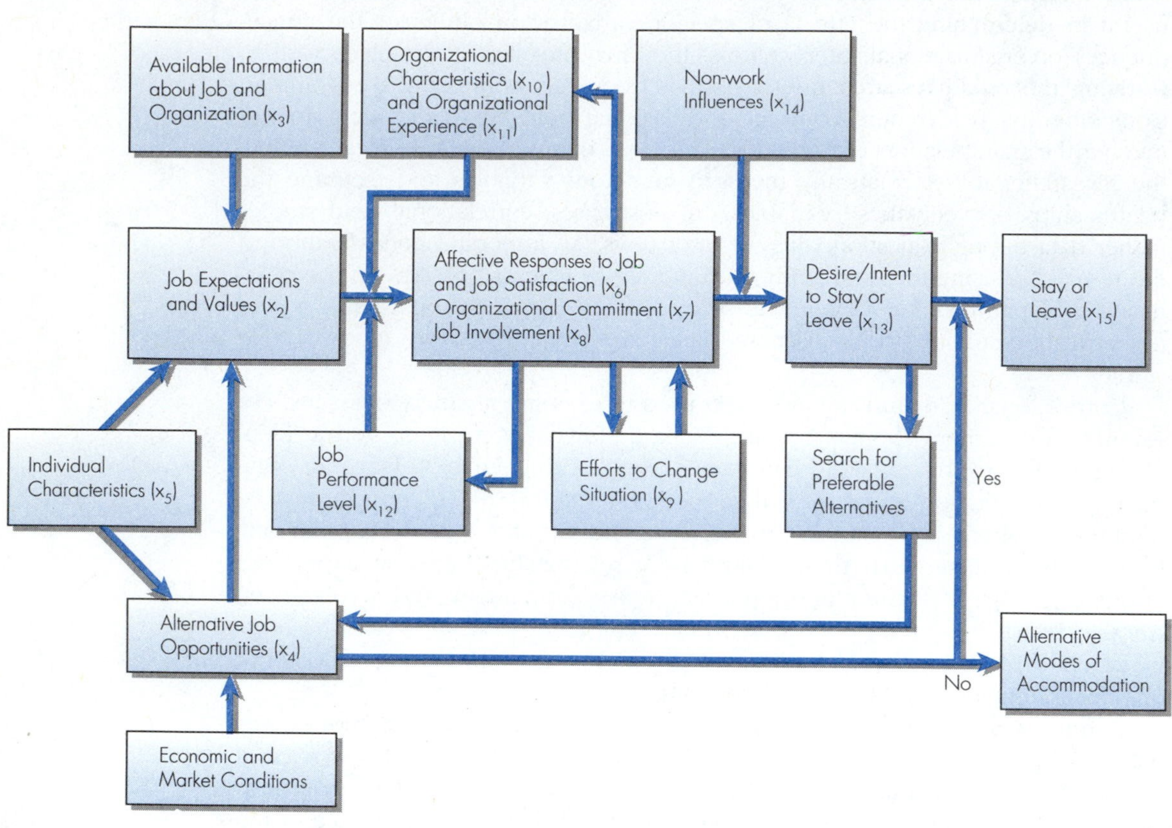

SOURCE: T. Lee and R. T. Mowday, "Voluntary Leaving an Organization: An Empirical Investigation of Steers and Mowday's Model of Turnover," *Academy of Management Journal* 30 (1987), 721–43.

ed interviews with human resource specialists to find out about benefits practices—life insurance, holidays, vacation, retirement and disability benefits, sick leave, insurance, and employee costs—in eight organizations. After determining the differences in benefits practices, the researchers surveyed employees in the agencies to determine their satisfaction with pay and benefits. Employees were also asked questions about their jobs and the level of benefits they received.

The study determined what average benefit levels were for the law enforcement agencies surveyed. Additionally, it showed that satisfaction with benefits increased as benefits coverage increased but decreased as employee costs associated with benefits increased. The study concluded that investments must be made in benefits programs to inform employees about the value of their benefits relative to the costs employees must pay.[12]

THE VALIDATION PROCESS

Regardless of the method or site used to study human resource issues, researchers need to be concerned about the reliability and validation of measurement devices. **Reliability** refers to the consistency of measurement, whereas **validity** relates to the truth or accuracy of measurement. The concept of a correlation coefficient is important to both reliability and validity.

Correlation Coefficient

Both reliability and validity are measured by a correlation coefficient (denoted by the symbol r),which is the degree to which two measurements covary. The correlation coefficient, which expresses the degree of linear relationship between two sets of scores, can range from positive to negative. A positive correlation exists when high values on one variable (e.g., job knowledge test) are associated with high values on another variable (e.g., overall ratings of job performance). A negative correlation exists when high values on one variable are associated with low values on another variable. The range is from + 1 (a perfect positive correlation coefficient) to – 1 (a perfect negative correlation coefficient). Several linear relationships represented by plotting actual data on personnel selection test–job performance relationship are shown in exhibit 14.3.

The correlation between scores on a predictor (x) and a criterion (y) is typically expressed for a sample as r_{xy}. If we did not have a sample but were able to compute our correlation on the population of interest, we would express the correlation as ρ_{xy} (where ρ is the Greek letter rho). In almost all cases, researchers do not have access to the population. Therefore, they must estimate the population correlation coefficient based on data from a sample of the population. For instance, an organization may desire to know the correlation between a computer programming ability test (scores on the predictor, x) and job performance (scores on a performance appraisal rating form, y) for all its computer programmers, but decides it cannot afford to test all computer programmers (i.e., the population of interest). Instead the organization may select a sample of computer programmers and estimate the correlation coefficient in the population (ρ_{xy}) with the observed correlation in the sample (r_{xy}).

Each scatterplot in exhibit 14.3 shows a solid line that best describes the linear relationship between the two variables. This line is described by the general

Exhibit 14.3

Scatterplots Indicating Possible Relationships between Personnel Selection Test Scores and Job Performance Scores

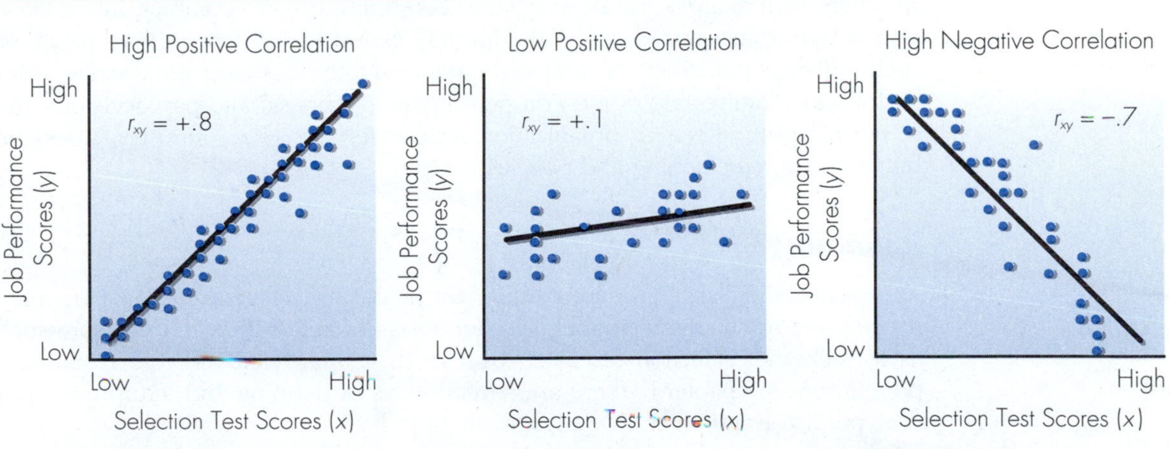

equation for a straight line ($y = ax + b$, where a is the slope of the line and b is the point at which the line intercepts the y axis). The importance of this general equation, or **prediction equation,** is that it allows personnel researchers to estimate values of y (the criterion) from the knowledge of x (the predictor). For example, we may conduct a study to determine the correlation between sales performance (i.e., dollar sales volume) and a predictor (such as a number of years of sales experience) for a group of current job incumbents. Once we have developed a prediction equation, we can then estimate how well a sales applicant might perform on the job.[13] For example, the equation might read

$sales/month = $50,290 + $2,000 (years of sales experience)

Therefore, a salesperson with ten years of experience could be expected to generate $70,290 a month in sales. A new salesperson with only one year of experience would be expected to generate only $52,290 a month in sales.

In many personnel research settings, researchers or decision makers often employ more than one predictor variable. For example, this would be the case when an organization uses a multiple predictor approach to make personnel selection and placement decisions. Similar to the single-predictor approach, the purpose of multiple prediction is the estimation of a criterion (y) from a linear combination of m predictor variables ($y = a + b_1x_1 + b_2x_2 + \ldots + b_mx_m$).[14] Such an equation provides a **multiple-prediction** or **multiple-regression** equation. The b's are the regression weights applied to the predictor variables. In addition, the relationship between the predictors and the criterion score is referred to as the **multiple-correlation coefficient.**

For example, if a manager believed that sales were a function of a salesperson's years of experience (exp), education level (ed), and gender (1 for females, 0 for males), information on each of these predictor variables could be collected along with outcome or criterion data. Using multiple regression, a regression equation such as the following could be generated:

$sales/month = $25,000 + $1,500 (exp) + $500(ed) – $25(gender)

This equation indicates that a female salesperson with ten years of experience and a college degree (sixteen years of schooling) would be expected to generate $47,975 in sales [$25,000 + 1500(10) + $500(16) – 25(1)].

Regression analysis has been used to determine how to combine information from multiple selection devices. Multiple regression has also been used to assess such things as the effects of rater and ratee characteristics (sex, experience, prior performance rating, rate of pay) on performance appraisal and pay decisions and to measure the effects of organizational characteristics (size, industry, sales) on human resource planning and policies.

Reliability

As noted earlier, an important component in the use of measures in personnel research—particularly personnel selection tests—is **reliability.** If a measure such as a personnel selection test is to be useful, it must yield reliable results. As pointed out in chapter 6, there are several ways of defining and interpreting test (i.e., predictor and criterion) reliability.

Each of these methods is based on the notion that observed scores (x) comprise true scores (T) plus some error (E), or $x = T + E$, where T is the expected score if there were no error in measurement.[15] To the extent that observed scores on a test are correlated with true scores, a test is said to be reliable. That is, if observed and true scores could be obtained for every individual who took a personnel selection test, the squared correlation between observed and true scores in the population (ρ^2_{xT}) would be called the reliability coefficient for that selection test.

One means of estimating reliability (ρ_{xx}) is **test-retest reliability.** This method is based on testing a sample of individuals twice with the same measure and then correlating the results to produce a reliability estimate. A potential major problem with the test-retest reliability estimate is the possibility of **carry-over effects** between the testing sessions: the second testing is influenced by the first testing. For instance, some people may improve between testing sessions. For example, students who retake the GMAT are likely to increase their scores by forty to eighty points merely because they have been exposed to test materials previously.

Another means of estimating the reliability of a measure is to correlate scores on alternate forms of the measure. **Alternate test forms** are any two test forms that have been constructed in an effort to make them parallel, and they may have equal (or very similar) observed score means, variances (i.e., a measure of the spread of scores about the means), and correlations with other measures.[16] They are also intended to be similar in content and are designed to measure the same traits. The use of alternate or parallel forms, however, does not necessarily eliminate the possibility of carryover effects related to response styles, moods, or attitudes.

A problem with test-retest reliability and alternate forms reliability is the necessity of testing twice. **Internal consistency reliability,** however, is estimated based on only one administration of a measure. The most common method, **coefficient** α (alpha), yields a **split-half reliability** estimate. That is, the measure (e.g., test) is divided into two parts, which are considered alternate forms of each other, and the relationship between these two halves is an estimate of the test's (i.e., the measure's) reliability. The major advantage of internal consistency reliability estimates is that the reliability of a measure can be estimated based on one administration of the measure.

Researchers are interested in assessing the reliability of measures based on one or more of the previous methods because reliability is a necessary condition for determining validity. The reliability of a measure sets an upper limit on how high the measure can correlate with another measure because it is highly unlikely that a measure will correlate more strongly with a different measure than with itself.

Validity

As defined in the *Principles for the Validation and Use of Personnel Selection Procedures* (American Psychological Association), validity is the degree to which inferences from scores on tests or assessments are supported by evidence. This definition implies that validity refers to the inferences made from use of a measure, not to the measure itself. Three primary strategies have been identified to gather evidence to support or justify the inferences made from scores on measures: criterion-related, content-oriented, and construct validation strategies.

Criterion-related strategy. A criterion-related strategy is an assessment of how well a measure (i.e., predictor) forecasts a criterion such as job performance. The two types of criterion-related validation strategies are concurrent and predictive—as shown in exhibit 14.4.

Concurrent validation evaluates the relationship between a predictor and a job criterion score for all employees in the study at the same time. For example, this strategy could be used to determine the correlation between years of experience and job performance. The HR department would collect from each person in the study information about years of experience and performance scores. All persons in the study would have to be working in similar jobs, generally in the same job family or classification. Then a correlation would be computed between the predictor scores and criterion scores.

The steps in determining predictive validity are similar, except that the predictor is measured sometime before the criterion is measured, as shown in exhibit 14.4. Thus, the **predictive validity** of a predictor could be determined by measuring an existing group of employees on a predictor and waiting to gather their criterion measures later.

The classic example of a predictive validation study is AT&T's Management Progress Study.[17] In that study, personnel researchers at AT&T administered an assessment center, similar to the one described in chapter 5, to 422 male employees, stored the results, and waited eight years before evaluating their predictions of how far these individuals would progress in AT&T's management hierarchy. For a group of college graduates, the predictions were highly accurate; a correlation of .71 was obtained between the assessment center predictions and level of management achieved. In addition, a twenty-year follow-up of the original predictions showed that the assessment center was still useful in predicting who would reach even higher levels in AT&T's management hierarchy.

Another more recent and controversial predictive validation study involving preemployment drug testing is being conducted at the U.S. Postal Service. The Postal Service has tested more than six thousand applicants for drug use and hired those who tested positive (as well as people who tested negative) as part

Exhibit 14.4
Criterion-Related Validation Strategies

Concurrent Study

Time 1	Time 1	Time 1
Test (predictor) scores are gathered	Criterion scores are gathered	Correlation between scores on predictor (x) and criterion (y), r_{xy}, is calculated

Predictive Study

Time 1	Time 2	Time 2
Test (predictor) scores are gathered	Criterion scores are gathered	Correlation between scores on predictor (x) and criterion (y), r_{xy}, is calculated

of their scientific study to see if past drug use correlates with poor job performance. Preliminary results indicate that there is no difference between the job performance of the identified drug users and that of hirees who did not test positive. It is likely that longitudinal predictive studies like this one at the U.S. Postal Service will yield more informative results than will concurrent validation studies. Unfortunately, the costs of longitudinal studies in terms of time, effort, and money often prohibit organizations from conducting such studies.[18]

Content-oriented strategy. On many occasions, employers are not able to obtain sufficient empirical data for a criterion-related study. Consequently, other methods of validation are useful. One of the most viable is **content-oriented validation.** It differs from a criterion-related strategy in that it estimates or judges the relevance of a predictor as a sample of the relevant situations (e.g., behaviors or tasks) that make up a job. According to the *Uniform Guidelines,* a selection procedure can be supported by a content validity strategy to the extent it is a representative sample of the content of the job. The administration of a typing test (actually a job sample test is used for typists) as a selection device for hiring typists is a classic example of a predictor judged to be content valid. In this case, the predictor is a skill related to a task that is actually part of the job. Thus, to employ a content validation strategy, one must know the duties of the actual job.[19] As discussed in chapter 4, information about job tasks and duties can be obtained using one or more job analysis procedures.

Construct validation strategy. Instead of showing a direct relationship between a predictor (test, education, experience) and a job criterion (performance, performance rating, turnover, absenteeism), it is sometimes useful to determine if an individual possesses abilities and characteristics (psychological traits) that are deemed necessary for successful job performance. These underlying psychological traits are called **constructs** and include such characteristics as intelligence, leadership ability, verbal ability, interpersonal sensitivity, integrity, and analytical ability. Constructs deemed necessary for doing well on job criteria are inferred from job behaviors and activities (duties) indicated in the job analysis.[20]

A **construct validation** study attempts to demonstrate that a relationship exists between a test or a measure of the construct and the psychological trait (construct) it seeks to measure. For example, does a reading comprehension test reliably and accurately measure how well people can read and understand what they read? To demonstrate construct validity, one would need data showing that high scorers on the test actually read more difficult material and are better readers than low scorers on the test. Other evidence that the test is measuring the relevant construct could be obtained based on its relationship to other measures that assess both similar and unrelated constructs. Generally, construct validity is not established with a single study. Rather, it is assessed based on the cumulation of a body of empirical evidence. This evidence is likely to include information gathered from both criterion-related and content-oriented validation studies.

Estimating Population Validity Coefficients

As discussed in the section on correlation coefficients, if we were able to assess the relationship between a predictor and criterion in a population of interest, with no measurement error, then we would have computed the true (population) correlation or validity coefficient, ρ_{xy}. Because we almost never have the population available and almost always have measurement error, our observed correlation coefficients (validity coefficients in personnel selection) underestimate the population validity coefficients between selection tests and job performance criteria.

Although predictor and criterion reliability have been noted as statistical artifacts that lower predictor-criterion relationships, other factors are also known to lower these estimated true relationships. Two other primary statistical artifacts which obscure true relationships are sampling error and range restriction. **Sampling error** refers to the inaccuracy in estimating the true population validity resulting from the use of a sample size that is less than the population when computing the validity coefficient. **Range restriction** relates to computing a correlation or validity coefficient between the predictor and criterion scores for a restricted group of individuals.[21] That is, the validity coefficient in personnel research is typically not computed on the entire range of scores for which the predictor will actually be used. This is evident when validity coefficients are based on a concurrent test validation study where only predictor scores obtained from the restricted group (i.e., current job incumbents as opposed to all job applicants) are used. We simply cannot hire all applicants and then relate their predictor scores to scores on a criterion measure such as job performance rating. As a consequence of range restriction, the observed validity coefficient typically underestimates the population validity coefficient.

Formulas have been developed to remove the effects of predictor unreliability, criterion unreliability, and range restriction, and for determining sampling error variance. That is, one would use the correction formulas to remove the influence of the previous statistical artifacts and, consequently, obtain a better idea of the predictor-criterion relationship in the relevant population. Recently, a number of studies have been conducted to examine the usefulness of these correction formulas in estimating population validity coefficients. These studies have examined the effects of variations in sample size, range restriction, and reliability on the size and variability of observed validity coefficient. These studies have improved our understanding of how observed validity coefficients are affected by measurement error and factors such as range restriction.[22]

Validity Generalization

Over the past fifty years, hundreds of validation studies have been conducted in organizations to determine the predictive effectiveness of personnel selection measures (e.g., ability tests) for selecting and placing individuals. Often the validity coefficients for the same or a similar predictor-criterion relationship differed substantially from one setting to another. Although personnel researchers were aware that these differences between the same or similar predictor-criterion relationships were affected by the statistical artifacts noted earlier (i.e., range restriction, predictor unreliability, criterion unreliability, and sampling error), only recently were corrections for these statistical artifacts integrated into systematic procedures for estimating to what degree true validity estimates for the same predictor-criterion relationship generalize across settings.

A series of studies has applied validity generalization procedures to validity coefficient data for clerical jobs, computer programming jobs, petroleum industry jobs, and so on.[23] In general, these investigations showed that the effects of criterion unreliability, predictor unreliability, range restriction, and sample size accounted for most of the observed variance in validity coefficients for the same or similar test-criterion relationship within an occupation (i.e., job grouping or job family). Thus, the estimated true validity coefficients (i.e., ρ_{xy} or corrected validity coefficients) were higher and less variable than were observed validity coefficients (i.e., r_{xy}s or observed validity coefficient not corrected for unreliability, range restriction, or sample size).

The implications of these findings are that inferences (predictions) from scores on personnel selection tests can be transported across situations for similar jobs. That is, if two similar jobs exist in two parts of an organization or in two different organizations, a given selection test should have approximately the same validity coefficients for both jobs. If validity generalization can be successfully argued, an organization can save a great deal of time and money developing valid, job-related predictors because the inferences from a predictor for a job have already been established. A validity generalization study of personality as a predictor of job performance is described in the Focus on Research: "Personalities: Important or Irrelevant?"

More recently, the concept of validity generalization (or what is also commonly referred to as **meta-analysis),** has been applied to other areas of personnel research.[24] This latter research has assisted the personnel and human resource field in gaining a better understanding of the effectiveness of interventions such as training programs, goal-setting programs, and performance measurement (appraisal) programs.

In addition to determining how well validity generalizes across settings, personnel researchers are interested in how stable their prediction equations are across samples. Cross-validation studies address this concern.

Cross-Validation

As discussed in the section on correlation coefficients, personnel researchers often develop prediction equations (or regression equations) with multiple predictors. For the prediction equations to be of any practical use, they must produce consistent results. **Cross-validation** is a procedure for determining the amount of capitalization on chance that has affected the prediction equation (the **regression weights**). As is the case in personnel selection, one is interested in how well the regression weights (the *b*'s noted earlier) estimated in a sample will predict the criterion value of new subjects (e.g., job applicants) not used in the estimation sample.

Traditional or empirical cross-validation typically involves holding out some of the data (sample). The equation developed in the initial sample could then be applied to the holdout sample to evaluate its stability. In general, however, this procedure has been shown to be less precise than formulas for estimating the stability of regression equations. The reason for the increased precision when using formula-based estimates is that all information (the total sample) is used at once in estimating the original weights.[25]

FOCUS ON RESEARCH

Personalities: Important or Irrelevant?

It's difficult to think about someone we know—a friend, family member, boss, or colleague—without conjuring up an image that reflects their personality. Introverts are easy to distinguish from extroverts. Friends who are "rock solid" provide sharp contrast to those who seem to ride an emotional roller coaster through life. And colleagues who can be counted on no matter what provide a standard we can hold up for those who are a bit more relaxed in this regard. Personality differences seem so clear in our everyday experience, they must surely be important predictors of job performance—right?

During the past three decades, over 200 studies of employees in occupations of all types have examined the linkage between a variety of personality dimensions and work-related behaviors. Among the many work-related behaviors studied have been performance in training programs, performance on the job, career progress, turnover and absenteeism. The great volume of research on this topic may be the best indication of how powerful our belief in the importance of personality actually is.

What have we learned from this great volume of research? Does personality predict work-related behaviors? And if so, what are the most important personality dimensions? These were the questions addressed by a recent quantitative review of existing findings. To bring order to this large volume of research, the researchers took advantage of the fact that there is a now growing consensus regarding a vocabulary for describing the key dimensions of personalities. Whereas our everyday vocabulary contains dozens of different words for describing personality, psychologists are concluding that there are only a few major dimensions of personality, which are called the "Big Five:" agreeableness, extraversion, conscientiousness, emotional stability, and openness to experience.

To find out if these personality dimensions are related to work behaviors, the researchers used the statistical techniques developed for assessing validity generalization. After combining quantitative results from thousands of employees, only one personality dimension appears to be consistently related to work-related outcomes across all of the occupational groups studied: conscientiousness. Conscientious people have a strong sense of purpose, obligation, and persistence, and it pays off in terms of higher job performance. Extroverts (who are gregarious, talkative, assertive, and active) are slightly better performers than introverts, but only in sales and management positions, where interaction with others is an important part of the job. Generally, emotional stability is not related to work outcomes, but there was an exception. For professionals, being slightly *low* on emotional stability was beneficial for performance, indicating that in these jobs performance is better among people who are a bit "high strung." Finally, openness to experience was associated with better performance in training programs only.

Is personality important at work? This study indicates the answer is a very hesitant "yes." Being conscientious is consistently beneficial, but the magnitude of its importance is actually quite small. Other personality traits are slightly beneficial in some occupations but not others, and sometimes in surprising ways. Thus, it seems that while "personality" has a powerful effect on the way we view people, it is only slightly related to how productive a person is. How can we explain this finding? What are its implications?

SOURCE: Based on M. R. Barrick and M. K. Mount, "The Big Five Personality Dimensions and Job Performance: A Meta-Analysis," *Personnel Psychology* 44 (1991), 1–26.

DETERMINING THE USEFULNESS OF HUMAN RESOURCE PROCEDURES

Armed with procedures to determine the reliability and validity of measurement devices, researchers have become concerned about demonstrating the usefulness of the methods and procedures they use. This is particularly important when human resource activities and programs are vying for scarce financial resources.

In order to justify funding, human resource activities must be cost effective. This section addresses the process used to determine the predictive usefulness of selection devices. Additionally, utility analysis, which assesses the costs and benefits of human resource programs, is discussed.

Predictive Usefulness of Selection Devices

An important application of validity and reliability is in selection decision making. By examining validity and reliability, as well as selection ratios and cutoff scores, the predictive usefulness of one selection device compared with another or with no selection device can be assessed.

Consider the diagram in exhibit 14.5. The vertical line labeled x_c divides the applicants based on scores on the predictor. Applicants who meet or exceed the cutoff score would be hired; those who score below the cutoff score would be rejected. For this example, 60 of 100 applicants would be hired. The horizontal line labeled x_y represents the division between successful and unsuccessful job performance. Using this cutoff score, if all 100 applicants were hired, only 45 would be successful. Thus, the **base rate** for this job is 45 percent. That is:

$$\text{Base rate of success} = \frac{\text{III} + \text{IV}}{\text{I} + \text{II} + \text{III} + \text{IV}} = \frac{35 + 10}{30 + 25 + 35 + 10} = .45$$

Quadrants I and III contain correct predictions made by the predictor. In Quadrant I, a low test score is related to low job performance. This is referred to as a **true negative** prediction. [The test predicted low (negative) job perfor-

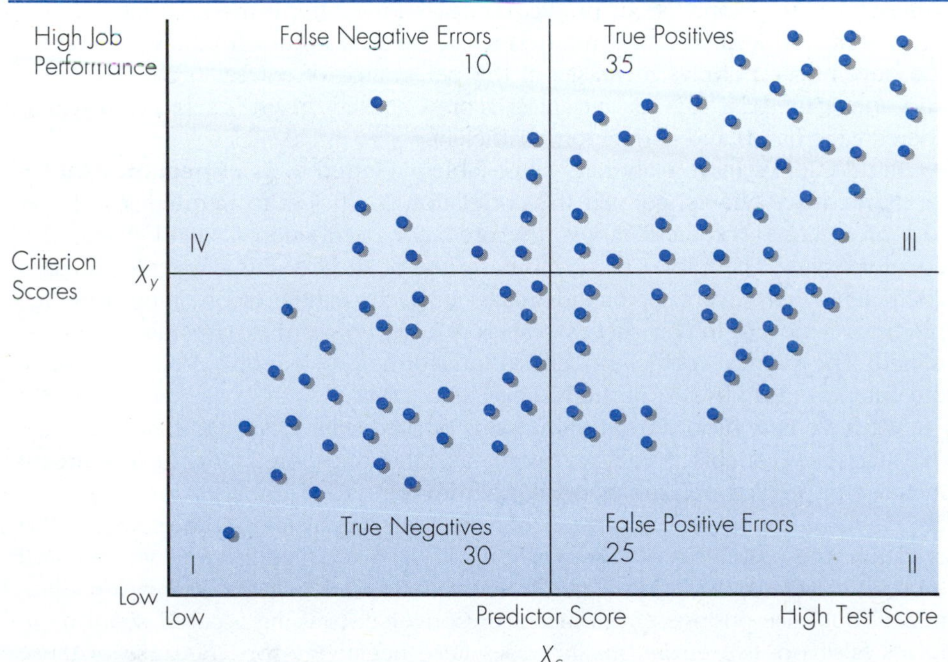

Exhibit 14.5
Scatter Diagram Showing Correct and Erroneous Selection Decisions (Based on a Selection Ratio of .60 and a Base Rate of .45)

mance, and it was true.] Quadrant III includes the scores of those applicants who scored above the cutoff score on the predictor and also were successful on the job. These judgments are referred to as **true positive** judgments. [The test predicted high (positive) job performance, and it was true.] The higher the number of true positives and true negatives relative to total applicants, the more accurate and useful is the selection device. In our example, the test made accurate predictions 65 percent of the time. This is a substantial improvement over selection by chance (45 percent).

However, because no selection device is perfect, errors in judgment occur. These fall into two categories. Quadrant II includes people who are hired based on their high scores but who are unsuccessful on the job. These are called **false positive** selection errors or erroneous acceptances. **False negative** selection errors (Quadrant IV) occur when individuals are not hired because they scored low on the test when actually they would have performed well. For the selection device shown in exhibit 14.5, there were 10 false negative selection errors and 25 false positive errors.

To determine the predictive usefulness of the selection device, the **predictor rate** (percentage of successful employees hired using the predictor) needs to be compared to this base rate. If the predictor is useful, it should produce an improvement in selection. As shown below, the predictor in exhibit 14.5 yields an improvement of .13 points over the base rate of .45:

$$\% \text{ increase in correct predictions} = \frac{\text{III}}{\text{III} + \text{II}} - \frac{\text{III} + \text{IV}}{\text{I} + \text{II} + \text{III} + \text{IV}} = .13$$

$$\frac{35}{35 + 25} - \frac{35 + 10}{30 + 25 + 35 + 10} = .13$$

where the first quantity is our predictor rate and the latter is the base rate.

A series of detailed tables referred to as the Taylor-Russell tables, named for the developers, portrays increases in the percentage of correct predictions over and above the base rate as the cutoff score is raised, given a selection **ratio** [26] (percentage hired) and correlation coefficient.[27]

In addition, a more elaborate set of tables, referred to as **expectancy tables** or **expectancy charts,** convert the correlation coefficient to frequencies of correct predictions. For these tables, the predictor distribution is divided into five equal intervals. Then, for a particular base rate of success and a specified validity coefficient, the percentage of individuals in each quintile (score range) on the predictor who fall in the success category (i.e., above the base rate) is determined. The validity coefficient can be transformed to its equivalent increase in the criterion mean by use of the Naylor-Shine tables.[28]

We have now moved from discussions of predictive validity to that of predictive accuracy. At this point, we might ask the question, "Does a 13-percent increase in predictive accuracy resulting from the use of any selection procedure always result in the same economic benefit to an organization?" In answer to this question, the usefulness of a selection device varies depending on where cutoff scores are set. By lowering a cutoff score, false and negative errors are minimized, but false positive errors increase. Conversely, raising a cutoff score minimizes false positive errors but increases false negative errors. Because of these trade-offs, an organization needs to carefully consider the cost of each type of error. Usually, false positive errors are the more costly because a poor performer is hired and trained and may have to be replaced. Still, as we will see next, the benefit of an increase in predictive accuracy is dependent on the costs to obtain it, as well as on the payoff associated with the correct predictions.[29] Thus, we now move from a concern with predictive accuracy to reasoning the costs and benefits of predictions.

Utility Analysis

In addition to assessing the usefulness of selection devices, correlation coefficients and validity information can also be used to conduct a utility analysis. Although it is not yet used by many organizations, **utility analysis** helps human resource managers determine the cost/benefit of one selection device over no selection device or over an alternate device. Utility analysis also can be used to determine the financial impact of human resource–related events (performance appraisal program, absenteeism, turnover, training program, compensation plan).[30]

Most applications of utility analysis are premised on the assumption that individuals who are familiar with a job (supervisors) can estimate the dollar value of performance associated with someone performing at the 50th percentile, the 85th percentile, and the 15th percentile. This is called the **standard deviation** (SD_y) of performance in dollars. Research indicates that the SD_y usually ranges from 16 to 70 percent of wages, with values most often being in the 40- to 60-percent range. This means that an estimate of SD_y for a job paying \$40,000 per year typically ranges from \$16,000 to \$24,000. Studies have been conducted in which supervisors have provided estimates of SD_y for such jobs as sales manager, computer programmer, insurance counselor, and entry-level park ranger.

In addition to estimating SD_y, utility analysis also considers other factors (e.g., number of employees, tax rates, and validity coefficient of the selection device) that affect the value or utility of a selection process. The following equation, which incorporates these economic concepts, can be employed when comparing two alternative selection procedures or other human resource options:

$$\Delta U = N_s \left[\sum_{t=1}^{T} (1/(1+i)^t)\, SD_y\, (1+V)\,(1-TAX)\,(\hat{\rho}_1 - \hat{\rho}_2)\bar{z}_s \right] - (C_1 - C_2)(1 - TAX)] \quad (14.1)$$

where

ΔU = total estimated dollar value of replacing one selection procedure (1) with another procedure (2) after variable costs, taxes, and discounting,

N_s = the number of employees selected,

T = the number of future time periods,

t = the time period in which a productivity increase occurs,

i = the discount rate,

SD_y = the standard deviation of job performance in dollars,

V = the proportion of SD_y represented by variable costs,

TAX = the organization's applicable tax rate,

$\hat{\rho}_1$ = the estimated population validity coefficient between scores on one selection procedure and the criterion,

$\hat{\rho}_2$ = the estimated population validity coefficient between scores on an alternative selection procedure and scores on the criterion,

$\bar{z}_s$ = the mean standard score on the selection procedure of those selected (this is assumed to be equal in the equation 14.1 for each selection procedure),

C_1 = the total cost of the first selection procedure, and

C_2 = the total cost of the alternative selection procedure.[31]

For illustration purposes, let us employ a portion of the utility analysis information collected at a large international manufacturing company, which we will call Company A. Company A undertook a utility analysis to obtain an estimate of the economic impact of its current procedure for selecting sales managers as compared with their previously used interviewing selection programs. The current selection procedure was a managerial assessment center. Although the assessment center had been in operation for seven years at the time of the utility analysis, a value for T of four years was used because this was the average time (tenure) for the 29 (N in equation 14.1) sales managers who had been selected from a pool of 132 candidates. A primary objective of the utility analysis at Company A was to compare the estimated dollar value of selecting 29 managers using the assessment center with what the economic gain would have been if 29 sales managers were selected by an interviewing program.

Company A employed an interdisciplinary approach when estimating the various components of equation 14.1. For instance, values of V and TAX were provided by the accounting and tax departments, respectively. These values were –.05 for V and .49 for TAX. V was considered the proportion of dollar sales volume as compared with operating costs. Because there was a positive relationship between combined operating costs (e.g., salary, benefits, supplies, automobile operations) and sales volume, a value for V of –.05 was used in equation 14.1. In addition, the value for i, .18, was based on an examination of corporate financial documentation. The accounting department also provided the figure for C_1 (the total cost of the assessment center), $263,636. Based on 29 selected individuals, the cost of selecting one district sales manager was computed to be about $9,091. The estimated total cost to select 29 sales managers by the previously used one-day interviewing program was $50,485 (i.e., the value for C_2 in equation 14.1). Let us now turn to the final four components of equation 14.1: $\hat{\rho}_1$, $\hat{\rho}_2$, $\bar{z}_s$, and SD_y.

The estimated population validity coefficient for the assessment center, $\hat{\rho}_1$, was obtained by correlating five assessment dimension scores (i.e., scores for planning and organizing, decision making, stress tolerance, sensitivity, and persuasiveness) with an overall performance rating. The multiple correlation between the measures was .61. Next, the population cross-validated multiple correlation was calculated, using the formulas mentioned above in the section on cross-validation. This resulting value of .41 was finally corrected for range restriction and criterion reliability to yield an estimated value of .59 for $\hat{\rho}_1$.

Because company A had not conducted a criterion-related validity study for the interviewing selection program, a value was obtained from the validity generalization literature.[32] The value of $\hat{\rho}_2$ for the interviewing program was .16. In addition, the standard score on the predictor $(\bar{z}_s)$ was determined to be .872. This value was assumed to be the same for both the assessment center and the interviewing program.

The final, and traditionally the most difficult, component to estimate in equation 14.1 has been SD_y. As indicated earlier, SD_y is an index of the variability of job performance in dollars in the relevant population. The relevant population or group for evaluating a selection procedure is the applicant group, the group with which the selection procedure is used. When evaluating the economic utility of organizational interventions, however, the relevant group is current employees. Because the intervention would be applied to current employees, the appropriate value of SD_y is for this group. In this latter case, if the SD_y were estimated from the applicant group, it could be an overestimate. Consequently, the approximate value for a sales manager, $30,000, will be used for SD_y in the present example.

Placing the previous values into the utility analysis equation would result in a value of approximately $316,460. This value represents the estimated present value, over a four-year time period, to the organization from the use of the assessment center in place of an interviewing program to select 29 sales managers. Although the cost of the interviewing program is only about one-fifth of the assessment center cost, the estimated dollar gain from use of the assessment center instead of the interviewing program is substantial. This result is primarily due to the greater predictive effectiveness (i.e., higher validity coefficient) of the assessment center.

As demonstrated, utility analysis makes it possible for human resource managers to estimate the dollar gains and losses that result from the use of employee selection practices. The same procedures can be, and have been, used to assess the usefulness of training programs to reduce absenteeism, safety and other human resource programs.

Although not discussed in detail here, utility analysis results need not be reported solely in dollars and cents. For many jobs it may make more sense to compute human resource management program utility in terms of percent improvement in output or some other understandable and/or comfortable measure, e.g., units of measured performance.[33] This can help get to the heart of increasing the potential usefulness of utility analysis, i.e., the need for HR managers to improve their communication of utility results to organizational decision makers.

Despite the potential usefulness of utility analysis, very few firms have adopted these procedures. There are several possible reasons for this. First, practice tends to lag theory. Because utility analysis is rather new, it may not yet have filtered down to organizations. Second, opponents of utility analysis question the viability of measuring the standard deviation of performance by using managerial estimates. The latter concern, however, may not be that problematic because of a new utility approach that does not require the direct estimation of SD_y.[34] Finally, it was noted in chapter 6 that validation studies were not conducted as often as they should be. Without information regarding the validity of selection, training, safety, or absenteeism programs, utility analysis cannot be conducted.

FOCUS ISSUES IN PERSONNEL AND HUMAN RESOURCE MANAGEMENT RESEARCH

In addition to assessing the economic utility of organizational interventions, human resource researchers and practitioners are making important progress in other research areas. Although many of these developments have been discussed in the chapters on job analysis, recruitment, selection, and compensation, four areas deserve discussion here: adaptive testing, procedural justice, mergers and acquisitions, and linking research to the business.

Adaptive Testing

One area of computer technology that is currently receiving increased research attention among HR professionals is that of tailored or adaptive testing. Tailored or adaptive testing refers to the situation in which the computer program adjusts the test difficulty to the ability of the individual being tested.

> A computer-assisted or adaptive test uses a multi-stage process to estimate a person's ability several times during the course of testing, and the selection of successive test items is based on those ability estimates. The person tested uses an interactive computer terminal to answer a test question. If the answer is correct, the next item will be more difficult; if not, an easier item follows. With each response, a revised and more reliable estimate is made of the person's ability. The test proceeds until the estimate reaches a specified level of reliability. Generally, the results are more reliable and require fewer items than a paper and pencil test.[35]

A few researchers have examined issues concerning the validity of computer-administered adaptive tests. One interesting study compared the Arithmetic Reasoning and Word Knowledge subtests of the Armed Services Vocational Aptitude Battery (ASVAB) with computer-administered adaptive tests as predictors of performance in an air force mechanic training course.[36] The study found that computer-administered adaptive tests that are one-third to one-half the length of conventional (i.e., paper-and-pencil) ASVAB tests could approximate the criterion-related validity coefficients of these conventional tests. The importance of these findings is even more impressive when one considers that adaptive tests administer different items to different individuals.

Others have pointed out that increased measurement accuracy is not the only benefit of computer-administered adaptive testing.[37] Additional benefits include reductions in testing time, fatigue, and boredom, as well as cost savings in some cases over conventional paper-and-pencil testing.[38] A study conducted within the U.S. Office of Personnel Management placed the cost of adaptive testing at less than that of paper-and-pencil testing.[39] Moreover, a report prepared for the Canadian government estimated that, even considering the capital investment in computer equipment, computer-administered adaptive tests could show a savings over conventional paper-and-pencil tests in one year.[40]

Although potential benefits are associated with computerized testing for making employment decisions, this form of assessment will probably be examined by the courts. Based on numerous and significant recent court decisions concerning employment testing,[41] continued legal scrutiny of employment practices is clearly a reality.

Procedural Justice

A research area that has been gaining in popularity concerns perceptions of justice and fair treatment at work. This line of research focuses on the process by which evaluation decisions (selection, performance appraisal, layoffs) or reward allocation decisions are made. In general, this research suggests that, even when employees are satisfied with a human resource outcome, they may or may not be satisfied with the process or procedures that were used to make the decision.

While research on procedural justice is just beginning, initial findings suggest that procedures that are open, are specified in advance, treat similarly situated people similarly, and allow input from employees are more likely to be perceived as fair than are those violating these principles. Procedural justice is of greatest concern when outcomes are unfavorable.

While early research was conducted in the laboratory, field research may be helpful to practitioners is several ways. According to a recent survey on the importance of human resource activities, policy adherence including assurances that proper administrative procedures have been followed in an equitable manner is one of the top four concerns of four human resource constituencies (executives, supervisors, professional employees, and hourly employees).[42]

As organizations strive to exist in an increasingly competitive global economy, it seems likely the fairness of procedures will become even more important. This is because allocation decisions will more often be unfavorable to employees. For this research to advance, practitioners need to team up with human resource researchers to explore the factors that influence perceptions of fairness.

Mergers, Acquisitions, and Downsizing

As noted in the initial chapters, many U.S. organizations have been forced to cut costs and reduce size—to become "lean and mean" in order to survive. At the same time, the rate of mergers and acquisitions has greatly increased. Both these trends have important implications for human resource practices and strategies. Because of the speed of these changes, research has lagged, rather than led, actions in the real world. Still, some knowledge has been acquired, and more can be expected about the changing structure of organizations.

Articles in practitioner journals on outplacement activities surfaced in the early 1980s and stimulated academic research on the consequences of job loss and job change. Some of this research has identified the conditions under which job loss is positive, leading to personal and career growth. Other research has focused on what organizations can do to reduce the stress associated with job loss or change through mergers and acquisitions.[43]

On the flip side of layoffs, knowledge is beginning to be amassed regarding the reactions of retained employees to reductions in force. Several studies have shown that "survivor guilt" can lead to increased performance among survivors of layoffs. For example, employees with a strong work ethic may increase their job involvement after even mild or temporary layoffs.[44]

Other research has identified the strategies used by organizations to reduce the size of the work force. For example, one study found that layoffs were by far the most common downsizing strategy used because personnel and human resource managers in the sample had less than two months, on average, in which to plan and carry out the reduction in employment levels. While research has not yet emerged, it would seem that personnel managers could become more expert and proactive in monitoring product life cycles, the business environment, and organizational strategy in order to anticipate needed staff changes. This is more likely to occur when human resource management is integrated in the planning process as described in chapter 4. There also is a need for more research on how downsizing is accomplished and on how employees respond before, during, and after the fact. Similar questions can be raised regarding mergers and acquisitions.

Linking Personnel and Human Resource Management Research to the Business

This focus issue brings us back to the opening features of this section, particularly those about Wayne Nelson and Bill Reffett. In both examples, research was used to gather information to improve specific conditions to improve the business.

In the case of Wayne Nelson, data were gathered from line managers indicating how the human resource department could better serve them so the line managers could manage their business more effectively. One consequence of this was the development of HR teams to work with the business unit managers. A result of this was the design and implementation of training programs that line managers really needed to help them.

In the case of Bill Reffett, data were gathered from Grand Union's customers, and this resulted in the firm's decision to upgrade its business strategy. This upgrade (see the discussion in chapter 13) required major changes in employee behavior and thus in the human resource practices of Grand Union.

In both cases research was linked closely with the needs of the business. Not surprisingly, this linkage is made possible working through the line managers. After all, they are the ones most directly in touch with the employees. Thus, helping them with human resource issues helps them manage their human resources more effectively. A good illustration of this is also provided in the "PHRM in the News: Measuring Matters at Mellon." At Mellon, research is used to ensure that the firm's performance appraisal system is used as effectively as possible. Thus, the research aids line managers in doing their jobs which, in turn, enhances employee performance.

SUMMARY

Human resource management research must be conducted in order to improve individual and organizational effectiveness, determine the success of human resource programs, and compete for scarce organizational financial resources. Emphasis here is placed on describing the steps in the empirical research process and on explaining research strategies. Laboratory research helps managers acquire basic knowledge, provided the setting is carefully designed to mimic organizational reality. While difficult to set up, field experiments involve the manipulation of specific variables in actual organizations.

By comparison, correlational field studies examine interrelationships between variables without assessing the effects of interventions. Underscoring the effectiveness of human resource management research are issues associated with reliability and validity, and the evaluation of the usefulness and economic utility of

PHRM IN THE NEWS

Measuring Matters at Mellon

"Our management reports used to be centered purely around profitability—now, we are also looking at how profitability is achieved," Candice Mendenhall, vice president, research, planning and information, Mellon Bank (Pittsburgh, PA) said.

"We began providing quarterly reports to senior management, consisting of corporate officers, legal entity presidents and department heads, on human resource management measures about one year ago. The reports are presented in aggregate form.

"We identify those departments doing exceptionally well in particular areas; for example, if a department's merit pay awards reflect performance appraisal ratings, we credit that department. We also identify general areas to probe into more deeply and provide assistance to those who want our help in addressing specific issues.

Impacts of Measurements

"We've found our reporting process has provided a high-visibility, powerful forum for emphasizing human resource management issues. We believe the responsibility for hr rests with line managers—but although you can encourage someone to manage according to the company's guidelines, it's sometimes tough to get things implemented. With measurements, the impact on the organization—and whether managers are carrying their share of the responsibility for hrm—becomes clear. Measuring is credible—managers are used to being measured, and they respond to measurement processes.

"Some of the impacts we've noticed include:

- Managers are incorporating our new management-by-objectives approach into their performance appraisals. This is not mandatory, but since we started measuring the number of such evaluations done on an annual basis, department heads are now acting.
- There's a healthy dialogue going on. We're asking more questions about the 'why's' behind the numbers we are generating. When we looked at the relationship of performance appraisal ratings to merit pay, we discovered we were not differentiating between levels of performance to the degree we'd like to be. Now, this issue is being addressed.

"We don't stress how this process is creating more of a demand for service from the hr department. In fact, our goal is to put ourselves out of business—to get to the point where line management is doing its own measuring, to where good hr management is part of the culture."

SOURCE: *HR Reporter* 4, no. 3 (April 1987). Used by permission.

personnel selection and organizational interventions. Recent issues in HR research relate to adaptive testing, procedural justice, mergers and acquisitions, and linking research with the business. Continued research efforts will further advance our knowledge of human resource activities as well as contribute to the effectiveness of managers, nonmanagers, and organizations.

WHERE WE ARE TODAY

1. Recent passage of the Civil Rights Act of 1991 and the Americans with Disabilities Act of 1990 provides further impetus for firms to conduct validation studies on their selection techniques.
2. Validation studies are important to conduct for legal purposes, but they also help the business by improving a firm's selection processes.

3. Validation studies can also be used to demonstrate the dollar value of using a particular selection technique, thereby increasing the possibility of getting organizational support for the selection technique.
4. Remember, the success of an empirical validation study often depends on the quality of the performance data that are collected, not just the quality of the predictor data that are gathered.
5. Computer technology enables organizations to offer adaptive testing, or testing that can be tailored to individual applicants. The technology also facilitates more rapid scoring of the tests.
6. Organizational surveys are certainly a means of communicating with employees, but they are also an important way of gathering research data to improve organizational conditions.
7. Increasingly, firms such as Blue Cross of Western Pennsylvania are also using surveys—both oral interview surveys and paper-and-pencil surveys—to improve the performance of the human resource department.
8. Research to improve the human resource department often leads to improvement in the effectiveness of line managers in their efforts to manage their people.
9. Human resource management research offers a systematic way of finding out what's going on inside the organization and outside the organization and what can be done to make the HR department and the organization more effective.
10. As the environment continues to become more competitive, firms will need to do everything to improve their effectiveness, thus increasing the need for systematic research.

DISCUSSION QUESTIONS

1. Discuss how the empirical research process can assist in finding solutions to organizational problems.
2. Describe three methods for assessing the reliability of measures, and evaluate the practicality of each method.
3. Discuss the importance of criterion-related validity in personnel selection test validation.
4. How should an organization evaluate the predictive effectiveness of a particular personnel selection test battery (i.e., series of tests) in another situation?
5. How does the concept of validity generalization relate to the documentation of ability-performance relationships?
6. How can firms use cross-validation to improve their selection process?
7. Discuss and apply the concepts of false positives and negatives, and true positives and negatives.
8. Describe the relationship between the predictor rate and base rate.
9. Discuss the potential benefits of computerized adaptive testing for both the HR department and the examinee.
10. How do organizational surveys serve as indicators of problems as well as criteria for evaluating the effectiveness of organizational interventions?

APPLIED PROJECTS

1. Obtain job descriptions for several jobs, preferably some simple, common jobs such as bus driver, and some more complex jobs such as computer programmer or personnel specialist. Develop job specifications for each job and selection procedures for each job. Discuss why you selected each selection procedure (e.g., the interview) and what specific information you will get from each procedure. State the cutoff scores or standards you would recommend for each selection procedure and describe how the procedures would be combined (e.g., multiple hurdles or in a compensatory manner). (Refer again to chapter 6.)
2. Construct a hypothetical selection situation in which one paper-and-pencil test is used to select job applicants. Report on the selection ratio (any you want to use), the base rate, and the validity of the test being used. You can make up all of the numbers you need, but show the numbers, plot the data (to show validation), and tell how you conducted the validation studies.

CASE STUDY

CompuTest, Inc: The Case of Alternative Personnel Selection Strategies

Fiscal 1985 was a landmark year of development and growth for CompuTest, Inc. As Jerome J. Rosner, president, indicated in a report to the stockholders, "Our company emerged to become a major force in the growing field of computerized psychological testing." It was a year that saw the company transform from 350 employees to over 460 employees. Although a number of personnel were added to the marketing, sales, and research operations, the largest number of employees were selected for clerical and administrative positions.

To date, the company has principally targeted its products at individual mental health practitioners, psychiatric hospitals, and other medical professionals. The company expects these specialized markets to continue to represent a substantial part of their revenue base through 1993. Thereafter, CompuTest expects its sources of revenue to shift as they aggressively enter the vast industrial market. In business and industry, thousands of psychological and ability tests are administered annually. In the past, these tests were given to employees and prospective employees by traditional paper-and-pencil methods—a long, cumbersome, and expensive process. As Paul Lefebre, the company's manager of personnel research states, "CompuTest's current and future testing products have the capability of revolutionizing the area of employee screening with new technologies never before available in the HR field."

One of the newest products developed for the industrial market is a comprehensive battery of computer-administered clerical tests. The company, however, does not want to introduce these tests into the market prior to gathering evidence concerning the predictive effectiveness of the tests. Paul Lefebre is currently searching for potential research sites to conduct a criterion-related validity study.

At present, Lane Carpenter, the director of human resources, has brought to the attention of President Rosner that many complaints are being raised about the quality of clerical personnel being selected with the company's verbal ability test. Lane has informed President Rosner that although 170 clerical and administrative personnel have been selected with this verbal ability test, the company has not conducted a criterion-related validation study to evaluate its usefulness. Because of the complaints and the need to select additional clerical personnel, President Rosner has called a meeting with Lane Carpenter and Paul Lefebre.

Jerome Rosner: As you both are aware, we are facing a number of complaints about the quality and quantity of clerical job performance throughout our company. In addition, I would like to bring to your attention that we have projected a need of fifty additional clerical personnel in our current job categories by the end of 1993. This situation requires us to closely examine our current clerical selection procedure and possibly consider viable alternatives. Furthermore, I would like us to reconsider the performance appraisal form we are currently using to evaluate clerical personnel. Our performance appraisal system does not seem to incorporate some of the major duties or tasks that our clerical personnel are being asked to perform. Lane, you have expressed some concerns about the currently used verbal ability test for selecting clerical personnel.

Lane Carpenter: Yes, I am concerned not only with how good this test is at screening potentially successful clerical personnel but also with how we would defend such a test if challenged in court. I assume you are aware that this test was developed and adopted only on the basis of a content-oriented validation study.

Jerome Rosner: Yes, Paul has informed me of the strategy used in developing the verbal ability test. Paul, you also mentioned in a previous discussion that we might be able to conduct another type of validation study for this test.

Paul Lefebre: We currently have a sufficient number of clerical personnel with verbal ability test scores and performance ratings to conduct a criterion-related validation study. In addition, since we have just completed a comprehensive job analysis of all clerical positions and expected openings within the company, we have the capability of revising our clerical performance appraisal system to more accurately reflect the tasks that they perform.

Jerome Rosner: Does this job analysis also indicate the necessary abilities to effectively perform these tasks?

Paul Lefebre: Yes, the job analysis clearly identified the required abilities. Furthermore, the job analysis indicated that although the major duties differed across some of our clerical jobs, the entry-level ability requirements for all of our clerical jobs were similar.

Lane Carpenter: If the ability requirements are similar across all clerical jobs, we might be able to conduct a criterion-related validation study for the verbal ability test with our current clerical employees.

Paul Lefebre: That would be a definite possibility. It might also be helpful for us to consider validating our newly developed computerized clerical ability test battery. That is, we could gather some evidence for its predictive effectiveness in our own company prior to marketing it to industry. Of course, my department would have to determine which tests were appropriate or should be considered for a validation study here

Jerome Rosner: Paul, that sounds like a good idea. If we are going to successfully market our computerized testing products to industry, we should also be willing to use them. An important question related to your suggestion is how our computer-administered clerical test battery would compare with our currently used verbal ability test. Would we be improving our predictions of who will turn out to be successful workers? If we decided to replace our current selection test with a battery of clerical tests, would it be cost beneficial? Paul, I would very much appreciate your preparing a proposal for how we might go about validating our currently used verbal ability test and the computer-administered clerical test battery and how we might compare these alternatives.

Case Questions

1. What is the difference between the test being developed on the basis of a content-oriented validation study vs. a criterion-related validity study?
2. Does CompuTest first have to change its performance appraisal form before doing a criterion-related validation study?
3. On what basis will Paul Lefebre go about determining the tests which would be appropriate to include in the computerized clerical test battery?
4. How should Paul Lefebre go about validating the firm's verbal ability test and the clerical test battery and comparing them?

NOTES

1. "HR on the First Team," *HR Reporter* (Feb. 1992): 1.
2. *Priorities for Competitive Advantage* (New York: IBM/Towers Perrin, 1992;) and *HR Reporter* (Feb. 1992): 1.
3. For a discussion of reasons for conducting organizational research, see J. E. Stone, *Research Methods in Organizational Behavior* (Santa Monica, Calif.: Goodyear, 1978).
4. This chapter was originally prepared and was updated by Michael J. Burke, Department of Psychology, Tulane University. For a discussion of reasons for conducting organizational research, see J. E. Stone, *Research Methods in Organizational Behavior* (Santa Monica, Calif.: Goodyear, 1978); M. W. McCall, Jr., "Research Methods in the Service of Discovery," in M. D. Dunnette and L. M. Hough, eds., *Handbook of Industrial and Organizational Psychology* (Palo Alto, Calif.: Consulting Psychologists Press, Inc.: 1990) 381-418; P. R. Sackett, "Research Strategies and Tactics in Industrial and Organizational Psychology," in *Handbook of Industrial and Organizational Psychology:*

419–90; N. W. Schmitt and R. J. Klimoski, *Research Methods in Human Resources Management* (Cincinnati, Ohio: South-Western Publishing Co., 1991); W R. Shadish, Jr., T. D. Cook, and L. C. Leviton, *Foundations of Program Evaluation: Theories of Practice* (Newbury Park, Calif.: Sage, 1990).

5. M. Neale and G. Northcraft, "Experience, Expertise, and Decision Bias in Negotiations: The Role of Strategic Conceptualization," in *Research in Bargaining and Negotiations,* 2d ed., ed. M. Bazerman and R. Lewicki (Greenwich, Conn.: JAI Press, 1989).
6. V. Huber, M. Neale, and G. Northcraft, "Decision Bias and Personnel Selection Strategies," *Organizational Behavior and Human Decision Processes* 40, (1987): 136–47; V. Huber, G. Northcraft, and M. Neale, "Effects of Decision Context and Anchoring on Selection Decisions," *Organizational Behavior and Human Decision Processes* 42 (1989).
7. V. Huber, M. Neale, and G. Northcraft, "Judgment by Heuristic Effects of Ratee and Rater Characteristics and Performance Standards on Performance-Related Judgments," *Organizational Behavior and Human Decision Processes* 40, (1987): 149–69.
8. S. Rynes and S. Lawler, "A Policy Capturing Investigation of the Role of Expectancies in Decisions to Pursue Job Alternatives," *Journal of Applied Psychology* 31 (1983): 353–64; S. Rynes, D. Schwab, and H. Heneman, "The Role of Pay and Market Pay Variability in Job Application Decisions," *Organizational Behavior and Human Decision Processes* 31 (1983): 353–64; P. Sherer, D. Schwab, and H. Heneman, "Managerial Salary-Raise Decisions: A Policy-Capturing Approach," *Personnel Psychology* 40 (1987): 27–38.
9. M. Gist, B. Rosen, and C. Schwoerer, "The Influence of Training Method and Trainee Age on the Acquisition of Computer Skills," *Personnel Psychology* 41 (1988): 255–67.
10. C. Frayne and G. Latham, "Application of Social Learning Theory to Employee Self-Management of Attendance," *Journal of Applied Psychology* 72 (1987): 387–92.
11. T. Lee and R. T. Mowday, "Voluntarily Leaving an Organization: An Empirical Investigation of Steers and Mowday's Model of Turnover," *Academy of Management Journal* 30 (1987): 721–43; B. Gerhart, "Voluntary Turnover and Alternative Job Opportunities," *Journal of Applied Psychology* 75, no. 5 (1990): 467–76; R. P. Steel and R. W. Griffeth, "The Elusive Relationship between Perceived Employment Opportunity and Turnover Behavior: A Methodological or Conceptual Artifact?" *Journal of Applied Psychology* 74, no. 6 (1989): 846–54; T. E. Becker, "Foci and Bases of Commitment: Are They Distinctions Worth Making?" *Academy of Management Journal* no. 1 (1992): 232–44; B. S. Romzek, "Personal Consequences of Employee Commitment," *Academy of Management Journal* 32, no. 3 (1989): 649–61.
12. G. Dreher, R. A. Ash, and R. D. Bretz, "Benefits Coverage and Employee Cost: Critical Factors in Explaining Compensation Satisfaction," *Personnel Psychology* 41 (1988): 237–54.
13. For a summary of the conditions under which each type of correlation coefficient is used, refer to M. J. Allen and W. M. Yen, *Introduction to Measurement Theory* (Monterey, Calif.: Brooks/Cole, 1979), 36-41.
14. G. V. Glass and J. C. Stanley, *Statistical Methods in Eduction and Psychology* (Englewood Cliffs, N.J.: Prentice-Hall, 1970).
15. F. M. Lord and M. R. Novick, *Statistical Theories of Mental Test Scores* (Reading, Mass.: Addison-Wesley, 1968).
16. E. E. Ghiselli, J. P. Campbell, and S. Zedeck, *Measurement Theory for the Behavioral Sciences* (San Francisco: Freeman, 1981).
17. A. Howard, "College Experience and Managerial Performance," *Journal of Applied Psychology* (1986): 530–52. For a discussion of the AT&T Management Progress Study, as well as an overview of assessment centers, see A. Howard, "An Assessment of Assessment Centers," *Academy of Management Journal* 17, no. 71 (1974): 115–34. A twenty-year follow-up study of AT&T's original Management Progress Study predictions was reported in A. Howard, "Cool at the Top: Personality Characteristics of Successful Executives," paper presented at the Annual Convention of the American Psychological Association, Aug. 1984, Toronto.
18. J. Normand, S. Salyards, and I. Mahoney, "An Evaluation of Preemployment Drug Testing," *Journal of Applied Psychology* 75 (1990): 629–39.
19. R. S. Barrett,"Is the Test Content-Valid: Or, Does It Really Measure Construct?" *Employee Relations Law Journal* 6, no. 3 (1981): 459–75; R. S. Barrett, "Is the Test Content-Valid: Or, Who Killed Cock Robin?" *Employee Relations Law Journal* 6, no. 4 (1981): 584–600.
20. A method for assessing construct validity based on correlation coefficients between the relevant construct measure (i.e., the measure being validated) and measures of similar and unrelated constructs is the multitrait-multimethod matrix. This method requires that at least two constructs be measured by minimally two methods. An assessment of construct validity is based on the degrees of convergence (i.e. the correlation coefficients between measures of the same construct) and divergence (i.e., judged by higher correlation coefficients between two methods of measuring the same construct in comparison with correlation coefficients of two constructs measured by the same method). For a discussion of the multitrait-multimethod matrix, refer to D. T. Campbell and D. W. Fiske, "Convergent and Discriminant Validation by the Multitrait-Multimethod Matrix," *Psychological Bulletin* 56 (1959): 81–105. A more concise discussion of the multitrait-multimethod matrix is present in A. Anastasi, *Psychological Testing* (New York: Macmillan, 1976): 156–58.
21. J. J. McHenry, L. M. Hough, J. L. Toquam, M. A. Hanson, and S. Ashworth, "Project A Validity Results: The Relationship Between Predictor and Criterion Domains," *Personnel Psychology* 43 (1990): 335–54; L. M. Hough, N. K. Eaton, M. D. Dunnette, J. D. Kamp, and R. A. McCloy, "Criterion-Related Validities of Personality Constructs and the Effect of Response Distortion on Those Validities," *Journal of Applied Psychology* 75, no. 5 (1990): 581–95; D. L. Deadrick and R. M. Madigan, "Dynamic Criteria Revisited: A Longitudinal Study of Performance Stability

and Predictive Validity," *Personnel Psychology* 43 (1990): 717–44; G. V. Barrett and R. A. Alexander, "Rejoinder to Austin, Humphreys, and Hulin: Critical Reanalysis of Barrett, Caldwell and Alexander," *Personnel Psychology* 42 (1989): 597–612; J. A. Austin, L. G. Humphreys, and C. L. Hulin, "Another View of Dynamic Criteria: A Critical Reanalysis of Barrett, Caldwell and Alexander," *Personnel Psychology* 42 (1989): 583-96; R. A. Alexander, G. M. Alliger, and P. J. Hanges, "Correcting for Range Restriction When the Population Variance is Unknown," *Applied Psychological Measurement* 8 (1984): 431–37; R. A. Forsyth and L. S. Feldt, "Investigation of Empirical Sampling Distributions and Correlations Corrected for Attenuation," *Educational and Psychological Measurement* 29 (1969): 61–71; R. L. Linn, D. L. Harnisch, and S. B. Dunbar, "Validity Generalization and Situational Specificity: An Analysis of the Prediction of First-Year Grades in Law School," *Applied Psychological Measurement* 5 (1981): 281–89.

22. P. Bobko, "An Analysis of Correlations Corrected for Attenuation and Range Restriction," *Journal of Applied Psychology* 68 (1983): 584–89; R. Lee, R. Miller, and W. Graham, "Corrections for Restriction of Range and Attenuation in Criterion-Related Validation Studies," *Journal of Applied Psychology* 67 (1982): 637–39.
23. For a review of validity generalization research, see M. J. Burke, "A Review of Validity Generalization Models and Procedures," in *Readings in Personnel and Human Resource Management,* 3d ed., R. S. Schuler, S. A. Youngblood, and V. L. Huber, eds. (St. Paul, Minn.: West, 1988). See also F. L. Schmidt and J. E. Hunter, "Development of a General Solution to the Problem of Validity Generalization," *Journal of Applied Psychology* 62 (1977): 529–40. Alternative validity generalization procedures have been presented in J. C. Callender and H. G. Osburn, "Development and Test of a New Model for Validity Generalization," *Journal of Applied Psychology* 65 (1980): 543–58; and N. S. Raju and M. J. Burke, "Two New Procedures for Studying Validity Generalization," *Journal of Applied Psychology* 68 (1983): 382–95.
24. G. V. Glass coined the term *meta-analysis* to refer to the statistical analysis of the findings of many individual studies in an article titled "Primary, Secondary, and Meta-Analysis of Research," *Educational Researcher* 5 (1976): 3–8. Although numerous articles and books are beginning to be written on the subject of meta-analysis (of which validity generalization can be considered a subset), two original and frequently cited texts, in this area are G. V. Glass, B. McGaw, and M. L. Smith, *Meta-Analysis in Social Research* (Beverly Hills, Calif.: Sage, 1981); and J. E. Hunter, F. L. Schmidt, and G. Jackson, *Meta-Analysis: Cumulating Research Findings Across Settings* (Beverly Hills, Calif.: Sage, 1982).
25. P. Cattin, "Estimations of the Predictive Power of a Regression Model," *Journal of Applied Psychology* 65 (1980): 407–14; J. G. Claudy, "Multiple Regression and Validity Estimation in One Sample," *Applied Psychological Measurement* 2 (1978): 595–607; K. R. Murphy, "Cost-Benefit Considerations in Choosing among Cross-Validation Methods," *Personnel Psychology* 37 (1984): 15–22.
26. The selection ratio refers to a population parameter representing the proportion of successful applicants or, more specifically, the proportion of individuals in the population scoring above a cutting score. Typically, the selection ratio is equated with the hiring rate (a sample description), which can lead to errors. For a discussion of the distinction between the terms *selection ratio* and *hiring rate,* see R. A. Alexander, G. V. Barrett, and D. Doverspike, "An Explication of the Selection Ratio and Its Relationship to Hiring Rate," *Journal of Applied Psychology* 68 (1983): 342–44.
27. H. C. Taylor and J. T. Russell, "The Relationship of Validity Coefficients to the Practical Validity of Tests in Selection: Discussion and Tables," *Journal of Applied Psychology* 23 (1939): 565–78.
28. J. Tiffin and E. J. McCormick, *Industrial Psychology,* 5th ed. (Englewood Cliffs, N.J.: Prentice-Hall, 1965).
29. H. E. Brogden, "On the Interpretation of the Correlation Coefficient as a Measure of Predictive Efficiency," *Journal of Educational Psychology* 37 (1946): 65–76; H. E. Brogden, "When Testing Pays Off," *Personnel Psychology* 2 (1949): 171–83. At a later point, the cost of testing was incorporated into the equations developed by Brogden in L. J. Cronbach and G. Gleser, *Psychological Tests and Personnel Decisions* (Urbana, Ill.: University of Illinois Press, 1965).
30. W. Cascio, *Costing Human Resource Management,* 3d ed. (Boston: PWS-Kent, 1991).
31. For more information on the economic components of this equation, see J. W. Boudreau. A study that has employed this full equation and provides useful information for estimating the economic components as well as the true validity coefficients is presented in M. J. Burke and J. T. Frederick, "A Comparison of Economic Utility Estimates for Alternative *SD,* Estimation Procedures," *Journal of Applied Psychology* 71 (1986): 334–39.
32. J. F. Binning and G. V. Barrett, "Validity of Personnel Decisions: A Conceptual Analysis of the Inferential and Evidential Bases," *Journal of Applied Psychology* 74, no. 3 (1989): 478–94; L. R. James, R. G. Demaree, S. A. Mulaik, and R. T. Ladd, "Validity Generalization in the Context of Situational Models," *Journal of Applied Psychology* 77, no. 1 (1992) 3–14; J. E. Hunter and R. F. Hunter, "Validity and Utility of Alternative Predictors of Job Performance," *Psychological Bulletin* 96 (1984): 72–98.
33. J. E. Hunter, F. L. Schmidt, and M. K. Judiesch, "Individual Differences in Output Variability as a Function of Job Complexity," *Journal of Applied Psychology* 75, no. 1 (1990): 28–42; L. L. Wise, J. McHenry, and J. P. Campbell, "Identifying Optimal Predictor Composites and Testing for Generalizability across Jobs and Performance Factors," *Personnel Psychology* 43 (1990): 355–66; J. P. Campbell, J. J. McHenry, and L. L. Wise, "Modeling Job Performance in a Population of Jobs," *Personnel Psychology* 43 (1990): 313–33; C. L. Hulin, R. A. Henry, and S. L. Noon, "Adding a Dimension: Time as a Factor in the Generalizability of Predictive Relationships," *Psychological Bulletin* 107, no. 3 (1990): 328–40; W. F. Cascio and J. R. Morris, "A Critical Reanalysis of Hunter, Schmidt, and Coggin's (1988) 'Problems and Pitfalls in Using Capital Budgeting and Financial

Accounting Techniques in Assessing the Utility of Personnel Programs,'" *Journal of Applied Psychology* 75, no. 4 (1990): 410–17.

34. N. S. Raju, M. J. Burke, and J. Normand, "A New Approach for Utility Analysis," *Journal of Applied Psychology* 75, no. 1 (1990): 3–12.
35. M. J. Burke, "Computerized Psychological Testing," in N. Schmitt and W. C. Borman, eds., *Personnel Selection* (San Francisco: Jossey-Bass, 1993). For summaries of research related to adaptive testing via the computer, see D. J. Weiss, "Improving Measurement Quality and Efficiency with Adaptive Testing," *Applied Psychological Measurement* 6 (1982): 473–92.
36. J. B. Sympson, D. J. Weiss, and M. J. Ree, *Predictive Validity of Conventional and Adaptive Tests in an Air Force Training Environment* (AFHRL 81–40), Brooks Air Force Base, Tex., Manpower and Personnel Division, Air Force Human Relations Laboratory.
37. C. L. Hulin, F. Drasgow, and C. K. Parsons, *Item Response Theory: Application to Psychological Measurement* (Homewood, Ill.: Dorsey, 1983).
38. For a critique of the espoused benefits and problems associated with not only adaptive testing but also computerized psychological testing in general, see M. J. Burke, and J. Normand, "Computerized Psychological Testing: An Overview and Critique," *Professional Psychology* 3 (1987): 42–51.
39. V. W. Urry, "Tailored Testing: A Successful Application of Latent Trait Theory," *Journal of Educational Measurement* 14 (1977): 181–96.
40. D. R. Budgell, "Preliminary Analysis of the Feasibility of Computerized Adaptive Testing and Item Banking in the Public Service," unpublished report, Public Service Commission Ottawa, Ont., Canada, 1982.
41. L. S. Kleiman and R. H. Faley, "The Implications of Professional and Legal Guidelines for Court Decisions Involving Criterion-Related Validity: A Review and Analysis," *Personnel Psychology* 38 (1985): 803–33. See also the January 1987 issue of *Personnel Administrator* for a series of articles on how recent court decisions have affected management policy.
42. R. Folger and M. Konovsky, "A Due Process Metaphor for Performance Appraisal," in Staw and Cummings, *Research in Organizational Behavior* (Greenwich, Conn.: JAI Press, 1993); M. Konovsky and S. Cropanzaño, "Perceived Fairness of Employee Drug Testing as a Predictor of Employee Attitudes and Job Performance," *Journal of Applied Psychology* (1991): 698–707; R. J. Bies and D. L. Shapiro, "Voice and Justification: Their Influence on Procedural Fairness Judgments," *Academy of Management Journal* 31 (1988): 676–85; J. Greenberg, "A Taxonomy of Organizational Justice Theories," *Academy of Management Review* 12 (1987): 9–22; J. Greenberg, "Reactions to Procedural Injustice in Payment Distributions: Do the Means Justify the Ends?" *Journal of Applied Psychology* 72 (1987): 55–61; B. H. Sheppard, R. J. Lewicki; and J. Minton, *Organizational Justice* (New York: Free Press, 1992).
43. R. D. Caplan, A. D. Vinokur, R. H. Price, and M. van Ryn, "Job Seeking, Reemployment, and Mental Health: A Randomized Field Experiment in Coping with Job Loss," *Journal of Applied Psychology* 74, no. 5 (1989): 759–69; R. C. Kessler, J. S. House, and J. B. Turner, "Unemployment and Health in a Community Sample," *Journal of Health and Social Behavior* (March 1987): 51–59; L. Greenhalgh, A. T. Lawrence, and R. I. Sutton, "Determinants of Work Force Reduction Strategies in Declining Organizations," *Academy of Management Review* 13 (1988): 241–54; A. Nahavandi and A. R. Malekzadeh, "Acculturation in Mergers and Acquisitions," *Academy of Management Review* 13 (1988): 79–90.
44. J. Brockner, "The Effects of Work Layoffs on Survivors: Research, Theory, and Practice," in *Research in Organizational Behavior,* vol. 10, B. M. Staw and L. L. Cummings, eds. (Greenwich, Conn.: JAI Press, 1988): 213–55; J. Brockner, S. L. Grover, and M. D. Blonder, "Predictors of Survivors' Job Involvement Following Layoffs: A Field Study," *Journal of Applied Psychology* 73 (1988): 436–42; J. Brockner, S. Grover, T. Reed, R. DeWitt, and M. Malley, "Survivors' Reactions to Layoffs: We Get By with a Little Help for Our Friends," *Administrative Science Quarterly* 32 (1987): 526–34.

END OF SECTION CASE STUDY

Peoples Trust Company

The Peoples Trust Company first opened its doors to the public on June 1, 1875, with a total salaried staff of eight members: a treasurer; a secretary; and six assistants (three of whom held the positions of day watchman, night watchman, and messenger). Located in a large, midwestern city, the original company had occupied the basement floor of a new five-story office building with an electric-bell system, steam heat, and steam-driven elevator.

During, its early years, the Trust Company had concentrated its activities on providing vault services to its customers for the safekeeping of tangible items and securities. Management had been able to develop the reputation of being a highly conservative trust company that concentrated on a relatively small and select market of wealthy individuals from the local area. In the years following, the vault service had been retained as an accommodation to its customers, but the company's emphasis had slowly shifted from vault service to a wider range of banking and trust services.

Until the early 1900s, banking services had overshadowed trust services in terms of asset volume. Following the turn of the century, trust assets had begun to grow at an increasing rate. Over the years, the company had been able to achieve an impressive record of sound and steady growth. According to a story often told in banking circles: "Peoples Trust was so conservative that they prospered even during the Depression!"

In 1963, with the appointment of a new president, a new era began for Peoples Trust Company. Between 1963 and 1978, trust assets under supervision rose by $145 million, while deposits increased by more than $20 million in savings deposits.

Accompanying this recent growth has been the company's desire to fashion a new image for itself. In 1979, Mr. Robert Toller assumed the presidency of Peoples Trust. In 1982, he remarked: "... it should be said that the old concept of a trust involving merely the regular payment of income and preservation of capital is largely obsolete." Accordingly, the Investment Division of the Company had been expanded and strengthened. Similar changes had been effected in the Trust and Estate Administrative Group and other customer services. Among these were the improvement of accounting methods and procedures, the installation of electronic data processing systems, and complete renovation of the company's eight-floor building and facilities. Most recently, the company has extended its services into the field of management consulting. This had been acknowledged as a "pioneer" step for a banking institution. The president recently characterized the company as "an organization in the fiduciary business."

At the time these data were gathered, the company had a total of 602 employees. Of this number, 109 were in what is considered the "officer-group"* positions of the company. The company's relations with its employees over the years have been satisfactory, and Peoples Trust is generally recognized by city residents and those in suburban areas as a good place to work. The company hires most of its employees from the local area.

In the period before 1980 Peoples Trust had provided satisfactory advancement opportunities for its employees, and it had been possible for a young, high-school graduate who showed promise on the job to work his way up gradually to officer status. Graduates of banking institutions were also sought for employment with the company. Ordinarily individuals were considered eligible for promotion to the jobs above them after they had thoroughly mastered the details of their present positions.

Prior to 1980 the total staff of the company was small enough so that there was no need to prepare official organization charts or job descriptions. Virtually all of the employees knew each other on a first-name basis, and they were generally familiar with each other's area of job responsibility. New employees were rapidly able to learn "whom you had to go to for what."

In 1980 the company management called in an outside consultant to appraise its organizational structure and operations and to confer on the rapid expansion and diversification of banking services that the company had planned. The presence of the consultants and the subsequent preparation of organization charts and job descriptions reportedly "shook up a lot of people"—many feared loss of their jobs or, at least, substantial changes in the nature of work and assignments. However, there was little overt reaction among the officer-level employees in terms of turnover and/or other indices of unrest.

Over the years it had been the policy of the company to pay wages that were at least average or a little above the average paid by comparable banking organizations in the area. This, combined with favorable employee relations and the stable and prestigious nature of the work, resulted in a low turnover of personnel. The bulk of employee turnover occurred among the younger employees who filled clerical positions throughout the company's various departments.

Since 1980, the personnel picture at Peoples Trust has been shifting. Several changes have taken place in the top management of the company. By adding several new customer services, the company has altered the very nature of its business. This has resulted in a trend toward "professionalization" of many of the officer-level positions in that these positions now require individuals with higher levels of education and broader abilities. The impact of these changes on current employees has been a matter of concern to several executives in the company, particularly to Mr. John Moore, Manager of the Organization Planning and Personnel Department. Mr. Moore described his picture of the situation to the researcher as follows:

Interview with John Moore, V.P., Organization Planning and Personnel

Our problem here is one of a changing image and along with it the changing of people. As a trust company, we had no other ties with an individual's financial needs ... we could only talk in terms of death. We wanted to be able to talk in terms of life, so we got active in the investment-advisory business.

The old wealth around here is pretty well locked up, so we wanted to provide services to new and growing organizations and to individuals who are accumulating wealth. Our problem is one of reorientation. We used to provide one service for one customer. We now want to enter new ventures, offer new services, attract new customers. The problem has become one of how to make the change ... do we have the talent and the people to make the change?

We have a "band" of people (see exhibits 1, 2, and note below) in our organization ... in the 35–50 age group who came in under the old hiring practices and ground rules. Given the new directions in which our company is moving and the changing job requirements, it's clear that, considering their current qualifications and capabilities, these individuals have nowhere to go. Some have been able to accept this; and this acceptance includes watching others move past them. Others have difficulty accepting it ... a few have left ... and we haven't discouraged anyone from leaving. For those who can't accept it, there is the problem of integrating their career strategy with ours. We've articulated our objectives clearly; now individuals need clarification of their own strategies.

As I see it, change caught up with these individuals. They had on-the-job training in their own areas, but that doesn't help them much to cope with the new demands. New functional areas are being melded on top of old ones. For example, marketing is new; so is electronic data processing. They both require qualities that our existing employee staff didn't have.

To date, we have not approached any of these people in an individual way to discuss their problems with them. Our objectives are to further develop these people, but we'll first have to get the support of the department managers who supervise them.

We want to find ways to further develop personnel of the kind represented by this group through a variety of approaches. I am thinking here not only of formal job training in management development, but also of management techniques that would help individuals identify new kinds of qualifications or possible new standards of performance they must take into consideration in planning their own personal growth.

We also have to find ways to provide more opportunities for minorities and women in the organization, particularly at the officer level. Although Peoples Trust is not a federal contractor, we would like to be seen as and be an affirmative action employer and an organization where everyone has an equal chance for employment and promotion.

We have to change the conditioning of old times throughout the company. A recently hired MBA is now an officer. Years ago that couldn't have happened so rapidly. And not everyone here is in agreement that the appointment I just mentioned *should* have happened the way it did. We have to develop support in our company for the new recruiting image.

There are two things which really concern me most about this whole problem:

1. We have a problem in under-utilization of resources.
2. There is a problem which is presented to the growth and development of the company in having some of the individuals I have been discussing settled into key spots.

The company really bears the responsibility for the current situation as I described it. In addition, what this all means to me is that our personnel function may change considerably over the coming year.

After this interview with Mr. Moore, the researcher talked with other company executives to learn their views of the problems outlined by Mr. Moore. The findings from these interviews are presented below.

Interview with Fred Bellows, Human Resource Planning

Historically we have been conservatively managed ... you might say "ultra-conservatively." But now we want

Exhibit 1
Key Personnel Needing Development

Name	Age	Education	Date of Hire	Positions Held
Linda Horn	37	2-year technical institute of business administration	1975	Messenger Clearance clerk Accounting clerk Unit head (working supervisor) Section head (supervisor)
Richard Gaul*	30	2-year junior college program in business administration	1977	Business machines operator Section head (supervisor) Operations officer
Fred James	35	B.A. degree local university American Institute of Banking	1976	Loan clerk Teller Accounting unit head (working supervisor) Section head (supervisor)
Fran Wilson*	35	1 year at local university	1981	Methods analyst Operations unit head (working supervisor) Systems programmer Property accounting dept. head
Martin Pfieffer*	32	Prep school	1977	Messenger Accounting clerk Section head (supervisor) Department head
James Klinger	38	B. A. degree from local university	1972	Messenger Accounting clerk Records clerk Unit head (working supervisor) Administrative specialist
Karen Kissler*	35	B.A. degree from local university co-op program	1974	Messenger Real property specialist Assistant estate officer
Charles Ferris	42	2-year jr. college program in business administration American Institute of Banking	1962	Messenger Deposit accounting section head (supervisor) Unit head (working supervisor)
William Jagger	54	High School	1949	Messenger Trust liaison clerk Accounting clerk Bookkeeping section head
Thomas Geoghigan*	42	2-year jr. college program in business administration	1969	Messenger Securities accountant Property custodian Office manager Assistant operations officer

* = Officer

to change that image. Several years ago there was a revolution in top management. In 1979, Mr. Toller took over and brought in young people, many not from the banking field but from other types of business and consulting organizations. Our employment philosophy may be stated as follows: "We want above-average people ... for above-average pay ... and we want to give them a chance to learn and grow and move with the organization." This applies mainly to those in whom we see management-level potential.

They are told in their employment interview that if they don't see opportunity with us, then they should leave. This is in contrast to the old philosophy that this is a secure place to work, that you can stay here by keeping your nose clean, and that you can sit and wait for pot luck to become a trust officer.

Many people are caught in this changing philosophy. A case in the Trust Administration Division is a good example. There we have an employee in a Grade 10 job who has been with the bank eight years.

Exhibit 2
Peoples Trust Company Organization Chart (June 1983)

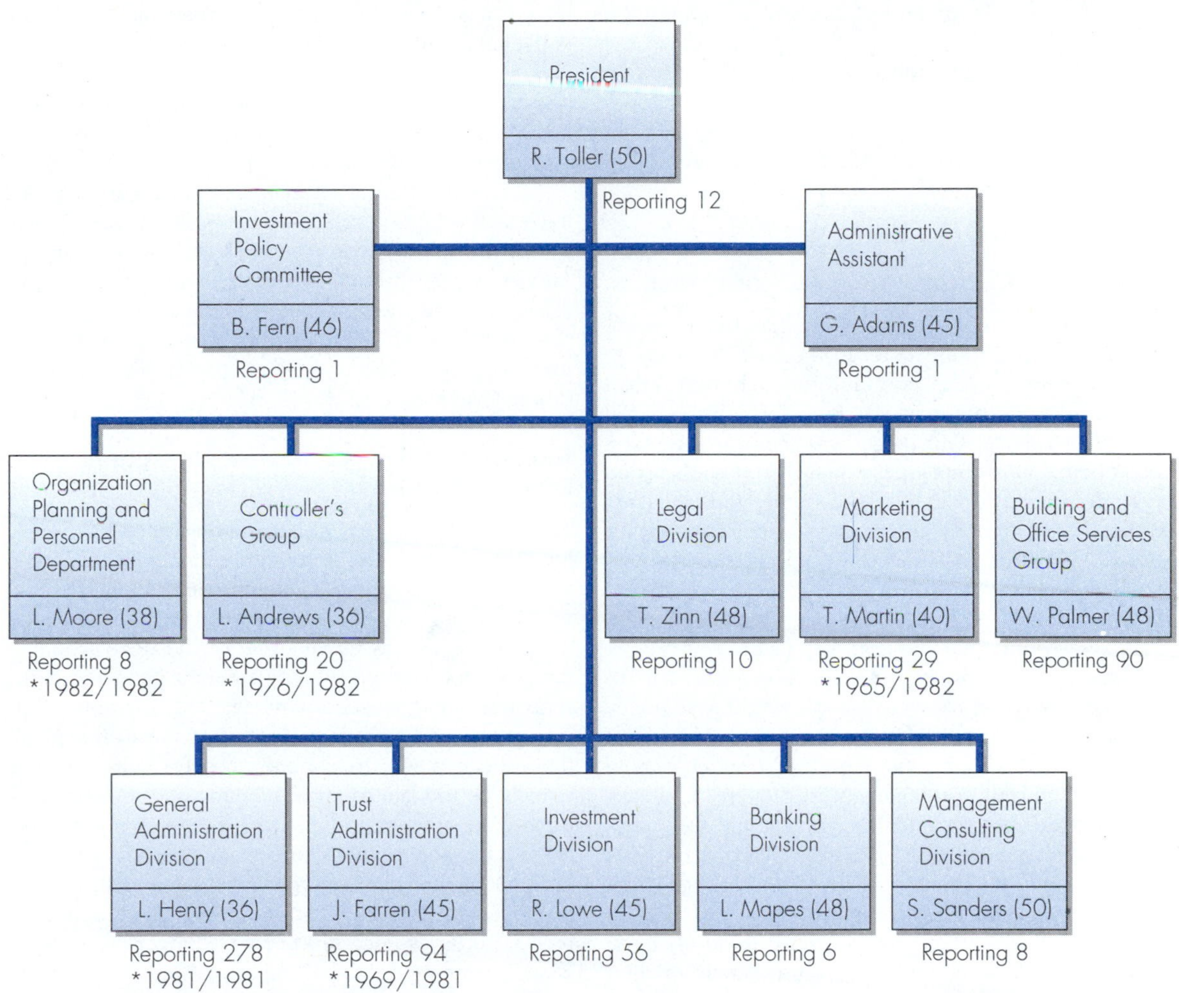

Note: Numbers in parentheses indicate manager's age. These are included for planning purposes only. Numbers below each position indicate number of subordinates.

*Indicates year in which manager joined the company and year in which he or she assumed current position. For example, Mr. Larry Andrews joined Peoples Trust Company in 1976 and became Controller in 1982.

We just hired a new person out of college who we put in that same Grade 10. Now they're both at the same level, but they're entirely different people in terms of education, social background, etc.

Now the Head of our Trust Division bucks this sort of thing. She argues that we don't need all "stars" in the company. Yet, the president wants young, dynamic individuals who can develop and be developed. So I'm trying to get the Trust Division to define: What does the job really require?

We have a number of people with two years of accounting training who have been with the company anywhere from six to nine years. Under our old system they'd be okay, but under the new system they're not. They're not realistic about their future. Our problem is that we're being honest, but few are getting the message.

We bring in a new individual ... ask others to train that person ... and then promote that person over their heads. We have people whose jobs we could get done for a lot less money. When, if ever, do we tell them to go elsewhere?

Interview with Larry Andrews, Controller

There is no question but that there has been a complete revolution around here. In the past, we were in business to serve the community; to handle small accounts; to help the small investor who needed investment service. Our motto was "help anyone who needs help." Our employees were geared to this kind of work orientation and felt at home with it. They could easily identify themselves with this sort of approach to doing business. Most people were quite comfortable; their personal goals coincided with the company goal.

But we found that we couldn't make any money conducting this kind of business. So, we've had to extend our services to attract people who have money and can afford our service. Now the company goal has changed. For example, the Trust Department is now concerned with the management of property in general. The "dead man's bank" has become the "live people's service organization." So we've had to create a kind of snob appeal that too many of our people can't identify with or don't believe in.

Many problems have emerged from these changes. Before, individuals' knowledge of the details of their jobs was their greatest asset. They worked to develop that knowledge and protected it. Now—and I'm speaking of supervisory jobs—the important factor is to have some familiarity with the work but to be able to work with people; to get others to do the detail. Too many of our people still don't understand this....

The route to the top is no longer clear. Over a five-year period this organization has changed. There have been reorganizations, new functions created, and some realignment of existing functions. Many who felt they had a clear line to something higher in the organization now find that that "something" isn't there anymore.

We've had lots of hiring-in at higher levels. Many old-timers have been bypassed. In some cases, the new, outside hirees came into jobs that never existed before, or were hired into a job that had previously existed, but which is now a "cut" above what it was before. What used to be a top job is now a second or third spot.

What we need now are people who are "professional managers"—by that I mean a supervisor versus a technical specialist. Years ago supervision could be concentrated in a few key individuals ... but in the past five years we've grown 20 percent to 30 percent and have a management hierarchy. A person used to be able to grow up as a technical specialist and develop managerial skills secondarily.

To a small extent it's a matter of personality too. We have a new president, and what is acceptable to him differs from what was acceptable to his predecessor. There's a new mix of personal favoritism that goes along with the new vogue. Technical specialists are "low need" as far as the company is concerned. I estimate we now have about 30 people in this category in officer-level jobs.

Interview with Tom Martin, Marketing Division Head

There have been many changes over the past six years. Mr. Toller took a look at the entire organization ... and then hired a consultant to do an organizational study. It was sort of an outside stamp of approval.

His hope was to move some of the dead wood ... the senior people who were past their peak and didn't represent what the company wanted anymore in its managerial and officer staff. Few of these individuals have the capacity to change, and for others it may already be too late to change. Many had leveled off in their development long before these changes came about, and the changes just made it more apparent. Early retirement has been given to some of those over 60. Others remained as titular head of their departments, but in essence report to a younger person who is really running the department.

Banking used to be a soft industry ... you were hired and never fired. If you were a poor performer, you were given a lousy job that you could stay at. No one was ever called in and told to shape up. The pay was so poor it attracted people who wanted to work in a sheltered area, and they were satisfied to try and build a career in that area. So it was a job with low pay, high prestige, and some opportunity.

Our biggest problem is to convince people that they are not technicians anymore, that they are to *supervise* their subordinates and work to develop them. Apparently, for many older individuals, and younger ones, too, this is an impossible assignment. They can do the jobs themselves, but having anyone else do it in any other way runs against their grain.

If our rate of personnel growth over the next ten years is as fast as the previous ten years, I'm afraid we can only absorb about 50 percent of our most promising people.

Interview with Jane Farren, Trust Administration Divisions Head

We have several people for whom there is very little opportunity anymore. We just don't see any potential in these people. There are about fifteen of them who are in their 40s and are really not capable of making any independent decisions. We're trying to get them to see other opportunities ... both inside and outside the company. For example, our Real Estate group was big in the 1960s and 1970s. We're trying to make it important again, and there may be some opportunities in that area.

To give you an idea of the problem we're faced with: One individual is really a personality problem. He's an attorney but he can't get along with others. He wants people to come to him; he focuses on detail too much; and he has great difficulty in telling others what to do and how to do it. He has to do the job all by himself.

Another individual: We gave him a section to supervise but he really hasn't measured up. But, he was the president's pet. I suppose we'll let him continue on ... he's 57 ... and then retire him early.

Interview with Mr. L. Henry, General Administration Division

The company has been undergoing basic change. In the past, if people demonstrated technical competence they were promoted, and that was fine while the company was a small, stable group, and everyone knew what the other was thinking. But then, many in the senior group began to retire. With this "changing of the guard" and the growth of the company, many of us have lost communication with our counterparts. Many of us are new in this field, new to this company, and, of course, new to each other. But we recognize this, so half the communication problem is solved. In a sense, we're not constrained by "how it was done before."

My people have reacted to all this change by sitting back and waiting, seeing which way things are going to go, then I guess deciding whether they are going to join you or not. Most of my people are relatively recent employees–as a matter of fact, of the 278 people in my division, only 11 have been with the company more than ten years. Conversion to EDP will really create a lot of changes in my area.

*Membership in the officer group is determined by an employee's being legally empowered to represent the company in a transaction.

Note: Mr. Moore drew from his files a list of ten individuals who he felt were representative of the group whose lack of appropriate experience or qualifications created a road block to their future development and advancement with the company. These individuals are described in exhibit 1.

SOURCE: This case was prepared by Hrach Bedrosian, New York University.

7

SECTION

Establishing and Maintaining Effective Work Relationships

Individuals want to be treated with respect and dignity. This is true whether they are at work or at home. This desire appears to be growing as employees today want to have more and more rights recognized by their employers. While there are many legal provisions for this, many areas are still not covered. However, in both the legally covered and the uncovered areas, employees think they have many rights that employers should recognize and honor; and because employees are increasingly gaining more legal rights, employment decisions such as discharges, layoffs, and demotions must be made with care and supported by evidence. Line managers must be aware of their employees' rights. Because of the importance of employee rights, they are the focus of the first of three chapters on establishing and maintaining effective work relationships.

Certainly important and vital concerns to employees are their health and safety. If employees do not believe that the work environment is safe or healthy, they may justifiably fail to make effective contributions to the organization. In fact, if the work environment is neither safe nor healthy, workers may not be *able* to make effective contributions. The increased attention and concern for workplace safety and health are important, so we discuss them at length in the second of the three chapters.

When employees feel that their rights are not being respected, that the work environment is neither safe nor healthy, or that wages and other working conditions are neither fair nor sufficient, they may seek to gather power in order to make changes. Gathering together to form a union or association is a result of this type of situation. The union is formed to represent the interests of the employees in discussions with the company. Contracts are established between the workers' union and the management of the company. These two parties negotiate and bargain over conditions of work and wages and benefits. The entire area of union-management relationships is an important one in establishing and maintaining effective work relationships; thus it is discussed in our final chapter in this final section of this book.

CHAPTER 15

Employee Rights

The sexual harassment case that brought Patricia Kidd a $300,000 jury verdict last year was an egregious one: Her supervisor at the District of Columbia's Department of Administrative Services, Melvin Carter, threatened to fire her if she would not have sex with him. Ms. Kidd, a single mother with two children, submitted.

—T. Lewin, *The New York Times*[1]

The issues surrounding sexual harassment captured national and international attention during the confirmation hearings of now Supreme Court Justice Clarence Thomas. While Anita Hill and Clarence Thomas did not invent sexual harassment, the hearings during the summer of 1991 increased awareness of it dramatically. The impact of these hearings carried far beyond the confirmation of Justice Thomas. Subsequent to the hearings, Congress passed the 1991 Civil Rights Act that included under its coverage victims of sexual discrimination. Since then there has been a substantial increase in the number of complaints filed and an increase in the number of employee rights seminars given across the country.[2]

This is not to say, however, that it will be easier for individuals to win decisions on their complaints. While the Equal Employment Opportunity guidelines say that sexual harassment is any kind of workplace sexual advance that is unwelcome, lawyers say that, to bring a successful lawsuit, a complainant has to prove that far more took place. The PHRM in the News: "Starting with a Compliment" *illustrates the emotions and challenges in Patricia Kidd's experience with the legalities of filing sexual harassment charges. Of course, the types of experiences undergone by Patricia Kidd prevent many cases of sexual harassment from ever getting to court. While the Thomas confirmation hearings and the Civil Rights Act of 1991 appear to be having a significant impact thus far—at least in terms of the number of complaints filed—you need to follow the news media to see what happens in terms of success at the court level.*

While sexual harassment is a serious issue in the area of employee rights, it is just one of several to be discussed in this chapter.

EMPLOYEE RIGHTS

Employee rights are regarded here as those rights that employees desire regarding the security of their jobs and the treatment administered by their employers while on the job, regardless of whether or not those rights are protected by law or collective bargaining agreements.

Employee rights cover much more than freedom from sexual harassment, including the right to a job under almost any conditions, and also the right to fair, just, and respectable treatment while on the job. More specific issues within these two broad areas include the right of plant closing notification; the right to refuse tests for substance abuse; the right against retaliation for whistle-blowing or filing complaints against the employer; due process treatment in discharge cases; the right to know about workplace hazards; freedom from discriminatory treatment based on sex, race, religion, or national origin; the right to be assisted in correcting ineffective performance; and the right to have personal records remain confidential. Some of these rights are protected by collective bargaining agreements; however, more than eighty percent of the work force is nonunionized and largely unprotected.[3]

As employee rights are recognized by employers, the extent of management rights and the prerogatives management has in dealing with its work force, such

IN THE NEWS

Starting with a Compliment

It began with Mr. Carter, her boss, complimenting her on her looks in June, 1987.

"I felt trouble from the outset, because this was a man who had pictures of nude women on his wall in his office," Ms. Kidd said. "I said, 'Let's keep this about work, let's keep this professional,' but he just went on like I hadn't said anything."

Over the next months his comments changed, she said. She said he began telling her that women who got to the top in District of Columbia government got there on their backs. He called her at home, she said, and propositioned her. Ms. Kidd secretly applied for a job in another department, but Mr. Carter found out about it and blocked it, she said.

The day after the office Christmas party, Mr. Carter called her at the office from a hotel a block away and told her to come join him. She hung up. But he called back and said he would fire her if she did not come, she said. She went.

"We were blessed, in this case, to have the hotel receipt, with phone logs showing both the calls to her at work and a phone call she made to her boyfriend afterwards, when she was still at the hotel and she needed someone to talk to," said Vicki Golden, the lawyer representing Ms. Kidd.

Complaint Mentioned No Sex

In 1988, Mr. Carter continued the harassment, Ms. Kidd said—once insisting that Ms. Kidd dine with him and another couple, and, another time, taking her to his house, where they again had sexual relations.

Ms. Kidd finally filed a formal complaint against Mr. Carter in May, citing harassment and unfair practices, but not mentioning sex. She got back a memo supporting Mr. Carter. In September she filed another complaint, with the Office of Human Rights, and this time she described the sex.

Mr. Carter denied having had sex with her but said he had taken her out to dinner. Fifteen months later, the human rights office ruled against Ms. Kidd, noting that she had not mentioned sex in her earlier complaints and that she had dined with Mr. Carter socially.

Mr. Carter continued his denials after Ms. Kidd filed suit, charging him and two of his supervisors with intentional infliction of emotional distress. At the trial, Mr. Carter called a psychiatrist to testify that Ms. Kidd had a personality disorder and that she had fabricated the entire story.

Continued

as employment-at-will, diminish. Thus, employee rights have significant impact on and importance for managing human resources effectively.

Employee–employer rights issues are wrapped in much legal regulation, so they could also be discussed in chapter 3. However, because they are so important and so extensive, it is more appropriate to devote an entire chapter to the discussion of employee–employer rights.

This chapter follows the conventional distinction found in research and practice and discusses employee rights in terms of two major headings: job security and rights on the job. After we define employee rights and their increasing importance in managing human resources, we then review major legislation and court decisions affecting these rights. A major on-the-job issue is an employee's right to privacy, especially electronic privacy. Other significant on-the-job issues involve access to employee records; cooperative acceptance, especially in regard to sexual harassment; and notification and assistance concerning plant or office closings. Employer success in ensuring employee rights in both job security and rights on the job depends on establishing more effective organizational communication as well as clear procedures for grievances, progressive discipline, privacy, and outplacement assistance.

"That just made the jury mad,"said Ms. Golden. She said she gets 10 calls a week from women with sexual harassment claims but takes on only about 5 percent of them.

Although cases where the victim has had sexual intercourse with the harasser are often difficult to win, Ms. Golden said, Ms. Kidd's case was a likely candidate because of both the telephone logs and the several corroborating witnesses, including the boyfriend and a son who had answered calls from Mr. Carter at home.

"It also helped us that, as it turned out, Pat was not the only woman this guy had harassed," said Ms. Golden. "There were complaints back to 1981".

Ms. Golden said she would usually not take a case without some corroboration but that co-workers can generally provide it.

Someone Usually Sees

"If you interview co-workers in these cases, there's usually someone who will come forward and testify that while they don't know exactly what happened, they saw the boss call the woman into his office a lot, or they noticed he was hanging around their section more than usual, or something," she said. "In Pat's case, she had complained administratively, and they retaliated by shipping her to a warehouse where she had another supervisor who came forward and testified on her behalf."

Ms. Kidd also clearly had damages, Ms. Golden said.

"She was very depressed and weepy and slept a lot," Ms. Golden said, "She had hair loss and ulcers, so she had seen a doctor, and she was seeing a shrink. This really messed up her life."

Despite the $300,000 verdict a year ago, Ms. Kidd's case might also serve as a cautionary tale on the perils of filing a sexual harassment claim.

The case is still on appeal, so she has not got any money yet. The city has not responded to the judge's suggestion that it find her a job in a different department. And while Mr. Carter and his two supervisors named as defendants in the lawsuit are no longer working for the city, Ms. Kidd says she still works, every day, with others who ignored her complaints and are now retaliating against her.

"They're punishing me left and right," she said. "I'm no more secure in my job than I was. I can't afford to quit. I can't get another job because they've blocked me everywhere I try. It's just outrageous."

SOURCE: T. Lewin, "A Case Study of Sexual Harassment and the Law," *The New York Times* (11 Oct. 1991): A17.

PURPOSES AND IMPORTANCE OF EMPLOYEE RIGHTS

The discussion on recruitment and selection in chapters 5 and 6 focused on getting job applicants into organizations; while some attention is given to individuals in the hiring process, primary attention now is directed toward establishing and maintaining relationships with the job applicants hired and terminating those not desired by the organization. Previous chapters stressed the importance of making sure employees (new and old) are informed about what is expected of them and what opportunities are available in the organization. This, after all, is part of the basis for an equitable employer-employee relationship.[4]

Treating employees fairly and with respect once they are hired is also important to organizations. Violation of legally protected employee rights—even when what is protected is not entirely clear—can result in severe penalties and fines. For example, in a recent case a jury awarded Valcar Bowman $1.2 million after finding that Mobil Corporation wrongfully fired him after he refused to violate environmental laws and policies:

> After a two-month trial in federal court in Newark, N.J., the jury ruled in favor of Valcar Bowman, Jr., the former manager for environmental affairs at the company's

> Mobil Chemical Co. unit. He claimed in his suit that he was fired in 1986 in retaliation for his refusal to remove environmental records from a Mobil plant in Bakersfield, Calif.
>
> The jury award consisted of $375,000 in compensatory damages, including lost wages and pain and suffering, and $1 million in punitive damages.[5]

Although failure to respect employee rights can be costly to organizations in terms of back-pay awards and fines, it can also be costly because of the increased difficulty in attracting and retaining good employees.[6] Thus, two other important purposes served by respecting employee rights are attracting and retaining good employees, making recruitment and selection more effective and their need less frequent. Additional purposes of respecting employee rights can be observed through their extensive relationships with the other human resource activities described in chapter 1 and illustrated in exhibit 15.1.

LEGAL CONSIDERATIONS IN EMPLOYEE RIGHTS

Because the entire activity of employee rights is filled with legal considerations, this section makes reference to numerous court cases and regulations. This section is followed by suggested human resource strategies to facilitate employer recognition of all the employee rights discussed in this chapter.

Employee Rights to Job Security

Over the years, the major limit on employee rights to job security has been the employer's right to terminate employees for any reason. This right is known as

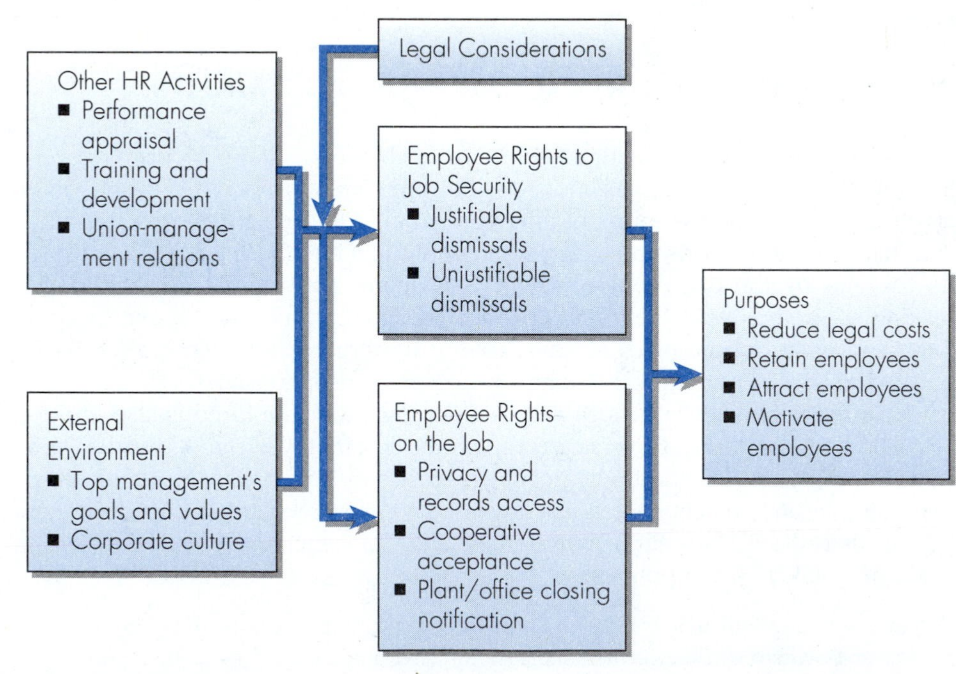

Exhibit 15.1
Components of Employee Rights

the **termination-at-will rule** (also referred to as the **employment-at-will rule**). The termination-at-will rule, which was developed in the United States more than 100 years ago, was explained by one Tennessee court in 1884 in this way: "All may dismiss their employee(s) at will, be they many or few, for good cause, for no cause, or even for cause morally wrong without being thereby guilty of legal wrong" (*Payne v. Western & A.R.R. Co., 1884).*

Limitations of termination. Although employers have relied on the termination-at-will rule over the years, it is proving to be less of a legally justifiable defense today because of several recent statutes (Title VII of the Civil Rights Act of 1964, the Age Discrimination in Employment Act of 1967, and the Rehabilitation Act of 1973) which are discussed in chapter 3.[7]

The National Labor Relations Act of 1935 prohibits discharge for union-organizing activities or for asserting rights under a union contract, even if the employee in question had a record of poor performance (*NLRB v. Transportation Management*, 1983).[8] When employees are represented by a union, the union contract replaces the termination-at-will doctrine and specifies the conditions under which an employee can be fired.

Such court decisions as the *Board of Regents of State Colleges v. Roth* (1972) protect workers from discharge when due process has not been given the employee. Various state acts, such as Montana's Maternity Leave Act that prohibits employers from terminating female employees because of pregnancy, also limit the employer's rights.

As stated in chapter 3, discharge is *not* a legitimate action under any circumstances for the following employee actions:

- Whistle-blowing (e.g., opposing and publicizing employer policies or practices that violate laws such as the antitrust, consumer protection, or environmental protection laws)[9]
- Garnishment for any one indebtedness
- Complaining or testifying about equal pay or wage/hour law violations
- Complaining or testifying about safety hazards and/or refusing an assignment because of the belief that the assignment is dangerous
- Engaging in union activities, provided there is no violence or unlawful behavior
- Engaging in concerted activity to protest wages, working conditions, or safety hazards
- Filing a workers' compensation claim
- Filing unfair labor practice charges with the NLRB or a state agency
- Filing discrimination charges with the Equal Employment Opportunity Commission (EEOC) or a state or municipal fair employment agency
- Cooperating in the investigation of a charge
- Reporting Occupational Safety and Health Administration (OSHA) violations[10]

Permissible termination. Although termination for good cause has not been an explicitly accepted doctrine for nonunion organizations, the decisions that courts are rendering suggest the safest (legal) grounds for discharge include the following:

- Incompetence in performance that does not respond to training or to accommodation
- Gross or repeated insubordination
- Too many unexcused absences
- Repeated lateness
- Verbal abuse
- Physical violence
- Falsification of records
- Drunkenness on the job
- Theft[11]

Firing or discharge, even under one of these nine conditions, should be the last step in a progressive discipline system.[12] Furthermore, all evidence and material relevant to each step and even any decision to discharge an employee should be documented and filed.

Even though an employer may have the right to fire an employee, the employer may be required to show evidence indicating that none of the protections against termination-at-will or for good-cause was violated.[13]

Employee Rights on the Job

Employee rights on the job include privacy and access to employment records, cooperative acceptance, freedom from sexual harassment, and plant/office closing notification.[14]

Rights to privacy and access to employment records. Recently, several lawsuits have been brought against organizations for invasion of privacy rights. The Privacy Act of 1974, which applies only to federal agencies, pertains to the verification of references in selection and employment decisions. This act allows individuals to determine which records pertaining to them are collected, used and maintained; to review and amend such records; to prevent unspecified use of such records; and to bring civil suit for damages against those intentionally violating the rights specified in the act.

The second federal privacy law is the Fair Credit and Reporting Act, which permits job applicants to know the nature and content of the credit file on them that is obtained by the organization. The third law is the Family Education Rights and Privacy Act, or the Buckley Amendment. This allows students to inspect their educational records and prevents educational institutions from supplying information without students' consent. If students do not provide this consent, potential employers are prevented from learning of their educational record. The fourth law is the Freedom of Information Act, which also pertains only to federal agencies. This act allows individuals to see all the material an agency uses in its decision-making processes.

While the four laws detailed above apply primarily to federal agencies, several states (e.g., California, Connecticut, Maine, Michigan, Oregon, and Pennsylvania) have enacted laws that give employees access to their personnel files and define what information employees are entitled and not entitled to see, as well as where, when, and under what circumstances the employees may see their files.[15]

In addition to these state and federal regulations, employees, their designated representatives, and OSHA have the right to access their on-the-job medical records and records that measure employee exposure to toxic substances. These rights are provided for by the Employee Exposure and Medical Records Regulation of 1980.

Employee rights to privacy have recently been extended to include the right not to be subjected to a polygraph test as a condition of employment (Employment Polygraph Protection Act of 1988) for most jobs.

Court rulings are also being applied in the area of drug testing (*O'Connor v. Ortega,* 1987). The area of drug testing raises several basically unresolved issues for employees and employers. On one hand, employees say they have a constitutional right to privacy and a right to have their "personal" (non-job-related) lives kept separate from their "workplace" lives. On the other hand, employers say they have a right to run their businesses safely and profitably, and they may require knowing whether or not their employees or job applicants are substance abusers, liars about their past, individuals who carry genetic traits making them susceptible to certain diseases, or individuals who have HIV or AIDS.[16]

While there is legal protection for individuals with HIV and AIDS and while the Polygraph Act protects individuals against the use of polygraph tests, in the area of the drug testing, courts appear to allow employers to test, particularly when public safety is an issue. An example is a program jointly developed between New York City and the Transit Authority union that allows random testing for drug and alcohol use.

> About 30,000 employees will be subject to the surprise tests, and about 10 percent of them will be tested each year, transit officials said.
>
> Workers subject to the random tests are in "safety sensitive" positions and have long been tested for drugs and alcohol on hiring and after incidents like accidents or prolonged absences. But Local 100 of the Transport Workers Union had opposed random testing, saying that it could be used for harassment.
>
> The union dropped its opposition in August [1991], a day after a Lexington Avenue express train crashed near Union Square, killing five people and injuring 200. The driver, Robert E. Ray, was charged with second-degree murder after he was found to have a high level of alcohol in his blood hours after the crash.
>
> Workers will be selected for testing at random by a computer, the Transit Authority said. Tests, which will be conducted at the transit agency's medical centers, will run round the clock seven days a week.[17]

The Americans with Disabilities Act of 1990 does not protect current drug users; however, anyone with a history of drug use who has successfully completed or is currently engaged in rehabilitation is covered. Furthermore, certain employers (e.g., law enforcement and transit agencies) "...may also be able to impose a qualification standard that excludes individuals with a history of illegal use of drugs if it can show that the standard is job-related and consistent with business necessity." Consequently, the act does not have a stand on drug testing.

Remember, however, it does have a stand on medical exams, indicating that they can be given only *after* a conditional job offer has been made.

Right to cooperative acceptance. The right of employees to be treated fairly and with respect, regardless of race, sex, national origin, physical disability, age, or religion, while *on the job* (as well as in obtaining a job and maintaining job security) is called **cooperative acceptance.**

Not only do employees have the right *not* to be discriminated against in employment practices and decisions, but also they have the right to be free of sexual harassment. The 1980 EEOC guidelines state that **sexual harassment** is a form of sex discrimination. According to the guidelines, verbal and physical conduct of a sexual nature is harassment under the following conditions:

- Submission to such conduct is either explicitly or implicitly made a term or condition of an individual's employment.
- Submission to or rejection of such conduct by an individual is used as the basis for employment decisions affecting such individuals.
- Such conduct has the purpose or effect of substantially interfering with an individual's work performance or creating an intimidating, hostile or offensive working environment.[18]

Numerous court decisions have also equated sexual harassment with sex discrimination under Title VII (*Tomkins v. Public Service Electric and Gas Company et al.*, 1977; *William v. Saxbe,* 1976; *Barnes v. Costle,* 1977; *Heelen v. Johns-Manville Corp.*, 1978; *Bellissimo v. Westinghouse,* 1984).[19]

A U.S. Supreme Court decision illustrates why employers should be especially concerned about the issue of sexual harassment (*Meritor Savings v. Vinson,* 1986):

> A bank teller's charge that her supervisor intimidated her into engaging in a sexual liaison led to a U.S. Supreme Court ruling that demonstrates just how vulnerable employers can be to charges of sexual harassment. The bank claimed that if, in fact, she had a sexual affair with her supervisor, she submitted voluntarily to his advances, and he never conditioned employment benefits on her participation in the affair. But the Supreme Court rejected those arguments. Even if the teller wasn't forced to participate in the alleged sexual liaison, she could still make a case if she could show that those advances were "unwelcome," ruled the Court. And though there was no evidence that her supervisor conditioned tangible job benefits on her participation in the alleged liaison, she could still sue by demonstrating that his conduct created an "intimidating, hostile, or offensive working environment."[20]

Finally, as our introductory story described, the Civil Rights Act of 1991 also protects victims of sexual harassment.[21]

Rights to plant/office closing notification. The employee's right to plant/office closing or relocation notification is an important one.[22] The suicide rate among displaced workers is almost thirty times the national average. The right of employers (where a union represents the workers) to move production facilities is greatly affected by federal labor law under the NLRA, Section 8(a). It has been clearly established that employers must bargain over the effects of a plant closing and relocation. The U.S. Supreme Court, however, ruled against the

NLRB in one case, saying that a corporate decision to close out a particular location or even a product line is not a subject that must be negotiated in advance with the union as long as it is for solely economic reasons (*First National Maintenance v. NLRB,* 1981). However, companies must negotiate with the union before they make a decision to move if there is no basic change in the nature of the employer's operation at the new location (*NLRB v. Dubuque Packing Company,* 1991).

Several states now recognize the importance of plant or office closings and relocations and are considering legislation to control them. Maine and Wisconsin require prenotification and penalize employers who move plants without doing so. At the federal level the Worker Adjustment and Retraining Notification Act took effect in 1989. It mandates that employers give employees 60 days' notice of layoffs of 50 or more employees in situations where the number constitutes one-third of the work force. It also requires employers to give prenotification of layoffs of 500 or more workers, regardless of the total number of workers at the company. All businesses are covered that employ 100 or more employees (excluding part-timers.)[22]

In addition to legal considerations in employee rights on the job, more "humane" considerations include outplacement assistance for employees who are no longer needed, even though they may be competent performers. Such circumstances may arise if a plant or office is moving or closing or if it must reduce its work force for economic reasons. [23]

STRATEGIES TO PRESERVE EMPLOYEE RIGHTS

Because of both legal and humane considerations, it is important that organizations develop and implement strategies for recognizing employee rights. Effectively implementing other human resource activities is one general way to help ensure that many of the legally sanctioned employee rights are recognized. In addition, organizations can implement specific employee programs such as privacy policies, assistance programs, outplacement activities, and sexual harassment prevention training.

Employer Strategies for Employee Job Security Rights

In addition to adhering to legal considerations applying to job security rights, employers should ensure fair and legal termination by communicating expectations and prohibitions, establishing grievance procedures and due process, and following progressive discipline procedures.

Communicate expectations and prohibitions. Although ignorance of rules is generally no excuse in society at large, it is in employment settings. Generally, employees may be disciplined only for conduct not in accordance with what they know or reasonably understand is prohibited or required (*Patterson v. American Tobacco Co.,* 1976, 1978; *Sledge v. J. P. Stevens & Co.,* 1978; and *Donaldson v. Pillsbury Co.,* 1975). Employers must, therefore, ensure that performance expectations are conveyed to employees along with information about what is prohibited. Employers can do this by developing and communicating written policy statements, job descriptions, and performance criteria. Written standards should also exist for promotions (*Rowe v. General Motors Corp.*, 1972; *Robinson v. Union Carbide Corp.*, 1976).

Treat employees equally. Equal treatment of employees is essential in ensuring that legally protected employee rights are upheld. For example, if the employer discharges one employee for five unexcused absences, then another employee with five unexcused absences must also be discharged. (*McDonald v. Santa Fe Trail Transportation Co.*, 1976). Periodic training for supervisors can help ensure that discharge policies are communicated and administered the same way by all supervisors. Employees value fairness in treatment and may react in unproductive ways, such as stealing, if they perceive unfairness, as discussed in the "Focus on Research."

Grievance procedures and due process. Not only should grievance procedures be established to ensure due process for employees, they should also be administered consistently and fairly. For example, evidence should be available to employee and employer, and both parties should have the right to call witnesses and refuse to testify against themselves.[24]

Furthermore, these grievance procedures should be clearly stated as company policy and communicated as such to employees. Increasingly organizations are using peer review panels to review employee grievances and appeals.

Establish progressive discipline procedures. A formal grievance policy should be accompanied by a progressive discipline policy. For most violations of company rules, firing should be the last step in a carefully regulated system of escalating discipline, often called progressive discipline. The steps possible in progressive discipline procedures include the following:

- Warning may be oral at first, but should then be written, and a copy with the employee's signature kept in the personnel files. Having that information in the personnel files is important when building a case for disciplinary discharge. Unfortunately, the information needed is often missing from the file. The biggest deficiencies in employment records often surface only after an employee challenges the legality of a discharge. Valid personnel files, along with a progressive discipline policy for discharge, can be the best defense according to several arbitration decisions regarding discharge for excessive absenteeism.
- Reprimand is official, in writing, and placed in the employee's file.
- Suspension can be for as short as part of a day or as long as several months without pay, depending on the seriousness of the employee's offense and the circumstances.
- Disciplinary transfer may take the pressure off a situation that might explode into violence, or one in which personality conflict is part of the disciplinary problem.
- Demotion can be a reasonable answer to problems of incompetence, or an alternative to layoff for economic reasons.

FOCUS ON RESEARCH

Who's Stealing from Whom? It's Not Such an Easy Call

A friend tells you she had her wallet stolen. Do you assume that the thief who did it is the guilty one and your friend is the innocent party? If employees are caught stealing company property, do you blame the employees or the company? Employers lose billions of dollars every year due to employee theft. Although it's easy to blame employees for this problem, the companies who are victims may be partly responsible.

When a large manufacturing company was forced to cut wages by 15%, one researcher had an opportunity to find out whether feeling unfairly treated might cause employees to steal from their employer. The company involved was a manufacturer of small mechanical parts used in the aerospace and automotive industries. Due to the loss of two contracts, temporary pay cuts were required at two of the company's three plants. Everyone at the plants affected, including management, took the same cut, which went into effect for 10 weeks. After management made the decision to cut pay, two plants were randomly assigned to two experimental conditions. The experiment involved giving the employees different explanations to justify the pay cuts, and then studying their reactions. Employees in the "adequate explanation" plant were told that the pay cuts would eliminate the need for layoffs; they were assured that no favoritism would occur and management attempted to seriously convey how much they regretted the pay cuts. At the meeting announcing the pay cuts, an hour was spent answering all of the employees' questions. In the "inadequate explanation" plant, the pay cut was announced at a 15 minute meeting with no apology and very little explanation.

Employee reactions were measured in three ways: theft rates, employee turnover, and survey responses. The results were clear. During the 10 weeks of pay cuts, theft level stayed the same at the plant that did not have to take a pay cut. For the two plants taking pay cuts, theft rates went up during the weeks the cuts were in effect, and then went down again when normal pay was restored. Furthermore, theft was much higher in the plant where employees were given an inadequate explanation. Whereas some employees responded by stealing from the company, others simply decided to leave. Turnover in the inadequate explanation plant soared, from 5% to 23%. Survey responses showed that employees in the plant given an inadequate explanation did not understand how their pay was determined during the pay cut and did not feel the pay they received was fair. These feelings of inequity are probably what led some employees to quit and others to retaliate by pilfering.

In times of economic adversity when cost-cutting takes on greater importance, employers may be forced to take actions that everyone will find disagreeable. But the negative side-effects of such actions can be minimized if employers make serious attempts to help employees understand why they are needed. Employers have the right to cut costs in order to ensure the survival of a company, but they should keep in mind that if employees are asked to make sacrifices, they are likely to feel it is their right to be informed about why.

SOURCE: Based on J. Greenberg, "Employee Theft as a Reaction to Underpayment Inequity: The Hidden Cost of Pay Cuts," *Journal of Applied Psychology* 75 (1990), 561–68.

- Discharge is the last resort, used only when all else has failed, although it might be a reasonable immediate response to violence, theft, or falsification of records. However, firing can be exceedingly painful, even though it is well organized and planned. In addition, many individuals are capable of effective performance but only in certain types of situations. Thus, some organizations carefully diagnose performance deficiencies, as discussed in chapter 8. Such a diagnosis may result in reassigning employees to different parts of the organization and trading top-level managers to other organizations.[25]

Another step in progressive discipline that may be added is the "last chance agreement." Before resorting to firing, an employer may be willing to grant an employee one more chance, but only with several stipulations. For example, instead of suspending or terminating an employee for excessive absenteeism, the employer may grant the employee one final fixed time period in which to improve. Employers may also wish to use several other positive strategies for improvement. These include positive reinforcement, employee assistance programs, and self-managed work teams. These are described in more detail in chapter 8 as strategies to improve the performance of individuals.

Even taking all of these steps does not ensure that the problem will be solved. Termination may still be necessary. The following advice may help in performing this difficult task:

> The terminational interview should be brief. Normally, a ten- to fifteen-minute meeting is sufficient. A longer meeting increases the opportunity for the company representative (in this case, you) to make a mistake. Some mistakes can be costly.
>
> It is best to conduct the termination meeting in that person's office or in some office other than your own. If conducted in your own office, you may be trapped into a lengthy harangue by a disgruntled individual who is using you to vent...hostility, anger, frustration.
>
> Many individuals hear very little after they understand they have lost their job. This is understandable. They often begin to think of their future [or] the anxiety and stress of having no job, and there is strong concern about their family, especially if the individual is the chief wage earner in the family.
>
> Hence, have a written description of benefits and/or salary continuation, if applicable. Also include how the individual is to be paid.
>
> It is a good idea to role play with someone before you actually do the termination. It is better yet if you can videotape the role play(s). Practice can help iron out the bugs and the discomfort and make it easier and less cumbersome in the actual termination meeting.[26]

Certainly a firm would not want to hurt an employee's chances of getting a job by defaming the person in any way. In fact, individuals can sue past employers in defamation cases, although their chances of winning appear minimal. Nonetheless, employers should be aware of its possible occurrence. Defamation may occur if any employer makes a statement regarding a former employee verbally in the presence of others, over the telephone, or in a writing that is read by others, when the statement is malicious or false (and made with knowledge of its falsity) and injures a person's character or reputation. For example, a jury awarded $1.9 million to a plaintiff after the former employer made statements to a prospective employer that implied he had been terminated for serious misconduct (*Frank B. Hall & Co. v. Buck*).

Employer Strategies for Employee Rights on the Job

To protect employee rights on the job, employers must develop effective policies, procedures, and programs in regard to privacy and records access, cooperative acceptance (particularly sexual harassment), and plant or office closings.

Employee privacy rights and record access. New since the 1960s is the concern for the privacy of personnel records and employee access to personnel files.[27] As discussed previously, privacy legislation generally does not cover private employer-employee relationships. Consequently, many companies such as General Foods and Chase Manhattan Bank have moved ahead on their own to establish policies and rules governing employee privacy and access rights.[28] While a few years ago only a few employers were attempting to define employee privacy, today almost fifty percent of the major companies have written policies regarding the privacy of personnel records. In addition, over eighty-five percent provide employees access to records containing information about themselves.[29] General Foods' (GF) privacy policy includes the following points:

- Employees who want to examine their personnel files must give the company advance notice and may review their files only during regular business hours in the presence of a management representative. Before employees are allowed to examine their personnel files, the company removes any information dealing with co-workers or the firm's activities or plans in such areas as investigations, litigation, and personnel or salary planning.
- Because release of employees' medical records can lead to problems, such as a worker's misinterpretation of health records, GF allows company physicians to make oral reports to workers and send written reports to their doctors. Medical information is regarded as confidential and is not released to a third party, except when an employee files an insurance claim.
- The company will release information in compliance with a subpoena without contesting the subpoena, but will advise the employee that the information was released, unless prohibited by law from doing so.
- When information is to be released within the company for reasons outside normal requirements, the employee is notified and given a chance to object to the release. For example, the United Givers Fund, a charity campaign within GF, requested payroll records showing charitable contributions. Before the information was supplied to the fund, workers were notified and given the option of keeping their payroll records confidential.[30]

Employer concerns about employee privacy rights are also influencing preemployment screening and the use of drug tests. Prehire practices are being examined to ensure that only job-related information is collected, because collecting nonjob information is now considered an unnecessary intrusion into the private lives of job applicants.[31] Wells Fargo has established an HIV policy, under the broader coverage of their AIDS policy, to help protect the rights of employees who have been infected with the Human Immunodeficiency Virus (HIV).

> Wells Fargo's AIDS policy was drafted and implemented in 1983, only two years after the disease was first identified. At the time, few companies had such a policy.
>
> Currently, only 4–10% of U.S. businesses have a written policy for employees who test HIV positive, according to Rosalind Brannigan, director of the Workplace Resource Center at the National Leadership Coalition on AIDS, in Washington, D.C.[32]

Wells Fargo's policy ensures that the rights of all employees are protected and that the individual with AIDS or HIV receives proper medical attention. Because of the seriousness of those diseases, more employers are likely to develop policies for them in the 1990s.

At Ciba-Geigy Corporation in the U.S., focus groups were formed to solicit employee opinions on drug problems. As a result, the company decided the following:

- To take an educational thrust to our program. We want supervisors and employees to recognize drug problems, and know what to do about them.
- To encourage employees and their families to ask for help when they need it—before there are problems. Our Employee Assistance Program is available on a confidential basis.
- To establish a positive tone program—not a punitive one. We offer a rehabilitation program through our Employee Assistance Program.
- To test when there [is] an accident or behaviorial indications of alcohol or drug use.
- To take a top-down approach to training, so everyone in management would learn how to handle abuse situations—both for alcohol and for drugs.
- To provide uniform training materials for each division, so there are consistent messages throughout the company.[33]

These practices of Ciba-Geigy closely parallel those outlined in the Drug-Free Workplace Act of 1988.

Employee rights to cooperative acceptance. Although many issues are associated with employee rights to cooperative acceptance, sexual harassment and smoking bans have recently become prominent concerns for many employees and employers.

What was once regarded by some employees as "good-natured fun" between supervisors (or managers) and employees may today constitute sexual harassment according to 1980 EEOC guidelines. Because sexual harassment creates an offensive and hostile work environment and can result in expensive financial settlements, and because employers are ultimately responsible, they need to be particularly concerned with developing strategies to prevent sexual harassment committed by their employees (*Meritor Savings v. Vinson,* 1986). The following steps constitute such a strategy.[34]

- Raise affirmatively the issue of harassment, and the fact that it exists, to the rest of the organization. The personnel and human resource manager should persuade top management to make it a rule that all discharges must be reviewed by a senior corporate officer or review board.
- Set up reporting (grievance) procedures for those who have been harassed. Because the employer is liable for sexual harassment, except where it can be shown that the organization took immediate and appropriate corrective action (when the offending individual is guilty), it pays to have an established policy and system in place.
- Establish procedures for corroborating a sexual harassment charge. That is, the HR manager should make sure that the person charged with sexual harassment has the right to respond immediately after charges are made by the alleged victim. Due process must be provided the alleged perpetrator as well as the victim.

- Specify a set of steps in a framework of progressive discipline for perpetrators of sexual harassment. These could be the same steps used by the organization in treating any violation of organization policies (see the progressive discipline procedures discussed earlier).
- Finally, make all employees aware of the company's position on sexual harassment. Provide support, such as training programs for managers and supervisors.

Although implementing these steps does not guarantee elimination of sexual harassment, it establishes a clear-cut company policy in this important human resource area.[35]

Rights to smoke-free workplace. Increasingly, employers are establishing bans against smoking during breaks, lunchtime, and even when at home as well as during work. They cite the following reasons for this action:

- Each smoking employee costs employers an estimated $1,000 per year through higher absenteeism, reduced productivity due to "smoking rituals," and higher health, fire and life insurance usage.
- Smoking controls will produce productivity losses—$867 per smoker by one estimate—by forcing employees to leave their work to take smoking breaks.
- Employers who resist smoking controls face increasing risks of legal action, including handicap discrimination claims from "smoke sensitive" employees who charge that employers are avoiding their legal obligation to provide a safe environment.

Some companies, however, have been hesitant to establish smoking bans because:

- Smoking controls themselves may produce legal action, including handicap claims by "addicted" smokers and possible racial discrimination charges based on the fact that black men are more likely to be smokers than white men.
- Smoking controls will be relaxed or repealed as their negative impact becomes evident.

> Adding to the confusion is the controversy over recently released official reports linking passive smoking—the breathing of cigarette smoke from others—to cancer and other life-threatening diseases....[36]

In an attempt to resolve existing conflicts, many employers have implemented one or more of the following policies: allowing smoking only during lunch or on breaks, staggering the break times of smokers and nonsmokers, segregating smokers and nonsmokers, installing more effective ventilation systems, designating certain areas for smoking or nonsmoking, instituting and encouraging participation in smoking cessation programs, and arranging for job transfers. These steps, although more expensive and administratively problematic than a total ban on smoking, involve less risk in terms of potential legal problems.[37]

Layoffs and plant closing notification. With the passage of the Worker Adjustment and Retraining Act, employers are obligated to notify employees in advance of a plant or office closing. However, layoffs that are temporary in nature or downsizings that are permanent but do not require complete shutdowns do not require advance notification. Regardless of the cause, the loss of a job can be traumatic for employees. To assuage the difficulty of this transition, organizations are pursuing several different strategies.[38]

Rather than terminating those with less seniority or poorly performing employees, some companies have initiated job-sharing programs. Job sharing involves reducing the employee's work week and pay. This helps the company cut labor costs and may actually lead to higher overall productivity because each employee is working more concentrated hours. One major disadvantage is that expenses per employee may increase because benefits are usually a function of the number of employees, not the number of hours worked or amount of pay. While few studies have investigated the payoffs of job sharing, Motorola found that job sharing, rather than layoffs, saved an average of $1,868 per employee or almost $1 million overall in one plant.[39]

While mandatory retirement at a specific age cannot be required for most employees, organizations are exploring early retirement for selected employees as a possible option to layoffs. Key to a successful early retirement program is to understand the needs of targeted employees and provide incentives that meet those needs. Incentives may include pension payments before and after age 62 when Social Security payments start, and company-paid health and life insurance. Alternatively, a company may maintain its current retirement program but lower the qualifying age. This increases the pool of potential retirees.

In setting up an early retirement program, an organization needs to determine:

- Who will be eligible?
- What incentives will be offered?
- How will early retirement benefits be calculated?
- What effect, if any, will incentives have on regular retirement benefits?
- What is the election period for participation?
- What source of funds will finance the early retirement obligations?

When early retirements fail to sufficiently reduce staffs, organizations may have no choice but to move to layoffs. However, humane employers are providing outplacement assistance to ease the strain of involuntary termination. Help ranges from providing severance pay and extending health care benefits to preparation of resumés, and providing job search information, secretarial and administrative support, and even letters of recommendation. The Bureau of National Affairs found that eighty percent of all firms continue health care benefits after plant closings. However, only half continue the benefits for more than five months—even when a new job has not been found.

Organizations can also ease the transition by providing severance pay based on seniority. For example, employees can be given one week's salary for one to four years of service; two weeks' salary for five to eight years of service; three weeks' for more than eight years of service. Severance pay becomes particularly critical for upper-level positions. One study found that for every $10,000 in salary, job search takes an additional month.

FOCUS ISSUES IN EMPLOYEE RIGHTS

A focus issue in employee rights is the use of computer technology and HRIS. The trend in computer technology is likely to provoke a great deal of interest and legal activity on the part of employees and employers due in part to the ethical issues raised by sophisticated computer usage.

Computer Technology, Ethics, and HRIS in Employee Rights

With computers and an HRIS, human resource departments can quickly generate confidential personnel information in a variety of formats. Thus, many copies of confidential information may exist at any one time, increasing the likelihood that some may be misplaced or even stolen. As a result, file security is of concern. Today's HRIS systems include access protectors that limit who can read or write to a file, and they can be designed to allow a single person or a group of individuals access or no access. While these systems reduce the threat of file invasion, most designers of "secure" systems build in back door entries. If discovered by an unauthorized user, the unauthorized user may gain access to the program.

At the same time, computer technology is also being used to ensure that employee policies are implemented fairly. Expert systems such as those developed by HumanTek, a San Francisco software company, guide managers with employee problems to solutions. By asking a series of questions, the computer steers the manager to organizational policies and precedents that relate to the specific performance problem. Some of the more sophisticated programs even give managers advice. According to Walter Ratcliff, HumanTek consultant, expert systems will be the best friend of tomorrow's manager. Rather than flipping through a human resource manual, a supervisor will turn on his or her computer for advice.

Computer technology is also being used to monitor the performance of employees, as described in chapter 7. The Office of Technology Assessment in Washington, D.C., estimates that up to ten million workers are regularly monitored at their computers:

> At hundreds of companies, the performance of data-entry clerks is judged by the speed of their computer-measured keystrokes. Directory-assistance operators at telephone companies are allotted 25 seconds or less to root out a number, however vague the request, and computers record their times.
>
> In supermarkets, computers measure the speed with which the checkout clerks sweep purchases over the optical scanners.
>
> In an office building in downtown St. Louis, customer-service representatives at Union Pacific Railroad offices who book shipments for companies that send their goods by rail work at the kind of pace that telephone operators and airline reservation agents do.
>
> "A customer calls in and says, 'I need two freezer cars to ship frozen french fries from American Falls, Idaho, to a warehouse in Kentucky,'" said Tracey Young, an official with the transportation and communication workers union. He said that computers track the origin, duration, and frequency of calls and that supervisors, secretly and at random, listen in.[40]

Here employees complain of their rights to privacy being violated, and the company states that it needs the information to be competitive. Meanwhile, the customer may claim the right to good service; and if computer monitoring is what it takes, then so be it.

At this time, regulations on the use of computer monitoring are basically in the development stage. Needless to say, it is an important employee rights issue that is likely to gain increased attention from its increased use in the 1990s.[41]

A related issue is the employer's access to employee work done on the computer. This is the issue called electronic privacy. The issue and its ethical dimensions are described in the PHRM in the News: "Do Employees Have a Right to Electronic Privacy?"

INTERNATIONAL COMPARISONS

Particularly for U.S. multinational corporations (MNCs), the issue of employee termination needs to be handled with an awareness of international differences.

Termination Liabilities

MNCs need to consider the strategic consequences of a decision to terminate overseas operations. Most countries have some traditional or legally required practices that come into play in the event of a plant closing or a substantial reduction of the work force.[42] In general, these practices create more extensive and costlier employer obligations than do layoffs in the U.S. and Canada. One of the most costly obligations is the payment of cash indemnities that are in addition to the individual termination payments that may be required by law, collective bargaining agreements, or individual contracts. These indemnities can range from as high as two years' pay in Mexico to a flat amount, adjusted for increases in the cost of living, in Belgium. In some countries, these costs are spelled out in collective agreements that may stipulate termination payments greater than those required by law. In other countries, the employer may have to negotiate the amounts with employees, unions, and often the government.

In many countries, a company that wishes to close down or curtail operations also must develop a "social plan" or its equivalent, typically in concert with unions and other interested parties. The "plan" may cover continuation of pay, benefit plan coverage, retraining allowances, relocation expenses, and supplementation of statutory unemployment compensation. Frequently, a company planning a partial or total plant closing must present its case to a government agency. Authorities in The Netherlands, for example, may deny permission for a substantial work force reduction in unless management is able to demonstrate that the cutback is absolutely necessary for economic reasons and that the company has an approved social plan.

Mexico. The Mexican Federal Labor Law governs all labor matters. The state labor boards oversee the enforcement of the law. These boards have representatives from the government, labor, and management. After hiring, the employer has 28 days to evaluate the employee's work ethics. After that period, the worker is granted job security and termination becomes difficult. This is especially true in terms of financial liability. For example, an employer who decides to fire a worker who has been with the company for six months could

IN THE NEWS

PHRM

Do Employees Have a Right to Electronic Privacy?

When Alana Shoars arrived for work at Epson America Inc. one morning in January 1990, she discovered her supervisor reading and printing out electronic mail messages between other employees. As electronic mail administrator, Ms. Shoars was appalled. When she had trained employees to use the computerized system, Ms. Shoars told them their mail was private. Now a company manager was violating that trust.

When she questioned the practice, Ms. Shoars said, she was told to mind her own business. A day later, she said she was fired for insubordination. She has since filed a $1 million wrongful termination suit.

A spokesman for Epson America, which is based in Torrance, Calif., refused to discuss Ms. Shoars account of the monitoring episode and insisted that her dismissal had nothing to do with her questioning of the electronic mail practice. He denied that Epson America, the United States marketing arm of a Japanese company, had a policy of monitoring electronic mail.

The Shoars case has brought attention not only to issues of technology and employee privacy, but also to broader questions of ethics among computer professionals. By taking a public stand, Ms. Shoars has become a visible exception in a profession that tends to ignore or avoid ethical issues, according to academics and consultants who monitor the field.

Although Ms. Shoars has found a new job as electronic mail administrator at Warner Brothers in Burbank, Calif., she still bristles about Epson: "You don't read other people's mail, just as you don't listen to their phone conversations. Right is right, and wrong is wrong."

Federal Express, American Airlines, Pacific Bell and United Parcel Service all have electronic-mail systems that automatically inform employees that the company reserves the right to monitor messages.

But many companies have yet to formulate clear policies or inform employees of those policies. "It's highly irresponsible for an employer not to have a policy," said Mitchell Kapor, the founder and former chairman of the Lotus Development Corporation, who left the company five years ago.

Some believe, however, that even if there is notice, the monitoring of electronic mail or searching through personal files is flat-out wrong. One who takes that position is Eugene Spafford, a computer science professor at Purdue University. He said: "Even if a company does post notice, is that something it should do? The legal question may be answered, but is it ethical? The company may say it is, but the employees say it isn't, and there's a conflict."

The Federal Electronic Communications Privacy Act of 1986 protects the privacy of electronic messages sent through public networks like Compuserve and MCI Mail to which individuals and companies subscribe. But the law does not apply to internal electronic mail within corporations. Formulating such a law for corporate settings would be virtually impossible, most experts believe.

Some information systems executives say that a code of ethics aimed at computing is unnecessary, that corporate codes of ethics encompass the work they do. But even if that were true, relying on corporate codes to cover technology might not be enough because not every company has one. A recent survey by Robert Half International Inc. found that only 44 percent of the largest companies in the United States had a written code of ethics. And even those with such policies rarely address technology issues.

Other computer professionals insist that ethics are simply not an issue. "In 28 years in this business, I could count on one hand the number of times I or somebody else had to point out ethical issues in information systems," said John Coman, manager of networks and information services at ARCO in Los Angeles.

But, in any case, "by and large, information systems professionals are taking a subservient role in the dialogue about the use of information," said H. Jeffrey Smith, assistant professor at Georgetown University's School of Business Administration. "Considering that many companies are using technology to gain a strategic advantage, that is particularly troubling."

Although many professional associations in the field have codes of ethics for their members, Mr. Parker insists that no new rules of conduct are needed because the golden rule still applies. "When people log onto a computer or network, they don't automatically turn off their ethical values," he said.

SOURCE: G. Rifkin, "Do Employees Have a Right to Electronic Privacy," *The New York Times* (8 Dec. 1991), F8.

be charged for an additional six weeks, plus vacation pay and bonuses. Therefore, it is important to screen employees before hiring.

An employee is considered tenured after one year of employment. This worker may be dismissed only for causes specifically set out in the Mexican Federal Labor Law. These causes include falsifying employment documents and committing dishonest or violent acts during working hours.

SUMMARY

Although many employers claim that essentially all their rights have been taken away, they still retain the right to terminate workers for poor performance, excessive absenteeism, unsafe conduct, and generally poor organizational citizenship. However, employers must maintain accurate records of these events for their employees and inform the employees of where they stand. To be safe, employers should also have a grievance process for employees to ensure that due process is respected. These practices are particularly useful in discharge situations that involve members of groups protected by the Civil Rights Act of 1991, Americans with Disabilities Act, and the Age Discrimination in Employment Act.

Today, keeping objective and orderly human resource files is more important than ever. They are critical evidence that employers have treated their employees fairly and with respect and have not violated any laws. Without these, organizations may get caught on the short end of a lawsuit. Although several federal laws influence record keeping, they are primarily directed at public employers. Nevertheless, many private employers are moving on their own initiative to give their employees the right to access their personnel files and to prohibit the file information from being given to others without employee consent. In addition, employers are casting out of their personnel files any non-job-related information and ending hiring practices that solicit that type of information.

Many employers now give their employees advance notification consistent with the Worker Adjustment and Retraining Notification Act. In addition to giving such notification, employers are implementing outplacement assistance programs. These offer employees retraining for new jobs, counseling and aid in finding new jobs or in getting transfers, severance pay, and even retention bonuses for those who stay until closing time. Closing a facility with notification and with outplacement assistance seems to produce positive results for the organization and to minimize the negative effects for employees.

Finally, in the area of employee rights to cooperative acceptance, employers must prevent sexual harassment. This can be done with top-management support, grievance procedures, verification procedures, training for all employees, and performance appraisal and compensation policies that reward those who practice antiharassment behavior and punish those who do not. Where appropriate, developing policies to prevent harassment in cooperation with the union is also useful. Union cooperation should be sought on many other issues, as well. The benefits of doing so can be substantial, as we will discuss in the last chapter.

WHERE WE ARE TODAY

1. While there are restrictions on the employer's ability to terminate employees, employers still retain significant rights to terminate employees for poor performance, excessive absenteeism, unsafe conduct, and any illegal behavior. Of course, it is important that employers maintain accurate records on employees to support these decisions.
2. Due process is a grievance procedure that gives an individual notice that his or her job is at risk. Due process enables the employee to appeal the case and to get his or her side heard by others regarding employment decisions such as layoffs and terminations. It also ensures the employee will get feedback regarding a reason for a decision.
3. Many employers are moving in the direction of giving employees access to their personnel files so the employees can see and, if necessary, correct employment information that the firm has in it records.
4. Regulations such as the Worker Adjustment and Retraining Notification Act encourage employers to plan their business and human resource activities rather than act in haste and perhaps terminate or lay off individuals who really might be necessary for the longer run survival of the firm.
5. As more women move into the work force, sexual harassment becomes a more pervasive employment concern. Firms are acting more aggressively to establish policies and procedures for dealing with workplace sexual harassment and to provide training programs to enable all employees to act in ways consistent with those policies.
6. Individuals who are victims of sexual harassment are urged to deal with it as quickly and directly as possible. Organizations are encouraged to act with confidentiality and with careful fact-finding.
7. Where appropriate, it is useful to develop policies and training programs to deal with sexual harassment in cooperation with the union. Of course, union involvement is also useful in developing other policies and procedures, such as those relevant to due process.
8. Some employers are moving to establish workplace policies and procedures regarding employee rights that are the same for all employee groups—managers as well as nonmanagers. Knowing that all employees are treated equally seems to be important to many employees today.
9. While employers have the right to terminate employees at will for many reasons, some employers find it more effective for the business to establish policies of employment security. In this way the employee becomes more focused on doing what's best for the business, and the employer becomes more focused on doing what's best for the employee.
10. The area of employee rights covers many employment activities. Some of them are legally defined and some are defined as being "good, humane, and ethical" things to do. It would appear that the more organizations act to do things because they are fair, humane and ethical, the less need there is apt to be for legal regulation.

DISCUSSION QUESTIONS

1. Identify and discuss four federal laws that have an impact on employee rights to privacy and access of employee records.
2. What is the bottom line in protection offered to employees concerning plant closing/relocation?
3. What is the employment-at-will doctrine? Why do you suppose courts in the late 1880s were more willing to uphold the doctrine than courts are today?
4. How would you distinguish a just from an unjust dismissal? Is this distinction easier to make for lower-level jobs than for upper-level or managerial jobs? Explain.
5. The industrial, occupational, and demographic composition of the labor force has shifted over the past twenty years. How might these specific shifts coincide with the heightened interest in employee rights in the 1990s?
6. Due process has been interpreted as the duty to inform an employee of a charge, solicit employee input, and provide the employee with feedback in regard to the employment decision. How can a grievance procedure ensure this type of due process for an employee accused of sexual harassment? How can the grievance procedure protect the victim of the alleged harassment.
7. Develop counterarguments for the following arguments in support of the termination-at-will doctrine:
   a. If the employee can quit for any reason, the employer can fire for any reason.
   b. Because of business cycles, employers must have flexibility to expand and contract their work force.
   c. Discharged employees are always free to find other employment.
   d. Employers have incentives not to unjustly discharge employees; therefore, their power to terminate should not be restricted.
8. What do you suppose are the most common reasons for termination decisions? How can HR departments prevent these causes of termination?
9. What potential employee rights violations could occur with an automated HRIS? How could you protect against these violations?
10. What kinds of behaviors might constitute sexual harassment? How does an organization prevent those types of behaviors from occurring?

APPLIED PROJECTS

1. Assess employers' responses to the AIDS (Acquired Immune Deficiency Syndrome) epidemic. The issue has become extremely controversial because some employers have fired workers who reveal they have the disease while others have embarked on AIDS screening procedures during employee selection. Key issues include: What are the rights of AIDS victims? What are the rights of non-AIDS-infected co-workers?
2. Find and interview an individual who has experienced sexual harassment on the job. Report to the class on the content of the interview including such things as: (1) Where did it take place; (2) who was involved; (3) how long did it last; (4) what did the person(s) do; (5) how did the person feel; and (6) what was the resolution or what is the person trying to do now to resolve the situation?

3. Consult BNA's *Fair Employment Practices* manual, *Labor Relations Reporter*, or *Labor Arbitration Reports* to find recent cases that involve a charge of unjust dismissal. Address the following issues: What type of job was involved? What are the characteristics of the discharged employee (age, sex, prior history with company)? Did the company have a grievance procedure? On what basis did the employee contest the discharge? What did the judge or arbitrator rule? Why? State whether you agree with the outcome of the cases, and why.

CASE STUDY

What's Wrong with What's Right?

Stuart Campbell, now 35, moved slowly down the front steps of the courthouse and squinted as the last rays of sunlight pierced through downtown Cleveland. It was a long day in the life of Stuart Campbell, who once again relived, before an Ohio State Court, a tortuous two years of his past. Stuart had spent the entire day in court recalling the details of his past employment with Nako Electronics, a major marketer of audio tapes in the United States. Nako Electronics had and still has a considerable stake in Stuart Campbell. Today, both sides made concluding arguments before the court in a trial initiated by Nako Electronics to overturn a private arbitrator's ruling that Nako had wrongfully terminated Stuart Campbell. The arbitrator's decision and the award of $500,000 plus interest of $82,0083.50 was a bitter pill for Nako to swallow for having terminated their Midwest sales representative.

Stuart hesitated for a moment at the foot of the courthouse steps and came back to the present; he had agreed to meet his attorney, Jim Baldwin, at the "Steak and Brew" for a couple of drinks and to unwind from the courtroom tension. His spirits began to pick up as he maneuvered through the city traffic, but he couldn't help thinking how within a year's time his good job had gone so bad on him.

Five years ago, Stuart Campbell was riding high as the Midwest representative for Nako covering Ohio, West Virginia, and Pennsylvania. Stuart, a hard driver, contracted with Nako Electronics and then boosted the sluggish sales of Nako audio tapes from less than $300,000 to a $2 million business in about 14 months. In fact, business was going so well for Stuart that he began driving a Mercedes-Benz 450 SEL. But that's when Mike Hammond, vice-president of marketing at Nako Electronics, took notice of Campbell. On one of his visits to Campbell's territory, Hammond commented to Stuart that he really liked his car. Mike remarked that he was making a trip to California soon. "I distinctly remember Mike saying he would like to have a Buick," Stuart testified. "He didn't want anything as fancy as I had, because a new Buick would be adequate and, after all, he wanted me to bear the expense!"

Mike Hammond unfortunately couldn't be in court that day to defend himself; Hammond died unexpectedly last year of a heart attack. During the trial, though, Nako Electronics had to defend a number of allegations made against Mike Hammond. It seems that some of Stuart Campbell's co-workers suffered a similar fate. Not only had Stuart refused to go along with Hammond's car scheme, but he also refused to invest in a phonograph cartridge business begun by Hammond, which Stuart believed was a phony. Hammond, in fact, had approached all the sales representatives of Nako Electronics to invest in the cartridge company at $1,250 a share, a company for which Hammond and two other associates paid $1 a share for 80 percent of the stock. Stuart's attorney, Jim Baldwin, made sure that two of Stuart's former fellow sales representatives testified at the court proceedings that they were mysteriously fired after refusing Mike Hammond's demands to invest in his side company.

In the year following Stuart's successful boost of sales of Nako audio tapes and Hammond's thwarted attempts at commercial shakedown, Nako increased Campbell's sales quota by more than 75 percent. As Campbell further testified, Nako sabotaged a substantial proportion of his sales by refusing to give his large customers promotional assistance. In the fall of that year, Nako fired Stuart without explanation, and the income from his sales dropped to zero. Nako argued in court that they didn't need a reason to fire Campbell and, besides, Campbell wasn't meeting his new, increased sales quota. Moreover, the company argued, Mr. Hammond could not very well defend himself against the charges of Campbell and others.

Stuart rehashed these details many times with his attorney both during the private arbitrator hearing and during numerous rehearsals for the trial. As he arrived at "Steak and Brew," he hoped he could put these memories behind him. After a few drinks, Jim summarized the day's proceedings and expressed cautious optimism for the final outcome. "But you know, Stuart," mused Jim, "If you would have kicked in the 10 or 15K that Hammond demanded, you would have outlived that old son-of-____, you'd have a business worth over $4 million in sales today, and we wouldn't be having this drink!"

SOURCE: Stuart A. Youngblood, Texas Christian University

Case Questions

1. Why did the arbitrator award Stuart so much money?
2. Was the arbitrator's decision a just and fair one?
3. Did Nako have to give Stuart a reason for firing him?
4. If his firing was due to his failure to invest in Hammond's side company, could this be defended in court?

NOTES

1. T. Lewin, "A Case Study of Sexual Harassment and the Law," *The New York Times* (11 Oct. 1991): A17.
2. "Sexual Harassment in the Workplace," *Personnel Journal* (Jan. 1992): 24; C. Marmer Solomon, "Sexual Harassment After the Thomas Hearings," *Personnel Journal* (Dec. 1991): 32–37; D. E. Terpstra and D. D. Baker, "Outcomes of Federal Court Decisions on Sexual Harassment," *Academy of Management Journal* 35, no.1 (1992): 181–90.
3. A. M. Zack, *A Handbook for Grievance Arbitration* (New York: Free Press, 1992).
4. S. Overman, "A Delicate Balance Protects Everyone's Rights," *HR Magazine* (Nov. 1990): 36–39.
5. A. D. Marcus and S. J. Adler, "Mobil Aide Wins Wrongful Firing Case," *The Wall Street Journal* (23 Nov. 1990): B2.
6. J. E. Jackson and W. T. Schantz, "A New Frontier in Wrongful Discharge," *Personnel Journal* (Jan. 1991): 101–104.
7. W. M. Bulkeley, "Nuns vs. the Bishop: Teachers' Dismissal Winds Up in Court," *The Wall Street Journal* (13 Sept. 1982): 1; E. L. Harrison, "Legal Restrictions on the Employer's Authority to Discipline," *Personnel Journal* (Feb. 1982): 136–46; W. L. Wall, "Firms Seek Aid on Avoiding Employee Suits," *The Wall Street Journal* (28 July 1982): 23; T. H. Williams, "Employment-at-Will," *Personnel Journal* (June 1985): 73–77; S. A. Youngblood and L Bierman, "Due Process and Employment-at-Will: A Legal and Behavioral Analysis," in *Research in Personnel and Human Resource Management,* vol. 3, K. Rowland and G. Ferris, eds. (Greenwich, Conn.: JAI Press, 1985): 185–230. See also A. T. Oliver, Jr., "The Disappearing Right to Terminate Employees at Will," *Personnel Journal* (Dec. 1982): 910–17; according to Oliver, two court decisions in California (*Cleary v. American Airlines, Inc.*, 1980; *Pugh v. See's Candies,* 1981) appear to have all but ended termination at will in that state. See also A. B. Krueger, "The Evolution of Unjust Dismissal Legislation in the United States," *Industrial and Labor Relations Review* (July 1991): 644–60.
8. B. B. Durling, "Retaliation: A Misunderstood Form of Employment Discrimination," *Personnel Journal* (July 1981): 555–58.
9. "Armor for Whistle-Blowers," *Business Week* (6 July 1981): 97–98; W. F. Westin, "Michigan's Law to Protect Whistle Blowers," *The Wall Street Journal* (13 April 1981): 1.
10. For further description of related cases and issues, see "Another View of Employment at Will," *Bulletin to Management* (12 Sept. 1985): 88; "Employment-at-Will Evolves," *Bulletin to Management* (5 April 1984); B. Keller, "Of Hearth and Home and the Right to Work," *The New York Times* (11 Nov. 1984): E8; "Mandatory Retirement," *FEP Guidelines* no. 225(H) (1984); B. S. Murphy, W. E. Barlow, and D. D. Hatch, "Constructive Discharge under Title VII," *Personnel Journal* (Feb. 1985): 17; *Yancey v. State Personnel Board,* 1985.
11. "Firing," *FEP Guidelines* no. 241(8) (1985): 3. See also "Discrimination Denied," *Bulletin to Management* (13 June 1985): 3.
12. However, if a union–management contract exists, an arbitrator may not uphold firing if based on false application information. J. N. Drazin, "Firing Over False Applications," *Personnel Journal* (June 1981): 433. See also D. L. Beacon and A. Gomez III, "How to Prevent Wrongful Termination Lawsuits," *Personnel* (Feb. 1988): 70–72: D. A. Bradshaw and B. C. Stikker, "Wrongful Termination: Keeping the Right to Fire At-Will," *Personnel Journal* (Sept. 1986): 45–47; B. S. Murphy, W. E. Barlow, and D. Hatch, "Constructive Discharge," *Personnel Journal* (Oct. 1986): 30–31; "RIFS, Exit Incentives, and the ADEA," *FEP Guidelines* no. 273 (4); "Wrongful Discharge," *FEP Guidelines* no. 275(6).
13. M. R. Buckley and W. Weitzel, "Employing at Will," *Personnel Administrator* (Aug. 1988): 78–82; M. Manley, "The Competitors Within," *INC.* (Sept. 1988): 137–138.
14. Other rights on the job that could be included here include the right to protection from retaliation. See B. B. Durling, "Retaliation: A Misunderstood Form of Employ-

ment Discrimination," *Fair Employment Guidelines* no. 188 (March 1981): 1–8.

15. For suggested courses of action, see I. M. Shepard and R. L. Duston, *Workplace Privacy* (Washington, D.C.: The Bureau of National Affairs, 1987); G. Henshaw and K. C. Youmans, "Employee Privacy in the Workplace and an Employer's Right to Conduct Workplace Searches and Surveillance," *Society for Human Resource Management* (Alexandria, Va.: Spring 1990); K. R. Murphy, G. C. Thornton III, and K. Prue, "Influence of Job Characteristics on the Acceptability of Employee Drug Testing," *Journal of Applied Psychology* 76, no. 3 (1991): 447–53; B. S. Klass and G. G. Dell'Omo, "The Determinants of Disciplinary Decisions: The Case of Employee Drug Use," *Personnel Psychology* 44 (1991): 813–35; J. Shedler and J. Block, "Adolescent Drug Use and Psychological Health," *American Psychologist* (May 1990): 612–30; D. L. Stone and D. A. Kotch, Individuals' Attitudes Toward Organizational Drug Testing Policies and Practices," *Journal of Applied Psychology* 74, no. 3 (1989): 518-21; J. D. Bible and D. A. McWhirter, *Privacy in the Workplace: A Guide for Human Resource Managers* (Westport, Conn.: Quorum Books, 1990); *Employee Access to Records* (Englewood Cliffs, N.J.: Prentice-Hall, 1984); see also R. J. Nobile, "Employee Searches in the Workplace: Developing a Realistic Search Policy, *Personnel Administrator* (May 1985): 89–98; and J. C. O'Meara, "The Emerging Law of Employees' Right to Privacy," *Personnel Administrator* (June 1985): 159–65; D. Bennett-Alexander, "Sexual Harassment in the Office," *Personnel Administrator* (June 1988): 174–88; S. R. Mendelsohn and K. K. Morrison, "Testing Applicants for Alcohol and Drug Abuse," *Personnel* (Aug. 1988): 57–60; J. Pereira, "Women Allege Sexist Atmosphere in Offices Constitutes Harassment," *The Wall Street Journal* (10 Feb. 1988): Sec. 2, 23; and I. M. Shepard and R. L. Duston, *Workplace Privacy* (Washington, D.C.: Bureau of National Affairs, 1988).
16. J. F. Steiner, *Industry, Society and Change: A Casebook* (New York: McGraw-Hill, 1991); S. M. Nkomo, M. D. Fottler, and R. B. McAfee, *Applications in Personnel/Human Resource Management: Cases, Exercises and Skill Builders* (Boston: PWS-Kent, 1988); "Privacy," *Business Week* (28 March 1988): 61–68; J. M. Jenks "Protecting Privacy Rights," *Personnel Journal* (Sept. 1987): 123, 126, 131; S. R. Mendelsohn and K. K. Morrison, "The Right to Privacy at the Workplace, Part 1: Employee Searches," *Personnel* (July 1988): 20–27; S. R. Mendelsohn and A. E. Libbin, "The Right to Privacy at the Workplace, Part 3: Employee Alcohol- and Drug-Testing Programs," *Personnel* (Sept. 1988): 65–72; A. E. Libbin and J. C. Stevens, "The Right to Privacy at the Workplace, Part 4: Employee Personal Information," *Personnel* (Oct. 1988): 56–60; A. E. Libbin, S. R. Mendelsohn, and D. P. Duffy, "The Right to Privacy at the Workplace, Part 5: Employee Medical and Honesty Testing," *Personnel* (Nov. 1988): 38–48; M. I. Finney, "The Right to be Tested," *Personnel Administrator* (March 1988): 74–75.
17. "Drug Testing to Start for Transit Workers," *The New York Times* (9 Nov. 1991): 28.
18. B. A. Gutek, A. G. Cohen, and A. M. Konrad, "Predicting Social-Sexual Behavior at Work: A Contact Hypothesis," *Academy of Management Journal* 33 no. 3 (1990): 560–77; K. M. York, "Defining Sexual Harassment in Workplaces: A Policy-Capturing Approach," *Academy of Management Journal* 32 no. 4 (1989): 830–850; C. K. Behrens, "Co-Worker Sexual Harassment: The Employer's Liability," *Personnel Journal* (May 1984): 12–14; "New Ruling on Sexual Harassment," *Management Review* (June 1985): 5: "Participation Bars Protest," *Fair Employment Practices* (12 Jan. 1984): 1; R. E. Quinn and P. L. Lees, "Attraction and Harassment: Dynamics of Sexual Politics in the Workplace," *Organizational Dynamics* (Autumn 1984): 35–46; "Retaliation," *FEP Guidelines* no. 237(4) (1985); S. Seymour, "The Case of the Mismanaged Ms.," *Harvard Business Review* (Nov./Dec. 1987): 77–87; "Sexual Harassment," *FEP Guidelines* no. 238(5) (1985); "Sexual Harassment: Prevention is the Key," *Fair Employment Practices* (18 Feb. 1988): 22; "What Makes an Environment 'Hostile'? Advice from Three Courts," *Fair Employment Practices* (23 June 1988): 78.
19. B. Southard Murphy, W. E. Barlow, and D. D. Hatch, "Court Broadens Scope of Sexual Harassment Law," *Personnel Journal* (April 1990): 24–31; J. K. Frierson, "Reduce the Costs of Sexual Harassment," *Personnel Journal* (Nov. 1989): 79–85; "Actions and Reactions in the Field of Fair Employment: Wrongful Discharge," *FEP Guidelines* no. 175 (1988); B. Southard Murphy, W. E. Barlow, and D. D. Hatch, "Wrongful Discharge: Recent Court Decisions," *Personnel Journal* (Nov. 1989): 18–19; "Ending Sexual Harassment: Business is Getting the Message," *Business Week* (18 March 1991): 98–100, 140; K. Flynn, "Preventive Medicine for Sexual Harassment," *HR Focus* (March 1991): 17; A. I. Fagin and M. D. Rumeld, "Employer Liability for Sexual Harassment," *Legal Report* of the Society for Human Resource Management (Fall 1991); "Sexual Harassment: Out of the Shadows," *Business Week* (28 Oct. 1991): 30–35; A. Deutschman, "Dealing with Sexual Harassment," *Fortune* (4 Nov. 1991): 145,148.
20. "Sexual Harassment after *Meritor Savings v. Vinson,"* FEP Guidelines 1, no. 264 (1987). Used by permission.
21. D. Bennett-Alexander, "Sexual Harassment in the Office," *Personnel Administrator* (June 1988): 174–87; P. J. Champagne and R. B. McAfee, "Auditing Sexual Harassment," *Personnel Journal* (June 1989): 124–140; G. Morgenson, "Watch That Leer, Stifle That Joke," *Forbes* (15 May 1989): 69–72: J. Pereira, "Women Allege Sexist Atmosphere in Offices Constitutes Harassment," *The Wall Street Journal* (10 Feb. 1988): 23; S. Seymour, "The Case of the Mismanaged Ms.," *Harvard Business Review* (Nov.-Dec. 1987): 77–87; T. Rendero, "Grievance Procedures for Nonunionized Employees," *Personnel* (Jan.-Feb. 1980): 4–10.
22. P. D. Staudohar, "New Plant Closing Law Aids Workers in Transition," *Personnel Journal* (Jan. 1989): 87–90; "WARN: One Year Later," *Bulletin to Management* (12 April 1990): 120.
23. "Current Wave of Layoffs Puts Employers at Risk," *FEP Guidelines* no. 304 (1990).
24. A. Bernstein and Z. Schiller, "'Tell It to the Arbitrator,'" *Business Week* (4 Nov. 1991): 109. Also see S. A. Youngblood, L. K. Trevino, and M. Favia, "Reactions to Unjust Dismissal and Third Party Dispute Resolution: A Justice Framework," *Employee Responsibilities & Rights Journal* (in press); J. M. Brett, S. B. Goldberg, and W. L. Ury, "Designing Systems for Resolving Disputes in Organizations," *American Psychologist* (Feb. 1990): 162–70; D. E. Conlon and P. M. Fasolo, "Influ-

ence of Speed of Third-Party Intervention and Outcome on Negotiator and Constituent Fairness Judgments," *Academy of Management Journal* 33, no. 4 (1990): 833–46; B. S. Klaas, "Managerial Decision Making about Employee Grievances: The Impact of the Grievant's Work History," *Personnel Psychology* 42 (1989): 53–68; R. H. Moorman, "Relationship Between Organizational Justice and Organizational Citizenship Behaviors: Do Fairness Perceptions Influence Employee Citizenship?" *Journal of Applied Psychology* 76, no. 6 (1991): 845–55; D. W. Organ and M. Konovsky, "Cognitive Versus Affirmative Determinants of Organizational Citizenship Behavior," *Journal of Applied Psychology* 74, no. 1 (1989): 157–64; J. Greenberg, "Looking Fair vs. Being Fair: Managing Impressions of Organizational Justice," *Research in Organizational Behavior* vol. 12 (1990): 111–57; A. Bernstein and Z. Schiller, "'Tell It to the Arbitrator,'" *Business Week* (4 Nov. 1991): 109; M. E. Gordon and R. L. Bowlby, "Reactance and Intentionality Attributions as Determinants of the Intent to File a Grievance," *Personnel Psychology* 42 (1989): 309–29; D W. Ewing, *Justice on the Job: Resolving Grievances in the Nonunion Workplace* (Boston, Mass.: Harvard Business School Press, 1989); B. S. Klaas, "Determinants of Grievance Activity and the Grievance System's Impact on Employee Behavior: An Integrative Perspective," *Academy of Management Review* 14, no. 3 (1989): 445–58; D. Lewin and R. B. Peterson, *The Modern Grievance Procedure in the United States* (Westport, Conn.: Quorum Books, 1988).

25. D. N. Adams, Jr., "When Laying Off Employees, the Word is 'Out-Training,'" *Personnel Journal* (Sept. 1980): 719–21.
26. L. D. Foxman and W. L. Polsky, "Ground Rules for Terminating Workers," *Personnel Journal* (July 1984): 32; A. Bequai, *Every Manager's Legal Guide to Firing* (Homewood, Ill.: Business One, 1991). Also see W. Freedman, *The Employment Contract: Rights and Duties of Employers and Employees* (Westport, Conn.: Quorum Books, 1989); C. A. B. Osigweh, ed., *Managing Employee Rights and Responsibilities* (Westport, Conn.: Quorum Books, 1989); D. T. Brodie, *Individual Employment Disputes: Definite and Indefinite Term Contracts* (Westport, Conn.: Quorum Books, 1991).
27. D. F. Linowes, "Update on Privacy Protection Safeguards: Is Business Giving Employees Privacy?" *Business and Society Review* (Winter 1979–80): 47–49; A. F. Westin, "What Should Be Done about Employee Privacy?" *Personnel Administrator* (March 1980): 27–30; *Employee Access to Records* (Englewood Cliffs, N.J.: Prentice-Hall/ASPA, 1984).
28. "Respecting Employee Privacy," *Business Week* (11 Jan. 1982): 130–31.
29. H. X. Levine, "Privacy of Employee Records," *Personnel* (May-June 1981): 4–11; J. A. Gildea, "Safety and Privacy: Are They Compatible?" *Personnel Administrator* (Feb. 1982): 78–83.
30. "Privacy Policy Approaches and Pointers," *Bulletin to Management* (20 Feb. 1986): 57. Reprinted by permission from *Bulletin to Management,* copyright 1986 by the Bureau of National Affairs, Inc., Washington, D.C. 20037.
31. J. A. Segal, "A Need Not To Know," *HR Magazine* (Oct. 1991): 85–86, 88, 90; "None of an Employer's Business," *The New York Times* (7 July 1991): E10; "Is Nothing Private?" *Business Week* (4 Sept. 1989): 74–77, 80–82; S. R. Mendelsohn and K. K. Morrison, "The Right to Privacy at the Workplace, Part 1: Employee Searches," *Personnel* (July 1988): 20–27; S. R. Mendelsohn and A. E. Libbin, "The Right to Privacy at the Workplace, Part 3: Employee Alcohol- and Drug-Testing Programs," *Personnel* (Sept. 1988): 65–70; A. E. Libbin and J. C. Stevens, "The Right to Privacy at the Workplace, Part 4: Employee Personal Information," *Personnel* (Oct. 1988): 56–60; A. E. Libbin, S. R. Mendelsohn, and D. P. Duffy, "The Right to Privacy at the Workplace, Part 5: Employee Medical and Honesty Testing," *Personnel* (Nov. 1988): 38–47; J. S. Franklin, "Undercover in Corporate America," *The New York Times* (29 Jan. 1989): 1, 6; "Privacy in the Workplace," *FEP Guidelines* no. 279 (1988).
32. J. L. Koch, "Wells Fargo's and IBM's HIV Policies Help Protect Employee's Rights," *Personnel Journal* (April 1990): 40–50.
33. "Soul-Searching at Ciba-Geigy," *HR Reporter* (May 1987): 5–6.
34. G. E. Biles, "A Program Guide for Preventing Sexual Harassment in the Workplace," *Personnel Administrator* (June 1981): 49–56; O. A. Ornati, "How to Deal with EEOC's Guidelines to Sexual Harassment," in *EEO Compliance Manual* (Englewood Cliffs, N.J.: Prentice-Hall, 1980): 377–80; R. H. Faley, "Sexual Harassment: A Critical Review of Legal Cases with General Principles and Practice Measures," *Personnel Psychology* 35 (1982): 583–600.
35. T. Segal and Z. Schiller, "Six Experts Suggest Ways to Negotiate the Minefield," *Business Week* (28 Oct. 1991): 33.
36. "Smoker's Rights vs. Health Concerns: Smoking Emerges as New Controversy," *Resource* (Feb. 1987): 3. Reprinted from the February 1987 issue of *Resource,* copyright 1987, The American Society for Personnel Administration, 606 North Washington Street, Alexandria, VA, 22314. See also "ASPA-BNA Survey No. 50, "Smoking in the Workplace," *Bulletin to Management* (12 June 1986); A. I. LaForge, "Snuffing Out Smoking in the Office," *The New York Times* (Feb. 22, 1987): F12–13.
37. "Do Employees Have the Right to Smoke?" *Personnel Journal* (April 1988): 72–81; L. Reibstein, "Forced to Consider Smoking Issue, Firms Produce Disparate Policies," *The Wall Street Journal* (10 Feb. 1987): 41; E. Schmitt, "The Last Refuge of Smokers May Be No Place but Home," *The New York Times* (27 Sept. 1987): E7; "Worksite Smoking: Need for Dual Accommodation," *Bulletin to Management* (25 June 1987): 201; S. F. Gambescia and W. T. Godshall, "Smokers Do Not Deserve a Special Status," *HR Focus* (Nov. 1991): 11; F. J. McManimon, "Employees Who Smoke Have a Right to Privacy, " *HR Focus* (Nov. 1991): 10.
38. J. B. Treece, "Doing It Right, Till the Last Whistle," *Business Week* (6 April 1992): 58–59; D. L. Worrell, W. N. Davidson III, and V. M. Sharma, "Layoff Announcements and Stockholder Wealth," *Academy of Management Journal* 34, no. 3 (1991): 662–78; P. D. Johnston, "Personnel Planning for a Plant Shutdown," *Personnel Journal* (Aug. 1981): 53–57.
39. T. Rendero, "Outplacement Practices," *Personnel* (July-Aug. 1980): 4–11; B. H. Millen, "Providing Assistance to Displaced Workers," *Monthly Labor Review* (May 1979): 17–22; "Outplacement Assistance," *Personnel Journal* (April 1981): 250; M. Elleinis, "Tips for Employers Shopping Around for a New Plant Site," *AMA Forum* (July 1982): 34; "Plant Closings: Problems and Panaceas," *Management Review* (July 1982): 55–57; "ITT's Early Retirement Package Fails to Achieve

Needed Staff Reductions," *Bureau of National Affairs White Collar Report* 60 (19 Nov. 1986); M. Harris, "A Lifetime at IBM Gets a Little Shorter for Some," *Business Week* (29 Sept. 1986): 40; J. Main, "Look Who Needs Outplacement," *Fortune* (9 Oct. 1989): 85–92; "Waivers and Releases," *FEP Guidelines* no. 285 (1989).

40. P. T. Kilborn, "Workers Using Computers Find a Supervisor Inside," *The New York Times* (23 Dec. 1990): 1, 18L. Also see "Surveillance and Searches: Reducing the Risks," *Bulletin to Management* (7 Nov. 1991): 345; *Federal Government Information Technology: Electronic Surveillance and Civil Liberties* (Washington, D.C.: Office of Technology Assessment, OTA-CIT-293, October 1985; *The Electronic Supervisor: New Technology, New Tensions, OTA-CIT-333* (Washington, D.C.: U.S. Government Printing Office, Sept. 1987).

41. *Ibid.* See note 40.

42. See R. L. Foltz and R. G. Foltz, "International Human Resource Management," in *Readings in Personnel and Human Resource Management,* 3d ed., R. S. Schuler, S. A. Youngblood, and V. L. Huber, eds. (St. Paul, Minn.: West Publishing Co., 1988); and P. Dowling and R. S. Schuler, *International Dimensions of Human Resource Management* (Boston: PWS-Kent, 1990).

CHAPTER 16

Occupational Safety and Health

Decisions about the welfare of future children must be left to the parents who conceive, bear, support, and raise them rather than to the employers who hire those parents.

—U.S. Supreme Court[1]

"Factory Fire Leaves Pall Over 'All-American City'" was the headline describing the feeling of Hamlet, North Carolina, one day after the fire at the Imperial Food Products plant that left 25 workers dead and 49 injured, September 3, 1991. According to John Brooks, the state's labor secretary, the tragedy was due to shortage of staff that left the federal Occupational Safety and Health Administration unable to hold his state to more stringent safety standards. Federal officials did deny this, but the percentage of the federal government's contribution to the state safety inspection program had been declining. This decline, accompanied by budget cutbacks at the state level, left Mr. Brooks with fewer inspectors than he had had ten years earlier. His assessment at that time was that federal guidelines would have required the state to have had 64 safety inspectors and 50 health inspectors, but that his state had only 6 health inspectors and between 6 and 12 safety inspectors—and this in a state that has the highest percentage of manufacturing employees and is the fourth-largest poultry producer in the country.[2]

This unfortunate tragedy in North Carolina brought to the attention of the entire country just how prevalent and how significant issues of safety and health still are in the American workplace. It has helped refocus the energies and concerns of employers and employees to being concerned and doing something about improving the workplace—factory or office, urban or rural.

OCCUPATIONAL SAFETY AND HEALTH

Occupational safety and health refers to the physiological/physical and sociopsychological conditions of an organization's work force resulting from the work environment. If an organization takes effective safety and health measures, fewer of its employees suffer harmful forms of these conditions.

Hazardous physiological/physical conditions caused by occupational diseases and accidents include actual loss of life or limb, cardiovascular diseases, various forms of cancer (such as of the lungs), emphysema, and arthritis. Other harmful conditions are leukemia, white lung disease, brown lung disease, black lung disease, sterility, central nervous system damage, and chronic bronchitis.

Hazardous sociopsychological conditions caused by occupational stress and low quality of work life include dissatisfaction, apathy, withdrawal, tunnel vision, forgetfulness, inner confusion about roles and duties, mistrust of others, vacillation in decision making, inattentiveness, irritability, procrastination, and a tendency to become distraught over trifles.

This chapter discusses the purposes and importance of occupational safety and health in organizations. Workplace hazards are divided into the accidents, conditions, and diseases that produce physiological/physical conditions and the stressors and low quality of work life that result in sociopsychological conditions. We briefly describe the role of the federal government in establishing and enforcing safety standards. We also discuss strategies to improve employee safety and health, including such measures as improved record keeping, job redesign, ergonomics, and educational programs.[3] You may also want to review the legal discussion of safety and health in chapter 3.

PURPOSES AND IMPORTANCE OF IMPROVING OCCUPATIONAL SAFETY AND HEALTH

The purposes of improving safety and health are to reduce the symptoms and costs of poor safety and health and make the work environment safer and healthier for all employees. Some employees, however, do appear to be more affected than others. For example,

> We've reached an accommodation with blue-collar death. Forget that a United States worker is five times more likely to die than a Swede ... Forget that a U.S. worker is three times more likely to die than a Japanese.
>
> The sad reality is that blue-collar blood pours too easily. [Occupational Safety and Health Administration] fines amount to mere traffic tickets for those who run our companies. The small fines are simply buried in the cost of production. Blood can be cash accounted, given a number, and factored with other costs....[4]

Of course, blue-collar workers are not the only ones to suffer from workplace hazards. Office workers—nonmanagers and managers alike—may also suffer. Their suffering, however, may be less physical and more psychological, namely due to stress.

> "Stress is the most pervasive and potent toxin in the workplace," says Leon J. Warshaw, executive director of the New York Business Group on Health, a coalition of businesses concerned about health care. In California, mental stress claims are the most rapidly increasing type of workers' compensation cases, having risen 700% in the past decade. And a poll earlier this year found that 25% of the employees surveyed at New Jersey businesses suffered from stress-induced ailments.[5]

Benefits of a Safe and Healthy Work Environment

If organizations can reduce the rates and severity of their occupational accidents, diseases, and stress and improve the quality of work life for their employees, they will be more effective. Fewer incidences of accidents and diseases, a reduced level of occupational stress, and improved quality of work life result in (1) more productivity due to fewer lost workdays for absenteeism; (2) increased efficiency for workers who are more involved with their jobs; (3) reduced medical and insurance costs; (4) lower workers' compensation rates and direct payments because of far fewer claims being filed; (5) greater flexibility and adaptability in the work force as a result of increased participation and sense of ownership in changes from quality-of-work-life projects; and (6) better selection ratios because of the increased attractiveness of the organization as a place to work.[6] As a consequence of all these factors, companies can increase their profits substantially. These benefits and the other components of safety and health described in this chapter are shown in exhibit 16.1.

Costs of an Unsafe and Unhealthy Work Environment

The nature of work engaged in by U.S. employees is continually changing. For example, the manufacturing sector of the economy is shrinking and the service sector is growing. These changes are associated with changing work conditions and new forms of occupational hazards. Unfortunately, the workplace does not appear to be getting safer, however, as one might expect.

> The number of workplace injuries and illnesses in the private sector rose to nearly 6.8 million in 1990—177,000 more than in 1989, the Bureau of Labor Statistics (BLS) says. The rate of occupational injuries and illnesses in 1990 increased to 8.8 per 100 full-time workers, compared with 8.6 in both 1988 and 1989.
>
> Of approximately 6.4 million job-related injuries reported in the private sector last year, about half were serious enough for the injured worker to lose work time, experience restricted work activity, or both. The manufacturing sector accounted for more than 33 percent of the total number of injuries in 1990 (2.2 million), although it employed only 20 percent of the private sector workforce. In contrast, the service industry accounted for about 30 percent of employment and 20 percent of the injuries (1.2 million).
>
> Nearly 332,000 new occupational illness cases were reported in 1990, up from 284,000 in 1989, BLS finds. Almost 60 percent of the 1990 cases were associated with repetitive motions, such as vibrations, repeated pressure, and carpal tunnel syndrome. The agency adds that the number of work-related illnesses is understated, due to difficulty in tracking long-term health effects.

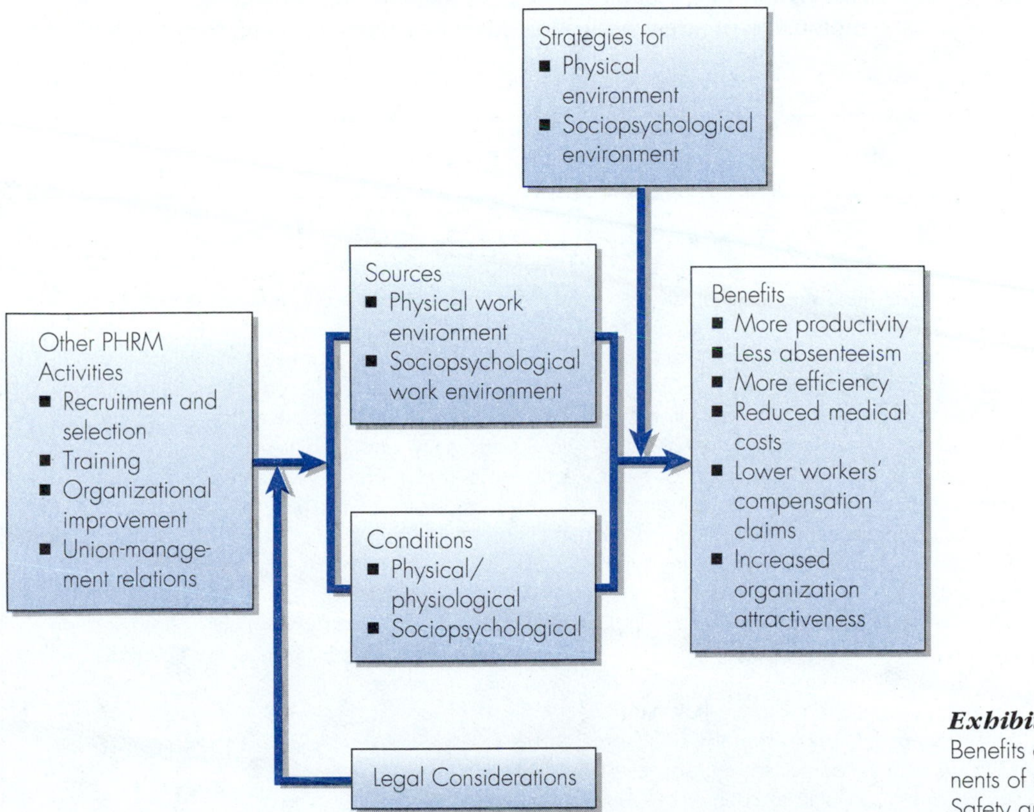

Exhibit 16.1
Benefits and Components of Occupational Safety and Health

BLS also expresses skepticism about the number of work-related deaths. While fatalities reported to the agency dropped from 3,600 in 1989 to 2,900 in 1990, BLS notes that other estimates range from 3,500 to 12,000 fatalities a year.[7]

Thus, while it is difficult to make accurate comparisons with work-related deaths from year-to-year, the human costs of work-related illnesses show a clear increase. Also showing a clear increase are the financial costs of work-related deaths and injuries.

> Work-related deaths and injuries cost the nation $48.5 billion in 1989, up more than a billion dollars from the previous year. The 1989 figure includes $8.3 billion in lost wages, $8.1 billion in medical costs, $6.1 billion in insurance administrative costs, $3.5 billion in fire loss, and an additional $22.5 billion in indirect costs, such as the time lost to investigate accidents.[8]

These are costs associated with all types of accidents and injuries; the numbers fail to identify the nature of our most prevalent work-related injuries—those associated with the back. The PHRM in the News: "My Aching Back" describes the nature of back injuries.

In addition to accidents, injuries and diseases generate enormous costs associated with organizational stress and a low quality of work life. For example, alcoholism, often the result of using drinking to cope with job pressures, costs organizations and society over $65 billion annually. Of this, $20 billion is attributed to lost productivity and the remainder to the direct costs of insurance, hospitalization, and other medical costs.[9] Perhaps more difficult to quantify, but just as symptomatic of stress and poor quality of work life, are workers' feelings of

PHRM IN THE NEWS

My Aching Back

Back injuries are the most prevalent of all workplace injuries. They also are the most enigmatic, since their exact causes and effects often remain a medical mystery.

Chronic back disorders can develop gradually as a result of repetitive activity over time. Because of the slow onset and insidious character of these internal injuries, the condition often may be ignored until the symptoms become chronic. Acute back injuries usually are the immediate result of improper lifting or too heavy loading. Injuries can arise in muscle, tendon, bursa, and ligaments, either singly or in combination.

An estimated 10 million employees in the United States every year encounter back pain that impairs their job performances. Approximately 1 million employees file workers' compensation claims for back injuries. Billions of dollars are spent each year to treat back pain—$5 billion in workers' compensation payments alone.

Back injuries are expensive for all concerned. Besides the cost of increased workers' compensation insurance claims and premiums, employers lose the productivity of skilled workers while they find and train replacements. Also suffering are the injured employees, who become separated from their sense of well being and livelihoods. Back injury prevention measures and injury management programs for injured workers can reduce the human and financial impact of back pain. These include injury prevention, post-incidence cost control, and back injury remedies.

SOURCE: "Back Injuries," *Bulletin to Management*, (9 Jan. 1992), 396.

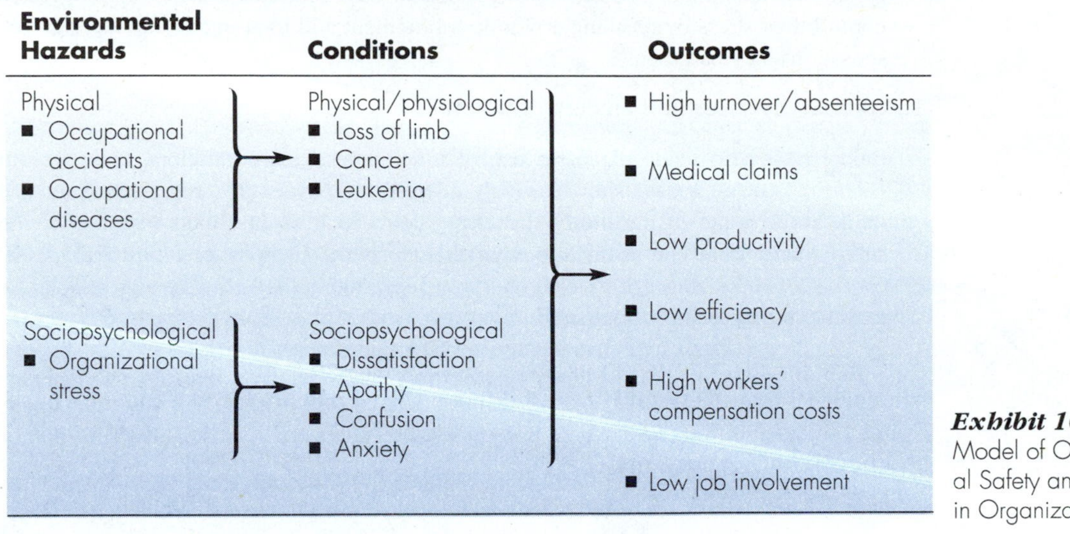

Exhibit 16.2
Model of Occupational Safety and Health in Organizations

lack of meaning and involvement in their work and loss of importance as individuals.

Sources of Conditions

The sources of these general conditions in organizations may be labeled as the *physical work environment* and the *sociopsychological work environment.* Keep in mind that all workers do not respond to their environment in the same way. What is harmful for one employee may not be for another. Together, the harmful physical/physiological and sociopsychological conditions, their sources, and their outcomes constitute a model of occupational health and safety in organizations. This model is shown in exhibit 16.2 and described in the next section.

HAZARDS TO OCCUPATIONAL SAFETY AND HEALTH

As exhibit 16.2 shows, both the physical and the sociopsychological aspects of the work environment are important components of occupational safety and health. Each aspect has its own hazards for health and safety. For the physical, it is diseases and accidents; for the sociopsychological, it is quality of work life and stress. Traditionally, the physical environment has received greater attention. Increasingly, however, both the Occupational Safety and Health Administration (OSHA) and companies are admitting to the impact of sociopsychological hazards on health and safety and are doing something about it. For example, in combatting stress and its symptoms,

> ... at Hoffman-LaRoche Inc., the Nutley, N. J.–based subsidiary of the Swiss pharmaceutical concern, employees receive after-hours instruction in a variety of stress man-

> agement methods. They include meditation, breathing exercises and a technique called "dot stopping." A form of biofeedback, the technique teaches employees to control their stress by recalling a wonderful moment and focusing on the feelings and sensations they had then.[10]

To combat the stress and anxiety of potential job loss,

> Citicorp has also made extensive use of lunch-time stress counselors. One, Dr. Art Ulene of NBC's "Today" show, recently advised employees "to change the way you think about some of the things that drive you crazy" as one method for lowering stress. Standing in line at the supermarket, which Dr. Ulene once found intolerable, can be less annoying if it's viewed as an opportunity to meet interesting people, he told the audience amid laughter.[11]

Consequently, efforts to improve occupational safety and health must include strategies to remove hazards from both aspects of the work environment. Developing effective strategies begins with understanding the factors affecting safety and health in organizations.

Factors Affecting Occupational Accidents

Certain organizations, and even certain departments within the same organization, have higher occupational accident rates than others. Several factors explain this difference.

Organizational qualities. Accident rates vary substantially by industry. For example, firms in the construction and manufacturing industries have higher incidence rates than firms in services, finance, insurance, and real estate; and when employees believe this, they tend to think things just can't be changed. According to Donald Brush, vice-president and general manager, the Barden Corporation, Danbury, Connecticut,

> Over the years, Barden employees assumed that, because we are a metal working shop, people were just going to get hurt. Several years ago we created a Safety and Health Committee that meets monthly to consider our safety and health performance and to effect improvements. More recently, we created a Safety Development Committee whose members included a line superintendent as chairman, the safety engineer, the plant chemist, the occupational health nurse, and the training coordinator—a nice mix of line, staff and human resource representation. This committee reports to the Safety and Health Committee. Its objective is to develop programs that strengthen safety awareness and performance. While it is too early to prepare a report card, early indications are that results will be favorably impressive. At about the same time, it became clear that the safety engineer was not producing the same results we wanted. After weighing the facts, we created something new and promising. We eliminated the safety engineering position as such and transferred its accountabilities to the Medical Department. The occupational health nurse had previously shown considerable knowledge about safety matters, and her aggressive investigation of accidents and near-misses prompted us to create a new position encompassing both the safety and the medical functions. The occupational health nurse has thus been promoted to a new position entitled Manager of Employee Health and Safety. We believe that this position is unique for a small company, and we are optimistic about results.[12]

Small and large organizations (those with fewer than a hundred employees or more than a thousand) have lower incidence rates than medium-sized organizations. This may be because supervisors in small organizations are better able to detect safety hazards and prevent accidents than those in medium-sized ones. On the other hand, larger organizations have more resources to hire staff specialists who can devote all their efforts to safety and accidents.

Safety programs. Organizations differ in the extent to which they develop techniques, programs, and activities to promote safety and prevent accidents. Johnson & Johnson, the New Brunswick, New Jersey, maker of Band-Aids and other health-care products, decided to become known as the safest firm:

> So, over a period of years, the company worked out tough workplace-safety rules. When any workplace accident causes a death, or an amputation, fracture, head injury or burn resulting in at least one lost workday, the head of the company unit involved must file a written report to the company's top management within 24 hours. The head person then has to travel to company headquarters in New Brunswick and personally explain, to a top-level management committee, what went wrong.
>
> The result of such efforts: Johnson & Johnson has slashed its annual lost workday incidence, or LWDI, rate per 100 workers to 0.14 last year from 1.81 in 1981. These are the rates of job-related injuries or illnesses that force employees to lose at least a full workday.
>
> By contrast, the lost workday case rate for 14 large competing pharmaceutical concerns in 1988 was 1.20. Overall rates for the pharmaceutical industry and the surgical appliances and supplies industry, in which Johnson & Johnson competes, were much higher than that, government reports show.[13]

The effectiveness of these techniques and programs may vary by the type of industry and size of organization. For example, in large chemical firms, greater expenditures for off-the-job safety, medical facilities and staff, safety training, and additional supervision are associated with decreased work-injury costs. On the other hand, work-injury costs have actually increased with additional expenditures for correction of unsafe physical conditions for safety staff, for employee orientation, and for safety records when these expenditures are applied ineffectively. As a result, some organizations in the same industry may have higher injury costs per employee than others; and, of course, organizations that have no safety programs generally have higher injury costs than similar companies that have implemented such programs.

The unsafe employee? Although organizational factors play an important role in occupational safety, some experts point to the employee as the cause of accidents. Accidents depend on the behavior of the person, the degree of hazard in the work environment, and pure chance. The degree to which the person contributes to the accident is often regarded as an indicator of proneness to accidents. Accident proneness cannot be considered a stable set of personal traits that always contribute to accidents. Nevertheless, certain psychological and physical characteristics seem to make some people more susceptible to accidents.

For example, employees who are emotionally "low" have more accidents than those who are emotionally "high," while employees who have had fewer accidents have been found to be more optimistic, trusting, and concerned for others than those who have had more accidents. Employees under greater stress are likely to have more accidents than those with poorer vision. Older workers are likely to be hurt less than younger workers. People who are quicker at recognizing visual patterns than at making muscular manipulations are less likely to have accidents than those who are just the opposite. Many psychological conditions probably related to accident proneness—for instance, hostility and emotional immaturity—may be temporary states. Thus, they are difficult to detect until after at least one accident.

Because none of these characteristics is related to accidents in all work environments, and because none is always present in employees, selecting and screening job applicants on the basis of accident proneness is difficult. Even if it were possible, aspects of the organization—such as its size, technology, management attitudes, safety programs, and quality of supervision—would still be important causes of accidents for those job applicants who are actually hired.

Factors Affecting Occupational Diseases

The potential sources of work-related diseases are as distressingly varied as the way they affect the human organism. Through the work of several federal agencies, the following workplace hazards have been detected: arsenic, asbestos, benzene, bichloromethylether, coal dust, coke-oven emissions, cotton dust, lead, radiation, and vinyl chloride. Workers likely to be exposed to these types of hazards include chemical and oil refinery workers, miners, textile workers, steelworkers, lead-smelters, medical technicians, painters, shoemakers, and plastics-industry workers.

The long-term consequences of these hazards have been linked to thyroid, liver, lung, brain, and kidney cancer; white, brown, and black lung disease; leukemia; bronchitis; emphysema; lymphoma; aplastic anemia; central nervous system damage; and reproductive disorders (for example, sterility, genetic damage, abortions, and birth defects). Continued research will no doubt uncover additional hazards that firms will want to diagnose and remedy for the future well-being of their work forces.

Categories of occupational diseases. A major category of occupational disease involves illnesses of the respiratory system. Chronic bronchitis and emphysema are among the fastest growing diseases in the country, doubling every five years since World War II, and they account for the second highest number of disabilities under Social Security.[14] Cancer, however, tends to receive the most attention, since it is a leading cause of death in the U.S. (second after heart disease). Many of the known causes of cancer are physical and chemical agents in the environment; and because these agents are theoretically more controllable than human behavior, OSHA places emphasis on eliminating them from the workplace.

OSHA's emphasis on health is not aimed solely at eliminating cancer and respiratory diseases, however. OSHA is concerned with all of the following categories of occupational diseases and illnesses on which employers are required to keep records: (1) occupation-related skin diseases and disorders; (2) dust diseases of the lungs; (3) respiratory conditions due to toxic agents; (4) poisoning (systemic effects of toxic materials); (5) disorders due to physical agents; (6) disorders associated with repeated trauma; and (7) all other occupational illnesses.[15]

Occupational groups at risk. Miners, construction and transportation workers, and blue-collar and lower-level supervisory personnel in manufacturing industries experience the bulk of both occupational disease and injury. The least safe occupations are mining, agriculture, and construction.

> Mining, agriculture, and construction...ranked as the most dangerous industries in 1989. While agriculture had the highest death rate in 1988—with 48 deaths per 100,000 workers—mining held that dubious distinction in 1989 with a death rate of 43. In 1989, deaths in the agricultural sector per 100,000 workers dipped to 40, and construction followed, with 32 per 100,000.[16]

In addition, large numbers of petrochemical and oil refinery workers, dye users, textile workers, plastics-industry workers, painters, and industrial chemical workers are also particularly susceptible to some of the most dangerous health hazards. Interestingly, skin diseases are the most common of all reported occupational diseases, with leather workers being the group most affected.

Of course, occupational diseases are not exclusive to the blue-collar workers and manufacturing industries. The "cushy office job" has evolved into a veritable nightmare of physical and psychological ills for white-collar workers in the increasingly growing service industries. Among the common ailments are varicose veins, bad backs (as described in the "PHRM in the News: My Aching Back"), deteriorating eyesight, migraine headaches, hypertension, coronary heart disorders, and respiratory and digestive problems. The causes of these in an office environment include the following:

- Too much noise
- Interior air pollutants such as cigarette smoke and chemical fumes—for example, from the copy machine
- Uncomfortable chairs
- Poor office design
- New office technology such as video display terminals[17]

In addition, dentists are routinely exposed to radiation, mercury, and anesthetics, and cosmetologists suffer from high rates of cancer and respiratory and cardiac diseases connected with their frequent use of chemicals.

Factors Affecting Low Quality of Work Life

For many workers a low quality of work life is associated with conditions in the organization that fail to satisfy important preferences and interests, such as a sense of responsibility, challenge, meaningfulness, self-control, recognition, achievement, fairness or justice, security, and certainty.[18] Common conditions in organizations causing these preferences and interests to remain unsatisfied include the following:

- Jobs with low significance, variety, identity, autonomy, and feedback and with qualitative underload
- Minimal involvement of employees in decision making and a great deal of one-way communication with employees

- Pay systems not based on performance or based on performance not objectively measured or under employee control
- Supervisors, job descriptions, and organizational policies that fail to convey to the employee what is expected and what is rewarded
- Human resource policies and practices that are discriminatory and of low validity
- Temporary employment conditions where employees are dismissed at will (employee rights do not exist)

Many conditions in organizations are associated with a low quality of work life. The same is true of organizational stress. Remember, however, that a condition causing stress or low quality of work life for one individual may not bother another because of differing preferences and interests and perceptions of uncertainty in the environment.

Factors Affecting Organizational Stress

A variety of factors can cause stress on the job. However, the most prevalent include organizational change, work pace, work overload, the physical environment, and job burnout. In addition several employee-specific factors cause stress.

Employee stressors. Referred to as the four S's, supervision, salary, job security, and safety often cause individual-specific stress.

The two major stressors that employees associate with the supervisor are petty work rules and relentless pressure for more production. Both deny workers fulfillment of their needs to control the work situation and to be recognized and accepted.

Salary is a stressor when it is perceived as being given unfairly. Many blue-collar workers believe that they are underpaid relative to their white-collar counterparts in the office. Teachers think they are underpaid relative to people with similar education who work in private industry.[19]

Employees experience stress when they are unsure whether they will have their jobs the next week, the next month, or even the next day. For many employees, lack of job security is even more stressful than jobs that are unsafe. With a lack of job security, employees are always in a state of uncertainty.[20]

Organizational change. Changes in organizational structure, job assignments, technology, and reporting relationships, as well as downsizings, mergers, and takeovers, are common in today's work world. Unfortunately, all these changes—even when they are for the organization's good—are stressful. The reason is that change often is accompanied by uncertainty and often occurs without advance warning. Even the rumors that precede change can cause stress as people speculate about whether and how the change will affect them. As a result, many employees suffer stress symptoms.[21]

Work pace. Work pacing, particularly who or what controls the pace of the work, is a potential stressor in organizations. **Machine pacing** removes control over the speed of the operation and the work output from the individual. Workers on machine-paced jobs reportedly feel exhausted at the end of the shift and are unable to relax soon after work because of increased adrenaline secretion on the job. In a study of twenty-three white- and blue-collar occupations, assembly workers reported the highest level of severe stress symptoms.

Jobs that entail unplanned interruptions also are stressful. For example, broadcast engineers must be able to make exacting repairs on telecommunication equipment at a moment's notice. If that is not bad enough, they make the repairs knowing that the station is losing viewers and money each second they are off the air. This type of work is far more stressful than work that involves planned cycles of peak activity with planned downtime in between.[22]

Physical environment. Although office automation (discussed in chapter 12) is a way to improve productivity, it has its stress-related drawbacks. One aspect of office automation with a specific stress-related drawback is the video display terminal (VDT). While findings are not complete, countries such as Sweden and Norway have taken more steps to deal with VDTs than has the U.S. Other aspects of the work environment associated with stress are crowding, lack of privacy, and lack of ability to change aspects of the environment (e.g. to move the desk or chairs or even to hang pictures in a work area in an effort to personalize it).[23]

Job burnout. A special type of organizational stress is called job burnout. This stress condition happens when people work in situations in which they have little control over the quality of their performance but feel personally responsible for their success or lack of it. People most susceptible to burnout include police officers, nurses, social workers, and teachers. When people begin to show burnout, they reveal three symptoms: (1) emotional exhaustion, (2) depersonalization, and (3) a sense of low personal accomplishment. Because this condition benefits neither the individual nor the organization, many programs have been designed to help people deal with burnout.[24]

STRATEGIES TO IMPROVE OCCUPATIONAL SAFETY AND HEALTH

Once the cause of stress is identified, strategies can be developed for eliminating or reducing it (see exhibit 16.3). to determine if the strategy was effective, organizations can compare the incidence, severity, and frequency of illness and accidents before and after the intervention. Methods to establish safety and health rates will be described first, and then strategies for improving accident and disease conditions will be presented.

Safety and Health Rates

OSHA requires organizations to maintain records of the incidence of injuries and illnesses. Some organizations also record the frequency and severity of each.

Incidence rate. The most explicit index of industrial safety is the incidence rate. It is calculated by the following formula:

Exhibit 16.3
Summary of Sources and Strategies for Occupational Safety and Health

	Physical Work Environment
Occupational accidents	Redesigning the work environment Setting goals and objectives Establishing safety committees Training Providing financial incentives
Occupational diseases	Measuring the work environment Setting goals and objectives
	Sociopsychological Work Environment
Organizational stress	Establishing organizational stress programs Establishing individual stress strategies

$$\text{Incidence rate} = \frac{\text{Number of injuries and illnesses x 200,000}}{\text{Number of employee hours worked}}$$

Suppose an organization had 10 recorded injuries and illnesses and 500 employees. To calculate the number of yearly hours worked, multiply the number of employees by 40 hours and by 50 work weeks: 500 x 40 x 50 = 1 million. Thus, in this case the incidence rate would be 2.

Severity rate. Strategies will vary depending on whether an organization is experiencing many minor safety problems or one or two major problems. The severity rate reflects the hours actually lost due to injury or illness. It recognizes that not all injuries and illnesses are equal. Four categories of injuries and illnesses have been established: deaths, permanent total disabilities, permanent partial disabilities, and temporary total disabilities. An organization with the same number of injuries and illnesses as another but with more deaths would have a higher severity rate. The severity rate is calculated by this formula:

$$\text{Severity rate} = \frac{\text{Total hours charged x 1 million}}{\text{Number of employee hours worked}}$$

Frequency rate. While similar to the incidence rate, the frequency rate reflects the number of injuries and illnesses per million hours worked rather than per year.[25] It is calculated thus:

$$\text{Frequency rate} = \frac{\text{Number of injuries and illnesses x 1 million}}{\text{Number of employee hours worked}}$$

Strategies to Control Accidents

Designing the work environment to make accidents difficult is perhaps the best way to prevent accidents and increase safety. Among the safety features that can be designed into the physical environment are guards on machines, handrails in stairways, safety goggles and helmets, warning lights, self-correcting mechanisms, and automatic shutoffs. The extent to which these features will actually reduce accidents depends on employee acceptance and use. For example, eye injuries will be reduced by the availability of safety goggles only if employees wear the goggles correctly. If employees are involved in the decision to make some physical change to improve safety, they are more likely to accept the decision than if they are not part of the decision-making process. This helps drive the success of DuPont in Canada. President and CEO Arthur Sawchuk describes his company's safety program in the PHRM in the News feature.

Ergonomics. Another way of improving safety is to make the job itself more comfortable and less fatiguing through ergonomics. Ergonomics considers changes in the job environment in conjunction with the physical and physiological capabilities and limitations of the employees.[26]

In an effort to reduce the number of back injuries, Ford Motor Company redesigns work stations and tasks that may be causing musculoskeletal problems for workers. For instance, lifting devices are being introduced on the assembly line to reduce back strain, and walking and working surfaces are being studied to see if floor mats can reduce body fatigue. Videotapes that feature Ford employees performing their jobs both before and after ergonomic redesign are used in training.[27]

In an effort to reduce cumulative trauma disorders, Perdue Farms, a large poultry producer in Salisbury, Maryland, established an extensive ergonomics plan for several of its plants.

> Perdue Farms Inc. will pay $39,690 in penalties and institute a comprehensive four-year program to reduce cumulative trauma disorders at its North Carolina poultry processing plants, under a settlement negotiated by the state's labor department, Perdue, and seven worker representatives.
>
> As part of the pact, which comes nearly a year-and-a-half after the state hit Perdue with precedent-setting citations for ergonomic hazards, the company agrees to issue a policy statement "demonstrating a personal concern for employee safety and health by placing a priority upon eliminating ergonomic hazards." Specifically, Perdue must investigate, study, and institute administrative controls intended to reduce exposure to ergonomic stress; implement a medical management program; and provide ergonomic awareness, training and education. The agreement requires that a symptom survey be completed by all plant employees annually, and that Perdue hire an ergonomics expert for the life of the pact.
>
> Additionally, the ergonomics program will include:
>
> - An employee complaint or suggestion procedure allowing workers to express their concerns without fear of reprisal.
> - A procedure for encouraging prompt and accurate reporting of signs and symptoms of cumulative trauma disorder.
> - Safety and health committees, with employee members randomly selected, which will recommend corrective action.
> - Ergonomic teams with the necessary skills to identify and analyze jobs for ergonomic stress and recommend solutions.[28]

PHRM IN THE NEWS

Safety is Our Mission

Du Pont Canada's Mission Statement begins: "Safety protection of the environment, concern and care for people and personal and corporate integrity are the company's highest values and we will not compromise them." It is not mere chance that safety is the first word in that statement.

At Du Pont employees understand that they bear the major responsibility for their own safety. This is even more important today, as Du Pont completes a decade of restructuring for future growth and globalization. The company has reduced its organizational levels—which means less supervision and a more participatory approach to management. With fewer supervisors and managers, there is a greater need for self-management and teamwork. Therefore, the onus is on the individual to assume more responsibility and work in a team to accomplish common objectives—including excellent safety performance.

Everyone is involved in protecting the safety and health of themselves and co-workers. This doesn't just happen. Every single employee must be encouraged to "buy in" to and accept that he or she is responsible for safety at all stages of developing, manufacturing, handling, distributing, using or disposing of the company's products. In the safety effort, managers establish priorities that best meet the needs of individual business operations and achieve corporate safety goals. And the line organization designs safety programs that are geared to each plant or office location. These include monthly safety promotions staged by employee groups, and at one plant, special scratch-and-win lottery tickets that are handed out to employees for using good safety practices and generally showing concern for their co-workers' well-being.

It is also critical that senior managers demonstrate their personal commitment to the safe, healthy workplace. The level of attention and priority that management gives to this issue has a direct influence on

Continued

Safety committee. Another strategy for accident prevention is the use of safety committees, as in the Barden Corporation described earlier. The human resource department can serve as a facilitator of the process, assisting in the collection of accident-related information.

The human resource department can also be instrumental by assisting the supervisors in their training efforts and by implementing safety motivation programs, such as contests and communications. Many organizations display signs indicating the number of days or hours worked without an accident or posters that read "Safety First." In safety contests, prizes or awards are given to individuals or departments with the best safety record. These programs seem to work best when employees are already safety conscious and when physical conditions of the work environment provide no extreme safety hazards.

Behavior modification. Reinforcing behaviors that reduce the likelihood of accidents can be highly successful. Reinforcers can range from nonmonetary reinforcers, such as feedback, to activity reinforcers, such as time off, to material reinforcers, such as company-purchased doughnuts during the coffee break, to financial rewards for attaining desired levels of safety.

The behavioral approach relies on measuring performance before and after the intervention, specifying and communicating the desired performance to employees, monitoring performance at unannounced intervals several times a week, and reinforcing desired behavior several times a week with performance feedback.

employees' safety motivation, knowledge and performance. For instance, managers are ready to take prompt action when safety or health might be threatened. Du Pont halted a polyethylene operation for several days when an employee found a faulty device that needed to be fixed; the company stopped using a dye in film processing when employees discovered it could be toxic to animals, and when some head office staff were concerned that the marble floors might be slippery, carpet was laid down in walkways and the company paid to have the heels of employees' shoes replaced with non-slip rubber.

Du Pont has found that a safety and health program can be successful only if a company: (1) demonstrates a sincere commitment by senior management; (2) involves all levels, from the president to the front-line employee, and (3) makes sure the effort is continuous and consistent throughout the organization.

Then, there are three necessary steps in setting up a program. (1) Establish firm objectives—just as for other important aspects of a business, like quality, cost, growth and return on investment. (2) Provide the resources and facilities that will help achieve the objectives—education and training tailored to real situations. (3) Demand results. At Du Pont, managers are held accountable for their groups' safety performance and this is an important factor in their personal performance appraisals. In other words, how their group performs in safety can directly affect their future careers and compensation. As well, regular impartial audits show if safety and health programs are effective and responding to changing needs.

One of the most important conclusions Du Pont reached about safety is that it is closely tied to business excellence and people excellence. People want to learn so they can continuously improve, and they want to personally influence the factors that affect performance, whether it is in productivity, quality—or safety.

SOURCE: From S. Dolan and R. Schuler, *Human Resource Management Canada* (Toronto: Nelson, 1993).

A behavior modification program was conducted to increase safe behavior in two food processing plants. Behavior was monitored for twenty-five weeks—before, during, and after a safety training program. Slides were used to illustrate safe and unsafe behavior. Employees also were given data on the percentage of safe behaviors in their departments. A goal of 90 percent safe behaviors was established. Supervisors were trained to give positive reinforcement when they observed safe behavior. Following the intervention, the incidence of safe behavior increased substantially—from an average of 70 percent to more than 95 percent in the wrapping department and from 78 percent to more than 95 percent in the make-up department. One year after the program, the incidence of lost-time injuries per million hours worked was fewer than 10, a substantial decline from the preceding year's rate of 53.8.[29]

Management by objectives programs. Behavior modification programs are often linked successfully to management-by-objectives programs that deal with occupational health. The seven basic steps of these programs are as follows:

1. Identify hazards and obtain information about the frequency of accidents.
2. Based on this information, evaluate the severity and risk of the hazards.
3. Formulate and implement programs to control, prevent, or reduce the possibility of accidents.

4. Set specific, difficult, but attainable goals regarding the reduction of accidents or safety problems.
5. Consistently monitor results.
6. Provide positive feedback for correct safety procedures.
7. Monitor and evaluate the program against the goals.[30]

Strategies to Reduce Occupational Diseases

More costly and harmful to organizations and employees, overall, than occupational accidents are occupational diseases. Because the causal relationship between the physical environment and occupational diseases is often far more subtle, developing strategies to reduce their incidence is generally more difficult.

Record keeping. At a minimum, OSHA requires that organizations measure the chemicals in the work environment and keep records on these measurements. Their records must also include precise information about ailments and exposures. Such information must be kept for as long a period as is associated with the incubation period of the specific disease—even as long as forty years. If the organization is sold, the new owner must assume responsibility for storing the old records and continuing to gather the required data. If the organization goes out of business, the administrative director of OSHA must be informed of the whereabouts of the records. Guidelines for recording are given in exhibit 16.4.

Communicating health and safety information. In addition to keeping records, the Access to Employee Exposure and Medical Records (AEEMR) regulation of 1980 requires organizations to show or give to employees, their designated representatives, and OSHA their on-the-job medical records of measurements of employee exposure to toxic substances. The employee's right to know has been further strengthened by the Hazard Communication Standard that went into effect in 1986, described in chapter 3. Among those points listed in chapter 3, the law requires that employees be trained prior to job assignment and retrained any time a new hazard is introduced into the work environment.

Monitoring exposure. While the obvious approach to controlling occupational illnesses is to rid the workplace of chemical agents or toxins, an alternative approach is to monitor and limit exposure to hazardous substances. For example, the nuclear industry recruits hundreds of "jumpers" who fix the aging innards of the nation's nuclear generating stations. The atmosphere is so radioactive that jumpers can only stay in about 10 minutes before they "burn out." Their exposure has to be closely monitored to ensure that it does not exceed more than 5,000 millirems (roughly 250 chest x-rays) annually.

Unfortunately, jumpers get rewarded for absorbing the maximum rather than a safe limit of radiation on any given job. Rather than twelve hours of pay for their ten minutes of work, jumpers get a bonus of several hundred dollars each time they "burn out" between jobs. Even with monitoring, it is estimated that 3 to 8 of 10,000 jumpers eventually will die as a result of the exposure.[31]

In addition to monitoring for radioactivity, some organizations now monitor genetic changes due to exposure to carcinogens (e.g., benzene, arsenic, ether,

Exhibit 16.4
OSHA Guidelines for Recording Cases

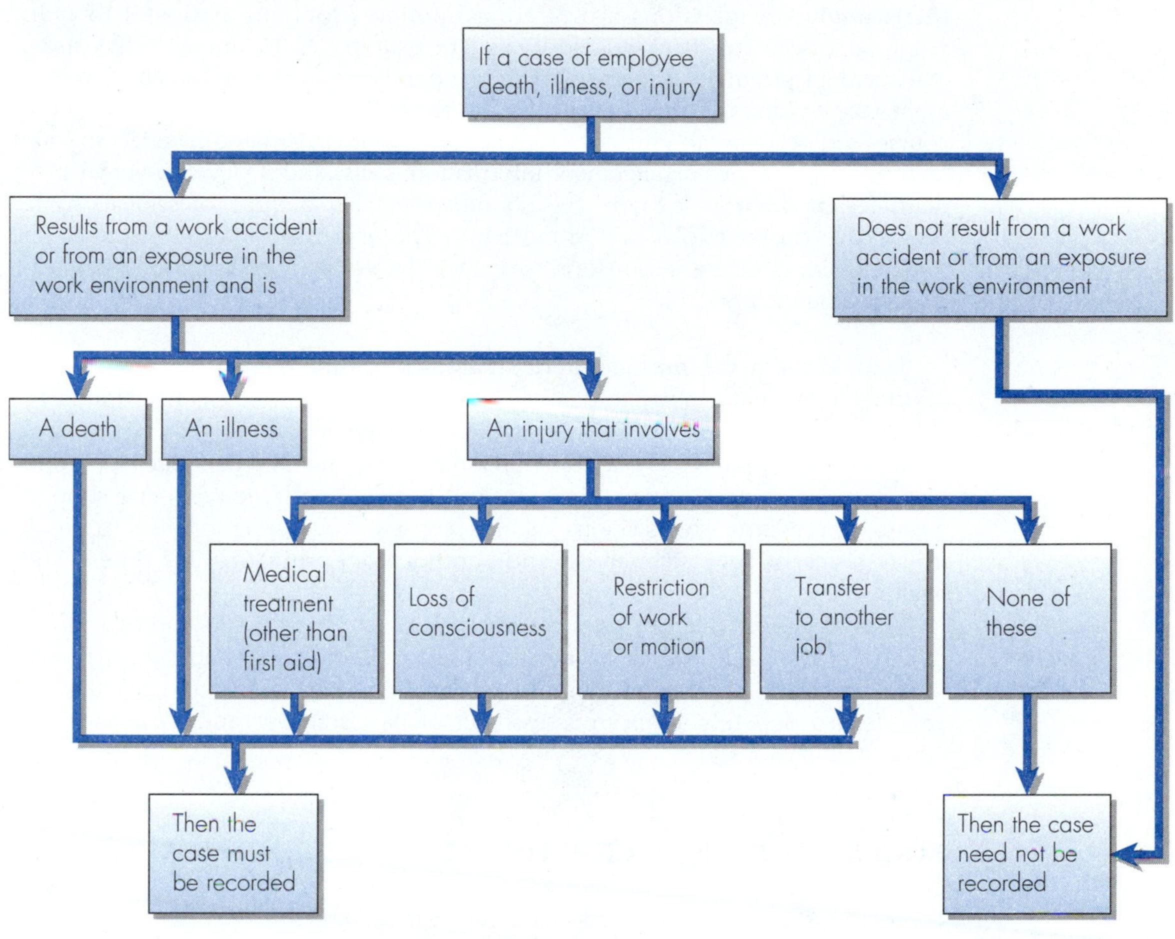

and vinyl chloride). Samples of blood are obtained from employees at fixed intervals in order to determine whether there has been damage to chromosomes. If damage has occurred, the employee is placed in a different job.

Genetic screening. Genetic screening is the most extreme, and consequently the most controversial, approach to controlling occupational disease. As noted in chapter 6, the genetic makeup of individuals makes them more or less predisposed to specific occupational diseases. By genetically screening out individuals who are susceptible to certain ailments, organizations lower their vulnerability to workers' compensation claims and problems. Opponents of genetic screening contend that genetic screening measures one's predisposition to disease, not the actual presence of disease; therefore, such testing violates an individual's rights.[32]

Strategies to Improve the Sociopsychological Work Environment

Increasingly organizations are offering training programs designed to help employees deal with work-related stress. For example, J. P. Morgan offers stress management programs as part of a larger supervisory and management development curriculum. Offered to supervisors, professional staff, and officers, these courses are designed to introduce supervisory and management material, specific technical supervisory/management information skills, and a developmental program designed to give experienced nonofficer managers and professionals some perspective on their roles within the bank. The emphasis here is on providing workers with concrete information to reduce the ambiguity associated with fast-paced changing work roles.[33]

Individual stress management strategies. Time management can be an effective individual strategy to deal with organizational stress. It is based in large part upon initial identification of an individual's personal goals. Other individual strategies that should be part of individual stress management include good diets, regular exercise, monitoring physical health, and building social support groups. Many large organizations such as Xerox encourage employees to enroll in programs of regular exercise and careful monitoring of their fitness and health.[34]

Thus, organizations can offer many activities or programs to improve physical and sociopsychological work conditions. Selecting the most appropriate activity depends upon a thorough diagnosis of existing safety and health hazards. It also depends upon an assessment of past activities and those used by other organizations.

FOCUS ISSUES IN OCCUPATIONAL SAFETY AND HEALTH

Three focus issues in occupational safety and health are occupational health policies, wellness programs, and ethics in shaping behavior.

Occupational Health Policies

As scientific knowledge accumulates and liabilities rise, more and more organizations are developing policy statements regarding occupational hazards. These policy statements grow out of concern that organizations should be proactive in dealing with occupational hazards. For example, Dow Chemical's policy states that "No employee, male or female, will knowingly be exposed to hazardous levels of materials known to cause cancer or genetic mutations in humans."[35]

One of the most recent clashes over health-care policies came from the debate over whether women of child-bearing age should be allowed to hold jobs in settings that could endanger fetuses. Johnson Controls, Milwaukee, Wisconsin, which makes lead automobile batteries for such customers as Sears and Goodyear, had restricted women's access to jobs in its Bennington, Vermont, plant. Johnson's management claimed that the factory's air contained traces of lead and lead oxide. While presumably not high enough to harm adults, the toxin levels are dangerous for children and fetuses. Thus, women were allowed to work in the plant, but only if they were unable to bear children (either because of surgery to prevent pregnancies or because they were too old to have children). According to the company, "the issue was protecting the health of unborn children."

Women's advocates and union leaders argued that the firm was guilty of sex discrimination. Specifically, they claimed that lead levels were too high for men as well, that the firm was making a decision *for* women rather than allowing women to decide whether to take the risk, that such rules invade women's privacy, and, finally, that the restrictions denied women access to high-paying jobs. A typical factory job in Bennington paid $6.35/hour versus $15.00/hour in the Johnson Controls plant.[36]

What made the situation more complex was that many workers were reluctant to leave jobs to avoid occupational exposure unless they were guaranteed that their income would not suffer. Some workers went so far as to have themselves sterilized to protect their jobs. When the Supreme Court heard this case, they ruled in favor of the workers, thus striking down the fetal protection policy of Johnson Controls (*United Auto Workers v. Johnson Controls,* 1991).

The policies of AT&T and Digital Equipment illustrate alternatives. Their policies provide for income protection for pregnant production workers who might be exposed to the toxic gases and liquids used to etch microscopic circuits onto silicon wafers. Other companies are obtaining signed, voluntary consent agreements from employees who choose to stay on hazardous jobs. While these statements can absolve employers from punitive damages in civil court, they do not alleviate liability under workers' compensation laws and civil disability suits.

Wellness Programs

Corporations increasingly are focusing on keeping employees healthy rather than helping them get well. They are investing in wellness programs at record rates.

> Their offerings range from the cheap and simple, like free raisins for morning snacks and scales in the bathrooms, to the expensive and technological, like corporate gymnasiums and computerized health-risk analyses. There are classes for quitting smoking, losing weight, eating better, exercising and managing stress. There are seat belt and drug-awareness campaigns, and tests for high blood pressure or diabetes.
>
> Part of the reason is spiraling costs of hospitalization, and of health insurance. "The bottom line for business is that it's been losing money on health care" said Benno Isaacs, a spokesman for the Health Insurance Association of America.
>
> Studies indicate that about half of worksites with more than 50 employees offer some form of wellness program. This year, IBM, one of the leaders in worksite health care, sponsored 1,800 wellness-oriented programs.[37]

Such programs appear to be paying off. A four-year study of 15,000 Control Data employees showed that employees who participate in only limited exercise spend 114 percent more on health insurance claims than co-workers who exercise more. Smokers and obese workers also had higher medical claims. Control Data, which has had its "Stay Well" program in place since the early 1980s, now markets its program to other firms such as Philip Morris and the National Basketball Association.[38]

Further issues are described in the Focus on Research: "Employee Health: Too High a Cost?"

FOCUS ON RESEARCH

Employee Health: Too High a Cost?

The rising costs of health insurance benefits and changing attitudes about the value of physical fitness have stimulated employers to consider programs for improving the health of their workforce. Health and wellness programs vary between those that simply screen out unhealthy job applicants to those that proactively seek to improve the health of all job incumbents. Examples include: using medical screening to select healthy applicants; prohibiting unhealthy behavior, such as smoking, in the workplace; monitoring to discourage unhealthy behavior, such as drug use, outside of work; offering health and safety education programs to employees; and providing physical fitness facilities.

Associated with the alternative approaches to employee health and wellness are differing philosophies about the responsibilities of employees and employers as well as differing costs and potential benefits. Employers who are willing to accept responsibility for improving employee health are most likely to consider the more costly approaches and will be particularly interested in selecting the most effective programs. But which programs are most effective? Does spending more on a program necessarily translate into the greatest health gains?

A recent three-year field experiment assessed the effectiveness of four alternative wellness programs. They expected to find that the keys to program effectiveness would be how extensive the reach of the program was and the amount of social support provided to employees for participating. Four manufacturing plants were randomly assigned to receive one of the following interventions: (1) health education only, which involved offering classes, distributing a newsletter, holding a health fair, occasional promotions, such as a Great American Low-Fat Pig-Out, and testing for such things as blood pressure and blood cholesterol; (2) health education *plus* follow-up, which included all the components of the "health education only" program and *also* included wellness counselors who contacted employees with identified health risks, counseled them regarding risk reduction strategies, and helped guide employees who wanted to make changes; (3) health education *plus* follow-up *plus* organizational strategies, which included the above components plus a few more proactive interventions intended to help employees change their daily behavior, such as setting up a one-mile walk-

Continued

Ethics in Shaping Behavior

Employers have known for a long time that a small percentage of their employees is responsible for the bulk of the health insurance claims. Originally they tried to encourage their employees to be healthy by offering to subsidize health club memberships and building exercise facilities and jogging trails, but the results were disappointing. Now it appears that many companies are implementing incentive-based health care programs.

While no ones denies the spiraling health care costs in the U.S., some question just how far companies should be allowed to go in "encouraging" their employees to shape up. How much should employers be allowed to know about what the employees do in their spare time? This is obviously the same question we asked in the previous chapter on employee rights. Is it possible that company policies and practices will become so financially attractive to employees that they will do things that they otherwise would not have done?

The potential for creating situations involving ethical or unethical behavior needs to be watched closely. It is too early to tell just how this situation will unfold. Doubtless, employers and employees are concerned about costs and health; perhaps creative solutions will save the day.[39] These might come from looking at events in other countries.

ing course and putting a buddy system in place for mutual support to encourage health-oriented behavioral changes; and (4) providing a full-scale fitness facility, which gave employees access to extensive aerobic and muscle-building equipment and was staffed by certified trainers, but included only limited educational and support activities.

Employees at the sites were screened on health indicators at the beginning of the study and again three years later. Program effectiveness was indicated by the degree of reduction in the four employee populations on several targeted risk factors, including blood pressure, body weight, smoking, and exercise. All programs resulted in substantial reductions in the risk factors measured, but interventions (2) and (3) led to roughly 10% more improvement than interventions (1) and (4). Costs associated with each type of program were analyzed also. Costs included pay for a health educator, medical staff and training costs for sites where screening and monitoring were conducted, company-paid costs for all health improvement programs, costs of all fitness equipment and attendants (but not the space used). For each site, operating costs were annualized and divided by the number of employees at each site. The average annual costs per employee were: (1) $17.68; (2) $30.96; (3) $38.57; and (4) $39.28.

The bottom line question in this study was, "Which approach is most cost-effective?" That is, which program results in the greatest risk reduction per dollar spent? The authors concluded that two very common programs were the least effective: Installing a fitness facility proved to be clearly the least cost effective—it was the most expensive and also the least effective intervention. The education only program was inexpensive but only slightly more effective than the fitness facility. Programs (2) and (3) were judged to be the most effective, costing only about $1 per year per employee to engage each additional 1% of the at-risk workforce in health improvement activities. The authors concluded that the key features of these successful programs were: a wellness screening component that identifies at-risk employees; follow-up outreach and counseling that provides information and support for behavior change; and offering a menu of health improvement programs, which allows employees to choose activities that best fit their needs and preferences.

SOURCE: Based on J. C. Erfurt, A. Foote and M. A. Heirich, "The Cost-Effectiveness of Worksite Wellness Programs for Hypertension Control, Weight Loss, Smoking Cessation, and Exercise," *Personnel Psychology* 45 (1992), 5–27.

INTERNATIONAL SAFETY AND HEALTH ISSUES

As consciousness of health and well-being has risen worldwide, pressures to improve health care in work environments have increased in some countries. In others, however, the trend is to ignore health hazards; by having lax safety standards, developing countries can lure large multinational firms to their shores.

Closer Monitoring of Foreign Firms

Following the leakage of lethal methyl isocyanate gas at Union Carbide's pesticide plant in Bhopal, India, which killed more than two thousand persons, India has formed committees in every state to identify potential hazards in factories. While foreign investments and technology are still welcome, the government now insists on knowing more about the potential as well as actual risks involved. New regulations in India require environmental impact studies for all new plants.[40]

By comparison, some countries have had workers' compensation programs and monitoring systems for years. For example, in 1972 New Zealand introduced a no-fault insurance program that covers job injuries. That same year, Finland passed an accident insurance act making it possible to compensate for muscular pain and tendonitis caused by one's work. In 1977, Sweden passed a law requiring employers to modify the work environment to meet the physical and psychological makeup of workers.

The response to health hazards has been quite different in Mexico. A disaster that killed more than five hundred people and wounded thousands at Pemex, a state-owned gas monopoly in Mexico, has had no noticeable effect on regulations. The situation is similar in other developing countries. These countries are often so in need of economic development that they may accept any industry—even those that have the potential for significant harm. This, of course, presents serious ethical questions to firms operating in the developing nations.

Repetitive Strain Injury in Australia

A computer-related health epidemic known as **repetitive strain injury** (RSI) is widespread in Australia and threatens to drown the country's workers' compensation system. RSI is a label given to a variety of painful, debilitating conditions believed to be caused by rapid, repetitive movements of the hands or arms. RSI appears most often in work involving rapid, repetitive movements, such as those associated with operating keyboards, cutting meat, or soldering circuits. It has also been found among such diverse groups as professional tennis players, journalists, court reporters, telephone operators, dog groomers, assembly-line workers, welders, and machinists.

One form of RSI that is particularly traumatic is **carpal tunnel syndrome**—a nerve blockage that occurs at the base of the palm of the hand between the thumb and little finger where the carpal ligament stretches between the two muscle groups. With excessive use, the ligament tightens and depresses the nerve into the carpal bones. The result is severe, sharp pain in the wrist that makes gripping impossible.

In the U.S., these clinical problems occur in less than one percent of the population. In contrast, it is estimated that half of all office workers in Australia suffer from some form of RSI. The Australian problem is exacerbated because a record number of workers' compensation claims (up more than 200 percent) and suits have been filed. In 1984, more than two billion Australian dollars were spent by private insurance programs to settle RSI claims. Additionally, labor-management disputes over RSI have skyrocketed.

There are several potential causes of RSI. Some researchers speculate that technological changes are responsible. When typewriters were used, there were breaks to insert paper, change margins, and adjust the platen. Now files are accessed through the computer rather than from filing cabinets. Employees don't even need to leave their work stations to hand in completed work. This can be accomplished through computer networks and electronic mail systems. Thus, there is no letup in the *pace* of work.

Ergonomists contend the problem is due to poorly designed equipment and tools. In response, the Australian Public Service Association has established detailed work station design principles. Some of the standards include footrests for short operators; identical viewing distance for screen, source document, and keyboard; a 38-degree angle of viewing; a 90-degree screen angle; and fully adjustable height and knee clearance of computer tables; still, the frequency of RSI is increasing.[41]

An alternative explanation is that repetitive, unrelieved work is part of otherwise unchallenging, dead-end, boring, and monotonous jobs. Therefore, it may be that people aren't getting sick from *doing* the job but from *having* a boring, colorless, dull job. It also seems possible that RSI claims in Australia can be understood as a labor relations and political issue, a form of economic and political resistance to conditions of work and society on the part of unions and feminists in Australia but not elsewhere. While researchers can't agree on the cause, RSI is costing the Australian government and firms billions of dollars annually.[42]

SUMMARY

The health of employees in organizations will become increasingly important in the years ahead. Employers are becoming more aware of the cost of ill health and the benefits of having a healthy work force. The federal government, through OSHA, is also making it more necessary for employers to be concerned with employee health. The government's current concern is primarily with employee health as related to occupational accidents and diseases, both aspects of the physical environment. However, organizations can choose to become involved in programs dealing with employee health and the workers' sociopsychological environment as well. If organizations choose not to become involved with improving the sociopsychological environment, the government may prescribe mandatory regulations. Thus, it pays for organizations to be concerned with both aspects of the work environment now. Effective programs for both environments can significantly improve both employee health and the effectiveness of the organization.

When adoption of programs for improvement is being considered, employee involvement is important. As with many quality-of-work-life programs being implemented in organizations, employee involvement in improving safety and health is not only a good idea but also one likely to be desired by the employees. Many things can be done to make work environments better, but it is important to distinguish two types of environments: the physical and the sociopsychological. Each is different and has its own unique subparts. Although some improvement strategies may work well for one part of the work environment, they will not work in other parts. Again, a careful diagnosis is required before programs are selected and implemented.

Assuming that a careful diagnosis indicates the need for a stress management program, the challenge is in deciding which program or strategy to select from the many organizational and individual stress management strategies currently available. Programs such as time management or physical exercise could be set up so employees could help themselves cope, or the organization could alter the conditions within the organization that are associated with stress. The latter requires a diagnosis of what is happening, where, and to whom before deciding how to proceed. Because so many possible sources of stress exist, and because not all people react the same way to them, implementing individual stress management strategies may be more efficient. However, if many people are suffering similar stress symptoms in a specific part of the organization, an organizational strategy is more appropriate.

Information regarding many aspects of safety and health is insufficient—either because it does not exist (e.g., knowledge of causes and effect) or because organizations are unwilling to gather or provide it. From a legal as well as ethical viewpoint, it is in the best interests of organizations to seek and provide more information so that more effective strategies for improving safety and health can be developed and implemented. Failure to do so may result in costly legal settlements against organizations or further governmental regulation of workplace safety and health. Effective strategies may result from concerted union-management efforts to improve workplace safety and health, as described in the next chapter.

WHERE WE ARE TODAY

1. As companies become more concerned with cost savings and competitiveness, we may see more, not less, emphasis on safety and health programs!
2. Companies appear to be just starting to move aggressively into incentive-based health care programs to reward employees for adopting and maintaining particular lifestyles.
3. Studies show that workers tend to minimize or at least discount the risks associated with jobs, particularly when they need the jobs for their livelihood.
4. Thus, workers might undertake tasks that are really too risky, and the organization might end up with increased rather than decreased rates of accidents, injuries, and illnesses, if it fails to assist workers in weighing or even reducing the risks involved in job assignments.
5. The issues involved in safety and health are significant. Thus, the balancing of who's right, who's responsible, and whose rights is an important individual, organizational, and societal concern.
6. As in many other human resource activities today, the greater the employee involvement in safety and health programs, the greater the ownership, understanding, and willingness to act—and the greater the success.
7. The Imperial Food Products plant disaster should serve as a watershed in gaining the country's attention and concern for workplace safety and health.
8. As organizations continue their efforts to reduce costs, they may locate in countries where wages are low and where working conditions are unsafe and unhealthy. On one hand, they will find the situation attractive; on the other hand, they will confront the questions of how much and to what extent they can help to improve working conditions.
9. Many countries have far better safety and health records than the U.S., so there is a lot we can learn in our process of globalization.
10. As the nation continues to shift from heavy manufacturing to light manufacturing and services, there is a risk that we will become too complacent regarding our concern for safety and health. The costs are too great for not doing everything we can to minimize this risk.

DISCUSSION QUESTIONS

1. In what ways can an organization prevent occupational accidents?
2. How can physical work environment strategies and sociopsychological work environment strategies be assessed?

3. The U.S. prides itself on freedom, democracy, and free labor markets. If this is true, why not make employees responsible for health and safety? In other words, employers who offer riskier employment will simply pay workers more for bearing the risk (a wage premium), and the workers can in turn buy more insurance coverage to cover this risk. Discuss the advantages and disadvantages of this approach.
4. Who is responsible for workplace safety and health? The employer? The employee? The federal government? Judges and juries? Explain.
5. How are physical hazards distinct from sociopsychological hazards? What implications does this have for programs to deal with these hazards?
6. Is there such a thing as an unsafe worker? Assuming that accident-prone workers exist, how can effective human resource activities address this problem?
7. Is accident proneness a reliable trait? If not, does that mean organizations cannot control it? Explain.
8. What incentives does OSHA provide the employer for promoting workplace safety? Explain.
9. How might a company's strategy to prevent occupational accidents differ from a program to prevent occupational disease? In what ways might the programs be similar?
10. Should all employers institute wellness programs for their employees?

APPLIED PROJECTS

1. Find out the *most* hazardous occupation or industry for workers. Data sources for this research might include *Vital Health Statistics,* BNA's *Occupational Safety and Health Reporter,* NIOSH reports, and Bureau of Labor Statistics Workers' Compensation data available in the library. Consider whether the data are congruent with workers' perceptions of "risky" occupations. For this you may want to interview some workers in particular occupations.

CASE STUDY

A Web of Danger

Appliance Park is located in Henderson, a small city in western Kentucky next to the Ohio River. Appliance Park is aptly named for the company, Appliance House, that created the 800 steady manufacturing jobs for this small community. Appliance House manufactures washing machines, dryers, and dishwashers at its Appliance Park location. As the major employer in this small river city, employment at Appliance Park varies between 600 and 1,100 hourly employees depending on the state of the economy and the housing market. Although new housing starts have slowed considerably in the past two years due to unusually high interest rates, employment at Appliance Park has stabilized and, if anything, is expected to increase as production picks up with the increase in housing starts.

Two weeks ago, a tragedy occurred at Appliance Park that was felt throughout the community. On May 2, 1992, Joe Kitner fell to his death at the east plant where washing machines are assembled. Joe, 24 years old, was a local football star in high school and had worked at Appliance Park full-time since his graduation from Henderson Central High School. An investigation of the accident was conducted by representatives of the corporate safety staff and Teamster local officials who represented the nonexempt workers at Appliance Park. Although not widely reported, a curious set of factors contributed to Joe's death.

The assembly line at the washing machine division occupies two stories within a large prefab building on the east side of the park. A rope net or mesh is suspended about 30 feet above the ground level floor to catch accessories and parts that drop from the upper conveyor system where some of the assembly of the washing machines is conducted. Periodically, when model changeovers are scheduled on the line, a changeover crew is assigned to switch the set-up of the various machines throughout the assembly line. One of Joe's jobs on the changeover crew was to climb out on the net and retrieve the parts that had dropped from the previous production run. The net, while tightly strung across the ceiling, did have a tear on one side where a bracket that had fallen previously cut part of the mesh. While it was the changeover crew's responsibility to inspect and repair the net, they often overlooked minor rips because of the production time lost in making repairs to the mesh net.

An autopsy of Joe Kitner revealed that he died of a brain hemorrhage suffered in the fall to the concrete floor below. The autopsy also revealed that Joe had a small but malignant brain tumor located near that part of the brain that controls the central nervous system. Whether the tumor was far enough along to affect his judgment or motor abilities was not stated by the medical examiner, but the other test result from the autopsy indicated that Joe had consumed alcohol a few hours before his death, probably at lunch. His blood alcohol level, however, was not high enough to have been ruled intoxication using the state DWI standard.

The changeover crew experienced some difficulty in replacing Joe Kitner. Because the plant was unionized, his job was open to bid, but no one would bid for the job. Under these circumstances, the company went by seniority to determine who would work the job among the assemblers. Luther Duncan was selected and he really didn't have much of a choice, because he was low man on the totem pole with only seven years seniority at the plant. Although the changeover job comprises several duties, inevitably Luther knew that he would be asked to climb out on the net.

Luther had been on the job for only eight days when his foreman ordered the assembly line shut down for a model changeover for the next production run. At first Luther decided not to think about what he eventually would have to do, but when his time came to scale the utility ladder to the rope net, Luther balked. No amount of encouragement, cajoling, or threatening would change Luther's mind; he simply wasn't going up that ladder with the memory of Joe's death fresh in his mind.

Stan Fryer, the Teamster steward, pulled Luther aside and pleaded with him to obey his foreman's order to complete the job. Stan even promised to file a grievance concerning the rip on the one side of the net which still had not been repaired. Luther stood firm and adamantly refused to proceed. Despite Stan's intervention, Luther's foreman suspended him for the remainder of the day and told him to report along with Stan Fryer immediately the next morning to the plant superintendent's office. Upon reporting to the superintendent's office the next day, Luther was informed of his dismissal for insubordination.

SOURCE: Stuart A. Youngblood, Texas Christian University.

Case Questions

1. If this was a case of insubordination, was Luther Duncan justified in refusing to work?
2. Was the company responsible for the death of Joe Kitner?
3. Should Joe also have refused to perform his job knowing the net had a tear on one side?
4. Was the "changeover job" an example of dangerous jobs that just have to exist or should they be eliminated?

NOTES

1. U.S. Supreme Court in its decision in *Automobile Workers v. Johnson Controls,* 1991. Under the Pregnancy Discrimination Act, "women as capable of doing their jobs as their male counterparts may not be forced to choose between having a child and having a job."
2. R. Smothers, "North Carolina Examines Inspection Lapses in Fire," *The New York Times* (5 Sept. 1991): D25; B. D. Ayres, Jr. "Factory Fire Leaves Pall Over 'All-American City'" *The New York Times* (5 Sept. 1991): D25. Plant owner, Emmett Roe, pleaded guilty to 25 counts of involuntary manslaughter and was sentenced to nearly 20 years in prison. *The New York Times* (15 Sept. 1992): A20.
3. R. S. Schuler, "Occupational Health in Organizations: A Measure of Personnel Effectiveness," in R. Schuler and

S. Youngblood, eds., *Readings in Personnel and Human Resource management,* 2d ed. (St. Paul, Minn.: West Publishing, 1984). Also see D. R. Ilgen, "Health Issues at Work: Opportunities for Industrial/Organizational Psychology," *American Psychologist* (Feb. 1990): 273–83.

4. J. A. Kinney, "Why Did Paul Die?" *Newsweek* (10 Sept. 1990): 11. Also see C. P. Hansen, "A Causal Model of the Relationship Among Accidents, Biodata, Personality, and Cognitive Factors," *Journal of Applied Psychology* 74, no. 1 (1989): 81–90.
5. T. F. O'Boyle, "Fear and Stress in the Office Take Toll," *The Wall Street Journal* (6 Nov. 1990): B1–2.
6. C. B. Wilson, "U.S. Businesses Suffer from Workplace Trauma," *Personnel Journal* (July 1991): 47–50; T. A. Beehr and R. S. Bhagat, eds., *Stress and Human Cognition* (New York: Wiley, 1984); T. A. Beehr and R. S. Schuler, "Stress in Organizations," in K. Rowland and G. Ferris, eds., *Personnel Management* (Boston, Mass.: Allyn & Bacon, 1982); R. S. Schuler and S. E. Jackson, "Managing Stress through PHRM Practices: An Uncertainty Interpretation," in K. Rowland and G. Ferris, eds., *Research in Personnel and Human Resources Management,* vol. 4 (Greenwich, Conn.: JAI Press, 1986).
7. *Bulletin to Management* (19 Dec. 1991): 396.
8. "Fewer Workers Killed on the Job Last Year," *Bulletin to Management* (27 Sept. 1990): 306.
9. These estimates should be regarded as conservative because they do not include the costs due to stress and health and accident costs associated with (caused by) low quality of work life.
10. O'Boyle, "Fear and Stress in the Office Takes Toll": B2.
11. See note 10.
12. From personal correspondence with Donald Brush, 8 March 1989.
13. C. S. Weaver, "Understanding Occupational Disease," *Personnel Journal* (June 1989): 86–94.
14. See note 13.
15. C. L. Wang, "Occupational Skin Disease Continues to Plague Industry," *Monthly Labor Review* (Feb. 1979): 17–22.
16. "Fewer Workers Killed…", 306.
17. K. R. Pelletier, "The Hidden Hazards of the Modern Office," *The New York Times* (8 Sept. 1985): F3; J. Hyatt, "Hazardous Effects of VDT Legislation," *Inc.* (March 1985): 27; W. L. Weis, "No Smoking," *Personnel Journal* (Sept. 1984): 53–58; "VDT Study: Safety Charges, Design Changes," *Bulletin to Management* (21 July 1983); "Office Hazard: Factory Environment can Boomerang," *Impact* (22 June 1983): 1.
18. "Charges of Emotional Distress: A Growing Trend," *FEP Guidelines* no. 284 (1989): 1–4; S. L. Sauter, L. R. Murphy, and J. J. Hurrell, Jr., "Prevention of Work-Related Psychological Disorders: A National Strategy Proposed by the National Institute for Occupational Safety and Health (NIOSH)," *American Psychologist* (Oct. 1990): 1146–56. Also see a set of references identifying and discussing each preference or interest listed here in R. S. Schuler, "Definition and Conceptualization of Stress in Organizations," *Organizational Behavior and Human Performance* 23 (1980): 184–215; R. S. Schuler, "An Integrative Transactional Process Model of Stress in Organizations," *Journal of Occupational Behavior* 3 (1982): 3–19.
19. A. B. Shostak, *Blue Collar Stress* (Reading, Mass.: Addison-Wesley, 1980).
20. R. C. Kessler, J. B. Turner, and J. S. House, "Unemployment and Health in a Community Sample," *Journal of Health and Social Behavior* 28 (1987): 51–59; R. C. Kessler, J. B. Turner, and J. S. House, "Intervening Processes in the Relationship between Unemployment and Health," *Psychological Medicine* 17 (1987): 949–61; R. D. Caplan, A. D. Vinokur, R. H. Price, and M. van Ryn, "Job Seeking, Reemployment and Mental Health: A Randomized Field Experiment in Coping with Job Loss," *Journal of Applied Psychology* 74 (1989): 759–69; S. J. Ashford, C. Lee, and P. Bobko, "Content, Causes, and Consequences of Job Insecurity: A Theory-Based Measure and Substantive Test," *Academy of Management Journal* 32, no. 4 (1989): 803–829; S. E. Markham and G. H. McKee, "Declining Organizational Size and Increasing Unemployment Rates: Predicting Employee Absenteeism from Within- and Between-Plant Perspectives," *Academy of Management Journal* 34, no. 4 (1991): 952–65; P. Cappelli, "Examining Managerial Displacement," *Academy of Management Journal* 35, no.1 (1992): 203–217; R. H. Price, "Psychological Impact of Job Loss on Individuals and Families," *Current Directions* (American Psychological Society, 1992); T. A. Beehr and R. S. Schuler, "Stress in Organizations," in *Personnel Management,* eds. K. M. Rowland and G. Ferris (Boston: Allyn & Bacon, 1982); A. P. Brief, R. S. Schuler, and M. Van Sell, *Managing Job Stress* (Boston: Little, Brown, 1980); R. S. Schuler and S. E. Jackson, "Managing Stress through PHRM Practices: An Uncertainty Interpretation," in *Research in Personnel and Human Resources Management,* vol. 4, ed. K. M. Rowland and G. Ferris (Greenwich, Conn.: JAI Press, 1986); D. S. Thelan, D. Ledgerwood, and C. F. Walters, "Health and Safety in the Workplace: A New Challenge for Business Schools, *Personnel Administrator* (Oct. 1985): 37–46.
21. A. Miller, K Springen, J. Gorgon, B. Cohn, L. Drew, and T. Barrett, "Stress on the Job," *Newsweek* (25 April 1988): 25; S. Swooplop, R. Rhein, Jr., and J. Weber, "Stress: The Test Americans are Failing," *Business Week* (18 April 1988): 75; L. Vallarosa, "Stressed-Out," *American Banker* (19 Oct. 1987): 38; M. O. Hatfield, "Stress and the American Worker," *American Psychologist* (Oct. 1990): 1162–64; A. O'Leary, "Stress, Emotion and Human Immune Function," *Psychological Bulletin* 108, no. 3 (1990): 363–82; G. W. Evans and S. Carrère, "Traffic Congestion, Perceived Control and Psychophysiological Stress among Urban Bus Drivers," *Journal of Applied Psychology* 76, no. 5 (1991): 658–63; D. C. Ganster, J. Schaubroeck, W. E. Sime, and B. T. Mayes, "The Nomological Validity of the Type A Personality Among Employed Adults," *Journal of Applied Psychology* 76, no. 1 (1991): 143-68; M. R. Frone and D. B. McFarlin, "Chronic Occupational Stressors, Self-Focused Attention, and Well-Being: Testing a Cybernetic Model of Stress," *Journal of Applied Psychology* 74, no. 6 (1989): 876–83; S. Cohen and G. M. Williamson, "Stress and Infectious Disease in Humans, " *Psychological Bulletin* 109, no. 1 (1991): 5–24; S. R. Barley and D. B.

Knight, "Toward a Cultural Theory of Stress Complaints," *Research in Organizational Behavior* vol. 14 (1992): 1–48; R. Martin and T. D. Wall, "Attentional Demand and Cost Responsibility as Stressors in Shopfloor Jobs," *Academy of Management Journal* 32, no. 1 (1989): 69–86; C. A. Higgins and L. E. Duxbury, "Work-Family Conflict in the Dual-Career Family," *Organizational Behavior and Human Decision Processes* 51 (1992): 51–75; S. Parasuraman, J. H. Greenhaus, S. Rabinowitz, A. G. Bedeian, and K. W. Mossholder, "Work and Family Variables as Mediators of the Relationship Between Wives' Employment and Husbands' Well-Being," *Academy of Management Journal* 32, no. 1 (1989): 185–201; B. A. Gutek, S. Searle, and L. Klepa, "Rational Versus Gender Role Explanations for Work-Family Conflict," *Journal of Applied Psychology,* 76, no. 4 (1991): 560–68; L. E. Duxbury and C. A. Higgins, "Gender Differences in Work-Family Conflict," *Journal of Applied Psychology* 76, no. 1 (1991): 60–74; K. J. Williams, J. Suls, G. M. Alliger, S. M. Learner, and C. K. Wan, "Multiple Role Juggling and Daily Mood States in Working Mothers: An Experience Sampling Study," *Journal of Applied Psychology* 76, no. 5 (1991): 664–74; M. F. Frone, M. Russell, and M. L. Cooper, "Antecedents and Outcomes of Work-Family Conflict: Testing a Model of the Work-Family Interface," *Journal of Applied Psychology* 77, no.1 (1992): 65–78.

22. M. Frankenhaeuser and B. Gardell, "Underload and Overload in Working Life: Outline of a Multidisciplinary Approach," *Journal of Human Stress* 2 (1976): 35–45; M. Pesci, "Stress Management: Separating Myth from Reality,"*Personnel Administrator* (Jan. 1982): 57–67; but even if individuals are under heavy work loads and stress, they may not necessarily want to eliminate them. See R. Richlefs, "Many Executives Complain of Stress, but Few Want Less-Pressured Jobs," *Wall Street Journal* (29 Sept. 1982): 35.
23. J. Hyatt, "Hazardous Effects of VDT Legislation," *INC.* (March 1985): 27; K. R. Pelletier, "The Hidden Hazards of the Modern Office," *New York Times* (8 Sept. 1985): F3; R. Sutton and A. Rafaeli, "Characteristics of Work Stations as Potential Occupational Stressors," *Academy of Management Journal* 30, no. 2 (June 1987): 260–76; "VDT Study: Safety Charges, Design Changes,"*Bulletin to Management* (21 July 1983): 27; W. L. Weis, "No Smoking," *Personnel Journal* (Sept. 1984): 53–58.
24. S. E. Jackson and R. S. Schuler, "Preventing Employee Burnout," *Personnel* (March-April 1983): 58–68; B. Dumaine, "Cool Cures for Burnout," *Fortune* (20 June 1986): 78–84.
25. H. J. Hilaski, "Understanding Statistics on Occupational Illnesses," *Monthly Labor Review* (March 1981): 25–29; R. A. Reber, J. A. Wallin, and J. S. Chhokar, "Reducing Industrial Accidents: A Behavioral Experiment," *Industrial Relations* (Winter 1984): 119–25.
26. For extensive discussion of office space and physical design issues, see L. Altman, "Some Who Use VDT's Miscarried, Study Says," *New York Times* (5 June 1988): 22; "Reproductive Hazards—How Employers Are Responding," *Fair Employment Practices* (29 Oct. 1987): 132; R. S. Schuler, L. R. Ritzman, and V. Davis, "Merging Prescriptive and Behavioral Approaches for Office Layout," *Production and Inventory Management Journal* 3 (1981): 131–42.
27. "National ASPA Conference Highlights," *Bulletin to Management* (28 July 1988): 239. Also see J. R. Hollenbeck, D. R. Ilgen, and S. M. Crampton, "Lower Back Disability in Occupational Settings: A Review of the Literature from a Human Resource Management View," *Personnel Psychology* 45, no. 2 (1992): 247–78.
28. *Bulletin to Management* (21 Feb. 1991): 50.
29. J. Komaki, K. D. Barwick, and L. Scott, "Pinpointing and Reinforcing Safe Performance in a Food Manufacturing Plant," *Journal of Applied Psychology* 63 (1978): 434–45.
30. H. M. Taylor, "Occupational Health Management-by-Objectives," *Personnel* (Jan.-Feb. 1980): 58–64.
31. M. Williams, "Ten Minutes Work for 12 Hours Pay? What's the Catch?" *The Wall Street Journal* (12 Oct. 1983): 19.
32. J. Olian, "New Approaches to Employment Screening," in *Readings in Personnel and Human Resource Management* 3d ed. (St. Paul, Minn.: West Publishing, 1988).
33. J. C. Erfurt, A. Foote, and M. A. Heirich, "The Cost-Effectiveness of Worksite Wellness Programs for Hypertension Control, Weight Loss, Smoking Cessation and Exercise,"*Personnel Psychology* 45 (1992): 5–27; D. L. Bebhardt and C. E. Crump, "Employee Fitness and Wellness Programs in the Workplace," *American Psychologist* (Feb. 1990): 262–72; M. R. Manning, J. S. Osland, and A. Osland, "Work-Related Consequences of Smoking Cessation," *Academy of Management Journal* 32 no. 3 (1989): 606–621.
34. O'Boyle, "Fear and Stress in the Office Take Toll": B2.
35. "Fetal Protection Policy Struck Down," *FEP Guidelines* (May 1991): 1–2; "Fetal Protection Ruling," *Fair Employment Practices* (28 March 1991): 31; S. Wermiel, "Justices Bar 'Fetal Protection' Policies," *The Wall Street Journal* (21 March 1991): B1; C. Trost, "Workplace Debate," *The Wall Street Journal* (8 Oct. 1990): 1; B. Meier, "Companies Wrestle with Threats to Workers' Reproductive Health," *The Wall Street Journal* (5 Feb. 1987): 25; L. Altman, "Some Who Use VDT's Miscarried, Study Says," *The New York Times* (5 June 1988): 22; "Reproductive Hazards—How Employers are Responding," *Fair Employment Practices* (29 Oct. 1987): 132.
36. From S. B. Garland, "A New Chief has OSHA Growing Again," *Business Week* (20 Aug. 1990): 57; P. T. Kilborn, "Who Decides Who Works at Jobs Imperiling Fetuses?" *The New York Times* (2 Sept. 1990): A1, 12; R. Winslow, "Air Polluted by Carbon Monoxide Poses Risk to Heart Patients, Study Shows," *The Wall Street Journal* (4 Sept. 1990): B4; R. Winslow, "Safety Group Cites Fatalities Linked to Work," *The Wall Street Journal* (31 Aug. 1990): B8; and C. Trost, "Business and Women Anxiously Watch Suit on 'Fetal Protection'" *The Wall Street Journal* (8 Oct. 1990): 1.
37. J. Hirsh, "What's New in Wellness Programs," *The New York Times* (5 Oct. 1986): F19.
38. F. B. James, "Study Lays Groundwork for Tying Health Costs to Workers' Behavior," *The Wall Street Journal* (14 April 1987): 37.
39. "Matching Life Styles to Benefits," *The New York Times* (1 March 1992).
40. P. R. Balgopal, C. Ramanathan, and M. Patchner, "Employee Assistance Programs: A Cross-Cultural Perspective," paper presented at the Conference on International Personnel and

Human Resource Management (Dec. 1987, Singapore); "Foreign Firms Feel the Impact of Bhopal Most," *The Wall Street Journal* (26 Nov. 1986): 24.

41. J. Saddler, "GM Agrees to Fight Repetitive-Motion Woes of Employees," *The Wall Street Journal* (21 Nov. 1990): C19; "An Invisible Workplace Hazard Gets Harder to Ignore," *Business Week* (30 Jan. 1989): 92–94, 104; "Repetitive Motion," *Bulletin to Management* (10 Aug. 1989): 256.
42. S. Kiesler and T. Finholt, "The Mystery of RSI," *American Psychologist* (Dec. 1988): 1004-15.

Unionization and Collective Bargaining

In some cases, [the union] was absolutely right. The protests refocused everyone to the sense of urgency to get the quality problems fixed.

—Richard G. (Skip) LeFauve, President, Saturn[1]

In the opening quotation, Skip LeFauve refers to the protests by the union workers at the General Motors Saturn plant in Spring Hill, Tennessee. GM's chairman, Robert Stempel, paid a visit to the plant in the autumn of 1991, and the workers, wearing black and orange armbands, launched a work slowdown. Another one of those strikes to get higher wages? In reality, it was a protest against the higher production quotas GM was trying to impose on the plant. While high quality and high quantity can go hand in hand when everything is working right, it is too much to expect in the early stages of operation. This being the early stage at the Saturn plant, the workers were more concerned about quality—about the car and the customer's satisfaction with the product—than they were with quantity of output. One could argue that the workers basically had no reason to go for quantity, since they get paid by the hour, not for the number of cars that go out the door (at least not in the short run). However, the same could be said for the workers' interest in quality.

Quality takes commitment, dedication, and training, and the United Automobile Workers (UAW) have never been known for being concerned about quality or quantity. However, these workers at the Spring Hill plant were concerned about quality. They believed quality was more critical than quantity for the longer term success of the company. One may say, "that's the only way they can keep their jobs," but this can be said for all workers.

The difference here is that the union workers at the Saturn plant were behaving contrary to the traditional stereotype of the union member in the auto industry. Why? Because management was behaving contrary to its *stereotype. Management was giving workers more say in the production of the automobile, treating workers as co-owners and as members of teams. Any employee who didn't want to fit into this new scheme of labor-management relationship in the auto business could collect a generous severance package ($15,000 to $50,000 depending upon length of service).*

Reflecting upon their original agreement, Robert Stempel and the GM management heard the concerns of the workers at the plant and gave them the benefit of any doubt. He and the others knew Saturn was the real test case for whether or not GM could build cars to compete directly with the top-selling Japanese cars, many of which are also made in the U.S., some by UAW members and some by nonmembers.[2]

These events at the Saturn plant highlight several important aspects of unionization and collective bargaining. One is that union members in the United Automobile Workers may indeed be more concerned about quality than anyone else. Another is that the degree of cooperation between the UAW and GM has been high at the Saturn plant, although somewhat less at other GM plants. Notable exceptions to this are the plants in Flint, Michigan, that form Buick City, the NUMMI joint venture in Fremont, California, and those in the Cadillac Division, winner of the prestigious Malcom Baldrige Award for quality in 1990.[3] Another aspect of these events at Saturn is that union-management cooperation can result in benefits to both workers and the company, such as improved quality, lower absenteeism, increased satisfaction, more employment security and training, and increased profitability. A final aspect is that union-management relationships are dynamic and changing all the time to reflect the changing conditions of the world.

As these conditions continue to change in the 1990s, expect the union-management relationships to also change. Changes are likely to occur both in unionization efforts of unions and in the bargaining relationships between existing unions and managements. For example, the UAW is extending its efforts to unionize nonteaching employees in universities. Changes are also occurring between the union itself and its membership as unions consider offering alternative forms of membership such as associate status.[4]

To put into perspective these aspects of union-management relationships, this chapter describes both the process of forming a union (unionization) and the characteristics of administering an agreement reached between the union and management (collective bargaining).

UNIONIZATION AND COLLECTIVE BARGAINING

Unionization is the effort by employees and outside agencies (unions or associations) to act as a single unit when dealing with management over issues relating to their work. When recognized by the National Labor Relations Board, a union has the legal authority to negotiate with the employer on behalf of employees—to improve wages, hours, and conditions of employment—and to administer the ensuing agreement.[5]

The core of union-management relations is **collective bargaining.** It generally includes two types of interaction. The first is the negotiation of work conditions that, when written up as the collective agreement (the contract), becomes the basis for employee–employer relationships on the job. The second includes activities related to interpreting and enforcing the collective agreement (contract administration) and resolving any conflicts arising out of it.[6]

These two activities are described in this chapter beginning with the processes of unionization. The second half is dedicated primarily to the process of collective bargaining. Because these processes are influenced by several aspects of the environment, such as top management's goals and values and legal and regulatory statutes, you may want to review those relevant sections of chapters 2 and 3 at this time.

PURPOSES AND IMPORTANCE OF UNIONIZATION

Unionization is important for both employers and employees. To employers, the existence of a union—or even the possibility of one—can significantly influence the ability of an organization to manage its vital human resources. To employees, unions can help them get what they want (for example, high wages and job security) from their employers.

Understanding the unionizing or organizing process, its causes, and its consequences is an important part of managing human resources effectively. Unionization may result in management having less flexibility in hiring, job assignments, and the introduction of new work methods such as automation; a loss of control; inefficient work practices; and inflexible job structure. Also, as indicated in chapter 15, unions obtain rights for their members that employees without unions do not legally have. This, of course, forces unionized companies to consider their employees' reactions to many more decisions. In some cases, however, employers who are nonunion and want to remain that way give more consideration and benefits to their employees. Consequently, the claim that it is more expensive for a company to operate with unionized rather than nonunionized employees is not always true.

Unions also assist employers through wage concessions or cooperation in joint workplace efforts, such as teamwork programs or Scanlon Plans, allowing employers to survive particularly difficult times and, in fact, remain profitable and competitive. This has been particularly true in the automobile and airline industries. Unions can also help identify workplace hazards and improve the quality of work life for employees. These ideas and the components of unionization to be discussed here are illustrated in exhibit 17.1

ATTRACTION OF UNIONIZATION

Unions were originally formed in response to the exploitation and abuse of employees by management. To understand the union movement today, we need to examine why employees decide to join unions and why they do not.

Decision to Join a Union

Three separate conditions strongly influence an employee's decision to join a union: dissatisfaction, lack of power, and union instrumentality.[7]

Dissatisfaction. When an individual takes a job, certain conditions of employment (wages, hours, and type of work) are specified in the employment contract. A psychological contract also exists between employer and employee, consisting of the unspecified expectation of the employee about reasonable working conditions, requirements of the work itself, the level of effort that should be expended on the job, and the nature of the authority the employer should have in directing the employee's work.[8] These expectations are related to the employee's desire to satisfy certain personal preferences in the workplace. The degree to which the organization fulfills these preferences determines the employee's level of satisfaction.

Dissatisfaction with the implicit terms and conditions of the employment **(the psychological contract)** will lead employees to attempt to improve the work situation, often through unionization. A major study found a very strong relationship between the level of satisfaction and the proportion of workers voting for a union. Almost all workers who were satisfied voted against the union.[9]

Thus, if management wants to make unionization less attractive to employees, it must make work conditions more satisfying. Management and the human resource department often contribute to the level of work dissatisfaction by doing the following:

- Giving unrealistic job previews that create expectations that cannot be fulfilled
- Designing jobs that fail to use the skills, knowledge, and abilities of employees and fail to satisfy their personalities, interests, and preferences

Exhibit 17.1
Components of the Unionization of Employees in the Union-Management Relationship

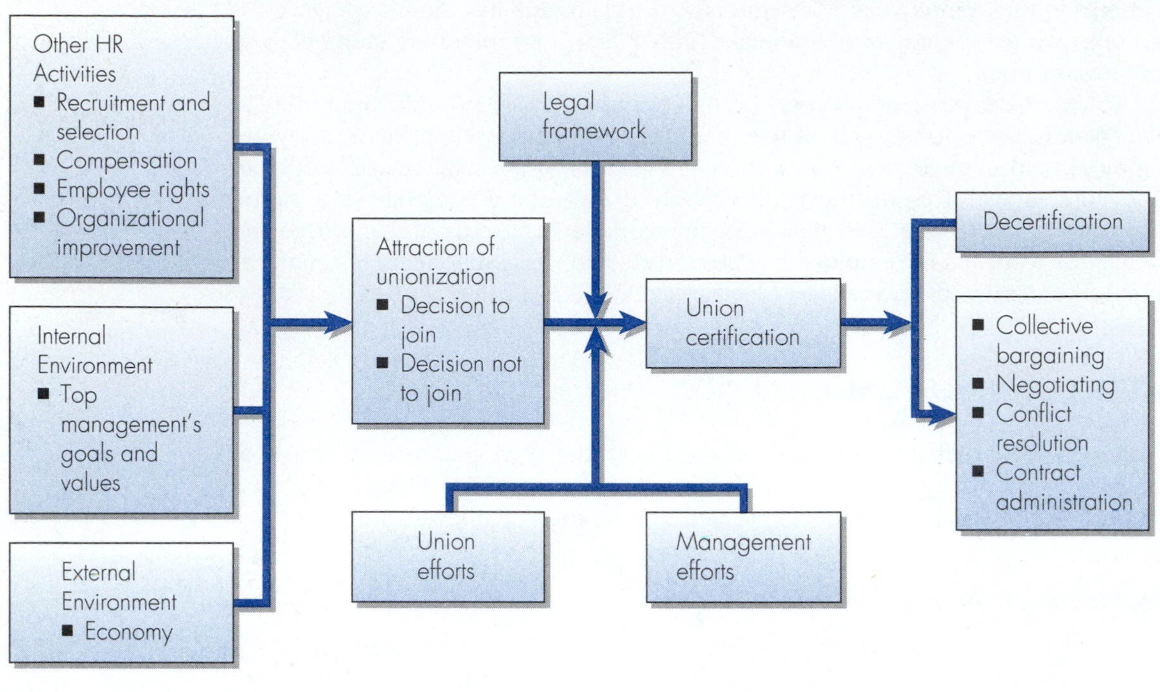

- Practicing poor day-to-day management and supervisory practices, including unfair treatment and one-way downward communication
- Failing to tell employees that management would prefer to operate without unions and that the organization is committed to treating employees with respect[10]

Lack of power. Unionization is seldom the first recourse of employees who are dissatisfied with some aspect of their job. The first attempt to improve the work situation is usually made by an individual acting alone. Someone who has enough power or influence can effect the necessary changes without collaborating with others. The amount of power the job holder has in the organization is determined by essentiality, or how important or critical the job is to the overall success of the organization, and exclusivity, or how difficult it is to replace the person. An employee with an essential task who is difficult to replace may be able to force the employer to make a change. If, however, the individual's task is not critical and the employee can easily be replaced, other means, including collective action, must be considered in order to influence the organization.[11]

In deciding whether collective action is appropriate, employees are also likely to consider whether a union could obtain the aspects of the work environment not now provided by the employer and to weigh those benefits against the costs of unionization. In other words, the employees would determine union instrumentality.[12]

Union instrumentality. Just as employees can be dissatisfied with many aspects of a work environment—such as pay, promotion opportunity, treatment by supervisor, the job itself, and work rules—employees can also perceive a union as being instrumental in removing these causes of dissatisfaction. The more that employees believe a union can obtain positive work aspects, the more instrumental employees perceive the union to be in removing the causes of dissatisfaction. The Focus on Research: "Where Did You Get That Attitude?" describes evidence that these perceptions are influenced early in life. If employees perceive unions as instrumental, then employees weigh the *value* of the benefits to be obtained through unionization against unionization's costs, such as the lengthy organizing campaign and the bad feelings among supervisors, managers, and other employees who may not want a union. Finally, the employees weigh the costs and benefits against the *likelihood* of a union being able to obtain the benefits—the perception of union instrumentality. When the benefits exceed the costs and union instrumentality is high, employees will be more willing to support a union.[13]

Exhibit 17.2 summarizes the reasons for deciding to join a union. In general, the expectation that work will satisfy personal preferences induces satisfaction or dissatisfaction with work. As the level of dissatisfaction increases, the individual workers seek to change their work situation. If they fail, and if the positive consequences of unionization seem to outweigh the negative ones, individuals will be inclined to join the union. This, however, will not always be the case. Employees may choose not to join a union.

Decision Not to Join a Union

The question of whether to join a union involves an assessment of the negative consequences of unionization. Employees may have misgivings about how effectively a union can improve unsatisfactory work conditions. Collective bargaining is not always successful; if the union is not strong, it will be unable to make an employer meet its demands. Even if an employer does respond to union demands, the workers may be affected adversely. The employer may not be able to survive when the demands of the unions are met, and thus the company may close down, costing employees their jobs. The organization may force the union to strike, inflicting economic hardship on employees who may not be able to afford being out of work; or it may in some cases attempt reprisals against pro-union employees, although this is illegal.[14]

Beyond perceptions of unions as ineffective in the pursuit of personal goals, employees may also resist unionization because of general attitudes toward unions. Employees may identify strongly with the company and have a high level of commitment to it. Therefore, they would tend to view the union as an adversary and be receptive to company arguments against unions. Employees may also perceive the goals of the union to be objectionable and likely to harm the company and the free enterprise system in general. They may object to the concept of seniority or even to the political activities of the unions. Moreover, certain employees—for example, engineers or scientists—view themselves as professionals and find collective action to be contrary to such professional ideals as independence and self-control.

There is another possible reason some persons will not be enthusiastic about the prospect of unionizing. Employees who possess individual bargaining power

FOCUS ON RESEARCH

Where Did You Get That Attitude?

The survival of unions depends, in part, on their ability to attract new members and convince employees to vote in favor of union certification. Consequently, numerous studies have examined why people choose to engage in pro-union behavior. The results consistently show that general positive attitudes about unions predict pro-union behaviors. Furthermore, people's general attitudes about unions are quite stable over long periods of time. Such results have led some researchers to conclude that attitudes about unions are formed early in life during a person's "impressionable years," prior to any specific personal experiences one has with a particular union or a particular employment situation.

A Canadian research team interested in understanding how family socialization experiences influence attitudes toward unions conducted a study of high school and university students. The study focused on two sources of unions attitudes: (a) fundamental work-related philosophies and beliefs, and (b) parents' union involvement and attitudes. Work-related philosophies were assessed by students' responses to questions that assessed Marxist work beliefs and Humanist work beliefs. For example, Marxist work beliefs would be held by students who agree with statements such as, "The work of the laboring class is exploited by the rich for their own benefit." Humanistic work beliefs would be held by students who agree with statements such as, "Work can be organized to allow for human fulfillment." The union involvement of each parent was determined by asking students about how often the parent attended meetings and other union-related activities as well as whether the parent was a union member, had ever gone out on strike, or was a union officer.

Students in this study reported that approximately 30% of their mothers and 30% of their fathers had been union members at some time. When asked whether they would be willing to join a union some day, about 40% of the students said "yes." Were students' attitudes a result of family socialization processes? Could students' attitudes be predicted from the attitudes and union involvement of their parents? To answer these questions, the researchers developed a statistical model to reflect the linkages between the union activities and attitudes of parents, on the one hand, and the work-related philosophies and union attitudes of their children, on the other hand. The analysis revealed several connections. Perhaps most important was a path that linked parents' participation in unions to their children's Marxist work beliefs, which in turn predicted the children's general attitudes toward unions and their willingness to join a union some day. The children's attitudes toward unions were also strongly related to parents' attitudes and weakly related to the children's own Humanistic work beliefs.

The results of this study clearly indicate that employees' attitudes about unions are determined partly by family socialization. This result, in combination with other studies that show attitudes toward unions are quite stable, suggests that union representatives and employers may have less power to change employees' attitudes than is often assumed. Furthermore, it suggests that as union participation declines in successive generations, the attitudes of the following generations are also likely to become less and less pro-union. Given the current pattern of declining union involvement in the U.S., can unions survive in the long run? Should they begin communicating with potential future members while these people are still children? If you were a union official, how would you react to the results from this study?

SOURCE: Based on J. Barling, E. K. Kelloway, and E. H. Bremermann, "Preemployment Predictors of Union Attitudes: The Role of Family Socialization and Work Beliefs." *Journal of Applied Psychology* 76 (1991), 725–31.

(e.g., craft workers in a unit that is being courted by an industrial union) may be unable to secure more favorable working conditions from the employer if those concessions conflict with the collective agreement.

The decision not to unionize can be influenced by management as well. Employers may influence the employees' decision not to join a union by establishing good management practices: fostering employee participation in planning and decision making, opening channels of communication, setting up processes for handling employee problems and grievances, developing employee trust, and offering competitive wages.[15]

It should be noted that some employers perceive that they may benefit from their employees unionizing. This is especially so when the union brings some certainty and discipline to the work force. In essence, a union can help manage the work force.[16] Organizations have seldom seen unions in this way, however. In fact, a review of the historical development of unionization in the U.S. may suggest exactly the opposite.

DEVELOPMENT AND STATE OF UNIONIZATION

A better understanding of the attitudes and behaviors of both unions and management can be gained through a knowledge of past union-management rela-

Exhibit 17.2
Processes in the Decision to Organize

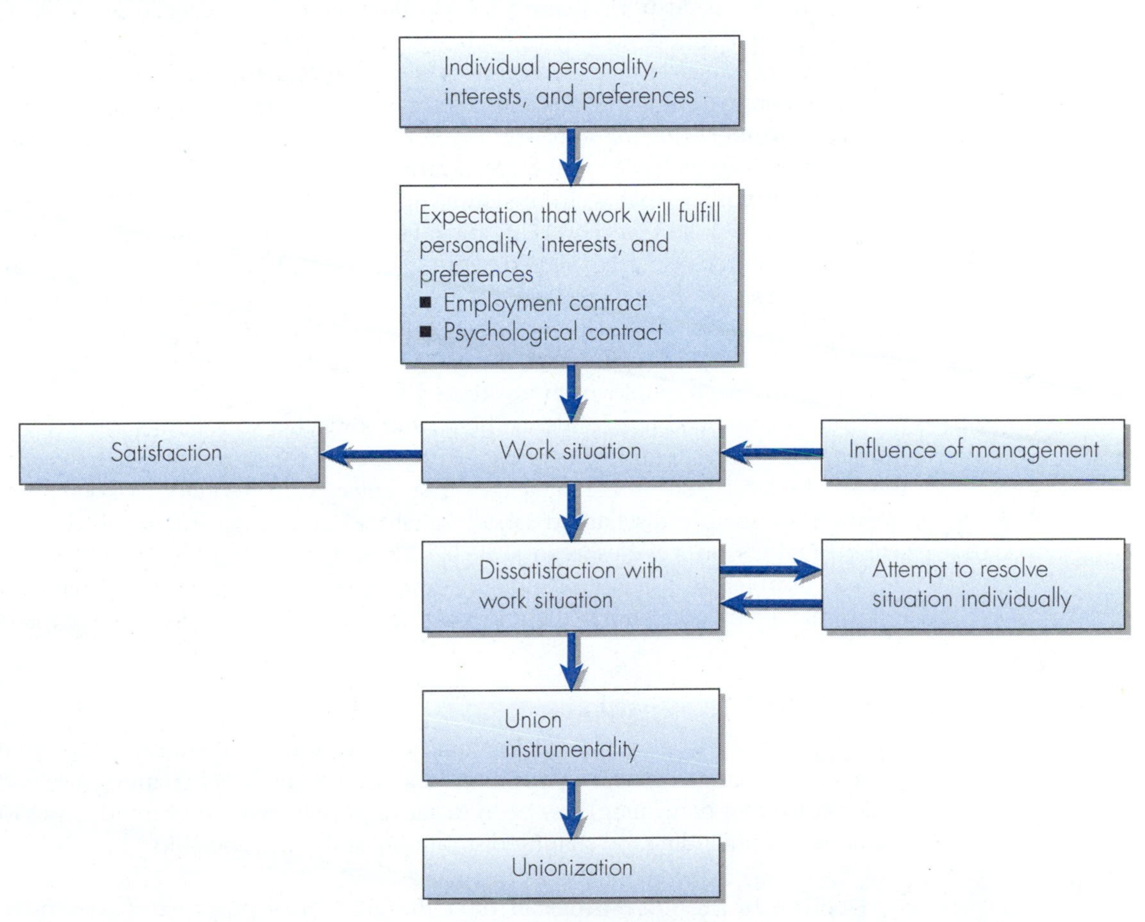

tions. The legal considerations discussed in chapter 3 form part of this historical context.

Early Days

Labor unions in the U.S. can be traced back to the successful attempt of journeymen printers to win a wage increase in 1778. By the 1790s, unions of shoemakers, carpenters, and printers had appeared in Boston, Baltimore, New York, and other cities. The Federal Society of Journeymen Cordwainers, for example, was organized in Philadelphia in 1794, primarily to resist employers' attempts to reduce wages. Other issues of concern to these early unions were **union shops** (companies using only union members) and the regulation of apprenticeships to prevent the replacement of journeymen employees.

The methods and objectives of early unions are still in evidence today. Although there was no collective bargaining, the unions did establish a price below which members would not work. Strikes were used to enforce this rate. These strikes were relatively peaceful and, for the most part, successful.

One negative characteristic of early unions was their susceptibility to depressions. Until the late 1800s, most unions thrived in times of prosperity but died off during depressions. Part of this problem may have been related to the insularity of the unions. Aside from sharing information on strike breakers or scabs, the unions operated independently of each other.

The work situation had undergone several important changes by the end of the Nineteenth Century. Transportation systems (canals, railroads, and turnpikes) expanded the markets for products and increased worker mobility. Increases in capital costs prevented journeymen from reaching the status of master craftsworker (that is, from setting up their own businesses), thereby creating a class of skilled workers. Unionism found its start in these skilled occupations, largely because "the skilled worker ... had mastered his craft through years of apprenticeship and was no longer occupationally mobile," and the alternatives were "to passively accept wage cuts, the competition of non-apprentice labor, and the harsh working conditions, or to join in collective action against such employer innovations."[17]

Unions continued to experience highs and lows that were largely tied to economic conditions. Employers took advantage of the depressions to combat unions: In "an all out frontal attack ... they engaged in frequent lockouts, hired spies ... summarily discharged labor 'agitators,' and [engaged] the services of strike breakers on a widespread scale."[18] These actions, and the retaliations of unions, established a tenor of violence and lent a strong adversarial nature to union-management relations, the residual effects of which are in evidence today.

Recent Days

Today the adversarial nature of the union-management relationship has been replaced to a certain extent by a more cooperative one. This change (discussed under collective bargaining) has been dictated in part by current trends in union membership, including the shifting distribution of the membership.

Decline in membership. In 1990, the number of private and government employees belonging to unions or employee associations was about 16 million.[19] The proportion of the labor force represented by unions has been declining steadily since the mid-1950s when 35 percent of the work force was unionized. In 1970, the percentage of unionized labor force was about 25 percent. In 1992, approximately 17 percent of all workers (twelve percent in the private sector) were represented by unions, down from 23 percent in 1980. Factors that contribute to the percentage decline include the increase in public-sector employment and white-collar jobs—both of which historically have had a low proportion of union members. Other contributing factors are the decline in employment in industries that are highly unionized, the high levels of unemployment, the increased decertification of unions, union leadership, union responsiveness to membership, and management initiatives.[20]

To gain more organizational ability, power, and financial strength, several unions have merged. Although mergers may not automatically increase membership, they can mean more efficiency in union-organizing efforts and an end to costly jurisdictional disputes among unions. Increased organizational strength from mergers may also enable unions to expand the coverage of their membership by unionizing industries and occupations previously underrepresented in union membership.

Distribution of membership. Historically, membership has been concentrated in a small number of large unions. In 1976, 16 unions represented 60 percent of union membership, and 85 unions represented just 2.4 percent. Similarly, the National Education Association accounted for 62 percent of all association members. Many employee associations are small because they are state organizations; therefore, their membership potential is limited.

Unions today are exhibiting a substantial and increasing amount of diversification of membership. For example, in 1958, at least four-fifths of union members in 73 percent of the unions embraced a single industry; this figure dropped to 55 percent by 1976. The most pronounced diversification has occurred in manufacturing. For example, of the 29 unions that represent workers in chemicals and allied products, 26 currently have less than 20 percent of their membership in a single industry.[21] With this understanding of union history and member characteristics, we can now examine the structure of unionization.

Structure of Unionization in the United States

The basic unit of labor unions in the U.S. is the national union (or international union), a body that organizes, charters, and controls member union locals. The national union develops the general policies and procedures by which locals operate and provides assistance to the locals in areas such as collective bargaining. National unions provide clout for the locals because they control a large number of employees and can influence large organizations through national strikes or slowdown activities.[22]

The major umbrella organization for national unions is the American Federation of Labor and Congress of Industrial Organizations **(AFL-CIO).** It represents about 85 percent of the total union membership and contains 90 national unions. The AFL-CIO is an important and powerful body.

Every two years the AFL-CIO holds a convention to develop policy and amend its constitution. Each national union is represented in proportion to its membership. Between conventions, an executive council (the governing body) and a general board direct the organization's affairs; a president is in charge of day-to-day operations.

The executive council's activities include evaluating legislation that affects labor and watching for corruption within the AFL-CIO. Standing committees are appointed to deal with executive, legislative, political, educational, organizing, and other activities. The department of organization and field services, for instance, focuses its attention on organizing activities. Outside of headquarters, three structures exist to organize the local unions. Many of the craft unions are organized into the trade department and the industrial department, which represent them in the national union. The remaining locals are organized directly as part of the national unions; they are affiliated with headquarters but retain independence in dealing with their own union matters.

Sixty-two national unions, representing 4.5 million workers, operate independently of the AFL-CIO. Although this separation is not considered desirable by the AFL-CIO, its impact has been diminished substantially since the Teamsters reaffiliated with the AFL-CIO in 1987.

At the heart of the labor movement are the 70,000 or so local unions, varying in size up to 40,000 members. The locals represent the workers at the workplace, where much of the day-to-day contact with management and the human resource department takes place. Most locals elect a president, a secretary-treasurer, and perhaps one or two other officers from the membership. In the larger locals, a business representative is hired as a full-time employee to handle grievances and contract negotiation. The other important member of the union local is the **steward,** an employee elected by his or her work unit to act as the union representative at the workplace and to respond to company actions against employees that may violate the labor agreement. The steward protects the rights of the worker by filing grievances when the employer has acted improperly.

Operations of Unions

Activities of union locals revolve around collective bargaining and handling grievances. In addition, locals hold general meetings, publish newsletters, and otherwise keep their members informed. Typically, however, the membership is apathetic about union involvement. Unless a serious problem exists, attendance at meetings is usually low, and even the election of officers often draws votes from less than one-fourth of the membership.[23]

At headquarters, the AFL-CIO staff and committees work on a wide range of issues, including civil rights, community service, economic policy, education, ethical practices, housing, international affairs, legislation, public relations, research, safety, Social Security, and veterans' affairs. A publications department also produces various literature for the membership and outsiders. National union headquarters also provides specialized services to regional and local bodies. People trained in organizing, strikes, legal matters, public relations, and negotiations are available to individual unions.

National unions and the AFL-CIO are also active in the political arena. Labor maintains a strong lobbying force in Washington, D.C., and is involved in political action committees at the state and local government level. A recent development has been the international political activities of some of the large national unions. For example, the United Auto Workers held discussions with Japanese car manufacturers concerning the level of imports into the U.S. and the construction of assembly plants here. They have also lobbied in Washington to restrict car imports in an attempt to bolster U.S. automakers and to increase jobs. Thus, to help their membership, unions are expanding their activities on all levels and, in some cases, working with other organizations to attain mutual goals.

THE ORGANIZING CAMPAIGN

One of the major functions of the National Labor Relations Board (NLRB) is to conduct the election of unions to represent nongovernment employees. This is accomplished through a certification election to determine if the majority of employees want the union. Under U.S. labor law, the union certified to represent a group of employees has sole and exclusive right to bargain for that group.

> The process by which a single union is selected to represent all employees in a particular unit is crucial to the American system of collective bargaining. If a majority of those voting opt for union representation, all employees are bound by that choice and the employer is obligated to recognize and bargain with the chosen union.[24]

Because unions may thereby acquire significant power, employers may be anxious to keep them out. Adding to this potential union-management conflict is the possibility of competition and conflict between unions if more than one union is attempting to win certification as the representative of a group of employees.

Several stages in the certification process can be identified: (1) a campaign to solicit employee support for union representation; (2) the determination of the appropriate group the union will represent; (3) the preelection campaign by unions and employers; (4) the election itself; and (5) the certification of a union.[25] These steps are outlined in exhibit 17.3. The next stage of the organizing process—negotiation of a collective bargaining agreement—is discussed in the next section of this chapter.

Exhibit 17.3
Certification Process

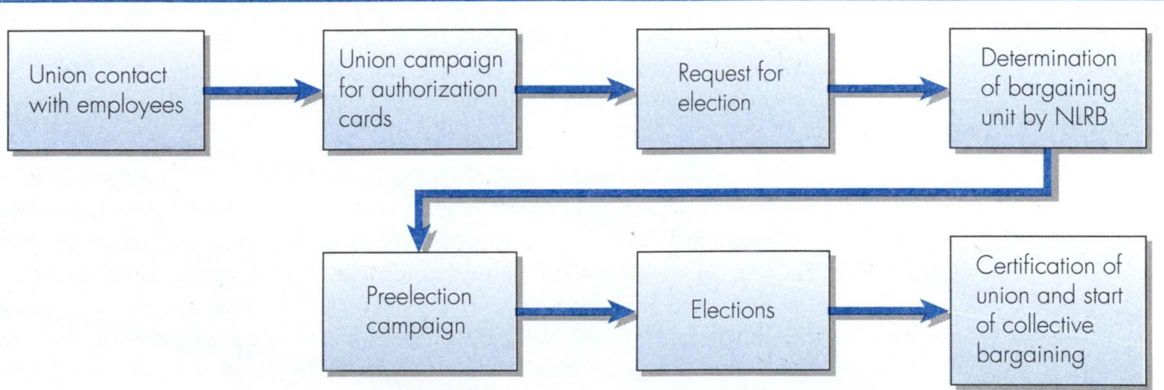

SOURCE: William D. Todor, Ohio State University.

Campaign to Solicit Employee Support

In the campaign to solicit employee support, unions generally attempt to contact the employees, obtain a sufficient number of authorization cards, and request an election from the NLRB.[26]

Establishing contact between the union and employees. Contact between the union and employees can be initiated by either party. National unions usually contact employees in industries or occupations in which they have an interest or are traditionally involved. The United Auto Workers, for example, would be likely to contact nonunion employees in automobile plants, as they have done for the new plants that have been built in the South. Another prominent example of union initiative was the attempt of two competing unions—the United Farm Workers and the Teamsters—to organize the agricultural workers in California. Often these unions were aggressive, even violent, during their campaigns for worker support. One consequence of their precertification activities, which included national boycotts of grapes and lettuce, was the California Agricultural Relations Act of 1975, which regulates union-management relations in the agriculture industry.

In many cases the union is approached by employees interested in union representation, and the union is usually happy to oblige. Employees may have strong reasons for desiring this affiliation—low pay, poor working conditions, and other factors relating to dissatisfaction. Because workers generally tend to be apathetic toward unions, however, their concern must become quite serious before they will take any action. At this point the company must be careful and must avoid committing unfair labor practices. Accordingly, **employers should not**

- Misrepresent the facts: Any information management provides about a union or its officers must be factual and truthful.
- Threaten employees: It is unlawful to threaten employees with loss of their jobs or transfers to less desirable positions, income reductions, or loss or reduction of benefits and privileges. Use of intimidating language to dissuade employees from joining or supporting a union also is forbidden. In addition, supervisors may not blacklist, lay off, discipline, or discharge any employee because of union activity.
- Promise benefits or rewards: Supervisors may not promise a pay raise, additional overtime or time off, promotions, or other favorable considerations in exchange for an employee's agreement to refrain from joining a union or signing a union card, vote against union representation, or otherwise oppose union activity.

Nor can the union promise benefits/rewards. It would be illegal for the local to bribe workers by offering to waive normal initiation fees for those who signed an authorization card prior to the election or to predict adverse consequences such as the loss of one's job for failure to join the union now (*NLRB v. Savair Mfg. Co.,* 1983). Free membership can be used as an organizing incentive so long as it extends to everyone who becomes a member up to the time that the first collective agreement is executed. Similarly, it is permissible to reimburse people for lost wages and out-of-pocket expenses incurred while participating in a campaign rally or being at an NLRB hearing. Attendance door prizes also are acceptable provided their value is not excessive.

The list of unfair labor practices management should avoid continues; **employers should not**

- Make unscheduled changes in wages, hours, benefits, or working conditions: Any such changes are unlawful unless the employer can prove they were initiated before union activity began.
- Conduct surveillance activities: Management is forbidden to spy on or request anti-union workers to spy on employees' union activities, or to make any statements that give workers the impression they are being watched. Supervisors also may not attend union meetings or question employees about a union's internal affairs. They also may not ask employees for their opinions of a union or its officers.
- Interrogate workers: Managers may not require employees to tell them who has signed a union card, voted for union representation, attended a union meeting, or instigated an organization drive.
- Prohibit solicitation: Employees have the right to solicit members on company property during their nonworking hours, provided this activity does not interfere with work being performed, and to distribute union literature in nonwork areas during their free time.[27]

Employers can, however,

- Discuss the history of unions and make factual statements about strikes, violence, or the loss of jobs at plants that have unionized.
- Discuss their own experiences with unions.
- Advise workers about the costs of joining and belonging to unions.
- Remind employees of the company benefits and wages they receive without having to pay union dues.
- Explain that union representation will not protect workers against discharge for cause.
- Point out that the company prefers to deal directly with employees, and not through a third party, in settling complaints about wages, hours, and other employment conditions.
- Tell workers that, in negotiating with the union, the company is not obligated to sign a contract or accept all the union's demands, especially those that aren't in its economic interests.
- Advise employees that unions often resort to work stoppages to press their demands and that such tactics can cost workers money.
- Inform employees of the company's legal right to hire replacements for workers who go out on strike for economic reasons.[28]

In regard to the employee's role in union solicitation, the interaction of two factors—type of communicator and format of the message—will dictate how much authority employers have to regulate the flow of pro-union communication on their premises. There are three categories of communicators: on-duty employees, off-duty employees, and nonemployees (union organizers). Workers are considered on-duty within the confines of their scheduled hours including breaks, lunch periods, and "free time" when they are physically present but not actively working. Off-duty employees are those who arrive well before or remain long after their slated work periods, as when individuals from one shift show up and attempt to interact with those who are working another shift.

On-duty employees do have the broadest set of communication rights. Employers can restrict the time, but not the place, of solicitation that is initiated by this group. They can restrict both time and place for *distributions* by on-duty employees. However, "place" in this instance refers to work areas *within the physical plant.* On-duty employees can be limited to handing out items in the cafeteria, locker room, hallways, or on the exterior grounds. Once workers go off-duty, "place" potentially includes being barred from the building entirely. The only exception here would be if employees were permitted back inside for any other reason once the workday has ended. Absent this, their only recourse for solicitation and distribution is the parking lot and exterior grounds.

Authorization cards and the request for elections. Once contact has been made, the union begins the campaign to collect sufficient **authorization cards,** or signatures of employees interested in having union representation. This campaign must be carried out within the constraints set by law. If the union obtains cards from thirty percent of an organization's employees, it can petition the National Labor Relations Board for an election. (Procedures in the public sector are similar.) If the NLRB determines there is indeed sufficient interest, it will schedule an election. If the union gets more than fifty percent of the employees to sign authorization cards, it may petition the employer as the bargaining representative. Usually employers refuse, whereupon the union petitions the NLRB for an election.

The employer usually resists the union's card-signing campaign. For instance, companies often prohibit solicitation on the premises.

Nevertheless, union organizers may earn the right to enter the property and even the building if (1) no other reasonable alternatives for contact exist or (2) the employer regularly permits representatives from other organizations to meet with the work force on the premises.

Employers are legally constrained from interfering with an employee's freedom of choice. However, union representatives have argued that employers ignore this law because the consequences are minimal—and, by doing so, employers can effectively discourage unionism.

During the union campaign and election process, it is important that the human resource manager caution the company against engaging in unfair labor practices. Unfair labor practices, when identified, generally cause the election to be set aside. Severe violations by the employer can result in certification of the union as the bargaining representative, even if it has lost the election. The local still must prove that a majority of the intended union supported it prior to the company's outrageous and pervasive violations. Since authorization cards are a common means of establishing this, one must know which type of card was originally signed. Single-purpose cards indicate that the person is authorizing the union to be his/her representative for collective bargaining outright. Dual-purpose cards express backing for an election and for bargaining. Single-purpose authorization cards have been accepted as evidence of majority status for bargaining orders; dual-purpose cards have not.

Determination of the Bargaining Unit

When the union has gathered sufficient signatures to petition for an election, the NLRB will make a determination of the **bargaining unit,** the group of employees that will be represented by the union. This is a crucial process, for it can determine the quality of labor-management relations in the future.

> At the heart of labor-management relations is the bargaining unit. It is all important that the bargaining unit be truly appropriate and not contain a mix of antagonistic interests or submerge the legitimate interests of a small group of employees in the interest of a larger group.[29]

In order to assure the fullest freedom of collective bargaining, legal constraints and guidelines exist for the unit. Professional and nonprofessional groups cannot be included in the same unit, and a craft unit cannot be placed in a larger unit unless both the professional and the craft units agree to it. Physical location, skill levels, degree of ownership, collective bargaining history, and extent of organization of employees are also considered.

From the union's perspective, the most desirable bargaining unit is one whose members are pro-union and will help win certification. The unit must also have sufficient influence in the organization to give the union some power once it wins representation. Employers generally want a bargaining unit that is least beneficial to the union; this will help maximize the likelihood of failure in the election and minimize the power of the unit.[30]

Pre-Election Campaign

After the bargaining unit has been determined, both union and employer embark on a pre-election campaign. Unions claim to provide a strong voice for employees, emphasizing improvement in wages and working conditions and the establishment of a grievance process to ensure fairness. Employers emphasize the costs of unionization—union dues, strikes, and loss of jobs.

The impact of pre-election campaigns is not clear. A study of thirty-one elections showed very little change in attitude and voting propensity after the campaign. People who will vote for or against a union before the election campaign generally vote the same way after. Severe violations of the legal constraints on behavior, such as using threats or coercion, are prevented by the NLRB, which watches the pre-election activity carefully.

Election, Certification and Decertification

Generally, elections are associated with the process of determining if the union will win the right to represent workers. Elections can also determine if the union will continue to have the right to represent a group of employees.

Election and certification. The NLRB conducts the certification election. If a majority votes for union representation, the union will be certified. If the union does not get a majority, another election will not be held for at least a year. In 1980, the NLRB held 7,200 elections in which 478,000 employees were eligible to vote. By contrast, in 1991 there were only 3,021 elections representing 183,987 employees. Generally, about one-third to one-half of the elections certify a union, with less union success in larger organizations. Once a union has been certified, the employer is required to bargain with that union.[31]

The success rate of union campaigns and the number of elections held is critical to the survival and growth of the union movement. On a national scale, however, union success in elections has declined dramatically. One notable reason for this decline are management's efforts to make unions less attractive.

Decertification elections. The NLRB also conducts decertification elections that can remove a union from representation. If thirty percent or more of the employees request such an election, it will be held. These decertification elections most frequently occur in the first year of a union's representation, when the union is negotiating its first contract. Union strength has not yet been established, and employees are readily discouraged about union behavior.

THE COLLECTIVE BARGAINING PROCESS

Collective bargaining is a complex process in which union and management negotiators maneuver to win the most advantageous contract. How the issues involved are settled depends on the following:

- Quality of the union-management relationship
- Processes of bargaining used by labor and management
- Management's strategies in the collective bargaining process
- Union's strategies in the collective bargaining process
- Joint union-management strategies

These critical determinants of the collective bargaining process are described in detail prior to the description of the negotiation process.

Union-Management Relationships

An understanding of union-management relationships is facilitated by seeing them within a labor relations system. The labor relations system is composed of three subunits—employees, management, and the union—with the government influencing the interaction among the three. Employees may be managers or union members, and some of the union members are part of the union management system (local union leaders). Each of the three interrelationships in the model is regulated by specific federal statutes: union and management by the National Labor Relations Act; management and employees by the National Labor Relations Act, Title VII of the Civil Rights Act of 1964, the Civil Rights Act of 1991, and the Americans with Disabilities Act of 1990; and union and employees by the Labor-Management Reporting and Disclosure Act, Title VII of the Civil Rights Act of 1964, and the Civil Rights Act of 1991.[32]

Each of the groups in the labor relations model has different goals. Workers are interested in improved working conditions, wages, and opportunities. Unions are interested in these as well as their own survival, growth, and acquisition of power, which depend on their ability to maintain the support of the employees by providing for their needs. Management has overall organizational goals (such as profit, market share, and growth) and also seeks to preserve managerial prerogatives to direct the work force and to attain the personal goals of the managers (promotion or achievement). Government is interested in a stable and healthy economy, protection of individual rights, and safety and fairness in the workplace.

Adversarial system. These goals were often seen as incompatible in most cases. Thus, an adversarial system emerged, with labor and management attempting to get a bigger cut of the pie while government oversaw its own interest. In an adversarial system of union-management relations, the union's role is to gain concessions from management during collective bargaining and to preserve those concessions through the grievance procedure. The union is an outsider and critic.[33]

Historically, unions have adopted an adversarial role in their interactions with management. Their focus has been on wages, hours, and working conditions as they attempted to get "more and better" from management. This approach works well in economic boom times but encounters difficulties when the economy is not healthy. High unemployment and the threat of continued job losses have recently induced unions to expand their role, especially since many of their traditional goals—better pay, hours, and working conditions—have already been achieved. Many unions have begun to enter into new, collaborative efforts with employers. The result of this can be described as a cooperative relationship.

Cooperative system. In a cooperative system, the union's role is that of a partner, not a critic, and the union is jointly responsible with management for reaching a cooperative solution. Thus, a cooperative system requires that union and management engage in problem solving, information sharing, and integration of outcomes.[34] Cooperative systems have not been a major component of labor relations in the U.S. Other countries—Sweden and Germany, for example—have built cooperative mechanisms into their labor systems.

Increasingly, U.S. management and labor are working together cooperatively. Management recognizes that most organization improvement programs they undertake need the acceptance of the union to be successful. Active involvement of the union is one of the best ways to gain this acceptance.[35]

An example of what this cooperation can bring is the worker participation and involvement project at Ford Motor's plant in Edison, New Jersey.

> The innovation at Edison—other Ford plants are installing the same concept—is only the most visible symbol of a near-revolution in labor-management relations that started five years ago and has since become entrenched. Ford and the United Auto Workers have established what may be the most extensive and successful worker participation process in a major, unionized company. Thousands of teams of workers and supervisors at eighty-six of Ford's ninety-one plants and depots meet weekly to deal with production, quality, and work-environment problems.[36]

As we discussed in chapter 13, teamwork is a critical component of efforts of firms to improve quality. Unions and firms such as Ford Motor and General Motors are recognizing how important quality is to survival. Consequently, they are working cooperatively to ensure that teamwork programs succeed. Of course, not all unions or firms are in favor of these "workplace reforms."[37]

In all fairness, it should be noted how difficult the transition from an adversarial to a cooperative relationship is for most unions as well as firms. The recent decision General Motors made to continue its Arlington, Texas plant and close its Willow Run, Michigan plant also illustrated that unions also may have their hands full dealing with locals that experiment more than the parent organization wants them to. For example, Stephen Yokich, a UAW vice president, assailed the union local at Arlington for its willingness to adjust its work schedule.[38]

Processes of Bargaining

The most widely used description of bargaining identifies five types of processes in contract negotiations: distributive bargaining, integrative bargaining, concessionary bargaining, continuous bargaining, and intraorganizational bargaining.

Distributive bargaining. Distributive bargaining takes place when the parties are in conflict over the issue, and the outcome represents a gain for one party and a loss for the other. Each party tries to negotiate for the best possible outcome. The process is outlined in exhibit 17.4.

On any particular issue, union and management negotiators each have three identifiable positions. The union has an **initial demand point,** which is generally more than it expects to get; a **target point,** which is its realistic assessment of what it may be able to get; and a **resistance point,** or the lowest acceptable level for the issue. Management has three similar points: an **initial offer,** which is usually lower than the expected settlement; a **target point,** at which it would like to reach agreement; and a **resistance point,** or its upper acceptable limit. If, as shown in exhibit 17.4, management's resistance point is greater than the union's, a **positive settlement range** exists where negotiation can take place.

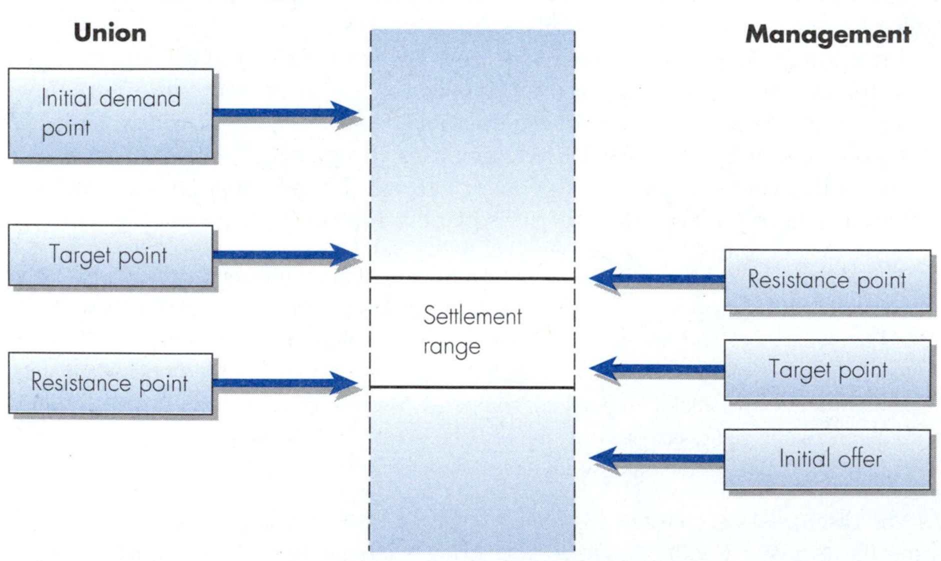

Exhibit 17.4
Negotiating Process

SOURCE: Adapted from R. Walton and R. B. McKersie, *A Behavioral Theory of Labor Negotiations* (New York: McGraw-Hill Book Company, 1965), 43.

The exact agreement within this range depends on the bargaining behavior of the negotiators. If, however, management's resistance point is below the union's, there is no common ground for negotiation. In such a situation, a **negative settlement range,** or bargaining impasse, exists.[39]

Using wages as an example, the union may have a resistance point of $8.40 per hour, a target of $8.60, and an initial demand point of $8.75. Management may offer $8.20 but have a target of $8.45 and a resistance point of $8.55. The positive settlement range is between $8.40 and $8.55, and this is where the settlement will likely be. However, only the initial wage demand and offer are made public at the beginning of negotiations.

Because many issues are involved in a bargaining session, the process becomes much more complicated. Although each issue may be described by the above model, in actual negotiations an interaction occurs among issues. Union concessions on one issue may be traded for management concessions on another. Thus, the total process is dynamic.

The ritual of the distributive bargaining process is well established, and deviations are often met with suspicion. the following story illustrates this point.

> A labor lawyer tells the story of a young executive who had just taken over the helm of a company. Imbued with idealism, he wanted to end the bickering he had seen take place during past negotiations with labor. To do this, he was ready to give workers as much as his company could afford. Consequently he asked some members of his staff to study his firm's own wage structure and decide how it compared with other companies, as well as a host of other related matters. He approached the collective bargaining table with a halo of goodness surrounding him. Asking for the floor, he proceeded to describe what he had done with a big smile on his face and made the offer.
>
> Throughout his entire presentation, the union officials stared at him in amazement. He had offered more than they had expected to secure. But no matter, as soon as he finished, they proceeded to lambaste him, denouncing him for trying to destroy collective bargaining and for attempting to buy off labor. They announced that they would not stand for any such unethical maneuvering, and immediately asked for 5 cents more than the idealistic executive had offered.[40]

Integrative bargaining. When there is more than one issue to be resolved, the potential exists to make trade-offs between the issues or to pursue integrative agreements. Integrative bargaining focuses on creative solutions to conflicts that reconcile (integrate) the parties' interests and yield high joint benefit. It can occur only when negotiators have an "expanding" pie perception—that is, when the two parties (union and management) value particular issues differently.[41]

Concessionary bargaining. While distributive and integrative bargaining represent the primary approaches to bargaining, concessionary bargaining often occurs within these two frameworks. Concessionary bargaining may be prompted by severe economic conditions faced by employers. Seeking to survive and prosper, employers seek givebacks or concessions from the unions, giving promises of job security in return. During the past few years, this type of bargaining has been particularly prevalent, especially in the smokestack industries, such as automobiles, steel, and rubber, and to some extent in the transportation industry. In these industries, concessions sought by management from the unions include wage freezes, wage reductions, change in or elimination of work rules, fringe-benefit reductions, delay or elimination of COLAs, and more hours of work for the same pay. Two-tier wage systems were tried in some industries, but problems of inequity and lower worker morale offset much of the savings from lower labor costs.[42] In addition, available evidence suggests that these agreements erode union solidarity, leadership credibility, and control, as well as union power and effectiveness.

Continuous bargaining. As affirmative action, safety and health requirements, and other government regulations continue to complicate the situation for both unions and employers, and as the rate of change in the environment continues to increase, some labor and management negotiators are turning to continuous bargaining. A joint committee meets on a regular basis to explore issues and solve problems of common interest. These committees have appeared in the retail food, over-the-road trucking, nuclear power, and men's garment industries.[43]

Several characteristics of continuous bargaining have been identified:

- Frequent meetings during the life of the contract
- Focus on external events and problem areas rather than on internal problems
- Use of outside experts in decision making
- Use of a problem-solving (integrative) approach[44]

The intention is to develop a union-management structure that is capable of adapting positively and productively to sudden changes in the environment. This continuous bargaining approach is different from, but an extension of, the emergency negotiations that unions have insisted on when inflation or other factors have substantially changed the acceptability of the existing agreement. Continuous bargaining is a permanent arrangement intended to help avoid the crises that often occur under traditional collective bargaining systems.

Although the selection and utilization of a bargaining strategy is important in determining the outcomes of collective bargaining, so, too, is the actual process of negotiation, or negotiating the agreement.

Intraorganizational bargaining. During negotiations, the bargaining teams from both sides may have to engage in intraorganizational bargaining—that is, conferring with their constituents over changes in bargaining positions. Management negotiators may have to convince management to change its position on an issue—for instance, to agree to a higher wage settlement. Union negotiators must eventually convince their members to accept the negotiated contract, so they must be sensitive to the demands of the membership as well as realistic. When the membership votes on the proposed package, it will be strongly influenced by the opinions of the union negotiators.

NEGOTIATING THE AGREEMENT

Once a union is certified as the representative of a bargaining unit, it becomes the only party that can negotiate an agreement with the employer for all members of that work unit, whether they are union members or not. Technically, however, individuals within the unit can still negotiate personal deals with the employer that convey *more* than the collective agreement awards to the unit, e.g., a highly skilled person strikes a deal to get paid higher than the wage rate lists for his job classification (*J. I. Case Co. v. NLRB,* 1944).

The union holds an important and potent position and serves as a critical link between employees and employer. The union is responsible to its members to negotiate for what they want, and it has the duty to represent all employees fairly. The quality of its bargaining is an important measure of union effectiveness.

Negotiating Committees

The employer and the union select their own representatives for the **negotiating committee.** Neither party is required to consider the wishes of the other. Management negotiators, for example, cannot refuse to bargain with representatives of the union because they dislike them or do not think they are appropriate.

Union negotiating teams typically include representatives of the union local—often the president and other executive staff members. In addition, the national union may send a negotiating specialist, who is likely to be a labor lawyer, to work with the team. The negotiators selected by the union do not have to be members of the union or employees of the company. The general goal is to balance bargaining skill and experience with knowledge and information about the specific situation.

At the local level, when a single bargaining unit is negotiating a contract, the company is usually represented by the manager and members of the labor relations or human resource staff. Finance and production managers may also be involved. When the negotiations are critical, either because the bargaining unit is large or because the effect on the company is great, specialists such as labor lawyers may be included on the team.

In national negotiations, top industrial-relations or human resource executives frequently head a team of specialists from corporate headquarters and perhaps managers from critical divisions or plants within the company. Again, the goal is to have expertise along with specific knowledge about critical situations.

The Negotiating Structure

Most contracts are negotiated by a single union and a single employer. In some situations, however, different arrangements can be agreed on. When a single union negotiates with several similar companies—for instance, firms in the construction industry or supermarkets—the employers may bargain as a group with the union. At the local level this is called **multiemployer bargaining,** but at the national level it is referred to as **industrywide bargaining.** Industrywide bargaining occurs in the railroad, coal, wallpaper, and men's suits industries. National negotiations result in contracts that settle major issues, such as compensation, whereas issues relating to working conditions are settled locally. This split bargaining style is common in Great Britain and has been used in the auto industry in the U.S. When several unions bargain jointly with a single employer, they engage in **coordinated bargaining.** Although not so common as the others, coordinated bargaining appears to be increasing, especially in the public sector.

One consequence of coordinated and industrywide bargaining is often **pattern settlements,** where similar wage rates are imposed on the companies whose employees are represented by the same union within a given industry. Pattern settlements can be detrimental because they ignore differences in the employers' economic condition and ability to pay. The result can be settlements that are tolerable for some companies but cause severe economic trouble for others. As a partial consequence of this, such pattern settlements have become less common.

A negotiating structure that exists in the contract construction industry is wide-area and multicraft bargaining. This bargaining structure arose in response to the need for unionized employers to be more price competitive and have fewer strikes and in response to the desire by construction trade unions to gain more control at the national level. Consequently, the bargaining is done on a regional (geographic) rather than a local basis. In addition, it covers several construction crafts simultaneously instead of one. The common contract negotiations resulting from **wide-area** and **multicraft bargaining** help lessen the opportunity for unions to whipsaw the employer. This technique uses one contract settlement as a precedent for the next, which then forces the employer to get all contracts settled in order to have all the employees working. As a result of **whipsawing,** an employer frequently agrees to more favorable settlements on all contracts, regardless of the conditions and merits of each one, just to get all employees back to work.[45]

Preparation for Bargaining

Prior to the bargaining session, management and union negotiators need to develop the strategies and proposals they will use.

Management strategies. In preparing for negotiations with the union, management needs to prepare in four different areas.

1. Preparation of specific proposals for changes in contract language
2. Determination of the general size of the economic package that the company anticipates offering during the negotiations
3. Preparation of statistical displays and supportive data that the company will use during negotiations
4. Preparation of a bargaining book for the use of company negotiators. This is a compilation of information on issues that will be discussed, giving an analysis of the effect of each clause, its use in other companies, and other facts[46]

An important part of this preparation is calculation of the cost of various bargaining issues or demands. The relative cost of pension contributions, pay increases, health benefits, and other provisions should be determined prior to negotiations. Other costs should also be considered. For instance, what is the cost to management—in its ability to do its job—of union demands for changes in grievance and discipline procedures or transfer and promotion provisions? The goal is to be as well-prepared as possible by considering the implications and ramifications of the issues that will be discussed and by being able to present a strong argument for the position management takes.

Union strategies. Like management, unions need to prepare for negotiations by collecting information. Because collective bargaining is the major means by which a union can convince its members that it is effective and valuable, this is a critical activity.

Unions collect information in at least these areas:

1. The financial situation of the company and its ability to pay
2. The attitude of management toward various issues, as reflected in past negotiations or inferred from negotiations in similar companies
3. The attitudes and desires of the employees

The first two areas give the union an idea of what demands management is likely to accept. The third area is important but it is sometimes overlooked. The union should be aware of the preferences of the membership. For instance, is a pension increase preferred over increased vacation or holiday benefits? The preferences will vary with the characteristics of the workers. Younger workers are more likely to prefer more holidays, shorter work weeks, and limited overtime, whereas older workers are more interested in pension plans, benefits, and overtime. The union can determine these preferences by using a questionnaire to survey its members.

Unions also gather information from parties outside the immediate environment. Locals often receive input from their parent internationals concerning the settlement patterns of other locals. The international may pressure a local to advance the larger aims of the union, even if those matters are not central to a particular office or plant. Interunion rivalries may serve as a catalyst for demands as well. Whether one labels it "orbits of coercive comparison" or "keeping up with the Joneses," gains achieved by one union challenge others to attain comparable or superior outcomes. The steelworkers will be very cognizant of the most recent advances that were obtained by the auto workers, who in turn may monitor what the Teamsters have won, and so on. Failure to keep stride may seriously diminish the stature of a local president or business agent, despite vast economic differences between industries.

Issues for Negotiation

The issues that can be discussed in collective bargaining sessions are specified by the Labor-Management Relations Act. This act has established three categories: mandatory issues, permissive issues, and prohibited issues.[47]

Employers and employee representatives (unions) are obligated to meet and discuss "wages, hours, and other terms and conditions of employment." These are the **mandatory issues.** These critical factors in the bargaining process include the issues that may affect management's ability to run the company efficiently or may clash with the union's desire to protect jobs and workers' standing in their jobs. Historically, the specific topics that fall into this category have been the subject of debate. The U.S. Supreme Court's decision in *Borg Warner Corporation v. NLRB* (1982) suggests that the distinction between mandatory and permissive bargaining issues is based on whether or not the topic regulates the relations between the employer and its employees. Any issue that changes the nature of the job itself or compensation for work must be discussed in collective bargaining. Mandatory issues, therefore, include subcontracting work, safety, changes of operations, and other actions management might take that will have an impact on employees' jobs, wages, and economic supplements. With the

Supreme Court decision in the *First National Maintenance* case in 1981, management's obligation to bargain over plant closings has been substantially reduced. In addition, NLRB's recent ruling has reduced management's obligation to bargain over plant relocations (*NLRB* v. *Dubuque Packing Company,* 1991).

Permissive issues are those that are neither mandatory nor illegal. They are issues not specifically related to the nature of the job but still of concern to both parties. For example, issues of price, product design, and decisions about new jobs may be subject to bargaining if the parties agree to it. Permissive issues usually develop when both parties see that mutual discussion and agreement will be beneficial, which may be more likely when a cooperative relationship exists between union and management. Management and union negotiators cannot refuse to agree on a contract if they fail to settle a permissive issue.[48]

Prohibited issues are those concerning illegal or outlawed activities, such as the demand that an employer use only union-produced goods or, where it is illegal, that it employ only union members. Such issues may not be discussed in collective bargaining sessions.

Although the actual issues for negotiation can be expected to vary in different instances of union-management bargaining, it is likely that the issues for negotiation are far more extensive than those brought out during the initial organizing campaign. In contrast to organizing, where the critical issues are grievances, economics, job security, and supervision, a multitude of mandatory issues exist for negotiation, not to mention the permissive issues.

Direct compensation. Wage conflicts are the leading cause of strikes. Difficulties arise here because a wage increase is a direct cost to the employer, as is a wage decrease to the employee. As discussed in chapters 9 and 10, rates of pay are influenced by a variety of factors including the going rate in an industry, the employer's ability to pay, the cost of living, and productivity. All of these are subjects often debated and discussed in negotiations.

Fringe benefits. Because the cost of fringe benefits now runs as high as forty-five percent of the total cost of wages, they are a major concern in collective bargaining. Benefit provisions are very difficult to remove once they are in place, so management tends to be cautious about agreeing to them. Still, some of the most commonly negotiated fringe benefits are:

- *Pensions.* Once management has decided to provide a pension plan, the conditions of the plan must be determined (when the benefits will be available, how much will be paid, and whether they become available according to age or years of service). Finally, the organization must decide how long employees must work for the company to receive minimum benefits (vesting) and whether the organization will pay the whole cost or whether the employees or the union will be asked to help.

- *Paid vacations.* Most agreements provide for paid vacations. Length of vacation is usually determined by length of service, up to some maximum. The conditions that qualify an individual for a vacation in a given year are also specified. Agreements occasionally specify how the timing of vacations will be determined.

- *Paid holidays.* Most agreements provide time off with pay on Independence Day, Labor Day, Thanksgiving, Christmas, New Year's Day, and Memorial Day. Several others may also be included.

- *Sick leave.* Unpaid sick leave allows the employee to take time off for sickness without compensation. Paid sick leave is usually accumulated while working. Typically one-half to one and one-half days of paid sick leave are credited for each month of work.
- *Health and life insurance.* The employer may be required to pay some or all of the costs of health and life insurance plans.
- *Dismissal or severance pay.* Occasionally employers agree to pay any employee who is dismissed or laid off because of technological changes or business difficulties.
- *Supplemental unemployment benefits.* In the mid-1950s, the United Auto Workers negotiated a plan to supplement state unemployment benefits and to make up the difference when these state benefits expired. Most contracts with this provision are found in the auto and steel industries, where layoffs are common, but workers in other industries are beginning to negotiate them as well.

Hours of employment. Finally, while organizations are required to pay overtime for work in excess of forty hours, unions continually try to reduce the number of hours worked each week. Negotiations focus on including lunch hours in the eight-hour-day requirement. Additionally, negotiations may focus on providing overtime after any eight-hour shift, rather than after forty hours.

Institutional issues. Some issues are not directly related to jobs but are nevertheless important to both employees and management. **Institutional issues** that affect the security and success of both parties include the following:

- *Union security.* About sixty-three percent of the major labor contracts stipulate that employees must join the union after being hired into its bargaining unit. However, twenty states that traditionally have had low levels of unionization have passed "right-to-work" laws outlawing union membership as a condition of employment.
- *Checkoff.* Unions have attempted to arrange for payment of dues through deduction from employees' paychecks. By law, employees must agree to dues checkoff in writing. About eighty-six percent of union contracts contain this provision.
- *Strikes.* The employer may insist that the union agree not to strike during the life of the agreement, typically when a cost-of-living clause has been included. The agreement may be unconditional, allowing no strikes at all, or it may limit strikes to specific circumstances.
- *Managerial prerogatives.* More than half the agreements today stipulate that certain activities are the right of management. In addition, management in most companies argues that it has "residual rights"—that all rights not specifically limited by the agreement belong to management.

Administrative issues. The last category of issues is concerned with the treatment of employees at work. Administrative issues include the following:

- *Breaks and cleanup time.* Some contracts specify the time and length of coffee breaks and meal breaks for employees. In addition, jobs requiring cleanup may have a portion of the work period set aside for this procedure.

- *Job security*. This is perhaps the issue of most concern to employees and unions. Employers are concerned with restriction of their ability to lay off employees. Changes in technology or attempts to subcontract work are issues that impinge on job security. A typical union response to technological change was the reaction of the International Longshoremen's Association in the late 1960s to the introduction of containerized shipping. The union operated exclusive hiring halls, developed complex work rules, and negotiated a guaranteed annual income for its members. Job security continues to be a primary issue for longshoremen, telephone workers, and most other blue-collar occupations.
- *Seniority*. Length of service is used as a criterion for many personnel decisions in most collective agreements. Layoffs are usually determined by seniority. "Last hired, first fired" is a common situation. Seniority is also important in transfer and promotion decisions. The method of calculating seniority is usually specified to clarify the relative seniority of employees.
- *Discharge and discipline*. This is a touchy issue and, even when an agreement addresses these problems, many grievances are filed concerning the way employees are disciplined or discharged.
- *Safety and health*. Although the Occupational Safety and Health Act specifically deals with worker safety and health, some contracts have provisions specifying that the company will provide safety equipment, first aid, physical examinations, accident investigations, and safety committees. Hazardous work may be covered by special provisions and pay rates. Often the agreement will contain a general statement that the employer is responsible for the safety of the workers, so the union can use the grievance process when any safety issues arise.
- *Production standards*. The level of productivity or performance of employees is a concern of both management and the union. Management is concerned with efficiency, but the union is concerned with the fairness and reasonableness of management's demands.
- *Grievance procedures*. This is a significant part of collective bargaining and is discussed in more detail later in this chapter.
- *Training*. The design and administration of training and development programs and the procedure for selecting employees for training may also be bargaining issues.
- *Duration of the agreement*. Agreements can last for one year or longer, with the most common period being three years.

Partly because there are so many issues over which to bargain, agreement and contract settlements are not always attained without conflict. When this occurs, forms of conflict resolution are utilized.

Factors Affecting Bargaining

The preceding discussion suggests that negotiations proceed in a rational manner and end in resolution when a **positive contract zone**—a set of outcomes that is preferred over the imposition of a strike—exists. Unfortunately, negotiators often fail to reach agreement, even when a positive contract zone exists.

Why? To fully understand the negotiation process, it is important to examine the decision processes of negotiators. If the biases of negotiators can be identified, then prescriptive approaches and training programs can be developed to improve negotiations. Discussed below are common cognitive limitations to negotiator judgments.[49]

Mythical fixed pie. All too frequently, negotiators believe that their interests automatically conflict with the other party's interests. In other words, what one side wins, the other side loses. However, most conflicts usually have more than one issue at stake, with the parties placing different values on the different issues. Consequently, the potential usually exists for integrative agreements. A fundamental task in training negotiators lies in identifying and eliminating this false "fixed pie" assumption and preparing them to look for trade-offs between issues of different value to each side.

Framing. Consider the following bargaining situation. The union claims its members need a raise to $12 an hour and that anything less will represent a loss due to inflation. Management argues that the company can't pay more than $10 an hour and that anything more would impose an unacceptable loss. If each side had the choice between settling at $11 an hour or going to binding arbitration, they would likely take the risk and move toward arbitration rather than settlement.

Changing the frame of the situation to a positive one results in a very different predicted outcome. If the union can view anything above $10 an hour as a gain, and if management can view anything under $12 as a gain, then a negotiated settlement is likely—at $11 dollars.

As the preceding example emphasizes, the frame (positive or negative) of negotiators can make the difference between settlement and impasse. One solution to impasses in bargaining, then, is to alter the frame of reference such that it is positive, rather than negative.[50]

CONFLICT RESOLUTION

Although the desired outcome of collective bargaining is agreement on the conditions of employment, on many occasions negotiators are unable to reach such an agreement at the bargaining table. In these situations several alternatives are used to break the deadlock. The most dramatic response is the strike or lockout, but third-party interventions such as mediation and arbitration are also common.

Strikes and Lockouts

When the union is unable to get management to agree to a demand it believes is critical, it may resort to a strike. A **strike** may be defined as the refusal by employees to work at the company. Management may refuse to allow employees to work, which is called a **lockout.**[51]

In order to strike if the negotiations are unsuccessful, the union usually holds a strike vote to gain members' approval. Strong membership support for a strike strengthens the union negotiators' position. If the strike takes place, union members picket the employer, informing the public about the existence of a labor dispute and preferably, from the union's point of view, convincing them to avoid this company during the strike. A common practice is the refusal of union members to cross the picket line of another striking union. This gives added support to the striking union.

Employers usually attempt to continue operations while the strike is in effect. They either run the company with supervisory personnel and people not in the bargaining unit or hire replacements for the employees. Although it appears that the company can legally hire replacements, the union reacts strongly to the use of "scabs," as the replacements are called, and they may be a cause of increasingly belligerent labor relations. At the conclusion of the strike, employers will be expected to (a) reinstate strikers in all of the positions that remain unfilled unless there are substantial business reasons for doing otherwise, and (b) establish a preferential hiring list for displaced strikers to facilitate their recall as new openings occur.

The success of a strike depends on its ability to cause economic hardship to the employer. Severe hardship usually causes the employer to concede to the union's demands.[52] Thus, from the union's point of view, it is paramount that the cost of this lack of production be high. The union, therefore, actively tries to prevent replacement employees from working. In addition, the timing of the strike is often critical. The union attempts to hold negotiations just prior to the period when the employer has a peak demand for its product or services, when a strike will have maximum economic impact.

Although strikes are common, they are costly to both the employer, who loses revenue, and employees, who face loss of income. If the strike is prolonged, it is likely that the cost to employees will never fully be recovered by the benefits gained. In part because of this, employers seek to avoid strikes. Moreover, the public interest is generally not served by strikes. They are often an inconvenience and can have serious consequences for the economy as a whole.

Slowdown. Short of an actual strike, unions may invoke a slowdown. The impact of slowdowns can be more effective than an actual strike. For example, the United Auto Workers recently orchestrated a work slowdown.

> In a contract dispute, union employees are refusing to install parts without blueprints, and they are working to the minimums of their job requirements. The union also is weighing a plan to stage mass grievances by having hundreds of workers blow whistles whenever a member has a complaint against a foreman.
>
> Although such tactics, viewed individually, might seem fairly mild, their cumulative effect has hurt the company and its earnings. Since the slowdown started, McDonnell Douglas has missed 10 delivery dates for MD-80 jets—though the company partly blames its production problems on parts shortages and the training of new workers. The union's actions have been "baffling and frustrating," says Sanford N. McDonnell, the company's chief executive, adding that he has fielded some phone calls from angry airline customers.[53]

Corporate campaigns. Another indirect tactic in the form of a secondary boycott is called a corporate campaign. In the corporate campaign a union may ask the public and other unions to write letters to a company asking it to change the way it bargains with the union.[54]

Conflict resolution that avoids work stoppages or slowdowns—which may occur regardless of the existence of no-strike clauses—by interventions such as mediation, arbitration, and injunctions may, therefore, be desirable from several perspectives.

Mediation

Mediation is a procedures in which a neutral third party assists the union and management negotiators in reaching voluntary agreement.[55] Having no power to impose a solution, the mediator attempts to facilitate the negotiations between union and management. The mediator may make suggestions and recommendations and perhaps add objectivity to the often emotional negotiations. To have any success at all, the mediator must have the trust and respect of both parties and have sufficient expertise and neutrality to convince the union and employer that he or she will be fair and equitable.

The U.S. government operates the Federal Mediation and Conciliation Service (FMCS) to make experienced mediators available to unions and companies. A program called Relationships by Objective is offered by the FMCS to eliminate the causes of recurrent impasses. It uses aspects of attitudinal structuring to increase the likelihood of a cooperative relationship between union and management.

Arbitration

Arbitration is a procedure in which a neutral third party studies the bargaining situation, listening to both parties and gathering information, and then makes recommendations that are binding on the parties. The arbitrator, in effect, determines the conditions of the agreement.[56] The arbitrator chooses between the final offer, on either the total package or on an issue-by-issue basis, of the union and the final offer of the employer. The arbitrator cannot alter these offers but must choose one as it stands. Since the arbitrator chooses the offer that appears most fair, and since losing the arbitration decision means settling for the other's offer, there is pressure to make as good an offer as possible. The intention of **final-offer arbitration** is to encourage the parties to make their best offer and to reach an agreement before arbitration becomes necessary. This is also true with respect to the use of **closed-offer arbitration.** Here the arbitrator receives information only on the parties' original positions without any information on the bargaining progress up to the time the arbitrator is selected.

Once the impasse is removed, union and management have a contract agreement. Abiding by it is the essence of contract administration; however, there are times when arbitration is again necessary, namely when a grievance is filed. This type of arbitration is referred to as rights or **grievance arbitration.** In contrast, the arbitration process that deals with the contract terms and conditions (described previously) is called **interest arbitration.** Although interest arbitration is relatively infrequent in the private sector, it is more common in the public sector, where it becomes a necessary *quid pro quo* for foregoing the strike option.[57] However, only about twenty states have compulsory interest arbitration procedures.

CONTRACT ADMINISTRATION

Once signed, the collective agreement becomes "the basic legislation governing the lives of the workers."[58] That is, the daily operation and activities in the organization are subject to the conditions of the agreement. Because of the difficulty of writing an unambiguous agreement anticipating all the situations that will occur over its life, disputes will inevitably occur over the contract's interpretation and application. The most common method of resolving these disputes is a **grievance procedure.** Virtually all agreements negotiated today provide for a grievance process to handle employee complaints.

Grievance Procedures

Basically, a **grievance** is a charge that the union-management contract has been violated.[59] A grievance may be filed by the union for employees or by employers, although management rarely does so. The grievance process is designed to investigate the charges and to resolve the problem.

The following sources of grievances have been identified:

- Outright violation of the agreement
- Disagreement over facts
- Dispute over the meaning of the agreement
- Dispute over the method of applying the agreement
- Argument over the fairness or reasonableness of actions[60]

In resolving these sources of conflict, the grievance procedure should serve three separate groups: the employers and unions, by interpreting and adjusting the agreement as conditions require; the employees, by protecting their contractual rights and providing a channel of appeal; and society at large, by keeping industrial peace and reducing the number of disputes in the courts.

Grievance procedures typically involve several stages. The collective bargaining agreement specifies the maximum length to be filed within five days of the incident that is the subject of dispute. The most common grievance procedure, shown in exhibit 17.5, involves four steps:

Step 1. An employee who feels that the labor contract has been violated usually contacts the union steward, and together they discuss the problem with the supervisor involved. If the problem is simple and straightforward, it is often resolved at this level. Many contracts require the grievance to be in written form at this first stage. However, cases may be resolved by informal discussion between the supervisor and the employee and, therefore, do not officially enter the grievance process.

Step 2. If agreement cannot be reached at the supervisor level, or if the employee is not satisfied, the complaint can enter the second step of the grievance procedure. Typically, a human resource representative of the company now seeks to resolve the grievance.

Step 3. If the grievance is sufficiently important or difficult to resolve, it may be taken to the third step. Although contracts vary, top-level management and union executives are usually involved at this stage. These people have the authority to make the major decisions that may be required to resolve the grievance.

Exhibit 17.5

Typical Union-Management Grievance Procedure

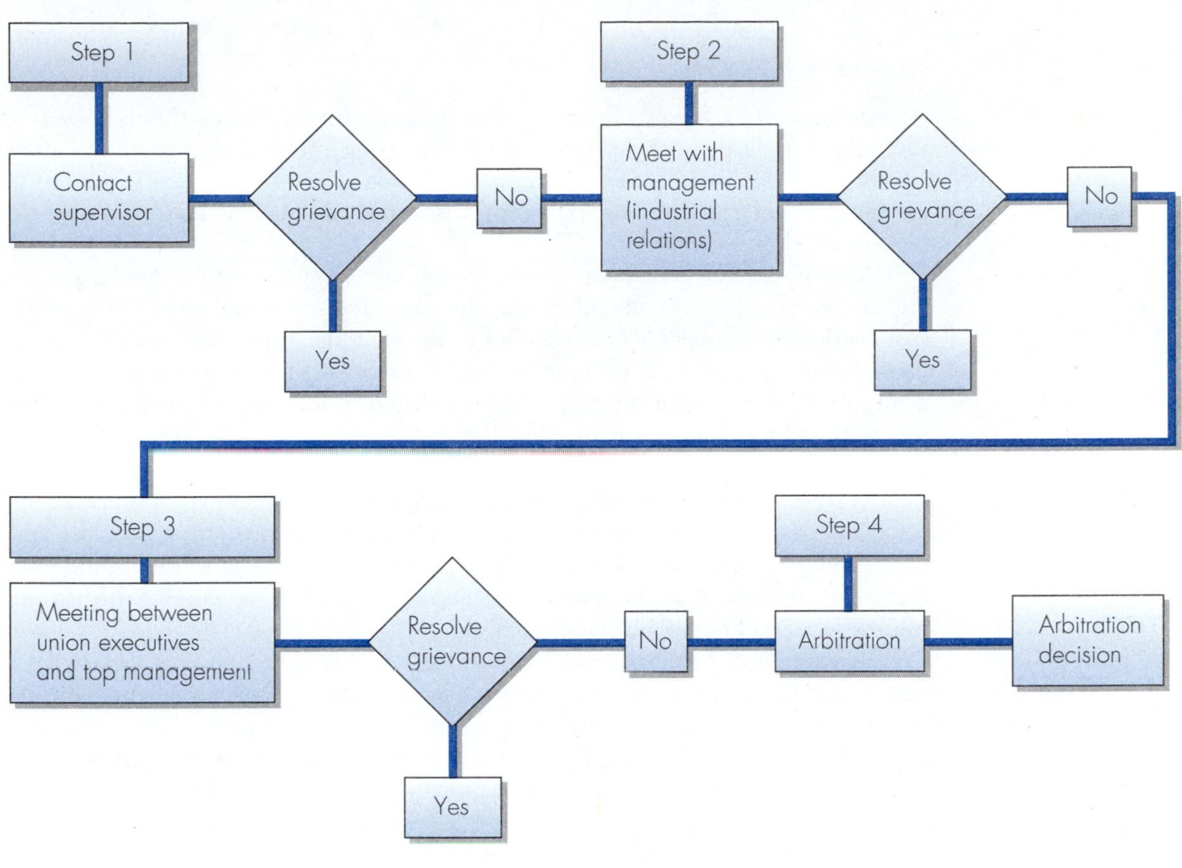

SOURCE: William D. Todor, Ohio State University.

Step 4. If a grievance cannot be resolved at this third step, most agreements require the use of an arbitrator to consider the case and reach a decision. The arbitrator is a neutral, mutually acceptable individual who may be provided by the FMCS or some private agency. The arbitrator holds a hearing, reviews the evidence, then rules on the grievance. The decision of the arbitrator is usually binding.

Since the cost of arbitration is shared by the union and employer, some incentive exists to settle the grievance before it goes to arbitration.[61] An added incentive in some cases is the requirement that the loser pays for the arbitration.[62] The expectation is that the parties will screen or evaluate grievances more carefully because pursuing a weak grievance to arbitration will be expensive.

Occasionally, the union will call a strike over a grievance in order to resolve it. This may happen when the issue at hand is so important that the union feels it cannot wait for the slower arbitration process, which sometimes takes more than 200 days.[63] This "employee rights" strike may be legal but, if the contract specifically forbids strikes during the tenure of the agreement, it is not legal and is called a **wildcat strike.** Wildcat strikes are not common, however, because most grievances are settled through arbitration.

Grievance Issues

Grievances can be filed over any issue relating to the workplace that is subject to the collective agreement, or they can be filed over interpretation and implementation of the agreement itself. The most common type of grievance reaching the arbitration stage involves discipline and discharge, although many grievances are filed over other issues.

Although it is accepted that absenteeism can be grounds for discharge, the critical issue is the determination that the absenteeism in question is excessive. Insubordination usually is either failure to do what the supervisor requests or the more serious problem of outright refusal to do it. If the supervisor's orders are clear and explicit, and if the employee is warned of the consequences, discipline for refusal to respond is usually acceptable. The exception is when the employee feels that the work endangers health.

Because seniority is usually used to determine who is laid off, bumped from a job to make way for someone else, or rehired, its calculation is of great concern to employees. Seniority is also used as one of the criteria to determine eligibility for promotions and transfers, so management must be careful in this area in order to avoid complaints and grievances.

Compensation for time away from work, vacations, holidays, or sick leave is also a common source of grievances. Holidays cause problems because special pay arrangements often exist for people working on those days.

Wage and work schedules may also lead to grievances. Disagreements often arise over interpretation or application of the agreement relating to such issues as overtime pay, pay for reporting, and scheduling. Grievances have been filed over the exercise of management rights—that is, its right to introduce technological changes, use subcontractors, or change jobs in other ways. This type of behavior may also be the source of charges of unfair labor practices, since these activities may require collective bargaining.

The Taft-Hartley Act gives unions the right to file grievances on their own behalf if they feel their rights have been violated. This act also gives unions access to information necessary to process the grievance or to make sure the agreement is not being violated. In addition, unions may file grievances for violations of union shop or check-off provisions. It might be useful to convey a sense of what unions *aren't* entitled to in the grievance process. For example, employees have the right to present their *own* grievances on an individual basis [Taft-Hartley, Section 9(a)], and the employer can adjust that grievance without the union's presence. The only qualifying items in the latter instance are that adjustments cannot abrogate the collective agreement, and the union must be given an opportunity to participate in the grievance proceedings at some point prior to the adjustment.

Occasionally, other activities prompt grievances. Wildcat strikes or behavior that is considered to be a strike (mass absences from work, for example) may result in a management grievance. The major focus of grievances, however, is in the administration of the conditions of the agreement.

Management Procedures

Management can significantly affect the grievance rate by adopting proper procedures when taking action against an employee. Two of the most important areas for such procedures are discipline and discharge. The issues of just cause and fairness are central to most discipline grievances. Employers must ensure that the employee is adequately warned of the consequences, that the rule involved is related to operation of the company, that a thorough investigation is undertaken, and that the penalty is reasonable. The following activities have been identified as being useful in meeting these considerations:

- Explanation of rules to employees
- Consideration of the accusations and facts
- Regular warning procedures, including written reports
- Involvement of the union in the case
- Examination of the employee's motives and reasons
- Consideration of the employee's past record
- Familiarization of all management personnel, especially supervisors, with disciplinary procedures and company rules

In areas outside of discipline and discharge, management can avoid some grievance problems by educating supervisors and managers about labor relations and about the conditions of the collective agreement. It has been found that supervisors with labor knowledge are an important factor in the reduction of grievances.

Union Procedures

The union has an obligation to its members to provide them fair and adequate representation and to speedily process and investigate grievances brought by its members (*Vaca v. Sipes,* 1967; *Hines v. Anchor Motor Freight,* 1976; *Smith v. Hussman Refrigerator Co. & Local 13889, United Steel Workers of America,* 1980). Thus, it should have a grievance-handling procedure that will aid in effectively processing grievances without being guilty of unfair representation.

Unfair representation, according to the NLRB, is usually related to one of four types of union behavior:

- *Improper motives or fraud.* The union cannot refuse to process a grievance because of the employee's race or sex or because of the employee's attitude toward the union.
- *Arbitrary conduct.* Unions cannot dismiss a grievance without investigating its merits.
- *Gross negligence.* The union cannot recklessly disregard the employee's interests.
- *Union conduct after filing the grievance.* The union must process the grievance to a reasonable conclusion.[64]

Because the employer can also be cited for unfair representation, management should attempt to maintain a fair grievance process. Company labor relations managers should avoid taking advantage of union errors in handling grievances so that this action does not affect fair representation.

Another important influence on the grievance process is the union steward. Since the union steward is generally the first person to hear about an employee's grievance, the steward has substantial influence on the grievance process. A steward can encourage an employee to file a grievance, can suggest that the problem is really not a grievance, or can informally resolve the problem outside the grievance procedure. Personality characteristics of stewards may, in fact, influence the number of grievances filed.[65] Because stewards are selected from the ranks of employees and may have little knowledge of labor relations, the union should provide training to improve their effectiveness. The company may also be liable in a fair-representation suit and, therefore, should support such training.

FOCUS ISSUES IN UNION-MANAGEMENT RELATIONSHIPS

Three focus issues in collective bargaining include union involvement in strategic issues of the firm, the future role of unions, and assessment of the effectiveness of the union-management relationship.[66]

Strategic Involvement

Labor costs are critical to the success of many companies vis-à-vis competitors. In many industries today, companies face possible bankruptcy because of high labor costs. Wage reductions reached between unions and management are helping to lower costs. During the 1980s, American Airlines, Greyhound, McDonnell Douglas, Boeing, and Ingersoll-Rand negotiated two-tiered wage systems to help reduce total costs by reducing labor costs. Without these jointly negotiated systems, these companies may not have survived. Thus, a company's relationship with its union can be critical to its survival, and the better its relationship, the more likely the company is to gain a competitive advantage.

Ford Motor Company has engaged in a program of more worker involvement and more cooperative labor relations with the United Auto Workers. The results of this program are higher product quality than its competitors and a marketing campaign centered on the slogan, "Quality is Job 1." This program of more worker involvement gains competitive advantage through higher product quality and improved efficiencies. Similar results of high product quality and efficiency have been obtained at Westinghouse Electric Corporation, Warner Gear Division of Borg-Warner Corporation, and the Mass Transportation Authority of Flint, Michigan. In these companies, gains in quality and efficiency have resulted from employee commitment associated with quality-circle programs. In addition to increased quality and efficiency, these companies have experienced fewer grievances, reduced absenteeism and turnover, lower design costs, higher engineering productivity, and fewer costly changes in design cycles.

What Should Unions Do?

The future role of the union is generating a great deal of discussion and speculation.[67] Some foresee a halt to the decline in union membership in the private sector. This is expected to follow from the decline in the numbers entering the work force and a subsequent tighter labor market; from more sophisticated and efficient organizing activities; from unions' rising appeal among less skilled workers; and from their ability and willingness to offer a broader array of consumer benefits and new forms of membership.[68]

All this needs to be put in the perspective of the environment. The U.S. economy will continue to globalize, and firms will continue to have available for their use high-quality, low-wage workers. The decline in mass production will continue at the same time as the skill levels of the work force increase. As Ray Marshall, former Secretary of Labor, describes it, "[E]conomic success will require new policies and high-performance systems more appropriate for a global, knowledge-intensive economic environment."[69] While Marshall meant this to describe the future of business, it could as easily be applied to the future of unions.[70]

A final perspective needs to be included here as well: The union movement will continue to be heterogenous. There will be differences within the movement, with some unions—such as the UAW—being more willing to enter into collaborative agreements and others less willing. Thus, we are likely to see several answers to the question, "What should unions do?"

Assessing the Collective Bargaining Process

The effectiveness of the entire collective bargaining process and of the union-management relationship can be measured by the extent to which each party attains its goals, but this approach has its difficulties. Because goals are in many cases incompatible and, therefore, can lead to conflicting estimates of effectiveness, a more useful measure may be the quality of the system used to resolve conflict. Conflict is more apparent in the collective bargaining process, where failure to resolve the issues typically leads to strikes. Another measure of effectiveness is the success of the grievance process, or the ability to resolve issues developing out of the bargaining agreement.

Effectiveness of negotiations. Because the purpose of negotiations is to achieve an agreement, this agreement becomes an overall measure of bargaining effectiveness. A healthy and effective bargaining process encourages the discussion of issues and problems and their subsequent resolution at the bargaining table. In addition, the effort required to reach agreement is a measure of how well the process is working. Some indications of this effort are the duration of negotiations, the outcome of member ratification votes, the frequency and duration of strikes, the use of mediation and arbitration, the need for government intervention, and the resulting quality of union-management relations (whether conflict or cooperation exists). Certainly, joint programs for productivity and quality-of-work-life improvements could be regarded as successes resulting from the quality of union-management relations.

Effectiveness of grievance procedures. How successful a grievance procedure is may be assessed from different perspectives. Management may view the number of grievances filed and the number settled in management's favor as measures of effectiveness. Unions may also consider the number of grievances but, from their point of view, a larger number, rather than a smaller number, may be considered more successful.

Although the views of management and the union may differ, an overall set of measures to gauge grievance procedure effectiveness may be related to the disagreements between managers and employees. Measures that might be included are frequency of grievances; the level in the grievance procedure at which grievances are usually settled; the frequency of strikes or slowdowns during the term of the labor agreements; the rates of absenteeism, turnover, and sabotage; and the necessity for government intervention.

The success of arbitration is often judged by the acceptability of the decisions, the satisfaction of the parties, the degree of innovation, and the absence of bias in either direction. The effectiveness of any third-party intervention rests, in part, on how successfully strikes are avoided because the motivation for such intervention is precisely to avert this extreme form of conflict resolution.

INTERNATIONAL COMPARISONS

Germany

The belief that workers' interests are best served if employees have a direct say in the management of the company is called *"Mitbestimmung"* (or *codetermination*). The original ideas about codetermination were conceived in Germany and are now spreading into many other European countries.

Codetermination means, for example, that unions are given seats on the boards of directors of corporations. In addition, managers are encouraged to consult with unions before making major organizational changes, whether they be mergers, investments, plant closings or relocations. If management disagrees with the union position, management prevails. However, unions may veto subcontracts by the company, and they have access to all company records.

Under the political leadership of the social-democratic government in Germany, consensus was reached during the early 1980s to promote international competitiveness through technological superiority and to overcome barriers to innovations by integrating the trade unions into the process of change. The German system of labor relations, with its key features of centralization, jurisdiction, and participation, seem to be functioning well, even in the face of changed socioeconomic conditions. The efficiency and legitimacy of collective bargaining seem also to hold given the codetermination practice and similar system flexibility. Low levels of conflict and commitment to cooperation characterize the labor relations system in Germany.

Since the unions' defeat in the 1930s, the German labor movement has consisted of unions with unitary structures that are a synthesis of traditional elements of the socialist and the Catholic labor movement. Although labor is dominated by social democracy, the Catholic influence on the development of such concepts as codetermination, social partnership, or capital formation for employees has become an integral part of the German trade unions' ideology. A second organizational principle of the trade unions in Germany is that they are organized on an industrial basis. The dominant labor organizations are seventeen trade unions affiliated with the DGB (Confederation of Trade Unions). The DGB sets the pattern in negotiating for the majority of the workers. The other trade union federations—the DBB (Association of Civil Servants), DAG (White Collar Association), and the CGB (Christian Trade Unions) lack significant bargaining power; hence, civil servants are not allowed to strike.

In the 1980s unionized employees who were members of DGB affiliates made up a third of the labor force. Nonetheless, their power and influence stretches significantly beyond their numbers. For example, employee support for unions far exceeds their readiness for unionization. In fact, during the election of workplace representatives, about eighty percent of all employees vote regularly for candidates who have been nominated by DGB unions. Another feature of the German unions is their centralized authority. Most of the internal decision-making takes place in the peak of the echelons of union bureaucracy.

German employers are also organized and centralized. There are employers' associations in several industries, often dominated by large-scale companies. The largest employers' umbrella organization is the BDA (Federation of German Employers' Association). The BDA coordinates various kinds of legally binding agreements for its members. For example, in 1978 it published a "taboo catalog" containing rules and provisions of the association designed to strengthen its bargaining power. It limited management compromise in bargaining; among its instructions was that Saturday, usually not a working day, should remain a working day in order to maximize the use of labor and machinery. Although this instruction was reversed in 1984, it illustrates the strategy of the employers' association to establish common policies. The notable efficiency of German HR practices could be explained by the strong connection of the major partners to the labor relations system and the adherence of the German employees to discipline, rules and regulations.[71]

Great Britain

The industrial relations system in Great Britain differs markedly from those in both the U.S. and other European countries. Traditionally, the framework of labor law in Britain has been noninterventionist, fostering an essentially voluntary system of industrial relations. Under this system, employers have had no general legal duty to recognize and bargain with their employees, while employees have had no legally protected rights to organize themselves in unions. Also, negotiated agreements signed between unions and employers are not enforceable as legal contracts. The collective agreements familiar to U.S. managers are more akin to gentleman's agreements in Britain and are based on social rather than on legal sanctions.

As with so many aspects of life in Britain, the explanation for this state of affairs is largely historical. The development of British labor law has progressed via the granting of immunities from existing restrictive statutes—such as immunity from prosecution for criminal conspiracy—rather than through the legislation of positive rights. Unlike their U.S. counterparts, British unions have not viewed the law as a positive and protective force guaranteeing their right to existence.

The tradition of legal nonintervention in industrial relations has, however, come under increasing challenge in recent years. Concern over the country's poor economic performance and a growing international reputation for labor strife sparked a vigorous debate among the major political parties in Britain during the 1960s and eventually led to the establishment of a royal commission of inquiry (the Donovan Commission). This commission, which reported in 1968, highlighted the growing importance of what it termed Britain's unofficial system of industrial relations. Under this system, terms and conditions of employment were increasingly being negotiated between local managers and informally elected shop stewards, rather than between management and paid full-time union officials.

Rejecting the Donovan Commission's recommendation that reform should be accomplished without destroying the tradition of keeping industrial relations out of the courts, a newly elected Conservative government made an ill-fated attempt in 1971 to reform Britain's voluntary system of industrial relations along U.S. lines. The Industrial Relations Act of 1971 included provisions to formalize the process of union certification through the establishment of bargaining units for which a designated union would be the sole bargaining agent. This reform was intended to replace the practice of voluntary recognition, which led to a complex pattern of multiunionism under which a single local management could find itself negotiating with as many as half a dozen unions at the same workplace. Provisions were also included to make collective agreements legally enforceable, unless the parties included a clause to the contrary. (In practice, most negotiators did include such a clause.)

The 1971 legislation also defined and strengthened a number of individual rights, including protection against unfair dismissal. The rationale for this legislation was not merely to redress a perceived inequality in the balance of power between the individual employee and a management able to fire at will. Rather, it was an attempt to limit the large number of unofficial wildcat strikes that were called, often with some success, to pressure management into reinstating a dismissed employee.

Active union hostility combined with management indifference to the 1971 legislation made it largely unworkable, and the act was repealed by a Labor government in 1974. Between 1974 and 1979, with the support of the unions, the Labor government introduced a number of pieces of legislation that took a significant step in the direction of creating more positive legal rights to protect and support trade union membership. Legislation also entrenched a variety of individual rights, including protection against unfair dismissal and discrimination on the basis of sex or race.

Many observers have seen this legislation as a form of *quid pro quo* for the cooperation of the Trade Union Council (TUC), the central umbrella organization for Britain's unions in the Labor government's incomes policy, which was in place between 1975 and 1978. Income policies in one form or another have acted as important constraints on management freedom in compensating employees in Britain during most of the 1960s and 1970s, but none has been based on the same degree of union cooperation.

By 1979, union power in Britain, measured by political influence and industrial strength as well as by membership, was undoubtedly at a postwar peak. Since the election of the Thatcher conservative government in 1979, however, the industrial relations climate has changed dramatically. A process of step-by-step reform, including laws against secondary picketing, restrictions on the operation of the closed shop, and the establishment of secret union ballots before strikes, has effectively shifted the balance of power back toward management. High levels of unemployment have further undermined union bargaining power. Between 1979 and 1985, the percentage of the labor force in unions fell by about one-fifth from its postwar peak of about fifty-five percent. Despite some highly publicized disputes, which give an unduly inflated impression of Britain's overall strike proneness, strike activity has also fallen to historically low levels.

The full, long-run consequences of these changes are difficult to predict with any certainty. Managers in Britain still face a work force that is highly unionized compared with that in the U.S., where less than seventeen percent of the labor force is currently in unions. Managers in many parts of British industry must also negotiate with a multiplicity of unions, the representational boundaries of which often owe more to craft tradition and the accidents of history than they do to the logic of efficient production. They must also operate on a day-to-day basis without the support of legally enforceable collective agreements. Important developments at the shop-floor level do, however, offer some clue to a changed future. On the union side, both the engineering and the electricians unions have been willing to sign single-union agreements that include no-strike clauses. They have also shown a preference for cooperative over confrontational relations with management. Perhaps significantly, the key movers on the management side of these innovative agreements have often been overseas companies setting up operations in Britain. Japanese companies such as Nissan, Hitachi, and Toshiba are notable examples, but innovative agreements have also been signed with some U.S. firms. This is a useful reminder that the behavior and attitudes of both sides determine the quality of labor-management relationships.

Other European Countries

Originally conceived in Germany, the codetermination philosophy of labor-management relations now exists in Sweden, The Netherlands, France, Norway, Denmark, Luxembourg, and Austria. Codetermination has sometimes caused unions to propose asset formation. Such proposals seek to place under the control of the union funds provided by the employer. At this time, however, these proposals have been rejected by management.

Although the European ideas of codetermination and union-controlled funds will probably not be applied in the U.S. in the 1990s, increased cooperation may occur between labor and management on issues of productivity and quality of work life. An issue on which cooperation has been less evident, in both Europe and the U.S., is that of the thirty-five-hour work week. The extent of union-management disagreement on this issue is particularly evident in Germany. In Sweden, however, some progress has been made in hours reduction.

Canada

Approximately one-third of the Canadian labor force is unionized. About three-fourths of the union members are affiliated with the Canadian Labor Congress (CLC). As in the U.S., the union local is the basic local unit. The CLC is the dominant labor group at the federal level. Its political influence may be compared with that of the AFL-CIO.

Although the labor laws in Canada are similar to those in the U.S., noteworthy differences do exist. Since 1925, the majority of Canadian workers have been covered by provincial, not federal, labor laws, whereas in the U.S. over ninety percent of the workers are covered by the National Labor Relations Act. The Canadian Industrial Relations Disputes and Investigation Act of 1973, on the other hand, covers less than ten percent of the labor force.

Canadian labor laws require frequent interventions by government bodies before a strike can take place. In the U.S., such intervention is largely voluntary.

Compulsory arbitration in Canada is governed by the Public Service Staff Relations Act of 1967. This law also allows nonmanagerial federal employees to join unions and bargain collectively.

The history of labor relations in Canada and the U.S. is similar because both nations follow British common law, except that provincial governments, rather than the federal government, have developed most of the Canadian labor laws. Since the decision in *Toronto Electric Commissioners v. Snider* (1925), Canadian workers have been governed primarily by provincial laws (except for employees working for the federal government and industries under federal coverage, as defined by amendments to the 1973 industrial relations act—for instance longshoring, seafaring, provincial railroads, Crown corporations, and airlines). Many of the features of the U.S. Taft-Hartley Act have been incorporated into the labor laws of the Canadian provinces.

For the union movement as a whole, the trend toward concessionary bargaining to avoid layoffs and plant closings appears to be less evident than it is in the U.S.[72] At the same time, Canadian labor organizations affiliated with unions dominated by labor organizations in the U.S. are becoming increasingly autonomous. This trend was recently highlighted when the United Auto Workers in Canada became independent from the same union in the U.S.

Japan

The third sacred treasure of the Imperial House of Japan is what is known as the enterprise union. Unlike in the U.S. and Europe, where unions are organized horizontally and industrywide, almost all trade unions in Japan are formed on a company-by-company, or enterprise, basis. In 1978, as many as 70,868 labor unions could be found in Japan, with one existing in practically every company or plant to conduct labor negotiations at that level. Enterprise unions today account for nearly ninety percent of all Japanese union organizations. Also, four principal industrywide federations of workers serve as coordinators, formulators of unified and reliable standards, and sources of information.

Although the enterprise concept received a fair amount of attention in the U.S. during the 1920s and 1930s, such unions collapsed, primarily as a result of excessive management involvement and their narrow field of interest. The success of the enterprise union in Japan is attributed to two major differences. The first of these is the allocation of financial responsibility between the enterprise union and the trade or regional organizations, which reflects a difference in the organizational roles of Japanese labor unions. In Western countries, where centralized union control and authority are predominant, the national union receives union dues, decides how they are to be used, and returns a portion to the local unions for expenses. In Japan, the enterprise union controls the dues, passing on ten percent or, at most, twenty percent to the federation.[73]

As a result of the enterprise union's role, problems in labor-management relationships can be dealt with more directly, without necessarily involving an outside body. The "mixed" union representation of all blue-collar and some white-collar workers also proves valuable in determining more representative concerns. As a result of greater union participation by employees of a given company, 15.7 percent of Japan's current top management have once been active labor union leaders. This should lead to better management understanding of the needs and interests of employees.

The second difference that accounts for the success of the enterprise union system in Japan is the greater company and national loyalty shown by each worker. Accordingly, workers do not look on the union solely as a negotiating body but use its structure to deal with such issues as industry and technical reforms, new plant and equipment investments, and matters of personnel and productivity development.

Australia

It is interesting to note that the institutional framework of both U.S. and Australian industrial relations evolved from similar historical circumstances: the need to compel strong employers to meet and deal with a weak labor union movement for collective bargaining purposes.[74] The legislative solutions to this situation that were enacted in each country were, however, quite different. American legislation in the 1930s carefully avoided imposing the decisions of a third party on labor and management by providing a detailed legal framework within which the parties were compelled to bargain in good faith with each other. In contrast, Australian legislation at the turn of the century provided government machinery for the making and enforcement of industrial awards.

Walker[75] has argued that the principal distinguishing features of the period that led to the establishment of the institutional framework of Australian industrial relations were as follows:

- The development of a strong and vigorous union movement that achieved industrial power and interunion solidarity earlier than in most countries. It is important to note that many of the Nineteenth-Century settlers who arrived in Australia had experienced the "dark Satanic mills" of industrial England, and some had been transported from Britain for participation in labor union activities.
- The complete defeat of the labor unions following nationwide strikes in the 1890s. This convinced the labor movement of the need for political representation and led to the formation of the Australian Labor Party (ALP), which rapidly became a major political party.
- The development of a labor movement which, despite its direct involvement in politics, was characterized by a pragmatic and nonrevolutionary ideology.
- Acceptance by the labor movement of the concept of compulsory arbitration of industrial disputes.

The results of this process were twofold. First, the notions of conciliation and arbitration were written into the Australian Constitution that was enacted in 1900. Section 51 (XXXV) of the constitution limits the role of the federal Parliament to making laws "with respect to conciliation and arbitration for the prevention and settlement of industrial disputes extending beyond the limits of any one state." Second, the Conciliation and Arbitration Act of 1904 established the institutional framework of Australian industrial relations that is still in place today, making this system of conciliation and arbitration the oldest national labor relations mechanism in the Western industrial democracies. The centerpiece of this legislation was the establishment of a federal tribunal known as the Australian Conciliation and Arbitration Commission (ACAC).

The constitutional limitation of federal government intervention in industrial relations issues and the emphasis on the role of a federal tribunal in the Conciliation and Arbitration Act combined to give the ACAC a leading role in Australian industrial relations. This system was explicitly designed to encourage union organization, and labor union membership rapidly increased from less than five percent to over fifty percent.[76] Employers who operated outside of the system were excluded from tariff protection—a major economic penalty. Faced with a rapidly growing labor movement and a centralized industrial relations system, employers developed strong associations to represent their interests before the federal and state tribunals, and this remains a distinctive feature of Australian industrial relations.

The Australian industrial relations system is now more than eighty years old. A strength of the present system is that the role of the ACAC allows for effective macro-wage policy implementation, but at the micro level serious labor market rigidities are apparent. For example, all companies in an industry face the same award, regardless of cost structure and market position, and individual companies cannot restructure a federal award through private negotiations with labor unions. The Business Council of Australia, one of the major employer representative bodies, has identified labor market failures as perhaps the single most important obstacle to improving the competitiveness of the Australian economy.[77]

In 1983, in recognition of these problems, the Labor federal government commissioned a committee of inquiry on industrial relations in Australia (generally referred to as the Hancock Committee in recognition of the chair, Professor Hancock). The Hancock Committee recommended a number of changes in the current system, such as the establishment of a new labor court and the extension of grievance procedures, but it did not recommend total deregulation of the current centralized system.[78] The federal government is clearly aware that change is necessary if Australia wishes to compete successfully for a share in the dynamic growth of the Pacific Basin. This awareness has been illustrated by such changes as the deregulation of the Australian financial markets in December, 1983.

After much debate and delay, the federal government's response to the recommendations of the Hancock Report was presented in the Industrial Relations Bill of 1988. Although the bill supports the need for increased flexibility in the industrial relations system, it presents a much diluted version of the original reforms recommended. The main elements of this bill include an updated name for the ACAC (to be known as the Industrial Relations Commission), which now has the power to hear unfair dismissal cases, and provisions for greater opportunities for enterprise-level negotiations. Despite the different approaches of labor unions and employer associations to industrial relations, both groups have advocated reforms that allow for decentralization and greater flexibility within the present system.[79]

Given the collectivist and centralist traditions of Australian labor relations, dramatic changes are unlikely, and any assumption of convergence over time to a system based solely on plant or enterprise collective bargaining, as in the U.S., would be unwarranted. Foreign companies doing business in Australia will still need to analyze the industrial relations implications of their business strategies in considerable detail.

SUMMARY

Employees are generally attracted to unionization because they are dissatisfied with work conditions and feel powerless to change these conditions. Some major sources of dissatisfaction are inequity in pay administration, poor communications, and poor supervisory practices. By correcting these, or by not allowing them to occur in the first place, organizations help prevent unions from becoming attractive. However, once a union-organizing campaign begins, a company can't legally stop it without committing an unfair labor practice.

Historically, unions and management have operated as adversaries because many of their goals are in conflict; but because conflict is detrimental to both management and unions, effective labor relations have been established to reduce this conflict. For instance, unions and management have begun to cooperate to achieve mutual goals. Although cooperation is not widespread, it may be the style of union-management relations in the future. Its effects are particularly apparent in collective bargaining, contract negotiation, and grievance processing.

In the U.S., collective bargaining relationships are currently at a critical crossroads. Global competition has brought about a greater emphasis on mutual survival. This has resulted in a shift from the traditional adversarial relationship between union and management toward cooperation. New bargaining strategies characterize this altered relationship. Productivity bargaining is an attempt to encourage increased effectiveness in the workplace by passing some of the economic savings of modernization or increased efficiency on to the employees. Another innovation is continuous bargaining, where a joint union-management committee meets on a regular basis to deal with problems.

Although obstacles exist to union-management cooperation—a history of adversarial relations, hesitancy on the part of the union to give up the traditional roles of labor, and both parties' fear of losing power—current economic conditions and the threat of an influx of foreign products are prompting many organizations to act for their mutual benefit.

The quality of the union-management relationship can have a strong influence on contract negotiations. Labor and management each select a bargaining committee to negotiate the new agreement. The negotiations may be between a single union and a single company or multiple companies, or between multiple unions and a single company. Bargaining issues are mandatory, permissive, or prohibited. Mandatory issues must be discussed, permissive issues can be discussed if both parties agree, and prohibited issues cannot be discussed. The issues can be grouped into wage issues, economic supplements issues, institutional issues, and administrative issues.

Almost all labor contracts outline grievance procedures for handling employee complaints. The most common grievance is related to discipline and discharge, although wages, promotions, seniority, vacations, holidays, and management and union rights are also sources of complaints. Management can influence the results of grievances by developing a procedure that ensures their actions are just and fair. Written records of actions taken are useful for potential arbitration. Unions have a legal responsibility to represent the employee fairly in grievances; therefore, they also need a grievance-handling procedure.

The effectiveness of collective bargaining and contract administration is usually assessed by measures of how well the process is working. Bargaining can be evaluated using measures such as the duration of negotiations, the frequency of strikes, the use of third-party intervention, and the need for government intervention. The effectiveness of the grievance process can be assessed by the number of grievances; the level in the grievance process at which settlement occurs; the frequency of strikes or slowdowns; the rates of absenteeism, turnover, and sabotage; and the need for government intervention.

Finally, as economic conditions in the world have changed substantially, so have union-management relations. There is much more cooperation. Management sees cooperative relationships as instrumental in the implementation of quality-improvement strategies. Unions see cooperative relationships as instrumental in protecting the jobs and incomes of their members. And society as a whole sees cooperative relationships as necessary and appropriate in these times of intense global competition. Thus, with some exceptions, we are likely to see cooperative relationships throughout the 1990s.

WHERE WE ARE TODAY

1. Given the opportunity, union and nonunion members respond to the call for quality and quantity—whatever it takes to be more competitive.
2. While there are certainly exceptions, the union movement as a whole still has reservations about the whole quality movement, particularly as it relates to employee empowerment, teamwork, and decision making. Work in these areas can make the union seem less relevant and necessary.
3. Nevertheless, UAW relationships with the Mazda plant in Michigan and the Saturn plant in Tennessee exemplify where the unions are behind the labor-management cooperative movement for quality improvement.
4. Even in England, where much of the labor-management relationship is still traditional, union workers have demonstrated their ability and interest in working in high-quality work environments such as those at the Nissan plant and the Komatsu plant in northern England.
5. Even so, the organized labor movement has diminished over the years, in the U.S. and around the world. Consequently, survival and then rebirth remain key concerns of the union movement.
6. Because of some growth of the union movement into the service sector, you will likely encounter union members in your career. You may even be in the position of joining a union or association someday.
7. In dealing with and understanding the union movement today, it is important to reflect on the history of the movement in the U.S. as well as around the world. Here you may also wish to review our discussion of the union movement in chapter 3.
8. In their attempts to rebuild membership, unions may find themselves creating alternative forms of membership, such as limited memberships at the individual level.
9. With the movement in the U.S. to cut costs, employers have created uncertainties and feelings of powerlessness among many workers. These conditions might provide fertile ground for the regrowth of union membership.
10. We are still to see final resolution on the legal standing of companies using work teams and empowering the work force to make decisions that have a tendency to affect wages and conditions of work.

DISCUSSION QUESTIONS

1. Identify and discuss the factors that make unionization attractive to employees. Are these factors different today than they were fifty years ago?

2. Briefly describe the history of the union movement.
3. What is a certification election? A decertification election? Who do you suppose wins the majority of certification elections today? Why has the rate changed over time?
4. What is the structure of unionization in the U.S. today?
5. What is a bargaining unit? Why is its formation important?
6. Why has there been a recent trend toward cooperation between unions and management?
7. What are the steps in a typical grievance procedure? Is this process formal or informal?
8. Distinguish unions' mandatory, permissive, and prohibited bargaining issues.
9. Distinguish mediation from arbitration. How does a grievance procedure differ from interest arbitration? What is final-offer arbitration?
10. How can unions assist organizations in organizational improvement plans?

APPLIED PROJECTS

1. Interview a union official. Ask about his or her views on plant closings and employee rights to learn about plant closings. Combine this with a library research project to find out what has been written about the topic.
2. Interview personnel and human resource managers on their views of unions. Visit union companies and nonunion companies. Interview union members, nonunion members, and even union officers to learn their views on unions. Present your findings to the class.

CASE STUDY

The Union's Strategic Choice

Maria Dennis sat back and thoughtfully read through the list of strategies the union's committee had given her that morning. If her union were to rebuild the power it had lost over the past few years, it was time to take drastic action. If the union continued to decline as it had been the last few years, it wouldn't be able to represent the members who had voted for it to be their exclusive bargaining representative.

Maria had been elected two years before at her union's convention to be the international president of the Newspaper Workers International Union (NWIU). At the time she knew it would not be an easy job, and she had eagerly looked forward to taking on a new challenge. But she had no idea during the election just how difficult it would be to get the union back on its feet again.

The NWIU had been founded in the late 1890s, made up of newspaper typographers who were responsible for such tasks as setting type on linotype machines, creating the layout of the newspaper, proofing the articles, and printing the newspaper. Members of the union typically completed a six-year apprenticeship, learning all the different tasks involved in the printing process. Prior to 1960 the printing profession had been considered to be the elite of the industrial work force. The craft demanded that typographers be literate at a time when even the middle and upper classes were not. The combination of this literacy with proficiency in a highly skilled, highly paid craft made printers the "status elite" of manual workers.

Since the 1970s, however, the union had begun to decline. Literacy was no longer a unique characteristic, and automation had led to a deskilling of the craft. The introduction of video display terminals, optical character recognition scanners, and computerized typesetting eliminated substantial composing room work, and the demand for skilled union workers was reduced. The union experienced its peak membership of 120,000 in 1965. During the 1970s, however, membership began a substantial decline, and in 1988 the total membership was only 40,000.

The union's reduced membership resulted in other problems for the union. First, there were fewer members to pay dues to the union, which was their main revenue-generating function. Consequently, the union was having some serious financial problems and was being forced to cut some of its services to the members.

Second, the union was experiencing a significant loss in bargaining power with newspaper management. In the past the printers had been fairly secure in their jobs because there was a good demand in the labor market for individuals who could run the complicated printing equipment. But the recent switch to automation had eliminated many jobs and had also made it possible for employers to easily replace union employees. Anyone could be trained in a short time to use the new printing equipment. Therefore, if union members decided to strike for better wages, hours, and working conditions, management could easily, and legally, find replacements for them. In essence, the union was unable to fulfill its main mission, which is to collectively represent those employees who had voted for it. To solve the current crisis, Maria was considering five options.

- Implement an associate member plan through which any individual could join the union for a fee of $50 a year. While these members would not be fully represented on the job, they would get an attractive package of benefits, such as low-cost home, health, and auto insurance.
- Attempt some cooperative labor-management relations programs, such as trying to get member representation on newspaper boards of directors or employee participation programs in the work place.
- Put more effort into political action. For example, lobby for labor law reform or for new laws more favorable to unions. Try to initiate action that would result in harsher penalties against employers that practice illegal union-avoidance activities, such as threatening to move the business if a union is voted in or firing pro-union employees.
- Appeal to community leaders to speak out in favor of the union in order to improve public relations, to help recruit new members, and to encourage employers to bargain fairly when negotiating with the union.
- Search for another union with which they might merge, thus increasing their membership, strengthening their finances, increasing their bargaining power, and obtaining economies of scale.

Maria realized each of the above options could have both positive and negative results and was unsure which strategy, if any, she should recommend for the union to pursue. In less than three hours, however, she would have to present the list to the council with her recommendations.

SOURCE: By Kay Stratton

Case Questions

1. What are the strengths and weaknesses of each strategy?
2. What strategies could be employed to get new bargaining units?
3. What other types of services could the union offer to its members?
4. What would your final recommendation be? Justify your response.

NOTES

1. "At Saturn, What Workers Want is ... Fewer Defects," *Business Week* (2 Dec. 1991): 117-18.
2. See note l.
3. "Highlights of GM/UAW Agreement," *Bulletin to Management* (11 Oct. 1990): 321. Information for the case was also taken from J. Zalusky, "Variable Pay: Labor Seeks Security, Not Bonuses," *Business Week* (Jan. 1991): 13; C. Brown and M. Reich, "When Does Union-Management Cooperation Work? A Look at NUMMI and GM–Van Nuys," *California Management Review* (Summer 1989): 27–44; "'The U.S. Must Do What GM has Done,' interview with Roger Smith, CEO of General Motors," *Fortune* (13 Feb. 1989): 70–73; G. A. Patterson, "GM's New Contract with UAW may be Ratified Sunday," *The Wall Street Journal* (28 Sept. 1990): A11; D. Woodruff, "It Looks as if the UAW is Drawing a Bead on GM," *Business Week* (20 Aug. 1990): 38; and D. Woodruff, "The UAW Veers Closer to Reality," *Business Week* (1 Oct. 1990): 33; W. Zellner, "Suddenly, the UAW is Raising its Voice at GM," *Business Week* (6 Nov. 1989): 96, 100; W. Zellner, "All the Ingredients for Disaster are There," *Business Week* (16 April 1990): 20–29.
4. "The Changing Situation of Workers and Their Unions," Report of the AFL-CIO Evolution of Work Committee

(Feb. 1985): 18–19; P. Jarley and J. Fiorito, "Associate Membership: Unionism or Consumerism?" *Industrial and Labor Relations Review* (Jan. 1990): 209–224.

5. For a more extensive discussion of unionization and the entire union-management relationship, see G. Strauss, D. G. Gallagher, and J. Fiorito, *The State of the Unions* (Madison, Wis.: Industrial Relations Research Association, University of Wisconsin, 1991); P. C. Weiler, *Governing the Workplace* (Cambridge., Mass.: Harvard University Press, 1990); H. J. Anderson, *Primer of Labor Relations,* 21st ed. (Washington, D.C.: Bureau of National Affairs, 1980); B. W. Justice, *Unions, Workers, and the Law* (Washington, D.C.: Bureau of National Affairs, 1983).
6. For an overview and in-depth discussion of collective bargaining, see L. Balliet, *Survey of Labor Relations* (Washington, D.C.: Bureau of National Affairs, 1981): J. A. Fossum, "Union-Management Relations," in *Personnel Management,* ed. K. M. Rowland and G. R. Ferris (Boston, Mass.: Allyn & Bacon, 1982): 420–60; J. A. Fossum, "Labor Relations," in *Human Resource Management in the 1980s,* ed. S. J. Carroll and R. S. Schuler (Washington, D.C.: Bureau of National Affairs, 1983); R. B. Freeman and J. L. Medoff, *What Do Unions Do?* (New York: Basic Books, 1984); R. J. Donovan, "Bringing America into the 1980s," *American Psychologist* (April 1984): 429–31.
7. J. Barling, E. K. Kelloway, and E. H. Bremermann, "Preemployment Predictors of Union Attitudes: The Role of Family Socialization and Work Beliefs," *Journal of Applied Psychology* 75, no. 5 (1991): 725–31; S. Mellor, "The Relationship Between Membership Decline and Union Commitment: A Field Study of Local Unions in Crisis," *Journal of Applied Psychology* 75, no. 3 (1990): 258–67; C. Fullagar and J. Barling, "A Longitudinal Test of a Model of the Antecedents and Consequences of Union Loyalty," *Journal of Applied Psychology* 74, no. 2 (1989): 213–27; S. P. Deshpande and J. Fiorito, "Specific and General Beliefs in Union Voting Models," *Academy of Management Journal* 32, no.4 (1989): 883–97; G. E. Fryxell and M. E. Gordon, "Workplace Justice and Job Satisfaction as Predictors of Satisfaction with Union and Management," *Academy of Management Journal* 32, no. 4 (1989): 851–66.
8. E. H. Schein, *Organizational Psychology* (Englewood Cliffs, N.J.: Prentice-Hall, 1965).
9. J. G. Getman, S. B. Goldberg, and J. B. Herman, *Union Representation Elections: Law and Reality* (New York: Russell Sage Foundation, 1976); "Employee Survey: Unionization and Attitude Measure," *Bulletin to Management* (24 April 1986): 133–34.
10. "The UAW vs. Japan: It's Showdown Time in Tennessee," *Business Week* (4 July 1989): 64–65; K. B. Noble, "Union Organizers' Task is Uphill at Nissan Point," *The New York Times* (3 April 1988): 18; D. P. Levin, "Nissan Workers in U.S. Test Union and Industry," *The New York Times* (12 Aug. 1989): 8; R. Kuttner, "A Beachhead for the Beleaguered Labor Movement," *Business Week* (17 July 1989): 14–15.
11. A. Ritter, "Are Unions Worth the Bargain?" *Personnel* (Feb. 1990): 12–14; Brett, "Behavioral Research on Unions," and Brett, "Why Employees Want Unions": 47–59.
12. S. A. Youngblood, A. D. DeNisi, J. Molleston, and W. H. Mobley, "The Impact of Work Attachment, Instrumentality Beliefs, Perceived Labor Union Image, and Subjective Norms on Union Voting Intentions and Union Membership," *Academy of Management Journal* (1984): 576–90.
13. T. Kochan, *Collective Bargaining and Industrial Relations* (Homewood, Ill.: Irwin, 1980); J. LeLouarn, *Proceedings of the 32nd Annual Meeting of the Industrial Relations Research Association* (1979): 72–82.
14. Getman, Goldman, and Herman, *Union Representation Elections.*
15. J. H. Hopkins and R. D. Binderup, "Employee Relations and Union Organizing Campaigns," *Personnel Administrator* (March 1980): 57–61.
16. Pro-union legislation in the 1920s and 1930s was favored by some pro-management groups because it was seen as a way to bring some degree of certainty and peace to union-management relationships. See Balliet, *Survey of Labor Relations:* 13–68.
17. A. A. Sloane and F. Witney, *Labor Relations,* 5th ed. (Englewood Cliffs, N. J.: Prentice-Hall, 1985): 57.
18. Sloane and Witney, *Labor Relations:* p. 62.
19. For an extensive presentation of union membership data, see C. Gifford, ed., *Directory of U.S. Labor Organizations, 1990-1991 Edition* (Washington, D.C.: Bureau of National Affairs, 1990); and "Union Membership in 1991," *Bulletin to Management Datagraph* (5 March 1992): 68–69; "Union Membership," *Bulletin to Management Datagraph* (28 Feb. 1991): 60–61.
20. "Union Membership," *Bulletin to Management Datagraph* (1 March 1990); "More Women Leading Unions," *Fair Employment Practices* (22 Nov. 1990): 141; J. G. Kilgour, "The Odds on White-Collar Organizing," *Personnel* (Aug. 1990): 29–34; S. R. Premeaux, R. W. Mondy, A. L. Bethke, and R. Comish, "Managing Tomorrow's Unionized Workers," *Personnel* (July 1989): 61–64; M. L. Colosi and W. A. Krupman, "Nurses: Supervisory Status or Union Solidarity?" *Personnel* (Sept. 1989): 13–18; "Professionals Not Ready for Union Organizing," *Bulletin to Management* (26 Oct. 1989): 337–38.
21. C. Gifford, *Directory of U.S. Labor Organizations 1990-1991 Edition* (Washington, D.C.: Bureau of National Affairs, Inc. 1990).
22. Getman, Goldberg, and Herman, *Union Representation Elections.*
23. Balliet, *Survey of Labor Relations:* 72–105.
24. Getman, Goldberg, and Herman, *Union Representation Elections:* 1.
25. Balliet, *Survey of Labor Relations:* 72–105.
26. For an extensive discussion of the organizing campaign, see J. A. Fossum, "Union-Management Relations," in *Personnel Management,* eds. K. M. Rowland and G. R. Ferris (Boston, Mass.: Allyn and Bacon, 1982); W. E. Fulmer, "Step by Step Through a Union Campaign," *Harvard Business Review* (July-Aug. 1981): 94–102.
27. "Dealing with Organizing: Do's and Don'ts," *Bulletin to Management* (7 March 1985): 8.
28. See note 27.
29. Twomey, *Labor Law and Legislation:* 134.

30. Getman, Goldberg, and Herman, *Union Representation Elections:* 72.
31. "Union Win Rate in 1991," *Bulletin to Management* (26 March 1992): 92–93.
32. "Do Union Contracts Conflict with ADA?" *Bulletin to Management* (19 Dec. 1991): 400.
33. J. Brett, "Behavioral Research on Unions and Union Management Systems," in eds. B. M. Staw and L. L. Cummings, *Research in Organizational Behavior,* vol. 2 (Greenwich, Conn.: JAI Press, 1980): 200
34. See N. Herrick, *Joint Management and Employee Participation: Labor and Management at the Crossroads* (San Francisco: Jossey-Bass, 1990); J. M. Brett, "Behavioral Research on Unions and Union-Management Systems, in eds. B. M. Staw and L. L. Cummings, *Research in Organizational Behavior,* vol. 2, (Greenwich, Conn.: JAI Press 1980); J. M. Brett, "Why Employees Want Unions, " *Organizational Dynamics* 8 (1980): 45–59; W. C. Hamner and F. J. Smith, "Work Attitudes as Predictors of Unionization Activity," *Journal of Applied Psychology* 63 (1978): 415–21; "Unions Are Turning to Polls to Read the Rank and File," *Business Week* (22 Oct. 1984): 66–67; W. Serrin, "Unions are Shifting Gears but Not Goals," *The New York Times* (31 March 1985): 2E.
35. D. Q. Mills, *The New Competitors* (New York: Free Press, 1985): 225–42; M. Schuster, "The Impact of Union-Management Cooperation on Productivity and Employment," *Industrial and Labor Relations Review* (April 1983): 415–30; H. C. Katz, T. A. Kochan, and K. R. Gobeille, "Industrial Relations Performance, Economic Performance, and QWL Programs: An Interplant Analysis," *Industrial and Labor Relations Review* (Oct. 1983): 3–17.
36. "What's Creating an 'Industrial Miracle' at Ford?" *Business Week* (30 July 1984): 80.
37. J. Hoerr, "The Strange Bedfellows Backing Workplace Reform," *Business Week* (20 April 1990): 57. Also see R. Koenig, "Quality Circles are Vulnerable to Union Tests," *The Wall Street Journal* (28 March 1990): B1; L. E. Hazzard, "A Union Says Yes to Attendance," *Personnel Journal* (Nov. 1990): 47–49.
38. T. Hayes, "Saving 3,727 GM Jobs in Texas," *The New York Times* (1 March 1992): F10.
39. J. Fossum, *Labor Relations: Development, Structure, Process,* 4th ed. (Plano, Tex.: Business Publications, 1988).
40. A Blum, "Collective Bargaining: Ritual or Reality?" *Harvard Business Review* (Nov.-Dec. 1961): 64.
41. M. Bazerman, *Judgment in Managerial Decision Making* (New York Wiley, 1986); M. Bazerman and J. S. Carroll, "Negotiator Cognition," in eds. L. Cummings and B. Staw, *Research in Organizational Behavior,* vol. 9 (Greenwich, Conn.: JAI Press, 1987); M. H. Bazerman, T. Magliozzi, and M. A. Neale, "The Acquisition of an Integrative Response in a Competitive Market, *Organizational Behavior and Human Decision Processes* 34 (1985): 294–313.
42. K. Jennings and E. Traynman, "Two-Tier Plans," *Personnel Journal* (March 1988): 56–58.
43. Sloan and Witney, *Labor Relations.*
44. Fossum, *"Labor Relations":* 395–96.
45. P. Hartman and W. Franke, "The Changing Bargaining Structure in Construction: Wide-Area and Multicraft Bargaining," *Industrial and Labor Relations Review* (Jan. 1980): 170–84.
46. Sloan and Witney, *Labor Relations:* 59.
47. Hartman and Franke, "The Changing Bargaining Structure in Construction..."
48. Fossum, *Labor Relations.*
49. M. Bazerman and M. A. Neale, "Heuristics in Negotiation: Limitations to Effective Dispute Resolution," in eds. M. Bazerman and R. Lewick, *Negotiating in Organizations* (Beverly Hills, Calif.: Sage, 1983): 51–67; M. Gordon, et al., "Laboratory Research in Bargaining and Negotiations: An Evaluation, *Industrial Relations* (Spring 1984): 218–23; R. E. Walton and R. B. McKersie, *A Behavioral Theory of Labor Negotiations* (New York: McGraw-Hill, 1965).
50. M. Neale, V. Huber, and G. Northcraft, "The Framing of Negotiations: Contextual versus Task Frame," *Organizational Behavior and Human Decision Processes* 39 (1987): 228–41.
51. L. Reynolds, "Management-Labor Tensions Spell Union Busting," *Personnel* (March 1991): 7–10; "Teamsters Hope Democracy Brings New Membership," *Personnel* (March 1991): 1–2; B. Schiffman, "Tougher Tactics to Keep Out Unions," *The New York Times* (3 March 1991): F8; "Lockout and Shutdowns," *Labor Relations Reporter* (Washington, D.C.: Bureau of National Affairs, 1985): 688–91.
52. D. Mitchell, "A Note on Strike Propensities and Wage Developments," *Industrial Relations* 20 (1981): 123–27; J. Kennan, "Pareto Optimality and the Economics of Strike Duration," *Journal of Labor Research* 1 (1980): 77–94.
53. A. Kotlowitz, "Labor's Shift: Finding Strikes Harder to Win: More Unions Turn to Slowdowns," *The Wall Street Journal* (22 May 1987): 1.
54. J. Tasini, "For the Unions, a New Weapon," *The New York Times Magazine* (12 June 1988): 24–25, 69–71.
55. S. Briggs, "Labor/Management Conflict and the Role of the Neutral," in eds. R. Schuler, S. Youngblood and V. Huber, *Personnel and Human Resource Management,* 3d ed. (St. Paul, Minn.: West Publishing, 1988).
56. "Judgment Day for Arbitrators," *Business Week* (19 April 1982): 66; R. Johnson, "Interest Arbitration Examined," *Personnel Administrator* (Jan. 1983): 53–59, 73; P. Compton-Forbes, "Interest Arbitration Hasn't Worked Well in the Public Sector," *Personnel Administrator* (Feb. 1984): 99–104.
57. Johnson, "Interest Arbitration Examined;" "Collective Bargaining Through Diplomacy," *Bulletin to Management* (25 Jan. 1990): 32.
58. R. L. Blevins, "Maximizing Company Rights Under the Contract," *Personnel Administrator* (June 1984): 75–82; and D. A. Hawver, "Plan Before Negotiating...and Increase Your Power of Persuasion," *Management Review* (Feb. 1984): 46–48; R. J. Colon, "Grievances Hinge on Poor Contract Language," *Personnel Journal* (Sept. 1990): 32–36.
59. S. Slichter, J. Healy, and E. Livernash, *The Impact of Collective Bargaining on Management* (Washington, D.C.: The Brookings Institution, 1960): 694.
60. See note 59: 694–96.

61. J. N. Draznin, "Labor Relations," *Personnel Journal* (July 1981): 528; J. N. Draznin, "Labor Relations," *Personnel Journal* (Aug. 1980): 625; B. A. Jacobs, "Don't Take 'No' for an Answer," *Industry Week* (26 Jan. 1981): 38–43; Kochan, *Collective Bargaining and Industrial Relations:* 385–86; I. Paster, Collective Bargaining: Warnings for the Novice Negotiator," *Personnel Journal* (March 1981): 203–206; M. H. Bazerman and M. A. Neale, *Negotiating Rationally* (New York: The Free Press, 1992).
62. B. Skeleton and P. Marett, "Loser Pays Arbitration," *Labor Law Journal* (May 1979): 302–309.
63. G. Bolander, "Fair Representation: Not Just a Union Problem," *Personnel Administrator* (March 1980): 39.
64. "Memorandum 79-55," National Labor Relations Board, July 1979.
65. D. Dalton and W. Todor, "Manifest Needs of Stewards: Propensity to File a Grievance," *Journal of Applied Psychology* (Dec. 1979): 654–59.
66. T. A. Kochan, R. B. McKersie, and P. Cappelli, "Strategic choice and Industrial Relations Theory," *Industrial Relations* (Winter 1984): 16–38; T. A. Kochan and J. Chalykoff, "Human Resource Management and Business Life Cycles: Some Preliminary Propositions," paper presented at UCLA Conference on Human Resources and Industrial Relations in High Technology Firms, 21 June 1985; D. Q. Mills, *The New Competitors:* 243–71.
67. J. Hoerr, "What Should Unions Do?" *Harvard Business Review* (May-June 1991): 30-45.
68. C. McDonald, "U.S. Union Membership in Future Decades: A Trade Unionist's Perspective," *Industrial Relations* (Winter 1992): 13–30; eds. A. Gladstone, et al., *Labour Relations in a Changing Environment* (New York: Walter de Gruyter, 1992); M Bognanno and M. Kleiner, "Introduction: Labor Market Institutions and the Future Role of Unions," *Industrial Relations* (Winter 1992): 1–12.
69. R. Marshall, "The Future Role of Government in Industrial Relations," *Industrial Relations* (Winter 1992): 31–49.
70. J. Reid, Jr., "Future Unions," *Industrial Relations* (Winter 1992): 122–36.
71. J. M. Markham,"German Workers Watch the Clock," *The New York Times* (13 May 1984); P. Revzin, "Swedes Gain Leisure, Not Jobs, by Cutting Hours," *The Wall Street Journal* (7 Jan. 1985): 10.
72. D. J. Schneider, "Canadian and U.S. Brands of Unionism Have Distinctly Different Nationalities," *Management Review* (Oct. 1983): 31–32.
73. M. S. O'Connor, *Report on Japanese Employee Relations Practices and Their Relation to Worker Productivity,* a report prepared for the Study Mission to Japan, (Nov. 1980): 8–23.
74. K. F. Walker, "The Development of Australian Industrial Relations in International Perspective," in *Perspectives on Australian Industrial Relations,* ed. W. A. Howard (Melbourne: Longman Cheshire, 1984).
75. For a comparison of laws governing union security in Australia and the United States, see B. Aaron, "Union Security in Australia and the United States," *Comparative Labor Law* 6 (1984): 415–41.
76. "Management Pressures for Change and the Industrial Relations System," Business Council of Australia submission to the Alternatives to the Present Arbitration System conference, Oct. 1984, Sydney.
77. *Report of the Committee of Review: Australia Industrial Relations Law and Systems* (Canberra: Australian Government Publishing Service, 1985).
78. For an analysis of these changes, see "Australia Vaults Ahead with Free Banking," *The Wall Street Journal* (4 Nov. 1985): 10, 26.
79. This observation was drawn from S. Deery and D. Plowman, *Australian Industrial Relations,* 3d ed. (Sydney: McGraw-Hill, 1985).

END OF SECTION CASE STUDY

QWL Startup: Is the Formula for Success Always the Same?

Alan is a third-level manager at a large public utility. In his organization, the Midwest Utility Company, Alan is a relatively young manager for somebody at the third-level of management. He received an MBA from a prestigious New England school where his training emphasized the development of non-traditional views regarding the role of management. Alan's job entailed responsibility for delivering his company's special services to the public. Customers would call Alan's offices and place orders for special services. Alan directly supervised four second-level managers who in turn supervised five first-level supervisors each. Each first-level supervisor had ten non-management, union-represented employees reporting to them. This resulted in a total of 20 first-level supervisors and 200 non-management employees within Alan's district. All these employees worked at one job site located in the suburb of a large metropolitan area. The non-management employees were represented by one local union of the Public Service Workers International (PSWI).

One chief steward represented all of Alan's non-management employees. This individual, Rita, came from a largely blue-collar, unionized background. When news spread of Alan's appointment, Rita was concerned. Having heard rumors about Alan's new ideas, she felt that Alan could create problems in an otherwise stable situation. The manager previous to Alan had been from the old line. He expressed much mistrust of the union, which was echoed by Rita in a mistrust of management. Both had learned to live together in a highly competitive atmosphere with a fragile truce. Under this truce, grievance activity was high as was the number of disciplinary actions filed by management.

Alan entered this job assignment with a perspective that varied from that of his predecessor and the majority of managers in his company. He believed that the only sensible approach to employee relations involved cooperation between union and management. Within the first week of this job assignment, Alan learned the history of the relationship between his predecessor and Rita. He determined that the most effective way to overcome the previous pattern of relationship would be to begin immediately with a new set of ground rules. As a first step, Alan invited Rita to a meeting, at a neutral off-site location, to become better acquainted with each other.

Rita was one of the few female chief stewards in her local union. She had moved through the union hierarchy by watching management carefully out of the corner of her eye. This behavior resulted in Rita winning several strategic victories on disputes with Alan's predecessor. In one instance, Rita won a grievance that shortened the workday of her employees by fifteen minutes through the implementation of a time allowance for travel to work. This particular victory entrenched Rita so firmly in her position that she had run for reelection uncontested in the last union election. Rita viewed any form of cooperation with management as a pitfall that could undermine the support she received from her constituency. Yet she did agree to Alan's meeting so as not to appear closed-minded to the new manager. Rita felt that she could use the meeting to probe Alan for weaknesses that could be used to her advantage at a later date.

At the meeting, Alan surprised Rita by not suggesting any radical changes in the operations of the department. Instead, Alan focused the meeting on pleasant discussion, with Alan probing Rita for her reactions to some of the more pressing problems employees experienced at the workplace. Rita was surprised to find that she and Alan shared some common perceptions of problems and the most effective solutions. The entire meeting went by without either party proposing any changes in the relationship. Both individuals felt positive about the experience but realized that the demands of the job could prevent any additional movement. At the conclusion of the meeting, Alan did suggest a follow-up meeting between himself, Rita, and the president and vice-president of her local union. Rita indicated that she would propose this to her officers but could not make any promises as to their receptivity.

Later that day, Rita met with her local officers and briefed them on the details of her meeting with Alan. Rita was surprised to find her officers receptive to pursuing this matter. In response to Alan's invitation, these officers found themselves in an unusually precarious situation. In the most recent contract negotiation, the international union negotiated a clause into the collective bargaining agreement urging cooperation between union and management to improve the quality of working lives of all employees. It had been a year since the contract was signed and no activity had been initiated anywhere in the company. The international was placing much pressure on the various locals to begin exercising this clause. These officers felt that they could win considerable points with their international by becoming the first local to move ahead with

Quality of Work Life (QWL) efforts. Another factor pressing in favor of Alan's invitation concerned the financial state of the Midwest Utility Company. The company was undergoing a financial crisis, tied to an economic recession, which was soon to result in a loss of jobs because of changing human resource needs. The officers realized that the maintenance of existing jobs could depend on changing the strategies they employed when dealing with management.

On the negative side, these officers were scared of QWL. They had become comfortable in their old patterns of behavior and the idea of changing created stress. Traditionally, these officers had resisted any form of cooperation between labor and management. They believed that any perception on the part of the rank and file that the officers were cooperating with management would undermine their authority. There was a very stiff anti-management contingent in the local that would pounce on any management cooperation. Already there were rumblings in the local about "selling out" to management that might strengthen the opposition in the upcoming union election.

It was with some degree of mixed emotions that the officers agreed to at least meet with Alan to hear what he had to say. The meeting took place at an off-site location. Ground rules that had been set in advance prohibited the discussion of particular problem issues (i.e., unresolved grievances) and encouraged discussion only of issues of mutual concern not specifically governed by the collective bargaining agreement. Rita was particularly uneasy regarding this meeting because she was seeing her officers in a different light. When she agreed to suggest the meeting to her officers, she expected a flat refusal. Instead, the offer was met with an almost immediate acceptance.

The actual meeting turned out to be more positive than any of the parties had expected. A number of areas of mutual concern that could be resolved through joint action were raised at the meeting. It was unanimous that further action was warranted and positive benefits to all parties might result. A tentative plan was developed to continue meeting and to hold further discussions. All parties agreed that no actions would be implemented immediately but future discussions would move slowly and involve more people.

The local officers decided that they would leave all future matters in Rita's hands. She was chief steward and the people involved looked to Rita for leadership. These leaders were playing a cautious hand by leaving themselves out of the direct action for several reasons: First, their direct involvement might be interpreted as an attempt to undermine and usurp Rita's authority. Second, if the attempt at QWL improvement turned into a disaster, they were leaving Rita to take the blame. Finally, if sentiments in the local ran anti-QWL involvement, they could claim that this was Rita's territory and they had no right to interfere. Rita thoroughly understood the vulnerable position she was being placed in and agreed to these terms. Rita was willing to risk the possibility of failure in return for the high potential payoff. Rita realized that since her people were involved, she should be the one to take the political risks. Rita reluctantly agreed to move ahead with further discussions. In return, the officers left all responsibility with Rita and agreed to act as unofficial resource people providing whatever informal support they could. Alan agreed to these terms and further proposed that sometime in the future a steering committee be established, jointly chaired by Rita and himself with an equal number of union and management representatives. His proposal was unanimously accepted.

Although reluctant, Rita treated this new change as a challenge. She felt that if successful this process could have a permanent and positive impact on her constituency. After several future discussions, Alan and Rita felt that it was time to move ahead. They determined that the next step would be to invite several "key people," both management and union, from the work district to a familiarization meeting. They invited all second-level managers, assistant chief stewards, and stewards to this meeting. In all, fourteen persons attended the meeting. Alan and Rita jointly presented the concept of QWL and their vision concerning what this might entail. Of the fourteen present, ten elected to move ahead and pursue the matter further.

Throughout a slow and arduous process lasting about eighteen months, Rita and Alan developed what many considered to be the organization's "showcase" QWL effort. QWL committees and teams had been established at all levels of the district. Employees became actively involved in the process. Many changes in work procedures were implemented that saved the company considerable money and made the work more interesting and challenging. Morale among employees was high and employees from all over the company were requesting transfers into the district. Alan gained a positive reputation as a manager who was willing to take risks and who could deliver results. Rita found herself besieged with requests to act as a union spokesperson for the benefits of QWL.

At this point, Alan received a change in job assignments. A new and unique position opened up in the company that called for a manager with new ideas who was not afraid to take risks. Because of his success with QWL, Alan had become quite visible and was placed in this new assignment. His new assignment entailed responsibility for 300 non-management and 45 management employees dispersed widely over a geographic region entailing an entire state. Alan was charged with supervising the work of 20 different offices with employee counts ranging from 5 to 50 employees at each location. These employees were represented by eight different local unions. This involved a significant job change for Alan, who had previously managed employees at one office who were represented by one local union.

Consistent with his past success, Alan decided that the most effective manner to approach his present job assignment was to implement QWL as a mechanism for managing his employees. This situation presented a unique challenge to Alan. The function his people were performing involved the marketing of new product lines to new customers. These services were recent additions to his company and had come about as a result of some technological advances. All the employees were new to their jobs. There were no standard practices, nor was there any type of history of union-management relationships. Alan was literally starting from scratch. His company did not even have the expertise in these services to provide training for his employees. Alan had to contract with an outside vendor for these services.

As a first step, Alan invited a representative of each local union to a preliminary meeting. Two of the locals refused to attend, wanting no part in any cooperation with management. Six locals did send representatives. In some cases, the president of the local attended, in other cases a chief steward attended. In addition to the union representatives, Alan invited his nine second-level managers, all of whom attended. These managers had just begun working for Alan and had heard of his penchant for union-management cooperation. Although several were distrustful and would rather not have attended, they did not want to risk making an unfavorable impression on their new supervisor. Total attendance at this meeting included 22 individuals.

From the very beginning, Alan encountered a host of problems that thwarted his progress. Even the scheduling of the initial meeting presented problems. With the wide geographic dispersion of his work locations, some locals represented as few as ten members while others represented as many as 70 employees. Ideally, Alan desired to create a steering committee with representation from each local. One of the smaller locals, representing ten employees, was located over 150 miles from the meeting place. This required the union representative to travel considerable distance and to spend considerable time to attend a meeting at which he represented only ten employees.

There was a wide variance among the locals in terms of their experience with QWL. Some locals were old hands while others were relative newcomers. Among those present at the meeting was Rita, who represented 20 employees in Alan's new district. Alan and Rita immediately started conversing and remarking at their excitement about working together again. The remainder of the initial meeting consisted of a two-way conversation between Alan and Rita concerning what they felt could be accomplished with this new and unique job situation. In their enthusiasm, Alan and Rita failed to notice that the representatives of the other locals were remaining quiet and not participating.

By the conclusion of the meeting, Alan and Rita had developed an action plan that included the development and administration of an extensive survey to measure the relevant attitudes of employees in the district. Within 60 days following the meeting, each employee would be asked to complete a survey. This data would then be used to facilitate the implementation of joint union-management QWL efforts. One of the union representatives present, Mark, was very upset at the pace of the meeting. Mark was a union president from an outstate location and had traveled 100 miles to attend this meeting. Only 15 of his members actually reported to Alan. Under normal circumstances, Mark would have sent his chief steward, but in this case he wanted to hear everything that transpired. He decided way in advance of the meeting that QWL and labor-management cooperation represented an unacceptable mode of operating. He attended the meeting because management was paying the expenses for his trip and he wanted to be informed concerning all goings on.

At the meeting, Mark only became more firm in his anti-cooperation attitudes. He believed that Alan was pressuring those in attendance into action before they had the opportunity to investigate alternatives. He was dismayed at the relationship between Rita and Alan. Upon leaving the meeting he was heard to comment that Rita's union had sold out to management. After returning to his local. Mark sent Alan a note indicating that his local would have no further involvement in QWL activities.

Aside from Mark, the other members of the steering committee agreed to go ahead with the implementation of QWL and specifically the survey. Many in attendance felt that Alan was moving too fast but did not express these sentiments. The chief steward of one of the larger locals, Steve, had no direct experience with QWL. He was friends with Rita and had heard many positive comments from her and from other local officers. Steve had been interested in getting started in some QWL activity for several months. Upon first receiving Alan's invitation to the meeting he was pleased that the opportunity to begin had presented itself. Although he voted to move ahead with QWL, Steve's enthusiasm fell off by the end of the meeting. He left feeling railroaded and disappointed that his input at the meeting had not been sought to a greater degree.

After the meeting Alan and Rita met for a debriefing. Both felt that something at the meeting was missing. They were disappointed and could not explain the unenthusiastic attitude expressed by those in attendance. Several months later Mark changed his negative attitude about QWL. He had come around to a more positive way of thinking about union-management cooperation. By the time he was ready to participate, the survey had already been administered and fed back. The steering committee was moving ahead with other projects. Mark's local had been left out of the action and nobody wanted to slow down to allow them to catch up.

SOURCE: Mitchell W. Fields, Texas A & M University; and James W. Thacker, University of Windsor. Printed by permission.

End of Text Summary Cases

THE BUZZY COMPANY DOWNTURN
NORTHEAST DATA RESOURCES, INC.

SUMMARY CASE

The Buzzy Company Downturn

The Challenge

During his regular weekly staff meeting, Mr. Topman, president of the Buzzy Company, expressed his serious concern over the report he had just received. "I have indications that there is not enough *enthusiasm* prevalent throughout the Buzzy plant," he stated emphatically. "We are not going to tolerate such an attitude," President Topman continued. "Buzzy people are always enthusiastic, and you, the staff members, are going to help me straighten this out!"

Most of the staff members realized that the recent business slowdown had necessitated a sizable reduction in workforce, causing many key people to personally question their own job security. To avoid the stigma of being laid off, many employees often actively sought and accepted positions in other companies. Those who remained were becoming conscious of protecting their job status. Established informal communication networks were being broken as a result of people leaving. Coupled with the fact that sales were down significantly from the previous year, many staff members wondered when they could expect Buzzy's employee and financial recovery.

Mr. Topman told his staff that this trend had to be reversed. Somehow, they would have to bring about a management renewal to ensure the successful achievement of their newly established company objectives. The president charged each member of his staff to carefully consider methods for overcoming their present dilemma.

Business Situation

Financially, the Buzzy Company had operated profitably over the years with about 80 percent of the business defense oriented. However, in 1979, changes in the defense market coupled with an altered economic environment began to reverse the trend. By 1982 consumer sales were up to 70 percent of total. Since 1988, however, an unexpected decrease in sales caused considerable alarm throughout the organization. In an effort to remain profitable in the face of declining sales, the company management found it necessary to make corresponding and significant reductions in force. In addition, wages became essentially frozen.

As viewed from top management levels, the business prospects for the future, by contrast, looked encouraging. In anticipation of improved business prospects, Mr. Topman redirected Buzzy's business objectives toward those opportunities that would most likely yield the highest return on investment.

Recognition of Problem

Mr. Topman and his immediate advisors recognized that the achievement of their newly established business objectives would require the support of an effective management organization to execute their carefully formulated plans. Unfortunately, the uncertainty that shrouded the general workforce was not seen by Mr. Topman as a major obstacle to achievement of company goals. This problem was the surprisingly sticky subject that generated considerable discussion at the next few weekly staff meetings. Many staff members thought that there was an insidious decay of personal motivation eating away at the vital elements of the organization. It finally became obvious to everyone that unless the current trends were reversed, the company would be faced with the prospect of replacing key individuals.

Because of the mounting concern expressed frequently by the members of his staff, Mr. Topman appointed a special task force to investigate the problem, to evaluate various alternative solutions, and to make appropriate recommendations. The task force consisted of the director of Industrial Relations, Mr. Peoples; the executive assistant to the president, Ms. Ryan; the director of Research and Development, Dr. Dees; the vice-president of Finance, Ms. Marcus; and the director of Business Planning, Mr. Guth. The makeup of the group was intended to represent a broad spectrum of company interests and talents.

Following the appointment of the task force, a series of meetings was held to accomplish their assigned task. It was decided that interviews with selected employees should be conducted to gather data relating to the problem. A reputable consultant firm was retained to assist in the investigation.

It was agreed that the survey data obtained from interviews throughout the company revealed at best an incomplete picture of the real problems facing the company. This was attributed to the fact that in this setting of uncertainty, people were reluctant to speak freely about their real concerns. As a consequence, the use of qualified interviewers from outside the company organization was seen by the task force as a mechanism for obtaining the data necessary for an intelligent definition of the problem.

Accordingly, the services of a reputable consulting firm, Burke and Associates, were obtained for the purposes of conducting confidential interviews, analyzing the data, and identifying pertinent problem areas. The results of this activity as summarized by, Burke and Associates, revealed that "... the central problem was communication throughout your organization—upward, downward, and laterally." This opinion expressed by the outside consultants was, of course, confirmed by the earlier reluctance of people to discuss their concern freely with company interviewers.

In addition, Burke and Associates interviews with many in management positions indicated a widespread desire to improve their management skills. For example, many managers indicated they would like to learn how to make better use of time in the execution of their assigned job.

Based on the findings of the consultants and their own independent investigations, the task force came to the conclusion that a management development program, specifically designed to address the identified problems and needs of the Buzzy organization, could contribute greatly toward the achievement of company objectives. Toward this end, the group then considered alternative methods of implementing such a program.

Consideration of Alternative Solutions

Three alternative approaches to implement the recommended management development program were considered by the task force. Identified as Plans A, B, and C, they are described briefly as follows:

Plan A–Existing In-House Talent

Adoption of this approach would involve the identification of individuals presently within the company who possess the unique talents required to implement such a program. The task force members agreed that the qualifications of the selected person (or persons) would have to include

- An advanced degree with at least a minor in education and/or psychology
- Previous related experience in the field of management development
- A keen appreciation of the unique problems and their relation to the company

Once selected, the individual(s) would become thoroughly familiar with the problems, investigate appropriate management training objectives directed toward the specific needs, and administer the resulting management development program.

Plan B—Hiring of a Professional Management Training Director

If this approach were recommended by the task force and adopted by the company, a lengthy sequence of activities and events would occur beginning with the preparation of a fairly comprehensive description of the job to be performed, not only in terms of the immediate problems at hand, but also the longer-range requirements associated with continuing management development training. Having established such a job description, the company would then advertise for prospective applicants. The qualifications and salary requirements would be carefully screened and the best qualified would be selected. Following his or her employment, the new management training director would begin an extensive orientation period during which he or she would become familiar with the company, its people, and their interrelated problems. Based on his or her perception of the situation and understanding of the assignment, the training director could select an appropriate management development program and administer it.

Plan C—Engagement of a Professional Consulting Firm

The third alternative solution considered by the task force would involve identification of the qualified professional consulting and/or management development firms. Having selected a firm whose capabilities best matched the specific needs of Buzzy, the company would then contract for services including the following:

- Confidential interviews with a representative sample of management and supervisory personnel
- An analysis of the results of these interviews to verify the previously identified problems
- Identification of other problem areas revealed by the interviews
- Proposal of a management development program
- If acceptable to the company, the execution of the program

Evaluation of Alternative Solutions

Having defined the alternative solutions described above, the task force then evaluated each of these in terms of their advantages and disadvantages, their respective probabilities of successfully achieving the specific objectives, and an analysis of required investment of resources versus the expected returns.

As seen by the task force, Plan A offered the unique advantage over the other plans that a qualified individual selected from within the company might already be well aware of the problems facing the company. Also, it was felt that such an insider would probably be more personally concerned than an outsider because of his or her established involvement with the company.

Several disadvantages were also recognized by the task force. It was generally conceded that it was not likely that the task force would find an individual employed by the company with the require qualifications. Even if identified, making this person available for this assignment would probably require the hiring of an individual to fill the vacant slot. Also, the reluctance on the part of potential trainees to respond openly during interviews would still exist to some degree and thereby diminish the effectiveness of the interview.

In general, it was believed by the members of the task force that Plan A had a low probability of successfully achieving the required objectives. Also, while the investment needed to implement the plan was thought to be the lowest, the expected results were similarly valued low.

Adoption of Plan B would afford the company an opportunity to more closely match the capabilities of the selected individual to the requirements of the job, thereby improving the probability of successfully achieving the objectives. Also, it was noted that this approach would have less impact on the existing operation than if an existing employee were transferred out of a critical position into the new slot.

On the minus side, the task force recognized that Plan B would require a considerable amount of time just getting to the point where the program could begin. Preparing the job description, advertising, screening applicants, selecting and hiring, orientation—all of these activities would have to precede the actual planning and execution of the program.

In considering the level of investment required for Plan B, the task force concluded that it probably would cost slightly more than Plan A and would more than likely yield a better result.

The advantages of Plan C were seen to include the following:

- The resulting management development program would be specifically tailored to the needs of Buzzy by qualified experienced professionals trained to recognize the critical problems and needs of the company.
- The time required to prepare and plan the selected management development program would be considerably shorter when compared with Plans A and B.
- Probability of successfully achieving objectives would be high based on the proven performance of the particular consulting firm selected.
- Minimal disruption of the routine company operations would occur since most of the effort would be performed by people external to the operation.

The only disadvantage seen by the task force was the somewhat higher ongoing cost of conducting the program compared with what it would cost using one of the so-called in-house plans.

Selection of Best Solution

Based on the foregoing evaluation of the alternative solutions considered, the task force selected Plan C, stating the following reasons orally to Mr. Topman at the next staff meeting:

- Shortest time to implement the program
- Highest probability of successfully achieving program objectives
- Least impact on routine company operations
- Most reasonable investment based on expected return

After considering several possible consulting firms for the Plan C assignment, the task force selected Burke and Associates based on their earlier involvement and their acknowledged reputation as a leader in their field.

Implementation of Selected Solution

Having arrived at a conclusion, the task force then wrote its report to Mr. Topman. The substance of their assignment was summarized briefly, followed by the problem definition, alternative solutions considered, their evaluation of the alternatives, and the conclusions and recommendations for subsequent action.

Mr. Topman accepted the conclusions and the recommendation of the task force, thanked them for their participation in this special assignment and relieved them of any further responsibilities. He then directed Mr. Peoples to proceed with the approach recommended by the task force.

Shortly thereafter, in response to a request from Mr. Peoples, Burke and Associates submitted its proposal for instituting a management development program at Buzzy. The program, to be coordinated and administered by the Industrial Relations Department, was designed for individuals responsible for developing strategies for human effectiveness within their organization. The program addressed five major areas of interest and concern:

1. *Communication Laboratory.* A one-day session aimed at solidifying the work group into a team. The method includes both structural and nonstructural techniques. Communication barriers are to be examined and approaches to alleviating the problems are developed.
2. *Managing Management Time.* A one-day seminar that examines the content of a manager's day as opposed to the efficiency with which he or she carries out activities. Special considerations include the art of delegation, the rightful assumption of responsibility, and the use of leverage in time management.
3. *Motivation and Job Enrichment.* A one-day seminar exploring a basic philosophy of management relating to people. Consideration to be given to those needs that on the surface appear to be motivational but are not. The actual motivation needs are to be explored with an eye to immediate practical application. The application of motivation concepts to the task of job enrichment will be featured.
4. *Managerial Performance Standards.* During this one-day seminar, managers will learn the technique of writing managerial performance standards. They will study the methods of determining with their supervisor how they will be quantifiably measured before the performance review takes place. Specific emphasis on effective performance review and controlling performance standards will be discussed.
5. *Development Sessions.* This series of development sessions will be conducted every fourth Friday covering such items as problem analysis, decision making, conference skills, managerial skills, technical skills as related to budgeting and finance, organization structures, and the like. These seminars will be given by individuals having expertise in these categories.

After reading this proposal, Mr. Peoples smiled to himself and began to prepare the necessary internal papers to begin the program.

SOURCE: By Bruce Evans and Hugh L. French, Jr. This case is reprinted from eds. R. S. Schuler and S. A. Youngblood, *Case Problems in Personnel and Human Resource Management* (St. Paul, Minn.: West Publishing Co., 1986).

SUMMARY CASES

Northeast Data Resources, Inc.

George Wellington closed the door behind him and slumped into his desk chair with an air of resignation. He had just returned from a meeting of the Executive Committee of Northeast Data Resources where personnel layoffs had been decided upon. As director of personnel at NDR, he realized that he would be responsible for both developing the process by which the layoffs would take place and assisting the managers responsible for the actual implementation. It wasn't a pleasant task, particularly in light of the human resources program that he had begun to implement over the past four years.

Wellington pulled out a pad of paper from the top desk drawer and began to scribble notes. He had found that in times of pressure it was best to get some perspective on the situation before taking action. The drastic character of this situation required a review of the growth of Northeast Data Resources from its inception in 1979 to the present. It was the first crisis the young company had been forced to face.

Background of the Company

In 1979, four young engineers formed a partnership to form the basis of NDR. Three of them had worked for a large, national data-processing company. They had recognized the high potential in the computer industry particularly for a product which filled a vital need in this growing field. Another engineer working in a research program with a large university was asked to join them because of his expertise in the computer field.

Jack Logan was the prime mover of the new company. He had been working for nearly five years on a project within the large company to develop ways to protect its computer systems from being copied by competitors. The primary objective in this project was to ensure that a customer would have to purchase the entire system rather than being able to make use of a number of different systems. Jack saw the opportunity to sell a service to customers that would do just the opposite—provide a mechanism that would link various competing systems into an integrated unit.

He and a colleague, Charlie Bonner, developed a "black box" which had the capacity to connect at least two types of computer systems already on the market. They had worked in Jack's basement over a two-year period to perfect this instrument. Another six months of testing found that it was very effective. The two other engineers had begun to work with them in order to expand the box to tie together three other systems with which they had experience.

The four men decided to strike out on their own and found that their innovation and daring paid off. The first two years were both exhilarating and demanding. NDR subcontracted the production of the black box to a small manufacturing company while the partners divided responsibilities between marketing and continuing research. Jack and Charlie carried the marketing and organizational functions while George Miller and Al Grant worked to streamline the instrument itself.

Early success in securing contracts with some key customers and fears about loss of the exclusive information about the unpatented invention led to a decision to go into full production. An old plant was leased and renovated and workers were hired to begin the process of building the black box for distribution. Within two years the company had grown from four partners to nearly 100 people. By 1989 NDR had expanded to about 700 people and had become the focus of attention for a number of investors. The invention, now dubbed Omega I, had become a product competitors emulated but with little success.

Logan assumed the responsibilities of chairman and president with Bonner as executive vice-president in charge of operations. Miller and Grant stayed in the lab with more interest in research and development, being willing to act more in advisory capacity on managerial decisions.

Logan saw the need to consolidate and expand the overall operations of the company. Production and distribution now overflowed into three buildings separated by nearly ten miles. He negotiated a contract with the economic development committee of Newbury, a New England town about 40 miles away, to help construct a new building to house headquarters and plant. The town agreed to help NDR through reduced taxes, water, and sewage hookups at a minimal charge, arrangements with local banks to secure a loan for construction of the plant, and development of a federal grant to train new workers at the plant. In exchange NDR agreed to move its entire operation to Newbury within the next two years. It helped Newbury in its search for new industry while assuring NDR of a secure base of operations for the future.

The Newbury headquarters was only 40 miles from the old facilities so NDR lost few of its present staff because of the change. But the growth in business demanded an increase in personnel. Engineers with sophisticated skills in computer science were hired to expand the system capability. Often, international engineers were the only ones available and the importation of English and Australians with a spattering of Europeans gave an international flair to the small company. New factory workers from Newbury and surrounding towns were hired so that the production shifts could be expanded from one to two. The training grants secured by the town helped to equip new workers and the integration with more experienced workers moved smoothly. Empty managerial slots required hiring from the outside mostly. A new vice-president of manufacturing came from a large industrial company in the Midwest. The new vice-president of finance had a solid resume which included most recently financial experience with a large conglomerate but before that two stints with growing companies much like NDR. The staffing of the growing company proceeded professionally.

Future of the Company

The phenomenal growth of NDR in old industrial New England rivaled the computer companies developing in California's Silicon Valley. The workforce had evolved from 4 in 1979 to 100 in 1981, 700 in 1986, and 1,350 by 1992. Sales increased from two small initial contracts in 1979 of $75,000 to nearly $20 million by 1992. The opening price of 7 moved to between 8 and 9 and hovered there in 1991. But a feature article in a national stock advisory report about NDR led to an upward move in the summer of 1992 to 15. Even without paying a dividend in its 13 years of existence, it had become an attractive investment.

Logan had taken time during the summer of 1992 to begin the process of strategic planning. Convinced that he and his executive committee could and should do this alone, he decided not to engage outside consultants to develop a costly set of plans. His projection was that the computer industry would grow nearly ten times in size over the next decade. Conservatively the company could expect to hold its share of the market which meant a doubling of sales in five years to $40 million and up to $70 million by 2004. Expansion was the key to maintaining market share and holding its own against the handful of competitors which had begun to appear by 1992.

In shaping the strategy, Logan began to map out a new marketing plan which would guarantee NDR's position in the national market instead of the eastern market alone. He saw new customer possibilities in the fields of insurance, financial institutions and state and local governments. He negotiated an option to buy the factory of a watch company moving South. Its building was about 35 miles away in the heart of another old industrial New England town with a pool of skilled workers available to be retrained. He began to develop some ideas about how many new staff would be needed and the kind of capital necessary to finance this expansion.

George Wellington's Career at NDR

George stopped his writing and reviewed the rapid growth of NDR up to this point. He remembered vividly his first few months at the company. He had moved to a nearby town to retire in the serenity of New England. His career had begun immediately after completing his MBA from a leading eastern university where he had concentrated on management and personnel. He had begun work in the personnel area with a major corporation located in New York. Six years in the field had led him next into marketing and then strategic planning with another company. The last seven years had been with a prestigious consulting firm in New York where he had focused on a variety of problems for a host of clients. His decision to retire had been prompted by a dislike for traveling and a desire to settle down in the area where his children had located.

While retirement continued to bring part-time consulting work, George still found the travel excessive. But his ideas of relaxation in retirement quickly exposed his own need to be fully active in business to be happy. His search for a part-time job was successful as Jack Logan met him at a Chamber of Commerce luncheon in Newbury and hired him as a consultant to help with the transition from the old to the new facilities. He remembered the challenges associated with coordinating not only the efforts of NDR personnel but outside contractors and town officials as well.

The flawless nature of the transition into the new plant made the president recognize that he needed George full-time. Wellington agreed to stay only another six months as a special assistant to Logan. He carried out a variety of projects for Logan and quickly became an integral part of the management team at NDR.

The president called in George one day and showed him an organization chart which he was reworking. "George, I know that your six months are nearly up but I need you around here on a permanent basis. I just don't know where to put you on this chart. How about becoming director of Personnel for NDR? That is the only important position which we haven't filled here in the past few months and it would allow me to have you close at hand for help on those big decisions."

George asked for some time to think through his decision and within a week agreed to a full-time position. While Logan still saw Personnel as a somewhat unnecessary staff function, there would be a chance for George to help him understand the importance of human resources to this company.

Wellington began immediately to develop a plan for human resources at NDR. Logan encouraged him but wasn't excited about the use of the term "human resources." "I don't understand why you have to complicate this whole business of Personnel with a new name. Why not still use the old 'Personnel' for the department?" Logan asked. George saw a futile battle in this naming process so he clearly defined his function as that of director of Personnel.

His plan for that function at NDR had three major elements.

1. The Program

- *Gathering employee information*
  He had his staff develop a file on each employee with a record of hiring date, previous experience and employers, salary, job title, etc. This was stored in a computer so that he could have rapid recall for evaluation.
- *Performance appraisal system*
  He developed a new appraisal system which incorporated a three-page form to be completed twice a year by immediate supervisors. The annual review was tied to salary and bonus decisions. He experimented with it in two engineering sections over a two-year period and then was able to get Logan to mandate it for all of NDR beginning in 1991. The results from the 1991–92 year were compiled and filed for future use.
- *Personnel policy manual*
  In 1991, a new personnel policy manual was developed that detailed the policies and procedures as well as benefits for all personnel at NDR. There was some initial negative reaction by those who had enjoyed a variety of benefits from the early days of the company. But the imprint of Logan on the manual quelled the complaints and ensured uniformity in the policies.
- *EEO and Affirmative Action (AA) program*
  The highly technical character of the NDR business and its presence in a small New England town made both EEO and AA difficult to pursue. A visit to Wellington by an EEO field investigator regarding the case of a former worker led him to move quickly to formulate this program. The data was gathered on minority hiring and promotion and then a plan designed for increasing the percentage of minorities in all categories and the number of women in management in particular. Logan resisted the immediate implementation of the program with the argument that the federal government would soft-pedal civil rights in employment so that business people did not need to worry. George accepted this decision with reluctance but got an agreement to update the plan periodically as well as pursue informally a goal of more integration of the workforce.
- *Management development program*
  The rapid growth of NDR created many new managerial positions. Hiring from the outside became one method by which to increase the number of managers, but George believed that the key to the company's future lay in developing them from within. He negotiated a contract with a professor of management at a local university to design and teach a course in management for selected employees. George and the professor team-taught a six-week course for 20 middle level managers in 1990. Its success led to an offering three times a year to both managers and potential managers.

2. The Staff

George became director of Personnel in the spring of 1989. He selected four professionals and two secretaries to work with him. Two professionals came from outside of NDR and two from within. All four had human resources management experience but needed more training. One was encouraged to enter an MBA program on a part-time basis with a concentration on human resource management. The other three were sent to local and national seminars to upgrade skills and understanding in the various areas of HRM. But at the heart of their training was George Wellington, drawing on his vast experience and encouraging his younger colleagues to learn through experimentation and discussion.

3. The Office Location

The final design of the NDR headquarters had not been decided when George became a consultant to the project so he had taken primary responsibility for the design of the corporate office area. Later, as director of Personnel, he negotiated some changes in the office assignments so that Personnel was located at one of the major entrances and exits of the building. It was a primary thoroughfare for engineers and managerial personnel arriving in the morning and leaving at night. It was also a stop along the way to the new cafeteria that had just opened.

George had chosen this location for a reason. He felt that human resource departments must have high visibility and availability. Being in the middle of a key thoroughfare allowed people to recognize the central function of personnel in the operation of NDR. It encouraged questions about policies and procedures. It also gave the HRM staff the chance to get to know all of the managers and professionals within a short period of time. This provided instant recognition and a capacity to deal with problems on a much more personal basis. George himself was always at his desk working before most of the staff arrived and usually left after 6:00 P.M. This gave him considerable visibility with managerial personnel who often worked late.

The images of the first few years were succeeded by thoughts about the past two months with his staff. He had begun to engage them in the planning process by asking them to think about NDR for the next five years. He had sketched out the growth projections of Logan and then provided some parameters within which to think about staffing. Each of his professional staff was to develop a short presentation on four consequences for HRM:

1. Impact of the size of our workforce
2. Impact on the mix of skills needed in the workforce
3. Impact on the recruitment efforts from outside NDR and development efforts from within
4. Impact on the working conditions within the company itself, both physically and organizationally

The first meeting four weeks ago had produced some very good reports. With one exception, the four had done a lot of homework and some imaginative thinking about the future with regard to how HRM plan would fit into the NDR overall strategic plan. George had collated and refined the projections and redistributed them to the professional staff asking for further thought and more specific targets for the next five years. He asked for input for his own report to the president, which he had hoped would be ready by December 1992.

The Present Dilemma

The work had now come to an abrupt halt although he had not alerted the staff to the discussion taking place within the executive committee until the day before. Logan's projections about the future had been overly optimistic.

Two weeks ago, Logan had asked George to meet him at 8:00 P.M. He laid out a report on the results from the first quarter of this fiscal year and then a chart which traced the sales of the last nine quarters. The last two quarters showed a significant decline. Logan indicated to George that, "The decline is now a trend and not simply a blip on the screen as I had thought." The loss of five key contracts totaling nearly $3 million over the past six months plus the entry of a new competitor in the southeastern market had been responsible for the dramatic sales drop. At the same time, profits had suffered as well because of the increased expenses from a decision to increase the size of the engineering and financial service departments. The president admitted that his projections had been too optimistic and that something had to be done immediately. The cash flow problem had emerged as the most important pressure in this situation. The budget had to be pared while efforts to increase revenue were intensified.

George studied the figures carefully and agreed reluctantly to both the conclusions and recommendations reached by Logan. The two men took some time to sort through the various options available but it always came back to drastic cuts in personnel. He urged Logan to call a meeting of the executive committee in the morning and provide the data to them with encouragement to diagnose the problem and solutions to it. He argued that any solution must be a product of consensus of the committee.

The meeting caught everybody by surprise as they had accepted the president's projections of growth despite a temporary decline in sales. Two weeks of intensive debate among the executives led to the meeting this morning which defined the exact personnel cuts to be made. It was agreed that 25 engineers, 50 production personnel (workers and supervisors), and 25 others from various departments would be laid off within the next two weeks. In addition, 15 new marketing and sales personnel would be added as soon as possible to carry out a new marketing thrust aimed at a different market segment.

There had been heated discussion about the exact number to be laid off and hired with considerable friction between the vice-presidents of production, engineering, and marketing. The blame for the crisis was shouldered by Logan who asked that the executives recognize that they had to work together to resolve this problem if the future of NDR was to be assured. Wellington as the director of Personnel was given the task of coordinating the identification of the people to be laid off although the actual decision would rest in the hands of the three vice-presidents. There were no criteria for the decisions although all agreed that loyal and trusted employees who had been with NDR for a number of years should be released only as a last resort.

The Director's Responsibility

The acrimonious debate of the morning still echoed in George's ears that afternoon. He tore the pages on which he had been writing off the pad and began a new one as he started to determine how the layoffs should be handled. It was a far cry from the exuberance with which he had begun the process of developing a five-year human resource plan just two months ago. Cutbacks in personnel demanded the same precision and careful thought in planning and action as hiring and promotion. There was less excitement about retrenching than growing because it affected the livelihood of so many people.

George jotted down the important questions in three different areas as he mapped out his thinking on this problem.

1. The Layoffs

- Criteria to be used?
- Data available on employees?
- Impact of EEO and AA on decisions?
- Severance pay and benefits?
- Procedure for layoffs?

2. The New Hires

- Skills needed in marketing and sales?
- Available resources for positions?
- Salary and benefit package?
- Procedure for hiring?

3. The HRM Plan

- Immediate impact on HRM five-year plan?
- What if only temporary reversal of growth trend? (Commitments to rehire or not?)
- Impact on employee morale now and in future?

George recognized that he had a lot of work to do. He struggled to regain his sense of professionalism as he began to detail the options available to each of the questions. His days as a consultant and manager had given him little experience in the arena of layoffs. But Logan had given him the responsibility and he knew that the future of NDR would depend heavily on how it handled this crisis.

SOURCE: This case was prepared by D. Jeffrey Lenn, The George Washington University. It is not meant to be an example of effective or ineffective human resource management but an example for teaching and discussion purposes.

APPENDIX A

Legislation, Court, and NRLB Decisions Affecting Personnel and Human Resource Management

LEGISLATION/BASIC PROVISIONS

Employment Legislation

Act	*Jurisdiction*	*Basic Provisions*
Fair Labor Standards Act (1938) and subsequent amendments—FLSA	Most interstate employers, certain types of employees, are exempt from overtime provisions—executive, administrative, and professional employees and outside salespeople	Establishes a minimum wage; controls hours through premium pay for overtime; controls working hours for children
Minimum Wage Law (1977)	Small businesses	Sets graduated increases in minimum wage rates
Equal Pay Act (1963 amendment to the FLSA)	Same as FLSA except no employees are exempt	Prohibits unequal pay for males and females with equal skill, effort, and responsibility working under similar working conditions
Civil Rights Act (1964) (amended by EEOA 1972)	Employers with fifteen or more employees, employment agencies, and labor unions	Prevents discrimination on the basis of race, color, religion, sex, or national origin; establishes EEOC
Civil Rights Act of 1991	Same as the Civil Rights Act of 1964	Protects groups against discrimination (as does the 1964 act), but makes provision for jury trials and punitive compensation
Equal Employment Opportunity Act (1972)—EEOA	Adds employees of state and local government and educational institutions; reduced number of employees required to fifteen	Amends Title VII; increases enforcement powers of EEOC
Executive Order 11246 (1965) as amended by Executive Order 11375 (1966)	Federal contractors and subcontractors with contracts over $50,000 and fifty or more employees	Prevents discrimination on the basis of race, color, religion, sex, or national origin; establishes Office of Federal Contract Compliance (OFCC)
Revised Order Number 4 (1971)	Federal contractors	Defines acceptable affirmative action program

Act	*Jurisdiction*	*Basic Provisions*
Executive Order 11478 (1969)	Federal agencies	Prevents discrimination on the basis of race, color, religion, sex, or national origin
Age Discrimination in Employment Act (1967)–revised 1978; 1986	Employers with more than twenty-five employees	Prevents discrimination against persons age forty and over, and states compulsory retirement for some workers
Rehabilitation Act (1973) as amended 1980	Government contractors and federal agencies	Prevents discrimination against persons with physical and/or mental handicaps and provides for affirmative action
Americans with Disabilities Act (1990)	Virtually all employers (15 or more employees by 1994)	Protects against discrimination against individuals with disabilities
Older Worker Benefit Protection Act of 1990	Same as the Age Discrimination in Employment Act as amended	Employers are prohibited from discriminating with regard to benefits on the basis of age
Immigration Act of 1990	Immigration Reform and Control Act of 1986—IRCA	Amends the employer-verification and unfair-immigration–related employment practices as defined by the IRCA
Prevailing wage laws—1. Davis-Bacon Act (1931) and 2. Walsh-Healey Act (1935)	Employers with government construction projects of $2,000 (Davis-Bacon) and government contracts of $10,000 or more	Guarantees prevailing wages to employees of government contractors
Legally required fringe benefits— 1. OASDHI (1935 and amendments)	Virtually all employers	Provides income and health care to retired employees and income to the survivors of employees who have died
2. Unemployment compensation (1935)	Virtually all employers	Provides income to employees who are laid off or fired
3. Workers' compensation (dates differ from state to state)	Virtually all employers	Provides benefits to employees who are injured on the job and to the survivors of employees who are killed on the job
Occupational Safety and Health Act (1970)—OSHA	Most interstate employers	Assures as far as possible every working man and woman in the nation safe and healthful working conditions and to preserve our human resources
Employee Retirement Income Security Act (1974)—ERISA	Most interstate employers with pension plans (no employer is required to have such a plan)	Protects employees covered by a pension plan from losses in benefits due to: ■ mismanagement ■ plant closings and bankruptcies ■ job changes

Act	*Jurisdiction*	*Basic Provisions*
Freedom of Information Act (1966)	Federal agencies only	Allows individuals to review employers' records on them and bring civil damages
The Pregnancy Discrimination Act of 1978	Same as Civil Rights Act (1964)	Pregnancy is a disability and, furthermore, must receive the same benefits as any other disability
Privacy Act of 1974 (Public Law 93-579)	Federal agencies only	Allows individuals to review employer's records on them and bring civil damages
Uniform Guidelines on Employee Selection Procedures (1978)	Same as EEOA (1972)	Updates EEOC 1970 guidelines to more clearly define adverse impact and test validation
Guidelines on Sexual Harassment (1980)	Same as EEOA (1972)	Defines standards for what constitutes harassment
Vietnam Era Veterans Readjustment Act (1974)	Government contractors with contracts in excess of $10,000	Provides for affirmative action in the employment of Vietnam era veterans
Civil Rights Act of 1866, Section 1981	All citizens	It gives all persons, regardless of race, age, and national origin, the same contractual rights as "white citizens." Does not apply to sex-based discrimination
Civil Rights Act of 1871, Section 1983	All citizens	As the Civil Rights Act of 1866 but does apply to sex-based discrimination
The First Amendment, U.S. Constitution	All citizens	Guarantees freedom of speech and religion
The Fifth Amendment	All citizens	No person shall be deprived of life, liberty, or property without the due process of law
The Fourteenth Amendment	All citizens	Prohibits abridgment of federally conferred privileges by actions of the state
Employee Polygraph Protection Act (1988)	Private Employers	Prohibits most employees from polygraph testing without reasonable suspicion
Drug-Free Workplace Act (1988)	Federal contractors with contracts exceeding $25,000	Requires employers to maintain drug-free workplace
Worker Adjustment and Retraining Notification Act of 1988	Employers with more than 100 employees	Requires 60 days notice of plant or office closing

Labor Relations Legislation: Private Sector

Railway Labor Act (1926)–RLA	Railroad workers and airline employees	Provides right to organize; provides majority choice of representatives; prohibits "yellow dog" contracts; outlines dispute settlement procedures
Norris-LaGuardia Act (1932)	All employers and labor organizations	No yellow dog contracts; no injunction for nonviolent activity of unions (strikes, picketing, and boycotts); limited union liability
National Labor Relations Act (1935)—Wagner Act	Nonmanagerial employees in private industry not covered by Railway Labor Act (RLA)	Provides right to organize; provides for collective bargaining; requires employers to bargain; unions must represent all members equally
Labor-Management Relations Act (1947)—Taft-Hartley	Nonmanagerial employees in private industry not covered by RLA	Prohibits unfair labor practices of unions; outlaws closed shop; prohibits strikes in national emergencies; requires both parties to bargain in good faith
Labor Management Reporting and Disclosure Act (1959)—Landrum-Griffin	Labor organizations	Outlines procedures for redressing internal union problems
Amendments to Taft-Hartley Act (1974)	Labor organizations	Specifies illegal activities within union

Labor Relations Legislation: Public Sector

Executive Order 10988 (1962)	Federal employees	Recognizes employee's right to join unions and bargain collectively; prohibits strikes. Requires agency to meet and confer with union on policy practices and working conditions
Executive Orders 11616 (1971) and 11838 (1975)	Federal employees	Expand EO 11491 to cover labor-management relations: cover disputes of bargaining rights; order elections; consolidate units; limit scope of grievance and arbitration procedures
Civil Service Reform Act (1978)	Federal employees	Defines grievance procedure and requirements for goal-type performance appraisals; establishes Senior Executive Service (SES)

COURT AND NLRB DECISIONS/BASIC PROVISIONS*

Title/Date

Stringfellow v. Monsanto Corporation (1970)
Established the precedent for giving credit to the employer for making performance appraisal–based decisions on the basis of evidence that the appraisal uses definite identifiable criteria based on the quality and quantity of an employee's work.

Phillips v. Martin Marietta Corp (1971)
Whether a BFOQ exists depends on whether it can be shown that the qualification is demonstrably more relevant to job performance for a woman than a man.

Diaz v. Pan American World Airways, Inc. (1971)
The primary function of an airline is to transport passengers safely from one point to another. Therefore, not hiring males for flight attendants is discriminatory. *Business necessity* is established.

Griggs v. Duke Power (1971)
Test for hiring cannot be used unless job related. Organizations must show evidence of job relatedness. Not necessary to establish intent to discriminate.

Board of Regents of State Colleges v. Roth (1972)
Protects workers from discharge when due process hasn't been given.

Richardson v. Hotel Corporation of America (1972)
Dismissal on grounds of conviction record resulted in adverse impact; but since conviction record argued (not shown) to be related to business necessity (not job performance), dismissal is okay.

Spurlock v. United Airlines (1972)
Use of college degree as a selection criterion valid because job related, even though no performance data provided.

Rowe v. General Motors Corporation (1972)
All white supervisory recommendations were based on subjective and vague standards which led to a lack of promotions for black employees. Identified five discriminatory factors.

Hodgson v. Robert Hall Clothes, Inc. (1973)
Pay differentials between salesmen and saleswomen justified on the basis of profitability of area in which employees work.

McDonnell Douglas Corporation v. Green (1973)
Employer's test device constitutes *prima facie* case of racial discrimination under four different criteria.

Brito v. Zia Company (1973)
Zia violated Title VII because they laid off a disproportionate number of a protected group on the basis of low performance scores on measures that were not validated.

Sugarman v. Dougal (1973)
The due process and equal protection clauses of the Fifth Amendment also apply to aliens in public employment.

Hodgson v. Greyhound Lines, Inc. (1974)
Could discriminate without empirical evidence on basis of age. Good faith used to show older people would make less safe drivers.

Corning Glass Works v. Brennan (1974)
The Equal Pay Act is violated by paying male inspectors on the night shift a higher base wage than female inspectors on the day shift.

Baxter v. Savannah Sugar Refining Co. (1974)
Subjective appraisal form is viewed as discriminatory.

Green v. Missouri Pacific R.R. Co. (1975)
Applying the lessons from *Griggs v. Duke Power,* the court and the EEOC have found it unlawful to refuse to hire job applicants because of their arrest record except for certain circumstances *(Richardson v. Hotel Corporation of America).*

Kirkland v. New York Department of Correctional Services (1975)
The use of quotas was rejected as a method of determining promotions except as an interim measure to be used until nondiscriminatory procedures to determine promotion are established.

Stamps (EEOC) v. Detroit Edison (1975)
Title VII does not provide for an award of punitive damages. Back pay and attorney fees are the explicit provisions of Title VII.

Rogers v. International Paper Company (1975)
Subjective criteria are not to be condemned as unlawful per se because some decisions about hiring and promotions in supervisory and managerial jobs cannot be made using objective standards alone. This opinion, however, is somewhat contrary to those in *Albemarle Paper Company v. Moody* (1973); *Baxter v. Savannah Sugar Refining Corporation* (1974); and *Rowe v. General Motors* (1972).

Albemarle v. Moody (1975)
Need to establish evidence that test is related to content of job. Could use job analysis to do so, but not evidence from global performance ratings made by supervisors.

McDonald v. Santa Fe Trail Transportation Co. (1976)
Requires consistency in dismissal policies due to absenteeism.

Mastie v. Great Lakes Steel Corporation (1976)
As with *Stringfellow,* the court said that the objectivity of evaluation can be established by demonstrating that the company performed and relied on a thorough evaluation process intended to be used fairly and accurately.

Smith v. Mutual Benefit Life Insurance Company (1976)
Employer is not discriminating if refusing to hire male appearing to be effeminate.

Chrysler Outboard v. Dept. of Industry (1976)
Employer refuses to hire a worker who had leukemia because he was prone to infection. Court said he had to be hired because he was qualified.

Watkins v. Scott Paper Company (1976)
Performance data to validate tests that are derived from graphic scales are too vague and easily subject to discrimination.

Robinson v. Union Carbide Corporation (1976)
These two require written standards for promotion to help prevent discrimination.

Wade v. Mississippi Cooperative Extension Service (1976)
Performance scores used to decide promotions and salary issues not valid because no job analysis.

Washington v. Davis (1976)
When a test procedure is challenged under constitutional law, intent to discriminate must be established. No need to establish intent if filed under Title VII, just show effects. Could use communication test to select applicants for police force.

Castaneda v. Partida (1977)
Prima facie evidence of discrimination established when evidence of both statistical dis-

parity and discriminatory selection procedures vis-à-vis the gross population figures.

General Foods Corp. (1977)
Corporatewide team program of employee-employer cooperation does not violate the National Labor Relations Act because program established to promote efficiency, not forestall unionization.

James v. Stockham Values and Fitting Company (1977)
An apprenticeship program was viewed as discriminatory since selections were made by supervisors who were given guidelines.

Barnes v. Costle (1977)
Sexual harassment is a form of sex discrimination under Title VII, and employer is responsible if takes no action on learning of events.

Mistretta v. Sandia Corporation (1977)
Employment decisions suspect when based on evaluations that reflect only best judgments and opinions of evaluators rather than identifiable criteria based on quality or quantity of work or specific performances that are supported by some kind of record.

Hazelwood School District v. U.S. (1977)
Labor market comparisons must be based on relevant labor market and not general labor market.

International Brotherhood of Teamsters v. United States (1977)
Bona fide seniority systems maintained without discriminatory intent are exempt from Title VII liability if established before 1964.

United Air Lines, Inc. v. McMann (1977)
Employer can force retirement before age of sixty-five if it has bona fide retirement plan.

Yukas v. Libbey-Owens-Ford (1977)
All practices against nepotism, especially close relatives and spouses, are nondiscriminatory, especially in same department and/or as in supervisor-subordinate relationship.

Flowers v. Crouch-Walter Corporation (1977)
Plaintiff established *prima facie* evidence that a discharge was discriminatory and not based on performance.

Donaldson v. Pillsbury Company (1977)
Requires clear establishment and communication of job requirements and performance standards.

James v. Stockman Values and Fittings Company (1977)
White supervisors without formal guidelines selecting applicants to apprenticeship program is discriminatory. Need more discrete performance appraisal.

Dothard v. Rawlinson (1977)
Height requirements not valid, therefore constitutes discriminatory practice.

Bakke v. Regents of the University of California (1978)
Reverse discrimination not allowed. Race, however, can be used in selection decisions. Affirmative action programs permissible when prior discrimination established.

United States v. City of Chicago (1978)
Specific promotion criteria must be used that are related to the job to which being promoted.

Detroit Police Officers Assn. v. Coleman Young (1979)
Court holds in favor of goals and quotas to reverse previous discrimination.

Oshiver v. Court of Common Pleas (1979)
Without objective or extrinsic documented evidence of poor performance or evidence not hastily developed, an employment decision is suspect if based on the notion of "poor performance."

Charles L. Maehren v. City of Seattle (1979)
Upheld practice of setting goals and quotas to reverse previous practices of discrimination.

Marshall v. Barlow's, Inc. (1979)
Employers are not required to let OSHA inspectors enter their premises unless they have search warrants.

Schultz v. Wheaton Glass (1979)
The employer's lower wage rate for women is in violation of the Equal Pay Act when the wage differentials are based on artificially created job classifications that differentiate otherwise equal jobs.

Steelworkers v. Weber (1979)
Quota system to admit employees into a training program may supersede seniority provisions as long as the program is a temporary one to correct past employment practices and does not trample the interests of the more senior employees.

State Division of Human Rights v. Rochester Housing Authority (1980)
Although religious preferences cannot be used for discrimination, an employer may defend not hiring an applicant because of religion by showing that a reasonable attempt was made to accommodate the applicant.

Fullilove v. Klutznick (1980)
Congress can impose racial quotas in handing out federal money (10 percent) to federal contractors who are minority owned (51 percent).

Ensley Branch NAACP v. Seibels (1980)
Training scores can only be used to screen out, not select job candidates.

City of St. Louis v. U.S. (1980)
Upheld use of quotas and goals.

EEOC v. United Virginia Bank (1980)
Prima facie evidence of discrimination established on the basis of statistical disparity vis-à-vis the relevant labor market (i.e., comparably qualified individuals).

Weahkee v. Perry (1978) and *Weahkee v. Norton* (1980)
Use of quotas in performance evaluation not objectively used or enforced so not justified in using if discrimination results. Weahkee was reinstated, but no finding of discrimination.

EEOC v. Sandia Corporation (1980)
Discrimination against employees protected by ADEA in regard to a decision on work force reduction required by budget restraints. Used a subjective (ranking) evaluation form for their scientists, engineers, and technical employees. Statistical impact and informal comments indicated bias.

Marshall v. Whirlpool (1980)
Employees have right to refuse job assignment if constitutes clear and present danger to life or limb. Employer, however, not required to pay if, as a result, employee sent home because of no work.

Backus v. Baptist Medical Center (1981)
A defense of bona fide occupational qualifications was extended to permit the hiring and staffing of only female nurses in an obstretics and gynecology department in a hospital.

NLRB v. Wright Line, Inc. (1981)
In cases where an employee is fired for what may appear to be union-related activities, the employer must show (to be vindicated in the dismissal) that the discipline imposed is the same as in other cases where union activity was not an issue.

American Textile Manufacturers Institute v. Donovan (1981)
OSHA need not do cost-benefit analyses before issuing working health standards.

Tooley v. Martin-Marietta Corporation (1981)
Must be religious accommodation for employees who object to union membership or support (as long as no undue hardship on union).

Los Angeles Dept. of Water v. Manhard (1981)
Rules against department rule of having female employees contribute more to a retirement plan than men.

Clayton v. United Auto Workers (1981)
When a union member feels unfairly represented and only the employer can grant the relief requested, the employee need not exhaust internal union remedies before suing the employer.

Lehman v. Yellow Freight System (1981)
Informal affirmative action not permissible although formal voluntary one such as *Weber* is okay.

Northwest Airlines, Inc. v. Transport Workers (1981)
An employer found guilty of job discrimination cannot force an employee's union to contribute to the damages, even though the union may have negotiated the unequal terms.

County of Washington, Oregon v. Gunther (1981)
It can be illegal (under Title VII and EPA 1963) to pay women unfairly low wages even if not doing same work as men (not a comparable worth case).

First National Maintenance v. NLRB (1981)
Management does not have to negotiate with unions in advance over closing plants or dropping lines.

Texas Department of Community Affairs v. Joyce Ann Burdine (1981)
A defendant in a job discrimination case need only provide a legitimate, nondiscriminatory explanation for not hiring or promoting a woman or minority, and need not prove that the white man hired was better qualified. The burden of proving intentional discrimination rests with the plaintiff.

Fernandez v. Wynn Oil Company (1981)
Title VII does not permit employers to use stereotypic impressions of male and female roles as a BFOQ defense to sex discrimination. Employer can't use customer preferences for working with male employees as a defense of discrimination.

Connecticut v. Teal (1982)
Employers must defend each part of a selection process against adverse impact and not just the end result of the entire process (the bottom line).

Spirit v. TIAA/CREF (1982)
Retirement annuities must be equal, regardless of sex.

Borg Warner Corp. v. NLRB (1982)
Distinction between mandatory and permissible. Terms depend on whether topic regulates the employer-employee relation.

American Tobacco v. Patterson (1982)
Bona fide seniority systems without discriminating intent are exempt from Title VII liability.

Newport News Shipbuilding and Dry Dock Co. v. EEOC (1983)
If an employer supplies any level of health benefits to female workers' husbands, the employer must also supply the same level of benefits to male workers' wives, and that includes pregnancy benefits. This, in effect, reverses the Supreme Court's ruling in *General Electric v. Gilbert,* where the court said that pregnancy benefits need not be given the same treatment by employers as other health and disability programs.

Arizona Governing Committee v. Norris (1983)
Pension payouts by employers should be equal for women and men, and past unequal treatment of women must be cured by retroactive funding of pensions. This decision is in essence the other half of the issue. The first half was rendered in the Supreme Court decision of *Los Angeles Department of Water and Power v. Manhart,* where the decision was made that requiring larger contributions by females than males into pension programs is discriminatory.

NLRB v. Transportation Management (1983)
Employees are protected by the NLRA when helping organize employees. If an employee claims to be fired for trying to organize a union but the employer claims it was poor performance, the employer has the burden of proof. In cases where such "mixed" motives for employer action may exist, the employer must prove the case.

Firefighters Local Union No. 1784 v. Stotts (1984)
In this decision, the Supreme Court upheld the bona fide seniority system over an affirmative action consent decree in a situation of layoffs. Thus, the employees most recently hired could be subject to layoff even though this action could compromise the affirmative action efforts.

Otis Elevator v. NLRB (1984)
Employees need not bargain over a transfer of operation if move is based on economics, not labor cost consideration.

AFSCME v. State of Washington (1985)
State had systematically paid jobs dominated by women less than their value according to job evaluation. Court of appeals overturned this decision saying state could not be forced "to eliminate an economic inequality that it did not create."

Pattern Makers' League v. NLRB (1985)
Employees may resign from a union at any time, even during a strike or when one is imminent.

Garcia v. San Antonio Transit Authority (1985)
Extends coverage of FLSA to state and local governments.

Scott v. Sears Roebuck (1985)
Woman unsuccessful in sex harassment suit based on acts by co-workers. Woman did not complain to supervisors. Court ruled only responsible for acts of co-workers if they knew or should have known of acts and took no action.

Horn v. Duke Homes (1985)
Court endorsed principle that employers have strict liability for sexual harassment by supervisors (company claimed that it was not liable because it was not aware of the behavior). Court supported full back pay (plaintiff had been terminated).

Glasgow v. Georgia Pacific Corp. (1985)
Court accepts sexual harassment argument on basis of creating hostile work environment (no *quid pro quo*). Company was found by Court to have made sexually harassing envi-

ronment a condition of employment because harassment went on for a long period of time with organization doing nothing. Court outlined four-point test for sexually harassing work environment.

1. Harassment was unwelcome
2. Harassment was because of sex
3. Harassment affected terms and conditions of employment
4. Knowledge of harassment is "imputed" to employer

Wygant v. Jackson Board of Education (1986)
The Court ruled that white teachers were illegally dismissed in order to hire minority teachers in the School Board's efforts to fulfill a voluntary affirmative action program.

Barns v. Washington Natural Gas (1986)
Employer fires an employee because he was believed to have epilepsy. Awarded two years back pay and reinstatement.

Local 28 of the Sheet Metal Workers v. Equal Employment Opportunity Commission (1986)
The Court approved a lower court order requiring a New York City sheet metal workers' local to meet a 29 percent minority membership goal by 1987. The Court also held that judges may order racial preferences in union membership and other context if necessary to rectify especially "egregious" discrimination.

Local 93 of the International Association of Firefighters v. City of Cleveland (1986)
The Court held that lower Federal courts have broad discretion to approve decrees in which employers, over the objections of white employees, settle discrimination suits by agreeing to preferential hiring or promotion of minority-group members. It upheld a decree in which Cleveland agreed to settle a job discrimination suit by African-American and Hispanic firefighters by temporarily promoting African-American and Hispanic workers ahead of whites who had more seniority and higher test scores.

Meritor Savings Bank v. Vinson (1986)
The Court held that sexual harassment is a form of sex discrimination prohibited by Title VII of the Civil Rights Act and that employers may be liable for condoning a hostile work environment. However, the Court made it clear that employers will not be automatically liable for sexual harassment by supervisors or employees.

Philbrook v. Ansonia Board of Education (1986)
An employer may choose its own method of religious accommodation over a plan suggested by the worker as long as the employer's plan is reasonable.

Johnson v. Transportation Agency, Santa Clara County (1987)
The U.S. Supreme Court ruled that the county was justified in giving a job to a woman who scored two points less on an exam than a man. The county had an affirmative action plan that was flexible, temporary, and designed to correct the imbalance of white males in the work force.

School Board of Nassau County, Fla. v. Arline (1987)
The U.S. Supreme Court ruled that contagious diseases are not automatically excluded from coverage of the handicap provisions of Section 504 of the 1973 Rehabilitation Act.

Luck v. Southern Pacific Transportation Company (1987)
The court ruled that the company wrongfully discharged Barbara Luck for refusing a drug test on the grounds that it violated her rights to privacy. Subsequently, the company stopped its random drug-testing program.

U.S. v. Paradise (1987)
The U.S. Supreme Court affirmed the affirmative action plan for the state troopers of Alabama in which promotion and hiring quotas were established in order to correct racial

imbalances even though it may result in discrimination against an individual because of race or color.

Chalk v. U.S. District Court for Central District of California (1987)
Although handicapped because of AIDS, the teacher was otherwise able to perform his job within the meaning of the Rehabilitation Act of 1973 and, therefore, should be allowed to teach.

O'Connor v. Ortega (1987)
Supreme Court recognized workplace privacy for the first time.

EEOC v. Commonwealth of Massachusetts (1987)
A Massachusetts law requiring entry-level motor vehicle examiners to be aged 35 or younger does not violate Age Discrimination in Employment Act because it is a bona fide occupational qualification (BFOQ).

Watson v. Fort Worth Bank and Trust (1988)
The U.S. Supreme Court held that all selection procedures—objective or subjective, scored or unscored—should be subject to adverse impact analysis, compelling a demonstration by the employer that the procedure is job related if adverse impact is shown.

Kraszewski v. State Farm (1988)
Out of court settlement. Firm agrees to set aside half of its new sales jobs to women for ten years and to pay damages and back pay.

Arrow Automotive Industries v. NLRB (1988)
Company does not have to bargain on plant closings even if based on labor-cost considerations.

Wards' Cove Packing v. Atonio (1989)
Concentration statistics were used to prove adverse impact. Court ruled that burden of proof should not shift to employer unless it can be proved that a specific policy created the disparity.

Hopkins v. Price Waterhouse (1989)
The court upheld the award of a partnership to the female accountant who successfully claimed that sexual sterotyping prevented her promotion.

Dimaranan v. Pomona Valley Hospital (1991)
The court essentially ruled that employers can restrict the use of foreign languages only when there is a compelling business-related necessity to do so.

EEOC v. Arabian American Oil Co. (1991)
The U.S. Supreme Court decided that Title VII has no application to U.S. employers employing U.S. citizens to work abroad. ADEA and the Civil Rights Act of 1991, however, have application.

*This set of court cases is meant to provide a sampling of those mentioned in the text. For descriptions of these and of other cases, see J. Ledvinka, and V. G. Scarpello *Federal Regulation of Personnel and Human Resource Management* 2nd ed. (Boston: Kent, 1991); J. Bernardin and W. Cascio, *Annotated Bibliography of Court Cases Relevant to Employment Decisions 1980–1984* (Boca Raton: Florida Atlantic University, 1984); M.D. Levin-Epstein, *Primer of Equal Employment Opportunity,* 3d ed. (Washington, D.C.: NA, 1984); M. McCarthy, ed., *Complete Guide to Employing Persons with Disabilities* (Albertson, N.Y.: National Center on Employment of the Handicapped at Human Resources Center, 1985); M. A. Player, *Federal Law of Employment Discrimination* (St. Paul: West Publishing, 1991).

Name Index

Subject Index